D0659091

America Firsthand

America Firsthand

FOURTH EDITION

Volume Two
Readings from Reconstruction to the Present

Robert D. Marcus
State University of New York College at Brockport

and

David Burner
State University of New York at Stony Brook

BEDFORD/ST. MARTIN'S
Boston ≈ New York

For Bedford/St. Martin's

President and Publisher: Charles H. Christensen
General Manager and Associate Publisher: Joan E. Feinberg
History Editor: Katherine E. Kurzman
Development Editor: Charisse Kiino
Managing Editor: Elizabeth M. Schaaf
Production Editor: Tony Perriello
Production Assistant: Deborah Baker
Copyeditor: David Bemelmans
Cover Design: Hannus Design Associates
Cover Art: Fifth Avenue in Winter, c. 1892, by Childe Hassam. Carnegie Museum of Art, Pittsburgh.

Library of Congress Catalog Card Number: 97–72373

Copyright © 1997 by Bedford Books

All rights reserved. No part of this book may be reproduced, stored in a retrieval system, or transmitted by any form or by any means, electronic, mechanical, photocopying, recording, or otherwise, except as may be expressly permitted by the applicable copyright statutes or in writing by the Publisher.

Manufactured in the United States of America.

1 0 9
f e d c b

For information, write: Bedford/St. Martin's, 75 Arlington Street, Boston, MA 02116
(617-426-7440)

ISBN: 0-312-15348–1

Acknowledgments
Bracketed numbers indicate selection numbers.
[3] "A Slaveholder's Journal at the End of the Civil War" from Arney Robinson Childs, ed., *The Private Journal of Henry William Ravenal, 1859–1887* (Columbia: The University of South Carolina Press, 1947), pp. 202–03, 206–07, 210–21 *passim*, 228–29, 237, and 239–40. Reprinted with the permission of the publishers.
[4] "African Americans During Reconstruction" from B. A. Botkin, ed., *Lay My Burden Down: A Folk History of Slavery* (Chicago: The University of Chicago Press, 1945), pp. 65–70, 223–24, 241–42, and 246–47. Copyright 1945 by B. A. Botkin. Reprinted by permission of Curtis Brown, Ltd.

Acknowledgments and copyrights are continued at the back of the book on page 335 which constitutes an extension of the copyright page. It is a violation of the law to reproduce these selections by any means whatsoever without the written permission of the copyright holder.

Preface

The fourth edition of *America Firsthand* aims to capture, through the variety of experiences it records, a lively picture of America and the diverse individual perspectives that comprise its history. Designed to supplement United States history survey textbooks, its two volumes give center stage to ordinary Americans who speak directly of their own lives. These include people from many groups whose experience until recently has been largely lost in mainstream history. As much as possible, individuals speak in their own words and in selections long enough to be memorable, personal, and immediate. The accounts of indentured servants, southern aristocrats, runaway slaves, factory workers, western explorers, civil rights activists, immigrants, and many others offer students opportunities to identify with a wide range of human experience.

Like their predecessors, these volumes respond to the increasing difficulty of teaching and learning American history, particularly the challenge of connecting traditional chronology with the new materials of social history. While the readings convey the experiences and force of specific personalities, *America Firsthand*, fourth edition, has retained the traditional markers of United States history by including accounts of people who acted in or responded to such events as the American Revolution, the western movement, the Civil War, Reconstruction, both World Wars, the Great Depression, the civil rights movement, and the war in Vietnam.

America Firsthand has been extensively revised in the fourth edition. We have retained readings that users wanted to continue teaching and have dropped less successful ones. Among many new readings in the first volume, students will find the diary of Hetty Shepard, a teenaged Puritan girl writing during King Philip's War, an account of the impact of the American Revolution on the slaves of Southern planter Landon Carter, and correspondence of Elizabeth Cady Stanton and Susan B. Anthony as they begin their long collaboration on women's rights. Fresh selections in the second volume include John Wesley Powell's diary of his party's dangerous exploration of the Grand Canyon, interviews of American soldiers who survived the Bataan death march during World War II, an account of how Odessa Williams raised grandchildren and great grandchildren on welfare in Philadelphia in the 1980s and 1990s, and the reflections of Katie Argyle on the death of a friend she had known only on the Internet.

The fourth edition has several new features intended to make it an even more effective teaching tool. The sections into which the book is divided have been brought closer to the typical organization of the standard American history textbook. Each part is organized around a general theme and begins with an introduction that announces the theme and briefly explains the relationship of each reading to it. Two "Points of View" then characterize the section theme by presenting an event from two different perspectives. Neither of the selections presents a simple pro or con position, nor do the critical thinking questions that follow them. By examining a single event that dramatically portrays the central theme of the section, they focus student attention, thereby allowing a deepening of perception and a more interesting probing of the past. Through the "Points of View" in Volume One, students will discover ways of thinking about the Pueblo Indian revolt of 1680, the Salem witchcraft trials, the Boston massacre, the battle of the Alamo, Nat Turner's slave rebellion, and the march of William T. Sherman's army through Georgia and the Carolinas. Volume Two "Points of View" engage students in consideration of a notorious Ku Klux Klan murder in South Carolina during Reconstruction, the battle of Little Big Horn, the Triangle Shirtwaist fire, the Scopes trial, the building of the atomic bomb, and the My Lai incident.

The headnotes preceding each selection have been revised and expanded to better prepare students for each reading by providing necessary background information without providing too much coaching. New questions immediately after the headnotes enable students and instructors to give attention to specific passages and issues that can provide points for discussion as well as material for testing or essays.

America Firsthand, fourth edition, presents the American experience through the perspectives of diverse people who have in common a vivid record of the world they inhabited and the times they experienced. We hope that the readings will serve as fertile ground in which students can begin to root their own interest in history and deepen their perception of the times in which they live.

Acknowledgments

Many fine teachers provided thoughtful criticism and good suggestions for the fourth edition of *America Firsthand*.

Our thanks to Irwin Klibaner, Madison Area Technical College; Dennis Deslippe, Shippensburg University; Norman L. Rosenberg, Macalester University; Ted Karamanski, Loyola University; Ruth Helm, University of Colorado at Boulder; Jean E. Friedman, University of Georgia; James S. Olson, Sam Houston State University; Anne S. Laszlo, Northern Essex Community

College; Jim Harper, Texas Tech University; Mark Newman, University of Illinois at Chicago; Sarah Deutsch, Clark University; Brian C. Hosmer, University of Delaware; James T. Moore, Virginia Commonwealth University; Janette Thomas Greenwood, Clark University; Margaret L. Brown, Brevard College; Rebecca S. Shoemaker, Indiana State University; Michael J. Shaff, Laramie County Community College; David Sloan, University of Arkansas; Wilma King, Michigan State University; Monys A. Hagen, Metropolitan State College of Denver; Susan Curtis, Purdue University; Gene A. Smith, Texas Christian University; David Dalton, College of the Ozarks; Nicolas Proctor, Emory University; Jeffrey S. Adler, University of Florida; and Susan Gray, Arizona State University.

We owe gratitude as well to the many people whose editorial work and judgment improved this edition. Phyllis Valentine and Charisse Kiino were both creative and good humored in keeping us in line through the long process of turning the third edition into the much altered fourth. Others at Bedford Books who played major roles have our thanks as well: Charles Christensen, Joan Feinberg, Katherine Kurzman, Elizabeth Schaaf, Tony Perriello, David Bemelmans, Susan Pace, Dick Hannus, and Fred Courtright. Outside the Bedford organization, Beth Donaldson did fine service in picture and other research and Elizabeth Marcus in modernizing seventeenth century prose. And Tom West remains for both of us the editors' editor.

Contents

Armed Alabama Klansmen posing in their disguises. In December 1868, *Harper's Weekly* used this photograph as the basis for an illustration.

PART ONE

The South after the Civil War

The Failure of Reconstruction

"I have vowed that if I should have children—the first ingredient of the first principle of their education shall be uncompromising hatred & contempt of the Yankee," declared a white Southerner toward the end of the Civil War. You will read a similar response from Caleb Forshey. "I'm free as a frog!" exulted one former slave, reacting like Felix Haywood and other black southerners to the prospect of a future without slavery. Great hopes or extreme bitterness, more common than the philosophical resignation of Henry Ravenel, some of whose journal you will read, promised a painful future for the South.

Wherever travelers went in the months following Appomattox, they saw abandoned fields, twisted rails, burned buildings, white men hobbling about on one leg or dangling an empty sleeve, and ex-slaves exploring their new freedom or searching for food, shelter, and work. Some things the war had settled: secession was impossible, slavery dead, and the South desperately impoverished, its prewar economy gone with the wind. Other outcomes the region and the United States struggle with still.

In particular, victory for the Union did not resolve questions about the role of African American men and women in the nation's life. The first attempts to secure rights for the ex-slaves, known as Reconstruction, produced the Thirteenth, Fourteenth, and Fifteenth Amendments to the Constitution which initiated a revolution that, more than a century later, is far from over. Beyond that, Reconstruction was largely defeated by determined opposition from white Southerners. Some of this resistance took nonviolent forms such as organizing politically, marshalling public opinion, and exercising economic power. But the resort to terror came early and continued in various forms for several generations. The Ku Klux Klan, arising soon after the war, quickly became an armed conspiracy that intimidated, assaulted, and killed African Americans and their white allies. The murder in 1871 of Jim Williams in South Carolina culminated the Klan's conquest of a whole section of a state and led to federal intervention, a story told in the first two readings.

Then in the 1880s, lynching, a new form of terror, swept the South. Ida B. Wells, whose account of the first lynchings in Memphis, Tennessee, you will read, became a leader in the battle against lynching, a battle dominated for most of its long history by women who recognized that using false accusations of rape as the shabby excuse for lynching was in fact a means of subjugating women as well as blacks.

The federal government and private Northerners took a major, if brief, role in attempting to reconstruct the southern states after the Civil War. For a few years, women like Sarah Foster attempted to educate the ex-slaves and enable them to improve their lives. But the South quickly resumed control of its own destiny and three institutions arose to manage race relations: in social affairs, Jim Crow or segregation; in politics, a whites-only Democratic Party; in economics, sharecropping. Arrangements such as the Grimes Sharecrop contract, offering neither full freedom to work where one chose nor slavery, marked the southern economy while parallel restrictions on free labor like the Swindell Brothers contract appeared in the North.

Points of View:
The Ku Klux Klan in South Carolina during Reconstruction (1871)

1

The Murder of Jim Williams

Rosy Williams et al.

There have been three distinct Ku Klux Klans: in the 1860s and 1870s, from the 1920s to the early 1940s, and from the 1950s through to the present. The first began as a fraternity in Tennessee in 1866 but soon turned into a terrorist organization dedicated to defeating Republican Reconstruction governments in the South and intimidating and controlling African Americans. In rural counties in many parts of the region, the Klan, its members sworn to secrecy on penalty of "death, death, death," sometimes controlled regions for months or even years, destroying the property of blacks or their white allies, driving people away, assaulting, and killing. Local governments and law enforcement agencies, dominated by or simply intimidated by the Klan, failed to stop these activities. Nationally, Republicans demanded action against the Klan while Democrats discounted its activities. In 1871, the Republicans, who then controlled both houses of Congress, established a joint House-Senate Committee chaired by Senator John Scott of Pennsylvania to investigate the Klan. Its report in twelve thick volumes is our main source of knowledge of the first Klan.

The climax of Klan activity came in 1871 with a reign of terror in a number of South Carolina counties. President Ulysses S. Grant, who since taking office had been reluctant to intervene in the South, requested from Congress a bill to put down the mounting atrocities in South Carolina and elsewhere. The result was the Ku Klux Act of 1871. It allowed the president to suspend the writ of habeas corpus, *which in turn enabled federal military authorities to arrest Klansmen when local authorities refused to do so. This was not, as some alleged, martial law, since all such prisoners were eventually tried in federal courts.*

The hanging on March 6, 1871, of Jim Williams, an outspoken enemy of the Klan who had been the captain of a black militia unit, became the single most famous event in the history of the South Carolina Klan. One of Yorkville's most prominent citizens, Dr. J. Rufus Bratton, was called to testify before the Committee, and was later accused of leading the raid. As soon as the suspension of habeas corpus *threatened his arrest, he fled to Canada, where he lived in exile until 1877, when President Rutherford B. Hayes, as part of the many deals that finally ended Reconstruction, dropped all charges against him. Bratton returned to Yorkville as something of a local hero. The Klan's day had ended but few Klansmen were ever punished for their actions.*

BEFORE YOU READ

1. What happened on the night of March 6, 1871, when Jim Williams was hanged? Piece together an account of events from the testimony.

2. What does this incident tell you about relations between blacks and whites in this part of South Carolina?

3. How widespread was membership in the Klan among whites in this area?

TESTIMONY OF MRS. ROSY WILLIAMS

Mrs. Rosy Williams, (colored,) widow of Jim Williams, was the eighth witness called for the prosecution. She was sworn, and testified as follows:

Direct examination by Mr. Corbin:

Question: Are you the wife of Jim Williams?

Answer: Yes, sir.

Question: Where do you live; where did you live when Jim Williams was living?

Answer: On Bratton's place.

Question: In what county, York County?

Answer: Yes, sir.

Question: When was Jim Williams killed—your husband?

Answer: The 7th of March.

United States, Cong., *Testimony Taken by the Joint Select Committee to Inquire into the Condition of Affairs in the Late Insurrectionary States, South Carolina,* vol. 3 [usually referred to as the *KKK Report*] (Washington: Government Printing Office, 1872), pp. 1720–21.

Question: Tell the court and jury all about it—all you know about it.

Answer: They came to my house about two o'clock in the night; came in the house and called him.

Question: Who came?

Answer: Disguised men. I can't tell who it was. I don't know any of them.

Question: What do you call them?

Answer: I call them Ku-Klux.

Question: How many came?

Answer: I don't know how many there was.

Question: How many do you think?

Answer: I reckon about nine or ten came into the house, as nigh as I can guess it.

Question: What did they do?

Answer: He went under the house before they came, and after they came in he came up in the house and gave them the guns; there were but two in the house, and then they asked him for the others, and cussed, and told him to come out. He told them he had never had any of the guns. He went with them, and after they had took him out-doors they came in the house after me, and said there were some guns hid. I told them there was not; and after I told them that they went out, and after they had went out there I heard him make a fuss like he was strangling.

Question: Who?

Answer: Williams. Then I went to the door and pulled the door open, and allowed to go down and beg them not to hurt him. They told me not to go out there. Well, I didn't go out. Then they told me to shut the door and take my children and go to bed. I shut the door but didn't go to bed. I looked out of the crack after them until they got under the shadows of the trees. I couldn't see them then.

Question: Did they take Jim Williams?

Answer: Yes, sir; but I couldn't tell him from the rest.

Question: Was that the last you ever saw him alive?

Answer: Yes, sir.

Question: Or did you see him again?

Answer: No, sir; the next morning I went and looked for him, but I didn't find him. I was scared, too. Then I went for my people, to get some one to go help me look for him; and I met an old man who told me they had found him, and said he was dead. They had hung him; but I didn't go out there until 12 o'clock.

Question: Did you go out there then—did you see him?

Answer: Yes, sir.

Question: What was his condition?

Answer: He was hung on a pine tree.

Question: With a rope around his neck?

Answer: Yes, sir.

Question: Dead?
Answer: Yes, sir; he was dead.

TESTIMONY OF JOHN CALDWELL

John Caldwell was the next witness called, who, being duly sworn, testified as follows:

Direct examination by Mr. Corbin:

Question: What is your name?
Answer: John Caldwell. . . .
Question: How long have you resided in York county?
Answer: Twenty-seven years. I was born and raised there.
Question: How old are you?
Answer: About twenty-seven years.
Question: In what portion of York county do you reside?
Answer: In the western portion.
Question: Have you ever been a member of the Ku-Klux organization in York County?
Answer: Yes, sir; I have.
Question: When did you join the order?
Answer: In 1868.
Question: Where was that?
Answer: At Yorkville.
Question: Who initiated you?
Answer: Major J. W. Avery.
Question: What was his relation to the order at that time?
Answer: He just came to me and asked me to walk up to his store. He took me into a room and said he wanted me to join an order. I asked him what he was getting it up for. He said it was in self-defense.
Question: Were you initiated by him then? Did he administer the oath? Can you tell us about what that oath was?
Answer: I cannot remember.
Question: Can you tell us the substance of it?
Answer: Only the last portion of it.
Question: What was that?
Answer: I understood that any person who divulged the secrets of the organization should "suffer death, death, death."
Question: Do you think you would recognize the oath were you to hear it again?
Answer: No, sir; only that portion of it. . . .

Question: Commence at the beginning and describe the raid on Jim Williams; when you got the order to go; where you went to muster; who took command of the men, and what road you traveled; what you did when you got to Jim Williams's house, and all about the matter.

Answer: The first I heard of it was at Yorkville; I was told there by Dr. Bratton that they were going down to McConnellsville; I asked him what he was going after; he said he was going for some guns; he asked me if I would go, and I said I would have nothing to do with it; I had never been on a raid; he asked me the name of the chief man in our county; I told him I understood it was William Johnson or Alonzo Brown was the leading man in our county.

Question: Do you mean in your portion of the county?

Answer: Yes, sir.

Question: Go on and tell all you know.

Answer: Johnson came to me and told me to meet him at the muster-patch; that was William Johnson.

Question: What is his relation to the order?

Answer: He was chief.

Question: Of what Klan?

Answer: Of the Rattlesnake Klan. I went out to the muster-ground that night; it is called the brier-patch; I met several men there. . . . Dr. Bratton came there, and Lindsay Brown and Rufus McLain.

Question: Did you put on your disguise at the brier-patch?

Answer: Yes, sir.

Question: What sort of disguises are they?

Answer: Most of them were black gowns, with heads and false-faces.

Question: What sort of heads were they?

Answer: They were made out of black cloth, or dark cloth.

Question: How were they ornamented?

Answer: Some had horns, and some had not.

Question: Had you horses there?

Answer: Yes, sir.

Question: Were the men armed?

Answer: No, sir. I don't believe I saw a gun in the party.

Question: Had they pistols?

Answer: I didn't see any pistols.

Question: Now tell us where they went.

Answer: We went down to the Pinckney road, and there we met another party of men. . . .

Question: What did they do there?

Answer: We stopped then, and there were four men initiated there. . . .

Question: Who was in command of the party?

Answer: Bratton was at the head of the party. He was riding in front.

Question: What Bratton was that?

Answer: Dr. J. Rufus Bratton, of Yorkville.

Question: Go on with what you had to say.

Answer: We went on then to McConnellsville; and about 200 or 300 yards from there we halted; and they said there were some guns down at that place, and they sent a party to search and get them. A man then came from the party that went forward and said, bring up the horses; and they took them down. They said there was a gun at Mr. Moore's; and they went up there for a black man; but I don't know who he was.

Question: At whose place was this?

Answer: They said it was Mr. Moore's place.

Question: What did they do with the black man?

Answer: They asked him about Jim Williams; how far away he lived. They asked him if he knew if Williams had any guns. He said he thought there were twelve or fifteen guns there. Then they took this black-masked man and mounted him on a horse or mule, and carried him a piece; then they halted and turned the black man loose, and he went back home. Then they went on from there about three miles, and stopped in a thicket, and a party of ten went off— I don't know whether there were more than ten—and were gone probably an hour.

Question: Can you describe the place?

Answer: It was in an old piney thicket on the side of a hill.

Question: What did you do?

Answer: I remained there with the horses. I was not well, and I just remained there with the horses.

Question: Did the party go forward?

Answer: Yes, sir. Before I got off my horse I heard some one call for ten men, and that party then went off. I saw them go off; and they were gone probably one hour when they returned.

Question: Did you hear anything of them while they were gone?

Answer: Not a word.

Question: Did the same crowd return?

Answer: Yes, sir.

Question: What was said by any of them as to what they had done?

Answer: I asked if they had found the black man Jim Williams, and if they saw him. I got no answer, and they just got on their horses to leave.

Question: Who ordered them?

Answer: I heard some man say, "Mount your horses," and then they mounted and took across over the fence, and I got up forward to the foremost man—Dr. Bratton. I asked him if he had found the negro. He said yes. Said I, "Where, where is he?" Said he, "He is in hell, I expect."

Question: What further was said?

Answer: I asked him, "You didn't kill him?" He said, "We hung him." I said, "Dr. Bratton, you ought not to have done that." He then pulled out his watch, and said, "We have no time to spare; we have to call on one or two more."

TESTIMONY OF DR. JAMES R. BRATTON

James R. Bratton sworn and examined.

By the Chairman:

Question: Do you reside in this place?

Answer: Yes, sir, and have been residing here for twenty-five years.

Question: Are you a native of this State?

Answer: Yes, sir; of this county.

Question: What is your occupation?

Answer: I have been practicing medicine here for twenty-five years.

Question: Have you had an opportunity of becoming acquainted with the people of this county generally?

Answer: Yes, sir, I think I have.

Question: Does your practice extend through the county?

Answer: Through the different sections of the county.

Question: Our purpose is to inquire into the security of life, person, and property through this county, and the manner in which the laws are executed. Have you any knowledge of any offenses against the law, or against the security of person and property, that have not been redressed in the ordinary courts of justice?

Answer: I have no personal knowledge of anything of the kind. I merely hear rumors and reports. Personally, I know nothing about it.

Question: Have you been called upon, as a physician, to either testify before, or certify upon, any inquests on the bodies of dead men?

Answer: I have not. I have only heard these reports from the coroner's inquests; that is the way I get my information about these cases.

Question: How many persons have you heard of who have been killed in this county within the last six or eight months?

Answer: There was a man up here named Tom Black, or Roundtree, that they say was killed — I cannot tell when. One report says he was killed by negroes for his money; another, that it was by white men in disguise. He had been to Charlotte a few days before that, to sell his cotton, and, when killed, his money could not be found; but who killed him I cannot tell. . . .

Question: Any others?

Answer: Yes, sir; a negro was hung about twelve miles below by some persons, who I cannot tell.

Question: What was his name?

Answer: Williams.

Question: Was he a militia captain?

Answer: He was.

Question: When was that?

Answer: That was some time in this year, in February or March; in the latter part of February or the first of March; I do not remember the date exactly.

Question: Do you recollect the day of the week?

Answer: No, sir, I do not remember it.

Question: Do you recollect the day you heard it?

Answer: No, sir; nor the day it was done; it was some time in the latter part of February or the first of March.

Question: Was that done by men in disguise?

Answer: Yes, sir, it was so reported; that was the testimony at the coroner's inquest.

Question: Were you at that inquest?

Answer: I was not; but it was so reported to me by the coroner.

Question: Was that in February or March?

Answer: Yes, sir.

Question: Are those the only cases you have known of?

Answer: I do not know any other cases that I can think of now. I have not fixed any other cases upon my mind. Let me see, there may have been other cases.

Question: Those are cases of actual death about which I am inquiring now?

Answer: What do you mean by that?

Question: Persons killed.

Answer: Those three are negroes killed. I do not know any other cases to my knowledge. . . .

Question: Do you discredit the statements of negroes who say they were whipped?

Answer: In many cases I do.

Question: Do you think the men who disguise themselves could be easily told?

Answer: I do not say that, but a great many of these people dislike to work, and if they can get the protection of the State or the United States to relieve them from work they will do it, and I have no faith in their testimony.

Question: In negro testimony?

Answer: I have not.

Question: Is there any concerted arrangement here for the purpose of intimidating the negroes either with regard to their political rights or their making complaints against those who have whipped them or otherwise committed violence upon them?

Answer: I know nothing of the kind. The truth is this, I think it is just the reverse. If ever our people were earnest in anything it is to teach the negro his duty to be quiet and passive and attend to his duty; to let public meetings alone; to go and vote as he pleases, allowing no man to interfere with him. I do not know any cases where a darkey has been interfered with at the polls.

Question: Is attendance at a political meeting considered imprudent or wrong in them?

Answer: When they attend in large numbers they create great confusion and annoyance; but I do not know a procession that has been interfered with.

Question: Is that the light in which the white people view that subject, that the negroes had better stay away altogether from political meetings?

Answer: Yes, sir. Our advice is "have as little to do with politics as possible; if you want to vote, vote, but vote for no dishonest, vicious, ignorant, and wicked man; vote for whom you please, so he is honest, whether a radical or a democrat." That has been my advice to them all.

Question: Do you know of no organization in this county intended to prevent negroes from voting as they saw proper?

Answer: I don't; and that has not been the case.

Question: Do you know anything of this organization commonly called Ku-Klux?

Answer: I am no member of the Ku-Klux, and know nothing of their proceedings. . . .

[Bratton is presented with an article on the Klan from the local newspaper.]

Question: Now, Doctor, having stated your belief that there is a Ku-Klux organization, since you saw this notice in the paper, state who in your belief compose it.

Answer: I cannot tell you that, sir.

Question: What class of people, sir?

Answer: I cannot tell you who compose that organization. I know nothing about them. I do not belong, and have no means of knowing.

Question: Have you no idea who compose it?

Answer: No, sir; I have no means of knowing. . . .

Question: Have you any knowledge of the men who participated in the hanging of Captain Williams?

Answer: I have no knowledge of that fact.

Question: Has no man said anything to you about it?

Answer: No, sir; no man has said, "I did it," or "he did." I know nothing about it as to who hung him.

Question: Either from those who participated in it or from any other person?

Answer: No, sir.

Question: Did you learn that he was hanged?

Answer: Yes, sir.

Question: That that was the mode of his killing—that he was hung?

Answer: Yes, sir.

Question: Were you upon the inquest of any one of these men who were murdered by violence in this county?

Answer: No, sir. I was engaged all the time in other business. Generally in these cases in the country they take the nearest physician. . . .

Question: What, in your opinion, have been the causes of whatever disturbances have occurred in this county within a year; what are the principal leading causes of any troubles that may have existed, whether breaking out by Ku-Klux acts or any other mode of proceeding?

Answer: Why, sir, my opinion is this: that these burnings of people's houses and barns and gin-houses produced this disturbance.

Question: Was that last summer?

Answer: That was last fall and winter, and this spring. I do not know that there were any burnings last summer that I remember. I think it was all this winter.

Question: You have given an estimate of the number of the whippings of negroes, whether by Ku-Klux or other negroes, or somebody else for private reasons, at twelve or fifteen. What is the probable number of burnings of gin-houses in this county in the last year?

Answer: I will have to count them up. Thomason, stables and barn; Warren, gin-houses; Miller, gin-house; Crosby, gin-house; Preacher Castle, barn; my brother's thrashing-house was burnt the other night. A boy confessed it afterward. He simply did it because my brother had told him not to go into his select orchard. He had a large orchard and told him that he and the rest of the colored people might go in there, but not in the garden. He did go into the garden. He caught him there and cursed him a little, and, in a few days, this fire took place. . . .

Question: Out of these six cases [of arson], is there any evidence to connect the negroes, as a class, with the burning?

Answer: No, sir.

Question: Yet you give these burnings as the outrages against the negroes?

Answer: That is the general impression among the people.

Question: What justice is there in charging the negroes, as a class, with burning, any more than the murderers who are operating through the country?

Answer: Let me tell you. These people are easily excited to action, and when we had the candidates last fall, strange to say, one candidate actually made this speech: "You have to succeed in this county if you have to burn every blade of grass," or something to that effect.

Question: Did you hear it?

Answer: No, sir.

Question: Who reported it to you?

Answer: I do not know.

Question: Who made the speech?

Answer: Doctor Neagle.

Question: Who heard it?

Answer: Almost any citizen you can take up.

Question: You cannot swear that he said it?

Answer: No, sir.

Question: You are willing to believe it?

Answer: Yes, sir.

Question: And that the negroes did these burnings, incited by that?

Answer: I am more disposed to think that the negroes did it than that white persons did it.

Question: And yet you have no opinion as to the murderers in this county?
Answer: No, sir.

2

Defeat of the Klan

Special Correspondent to the *New York Tribune* and Senator John Scott

Suspending habeas corpus *is a dramatic act. Abraham Lincoln did so during the Civil War and opponents of the Union were arrested. Democrats called him a tyrant for it. Before Grant finally and with obvious reluctance suspended the writ in the counties around Yorkville, South Carolina, the Klan's activities there had already become a subject of national concern. Like many other Republicans, Senator John Scott of Pennsylvania, chairman of the Joint Select Committee investigating the Klan, viewed the organization as a political conspiracy aimed at bringing the Democratic Party back to power not only in the southern states but nationally as well.*

Democrats, on the other hand, insisted that the Klan lacked any central direction or leadership and was really a number of loosely connected local Klans. With melodramatic names like the "Black Panthers" or the "Avengers," these night riders were poor, uneducated, unruly, rural whites acting on their own. The higher social classes, claimed the political leaders of the South, did not do such things. And the federal government and its army had no business interfering in the purely internal affairs of sovereign states.

The Seventh Cavalry, later made famous under General George Custer, had three companies of troops in the Yorkville area commanded by a determined and highly capable officer, Major Lewis M. Merrill. Once habeas corpus *had been suspended, Merrill quickly rounded up and secured confessions from hundreds of Klansmen. This enabled the federal attorney to indict a number of Klan leaders including Dr. J. Rufus Bratton, who was charged with the murder of Jim Williams.*

The Yorkville situation by now commanded national attention. Senator Scott, in his speech calling for the extension of the Ku Klux Act, many of whose provisions (including the power to suspend habeas corpus*) were about to expire, called special attention to the Williams case. And the* New York Tribune, *long concerned about Klan atrocities, sent a correspondent to the region who telegraphed stories for a number of weeks* *in the fall of 1871. The defeat of the Klan, while it did not mean the success of Re-publican Reconstruction policies, was a major story.*

BEFORE YOU READ

1. What argument did Scott make in his speech and how did he use the Williams case to bolster his position?
2. What was Major Merrill's role and how did he justify it?
3. What view of the Klan did the *Tribune* correspondent have?
4. What was his opinion of this part of the South?
5. How much credence do you give his account?

SOUTH CAROLINA KU-KLUX

Confessions of Members of the Klan.

*Complete exposure of the character, strength,
and purpose of the infamous order—over
300 men confess themselves KU-KLUX.
[From the special correspondent of the* Tribune.]

Yorkville, S. C., Nov. 10.—Every day there is a fresh arrival of frightened and repentant Ku-Klux from the country, who come in on foot, on horseback, or in wagons drawn by mules, to report themselves to Major Merrill, make confession of all or a part of what they know about the Klan, and ask leave to go home, promising not to run away, and to report again whenever sent for. The number paroled in this manner is now over 300. The parting injunction these men get from the Major or District Attorney is usually, "You go home, and stay there, and mind your own business, and when you're wanted you'll be sent for. If you haven't told all you know it will be the worse for you, for it will all come out before we get through." The troubled Ku-Klux is usually much relieved at this. He says, "Thank you, Major," and shuffles to the door, fumbling his dirty old slouched hat, and starts for home with a great weight off his mind. When he left his log cabin in the morning, he feared he might sleep in the jail that night, and many nights to come, and he goes back to his slatternly, snuff-dipping wife, and troop of ragged, dirty, yellow-faced children, with a lighter heart than he has had for the past three weeks.

Occasionally a man does not escape so easily. Previous confessions show that he has not told the truth, and that instead of having been only a passive member of the order, obliged to join for his own protection, he has been actively engaged in raiding. The Major says, quietly, "I am very sorry, Sir, but I shall have to send you to jail. I know more about your doings than you seem to yourself," and he steps to the door, calls a guard, and says, "Corporal, take this man to jail and deliver him to Capt. Ogden." The Ku-Klux is marched off, and a visible gloom comes over the countenances of his friends waiting outside, as he passes through their midst. It sometimes happens that a man who comes in with a plausibly made up story is astonished to find that Major Merrill knows his whole history, the names of all his acquaintances, and of every member of the Klan to which he belonged. No sooner has he told his name than the Major talks to him somewhat in this way: "You are the man I have been wanting to see for some time. You live on the Howell's Ferry road, and belong to the Rattlesnake Klan. You were in the raid when Jim Williams was killed. Now I don't ask you to tell anything or make any promises, but if you wish to make a statement you can do so." The poor devil forgets the lies he had invented and blurts out the truth.

There are hundreds of men, however, who were forced into the order against their will. Some were brutally whipped before they could be made to join. One man was set astride a steer and whipped for five miles along the road to the gathering place of the Klan. By the time he arrived there he was ready to take the oath. A great many of the confessions are like this:

> The whippings and killings were goin' on all about our part of the country, and it jis' 'peared like as if no man was safe. I was mighty skeered for fear they'd come on me, for there'd been threats made agin me, and one night Jim Brown he come to my house and said as how if I didn't join the Ku-Klux they was a goin' to make a raid on me, and I'd git used mighty rough; so I done joined so as I could live in peace. But, Major, I never believed in it nohow, and I never went on no raid. 'Pears like as though they didn't trust me or want me along when any devilment was goin' on.

They are a hard-looking set of men, these self-convicted Ku-Klux that throng about the Post Commander's office; but they are not near as ill-looking as their comrades in jail, who will not confess; who insist that they are "as innocent as the dead," and who never heard there was any such thing as Ku-Klux until they were arrested. The average White man of South Carolina is the poorest specimen of the Caucasian race I have ever seen on either side of the Atlantic. The most discouraging feature about him is that he shows no desire to improve his condition. What can be expected from a man who will not take the trouble to put a window in his house, and who keeps his door shut by putting a "chunk" of wood against it, because he is too shiftless to whittle out a latch or a button. Brutal, cowardly, and inconceivably ignorant, he is a Ku-Klux by nature. There are, of course, a few intelligent and worthy men sprinkled over the country, or the semblance of civilized society would not have been possible; and these men in the old time controlled the lower orders as absolutely as did the Scottish chiefs their clans. Whenever, in this State, such men have opposed the Ku-Klux organization it has never had any headway. Unfortunately, in this county, and in Spartanburg, Union, and Chester, these men, with exceptions so few as not to be worth mentioning, all joined the order—some from choice, others through fear. . . .

. . . Forty-five Klans are known to have existed in York County. Some of these have fanciful or ferocious names, such as the Rattlesnakes, the Tigers, the

White Panthers, the Black Panthers, the White Rangers, the Pilots, the Avengers, &c., and others took the names of their Chiefs or of the localities where they were formed. Each Klan elected its own chief, his lieutenant, and two or three "night-hawks," who were couriers to notify to the members gatherings of the Klan, and to communicate with the central authority in Yorkville. All the members had pistols and guns, many had Winchester repeating rifles, which, there is reason to believe, were bought in New York, with funds raised there for the purpose. Eight thousand of these arms are known to have been brought to South Carolina since the Ku-Klux troubles began. Most of the men who now possess these guns never in their lives had money enough at one time to buy one, for they cost $40 or $50 each, and it is certain that those that were not stolen from the negro militia were given to them by somebody. They were all well-supplied with the peculiar ammunition the guns required. The discipline of the Klans was severe. At Limestone Spring, in Spartanburg County, a whipping-post was set up, where disobedient members were flogged. The word of the Chief was law to his Klan, and the order of the Grand Chief was law to his chiefs. In all ordinary cases of whipping and abusing negroes, and disciplining their Klans, the chiefs acted on their own responsibility; but when any important enterprise was contemplated the plot was laid by the Grand Chief and his Council, and orders dispatched by "night hawks" to the chiefs, who were required to coöperate, to make a detail from their Klans and march to the rendezvous at an hour appointed. . . . When Capt. Jim Williams was hung in this County, three Klans were ordered to commit the murder. They met at the rendezvous in an "old pine field," and when they were assembled, Dr. Bratton of this village appeared with orders from the Grand Chief to take command. No one but himself and the Chiefs knew what was to be done, or where they were to go. He marched the party to Williams's house, and when the poor victim was taken from the arms of his shrieking wife, ordered the men to hang him, and produced the rope brought along for the purpose. Williams was an honest, intelligent, hard-working negro, who was murdered because he had been Captain of a militia Company. Bratton was a "highly respectable" practicing physician in Yorkville. He fled the country as soon as the President's proclamation [suspending *habeas corpus*] was issued. . . .

The confessing Ku-Klux agree in the main as to what they understood were the purposes of the organization. One man says he was told it was to "suppress lawlessness and support the Democratic party;" another that he understood it was to "put down the Radical Government;" another that it was to "keep the negroes from rising;" another that the purpose was to "keep fusses down and colored men and white women apart;" and so on through many variations of the same purpose, understood by all, namely, hostility to the negroes and to the Republican party. A considerable portion of Ku-Klux were too ignorant to know much of politics or parties, but they were not slow to see the advantages of being able to abuse with impunity the black men and women who lived in their neighborhood. The aim of the intelligent was to control this poor white element for their political advantage, and to thoroughly crush the spirit of the ncgroes, so that they could be made to work without wages and vote as they were told.

SPEECH OF SENATOR JOHN SCOTT, REPUBLICAN OF PENNSYLVANIA, ON EXTENDING THE KU KLUX ACT, MAY 17, 1872

The testimony taken by the joint committee clearly establishes that the same organization [the Ku Klux Klan], pursuing the same purposes and seeking to accomplish them by the same means, has existed, and been active since 1868, in the States of North and South Carolina, Georgia, Florida, Alabama, and Mississippi. There can be no reasonable doubt of its existence still in Tennessee and in most of the other States where it is for the present quiet but ready to act whenever it may be deemed necessary or prudent to do so. Its recent character is better fixed, however, by the evidence furnished from the organization itself, evidence which stamps it as one of the foulest blots upon the civilization of this century. At the trials in Columbia, South Carolina, the constitution of the Ku Klux in that State was given in evidence, having been found in possession of one Samuel Brown, esq., a man of wealth and standing in York county, who was chief of a Klan, and is now expiating his offense in the Albany penitentiary, sentenced upon his own confession. . . .

. . . The oath administered was as follows:

Obligation.

I, [name,] before the immaculate Judge of heaven and earth, and upon the holy Evangelists of Almighty God, do, of my own free will and accord, subscribe to the following sacredly binding obligation:

1. We are on the side of justice, humanity, and constitutional liberty, as bequeathed to us in its purity by our forefathers.

2. We oppose and reject the principles of the Radical party.

3. We pledge mutual aid to each other in sickness, distress, and pecuniary embarrassment.

4. Female friends, widows, and their households shall ever be special objects of our regard and protection.

Any member divulging, or causing to be divulged, any of the foregoing obligations shall meet the fearful penalty and traitor's doom, which is death, death, death.

Organized under such a constitution and bound by such an oath the proceedings of its members in the northern counties of South Carolina after the election of 1870 and until the spring and summer of 1871, as well as in the southern portion of North Carolina, were of the most lawless and desperate character. I do not propose to attempt a recital of them. They embrace indignity, outrage, and murder. They were inflicted principally upon the negroes, but in many instances also upon white men, and of the highest respectability. I give several instances as showing the character of all.

Congressional Globe, 42nd Congress, 2nd Session. Washington, D.C.: pp. 3580–85.

[Several incidents of terror, beatings, lynchings, and other crimes are described in some detail.]

... The occurrences in South Carolina to which I have referred had taken place before the sub-committee visited that State. When there, ascertaining the fearful extent to which these lawless acts had been perpetrated with impunity, members of that sub-committee were impressed with the belief that if, after the community was made aware of them, there was any recurrence of violence, no other remedy than the most stringent one would suffice to bring the perpetrators to justice, and to prevent scenes of bloody retaliation.

[After a dedicated officer, Colonel Lewis M. Merrill, gathered extensive evidence to supplement the findings of the Select Committee, President Ulysses S. Grant suspended the writ of *habeas corpus* in a number of South Carolina counties, and the federal judicial system moved against the Klan.] The presiding judge of that circuit, Judge Thomas, had requested of me as the chairman of the committee the information communicated to the President as to York county. I referred him to Major Merrill, the commander of the United States troops at Yorkville, and requested him to give all the aid in his power to any investigation directed by the court. I regret that I cannot incorporate here the whole report of Major Merrill made to his superior officer, but his account of the proceedings of the court, of the suspension of the writ, and of the scenes which followed it, gives a better idea of the true state of facts than any words of mine can give, and I make room for an extract. ...

> If any other evidence were needed of the fact that the body of the local civil authorities is either in complicity with the Ku Klux conspiracy or intimidated by it, it is to be found in the fact, which now appears, that at least three of the justices of the peace (called trial justices) have been members of the Ku Klux, and that at least one third of the white members of the grand and petit juries at the last term of court were members, and among the number some who were officers of high grade in the order, and at least two of the number having been accessory to Ku Klux murders.
>
> In view of this, it is small wonder that eleven murders, and more than six hundred cases of whipping, and other brutal outrages by the Ku Klux, have to this day gone unnoticed, and their authors unwhipped of justice, so far as any serious effort of the local authorities has been concerned.
>
> Immediately subsequent to the adjournment of the court, I went to Columbia, to confer with the district attorney, and endeavor to concert some means of bringing better things about in this section. ...
>
> Those arrested and those who have surrendered are of every social grade, from the highest to the lowest, including representatives of all the liberal professions, even ministers of the gospel. When it is stated that these men among their number include those who confessed every crime known to the law, the state of society in which such facts are possible must be left to the imagination to depict: it is impossible to describe it.
>
> In short, the conspiracy may be stated to have practically included the whole white community within the ages when active participation in public affairs was possible. ...

The total white voters of the county are about twenty-three hundred, of whom a small majority live in that part of the county from which most of the surrenders have come.

From these facts, I think the number of sworn members of the organization in the whole county is underestimated when placed at eighteen hundred.

Such a state of facts shows that at the time of the suspension of the writ, York county was in point of fact an armed camp, and that it was not for want of power to do it, but because the flight of the leaders made organized resistance hopeless, that danger of this kind was not encountered. Had it been attempted, and the organization used its strength, with its leaders present to direct it, while there could be no question as to the final event, there would have been needed much more force than I had at command to enforce any arrests that might have been attempted.

I am convinced, too, that the moral effect of the suspension of the writ had much to do with the complete collapse of the organization.

At that term of the court true bills were found against seven hundred and eighty-five defendants, there being about five hundred defendants in all, as some of them were named in several bills. Of these, five were convicted upon trial; fifty-three pleaded guilty, and the others could not be tried and were held over. Several of them have since been tried and others have pleaded guilty, as I am informed, at Charleston in the circuit court. The evidence elicited at those trials leaves no doubt of the existence of the order, and its purposes as elsewhere described, and also of the intercourse of its members through the several States. . . .

The cases I have given and this testimony show the effect of this organization upon its victims. Now, I desire very briefly to call attention to its effects upon its members, and I do it in but one case; but it will, I think, satisfy any one that it is idle to talk about demoralization and corruption in the southern States among the negroes or in any party, when it is apparent that in South Carolina and in a number of these States there is an organization which in its consequences would lead every man to distrust his neighbor and destroy all confidence in every judicial tribunal. I refer to the printed testimony on page 1342 for the purpose of making two or three very brief extracts from the evidence of a Dr. Bratton. Dr. Bratton, let me state, was the leading physician in York county, South Carolina. He had the largest practice of any physician in the county; a man of culture, a man of intelligence, a man probably, according to my recollection of his appearance, from forty to forty-five years of age. He was called before the committee when they were in York. . . .

Bear in mind he denied all personal knowledge of a single Ku Klux outrage in that county, in which there were eleven murders and over six hundred whippings. He denied that he knew anything of the organization. He denied all knowledge, in short, of its operations except what he gathered from common rumor. Bear in mind the character of the man. Bear in mind that it is said that no man of respectability or character had any part in these outrages, much less countenanced them. Now, sir, when the proclamation was made that the writ of *habeas corpus* would be suspended, Dr. Bratton fled, and my information is that he has never been back in York county since. Several of the men who hanged a man named Jim Williams, a militia captain, were arraigned and tried at Columbia for that offense, and the testimony upon that occasion proved that this Dr. Bratton, who thus swore, was the leader of the band; that he provided himself with a rope in the town of Yorkville and carried it on his saddle-bow out to the cabin of that man, Jim Williams, and with his own hand put the rope around Williams's neck and hanged him. . . .

. . . Talk about corruption; talk about demoralization in Legislatures under the negroes, when the leaders of society are not only themselves murderers, but come before the country and deny it by perjury!

I have thus given in some detail the proceedings in South Carolina, because there the evidence of the existence of the organization and its purposes and acts is beyond controversy, and it is only necessary to apply the same evidence to other localities infested by the organization to appreciate the condition of the poor and defenseless, who are the objects of its attacks, and to show the necessity of the exercise of power by the strong arm of the Federal Government to suppress this monstrous conspiracy.

FOR CRITICAL THINKING

1. Was the Klan a conspiracy? What evidence for organized, concerted actions do you find in any of the readings in this or the previous selection?

2. Although Klan activities generally ceased after the South Carolina prosecutions, other means of intimidation continued, contributing to the collapse of Reconstruction. How does what you have read about the Klan and what was required to end its activities make such an outcome understandable?

3

A Slaveowner's Journal at the End of the Civil War

Henry William Ravenel

In a letter of August 26, 1865, Henry William Ravenel summarized the immediate effects of the collapse of the Confederacy as well as anyone ever has:

> A new era opens before us, but alas! with what great changes. Our country is in ruins, and our people reduced to poverty. . . . We had no money but Confederate and that is now worthless . . . all our securities and investments are bankrupt. . . . There is little money in the country, little cotton and other produce, so there is no business or employment for those who are anxiously seeking to make a living. . . .

Emancipation had altered social relations; the collapse of the Confederacy and then Reconstruction were transforming southern politics; the war and emancipation had upset every economic arrangement making currency worthless, land unsalable, and credit—previously based on chattel mortgages on slave "property"—scarcely to be obtained.

Ravenel was born in 1814 to a prominent South Carolina slaveholding family. In addition to managing a plantation, he was also to become an important self-trained naturalist whose studies of American fungi achieved international renown. After the war he supported his family by selling seeds and parts of his collections of fungi to collectors and later worked as a naturalist for the U.S. Department of Agriculture. After his death, Ravenel's botanical collections were sold to the British Museum.

Ravenel began his journal in 1859 and continued it to within weeks of his death in 1887. The journal shows how one thoughtful and well-placed member of the southern elite struggled to understand the collapse of his familiar world.

BEFORE YOU READ

1. How did Ravenel interpret the causes and outcome of the Civil War?
2. What did he expect to happen to the ex-slaves and how did he explain their behavior?
3. Are his reactions what you expected of a slaveholder or are there any surprises in what he writes in his journal?

November [1864]

F. 18   The Augusta paper of this morning has startling intelligence from Atlanta. There is no doubt that Sherman has burned Rome, Decatur & Atlanta, & has commenced a move with 4 or 5 army corps (40 to 50000) in the

Arney Robinson Childs, ed., *The Private Journal of Henry William Ravenel, 1859–1887* (Columbia: University of South Carolina Press, 1947), pp. 202–03, 206–07, 210–21 passim, 228–29, 237, 239–40.

direction of Macon & Augusta. The Northern papers say his intention is to move through to Charleston & Mobile, destroy the rail road & bridges behind him & feed his army from the country. I have been apprehending just such a move since Hood's army was withdrawn. It is a bold stroke, & if successful, would bring untold evils upon us, in the destruction of property & the means of subsistance. . . .

Sunday 20 Beauregard telegraphs the people to be firm & resolute—to obstruct his passage by cutting the woods in his front & flank—to destroy all provisions which cannot be carried away—to remove all negroes, horses & cattle, & leave a scene of desolation in his front, instead of in his rear as it would be if he passed. . . . Should Sherman succeed in taking Augusta, his march will be onward toward Charleston, & his track will be a scene of desolation. I await the developments of the next few days with anxiety, chiefly on account of my negroes. If I send them away & the farm & house is left without protection, my house will be robbed & despoiled of every thing, whether the enemy passes here or not. I must wait before removing them, until I am very sure the enemy will succeed in his designs upon Augusta—& then perhaps it may be too late.

M. 21 I have had a talk with my negroes on the subject, & explained to them the true state of affairs—that should the enemy pass through this place they must escape & take care of themselves for a while until the danger is passed. I am well satisfied from their assurances, that they are really alarmed at the idea of being seized & taken off by the Yankees, & that they will not desert me.

F. 25 We are now at the gloomiest period of the war which for nearly four years has afflicted our land. I cannot conceal from myself the many discouraging features of our situation & the perilous straits in which we stand.

1st Our Finances are in such a condition that universal discontent & real suffering exists. The currency is so much depreciated, that for the ordinary & necessary articles of subsistance, it requires an outlay beyond the means of most people. This involves privation & suffering. There is a want of confidence in the ability of the Govt. to redeem its credits, founded partly on their great amount & partly on the precarious condition of our affairs. If our cause fails the whole Govt. credits are lost, & doubtless this consideration has its weight among capitalists in producing distrust.

Sunday 8 Samuel Ravenel at home on furlough from Measles was here this morning. He told me that the Post Surgeon had offered Harry & himself & three other boys, exemptions on account of their age & size, & that two had accepted. He & Harry & another had declined. I was gratified to hear that our boys took such high views of their duty. Sam says they have no tents, & have to lie on the bare ground, or with such protection as a few bushes or straw can give. They do picket & *vidette* duty in sight & hearing of the enemy, see them drill & enjoy the music from their bands every day. . . .

M. 9   Sent off two boxes bacon today to the Depot for Aiken via Charleston. I hope these supplies may not be caught in Charleston or intercepted by the enemy on the way. We are in a quandary what to do. I am buying hogs down here, & at the same time sending supplies hurriedly to Aiken. . . .

January [1865]

Sunday 15   My claim for compensation for slave (Jim) lost in Confed. service, has passed the Legislature & $2000 are allowed. I am to send James Wilson a power of attorney to receive it. They have commenced to fortify Columbia. . . .

M. 23   Our currency still continues to depreciate, as is shown by the increasing prices of all articles. . . .

February [1865]

S. 18   It is reported that Columbia has fallen - - - - No mail from Charleston. We are now closed in & cut off from all news from the outside world. . . . We are now virtually in the enemy's lines. I am in doubt what to do with Harry. He is very weak & just able to walk about. If he remains, he may be captured as prisoner of war—if I undertake to carry him away, I then leave my family never to see them until the war is over. I would not hesitate about leaving my family if they were in a region where they needed no protection & could get subsistance—but the thoughts of deserting them here is very distressing to me.

Sunday 19   Dr. Frank Porcher dined here today. He thinks we should remain where we are. The upper country is in danger of famine, & will soon be without salt, now the coast is given up. . . . Charleston was occupied by the enemy yesterday at 10 A.M.—Columbia has been captured. We hear of a great fire in Charleston yesterday, but no particulars yet. Exciting times!

M. 20   In a few days the last of our army will have crossed the Santee, the bridge burnt behind them—& we then become an evacuated & conquered region. We fall under Yankee rule & the laws & authority of the U. States are established during the continuance of the war. What new relations between us & our negroes will be established we cannot tell but there is no doubt it will be a radical change. I do not apprehend destructive raids, or personal violence to citizens who remain, but we will be compelled to conform to the new conditions under which we are placed, as a conquered people. I suppose all the cotton will be seized & confiscated to the use of the U. S. govt,—& probably a system of culture will be adopted & enforced the profits from which will accrue to them. I think it the duty of all slave owners & planters who remain, to be with their negroes. They have been faithful to the last, & they deserve in turn, confidence from him, protection, attention & care. . . .

T. 21   I think masters who are within these lines of the enemy, should remain on their plantations among their negroes;—the first change of conditions should not be volunteered by us. We have always believed we were right in maintaining the relation of master & slave for the good of the country & also for the benefit of the negro. If we have believed firmly in the Divine sanction which the Bible affords to this relation, we should not be the first to sever it, by abandoning them. They have grown up under us, they look to us for support, for guidance & protection—They have faithfully done their duty during this trying time, when the great temptations were offered to leave us. In the sight of God, we have a sacred duty to stand by them as long as they are faithful to us. We know that if left to themselves, they cannot maintain their happy condition. We must reward their fidelity to us by the same care & consideration we exercised when they were more useful. . . .

T. 28 David returned with a cart from PineVille last night, & said Rene told him the Yankees had been, or were, in PineVille, taking poultry & whatever they wanted. The negroes on many places have refused to go to work. . . . I have spoken to some of them here & intend to give them advice as a friend to continue on the plantation, & work—Of course there must be great care & judgement used in preserving discipline & I have advised with the overseer. I think for their own good & the good of the country, it would be best for the present organization of labor to go on, so that all may get a subsistance, the old & young, the sick & disabled, & the other non producers. . . . The freed & idle negroes who are not kept now under discipline or fear will give us trouble. I feel great anxiety for the future. . . .

March [1865]

Th. 2 Half past two o'clock A.M. Night of horrors! How can I describe the agonizing suspense of the past six hours! Thank God who has protected us all we are still alive & have lost nothing but property.—About half past 8 oclock I was standing in the back piazza, when I heard the discharge of 3 or 4 fire arms. The negroes soon came running up to inform us that the Yankees were in the negro yard. They soon after entered the house, (4 or 5 colored men) armed & demanded to see the owner of the house. I called to Pa & he walked up to the back door where they were. They told him that they had come for provisions, corn, bacon, poultry & whatever they wanted—demanded his horses & wagons, his guns, wine &c. That they had come to tell the negroes they were free & should no longer work for him. They used very threatening language with oaths & curses. They then proceeded to the stable & took my pair & Renes horse—Took the 2 sets harness & put in the horses, into the two wagons & Lequeax buggy. They then emptied the smoke house, store room & meat house, giving to the negroes what they did not want. They then took from the fowl house what poultry they wanted, took the two plantation guns, & used great threats about the wine & brandy. To our great relief they did not enter the house again, & at 1.30 A.M. drove off. They told the negroes if they worked for their master again they would shoot them when they came back. What the future is to be to us God only knows. I feel that my trust is still unshaken in his all protecting Providence. I have all confidance in the fidelity of the negroes & their attachment to us if they are not restrained from showing it. We are all up for the night as the excitement is too great to permit sleep - - - - - 9 A M at the usual hour this morning the house negroes came in— They seemed much distressed & said the troops told them last night if they came to the yard or did anything for us, they would shoot them—That a large troop would come today. We told them to go back & not bring trouble upon themselves, until we could see the Commanding officer. The fidelity & attachment of some who have come forward is very gratifying. The girls have been cooking our simple breakfast & we have taken our first meal under the new regime. I long for a visit from some officer in authority, that we may know our future condition & whether the negroes will be allowed to hire themselves to us or not. I know if they are not restrained there are many who would willingly & gladly help us. I had heard often of insurrectionary feelings among the negroes, but I never believed they would be brought to it of their own accord. The experience of this war, & especially of last night all tend to confirm that conviction. Even when compelled by intimidation, & fear of the consequences to their lives, many of them evince real distress, & not one has yet joined in any language or act of defiance. Their fidelity & attachment is amazing with the temptations before them. Those who were engaged in the sacking of the store room & meat house, did so stealthily & I believe not until they were commanded to help themselves.

S. 4   Inauguration of Presdt. Lincoln today for his 2d term of 4 years. Will any thing come out of it in respect to the war? The negroes are completely bewildered at the change of their condition. Many are truly distressed, some of the younger ones delirious with the prospect of good living & nothing to do. Some are willing to remain & work, but object to gang work,—all is in a chaotic state. When they were told that they were free, some said they did not wish to be free, & they were immediately silenced with threats of being shot. I fear this region will be a desolate waste in one year hence, if this state of things continue - - On Thursday night when the army was camped here, their troops were among our negroes, distributing sugar, coffee, meats & bread in profusion—they killed 8 or 10 of the sheep & had them cooked in the negro yard. This was all intended as an earnest of the good things which followed their freedom. . . .

M. 6   The events of the past week have brought up vividly before us the horrors of the French Revolution—& those startling scenes which Dickens describes in his "Tale of two cities". We are in a fearful & trying crisis. If those who had unsettled the present order of things in the name of Humanity, were consistent, they would make some effort to order the freed negroes for their good, & ought to take some steps toward restoring order & recommanding & enforcing some plan by which such a large number may escape the horrors of insubordination, violence & ultimately starvation. The negroes are intoxicated with the idea of freedom. Many of them are deluded into the hope that their future is to be provided for by the U S. Govt. —& hence they do not feel the necessity of work. Many are disposed to remain, but perhaps will insist on terms which are incompatable with discipline & good management. It is a fearful crisis.

T. 7   No disposition evinced among the negroes to go to work. There seems to be sullenness which I dislike to see. I think those who are disposed to work or to do for us, are restrained. I hear that many of the negroes are armed with pistols & guns. Some were at Black Oak last night firing off pistols. This is a bad feature in this fearful period. — Oh, Humanity! what crimes are committed in thy name. One week ago we were in the midst of a peaceful, contented & orderly population — now all is confusion, disorder, discontent, violence, anarchy. If those who uprooted the old order of things had remained long enough to reconstruct another system in which there should be order restored, it would have been well, but they have destroyed our system & left us in the ruins — "God is our refuge & strength, a very present help in trouble" - - - - The negroes are rambling about the country. This morning 4 mounted on horses & mules rode through the negro yard, stopping for a while, & some have passed through in vehicles. It is said they were told to go to St Stephens for horses which the army left behind.

W. 8   We heard guns again last night, but cannot learn from the negroes who fired them. The disordered state of affairs keeps us anxious. . . . On this day a week ago the old system of slave labour was in peaceful operation. The breath of Emancipation has passed over the country, & we are now in that transition state between the new & the old systems — a state of chaos & disorder. Will the negro be materially benefitted by the change? Will the condition of the country in its productive resources, in material prosperity be improved? Will it be a benefit to the landed proprietors? These are questions which will have their solution in the future. They are in the hands of that Providence which over-ruleth all things for good. It was a strong conviction of my best judgement that the old relation of master & slave, had received the divine sanction & was the best condition in which the two races could live together for mutual benefit. There were many defects to be corrected & many abuses to be remedied, which I think would have been done if we had gained our independence & were freed from outside pressure. Among these defects I will enumerate the want of legislation to make the marriage contract binding — to prevent the separation of families, & to restrain the cupidity of cruel masters. Perhaps it is for neglecting these obligations that God has seen fit to dissolve that relation. I believe the negro must remain in this country & that his condition although a freed-man, must be to labour on the soil. Nothing but necessity will compel him to labour. Now the question is, will that necessity be so strong as to compel him to labour, which will be profitable to the landed proprietors. Will he make as much cotton, sugar, rice & tobacco for the world as he did previously? They will now have a choice *where* to labour. This will ensure good treatment & the best terms. The most humane, the most energetic & the most judicious managers have the best chances in the race for success. I expect to see a revolution in the ownership of landed estates. Those only can succeed who bring the best capacity for the business. Time will show. . . .

Sunday 12   Some of the very peculiar traits of negro character are now exhibited. John & Solomon left Morefield on Thursday with the black troops wild with excitement & probably drunk—In all this reign of disorder & anarchy I have not seen or heard of any violence or even of rudeness or incivility from the plantation negroes. Docility & submissiveness still prevail. There are two exhibitions of character which have surprised us, & which were never anticipated. 1st. On many places where there was really kind treatment & mutual attachment, the exciting events of the last week or two, & the powerful temptations brought to bear upon them, have seemed to snap the ties suddenly. Some have left their comfortable homes & kind masters & friends, & gone off with the army, thinking to better their conditions. We must be patient & charitable in our opinions—They are ignorant of what they have to encounter, mere children in knowledge & experience, excitable, impulsive & have fallen under the tempting delusions presented to them in such glowing terms—Some who are disposed to take a proper view of their condition, & to return to work, are intimidated & kept back by threats from the more strong & overbearing. They do not clearly comprehend this situation—they have been told they are free, & their idea of freedom is associated with freedom from work & toil. In many places there was bad discipline & little care for the negroes. These are generally the foremost in all the acts of disorder, — & their example & word keep back others. We are astonished at this defection when we do not expect it, but on reflection the causes at work are sufficient to account for it. 2nd. Had we been told four years ago, that our negroes would have withstood the temptation to fidelity which have been constantly before them during the war, we would have doubted the possibility—& had we been told further of the events of the last two weeks, the incitements to acts of violence both by the example & the precepts of the black troops all throughout this region, we would have shuddered for the consequences. Except from the black soldiers, I have not heard of a single act of violence, or even of rude or uncivil language. Their behaviour is perfectly civil so far, & I believe, with a judicous course on the part of the whites, will continue so. This whole revolution from its commencement has developed in its progress, a course of events which no human sagacity on either side, ever foresaw. We are carried along by an inscrutable providence to the consummation of great & radical changes, — we are the actors in a Great Revolution where, not civil institutions only, but social polity, must be reconstructed & re-organized. . . .

May [1865]

May M. 1   Gen Lees surrender took place on the 9th.ult, but it only reached us through our papers & the returning prisoners about a week ago. . . . [This] means the loss of our Independence for which we have been struggling for four years with immense loss of life & property. But the fate of nations is controlled & over-ruled by a wise Providence, which sees the end from the beginning, & orders all things in the highest wisdom. Whatever therefore may be the will of God regarding our destiny, I accept His decision as final & as eminently good. I have honestly believed we were right in our revolution, & would receive the divine sanction—if I have erred, I pray God to forgive me the error, & I submit with perfect satisfaction to His decree, knowing that He cannot err.

M. 22. We begin now to realize the ruin to property which the war has entailed upon us. All classes & conditions of men will suffer who had property, except the small farmers who owned no negroes. Confederate securities, I consider a total loss. Bank stock, confederation & private bonds, are all more or less dependent for their availability upon Confed securities, & upon the value of negro property; both of which are lost. The Rail road companies are nearly all ruined by the destruction of their roads & the heavy debt they must incur to rebuild. The only money now in possession of our people is coin in small quantities which had been hoarded through the war, & some bills of the local banks. There will be but little means of increasing this amount for some time to come, as provisions are scarce, & the cotton has been mostly burnt, captured or sold. The financial prospect is a gloomy one, & there will be much distress before our conditions can improve. . . .

M. 29 I went in to Aiken this morning & called at the hotel to inquire if any officer in Aiken was authorized to administer the Oath of Allegiance. They expected in a day or two to have it done here. It is necessary now in order to save property, have personal protection, or exercise the rights of citizenship, or any business calling. Every one who is allowed, is now taking the oath, as the Confederate govt. is annulled, the state govt. destroyed, & the return into the Union absolutely necessary to our condition as an organized community. As Gen. Gillmore's order based upon Chief Justice Chase's opinion announces the freedom of the negroes there is no further room to doubt that it is the settled policy of the country. I have today formally announced to my negroes the fact, & made such arrangements with each as the new relation rendered necessary. Those whose whole time we need, get at present clothes & food, house rent & medical attendance. The others work for themselves giving me a portion of their time on the farm in lieu of house rent. Old Amelia & her two grandchildren, I will spare the mockery of offering freedom to. I must support them as long as I have any thing to give.

T. 30 My negroes all express a desire to remain with me. I am gratified at the proof of their attachment. I believe it to be real & unfeigned. For the present they will remain, but in course of time we must part, as I cannot afford to keep so many, & they cannot afford to hire for what I could give them. As they have always been faithful & attached to us, & have been raised as family servants, & have all of them been in our family for several generations, there is a feeling towards them somewhat like that of a father who is about to send out his children on the world to make their way through life. Those who have brought the present change of relation upon us are ignorant of these ties.

They have charged us with cruelty. They call us, man stealers, robbers, tyrants. The indignant denial of these changes & the ill feelings engendered during 30 years of angry controversy, have culminated at length in the four years war which has now ended. It has pleased God that we should fail in our efforts for independance—& with the loss of independance, we return to the Union under the dominion of the abolition sentiment. The experiment is now to be tried. The negro is not only to be emancipated, but is to become a citizen with all the right & priviledges! It produces a financial, political & social revolution at the South, fearful to contemplate in its ultimate effects. Whatever the result may be, let it be known & remembered that neither the negro slave nor his master is responsible. It has been done by those who having political power, are determined to carry into practice the sentimental philanthropy they have so long & angrily advocated. Now that is fixed. I pray God for the great issues at stake, that he may bless the effort & make it successful—make it a blessing & not a curse to the poor negro.

4

African Americans During Reconstruction
Felix Haywood et al.

The Thirteenth, Fourteenth, and Fifteenth Amendments to the U.S. Constitution decreed an equality between the races that did not become a reality in African Americans' daily lives. At first the federal government through the Freedman's Bureau and support for Reconstruction governments in southern states made vigorous efforts to help the freed slaves gain education, legal and medical services, reasonable employment contracts, and a measure of political power. But within about a decade those efforts were abandoned as the northern public, tired of disorder in the South and wary of government intervention, abandoned the ex-slaves to their ex-masters. The newly freed African Americans were soon left to respond however they could to the social revolution brought about by emancipation, the war's impoverishment of the South, and the violence of groups like the Ku Klux Klan. Historians have pieced together the story of their actions from a multiplicity of sources. Interviews with ex-slaves collected in the 1930s, of which you will here read a sample, are one important source.

BEFORE YOU READ

1. What, judging from these accounts, were the major problems the ex-slaves faced after the war?
2. What did these ex-slaves expect of freedom?
3. What role did the Ku Klux Klan play in ex-slaves' lives?
4. Why did some freedmen continue to work for their former masters?

FELIX HAYWOOD

San Antonio, Texas. Born in Raleigh,
North Carolina. Age at interview: 88.

The end of the war, it come just like that—like you snap your fingers. . . . How did we know it! Hallelujah broke out—

> Abe Lincoln freed the nigger
>   With the gun and the trigger;
> And I ain't going to get whipped any more.
>   I got my ticket,
> Leaving the thicket,
>   And I'm a-heading for the Golden Shore!

Soldiers, all of a sudden, was everywhere—coming in bunches, crossing and walking and riding. Everyone was a-singing. We was all walking on golden clouds. Hallelujah!

Union forever,
    Hurrah, boys, hurrah!
Although I may be poor,
    I'll never be a slave—
Shouting the battle cry of freedom.

Everybody went wild. We felt like heroes, and nobody had made us that way but ourselves. We was free. Just like that, we was free. It didn't seem to make the whites mad, either. They went right on giving us food just the same. Nobody took our homes away, but right off colored folks started on the move. They seemed to want to get closer to freedom, so they'd know what it was — like it was a place or a city. Me and my father stuck, stuck close as a lean tick to a sick kitten. The Gudlows started us out on a ranch. My father, he'd round up cattle—unbranded cattle—for the whites. They was cattle that they belonged to, all right; they had gone to find water 'long the San Antonio River and the Guadalupe. Then the whites gave me and my father some cattle for our own. My father had his own brand—7 B)—and we had a herd to start out with of seventy.

We knowed freedom was on us, but we didn't know what was to come with it. We thought we was going to get rich like the white folks. We thought we was going to be richer than the white folks, 'cause we was stronger and knowed how to work, and the whites didn't, and they didn't have us to work for them any more. But it didn't turn out that way. We soon found out that freedom could make folks proud, but it didn't make 'em rich.

Did you ever stop to think that thinking don't do any good when you do it too late? Well, that's how it was with us. If every mother's son of a black had thrown 'way his hoe and took up a gun to fight for his own freedom along with the Yankees, the war'd been over before it began. But we didn't do it. We couldn't help stick to our masters. We couldn't no more shoot 'em than we could fly. My father and me used to talk 'bout it. We decided we was too soft and freedom wasn't going to be much to our good even if we had a education.

WARREN McKINNEY

Hazen, Arkansas. Born in South Carolina.
Age at interview: 85.

I was born in Edgefield County, South Carolina. I am eighty-five years old. I was born a slave of George Strauter. I remembers hearing them say, "Thank God, I's free as a jay bird." My ma was a slave in the field. I was eleven years old when freedom was declared. When I was little, Mr. Strauter whipped my ma. It hurt me bad as it did her. I hated him. She was crying. I chunked him with rocks. He run after me, but he didn't catch me. There was twenty-five or thirty hands that worked in the field. They raised wheat, corn, oats, barley, and cotton. All the children that couldn't work stayed at one house. Aunt Mat kept the babies and small children that couldn't go to the field. He had a gin and a shop. The shop was at the fork of the roads. When the war come on, my papa went to built forts. He quit Ma and took another woman. When the war close, Ma took her four children, bundled 'em up and went to Augusta. The government give out rations there. My ma washed and ironed. People died in piles. I don't know till yet what was the matter. They said it was the change of living. I seen five or six wooden, painted coffins piled up on wagons pass by our house. Loads passed every day like you see cotton pass here. Some said it was cholera and some took consumption. Lots of the colored people nearly starved. Not much to get to do and not much houseroom. Several families had to live in one house. Lots of the colored folks went up North and froze to death. They couldn't stand the cold. They wrote back about them dying. No, they never sent them back. I heard some sent for money to come back. I heard plenty 'bout the Ku Klux. They scared the folks to death. People left Augusta in droves. About a thousand would all meet and walk going to hunt work and new homes. Some of them died. I had a sister and brother lost that way. I had another sister come to Louisiana that way. She wrote back.

I don't think the colored folks looked for a share of land. They never got nothing 'cause the white folks didn't have nothing but barren hills left. About all the mules was wore out hauling provisions in the army. Some folks say they ought to done more for the colored folks when they left, but they say they was broke. Freeing all the slaves left 'em broke.

That reconstruction was a mighty hard pull. Me and Ma couldn't live. A man paid our ways to Carlisle, Arkansas, and we come. We started working for Mr. Emenson. He had a big store, teams, and land. We liked it fine, and I been here fifty-six years now. There was so much wild game, living was not so hard. If a fellow could get a little bread and a place to stay, he was all right. After I come to this state, I voted some. I have farmed and worked at odd jobs. I farmed mostly. Ma went back to her old master. He persuaded her to come back home. Me and her went back and run a farm four or five years before she died. Then I come back here.

LEE GUIDON

South Carolina. Born in South Carolina.
Age at interview: 89.

Yes, ma'am, I sure was in the Civil War. I plowed all day, and me and my sister helped take care of the baby at night. It would cry, and me bumping it [in a straight chair, rocking.] Time I git it to the bed where its mama was, it wake up and start crying all over again. I be so sleepy. It was a puny sort of baby. Its papa was off at war. His name was Jim Cowan, and his wife Miss Margaret Brown 'fore she married him. Miss Lucy Smith give me and my sister to them. Then she married Mr. Abe Moore. Jim Smith was Miss Lucy's boy. He lay out in the woods all time. He say no need in him gitting shot up and killed. He say let the slaves be free. We lived, seemed like, on 'bout the line of York and

Union counties. He lay out in the woods over in York County. Mr. Jim say all the fighting 'bout was jealousy. They caught him several times, but every time he got away from 'em. After they come home Mr. Jim say they never win no war. They stole and starved out the South. . . .

After freedom a heap of people say they was going to name theirselves over. They named theirselves big names, then went roaming round like wild, hunting cities. They changed up so it was hard to tell who or where anybody was. Heap of 'em died, and you didn't know when you hear about it if he was your folks hardly. Some of the names was Abraham, and some called theirselves Lincum. Any big name 'cepting their master's name. It was the fashion. I heard 'em talking 'bout it one evening, and my pa say, "Fine folks raise us and we gonna hold to our own names." That settled it with all of us. . . .

I reckon I do know 'bout the Ku Kluck. I knowed a man named Alfred Owens. He seemed all right, but he was a Republican. He said he was not afraid. He run a tanyard and kept a heap of guns in a big room. They all loaded. He married a Southern woman. Her husband either died or was killed. She had a son living with them. The Ku Kluck was called Upper League. They get this boy to unload all the guns. Then the white men went there. The white man give up and said, "I ain't got no gun to defend myself with. The guns all unloaded, and I ain't got no powder and shot." But the Ku Kluck shot in the houses and shot him up like lacework. He sold fine harness, saddles, bridles — all sorts of leather things. The Ku Kluck sure run them outen their country. They say they not going to have them round, and they sure run them out, back where they came from. . . .

For them what stayed on like they were, Reconstruction times 'bout like times before that 'cepting the Yankee stole out and tore up a scandalous heap. They tell the black folks to do something, and then come white folks you live with and say Ku Kluck whup you. They say leave, and white folks say better not listen to them old yankees. They'll git you too far off to come back, and you freeze. They done give you all the use they got for you. How they do? All sorts of ways. Some stayed at their cabins glad to have one to live in and farmed on. Some running round begging, some hunting work for money, and nobody had no money 'cepting the Yankees, and they had no homes or land and mighty little work for you to do. No work to live on. Some going every day to the city. That winter I heard 'bout them starving and freezing by the wagon loads. I never heard nothing 'bout voting till freedom. I don't think I ever voted till I come to Mississippi. I votes Republican. That's the party of my color, and I stick to them as long as they do right. I don't dabble in white folks' business, and that white folks' voting is their business. If I vote, I go do it and go on home.

I been plowing all my life, and in the hot days I cuts and saws wood. Then when I gets outa cotton-picking, I put each boy on a load of wood and we sell wood. The last years we got $3 a cord. Then we clear land till next spring. I don't find no time to be loafing. I never missed a year farming till I got the

Bright's disease [one of several kinds of kidney ailments] and it hurt me to do hard work. Farming is the best life there is when you are able. . . .

When I owned most, I had six head mules and five head horses. I rented 140 acres of land. I bought this house and some other land about. The anthrax killed nearly all my horses and mules. I got one big fine mule yet. Its mate died. I lost my house. My son give me one room, and he paying the debt off now. It's hard for colored folks to keep anything. Somebody gets it from 'em if they don't mind.

The present times is hard. Timber is scarce. Game is about all gone. Prices higher. Old folks cannot work. Times is hard for younger folks too. They go to town too much and go to shows. They going to a tent show now. Circus coming, they say. They spending too much money for foolishness. It's a fast time. Folks too restless. Some of the colored folks work hard as folks ever did. They spends too much. Some folks is lazy. Always been that way.

I signed up to the government, but they ain't give me nothing 'cepting powdered milk and rice what wasn't fit to eat. It cracked up and had black something in it. A lady said she would give me some shirts that was her husband's. I went to get them, but she wasn't home. These heavy shirts give me heat. They won't give me the pension, and I don't know why. It would help me buy my salts and pills and the other medicines like Swamp Root. They won't give it to me.

TOBY JONES

Madisonville, Texas. Born in South Carolina.
Age at interview: 87.

I worked for Massa 'bout four years after freedom, 'cause he forced me to, said he couldn't 'ford to let me go. His place was near ruint, the fences burnt, and the house would have been, but it was rock. There was a battle fought near his place, and I taken Missy to a hideout in the mountains to where her father was, 'cause there was bullets flying everywhere. When the war was over, Massa come home and says, "You son of a gun, you's supposed to be free, but you ain't, 'cause I ain't gwine give you freedom." So I goes on working for him till I gits the chance to steal a hoss from him. The woman I wanted to marry, Govie, she 'cides to come to Texas with me. Me and Govie, we rides the hoss 'most a hundred miles, then we turned him a-loose and give him a scare back to his house, and come on foot the rest the way to Texas.

All we had to eat was what we could beg, and sometimes we went three days without a bite to eat. Sometimes we'd pick a few berries. When we got cold we'd crawl in a brushpile and hug up close together to keep warm. Once in a while we'd come to a farmhouse, and the man let us sleep on cottonseed in his barn, but they was far and few between, 'cause they wasn't many houses in the country them days like now.

When we gits to Texas, we gits married, but all they was to our wedding am we just 'grees to live together as man and wife. I settled on some land, and we cut some trees and split them open and stood them on end with the tops together for our house. Then we deadened some trees, and the land was ready to farm. There was some wild cattle and hogs, and that's the way we got our start, caught some of them and tamed them.

I don't know as I 'spected nothing from freedom, but they turned us out like a bunch of stray dogs, no homes, no clothing, no nothing, not 'nough food to last us one meal. After we settles on that place, I never seed man or woman, 'cept Govie, for six years, 'cause it was a long ways to anywhere. All we had to farm with was sharp sticks. We'd stick holes and plant corn, and when it come up we'd punch up the dirt round it. We didn't plant cotton, 'cause we couldn't eat that. I made bows and arrows to kill wild game with, and we never went to a store for nothing. We made our clothes out of animal skins.

WHY ADAM KIRK WAS A DEMOCRAT

(House Report No. 262, 43 Cong., 2 Sess., p. 106.
Statement of an Alabama Negro [1874].)

A white man raised me. I was raised in the house of old man Billy Kirk. He raised me as a body servant. The class that he belongs to seems nearer to me than the northern white man, and actually, since the war, everything I have got is by their aid and their assistance. They have helped me raise up my family and have stood by me, and whenever I want a doctor, no matter what hour of the day or night, he is called in whether I have got a cent or not. And when I want any assistance I can get it from them. I think they have got better principles and better character than the republicans.

5

White Southerners' Reactions to Reconstruction

Caleb G. Forshey and Reverend James Sinclair

The Congressional Joint Committee of Fifteen, assembled to examine Southern representation in Congress, was named in December 1865 as part of the Republican Congress's response to President Andrew Johnson's plan of Reconstruction. In 1866, the committee held hearings as part of its effort to develop the Fourteenth Amendment. Despite the president's veto, Congress had already enlarged the scope of the Freedmen's Bureau to care for displaced ex-slaves and to try by military commission those accused of depriving freedmen of civil rights. Republicans in Congress, in opposition to the Johnson administration, would continue to evolve a Reconstruction policy that attempted to protect the ex-slaves' rights.

Of the two white Southerners whose interviews with the committee you will read here, Caleb G. Forshey had supported secession while James Sinclair, although a slaveholder, had opposed it. A Scottish-born minister who had only moved to North Carolina in 1857, Sinclair's Unionist sentiments had led to the loss of his church and then to his arrest during the war. In 1865 he served on the Freedmen's Bureau.

BEFORE YOU READ

1. What effect did Caleb Forshey anticipate from military occupation of southern states?
2. What was his evaluation of the Freedmen's Bureau?
3. What were Forshey's beliefs about African Americans?
4. What were the strengths and weaknesses of the Freedmen's Bureau according to James Sinclair?
5. How does Sinclair's view of southern opinion differ from Forshey's?

CALEB G. FORSHEY

Washington, D.C., March 28, 1866

Question: Where do you reside?
Answer: I reside in the State of Texas.
Question: How long have you been a resident of Texas?
Answer: I have resided in Texas and been a citizen of that State for nearly thirteen years.
Question: What opportunities have you had for ascertaining the temper and disposition of the people of Texas towards the government and authority of the United States?

Answer: For ten years I have been superintendent of the Texas Military Institute, as its founder and conductor. I have been in the confederate service in various parts of the confederacy; but chiefly in the trans-Mississippi department, in Louisiana and Texas, as an officer of engineers. I have had occasion to see and know very extensively the condition of affairs in Texas, and also to a considerable extent in Louisiana. I think I am pretty well-informed, as well as anybody, perhaps, of the present state of affairs in Texas.

Question: What are the feelings and views of the people of Texas as to the late rebellion, and the future condition and circumstances of the State, and its relations to the federal government?

Answer: After our army had given up its arms and gone home, the surrender of all matters in controversy was complete, and as nearly universal, perhaps, as anything could be. Assuming the matters in controversy to have been the right to secede, and the right to hold slaves, I think they were given up tee-totally, to use a strong Americanism. When you speak of feeling, I should discriminate a little. The feeling was that of any party who had been cast in a suit he had staked all upon. They did not return from feeling, but from a sense of necessity, and from a judgment that it was the only and necessary thing to be done, to give up the contest. But when they gave it up, it was without reservation; with a view to look forward, and not back. That is my impression of the manner in which the thing was done. There was a public expectation that in some very limited time there would be a restoration to former relations. . . . It was the expectation of the people that, as soon as the State was organized as proposed by the President, they would be restored to their former relations, and things would go on as before.

Question: What is your opinion of a military force under the authority of the federal government to preserve order in Texas and to protect those who have been loyal, both white and black, from the aggressions of those who have been in the rebellion?

Answer: My judgment is well founded on that subject: that wherever such military force is and has been, it has excited the very feeling it was intended to prevent; that so far from being necessary it is very pernicious everywhere, and without exception. The local authorities and public sentiment are ample for protection. I think no occasion would occur, unless some individual case that our laws would not reach. We had an opportunity to test this after the surrender and before any authority was there. The military authorities, or the military officers, declared that we were without laws, and it was a long time before the governor appointed arrived there, and then it was sometime before we could effect anything in the way of organization. We were a people without law, order, or anything; and it was a time for violence if it would occur. I think it is a great credit to our civilization that, in that state of affairs, there was nowhere any instance of violence. I am proud of it, for I expected the contrary; I expected that our soldiers on coming home, many of them, would be dissolute, and that many of them would oppress the class of men you speak of; but it did not occur. But afterwards, wherever soldiers have been sent, there have been little troubles, none of them large; but personal collisions between soldiers and citizens.

Question: What is your opinion as to the necessity and advantages of the Freedmen's Bureau, or an agency of that kind, in Texas?

Answer: My opinion is that it is not needed; my opinion is stronger than that—that the effect of it is to irritate, if nothing else. While in New York city recently I had a conversation with some friends from Texas, from five distant points in the State. We met together and compared opinions; and the opinion of each was the same, that the negroes had generally gone to work since January; that except where the Freedmen's Bureau had interfered, or rather encouraged troubles, such as little complaints, especially between negro and negro, the negro's disposition was very good, and they had generally gone to work, a vast majority of them with their former masters. . . . The impression in Texas at present is that the negroes under the influence of the Freedmens's Bureau do worse than without it.

I want to state that I believe all our former owners of negroes are the friends of the negroes; and that the antagonism paraded in the papers of the north does not exist at all. I know the fact is the very converse of that; and good feeling always prevails between the masters and the slaves. But the negroes went off and left them in the lurch; my own family was an instance of it. But they came back after a time, saying they had been free enough and wanted a home.

Question: Do you think those who employ the negroes there are willing to make contracts with them, so that they shall have fair wages for their labor?

Answer: I think so; I think they are paid liberally, more than the white men in this country get; the average compensation to negroes there is greater than the average compensation of free laboring white men in this country. It seems to have regulated itself in a great measure by what each neighborhood was doing; the negroes saying, "I can get thus and so at such a place." Men have hired from eight to fifteen dollars per month during the year, and women at about two dollars less a month; house-servants at a great deal more.

Question: Do the men who employ the negroes claim to exercise the right to enforce their contract by physical force?

Answer: Not at all; that is totally abandoned; not a single instance of it has occurred. I think they still chastise children, though. The negro parents often neglect that, and the children are still switched as we switch our own children. I know it is done in my own house; we have little house-servants that we switch just as I do our own little fellows.

Question: What is your opinion as to the respective advantages to the white and black races, of the present free system of labor and the institution of slavery?

Answer: I think freedom is very unfortunate for the negro; I think it is sad; his present helpless condition touches my heart more than anything else I ever contemplated, and I think that is the common sentiment of our slaveholders. I have seen it on the largest plantations, where the negro men had all left, and where only women and children remained, and the owners had to keep them and feed them. The beginning certainly presents a touching and sad spectacle. The poor negro is dying at a rate fearful to relate.

I have some ethnological theories that may perhaps warp my judgment; but my judgment is that the highest condition the black race has ever reached or can reach, is one where he is provided for by a master race. That is the result of a great deal of scientific investigation and observation of the negro character by me ever since I was a man. The labor question had become a most momentous one, and I was studying it. I undertook to investigate the condition of the negro from statistics under various circumstances, to treat it purely as a matter of statistics from the census tables of this country of ours. I found that the free blacks of the north decreased 8 per cent.; the free blacks of the south increased 7 or 8 per cent., while the slaves by their sides increased 34 per cent. I inferred from the doctrines of political economy that the race is in the best condition when it procreates the fastest; that, other things being equal, slavery is of vast advantage to the negro. I will mention one or two things in connexion with this as explanatory of that result. The negro will not take care of his offspring unless required to do it, as compared with the whites. The little children will die; they do die, and hence the necessity of very rigorous regulations on our plantations which we have adopted in our nursery system.

Another cause is that there is no continence among the negroes. All the continence I have ever seen among the negroes has been enforced upon plantations, where it is generally assumed there is none. For the sake of procreation, if nothing else, we compel men to live with their wives. The discipline of the plantation was more rigorous, perhaps, in regard to men staying with their wives, than in regard to anything else; and I think the procreative results, as shown by the census tables, is due in a great measure to that discipline. . . .

Question: What is the prevailing inclination among the people of Texas in regard to giving the negroes civil or political rights and privileges?

Answer: I think they are all opposed to it. There are some men—I am not among them—who think that the basis of intelligence might be a good basis for the elective franchise. But a much larger class, perhaps nine-tenths of our people, believe that the distinctions between the races should not be broken down by any such community of interests in the management of the affairs of the State. I think there is a very common sentiment that the negro, even with education, has not a mind capable of appreciating the political institutions of the country to such an extent as would make him a good associate for the white man in the administration of the government. I think if the vote was taken on the question of admitting him to the right of suffrage there would be a very small vote in favor of it—scarcely respectable: that is my judgment.

REVEREND JAMES SINCLAIR

Washington, D.C., January 29, 1866

Question: What is generally the state of feeling among the white people of North Carolina towards the government of the United States?

Answer: That is a difficult question to answer, but I will answer it as far as my own knowledge goes. In my opinion, there is generally among the white people not much love for the government. Though they are willing, and I believe determined, to acquiesce in what is inevitable, yet so far as love and affection for the government is concerned, I do not believe that they have any of it at all, outside of their personal respect and regard for President Johnson.

Question: How do they feel towards the mass of the northern people—that is, the people of what were known formerly as the free States?

Answer: They feel in this way: that they have been ruined by them. You can imagine the feelings of a person towards one whom he regards as having ruined him. They regard the northern people as having destroyed their property or taken it from them, and brought all the calamaties of this war upon them.

Question: How do they feel in regard to what is called the right of secession?

Answer: They think that it was right . . . that there was no wrong in it. They are willing now to accept the decision of the question that has been made by the sword, but they are not by any means converted from their old opinion that they had a right to secede. It is true that there have always been Union men in our State, but not Union men without slavery, except perhaps among Quakers. Slavery was the central idea even of the Unionist. The only difference between them and the others upon that question was, that they desired to have that institution under the aegis of the Constitution, and protected by it. The secessionists wanted to get away from the north altogether. When the secessionists precipitated our State into rebellion, the Unionists and secessionists went together, because the great object with both was the preservation of slavery by the preservation of State sovereignty. There was another class of Unionists who did not care anything at all about slavery, but they were driven by the other whites into the rebellion for the purpose of preserving slavery. The poor whites are to-day very much opposed to conferring upon the negro the right of suffrage; as much so as the other classes of the whites. They believe it is the intention of government to give the negro rights at their expense. They cannot see it in any other light than that as the negro is elevated they must proportionately go down. While they are glad that slavery is done away with, they are bitterly opposed to conferring the right of suffrage on the negro as the most prominent secessionists; but it is for the reason I have stated, that they think rights conferred on the negro must necessarily be taken from them, particularly the ballot, which was the only bulwark guarding their superiority to the negro race.

Question: In your judgment, what proportion of the white people of North Carolina are really, and truly, and cordially attached to the government of the United States?

Answer: Very few, sir; very few. . . .

Question: Is the Freedmen's Bureau acceptable to the great mass of the white people in North Carolina?

Answer: No, sir; I do not think it is; I think the most of the whites wish the bureau to be taken away.

Question: Why do they wish that?

Answer: They think that they can manage the negro for themselves: that they understand him better than northern men do. They say, "Let us understand what you want us to do with negro — what you desire of us; lay down your conditions for our readmission into the Union, and then we will know what we have to do, and if you will do that we will enact laws for the government of these negroes. They have lived among us, and they are all with us, and we can manage them better than you can." They think it is interfering with the rights of the State for a bureau, the agent and representative of the federal government, to overslaugh the State entirely, and interfere with the regulations and administration of justice before their courts.

Question: Is there generally a willingness on the part of the whites to allow the freedmen to enjoy the right of acquiring land and personal property?

Answer: I think they are very willing to let them do that, for this reason; to get rid of some portion of the taxes imposed upon their property by the government. For instance, a white man will agree to sell a negro some of his land on condition of his paying so much a year on it, promising to give him a deed of it when the whole payment is made, taking his note in the mean time. This relieves that much of the land from taxes to be paid by the white man. All I am afraid of is, that the negro is too eager to go into this thing; that he will ruin himself, get himself into debt to the white man, and be forever bound to him for the debt and never get the land. I have often warned them to be careful what they did about these things.

Question: There is no repugnance on the part of the whites to the negro owning land and personal property?

Answer: I think not.

Question: Have they any objection to the legal establishment of the domestic relations among the blacks, such as the relation of husband and wife, of parent and child, and the securing by law to the negro the rights of those relations?

Answer: That is a matter of ridicule with the whites. They do not believe the negroes will ever respect those relations more than the brutes. I suppose I have married more than two hundred couples of negroes since the war, but the whites laugh at the very idea of the thing. Under the old laws a slave could not marry a free woman of color; it was made a penal offence in North Carolina for any one to perform such a marriage. But there was in my own family a slave who desired to marry a free woman of color, and I did what I conceived to be my duty, and married them, and I was presented to the grand jury for doing so, but the prosecuting attorney threw out the case and would not try it. In former times the officiating clergyman marrying slaves, could not use the usual formula: "Whom God has joined together let no man put asunder"; you could not say, "According to the ordinance of God I pronounce you man and wife; you are no longer two but one." It was not legal for you to do so.

Question: What, in general, has been the treatment of the blacks by the whites since the close of hostilities?

Answer: It has not generally been of the kindest character, I must say that; I am compelled to say that.

Question: Are you aware of any instance of personal ill treatment towards the blacks by the whites?

Answer: Yes, sir.

Question: Give some instances that have occurred since the war.

Answer: [Sinclair describes the beating of a young woman across her buttocks in graphic detail.]

Question: What was the provocation, if any?

Answer: Something in regard to some work, which is generally the provocation.

Question: Was there no law in North Carolina at that time to punish such an outrage?

Answer: No, sir; only the regulations of the Freedmen's Bureau; we took cognizance of the case. In old times that was quite allowable; it is what was called "paddling."

Question: Did you deal with the master?

Answer: I immediately sent a letter to him to come to my office, but he did not come, and I have never seen him in regard to the matter since. I had no soldiers to enforce compliance, and I was obliged to let the matter drop.

Question: Have you any reason to suppose that such instances of cruelty are frequent in North Carolina at this time—instances of whipping and striking?

Answer: I think they are; it was only a few days before I left that a woman came there with her head all bandaged up, having been cut and bruised by her employer. They think nothing of striking them.

Question: And the negro has practically no redress?

Answer: Only what he can get from the Freedmen's Bureau.

Question: Can you say anything further in regard to the political condition of North Carolina—the feeling of the people towards the government of the United States?

Answer: I for one would not wish to be left there in the hands of those men; I could not live there just now. But perhaps my case is an isolated one from the position I was compelled to take in that State. I was persecuted, arrested, and they tried to get me into their service; they tried everything to accomplish their purpose, and of course I have rendered myself still more obnoxious by accepting an appointment under the Freedmen's Bureau. As for myself I would not be allowed to remain there. I do not want to be handed over to these people. I know it is utterly impossible for any man who was not true to the Confederate States up to the last moment of the existence of the confederacy, to expect any favor of these people as the State is constituted at present.

Question: Suppose the military pressure of the government of the United States should be withdrawn from North Carolina, would northern men and true Unionists be safe in that State?

Answer: A northern man going there would perhaps present nothing obnoxious to the people of the State. But men who were born there, who have been true to the Union, and who have fought against the rebellion, are worse off than northern men. . . .

Question: In your judgment, what effect has been produced by the liberality of the President in granting pardons and amnesties to rebels in that State — what effect upon the public mind?

Answer: On my oath I am bound to reply exactly as I believe; that is, that if President Johnson is ever a candidate for re-election he will be supported by the southern States, particularly by North Carolina; but that his liberality to them has drawn them one whit closer to the government than before, I do not believe. It has drawn them to President Johnson personally, and to the Democratic party, I suppose.

6

Teacher of the Freedmen
Sarah Jane Foster

With the ending of the Civil War, many Northerners journeyed south seeking a wide range of personal goals. Some sought political power in the newly organized southern Republican Party or economic opportunity in what they hoped would be a moderniz- ing South. Others pursued far more idealistic goals. Sarah Jane Foster's diary and let- ters are among the few autobiographical writings supplying the personal dimension to the great story of the hundreds of Northerners—the majority of them women—who went south during and after the Civil War to educate former slaves. Foster, born in a country town in Maine in 1839, struggled as an educator and missionary in Mar- tinsburg, West Virginia, and Harper's Ferry, Virginia, to win over both blacks and whites. She struggled with rowdies and vandals who attacked her school and was crit- icized even by her missionary brethren for turning for protection to the African Amer- ican men who accompanied her through the streets after school or religious services. We have no later reflections from Foster about how her experiences in the South affected her because she died of yellow fever in 1868.

BEFORE YOU READ

1. How would you describe Foster's attitude toward her black students?
2. What evidence can you find in her letters of white attitudes toward her work in Martinsburg?
3. Why did Foster and the farm woman who gave her party water have such dif- ferent attitudes toward the battlefield at Antietam?
4. How did Foster's perceptions of both whites and blacks change while teaching in the South?

Martinsburg, West Va., Feb. 11th, 1866
Dear Advocate [a Maine Newspaper]:—

My day school . . . is growing larger. Its list is now seventy, while the night list approaches fifty. By the aid of the older scholars I have succeeded in cutting off about an hour and a half from my daily labors, but, even then, I spend not less than forty-two hours per week in the school-room, counting my Sabbath school and the meetings that I attend. Yet I am wonderfully sustained.—With all the changefulness of the climate and the humidity of the air, I find the place healthy, and never enjoyed better health anywhere. There has been no further disturbance, and I now walk home alone though the soldiers are yet in town, for I think it better to show no distrust. I understand that it was reported in the Baltimore American that our school was disturbed by returned rebel soldiers. I am not aware that such was in any instance the case, and think it but just to say I anticipate no trouble from them.

I spoke of good spelling in my last letter. Week before last a boy of sixteen, named Willoughby Fairfax, who chanced to recite alone, spelled seventy-five long words and only missed *two*. At the beginning of the year he was in words of four letters. He is one of my best pupils but not the best in spelling as good as he is. A girl of thirteen bears off the palm in that branch.

I now have several who are making creditable progress in cyphering, not to mention the boys who do easy sums on their slates, which I set to relieve the tedium of study. I have also several very good pupils in Geography, and actually hear some as good map lessons as I could expect to at home. Quite a number are learning fast to write. A great many are in Mental Arithmetic. I even have one small class in the night school who recite in the old but good Colburn's Arithmetic, which quite carries me back to my early school-days again. I have met with two copies each of Webster's and Town's spelling Books. Those most common are Comly's, which are not so good as either of the above. But, in spite of all the disadvantages, the scholars are bound to prove their capacity to learn. They are usually fond of school, and punctual in attendance, and, as a class, orderly on the street.

I daily become more and more interested in the school, and in all that concerns the welfare of the colored people here.

Martinsburg, W. Va., Feb. 28th, 1866

Dear Advocate:—Again I snatch a few minutes to pen a short report of my school and its affairs. We are having now I judge about the fullest school that we shall have at all. The weather of late has been such as to allow the small children to come, and young men and women, who will soon be out at service for the summer, are now improving the time to come to school for a while. Even now the schools begin to change a little. The day school for a week or two has diminished a little, and the other has proportionately increased. One after another they come to me with the remark "Miss Jenny, I can't come to day-school anymore, I'm going to work, but I'll come at night," and they do so all that they can. The boy to whose spelling I alluded in my last will not be able to come any more than this week, for his father has bought a farm in the country and has work for him now: I regret to lose so good a scholar, but he will not fail to do well anywhere.

The cognomen[1] of "nigger teacher" seems to have died out, and I occasionally hear my own name as I pass in the street, or, more frequently some person is notified that "there goes the Freedmen's Bureau." I have not met with any annoyance on the street but once, and then a white man addressed an insolent remark to me as I was going into the school-room door. I don't mind such things at all. Report has married or engaged me several times to men connected with the school, and, Mrs. Vosburgh was actually asked by a neighbor the day I was there "if I was not part nigger." I hope they will believe it, for

1. **cognomen:** nickname.

then surely they could not complain of my teaching the people of my own race. But Rev. Mr. Osborne preaches at our school room tonight, and I must prepare to go.

In haste, Sarah J. Foster

Diary, 1866

Thursday, March 1

I have enjoyed today very much, for the air has been mild and springlike. People are working their gardens. My school glides along smoothly too. Tonight Mary Brown came in to school to see me. Waited half an hour to talk with me afterward. We did not walk together on the street but she came after me and stopped at the shop window to call out Isaac. A lady(?) called out "Is that a 'nigger' or a white woman?" just as I passed her referring to Mary at the shop.

Friday, March 2

A springlike overcast day. I fear it will rain tomorrow. My day and evening in school were as usual pleasant. Will Fairfax has done coming for now. He must work. I gave him a nice book. He seemed glad of it. I also gave him my last Advocate letter in which I had praised him.

Tonight two white men came in to school for about twenty minutes. They were civil, but will doubtless go off and be as hard as they can.

Yesterday we made up a party for the Antietam battle-ground. We had a sky blue U.S. wagon, with a black oil-cloth cover that would roll up at the sides. That was filled and the rest of the party went on horseback. The party included Mr. and Mrs. Brackett, Mr. Given, the Misses Dudley, Wright, Gibbs and Libby, Mrs. Smith and myself, besides a Mr. Ames formerly of Massachusetts — now trading here, and a Mrs. Clemmen and her daughter also from Massachusetts, a young colored man named Keyes, invited to go as a friend and to point out localities, and our sable driver. Mr. Ames and Mr. and Mrs. Brackett rode horseback all the way, and Miss Clemmen nearly all, while Mr. Given and Mr. Keyes alternated with each other. We made a merry party, and seemed to attract a great deal of attention. We first visited the Burnside bridge near which we lunched on the grass, drinking from a cold spring that has doubtless slaked the thirst of many a wounded and dying soldier. Then we moved over to the place where the Irish Brigade fought. — Dismounting we walked about among the trees which bore many scars of shot and shell — bits of shell yet remaining in some of them. Mr. Keyes got our party some water at a house not far beyond the battle field. They inquired where we were from. He told them from New England, and that we came to visit the battle ground. They seemed to think us a long way from home, and he did not correct the impression that we came on purpose to see Antietam. The lady of the house said that eight thousand dead bodies were interred on her farm, and previously Mr. Keyes had pointed out a large field, once filled with graves, now cultivated over. The lady spoke of it without seeming conscious of the horrible sacrilege of thus utilizing a nation's hallowed ground. We soon turned back from the plough polluted graveyard, and, coming to Bloody Lane, drove up it a little way, trying to fancy what it must have been when piled with reeking corpses, but the horror of the field beyond yet clung to us and no one alighted to search for relics. The place seemed too awful for tarrying.

Letter from Virginia

Harper's Ferry, April 20th, 1866

Dear Advocate:—it is now two weeks since I opened school here. Miss Gibbs retains the school that she has had from the first, except that a few of the poorest scholars have been put in the other department. So she has a fine school, while mine are yet in the earliest stages of reading, or else unable to read at all. The coloured people here are scattered, and many of them in very destitute circumstances. They do not now come into school so well as they did last term. The older ones are gone out at service and smaller ones, who have long distances to come, fear to do so without protection; for the white boys will molest them when they find an opportunity. The boys of both races seem rather pugilistic[2] about here. They have had several battles for the possession of this hill as a playground. The weapons were stones, and both parties were in earnest. My scholars at Martinsburg, though not destitute of spirit and courage, had the good sense to avoid collisions with the white boys, who often played marbles before the door. Jefferson County is much more aristocratic than Berkeley, and, as a consequence, the coloured people seem much more degraded as a class here than they are there. Here is a field for much mission labor. In Berkeley County there are more of the blacks who are competent to care for the interests of their race. But they are not dull here. Several children, who two weeks ago did not know the alphabet, are now reading in words of three letters. In the short time that we have taught out here, many, who did not know a letter, have learned to read in the Testament, and to spell well. The united testimony from all our schools is, that color is no barrier to progress.

I have four boys in my school who are so white that I should not suspect their lineage elsewhere. One has straight, light hair, and all are fine looking. Miss Gibbs has several little girls who are even whiter, or "brighter," as they call it here. One in particular, very appropriately named Lillie, has flaxen hair and grey blue eyes. One white boy comes to my school. His brother lives in the chambers here, and very wisely discards prejudice that he may have the benefit of a free school.

Last Sabbath our Sabbath school was reorganized here, some colored teachers being appointed; as Mr. Brackett wishes to get them prepared to continue the school after we go home in hot weather. Each of us takes a class. I do not know personally a member of mine, but hope to get acquainted.

2. **pugilistic:** fighting.

Letter from Virginia

Harper's Ferry, May 2d, 1866

Dear Advocate: — When I last wrote to you I thought it possible that I might be sent to Smithfield, but now my school has come up to a list of forty, with a prospect of nearly thirty daily in fair weather. As I have thirteen in the alphabet, and all are beginners in reading, I find enough to do. I have now got the school classified and systematized, and taught to come and go by strokes of the bell. The colored children fall into systematic regulations quite well, and seem to like them too. They annoy us most of all by whispering and laughing. The little ones will forget and whisper, and all laugh easily. They improve in that however. I sometimes use their laughter as a sort of spur to dull scholars, letting them laugh at their blunders, and it works well, for they are sensitive to ridicule. We have to use all ways and means to keep up their ambition and to encourage them to study. I tried, when I first began at Martinsburg, to avoid corporeal punishment. I found it impossible, but yet, by due severity when forced to punish, I did not have it to do very often. The fact is, the colored people are practical followers of Solomon. They show very great attachment to their children, making great efforts to reclaim them if they have been sold away, but they are very severe in governing them. They expect a teacher to be so too, and the children are of the same opinion. They really like a teacher better who compels them to perfect obedience. I followed the theory at once on acquaintance, and it worked well. I grew to like some of my pupils very much, and the attachment was mutual.

I spoke of the efforts of parents to recover children who had been sold away. One woman here has exerted herself to find her four children at great expense, though dependent on her own labor altogether. She has only been able to recover two, though she has made a journey to Richmond and back to try and obtain the others, who were sold away in that vicinity. Not only has she found those two, but she has bought clothing for them, and has never drawn a ration from the Bureau, though supporting her mother also. I know two young men who have gathered together their father and mother, a sister and two infant children, and four nephews and nieces from seven to fourteen years of age. By joint efforts the family dress neatly and live entirely unaided. Where are the white men who could voluntarily burden themselves with the children of deceased relatives, while young, single, and dependent on their daily labor? I think that parallel cases among us are rare, and yet we have been asked to believe that this race are only fit for chattels, and that they felt separation as little as the brutes. A deeper, darker falsehood was never palmed upon the public. It contradicts itself at every stage of our acquaintance with them. Stronger domestic affection I never saw than some of them exhibit.

I have spoken of the variations of some familiar hymns. One occurs to me now, It is this:

> Jesus my all to heaven is gone, —
> He's coming again by and by —

> He whom I've fixed my hopes upon—
> He's coming again by and by.
> Christ's coming again, Christ's coming again,
> He's coming again by and by,
> He'll come this time, and He'll come no more,
> He's coming again by and by.

And that is about the style of their peculiar hymns. They are nearly all chorus, but I like to hear them. They can all come in on the chorus after one or two repetitions, and, in a full meeting, the effect of their full melodious voices is thrilling and inspiring. As they sing they sway back and forth in time to the music, and some even step to it in a way that seems like dancing, only the whole body is in a quiver of excitement. At a meeting when a number are seeking the Savior, they will make a circle at the close around the "mourner's bench," where the seekers kneel meeting after meeting till they find peace. The circle then join hands, taking also the hands of their kneeling friends, and begin to sing, swaying as I have described, or lifting and dropping their hands in regular time. They will sing hymn after hymn with increasing earnestness, till the more excitable singers, and very likely some of the mourners, are shouting. The jumping, leaping and bodily contortions of a "shout" are beyond all description. They must be seen to be understood. For a long time I saw none of this at Martinsburg, and indeed the leading members there never practiced it, but they seem to think that converts can be brought out in no other way.

"They're going to sing over Isaac," said a colored woman to me, as I looked a little surprised to see them grouping around the bench at which one of my schoolboys was kneeling. I found that nearly all thought that the way to be "brought through." Some never yielded to it, and I am satisfied that none ever affected the emotion that convulsed those who were influenced by it. Even the white Methodists are very much the same about here; so it is not to be wondered at at all. On Saturday night we had here the most magnificent thunder shower that it was ever my lot to witness. The effect of the lightning, as the vivid chains lit up the darkness and played over the Heights, was sublime and awe-inspiring. It is quite chilly here now much of the time. We have needed a fire all day to-day. We have had some quite warm weather a day or two at a time, however, but we did not realize it much except when we descended to the village below the Hill. Here there is usually a breeze, and we can keep quite cool, I think, as long as we shall stay.

Some collisions are constantly occurring around here between the "chivalry"[3] and the colored people. A sister of Mr. Keyes had an amusing triumph recently. A poor white neighbor struck her with no reasonable provocation, the fault being wholly her own. At first Mrs. Poles did not resent, but when the beating was recommenced, she retaliated in self-defense. The woman had her arrested, seeming not to know that a colored woman could have a right

---

3. **chivalry:** Southern gentry.

to defend herself, or that she was amenable to the law for having struck first. When the case was tried before a Justice in Bolivar, she gained a little valuable experience, and had the privilege of paying the costs. The justice, I learn, referred to the Civil Rights Bill, and also intimated that the Bureau had an influence upon his decision. Well it might here, for Major Welles is an excellent and efficient officer. Only this week a colored man was knocked down for remonstrating a little because some white men had broken open his stable, taking his horse to plow with, and refusing to give it back at his request. The Justice simply made them deliver up the horse, but he designs to bring a suit for assault, to see what will be done about it. An aggravated case of assault took place in Charlestown, the particulars of which I have not yet learned. I think that some test cases will have to be brought up to prove the extent and validity of the Civil Rights Bill. The Bureau officers will probably look out for that, and may thus benefit the Freedmen a great deal.

7

Work Under Sharecropper
and Labor Contracts

Grimes Family
and Swindell Brothers

The end of slavery and the impoverishment of the South in the aftermath of the Civil War seriously disrupted southern agriculture. Five years after the war's end, southern cotton production was still only about half of what it had been in the 1850s. The large plantations, no longer tended by gangs of slaves or hired freedmen, were broken up into smaller holdings, but the capital required for profitable agriculture meant that control of farming remained centralized in a limited elite of merchants and larger landholders.

Various mechanisms arose to finance southern agriculture. Tenants worked on leased land and small landowners gave liens on their crops to get financing. But the most common method of financing agriculture was sharecropping. Agreements like the Grimes family's sharecrop contract determined the economic life of thousands of poor rural families in the southern United States after the Civil War. Families, both African American and white, lacking capital for agriculture were furnished the seed, implements, and a line of credit for food and other necessities to keep them through the growing season. Accounts were settled in the winter after crops were in. Under these conditions a small number of farmers managed to make money and eventually became landowners, but the larger part found themselves in ever deeper debt at the end of the year, with no choice but to contract again for the next year.

Another form of labor contract was the agreement, like that of the Swindell Brothers firm, to pay the passage to America for immigrants with needed skills in return for their agreeing to work for a fixed period of time. Under pressure from labor organizations, this form of labor recruitment, legalized during the Civil War, was banned in 1885.

BEFORE YOU READ

1. What restrictions on the freedom of sharecroppers were built into the contract?
2. Which restrictions might have been the most significant in preventing croppers from achieving independence?
3. Why would labor organizations object to agreements like the Swindell contract?
4. What would motivate workers to enter into such contracts?

GRIMES FAMILY PAPERS

To every one applying to rent land upon shares, the following conditions must be read, and *agreed to.*

To every 30 or 35 acres, I agree to furnish the team, plow, and farming implements, except cotton planters, and I *do not* agree to furnish a cart to every cropper. The croppers are to have half of the cotton, corn and fodder (and peas and pumpkins and potatoes if any are planted) if the following conditions are compiled with, but—if not—they are to have only two fifths (2/5). Croppers are to have no part or interest in the cotton seed raised from the crop planted and worked by them. No vine crops of any description, that is, no watermelons, muskmelons, . . . squashes or anything of that kind, except peas and pumpkins, and potatoes, are to be planted in the cotton or corn. All must work under my direction. All plantation work to be done by the croppers. My part of the crop to be *housed* by them, and the fodder and oats to be hauled and put in the house. All the cotton must be topped about 1st August. If any cropper fails from any cause to save all the fodder from his crop, I am to have enough fodder to make it equal to one half of the whole if the whole amount of fodder had been saved.

For every mule or horse furnished by me there must be 1000 good sized rails . . . hauled, and the fence repaired as far as they will go, the fence to be torn down and put up from the bottom if I so direct. All croppers to haul rails and work on fence whenever I may order. Rails to be split when I may say. Each cropper to clean out every ditch in his crop, and where a ditch runs between two croppers, the cleaning out of that ditch is to be divided equally between them. Every ditch bank in the crop must be shrubbed down and cleaned off before the crop is planted and must be cut down every time the land is worked with his hoe and when the crop is "laid by," the ditch banks must be left clean of bushes, weeds, and seeds. The cleaning out of all ditches must be done by the first of October. The rails must be split and the fence repaired before corn is planted.

Each cropper must keep in good repair all bridges in his crop or over ditches that he has to clean out and when a bridge needs repairing that is outside of all their crops, then any one that I call on must repair it.

Fence jams to be done as ditch banks. If any cotton is planted on the land outside of the plantation fence, I am to have *three fourths* of all the cotton made in those patches, that is to say, no cotton must be planted by croppers in their home patches.

All croppers must clean out stables and fill them with straw, and haul straw in front of stables whenever I direct. All the cotton must be manured, and enough fertilizer must be brought to manure each crop highly, the croppers to pay for one half of all manure bought, the quantity to be purchased for each crop must be left to me.

No cropper to work off the plantation when there is any work to be done on the land he has rented, or when his work is needed by me or other croppers. Trees to be cut down on Orchard, House field & Evanson fences, leaving such as I may designate.

Road field to be planted from the *very edge of the ditch to the fence*, and all the land to be planted close up to the ditches and fences. *No stock of any kind* belonging to croppers to run in the plantation after crops are gathered.

If the fence should be blown down, or if trees should fall on the fence outside of the land planted by any of the croppers, any one or all that I may call upon must put it up and repair it. Every cropper must feed, or have fed, the team he works, Saturday nights, Sundays, and every morning before going to work, beginning to feed his team (morning, noon, and night *every day* in the week) on the day he rents and feeding it to and including the 31st day of December. If any cropper shall from any cause fail to repair his fence as far as 1000 rails will go, or shall fail to clean out any part of his ditches, or shall fail to leave his ditch banks, any part of them, well shrubbed and clean when his crop is laid by, or shall fail to clean out stables, fill them up and haul straw in front of them whenever he is told, he shall have only two-fifths (2/5) of the cotton, corn, fodder, peas and pumpkins made on the land he cultivates.

If any cropper shall fail to feed his team Saturday nights, all day Sunday and all the rest of the week, morning/noon, and night, for every time he so fails he must pay me five cents.

No corn nor cotton stalks must be burned, but must be cut down, cut up and plowed in. Nothing must be burned off the land except when it is *impossible* to plow it in.

Every cropper must be responsible for all gear and farming implements placed in his hands, and if not returned must be paid for unless it is worn out by use.

Croppers must sow & plow in oats and haul them to the crib, but *must have no part of them*. Nothing to be sold from their crops, nor fodder nor corn to be carried out of the fields until my rent is all paid, and all amounts they owe me and for which I am responsible are paid in full.

I am to gin & pack all the cotton and charge every cropper an eighteenth of his part, the cropper to furnish his part of the bagging, ties, & twine.

The sale of every cropper's part of the cotton to be made by me when and where I choose to sell, and after deducting all they owe me and all sums that I may be responsible for on their accounts, to pay them their half of the net proceeds. Work of every description, particularly the work on fences and ditches, to be done to my satisfaction, and must be done over until I am satisfied that it is done as it should be.

No wood to burn, nor light wood, nor poles, nor timber for boards, nor wood for any purpose whatever must be gotten above the house occupied by Henry Beasley—nor must any trees be cut down nor any wood used for any purpose, except for firewood, without my permission.

SWINDELL BROTHERS CONTRACT

Antwerp, Dec. 15, 1882

Agreement between the firm of Swindell Bros. of the first part, and John Schmidt, gatherer, and Carl Wagner, blower, of the second part.

The undersigned, of the second part, covenants and agrees with the party of the first part that they will for two consecutive years, beginning January 1, 1882, work and duly perform such duties as instructed by the party of the first part or his superintendents. The party of the first part covenants and agrees to pay the undersigned, who may duly perform their duties, the price generally paid by Baltimore manufacturers for the size of 16 by 24 inches, and all sheets shall be estimated at eight sheet of 36 by 54 inches for 100 square feet. The party of the first part covenants and agrees that the wages of each glassblower shall be an average of $80 per calendar month, on condition that he makes 180 boxes of 100 square feet per calendar month.

The gatherer shall receive 65 percent of the sum paid the blower for wages per calendar month for actual work performed during the fire. It is agreed that the party of the first part shall retain 10 percent of the wages of each and every workman until the expiration of this contract as a guarantee of the faithful performance of the provisions of this contract. The aforesaid 10 percent shall be forfeited by each and every workman who shall fail to comply with the provisions of this contract.

It is further agreed that the party of the first part shall advance the passage money for the parties of the second part.

It is further agreed that the party of the first part have the right to discharge any of the workmen for drunkenness or neglect of duty, or for disturbing the peace, or creating dissatisfaction among them, or for joining any association of American workmen.

The said Swindell Bros., their heirs, and assigns, shall be considered the parties of the first part, and they agree to pay each blower $12 per week and the gatherer $9.00 per week, on condition that each perform his work faithfully at every blowing. The parties of the first part agrees to make monthly settlements for the parties of the second part, after the advances for the passage, etc., shall have been repaid. Provided you faithfully perform your work for the term of contract (two years), we will pay back the passage money from Europe to America.

Swindell Bros.
Yohonn Schmidt, *Gatherer*
Carl Wagener, *Blower*

8

Anti-Lynching Campaign in Tennessee
Ida B. Wells

Lynching—the murder of a person accused of some offense, real or imagined, by a mob—is an old crime in the United States. The word can be traced back to the way Colonel Charles Lynch and his fellow Patriots in revolutionary Virginia dealt with suspected Tories. Lynchings, especially of blacks, began to increase in the 1880s and peaked in 1892, the worst year in American history for this particularly brutal crime.

Thomas Moss, Calvin McDowell, and Henry Stewart, friends of Wells's and respectable and successful members of the Memphis African American community, were among the approximately two hundred fifty people whose lynchings were recorded in 1892. (There were doubtless more of which no record was made.) The murder of her friends changed Wells's entire life. Already well known as a leading African American journalist and reformer—she had sued a railroad company in 1883 for forcing her to leave a "whites-only" car—she left Memphis after her angry editorial on the lynchings put her life in danger, and she became a life-long activist against the crime. Her campaign helped make opposition to lynching a leading cause among African American activists until World War II, when lynchings largely—but not completely—ceased. (The murders in 1964 of civil rights workers James Chaney, Andrew Goodman, and Michael Schwerner were lynchings.)

In answering the accusation that lynching was the response to "The New Negro Crime"—the propensity of black men to rape white women—Wells researched in detail the circumstances of the 728 lynchings of the previous ten years that she was able to authenticate. Her evidence refuted the excuse that the victims had committed rape. Only a third of black lynching victims were even accused of rape. Many died for crimes like "race prejudice," "making threats," or "quarreling with whites." Some of the victims were women and even children.

BEFORE YOU READ

1. How did Wells explain the lynchings of her friends and others? Do you agree with her?

2. What was Wells's strategy for Memphis African Americans to respond to the lynchings? What do you think of it?

3. Do you agree with Wells that "every white man in Memphis who consented" to the lynchings and rioting "is as guilty as those who fired the guns"?

While I was thus carrying on the work of my newspaper, happy in the thought that our influence was helpful and that I was doing the work I loved and had

Alfreda M. Duster, ed., *Crusade for Justice: The Autobiography of Ida B. Wells* (Chicago: University of Chicago Press, 1970), pp. 47–52.

proved that I could make a living out of it, there came the lynching in Memphis which changed the whole course of my life. . . .

Thomas Moss, Calvin McDowell, and Henry Stewart owned and operated a grocery store in a thickly populated suburb [of Memphis]. Moss was a letter carrier and could only be at the store at night. Everybody in town knew and loved Tommie. An exemplary young man, he was married and the father of one little girl, Maurine, whose godmother I was. He and his wife Betty were the best friends I had in town. And he believed, with me, that we should defend the cause of right and fight wrong wherever we saw it.

He delivered mail at the office of the *Free Speech,* and whatever Tommie knew in the way of news we got first. He owned his little home, and having saved his money he went into the grocery business with the same ambition that a young white man would have had. He was the president of the company. His partners ran the business in the daytime.

They had located their grocery in the district known as the "Curve" because the streetcar line curved sharply at that point. There was already a grocery owned and operated by a white man who hitherto had had a monopoly on the trade of this thickly populated colored suburb. Thomas's grocery changed all that, and he and his associates were made to feel that they were not welcome by the white grocer. The district being mostly colored and many of the residents belonging either to Thomas's church or to his lodge, he was not worried by the white grocer's hostility.

One day some colored and white boys quarreled over a game of marbles and the colored boys got the better of the fight which followed. The father of the white boys whipped the victorious colored boy, whose father and friends pitched in to avenge the grown white man's flogging of a colored boy. The colored men won the fight, whereupon the white father and grocery keeper swore out a warrant for the arrest of the colored victors. Of course the colored grocery keepers had been drawn into the dispute. But the case was dismissed with nominal fines. Then the challenge was issued that the vanquished whites were coming on Saturday night to clean out the People's Grocery Company.

Knowing this, the owners of the company consulted a lawyer and were told that as they were outside the city limits and beyond police protection, they would be justified in protecting themselves if attacked. Accordingly the grocery company armed several men and stationed them in the rear of the store on that fatal Saturday night, not to attack but to repel a threatened attack. And Saturday night was the time when men of both races congregated in their respective groceries.

About ten o'clock that night, when Thomas was posting his books for the week and Calvin McDowell and his clerk were waiting on customers preparatory to closing, shots rang out in the back room of the store. The men stationed there had seen several white men stealing through the rear door and fired on them without a moment's pause. Three of these men were wounded, and others fled and gave the alarm.

Sunday morning's paper came out with lurid headlines telling how officers of the law had been wounded while in the discharge of their duties, hunting up criminals whom they had been told were harbored in the People's Grocery Company, this being "a low dive in which drinking and gambling were carried on: a resort of thieves and thugs." So ran the description in the leading white journals of Memphis of this successful effort of decent black men to carry on a legitimate business. The same newspaper told of the arrest and jailing of the proprietor of the store and many of the colored people. They predicted that it would go hard with the ringleaders if these "officers" should die. The tale of how the peaceful homes of that suburb were raided on that quiet Sunday morning by police pretending to be looking for others who were implicated in what the papers had called a conspiracy, has been often told. Over a hundred colored men were dragged from their homes and put in jail on suspicion.

All day long on that fateful Sunday white men were permitted in the jail to look over the imprisoned black men. Frenzied descriptions and hearsays were detailed in the papers, which fed the fires of sensationalism. Groups of white men gathered on the street corners and meeting places to discuss the awful crime of Negroes shooting white men.

There had been no lynchings in Memphis since the Civil War, but the colored people felt that anything might happen during the excitement. Many of them were in business there. Several times they had elected a member of their race to represent them in the legislature in Nashville. And a Negro, Lymus Wallace, had been elected several times as a member of the city council and we had had representation on the school board several times. Mr. Fred Savage was then our representative on the board of education.

The manhood which these Negroes represented went to the county jail and kept watch Sunday night. This they did also on Monday night, guarding the jail to see that nothing happened to the colored men during this time of race prejudice, while it was thought that the wounded white men would die. On Tuesday following, the newspapers which had fanned the flame of race prejudice announced that the wounded men were out of danger and would recover. The colored men who had guarded the jail for two nights felt that the crisis was past and that they need not guard the jail the third night.

While they slept a body of picked men was admitted to the jail, which was a modern Bastille. This mob took out of their cells Thomas Moss, Calvin Mc-Dowell, and Henry Stewart, the three officials of the People's Grocery Company. They were loaded on a switch engine of the railroad which ran back of the jail, carried a mile north of the city limits, and horribly shot to death. One of the morning papers held back its edition in order to supply its readers with the details of that lynching.

From its columns was gleaned the above information, together with details which told that "It is said that Tom Moss begged for his life for the sake of his wife and child and his unborn baby"; that when asked if he had anything to say, told them to "tell my people to go West—there is no justice for them here"; that Calvin McDowell got hold of one of the guns of the lynchers and because they could not loosen his grip a shot was fired into his closed fist. When the three bodies were found, the fingers of McDowell's right hand had been shot to pieces and his eyes were gouged out. This proved that the one who wrote that news report was either an eyewitness or got the facts from someone who was.

The shock to the colored people who knew and loved both Moss and Mc-Dowell was beyond description. Groups of them went to the grocery and elsewhere and vented their feelings in talking among themselves, but they offered no violence. Word was brought to the city hall that Negroes were massing at the "Curve" where the grocery had been located. Immediately an order was issued by the judge of the criminal court sitting on the bench, who told the sheriff to "take a hundred men, go out to the Curve at once, and shoot down on sight any Negro who appears to be making trouble."

The loafers around the courts quickly spread the news, and gangs of them rushed into the hardware stores, armed themselves, boarded the cars and rushed out to the Curve. They obeyed the judge's orders literally and shot into any group of Negroes they saw with as little compunction as if they had been on a hunting trip. The only reason hundreds of Negroes were not killed on that day by the mobs was because of the forebearance of the colored men. They realized their helplessness and submitted to outrages and insults for the sake of those depending upon them.

This mob took possession of the People's Grocery Company, helping themselves to food and drink, and destroyed what they could not eat or steal. The creditors had the place closed and a few days later what remained of the stock was sold at auction. Thus, with the aid of the city and county authorities and the daily papers, that white grocer had indeed put an end to his rival Negro grocer as well as to his business.

As said before, I was in Natchez, Mississippi, when the worst of this horrible event was taking place. Thomas Moss had already been buried before I reached home. Although stunned by the events of that hectic week, the *Free Speech* felt that it must carry on. Its leader for that week said:

> The city of Memphis has demonstrated that neither character nor standing avails the Negro if he dares to protect himself against the white man or become his rival. There is nothing we can do about the lynching now, as we are outnumbered and without arms. The white mob could help itself to ammunition without pay, but the order was rigidly enforced against the selling of guns to Negroes. There is therefore only one thing left that we can do; save our money and leave a town which will neither protect our lives and property, nor give us a fair trial in the courts, but takes us out and murders us in cold blood when accused by white persons.

This advice of the *Free Speech*, coupled with the last words of Thomas Moss, was taken up and reechoed among our people throughout Memphis. Hundreds disposed of their property and left. Rev. R. N. Countee and Rev. W. A. Brinkley, both leading pastors, took their whole congregations with them as they, too, went West. Memphis had never seen such an upheaval among colored people. Business was practically at a standstill, for the Negro was famous then, as now, for spending his money for fine clothes, furniture, jewelry, and pianos and other musical instruments, to say nothing of good things to eat. Music houses had more musical instruments, sold on the installment plan, thrown back on their hands than they could find storage for.

Six weeks after the lynching the superintendent and treasurer of the City Railway Company came into the office of the *Free Speech* and asked us to use our influence with the colored people to get them to ride on the streetcars again. When I asked why they came to us the reply was that colored people had been their best patrons, but that there had been a marked falling off of their patronage. There were no jim crow streetcars in Memphis then. I asked what they thought was the cause. They said they didn't know. They had heard Negroes were afraid of electricity, for Memphis already had streetcars run by electricity in 1892. They wanted us to assure our people that there was no danger and to tell them that any discourtesy toward them would be punished severely.

But I said that I couldn't believe it, because "electricity has been the motive power here for over six months and you are just now noticing the slump. How long since you have observed the change?" "About six weeks," said one of them. "You see it's a matter of dollars and cents with us. If we don't look after the loss and remedy the cause the company will get somebody else who will."

"So your own job then depends on Negro patronage?" I asked. And although their faces flushed over the question they made no direct reply. "You see it is like this," said the superintendent. "When the company installed electricity at a cost of thousands of dollars last fall, Negro labor got a large share of it in wages in relaying tracks, grading the streets, etc. And so we think it is only fair that they should give us their patronage in return."

Said I, "They were doing so until six weeks ago, yet you say you don't know the cause of the falling off. Why, it was just six weeks ago that the lynching took place." "But the streetcar company had nothing to do with the lynching," said one of the men. "It is owned by northern capitalists." "And run by southern lynchers," I retorted. "We have learned that every white man of any standing in town knew of the plan and consented to the lynching of our boys. Did you know Tom Moss, the letter carrier?" "Yes," he replied.

"A finer, cleaner man than he never walked the streets of Memphis," I said. "He was well liked, a favorite with everybody; yet he was murdered with no more consideration than if he had been a dog, because he as a man defended his property from attack. The colored people feel that every white man in Memphis who consented to his death is as guilty as those who fired the guns which took his life, and they want to get away from this town.

"We told them the week after the lynching to save their nickels and dimes so that they could do so. We had no way of knowing that they were doing so before this, as I have walked more than I ever did in my life before. No one has been arrested or punished about that terrible affair nor will they be because all are equally guilty."

"Why don't the colored people find the guilty ones?" asked one of them. "As if they could. There is strong belief among us that the criminal court judge himself was one of the lynchers. Suppose we had the evidence; could we get it before that judge? Or a grand jury of white men who had permitted it to be? Or force the reporter of the *Appeal* to tell what he saw and knows about that night? You know very well that we are powerless to do any of these things."

"Well we hope you will do what you can for us and if you know of any discourtesy on the part of our employees let us know and we will be glad to remedy it."

When they left the office I wrote this interview for the next issue of the *Free Speech* and in the article told the people to keep up the good work. Not only that, I went to the two largest churches in the city the next Sunday, before the paper came out, and told them all about it. I urged them to keep on staying off the cars.

Every time word came of people leaving Memphis, we who were left behind rejoiced. Oklahoma was about to be opened up, and scores sold or gave away property, shook Memphis dust off their feet, and went out West as Tom Moss had said for us to do.

This detail of an Indian drawing, called a pictograph, by Kicking Bear, recalls the defeat of George Armstrong Custer's force at the battle of the Little Big Horn, June 25, 1876.

PART TWO

Western Settlement

Winners and Losers

The West has always been—and continues to be—among the most polyglot regions of the United States, uneasily shared by people of Mexican, Anglo-American, Chinese, and an extremely wide range of Native American backgrounds. While the Mexican War had earlier ensured Anglo-American dominance of the West, it was like deserts and semiarid regions all over the world in having always been sparsely populated. But the renewed westward movement of Anglo-Americans and some African Americans after the Civil War fundamentally altered the region. Now a substantial number of people, supported by sophisticated technologies for transportation, farming, mining, and defending this difficult environment, streamed into the West. The building of the transcontinental railroads not only sped this westward migration, it also encouraged immigrants from the other East—tens of thousands of Chinese workers who, as James Rusling describes, built railroads and contributed to virtually every part of western society. Within a generation, the region had become an important supplier of raw materials for the vast American industrial empire that developed across the continent in the years after the Civil War. The last forbidding corners of this rugged world were finally mapped in this era, exacting daily feats of death-defying heroism such as those of John Wesley Powell and the members of his expedition through the Grand Canyon.

The heroic venture of moving westward has dominated the American imagination. Within this triumphal story, Americans have often been generous in remembering—with whatever distortions of myth—the losers as well as the winners. This is especially true of the Indian resistance to this westward sweep. The Plains Indians who defeated George Armstrong Custer at the battle of the Little Big Horn epitomize in most American minds the whole history of native America. The Points of View readings on this battle will help you penetrate the mists of legend and assess the event in its time and place. And the experience of western Indians after the heroic age can be viewed in the writings of Zitkala-Sä, a Lakota Sioux woman who discovered the ironies of assimilation.

The West in the twentieth century has lost some of its air of triumph. California, long imagined as the destination for those pursuing the American dream, has seen extensive outmigration in recent years. The plains states have seen declines in rural population for a generation, but remarkably, a comeback for the American bison and a flourishing of Native American cultures. The harsh climate has proven as inhospitable as the banks and railroads of the 1880s and 1890s to the dreams that Luna Kellie and her family brought to the Great Plains.

Points of View: The Battle of the Little Big Horn (1876)

9

Vengeance Against "Long Hair"

She Walks with Her Shawl and One Bull

Americans vividly remember the Plains Indians, whose last great victory came at the Little Big Horn in 1876, the "feather-streaming, buffalo-chasing, wild-riding, recklessly fighting Indian of the plains," as the historian William Brandon describes their young male warriors. In most American imaginations they are the archetype of the American Indian.

The reality is far more complex, however. The religion, elaborate warrior code, fierce grief for the dead, and stunning rituals and visions of other worlds were largely borrowed from the many Indian cultures these nomads briefly conquered as they swept across the plains in the eighteenth and nineteenth centuries on horses first brought to the Americas by the Spanish conquistadors. Not the tomahawk but the rifle, acquired from French, English, and, later, American traders, was their main weapon. And the beads were all from Europe. Anthropologists use the term syncretic *to describe the culture of nomadic Plains Indians like the Lakota Sioux: a magnificent amalgam of all the peoples they had encountered. Native American, surely, but in this they were also quintessentially American.*

The horse and rifle brought wealth and military might. The plains became a terrain of ritual hunting and warfare, and prosperity permitted extensive trade and the elaboration of Indian cultures. For about a century, competing powers hindered white conquest. But over time the French, Spanish, English, and Mexicans ceased to be counterweights to the rising power of the Anglo-Americans. Emigrants to the West Coast and then settlers disrupted Indian life, and the Civil War divided and weakened the western Indians even as it strengthened the federal government. Then came the wasteful white buffalo hunters, the miners, the railroads, rushes of settlers, and a determined U.S. Army. A series of Indian wars, beginning during the Civil War, rapidly pushed into reservations all but a few Plains Indians.

By 1876 the great western saga, "America's Iliad" as Brandon calls it, appeared about over. But thousands of Sioux and Northern Cheyenne, still off of or escaping from the reservations, gathered briefly at the Little Big Horn to enjoy religious rituals, hunting, and their defiance of the U.S. Army. George Armstrong Custer and his premier Indian fighters, the Seventh Cavalry, found them there and promptly attacked.

We see the ensuing battle through the eyes of a Hunkpapa Lakota woman, She Walks with Her Shawl, and a Minneconjou Lakota man, One Bull, the adopted son of Sitting Bull. Keep in mind that both accounts are filtered through white interviewers.

BEFORE YOU READ

1. Observe in each account how these informants reacted to the battle. What role did each assume? What can you learn about Lakota culture from their actions?

2. What can you infer about Sitting Bull's role from One Bull's account?

3. On the basis of these accounts, does the usual characterization of the battle as a "massacre" seem accurate? Why or why not?

SHE WALKS WITH HER SHAWL
(HUNKPAPA LAKOTA)

Account given to Walter S. Campbell in 1931

I was born seventy-seven winters ago, near Grand River, [in present] South Dakota. My father, Slohan, was the bravest man among our people. Fifty-five years ago we packed our tents and went with other Indians to Peji-slawakpa (Greasy Grass). We were then living on the Standing Rock Indian reservation [Great Sioux Reservation, Standing Rock Agency]. I belonged to Sitting Bull's band. They were great fighters. We called ourselves Hunkpapa. This means confederated bands. When I was still a young girl (about seventeen) I accompanied a Sioux war party which made war against the Crow Indians in Montana. My father went to war 70 times. He was wounded nearly a dozen times.

But I am going to tell you of the greatest battle. This was a fight against Pehin-hanska (General Custer). I was several miles from the Hunkpapa camp when I saw a cloud of dust rise beyond a ridge of bluffs in the east. The morning was hot and sultry. Several of us Indian girls were digging wild turnips. I was then 23 years old. We girls looked towards the camp and saw a warrior ride

Jerome A. Greene, ed., *Lakota and Cheyenne, Indian Views of the Great Sioux War, 1876–1877* (Norman: University of Oklahoma Press, 1994), 42–46, 54–59.

swiftly, shouting that the soldiers were only a few miles away and that the women and children including old men should run for the hills in an opposite direction.

I dropped the pointed ash stick which I had used in digging turnips and rans towards my tipi. I saw my father running towards the horses. When I got to my tent, mother told me that news was brought to her that my brother had been killed by the soldiers. My brother had gone early that morning in search for a horse that strayed from our herd. In a few moments we saw soldiers on horseback on a bluff just across the Greasy Grass (Little Big Horn) river. I knew that there would be a battle because I saw warriors getting their horses and tomahawks.

I heard Hawkman shout, Ho-ka-he! Ho-ka-he! (Charge.) The soldiers began firing into our camp. Then they ceased firing. I saw my father preparing to go to battle. I sang a death song for my brother who had been killed.

My heart was bad. Revenge! Revenge! For my brother's death. I thought of the death of my young brother, One Hawk. Brown Eagle, my brother's companion on that morning had escaped and gave the alarm to the camp that the soldiers were coming. I ran to a nearby thicket and got my black horse. I painted my face with crimson and unbraided my black hair. I was mourning. I was a woman, but I was not afraid.

By this time the soldiers (Reno's men) were forming a battle line in the bottom about a half mile away. In another moment I heard a terrific volley of carbines. The bullets shattered the tipi poles. Women and children were running away from the gunfire. In the tumult I heard old men and women singing death songs for their warriors who were now ready to attack the soldiers. The chanting of death songs made me brave, although I was a woman. I saw a warrior adjusting his quiver and grasping his tomahawk. He started running towards his horse when he suddenly recoiled and dropped dead. He was killed near his tipi.

Warriors were given orders by Hawkman to mount their horses and follow the fringe of a forest and wait until commands were given to charge. The soldiers kept on firing. Some women were also killed. Horses and dogs too! The camp was in great commotion.

Father led my black horse up to me and I mounted. We galloped towards the soldiers. Other warriors joined in with us. When we were nearing the fringe of the woods an order was given by Hawkman to charge. Ho-ka-he! Ho-ka-he! Charge! Charge! The warriors were now near the soldiers. The troopers were all on foot. They shot straight, because I saw our leader killed as he rode with his warriors.

The charge was so stubborn that the soldiers ran to their horses and, mounting them, rode swiftly towards the river. The Greasy Grass river was very deep. Their horses had to swim to get across. Some of the warriors rode into the water and tomahawked the soldiers. In the charge the Indians rode among the troopers and with tomahawks unhorsed several of them. The soldiers were very excited. Some of them shot into the air. The Indians chased the soldiers across the river and up over a bluff.

Then the warriors returned to the bottom where the first battle took place. We heard a commotion far down the valley. The warriors rode in a column of fives. They sang a victory song. Someone said that another body of soldiers were attacking the lower end of the village. I heard afterwards that the soldiers were under the command of Long Hair (Custer). With my father and other youthful warriors I rode in that direction.

We crossed the Greasy Grass below a beaver dam (the water is not so deep there) and came upon many horses. One soldier was holding the reins of eight or ten horses. An Indian waved his blanket and scared all the horses. They got away from the men (troopers). On the ridge just north of us I saw blue-clad men running up a ravine, firing as they ran.

The dust created from the stampeding horses and powder smoke made everything dark and black. Flashes from carbines could be seen. The valley was dense with powder smoke. I never heard such whooping and shouting. "There was never a better day to die," shouted Red Horse. In the battle I heard cries from troopers, but could not understand what they were saying. I do not speak English.

Long Hair's troopers were trapped in an enclosure. There were Indians everywhere. The Cheyennes attacked the soldiers from the north and Crow King from the South. The Sioux Indians encircled the troopers. Not one got away! The Sioux used tomahawks. It was not a massacre, but [a] hotly contested battle between two armed forces. Very few soldiers were mutilated, as oft has been said by the whites. Not a single soldier was burned at the stake. Sioux Indians do not torture their victims.

After the battle the Indians took all the equipment and horses belonging to the soldiers. The brave men who came to punish us that morning were defeated; but in the end, the Indians lost. We saw the body of Long Hair. Of course, we did not know who the soldiers were until an interpreter told us that the men came from Fort Lincoln, then [in] Dakota Territory. On the saddle blankets were the cross saber insignia and the letter seven.

The victorious warriors returned to the camp, as did the women and children who could see the battle from where they took refuge. Over sixty Indians were killed and they were also brought back to the camp for scaffold-burial. The Indians did not stage a victory dance that night. They were mourning for their own dead. . . .

ONE BULL (MINNECONJOU LAKOTA)

Account given to John P. Everett in the 1920s

I was in Sitting Bull's camp on [Little] Big Horn River, One Horn Band Hinkowoji [Minneconjou] Tepee. They were called that because they planted their gardens near the river. Itazipco (Without Bow [Sans Arc]) was another band. Ogalala [Oglala] was the Red Cloud band. Another band, Schiyeio means Cheyenne. They were a different tribe, not Lakota. They were friends of Lakota.

Pizi (Gall) had another band. All the different bands camped together. There were many other chiefs with their bands. Four Horn and Two Moon and many others. Whenever the chiefs held a council they went to Sitting Bull's camp because he was a good medicine man.

Lakota and Cheyennes had gone to this camp to look after their buffalo and so young men and women could get acquainted. White men had driven our buffalo away from Lakota land. So we went where buffalo were to take care of them and keep white men away.

I was a strong young man 22 years old. On the day of the fight I was sitting in my tepee combing my hair. I don't know what time it was. About this time maybe. (Two P.M.) Lakota had no watches in those days. I had just been out and picketed my horses and was back in my tepee. I saw a man named Fat Bear come running into camp and he said soldiers were coming on the other side of the river and had killed a boy named Deeds who went out to picket a horse. Then I came out of my tepee and saw soldiers running their horses toward our camp on same side of the river. We could hear lots of shooting. I went to tepee of my uncle, Sitting Bull, and said I was going to go take part in the battle. He said, "Go ahead, they have already fired."

I had a rifle and plenty of shells, but I took that off and gave it to Sitting Bull and he gave me a shield. Then I took the shield and my tomahawk and got on my horse and rode up to where the soldiers were attacking us. They were firing pretty heavy. They were all down near the river in the timber. Lakota were riding around fast and shooting at them. I rode up to some Lakota and said, "Let's all charge at once." I raised my tomahawk and said, "Wakontanka help me so I do not sin but fight my battle." I started to charge. There were five Lakota riding behind me. We charged for some soldiers that were still fighting and they ran to where their horses were in the timber. Then the soldiers all started for the river. I turned my horse and started that way too and there was a man named Mato Washte (Pretty Bear) right behind me and he and his horse were shot down. I followed the soldiers. They were running for the river. I killed two with my tomahawk. Then the soldiers got across the river. I came back to where Pretty Bear was and got him up on my horse. He was wounded and covered with blood. I started my horse toward the river where the soldiers were, trying to get across.

Then I let Pretty Bear get off my horse and I went across the river after the soldiers. I killed one more of them with my tomahawk.

Then I saw four soldiers ahead of me running up the hill. I was just about to charge them when someone rode along beside me and said, "You better not go any farther. You are wounded." That was Sitting Bull. I was not wounded but I was all covered with blood that got on me when I had Pretty Bear on my horse. So I did what Sitting Bull told me. Then Sitting Bull rode back but I went on. Another Lakota went after these four soldiers. He had a rifle and shot one of them off his horse. One of the soldiers kept shooting back but without hitting us. The man that was with me was a Lakota but I did not know who he was. Now the soldiers were getting together up on the hill and we could see the other soldiers coming with the pack mules a long way off.

Then I went back across the river and rode down it a way, then I rode with the man who was shooting at the four soldiers and we crossed the river again just east of Sitting Bull's camp. We saw a bunch of horsemen up on a hill to the north and they were Lakotas. We rode up to them and I told them I had killed a lot of soldiers and showed them my tomahawk. Then I said I was going up and help kill Custer's soldiers, but Sitting Bull told me not to go so I didn't go but we rode up where we could see the Lakotas and Cheyennes killing Custer's men. They had been shooting heavy but the Indians charged them straight from the west and then some rode around them shooting and the Indians were knocking them off their horses and killing them with tomahawks and clubs. THEY WERE ALL KILLED. There were a lot of Sioux killed. The others were picking them up on their horses and taking them back to camp.

Then we had a war dance all night and in the morning we heard that the soldiers with the pack mules were up on the hill and the Sioux started up after them. I went with Sitting Bull and volunteered to go help kill these soldiers but Sitting Bull said no. So we watched the fight from a hill. I didn't have my rifle with me then, just my tomahawk. The Sioux surrounded them and they fought that way all day. The soldiers had ditches dug all around the hill. Then along towards sundown the Sioux broke camp and went [south] to the mountains.

The Sioux did not take any prisoners that I know of. I didn't see any. I don't know how many Indians there were, but it was a very big band. Many bands together. The Indians had rifles with little short cartridges. I didn't use mine.

After the fight we all stayed in the Big Horn Mountains about ten days. After that they broke camp and went north following along the Tongue River. Then we went to the Little Missouri, and we found a place where there must have been some soldiers for we found a lot of sacks of yellow corn piled up. Then some of the bands went one way and some went another. One little band went to Slim Buttes and they were all killed by soldiers.

I was with Sitting Bull all the time we were in camp on the [Little] Big Horn and saw him during the battle. He was telling his men what to do. The first I knew of any soldiers was when they killed the boy who went to picket his horse across the river from Sitting Bull's camp. Before we broke camp that night we saw the walking soldiers coming from down the river but my uncle said, "We won't fight them. We have killed enough. We will go. . . ."

10

So Preposterous an Idea

Holmes Offley Paulding

The battle of the Little Big Horn spoiled a national party. On June 25, 1876, the day that Alexander Graham Bell was demonstrating the telephone at the Centennial Exposition in Philadelphia, a massive gathering of Northern Plains Indians destroyed George Armstrong Custer's Seventh Cavalry. Eastern newspapers received the story only in time to publish it on July 5, 1876, one day after what had been designated as the nation's centennial. That a crack regiment like the Seventh Cavalry could be completely wiped out by Indians at such a moment in the development of a mighty industrial nation was, as Holmes Offley Paulding said, "preposterous." Yet it had happened.

After a lengthy period of pushing eastern Indians westward, forcing them to compete with the older Plains Indian tribes, the United States in the decade before the Civil War had begun pressuring all the Indians on the Great Plains to settle into reservations. That would remove them from areas desired by white miners and settlers and keep them from interfering with the trail routes and later the railroad routes to the West Coast. This required treaties setting aside Indian lands, armies to protect them from both white and Indian intruders, compensation for lands taken, and defined hunting and other rights. While several such treaties succeeded in bringing brief eras of peace, the relentless pressure of white settlement, conflicts between whites and Indians as well as among tribes, new gold and silver discoveries, the decimation of the buffalo herds, and the construction of railroads eventually brought renewed demands for Indian land and fresh clashes. This cycle of violence culminated with the Sioux War of 1876–1877, when the U.S. Army steadily conquered and forced onto reservations all the Plains Indians. The Lakota Sioux and a few other northern tribes were among the last to surrender their nomadic ways.

Holmes Offley Paulding, who considered Custer a "dear friend," was born in Washington, D.C., in 1852. He studied medicine and became a field surgeon with the Montana column, one of the armies pursuing the Sioux that fateful summer. Arriving at the Little Big Horn two days after the battle, Paulding in a letter to his mother describes what he saw.

BEFORE YOU READ

1. What was Paulding's attitude toward the Sioux?
2. Why did he and his fellow officers consider the idea of "any number of Sioux whipping that gallant regiment" so preposterous?
3. How did Paulding explain Custer's defeat?

A SURGEON AT THE LITTLE BIG HORN

April 21, 1876

The morning of May 23, a war party came over this side of the river & caught 3 of our men near the bluffs. They killed & mutilated these men and then rode off pursued by a party of our Cavalry, but they might as well hunt for a needle in a hay stack as Indians in the bad lands. I was sent out with a small party to bring in the bodies and we buried them in camp just after sunset.

During the ceremony there were about 200 Sioux on the bluffs across the river watching us & riding around in plain sight. A large camp was found up

Thomas R. Buecker, "A Surgeon at the Little Big Horn," *The Great Sioux War 1876–1877*, ed. Paul L. Hedren (Helena: Montana Historical Society Press, 1991), pp. 131–45.

the Rosebud about 18 miles off, but our genial C. O. did not deem it advisable to attack it, a chance any other commander would give any price for, and after laying there for 10 days with the Indians showing themselves everyday in plain sight, as though they knew what a harmless concern they were dealing with, he at last began to do something. *not* to cross the command in boats & attack— but to *go away.* and this he did, keeping on down the river till we met Terry & were turned back as soon as he heard of it.

Our C. O.'s excuse was that he had rec'd orders from St. Paul to guard *this* side of the Yellowstone. There's literal obedience for you. This whole trip has been a miserable farce and everything has been as disagreeable as idiotic, pig headed stupidity could make it. . . .

So far we have lost as many men doing nothing as Crook did in his winter campaign & a hard fight.

July 2, 1876

. . . Gen. Terrys staff went ahead with the Cavalry. It soon began to rain and as we marched into camp, nearly dark, we could see the Cavalry moving about for a night march undertaken on account of our scouts having come in with a report that there was a big smoke about 20 miles up the Little Horn river whose mouth was 16 miles above our camp.

Three [scouts] . . . had tried to get into camp the night before but had been driven away by the sentries who thought them hostile and had swum across the Big Horn where they were at that time opposite to us. Our remaining scouts tried to induse them to recross & deliver any word from Custer, but they said they were tired, sick and very much afraid and wouldn't come over. They yelled across the river that the day before Custer had attacked a village 14 or 15 miles up the Little Horn, where we could see the several immense columns of smoke, that he had been led into a trap & surrounded. The village consisting of 1900 lodges & over 8000 warriors, who had whipped him, shot down his men like buffalo & that there were no white men left except for a few who had got into the heavy brush and timber & that the Indians had set fire to it to drive them out or burn them & that they did not think any one was left, also that these Indians would come on down & attack us and do the same with us as they had with Custer who had twice as many men as our column, the whole 12 Cos. of the 7th Cavalry being with him for the first time in the history of the regiment, united, all newly remounted & splendidly equipped.

We of course could not credit so preposterous an idea as that, of any number of Sioux whipping that gallant regiment, so concluded that he had been trying to surprise the camp, perhaps 200 or 250 lodges, and while sneaking down some ravine at night without flankers had been discovered & had a volley poured in from the sides of the ravine above, which would have killed some of his advance guard & would perhaps have driven him back on his main column. But that as a matter of course they had gone in & cleaned out the village, and that the smoke we saw was from the burning up of lodges and plunder. We expected to find a guard left behind with my dear old friend Dr. Lord in charge of the wounded & Williams & I pictured to ourselves how glad he would be to have us come in and help him through. Custer, we supposed would be scattered over the country pursuing the fugitives.

Our scouts (20) however, had a big scare on & said they were afraid to go ahead, or even ride with the advance guard with Terry and the staff. They were ordered to the rear, and after talking together for a few minutes, turned tail and galloped off deserting us entirely.

We thought at the very worse Custer might have underestimated the force he was attacking & had perhaps fortified to await reinforcements, so we pushed ahead, sweeping up the valley as fast as we could go with the Inf'y (which is simply an encumbrance of the worst kind in chasing Indians)

We marched ahead nearing the fires until within 8 miles of them when we had gone nearly 26 miles, and at that point two men were sent out to try and communicate with Custer under a reward of $200 each in case of success. . . . Then about 5 miles ahead of us & opposite the fires (which we could see were burning timber but no lodges in sight) three large bodies of men, maybe 300 in all, rose up on the edge of the bluff and rested there, just on the crest, closely huddled together & looking in the distance like squadrons of cavalry, only seeming to me, larger in number & disposed rather more irregularly than usual with animals galloping up & down the line.[1] Behind the main body & scattered over the plain for more than a mile, but so nearly on a level with us as hardly to be distinguished were other animals, moving slowly & raising considerable dust. The question now was whether what we saw meant Indians or soldiers. As to those nearest us, the small scattered bands; there was no doubt they were Sioux, hanging about to annoy & pick up ponies &c. . . .

Early next morning—the 27th, we moved on over the bluffs, the entire command, toward the village, or what was left of it. It was but a few miles away & of course on reaching it, not an Indian was seen, all having got away during the night. When we got there we found ourselves on the side of an immense village that had covered the valley for at least 8 miles up & 2 or 3 miles across. It had been hastily abandoned the night before from appearances. Where each tepee had been were left piles of undressed robes, hatchets, axes, tin cups, camp & equipage such as is used by soldiers, Indian & Cavalry saddles, spurs, hobbles, cut up blue clothing, dead ponies & a good many wounded cavalry horses limping around. Two lodges had been left up and were filled with 16 dead Indians. Most of them seemingly Chiefs & other Indian bodies had been recently buried around the outskirts of the village & in scaffolds, with their ponies killed near them. Some bodies of white men were also found and also heads (which had been cut off and dragged around by throngs [sic]). I rode on one flank and picked up part of a buckskin jacket marked "Porter," a bullet hole under the right shoulder, from which the blood had streamed down told the fate, a pair of gloves marked "Yates" 7th Cav.," the under clothing of Lieut. Sturgis & other things. Feeling sick at heart we went on caring little how soon we shared the same fate. No signs of a fight having occurred *in the village* were

1. Apparently these were Indians dressed in the clothing of Custer's men.

to be seen, but Lieut. Bradley in ascending with a scouting party the ridge, across the Little Horn from us, send over word he had found 200 dead bodies of white men along the crest and in looking with our glasses we could see the remains of about 40 horses & men in a little clump on top of a knoll, where they had made their last stand. Custer was among the party. We found our Indians had told us what they thought the truth. Keeping on up the valley with scouts ahead, we were soon met by Lieut. Hare and 2 other officers of the 7th Cav. & learned from them the particulars as to Reno's charge & conflict on the plains: While Custer was attacking with 5 cos. from the other side that they had been driven back across the river & up the bluffs & corralled there where they still remained with the remnants of the other 7 cos. & pack animals. They had heard nothing from Custer from the time he made his charge, about noon on the 25th to that time (morning of the 27th) that they had plenty of food but were getting short of ammunition and that until the night before they had got no water being under constant fire for two days & away up on high steep bluffs under which the river ran whose opposite bank was lined with riflemen to keep them from getting down. They had been surrounded by a body of Indians numbering 3000 or 3500 men and there was no chance of escape. Indeed they could not show their heads above ground without being shot at from the surrounding hillocks. It seems that the night before the Indians had suddenly drawn off & allowed them to get water & a little sleep & to attend to their wounded of whom there were about 50 on the hill. Our coming explained why the Indians had left. They must have run short of ammunition from the terrific fire they kept up for 2 days and were afraid to await our attack. Dr. Williams & I were ordered up to Reno's position immediately to give Dr. Porter who had accompanied the expedition from Bismarck, relief. He was the only one of the 3 M.D.s surviving and we found a horrible sight & did all we could for the wounded of whom only 50 had got in, the rest being killed or carried off by the Sioux. None of the officers knew what had become of Custer, his staff & 5 cos. with him until we told them that *all* had been killed, not a man escaping to tell the story. They had lost more than ½ their regiment, about 330 men & 14 officers. How we got away with the remainder & the wounded I will have to defer until another chance arrives to write a letter. We are back at a safe place now and are all played out, myself included and everything is going on as though nothing had happened. Of course we dont realize what has occurred yet. We have made forced night marches and are entirely wore out and it has been with great effort I have written what you will find here.

July 8, 1876

. . . We were shortly after met by Lts. Hare and Wallace of the 7th Cav. who rode down to us and shook hands and from them learned the particulars of the whole thing, or such as they themselves knew at that time. Major Reno, to whose battalion they belonged, was at the time we arrived corralled on the summit of the bluffs across the river about 3 miles or more from where Custer had fought, having been driven there on the first day of the fight, and had with him 7 companies, or what was left of them. The particulars are brief as we learned them from these officers & from one of our Crow scouts named "Curley" who had been with Custer until the fight was over or nearly so, and who had escaped by mixing with Sioux after all the Whites were killed but 5, one of whom was then wounded, were about as follows. Custer with his regiment had been marching with a pack train up the Yellowstone but 20 or 30 miles back near the mountains where he could cross all the streams near their head and scout them. He was to meet our column at the mouth of the Little Horn on the 27th but on the 23rd struck a fresh trail of Indians moving & lit out after them, instead of waiting as they should have done to strike when we should be near enough to help if it should be necessary. I dare say he thought his regiment capable of whipping any number of Indians (a common error) & wanted it all to himself. Anyhow he marched his regiment 75 miles in 36 hours, resting about 5 hours so for 31 hours his men were in the saddle with but one interval. They were then, about 8 A.M. of the 25th where they could see the smoke of a big Indian Camp on the Little Horn, and very soon after, Custer, becoming satisfied that he was discovered, determined to attack at once so as to give them no chance to leave. He ordered Captain Benteen with 4 companies to guard the pack train and proceed toward the bluffs while he with 5 companies attacked from one end of the village & Reno with I believe, 3 companies was to charge down toward Custer from the other. Before making his final disposition, he sent a scout ahead to find out where the tepees (lodges) were the thickest, as there was where he would charge. The scout returned & it is said that when he reported told Custer with perfect terror, that there were lodges as thick as the grass & begged him not to fight so many. Custer merely said with a laugh that he was glad they were all there. Then giving his orders to Reno & Benteen, he left them.

Where he charged from was very bad ground, from the top of the bluffs to the river was a slope of about 2 miles [probably from where they first clearly saw the village], the village lying in the valley across the stream in plain sight the whole length of the slope. Custer and these men gave their yell and charged down for a ford. They did not strike it exactly—but had to move along a cut bank for some distance, under heavy fire from the timber opposite. Finally on reaching the ford they were met by an immense body of Indians fighting on foot. They crossed in the face of this terrible fire but were driven back, dismounted & put in one or two volleys, remounted & retreated alternately, until what was left of them reached the summit of the bluffs. At this point they were met by another large body of Indians who had swept around behind them and here surrounded by about 2500 or more warriors they fought to the death.

One Indian "Curley" says they began to fight before the sun was yet in the middle of the sky & when he got away it was nearly half behind the bluffs — about 8 o'clock. They must have fought with desperation & it is thought they must have killed right there more than the entire number of soldiers in the outfit.

Indeed they must have been so thick & in such short range that it must have been almost impossible to shoot without hitting someone. There was not a white man escaped out of about 250 with Custer, some 20 or so cannot be accounted for except by the fear that they were carried off alive or dead. Among those whose bodies were not positively identified were Dr. Lord & Lt. Sturgis. Their under clothing found in the camp Sturgis with a bullet hole through the under shirt, show that they are gone. The dead were, when found, almost entirely stripped, slashed up and mutilated so as to be hardly recognized.

The officers were Gen. Custer—Capts. Keogh, Cooke, Smith, Yates & Custer—Boston Custer, Lts. Porter, Sturgis, Riley, Harrington, Crittenden & Calhoun, Dr. Lord—a friend of Gen. Custers, Mr. Reed & the Herald reporter Mr. Kellogg. I did not see any of these as they were buried where they fell & during the 2 or 3 days we were there I was too busy with the wounded from Reno's party. . . .

[Paulding describes Reno's hospital.] They dug out small holes with their tin cups in the best place they could find and make barricades of their packs, cracker boxes & dead animals. Dr. de Wolf was shot going up the hill but it left one surgeon, an acting Assistant Surgeon from Bismark, a Dr. Porter, whom I knew very well at Lincoln. The mules were put in a circle with the "hospital" in the middle & every now and then a mule would drop into the ring, shot. They found it impossible to get water for 2 days, all day of the 26th they kept up a fight from different spots where the Indians had taken positions. The Indians charged their works but were repulsed & Benteen made a counter charge. This fight kept up all day of the 26th letting up about noon as they think from the Sioux running short of ammunition. A party of men undertook to crawl down a ravine hoping to reach water under the concealment by the bluffs on each side of the ravine, & the smoke from the burning timber on the opposite bank set fire to drive out some of our men who had taken refuge there. They got some water although some were killed and some badly shot in the effort owing to their having to run the gauntlet of 20 or 30 feet to the river & back into the ravine. The Indians hauled off on the evening of the 26th & then they got water—all they wanted. We (Gen. Gibbons column) were lying quietly in camp about 8 miles off when the Indians left. Dr. Williams and myself were ordered ahead to Reno's position as soon as it was discovered & when we got there they did not know where Custer was. Varnum (whom I thought was dead & who was with me last year on the White River) came up & shook hands. He said "Where is Custer? is he coming up with your column? ["] & when I told him he turned, broken down completely, crying like a baby. All the officers & men were when I got there, in spite of hardships & suffering, cheerful & apparently cool and nonchalant as though nothing much had happened & tho. The announcement of Custers fate fell on them like an unexpected shock they soon rallied. The fact is that now we are quietly lying in camp they appear to be just beginning to realize what it all means. For the next day or two we were busy enough caring for the wounded of whom there were 50 left. Lt. Hodgson died this morning. Lt. MacIntosh was killed in the 2nd charge and the total loss of this part of the regiment was then 41 killed in the charges & during the fights of the 25th & 26th: several of the wounded 2 or 3 have since died. The rest were sent down the river in the steamer "Far West" with my last letter of the 2nd. We had a hard job carrying off the wounded, marching during the late afternoon & nearly all night of the 28th carrying them in hand litters. This was slow and exhausting, and next day (we had'nt marched over 6 miles the night before) Doane of the 2nd went to work and made mule litters from timber frames with throngs [*sic*] of raw hide cut from some of the wounded horses we found in the camp & among the timber & which we killed & skinned for the purpose. . . .

On returning here we found information in the papers of which we knew nothing before starting & *they* knew what we did not dream — that there were between 3000 & 4000 warriors in the band & also pretty definately their where abouts. It came too late for us.

FOR CRITICAL THINKING

1. What really happened at the battle of the Little Big Horn? Did Custer make a classic blunder or did Sitting Bull simply out-general him? Using all the sources before you, analyze the battle and then create a narrative — that is, tell the story, making your analysis clear to the listener or reader.

2. If Holmes Offley Paulding were asked to comment on the accounts by She Walks with Her Shawl and One Bull of the events at the Little Big Horn, what would he say? What parts of their accounts would he be likely to accept and what would he reject?

3. If She Walks with Her Shawl or One Bull were to comment on Holmes Offley Paulding's account of what happened at the Little Big Horn, what would she or he say? What parts of his account would either of them be likely to accept or reject?

11

First Descent Down the Colorado River

John Wesley Powell

John Wesley Powell, while not famous in popular western lore, is surely one of the great heroes of the American West. A child of the frontier, he was born in Mount Morris in western New York on March 24, 1834, and moved with his family to Wisconsin and then Illinois. In 1855 he spent four months walking across Wisconsin. Two years later he floated down the Ohio River from Pittsburgh to St. Louis, gathered fossils in Missouri, then rowed and portaged[1] to Iowa. That early combination of science and adventure presaged the remainder of Powell's life.

Serving in the Union army, Powell lost an arm at Shiloh—the raw nerve endings hurt for the rest of his life. He tried college teaching but felt drawn to the high plateau lands of Colorado, Utah, Arizona, New Mexico, and Nevada. In May 1869 he launched the Powell Geographic Expedition on behalf of the Smithsonian Institution: four little wooden dories ranging from fifteen to twenty-one feet to explore the Colorado River's rapids and canyons, most never before visited by whites. Each night Powell carefully recorded what he had seen. Like a hero out of Greek mythology, he gave names to the points he passed: Glen Canyon, Marble Canyon, Soap Creek, Badger Creek, Crystal Creek, Lava Falls, Grand Canyon. With Powell lashed to a pole to keep his balance, the party navigated the biggest set of rapids in the United States except for the Niagara River, the dories taking such a pounding that they required recaulking every day. The story is before you to read: The expedition reaches a depth of one mile below tree level; help is hundreds of miles off; supplies run low; boats are wrecked; several in the party reach the point where they refuse to go on and climb the canyon wall rather than continue.

On Powell's subsequent trips west he watched the Great Plains and the basin country fill with settlers. He saw the dust of the cattle drives and understood its ecological meaning as his contemporaries did not. He witnessed the fraudulent land claims under the Desert Land Act. His insights came together in a remarkable book, A Report on the Lands of the Arid Region of the United States, *published in 1876. He explained the cyclical character of rainfall in the region, argued that barely 3 percent of the region's land could be farmed even with irrigation, and called for limiting population and pulling the region's economy more toward grazing than farming—its direction in the present.*

BEFORE YOU READ

1. As you read Powell's account of descending the Colorado, ask yourself why he and his men were doing this. What characteristics do you find in Powell that enabled him to make this astonishing journey?

---

1. **portage:** carrying boats by land.

2. Why do you think no one was willing to listen to Powell's recommendations about how the semiarid areas of the West should be settled?

THE GRAND CANYON OF THE COLORADO

August 13

We are now ready to start on our way down the Great Unknown. Our boats, tied to a common stake, are chafing each other, as they are tossed by the fretful river. They ride high and buoyant, for their loads are lighter than we could desire. We have but a month's rations remaining. The flour has been resifted through the mosquito-net sieve; the spoiled bacon has been dried, and the worst of it boiled; the few pounds of dried apples have been spread in the sun, and reshrunken to their normal bulk; the sugar has all melted, and gone on its way down the river; but we have a large sack of coffee. The lighting of the boats has this advantage: they will ride the waves better, and we shall have but little to carry when we make a portage.

We are three-quarters of a mile in the depths of the earth, and the great river shrinks into insignificance, as it dashes its angry waves against the walls and cliffs, that rise to the world above; they are but puny ripples, and we but pigmies, running up and down the sands, or lost among the boulders.

We have an unknown distance yet to run; an unknown river yet to explore. What falls there are, we know not; what rocks beset the channel, we know not; what walls rise over the river, we know not. Ah, well! we may conjecture many things. The men talk as cheerfully as ever; jests are bandied about freely this morning; but to me the cheer is somber and the jests are ghastly.

With some eagerness, and some anxiety, and some misgiving, we enter the canyon below, and are carried along by the swift water through walls which rise from its very edge. They have the same structure as we noticed yesterday — tiers of irregular shelves below, and above these, steep slopes to the foot of marble cliffs. We run six miles in a little more than half an hour. . . .

August 14

At daybreak we walk down the bank of the river, on a little sandy beach, to take a view of a new feature in the canyon. Heretofore, hard rocks have given us bad river; soft rocks, smooth water; and a series of rocks harder than any we have experienced sets in. The river enters the granite!

We can see but a little way into the granite gorge, but it looks threatening. . . .

As we proceed, the granite rises higher, until nearly a thousand feet of the lower part of the walls are composed of this rock.

John Wesley Powell, "Diary of the First Trip Through the Grand Canyon, 1869," *Exploration of the Colorado River of the West, and its tributaries. Explored in 1869, 1870, 1871, and 1872, under the direction of the secretary of the Smithsonian Institution* (Washington: Government Printing Office, 1875), pp. 81–103.

About eleven o'clock we hear a great roar ahead, and approach it very cautiously. The sound grows louder and louder as we run, and at last we find ourselves above a long, broken fall, with ledges and pinnacles of rock obstructing the river. There is a descent of, perhaps, seventy-five or eighty feet in a third of a mile, and the rushing waters break into great waves on the rocks, and lash themselves into a mad, white foam. We can land just above, but there is no foothold on either side by which we can make a portage. It is nearly a thousand feet to the top of the granite, so it will be impossible to carry our boats around, though we can climb to the summit up a side gulch, and, passing along a mile or two, can descend to the river. This we find on examination; but such a portage would be impracticable for us, and we must run the rapid, or abandon the river. There is no hesitation. We step into our boats, push off and away we go, first on smooth but swift water, then we strike a glassy wave, and ride to its top, down again into the trough, up again on a higher wave, and down and up on waves higher and still higher, until we strike one just as it curls back, and a breaker rolls over our little boat. Still, on we speed, shooting past projecting rocks. . . .

The walls, now, are more than a mile in height—a vertical distance difficult to appreciate. . . .

A thousand feet of this is up through granite crags, then steep slopes and perpendicular cliffs rise, one above another, to the summit. The gorge is black and narrow below, red and gray and flaring above, with crags and angular projections on the walls, which, cut in many places by side canyons, seem to be a vast wilderness of rocks. Down in these grand, gloomy depths we glide, ever listening, for the mad waters keep up their roar; ever watching, ever peering ahead, for the narrow canyon is winding, and the river is closed in so that we can see but a few hundred yards, and what there may be below we know not; but we listen for falls, and watch for rocks, or stop now and then, in the bay of a recess, to admire the gigantic scenery. And ever, as we go, there is some new pinnacle or tower, some crag or peak, some distant view of the upper plateau, some strange-shaped rock, or some deep, narrow side canyon. Then we come to another broken fall, which appears more difficult than the one we ran this morning.

August 15

This morning we find we can let down for three or four hundred yards, and it is managed in this way: We pass along the wall, by climbing from projecting point to point, sometimes near the water's edge, at other places fifty or sixty feet above, and hold the boat with a line, while two men remain aboard, and prevent her from being dashed against the rocks, and keep the line from getting caught on the wall. In two hours we had brought them all down, as far as it is possible, in this way. A few yards below, the river strikes with great violence against a projecting rock, and our boats are pulled up in a little bay above. We must now manage to pull out of this, and clear the point below. The little boat is held by the bow obliquely up the stream. We jump in, and pull out only a few strokes, and sweep clear of the dangerous rock. The other boats follow in the same manner, and the rapid is passed. . . .

Early in the afternoon, we discover a stream, entering from the north, a clear, beautiful creek, coming down through a gorgeous red canyon. We land, and camp on a sand beach, above its mouth, under a great, overspreading tree, with willow-shaped leaves.

This stream heads away back, under a line of abrupt cliffs, that terminates the plateau, and tumbles down more than four thousand feet in the first mile or two of its course; then runs through a deep, narrow canyon, until it reaches the river.

Late in the afternoon I return, and go up a little gulch, just above this creek, about two hundred yards from camp, and discover the ruins of two or three old houses, which were originally of stone, laid in mortar. Only the foundations are left, but irregular blocks, of which the houses were constructed, lie scattered about. In one room I find an old mealing stone, deeply worn, as if it had been much used. A great deal of pottery is strewn around, and old trails, which in some places are deeply worn into the rocks, are seen.

It is ever a source of wonder to us why these ancient people sought such inaccessible places for their homes. They were, doubtless, an agricultural race, but there are no lands here, of any considerable extent, that they could have cultivated. To the west of Oraiby, one of the towns in the "Province of Tusayan," in Northern Arizona, the inhabitants have actually built little terraces along the face of the cliff, where a spring gushes out, and thus made their sites for gardens. It is possible that the ancient inhabitants of this place made their agricultural lands in the same way. But why should they seek such spots? Surely, the country was not so crowded with population as to demand the utilization of so barren a region. The only solution of the problem suggested is this: We know that, for a century or two after the settlement of Mexico, many expeditions were sent into the country, now comprised in Arizona and New Mexico, for the purpose of bringing the town-building people under the dominion of the Spanish government. Many of their villages were destroyed, and the inhabitants fled to regions at that time unknown; and there are traditions, among the people who inhabit the *pueblos* that still remain, that the canyons were these unknown lands. Maybe these buildings were erected at that time; sure it is that they have a much more modern appearance than the ruins scattered over Nevada, Utah, Colorado, Arizona, and New Mexico.

August 17

Our rations are still spoiling. . . . We have now only musty flour sufficient for ten days, a few dried apples, but plenty of coffee. We must make all haste possible. If we meet with difficulties, as we have done in the canyon above, we may be compelled to give up the expedition, and try to reach the Mormon settlements to the north. Our hopes are that the worst places are passed, but our barometers are all so much injured as to be useless, so we have lost our reckoning in altitude, and know not how much descent the river has yet to make. . . .

August 18

The day is employed in making portages, and we advance but two miles on our journey. Still it rains.

While the men are at work making portages, I climb up the granite to its summit, and go away back over the rust-colored sandstones and greenish-yellow shales, to the foot of the marble wall. I climb so high that the men and boats are lost in the black depths below, and the dashing river is a rippling brook; and still there is more canyon above than below. All about me are interesting geological records. The book is open, and I can read as I run. All about me are grand views, for the clouds are playing again in the gorges. But somehow I think of the nine days' rations, and the bad river, and the lesson of the rocks, and the glory of the scene is but half seen. . . .

August 19

. . . Soon we find a little beach, with just room enough to land. Here we camp, but there is no wood. Across the river, and a little way above, we see some drift-wood lodged in the rocks. So we bring two boat loads over, build a huge fire, and spread everything to dry. It is the first cheerful night we have had for a week; a warm, drying fire in the midst of the camp, and a few bright stars in our patch of heavens overhead. . . .

August 26

. . . Since we left the Colorado Chiquito, we have seen no evidences that the tribe of Indians inhabiting the plateaus on either side ever come down to the river; but about eleven o'clock today we discover an Indian garden, at the foot of the wall on the right, just where a little stream, with a narrow flood-plain, comes down through a side canyon. Along the valley, the Indians have planted corn, using the water which burst out in springs at the foot of the cliff, for irrigation. The corn is looking quite well, but is not sufficiently advanced to give us roasting ears; but there are some nice, green squashes. We carry ten or a dozen of these on board our boats, and hurriedly leave, not willing to be caught in the robbery, yet excusing ourselves by pleading our great want. We run down a short distance, to where we feel certain no Indians can follow; and what a kettle of squash sauce we make! True, we have no salt with which to season it, but it makes a fine addition to our unleavened bread and coffee. Never was fruit so sweet as these stolen squashes.

August 27

. . . About eleven o'clock we come to a place in the river where it seems much worse than any we have yet met in all its course. A little creek comes down from the left. We land first on the right, and clamber up over the granite pinnacles for a mile or two, but can see no way by which we can let down, and to run it would be sure destruction. After dinner we cross to examine it on the left. High above the river we can walk along on the top of the granite, which is broken off at the edge, and set with crags and pinnacles, so that it is very difficult to get a view of the river at all. In my eagerness to reach a point where I can see the roaring fall below, I go too far on the wall, and can neither advance nor retreat. I stand with one foot on a little projecting rock, and cling with my hand fixed in a little crevice. Finding I am caught here, suspended 400 feet above the river, into which I should fall if my footing fails, I call for help. The men come, and pass me a line, but I cannot let go of the rock long enough to take hold of it. Then they bring two or three of the largest oars. All this takes time which seems very precious to me; but at last they arrive. The blade of one of the oars is pushed into a little crevice in the rock beyond me, in such a manner that they can hold me pressed against the wall. Then another is fixed in such a way that I can step on it, and thus I am extricated. . . .

After supper Captain Howland asks to have a talk with me. We walk up the little creek a short distance, and I soon find that his object is to remonstrate against my determination to proceed. He thinks that we had better abandon the river here. Talking with him, I learn that his brother, William Dunn, and himself have determined to go no farther in the boats. So we return to camp. Nothing is said to the other men. . . .

We have another short talk about the morrow, and he lies down again; but for me there is no sleep. All night long, I pace up and down a little path, on a few yards of sand beach, along by the river. Is it wise to go on? I go to the boats again, to look at our rations. I feel satisfied that we can get over the danger immediately before us; what there may be below I know not. From our outlook yesterday, on the cliffs, the canyon seemed to make another great bend to the south, and this, from our experience heretofore, means more and higher granite walls. I am not sure that we can climb out of the canyon here, and, when at the top of the wall, I know enough of the country to be certain that it is a desert of rock and sand, between this and the nearest Mormon town, which, on the most direct line, must be seventy-five miles away. True, the late rains have been favorable to us, should we go out, for the probabilities are that we shall find water still standing in holes, and, at one time, I almost conclude to leave the river. But for years I have been contemplating the trip. To leave the exploration unfinished, to say that there is a part of the canyon which I cannot explore, having already almost accomplished it, is more than I am willing to acknowledge, and I determine to go on.

I wake my brother, and tell him of Howland's determination, and he promises to stay with me; then I call up Hawkins, the cook, and he makes a like promise; then Sumner, and Bradley, and Hall, and they all agree to go on.

August 28

At last daylight comes, and we have breakfast, without a word being said about the future. The meal is solemn as a funeral. After breakfast, I ask the three men if they still think it best to leave us. The elder Howland thinks it is, and Dunn agrees with him. The younger Howland tries to persuade them to go on with the party, failing in which, he decides to go with his brother. . . .

Two rifles and a shot gun are given to the men who are going out. I ask them to help themselves to the rations, and take what they think to be a fair share. This they refuse to do, saying they have no fear but that they can get something to eat; but Billy, the cook, has a pan of biscuits prepared for dinner, and these he leaves on a rock.

Before starting, we take our barometers, fossils, the minerals, and some ammunition from the boat, and leave them on the rocks. We are going over this place as light as possible. The three men help us lift our boats over a rock twenty-five or thirty feet high, and let them down again over the first fall, and now we are all ready to start. The last thing before leaving, I write a letter to my wife, and give it to Howland. Sumner gives him his watch, directing that it be sent to his sister, should he not be heard from again. The records of the expedition have been kept in duplicate. One set of these is given to Howland, and now we are ready. For the last time, they entreat us not to go on, and tell us that it is madness to set out in this place; that we can never get safely through it. . . . Some tears are shed; it is rather a solemn parting; each party thinks the other is taking the dangerous course. . . .

August 29

We start very early this morning. The river still continues swift, but we have no serious difficulty, and at twelve o'clock emerge from the Grand Canyon of the Colorado. . . . Tonight we camp on the left bank, in a *mesquite* thicket. . . .

The river rolls by us in silent majesty; the quiet of the camp is sweet; our joy is almost ecstasy. We sit till long after midnight, talking of the Grand Canyon, talking of home, but chiefly talking of the three men who left us. Are they wandering in those depths, unable to find a way out? are they searching over the desert lands above for water? are they nearing the settlements?[2]

---

2. Above the place in the river where the three men left the Powell party—which Powell named Separation Rapids—visitors will find a bronze plaque answering Powell's questions: "Seneca Howland, O. G. Howland, and William Dunn separated from the Original Powell Party, climbed to the North Rim, and were killed by the Indians."

12

The Chinese in the Far West
James F. Rusling

In the nineteenth century, many Chinese, particularly in the region around Canton, fled the country to escape civil war and economic decline. Most migrated to southeast Asia and the Philippines and other Pacific islands, but about one in a hundred came to California. Like other migrants there, they sought the gold that had been discovered in 1849. After Anglo-Americans, immigrant Chinese were the largest group in the gold fields, comprising about one-quarter of all miners. A little later large numbers of Chinese, called at that time "Celestials" or "John Chinaman" (often shortened to "John"), became the principal work force constructing the Central Pacific Railroad from San Francisco eastward into Utah. By the 1870s they were present all over the West, as James F. Rusling wrote, in "pretty much all occupations except the highest." Yet prejudice against the Chinese was intense. In a typical instance, a California judge ruled in 1854 that "Asiatics" were Indians and could not testify against whites in court.

In 1866–67 Rusling, an officer in the Army Quartermaster Department, traveled throughout the West by steamer, stagecoach, railroad, wagon, and horseback on a fifteen thousand-mile tour of inspection for the Quartermaster-General. He boasts of being "about the last if not the last" person to make such a tour before the transcontinental railroad, completed in 1869, drastically shortened and simplified such adventures.

BEFORE YOU READ

1. What did Rusling think that the Chinese have contributed to the development of the western United States?
2. What did he admire about them?
3. In what ways did he look down on them?
4. What did Rusling think the future of the American Chinese will be?

We found the Chinese everywhere on the street and in the houses, in pretty much all occupations except the highest, and were constantly amazed at their general thrift and intelligence. . . .

All wore the collarless Chinese blouse, looped across the breast, not buttoned—that of the poorer classes of coarse blue stuff, but of the richer of broadcloth. Otherwise, they dressed outwardly chiefly as Americans. Here and there a Chinese hat, such as you see in the tea-prints, appeared, but not often—the American felt-hat being the rule, stove-pipes never. A good many still wore the Chinese shoe, wooden-soled, with cotton uppers; but the American boot and shoe were fast supplanting this, especially among the out-door classes, such

James F. Rusling, *Across America* (New York: Sheldon, 1874), pp. 225–26, 300–18.

as mechanics and laborers. Pig-tails were universal, generally hanging down, but often coiled about the head, under the hat, so as to be out of the way and attract less attention. In features, of course, they were all true Mongolians; but here and there were grand faces, worthy of humanity anywhere. Their food consists chiefly of fish and rice; but the wealthier classes indulge freely in poultry and beef, and the Chinese taste for these was constantly on the increase. The old stories of their dog and rat diet are evidently myths, at least here in America. Intelligent Californians laugh at such reports as antediluvian, and say their Chinese neighbors are only too glad to eat the very best, if they can only get it.

Everybody gave them credit for sobriety, intelligence, and thrift, the three great master qualities of mankind, practically speaking; and without them the industry of the Pacific Coast, it was conceded, would soon come to a stand-still. All are expert at figures, all read and write their own tongue, and nearly all seemed intent on mastering English, as quickly and thoroughly as possible. When not at work or otherwise occupied, they were usually seen with a book in their hands, and seemed much given to reading and study.

Their chief vices were gambling, and opium-smoking, but these did not seem to prevail to the extent we had heard, and appeared really less injurious, than the current vices of other races on the Coast, all things considered. The statistics of the city and Coast somehow were remarkably in their favor, showing a less percentage of vagrancy and crime among these heathens, than any other part of the population, notwithstanding the absurd prejudices and barbarous discriminations against them.

Their quickness to learn all American ways, even when not able to speak our tongue, was very surprising. They engaged in all household duties, ran errands, worked at trades, performed all kinds of manual labor, and yet as a rule, their only dialect was a sort of chow-chow or "Pigeon English." "Pigeon" is said to be the nearest approach a Chinaman can make to *"business,"* and hence "Pigeon English" really means *business* English. Most of the words are English, more or less distorted; a few, however, are Chinese Anglicized. They always use *l* for *r*—thus *lice* for "rice"; *mi* for "I," and abound in terminal "ee's." *Chop-chop* means "very fast"; *maskee*, "don't mind." If you call on a lady, and inquire of her Chinese servant, "Missee have got?" he will reply, if she be up and about, "Missee hab got topside"; or if she be still asleep, "Missee hab got, wakee sleepee." Not wishing to disturb her, you hand him your card, and go away with, "maskee, maskee; no makee bobbery!"

We had seen a good deal of the Chinese generally, but on the evening of Dec. 31st were so fortunate as to meet most of their leading men together. The occasion was a grand banquet at the *Occidental*, given by the merchants of San Francisco, in honor of the sailing of the *Colorado*, the first steamer of the new monthly line to Hong-Kong. All the chief men of the city—merchants, lawyers, clergymen, politicians—were present, and among the rest some twenty or more Chinese merchants and bankers. The Governor of the State presided, and the military and civil dignitaries most eminent on the Coast were all there. The magnificent Dining-Room of the *Occidental* was handsomely decorated

with festoons and flowers, and tastefully draped with the flags of all nations—
chief among which, of course, were our own Stars and Stripes, and the Yellow-
Dragon of the Flowery Empire. A peculiar feature was an infinity of bird-cages
all about the room, from which hundreds of canaries and mocking-birds dis-
coursed exquisite music the livelong evening. The creature comforts disposed
of, there were eloquent addresses by everybody, and among the rest one by Mr.
Fung Tang, a young Chinese merchant, who made one of the briefest and most
sensible of them all. It was in fair English, and vastly better than the average of
post-prandial[1] discourses. This was the only set speech by a Chinaman, but the
rest conversed freely in tolerable English, and in deportment were certainly perfect Chesterfields of courtesy and propriety. They were mostly large, dignified,
fine-looking men, and two of them—Mr. Hop Kee, a leading tea-merchant,
and Mr. Chy Lung, a noted silk-factor—had superb heads and faces, that would
have attracted attention anywhere. They sat by themselves; but several San
Franciscans of note shared their table, and everybody hob-nobbed with them,
more or less, throughout the evening. These were the representatives of the
great Chinese Emigration and Banking Companies, whose checks pass current
on 'Change in San Francisco, for a hundred thousand dollars or more any day,
and whose commercial integrity so far was unstained. There are five of these
Companies in all, the Yung-Wo, the Sze-Yap, the Sam-Yap, the Yan-Wo, and
the Ning-Yung. They contract with their countrymen in China to transport
them to America, insure them constant work while here at fixed wages, and at
the expiration of their contract return them to China again, dead or alive, if so
desired. They each have a large and comfortable building in San Francisco,
where they board and lodge their members, when they first arrive, or when sick,
or out of work, or on a visit from the interior. Chinese beggars are rare on the
Coast, and our public hospitals contain no Chinese patients, although John before landing has always to pay a "hospital-tax" of ten dollars. This is what it is
called out there; but, of course, it is a robbery and swindle, which the Golden
State ought promptly to repeal. These great Companies also act, as express-
agents and bankers, all over the Coast. In all the chief towns and mining districts, wherever you enter a Chinese quarter or camp, you will find a representative of one or more of them, who will procure anything a Chinaman needs,
from home or elsewhere; and faithfully remit to the Flowery Kingdom whatever he wants to send, even his own dead body. Both parties appear to keep their
contracts well—a breach of faith being seldom recorded. Here, surely, is evidence of fine talent for organization and management—the best tests of human
intellect and capacity—and a hint at the existence of sterling qualities, which
the English-speaking nations are slow to credit other races with. Such gigantic
schemes, such far-reaching plans, such harmonious workings, and exact results,
imply a genius for affairs, that not even the Anglo-Saxon can afford to despise,
and which all others may ponder with profit. A race that can plan and execute
such things as these, must have some vigor and virility in it, whatever its other
peculiarities.

  1. **post-prandial:** after-dinner.

Some days after the Banquet, we were driven out to the Mission Woolen Mills, where Donald McLennan, a Massachusetts Scotch-Yankee, was converting California wool into gold. The climate being so favorable to sheep, the wool-product of the coast was already large, and everywhere rapidly increasing. I mention all these things in order to emphasize the fact, that out of the 450 persons then employed about these Mills, 350 were Chinamen. For the heavier work, Americans or Europeans were preferred; but the more delicate processes, we were assured, Chinamen learned more quickly and performed more deftly, besides never becoming drunk, or disorderly, or going on a "strike." We saw them at the looms, engaged in the most painstaking and superb pieces of workmanship, and they could not have been more attentive and exact, if they had been a part of the machinery itself. And yet, these one hundred Anglo-Saxons were paid $2,95 per day, coin, while the three hundred and fifty Chinamen received only $1,10 per day, coin, though the average work of each was about the same. Without this cheap labor of John Chinaman, these Mills would have had to close up; with it, they were run at a profit, and at the same time were a great blessing and credit to the Pacific Coast in every way. So, also, the Central Pacific Railroad was then being pushed through and over the Sierra Nevadas, by some ten thousand Chinamen, working for one dollar per day each, in coin, and finding themselves, when no other labor could be had for less than two dollars and a half per day, coin. It was simply a question with the Central directors, whether to build the road or not. Without John, it was useless to attempt it, as the expense would have bankrupted the company, even if other labor could have been had, which was problematical. With him, the road is already a fact accomplished; and in view of possible contingencies, nationally and politically, who shall say we have completed it an hour too soon? Here are practical results, not shadowy theories—of such a character, too, as should give one pause, however anti-Chinese, and ought to outweigh a world of prejudices.

Not long afterwards, we were invited to join a party of gentlemen, and make a tour of the Chinese quarter. Part were from the East, like ourselves, bent on information, and the rest Pacific-Coasters. We started early in the evening, escorted by two policemen, who were familiar with the ins and outs of Chinadom, and did not reach the *Occidental* again until long after midnight. We went first to the Chinese Theatre, an old hotel on the corner of Jackson and Dupont streets, that had recently been metamorphosed into an Oriental playhouse. We found two or three hundred Chinese here, of both sexes, but mainly males, listening to a play, that required eighty weeks or months—our informants were not certain which—to complete its performance. Here was drama for you, surely, and devotion to it! It was a history of the Flowery Kingdom, by some Chinese Shakespeare—half-tragedy, half-comedy, like most human history—and altogether was a curious medly. The actors appeared to be of both sexes, but we were told were only men and boys. Their dresses were usually very rich, the finest of embroidered silks, and their acting quite surprised us. Their pantomime was excellent, their humor irresistible, and their love-passages a good reproduction of the grand passion, that in all ages "makes the world go round." But it is to be doubted, if the Anglo-Saxon ear will ever become quite reconciled to John's orchestra. This consisted of a rough drum, a rude banjo or guitar, and a sort of violin, over whose triple clamors a barbarous clarionet squeaked and squealed continually. Japanese music, as rendered by Risley's troupe of "Jugglers," is much similar to it; only John's orchestra is louder, and more hideous. Much of the play was pantomime, and much opera; some, however, was common dialogue, and when this occurred, the clash and clang of the Chinese consonants was something fearful. Every word seemed to end in "ng," as Chang, Ling, Hong, Wung; and when the parts became animated, their voices roared and rumbled about the stage, like Chinese gongs in miniature. The general behavior of the audience was good; everybody, however, smoked — the majority cigars and cigarritos, a very few opium. Over the theatre was a Chinese lottery-office, on entering which the Proprietor tendered you wine and cigars, like a genuine Californian. He himself was whiffing away at a cigarrito, and was as polite and politic, as a noted New York ex-M.C. in the same lucrative business. Several Chinamen dropped in to buy tickets, while we were there; and the business seemed to be conducted on the same principle, as among Anglo-Saxons elsewhere.

Next we explored the famous Barbary Coast,[2] and witnessed scenes that Charles Dickens never dreamed of, with all his studies of the dens and slums of London and Paris. Here in narrow, noisome alleys are congregated the wretched Chinese women, that are imported by the ship-load, mainly for infamous purposes. As a class, they are small in stature, scarcely larger than an American girl of fourteen, and usually quite plain. Some venture on hoops and crinoline, but the greater part retain the Chinese wadded gown and trousers. Their chignons are purely Chinese — huge, unique, indescribable — and would excite the envy even of a Broadway belle. They may be seen on the street any day in San Francisco, bonnet-less, fan in hand, hobbling along in their queer little shoes, perfect fac-similes of the figures you see on lacquered were imported from the Orient. They are not more immodest, than those of our own race, who ply the same vocation in Philadelphia and New York; and their fellow-countrymen, it seemed, behaved decently well even here. But here is the great resort of sailors, miners, 'long-shoremen, and the floating population generally of San Francisco, and the brutality and bestiality of the Saxon and the Celt here all comes suddenly to the surface, as if we were fiends incarnate. Here are the St. Giles[3] of London and the Five Points[4] of New York, magnified and intensified (if possible), both crowded into one, and what a hideous example it is for Christendom to set to Heathendom! San Francisco owes it to herself, and to our boasted civilization, to cleanse this Augean stable — to obliterate, to stamp out this plaguespot — to purge it, if need be, by fire — and she has not a day to lose in doing it. It is the shameful spectacle, shocking alike to gods and men, of a strong race trampling a weaker one remorselessly in the mud; and justice will not sleep forever, confronted by such enormities.

2. **Barbary Coast:** vice district of San Francisco.
3. **St. Giles:** vice district of London.
4. **Five Points:** vice district of New York.

The same evening we took a turn through the Chinese gambling-houses, but did not find them worse than similar institutions elsewhere. Indeed, they were rather more quiet and respectable, than the average of such "hells" in San Francisco. They were frequented solely by Chinamen, and though John is not averse to "fighting the tiger," he proposes to do it in his own *dolce far niente* way. They seemed to have only one game, which consisted in betting whether in diminishing steadily a given pile of perforated brass-coins, an odd or even number of them would at last be left. The banker with a little rod, drew the coins, two at a time, rapidly out of the pile towards himself, and when the game was ended all parties cheerfully paid up their losses or pocketed their gains. The stakes were small, seldom more than twenty-five or fifty cents each, and disputes infrequent. A rude idol or image of Josh, with a lamp constantly burning before it, appeared in all these dens, and indeed was universal throughout the Chinese quarter.

The Chinese New Year comes in February, and is an occasion of rare festivities. It began at midnight on the 4th that year, and was ushered in with a lavish discharge of fire-crackers and rockets, to which our usual Fourth of July bears about the same comparison as a minnow to a whale. The fusilade of crackers continued, more or less, for a day or two, until the whole Chinese quarter was littered with the remains. It takes them three days to celebrate this holiday, and during all this period there was a general suspension of business, and every Chinaman kept open house. Their leading merchants welcomed all "Melican" men who called upon them, and the Celestials themselves were constantly passing from house to house, exchanging the compliments of the season. I dropped in upon several, whom I had met at the Banquet, and now have lying before me the unique cards of Mr. Hop Kee, Mr. Chy Lung, Mr. Fung Tang, Messrs. Tung Fu and Co., Messrs. Kwoy Hing and Co., Messrs. Sun Chung Kee and Co., etc. Several of these understood and spoke English very well, and all bore themselves becomingly, like well-to-do gentlemen. Like the majority of their countrymen, many were small; but some were full-sized, athletic men, scarcely inferior, if at all, to our average American. Their residences were usually back of their stores, and here we everywhere found refreshments set out, and all invited to partake, with a truly Knickerbocker hospitality. Tea, sherry, champagne, cakes, sweetmeats, cigars, all were offered without stint, but never pressed unduly. For three days the whole Chinese quarter was thus given up to wholesale rejoicing, and hundreds of Americans flocked thither, to witness the festivity and fun. John everywhere appeared in his best bib and tucker, if not with a smile on his face, yet with a look of satisfaction and content; for this was the end of his debts, as well as the beginning of a new year. At this period, by Chinese custom or law, a general settlement takes place among them, a balance is struck between debtor and creditor, and everything starts afresh. If unable to pay up, the debtor surrenders his assets for the equal benefit of his creditors, his debts are sponged out, and then with a new ledger and a clean conscience he "picks his flint and tries it again." This is the merciful, if not sensible, Bankrupt Law of the Chinese, in force among these heathen for thousands of years — "for a time whereof the memory of man runneth not to the contrary"—and its humane and wise provisions suggest, whether our Christian legislators, after all, may not have something to learn, even from Pagan Codes.

The Chinese temple, synagogue, or "Josh House," of which we had heard such conflicting reports, stands near the corner of Kearney and Pine streets, in the heart of the city. It is a simple structure of brick, two or three stories high, and would attract little or no attention, were it not for a plain marble slab over the entrance, with "Sze-Yap Asylum" carved upon it, in gilt letters, and the same repeated in Chinese characters. It was spoken of as a "Heathen Synagogue," a "Pagan Temple," etc., and we had heard much ado about it, from people of the William Nye[5] school chiefly, long before reaching San Francisco. But, in reality, it appeared to be only an asylum or hospital, for the unemployed and infirm of the Sze-Yap Emigration Company; with a small "upper chamber," set apart for such religious services, as to them seemed meet. The other companies all have similar hospitals or asylums, but we visited only this one. The first room on the ground-floor seemed to be the business-room or council-chamber of the company, and this was adorned very richly with crimson and gold. Silk-hangings were on the walls, arm-chairs elaborately carved along the sides, and at the end on a raised platform stood a table and chair, as if ready for business. The room adjoining seemed to be the general smoking and lounging room of the members of the company. Here several Chinamen lay stretched out, on rude but comfortable lounges, two smoking opium, all the rest only cigarritos—taking their afternoon siesta. Back of this were the dining-room, kitchen, etc., but we did not penetrate thither. A winding stairs brought us to the second floor, and here was the place reserved for religious purposes,—an "upper chamber" perhaps twenty by thirty feet, or even less. Its walls and ceiling were hung with silk, and here and there were placards, inscribed with moral maxims from Confucius and other writers, much as we suspend the same on the walls of our Sunday-school rooms, with verses on them from *our* Sacred writings. These mottoes, of course, were in Chinese; but they were said to exhort John to virtue, fidelity, integrity, the veneration of ancestors, and especially to admonish the young men not to forget, that they were away from home, and to do nothing to prejudice the character of their country in the eyes of foreigners. A few gilded spears and battle-axes adorned either side, while overhead hung clusters of Chinese lanterns, unique and beautiful. Flowers were scattered about quite profusely, both natural and artificial—the latter perfect in their way. At the farther end of the room, in "a dim religious light," amid a barbaric array of bannerets and battle-axes, stood their sacred Josh—simply a Representative Chinaman, perhaps half life-size, with patient pensive eyes, long drooping moustaches, and an expression doubtless meant for sublime repose or philosophic indifference. Here all orthodox Chinamen in San Francisco, connected with the Sze-Yap company, were expected to come at least once a year, and propitiate the deity by burning a slip of paper before

5. **William Nye:** humorist and popular writer.

his image. There was also some praying to be done, but this was accomplished by putting printed prayers in a machine run by clock-work. Tithes there were none—at least worth mentioning. Altogether, this seemed to be a very easy and cheap religion; and yet, easy as it was, John did not seem to trouble himself much about it. The place looked much neglected, as if worshippers were scarce, and devotees infrequent. A priest or acolyte, who came in and trimmed the ever-burning lamp, without even a bow or genuflection to Josh, was the only person about the "Temple," while we were there. The dormitories and apartments for the sick and infirm, we were told, were on this same floor and above; but we did not visit them. This Josh-worship, such as it is, seemed to be general among the Chinese, except the handful gathered into the various Christian churches; but it did not appear to be more than a ceremony. The truth is, John is a very practical creature, and was already beginning to understand, that he is in a new land and among new ideas. Surely, our vigorous, aggressive California Christians stand in no danger from such Pagan "Temples," and our all-embracing nationality can well afford to tolerate them, as China in turn tolerates ours.

13

School Days of an Indian Girl
Zitkala-Sä (Gertrude Simmons Bonnin)

From the mid-1880s to the 1930s, the thrust of American Indian policy was to assimilate native Americans into the larger society. Boarding schools for Native American children became a common strategy for inducting promising young Native Americans into white culture. Officials were particularly eager to educate girls, hoping to alter the domestic culture of the Indians.

Zitkala-Sä, or Red Bird (1876–1938), a Sioux from the Yankton reservation in South Dakota, described in a series of articles in the Atlantic Monthly *in 1900 her experiences at a Quaker missionary school for Native Americans in Wabash, Indiana, which she attended from age eight to eleven. She remarked ironically that she returned to the reservation "neither a wild Indian nor a tame one."*

Red Bird returned to the school four years later to complete the course of study and then attended Earlham College in Richmond, Indiana, somehow acquiring the capacity to succeed in the white world without losing her Native American heritage. She wrote of her experience in a series of magazine articles, as well as a book, Old Indian Legends. *After returning to the Sioux country, she married a Sioux, and began a lifetime of work to improve the status and condition of Native Americans. In a long career that ended with her death in 1938, she played an influential role in the organization of Native American communities, which led to major reforms in the New Deal era of the 1930s.*

BEFORE YOU READ

1. What do you think Zitkala-Sä meant when she said she returned to the reservation "neither a wild Indian nor a tame one"? What did she reject and what did she accept about her education?

2. Given the pain of her school experience, what reasons can you suggest for Zitkala-Sä's return to school?

3. What did Zitkala-Sä mean by her final comment about the Indian schools: "[F]ew there are who have paused to question whether real life or long-lasting death lies beneath this semblance of civilization"?

The first turning away from the easy, natural flow of my life occurred in an early spring. It was in my eighth year; in the month of March, I afterward learned. At this age I knew but one language, and that was my mother's native tongue. . . .

"Mother, my friend Judéwin is going home with the missionaries. She is going to a more beautiful country than ours; the palefaces told her so!" I said wistfully, wishing in my heart that I too might go.

Mother sat in a chair, and I was hanging on her knee. Within the last two seasons my big brother Dawée had returned from a three years' education in the East, and his coming back influenced my mother to take a farther step from her native way of living. First it was a change from the buffalo skin to the white man's canvas that covered our wigwam. Now she had given up her wigwam of slender poles, to live, a foreigner, in a home of clumsy logs.

"Yes, my child, several others besides Judéwin are going away with the palefaces. Your brother said the missionaries had inquired about his little sister," she said, watching my face very closely.

My heart thumped so hard against my breast, I wondered if she could hear it.

"Did he tell them to take me, mother?" I asked, fearing lest Dawée had forbidden the palefaces to see me, and that my hope of going to the Wonderland would be entirely blighted.

With a sad, slow smile, she answered: "There! I knew you were wishing to go, because Judéwin has filled your ears with the white men's lies. Don't believe a word they say! Their words are sweet, but, my child, their deeds are bitter. You will cry for me, but they will not even soothe you. Stay with me, my little one! Your brother Dawée says that going East, away from your mother, is too hard an experience for his baby sister."

Thus my mother discouraged my curiosity about the lands beyond our eastern horizon; for it was not yet an ambition for Letters that was stirring me. But on the following day the missionaries did come to our very house. I spied them coming up the footpath leading to our cottage. A third man was with them, but he was not my brother Dawée. It was another, a young interpreter, a paleface who had a smattering of the Indian language. I was ready to run out to meet them, but I did not dare to displease my mother. With great glee, I jumped up and down on our ground floor. I begged my mother to open the door, that they would be sure to come to us. Alas! They came, they saw, and they conquered!

Judéwin had told me of the great tree where grew red, red apples; and how we could reach out our hands and pick all the red apples we could eat. I had never seen apple trees. I had never tasted more than a dozen red apples in my life; and when I heard of the orchards of the East, I was eager to roam among them. The missionaries smiled into my eyes, and patted my head. I wondered how mother could say such hard words against them.

"Mother, ask them if little girls may have all the red apples they want, when they go East," I whispered aloud in my excitement.

The interpreter heard me, and answered: "Yes, little girl, the nice red apples are for those who pick them; and you will have a ride on the iron horse if you go with these good people."

I had never seen a train, and he knew it.

"Mother, I'm going East! I like big red apples, and I want to ride on the iron horse! Mother, say yes!" I pleaded.

My mother said nothing. The missionaries waited in silence; and my eyes began to blur with tears, though I struggled to choke them back. The corners of my mouth twitched, and my mother saw me.

"I am not ready to give you any word," she said to them. "Tomorrow I shall send you my answer by my son."

With this they left us. Alone with my mother, I yielded to my tears, and cried aloud, shaking my head so as not to hear what she was saying to me. This was the first time I had ever been so unwilling to give up my own desire that I refused to hearken to my mother's voice.

There was a solemn silence in our home that night. Before I went to bed I begged the Great Spirit to make my mother willing I should go with the missionaries.

The next morning came, and my mother called me to her side. "My daughter, do you still persist in wishing to leave your mother?" she asked.

"Oh, mother, it is not that I wish to leave you, but I want to see the wonderful Eastern land," I answered.

My dear old aunt came to our house that morning, and I heard her say, "Let her try it."

I hoped that, as usual, my aunt was pleading on my side. My brother Dawée came for mother's decision. I dropped my play, and crept close to my aunt.

"Yes, Dawée, my daughter, though she does not understand what it all means, is anxious to go. She will need an education when she is grown, for then there will be fewer real Dakotas, and many more palefaces: This tearing her away, so young, from her mother is necessary, if I would have her an educated woman. The palefaces, who owe us a large debt for stolen lands, have begun to pay a tardy justice in offering some education to our children. But I know my daughter must suffer keenly in this experiment. For her sake, I dread to tell you my reply to the missionaries. Go, tell them that they may take my little daughter, and that the Great Spirit shall not fail to reward them according to their hearts." . . .

THE CUTTING OF MY LONG HAIR

The first day in the land of apples was a bitter-cold one; for the snow still covered the ground, and the trees were bare. A large bell rang for breakfast, its loud metallic voice crashing through the belfry overhead and into our sensitive ears. The annoying clatter of shoes on bare floors gave us no peace. The constant clash of harsh noises, with an undercurrent of many voices murmuring an unknown tongue, made a bedlam within which I was securely tied. And though my spirit tore itself in struggling for its lost freedom, all was useless.

A paleface woman, with white hair, came up after us. We were placed in a line of girls who were marching into the dining room. These were Indian girls, in stiff shoes and closely clinging dresses. The small girls wore sleeved aprons and shingled hair. As I walked noiselessly in my soft moccasins, I felt like sinking to the floor, for my blanket had been stripped from my shoulders. I looked hard at the Indian girls, who seemed not to care that they were even more immodestly dressed than I, in their tightly fitting clothes. While we marched in, the boys entered at an opposite door. I watched for the three young braves who came in our party. I spied them in the rear ranks, looking as uncomfortable as I felt.

A small bell was tapped, and each of the pupils drew a chair from under the table. Supposing this act meant they were to be seated, I pulled out mine and at once slipped into it from one side. But when I turned my head, I saw that I was the only one seated, and all the rest at our table remained standing. Just as I began to rise, looking shyly around to see how chairs were to be used, a second bell was sounded. All were seated at last, and I had to crawl back into my chair again. I heard a man's voice at one end of the hall, and I looked around to see him. But all the others hung their heads over their plates. As I glanced at the long chain of tables, I caught the eyes of a paleface woman upon me. Immediately I dropped my eyes, wondering why I was so keenly watched by the strange woman. The man ceased his mutterings, and then a third bell was tapped. Every one picked up his knife and fork and began eating. I began crying instead, for by this time I was afraid to venture anything more.

But this eating by formula was not the hardest trial in that first day. Late in the morning, my friend Judéwin gave me a terrible warning. Judéwin knew a few words of English; and she had overhead the paleface woman talk about cutting our long, heavy hair. Our mothers had taught us that only unskilled warriors who were captured had their hair shingled by the enemy. Among our people, short hair was worn by mourners, and shingled hair by cowards!

We discussed our fate some moments, and when Judéwin said, "We have to submit, because they are strong," I rebelled.

"No, I will not submit! I will struggle first!" I answered.

I watched my chance, and when no one noticed I disappeared. I crept up the stairs as quietly as I could in my squeaking shoes,—my moccasins had been exchanged for shoes. Along the hall I passed, without knowing whither I was going. Turning aside to an open door, I found a large room with three white beds in it. The windows were covered with dark green curtains, which made the room very dim. Thankful that no one was there, I directed my steps toward the corner farthest from the door. On my hands and knees I crawled under the bed, and cuddled myself in the dark corner.

From my hiding place I peered out, shuddering with fear whenever I heard footsteps near by. Though in the hall loud voices were calling my name, and I knew that even Judéwin was searching for me, I did not open my mouth to answer. Then the steps were quickened and the voices became excited. The sounds came nearer and nearer. Women and girls entered the room. I held my breath and watched them open closet doors and peep behind large trunks. Some one threw up the curtains, and the room was filled with sudden light. What caused them to stoop and look under the bed I do not know. I remember being dragged out, though I resisted by kicking and scratching wildly. In spite of myself, I was carried downstairs and tied fast in a chair.

I cried aloud, shaking my head all the while until I felt the cold blades of the scissors against my neck, and heard them gnaw off one of my thick braids. Then I lost my spirit. Since the day I was taken from my mother I had suffered extreme indignities. People had stared at me. I had been tossed about in the air like a wooden puppet. And now my long hair was shingled like a coward's! In my anguish I moaned for my mother, but no one came to comfort me. Not a soul reasoned quietly with me, as my own mother used to do; for now I was only one of many little animals driven by a herder.

IRON ROUTINE

A loud-clamoring bell awakened us at half past six in the cold winter mornings. From happy dreams of Western rolling lands and unlassoed freedom we tumbled out upon chilly bare floors back again into a paleface day. We had short time to jump into our shoes and clothes, and wet our eyes with icy water, before a small hand bell was vigorously rung for roll call. . . .

A paleface woman, with a yellow-covered roll book open on her arm and a gnawed pencil in her hand, appeared at the door. Her small, tired face was coldly lighted with a pair of large gray eyes. . . .

Relentlessly her pencil black-marked our daily records if we were not present to respond to our names, and no chum of ours had done it successfully for us. No matter if a dull headache or the painful cough of slow consumption had delayed the absentee, there was only time enough to mark the tardiness. It was next to impossible to leave the iron routine after the civilizing machine had once begun its day's buzzing; and as it was inbred in me to suffer in silence rather than to appeal to the ears of one whose open eyes could not see my pain, I have many times trudged in the day's harness heavy-footed, like a dumb sick brute. . . .

I grew bitter, and censured the woman for cruel neglect of our physical ills. I despised the pencils that moved automatically, and the one teaspoon which dealt out, from a large bottle, healing to a row of variously ailing Indian children. I blamed the hard-working, well-meaning, ignorant woman who was inculcating in our hearts her superstitious ideas. Though I was sullen in all my little troubles, as soon as I felt better I was ready again to smile upon the cruel woman. Within a week I was again actively testing the chains which tightly bound my individuality like a mummy for burial. . . .

INCURRING MY MOTHER'S DISPLEASURE

In the second journey to the East I had not come without some precautions. I had a secret interview with one of our best medicine men, and when I left his wigwam I carried securely in my sleeve a tiny bunch of magic roots. This possession assured me of friends wherever I should go. So absolutely did I believe in its charms that I wore it through all the school routine for more than a year. Then, before I lost my faith in the dead roots, I lost the little buckskin bag containing all my good luck.

At the close of this second term of three years I was the proud owner of my first diploma. The following autumn I ventured upon a college career against my mother's will.

I had written for her approval, but in her reply I found no encouragement. She called my notice to her neighbors' children, who had completed their education in three years. They had returned to their homes, and were then talking English with the frontier settlers. Her few words hinted that I had better give up my slow attempt to learn the white man's ways, and be content to roam over the prairies and find my living upon wild roots. I silenced her by deliberate disobedience.

Thus, homeless and heavy-hearted, I began anew my life among strangers.

As I hid myself in my little room in the college dormitory, away from the scornful and yet curious eyes of the students, I pined for sympathy. Often I wept in secret, wishing I had gone West, to be nourished by my mother's love, instead of remaining among a cold race whose hearts were frozen hard with prejudice.

During the fall and winter seasons I scarcely had a real friend, though by that time several of my classmates were courteous to me at a safe distance. . . .

. . . I appeared as the college representative in [an oratorical] contest. This time the competition was among orators from different colleges in our state. It was held at the state capital, in one of the largest opera houses.

Here again was a strong prejudice against my people. In the evening, as the great audience filled the house, the student bodies began warring among themselves. Fortunately, I was spared witnessing any of the noisy wrangling before the contest began. The slurs against the Indian that stained the lips of our opponents were already burning like a dry fever within my breast.

But after the orations were delivered a deeper burn awaited me. There, before that vast ocean of eyes, some college rowdies threw out a large white flag, with a drawing of a most forlorn Indian girl on it. Under this they had printed in bold black letters words that ridiculed the college which was represented by a "squaw." Such worse than barbarian rudeness embittered me. While we waited for the verdict of the judges, I gleamed fiercely upon the throngs of palefaces. My teeth were hard set, as I saw the white flag still floating insolently in the air.

Then anxiously we watched the man carry toward the stage the envelope containing the final decision.

There were two prizes given, that night, and one of them was mine!

The evil spirit laughed within me when the white flag dropped out of sight, and the hands which furled it hung limp in defeat.

Leaving the crowd as quickly as possible, I was soon in my room. The rest of the night I sat in an armchair and gazed into the crackling fire. I laughed no more in triumph when thus alone. The little taste of victory did not satisfy a hunger in my heart. In my mind I saw my mother far away on the Western plains, and she was holding a charge against me.

RETROSPECTION

Leaving my mother, I returned to the school in the East. As months passed over me, I slowly comprehended that the large army of white teachers in Indian schools had a larger missionary creed than I had suspected.

It was one which included self-preservation quite as much as Indian education. When I saw an opium-eater holding a position as teacher of Indians, I did not understand what good was expected, until a Christian in power replied that this pumpkin-colored creature had a feeble mother to support. An inebriate paleface sat stupid in a doctor's chair, while Indian patients carried their ailments to untimely graves, because his fair wife was dependent upon him for her daily food. . . .

My illness, which prevented the conclusion of my college course, together with my mother's stories of the encroaching frontier settlers, left me in no mood to strain my eyes in searching for latent good in my white co-workers.

At this stage of my own evolution, I was ready to curse men of small capacity for being the dwarfs their God had made them. In the process of my education I had lost all consciousness of the nature world about me. Thus, when a hidden rage took me to the small white-walled prison which I then called my room, I unknowingly turned away from my one salvation.

Alone in my room, I sat like the petrified Indian woman of whom my mother used to tell me. I wished my heart's burdens would turn me to unfeeling stone. But alive, in my tomb, I was destitute!

For the white man's papers I had given up my faith in the Great Spirit. For these same papers I had forgotten the healing in trees and brooks. On account of my mother's simple view of life, and my lack of any, I gave her up, also. I made no friends among the race of people I loathed. Like a slender tree, I had been uprooted from my mother, nature, and God. I was shorn of my branches, which had waved in sympathy and love for home and friends. The natural coat of bark which had protected my oversensitive nature was scraped off to the very quick.

Now a cold bare pole I seemed to be planted in a strange earth. Still, I seemed to hope a day would come when my mute aching head, reared upward to the sky, would flash a zigzag lightning across the heavens. With this dream of vent for a long-pent consciousness, I walked again amid the crowds.

At last, one weary day in the schoolroom, a new idea presented itself to me. It was a new way of solving the problem of my inner self. I liked it. Thus I resigned my position as teacher; and now I am in an Eastern city, following the long course of study I have set for myself. Now, as I look back upon the recent past, I see it from a distance, as a whole. I remember how, from morning till evening, many specimens of civilized peoples visited the Indian school. The city folks with canes and eyeglasses, the countrymen with sunburnt cheeks and clumsy feet, forgot their relative social ranks in an ignorant curiosity. Both sorts of these Christian palefaces were alike astounded at seeing the children of savage warriors so docile and industrious.

As answers to their shallow inquiries they received the students' sample work to look upon. Examining the neatly figured pages, and gazing upon the Indian girls and boys bending over their books, the white visitors walked out of the schoolhouse well satisfied: they were educating the children of the red man! They were paying a liberal fee to the government employees in whose able hands lay the small forest of Indian timber.

In this fashion many have passed idly through the Indian schools during the last decade, afterward to boast of their charity to the North American Indian. But few there are who have paused to question whether real life or long-lasting death lies beneath this semblance of civilization.

14

A Prairie Populist
Luna Kellie

*Luna Kellie's account of the Nebraska frontier in the last quarter of the nineteenth cen-
tury is one among several memoirs of rural American women that historians have re-
discovered in recent years. Farm women like Luna Kellie, as the historian Albert E.
Stone has written, "were at once pioneer travelers, wives and mothers, educators and
caregivers, and cocreators with men of a social order that both supported and both came
to criticize for betraying their dreams of a better life." In addition to providing a
graphic picture of the hardships and the rewards of rural life, Kellie's memoirs also re-
count the story of a pioneer woman reformer and political activist whose writings,
speeches, and songs sustained the Nebraska Farmers' Alliance through the 1890s.*

*Kellie, born Luna Elizabeth Sanford in 1857, and her husband, J. T. Kellie,
farmed the prairie land during the hard years of the last quarter of the nineteenth
century. Struggling through drought, plagues of locusts, high freight rates, slump-
ing farm prices, and the depressing environment of a sod house, Luna and her husband raised a large family, surviving as best they could, with Luna contributing
greatly to the family's income by selling eggs and the chickens she raised. Both J. T.
and Luna became active in the Nebraska Alliance, remaining with the "Middle-of-
the-Road" faction, which rejected fusion in 1896 with the Democratic Party's standard bearer, William Jennings Bryan. Luna's speech "Stand Up for Nebraska" and
the song that accompanied it brought her local fame, and she served as state secretary
of the Alliance and editor of the official Alliance newspaper,* Prairie Home, *which
she not only edited but also printed from her home from 1896 to 1901. By then a
measure of agricultural prosperity was returning to the prairie states, and the
prospects for agrarian radicalism appeared hopeless. "So," she wrote at the end of her
memoirs, "I busy myself with my garden and chickens and have given up all hope of
making the world any better."*

BEFORE YOU READ

1. What led Luna Kellie and her husband to migrate to Nebraska?
2. How did their expectations lead to the disappointments Kellie recounts?
3. What did Kellie's own experience teach her about the problem of expensive
credit, which was a chief issue for the Alliance?

[Nebraska]

The sun was very hot and bright. The prairie had all been burnt and grass just
starting [and] not one spear seemed to dare to grow an inch higher than an-

other. Not a tree a shrub or even a gooseberry bush to be seen all the way and not many houses and most of them sod. The first one I saw I said "But it is most black." Pa said "What color did you think a sod house would be?" "Oh nice and green and grassy" I said "not such a dirty looking thing." "Well" he said "it is dirty looking because it is made of dirt." Really I had thought a sod house would be kind of nice but the sight of the first one sickened me. The bright sun in our faces soon gave me a terrific headache which is the most I remember of the ride except there was hardly anything to call a road. We went down all the little ditches and up again, no culverts or anything. I was so frighted I thought I would stay still when I got there. . . .

The glowing accounts of the golden west sent out by the R.R. company remained in my mind and I had a vague idea being only 14 years old that they were doing a noble work to let poor people know there was such a grand haven they could reach. It was quite a number of years afterwards that I saw a statement in a Boston paper from one of the R.R. officials saying how profitable the advertising had been and that they estimated that they had cleared $1500 from each emigrant they had obtained. Well that was a low estimate I know now though I did not see it even at the time, for the minute you crossed the Missouri River your fate both soul and body was in their hands. What you should eat and drink, what you should wear, everything was in their hands and they robbed us of all we produced except enough to keep body and soul together and many many times not that as too many of the early settlers filled early graves on account of being ill nourished and ill clad while the wealth they produced was being coldly calculated as paying so much per head. But more of that later as it was many years before the situation became clear to us and I am glad of it for during those years we had youth and *hope* which means happiness and we worked ourselves harder than slaves were ever worked to be able to fulfill our hopes.

When I think back now to the little girl I really was when I came to Nebraska not quite 19 years old with a dearly loved husband left behind and a bright healthy baby boy who lived entirely on his mother's milk, it does not seem strange that I was unnaturally homesick and nothing around seemed good to me. Of course I was very glad to see my father and brothers and sister again but to see them in such wretched circumstances made me heartsick indeed and I would not go to any of the neighbors' for some time and felt most wretched when any of them came there as I could not realize that they were no better off and indeed many of them not nearly so well off as we were. For instance our dugout had two rooms and I had the inner one which was as private as need be while many perhaps most of the sod houses only had one room. Then we had a very good cave by the house and many things were kept in it that others had to crowd in their one room. Then our roof did not leak and most of them did but Father had used large logs in the roof so he was able to pile on enough dirt to keep it from leaking which most of them could not do, but I did not realize any of these blessings until time had gone on and I was deprived of them.

It was not hard to get ventilation those days. It seemed to be always blowing some way. I had kept close in the house all winter and now the awful wind made me feel I never wanted to go out of doors. It seemed to blow from the north until it was blown out and then turn around and blow it all back again. The others did not seem to mind it but it was a real misery to me and I hardly seemed that first summer to get the real charm of the Prairie at all.

The days seemed very long with just Susie 5 years old and baby and I. There was nothing to read. There were few weeds in the garden on the new sod and no material to sew, only some patching. When it began to get dark we used to go and sit on the cave where we could see all around and the little owls used to hoot so lonesome and sometime the coyotes would howl, and I used to be sure at times it was Indians signalling to one another off in the sand hills south and west of us for there were no houses in sight and it seemed like the end of the world. But most every night when we sat alone some little antelopes would come and look at us with great curiosity and come a little nearer and nearer till sometimes they got real close just a few rods but they always went away before Pa and the boys came. They were pretty and graceful little things and they seemed to want to know us but as soon as the wagon rattled in the distance, a flash, and they were gone. I never can hear a coyote or hoot owl now without seeming to see a picture of us there grouped on top of the cave because we were afraid to stay in the house as it had only one outside door and if Indians or anything came in that door we could not get away. So though sometimes the nights were chilly we wrapped something around us and cuddled close together and I kept close watch and listened for the least noise, for I had the idea that out there if Indians came we might run and hide out in the corn or grass and not be caught in a trap.

Well there were no Indians anywhere around and I did not see one for 20 years when I saw one at the depot in Omaha but the fear was as dreadful to me as if they were really there and I guess no one knew for sure but they might be. For that was the summer of the Custer massacre [1876] and the plains Indians were all off their regular hunting grounds.

Although only one year from sod the garden spot where the fruit trees and bushes were planted had by repeated plowing and harrowing been so pulverized that we had a really fine garden with very few weeds. We all took a great interest and pride in it and very soon it made a lot of difference in our table. I then learned as I had not realized before what a difference a few fresh vegetables can make in the appearance of the table as well as the satisfaction of the appetite; and I resolved always to have abundance of them in season and a cellar full for winter, which resolve has been pretty fully carried out to a great advantage both to pocket book and health. I am convinced that nothing else equals an early hour or two in the garden with hoe and rake to keep an *overworked* housewife equal to her duties. She comes back to the dishes and cooking with lungs full of fresh air which could not be got by simply walking or riding around, and the outdoor interest brightens the day, and makes the indoor work more pleasing. I always began to feel more fit in the spring as soon as I could get out to work in the dirt.

While Father and the boys had been off harvesting the year before, the grasshoppers had "lit" where they were at work, and ending all need of work had harvested everything themselves, even the grain already shocked. So the boys were often talking about it and wishing I could have seen them and wondering when they would come again. I had seen a few hoppers I thought all my life and could not realize how they could do all the damage they did in so short a time but one clear afternoon about 3 o'clock Johnny came to the dugout door and hollered "Luna come out here and see the grasshoppers flying over."

I came out and looked around but did not see any hoppers. Looked up and did not see any.

"Why there are no hoppers" I said.

"Yes that cloud is hoppers" said John.

"No that is just a cloud" I said. "See, it is going to rain."

"Yes I am afraid it will rain hoppers" said John. "Can't you see them?"

"No."

"Come here" he said. "Now get the edge of the roof between you and the sun and look."

As I did so I exclaimed "Oh John it is going to snow. The air up there is full of snow, big white flakes of snow. Lots of it is beginning to come down."

"Yes" said John "they are starting to light. What can we do, what can we save? Let us go to the garden and get what we can. We can put some things in the cellar."

And off he ran for [a] box or sack to gather something in. I was slower as I did not see the need to gather green and perishable garden stuff until something was destroying it but by the time I could get out the things were already gray with locusts and the air full of more coming down. They lit on me my head my dress my hands and no place to put my feet except as they hopped up probably onto me. John was frantically pulling young beets and carrots and onions but he shouted to me to go back and try and keep them out of the house. He could save what we could use of the green stuff before it spoiled.

The sweet corn was just getting big enough to begin using but now no corn could be seen. The green was all covered with gray hoppers and where the ears were was simply a large cluster of hoppers while between the rows they were several hoppers deep waiting for a chance to feed. And the noise. Who could believe a grasshopper feeding made a noise but the whole army of them made a noise as of a bunch of hogs chanking. I was glad to get back in the house but found the entry way well stacked with hoppers so it was hard to shake them off my clothes and get in without a lot of them going in also and I had no desire to go out among them again. They still kept slowly coming down, coming down looking like snow till nearly down they changed to gray. Finally John gave up and came in and we sure felt pretty blue.

"That is the end of all our fruit trees and berries" said John "as well as the corn and potatoes."

"Oh surely they can't eat the potatoes John."

"Well they will eat all the tops and all that are near the top and they are so green they will rot in the ground." John had brought the shovel in the house when he came and I now saw why as he opened the door and went out and shovelled the hoppers out of the entry way to the dugout. This he did every little while and between times he chased and threw out those that had got in the house so he kept pretty busy and when he went after a bucket of water he took a big cloth to tie over the pail so he could get it home without half hoppers as he said. Night came. Father and Fred came home and we went to bed but could still hear the hoppers chanking chanking.

The next morning the hoppers were still there though the chanking was not so loud as most of the green stuff was eaten. I think that towards night they rose up and left as suddenly as they came though it may have been the morning after.

Anyway when they said they were gone I went out of the house and to the garden to see what was left. Desolation only. Where the onions carrots beets and sweet potatoes had been was not a single thing, no sign of leaf or stem, only holes in the ground where they had eaten down and eaten out every bit of vegetable fiber. The fruit trees had all the small limbs completely eaten away and all the bark from the entire tree and if they had stayed a few hours longer I suppose there would have been only holes in the ground where roots were eaten out. The corn was eaten off completely, nothing to tell there had been a corn field there. Also, on going out to the road and onto the prairie [I saw] all the grass eaten down into the roots.

Well we knew of course one of the first things to do was to raise our own meat and we must get started in hogs. John Ellis had an old chicken-eating razor back sow he had brought from Illinois and she pestered me to distraction by coming up and catching my chickens. She would come on a lope as far as I could see her and spite of all I could do to head her off would run around and around the house till [she] tired out when I would chase her home. She seemed fairly crazy to catch chickens. Well she had a litter of pigs and John sold one to J. T. for $2.00 as soon as it was two weeks old. I did not like the breed [and] feared it would be like its mother but J. T. said he did not know where we could get another and it would probably be all right if we did not let it get a taste of chicken. But no sir, no sooner had it come than it began to chase chickens and it kept me busy watching it. It was rather a cute little pig for that and we gave it a good deal of our milk but nothing would satisfy it but to smell chickens and run after them and in spite of me it got one occasionally. We had no pen for it and nothing to make one of but shut it in a little box at night. It soon became the pest of my life and when we had had it about 4 weeks I went to the garden one day. At such times I would get Willie to play with it or shut it in the box but this time I was coming right back so put it and Willie in the house. Some way I felt very uneasy and ran back as fast as I could and on opening the door got an awful shock. There lay Willie flat on his back, the pig standing on his chest with its snout in his mouth and the blood running freely down both sides of Willie's face. He could not make a noise as his mouth was full of pig's snout. Of course I grabbed the pig but it was fairly crazed to get back for more blood but I finally threw it out the door.

Willie had found his voice by that time and was so covered with blood it took some time washing him to see how bad he was hurt. Finally found big gashes inside of his lip and in his tongue on the underside mostly. I was terribly frightened but there was no one near so after a while it stopped bleeding and while he had a very sore mouth for some time no great harm was done.

If anyone needed money to buy seed or grains or anything which was needed to farm with the town was full of money lenders the most of whom took 10 times the needful security and as a great favor procured your money "from a friend in the east" at never less than 2 come 10 and I have known the Updike Brothers to charge 7 come 10 interest. Three per cent come was the usual charge if you were not too hard up and it meant that to borrow a hundred dollars for seed or harvest hands or anything you gave a mortgage on everything you had and all your future prospects for $100 at 10% interest. Then if it was to run 6 months 3% a month or $18 was kept back. The note was made for 100 and 10% interest but you only got 82 dollars. This was the business that started a number of soon wealthy families and they were known as 3 come 10ers. At the time the Updikes tried to charge us 7 come 10 they assured us there was more demand for their money at that rate than they could supply. As this was needed to farm with and in the spring we could have afforded to pay any reasonable interest but for 6 months we would only have received 58 dollars and given note for 100 and 10% interest, no wonder the Updikes soon became millionaires and great ones on the Chicago board of trade.

There was a good deal of sickness among the babies in the neighborhood but we stayed at home. Fred came to help harvest and though we knew Jimmie was not well we did not think it anything serious till one day all of a sudden we got scared and sent Juniata for Dr. Ackley and when he came and looked him over baby looked up at him and smiled and I thought he would say we did not need to call him but he said "I am sorry but it is too late to do anything now."

We were dumbfounded stupefied and as he was a young doctor then we thought he did not know. He left us something of course and said something about while there was life there was always a little hope and went away. But alas he knew too well. Old Lady Strohl, Jim's mother, came up to stay with us. I suppose Fred went home and told them on the way how sick the baby was. I could not let him out of my arms all night and in the morning with a look of love and [a] bright smile he was gone. He looked in my eyes and smiled and looked up over my head and smiled as if he saw something fine and I felt that he went from my arms to my mother's. I told Mrs. Strohl and she said "Might

be, might be." She wanted to wash and dress him but I could not allow anyone else to touch my baby and so washed dressed him for the last time putting
on him a little embroidered dress and skirt my mother made for me. Without
my knowing it Aunt Hattie, I suppose, cut a piece out of the back of each and
gave me afterwards which I still have.

We buried him in the yard. We could not take our baby away too far and a
great many came to the burial that I never saw before or since. It seemed to me
many thought it a holiday of some sort and the women acted very curious regarding everything in the house. I had a fine bedspread my mother had made
on the bed and everything fixed up as good as possible and I guess they meant
all right but to me nothing mattered but that the baby was gone from our
lives and I could not bear to see folks act so concerned with every little thing.
I soon found I could not stand up. My limbs would not support me and I had
to spend several days in bed while the men folks got along with the harvest and
cows and made out the best they could.

Women trapped in the Triangle Shirtwaist fire on March 25, 1911, had to choose between being burned alive or jumping to near-certain death from upper-story windows. The disaster took 146 lives.

PART THREE

Industrial America

Opportunity and Exploitation

The United States, already a very rich nation in 1860, still mostly produced food and raw materials for its own people and for consumers elsewhere in the Atlantic world. In the half century that followed, it became the world's largest industrial power. This remarkable economic growth affected virtually every American's life, offering both hardships and opportunities.

Working conditions at the Triangle Shirtwaist Company, whose workers faced mostly adversity, aptly illustrate the ironies of progress. By the time the Triangle fire occurred, American society was only beginning to recognize the new workers in their midst and the peculiar dangers they faced. Sewing garments that defined the new middle-class style in high-rise factory buildings, these young immigrant women were risking their lives in unsafe conditions for low wages.

Andrew Carnegie was the era's chief illustration of the opportunities the new order offered to those able to seize them. His advice to young men was undoubtedly practical. Yet Carnegie's own career illustrated a major force that limited opportunity for others: the rise of vast corporations dominating whole industries. Men like George Rice discovered how such corporate trusts limited opportunity and began to develop the means to fight against them.

The life of Rose Pastor Stokes reflects both the opportunities and the misfortunes of rapid industrialization. Struggling as a child laborer in cigar factories with enormous family responsibilities, Stokes nonetheless succeeded in becoming a journalist and a radical reformer. It is a mark of the fluidity of American society that she married a man of great wealth and social background. That Upton Sinclair, dreaming of alleviating the misery of working people, managed instead to improve the health of the American public illustrates both the capacity of American society to respond to social problems and the limits of that capacity. And nowhere were the perils and promises of the time more inextricably mixed than in the lives of new immigrants like those who wrote to "A Bintel Brief," a regular feature of the *Jewish Daily Forward*, about their struggles to adjust to and succeed in a new society.

Points of View:
The Triangle Shirtwaist Fire (1911)

15

Conditions at the
Triangle Shirtwaist Company

Pauline Newman et al.

"I think if you want to go into the . . . twelve-, fourteen- or fifteen-story buildings they call workshops," New York City's fire chief testified in 1910, "you will find it very interesting to see the number of people in one of these buildings with absolutely not one fire protection, without any means of escape in case of fire." At the time, over half a million New Yorkers worked eight or more floors above ground level, beyond the eighty-five-foot reach of the fire fighters' ladders. When the shirtwaist makers struck in 1909, they demanded improved safety and sanitary conditions as well as better wages. The strikers did not win most of their demands, and fire safety in particular did not improve.

On Saturday, March 25, 1911, the issues of the strike received renewed meaning when fire broke out in the shop of the Triangle Shirtwaist Company, on the eighth, ninth, and tenth floors of a modern, fireproof loft building in lower Manhattan. The number of exits was inadequate, doors were locked to prevent pilfering, other doors opened inward, and the stairwell had no exit to the roof. Hundreds of workers were trapped; within half an hour, 146 of them, mostly young immigrant women, had died. The owners of the Triangle Shirtwaist Company were later tried for manslaughter, found not guilty, and collected insurance to replace their factory.

The fire evoked a public cry for labor reform. More than 120,000 people attended a funeral for the unclaimed dead. The International Ladies Garment Workers Union and the Women's Trade Union League, both supporters of previous strikes and safety protests, were now joined by the city's leading civic organizations in protest meetings and demands—eventually heeded by the New York state legislature—for factory safety legislation.

In a speech many years later to a group of trade union women, Pauline Newman, who became the first woman organizer for the International Ladies Garment Workers Union, recounts what it was like to work at the Triangle Company. Kate Alterman, Ann Gullo, and Ida Nelson testified at the company owners' trial about their experience during that terrible half hour. Rose Schneiderman's speech at the fashionable memorial meeting at the Metropolitan Opera House held commemorating the victims created a sensation and began the twenty-nine-year-old Schneiderman's career in labor reform.

BEFORE YOU READ

1. What were the main abuses that Newman reported?
2. How did Kate Alterman, Ann Gullo, and Ida Nelson manage to survive the fire?
3. Would a speech like Rose Schneiderman's help the cause of factory safety or would it alienate potential supporters?

PAULINE NEWMAN

I'd like to tell you about the kind of world we lived in 75 years ago because all of you probably weren't even born then. Seventy-five years is a long time, but I'd like to give you at least a glimpse of that world because it has no resemblance to the world we live in today, in any respect.

That world 75 years ago was a world of incredible exploitation of men, women, and children. I went to work for the Triangle Shirtwaist Company in 1901. The corner of a shop would resemble a kindergarten because we were young, eight, nine, ten years old. It was a world of greed; the human being didn't mean anything. The hours were from 7:30 in the morning to 6:30 at night when it wasn't busy. When the season was on we worked until 9 o'clock. No overtime pay, not even supper money. There was a bakery in the garment center that produced little apple pies the size of this ashtray [*holding up ashtray for group to see*] and that was what we got for our overtime instead of money.

My wages as a youngster were $1.50 for a seven-day week. I know it sounds exaggerated, but it isn't; it's true. If you worked there long enough and you were satisfactory you got 50 cents a week increase every year. So by the time I left the Triangle Waist Company in 1909, my wages went up to $5.50, and that was quite a wage in those days.

All shops were as bad as the Triangle Waist Company. When you were told Saturday afternoon, through a sign on the elevator, "If you don't come in on Sunday, you needn't come in on Monday," what choice did you have? You had no choice.

I worked on the 9th floor with a lot of youngsters like myself. Our work was not difficult. When the operators were through with sewing shirtwaists, there was a little thread left, and we youngsters would get a little scissors and trim the threads off.

And when the inspectors came around, do you know what happened? The supervisors made all the children climb into one of those crates that they ship material in, and they covered us over with finished shirtwaists until the inspector had left, because of course we were too young to be working in the factory legally.

Barbara Mayer Wertheimer, *We Were There: The Story of Working Women in America* (New York: Pantheon, 1977), pp. 294–295.

The Triangle Waist Company was a family affair, all relatives of the owner running the place, watching to see that you did your work, watching when you went into the toilet. And if you were two or three minutes longer than foreman or foreladies thought you should be, it was deducted from your pay. If you came five minutes late in the morning because the freight elevator didn't come down to take you up in time, you were sent home for half a day without pay.

Rubber heels came into use around that time and our employers were the first to use them; you never knew when they would sneak up on you, spying, to be sure you did not talk to each other during working hours.

Most of the women rarely took more than $6.00 a week home, most less. The early sweatshops were usually so dark that gas jets (for light) burned day and night. There was no insulation in the winter, only a pot-bellied stove in the middle of the factory. If you were a finisher and could take your work with you (finishing is a hand operation) you could sit next to the stove in winter. But if you were an operator or a trimmer it was very cold indeed. Of course in the summer you suffocated with practically no ventilation.

There was no drinking water, maybe a tap in the hall, warm, dirty. What were you going to do? Drink this water or none at all. Well, in those days there were vendors who came in with bottles of pop for 2 cents, and much as you disliked to spend the two pennies you got the pop instead of the filthy water in the hall.

The condition was no better and no worse than the tenements where we lived. You got out of the workshop, dark and cold in winter, hot in summer, dirty unswept floors, no ventilation, and you would go home. What kind of home did you go to? You won't find the tenements *we* lived in. Some of the rooms didn't have any windows. I lived in a two-room tenement with my mother and two sisters and the bedroom had no windows, the facilities were down in the yard, but that's the way it was in the factories too. In the summer the sidewalk, fire escapes, and the roof of the tenements became bedrooms just to get a breath of air.

We wore cheap clothes, lived in cheap tenements, ate cheap food. There was nothing to look forward to, nothing to expect the next day to be better.

Someone once asked me; "How did you survive?" And I told him, what alternative did we have? You stayed and you survived, that's all.

KATE ALTERMAN

At the Fire

Then I went to the toilet room. Margaret [Schwartz] disappeared from me and I wanted to go up Greene Street side, but the whole door was in flames, so I went and hid myself in the toilet rooms and bent my face over the sink, and then I ran to the Washington side elevator, but there was a big crowd and I couldn't

Leon Stein, *The Triangle Fire* (Philadelphia: Lippincott, 1962), pp. 55–56, 59–60, 144–45, 191–92.

pass through there. Then I noticed someone, a whole crowd around the door and I saw Bernstein, the manager's brother, trying to open the door, and there was Margaret near him. Bernstein tried the door, he couldn't open it.

And then Margaret began to open the door. I take her on one side—I pushed her on the side and I said, "Wait, I will open that door." I tried, pulled the handle in and out, all ways and I couldn't open it. She pushed me on the other side, got hold of the handle and then she tried. And then I saw her bending down on her knees, and her hair was loose, and the trail of her dress was a little far from her, and then a big smoke came and I couldn't see.

I just know it was Margaret, and I said, "Margaret," and she didn't reply. I left Margaret, I turned my head on the side and I noticed the trail of her dress and the ends of her hair begin to burn. Then I ran in, in a small dressing room that was on the Washington side, there was a big crowd and I went out from there, stood in the center of the room, between the machines and between the examining tables.

I noticed afterwards on the other side, near the Washington side windows, Bernstein, the manager's brother throwing around like a wildcat at the window, and he was chasing his head out of the window, and pull himself back in—he wanted to jump, I suppose, but he was afraid. And then I saw the flames cover him. I noticed on the Greene Street side someone else fell down on the floor and the flames cover him.

And then I stood in the center of the room, and I just turned my coat on the left side with the fur to my face, the lining on the outside, got hold of a bunch of dresses that was lying on the examining table not burned yet, covered my head and tried to run through the flames on the Greene Street side. The whole door was a red curtain of fire, but a young lady came and she wouldn't let me in. I kicked her with my foot and I don't know what became of her.

I ran out through the Greene Street side door, right through the flames on to the roof.

ANNA GULLO

At the Fire

[T]he flames came up higher. I looked back into the shop and saw the flames were bubbling on the machines. I turned back to the window and made the sign of the cross. I went to jump out of the window. But I had no courage to do it. . . .

. . . I had on my fur coat and my hat with two feathers. I pulled my woolen skirt over my head. Somebody had hit me with water from a pail. I was soaked.

At the vestibule door there was a big barrel of oil. I went through the staircase door. As I was going down I heard a loud noise. Maybe the barrel of oil exploded. I remember when I passed the eighth floor all I could see was a mass of flames. The wind was blowing up the staircase.

When I got to the bottom I was cold and wet. I was crying for my sister. I remember a man came over to me. I was sitting on the curb. He lifted my head and looked into my face. It must have been all black from the smoke of the fire. He wiped my face with a handkerchief. He said, 'I thought you were my sister.' He gave me his coat.

I don't know who he was. I never again found my sister alive. I hope he found his.

IDA NELSON

At the Fire

I don't know what made me do it but I bent over and pushed my pay into the top of my stocking. Then I ran to the Greene Street side and tried to get into the staircase. . . .

[But where Anna Gullo had just exited, there was now a wall of fire.] I couldn't get through. The heat was too intense.

I ran back into the shop and found part of a roll of piece goods. I think it was lawn; it was on the bookkeeper's desk. I wrapped it around and around me until only my face showed.

Then I ran right into the fire on the stairway and up toward the roof. I couldn't breathe. The lawn caught fire. As I ran, I tried to keep peeling off the burning lawn, twisting and turning as I ran. By the time I passed the tenth floor and got to the roof, I had left most of the lawn in ashes behind me. But I still had one end of it under my arm. That was the arm that got burned.

ROSE SCHNEIDERMAN

At the Memorial Meeting
at the Metropolitan Opera House

I would be a traitor to those poor burned bodies if I were to come here to talk good fellowship. We have tried you good people of the public—and we have found you wanting.

The old Inquisition had its rack and its thumbscrews and its instruments of torture with iron teeth. We know what these things are today: the iron teeth are our necessities, the thumbscrews are the high-powered and swift machinery close to which we must work, and the rack is here in the firetrap structures that will destroy us the minute they catch fire.

This is not the first time girls have been burned alive in this city. Every week I must learn of the untimely death of one of my sister workers. Every year thousands of us are maimed. The life of men and women is so cheap and property is so sacred! There are so many of us for one job, it matters little if 140-odd are burned to death.

We have tried you, citizens! We are trying you now and you have a couple of dollars for the sorrowing mothers and brothers and sisters by way of a charity gift. But every time the workers come out in the only way they know to protest against conditions which are unbearable, the strong hand of the law is allowed to press down heavily upon us.

Public officials have only words of warning for us—warning that we must be intensely orderly and must be intensely peaceable, and they have the work-house just back of all their warnings. The strong hand of the law beats us back when we rise—back into the conditions that make life unbearable.

I can't talk fellowship to you who are gathered here. Too much blood has been spilled. I know from experience it is up to the working people to save themselves. And the only way is through a strong working-class movement.

16

A Fire Trap

William Gunn Shepherd

On the afternoon of March 25, 1911, when fire broke out in the loft building at Wash-ington Place and Greene Street in lower Manhattan that housed the Triangle Shirt-waist Company, the New York World *reporter William Gunn Shepherd happened to be in the vicinity. Finding a telephone in a store across the street, he reported the scene before him to a relay of four men at the newspaper. Then the exhausted Shep-herd returned to the* World *building further downtown at Park Row to rewrite his dispatches. Accompanying his story were pictures, diagrams of the scene, reports from other journalists, and a list of the dead. The first six pages of the newspaper's next edi-tion were wholly given over to the fire.*

This article is a remarkably complete eyewitness account of a great public disaster. Given that it appeared in a conservative and respected newspaper, it suggests—both by what it says and what it does not—a great deal about how respectable people of the period thought about the victims and heroes of such an event.

Before You Read
1. Did Shepherd connect the fire to concerns that had led to the earlier strike?
2. How did he deal with the issue of criminal liability?
3. What picture do you get of the men and women involved?
4. How does this report compare to the survivors' accounts?

At 4.35 o'clock yesterday afternoon fire springing from a source that may never be positively identified was discovered in the rear of the eighth floor of

New York World, March 26, 1911.

the ten-story building at the northwest corner of Washington place and Greene street, the first of three floors occupied as a factory of the Triangle Waist Company.

At 11.30 o'clock Chief Croker made this statement:

> Every body has been removed. The number taken out, which includes those who jumped from the windows, is 141. The number of those that have died so far in the hospitals is seven, which makes the total number of deaths at this time 148.

At 2 o'clock this morning Chief Croker estimated the total dead as one hundred and fifty-four. He said further: "I expected something of this kind to happen in these so-called fire-proof buildings, which are without adequate protection as far as fire-escapes are concerned."

More than a third of those who lost their lives did so in jumping from windows. The firemen who answered the first of the four alarms turned in found 30 bodies on the pavements of Washington place and Greene street. Almost all of these were girls, as were the great majority of them all.

A single fire escape, a single stairway, one working passenger elevator and one working freight elevator offered the only means of escape from the building. A loft building under the specifications of the law, no other ways of egress were required, and to this fact, which also permitted the use of the building as a factory, the dreadful toll may be traced. Two other elevators were there, but were not in operation.

The property damage resulting from the fire did not exceed $100,000.

To accommodate the unprecedented number of bodies, the Charities pier at the foot of East Twenty-sixth street was opened, for the first time since the Slocum disaster, with which this will rank, for no fire in a building in New York ever claimed so many lives before.

Inspection by Acting Superintendent of Buildings Ludwig will be made the basis for charges of criminal negligence on the ground that the fire-proof doors leading to one of the inclosed tower stairways were locked.

The list of dead and injured will be found on page 4.

STREETS LITTERED WITH BODIES OF MEN AND WOMEN

It was the most appalling horror since the Slocum disaster and the Iroquois Theatre fire in Chicago. Every available ambulance in Manhattan was called upon to cart the dead to the Morgue—bodies charred to unrecognizable blackness or reddened to a sickly hue—as was to be seen by shoulders or limbs protruding through flame eaten clothing. Men and women, boys and girls were of the dead that littered the street; that is actually the condition—the streets were littered.

The fire began in the eighth story. The flames licked and shot their way up through the other two stories. All three floors were occupied by the Triangle Waist Company. The estimate of the number of the employees at work is made by Chief Croker at about 1,000. The proprietors of the company say 700 men and girls were in their place.

Whatever the number, they had no chance of escape. Before smoke or flame gave signs from the windows the loss of life was fully under way. The first signs that persons in the street knew that these three top stories had turned into red furnaces in which human creatures were being caught and incinerated was when screaming men and women and boys and girls crowded out on the many window ledges and threw themselves into the streets far below.

They jumped with their clothing ablaze. The hair of some of the girls streamed up of flame as they leaped. Thud after thud sounded on the pavements. It is the ghastly fact that on both the Greene street and the Washington place sides of the building there grew mounds of the dead and dying.

And the worst horror of all was that in this heap of the dead now and then there stirred a limb or sounded a moan.

Within the three flaming floors it was as frightful. There flames enveloped many so that they died instantly. When Fire Chief Croker could make his way into the three floors he found sights that utterly staggered him—that sent him, a man used to viewing horrors, back and down into the street with quivering lips.

The floors were black with smoke. And then he saw as the smoke drifted away bodies burned to bare bones. There were skeletons bending over sewing machines.

The elevator boys saved hundreds. They each made twenty trips from the time of the alarm until twenty minutes later when they could do no more. Fire was streaming into the shaft, flames biting at the cables. They fled for their own lives.

Some—about seventy—chose a successful avenue of escape. They clambered up a ladder to the roof. A few remembered the fire escape. Many may have thought of it, but only as they uttered cries of dismay.

Wretchedly inadequate was this fire escape—a lone ladder running down a rear narrow court, which was smoke filled as the fire raged, one narrow door giving access to the ladder. By the scores they fought and struggled and breathed fire and died trying to make that needle-eye road to self-preservation.

Those who got the roof—got life. Young men of the University of New York Commercial and Law School, studious young fellows who had chosen to spend their Saturday afternoon in study, answered the yells for aid that came from the smoking roof by thrusting ladders from the upper windows of their class rooms to the frantic men and women on the roofs.

None of the fire-besieged hesitated an instant. In going down on all fours and struggling across these slender bridges—eighty feet above the paved court—to the out-thrust arms of the students. It is a fact that none of the men on the roof, wild with excitement as they were, made a movement toward the ladder till the girls had crossed to safety.

Those who did make the fire escape—and these were but the few who had, in spite of panic, first thought of it—huddled themselves into what appeared as bad a trap as the one from which they had escaped. They found themselves let down into an absolutely closed court; and when through the cellar of the Asch Building they sought to make their way to the street, they encountered on the ground floor iron shutters securely clamped into place.

For a time they stood around or knelt in prayer, not knowing when the burning building might crash in upon them. Some of these dashed back and screamed, in the hope of attracting the attention of the law students in the university building. But there were so many agonized cries ringing in the air that the youths never heard the shouts from below.

Those who had got down the fire escape and found themselves cut off from the street by the iron shutters rushed frantically back to the court and ran around distraught, until firemen putting their implements to the iron shutters rushed through the Greene street entrance. They herded the wild-eyed group to the street.

Shivering at the chasm below them, scorched by the fire behind, there were some that still held positions on the window sills when the first squad of the firemen arrived.

The nets were spread below with all promptness. Citizens were commandeered into the service—as the firemen necessarily gave their attention to the one engine and hose of the force that first arrived.

The catapult force that the bodies gathered in the long plunges made the nets utterly without avail. Screaming girls and men, as they fell, tore the nets from the grasp of the holders and the bodies struck the sidewalks and lay just as they fell. Some of the bodies ripped big holes through the life-nets.

The curious, uncanny feature about this deadly fire is that it was not spectacular from flame and smoke. The city had no sign of the disaster that was happening. The smoke of the fire scarcely blackened the sky. No big, definite clouds arose to blot out the sunshine and the springtime brightness of the blue above.

Concentrated, the fire burned within. The flames caught all the flimsy lace stuff and linens that go into the making of spring and summer shirt-waists and fed eagerly upon the rolls of silk.

The cutting room was laden with the stuff on long tables. The employees were toiling over such material at the rows and rows of machines. Sinisterly the spring day gave aid to the fire. Many of the window panes facing south and east were drawn down. Draughts had full play.

It was the first fire with heavy loss of life in a skyscraper factory building in this city, but it bore out Fire Chief Croker's predictions of several years' standing. These were that such a fire would absolutely mean disaster! The walls of such buildings are fireproof, but the contents of the buildings—as in this case—are highly inflammable. The fire, having no manner of eating into the walls, concentrates on all the food it can find in the interior. The result is a furnace, with the flames fighting upward till they strike the roof. Then the fire mushrooms and starts back down the walls.

This is what happened in the Asch Building yesterday. Before a curl of smoke sifted outward through the windows the flames had swept and swirled around the rooms and mercilessly killed.

FOUR THOUSAND OUT BEFORE THE FIRE

Four thousand workers most fortunately had left the building about an hour and a half before—had tripped along toward the east side laughingly, buoyantly. For this was their fine day—pay day. These were the girls and boys and men and women from the factories and waterooms on the seven lower floors and the shipping departments in the basement.

All the places except the Triangle Waist Company's factory closed down at 3 o'clock yesterday. The Triangle Waist Company does not recognize the union. Around their big shop a strike centered not long ago. The delay in the filling of orders caused by the strike had made it necessary for the toilers to work overtime. That was why they sat bent over their machines and otherwise were busy at their tasks yesterday afternoon.

Those of the Triangle factory had, many of them, drawn their pay. Detectives were placed on guard over the bodies till they were taken to the Morgue, lest vandals should seek to rob. But no such creature appeared on the scene of the disaster. When darkness came upon the rows of bodies huddled under brown tarpaulins the vigilance was renewed. But no ghoul attempted to prowl among the dead.

So swift and unwarningly did the fire come that the first man on the street aware of it saw no smoke at all. He saw only a girl standing on a window ledge on the ninth floor of the building, waving her arms and shrieking that she was going to jump. He yelled back at her to stand where she was. And then as he stared, wonderingly, he saw a mere puff of smoke, such as a man might blow from a cigarette.

This man, John Maron of No. 116 Waverly Place, suddenly took panic as he saw the girl lean far over the sill and come tumbling down, with a flutter of her skirts. He saw her fall past floor after floor and strike the pavement on her head.

A man who later gave his name as R. Garner, but would not tell his address, had seen Maron and heard him shout, without realizing what it meant until the girl's body on the pavement came across his vision. Then he too looked upward.

What he saw made him rush for the nearest fire box at an opposite corner, about one hundred feet away. He had seen countless windows crowded with white faces and he had heard a frantic, swelling call for help.

He tore at the key of the fire box. And he said last night that somehow before he turned he became conscious that there was a frightful rain of bodies from the windows.

The first fireman to arrive took but a single glance at the tall building, saw with a gasp the heap of bodies and rushed to summon all the help available. Police whistles began to shrill their calls, and from opposite buildings hundreds were leaning out of windows, shouting insanely in their agony at the sight.

It seemed a long time to the helpless watchers before wailing sirens of many fire engines, the rattling bells of patrol wagons and ambulances sounded near by. Reserve after reserve squad of police from everywhere in the city were shunted to the neighborhood. Fifteen ambulances took stations along Washington Place. Calls for more ambulances went out.

In less than half an hour ten thousand persons were pressing the swiftly constructed police lines. Thousands ran down the side streets from Broadway. A huge crowd lined along the lawns of Washington Square, peering down Washington Place. For the most part the crowd could barely see the evidence of the horror that had happened—could make out but vaguely the black objects on the water blackened sidewalks.

WOMEN GOT FIRST CHANCE
AT THE WINDOWS

From all that could be learned it appears that the men among these shirt waist workers were really men—pallid faced weaklings as they might have appeared as they threaded their way to the shop early yesterday morning. It appears that even the boys acted in fine, manly fashion.

Eye witnesses of those who saw the wild leaps from the windows declared that the girls were given first chance at even this miserable prospect of saving their lives. Men could be seen in the reddening rooms helping the girls to the window sills for a final breath of life sustaining air.

On the ledge of a ninth story window two girls stood silently watching the arrival of the first fire apparatus. Twice one of the girls made a move to jump. The other restrained her, tottering in her foothold as she did so. They watched firemen rig the ladders up against the wall. They saw the last ladder lifted and pushed into place. They saw that it reached only the seventh floor.

For the third time the more frightened girl tried to leap. The bells of arriving fire wagons must have risen to them. The other girl gesticulated in the direction of the sounds. But she talked to ears that could no longer hear. Scarcely turning, her companion dived head first into the street.

The other girl drew herself erect. The crowd in the street were stretching their arms up at her shouting and imploring her not to leap. She made a steady gesture, looking down as if to assure them she would remain brave.

But a thin flame shot out of the window at her back and touched her hair. In an instant her head was aflame. She tore at her burning hair, lost her balance and came shooting down upon the mound of bodies below.

ELEVATOR BOYS MADE TWENTY TRIPS

If it had not been for the courage of the elevator boys the disaster might have been doubly if not trebly appalling. These young men, John Vito and Joseph Gasper, ran their cars up and down until the shafts were ablaze. Each made no less than twenty trips up and down after the first alarm was given.

And Vito attributes fine heroism to Maurice Blanck and Isaac Harris, the owners of the Triangle Waist Company. He says the partners stood by the shafts, holding back men who would have pressed forward and calling to him to take only the women down. Vito showed bloody hands to indicate how he had fought back the few cowardly men who had tried to overrun the women.

Blanck's two little children and their governess were with him when the alarm came. He had just ordered a taxicab and was awaiting its arrival before starting for his home. Blanck and his children and his partner, Harris managed afterward to make their way to the roof and the men handed the governess and the children over the ladder to the students of the University Law School and then themselves crawled to safety

FOR CRITICAL THINKING

1. How would a present-day event similar to the Triangle Shirtwaist fire be covered on television news? How would its tone and attitude be different from that of the *New York World* story? Would present-day journalists delve into aspects of the story that their 1911 counterparts would not?

2. The role of government in regulating working conditions was controversial in 1911 when the Triangle Shirtwaist fire occurred, and it remains controversial in the present as indicated by extensive criticism of the Occupational Safety and Health Administration (OSHA) for restricting economic growth. Should local, state, and federal government have the responsibility to inspect and regulate working conditions at privately owned enterprises or should this be an issue between workers and management?

17

Lecture to Young Men
Andrew Carnegie

Historians who have studied the captains of industry who emerged during and after the Civil War have found that such men overwhelmingly came from comfortable or even wealthy backgrounds. Andrew Carnegie (1835–1919) was the rare exception: He actually began poor and without social connections became very rich. His family migrated from Scotland when Carnegie was twelve, settling in Pittsburgh. Working as a telegraph operator for the Pennsylvania Railroad, Carnegie won the favor of a senior official of the railroad, Thomas A. Scott, who sponsored his rise in the company and guided him into a variety of entrepreneurial and investment opportunities. Like many of his contemporaries, Carnegie became rich during the 1860s, avoiding the military draft during the Civil War (for three hundred dollars a man could legally buy his way out of serving). In the 1870s he focused on the steel business. Using the advanced business techniques he had learned in railroading and ruthlessly holding wages down, Carnegie soon dominated the industry and emerged as one of the world's richest men.

The remainder of Carnegie's long life was at least as interesting and unusual as his business career. He virtually created the modern role of philanthropist, giving away his money with the same planning and care that had amassed his fortune. Most famous for building thousands of libraries, Carnegie also supported efforts toward world peace, endowed universities, and built concert halls.

Carnegie delivered this address in 1885 to a group of young men at a business school in Pittsburgh. (Like the rest of his contemporaries, he never thought of sharing his message with young women.) Its optimism and emphasis on character make it typical of American success literature from Benjamin Franklin's autobiography to present-day motivational literature.

BEFORE YOU READ

1. What, according to Carnegie, did young men need to do to succeed?
2. What were the main temptations they must avoid?
3. How does this advice compare to what you have heard about prospects for success in the present? What emphases are different and what present-day considerations were absent in Carnegie's time?

THE ROAD TO BUSINESS SUCCESS: A TALK TO YOUNG MEN

It is well that young men should begin at the beginning and occupy the most subordinate positions. Many of the leading business men of Pittsburgh had a serious responsibility thrust upon them at the very threshold of their career.

From an address to Curry Commercial College, Pittsburgh, June 23, 1885. Published in Andrew Carnegie, *The Empire of Business* (New York: Doubleday, Page, and Co., 1902), pp. 3–18.

They were introduced to the broom, and spent the first hours of their business lives sweeping out the office. I notice we have janitors and janitresses now in offices, and our young men unfortunately miss that salutary branch of a business education. But if by chance the professional sweeper is absent any morning the boy who has the genius of the future partner in him will not hesitate to try his hand at the broom. The other day a fond fashionable mother in Michigan asked a young man whether he had ever seen a young lady sweep in a room so grandly as her Priscilla. He said no, he never had, and the mother was gratified beyond measure, but then said he, after a pause, "What I should like to see her do is sweep out a room." It does not hurt the newest comer to sweep out the office if necessary. I was one of those sweepers myself, and who do you suppose were my fellow sweepers? David McCargo, now superintendent of the Alleghany Valley Railroad; Robert Pitcairn, Superintendent of the Pennsylvania Railroad, and Mr. Moreland, City Attorney. We all took turns, two each morning did the sweeping; and now I remember Davie was so proud of his clean white shirt bosom that he used to spread over it an old silk bandana handkerchief which he kept for the purpose, and we other boys thought he was putting on airs. So he was. None of us had a silk handkerchief.

Assuming that you have all obtained employment and are fairly started, my advice to you is "aim high." I would not give a fig for the young man who does not already see himself the partner or the head of an important firm. Do not rest content for a moment in your thoughts as head clerk, or foreman, or general manager in any concern, no matter how extensive. Say each to yourself. "My place is at the top." *Be king in your dreams.* Make your vow that you will reach that position, with untarnished reputation, and make no other vow to distract your attention, except the very commendable one that when you are a member of the firm or before that, if you have been promoted two or three times, you will form another partnership with the loveliest of her sex—a partnership to which our new partnership act has no application. The liability there is never limited.

Let me indicate two or three conditions essential to success. Do not be afraid that I am going to moralize, or inflict a homily upon you. I speak upon the subject only from the view of a man of the world, desirous of aiding you to become successful business men. You all know that there is no genuine, praiseworthy success in life if you are not honest, truthful, fair-dealing. I assume you are and will remain all these, and also that you are determined to live pure, respectable lives, free from pernicious or equivocal associations with one sex or the other. There is no creditable future for you else. Otherwise your learning and your advantages not only go for naught, but serve to accentuate your failure and your disgrace. I hope you will not take it amiss if I warn you against three of the gravest dangers which will beset you in your upward path.

The first and most seductive, and the destroyer of most young men, is the drinking of liquor. I am no temperance lecturer in disguise, but a man who knows and tells you what observation has proved to him; and I say to you that you are more likely to fail in your career from acquiring the habit of drinking liquor than from any, or all, the other temptations likely to assail you. You may

yield to almost any other temptation and reform—may brace up, and if not recover lost ground, at least remain in the race and secure and maintain a respectable position. But from the insane thirst for liquor escape is almost impossible. I have known but few exceptions to this rule. First, then, you must not
drink liquor to excess. Better if you do not touch it at all—much better; but
if this be too hard a rule for you then take your stand firmly here:—Resolve
never to touch it except at meals. A glass at dinner will not hinder your advance
in life or lower your tone; but I implore you hold it inconsistent with the dignity and self-respect of gentlemen, with what is due from yourselves to your-
selves, being the men you are, and especially the men you are determined to
become, to drink a glass of liquor at a bar. Be far too much of the gentleman
ever to enter a bar-room. You do not pursue your careers in safety unless you
stand firmly upon this ground. Adhere to it and you have escaped danger from
the deadliest of your foes.

The next greatest danger to a young business man in this community I believe to be that of speculation. When I was a telegraph operator here we had
no Exchanges in the City, but the men or firms who speculated upon the Eastern Exchanges were necessarily known to the operators. They could be
counted on the fingers of one hand. These men were not our citizens of first
repute: they were regarded with suspicion. I have lived to see all of these speculators irreparably ruined men, bankrupt in money and bankrupt in character.
There is scarcely an instance of a man who has made a fortune by speculation
and kept it. Gamesters die poor, and there is certainly not an instance of a speculator who has lived a life creditable to himself, or advantageous to the community. The man who grasps the morning paper to see first how his specula-
tive ventures upon the Exchanges are likely to result, unfits himself for the
calm consideration and proper solution of business problems, with which he
has to deal later in the day, and saps the sources of that persistent and concentrated energy upon which depend the permanent success, and often the
very safety, of his main business.

The speculator and the business man tread diverging lines. The former depends upon the sudden turn of fortune's wheel; he is a millionaire to-day, a
bankrupt to-morrow. But the man of business knows that only by years of patient, unremitting attention to affairs can he earn his reward, which is the result, not of chance, but of well-devised means for the attainment of ends. During all these years his is the cheering thought that by no possibility can he
benefit himself without carrying prosperity to others. The speculator on the
other hand had better never have lived so far as the good of others or the good
of the community is concerned. Hundreds of young men were tempted in this
city not long since to gamble in oil, and many were ruined; all were injured
whether they lost or won.

The third and last danger against which I shall warn you is one which has
wrecked many a fair craft which started well and gave promise of a prosperous
voyage. It is the perilous habit of indorsing—all the more dangerous, inas-

much as it assails one generally in the garb of friendship. It appeals to your generous instincts, and you say, "How can I refuse to lend my name only, to assist a friend?" It is because there is so much that is true and commendable in that view that the practice is so dangerous. Let me endeavor to put you upon safe honourable grounds in regard to it. I would say to you to make it a rule now, *never indorse:* but this is too much like never taste wine, or never smoke, or any other of the "nevers." They generally result in exceptions. You will as business men now and then probably become security for friends. Now, here is the line at which regard for the success of friends should cease and regard for your own honour begins.

If you owe anything, all your capital and all your effects are a solemn trust in your hands to be held inviolate for the security of those who have trusted you. Nothing can be done by you with honour which jeopardizes these first claims upon you. When a man in debt indorses for another, it is not his own credit or his own capital he risks, it is that of his own creditors. He violates a trust. Mark you then, never indorse until you have cash means not required for your own debts, and never indorse beyond those means.

I beseech you avoid liquor, speculation and indorsement. Do not fail in either, for liquor and speculation are the Scylla and Charybdis[1] of the young man's business sea, and indorsement his rock ahead.

Assuming you are safe in regard to these your gravest dangers, the question now is how to rise from the subordinate position we have imagined you in, through the successive grades to the position for which you are, in my opinion, and, I trust, in your own, evidently intended. I can give you the secret. It lies mainly in this. Instead of the question, "What must I do for my employer?" substitute "What can I do?" Faithful and conscientious discharge of the duties assigned you is all very well, but the verdict in such cases generally is that you perform your present duties so well that you had better continue performing them. Now, young gentlemen, this will not do. It will not do for the coming partners. There must be something beyond this. We make Clerks, Bookkeepers, Treasurers, Bank Tellers of this class, and there they remain to the end of the chapter. The rising man must do something exceptional, and beyond the range of his special department. *He must attract attention.* A shipping clerk, he may do so by discovering in an invoice an error with which he has nothing to do, and which has escaped the attention of the proper party. If a weighing clerk, he may save for the firm by doubting the adjustment of the scales and having them corrected, even if this be the province of the master mechanic. If a messenger boy, even he can lay the seed of promotion by going beyond the letter of his intructions in order to secure the desired reply. There is no service so low and simple, neither any so high, in which the young man of ability and willing disposition cannot readily and almost daily prove himself capable of greater trust and usefulness, and, what is equally important, show his

---

1. **Scylla and Charybdis:** dangers on both sides.

invincible determination to rise. Some day, in your own department, you will be directed to do or say something which you know will prove disadvantageous to the interest of the firm. Here is your chance. Stand up like a man and say so. Say it boldly, and give your reasons, and thus prove to your employer that, while his thoughts have been engaged upon other matters, you have been studying during hours when perhaps he thought you asleep, how to advance his interests. You may be right or you may be wrong, but in either case you have gained the first condition of success. You have attracted attention. Your employer has found that he has not a mere hireling in his service, but a man; not one who is content to give so many hours of work for so many dollars in return, but one who devotes his spare hours and constant thought to the business. Such an employee must perforce be thought of, and thought of kindly and well. It will not be long before his advice is asked in his special branch, and if the advice given be sound, it will soon be asked and taken upon questions of broader bearing. This means partnership; if not with present employers then with others. Your foot, in such a case, is upon the ladder; the amount of climbing done depends entirely upon yourself.

One false axiom you will often hear, which I wish to guard you against: "Obey orders if you break owners." Don't you do it. This is no rule for you to follow. Always break orders to save owners. There never was a great character who did not sometimes smash the routine regulations and make new ones for himself. The rule is only suitable for such as have no aspirations, and you have not forgotten that you are destined to be owners and to make orders and break orders. Do not hesitate to do it whenever you are sure the interests of your employer will be thereby promoted and when you are so sure of the result that you are willing to take the responsibility. You will never be a partner unless you know the business of your department far better than the owners possibly can. When called to account for your independent action, show him the result of your genius, and tell him that you knew that it would be so; show him how mistaken the orders were. Boss your boss just as soon as you can; try it on early. There is nothing he will like so well if he is the right kind of boss; if he is not, he is not the man for you to remain with—leave him whenever you can, even at a present sacrifice, and find one capable of discerning genius. Our young partners in the Carnegie firm have won their spurs by showing that we did not know half as well what was wanted as they did. Some of them have acted upon occasion with me as if they owned the firm and I was but some airy New Yorker presuming to advise upon what I knew very little about. Well, they are not interfered with much now. They were the true bosses—the very men we were looking for.

There is one sure mark of the coming partner, the future millionaire; his revenues always exceed his expenditures. He begins to save early, almost as soon as he begins to earn. No matter how little it may be possible to save, save that little. Invest it securely, not necessarily in bonds, but in anything which you have good reason to believe will be profitable, but no gambling with it, remember. A rare chance will soon present itself for investment. The little you have saved will prove the basis for an amount of credit utterly surprising to you. Capitalists trust the saving young man. For every hundred dollars you can produce as the result of hard-won savings, Midas, in search of a partner, will lend or credit a thousand; for every thousand, fifty thousand. It is not capital that your seniors require, it is the man who has proved that he has the business habits which create capital, and to create it in the best of all possible ways, as far as self-discipline is concerned, is, by adjusting his habits to his means. Gentlemen, it is the first hundred dollars saved which tells. Begin at once to lay up something. The bee predominates in the future millionaire.

Of course there are better, higher aims than saving. As an end, the acquisition of wealth is ignoble in the extreme; I assume that you save and long for wealth only as a means of enabling you the better to do some good in your day and generation. Make a note of this essential rule: Expenditure always within income.

You may grow impatient, or become discouraged when year by year you float on in subordinate positions. There is no doubt that it is becoming harder and harder as business gravitates more and more to immense concerns, for a young man without capital to get a start for himself, and in this city especially where large capital is essential, it is unusually difficult. Still, let me tell you for your encouragement, that there is no country in the world, where able and energetic young men can so readily rise as this, nor any city where there is more room at the top. Young men give all kinds of reasons why in their cases failure was clearly attributable to exceptional circumstances which render success impossible. Some never had a chance, according to their own story. This is simply nonsense. No young man ever lived who had not a chance, and a splendid chance, too, if he ever was employed at all.

The young man who never had a chance is the same young man who has been canvassed over and over again by his superiors, and found destitute of necessary qualifications, or is deemed unworthy of closer relations with the firm, owing to some objectionable act, habit, or association, of which he thought his employers ignorant.

And here is the prime condition of success, the great secret: Concentrate your energy, thought, and capital exclusively upon the business in which you are engaged. Having begun in one line, resolve to fight it out on that line, to lead in it; adopt every improvement, have the best machinery, and know the most about it.

The concerns which fail are those which have scattered their capital, which means that they have scattered their brains also. They have investments in this, or that, or the other, here, there and everywhere. "Don't put all your eggs in one basket" is all wrong. I tell you "put all your eggs in one basket, and then watch that basket." Look round you and take notice; men who do that do not often fail. It is easy to watch and carry the one basket. It is trying to carry too many baskets that breaks most eggs in this country. He who carries three baskets must put one on his head, which is apt to tumble and trip him up. One fault of the American business man is lack of concentration.

To summarize what I have said: Aim for the highest; never enter a bar-room; do not touch liquor, or if at all only at meals; never speculate; never in-dorse beyond your surplus cash fund; make the firm's interest yours; break or-ders always to save owners; concentrate; put all your eggs in one basket, and watch that basket; expenditure always within revenue; lastly, be not impatient, for, as Emerson says, "no one can cheat you out of ultimate success but your-selves."

18

George Rice Loses Out to Standard Oil
New York World

Even the optimistic Andrew Carnegie noted in his lecture to young men that "as business gravitates more and more to immense concerns," opportunity might be threatened. George Rice (1835–1905) did all that Carnegie would have suggested. Entering the oil business early, he kept, as Carnegie advised, all his eggs in one basket, and watched the basket closely. What he saw was the Standard Oil Company under John D. Rockefeller undercut his operation and eventually drive him out of business.

Rice's legal and intellectual counterattack on Standard Oil led the charge against "the trusts." He supplied information to two of the major writers on that corporation, Henry Demerest Lloyd and Ida Tarbell, whose books and articles encouraged antitrust legislation. And he spent much of his life in legal pursuit of Standard Oil, a quest that never met with success during his lifetime but that eventually inspired efforts that led to the breakup of the giant corporation in 1911.

After a dramatic personal encounter with John D. Rockefeller during depositions for one of Rice's many suits against Standard Oil, a reporter for the New York World *interviewed him. Here is his explanation of how Standard Oil operated.*

BEFORE YOU READ

1. How, according to Rice, did Standard Oil undercut its competitors?
2. Do you agree with Rice that this constituted unfair competition?
3. What was Rice's attitude toward large corporations and how did it reflect popular feelings?

"I have been twenty years fighting John D. Rockefeller and the Standard Oil Trust, and I am not through yet."

The man who said this was George Rice, of Marietta, O. He is the man who told John D. Rockefeller to his face last Wednesday in the New Netherland Hotel, where Mr. Rockefeller had been testifying before the State Commission sent from Ohio to get evidence in proceedings intended to prove him guilty of contempt of the Ohio Supreme Court, that his great wealth was built on wrecks of other men's business.

It was a dramatic scene. Mr. Rockefeller and Mr. Rice have known each other well for a generation. In a twenty-year fight men are apt to get well acquainted.

But when the great multi-millionaire walked across the parlor, and, extending his hand—which was not taken—said to George Rice in a suave tenor voice:

New York World, October 16, 1898: 25.

"HOW ARE YOU, GEORGE! WE ARE GETTING TO BE GRAY-HAIRED MEN NOW, AIN'T WE? DON'T YOU WISH YOU HAD TAKEN MY ADVICE YEARS AGO?" the group of onlookers were not prepared for what followed.

George Rice drew himself up to his full height, which is about 6 feet 2 inches, his bright gray eyes flashed fire, and his massive frame visibly vibrated with suppressed anger, as he looked the great oil magnate straight in the face and said: "Perhaps it would have been better for me if I had. YOU HAVE CERTAINLY RUINED MY BUSINESS, AS YOU SAID YOU WOULD."

Mr. Rockefeller recoiled and his face showed a shade of pallor. The words of Rice had evidently stung him. Quickly recovering himself he turned from his accuser, saying, "Oh, pshaw, that isn't so, George!"

"But I say it is so," was the instant rejoinder of George Rice, and, raising his voice so that everybody in the room could hear him, he pointed his index finger at the Oil King, and added: "You know well that by the power of your great wealth you have ruined my business, and you cannot deny it."

MR. RICE TELLS HIS EXPERIENCE
TO THE WORLD

This ended the episode in the hotel parlor. A few hours later, sitting in his private room, Mr. Rice gave to a World representative the full story of how he was ruined as an oil refiner by the machinations of the great Standard Oil Laocoon in whose coils an uncounted multitude of competitors have been crushed to death.

"I am but one of many victims of Rockefeller's colossal combination," said Mr. Rice, "and my story is not essentially different from the rest. You ask me to tell you what I meant by telling Mr. Rockefeller, as I did publicly to-day, that he had ruined my business. The whole story, with all its inside details of intrigue and conspiracy, would require a volume to tell. I will tell you as much of it as you choose to ask me for. What particular phase of my experience do you care to have me relate?"

"Give me your personal story, Mr. Rice—just what happened to you in your own business."

"Well, I went into the oil-producing business in West Virginia in 1872, and in 1876 I went into the oil-refining business. Immediately I did that my fight with the Standard Oil people began. I established what was known as the Ohio Oil Works, which had a capacity of about 100,000 barrels of crude oil per annum. I found to my surprise at first, though I afterward understood it perfectly, that the Standard Oil Company was offering the same quality of oil at much lower prices than I could do—from one to three cents a gallon less than I could possibly sell it for.

"I sought for the reason and found that the railroads were in league with the Standard Oil concern at every point, giving it discriminating rates and privileges of all kinds as against myself and all outside competitors.

"For instance, I found that the railroads would not furnish tank-cars to any competitors, while the Standard combination was able by its immense wealth to buy its own cars. It owns from 8,000 to 10,000 tank-cars, and the railroads pay them sufficient mileage on the use of those Standard Oil cars to pay for the first cost of the cars inside of three years. A tank-car, when it comes back empty, cannot bring any goods. The transcontinental lines charge $105 to return an empty cylinder tank-car from the Pacific coast to the Missouri River, while they charge the trust nothing at all for the return of their own exclusive box tank-cars. This gives the trust an advantage of over $100 a car.

"Again, the independent competitor, like myself, was obliged to ship his oil in box-cars and pay 25 per cent more freight on the weight of the wooden barrels, while no charge at all was made to the Standard Oil Trust on the weight of the iron cylinders.

"Again, the railroads deduct 63 gallons (or over 400 pounds) from the filled capacity of each Standard Oil tank-car, which is the same as carrying 1 1/4 per cent of their rail products entirely free of cost. This went on up to March 15, 1890, and was one of the things that helped to wreck my business. Yet another thing helped to ruin me. The railroads allowed the trust to deliver its oils in less than carload quantities at the same rates as for full carloads. They allowed the trust to stop its cars, whether carrying oil in bulk or barrels, at different stations and take it off in small quantities without paying the higher rates which independent competitors were always charged for small quantities thus delivered. Of course, against such discriminations as these the independent competitor of moderate capital could not contend. He was driven to the wall every time, as I was."

MIGHT HAVE BEEN WORTH
A MILLION

"My refinery," continued Mr. Rice, "has been shut down for two years. If I had had a fair and equal show with the railroads my refinery plant to-day would have been easily worth a million dollars and would have been growing all the time. As it is, I am out of the business, my plant is worthless and the men whom it would have employed are either idle or finding other work. These discriminations of which I have spoken are as bad to-day as they have ever been. The public needs to understand that the railroads and Standard Oil monopoly are really one and the same thing. The officers and directors of the Oil Trust are also the presidents and directors of one-fifth of the total railroad mileage of the United States. This is no mere statement of mine. It is proved by Poor's Manual.

"The trust was formed in January, 1882, and from that time the lines were drawn tighter and tighter to oppress and strangle every competitor. It was the highwayman's policy of 'stand and deliver.' I had my choice offered me to either give up my business at a price far less than I knew it to be worth, or to be robbed of it under forms of law. I chose not to accept the price and my business was destroyed. The threat of the trust was made good, and I suppose that is what John D. Rockefeller must have meant when he asked me if I didn't wish I had been wiser and listened to him years ago."

"Well, do you now wish, Mr. Rice, that you had knuckled to the trust and saved your money?"

"Not a bit of it," replied the "ruined" but plucky oil refiner of Marietta. "I have made a fight for principle, and I am neither sorry for it nor ashamed of it. I have been before the courts many times; I have been before Congressional committees; and I have appeared time and time again before the Interstate Commerce Commission, all the time trying to get relief from these gross discriminations. I confess I have made very little headway as yet. I shall go on with the fight as long as I live, and it may be that I shall never win. But, sooner or later, in my lifetime or afterward, the people of this country will surely take up this fight as their own and settle the question of whether they will rule the railroads and the trusts or be ruled by them."

LAWS NOT ENFORCED

"I have made a mistake, apparently, in supposing that the laws of our country could and would be enforced. I supposed the courts and the other authorities of the land would support me in my right to a free and equal chance in business with all my fellow-citizens, John D. Rockefeller included. But I have learned by long years of conflict and trial and tribulation, which have cost me untold worry and a lot of money, that this is not so; that I have no business rights which the railroads and this great trust can be made to respect.

"The Interstate Commerce Commission is all right in theory, but it does not have the courage of its powers; it suffers from the paralysis of political influences. The laws are neither feared nor respected by the men of many millions."

"Tell me just how the shoe was made to pinch you personally. How did the trust manage to close your refinery at Marietta?"

"Why, that's easy to tell. Every car of oil that I sent into any part of the United States the trust would jump on it and cut the life out of it. I mean to say that as soon as my oil arrived at the point to which it was shipped the trust would cut the price, so that the man who bought my oil lost money on the sale of it. They would not cut the prices to the whole town, but only to my one customer, and the whole town knew of this man's having lost money by trading with me. From that time forward, of course, I could get no orders in that town. . . .

"In 1872, the trunk lines of railroads made a contract with a corporation called 'The South Improvement Company,' which was only another name for the Standard Oil Company, under which the Standard Oil Company was allowed the most outrageous discriminating freight rates. It seems incredible that these contracts should have been made. They not only gave the Standard

Oil Company heavy rebates on their own shipments of oil, but gave them rebates on the shipments of their competitors. At that time the Standard Oil
Company only had 10 per cent of the petroleum industry of the country, while
their competitors had 90 per cent. The rebates allowed to the Standard people
were from 40 cents to $1.06 per barrel on crude petroleum, and from 50 cents
to $1.32 per barrel on refined petroleum. Thus the Standard Oil Company re-
ceived nine times as much for rebates on the shipments of its competitors than
it did on its own.

"In 1874," continued Mr. Rice, "the railroads forced the independent pipe
lines of the country to sell out their plants to the Standard Oil Company at the
price of old junk, and gave to the latter, besides, still further discriminating rebates on freight. A circular was issued on Sept. 9, 1874, known as "The Rut-
ter Circular," from the freight office of the New York Central and Rudson
River Railroad Company, establishing new rates on refined and crude oil.
Under this circular the Standard Oil Company was given an advantage of 20
cents a barrel in the freight charges on crude oil connected with its pipe-line
system, which the independent refineries did not have. In that same year the
Standard company secured the railroad terminal oil facilities of all the trunk
lines centering in New York City. Many fortunes invested in the independent
pipe lines were wrecked by that move, through no fault of their managers and
no lack of business skill, but simply because the Standard Oil officials, acting
in collusion with the railroad officials, had established these unfair discriminations in freight rates between the oil that came through the Standard pipes
and that which came through other pipes.

"To show you how the rebate system worked in my own case, let me say that
in 1885, I was charged 25 cents a barrel for carrying oil from Macksburg to
Marietta, a distance of twenty-five miles, while the Standard Oil Company
only paid 10 cents a barrel for the same distance. More than this, out of the 35
cents a barrel that I paid the trust actually received 25 cents. In other words,
the trust received about two-thirds of all the money I paid for freight."

TRUST "GREATER" THAN THE COURTS
OR THE COUNTRY

"You spoke of your having fought the trust for twenty years. Give me a general outline of your encounter with it."

"Well, about 1879 or 1880 I, with others, brought about a public investigation by the Legislature of Ohio as to the discriminations by the railroads of
which I have spoken. Nothing came of that investigation except that we proved
any number of facts on which further agitation and action was based. I have
gone before the Interstate Commerce Commission in many cases trying to get
these discriminations stopped. I brought an action through the Attorney-
General of Ohio in 1887 to forfeit the charters of two railroads for gross dis-

crimination, and I proved my case. The courts decided, clear up to the highest court, that these two railroads could not make those discriminating charges.

"I obtained at great cost a decree of the Court to that effect. Apparently it was a conclusive victory. In reality it was of no account. The discriminating rates went on as before, and they are still going on to-day. There is no use in trying to stop it. In March, 1892, the Ohio Supreme Court rendered a judgment against the Standard Oil Company, of Ohio, ordering it to discontinue all business relations with the trust.

"The company has pretended to comply with the decree. In fact the trust still exists and the Standard Oil Company, of Ohio, is still a part of it. The way they have got around it is this: On March 21, 1892, the trust resolved on paper to wind up its affairs, and trustees were appointed for that purpose. Then they issued another kind of trust certificate, called an 'Assignment of Legal Title,' which they made marketable and allowed to be transferred from one holder to another on their trust transfer books, which makes this certificate just as negotiable and salable as the old original trust certificate."

$140,060,000 PROFITS IN SIX YEARS.

"In this way the trust is still kept intact. In proof of this fact the trust is known to have declared and paid since March, 1892, up to September of this year, 26 regular quarterly dividends of 3 per cent., and 59 per cent. besides in special dividends, or a total of 137 per cent.—dividends, which, based on their reported capitalization of $102,230,700, amounts to $140,060,000 paid in dividends since its pretended dissolution. No more proof is required that the trust has not been dissolved and that the decree of the Supreme Court of Ohio has been treated with contempt."

"But while you have been ruined, Mr. Rice, it is said, you know, that the mass of consumers have gained—that the price of oil is cheaper, because of the trust. What do you say to this suggestion that you, and others like you, have been crushed for the general good?"

"It is a trust lie," replied Mr. Rice warmly. "There is not the least truth in it. Refined oil for general consumption is as much higher in price as these gross rebates and discriminations amount to, because it is fair to assume, on general principles, that the railroads are making money on the transportation of Standard oil. It only costs three-eighths of a cent a gallon to refine oil. The Standard Oil Trust may possibly save one-eighth of a cent on that, but not more. How much does that amount to in the problem of the cost of oil to the retail consumer?

"Refined oil would certainly have been cheaper right along for the last twenty years but for the Standard combination. If the railroad rates had been honest, and the allowances for rebate had been fair and square to all oil producers and refiners, the mass of the people must and would have got the benefit of it. There is no question that the people have paid millions more for oil than they would have done if the laws against conspiracies and combinations in restriction of fair trade could have been enforced. The price of refined oil is notoriously high to-day compared with the low price of crude oil. There is a difference of from 100 to 300 per cent between crude and refined oil prices, when we all know that crude oil can be turned into refined oil and sold all within thirty days."

"Do you see no remedy ahead for the condition of things which ruined your business as a refiner?"

THE REMEDY—ENFORCE THE LAW

"No, I see no remedy, so long as the railroads are under their present management. I have myself tried every known avenue of relief, and my experience has satisfied me that Blackstone did not foresee the conditions of law and justice now prevailing in this country when he wrote his famous maxim, "There is no wrong without a legal remedy." There is no relief for present conditions in this country except by the Government's acquiring ownership of the railroads. There is plenty of law existing now, but it cannot be enforced. It is a dead letter. The Interstate Commerce act has been law for ten years, and the penalty for the violation of it is a fine of $500 and two years in the State prison. It is violated every day, and it has been violated every day for ten years past, but I observe that no one has yet been sent to prison, and I do not believe that any violator of this law ever expects to be."

Speaking of Mr. Rockefeller, the man who said to him at the public hearing at the New Netherland Hotel, Thursday: "We are getting to be gray-haired men now, aren't we, George? Don't you wish you had taken my advice years ago?" Mr. Rice said: "There is no doubt whatever that Mr. Rockefeller, through the operations of the Standard Oil Trust, is the richest man in the world to-day. I know their business, because it is also mine, and I believe that the Rockefellers are now worth $200,000,000.

"John D. Rockefeller's personal income from the trust and other sources has for several years exceeded $12,000,000 per annum."

19

Part of the Working Class

Rose Pastor Stokes

The emphatic title of Rose Pastor Stokes's unfinished autobiography, I Belong to the Working Class, *reflects the zigs and zags in the life of this remarkable woman, born Rose Harriet Wieslander in Poland in 1879. Migrating with her mother to London in 1882 and then to Cleveland, Ohio, in 1890, Stokes, as this excerpt describes, knew desperate poverty and early years of hard labor as a cigar maker. After the part English, part Yiddish* Jewish Daily News *accepted some articles she had submitted, she and her mother moved to New York City and she became a journalist on the paper's staff. Her life for a time seemed a quintessential American success story. She wed the progressive James Graham Phelps Stokes, son of one of New York's wealthiest families. The* New York Times *in 1910 described Mr. Stokes as "the hero of our greatest social romance" for choosing "for his wife, a few years ago, a Jewish cigarette girl, Rose Pastor." In an almost too pat parallelism between personal and political history, their mutual socialism brought them together, but their opposite positions on American entry into World War I and the Bolshevik revolution drove them apart.*

Passionate in her politics, Rose Pastor Stokes actively supported major strikes of the era: the shirtwaist-makers in 1909, the hotel workers in 1912, the Paterson silk workers in 1913. She challenged federal law by disseminating birth control information, and the Espionage Act by denouncing the war. Finally, she was a founding member of the American Communist Party and played an important role in defining its stance on what was then called "the Negro question." She died in Germany in 1933, leaving an unfinished autobiography that was not published until 1992.

Stokes in her early years experienced firsthand many of the labor conditions of the age of industrialization. This excerpt offers a dramatic account of the struggles of immigrant workers.

BEFORE YOU READ

1. Why did families send children to work so early?
2. What was the impact of the depression of 1893 on Stokes's stepfather's business?
3. What were the main complaints that drove workers in the cigar factories to attempt to organize unions?
4. What made Stokes a "socialist by instinct"?

Our lives were like our neighbors' lives. The Installment man came Monday mornings. There was not always the dollar to give him. We would take the money from the bread we needed, to pay for the blankets we needed as much. The same blankets, in the store, were half the price. All the neighbors knew it. My mother discovered it for herself. She raged against the Installment Robbers. "But how many poor workers are there who can buy for cash? Yes! That's why these leeches can drain our blood on the Installment Plan!"

[My stepfather] loved my mother. He would have given her the moon and stars for playthings had he been able. The least he could bear to let her have were the few cheap new things he was paying on. His work kept him driving his horse and wagon about the city—often, in the avenues of the wealthy. Sometimes he'd be called into the homes of the rich to cart away old magazines, or bottles, or rags, or old plumbing material, or discarded what-not. He knew the beautiful things the rich lived with.

My step-father's gains were uncertain. Some days he'd clear two or three or three and a half dollars. On other days there would be no gains at all. There would even be losses through a bad "buy." Or he would be cheated in the sale of his load. On such days the horse had to get his feed as when he salvaged two or three dollars from his labor. I brought home little enough, that first winter: between one and two dollars a week, at first. After that, from two and a half to three and a half dollars a week; and toward the end of the winter nearer four.

Food became so scarce in our cupboard that we almost measured out every square inch of bread. There was nothing left for clothing and shoes. I wore mine till the snow and slush came through. I had often to sit all day at my bench with icy feet in wet leather.

I was working ten or eleven hours a day [at cigar making] with swift, sure hands. Mr. Wertheim had said, one morning: "Rose Pastor, you're the quickest and best worker in the shop!" I didn't know or think how much I was earning for Mr. Wertheim, but I knew I was getting hunger and cold for my portion.

All winter long I wore the gingham dress and thin jacket. Every morning of that winter, when my mother tucked my lunch of bread and milk and an apple—or orange—or banana—newspaper-wrapped under my arm and opened the door to let me out into the icy dawn, I felt the agony that tugged at her mother-heart. "Walk fast," she would always say, "walk as fast as you can, Rosalie. Remember, it is better to walk fast in the cold."

After the long day in the stogie factory, and after supper and the chores for mother, there was my book—there were Lamb's *Tales*—the magic of words . . . Before the kitchen stove, when the house was asleep, I'd throw off my shoes, thaw out the icy tissues that bit all day into my consciousness, and lose myself in the loves and losses, the sorrows and joys, the gore-dripping tragedies and gay comedies of kings and queens, lords and ladies of olden times. I read and re-read the "Tales" with never-flagging interest. But (and this is perhaps a noteworthy fact) with complete detachment. Not then, nor later, when I read Shakespeare in the text did I ever, for even a fleeting moment identify myself with the people of Shakespeare's dramas. The rich lords and ladies, the ruling kings and queens of whom the supreme dramatist wrote in such noble strain, were alien to me. They moved in a different world. On the other hand, there lurked in my heart an undefined feeling of resentment over the fact that his clowns were always poor folk. He seemed never to draw a poor man save to make him an object of ridicule. Instinctively, I identified myself with his poor.

At the end of winter I had quit the shop under the viaduct, and Spring found me in Mr. Brudno's "factory." Mr. Brudno ran what cigar makers in Ohio called a "buckeye." A "buckeye" is a cigar "factory" in a private home. In other words, it was a sweat shop.

In the three small rooms that comprised Mr. Brudno's stogie "factory" were a dozen scattered benches. Of the dozen workers at the bench not counting strippers, bookers, and packers, six were Brudno's very own: four sons and two daughters. Several others were blood-relations — first cousins; and still another was a distant connection by marriage. The remaining few were "outsiders"; young girls and boys and — I — came to fill the last unoccupied bench.

Mr. Brudno was a picturesque patriarch, with his long black beard, and his tall black skull-cap. He had come from the old country with a little money (not acquired through toil, rumor had it) and was determined to get rich quick in America. With money and six grown children, and the persuasive need of his poverty-stricken relatives and compatriots here and in the old world, he had an undoubted advantage over the rest of us. He put his children to work, and drew in his poor relations. In this godless America he would give them plenty of work in a shop where the Sabbath was kept holy! It was his strength, for they would work in no shop where the Sabbath was not kept holy. Their learner's period to be stretched out far beyond the usual time limit, thus adding much to his profits. The "outsiders" were young children. He hired them and drove them, and kept reducing their pay.

He would go about the "buckeye" dreaming aloud . . . This was his first sweatshop. By-and-bye he'd have a bigger place — a real stogie factory with dozens of new workers. His children would do all the work of foremen and watchers, and work at the bench too. Soon there would be a big factory building all his own. . . .

In the six years, off and on, that I worked for Mr. Brudno, his dream grew to reality. He did everything a boss could do to make his dream come true. Beginning in a little "buckeye," he soon moved to an enormous loft, where the dozen benches he started with, were many times multiplied. There his factory hummed with the industry of boys and girls, of men, women, and young children. The stripping and the bunch-making were concentrated in one end of the vast room where the rolling was done. The raw material was unpacked and sorted, the drying, storing, and other processes carried on in another room. Driven by Mr. Brudno and our own need, we piled up stogies rapidly. Brudno paid miserably little for our labor, and always complained that we were getting too much. But before long, he was able to rear a factory building of his own, on a very desirable site on Broadway. It was of red brick — and several stories high. There he drove us harder than ever, and in time added another story to his Broadway structure. Now he was a big "manufacturer"; he strutted about and watched us manufacture.

When the "buckeye" moved to the big loft and became a factory, Mr. Brudno announced a cut. The stogie-rollers were getting fourteen cents a hundred. Now it would be thirteen. We took the cut in silence. We were for the most part poor little child slaves, timid and unorganized. The thought of union never occurred to us. There was no strength in us or behind us. It was each one by his lone self. Not one of us would have ventured to pit his little self against the boss. We merely looked into one another's faces. No words. But each had the same thought in mind: Now there would be less of something that was already scarce: Bread, milk, or coal. Mr. Brudno owned the factory and we were his workers. Nothing could be done about it. So we raced some more . . . and still more, and more!

It never occurred to me that I was being used by the boss to set the pace in his stogie factory. . . . And that one cut would follow another, as our speed in-creased. . . .

A cut came the week that the new baby came.

"Rosalie!"

My step-father's voice, tense and unnatural with excitement, shook me out of sleep.

I heard my mother's shriek piercing the deep night, and rushed into the room next to mine.

"Mother! Oh, my mother!" What could be wrong with my mother?

My step-father rushed after me, and snatched me out of the room.

"Rosalie, run to the midwife! Say she's to come right away. Mother's giving birth. Quick!"

"Giving birth?" A new baby coming! . . . Out into the dark, chill, deserted streets I went, shoes unbuttoned, hair loose in the wind, feet flying. . . .

It was hard enough to scrape together the ten dollars for the midwife. To get help for the two weeks of confinement was out of the question. For those two weeks, after shop, I did the work at home. There was no water in the flat on Liberal Street. I had to carry pails of water from the pump in the yard to fill the wash tubs upstairs and take the water down to spill. How heavy the sheets were, and how hard to rub clean! . . . Every day of the two weeks, I washed: Diapers, sheets, other "linens," carrying water up and down, up and down, till all was washed and rinsed, and the white things hanging out on the line in the yard.

Something was in the air. Not only at Brudno's, but everywhere. Our little world of working fathers, dependent mothers, and young bread-winners was tense with an apprehension never felt before.

We were always hanging over a precipice. But now we felt that something was going to break; that the precarious bit of shale we called "life" to which we clung in such desperation would give way; and that we—all of us—with our poverty and our crust of bread, would go crashing down to disaster! This was the beginning of the crisis of 1893.

My step-father, though no worker in a factory, felt the effects of the crisis along with the rest of our class. His horse and wagon now carried fewer and fewer of the loads that gave a precarious living. At the week's end, after all was paid—feed and stall for the horse and shed-rent for the wagon—he would find only four or five dollars clear.

He worked harder now and cleared less. He would bring his diminishing loads to the warehouses, and get smaller return for them with every passing day. A deep depression settled upon him.

My own work too fell off. Most of the workers at Brudno's were sent home. A few were kept on part-time. These were the quickest and best workers—the most profitable to him in busy season—the boss preferred not to lose them. He pretended to be generous in keeping us on the payroll.

The three or three-and-a-half dollars I brought, when added to the miserable little that my poor step-father was able to bring in, spelled deeper need for us.

Mr. Brudno was often in a genial mood now, but not too often. Frequently he was morose; at times, vindictive. His black skull-cap announced the mood. If he came through the swinging doors with the cap to his right or left ear we expected taciturnity or jest. If the cap sat against the back of his skull we looked for trouble. Then no work he examined was good enough for him. He would go from rack to rack; picking up handfuls of stogies. A mis-roll or two, a head or two badly sealed; a slight unevenness in length would call forth a violent fit of temper. He would hurl curses at the workers, break and twist the stogies out of shape, and throw them into the drawer of waste cuttings! A morning's work gone to the scrap-pile!

The most intolerable fines were inflicted upon us. For example, the leaf tobacco in which we rolled our "bunches" was often so rotted that we were forced to re-roll our stogies several times, each time removing the worthless piece to try another. Or, the leaf would be so badly wormeaten we could not cover a third of the required number of stogies. This bad stock retarded the work. It meant rolling two or three hundred less in a day; it meant beside, unusual effort; increased care and anxiety; and a nervous strain that sent us home trembling from head to feet. Yet for this stock Mr. Brudno demanded the same standard of workmanship and the same number of stogies to the pound that was set for the finest leaf tobacco, and docked us heavily for the inescapable failure. When we opened our slim pay envelopes, we would often find from fifty cents to one dollar and fifty cents deducted, out of a possible five dollars. When driven too hard, some one of us would venture to complain in a timid voice: "But look at this stock. Mr. Brudno. How can you expect the same work out of such rotten leaf tobacco? See this and this and this!—and look at the holes in these. . . . Look! look! I just brought this pound from the stripping room. We can't do the impossible!"

"Well, what's wrong with this stock anyway? A little hole, here and there— that's nothing. Rotten? That ain't rotten. You pull too hard, so it tears. Don't pull, or you'll go home."

"Ask your own sons and daughters; they'll tell you what sort of stock it is."

But if he ever asked them we were not told. The fines were taken out of our pay often without any previous warning; and those who complained too disrespectfully were "fired."

If a period of good stock followed, we would race madly. Now is the time to make up for the bad weeks! If then we succeeded—if we increased our speed and turned out a few hundred stogies more than usual at the week's end, Mr. Brudno would announce a reduction of a cent or two on the hundred. Before these attacks we were helpless sheep. We knew nothing of organizing protest. A few of us dreamed. . . . But nothing came of our dreams.

Brudno's shop, however, was to have a strike—a curious strike confined to his relatives. One morning, at daybreak, I was roused by a sharp rap at our door. It was Lyoti, one of that group of blood relations whom Brudno drew from the old country with tales of work and freedom, in a shop that kept the Sabbath holy.

"I came to beg you please, not to go back to the shop, this morning!" he said, "We are on strike."

"We? Who?"

"The boss's relations," he explained. "We can't do the special work he gives us to do, and live on the pay. It is impossible."

I roused my sleeping mother. The children woke. They ran or toddled to the door of the tiny frame house on Orange Street where we now lived; half-naked; sleepy, yet curious.

I kissed my mother, kissed each child in turn, and forgot for the moment that our father, in despair, had left home the week before and had not been heard from since. A strike at Brudno's shop! Every outraged feeling in me broke into exultant rebellion.

"I'll stay out even if we starve altogether! Eh, Mamele?" My mother kissed me and nodded assent. There were shadows as we contemplated the children. "But a strike is a strike," said my mother. And Lyoti explained, "If we win you win too. If we win the boss will not dare to press you harder than he is already pressing you. He will not dare to take another cent off the hundred from anybody."

My first strike—a sympathy strike! I visited workers in their homes that early morning and got them to stay out. I picketed the shop. Lyoti turned to me for many strike activities. I did as directed and drew in others. At the end of some ten or twelve days the men returned in triumph. The boss had yielded to their demands, and the rest of us who appeared to have gained nothing, felt stronger—even a bit audacious in the presence of the boss. The old timidity never again quite overcame any of us—for was he not beaten in our sight?

With the monopoly of the newly-invented suction machine, by which a worker could turn out many times the number of cigars made by skilled hand labor, the Cigar Trust came into existence. It was spreading westward from New York. It needed workers to operate the new machines. A Mr. Young, foreman at Baer's, had shown off my skill, economy of motion, and economical use of material, to visiting buyers and "manufacturers." Mr. Young it was who was now engaged by the trust to start their Cleveland factory, and who, in turn, engaged me to learn the suction-machine method, and to teach it to other workers. Soon I was given charge of an entire floor, at fifteen dollars a week.

But my job lasted only a few weeks. A Mr. Weiss, vice-president of the newly-formed trust, was making a tour of inspection of their factories, and came to Cleveland. Early one morning the elderly superintendent of the building stopped me on my way up to the loft: "I'm sorry, Miss Pastor, but you can't go up to the suction-room." His words were like a blow. I could only stammer: "Why—why—what have I done?" "Mr. Weiss was here," said the superintendent. "He opened your desk, and found a book—" Yes, I understood. I had been reading a book, Vandervelde's *Collectivism*. I went back to the bench where, by terrific driving, I earned between six and seven dollars a week. But the lesson in the antagonism between Capital and Labor sank deep.

I remained a "socialist by instinct." However, within the limited franchise for women I voted for socialist candidates (for school offices) when I became of voting age and went about with the vague notion that some day, in some way, we workers would abolish wage-slavery. When the local political boss, who had a saloon on Orange Street, asked me to "vote Democrat," I proudly announced that I was a socialist and would vote for socialist candidates only. Although friends had warned me that "without this man's good-will no good can come to anybody in the entire neighborhood."

An attempt was made to organize several of the stogie factories. We hired a little hall, got the workers to attend several times; speeches were made; the group held together. But when we applied for membership in the Cigar Makers Union, we were told by the American Federation of Labor that there was no room in the union for unskilled workers.

20

A Bintel Brief

Abraham Cahan

Years before Ann Landers and Dear Abby, there was "A Bintel Brief." In 1906 the Jewish Daily Forward, a Yiddish-language newspaper addressing the more than half-million Jewish immigrants in New York City, began running an advice column under a title that translates as "a bundle of letters." The column spoke to Jews from Russia, Hungary, Poland, Romania, and the Middle East, with different traditions and dialects as well as skills and opportunities, struggling with each other as well as their new circumstances in some of the most crowded urban neighborhoods in the world.

The paper's editor was Abraham Cahan, who also wrote several novels about immigrant life. Cahan contributed some of the letters as well as the responses. "A Bintel Brief" gave advice on all kinds of personal problems. These excerpts from the early years of the column offer fascinating glimpses into Jewish immigrant life at the turn of the century and speak of issues central to the experiences of most immigrants.

BEFORE YOU READ

1. What are the major tensions of immigrant life as revealed in the letters?
2. What values did Cahan represent in his answers?
3. How does Cahan's advice compare to that given today in similar newspaper columns and on daytime talk shows?

Worthy Editor,

We are a small family who recently came to the "Golden Land." My husband, my boy and I are together, and our daughter lives in another city.

I had opened a grocery store here, but soon lost all my money. In Europe we were in business; we had people working for us and paid them well. In short, there we made a good living but here we are badly off.

My husband became a peddler. The "pleasure" of knocking on doors and ringing bells cannot be known by anyone but a peddler. If anybody does buy anything "on time," a lot of the money is lost, because there are some people who never intend to pay. In addition, my husband has trouble because he has a beard, and because of the beard he gets beaten up by the hoodlums.

Also we have problems with our boy, who throws money around. He works every day till late at night in a grocery for three dollars a week. I watch over him and give him the best because I'm sorry that he has to work so hard. But he costs me plenty and he borrows money from everybody. He has many friends and owes them all money. I get more and more worried as he takes here and borrows there. All my talking doesn't help. I am afraid to chase him away from home because he might get worse among strangers. I want to point out that he is well versed in Russian and Hebrew and he is not a child any more, but his behavior is not that of an intelligent adult.

I don't know what to do. My husband argues that he doesn't want to continue peddling. He doesn't want to shave off his beard, and it's not fitting for such a man to do so. The boy wants to go to his sister, but that's a twenty-five-dollar fare. What can I do? I beg you for a suggestion.

> Your Constant reader,
> F. L.

Answer:

Since her husband doesn't earn a living anyway, it would be advisable for all three of them to move to the city where the daughter is living. As for the beard, we feel that if the man is religious and the beard is dear to him because the Jewish law does not allow him to shave it off, it's up to him to decide. But if he is not religious, and the beard interferes with his earnings, it should be sacrificed.

Dear Editor,

For a long time I worked in a shop with a Gentile girl, and we began to go out together and fell in love. We agreed that I would remain a Jew and she a Christian. But after we had been married for a year, I realized that it would not work.

I began to notice that whenever one of my Jewish friends comes to the house, she is displeased. Worse yet, when she sees me reading a Jewish newspaper her face changes color. She says nothing, but I can see that she has changed. I feel that she is very unhappy with me, though I know she loves me. She will soon become a mother, and she is more dependent on me than ever.

She used to be quite liberal, but lately she is being drawn back to the Christian religion. She gets up early Sunday mornings, runs to church and comes home with eyes swollen from crying. When we pass a church now and then, she trembles.

Dear Editor, advise me what to do now. I could never convert, and there's no hope for me to keep her from going to church. What can we do now?

> Thankfully,
> A Reader

Answer:

Unfortunately, we often hear of such tragedies, which stem from marriages between people of different worlds. It's possible that if this couple were to move to a Jewish neighborhood, the young man might have more influence on his wife.

Dear Editor,

I am a girl from Galicia and in the shop where I work I sit near a Russian Jew with whom I was always on good terms. Why should one worker resent another?

But once, in a short debate, he stated that all Galicians were no good. When I asked him to repeat it, he answered that he wouldn't retract a word, and that he wished all Galician Jews dead.

I was naturally not silent in the face of such a nasty expression. He maintained that only Russian Jews are fine and intelligent. According to him, the *Galitzianer* are inhuman savages, and he had the right to speak of them so badly.

Dear Editor, does he really have a right to say this? Have the Galician Jews not sent enough money for the unfortunate sufferers of the pogroms in Russia? When a Gentile speaks badly of Jews, it's immediately printed in the newspapers and discussed hotly everywhere. But that a Jew should express himself so about his own brothers is nothing? Does he have a right? Are Galicians really so bad? And does he, the Russian, remain fine and intelligent in spite of such expressions?

As a reader of your worthy newspaper, I hope you will print my letter and give your opinion.

> With thanks in advance,
> B. M.

Answer:

The Galician Jews are just as good and bad as people from other lands. If the Galicians must be ashamed of the foolish and evil ones among them, then the Russians, too, must hide their heads in shame because among them there is such an idiot as the acquaintance of our letter writer.

Worthy Editor,

I am eighteen years old and a machinist by trade. During the past year I suffered a great deal, just because I am a Jew.

It is common knowledge that my trade is run mainly by the Gentiles and, working among the Gentiles, I have seen things that cast a dark shadow on the American labor scene. Just listen:

I worked in a shop in a small town in New Jersey, with twenty Gentiles. There was one other Jew besides me, and both of us endured the greatest hardships. That we were insulted goes without saying. At times we were even beaten up. We work in an area where there are many factories, and once, when we were leaving the shop, a group of workers fell on us like hoodlums and beat us. To top it off, we and one of our attackers were arrested. The hoodlum was let out on bail, but we, beaten and bleeding, had to stay in jail. At the trial, they fined the hoodlum eight dollars and let him go free.

After that I went to work on a job in Brooklyn. As soon as they found out that I was a Jew they began to torment me so that I had to leave the place. I have already worked at many places, and I either have to leave, voluntarily, or they fire me because I am a Jew.

Till now, I was alone and didn't care. At this trade you can make good wages, and I had enough. But now I've brought my parents over, and of course I have to support them.

Lately I've been working on one job for three months and I would be satisfied, but the worm of anti-Semitism is beginning to eat at my bones again. I
go to work in the morning as to Gehenna,[1] and I run away at night as from a
fire. It's impossible to talk to them because they are common boors, so-called
"American sports." I have already tried in various ways, but the only way to
deal with them is with a strong fist. But I am too weak and there are too many.

Perhaps you can help me in this matter. I know it is not an easy problem.

Your reader,
E. H.

Answer:

In the answer, the Jewish machinist is advised to appeal to the United Hebrew
Trades and ask them to intercede for him and bring up charges before the Ma-
chinists Union about this persecution. His attention is also drawn to the fact
that there are Gentile factories where Jews and Gentiles work together and get
along well with each other.

Finally it is noted that people will have to work long and hard before this
senseless racial hatred can be completely uprooted.

Worthy Editor,

I was born in America and my parents gave me a good education. I studied Yiddish and Hebrew, finished high school, completed a course in bookkeeping and
got a good job. I have many friends, and several boys have already proposed to
me.

Recently I went to visit my parents' home in Russian Poland. My mother's
family in Europe had invited my parents to a wedding, but instead of going
themselves, they sent me. I stayed at my grandmother's with an aunt and uncle
and had a good time. Our European family, like my parents, are quite well off
and they treated me well. They indulged me in everything and I stayed with
them six months.

It was lively in the town. There were many organizations and clubs and they
all accepted me warmly, looked up to me — after all, I was a citizen of the free
land, America. Among the social leaders of the community was an intelligent
young man, a friend of my uncle's, who took me to various gatherings and affairs.

He was very attentive, and after a short while he declared his love for me in
a long letter. I had noticed that he was not indifferent to me, and I liked him
as well. I looked up to him and respected him, as did all the townsfolk. My family became aware of it, and when they spoke to me about him, I could see they
thought it was a good match.

He was handsome, clever, educated, a good talker and charmed me, but I
didn't give him a definite answer. As my love for him grew, however, I wrote
to my parents about him, and then we became officially engaged.

A few months later we both went to my parents in the States and they received him like their own son. My bridegroom immediately began to learn

1. **Gehenna:** hell.

English and tried to adjust to the new life. Yet when I introduced him to my friends they looked at him with disappointment. "This 'greenhorn'[2] is your fiancé?" they asked. I told them what a big role he played in his town, how everyone respected him, but they looked at me as if I were crazy and scoffed at my words.

At first I thought, Let them laugh, when they get better acquainted with him they'll talk differently. In time, though, I was affected by their talk and began to think, like them, that he really was a "greenhorn" and acted like one.

In short, my love for him is cooling off gradually. I'm suffering terribly because my feelings for him are changing. In Europe, where everyone admired him and all the girls envied me, he looked different. But, here, I see before me another person.

I haven't the courage to tell him, and I can't even talk about it to my parents. He still loves me with all his heart, and I don't know what to do. I choke it all up inside myself, and I beg you to help me with advice in my desperate situation.

Respectfully,
A Worried Reader

Answer:

The writer would make a grave mistake if she were to separate from her bridegroom now. She must not lose her common sense and be influenced by the foolish opinions of her friends who divided the world into "greenhorns" and real Americans.

We can assure the writer that her bridegroom will learn English quickly. He will know American history and literature as well as her friends do, and be a better American than they. She should be proud of his love and laugh at those who call him "greenhorn."

Dear Editor,

Since I do not want my conscience to bother me, I ask you to decide whether a married woman has the right to go to school two evenings a week. My husband thinks I have no right to do this.

I admit that I cannot be satisfied to be just a wife and mother. I am still young and I want to learn and enjoy life. My children and my house are not neglected, but I go to evening high school twice a week. My husband is not pleased and when I come home at night and ring the bell, he lets me stand outside a long time intentionally, and doesn't hurry to open the door.

Now he has announced a new decision. Because I send out the laundry to be done, it seems to him that I have too much time for myself, even enough to go to school. So from now on he will count out every penny for anything I have to buy for the house, so I will not be able to send out the laundry any

---

2. **greenhorn:** newly arrived immigrant.

more. And when I have to do the work myself there won't be any time left for such "foolishness" as going to school. I told him that I'm willing to do my own washing but that I would still be able to find time for study.

When I am alone with my thoughts, I feel I may not be right. Perhaps I should not go to school. I want to say that my husband is an intelligent man and he wanted to marry a woman who was educated. The fact that he is intelligent makes me more annoyed with him. He is in favor of the emancipation of women, yet in real life he acts contrary to his beliefs.

Awaiting your opinion on this, I remain,

Your reader,
The Discontented Wife

Answer:

Since this man is intelligent and an adherent of the women's emancipation movement, he is scolded severely in the answer for wanting to keep his wife so enslaved. Also the opinion is expressed that the wife absolutely has the right to go to school two evenings a week.

Dear Editor,

I plead with you to open your illustrious newspaper and take in my "Bintel Brief" in which I write about my great suffering.

A long gloomy year, three hundred and sixty-five days, have gone by since I left my home and am alone on the lonely road of life. Oh, my poor dear parents, how saddened they were at my leaving. The leave-taking, their seeing me on my way, was like a silent funeral.

There was no shaking of the alms box, there was no grave digging and no sawing of boards, but I, myself, put on the white shirt that was wet with my mother's tears, took my pillow, and climbed into the wagon. Accompanying me was a quiet choked wail from my parents and friends.

The wheels of the wagon rolled farther and farther away. My mother and father wept for their son, then turned with heavy hearts to the empty house. They did not sit shive[3] even though they had lost a child.

I came to America and became a painter. My great love for Hebrew, for Russian, all of my other knowledge was smeared with paint. During the year that I have been here I have had some good periods, but I am not happy, because I have no interest in anything. My homesickness and loneliness darken my life.

Ah, home, my beloved home. My heart is heavy for my parents whom I left behind. I want to run back, but I am powerless. I am a coward, because I know that I have to serve under *"Fonie"* [the Czar] for three years.

---

3. **shive:** period of mourning.

I am lonely in my homesickness and I beg you to be my counsel as to how to act.

Respectfully,
V. A.

Answer:

The answer states that almost all immigrants yearn deeply for dear ones and home at first. They are compared with plants that are transplanted to new ground. At first it seems that they are withering, but in time most of them revive and take root in the new earth.

The advice to this young man is that he must not consider going home, but try to take root here. He should try to overcome all these emotions and strive to make something of himself so that in time he will be able to bring his parents here.

21

Conditions at the Slaughterhouse

Upton Sinclair

Exposing the meat-packing industry was not Upton Sinclair's main purpose in writing The Jungle. *A recent convert to socialism, Sinclair (1878–1968) had received a five hundred-dollar advance from* The Appeal to Reason, *the nation's leading socialist newspaper. Choosing to write about packinghouse workers who had recently lost a labor strike in the summer of 1904, he went to Chicago, infiltrated the stockyards, and wrote a novel exposing the miseries of the workers there.*

The publication of The Jungle *in 1906 was one of the major events of the Progressive Era. Intended as a plea for socialism, the book was read by a shocked public as an exposé not of the economic system but of the sanitary conditions in Chicago meat-packing houses. Sinclair himself said that he had taken aim at America's heart and hit instead its stomach. Evidently the empty stomachs of the book's immigrant workers Jurgis and Ona mattered less to the public than its own, which it feared might be filled with packinghouse wastes mixed with food. Sinclair's book and President Theodore Roosevelt's leadership persuaded Congress to enact the nation's first national drug and meat inspection and pure-food laws.*

BEFORE YOU READ

1. What comparison did Sinclair make between the animals and the workers in the slaughterhouse?

2. What are the psychological effects of the work on Jurgis and Ona?

3. Why do you think the account of sanitary conditions impressed the public so much more sharply than the account of workers' lives?

Entering one of the Durham buildings, they found a number of other visitors waiting; and before long there came a guide, to escort them through the place. They make a great feature of showing strangers through the packing plants, for it is a good advertisement. But *ponas* Jokubas whispered maliciously that the visitors did not see any more than the packers wanted them to.

They climbed a long series of stairways outside of the building, to the top of its five or six stories. Here was the chute, with its river of hogs, all patiently toiling upward; there was a place for them to rest to cool off, and then through another passageway they went into a room from which there is no returning for hogs.

It was a long, narrow room, with a gallery along it for visitors. At the head there was a great iron wheel, about twenty feet in circumference, with rings here and there along its edge. Upon both sides of this wheel there was a narrow space, into which came the hogs at the end of their journey; in the midst of them stood a great burly Negro, bare-armed and bare-chested. He was resting for the moment, for the wheel had stopped while men were cleaning up. In a minute or two, however, it began slowly to revolve, and then the men upon each side of it sprang to work. They had chains which they fastened about the leg of the nearest hog, and the other end of the chain they hooked into one of the rings upon the wheel. So, as the wheel turned, a hog was suddenly jerked off his feet and borne aloft.

At the same instant the ear was assailed by a most terrifying shriek; the visitors started in alarm, the women turned pale and shrank back. The shriek was followed by another, louder and yet more agonizing—for once started upon that journey, the hog never came back; at the top of the wheel he was shunted off upon a trolley, and went sailing down the room. And meantime another was swung up, and then another, and another, until there was a double line of them, each dangling by a foot and kicking in frenzy—and squealing. The uproar was appalling, perilous to the eardrums; one feared there was too much sound for the room to hold—that the walls must give way or the ceiling crack. There were high squeals and low squeals, grunts, and wails of agony; there would come a momentary lull, and then a fresh outburst, louder than ever, surging up to a deafening climax. It was too much for some of the visitors—the men would look at each other, laughing nervously, and the women would stand with hands clenched, and the blood rushing to their faces, and the tears starting in their eyes.

Meantime, heedless of all these things, the men upon the floor were going about their work. Neither squeals of hogs nor tears of visitors made any difference to them; one by one they hooked up the hogs, and one by one with a swift stroke they slit their throats. There was a long line of hogs, with squeals and lifeblood ebbing away together; until at last each started again, and vanished with a splash into a huge vat of boiling water.

It was all so very businesslike that one watched it fascinated. It was porkmaking by machinery, porkmaking by applied mathematics. And yet somehow the most matter-of-fact person could not help thinking of the hogs. . . .

One could not stand and watch very long without becoming philosophical, without beginning to deal in symbols and similes, and to hear the hog squeal of the universe. Was it permitted to believe that there was nowhere upon the earth, or above the earth, a heaven for hogs, where they were requited for all this suffering? Each one of these hogs was a separate creature. Some were white hogs, some were black; some were brown, some were spotted; some were old, some young; some were long and lean, some were monstrous. And each of them had an individuality of his own, a will of his own, a hope and a heart's desire; each was full of self-confidence, of self-importance, and a sense of dignity. And trusting and strong in faith he had gone about his business, the while a black shadow hung over him and a horrid Fate waited in his pathway. Now suddenly it had swooped upon him, and had seized him by the leg. Re-

lentless, remorseless, it was; all his protests, his screams, were nothing to it—
it did its cruel will with him, as if his wishes, his feelings, had simply no existence at all; it cut his throat and watched him gasp out his life. And now was
one to believe that there was nowhere a god of hogs, to whom this hog personality was precious, to whom these hog squeals and agonies had a meaning?
Who would take this hog into his arms and comfort him, reward him for his
work well done, and show him the meaning of his sacrifice? Perhaps some
glimpse of all this was in the thoughts of our humble-minded Jurgis, as he
turned to go on with the rest of the party, and muttered: *"Dieve*—but I'm glad
I'm not a hog!"

The carcass hog was scooped out of the vat by machinery, and then it fell
to the second floor, passing on the way through a wonderful machine with numerous scrapers, which adjusted themselves to the size and shape of the animal, and sent it out at the other end with nearly all of its bristles removed. It
was then again strung up by machinery, and sent upon another trolley ride; this
time passing between two lines of men, who sat upon a raised platform, each
doing a certain single thing to the carcass as it came to him. One scraped the
outside of a leg; another scraped the inside of the same leg. One with a swift
stroke cut the throat; another with two swift strokes severed the head, which
fell to the floor and vanished through a hole. Another made a slit down the
body; a second opened the body wider; a third with a saw cut the breastbone;
a fourth loosened the entrails; a fifth pulled them out—and they also slid
through a hole in the floor. There were men to scrape each side and men to
scrape the back; there were men to clean the carcass inside, to trim it and wash
it. Looking down this room, one saw, creeping slowly, a line of dangling hogs
a hundred yards in length; and for every yard there was a man, working as if a
demon were after him. At the end of this hog's progress every inch of the carcass had been gone over several times; and then it was rolled into the chilling
room, where it stayed for twenty-four hours, and where a stranger might lose
himself in a forest of freezing hogs.

Before the carcass was admitted here, however, it had to pass a government
inspector, who sat in the doorway and felt of the glands in the neck for tuberculosis. This government inspector did not have the manner of a man who was
worked to death; he was apparently not haunted by a fear that the hog might
get by him before he had finished his testing. If you were a sociable person, he
was quite willing to enter into conversation with you, and to explain to you the
deadly nature of the ptomaines[1] which are found in tubercular pork; and while
he was talking with you you could hardly be so ungrateful as to notice that a
dozen carcasses were passing him untouched. This inspector wore a blue uniform, with brass buttons, and he gave an atmosphere of authority to the scene,
and, as it were, put the stamp of official approval upon the things which were
done in Durham's.

Jurgis went down the line with the rest of the visitors, staring open-

---

1. **ptomaines:** bacteria causing food poisoning.

mouthed, lost in wonder. He had dressed hogs himself in the forest of Lithuania; but he had never expected to live to see one hog dressed by several hundred men. It was like a wonderful poem to him, and he took it all in guilelessly—even to the conspicuous signs demanding immaculate cleanliness of the employees. Jurgis was vexed when the cynical Jokubas translated these signs with sarcastic comments, offering to take them to the secret rooms where the spoiled meats went to be doctored.

The party descended to the next floor, where the various waste materials were treated. Here came the entrails, to be scraped and washed clean for sausage casings; men and women worked here in the midst of a sickening stench, which caused the visitors to hasten by, gasping. To another room came all the scraps to be "tanked," which meant boiling and pumping off the grease to make soap and lard; below they took out the refuse, and this, too, was a region in which the visitors did not linger. In still other places men were engaged in cutting up the carcasses that had been through the chilling rooms. First there were the "splitters," the most expert workmen in the plant, who earned as high as fifty cents an hour, and did not a thing all day except chop hogs down the middle. Then there were "cleaver men," great giants with muscles of iron; each had two men to attend him—to slide the half carcass in front of him on the table, and hold it while he chopped it, and then turn each piece so that he might chop it once more. His cleaver had a blade about two feet long, and he never made but one cut; he made it so neatly, too, that his implement did not smite through and dull itself—there was just enough force for a perfect cut, and no more. So through various yawning holes there slipped to the floor below—to one room hams, to another forequarters, to another sides of pork. One might go down to this floor and see the pickling rooms, where the hams were put into vats, and the great smoke rooms, with their airtight iron doors. In other rooms they prepared salt pork—there were whole cellars full of it, built up in great towers to the ceiling. In yet other rooms they were putting up meat in boxes and barrels, and wrapping hams and bacon in oiled paper, sealing and labeling and sewing them. From the doors of these rooms went men with loaded trucks, to the platform where freight cars were waiting to be filled; and one went out there and realized with a start that he had come at last to the ground floor of this enormous building.

Then the party went across the street to where they did the killing of beef—where every hour they turned four or five hundred cattle into meat. Unlike the place they had left, all this work was done on one floor; and instead of there being one line of carcasses which moved to the workmen, there were fifteen or twenty lines, and the men moved from one to another of these. This made a scene of intense activity, a picture of human power wonderful to watch. It was all in one great room, like a circus amphitheater, with a gallery for visitors running over the center.

The visitors were taken there and shown them, all neatly hung in rows, labeled conspicuously with the tags of the government inspectors—and some, which had been killed by a special process, marked with the sign of the *kosher* rabbi, certifying that it was fit for sale to the orthodox. And then the visitors were taken to the other parts of the building, to see what became of each particle of the waste material that had vanished through the floor; and to the pickling rooms, and the salting rooms, the canning rooms, and the packing rooms, where choice meat was prepared for shipping in refrigerator cars, destined to be eaten in all the four corners of civilization. Afterward they went outside, wandering about among the mazes of buildings in which was done the work auxiliary to this great industry.

There were the men in the pickle rooms, for instance, where old Antanas had gotten his death; scarce a one of these that had not some spot of horror on his person. Let a man so much as scrape his finger pushing a truck in the pickle rooms, and he might have a sore that would put him out of the world; all the joints in his fingers might be eaten by the acid, one by one. Of the butchers and floorsmen, the beef-boners and trimmers, and all those who used knives, you could scarcely find a person who had the use of his thumb; time and time again the base of it had been slashed, till it was a mere lump of flesh against which the man pressed the knife to hold it. The hands of these men would be criss-crossed with cuts, until you could no longer pretend to count them or to trace them. They would have no nails,—they had worn them off pulling hides; their knuckles were swollen so that their fingers spread out like a fan. There were men who worked in the cooking rooms, in the midst of steam and sickening odors, by artificial light; in these rooms the germs of tuberculosis might live for two years, but the supply was renewed every hour. There were the beef-luggers, who carried two-hundred-pound quarters into the refrigerator-cars; a fearful kind of work, that began at four o'clock in the morning, and that wore out the most powerful men in a few years. There were those who worked in the chilling rooms, and whose special disease was rheumatism; the time limit that a man could work in the chilling rooms was said to be five years. There were the wool-pluckers, whose hands went to pieces even sooner than the hands of the pickle men; for the pelts of the sheep had to be painted with acid to loosen the wool, and then the pluckers had to pull out this wool with their bare hands, till the acid had eaten their fingers off. There were those who made the tins for the canned meat; and their hands, too, were a maze of cuts, and each cut represented a chance for blood poisoning. Some worked at the stamping machines, and it was very seldom that one could work long there at the pace that was set, and not give out and forget himself, and have a part of his hand chopped off. There were the "hoisters," as they were called, whose task it was to press the lever which lifted the dead cattle off the floor. They ran along upon a rafter, peering down through the damp and the steam; and as old Durham's architects had not built the killing room for the convenience of the hoisters, at every few feet they would have to stoop under a beam, say about four feet above the one they ran on; which got them into the habit of stooping, so that in a few years they would be walking like chimpanzees. Worst of any, however, were the fertilizer men, and those who served in the cooking rooms. These people could not be shown to the visitor,—for the odor of a fertilizer man would scare any ordinary visitor at a hundred yards, and as for the other men, who worked in tank rooms full of steam, and in some of which there were open vats near the level of the floor, their peculiar trouble was that they fell into the vats; and when they were fished out, there was never enough of them left to be worth exhibiting,—sometimes they would be overlooked for days, till all but the bones of them had gone out to the world as Durham's Pure Leaf Lard!

It was only when the whole ham was spoiled that it came into the department of Elzbieta. Cut up by the two-thousand-revolutions-a-minute flyers, and mixed with half a ton of other meat, no odor that ever was in a ham could make any difference. There was never the least attention paid to what was cut up for sausage; there would come all the way back from Europe old sausage that had been rejected, and that was moldy and white—it would be dosed with borax and glycerine, and dumped into the hoppers, and made over again for home consumption. There would be meat that had tumbled out on the floor, in the dirt and sawdust, where the workers had tramped and spit uncounted billions of consumption germs. There would be meat stored in great piles in rooms; and the water from leaky roofs would drip over it, and thousands of rats would race about on it. It was too dark in these storage places to see well, but a man could run his hand over these piles of meat and sweep off handfuls of the dried dung of rats. These rats were nuisances, and the packers would put poisoned bread out for them; they would die, and then rats, bread, and meat would go into the hoppers together. This is no fairy story and no joke; the meat would be shoveled into carts, and the man who did the shoveling would not trouble to lift out a rat even when he saw one—there were things that went into the sausage in comparison with which a poisoned rat was a tidbit. There was no place for the men to wash their hands before they ate their dinner, and so they made a practice of washing them in the water that was to be ladled into the sausage. There were the butt-ends of smoked meat, and the scraps of corned beef, and all the odds and ends of the waste of the plants, that would be dumped into old barrels in the cellar and left there. Under the system of rigid economy which the packers enforced, there were some jobs that it only paid to do once in a long time, and among these was the cleaning out of the waste barrels. Every spring they did it; and in the barrels would be dirt and rust and old nails and stale water—and cartload after cartload of it would be taken up and dumped into the hoppers with fresh meat, and sent out to the public's breakfast. Some of it they would make into "smoked" sausage—but as the smoking took time and was therefore expensive, they would call upon their chemistry department, and preserve it with borax and color it with gelatine to make it brown. All of their sausage came out of the same bowl, but when they came to wrap it they would stamp some of it "special," and for this they would charge two cents more a pound.

Such were the new surroundings in which Elzbieta was placed, and such was the work she was compelled to do. It was stupefying, brutalizing work; it left her no time to think, no strength for anything. She was part of the machine she tended, and every faculty that was not needed for the machine was doomed to be crushed out of existence. There was only one mercy about the cruel grind—that it gave her the gift of insensibility. Little by little she sank into a torpor—she fell silent. She would meet Jurgis and Ona in the evening, and the three would walk home together, often without saying a word. Ona, too, was falling into a habit of silence—Ona, who had once gone about singing like a bird. She was sick and miserable, and often she would barely have strength enough to drag herself home. And there they would eat what they had to eat, and afterward, because there was only their misery to talk of, they would crawl into bed and fall into a stupor and never stir until it was time to get up again, and dress by candlelight, and go back to the machines. They were so numbed that they did not even suffer much from hunger, now; only the children continued to fret when the food ran short.

Yet the soul of Ona was not dead—the souls of none of them were dead, but only sleeping; and now and then they would waken, and these were cruel times. The gates of memory would roll open—old joys would stretch out their arms to them, old hopes and dreams would call to them, and they would stir beneath the burden that lay upon them, and feel its forever immeasurable weight. They could not even cry out beneath it; but anguish would seize them, more dreadful than the agony of death. It was a thing scarcely to be spoken—a thing never spoken by all the world, that will not know its own defeat.

They were beaten; they had lost the game, they were swept aside. It was not less tragic because it was so sordid, because it had to do with wages and grocery bills and rents. They had dreamed of freedom; of a chance to look about them and learn something; to be decent and clean, to see their child grow up to be strong. And now it was all gone—it would never be! They had played the game and they had lost. Six years more of toil they had to face before they could expect the least respite, the cessation of the payments upon the house; and how cruelly certain it was that they could never stand six years of such a life as they were living! They were lost, they were going down—and there was no deliverance for them, no hope; for all the help it gave them the vast city in which they lived might have been an ocean waste, a wilderness, a desert, a tomb. So often this mood would come to Ona, in the nighttime, when something wakened her; she would lie, afraid of the beating of her own heart, fronting the blood-red eyes of the old primeval terror of life. Once she cried aloud, and woke Jurgis, who was tired and cross. After that she learned to weep silently—their moods so seldom came together now! It was as if their hopes were buried in separate graves.

Jurgis, being a man, had troubles of his own. There was another specter following him. He had never spoken of it, nor would he allow any one else to speak of it—he had never acknowledged its existence to himself. Yet the battle with it took all the manhood that he had—and once or twice, alas, a little more. Jurgis had discovered drink.

He was working in the steaming pit of hell; day after day, week after week—

until now there was not an organ of his body that did its work without pain, until the sound of ocean breakers echoed in his head day and night, and the buildings swayed and danced before him as he went down the street. And from all the unending horror of this there was a respite, a deliverance—he could drink! He could forget the pain, he could slip off the burden; he would see clearly again, he would be master of his brain, of his thoughts, of his will. His dead self would stir in him, and he would find himself laughing and cracking jokes with his companions—he would be a man again, and master of his life.

This *Chicago Tribune* cartoon, captioned "He's Always Seeing Things," belittled William Jennings Bryan, three-time Democratic presidential candidate, who defended the Tennessee law that forbade the teaching of evolution.

PART FOUR

War and Its Aftermath

A New Society

Although all wars generate uncertainty and turmoil, some in American history have consolidated a sense of national mission and purpose. World War I, however, like the Korean and Vietnamese Wars, encouraged social discontent. The war had to be "sold" to the American people; it raised the questions of who was a hyphenated American (Irish-American, German-American, and so on), who was loyal and who was not. While some soldiers such as Louis F. Ranlett went to war rather innocently, they came back less innocent. At home, the argument over the meaning of the war and of American loyalty engaged much of American society.

The First World War brought other major domestic changes. Fresh opportunities in war industries, combined with the depredations of the boll weevil on cotton crops, stimulated the great migration of African Americans to the northern cities, a migration that would be further fueled by the next great war and the era of Cold War prosperity that followed it. World War I was one of many forces inducing a higher degree of economic organization in American society as it moved into the "consumer" age. Americans reveled in such new consumer goods as automobiles and developed doubts about whether what had worked for a previous generation would work for them. These doubts fueled modern movements in society, literature, and the arts, as well as powerful reactions to them in the defensive reassertion of traditional values. These conflicting values were played out in many arenas. Margaret Sanger's crusade for birth control challenged traditional attitudes in the sensitive areas of family and sexuality. The Scopes trial, pitting William Jennings Bryan, the hero of rural America, against Clarence Darrow and other champions of modernism like Henry Louis Mencken, revealed the chasm in religious and social values between fundamentalists and modernists. And the Harlem Renaissance, which brought Zora Neale Hurston to New York City, revealed new possibilities in race relations exhilarating to some Americans but frightening to many others.

The assumption that American life meant unending growth, expansion, and prosperity came into question once again during the Great Depression of the 1930s. Although everyone was reacting to the same overwhelming set of events, the degree to which different people were affected by the Depression was quite variable. Some people ruminated over lost fortunes on the stock markets; others organized workers; still others drifted from place to place. Many wrote plaintive letters to the president and the first lady.

Points of View: The Scopes Trial (1925)

22

In Defense of the Bible

William Jennings Bryan
and Clarence Darrow

In July 1925 John T. Scopes was tried for teaching the theory of evolution in the Dayton, Tennessee, high school. The first trial in American history to be broadcast nationally, it was "monkey business" to some and "the trial of the century" to others. A writer in the Moody Bible Institute Monthly *considered the case "the mightiest issue that has ever been joined since the trial of Jesus Christ before Pontius Pilate."*

The Tennessee legislature in March 1925 had passed the Butler Act making it a crime to teach in any state-supported school (including universities) "any theory that denies the story of the Divine Creation of man as taught in the Bible, and to teach instead that man has descended from a lower order of animals." Almost on a whim, a few Daytonians decided to test the law and persuaded local high-school biology teacher John T. Scopes to become the defendant.

Larger forces, however, were at work. The Protestant churches were even then sharply dividing between fundamentalists who believed in the literal truth of the Bible and liberals who accepted the changes brought about by the development of scientific understanding. The split corresponded to a division between urban and rural values, a division that was also sharply reflected in national, and especially Democratic Party, politics. The South was a stronghold of fundamentalism and laws like the Butler Act had much support throughout the region.

A famous orator led each legal team. William Jennings Bryan, long identified with the values of the countryside, had been the Democratic Party candidate for president in 1896, 1900, and 1908, and had served as Woodrow Wilson's first secretary of state. Clarence Darrow was nationally famous both as a trial lawyer and as a lecturer speaking for evolution, the scientific outlook, and various reforms. When the presiding judge, John T. Raulston, banned the use of expert witnesses on the theory of evolution, Darrow called Bryan himself to the stand as an authority on the Bible. Bryan agreed to mount the witness box and the judge permitted the testimony to proceed, but without the jury — which, the judge had ruled, was not to decide matters of the truth of either evolution or the Bible, but only whether Scopes had taught evolution to his high-school class. Yet Darrow made it seem as if Bryan, fundamentalism, and perhaps even the Bible were on trial. The following day the judge changed his mind, expunged all of Bryan's testimony, and sent the case to the jury for the inevitable finding of Scopes's admitted guilt.

Before You Read

1. Why do you think Bryan agreed to testify?
2. Was Darrow's questioning fair?
3. Could Bryan have made his arguments stronger?
4. What values was he defending?
5. What do you think of Darrow's performance? Was he, as some have said, putting the Bible on trial?

The Court: The question is whether or not Mr. Scopes taught man descended from the lower order of animals.

Examination of W. J. Bryan by Clarence Darrow, counsel for the Defense

Q: You have given considerable study to the Bible, haven't you, Mr. Bryan?

A: Yes, sir, I have tried to.

Q: Well, we all know you have; we are not going to dispute that at all. But you have written and published articles almost weekly, and sometimes have made interpretations of various things.

A: I would not say interpretations, Mr. Darrow, but comments on the lesson.

Q: If you comment to any extent these comments have been interpretations?

A: I presume that any discussion might be to some extent interpretations, but they have not been primarily intended as interpretations.

Q: Then you have made a general study of it?

A: Yes, I have; I have studied the Bible for about fifty years, or some time more than that, but, of course, I have studied it more as I have become older than when I was but a boy.

Q: Do you claim that everything in the Bible should be literally interpreted?

A: I believe everything in the Bible should be accepted as it is given there; some of the Bible is given illustratively. For instance: "Ye are the salt of the earth." I would not insist that man was actually salt, or that he had flesh of salt, but it is used in the sense of salt as saving God's people.

Q: You believe the story of the flood to be a literal interpretation?

A: Yes, sir.

Sheldon Norman Grebstein, ed., *Monkey Trial: The State of Tennessee vs. John Thomas Scopes* (Boston: Houghton, Mifflin Company 1960).

Q: When was that flood?

A: I would not attempt to fix the date. The date is fixed, as suggested this morning.

Q: About 4004 B.C.?

A: That has been the estimate of a man that is accepted today. I would not say it is accurate.

Q: That estimate is printed in the Bible?

A: Everybody knows, at least, I think most of the people know, that was the estimate given.

Q: But what do you think that the Bible, itself, says? Don't you know how it was arrived at?

A: I never made a calculation.

Q: What do you think?

A: I do not think about things I don't think about.

Q: Do you think about things you do think about?

A: Well, sometimes.

The Bailiff: Let us have order.

Mr. Darrow: Mr. Bryan, you have read these dates over and over again?

A: Not very accurately; I turn back sometimes to see what the time was.

Q: You want to say now you have no idea how these dates were computed?

A: No, I don't say, but I have told you what my idea was. I say I don't know how accurate it was.

Q: You say from the generation of man —

Gen. Stewart: I am objecting to his cross-examining his own witness.

Mr. Darrow: He is a hostile witness.

The Court: I am going to let Mr. Bryan control —

The Witness: I want him to have all the latitude he wants, for I am going to have some latitude when he gets through.

Mr. Darrow: You can have latitude and longitude.

The Court: Order.

Gen. Stewart: The witness is entitled to be examined as to the legal evidence of it. We were supposed to go into the argument today, and we have nearly lost the day, your Honor.

Mr. McKenzie: I object to it.

Gen. Stewart: Your Honor, he is perfectly able to take care of this, but we are attaining no evidence. This is not competent evidence.

The Witness: These gentlemen have not had much chance — they did not come here to try this case. They came here to try revealed religion. I am here to defend it, and they can ask me any question they please.

The Court: All right.

Mr. Darrow: Great applause from the bleachers.

The Witness: From those whom you call "yokels."

Mr. Darrow: I have never called them yokels.

The Witness: That is the ignorance of Tennessee, the bigotry.

Mr. Darrow: You mean who are applauding you?

The Witness: Those are the people whom you insult.

Mr. Darrow: You insult every man of science and learning in the world because he does not believe in your fool religion.

The Court: I will not stand for that.

Mr. Darrow: For what he is doing?

The Court: I am talking to both of you.

Gen. Stewart: This has gone beyond the pale of a lawsuit, your Honor. I have a public duty to perform under my oath, and I ask the Court to stop it. Mr. Darrow is making an effort to insult the gentleman on the witness stand and I ask that it be stopped, for it has gone beyond the pale of a lawsuit.

The Court: To stop it now would not be just to Mr. Bryan. He wants to ask the other gentleman questions along the same line.

Gen. Stewart: It will all be incompetent.

The Witness: The jury is not here.

The Court: I do not want to be strictly technical.

Mr. Darrow: Then your Honor rules, and I accept.

Gen. Stewart: The jury is not here.

Mr. Darrow: How long ago was the flood, Mr. Bryan?

A: Let me see Ussher's calculation about it?

Mr. Darrow: Surely.

A: I think this does not give it.

Q: It gives an account of Noah. Where is the one in evidence? I am quite certain it is there.

The Witness: Oh, I would put the estimate where it is, because I have no reason to vary it. But I would have to look at it to give you the exact date.

Q: I would, too. Do you remember what book the account is in?

A: Genesis.

Mr. Hays: Is that the one in evidence?

Mr. Neal: That will have it; that is the King James Version.

Mr. Darrow: The one in evidence has it.

The Witness: It is given here, as 2348 years B.C.

Q: Well, 2348 years B.C. You believe that all the living things that were not contained in the ark were destroyed.

A: I think the fish may have lived.

Q: Outside of the fish?

A: I cannot say.

Q: You cannot say?

A: No, I accept that just as it is; I have no proof to the contrary.

Q: I am asking you whether you believe?

A: I do.

Q: That all living things outside of the fish were destroyed?

A: What I say about the fish is merely a matter of humor.

Q: I understand.

The Witness: Due to the fact a man wrote up here the other day to ask whether all the fish were destroyed, and the gentleman who received the letter told him the fish may have lived.

Q: I am referring to the fish, too.

A: I accept that as the Bible gives it and I have never found any reason for denying, disputing, or rejecting it.

Q: Let us make it definite, 2,348 years?

A: I didn't say that. That is the time given there [*indicating the Bible*] but I don't pretend to say that is exact.

Q: You never figured it out, these generations, yourself?

A: No, sir; not myself.

Q: But the Bible you have offered in evidence says 2,340 something, so that 4,200 years ago there was not a living thing on the earth, excepting the people on the ark and the animals on the ark and the fishes?

A: There have been living things before that.

Q: I mean at that time.

A: After that.

Q: Don't you know there are any number of civilizations that are traced back to more than 5,000 years?

A: I know we have people who trace things back according to the number of ciphers they have. But I am not satisfied they are accurate.

Q: You are not satisfied there is any civilization that can be traced back 5,000 years?

A: I would not want to say there is because I have no evidence of it that is satisfactory.

Q: Would you say there is not?

A: Well, so far as I know, but when the scientists differ from 24,000,000 to 306,000,000 in their opinion as to how long ago life came here, I want them to be nearer, to come nearer together, before they demand of me to give up my belief in the Bible.

Q: Do you say that you do not believe that there were any civilizations on this earth that reach back beyond 5,000 years?

A: I am not satisfied by any evidence that I have seen.

Q: I didn't ask you what you are satisfied with. I asked you if you believe it?

The Witness: Will you let me answer it?

The Court: Go right on.

The Witness: I am satisfied by no evidence that I have found that would justify me in accepting the opinions of these men against what I believe to be the inspired Word of God.

Q: And you believe every nation, every organization of men, every animal, in the world outside of the fishes—

The Witness: The fish, I want you to understand, is merely a matter of humor.

Q: You believe that all the various human races on the earth have come into being in the last 4,000 years or 4,200 years, whatever it is?

A: No, it would be more than that.

[Here Bryan and Darrow engaged in some calculations as to when man was created, according to the chronology Bryan was defending.]

Q: That makes 4,262 years. If it is not correct, we can correct it.

A: According to the Bible there was a civilization before that, destroyed by the flood.

Q: Let me make this definite. You believe that every civilization on the earth and every living thing, except possibly the fishes, that came out of the ark were wiped out by the flood?

A: At that time.

Q: At that time. And then whatever human beings, including all the tribes, that inhabited the world, and have inhabited the world, and who run their pedigree straight back, and all the animals, have come onto the earth since the flood?

A: Yes.

Q: Within 4,200 years. Do you know a scientific man on the face of the earth that believes any such thing?

A: I cannot say, but I know some scientific men who dispute entirely the antiquity of man as testified to by other scientific men.

Q: Oh, that does not answer the question. Do you know of a single scientific man on the face of the earth that believes any such thing as you stated, about the antiquity of man?

A: I don't think I have ever asked one the direct question.

Q: Quite important, isn't it?

A: Well, I don't know as it is.

Q: It might not be?

A: If I had nothing else to do except speculate on what our remote ancestors were and what our remote descendants have been, but I have been more interested in Christians going on right now to make it much more important than speculation on either the past or the future.

Q: You have never had any interest in the age of the various races and people and civilization and animals that exist upon the earth today, is that right?

A: I have never felt a great deal of interest in the effort that has been made to dispute the Bible by the speculations of men, or the investigations of men.

Q: Are you the only human being on earth who knows what the Bible means?

Gen. Stewart: I object.

The Court: Sustained.

Mr. Darrow: You do know that there are thousands of people who profess to be Christians who believe the earth is much more ancient and that the human race is much more ancient?

A: I think there may be.

Q: And you never have investigated to find out how long man has been on the earth?

A: I have never found it necessary—

Q: For any reason, whatever it is?

A: To examine every speculation; but if I had done it I never would have done anything else.

Q: I ask for a direct answer.

A: I do not expect to find out all those things, and I do not expect to find out about races.

Q: I didn't ask you that. Now, I ask you if you know if it was interesting enough or important enough for you to try to find out about how old these ancient civilizations were?

A: No; I have not made a study of it.

Q: Don't you know that the ancient civilizations of China are 6,000 or 7,000 years old, at the very least?

A: No; but they would not run back beyond the creation, according to the Bible, 6,000 years.

Q: You don't know how old they are, is that right?

A: I don't know how old they are, but probably you do. [*Laughter in the courtyard.*] I think you would give preference to anybody who opposed the Bible, and I give the preference to the Bible.

Q: I see. Well, you are welcome to your opinion. Have you any idea how old the Egyptian civilization is?

A: No.

Q: Do you know of any record in the world, outside of the story of the Bible, which conforms to any statement that it is 4,200 years ago or thereabouts that all life was wiped off the face of the earth?

A: I think they have found records.

Q: Do you know of any?

A: Records reciting the flood, but I am not an authority on the subject.

Q: Now, Mr. Bryan, will you say if you know of any record, or have ever heard of any records, that describe that a flood existed 4,200 years ago, or about that time, which wiped all life off the earth?

A: The recollection of what I have read on that subject is not distinct enough to say whether the records attempted to fix a time, but I have seen in the discoveries of archaeologists where they have found records that described the flood.

Q: Mr. Bryan, don't you know that there are many old religions that describe the flood?

A: No, I don't know.

Q: You know there are others besides the Jewish?

A: I don't know whether these are the record of any other religion or refer to this flood.

Q: Don't you ever examine religion so far to know that?

A: Outside of the Bible?

Q: Yes.

A: No; I have not examined to know that, generally.

Q: You have never examined any other religions?

A: Yes, sir.

Q: Have you ever read anything about the origins of religions?

A: Not a great deal.

Q: You have never examined any other religion?

A: Yes, sir.

Q: And you don't know whether any other religion ever gave a similar account of the destruction of the earth by the flood?

A: The Christian religion has satisfied me, and I have never felt it necessary to look up some competing religions.

Q: Do you consider that every religion on earth competes with the Christian religion?

A: I think everybody who does not believe in the Christian religion believes so—

Q: I am asking what you think?

A: I do not regard them as competitive because I do not think they have the same sources as we have.

Q: You are wrong in saying "competitive"?

A: I would not say competitive, but the religious unbelievers.

Q: Unbelievers of what?

A: In the Christian religion.

Q: What about the religion of Buddha?

A: I can tell you something about that, if you want to know.

Q: What about the religion of Confucius or Buddha?

A: Well, I can tell you something about that, if you would like to know.

Q: Did you ever investigate them?

A: Somewhat.

Q: Do you regard them as competitive?

A: No, I think they are very inferior. Would you like for me to tell you what I know about it?

Q: No.

A: Well, I shall insist on giving it to you.

Q: You won't talk about free silver, will you?

A: Not at all. . . .

23

To Expose a Fool

H. L. Mencken

Henry L. Mencken (1880–1956) was one of the most controversial figures of the 1920s. The acid pen of this journalist and author championed science, modern literature, and urban sophistication while attacking religion and democracy in general and fundamentalism and political reform in particular. Beloved of college students who sought to shed the previous generation's Victorian values and described in 1926 as "the most powerful personal influence on this whole generation of educated people," Mencken was also roundly hated by representatives of older, rural values and of fundamentalism, the people who rallied behind William Jennings Bryan. "If a buzzard had laid an egg in a dunghill," wrote a minister in the Gospel Call, *"and the sun had hatched a thing like Mencken, the buzzard would have been justly ashamed of its offspring."*

It was Mencken who persuaded Clarence Darrow to enter the Scopes trial. "Nobody gives a damn about that yap schoolteacher," Mencken asserted. "The thing to do is make a fool out of Bryan." Darrow, who had earlier tangled with Bryan in newspaper debates over evolution, was pleased to oblige. Mencken supported the cause—and scandalized the locals—by reporting on the case from Dayton. Unfortunately, the responsibilities of editing his magazine, the American Mercury, *brought him back to Baltimore the weekend before Darrow's famous questioning of Bryan. But Mencken recovered from this missed opportunity a few days later when Bryan died in his sleep at Dayton. Mencken's perspective on the case is presented in this savage obituary. In private conversation, he was even more direct in assessing Bryan's death: "Well, we killed the son-of-a-bitch."*

BEFORE YOU READ

1. How would you describe Mencken's view of Bryan? Can you arrive at an adjective to characterize it?

2. How did Mencken's literary style reinforce his views of society? Why, for example, does he refer to country wives as "unyieldingly multiparous," or to religion as "purely ghostly concerns," or to conversation in small towns as "simian gabble"?

3. How serious do you think Mencken was about the danger of fundamentalism?

4. Was Mencken more cosmopolitan than Bryan or simply provincial in another way?

Has it been marked by historians that the late William Jennings Bryan's last secular act on this earth was to catch flies? A curious detail, and not without its sardonic overtones. He was the most sedulous flycatcher in American history, and by long odds the most successful. His quarry, of course, was not *Musca domestica* but *Homo neandertalensis*. For forty years he tracked it with snare and blunderbuss, up and down the backways of the Republic. Wherever the flambeaux of Chautauqua smoked and guttered, and the bilge of Idealism ran in the veins, and Baptist pastors dammed the brooks with the saved, and men gathered who were weary and heavy laden, and their wives who were unyieldingly multiparous and full of Peruna—there the indefatigable Jennings set up his traps and spread his bait. He knew every forlorn country town in the South and West, and he could crowd the most remote of them to suffocation by simply winding his horn. The city proletariat, transiently flustered by him in 1896, quickly penetrated his buncombe and would have no more of him; the gallery jeered him at every Democratic National Convention for twenty-five years. But out where the grass grows high, and the horned cattle dream away the lazy days, and men still fear the powers and principalities of the air—out there between the corn-rows he held his old puissance to the end. There was no need of beaters to drive in his game. The news that he was coming was enough. For miles the flivver dust would choke the roads. And when he rose at the end of the day to discharge his Message there would be such breathless attention, such a rapt and enchanted ecstasy, such a sweet rustle of amens as the world had not known since Johanan fell to Herod's headsman.

There was something peculiarly fitting in the fact that his last days were spent in a one-horse Tennessee village, and that death found him there. The man felt at home in such scenes. He liked people who sweated freely, and were not debauched by the refinements of the toilet. Making his progress up and down the Main Street of little Dayton, surrounded by gaping primates from the upland valleys of the Cumberland Range, his coat laid aside, his bare arms and hairy chest shining damply, his bald head sprinkled with dust—so accoutred and on display he was obviously happy. He liked getting up early in the morning, to the tune of cocks crowing on the dunghill. He liked the heavy, greasy victuals of the farmhouse kitchen. He liked country lawyers, country pastors, all country people. I believe that this liking was sincere—perhaps the only sincere thing in the man. His nose showed no uneasiness when a hillman in faded overalls and hickory shirt accosted him on the street, and besought him for light upon some mystery of Holy Writ. The simian gabble of a country town was not gabble to him, but wisdom of an occult and superior sort. In the presence of city folks he was palpably uneasy. Their clothes, I suspect, annoyed him, and he was suspicious of their too delicate manners. He knew all the while that they were laughing at him—if not at his baroque theology, then at least at his alpaca pantaloons. But the yokels never laughed at him. To them he was not the huntsman but the prophet, and toward the end, as he gradually forsook mundane politics for purely ghostly concerns, they began to elevate him in their hierarchy. When he died he was the peer of Abraham. Another curious detail: his old enemy, Wilson, aspiring to the same white and shining robe, came down with a thump. But Bryan made the grade. His place in the Tennessee hagiocracy is secure. If the village barber saved any of his hair, then it is curing gall-stones down there today.

II

But what label will he bear in more urbane regions? One, I fear, of a far less flattering kind. Bryan lived too long, and descended too deeply into the mud, to be taken seriously hereafter by fully literate men, even of the kind who write school-books. There was a scattering of sweet words in his funeral notices, but it was no more than a response to conventional sentimentality. The best verdict the most romantic editorial writer could dredge up, save in the eloquent South, was to the general effect that his imbecilities were excused by his earnestness— that under his clowning, as under that of the juggler of Notre Dame, there was the zeal of a steadfast soul. But this was apology, not praise; precisely the same thing might be said of Mary Baker G. Eddy, the late Czar Nicholas, or Czolgosz. The truth is that even Bryan's sincerity will probably yield to what is called, in other fields, definitive criticism. Was he sincere when he opposed imperialism in the Philippines, or when he fed it with deserving Democrats in Santo Domingo? Was he sincere when he tried to shove the Prohibitionists under the table, or when he seized their banner and began to lead them with loud whoops? Was he sincere when he bellowed against war, or when he dreamed of himself as a tin-soldier in uniform, with a grave reserved among the generals? Was he sincere when he denounced the late John W. Davis, or when he swallowed Davis? Was he sincere when he fawned over Champ Clark, or when he betrayed Clark? Was he sincere when he pleaded for tolerance in New York, or when he bawled for the fagot and the stake in Tennessee?

This talk of sincerity, I confess, fatigues me. If the fellow was sincere, then so was P. T. Barnum. The word is disgraced and degraded by such uses. He was, in fact, a charlatan, a mountebank, a zany without shame or dignity. What animated him from end to end of his grotesque career was simply ambition— the ambition of a common man to get his hand upon the collar of his superiors, or, failing that, to get his thumb into their eyes. He was born with a roaring voice, and it had the trick of inflaming half-wits. His whole career was devoted to raising these half-wits against their betters, that he himself might shine. His last battle will be grossly misunderstood if it is thought of as a mere exercise in fanaticism—that is, if Bryan the Fundamentalist Pope is mistaken for one of the bucolic Fundamentalists. There was much more in it than that, as everyone knows who saw him on the field. What moved him, at bottom, was simply hatred of the city men who had laughed at him so long, and brought him at last to so tatterdemalion an estate. He lusted for revenge upon them. He yearned to lead the anthropoid rabble against them, to set *Homo neandertalensis* upon them, to punish them for the execution they had done upon him by attacking the very vitals of their civilization. He went far beyond the bounds of any merely religious frenzy, however inordinate. When he began denouncing the notion that man is a mammal even some of the hinds at Dayton were agape. And when, brought upon Darrow's cruel hook, he writhed and tossed in a very fury of malignancy, bawling against the baldest elements of sense and decency like a man frantic—when he came to that tragic climax there were snickers among the hinds as well as hosannas.

Upon that hook, in truth, Bryan committed suicide, as a legend as well as in the body. He staggered from the rustic court ready to die, and he staggered from it ready to be forgotten, save as a character in a third-rate farce, witless and in execrable taste. The chances are that history will put the peak of democracy in his time; it has been on the downward curve among us since the campaign of 1896. He will be remembered, perhaps, as its supreme impostor, the *reductio ad absurdum* of its pretension. Bryan came very near being President of the United States. In 1896, it is possible, he was actually elected. He lived long enough to make patriots thank the inscrutable gods for Harding, even for Coolidge. Dulness has got into the White House, and the smell of cabbage boiling, but there is at least nothing to compare to the intolerable buffoonery that went on in Tennessee. The President of the United States doesn't believe that the earth is square, and that witches should be put to death, and that

Jonah swallowed the whale. The Golden Text is not painted weekly on the White House wall, and there is no need to keep ambassadors waiting while Pastor Simpson, of Smithsville, prays for rain in the Blue Room. We have escaped something—by a narrow margin, but still safely.

III

That is, so far. The Fundamentalists continue at the wake, and sense gets a sort of reprieve. The legislature of Georgia, so the news comes, has shelved the anti-evolution bill, and turns its back upon the legislature of Tennessee. Elsewhere minorities prepare for battle—here and there with some assurance of success. But it is too early, it seems to me, to send the firemen home; the fire is still burning on many a far-flung hill, and it may begin to roar again at any moment. The evil that men do lives after them. Bryan, in his malice, started something that it will not be easy to stop. In ten thousand country towns his old heelers, the evangelical pastors, are propagating his gospel, and everywhere the yokels are ready for it. When he disappeared from the big cities, the big cities made the capital error of assuming that he was done for. If they heard of him at all, it was only as a crimp for real-estate speculators—the heroic foe of the unearned increment hauling it in with both hands. He seemed preposterous, and hence harmless. But all the while he was busy among his old lieges, preparing for a *jacquerie* that should floor all his enemies at one blow. He did the job competently. He had vast skill at such enterprises. Heave an egg out of a Pullman window, and you will hit a Fundamentalist almost anywhere in the United States today. They swarm in the country towns, inflamed by their pastors, and with a saint, now, to venerate. They are thick in the mean streets behind the gasworks. They are everywhere that learning is too heavy a burden for mortal minds, even the vague, pathetic learning on tap in little red schoolhouses. They march with the Klan, with the Christian Endeavor Society, with the Junior Order of United American Mechanics, with the Epworth League, with all the rococo bands that poor and unhappy folk organize to bring some light of purpose into their lives. They have had a thrill, and they are ready for more.

Such is Bryan's legacy to his country. He couldn't be President, but he could at least help magnificently in the solemn business of shutting off the presidency from every intelligent and self-respecting man. The storm, perhaps, won't last long, as time goes in history. It may help, indeed, to break up the democratic delusion, now already showing weakness, and so hasten its own end. But while it lasts it will blow off some roofs and flood some sanctuaries.

For Critical Thinking

1. Bryan, in agreeing to testify at the Scopes trial, had reserved the right similarly to question Darrow. What questions might Bryan have asked? Construct a set of ques-

tions and answers between the two men with Darrow in the witness box and Bryan doing the questioning.

2. Was the Scopes trial really "the trial of the century"? Which issues of the trial are still matters of debate today? In what ways does discussion of these issues today resemble or differ from arguments at the Scopes trial?

3. Imagine yourself a supporter of Bryan and an opponent of evolution. Write an editorial objecting to H. L. Mencken's obituary of William Jennings Bryan.

24

Letters from the Great Migration
Emmett J. Scott et al.

These letters, collected by the distinguished African American educator and editor Emmett J. Scott, reflect one of the most important events of American social history, the "great migration" of about half a million African Americans largely from the rural South to northern cities early in the twentieth century. World War I, both by stimulating business and by cutting off immigration from Europe, created opportunities such as had never before existed for African Americans. The widespread circulation of Chicago newspapers throughout the South, particularly the Defender, gave southern African Americans a picture of the thriving economies and available jobs in Chicago and other northern cities.

Reasons for leaving the South were endless: Jim Crow, political disenfranchisement, lynching and other forms of mob violence, and more immediately, injury to the rural economy from floods and boll weevil infestations. The migration northward was a great, leaderless folk movement—the individual decisions of hundreds of thousands to flee the South by whatever means they could find in search of a world offering better schools, greater personal safety and dignity, and the chance for economic improvement.

The migration had enormous long-term effects. In the next half century, six million African Americans left the South, most moving to cities. The migration brought political power and cultural authority to black America and moved large numbers into the American middle class. It also provoked race riots, created vast ghettoes, and influenced white movement to segregated suburbs.

BEFORE YOU READ

1. What were the main purposes of the letters to the *Defender*?
2. What were the hopes of these letter writers?
3. To what extent do you think these hopes were realistic?

Sherman, Ga., Nov. 28, 1916.

Dear Sir: This letter comes to ask for all infirmations concerning employment in your connection in the warmest climate. Now I am in a family of (11) eleven more or less boys and girls (men and women) mixed sizes who want to go north as soon as arrangements can be made and employment given places for shelter and so on (etc) now this are farming people they were raised on the farm and are good farm hands I of course have some experience and qualefication as a coman school teacher and hotel waiter and along few other lines.

I wish you would write me at your first chance and tell me if you can give us employment at what time and about what wages will you pay and what kind of arrangement can be made for our shelter. Tell me when can you best use us now or later.

Will you send us tickets if so on what terms and at what price what is the cost per head and by what route should we come. We are Negroes and try to show ourselves worthy of all we may get from any friendly source we endeavor to be true to all good causes, if you can we thank you to help us to come north as soon as you can.

Sanford, Fla., April 27, 1917.

Dear Sir: I have seen through the Chicago Defender that you and the people of Chicago are helping newcomers. I am asking you for some information about conditions in some small town near Chicago.

There are some families here thinking of moving up, and are desirous of knowing what to expect before leaving. Please state about treatment, work, rent and schools. Please answer at some spare time.

Anniston, Ala., April 23, 1917.

Dear Sir: Please gave me some infamation about coming north i can do any kind of work from a truck gardin to farming i would like to leave here and i cant make no money to leave I ust make enough to live one please let me here from you at once i want to get where i can put my children in schol.

Cedar Grove, La., April 23, 1917.

Dear sir: to day I was advise by the defendent offices in your city to communicate with you in regards to the labor for the colored of the south as I was lead to beleave that you was in position of firms of your city & your near by surrounding towns of Chicago. Please state me how is the times in & around Chicago place to locate having a family dependent on me for support. I am informed by the Chicago Defender a very valuable paper which has for its purpose the Uplifting of my race, and of which I am a constant reader and real lover, that you were in position to show some light to one in my condition.

Seeking a Northern Home. If this is true Kindly inform me by next mail the next best thing to do Being a poor man with a family to care for, I am not coming to live on flowry Beds of ease for I am a man who works and wish to make the best I can out of life I do not wish to come there hoodwinked not knowing where to go or what to do so I Solicite your help in this matter and thanking you in advance for what advice you may be pleased to Give I am yours for success.

P. S. I am presently imployed in the I C RR. Mail Department at Union Station this city.

Brookhaven, Miss., April 24, 1917.

Gents: The cane growers of Louisiana have stopped the exodus from New Orleans, claiming shortage of labor which will result in a sugar famine.

Now these laborers thus employed receive only 85 cents a day and the high cost of living makes it a serious question to live.

There is a great many race people around here who desires to come north but have waited rather late to avoid car fare, which they have not got. isnt there some way to get the concerns who wants labor, to send passes here or elsewhere so they can come even if they have to pay out of the first months wages? Please done publish this letter but do what you can towards helping them to get away. If the R. R. Co. would run a low rate excursion they could leave that way. Please ans.

Savannah, Ga., April 24, 1917.

Sir: I saw an advertisement in the Chicago Ledger where you would send tickets to any one desireing to come up there. I am a married man with a wife only, and I am 38 years of age, and both of us have so far splendid health, and would like very much to come out there provided we could get good employment regarding the advertisement.

Fullerton, La., April 28, 1917.

Dear sir: I was reading about you was neading labor ninety miles of Chicago what is the name of the place and what R R extends ther i wants to come north and i wants a stedy employment ther what doe you pay per day i dont no anything about molding works but have been working around machinery for 10 years. Let me no what doe you pay for such work and can you give me a job of that kind or a job at common labor and let me no your prices and how many hours for a day.

De Ridder, La., April 29, 1917.

Dear sir: there is lots of us southern mens wants transportation and we want to leave ratway as soon as you let us here from you some of us is married mens who need work we would like to bring our wife with us there is 20 head of good mens want transportation and if you need us let us no by return mail we all are redy only wants here from you there may be more all of our peoples wont to leave here and i want you to send as much as 20 tickets any way I will get you up plenty hands to do most any kind of work all you have to do is to send for them. looking to here from you. This is among us collerd.

Atlanta, Ga., April 30, 1917.

Dear Sir: In reading the Chicago Defender I find that there are many jobs open for workmen, I wish that you would or can secure me a position in some of the northern cities; as a workman and not as a loafer. One who is willing to do any kind of hard in side or public work, have had broad experience in machinery and other work of the kind. A some what alround man can also cook, well trained devuloped man; have travel extensively through the western and southern states; A good strong *morial religious* man no habits. I will accept transportation on advance and deducted from my wages later. It does not matter where, that is; as to city, country, town or state since you secure the positions. I am quite sure you will be delighted in securing a position for a man of this description. I'll assure you will not regret of so doing. Hoping to hear from you soon.

Houston, Tx. April 30, 1917.

Dear Sir: wanted to leave the South and Go any Place where a man will be any thing Except a Ker I thought would write you for Advise as where would be a Good Place for a Comporedly young man That want to Better his Standing who has a very Promising young Family.

I am 30 years old and have Good Experience in Freight Handler and Can fill Position from Truck to Agt.

would like Chicago or Philadelphia But I dont Care where so long as I Go where a man is a man.

Beaumont, Texas, May 7, 1917.

Dear Sir: I see in one of your recent issue of collored men woanted in the North I wish you would help me to get a position in the North I have no trade I have been working for one company eight years and there is no advancement here for me and I would like to come where I can better my condition I woant work and not affraid to work all I wish is a chance to make good. I believe I would like machinist helper or Molder helper. If you can help me in any way it will be highly appreciate hoping to hear from you soon

25

Life in the Trenches—France
Louis Felix Ranlett

Writing in 1927, Louis Felix Ranlett admitted that few people want to hear about World War I. The "Great War" had revealed the weaknesses that underlay the glittering civilization of Europe and destroyed faith in progress and enlightenment. "They at once interrupt with 'It's all too dreadful'; or, 'How can you think of it?' or, 'I can't imagine such things.'"

Yet Ranlett's story is typical of American memoirs of World War I: "In it," he writes, "you will find more sunshine than you do mud." Unlike European soldiers who often spent years in trench warfare punctuated by massive, apparently pointless slaughter during the occasional offensives, American soldiers, arriving late in the war, spent little time in trenches. For most, the experience of battle was brief. While, as in all wars, too many returned maimed, for most of them it was a great adventure, the most exciting time of their lives. They objected to authority, not to war, and most became disillusioned more by the results of the war than by their experiences of it.

Ranlett was a Harvard undergraduate who took "military courses" at the college. He became the sole freshman among a group of fifty-one Harvard men given officer training at Camp Upton on eastern Long Island. At the time he writes of here, the summer of 1918, Ranlett was still a sergeant (he soon became a second lieutenant), fighting with the 77th Division near Nancy in Lorraine in northern France.

BEFORE YOU READ

1. What attitude did Ranlett assume about his service in the war? What adjective would you use to describe his tone?

2. What lessons did Ranlett learn about leadership from his experience?

Suddenly the dugout, deep underground though it was, trembled and shook as a ship might striking a rock; a heavy crust of dirt, from the bunks above, fell in my face, and the rat that had been exploring along the beam close by plumped on his back beside my head, writhed for a moment, squirmed over onto his feet, and darted off screeching. An all-enveloping blanket of heavy, rumbling sound fell about the dugout, and the roar of bursting shells outside merged in one grand clamor that hurled every occupant of the tiny space instantly into stunned wakefulness.

"What is it? What is it?" some one called in a strained, pleading voice, for he, like the rest of us, was too startled to understand. "An earthquake?"

"No! A barrage! Get dressed! Put 'em on!"

Each man started fumbling with his shoes and leggins, working in hurried helplessness.

I can only tell how I felt, but I believe that my comrades all experienced the same sensations. My whole body trembled convulsively as in a violent chill, my knees shook, my fingers and hands moved purposelessly. I seemed deprived of strength, almost of power to control my limbs, as a man struggling against a monster in a dream. I was afraid—and I admit it shamelessly, as every one of my comrades did—scared "into jelly." It was not the fear of any specific injury that I experienced, just an overpowering sense of the terrible unusual, the unknown that might happen. My voice was, can I say, staring, strained, unnatural—high-pitched and helpless.

I crammed on my helmet and grabbed my rifle, with bayonet fixed, from its nail on the wall. The others finally got themselves together, literally, and sat on the edge of their bunks talking rapidly and aimlessly, without listening to each other, to conceal their fear. The candles were burning low, and as we noticed it we whiffed out all but one to preserve them, for we were suddenly struck by an additional terror of being left in darkness.

Norton, the gas sentinel, with more courage than the rest of us, perhaps because he could see what was going on, remained silent at his post inside the dugout door, until, as he told me later, he saw, in the dim light made by the moon behind thin clouds, a gray haze settling down the steps above him. He stuck his head inside and remarked in an almost matter-of-fact way, "Gas, boys, gas!" He ducked inside, rolling down the double blankets, and hurried to the other door which he closed likewise. Since the stovepipe was already plugged, this made the dugout supposedly gas-proof, but we were taking no chances with the most dreaded of weapons.

We bounced off our helmets, dove into our masks, which had been close tied under our chins for the last four days, and then fumbled on the floor again for the suddenly discarded headgear. The masks shut us off from everything even more than the terrific sound which still eddied about us, and instinctively seeking contact with each other we drew in around the one candle where it sputtered on the edge of the bunk. I held two fingers together against it to measure the length, and wondered how many more minutes it could hold out. As it shrank and flickered, we crowded closer together.

Looking out through the steamed eye-pieces of the mask I saw a sight that instantly reminded me of some of the pictures of Captain Nemo and his faithful followers gathered about some treasure chest on the sea bottom. Just at the edge of the little circle of light ranged a row of huge staring eyes in black, pointed faces from the snouts of which a shaking pipe led down into the darkness. The mud-colored helmets hid the men's foreheads. Only their ears, white and large, projected out on either side of the weird mask faces. Conversation was reduced to a mere series of gurgles.

Sergeant Loffman had alone remained lying on the bunk in almost his characteristically undisturbed and somnolent state. Finally out of the recesses of his mask he called, "Load up your pockets with these shells!"

The crowd attacked the pile of French cartridges and divided them rapidly. The idea was good in that it kept the men busy and hence helped to reduce their fear, but had no other value, for the shells would fit only the auto-rifles of which there was not one in the dugout.

A half-hour went by, and finally, to my infinite relief, I heard Straight's voice outside.

"Ranlett, are you there?" he called.

"Yes."

"Come on out."

I pushed aside the blankets and found him at the top of the steps.

"Take your mask off, it's all safe now," he said. I obeyed.

"Get 'em all out quick! Stand to!" he cried when I was free of the mask.

I jumped down the steps, shouting, "Take 'em off, boys! It's all right. Come on out!"

"Go on out," called Loffman in his usual nonchalant tone of voice. A few of the men stepped out warily, and when they found that the racket had greatly diminished tried to persuade the rest to follow. All, however, still wore their masks.

"It's safe!" I called, rushing in. "I've got mine off."

When those inside saw me alive without a mask, some of their courage returned and, snatching off their face-pieces, they tumbled out, but balked at ascending the steps, for the shells were still bursting, though not in full chorus.

Lieutenant Bishop, his mask dangling from its satchel and his face pale but covered with sweat, was suddenly seen standing on the trench parados, a smoking automatic in his hand.

The sight brought courage with the thought, "If he can get away with it up there, I'm safe enough here," and each man hurried confidently to his post in the trenches. Thus by an exhibition of thoughtless, and what some would call foolhardy, courage, the lieutenant instantly transformed us all from scared creatures into fighting men. It was a lesson in leadership which I shall not forget, and for which he deserves much credit, though he maintained later that his only purpose in exposing himself was to see whether the Boches[1] were coming, and that he had fired his automatic merely to make sure it would work.

"Come out to Duffy's with me," shouted Straight. "I've been everywhere else. Zitto was hit. Plane flew along the trench and bullet came through the shelter roof. Got him in the back. He's patched up now and down at the station."

I hurried along behind him. In a depression we smelled a strong breath of gas and plunged into our masks again. Almost trotting through the dark trench in the steamed mask was like running in a dream. Straight had been on the move ever since the barrage started while I had been safe in the dugout, and now he was nearly overcome by exhaustion, the heat of his mask, and its pressure on his temples. He sat down on the fire step while I bathed his face around the edge of his mask with water from my canteen, until he could proceed. At last we reached Duffy's post which had been beyond the concentration of fire

---

1. **Boches:** Germans.

and found his crew, scared like the rest of us, but very thankful to know that the platoon was not wiped out leaving them alone in their isolated position.

Gradually the noise died down, and at last, an hour after it had begun, was suddenly cut off like the din of a shop at the closing gong. The Boches did not come over against us.

At six o'clock a horribly pale Frenchman, spitting green slime, almost speechless, and gasping frantically for every breath, struggled into our trench looking for the dugout where his sergeant had stayed with our lieutenant for the first night. He brought the news that the dugout we had given up that evening had been directly hit by a big shell, that his *sous-lieutenant* had been killed, and that all the platoon were casualties by gas or by the collapse of their shelter. The sergeant, assuring us that the barrage, of many caliber shells and all types of projector and shell gas, had been worse than any concentration of fire he had seen even at Verdun, hurried off to his mates, apparently little excited at their reported fate, though we could not help remarking on our good fortune in having changed dugouts.

By eight o'clock the two men from our platoon who had been gassed were carried to the dressing-station and a new schedule of watches was put into effect, with the resumption of the old quiet of trench life. At eight-thirty sad news came from the rear. The company kitchen had been struck by the first shell of the barrage, which had gone clean through the roof of the *abri*, ruining the stove and destroying all the provisions. The reserve platoon had suffered several gas casualties; one of the cooks was gassed to death through a failure to get the elastics of his mask untangled from the mouthpiece and several others were so badly affected that they died later. Lieutenant Miles's platoon, in the exposed trench of our former night position, suffered about twenty-five casualties by gas and fragments of H.E. (high explosive), several men being killed outright; and Sergeant Mitchell's platoon fared only a little better. It had been a severe first time under fire.

We later learned that the barrage had fallen for an hour upon the whole front of the Seventy-Seventh Division, which served to conceal the true purpose of the Boches. One of the front-line platoons of 'A' Company, about a half-mile to our left, directly in front of Badonviller, was surrounded by a box barrage which cut it off from the rear. A line of skirmishers advanced on its front, drawing the fire of the terrified men, so that a platoon column of enemy crept in on either flank unobserved and attacked with terrible success, taking several prisoners, killing many, and breaking up the whole platoon.

But none of these happenings touched us so much at the time — such was our already well-developed military callousness — as the fact that we should have no hot breakfast. The emergency ration proved its worth, everybody drawing a half-box of biscuits from the supply, so that life was made tolerable, but we missed our hot coffee and beans.

During the morning three more members of the platoon complained of gassing and were taken to the first-aid station. Just as the last of these men was removed, Corporal Nolan, always a nervous and depressed man, who had been becoming more and more silent and white-faced ever since the terrible night ordeal in the exposed trench, when the cold fingers of fear had clutched at all, seemed suddenly changed. He leaped up from his post and began running about the trench, tapping his companions as if in a game of tag. His eyes strained forward curiously in their sockets, his fingers twitched rapidly, and he jabbered incoherently. Loffman, who was near, grappled with him, and others came to his assistance to restrain the madman, overcome by shell shock and fear. We laid him upon a stretcher and held him down, while Lieutenant Bishop tried to quiet him.

"Don't you recognize me, Tom? Tom!—answer!"

Tom writhed on, frothing at the mouth.

"Be quiet, Tom! Keep still."

It was like a person soothing a crying child. Gradually Nolan became still and could be carried away.

I obtained an empty stretcher and putting it on the parapet where I should be undisturbed and could have plenty of fresh air, made up my two days' sleep in two hours.

That afternoon we made elaborate preparations in apprehension of an attack during the coming night, distributing much ammunition from the ammunition dugout and laying all the auto-rifles carefully. A new kitchen was installed at the P.C., and by supper the succession of luxurious meals was resumed. At one noon meal we had baked kidney beans, steak, boiled potatoes, coffee, cabbage, hot cakes, bread, rice pudding, and corn syrup. Our rationing in the trenches was more hearty, varied, and wholly satisfying than it had been at any time since we left Camp Upton, and was in every way a success. Sweets were supplied us in abundance in the form of syrup. Gallon cans of the pleasant syrup stood in every dugout, for we had more than we could use at any one meal. Candles, which were ordinarily issued with the ration, were, however, scarce when they were most needed, and matches were counted more carefully than franc pieces, so that we had to get on with a minimum of light.

Though food was abundant, water, which had to be carried just like food, was comparatively scarce. One was fortunate if he got a canteen full a day for all purposes: drinking, washing, and cleaning his messkit. The kits were more often scoured with mud and wiped with paper than washed, and each man's small dishtowel became even more grease-encrusted than usual. There was hardly any water for toilet purposes; I shaved once during the week, using as a shaving-mug my canteen cup from which I ordinarily drank my coffee or ate my rice pudding, and washing my face and hands from the same cup full. Many of the men used coffee for shaving, both because it was hot and because it was more abundant than plain water. The order which made clear that a cake of issue soap was all that was necessary to keep one's uniform free from spots "under all conditions" could not have contemplated such a scarcity.

On Tuesday we continued our preparations for a warm reception. My training in map-sketching served me in good stead, for I was able to make a map of the sector to aid us in laying the lines of fire, and to serve as a guide to the platoon which should relieve us. The machine-gun company moved a gun into our position, and a night patrol was sent out to examine the area in front of us.

Wednesday night at eleven, when my turn to sleep was up, I scrambled from the bench in the mess shelter where I slept on my back on the single board, wedged in between the wall and the legs of the table, and began my rounds in the trenches. Way out in the long, unguarded section of line between Eulert's and Duffy's posts I saw the nodding line of helmets of the French visiting patrol coming toward me in the half-moonlight. Since safety demanded that we halt all persons passing through the trench, whether we thought we knew them or not, I halted and raised the loaded automatic which I was carrying in my hand, in welcome. The leading sergeant stopped at my tensely whispered "Halt!"

"Give the countersign."

"*Comment?*"

"The password."

"*Pas comprend.*"

I was getting worried, and could not think of what to say next. Hah! I made a wild guess.

"*Le mot de passe.*"

"*Ah! Oui!*—" he burst out delightedly, but stopped, for he had been drinking and was not wholly steady. He did not know the password.

This was bad. Perhaps I had really stopped a German patrol. What should I do? There was my automatic, but I was alone and a dark line of figures stretched away around the traverse beyond the sergeant, who was now fumbling in his coat with one hand and with the other scratching his head under the edge of his tilted helmet as if to stimulate thought.

I waited. At last he found the object of his search—a piece of paper with the list of the daily passwords for the week. He picked out the right one and gave it to me—"*Châlòns!*" What a relief!

Friday evening, a week after we had entered the line, came the word that we were to go into reserve. Saul, who had been through the *boyau* to the P.C. many times, was to guide us out after dark. At ten o'clock the first members of the relief arrived, under Sergeant Kimball, and I set out with a party for the rear. Saul became confused in the dark at the first trench crossing and gave up helplessly.

"Let me take it," I said, forcing my way to the head of the column. I had not been down that particular trench, but, having mapped our platoon sector and having seen the other end of the *boyau* at the P.C., thought I could lead the crowd out.

As I proceeded clamors of protest arose behind:

"You'll get us into the Boche lines!—We've gone twice the distance already!—Stop and wait.—Go ahead yourself and find out whether you are right!"

I did not heed them, and in ten minutes, though it seemed an hour, we came out at the P.C. dugout and were assigned to an *abri* in the roadside, where we lit our candles and began reading the inscriptions left by the Iowa troops of the Forty-Second Division.

The relief was completed at eleven o'clock and we had just settled down with a gas sentinel near the big bell, for what we hoped might be our first good sleep in a week, when the inevitable happened. Hooper, the first sergeant, appeared at the door. "Hi, Ranlett, pick out a detail to carry coffee." I had the usual unpleasant job of trying to decide who had done the least work lately and would consequently be in line for assignment to the detail. Jolly little Corporal Lorier and five men "drew the unlucky numbers" and went out on a hard round.

On Saturday night, June 29th, ten days after we had entered the front-line position, the company was relieved. At eleven o'clock, in the utter blackness of an overcast night, we took the road in section columns of twos with single connecting files at twenty-five-yard intervals between them. I was marching alone in this capacity, the rattle and bang of my equipment being the only sound that broke the stillness, when the low hum of a distant Boche plane struck my ears. It grew louder and louder, evidently approaching, but the plane was entirely invisible in the gloom. Suddenly a long stream of sparkling fire shot out of the night ahead and curved crackling to earth in short bursts. Fritz was peppering the road with tracer bullets. We dove for the grass ditch at the side, now that we knew where he was, for a mass of men on the white surface of the road would show clearly from above, while against the dark hue of the grass they would be hidden. Ahead of us and approaching swiftly darted the fearful stream of fire accompanied by the pulsing roar of the motor, but in an instant, directly over our heads, the thunder of another plane burst out and the hanging wheels of the night terror that had stolen up on us with motor shut off, under the diversion created by his comrade, appeared barely skirting the tree-tops.

He opened fire with a rush, the whizzing, flaming bullets spattering the hard surface of the road and dislodging bits of stone in the wreckage of the house against which I was crouching. On he swept—and as the stream of fire disappeared in the dark again, no one stirred.

Five minutes passed, but the planes did not return. I breathed again.

"Hi! Did he get you?" called Duffy, running up from behind.

"No. They went into the rocks there."

"Gee! He fired at you!"

"No!"

"He did. I saw it."

"Well, I was here. I ought to know."

"Lucky kid. Too close for me. He didn't miss any of us by much. Some stunt. Nice fellow."

26

Memories of College Days
Zora Neale Hurston

Zora Neale Hurston's remarkably sunny view of her education hides, in her typical way, a world of difficulties surmounted. Her autobiography, Dust Tracks on a Road, *sets her birth at January 7, 1903, in Eatonville, Florida. Scholars have discovered, however, that she was born in Notasulga, Alabama, in 1891. This enormous discrepancy represented more than vanity about age: It masked the painful years after her mother's death in 1904 during which Hurston was shuttled between relatives' houses and prevented from pursuing her education. Like so many older students since, once gaining the opportunity for education, she made the most of it.*

While at Barnard College, Hurston came under the influence of the foremost anthropologist of the age, Franz Boas, who launched her career as a folklorist. Many trips to the South and the Caribbean gave back to Hurston in a new form the world she had lost when her mother died. This was the world of Eatonville, Florida, the first incorporated all-black town in the United States, "a pure Negro town—charter mayor, council, town marshal and all," as she later described it. Encouraged by the emergence of black writers and artists in the 1920s, a period called the "Harlem Renaissance," to which she made important contributions, Hurston turned to drama and fiction, publishing several novels. Well received in her day, they were soon forgotten. She died in a country welfare home in 1960.

The civil rights and women's movements in the 1970s revived interest in her work. Alice Walker, who first called renewed attention to her, praised her work for its "racial health—a sense of black people as complete, complex, undiminished *human beings, a sense that is lacking in so much black writing and literature." All of her major books are now back in print and one of them,* Their Eyes Were Watching God, *is recognized as among the masterpieces of American literature.*

BEFORE YOU READ

1. How did Zora Neale Hurston deal with racial prejudice? What lesson did she draw from the incident in the barber shop?
2. How does the discrepancy in her age affect the way you read her story?
3. Why do you think she felt so readily accepted in New York City?

Now as everyone knows, Howard University is the capstone of Negro education in the world. There gather Negro money, beauty, and prestige. It is to the

David Levering Lewis, ed., *The Portable Harlem Renaissance Reader* (New York: Viking, 1994), pp. 142–43, 144–45, 147–52.

Negro what Harvard is to the whites. They say the same thing about a Howard man that they do about Harvard—you can tell a Howard man as far as you can see him, but you can't tell him much. He listens to the doings of other Negro schools and their graduates with bored tolerance. Not only is the scholastic rating at Howard high, but tea is poured in the manner!

I had heard all about the swank fraternities and sororities and the clothes and everything, and I knew I could never make it. I told Mae that.

"You can come and live at our house, Zora," Bernice offered. At the time, her parents were living in Washington, and Bernice and Gwendolyn were in the boarding department at Morgan. "I'll ask Mama the next time she comes over. Then you won't have any room and board to pay. We'll all get together and rustle you up a job to make your tuition."

So that summer I moved on to Washington and got a job. First, as a waitress in the exclusive Cosmos Club downtown, and later as a manicurist in the G Street shop of Mr. George Robinson. He is a Negro who has a chain of white barber shops in downtown Washington. I managed to scrape together money for my first quarter's tuition, and went up to register.

I shall never forget my first college assembly, sitting there in the chapel of that great university. I was so exalted that I said to the spirit of Howard, "You have taken me in. I am a tiny bit of your greatness. I swear to you that I shall never make you ashamed of me."

It did not wear off. Every time I sat there as part and parcel of things, looking up there at the platform crowded with faculty members, the music, the hundreds of students about me, it would come down on me again. When on Mondays we ended the service by singing Alma Mater, I felt just as if it were the Star Spangled Banner:

> Reared against the eastern sky
> Proudly there on hill-top high
> Up above the lake so blue
> Stands Old Howard brave and true.
> There she stands for truth and right,
> Sending forth her rays of light,
> Clad in robes of majesty
> Old Howard! We sing of thee.

My soul stood on tiptoe and stretched up to take in all that it meant. So I was careful to do my classwork and be worthy to stand there under the shadow of the hovering spirit of Howard. I felt the ladder under my feet.

Mr. Robinson arranged for me to come to work at 3:30 every afternoon and work until 8:30. In that way, I was able to support myself. Soon, most of the customers knew I was a student, and tipped me accordingly. I averaged twelve to fifteen dollars a week.

Mr. Robinson's 1410 G Street shop was frequented by bankers, Senators, Cabinet Members, Congressmen, and gentlemen of the Press. The National Press Club was one block down the same street, the Treasury Building was one block up the street and the White House not far away.

I learned things from holding the hands of men like that. The talk was of world affairs, national happenings, personalities, the latest quips from the cloakrooms of Congress and such things. I heard many things from the White House and the Senate before they appeared in print. They probably were bursting to talk to somebody, and I was safe. If I told, nobody would have believed me anyway. Besides, I was much flattered by being told and warned not to repeat what I had heard. Sometimes a Senator, a banker, a newspaper correspondent attached to the White House would all be sitting around my table at one time. While I worked on one, the others waited, and they all talked. Sometimes they concentrated on teasing me. At other times they talked about what had happened, or what they reasoned was bound to happen. Intimate stories about personalities, their secret love affairs, cloakroom retorts, and the like. Soon they took me for granted and would say, "Zora knows how to keep a secret. She's all right." Now, I know that my discretion really didn't matter. They were relieving their pent-up feelings where it could do no harm.

Some of them meant more to me than others because they paid me more attention. Frederick William Wile, White House correspondent, used to talk to me at times quite seriously about life and opportunities and things like that. He had seen three presidents come and go. He had traveled with them, to say nothing of his other traveling to and fro upon the earth. He had read extensively. Sometimes he would be full of stories and cracks, but at other times he would talk to me quite seriously about attitudes, points of view, why one man was great and another a mere facile politician, and so on.

There were other prominent members of the press who would sit and talk longer than it took me to do their hands. One of them, knowing that certain others sat around and talked, wrote out questions two or three times for me to ask and tell him what was said. Each time the questions were answered, but I was told to keep that under my hat, and so I had to turn around and lie and say the man didn't tell me. I never realized how serious it was until he offered me twenty-five dollars to ask a certain Southern Congressman something and let him know as quickly as possible. He sent out and bought me a quart of French ice cream to bind the bargain. The man came in on his regular time, which was next day, and in his soft voice, began to tell me how important it was to be honorable at all times and to be trustworthy. How could I ask him then? Besides, he was an excellent Greek scholar and translated my entire lesson for me, which was from Xenophon's *Cyropædeia*, and talked at length on the ancient Greeks and Persians. The news man was all right. He had to get his information the best way he could, but, for me, it would have been terrible to do that nice man like that. I told the reporter how it was and he understood and never asked me again.

An incident happened that made me realize how theories go by the board when a person's livelihood is threatened. A man, a Negro, came into the shop one afternoon and sank down in Banks's chair. Banks was the manager and had the first chair by the door. It was so surprising that for a minute Banks just looked at him and never said a word. Finally, he found his tongue and asked, "What do you want?"

"Hair-cut and shave," the man said belligerently.

"But you can't get no hair-cut and shave here. Mr. Robinson has a fine shop for Negroes on U Street near Fifteenth," Banks told him.

"I know it, but I want one here. The Constitution of the United States—"

But by that time, Banks had him by the arm. Not roughly but he was helping him out of his chair, nevertheless.

"I don't know how to cut your hair," Banks objected. "I was trained on straight hair. Nobody in here knows how."

"Oh, don't hand me that stuff!" the crusader snarled. "Don't be such an Uncle Tom."

"Run on, fellow. You can't get waited on in here."

"I'll stay right here until I do. I know my rights. Things like this have got to be broken up. I'll get waited on all right, or sue the place."

"Go ahead and sue," Banks retorted. "Go on uptown, and get your hair cut, man. Don't be so hardheaded for nothing."

"I'm getting waited on right here!"

"You're next, Mr. Powell," Banks said to a waiting customer. "Sorry, mister, but you better go on uptown."

"But I have a right to be waited on wherever I please," the Negro said, and started towards Updyke's chair which was being emptied. Updyke whirled his chair around so that he could not sit down and stepped in front of it. "Don't you touch *my* chair!" Updyke glared. "Go on about your business."

But instead of going, he made to get into the chair by force.

"Don't argue with him! Throw him out of here!" somebody in the back cried. And in a minute, barbers, customers all lathered and hair half cut, and porters, were all helping to throw the Negro out.

The rush carried him way out into the middle of G Street and flung him down. He tried to lie there and be a martyr, but the roar of oncoming cars made him jump up and scurry off. We never heard any more about it. I did not participate in the mêlée, but I wanted him thrown out, too. My business was threatened.

It was only that night in bed that I analyzed the whole thing and realized that I was giving sanction to Jim Crow, which theoretically, I was supposed to resist. But here were ten Negro barbers, three porters and two manicurists all stirred up at the threat of our living through loss of patronage. Nobody thought it out at the moment. It was an instinctive thing. That was the first time it was called to my attention that self-interest rides over all sorts of lines. I have seen the same thing happen hundreds of times since, and now I understand it. One sees it breaking over racial, national, religious and class lines. Anglo-Saxon against Anglo-Saxon, Jew against Jew, Negro against Negro, and all sorts of combinations of the three against other combinations of the three. Offhand, you might say that we fifteen Negroes should have felt the racial thing and served him. He was one of us. Perhaps it would have been a beautiful thing if Banks had turned to the shop crowded with customers and announced that this man was going to be served like everybody else even at the risk of losing their patronage, with all of the other employees lined up in the center of the floor shouting, "So say we all!" It would have been a stirring gesture, and made the headlines for a day. Then we could all have gone home to our unpaid rents and bills and things like that. I could leave school and begin my wanderings again. The "militant" Negro who would have been the cause of it all, would have perched on the smuddled-up wreck of things and crowed. Nobody ever found out who or what he was. Perhaps he did what he did on the spur of the moment, not realizing that serving him would have ruined Mr. Robinson, another Negro who had got what he had the hard way. For not only would the G Street shop have been forced to close, but the F Street shop and all of his other six downtown shops. Wrecking George Robinson like that on a "race" angle would have been ironic tragedy. He always helped out any Negro who was trying to do anything progressive as far as he was able. He had no education himself, but he was for it. He would give any Howard University student a job in his shops if they could qualify, even if it was only a few hours a week.

So I do not know what was the ultimate right in this case. I do know how I felt at the time. There is always something fiendish and loathsome about a person who threatens to deprive you of your way of making a living. That is just human-like, I reckon.

At the University, I got on well both in class-work and the matter of making friends. I could take in but so many social affairs because I had to work, and then I had to study my lessons after work hours at night, and I was carrying a heavy program.

The man who seemed to me to be most overpowering was E. C. Williams, Librarian and head of the Romance Language department. He was cosmopolitan and world-traveled. His wit was instant and subtle. He was so inaccessible in a way, too. He told me once that a flirtation with a co-ed was to him like playing with a teething-ring. He liked smart, sophisticated women. He used to lunch every day with E. D. Davis, head of the Greek and German department. Davis was just the antithesis of Williams, so shy, in the Charles S. Johnson manner, in spite of his erudition. They would invite me to come along and would pay for my milk and pie. Williams did most of the talking. I put in something now and then. Davis sat and smiled. Professor Williams egged me on to kiss him. He said that Davis would throw a fit, and he wanted to be present to see it. He whispered that Davis liked to have me around, but from what he ever said, I couldn't notice. When I was sick, Professor Davis came to see me and brought an arm-load of roses, but he sat there half an hour and scarcely said a word. He just sat there and smiled now and then.

All in all, I did a year and a half of work at Howard University. I would have done the two full years, but I was out on account of illness, and by the time that was over, I did not have the money for my tuition.

I joined the Zeta Phi Beta Sorority, took part in all the literary activities on the campus, and made The Stylus, the small literary society on the hill. I named the student paper *The Hill Top*. The Stylus was limited to nineteen members, two of them being faculty members. Dr. Alain Leroy Locke was the presiding genius and we had very interesting meetings.

My joining The Stylus influenced my later moves. On account of a short story which I wrote for The Stylus, Charles S. Johnson, who was just then founding *Opportunity Magazine*, wrote to me for material. He explained that he was writing to all of the Negro colleges with the idea of introducing new writers and new material to the public. I sent on *Drenched in Light* and he published it. Later, he published my second story *Spunk*. He wrote me a kind letter and said something about New York. So, beginning to feel the urge to write, I wanted to be in New York.

This move on the part of Dr. Johnson was the root of the so-called Negro Renaissance. It was his work, and only his hush-mouth nature has caused it to be attributed to many others. The success of *Opportunity* Award dinners was news. Later on, the best of this material was collected in a book called *The New Negro* and edited by Dr. Alain Locke, but it was the same material, for the most part, gathered and published by Dr. Charles Spurgeon Johnson, now of the Department of Social Sciences, Fisk University, Nashville.

Being out of school for lack of funds, and wanting to be in New York, I decided to go there and try to get back in school in that city. So the first week of January, 1925, found me in New York with $1.50, no job, no friends, and a lot of hope.

The Charles Johnsons befriended me as best they could. I could always find something to eat out at their house. Mrs. Johnson would give me carfare and encouragement. I came to worship them really.

So I came to New York through *Opportunity*, and through *Opportunity* to Barnard. I won a prize for a short story at the first Award dinner, May 1, 1925, and Fannie Hurst offered me a job as her secretary, and Annie Nathan Meyer offered to get me a scholarship to Barnard. My record was good enough, and I entered Barnard in the fall, graduating in 1928.

I have no lurid tales to tell of race discrimination at Barnard. I made a few friends in the first few days. Eleanor Beer, who lived on the next chair to me in Economics, was the first. She was a New York girl with a sumptuous home down in West 71st Street, near the Hudson. She invited me down often, and her mother set out to brush me up on good manners. I learned a lot of things from them. They were well traveled and cosmopolitan. I found out about forks, who entered a room first, sat down first, and who offered to shake hands. A great deal more of material like that. These people are still lying very close to my heart. I was invited to Eleanor's wedding when she married Enzo de Chetalat, a Swiss mining engineer, but I was down in Florida at the time. So I sent her a hat-box full of orange blossoms for the occasion, so she could know how I felt.

The Social Register crowd at Barnard soon took me up, and I became Barnard's sacred black cow. If you had not had lunch with me, you had not shot from taw.[1] I was secretary to Fannie Hurst and living at her 67th Street duplex apartment, so things were going very well with me.

Because my work was top-heavy with English, Political Science, History and Geology, my adviser at Barnard recommended Fine Arts, Economics, and Anthropology for cultural reasons. I started in under Dr. Gladys Reichard, had a term paper called to the attention of Dr. Franz Boas and thereby gave up my dream of leaning over a desk and explaining Addison and Steele to the sprouting generations.

I began to treasure up the words of Dr. Reichard, Dr. Ruth Benedict, and Dr. Boas, the king of kings.

That man can make people work the hardest with just a look or a word, than anyone else in creation. He is idolized by everybody who takes his orders. We all call him Papa, too. One day, I burst into his office and asked for "Papa Franz" and his secretary gave me a look and told me I had better not let him hear me say that. Of course, I knew better, but at a social gathering of the Department of Anthropology at his house a few nights later, I brought it up.

"Of course, Zora is my daughter. Certainly!" he said with a smile. "Just one of my missteps, that's all." The sabre cut on his cheek, which it is said he got in a duel at Heidelberg, lifted in a smile.

Away from his office, Dr. Boas is full of youth and fun, and abhors dull, stodgy arguments. Get to the point is his idea. Don't raise a point which you cannot defend. He wants facts, not guesses, and he can pin you down so expertly that you soon lose the habit of talking all over your face. Either that, or you leave off Anthropology.

I had the same feeling at Barnard that I did at Howard, only more so. I felt that I was highly privileged and determined to make the most of it. I did not resolve to be a grind, however, to show the white folks that I had brains. I took it for granted that they knew that. Else, why was I at Barnard? Not everyone who cries, "Lord! Lord!" can enter those sacred iron gates. In her high scholastic standards, equipment, the quality of her student-body and graduates, Barnard has a right to the first line of Alma Mater. "Beside the waters of the Hudson, Our Alma Mater stands serene!" Dean Gildersleeve has that certain touch. We know there are women's colleges that are older, but not better ones.

So I set out to maintain a good average, take part in whatever went on, and just be a part of the college like everybody else. I graduated with a *B* record, and I am entirely satisfied.

1. **taw:** a large marble.

Mrs. Meyer, who was the moving spirit in founding the college and who is still a trustee, did nobly by me in getting me in. No matter what I might do for her, I would still be in her debt.

Two weeks before I graduated from Barnard, Dr. Boas sent for me and told me that he had arranged a fellowship for me. I was to go south and collect Negro folklore. Shortly before that, I had been admitted to the American Folk-Lore Society. Later, while I was in the field, I was invited to become a member of the American Ethnological Society, and shortly after the American Anthropological Society.

Booker T. Washington said once that you must not judge a man by the heights to which he has risen, but by the depths from which he came. So to me these honors meant something, insignificant as they might appear to the world. It was a long step for the waif of Eatonville. From the depth of my inner heart I appreciated the fact that the world had not been altogether unkind to Mama's child.

27

My Fight for Birth Control

Margaret Sanger

Margaret Sanger (1879–1966) was not the first champion of the right of contraception, but she was an important organizer of the twentieth-century movement to make "birth control"—an expression she coined in 1914—legal and widely available. Her account of the life and death of Sadie Sacks, presented here as written in her autobiography, she told in countless speeches throughout her career. While the incident did not initiate her concern for birth control access or for the plight of poor women, it did fix her decision to focus her work on this issue, as she did for the rest of her life.

In 1873 Congress had passed the Comstock Act, which imposed fines and imprisonment for providing information to another person "for the prevention of conception or procuring of abortion." The state of New York had a similar statute. So virtually all Sanger's activities to further her cause were against the law. Opening a birth control clinic in 1916 was an act of civil disobedience—much like the acts practiced by the civil rights movement half a century later. Sanger, by violating the law, forced changes in it.

While contraception was to remain illegal in some states into the 1960s, this determined reformer brought about a major change. When she began her crusade, middle-class women had informal access to birth control information and devices but poor women generally did not. By 1921 when she formed the American Birth Control League—which in 1942 would become Planned Parenthood—courts had already begun to allow doctors to disseminate birth control information and devices to married women and prosecutions under the Comstock Act virtually ceased.

BEFORE YOU READ

1. Is it, as Margaret Sanger wrote at the beginning of this selection, "futile and useless to relieve . . . misery" if you do not get to its root?

2. When she had her revelation after Mrs. Sacks's death, she wrote, "I could now see clearly the various social strata of our life; all its mass problems seemed to be centered around uncontrolled breeding." Do you agree with this? What are the merits and the dangers of such an argument?

3. What was Sanger's motive for opening the birth control clinic in Brooklyn?

Early in the year 1912 I came to a sudden realization that my work as a nurse and my activities in social service were entirely palliative and consequently futile and useless to relieve the misery I saw all about me. . . .

Margaret Sanger, *My Fight for Birth Control* (New York: Farrar-Rinehart, 1931), pp. 46–56, 152–60.

Were it possible for me to depict the revolting conditions existing in the homes of some of the women I attended in that one year, one would find it hard to believe. There was at that time, and doubtless is still today, a sub-stratum of men and women whose lives are absolutely untouched by social agencies.

The way they live is almost beyond belief. They hate and fear any prying into their homes or into their lives. They resent being talked to. The women slink in and out of their homes on their way to market like rats from their holes. The men beat their wives sometimes black and blue, but no one inter-feres. The children are cuffed, kicked and chased about, but woe to the child who dares to tell tales out of the home! Crime or drink is often the source of this secret aloofness, usually there is something to hide, a skeleton in the closet somewhere. The men are sullen, unskilled workers, picking up odd jobs now and then, unemployed usually, sauntering in and out of the house at all hours of the day and night.

The women keep apart from other women in the neighborhood. Often they are suspected of picking a pocket or "lifting" an article when occasion arises. Pregnancy is an almost chronic condition amongst them. I knew one woman who had given birth to eight children with no professional care what-ever. The last one was born in the kitchen, witnessed by a son of ten years who, under his mother's direction, cleaned the bed, wrapped the placenta and soiled articles in paper, and threw them out of the window into the court below. . . .

In this atmosphere abortions and birth become the main theme of conver-sation. On Saturday nights I have seen groups of fifty to one hundred women going into questionable offices well known in the community for cheap abor-tions. I asked several women what took place there, and they all gave the same reply: a quick examination, a probe inserted into the uterus and turned a few times to disturb the fertilized ovum, and then the woman was sent home. Usu-ally the flow began the next day and often continued four or five weeks. Some-times an ambulance carried the victim to the hospital for a curetage, and if she returned home at all she was looked upon as a lucky woman.

This state of things became a nightmare with me. There seemed no sense to it all, no reason for such waste of mother life, no right to exhaust women's vitality and to throw them on the scrap-heap before the age of thirty-five.

Everywhere I looked, misery and fear stalked—men fearful of losing their jobs, women fearful that even worse conditions might come upon them. The menace of another pregnancy hung like a sword over the head of every poor woman I came in contact with that year. The question which met me was al-ways the same: What can I do to keep from it? or, What can I do to get out of this? Sometimes they talked among themselves bitterly.

"It's the rich that know the tricks," they'd say, "while we have all the kids." Then, if the women were Roman Catholics, they talked about "Yankee tricks," and asked me if I knew what the Protestants did to keep their families down. When I said that I didn't believe that the rich knew much more than they did I was laughed at and suspected of holding back information for money. They would nudge each other and say something about paying me before I left the case if I would reveal the "secret." . . .

Finally the thing began to shape itself, to become accumulative during the three weeks I spent in the home of a desperately sick woman living on Grand Street, a lower section of New York's East Side.

Mrs. Sacks was only twenty-eight years old; her husband, an unskilled worker, thirty-two. Three children, aged five, three and one, were none too strong nor sturdy, and it took all the earnings of the father and the ingenuity of the mother to keep them clean, provide them with air and proper food, and give them a chance to grow into decent manhood and womanhood.

Both parents were devoted to these children and to each other. The woman had become pregnant and had taken various drugs and purgatives, as advised by her neighbors. Then, in desperation, she had used some instrument lent to her by a friend. She was found prostrate on the floor amidst the crying children when her husband returned from work. Neighbors advised against the ambulance, and a friendly doctor was called. The husband would not hear of her going to a hospital, and as a little money had been saved in the bank a nurse was called and the battle for that precious life began.

It was in the middle of July. The three-room apartment was turned into a hospital for the dying patient. Never had I worked so fast, never so concentratedly as I did to keep alive that little mother. Neighbor women came and went during the day doing the odds and ends necessary for our comfort. The children were sent to friends and relatives and the doctor and I settled ourselves to outdo the force and power of an outraged nature.

Never had I known such conditions could exist. July's sultry days and nights were melted into a torpid inferno. Day after day, night after night, I slept only in brief snatches, ever too anxious about the condition of that feeble heart bravely carrying on, to stay long from the bedside of the patient. . . .

At the end of two weeks recovery was in sight, and at the end of three weeks I was preparing to leave the fragile patient to take up the ordinary duties of her life, including those of wifehood and motherhood. Everyone was congratulating her on her recovery. All the kindness of sympathetic and understanding neighbors poured in upon her in the shape of convalescent dishes, soups, custards, and drinks. Still she appeared to be despondent and worried. She seemed to sit apart in her thoughts as if she had no part in these congratulatory messages and endearing welcomes. I thought at first that she still retained some of her unconscious memories and dwelt upon them in her silences.

But as the hour for my departure came nearer, her anxiety increased, and finally with trembling voice she said: "Another baby will finish me, I suppose."

"It's too early to talk about that," I said, and resolved that I would turn the question over to the doctor for his advice. When he came I said: "Mrs. Sacks is worried about having another baby."

"She well might be," replied the doctor, and then he stood before her and said: "Any more such capers, young woman, and there will be no need to call me."

"Yes, yes—I know, Doctor," said the patient with trembling voice, "but," and she hesitated as if it took all of her courage to say it, *"what* can I do to prevent getting that way again?"

"Oh ho!" laughed the doctor good naturedly. "You want your cake while you eat it too, do you? Well, it can't be done." Then, familiarly slapping her on the back and picking up his hat and bag to depart, he said: "I'll tell you the only sure thing to do. Tell Jake to sleep on the roof!"

With those words he closed the door and went down the stairs, leaving us both petrified and stunned.

Tears sprang to my eyes, and a lump came in my throat as I looked at that face before me. It was stamped with sheer horror. I thought for a moment she might have gone insane, but she conquered her feelings, whatever they may have been, and turning to me in desperation said: "He can't understand, can he?—he's a man after all—but you do, don't you? You're a woman and you'll tell me the secret and I'll never tell it to a soul."

She clasped her hands as if in prayer, she leaned over and looked straight into my eyes and beseechingly implored me to tell her something—something *I really did not know.* It was like being on a rack and tortured for a crime one had not committed. To plead guilty would stop the agony; otherwise the rack kept turning.

I had to turn away from that imploring face. I could not answer her then. I quieted her as best I could. She saw that I was moved by the tears in my eyes. I promised that I would come back in a few days and tell her what she wanted to know. The few simple means of limiting the family like *coitus interruptus* or the condom were laughed at by the neighboring women when told these were the means used by men in the well-to-do families. That was not believed, and I knew such an answer would be swept aside as useless were I to tell her this at such a time.

A little later when she slept I left the house, and made up my mind that I'd keep away from those cases in the future. I felt helpless to do anything at all. I seemed chained hand and foot, and longed for an earthquake or a volcano to shake the world out of its lethargy into facing these monstrous atrocities.

The intelligent reasoning of the young mother—how to *prevent* getting that way again—how sensible, how just she had been—yes, I promised myself I'd go back and have a long talk with her and tell her more, and perhaps she would not laugh but would believe that those methods were all that were really known.

But time flew past, and weeks rolled into months. That wistful, appealing face haunted me day and night. I could not banish from my mind memories of that trembling voice begging so humbly for knowledge she had a right to have. I was about to retire one night three months later when the telephone rang and an agitated man's voice begged me to come at once to help his wife who was sick again. It was the husband of Mrs. Sacks, and I intuitively knew before I left the telephone that it was almost useless to go.

I dreaded to face that woman. I was tempted to send someone else in my place. I longed for an accident on the subway, or on the street—anything to prevent my going into that home. But on I went just the same. I arrived a few minutes after the doctor, the same one who had given her such noble advice. The woman was dying. She was unconscious. She died within ten minutes after my arrival. It was the same result, the same story told a thousand times before—death from abortion. She had become pregnant, had used drugs, had then consulted a five-dollar professional abortionist, and death followed.

After I left that desolate house I walked and walked and walked; for hours and hours I kept on, bag in hand, thinking, regretting, dreading to stop; fearful of my conscience, dreading to face my own accusing soul. At three in the morning I arrived home still clutching a heavy load the weight of which I was quite unconscious.

I entered the house quietly, as was my custom, and looked out of the window down upon the dimly lighted, sleeping city. . . .

. . . For hours I stood, motionless and tense, expecting something to happen. I watched the lights go out, I saw the darkness gradually give way to the first shimmer of dawn, and then a colorful sky heralded the rise of the sun. I knew a new day had come for me and a new world as well.

It was like an illumination. I could now see clearly the various social strata of our life; all its mass problems seemed to be centered around uncontrolled breeding. There was only one thing to be done: call out, start the alarm, set the heather on fire! Awaken the womanhood of America to free the motherhood of the world! I released from my almost paralyzed hand the nursing bag which unconsciously I had clutched, threw it across the room, tore the uniform from my body, flung it into a corner, and renounced all palliative work forever.

I would never go back again to nurse women's ailing bodies while their miseries were as vast as the stars. I was now finished with superficial cures, with doctors and nurses and social workers who were brought face to face with this overwhelming truth of women's needs and yet turned to pass on the other side. They must be made to see these facts. I resolved that women should have knowledge of contraception. They have every right to know about their own bodies. I would strike out—I would scream from the housetops. I would tell the world what was going on in the lives of these poor women. I *would* be heard. No matter what it should cost. *I would be heard.*

[1916]

The selection of a place for the first birth control clinic was of the greatest importance. No one could actually tell how it would be received in any neighborhood. I thought of all the possible difficulties: The indifference of women's organizations, the ignorance of the workers themselves, the resentment of social agencies, the opposition of the medical profession. Then there was the law—the law of New York State.

Section 1142 was definite. It stated that *no one* could give information to prevent conception to *anyone* for any reason. There was, however, Section

1145, which distinctly stated that physicians *(only)* could give advice to prevent conception for the cure or prevention of disease. I inquired about the section, and was told by two attorneys and several physicians that this clause was an exception to 1142 referring only to venereal disease. But anyway, as I was not a physician, it could not protect me. Dared I risk it?

I began to think of the doctors I knew. Several who had previously promised now refused. I wrote, telephoned, asked friends to ask other friends to help me find a woman doctor to help me demonstrate the need of a birth control clinic in New York. None could be found. No one wanted to go to jail. No one cared to test out the law. Perhaps it would have to be done without a doctor. But it had to be done; that I knew.

Fania Mindell, an enthusiastic young worker in the cause, had come on from Chicago to help me. Together we tramped the streets on that dreary day in early October, through a driving rainstorm, to find the best location at the cheapest terms possible. . . .

Finally at 46 Amboy Street, in the Brownsville section of Brooklyn, we found a friendly landlord with a good place vacant at fifty dollars a month rental; and Brownsville was settled on. It was one of the most thickly populated sections. It had a large population of working class Jews, always interested in health measures, always tolerant of new ideas, willing to listen and to accept advice whenever the health of mother or children was involved. I knew that here there would at least be no breaking of windows, no hurling of insults into our teeth; but I was scarcely prepared for the popular support, the sympathy and friendly help given us in that neighborhood from that day to this.

With a small bundle of handbills and a large amount of zeal, we fared forth each morning in a house-to-house canvass of the district in which the clinic was located. Every family in that great district received a "dodger" printed in English, Yiddish and Italian. . . .

It was on October 16, 1916, that the three of us—Fania Mindell, Ethel Byrne and myself—opened the doors of the first birth control clinic in America. I believed then and do today, that the opening of those doors to the mothers of Brownsville was an event of social significance in the lives of American womanhood.

News of our work spread like wildfire. Within a few days there was not a darkened tenement, hovel or flat but was brightened by the knowledge that motherhood could be voluntary; that children need not be born into the world unless they are wanted and have a place provided for them. For the first time, women talked openly of this terror of unwanted pregnancy which had haunted their lives since time immemorial. The newspapers, in glaring headlines, used the words "birth control," and carried the message that somewhere in Brooklyn there was a place where contraceptive information could be obtained by all overburdened mothers who wanted it.

Ethel Byrne, who is my sister and a trained nurse, assisted me in advising, explaining, and demonstrating to the women how to prevent conception. As all of our 488 records were confiscated by the detectives who later arrested us for violation of the New York State law, it is difficult to tell exactly how many more women came in those few days to seek advice; but we estimate that it was far more than five hundred. As in any new enterprise, false reports were maliciously spread about the clinic; weird stories without the slightest foundation of truth. We talked plain talk and gave plain facts to the women who came there. We kept a record of every applicant. All were mothers; most of them had large families.

It was whispered about that the police were to raid the place for abortions. We had no fear of that accusation. We were trying to spare mothers the necessity of that ordeal by giving them proper contraceptive information. It was well that so many of the women in the neighborhood knew the truth of our doings. Hundreds of them who had witnessed the facts came to the courtroom afterward, eager to testify in our behalf.

One day a woman by the name of Margaret Whitehurst came to us. She said that she was the mother of two children and that she had not money to support more. Her story was a pitiful one — all lies, of course, but the government acts that way. She asked for our literature and preventives, and received both. Then she triumphantly went to the District Attorney's office and secured a warrant for the arrest of my sister, Mrs. Ethel Byrne, our interpreter, Miss Fania Mindell, and myself.

I refused to close down the clinic, hoping that a court decision would allow us to continue such necessary work. I was to be disappointed. Pressure was brought upon the landlord, and we were dispossessed by the law as a "public nuisance." In Holland the clinics were called "public utilities."

When the policewoman entered the clinic with her squad of plain clothes men and announced the arrest of Miss Mindell and myself (Mrs. Byrne was not present at the time and her arrest followed later), the room was crowded to suffocation with women waiting in the outer room. The police began bullying these mothers, asking them questions, writing down their names in order to subpoena them to testify against us at the trial. These women, always afraid of trouble which the very presence of a policeman signifies, screamed and cried aloud. The children on their laps screamed, too. It was like a panic for a few minutes until I walked into the room where they were stampeding and begged them to be quiet and not to get excited. I assured them that nothing could happen to them, that I was under arrest but they would be allowed to return home in a few minutes. That quieted them. The men were blocking the door to prevent anyone from leaving, but I finally persuaded them to allow these women to return to their homes, unmolested though terribly frightened by it all.

Crowds began to gather outside. A long line of women with baby carriages and children had been waiting to get into the clinic. Now the streets were filled, and police had to see that traffic was not blocked. The patrol wagon came rattling through the streets to our door, and at length Miss Mindell and I took our seats within and were taken to the police station.

28

Down and Out in the Great Depression

Anonymous

President Franklin D. Roosevelt, in his famous "fireside chats," was the first president effectively to use radio to communicate directly to the nation. And Eleanor Roosevelt was different from all previous first ladies in her independent public role of champion of the underdog. Victims of the Great Depression of the 1930s sometimes wrote to the president, to Mrs. Roosevelt, or to the various agencies and administrators responsible for carrying out government-sponsored plans for relief. This was largely a new phenomenon in American life. President Hoover employed one secretary to answer mail from the public; the Roosevelt White House needed fifty.

The archives of the New Deal era contain tens of millions of letters from ordinary people expressing their concerns and frequently asking for help. This trove of information about the forgotten men and women of the 1930s reveals attitudes about government, wealth and poverty, opportunity, and patriotism. Unlike many secondary sources for understanding the ways events affected everyday people, these letters are not filtered through the perception of some interviewer nor are they time-beclouded memoirs written long after the events.

Robert S. McElvaine, who edited these letters in Down and Out in the Great Depression, *published in 1983, uses them to get closer to the real experience of unemployment and destitution in the 1930s.*

BEFORE YOU READ

1. What attitudes toward the government did these people writing to the Roosevelts have?

2. What attitudes about social class do you find in the letters?

3. Can you identify the prejudices these people had? Toward whom and for what reasons?

4. What can you infer about the successes and failures of the New Deal from these letters?

[Oil City, Penn.
December 15, 1930]

Col Arthur Woods
Director, Presidents Committee
Dear Sir:

. . . I have none of these things [that the rich have], what do they care how much we suffer, how much the health of our children is menaced. Now I happen to know there is something can be done about it and Oil City needs to be awakened up to that fact and compelled to act.

Now that our income is but $15.60 a week (their are five of us My husband Three little children and myself). My husband who is a world war Veteran and saw active service in the trenches, became desperate and applied for Compensation or a pension from the Government and was turned down and that started me thinking. . . . [There should be] enough to pay all world war veterans a pension, dysabeled or not dysabeled and there by relieve a lot of suffering, and banish resentment that causes Rebellions and Bolshevism. Oh why is it that it is allways a bunch of overley rich, selfish, dumb, ignorant money hogs that persist in being Senitors, legislatures, representitives? Where would they and their possessions be if it were not for the Common Soldier, the common laborer that is compelled to work for a starvation wage. for I tell you again the hog of a Landlord gets his there is not enough left for the necessaries if a man has three or more children. Not so many years ago in Russia all the sufferings of poverty (and you can never feel them you are on the other side of the fence but try to understand) conceived a child, that child was brought forth in agony, and its name was Bolshevism. I am on the other side of the fence from you, you are not in a position to see, but I, I can see and feel and understand. I have lived and suffered too. I know, and right now our good old U. S. A. is sitting on a Seething Volcano. In the Public Schools our little children stand at salute and recite a "rig ma role" in which is mentioned "Justice to all." What a lie, what a naked lie, when honest, law abiding citizens, decendents of Revilutionary heros, Civil War heros, and World war heros are denied the priviledge of owning their own homes, that foundation of good citizenship, good morals, and the very foundation of good government the world over. Is all that our Soldiers of all wars fought bled and died for to be sacrificed to a God awful hideious Rebellion? in which all our Citizens will be involved, because of the dumb bungling of rich politicians? Oh for a few Statesmen, oh for but one statesman, as fearless as Abraham Lincoln, the amancipator who died for us. and who said, you can fool some of the people some of the time, But you can't fool all of the people all of the time. Heres hoping you have read this to the end and think it over. I wish you a Mery Christmas and a Happy New Year.

Very Truly Yours
Mrs. M. E. B

Phila., Pa.
November 26, 1934

Honorable Franklin D. Roosevelt
Washington, D. C.
Dear Mr. President:

I am forced to write to you because we find ourselves in *a very serious condition*. For the last three or four years we have had depression and *suffered* with my *family* and little children *severely*. Now Since the Home Owners Loan Corporation opened up, I have been going there in order to save my home, because there has been unemployment in my house for more than three years. You can imagine that I and my family have suffered from lack of water supply in my house for more than two years. Last winter I did not have coal and the pipes burst in my house and therefore could not make heat in the house. Now winter is here again and we are suffering of cold, no water in the house, and we are facing to be forced out of the house, because I have no money to move or pay so much money as they want when after making settlement I am mother of little children, am sick and losing my health, and we are eight people in the family, and where can I go when I don't have money because no one is working in my house. The Home Loan Corporation wants $42. a month rent or else we will have to be on the street. I am living in this house for about ten years and when times were good we would put our last cent in the house and now I have *no money, no home* and *no wheres to go.* I beg of you to please help me and my family and little children for the sake of a sick mother and suffering family to give this your immediate attention so we will not be forced to move or put out in the street.

Waiting and Hoping that you will act quickly.

Thanking you very much I remain

Mrs. E. L.

Lincoln Nebraska.
May 19/ 34.

Mrs Franklin D. Roosevelt
Washington, D. C.
Dear Mrs Roosevelt;

Will you be kind enough to read the following as it deals with a very important subject which you are very much interested in as well as my self.

In the Presidents inaugral adress delivered from the capitol steps the afternoon of his inauguration he made mention of The Forgotten Man, and I with thousands of others am wondering if the folk who was borned here in America some 60 or 70 years a go are this Forgotten Man, the President had in mind, if we are this Forgotten Man then we are still Forgotten.

We who have tried to be diligent in our support of this most wonderful nation of ours boath social and other wise, we in our younger days tried to do our duty without complaining.

We have helped to pay pensions to veterans of some thre wars, we have raised the present young generation and have tried to train them to honor and support this our home country.

And now a great calamity has come upon us and seamingly no cause of our own it has swept away what little savings we had accumulated and we are left in a condition that is imposible for us to correct, for two very prominent reasons if no more.

First we have grown to what is termed Old Age, this befalls every man.

Second as we put fourth every effort in our various business lines trying to rectify and reestablish our selves we are confronted on every hand with the young generation, taking our places, this of corse is what we have looked forward to in training our children. But with the extra ordinary crisese which left us helpless and placed us in the position that our fathers did not have to contend with.

Seamingly every body has been assisted but we the Forgotten Man, and since we for 60 years or more have tried to carry the loan without complaining, we have paid others pensions we have educated and trained the youth, now as we are Old and down and out of no reason of our own, would it be asking to much of our Government and the young generation to do by us as we have tried our best to do by them even without complaint.

We have been honorable citizens all along our journey, calamity and old age has forced its self upon us please donot send us to the Poor Farm but instead allow us the small pension of $40.00 per month and we will do as we have done in the past (not complain).

I personly Know of Widows who are no older than I am who own their own homes and draw $45,00 per month pension, these ladies were born this side of the civil war the same as I, therefore they never experianced war trouble.

Please donot think of us who are asking this assitsnce as Old Broken down dishonorable cotizens, but we are of those borned in this country and have done our bit in making this country, we are folk in all walks of life and businesse.

For example I am an architect and builder I am not and old broken down illiterate dishonorable man although I am 69 years old, but as I put forth every effort to regain my prestage in business I am confronted on every side by the young generation taking my place, yes this is also the case even in the effort of the government with its recovery plan, even though I am qualifyed to suprentend any class of construction but the young man has captured this place also.

What are we to do since the calamity has swept our all away,? We are just asking to be remembered with a small part as we have done to others $40,00 a month is all we are asking.

Mrs. Roosevelt I am asking a personal favor of you as it seems to be the only means through which I may be able to reach the President, some evening very soon, as you and Mr. Roosevelt are having dinner together privately will you ask him to read this. And we American citizens will ever remember your kindness.

Yours very truly.

R. A. [male]

[February, 1936]

Mr. and Mrs. Roosevelt.
Wash. D. C.
Dear Mr. President:

I'm a boy of 12 years. I want to tell you about my family. My father hasn't worked for 5 months. He went plenty times to relief, he filled out application. They won't give us anything. I don't know why. Please you do something. We haven't paid 4 months rent, Everyday the landlord rings the door bell, we don't open the door for him. We are afraid that we will be put out, been put out before, and don't want to happen again. We haven't paid the gas bill, and the electric bill, haven't paid grocery bill for 3 months. My brother goes to Lane Tech. High School. he's eighteen years old, hasn't gone to school for 2 weeks because he got no carfare. I have a sister she's twenty years, she can't find work. My father he staying home. All the time he's crying because he can't find work. I told him why are you crying daddy, and daddy said why shouldn't I cry when there is nothing in the house. I feel sorry for him. That night I couldn't sleep. The next morning I wrote this letter to you. in my room. Were American citizens and were born in Chicago, Ill. and I don't know why they don't help us Please answer right away because we need it. will starve Thank you.

God bless you.

[Anonymous]
Chicago, Ill.

Dec. 14—1937.
Columbus, Ind.

Mrs. F. D. Roosevelt,
Washington, D. C.

Mrs. Roosevelt: I suppose from your point of view the work relief, old age pensions, slum clearance and all the rest seems like a perfect remedy for all the ills of this country, but I would like for you to see the results, as the other half see them.

We have always had a shiftless, never-do-well class of people whose one and only aim in life is to live without work. I have been rubbing elbows with this class for nearly sixty years and have tried to help some of the most promising and have seen others try to help them, but it can't be done. We cannot help those who will not try to help themselves and if they do try a square deal is all they need, and by the way that is all this country needs or ever has needed: a square deal for all and then, let each one paddle their own canoe, or sink.

There has never been any necessity for any one who is able to work, being on relief in this locality, but there have been many eating the bread of charity and they have lived better than ever before. I have had taxpayers tell me that their children came from school and asked why they couldn't have nice lunches like the children on relief.

The women and children around here have had to work at the fields to help save the crops and several women fainted while at work and at the same time we couldn't go up or down the road without stumbling over some of the reliefers, moping around carrying dirt from one side of the road to the other and back again, or else asleep. I live alone on a farm and have not raised any crops for the last two years as there was no help to be had. I am feeding the stock and have been cutting the wood to keep my home fires burning. There are several reliefers around here now who have been kicked off relief, but they refuse to work unless they can get relief hours and wages, but they are so worthless no one can afford to hire them.

As for the clearance of the real slums, it can't be done as long as their inhabitants are allowed to reproduce their kind. I would like for you to see what a family of that class can do to a decent house in a short time. Such a family moved into an almost new, neat, four-room house near here last winter. They even cut down some of the shade trees for fuel, after they had burned everything they could pry loose. There were two big idle boys in the family and they could get all the fuel they wanted, just for the cutting, but the shade trees were closer and it was taking a great amount of fuel, for they had broken out several windows and they had but very little bedding. There were two women there all the time and three part of the time and there was enough good clothing tramped in the mud around the yard to have made all the bedclothes they needed. It was clothing that had been given them and they had worn it until it was too filthy to wear any longer without washing, so they threw it out and begged more. I will not try to describe their filth for you would not believe me. They paid no rent while there and left between two suns owing everyone from whom they could get a nickels worth of anything. They are just a fair sample of the class of people on whom so much of our hard earned tax-money is being squandered and on whom so much sympathy is being wasted.

As for the old people on beggars' allowances: the taxpayers have provided homes for all the old people who never liked to work, where they will be neither cold nor hungry: much better homes than most of them have ever tried to provide for themselves. They have lived many years through the most prosperous times of our country and had an opportunity to prepare for old age, but they spent their lives in idleness or worse and now they expect those who have worked like slaves, to provide a living for them and all their worthless descendants. Some of them are asking for from thirty to sixty dollars a month when I have known them to live on a dollar a week rather than go to work. There is many a little child doing without butter on its bread, so that some old sot can have his booze and tobacco: some old sot who spent his working years loafing around pool rooms and saloons, boasting that the world owed him a living.

Even the child welfare has become a racket. The parents of large families are getting divorces, so that the mothers and children can qualify for aid. The children to join the ranks of the "unemployed" as they grow up, for no child that has been raised on charity in this community has ever amounted to anything.

You people who have plenty of this worlds goods and whose money comes easy, have no idea of the heart-breaking toil and self-denial which is the lot of the working people who are trying to make an honest living, and then to have to shoulder all these unjust burdens seems like the last straw. During the worst of the depression many of the farmers had to deny their families butter, eggs, meat etc. and sell it to pay their taxes and then had to stand by and see the dead-beats carry it home to their families by the arm load, and they knew their tax money was helping pay for it. One woman saw a man carry out eight pounds of butter at one time. The crookedness, shelfishness, greed and graft of the crooked politicians is making one gigantic racket out of the new deal and it is making this a nation of dead beats and beggars and if it continues the people who will work will soon be nothing but slaves for the pampered poverty rats and I am afraid these human parasites are going to become a menace to the country unless they are disfranchised. No one should have the right to vote theirself a living at the expense of the tax payers. They learned their strength at the last election and also learned that they can get just about what they want by "voting right." They have had a taste of their coveted life of idleness, and at the rate they are increasing, they will soon control the country. The twentieth child arrived in the home of one chronic reliefer near here some time ago.

Is it any wonder the taxpayers are discouraged by all this penalizing of thrift and industry to reward shiftlessness, or that the whole country is on the brink of chaos?

M. A. H. [female]
Columbus, Ind.

[no address]
Jan. 18, 1937

[Dear Mrs. Roosevelt:]

I . . . was simply astounded to think that anyone could be nitwit enough to wish to be included in the so called social security act if they could possibly avoid it. Call it by any name you wish it, in my opinion, (and that of many people I know) is nothing but downright stealing. . . .

Personally, I had my savings so invested that I would have had a satisfactory provision for old age. Now thanks to his [F.D.R.'s] desire to "get" the utilities I cannot be sure of anything, being a stockholder, as after business has survived his merciless attacks (*if* it does) insurance will probably be no good either.

[She goes on to complain about the lack of profits.]

Then the president tells them they should hire more men and work shorter hours so that the laborers, who are getting everything now raises etc. can have a "more abundant life." That simply means taking it from the rest of us in the form of taxes or otherwise. . . .

Believe me, the only thing we want from the president, unless or if you except Communists and the newly trained chiselers, is for him to balance the budget and reduce taxes. That, by the way, is a "mandate from the people" that isn't getting much attention.

I am not an "economic royalist," just an ordinary white collar worker at $1600 per. Please show this to the president and ask him to remember the wishes of the forgotten man, that is, the one who dared to vote against him. We expect to be tramped on but we do wish the stepping would be a little less hard.

Security at the price of freedom is never desired by intelligent people.

M. A. [female]

[Mr. Harry Hopkins
Washington, D. C.]
[Dear Mr. Hopkins:]

Will you please investigate the various relief agencies in many cities of the United States. The cities where there are a large foreign and jewish population. No wonder the cities are now on the verge of bankruptcy because we are feeding a lot of ignorant foreigners by giving them relief. And, they are turning against us every day. I would suggest to deport all foreigners and jews who are not citizens over the United States back to any land where they choose to go and who will admit them. As America is now over crowded with too much immigration and it can not feed even its own citizens without feeding the citizens of other foreign nations. I have found out after careful investigation that we are feeding many foreigners who send out their wives to work and who have money in the bank. While the men drink wine and play cards in saloons and cafes. I have spoken to one Italian whom I met. And I ask him what he was doing for a living. He said me drinka da dago red wine and play cards and send the wife out to work. Isn't a very good thing for us to support them. No wonder the taxpayers are grumbling about taxes. Most of them are a race of black hands murders boot leggers bomb throwers. While most of the sheeney jews as they are called are a race of dishonest people who get rich by swindling, faking and cheating the poor people. Besides the jews are responsible by ruining others in business by the great amount of chisling done. And selling even below the cost prices, in order to get all the others business. The foreigners and jews spend as little as they can to help this country. And, they live as cheap as they can. And, work as cheap as they can, and save all the money they can. And when they have enough they go back to their country. Why don't we deport them under the section of the United States Immigration Laws which relates to paupers and those who become a public charge. The Communist Party is composed mostly by foreigners and jews. The jews are the leaders of the movement and urge the downfall of this government. . . .

A Taxpayer

J. Robert Oppenheimer, scientific director of the Manhattan Project, and General Leslie R. Groves, its military director, at ground zero sometime after the first test explosion of a nuclear device at Alamogordo, New Mexico, on July 16, 1945.

PART FIVE

Global Reach

War, Affluence, and Uncertainty

World War II affected virtually every part of American life. Problems of economic depression vanished with the growth of war industries and—to the surprise of most economists—did not return after the war. The size and scope of government swelled, particularly the federal government, never to shrink to its previous size. Family life changed dramatically: fathers absent, families moving toward crowded centers of war industry, mothers working, consumer goods rationed or unavailable, divorce *and* birth rates both soaring. Science was transformed both by its scale of activities and by its subjection to government control and security regulations. Loyalties and antipathies shifted in extraordinary ways: The Communist U.S.S.R. became one of our most important allies, bearing the brunt of the war, while German and Italian Americans became suspect and Japanese Americans were locked in internment camps.

The readings in Part Five sample some of the drama of World War II. J. Robert Oppenheimer, who directed scientific work at Los Alamos National Laboratory, recounts the creation of the atomic bomb. Phyllis Fisher, for whom Los Alamos was a totally unexpected part of life, recounts the experience of living under the strange new routines of science. Fanny Christina Hill was one of the many women, collectively named "Rosie the Riveter," who found new opportunities in the war industries. Ben Yorita and Philip Hayasaka describe the internment camps where they and their families were forced to endure much of the war. Several American soldiers remember how they suffered at the hands of the Japanese during the Bataan death march.

Victory in the war planted seeds of both hope and fear. Uncertainties about the future of the United States were accompanied by ideological quarrels with the Soviet Union. The anxious transition to a peacetime economy and then back to the quasiwarfare of the Cold War provoked the Red Scare with which Mark Goodson and his conscience struggled. But as war was replaced not with renewed depression but with a widespread prosperity unknown in previous human history, the nation's confidence awakened.

People were determined that the years ahead would be, in *the words from* the title of a distinguished motion picture of the time, "the best years of our lives." Millions of Americans, like the man in the gray flannel suit and his family, sought the good life of high consumption in the new suburbs and the vastly successful corporations that came to define home and work in the postwar American imagination. Both the suburbs and the opportunities were for whites only. But pioneers of the civil rights movement like Jo Ann Gibson Robinson were ready to risk all they had to overcome that injustice and achieve their rightful dignity.

Points of View: Building an Atomic Bomb (1942–45)

29

Letters from Los Alamos

Phyllis Fisher

"My two great loves," J. Robert Oppenheimer often told friends, "are physics and New Mexico. It's a pity they can't be combined." Oppenheimer had first visited the Pajarito Plateau in New Mexico in 1922 just before he began college. Two decades later, the need for secrecy and his longtime affection for the area made it the appropriate site of a great adventure for many physicists and their families.

At Los Alamos, scientists who were accustomed to open communications and sophisticated academic communities lived under the rule of secrecy and military security. They could not tell relatives where they were going or what they were doing, and even their spouses might not have known what the laboratory's mission was. Often they did not know what those in other units in the laboratory were doing, and many workers were not briefed on the ultimate objective of the project.

Leon Fisher, a physicist, his wife Phyllis, and their son, Bobby, came to Los Alamos in October 1944. All mail was censored, so Phyllis Fisher's frequent letters to her parents could not reveal where she was. The first successful explosion of a nuclear device on July 16, 1945, at the "Trinity site" at Alamogordo, New Mexico, had to pass unnoticed in her letters. But after August 6, 1945, when an atomic bomb was dropped on Hiroshima, she could freely write what she thought about the atomic bomb and how scientists at Los Alamos reacted to it.

BEFORE YOU READ

1. What was life like at Los Alamos? What adjustments did people have to make to live there?

2. What was Phyllis Fisher's reaction to the dropping of the atomic bombs in Japan? What do you think of it?

October 4, 1944

We're moving! Believe me, you're not any more surprised than I am! You'd like to know where we're going? So would we! And it isn't that Lee won't tell me. It's hard to believe, but he doesn't know either. The only encouraging thing he could say was that we'll know where we are when we get there. Great!

Lee came home from the university early this afternoon, tossed his briefcase on the couch and said, "Sit down, Phyllis, we've really got to talk." He was so serious that he ignored Bobby, who had toddled across the floor to greet him. He told me of an important phone call that he had made earlier in the afternoon, which really leaves us no choice and which will result in our making this sudden move.

Here's what I can tell you. We'll be going "there" next week (less than a day's trip from Albuquerque) to select our living quarters, and we will move "there" sometime between the 26th and 30th of this month. We have been directed to drive to a certain city and report to an inconspicuous address where we will be given further instructions. It's alright with me, so long as we're not met by a bearded mystic, given a piece of thread and instructed to follow it to its end. At this point, nothing would surprise me. . . .

For the time being, let's call the place Shangri-La or Sh-La for short. I'm tired of writing "there" and "the place," and I don't know what to call it. I couldn't tell you its real name if I knew it. Please don't say anything to anyone yet, at least until I tell you what you can or should say. I'll write all I can about Sh-La. Please understand that if I don't answer your questions, there is a reason. I have been told that our mail, both incoming and outgoing, will be censored. If my letters have less coherence than usual, please blame it on the rules and regulations of our future home.

Well, here we go, two so-called adults, one baby and one fox-terrier, heading off to play "hide and seek" for the duration. I'm pretty excited about it, but I'm frightened too. It's very much like stepping off into space and I just hope we land on our feet.

Phyllis Fisher, *The Los Alamos Experience* (Tokyo: Japan Publications Inc., 1985), pp. 24–27, 29–30, 32, 46–50, 115–17, 121, 122, 145.

[October, 1944]

Authoritative books on child-rearing warn me that when Bobby is three (or is it four?) he'll ask countless questions, many of them unanswerable. Well, it will take him a full year to ask as many questions as you did in your last letter. The worst of it is, I can't answer anything! I don't know the answers and I couldn't tell you if I did! No, we can never give you the size of the project. They take precautions that this information not be known. For example, we have been told not to transfer what they flatteringly term our "entire bank account" to a bank nearer the project. And, "What kind of work will Leon do?" and "Is it dangerous?" Mom! How can I answer you? Then you ask, "Can you assure us you will stay in New Mexico or, at least in continental U.S.A.?" I can tell you're both worried. I don't know what to say to you.

October 11, 1944

I'm breathless! We've been "there"! Shangri-La is super! We drove up yesterday and stayed just long enough to tour the place, pick out our house and learn some of the rules, regulations and by-laws of this Never-Never-Land. Naturally, the day was not uneventful. In fact, Lee and I are still blushing over our latest butch.

I wrote you that we were given an address in Santa Fe from which we were to receive further instructions. We dutifully followed our little map, found the address alright and stared at it in amazement. The place was a bakery! Once in, we didn't know what to do. A girl behind the counter asked if she could help us and we boobs were tongue-tied. Lee finally stated that we were "told to come here." Silence reigned. More silence. Believe me, I fully expected the girl to break open a loaf of bread, surreptitiously extract from it a message written in code and slyly slip it to us. Instead, a bored voice from the other side of the room said, "You must be looking for the office down the way; people are going in and out of there all the time." We felt like four cents, said our thanks and meekly ambled out. Fine beginning! The office down the way was presided over by Dorothy, a genial, relaxed woman from whom we learned that we were expected and were given our directions to Sh-La. Then we started out on a most spectacularly beautiful drive.

Shangri-La is a streamlined, alpine settlement, size unmentionable, location unmentionable, altitude unmentionable. But it's very complete. We found theater, sports field, playground, and a school. There is even a radio station that picks up programs and adds music. Apparently, we will live in a spot where ordinary radio reception is extremely poor.

Anyway, the inmates assure us that there is plenty here to compensate for the very extreme isolation. We saw notices of picnics, dances, bridge parties, etc. If we get tired of my cooking, and that's entirely possible, we can eat out at the mess hall. We are entitled to use the Army commissary and PX, and they seem quite adequate.

Lee and I were lectured briefly on the importance of developing an anti-social outlook. We're not to be friendly with residents of nearby towns. (I hadn't noticed any nearby towns.) If we go to Santa Fe (which isn't my idea of nearby) we are to keep to ourselves and not talk to outsiders unless it is necessary in the transaction of business, etc. However, we are allowed a half-smile and a slight nod to persons we already know there. "Only this and nothing more." . . .

October 27, 1944

. . . You can tear up the floor plan I sent you. Any resemblance between it and the place we're living in is purely coincidental. Our belongings were unceremoniously dumped in the wrong house, a smaller place (classification: garage style) at about six o'clock this evening. Our chosen home, we were told by a WAC *[Women's Army Corps member]* in the housing office, had been assigned by mistake to someone else. Instead, after a great deal of scurrying around, we were deposited here to remain until another batch of houses can be built. The WAC tried to be comforting, assuring us in her most languid southern accent, that it would be but a week or so before these next prefabs would be tossed together, and we could move.

November, 1944

Now, listen to this very carefully and try to understand. I can't. We have a gate here that isn't a gate at all. It consists of a guardhouse and an unfriendly signpost surrounded by sentries. Regulations governing passage of said "gate" top any screwy regulation of any Army post anywhere. It seems that you can drive past it in an automobile without showing a pass, but you can't walk past it. Pedestrians must show passes. No exceptions.

I drove past the gate (to the vet's) with Fawn and, naturally, wasn't stopped. The veterinary hospital is only about 100 yards beyond and is visible from the gate. After our visit to the vet, I rushed out with my shivering dog, climbed into the car to start back, and—you guessed it—the car wouldn't start. By this time, it was snowing. I began to run as best I could, with Fawn held securely inside my coat. Of course, I was promptly stopped at the gate. I had no pass! In my rush to get Fawn to the vet's and back, I had neglected to take it. I explained to the sentries that my car wouldn't start. I had to get back. My husband had to get to work. My baby would be alone! My dog was dying! None of which made any difference. Only one word seemed to have meaning, the word "regulations." There were, it seemed, no provisions for someone who drove out the gate and had to walk back through it. Too bad. By then the snow was slanting and spinning angrily, and I wasn't getting any warmer. Fawn wasn't getting any lighter. They could see my car standing there, but that didn't make any difference. One MP suggested that I phone someone who could come out and identify me. Fine help! No one I knew had a phone. Lee couldn't be reached by phone until he left Bobby and went to work. And he wouldn't do that (I certainly hope he wouldn't do that) until I was safely home. What to do?

Then through the gloom and the swirling snow, there appeared a jeep, with driver, of course. Through chattering teeth, and right in front of the MPs, I asked the stranger for a lift. He agreed. I climbed into the jeep and in we went with full permission of the guards at the gate!

[November, 1944]

. . . Our guests were two completely balmy SEDs *[Special Engineering Detachment members]*, Bob and Norman. Bob, an attractive fellow with a nice smile, was in high spirits. He told us that next Wednesday he is going to fall madly in love with a girl named Shirley. A whirlwind romance will follow, culminating in marriage sometime in December. I was most impressed, but a little baffled by it all. But there is an explanation. Military regulations here forbid the wife of an enlisted man to come to live in Sh-La. If Bob goes home to marry his Shirley, he'll have to leave her and return to our little exile alone. However, if Shirley qualifies for a position here, meets Bob here, falls in love here, marries here, why then, she can stay. In fact, she has to stay! Hence the plotted romance. See? And Shirley has already been hired by the project and will arrive next Wednesday.

[November, 1944]

This evening we were invited to dinner with friends. It was the sort of evening one learns to expect around these parts. Dinner is eaten in a mad rush. The men dash back to work. The wives do the dishes and chat a while. At ten o'-clock the men return jabbering a strange language most nearly identified as "scientese." Tonight it was particularly pleasant. We discovered we had many interests in common. In other words, we all are very fond of Mozart and heartily dislike Dewey *[Republican presidential candidate]*.

This afternoon a group of Leon's co-workers dropped in. Apparently, they are very charming and comical as well as very bright and interesting. You'll have to take Lee's word for it. You see, they, too, speak little English, but mostly "scientese." The only conversation directed my way was "Hello" and "Goodbye" and oft-repeated moanings about dreading Thanksgiving dinner at the mess hall. Hint, hint.

Monday, August 6, 1945

Please note——LOS ALAMOS, NEW MEXICO

Well, today's news makes everything else seem pretty unimportant! You can't possibly imagine how strange it is to turn on the radio and hear the outside world talking about us today! After all the extreme secrecy, it seems positively unreal to hear stories about the bomb, the site, and everything.

The "gadget" worked better (!) than anyone dare to expect, and Hiroshima, a city we have never heard of, and its population of 350,000 has been wiped out. The radio announcers could hardly control their voices. They told the whole story. How had they gotten the information so quickly? They named names! Who had told them? They described our hill, our hill. They located us on a barren plateau in the mountains north and west of Santa Fe.

They identified us as LOS ALAMOS!

We couldn't believe what we heard! "Over one hundred thousand Japs killed by one bomb," the announcers bragged. They ticked off the figures as though they were reporting scores at a sporting event. But, hey, those are people! A radius of one mile vaporized, they cheered as I shuddered. They are talking about a populated target, a city. And part of me keeps saying, "This can't be real." It's also actually unreal to hear names connected with the project, names like Oppenheimer, Segre, Fermi, Bohr, and others. After months of caution and secrecy, it's too much.

Kaltenborn *[a news commentator]* somehow seemed more detached and more objective than the others. He took time, in spite of the hysteria, to consider the bomb's potential for good or evil. Then he described the first test atomic explosion in the southern "arid part of the state" in New Mexico and named the date, the place, and even the code name, "Trinity."

After "Trinity," days went by while we waited to hear how and when the gadget (maybe I'd better get used to writing the word "bomb") would be used. Which brings us up to today. By comparison the excitement on the hill today has put that of July 16th far down the scale of insane rejoicing. You can't imagine it. I can't describe it. I'm certain that it will take time for the emotional bits in all of us that were triggered by "Trinity" and that blew up with the bomb to settle down into place.

August 10, 1945

Now I am upset! Yesterday's bombing of Nagasaki was shocking! I cannot understand the necessity of a second bomb. The Japanese were known to be suing for peace and trying to negotiate terms that they could accept. Why destroy another city and its inhabitants? Why couldn't both bombs have been dropped over some unimportant unpopulated island as a demonstration of what could happen to Japan?

[August, 1945]

I almost fainted when a traveling salesman knocked at my door. There has never been one here before. He had gotten a temporary pass. Amazing! I was so busy questioning him that he had trouble telling me what he had for sale.

[The following paragraphs describe varying reactions to the success of the project. Some were on the verge of hysteria; others took it more calmly.]

. . . for instance, yesterday, Scotty *[who works in the tech area and]* who lives across the street, called to me at around 9:00 A.M. I went over to his house, found him in bed sobbing convulsively into his pillow. He had turned on his heater, which had exploded and burned about a square inch on his arm and spread soot around the living room. It was just too much and the poor guy was nauseated, dizzy, and completely hysterical. I got him quieted down somewhat, notified his wife, who *[also]* works in the tech area, and called a doctor.

Lee goes around with a "Cheshire Cat" grin that won't wipe off. He is very tired and has gotten little sleep. He gets up and wanders around at night when he should be sleeping. And I've lost four pounds in all the excitement.

[In October, J. Robert Oppenheimer spoke to the scientists and their families.]

[October, 1945]

. . . And what he *[Oppenheimer]* said was so exactly what I've been feeling but have been unable to express. His talk was short, even faltering. He told us that the whole world must unite or perish. He felt that unless there is a way to prevent wars, the pride we are feeling today will give way to concern and fear for the future. He said that the day may come when "mankind will curse the names of Los Alamos and Hiroshima."

30

To Build a Bomb

J. Robert Oppenheimer

The 1920s were a golden age in theoretical physics. Brilliant and dedicated physicists like J. Robert Oppenheimer ignored society and politics, living in a separate world of new theories and discoveries in relativity and quantum theory that transformed classic Newtonian physics. Then in the early 1930s, with the rise of dictators such as Hitler, Mussolini, and Stalin, politics began noticeably to intrude even on sciences as remote as theoretical physics. And, far harder to notice, scientific theories and discoveries began ever so slowly to intrude on politics. James Chadwick's discovery of the neutron in 1932 or Albert Einstein's emigration from Germany to the United States in 1933 seemed far less important than the rise of Adolf Hitler or the election of Franklin Roosevelt. Yet by 1938, when scientists in Germany at last figured out that neutrons could "split" certain atoms and release great quantities of energy, the fate of people and nations suddenly hung in the balance.

Germany had long been the center of the new physics; scientists in Great Britain and the United States could only speculate on what progress Hitler's scientists might have been making in harnessing nuclear fission. In June 1942, American and British scientists developed plans for a uranium-based atomic bomb. Full-scale efforts to construct such a bomb, code named the "Manhattan Project," thus began in the shadow of Germany's head start.

The Manhattan Project was actually an activity of the Army Corps of Engineers. Under the direction of General Leslie R. Groves, massive facilities in Los Alamos, New Mexico, Oak Ridge, Tennessee, and Hanford, Washington, were built, involving about a hundred twenty-five thousand workers and costing $2 billion. Los Alamos — chosen by Oppenheimer — was the scientific capital of the project and was kept relatively independent of the military despite its strict security. Oppenheimer, no longer the de-

tatched scholar of the 1920s, recruited scientists worldwide and directed their work in ways they were completely unaccustomed to. Collaborating with larger groups of scientists than had ever gathered before, they worked to the tightest of deadlines: beating the Germans to the bomb. Their success, and the ironies of that success, are the subjects of Oppenheimer's autobiographical sketch and his November 1945 speech.

BEFORE YOU READ

1. What changed Oppenheimer from an unworldly scientist to a man who could direct so large and important an enterprise?

2. What responsibilities did he see for scientists after the war?

3. After he opposed the development of the hydrogen bomb, Oppenheimer lost his security clearance to engage in or advise government research on nuclear weapons. What foreshadowings of his doubts about nuclear weapons do you see in Oppenheimer's speech?

AUTOBIOGRAPHICAL SKETCH (1954)

I was born in New York in 1904. My father had come to this country at the age of 17 from Germany. He was a successful businessman and quite active in community affairs. My mother was born in Baltimore and before her marriage was an artist and teacher of art. I attended Ethical Culture School and Harvard College, which I entered in 1922. I completed the work for my degree in the spring of 1925. I then left Harvard to study at Cambridge University and in Goettingen, where in the spring of 1927 I took my doctor's degree. The following year I was national research fellow at Harvard and at the California Institute of Technology. In the following year I was fellow of the international education board at the University of Leiden and at the Technical High School in Zurich.

In the spring of 1929, I returned to the United States. I was homesick for this country, and in fact I did not leave it again for 19 years. I had learned a great deal in my student days about the new physics; I wanted to pursue this myself, to explain it and to foster its cultivation. I had had many invitations to university positions, 1 or 2 in Europe, and perhaps 10 in the United States. I accepted concurrent appointments as assistant professor at the California Institute of Technology in Pasadena and at the University of California in Berkeley. For the coming 12 years, I was to devote my time to these 2 faculties.

Starting with a single graduate student in my first year in Berkeley, we gradually began to build up what was to become the largest school in the country of graduate and postdoctoral study in theoretical physics, so that as time went on, we came to have between a dozen and 20 people learning and adding to quantum theory, nuclear physics, relativity and other modern physics.

Jonathan F. Fanton, R. Hae Williams, and Michael B. Stoff, eds., *The Manhattan Project: A Documentary Introduction to the Atomic Age* (New York: McGraw-Hill, 1991), pp. 29–32.

My friends, both in Pasadena and in Berkeley, were mostly faculty people, scientists, classicists, and artists. I studied and read Sanskrit with Arthur Rider. I read very widely, mostly classics, novels, plays, and poetry; and I read something of other parts of science. I was not interested in and did not read about economics or politics. I was almost wholly divorced from the contemporary scene in this country. I never read a newspaper or a current magazine like *Time* or *Harper's*; I had no radio, no telephone; I learned of the stock-market crash in the fall of 1929 only long after the event; the first time I ever voted was in the presidential election of 1936. To many of my friends, my indifference to contemporary affairs seemed bizarre, and they often chided me with being too much of a highbrow. I was interested in man and his experience; I was deeply interested in my science; but I had no understanding of the relations of man to his society.

Beginning in late 1936, my interests began to change. These changes did not alter my earlier friendships, my relations to my students, or my devotion to physics; but they added something new. I can discern in retrospect more than one reason for these changes. I had had a continuing, smoldering fury about the treatment of Jews in Germany. I had relatives there, and was later to help in extricating them and bringing them to this country. I saw what the depression was doing to my students. Often they could get no jobs, or jobs which were wholly inadequate. And through them, I began to understand how deeply political and economic events could affect men's lives. I began to feel the need to participate more fully in the life of the community. But I had no framework of political conviction or experience to give me perspective in these matters. . . .

Ever since the discovery of nuclear fission, the possibility of powerful explosives based on it had been very much in my mind, as it had in that of many other physicists. We had some understanding of what this might do for us in the war, and how much it might change the course of history. In the autumn of 1941, a special committee was set up by the National Academy of Sciences under the chairmanship of Arthur Compton to review the prospects and feasibility of the different uses of atomic energy for military purposes. I attended a meeting of this committee; this was my first official connection with the atomic-energy program.

After the academy meeting, I spent some time in preliminary calculations about the consumption and performance of atomic bombs, and became increasingly excited at the prospects. At the same time I still had a quite heavy burden of academic work with courses and graduate students. I also began to consult, more or less regularly, with the staff of the Radiation Laboratory in Berkeley on their program for the electromagnetic separation of uranium isotopes. I was never a member or employee of the laboratory; but I attended many of its staff and policy meetings. With the help of two of my graduate students, I developed an invention which was embodied in the production plants at Oak Ridge. I attended the conference in Chicago at which the Metallurgical Laboratory (to produce plutonium) was established and its initial program projected.

In the spring of 1942, Compton called me to Chicago to discuss the state of work on the bomb itself. During this meeting Compton asked me to take the responsibility for this work, which at that time consisted of numerous scattered experimental projects. Although I had no administrative experience and was not an experimental physicist, I felt sufficiently informed and challenged by the problem to be glad to accept. At this time I became an employee of the Metallurgical Laboratory.

After this conference I called together a theoretical study group in Berkeley, in which Hans Bethe, Emil Konopinski, Robert Serber, Edward Teller, John H. Van Vleck, and I participated. We had an adventurous time. We spent much of the summer of 1942 in Berkeley in a joint study that for the first time really came to grips with the physical problems of atomic bombs, atomic explosions, and the possibility of using fission explosions to initiate thermonuclear reactions. I called this possibility to the attention of Dr. Vannevar Bush during the late summer; the technical views on this subject were to develop and change from then until the present day.

After these studies there was little doubt that a potentially world-shattering undertaking lay ahead. We began to see the great explosion at Alamogordo[1] and the greater explosions at Eniwetok[2] with a surer foreknowledge. We also began to see how rough, difficult, challenging, and unpredictable this job might turn out to be. . . .

In later summer, after a review of the experimental work, I became convinced, as did others, that a major change was called for in the work on the bomb itself. We needed a central laboratory devoted wholly to this purpose, where people could talk freely with each other, where theoretical ideas and experimental findings could affect each other, where the waste and frustration and error of the many compartmentalized experimental studies could be eliminated, where we could begin to come to grips with chemical, metallurgical, engineering, and ordnance problems that had so far received no consideration. We therefore sought to establish this laboratory for a direct attack on all the problems inherent in the most rapid possible development and production of atomic bombs.

In the autumn of 1942 General Leslie R. Groves assumed charge of the Manhattan Engineer District. I discussed with him the need for an atomic bomb laboratory. There had been some thought of making this laboratory a part of Oak Ridge. For a time there was support for making it a Military Establishment in which key personnel would be commissioned as officers; and in preparation for this course I once went to the Presidio to take the initial steps toward obtaining a commission. After a good deal of discussion with the personnel who would be needed at Los Alamos and with General Groves and his advisers, it was decided that the laboratory should, at least initially, be a civilian establishment in a military post. While this consideration was going on, I had showed General Groves Los Alamos; and he almost immediately took steps to acquire the site.

1. **Alamogordo:** New Mexico site of first detonation of an atomic device.
2. **Eniwetok:** Pacific island used as an atomic test site.

In early 1943, I received a letter signed by General Groves and Dr. James B. Conant, appointing me director of the laboratory, and outlining their conception of how it was to be organized and administered. The necessary construction and assembling of the needed facilities were begun. All of us worked in close colloboration with the engineers of the Manhattan District.

The site of Los Alamos was selected in part at least because it enabled those responsible to balance the obvious need for security with the equally important need of free communication among those engaged in the work. Security, it was hoped, would be achieved by removing the laboratory to a remote area, fenced and patrolled, where communication with the outside was extremely limited. Telephone calls were monitored, mail was censored, and personnel who left the area—something permitted only for the clearest of causes— knew that their movements might be under surveillance. On the other hand, for those within the community, fullest exposition and discussion among those competent to use the information was encouraged.

The last months of 1942 and early 1943 had hardly hours enough to get Los Alamos established. The real problem had to do with getting to Los Alamos the men who would make a success of the undertaking. For this we needed to understand as clearly as we then could what our technical program would be, what men we would need, what facilities, what organization, what plan.

The program of recruitment was massive. Even though we then underestimated the ultimate size of the laboratory, which was to have almost 4,000 members by the spring of 1945, and even though we did not at that time see clearly some of the difficulties which were to bedevil and threaten the enterprise, we knew that it was a big, complex and diverse job. Even the initial plan of the laboratory called for a start with more than 100 highly qualified and trained scientists, to say nothing of the technicians, staff, and mechanics who would be required for their support, and of the equipment that we would have to beg and borrow since there would be no time to build it from scratch. We had to recruit at a time when the country was fully engaged in war and almost every competent scientist was already involved in the military effort.

The primary burden of this fell on me. To recruit staff I traveled all over the country talking with people who had been working on one or another aspect of the atomic-energy enterprise, and people in radar work, for example, and underwater sound, telling them about the job, the place that we were going to, and enlisting their enthusiasm.

In order to bring responsible scientists to Los Alamos, I had to rely on their sense of the interest, urgency, and feasibility of the Los Alamos mission. I had to tell them enough of what the job was, and give strong enough assurance that it might be successfully accomplished in time to affect the outcome of the war, to make it clear that they were justified in their leaving other work to come to this job.

The prospect of coming to Los Alamos aroused great misgivings. It was to be a military post; men were asked to sign up more or less for the duration; restrictions on travel and on the freedom of families to move about to be severe; and no one could be sure of the extent to which the necessary technical freedom of action could actually be maintained by the laboratory. The notion of disappearing into the New Mexico desert for an indeterminate period and under quasi military auspices disturbed a good many scientists, and the families of many more. But there was another side to it. Almost everyone realized that this was a great undertaking. Almost everyone knew that if it were completed successfully and rapidly enough, it might determine the outcome of the war. Almost everyone knew that it was an unparalleled opportunity to bring to bear the basic knowledge and art of science for the benefit of his country. Almost everyone knew that this job, if it were achieved, would be a part of history. This sense of excitement, of devotion and of patriotism in the end prevailed. Most of those with whom I talked came to Los Alamos. Once they came, confidence in the enterprise grew as men learned more of the technical status of the work; and though the laboratory was to double and redouble its size many times before the end, once it had started it was on the road to success.

We had information in those days of German activity in the field of nuclear fission. We were aware of what it might mean if they beat us to the draw in the development of atomic bombs. The consensus of all our opinions, and every directive that I had, stressed the extreme urgency of our work, as well as the need for guarding all knowledge of it from our enemies. . . .

The story of Los Alamos is long and complex. Part of it is public history. For me it was a time so filled with work, with the need for decision and action and consultation, that there was room for little else. I lived with my family in the community which was Los Alamos. It was a remarkable community, inspired by a high sense of mission, of duty and of destiny, coherent, dedicated, and remarkably selfless. There was plenty in the life of Los Alamos to cause irritation; the security restrictions, many of my own devising, the inadequacies and inevitable fumblings of a military post unlike any that had ever existed before, shortages, inequities and in the laboratory itself the shifting emphasis on different aspects of the technical work as the program moved forward; but I have never known a group more understanding and more devoted to a common purpose, more willing to lay aside personal convenience and prestige, more understanding of the role that they were playing in their country's history. Time and again we had in the technical work almost paralyzing crises. Time and again the laboratory drew itself together and faced the new problems and got on with the work. We worked by night and by day; and in the end the many jobs were done. . . .

SPEECH TO THE ASSOCIATION
OF LOS ALAMOS SCIENTISTS

Los Alamos, November 2, 1945

I am grateful to the Executive Committee for this chance to talk to you. I should like to talk tonight—if some of you have long memories perhaps you will regard it as justified—as a fellow scientist, and at least as a fellow worrier about the fix

Alice Kimball Smith and Charles Weiher, eds., *Robert Oppenheimer: Letters and Recollections* (Cambridge: Harvard University Press, 1980), pp. 315–20, 324–25.

we are in. I do not have anything very radical to say, or anything that will strike most of you with a great flash of enlightenment. I don't have anything to say that will be of an immense encouragement. In some ways I would have liked to talk to you at an earlier date—but I couldn't talk to you as a Director. I could not talk, and will not tonight talk, too much about the practical political problems which are involved. . . . I don't think that's important. I think there are issues which are quite simple and quite deep, and which involve us as a group of scientists—involve us more, perhaps than any other group in the world. I think that it can only help to look a little at what our situation is—at what has happened to us—and that this must give us some honesty, some insight, which will be a source of strength in what may be the not-too-easy days ahead.

The real impact of the creation of the atomic bomb and atomic weapons—to understand that one has to look further back, look, I think, to the times when physical science was growing in the days of the renaissance, and when the threat that science offered was felt so deeply throughout the Christian world. The analogy is, of course, not perfect. You may even wish to think of the days in the last century when the theories of evolution seemed a threat to the values by which men lived. The analogy is not perfect because there is nothing in atomic weapons—there is certainly nothing that we have done here or in the physics or chemistry that immediately preceded our work here—in which any revolutionary ideas were involved. I don't think that the conceptions of nuclear fission have strained any man's attempts to understand them, and I don't feel that any of us have really learned in a deep sense very much from following this up. It is in a quite different way. It is not an idea—it is a development and a reality—but it has in common with the early days of physical science the fact that the very existence of science is threatened, and its value is threatened. This is the point that I would like to speak a little about.

I think that it hardly needs to be said why the impact is so strong. There are three reasons: one is the extraordinary speed with which things which were right on the frontier of science were translated into terms where they affected many living people, and potentially all people. Another is the fact, quite accidental in many ways, and connected with the speed, that scientists themselves played such a large part, not merely in providing the foundation for atomic weapons, but in actually making them. In this we are certainly closer to it than any other group. The third is that the thing we made—partly because of the technical nature of the problem, partly because we worked hard, partly because we had good breaks—really arrived in the world with such a shattering reality and suddenness that there was no opportunity for the edges to be worn off.

But when you come right down to it the reason that we did this job is because it was an organic necessity. If you are a scientist you cannot stop such a thing. If you are a scientist you believe that it is good to find out how the world works; that it is good to find out what the realities are; that it is good to turn over to mankind at large the greatest possible power to control the world and to deal with it according to its rights and its values.

There are many people who try to wiggle out of this. They say the real importance of atomic energy does not lie in the weapons that have been made; the real importance lies in all the great benefits which atomic energy, which the various radiations, will bring to mankind. There may be some truth in this. I am sure that there is truth in it, because there has never in the past been a new field opened up where the real fruits of it have not been invisible at the beginning. I have a very high confidence that the fruits—the so-called peacetime applications—of atomic energy will have in them all that we think, and more. There are others who try to escape the immediacy of this situation by saying that, after all, war has always been very terrible; after all, weapons have always gotten worse and worse; that this is just another weapon and it doesn't create a great change; that they are not so bad; bombings have been bad in this war and this is not a change in that—it just adds a little to the effectiveness of bombing; that some sort of protection will be found. I think that these efforts to diffuse and weaken the nature of the crisis make it only more dangerous. I think it is for us to accept it as a very grave crisis, to realize that these atomic weapons which we have started to make are very terrible, that they involve a change, that they are not just a slight modification: to accept this, and to accept with it the necessity for those transformations in the world which will make it possible to integrate these developments into human life.

. . . It is a new field, in which the position of vested interests in various parts of the world is very much less serious than in others. It is serious in this country, and that is one of our problems. It is a new field, in which the role of science has been so great that it is to my mind hardly thinkable that the international traditions of science, and the fraternity of scientists, should not play a constructive part. It is a new field, in which just the novelty and the special characteristics of the technical operations should enable one to establish a community of interest which might almost be regarded as a pilot plant for a new type of international collaboration. I speak of it as a pilot plant because it is quite clear that the control of atomic weapons cannot be in itself the unique end of such operation. The only unique end can be a world that is united, and a world in which war will not occur. But those things don't happen overnight, and in this field it would seem that one could get started, and get started without meeting those insuperable obstacles which history has so often placed in the way of any effort of cooperation. Now, this is not an easy thing, and the point I want to make, the one point I want to hammer home, is what an enormous change in spirit is involved. There are things which we hold very dear, and I think rightly hold very dear; I would say that the word democracy perhaps stood for some of them as well as any other word. There are many parts of the world in which there is no democracy. There are other things which we hold dear, and which we rightly should. And when I speak of a new spirit in international affairs I mean that even to these deepest of things which we cherish, and for which Americans have been willing to die—and certainly most of us would be willing to die—even in these deepest things, we realize that there is something more profound than that; namely, the common bond with other men everywhere. It is only if you do that that this makes sense; because if you approach the problem and say, "We know what is right and we would like to use the atomic bomb to persuade you to agree with us," then you are in a very weak position and you will not succeed, because under those conditions you will not succeed in delegating responsibility for the survival of men. It is a purely unilateral statement; you will find yourselves attempting by force of arms to prevent a disaster.

I don't have very much more to say. There are a few things which scientists perhaps should remember, that I don't think I need to remind us of; but I will, anyway. One is that they are very often called upon to give technical information in one way or another, and I think one cannot be too careful to be honest. And it is very difficult, not because one tells lies, but because so often questions are put in a form which makes it very hard to give an answer which is not misleading. I think we will be in a very weak position unless we maintain at its highest the scrupulousness which is traditional for us in sticking to the truth, and in distinguishing between what we know to be true from what we hope may be true.

The second thing I think it right to speak of is this: it is everywhere felt that the fraternity between us and scientists in other countries may be one of the most helpful things for the future; yet it is apparent that even in this country not all of us who are scientists are in agreement. There is no harm in that; such disagreement is healthy. But we must not lose the sense of fraternity because of it; we must not lose our fundamental confidence in our fellow scientists.

I think that we have no hope at all if we yield in our belief in the value of science, in the good that it can be to the world to know about reality, about nature, to attain a gradually greater and greater control of nature, to learn, to teach, to understand. I think that if we lose our faith in this we stop being scientists, we sell out our heritage, we lose what we have most of value for this time of crisis.

But there is another thing: we are not only scientists; we are men, too. We cannot forget our dependence on our fellow men. I mean not only our material dependence, without which no science would be possible, and without which we could not work; I mean also our deep moral dependence, in that the value of science must lie in the world of men, that all our roots lie there. These are the strongest bonds in the world, stronger than those even that bind us to one another, these are the deepest bonds — that bind us to our fellow men.

FOR CRITICAL THINKING

1. Joseph Rothblat, a Polish scientist recruited to work at Los Alamos, insisted on leaving the project at the end of 1944 when it became apparent that there was no danger of any other nation's building a nuclear weapon before the United States. What do you think of his decision? Should other scientists have followed his lead? Why or why not?

2. What are the dangers to scientists and scientific research posed by the sort of secrecy under which work at Los Alamos was done? Did this set a dangerous precedent for the future? Should scientists agree to do work that cannot be freely published? Does this violate a central ethic of science?

3. What role should scientists play in influencing public policies that directly stem from their work, such as the policy regarding the use of nuclear weapons? What similar issues are important today and what role should scientists play in them?

31

Rosie the Riveter
Fanny Christina Hill

In 1940, 11.5 million women were employed outside the home, principally single women, widows, and wives from poor families. African American women like Fanny Christina Hill expected to work in whatever jobs were available to them—most commonly domestic service. World War II brought massive needs for additional labor. Millions of men were under arms and the United States, billing itself the "Arsenal of Democracy" for the Allied forces, strove for giant increases in the production of planes, ships, trucks, tanks, armaments, food and clothing, and all the other supplies that fuel a major war. On Columbus Day 1942, President Franklin D. Roosevelt called for a new attitude in the workplace: "In some communities employers dislike to hire women. In others they are reluctant to hire Negroes. We can no longer afford to indulge such prejudices." Soon women like Fanny Hill shifted from "women's jobs" to defense work, prompting women who previously had not worked into these new roles as well.

War production peaked in 1944. By the middle of that year, a reverse pressure on women to return to the home as soon as the war ended had begun. Defense plant newspapers replaced features on women production workers with "cheesecake" contests. Tales of neglected children became a theme of popular journalism. Yet 75 percent of women surveyed in 1944 and 1945 expressed the desire to continue working after the war. A cultural battle had begun that would outlast the war.

BEFORE YOU READ

1. How was Fanny Christina Hill's life affected by her work during the war?
2. Why did she continue working after the war? Was she influenced by the pressure to cease working after the war?
3. What examples of prejudice affecting her life do you find? How did she deal with them?

I'll never forget, my grandmother on my father's side was telling me that she was a little girl when the slaves was freed. The master's wife told her mother, which was my great-grandmother, "Nancy, now you come in the house and you get you some of the dishes and things because you're going to have to be keeping house of your own and I want you to have something that you're familiar with." She gave my great-grandmother that bowl. That thing is over a hundred years old, passed down from one family to the other. My great-grandmother gave it to her girl, which was my grandmother; my father was next and then I'm next; then Beverly and then the little baby.

Sherna Berger Gluck, *Rosie the Riveter Revisited* (Boston: Twayne, 1987), pp. 28–33, 35–38, 40–45, 48–49.

My great-grandfather was named Crawford and he went by his own name; he didn't use the master's name. He was working as a carpenter during the slavery time, and he did all the building around the plantation. He had saved enough money to buy his freedom and he had half enough to buy his wife's freedom and then he was going to buy his little girl's freedom, which was my grandmother. But then they came along and freed the slaves, so he didn't have to buy them. He took that money and bought seventy acres of land right off of the plantation. He built them a house and they farmed that little seventy acres.

My mother didn't come from this same group of people. I don't know too much about her parents because she doesn't know too much about them herself. She said they was cousins to the ones up there where my grandmother lived. The white people was almost like the Negroes: if they wasn't kin by marriage, they was kin by blood. So they were sort of the same kin in there somehow or the other. My mother was a very light-skinned woman and I know she got a lot of favors just by being that. From the black people, as well. She was almost as light as my grandbaby. And you see how dark I am? Because my father was dark.

She married my father when she was about sixteen, so from about sixteen until, oh, about thirty—I think that's how old she was when my father died. Then she was out there on her own with five children: one boy and four girls. I'm the youngest. I was born January 9, 1918.

My father was supposed to have been a farmer, but he just got by by doing a little bit of nothing. Some men are like that. Mama went to work and supported us the best she could. There were times we wouldn't have anything to eat if Mama hadn't gone to work. That's why you talk about women liberation and women go out to work? The black woman has worked all of her life and she really was the first one to go out to work and know how to make ends meet, because it was forced on her.

My mother worked for this lady. . . . This lady thought so much of my mama and she treated us fairly good. She always looked after me. A lot of times I didn't go home. I slept right beside the fireplace at night to keep warm. Mama said I was just like she left me: when she'd come back the next morning, I would be right there. Sometimes I'd have the same diaper on and sometimes I wouldn't. So you often think about white people not being nice to you, but that woman changed my diapers. Nevertheless, my mama was her servant.

I decided I wanted to make more money, and I went to a little small town—Tyler, Texas. . . . And the only thing I could do there for a living was domestic work and it didn't pay very much. So I definitely didn't like it.

But I left Tyler. I was saying, "I don't like it here because you can't make any money." I discovered I didn't have any trade. I had nothing I could do other than just that, and that wasn't what I wanted. So I decided I'd better get out of this town. I didn't like Dallas because that was too rough. Then someone told me, "Well, why don't you try California?" So then I got Los Angeles in my mind. I was twenty and I saved my money till I was twenty-one. In August 1940, I came here.

When I first came, when my aunt met me down at the station, I had less then ten dollars. I went on to her house and stayed. In less than ten days I had found a job living on the place doing domestic work. I stayed there from some time in August until Christmas. I was making thirty-five dollars a month. That was so much better than what I was making at home, which was twelve dollars a month. I saved my money and I bought everybody a Christmas present and sent it. Oh, I was the happiest thing in the world!

I liked to go on outings a lot. So when I first came to California, when I'd have my day off, I'd go to the parks and to the beach and museum. Just go sightseeing; walking and look in the windows. Sometimes my aunt would go along with me or I'd find another girlfriend. But then I had a sister here pretty soon.

Los Angeles was a large city but I adjusted to it real well. It didn't take me long to find a way about it. I knew how to get around, and I knew how to stay out of danger and not take too many chances. I read the *Eagle* and I still get the *Sentinel* once in a while. [The *California Eagle* and the *Los Angeles Sentinel* were local black newspapers.] I have to get it to keep up with what the black people are doing. I used to read those papers when I was a child back home. That's what give me a big idea. I used to read a little paper called the *Kansas City Call*, and they had a *Pittsburgh Courier* that all the Negroes read.

[She returns to Texas to get married.] I stayed there for about nine months until he went into the service. Then I came to Los Angeles. I told my sister, "Well, I better get me a good job around here working in a hotel or motel or something. I want to get me a good job so when the war is over, I'll have it." And she said, "No, you just come on out and go in the war plants and work and maybe you'll make enough money where you won't have to work in the hotels or motels." . . .

I don't remember what day of the week it was, but I guess I must have started out pretty early that morning. When I went there, the man didn't hire me. They had a school down here on Figueroa and he told me to go to the school. I went down and it was almost four o'clock and they told me they'd hire me. You had to fill out a form. They didn't bother too much about your experience because they knew you didn't have any experience in aircraft. Then they give you some kind of little test where you put the pegs in the right hole.

There were other people in there, kinda mixed. I assume it was more women than men. Most of the men was gone, and they weren't hiring too many men unless they had a good excuse. Most of the women was in my bracket, five or six years younger or older. I was twenty-four. There was a black girl that hired in with me. I went to work the next day, sixty cents an hour.

I think I stayed at the school for about four weeks. They only taught you shooting and bucking rivets and how to drill the holes and to file. You had to use a hammer for certain things. After a couple of whiles, you worked on the real thing. But you were supervised so you didn't make a mess.

When we went into the plant, it wasn't too much different than down at the school. It was the same amount of noise; it was the same routine. One difference was there was just so many more people, and when you went in the door you had a badge to show and they looked at your lunch. I had gotten accustomed to a lot of people and I knew if it was a lot of people, it always meant something was going on. I got carried away: "As long as there's a lot of people here, I'll be making money." That was all I could ever see.

I was a good student, if I do say so myself. But I have found out through life, sometimes even if you're good, you just don't get the breaks if the color's not right. I could see where they made a difference in placing you in certain jobs. They had fifteen or twenty departments, but all the Negroes went to Department 17 because there was nothing but shooting and bucking rivets. You stood on one side of the panel and your partner stood on this side, and he would shoot the rivets with a gun and you'd buck them with the bar. That was about the size of it. I just didn't like it. I didn't think I could stay there with all this shooting and a'bucking and a'jumping and a'bumping. I stayed in it about two or three weeks and then I just decided I did *not* like that. I went and told my foreman and he didn't do anything about it, so I decided I'd leave.

While I was standing out on the railroad track, I ran into somebody else out there fussing also. I went over to the union and they told me what to do. I went back inside and they sent me to another department where you did bench work and I liked that much better. You had a little small jig that you would work on and you just drilled out holes. Sometimes you would rout them or you would scribe them and then you'd cut them with a cutters.

I must have stayed there nearly a year, and then they put me over in another department, "Plastics." It was the tail section of the B-Bomber, the Billy Mitchell Bomber. I put a little part in the gun-sight. You had a little ratchet set and you would screw it in there. Then I cleaned the top of the glass off and put a piece of paper over it to seal it off to go to the next section. I worked over there until the end of the war. Well, not quite the end, because I got pregnant, and while I was off having the baby the war was over.

Some weeks I brought home twenty-six dollars, some weeks sixteen dollars. Then it gradually went up to thirty dollars, then it went up a little bit more and a little bit more. And I learned somewhere along the line that in order to make a good move you gotta make some money. You don't make the same amount everyday. You have some days good, sometimes bad. Whatever you make you're supposed to save some. I was also getting that fifty dollars a month from my husband and that was just saved right away. I was planning on buying a home and a car. And I was going to go back to school. My husband came back, but I never was laid off, so I just never found it necessary to look for another job or to go to school for another job.

I was still living over on Compton Avenue with my sister in this small little back house when my husband got home. Then, when Beverly was born, my sister moved in the front house and we stayed in the back house. When he came back, he looked for a job in the cleaning and pressing place, which was just plentiful. All the people had left these cleaning and pressing jobs and every other job; they was going to the defense plant to work because they was paying good. But in the meantime he was getting the same thing the people out there was getting, $1.25 an hour. That's why he didn't bother to go out to North American. But what we both weren't thinking about was that they did have better benefits because they did have an insurance plan and a union to back you up. Later he did come to work there, in 1951 or 1952.

I worked up until the end of March and then I took off. Beverly was born the twenty-first of June. I'd planned to come back somewhere in the last of August. I went to verify the fact that I did come back, so that did go on my record that I didn't just quit. But they laid off a lot of people, most of them, because the war was over.

It didn't bother me much—not thinking about it jobwise. I was just glad that the war was over. I didn't feel bad because my husband had a job and he also was eligible to go to school with his GI bill. So I really didn't have too many plans—which I wish I had had. I would have tore out page one and fixed it differently; put my version of page one in there.

I went and got me a job doing day work. That means you go to a person's house and clean up for one day out of the week and then you go to the next one and clean up. I did that a couple of times and I discovered I didn't like that so hot. Then I got me a job downtown working in a little factory where you do weaving—burned clothes and stuff like that. I learned to do that real good. It didn't pay too much but it paid enough to get me going, seventy-five cents or about like that.

When North American called me back, was I a happy soul! I dropped that job and went back. That was a dollar an hour. So, from sixty cents an hour, when I first hired in there, up to one dollar. That wasn't traveling fast, but it was better than anything else because you had hours to work by and you had benefits and you come home at night with your family. So it was a good deal.

It made me live better. I really did. We always say that Lincoln took the bale off of the Negroes. I think there is a statue up there in Washington, D.C., where he's lifting something off the Negro. Well, my sister always said—that's why you can't interview her because she's so radical—"Hitler was the one that got us out of the white folks' kitchen."

[She recalls the discrimination faced by black workers at North American Aircraft.] But they had to fight. They fought hand, tooth, and nail to get in there. And the first five or six Negroes who went in there, they were well educated, but they started them off as janitors. After they once got their foot in the door and was there for three months—you work for three months before they say you're hired—then they had to start fighting all over again to get off of that broom and get something decent. And some of them did.

But they'd always give that Negro man the worst part of everything. See, the jobs have already been tested and tried out before they ever get into the department, and they know what's good about them and what's bad about them. They always managed to give the worst one to the Negro. The only reason why the women fared better was they just couldn't quite give the woman as tough a job that they gave the men. But sometimes they did.

There were some departments, they didn't even allow a black person to walk through there let alone work in there. Some of the white people did not want to work with the Negro. They had arguments right there. Sometimes they would get fired and walk on out the door, but it was one more white person gone. I think even to this very day in certain places they still don't want to work with the Negro. I don't know what their story is, but if they would try then they might not knock it.

But they did everything they could to keep you separated. They just did not like for a Negro and a white person to get together and talk. Now I am a person that you can talk to and you will warm up to me much better than you can a lot of people. A white person seems to know that they could talk to me at ease. And when anyone would start—just plain, common talk, everyday talk—they didn't like it.

And they'd keep you from advancing. They always manage to give the Negroes the worst end of the deal. I happened to fall into that when they get ready to transfer you from one department to the next. That was the only thing that I ever ran into that I had to holler to the union about. And once I filed a complaint downtown with the Equal Opportunity.

The way they was doing this particular thing—they always have a lean spot where they're trying to lay off or go through there and see if they can curl out a bunch of people, get rid of the ones with the most seniority, I suppose. They had a good little system going. All the colored girls had more seniority in production than the whites because the average white woman did not come back after the war. They thought like I thought: that I have a husband now and I don't have to work and this was just only for the war and blah, blah, blah. But they didn't realize they was going to need the money. The average Negro was glad to come back because it meant more money than they was making before. So we always had more seniority in production than the white woman.

All the colored women in production, they was just one step behind the other. I had three months more than one, the next one had three months more than me, and that's the way it went. So they had a way of putting us all in Blueprint. We all had twenty years by the time you got in Blueprint and stayed a little while. Here come another one. He'd bump you out and then you went out the door, because they couldn't find nothing else for you to do—so they said. They just kept doing it and I could see myself: "Well, hell, I'm going to be the next one to go out the door!"

So I found some reason to file a grievance. I tried to get several other girls: "Let's get together and go downtown and file a grievance" [a discrimination complaint with the Equal Opportunities Employment Commission]. I only got two girls to go with me. That made three of us. I think we came out on top, because we all kept our jobs and then they stopped sending them to Blueprint, bumping each other like that. So, yeah, we've had to fight to stay there.

When I bought my house in '49 or '48, I went a little further on the other side of Slauson, and I drove up and down the street a couple of times. I saw one colored woman there. I went in and asked her about the neighborhood. She said there was only one there, but there was another one across the street. So I was the third one moved in there. I said, "Well, we's breaking into the neighborhood."

I don't know how long we was there, but one evening, just about dusk, here comes this woman banging on my door. I had never seen her before. She says, "I got a house over here for sale, you can tell your friends that they can buy it if they want to." I thought to myself, "What in the hell is that woman thinking about?" She was mad because she discovered I was there. Further down, oh, about two streets down, somebody burned a cross on a lawn.

Then, one Sunday evening, I don't know what happened, but they saw a snake in the yard next door to us. Some white people were staying there and the yard was so junky, I tell you. Here come the snake. We must have been living there a good little while, because Beverly was old enough to bring the gun. Everybody was looking and they had a stick or something. I don't know how, but that child came strutting out there with the gun to shoot the snake. My husband shot the snake and from that point on, everybody respected us— 'cause they knew he had a gun and could use it.

I was talking to a white person about the situation and he said, "Next time you get ready to move in a white neighborhood, I'll tell you what you do. The first thing you do when you pull up there in the truck, you jump out with your guns. You hold them up high in the air." He says, "If you don't have any, borrow some or rent 'em, but be sure that they see you got a gun. Be sure one of them is a shotgun and you go in there with it first. They going to be peeping out the window, don't you worry about it. They going to see you. But if they see those guns going in first, they won't ever bother you."

I did like he said, moved in here with some guns, and nobody come and bothered me. Nobody said one word to me.

Working at North American was good. I did make more money and I did meet quite a few people that I am still friends with. I learned quite a bit. Some of the things, I wouldn't want to go back over. If I had the wisdom to know the difference which one to change and which one not to, I would. I would have fought harder at North American for better things for myself.

I don't have too many regrets. But if I had it to do over again, if I had to tamper with page one, I would sure get a better education. I would never have stopped going to school. I took several little classes every so often—cosmetology, photography, herbs. For a little while, I did study nursing. I would have finished some of them. I would have went deeper into it.

We always talking about women's lib and working. Well, we all know that the Negro woman was the first woman that left home to go to work. She's been working ever since because she had to work beside her husband in slavery—against her will. So she has always worked. She knows how to get out there and work. She has really pioneered the field. Then after we've gotten out here and proved that it can be done, then the white woman decided: "Hey, I don't want to stay home and do nothing." She zeroed in on the best jobs. So we're still on the tail-end, but we still back there fighting.

32

Memories of the Internment Camp
Ben Yorita and Philip Hayasaka

During World War II, the United States was more careful about protecting the civil liberties of its citizens than it had been after its entrance into World War I. There was, however, one glaring exception: the internment of 110,000 Japanese Americans in camps euphemistically called "relocation centers." (A similar attempt to relocate Italian and German Americans from areas along the West Coast was quickly recognized as impractical and soon abandoned.) The military director of the internment program declared that the "Japanese race is an enemy race and while many second and third generation Japanese born on United States soil, possessed of United States Citizenship, have become Americanized, the racial strains are undiluted. . . . It, therefore, follows that along the vital Pacific coast over 112,000 potential enemies, of Japanese extraction, are at large today." These people, seventy thousand of them native-born citizens of the United States, were forced to evacuate their homes within forty-eight hours (losing about $500 million in property along with their jobs) and made to live for long periods of time in tar-papered barracks behind barbed wire.

The Supreme Court of the United States, in two major decisions, supported the constitutionality of internment. Justice Robert Jackson warned in a dissenting opinion that the case established a precedent that "lays about like a loaded weapon." In 1988, however, Congress, in recognition of the wrong that the government inflicted, appropriated compensation for internees.

This reading, from interviews conducted by Archie Satterfield in the 1970s, is about the experience of two Japanese Americans who had suffered through this mockery of American justice.

BEFORE YOU READ

1. What were the main fears aroused among Japanese Americans by the internment?
2. What did Japanese Americans lose by the internment?
3. What were the chief effects on Japanese Americans of the internment?
4. Compare the treatment of Japanese Americans in the United States with that of Jews in Germany. What was similar? What was different?

BEN YORITA

"Students weren't as aware of national politics then as they are now, and Japanese-Americans were actually apolitical then. Our parents couldn't vote, so we simply weren't interested in politics because there was nothing we could do about it if we were.

"There were two reasons we were living in the ghettos: Birds of a feather flock together, and we had all the traditional aspects of Japanese life—Japanese restaurants, baths, and so forth; and discrimination forced us together. The dominant society prevented us from going elsewhere.

"Right after Pearl Harbor we had no idea what was going to happen, but toward the end of December we started hearing rumors and talk of the evacuation started. We could tell from what we read in the newspapers and the propaganda they were printing—guys like Henry McLemore, who said he hated all Japs and that we should be rounded up, gave us the idea of how strong feelings were against us. So we were expecting something and the evacuation was no great surprise.

"I can't really say what my parents thought about everything because we didn't communicate that well. I never asked them what they thought. We communicated on other things, but not political matters.

"Once the evacuation was decided, we were told we had about a month to get rid of our property or do whatever we wanted to with it. That was a rough time for my brother, who was running a printshop my parents owned. We were still in debt on it and we didn't know what to do with all the equipment. The machines were old but still workable, and we had English type and Japanese type. Japanese characters had to be set by hand and were very hard to replace. Finally, the whole works was sold, and since nobody would buy the Japanese type, we had to sell it as junk lead at 50¢ a pound. We sold the equipment through newspaper classified ads: 'Evacuating: Household goods for sale.' Second-hand dealers and everybody else came in and bought our refrigerator, the piano, and I had a whole bunch of books I sold for $5, which was one of my personal losses. We had to sell our car, and the whole thing was very sad. By the way, it was the first time we had ever had a refrigerator and it had to be sold after only a few months.

"We could take only what we could carry, and most of us were carrying two suitcases or duffel bags. The rest of our stuff that we couldn't sell was stored in the Buddhist church my mother belonged to. When we came back, thieves had broken in and stolen almost everything of value from the church.

"I had a savings account that was left intact, but people who had their money in the Japanese bank in Seattle had their assets frozen from Pearl Harbor until the late 1960s, when the funds were finally released. They received no interest.

"They took all of us down to the Puyallup fairgrounds, Camp Harmony, and everything had been thrown together in haste. They had converted some of the display and exhibit areas into rooms and had put up some barracks on the parking lot. The walls in the barracks were about eight feet high with open space above and with big knotholes in the boards of the partitions. Our family was large, so we had two rooms.

"They had also built barbed-wire fences around the camp with a tower on each corner with military personnel and machine guns, rifles, and searchlights. It was terrifying because we didn't know what was going to happen to us. We didn't know where we were going and we were just doing what we were told. No questions asked. If you get an order, you go ahead and do it.

"There was no fraternization, no contact with the military or any Caucasian except when we were processed into the camp. But the treatment in Camp Harmony was fairly loose in the sense that we were free to roam around in the camp. But it was like buffalo in cages or behind barbed wire.

"There was no privacy whatsoever in the latrines and showers, and it was humiliating for the women because they were much more modest then than today. It wasn't so bad for the men because they were accustomed to open latrines and showers.

"We had no duties in the sense that we were required to work, but you can't expect a camp to manage itself. They had jobs open in the kitchen and stock room, and eventually they opened a school where I helped teach a little. I wasn't a qualified teacher, and I got about $13 a month. We weren't given an allowance while we were in Camp Harmony waiting for the camp at Minidoka to be finished, so it was pretty tight for some families.

"From Camp Harmony on, the family structure was broken down. Children ran everywhere they wanted to in the camp, and parents lost their authority. We could eat in any mess hall we wanted, and kids began ignoring their parents and wandering wherever they pleased.

"Eventually they boarded us on army trucks and took us to trains to be transported to the camps inland. We had been in Camp Harmony from May until September. There was a shortage of transportation at the time and they brought out these old, rusty cars with gaslight fixtures. As soon as we got aboard we pulled the shades down so people couldn't stare at us. The cars were all coaches and we had to sit all the way to camp, which was difficult for some of the older people and the invalids. We made makeshift beds out of the seats for them, and did the best we could.

"When we got to Twin Falls, we were loaded onto trucks again, and we looked around and all we could see was that vast desert with nothing but sagebrush. When the trucks started rolling, it was dusty, and the camp itself wasn't completed yet. The barracks had been built and the kitchen facilities were there, but the laundry room, showers, and latrines were not finished. They had taken a bulldozer in the good old American style and leveled the terrain and then built the camp. When the wind blew, it was dusty and we had to wear face masks to go to the dining hall. When winter came and it rained, the dust turned into gumbo mud. Until the latrines were finished, we had to use outhouses.

"The administrators were civilians and they tried to organize us into a chain of command to make the camp function. Each block of barracks was told to appoint a representative, who were called block managers. Of course we called them the Blockheads.

"When winter came, it was very cold and I began withdrawing my savings to buy clothes because we had none that was suitable for that climate. Montgomery Ward and Sears Roebuck did a landslide business from the camps because we ordered our shoes and warm clothing from them. The people who didn't have savings suffered quite a bit until the camp distributed navy pea coats. Then everybody in camp was wearing outsize pea coats because we were such small people. Other than army blankets, I don't remember any other clothing issues.

"The barracks were just single-wall construction and the only insulation was tar paper nailed on the outside, and they never were improved. The larger rooms had potbellied stoves, and we all slept on army cots. Only the people over sixty years old were able to get metal cots, which had a bit more spring to them than the army cots, which were just stationary hammocks.

"These camps were technically relocation centers and there was no effort to hold us in them, but they didn't try actively to relocate us until much later. On my own initiative I tried to get out as soon as I could, and started writing letters to friends around the country. I found a friend in Salt Lake City who agreed to sponsor me for room and board, and he got his boss to agree to hire me. I got out in May 1943, which was earlier than most. In fact, I was one of the first to leave Minidoka.

"Of course I had to get clearance from Washington, D. C., and they investigated my background. I had to pay my own way from Twin Falls to Salt Lake City, but after I left, the government had a program of per diem for people leaving.

"I got on the bus with my suitcase, all by myself, my first time in the outside world, and paid my fare and began looking for a seat, then this old guy said: 'Hey, Tokyo, sit next to me.'

"I thought, Oh, my God, Tokyo! I sat next to him and he was a friendly old guy who meant well."

Yorita's friend worked in a parking garage across the street from the Mormon tabernacle, and the garage owner let them live in the office, where the two young men cooked their own meals. One nearby grocery-store owner wouldn't let them buy from him, and a barber in the neighborhood hated them on sight. Yorita parked a car once that had a rifle and pair of binoculars in the back seat, and he and his friend took the binoculars out and were looking through them when the barber looked out and saw them studying the Mormon tabernacle. He called the FBI, and two agents were soon in the garage talking to the young men.

Yorita wasn't satisfied with his job in Salt Lake City, and soon left for Cincinnati, then Chicago, which he enjoyed because most Chicago people didn't care what nationality he was. He and a brother were able to find good jobs and a good place to live, and they brought their parents out of the Idaho camp to spend the rest of the war in Chicago.

PHILIP HAYASAKA

Philip Hayasaka was a teen-ager when Pearl Harbor was attacked. Unlike most Japanese-Americans, his parents had been able to find a home in a predominantly Caucasian neighborhood because his father was a wholesale produce dealer and most of his business was conducted with Caucasians. Consequently, when the family was interned, Hayasaka was a stranger to most of the other families.

Still, he and his family understood well the rationale of the Little Tokyos along the West Coast.

"If you could become invisible, you could get along. We were forced into a situation of causing no trouble, of being quiet, not complaining. It was not a matter of our stoic tradition. I've never bought that. We did what we had to do to survive.

"There was a lot of hysteria at the time, a lot of confusion, and the not knowing what was going to happen created such a fear that we became supercautious. We would hear that the FBI was going into different houses and searching, and we would wonder when they were coming to our house. We just knew that they were going to come and knock on the door and that we wouldn't know what to do when they came.

"A lot of people were burning things that didn't need to be burned, but they were afraid suspicion would be attached to those things. All those wonderful old calligraphies were destroyed, priceless things, because they thought someone in authority would believe they represented allegiance to Japan. One time I was with my mother in the house, just the two of us, and there was a knock on the door. My mother had those rosary-type beads that the Buddhists use for prayer, and she put them in my pocket and sent me outside to play and stay out until whoever was at the door left. She was afraid it was the FBI and they would take them away from us. It sounds silly now, but that kind of fear was pervasive then. It was tragic.

"When this happened, my dad's business went to hell. Suddenly all his accounts payable were due immediately, but all the accounts receivable weren't. People knew the guy wasn't going to be around much longer, so they didn't pay him. I knew at one time how much he lost that way—we had to turn in a claim after the war—but I've forgotten now. But it was a considerable amount. Those claims, by the way, didn't give justice to the victims; it only legitimized the government. We got about a nickel on the dollar.

"It was kind of interesting how different people reacted when they came to Camp Harmony to see friends, and how we reacted in return. Friends from Seattle would come down to see me, and we had to talk through the barbed-wire fences. [Note: Nobody was permitted to stand closer than three feet to the fence, which meant conversations were held at least six feet from each other, with people standing and watching.] There was one instance when I saw a close friend from high school just outside the fence, and he had come down to see me. He hadn't seen me inside, so I hid rather than going out to see him. The whole evacuation did funny things to your mind.

"All the leaders of the community were taken away, and my dad was interned before we were and taken to the interrogation camp in Missoula. It was one of the greatest shocks of my life when the FBI came and picked him up. Here was a guy who had followed all the rules, respected authority, and was a leader in the company. And all of the sudden he was behind bars for no reason. He stayed there several months before they let him join us at Minidoka."

When the war ended and the camps were closed, about the only people left in them were young children and the elderly. All who could leave for jobs did so, and the experience had a scattering effect on the Japanese-American communities across the Pacific Coast. Several families settled on the East Coast and in the Midwest, and when those with no other place to go, or who didn't want to migrate away from the Coast, returned to their hometowns, they usually found their former ghettos taken over by other minority groups. Consequently, whether they wanted to or not, they were forced to find housing wherever it was available. It was difficult returning to the cities, however. Everybody dreaded it, and some of the elderly people with no place to go of their own were virtually evacuated from the camps. They had become accustomed to the life there and were afraid to leave.

Some Caucasians, such as Floyd Schmoe and the Reverend Emory Andrews, worked with the returning outcasts to help them resettle as smoothly as possible. A few farms had been saved for the owners, but four years of weeds and brush had accumulated. Schmoe was back teaching at the University of Washington by that time, and he organized groups of his students to go out on weekends and after school to help clear the land for crops again. Some people returning found their former neighbors had turned against them in their absence, and grocery-store owners who had become Jap-haters during the war would not sell them food.

The farmers who did get their crops growing again were often so discriminated against that they could not sell their produce, or get it delivered into the marketplace. Schmoe was able to solve this problem for one farmer by talking a neighbor, a Filipino, into taking the Japanese-American's produce and selling it as his own. Hayasaka's father was able to get back into the wholesale produce business by becoming partners with a young Japanese-American veteran of the famed 442d Regiment, the most highly decorated group in the war. The veteran put up a sign over the office saying the business was operated by a veteran, which made it difficult for buyers to avoid it.

BEN YORITA

"The older people never recovered from the camps. The father was the traditional breadwinner and in total command of the family. But after going into the camps, fathers were no longer the breadwinners; the young sons and daughters were. Most of them couldn't even communicate in English, so all the burdens fell on the second generation. And most of us were just kids, nineteen or twenty. Consequently there was a big turnover of responsibility and authority, and the parents were suddenly totally dependent on their children. When we returned to the cities after the war, it was the second generation again that had to make the decisions and do all the negotiating with landlords, attorneys, and the like."

33

The Bataan Death March
Blair Robinett et al.

In the months immediately after the attack on Pearl Harbor—as Japanese Americans were being herded into internment camps—the Axis powers seemed nearly invincible. Hitler's armies threatened Moscow and the Suez Canal while his submarine navy was sinking British and American ships far more rapidly than they could be replaced: nearly seven hundred fifty thousand tons a month. In the Pacific, Japan captured the key British naval base of Singapore as well as Burma, most of the East Indies, and the Philippines, where General Douglas MacArthur directed troops in a gallant but futile defense.

When the Philippine stronghold of Bataan fell on April 9, 1942, after a three-month siege, Japanese soldiers forced their prisoners—about seventy thousand Americans and Filipinos—to evacuate quickly and without adequate food or water. Thousands died on this infamous Bataan death march amid tortures and horrors that the selections only begin to describe.

The death march joined the sneak attack on Pearl Harbor as a focus for many Americans' hatred of all things Japanese. Most Americans believed that the cruelty was deliberate and planned. In reality, as the historian John Toland has written, "There had been no plan at all. About half of the prisoners rode in trucks . . . and suffered little. Some who walked saw almost no brutalities and were fed, if not well, at least occasionally. Yet others a mile behind were starved, beaten and killed by brutal guards." Perhaps seven to ten thousand men died on the march, about 2,330 of them Americans. The Japanese generals, in Toland's view, had seriously underestimated how many soldiers had surrendered as well as how sick and near starvation the prisoners already were. Their responsibility for the general misery as well as the gratuitous violence inflicted upon the prisoners stemmed not from some deliberate plan but from indifference to suffering, the habitual brutality of the Japanese army (officers routinely beat enlisted men), and their lack of control over their own soldiers.

BEFORE YOU READ

1. What evidence can you find in the readings to corroborate or disprove Toland's view of how the death march occurred?

2. How would you try to explain the way the guards acted?

3. How did the prisoners whose accounts you will read survive the march?

PFC. BLAIR ROBINETT

Company C, 803d Engineers

My group came up the road from Mariveles another half mile or so when a Jap soldier stepped out, came across, and took my canteen out of its cover. He took a drink, filled his canteen out of mine, poured the rest of my water on the ground, and dropped the canteen at my feet. I thought he was going to walk back to the line of Jap troops standing across the road, so I bent over to pick up my canteen. But he turned around and hit me on the head with his rifle butt. Put a crease in the top of my head that I still have. I fell face down on the cobblestones. I crawled back up to my knees, debating whether to pick up the canteen again. I figured the best course of action was to stand up and leave the canteen alone. Soon as the Jap troops moved off, I squatted down and picked it up. A little later a Jap soldier came over to one of the lieutenants out of our company, and when he found out his canteen was empty he beat the lieutenant to his knees with the canteen. Just kept slapping him back and forth across the face.

We moved down the ridge a ways when we saw this GI. He was sick. I figured he had come out of the hospital that was in tents out under the trees. He was wobbling along, uneasy on his feet. There were Japanese infantry and tanks coming down the road alongside us. One of these Jap soldiers, I don't know whether he was on our side or if he deliberately came across the road, but he grabbed this sick guy by the arm and guided him to the middle of the road. Then he just flipped him out across the road. The guy hit the cobblestone about five feet in front of a tank and the tank pulled on across him. Well, it killed him quick. There must have been ten tanks in that column, and every one of them came up there right across the body. When the last tank left there was no way you could tell there'd ever been a man there. But his uniform was embedded in the cobblestone. The man disappeared, but his uniform had been pressed until it had become part of the ground.

Now we knew, if there had been any doubts before, we were in for a bad time.

CAPT. MARION LAWTON

1st Battalion, 31st Regiment, Philippine Army

When we had marched several kilometers, we came to a large group of prisoners who were all Americans. My little group had increased to about fifty by then. There I found my commanding officer, Colonel Erwin. He was a large fellow, a little over six feet tall and weighed probably 240 pounds. He was the type who believed in having an abundance of everything. I noticed he had a heavy barracks bag with him. I'd thrown away everything except a change of socks, underwear, and toilet articles, because I knew I couldn't carry a lot of stuff. Knowing how heavy Colonel Erwin's bag was, I volunteered to help

Donald Knox, *Death March: The Survivors of Bataan* (New York: Harcourt Brace Jovanovich, 1981), pp. 122–39.

him, but I warned him that I felt it was a mistake to carry that much. "Oh, no," he said, "I might need this gear." He had extra shoes and uniforms and who knows what else. Hadn't been looted either.

The Japs put us in groups of a hundred, columns of four, and marched us out by groups. I managed to stick with Colonel Erwin. This was April 9, the actual day of surrender. It was as hot as the dickens. The Jap trucks started coming in. And there was just clouds of dust. We started marching. I can't remember hours or specific days, but as we moved on it got hotter and we got more fatigued. After a couple of hours people started faltering. Thirsty, tired, some, like me, already sick. Most everyone was suffering from malaria and diarrhea, all hungry. I'd been pretty well fed, but a lot of these fellows had been on half rations since January and, on top of that, in the confusion of the last few days they had eaten nothing at all. So we were hungry, plus being under pressure of combat. We were emotionally spent, so horribly frightened and depressed and distressed, not knowing what was going to happen to us.

About midday Colonel Erwin, still holding his bag, started slowing down and gradually dropping back. Soon I lost sight of him. I got reports later of what happened. He finally dropped back to the tail of the column and the guards back there started prodding him. He drifted on back further still, until one of the guards stuck him with a bayonet. I guess he was delirious and fevered and exhausted. Finally, a guard pushed him to the side of the road and put his rifle muzzle to his back and pulled the trigger. He was one of the early casualties.

With this exception I didn't see many atrocities, other than people being hit or bayonet prodded. See, I was among the first groups out and all the killings and beatings took place in the later groups, those who were one to three days hungrier and weaker.

CPL. HUBERT GATER

200th Coast Artillery (AA)

Suddenly the hill rocked under us. There was a roar to the left, to the right, and then several back to our rear. The Japs had moved their field guns into position around us on Cabcaben Field.

"Why the dirty bastards!" the man next to me said. "They're using us as a shield to fire on Corregidor." It was true. We should have realized then what to expect as their prisoners.

A flight of Jap bombers were flying over Corregidor. Our officers cautioned us not to watch them because if our anti-aircraft fire hit any of them we would cheer in spite of ourself. Our chief worry was, would Corregidor return fire on the guns that surrounded us?

Corregidor didn't, but a gunboat out in the Bay did. I don't know the size of the shells; they were some smaller than our 3-inch. The first shell was to our right. Apparently, a dud. It skidded through the grass and set it on fire. Some of the men flattened out; others stood up ready to run to cover. Our officers motioned us down. There were a lot of Japs around us now.

The second shell burst to the rear and center of us. At the time I thought it had hit some of our men. A Jap soldier got part of his chin tore off. He was a terrible looking sight running around, evidently half out of his mind. From chin to waist he was covered with blood.

A young Jap officer who had been silently watching us motioned with his hand for us to take cover. About 300 of us ran across Cabcaben Field to get behind a hill. The rest ran the other way, up the road.

CPL. HUBERT GATER

200th Coast Artillery (AA)

Night came. We had moved across the road into a rice field. Jap soldiers, tanks, big field guns, and horses went by in a steady stream. Occasionally, a Jap would run out and hit one of us with his rifle. No one slept. Most of the night Corregidor was firing their big guns. The only way to describe it—it sounded like freight trains going through the air over our heads. They were firing into the area that the Japanese would use to invade Bataan. During the night a man was sent with some canteens for water. The canteens were taken and he was beat up.

The next morning a steady stream of Filipino civilians began to go by, moving out of Bataan. Old and young, many were evidently sick. I didn't realize so many of them had been trapped on Bataan.

SGT. RALPH LEVENBERG

17th Pursuit Squadron

Eventually they started to systematically put us in groups of about 100 or so and marched us off. There were one, two, sometimes four guards, you never knew.

I was fortunate in two respects. First, I had a new pair of shoes, and second, I had some chlorine pills. The shoes I had kept with me ever since we left the barracks outside Manila, and the chlorine I had just managed to pick up. I don't know why, maybe because of my upbringing, I was taught to be protective of my physical being. I was therefore able from time to time, when we stopped near a creek which had dead bodies and horses floating in it, to get some water and purify it with the chlorine.

One of the tricks the Japs played on us—thought it was funny, too—was when they would be riding on the back of a truck, they would have these long black snake whips, and they'd whip that thing out and get some poor bastard by the neck or torso and drag him behind their truck. 'Course if one of our guys was quick enough he didn't get dragged too far. But, if the Japs got a sick guy. . . .

CAPT. MARK WOHLFELD

27th Bombardment Group (L)

We were all mixed up—privates, officers, Scout officers, 31st Infantry, 192d Tank Battalion, 200th New Mexico Coast Artillery—just a jumbled mass of humanity.

My group stopped at a small bridge up above Cabcaben to let some Jap horse artillery through. They were in a real hurry to get these guns in place and start on Corregidor. Right behind the artillery there arrived a great big 1942 Cadillac equipped with a freshly cut wooden camera platform attached to the roof. As soon as they saw us they stopped and the cameraman jumped out and placed his tripod and camera on the platform. He had his big box camera which he looked down into. A white-shirted Japanese interpreter staged us for the cameraman. He told us to line up and put our hands over our heads. We should look depressed and dejected. That wasn't hard. The cameraman took his pictures and started back down the road in his Cadillac towards Corregidor, while we started marching in the other direction. That picture eventually appeared in *Life* magazine.

An hour or so later we halted and fell out near a ditch where there were about five dead Filipinos lying around. They looked like swollen rag dolls. I used a handkerchief knotted at the four corners to keep the sun from my head. I asked the Japanese guard, part talk, part pantomime, "Can I have a helmet? Dead, Filipino. Sun, hot, hot." He finally gave in, but I wondered whether he'd shoot me when I got as far as the ditch: "Fuck it, I'll try it." There was this dead Filipino lying there, and because his face was so puffed up I could only barely manage to get the chin strap off. He was full of maggots and flies. I finally got the helmet off and wiped out the inside with a part of his uniform that wasn't soiled. Then I hung it from my belt so it would dry. Who cared for germs at a time like that? I came back from the ditch and sat next to Major Small. "Boy," he said, "could I stand a Coca-Cola now." I started thinking about my girlfriend then. She worked in Grand Central Station in a real estate office, and I knew she used to go downstairs on her break and get a nice Coke with lots of ice chips in it. I started to take the helmet off my belt and put it on my head, when I noticed the dead Filipino had scratched the name Mary in his helmet liner. The amazing thing was my girlfriend's name was also Mary!

After a column of trucks carrying landing craft passed us, we resumed our march. We fell in behind another group marching out. We'd gone a little farther when we pulled off to the side of the road again to let some trucks roll by. Some of our young guys started asking the Japs whether they could have a drink of water. I looked to my right and saw a buffalo wallow about fifty yards off the road. It looked like green scum. The guards started to laugh and said. "O.K., O.K." So all these kids, eighteen or nineteen year old enlisted men, run for the water and began drowning each other trying to get a drink. The Japs thought it was hilarious. I noticed at the end of the scum some others drinking through handkerchiefs, thinking that would filter the bacteria out. Finally, a Japanese officer came along and began shouting at the men in the water. There must have been fifty of them, and they scattered and ran back for the road. That wasn't the end of it. This officer found some Jap soldiers who had been watching us and ordered them to pull out of the line any Americans who had water stains on their uniforms. When we marched out, after a short while we heard shooting behind us.

That night when we stopped, most of us had had no water all day. Our tongues were thick with dust. We had come into this abandoned barrio and were now sitting in a field. My small group was made up of some senior officers, even a few full colonels. I noticed one, Col. Edmund Lillie, who had been my reserve unit instructor back in the States ten years before. I went up to him, but of course he didn't remember me. We started to talk and began wondering how we could get some water. There was an artesian well near us that had water dribbling out of it, but we were afraid that we'd be shot if we went to get any. Desperate as we were, Colonel Lillie asked a guard whether we could go and get water. The Jap agreed. Most of these officers did not have canteens, but I spotted an old pail, and since I was only a captain, I went over to get it. Inside the pail, stuck to the bottom, was some dried manure. "Maybe I can rinse it out," I said. Lillie told me, "Don't waste the water rinsing it, just fill it up." When I got to the well, one of the Jap guards kept urging me to hurry up. As soon as I got as much as I could, without running the risk of being bayoneted, I came back to the group. There wasn't much water in the pail, but it was something. Lillie told us we could each have only one full mouthful before we passed the pail to the next man. In those days an officer's word meant something, so that's just what we did. Each of us took one full gulp. That way there was enough for everyone.

CAPT. LOYD MILLS

Company C, 57th Infantry, Philippine Scouts

The nights were the worst times for me. We walked all day, from early morning until dusk. Then we were put into barbed-wire enclosures in which the conditions were nearly indescribable. Filth and defecation all over the place. The smell was terrible. These same enclosures had been used every night, and when my group got to them, they were covered by the filth of five or six nights.

I had dysentery pretty bad, but I didn't worry about it because there wasn't anything you could do about it. You didn't stop on "the March" because you were dead if you did. They didn't mess around with you. You didn't have time to pull out and go over and squat. You would just release wherever you were. Generally right on yourself, or somebody else if they happened to be in your way. There was nothing else to do. Without food it was water more than anything. It just went through me . . . bang.

I was in a daze. One thing I knew was that I had to keep going. I was young, so I had that advantage over some of the older men. I helped along the way. If someone near you started stumbling and looked like he was going to fall, you would try to literally pick him up and keep him going. You always talked to them. Tried to make them understand that if they fell they were gone. 'Course, there was nothing you could do about the people who fell in the back.

STAFF SGT. HAROLD FEINER

17th Ordnance Company, Provisional Tank Group

I don't know if the guards were Korean or Taiwanese. I was so miserable on that Death March that I couldn't tell you what they were. I know one thing about them, though — they were mean, sadistic, brutal. And yet, on "the March" I was befriended.

I had been hit at Cabcaben and had a piece of Corregidor shrapnel in my leg. It was the size of a piece of pencil lead and was laying along my shinbone. I had wrapped an old white towel around it and had managed to walk about fifteen miles, but I was getting weaker and more feverish the further I went. I was in bad shape. Guys had to help me. They would kind of hold onto me. If you fell, you were dead. They bayoneted you right away. No bullshit! If you fell, bingo, you were dead.

We finally stopped for the night near a small stream and I laid down. About an hour later this guy comes crawling along. He looked like an Italian, swarthy, kind of muscular. "Hey, fellows, any of you guys need any help?" he was whispering. "I'm a doctor." Didn't give us his name. When he got to me, he stopped and I told him about my leg. Just then a young guard saw us and came over. The first thing they did was hit you with their rifle butts. He spoke atrocious English and he yelled for us to separate. The doctor kept talking, and asked him would it be all right if he took the shrapnel out of my leg. "Wait, wait, wait," and he ran out into the road to see if anyone was coming. Then he came back and said, "Hurry, hurry." I remember the doctor saying, "Soldier, this is going to hurt. If you can take it, I'll get it out." He never had to worry about me hurting. As soon as he touched it, bam, I passed out. He took it out and wrapped a hand towel around my shin. When he left he said, "Yeah, well, I hope to God you make it. God bless you." He disappeared and I never got to know his name.

The Jap guard came up to me during the night and gave me a cup of sweetened chocolate, tasted like milk. I hadn't had any food and no water for days. I didn't speak one single word of Japanese then, but he could speak a little English, but with a really horrible accent. "Someday me go Hollywood, me going to be movie star." That's the way he talked. He made me laugh. All through the night he gave me something, because he knew I needed strength. In the morning he was gone. His squad had been replaced by another. The orders were given, "Everybody up, up, up." We got in line and I found I couldn't walk. My leg hurt so much. Some guys held me up and I was carried about 100 feet to the road. There we were told to stop and sit down. Then we were told to get up. We waited about a half an hour before we were permitted to sit down again. Then we were turned around and marched back to where we started. Wait . . . rest . . . wait . . . march . . . turn around . . . go back. We did this the whole day. I never had to walk, and by the time we started out the next day I had enough strength to limp along on my own. I'm not a religious man, but God said keep those men there, we want to save that man. I don't know what it was. I know I wouldn't have made it, if I had to march that day.

Maybe a day or so later we came to a river. I was still in fairly bad shape. There were a lot of little rivers, and because it was the dry season, they were shallow. The bridge had been knocked out and the Japanese had reconstructed an engineering bridge. Since their troops were crossing it when we arrived, we were made to march down the bank, cross the river, and march up the other side. Sounds simple. We were told not to touch the water. Some of the guys managed to drag their towels in the water and got some water that way. One man, however, reached over and tried to cup his hands and drink some. He was twelve feet from me. They shot him. Some guards on the bridge just popped him off. Going up the other side was hard for me with my leg. I kept sliding on the slimy clay. Finally some guys helped me up.

When we got to the top of the bank, there was a little bend in the road before it crossed the bridge. At that point some Jap sentries were stationed and they were laughing at our struggles. When I got to the top—mind you, I was still crippled—for some reason, maybe because I needed help, one of the sentries took his rifle by the barrel and swung it at me and broke the ribs on my right side. Then I walked with broken ribs and a wounded leg. But I got to San Fernando. Had lots of help. But, hell, guys got there with less than me.

34

Post-World War II "Red Scare"

Mark Goodson

Following each of the world wars of the twentieth century, American politics shifted from progressive to conservative and went through a Red Scare. While there were real reasons that provoked America's confrontation with the Soviet Union, this readiness to attribute all evil, perhaps all social change, to a malevolent force emanating from Moscow remains one of the mysteries of American life.

The Truman administration conducted a rigid internal security program to weed out disloyal or potentially subversive federal employees (although it fired far more homosexuals than political activists). And Truman pursued a foreign policy of unparalleled aggressiveness against the Soviet Union. Yet he was successfully attacked by Republicans as "soft" on communism. Espionage cases from World War II and even earlier stirred fears, but not a single case of any attempt by communists in the postwar years to commit espionage was ever proved. Teachers and professors were fired for political reasons, but no case of communist indoctrination in the classroom ever emerged in these years. Several state commissions and committees branded the National Association for the Advancement of Colored People an instrument of international communism. And the landmark decision in Brown v. Board of Education, *which paved the way for the integration of public schools, was regularly cited across the South as evidence of communist infiltration of the U.S. Supreme Court.*

The Red Scare affected the entertainment industry particularly. Both Hollywood and New York had been centers of radicalism in the 1930s and during the war. A highly organized effort to control the product and personnel of the entertainment industry was carried out through the blacklisting of writers, directors, and actors, among others. This greatly influenced what Americans did and did not see when they watched television or went to the movies. Mark Goodson, who died in 1992 at the age of seventy-seven, was a television producer of highly successful game shows such as What's My Line, To Tell the Truth, I've Got a Secret, Password, *and* Family Feud. *His recollections of the era explain how the system of blacklisting worked and illustrate how extensive its influence was.*

BEFORE YOU READ

1. Ask your parents or grandparents about Mark Goodson's quiz shows. Did they have any political content? What purpose was served by keeping certain people off them?

2. Consider the cases of Anna Lee and Abe Burrows. What recourse was there against the blacklists?

I'm not sure when it began, but I believe it was early 1950. At that point, I had no connection with the blacklisting that was going on, although I had heard about it in the motion picture business and heard rumors about things that had happened on other shows, like *The Aldrich Family*. My first experience really was when we settled into a fairly regular panel on *What's My Line?* in mid-1950. The panel consisted of the poet Louis Untermeyer, Dorothy Kilgallen, Arlene Francis, and Hal Block, a comedy writer. Our sponsor was Stopette, a deodorant.

A few months into the show, I began getting mail on Louis Untermeyer. He had been listed in *Red Channels*. He was one of those folks who had supported the left-wing forces against Franco in Spain. I know that he also had allowed his name to be affiliated with the Joint Anti-Fascist Refugee Committee and had been a sponsor of the 1948 May Day parade. Back in the early 1920s,[1] he had written articles for *The Masses*. But he was certainly not an active political person, at least as far as I knew.

CBS and Stopette also began receiving letters of protest. First, it was just a few postcards. Then it grew. Members of the Catholic War Veterans put stickers on drugstore windows, red, white, and blue stickers, warning, "Stop Stopette Until Stopette Stops Untermeyer."

We didn't pay too much attention until we got the call from CBS. Untermeyer and I were summoned to Ralph Colin's office, who was the general counsel for CBS at the time. Louis and Colin knew each other. Ralph asked him why he lent his name to the group. "I thought it was a good cause," Untermeyer said. "Louis, you're being very naive. These are very difficult times and you've put us in a bad spot. We're going to have to drop you." Untermeyer was very apologetic, but the decision had been made. He was let go.

I remember leaving that office feeling embarrassed. Untermeyer was in his sixties, a man of considerable dignity. He was a good American poet and I liked him; he was funny and articulate on the show. What's more, I had no political ax to grind.

That was the last of that kind of meeting. Soon afterwards, CBS installed a clearance division. There wasn't any discussion. We would just get the word— "Drop that person"—and that was supposed to be it. Whenever we booked a guest or a panelist on *What's My Line?* or *I've Got a Secret*, one of our assistants would phone up and say, "We're going to use so-and-so." We'd either get the okay, or they'd call back and say, "Not clear," or "Sorry, can't use them." Even advertising agencies—big ones, like Young & Rubicam and BBD&O—had

Griffin Fariello, *Red Scare: Memories of the American Inquisition: An Oral History* (New York: Norton, 1995), pp. 320–26.

1. Louis Untermeyer (1885–1977) began publishing his poetry in *The Masses* in 1913. During World War One, the magazine's antiwar position ran afoul of the Postmaster General, who revoked its mailing license under the Espionage Act of 1917. *The Masses'* editors were vindicated in court, but lost access to the mails through a legal technicality. The magazine was succeeded by the *Liberator*, which ran until 1924. [Goodson's note.]

their own clearance departments. They would never come out and say it. They would just write off somebody by saying, "He's a bad actor." You were never supposed to tell the person what it was about; you'd just unbook them. They never admitted there was a blacklist. It just wasn't done.

Some fairly substantial names were off-limits—big stars like Leonard Bernstein, Harry Belafonte, Abe Burrows, Gypsy Rose Lee, Judy Holliday, Jack Gilford, Uta Hagen, and Hazel Scott. Everyone, from the stars to the bit-part actors, was checked. We once did a show in California called *The Rebel*, and we used wranglers to take care of the horses—we had to clear all of their names. CBS, in particular, asked for loyalty oaths to be signed by everybody, making sure that you were not un-American. So far as I know, no one ever refused.

In 1952, *I've Got a Secret* got a new sponsor, R. J. Reynolds Tobacco Company, with its advertising agency, William Este. When they came aboard, someone from the agency called me and said, "Please get rid of Henry Morgan," one of the regular panelists on the show. Morgan had been named in *Red Channels*. I had known Henry for a long time; he was one of those young curmudgeons who was acidic at times, but he was by no means a communist. His wife was involved with radical politics, but they were getting a divorce, and to some extent his name was just smeared.

I went to the agency and told them that they were crazy to try and get rid of Henry Morgan. They agreed that the charge in *Red Channels* was absurd, but they said they couldn't take the risk. That was the main thing—mail accusing them of being pro-communist was not going to sell cigarettes. They gave me an ultimatum: dump Morgan or face the show's cancellation.

So I went to Garry Moore, the MC of the show and an established comedian. He was a conservative, a Republican from Maryland. I knew that he liked Morgan. I said that if he'd be willing to back me up, I'd tell the agency I'd do the show without a sponsor. He agreed without hesitation. I phoned up William Este and said, "We're not going to do the show without Henry." The people at the agency were flabbergasted. It was virtually unheard-of to have this kind of confrontation. They told me they'd think about it, and in the end, they actually backed down. The show was not canceled, and some weeks later Morgan's name simply vanished from *Red Channels*.

Morgan never even knew. When I wrote the article about my experience,[2] Henry called me. "I did not know that I was about to be dropped," he said. "I knew I was in *Red Channels* and I was outraged about that, but I didn't know I was about to be dropped." It was a revelation for him.

The Morgan episode was my first act of resistance. It was not something my lawyers ever encouraged. The watchword in the business is "Don't make waves."

The studios and the advertising agencies didn't have to subscribe to *Red Channels*. It was one of about a dozen publications. There were several private

2. *New York Times Magazine*, January 13, 1991. [Goodson's note.]

lists, and the major agencies and networks exchanged lists, most of which had several names each. I'd help you out by giving you my list and you'd help me out by giving me your list. There was a big interchange of listings. A fellow called Danny O'Shea was in charge of the listings at CBS, an ex-FBI man. *Red Channels* would maybe have a couple of hundred names, but there might be on the other list at CBS several hundred more. Anybody could show up on a list, stars, technicians, cowboys.

Faye Emerson was a regular panelist on *I've Got a Secret* around the same time. Faye was a liberal, very attractive actress who was also hostessing a show called *Author Meets the Critics*. It was a show like *Meet the Press*, with a series of critics dealing with a book. On one episode, they discussed a book that advocated the United States' possible recognition of Red China. For the most part, the critics agreed with the author. The show went on the air live. The very next day I got a call from the William Este Agency, the same people who had protested Morgan. They told me to drop Faye Emerson, that, because of what she had said, she was a Red China sympathizer. I said, "It doesn't make any sense. We have no control over what Faye Emerson says on a different show." We stood up and said, "No, we won't drop her." And for some reason, they ended up listening to us. But she could very easily have been cut.

Anna Lee was an English actress on a later show of ours called *It's News to Me*. The sponsor was Sanka Coffee, a product of General Foods. The advertising agency was Young & Rubicam. One day, I received a call telling me we had to drop one of our panelists, Anna Lee, immediately. They said she was a radical, that she wrote a column for the *Daily Worker.* They couldn't allow that kind of stuff on the air. They claimed they were getting all kinds of mail. It seemed incongruous to me that this little English girl, someone who seemed very conservative, would be writing for a communist newspaper. It just didn't sound right.

I took her out to lunch. After a little social conversation, I asked her about her politics. She told me that she wasn't political, except she voted Conservative in England. Her husband was a Republican from Texas.

I went back to the agency and said, "You guys are really off your rocker. Anna Lee is nothing close to a liberal." They told me, "Oh, you're right. We checked on that. It's a different Anna Lee who writes for the *Daily Worker.*" I remember being relieved and saying, "Well, that's good. You just made a mistake. Now we can forget this." But that wasn't the case. They told me, "We've still got to get rid of her, because the illusion is just as good as the reality. If our client continues to get the mail, no one is going to believe him when he says there's a second Anna Lee." At that point I lost it. I told them their demand was outrageous. They could cancel the show if they wanted to, but I would not drop somebody whose only crime was sharing a name. When I got back to my office, there was a phone call waiting for me. It was from a friend of mine at the agency. He said, "If I were you, I would not lose my temper like that. If you want to argue, do it quietly. After you left, somebody said, 'Is Goodson a pinko?' You could get yourself a very bad label around town." That would have caused me a lot of trouble. All I had to be was in *Red Channels* myself.

Abe Burrows was a regular panelist on *The Name's the Same*, a show we had on ABC in 1952. The sponsor was the Swanson Foods Company. Burrows was a brilliant comedy writer, a nice round-faced fellow whose big hit was a radio show called *Duffy's Tavern*. During the war years Burrows had apparently taken part in cultural activities sponsored by communists in California. To clear his name, he appeared twice before the House Un-American Activities Committee. They released him from further questioning, apparently cleared. But when he went down to testify, it made headlines, and if you made headlines, you got in *Red Channels*. It wasn't long after we booked him on the show that the protest mail began to roll in.

ABC was a brand-new network at the time and didn't have a clearance department. So I would just take the mail and quietly throw it away. One day I got a call from one of the Swanson brothers. He asked if we were getting mail on Burrows. I said we were. He said they were getting a lot of mail. I said we were getting some. He asked if Burrows was a communist. I said, "I don't think so." "Then why is he in *Red Channels?* Why is he getting this mail?" I said, "I think that a long time ago, during the war, he wrote some stuff that was pro-Russian and once belonged to some very liberal groups." Swanson sounded relieved. "If he's not a communist now, then forget it," he said.

Six months later, he called me back. He said, "Are you familiar with the Johnson Supermarkets up in Syracuse, New York?" I had heard about them. Although Mr. Johnson only owned three markets, he was famous for influencing policy throughout the country in the grocery business.[3] Whenever a "controversial" performer appeared on television, he hung signs over the sponsoring company's goods, warning the public that they employed subversives. Swanson told me that Johnson had put out ballots in the store that said, "Do you want any part of your purchase price of Swanson Foods to be used to hire communist fronters? Vote yes or no." Of course, nobody said yes. They took the ballot and marked no. Then Johnson gathered all these ballots together and sent copies of them to stores all over the country. They began getting rid of all Swanson Foods products.

---

3. By the early 1950s no one worked in radio or television without the consent of Laurence A. Johnson. He and his family monitored all network programming and took down the names of those actors, writers, and directors whose politics were considered offensive. Working in concert with a local American Legion post, Johnson threatened the sponsors of the programs with a consumer boycott of their products unless the artists he named were fired. It was the implied support of the American Legion (and its millions of members) that made him such a powerful figure. Johnson died in 1962 at the age of seventy-three, a few days before the courts awarded radio personality John Henry Faulk $3.5 million in a suit against him and Aware, Inc. [Goodson's note.]

Swanson said, "Look, we love you, we love Burrows. We would like to be liberal, but we're not going to let our business go down the drain for one man." I said, "I understand." That was the end of Abe Burrows, at least on television. Abe understood completely. Luckily for him, he had a major Broadway hit at the time called *Guys and Dolls*, so he did not suffer. The people who suffered the most were the ones who had little or no names. Every once in a while, they'd get a part in a theater on Broadway, but basically they just vanished.

It was difficult to get people to stand up against this. The people who did stand up were your conservative friends, like Garry Moore and in the beginning, the Swanson brothers. I can understand that. The more liberal the network, the more frightened they were. CBS, after all, was concerned because in Congress, CBS was being called the Communist Broadcasting System. All three networks were run by Jewish Americans. They were concerned with being thought of as un-American. The first major company to break the blacklist was Ford Motors, with a broadcast of a Leonard Bernstein concert. They were strong enough and conservative enough that nobody could accuse them of anything.

I think it's very important to note that I was not really dealing with communists. I was dealing with people who were being tarred with the brush at a time when it was dangerous to be liberal. That was basically it. Whether I would actually have gone to bat for someone like Paul Robeson, an avowed communist at the time, I don't know.[4]

My life had been apolitical, I had never been involved. I was just operating out of a sense of not wanting to see people pushed around. I did not do it from any ideological point of view, except out of a fairly liberal, centrist position. My lawyers, nice liberal guys, certainly did not advise me to stand up and get involved. Most people looked at the names in *Red Channels* and said, "Somebody says they're left-wing and that's that. We don't want to get into trouble."

You can't know what it was like. Nobody today has any feeling of what the atmosphere was like then, to know that one remark in Jack O'Brien's television column in the *Journal-American* could hurt somebody badly. We were all scared.

4. Robeson, although very close to the Party and to the Soviet Union, denied under oath in 1946 that he was a member. [Goodson's note.]

35

Life in Gray Flannel
Sloan Wilson

In 1945, twelve million GIs were demobilized. Returning to a nation that had built few new residences during fifteen years of depression and war, they and their families faced a formidable housing shortage. Abundant land and equally abundant techno- logical ingenuity pointed to the answer: the mass-produced suburb. The new suburbs supported a new prosperity, based largely on construction and automobile manufac- turing—along with revived defense industries a few years later. Suburban houses, the automobiles essential to live in them, plentiful food and clothing, appliances, and gad- gets defined the greatly enlarged postwar white middle class.

The Man in the Gray Flannel Suit became in the mid-1950s a catch phrase for the struggling, security-oriented male suburbanite and corporate climber. These first pages from Sloan Wilson's 1955 novel—made into a movie starring Gregory Peck and Jennifer Jones—present Tom Rath and his wife, Betsy, who are caught between their ideals and the materialism that has marked the suburbanization of American life.

Later in the novel, Tom gets the job he applies for at the United Broadcasting Cor- poration, the job that makes him another man in a gray flannel suit. Then, incidents from his experiences in World War II, briefly alluded to in this excerpt, come back to haunt him.

BEFORE YOU READ

1. The Raths hate their house. What does this indicate about conflicts they expe- rience about their values?
2. Why is Tom Rath unwilling to write an autobiography to get the job he wants?
3. He is hired anyway. What does this suggest about the values of his new company?
4. Do conflicts such as the Raths experience exist today?

By the time they had lived seven years in the little house on Greentree Avenue in Westport, Connecticut, they both detested it. There were many reasons, none of them logical, but all of them compelling. For one thing, the house had a kind of evil genius for displaying proof of their weaknesses and wiping out all traces of their strengths. The ragged lawn and weed-filled garden pro- claimed to passers-by and the neighbors that Thomas R. Rath and his family disliked "working around the place" and couldn't afford to pay someone else

Sloan Wilson, *The Man in the Gray Flannel Suit* (New York: Simon and Schuster, 1955), pp. 3–17.

to do it. The interior of the house was even more vengeful. In the living room there was a big dent in the plaster near the floor, with a huge crack curving up from it in the shape of a question mark. That wall was damaged in the fall of 1952, when, after struggling for months to pay up the back bills, Tom came home one night to find that Betsy had bought a cut-glass vase for forty dollars. Such an extravagant gesture was utterly unlike her, at least since the war. Betsy was a conscientious household manager, and usually when she did something Tom didn't like, they talked the matter over with careful reasonableness. But on that particular night, Tom was tired and worried because he himself had just spent seventy dollars on a new suit he felt he needed to dress properly for his business, and at the climax of a heated argument, he picked up the vase and heaved it against the wall. The heavy glass shattered, the plaster cracked, and two of the lathes behind it broke. The next morning, Tom and Betsy worked together on their knees to patch the plaster, and they repainted the whole wall, but when the paint dried, the big dent near the floor with the crack curving up from it almost to the ceiling in the shape of a question mark was still clearly visible. The fact that the crack was in the shape of a question mark did not seem symbolic to Tom and Betsy, nor even amusing — it was just annoying. . . .

The crack in the living room was not the only reminder of the worst. An ink stain with hand marks on the wallpaper in Janey's room commemorated one of the few times Janey ever willfully destroyed property, and the only time Betsy ever lost her temper with her and struck her. Janey was five, and the middle one of the three Rath children. She did everything hard: she screamed when she cried, and when she was happy her small face seemed to hold for an instant all the joy in the world. Upon deciding that she wanted to play with ink, she carefully poured ink over both her hands and made neat imprints on the wallpaper, from the floor to as high as she could reach. Betsy was so angry that she slapped both her hands, and Janey, feeling she had simply been interrupted in the midst of an artistic endeavor, lay on the bed for an hour sobbing and rubbing her hands in her eyes until her whole face was covered with ink. Feeling like a murderess, Betsy tried to comfort her, but even holding and rocking her didn't seem to help, and Betsy was shocked to find that the child was shuddering. When Tom came home that night he found mother and daughter asleep on the bed together, tightly locked in each other's arms. Both their faces were covered with ink. All this the wall remembered and recorded.

The Raths had bought the house in 1946, shortly after Tom had got out of the Army and, at the suggestion of his grandmother, become an assistant to the director of the Schanenhauser Foundation, an organization which an elderly millionaire had established to help finance scientific research and the arts. They had told each other that they probably would be in the house only one or two years before they could afford something better. It took them five years to realize that the expense of raising three children was likely to increase at least as fast as Tom's salary at a charitable foundation. If Tom and Betsy had been entirely reasonable, this might have caused them to start painting the place like crazy, but it had the reverse effect. Without talking about it much, they both began to think of the house as a trap, and they no more enjoyed refurbishing it than a prisoner would delight in shining up the bars of his cell. Both of them were aware that their feelings about the house were not admirable.

"I don't know what's the matter with us," Betsy said one night. "Your job is plenty good enough. We've got three nice kids, and lots of people would be glad to have a house like this. We shouldn't be so *discontented* all the time."

"Of course we shouldn't!" Tom said.

Their words sounded hollow. It was curious to believe that that house with the crack in the form of a question mark on the wall and the ink stains on the wallpaper was probably the end of their personal road. It was impossible to believe. Somehow something would have to happen.

Tom thought about his house on that day in June 1953, when a friend of his named Bill Hawthorne mentioned the possibility of a job at the United Broadcasting Corporation. Tom was having lunch with a group of acquaintances in The Golden Horseshoe, a small restaurant and bar near Rockefeller Center.

"I hear we've got a new spot opening up in our public-relations department," Bill, who wrote promotion for United Broadcasting, said. "I think any of you would be crazy to take it, mind you, but if you're interested, there it is. . . ."

Tom unfolded his long legs under the table and shifted his big body on his chair restlessly. "How much would it pay?" he asked casually.

"I don't know," Bill said. "Anywhere from eight to twelve thousand, I'd guess, according to how good a hold-up man you are. If you try for it, ask fifteen. I'd like to see somebody stick the bastards good."

It was fashionable that summer to be cynical about one's employers, and the promotion men were the most cynical of all.

"You can have it," Cliff Otis, a young copy writer for a large advertising agency, said. "I wouldn't want to get into a rat race like that."

Tom glanced into his glass and said nothing. Maybe I could get ten thousand a year, he thought. If I could do that, Betsy and I might be able to buy a better house.

The next morning, Tom put on his best suit, a freshly cleaned and pressed gray flannel. On his way to work he stopped in Grand Central Station to buy a clean white handkerchief and to have his shoes shined. During his luncheon hour he set out to visit the United Broadcasting Corporation. As he walked across Rockefeller Plaza, he thought wryly of the days when he and Betsy had assured each other that money didn't matter. They had told each other that when they were married, before the war, and during the war they had repeated it in long letters. "The important thing is to find a kind of work you really like, and something that is useful," Betsy had written him. "The money doesn't matter."

The hell with that, he thought. The real trouble is that up to now we've been kidding ourselves. We might as well admit that what we want is a big house and a new car and trips to Florida in the winter, and plenty of life insurance. When you come right down to it, a man with three children has no damn right to say that money doesn't matter.

There were eighteen elevators in the lobby of the United Broadcasting building. They were all brass colored and looked as though they were made of money. The receptionist in the personnel office was a breathtakingly beautiful girl with money-colored hair—a sort of copper gold. "Yes?" she said.

"I want to apply for a position in the public-relations department."

"If you will sit down in the reception room, I'll arrange an interview for you," she said.

The company had a policy of giving all job applicants an interview. Every year about twenty thousand people, most of them wildly unqualified, applied for jobs there, and it was considered poor public relations to turn them away too abruptly. Beyond the receptionist's desk was a huge waiting room. A rich wine-red carpet was on the floor, and there were dozens of heavy leather armchairs filled with people nervously smoking cigarettes. On the walls were enormous colored photographs of the company's leading radio and television stars. They were all youthful, handsome, and unutterably rich-appearing as they smiled down benignly on the job applicants. Tom picked a chair directly beneath a picture of a big-bosomed blonde. He had to wait only about twenty minutes before the receptionist told him that a Mr. Everett would see him. Mr. Everett's office was a cubicle with walls of opaque glass brick, only about three times as big as a priest's confessional. Everett himself was a man about Tom's age and was also dressed in a gray flannel suit. The uniform of the day, Tom thought. Somebody must have put out an order.

"I understand that you are interested in a position in the public-relations department," Everett said.

"I just want to explore the situation," Tom replied. "I already have a good position with the Schanenhauser Foundation, but I'm considering a change."

It took Everett only about a minute to size Tom up as a "possibility." He gave him a long printed form to fill out and told him he'd hear from the United Broadcasting Corporation in a few days. Tom spent almost an hour filling out all the pages of the form, which, among other things, required a list of the childhood diseases he had had and the names of countries he had visited. When he had finished, he gave it to the girl with the hair of copper gold and rang for one of the golden elevators to take him down.

Five days later Tom got a letter from Everett saying an interview had been arranged for him with Mr. Gordon Walker in Room 3672 the following Monday at 11:00 A.M. In the letter Walker was given no title. Tom didn't know whether he were going to have another routine interview, or whether he were actually being considered for a position. He wondered whether he should tell

Dick Haver, the director of the Schanenhauser Foundation, that he was looking for another job. The danger of not telling him was that broadcasting company might call him for references any time, and Dick wouldn't be pleased to
find that Tom was applying for another job behind his back. It was important
to keep Dick's good will, because the broadcasting company's decision might
depend on the recommendation Dick gave him. In any one of a thousand
ways, Dick could damn him, without Tom's ever learning about it. All Dick
would have to do when the broadcasting company telephoned him would be
to say, "Tom Rath? Well, I don't know. I don't think I'd want to go on record
one way or the other on Mr. Rath. He's a nice person, you understand, an aw-
fully nice person. I'd be perfectly willing to say that!"

On the other hand, it would be embarrassing to tell Dick he was seeking another job and then be unable to find one. Tom decided to delay seeing Dick
until after he had had his next interview.

Walker's outer office was impressive. As soon as Tom saw it, he knew he was
being seriously considered for a job, and maybe a pretty good one. Walker had
two secretaries, one chosen for looks, apparently, and one for utility. A pale-
yellow carpet lay on the floor, and there was a yellow leather armchair for
callers. Walker himself was closeted in an inner office which was separated
from the rest of the room by a partition of opaque glass brick.

The utilitarian secretary told Tom to wait. It was extremely quiet. Neither
of the two girls was typing, and although each had two telephones on her desk
and an interoffice communication box, there was no ringing or buzzing. Both
the secretaries sat reading typewritten sheets in black notebooks. After Tom
had waited about half an hour, the pretty secretary, with no audible or visible
cue, suddenly looked up brightly and said, "Mr. Walker will see you now. Just
open the door and go in."

Tom opened the door and saw a fat pale man sitting in a highbacked up-
holstered chair behind a kidney-shaped desk, with nothing on it but a blotter
and pen. He was in his shirt sleeves, and he weighed about two hundred and
fifty pounds. His face was as white as a marshmallow. He didn't stand up when
Tom came in, but he smiled. It was a surprisingly warm, spontaneous smile, as
though he had unexpectedly recognized an old friend. "Thomas Rath?" he
said. "Sit down! Make yourself comfortable! Take off your coat!"

Tom thanked him and, although it wasn't particularly warm, took off his
coat. There wasn't anyplace to put it, so, sitting down in the comfortable chair
in front of Walker's desk, he laid the coat awkwardly across his lap.

"I've read the application forms you filled out, and it seems to me you might
be qualified for a new position we may have opening up here," Walker said.
"There are just a few questions I want to ask you." He was still smiling. Suddenly he touched a button on the arm of his chair and the back of the chair
dropped, allowing him to recline, as though he were in an airplane seat. Tom
could see only his face across the top of the desk.

"You will excuse me," Walker said, still smiling. "The doctor says I must get
plenty of rest, and this is the way I do it."

Tom couldn't think of anything more appropriate to say than "It looks comfortable. . . ."

"Why do you want to work for the United Broadcasting Corporation?" Walker asked abruptly.

"It's a good company . . ." Tom began hesitantly and was suddenly impatient at the need for hypocrisy. The sole reason he wanted to work for United Broadcasting was that he thought he might be able to make a lot of money there fast, but he felt he couldn't say that. It was sometimes considered fashionable for the employees of foundations to say that they were in it for the money, but people were supposed to work at advertising agencies and broadcasting companies for spiritual reasons.

"I believe," Tom said, "that television is developing into the greatest medium for mass education and entertainment. It has always fascinated me, and I would like to work with it. . . ."

"What kind of salary do you have in mind?" Walker asked. Tom hadn't expected the question that soon. Walker was still smiling.

"The salary isn't the primary consideration with me," Tom said, trying desperately to come up with stock answers to stock questions. "I'm mainly interested in finding something useful and worth while to do. I have personal responsibilities, however, and I would hope that something could be worked out to enable me to meet them. . . ."

"Of course," Walker said, beaming more cheerily than ever. "I understand you applied for a position in the public-relations department. Why did you choose that?"

Because I heard there was an opening, Tom wanted to say, but quickly thought better of it and substituted a halting avowal of lifelong interest in public relations. "I think my experience in working with *people* at the Schanenhauser Foundation would be helpful," he concluded lamely.

"I see," Walked said kindly. There was a short silence before he added, "Can you write?"

"I do most of the writing at the Schanenhauser Foundation," Tom said. "The annual report to the trustees is my job, and so are most of the reports on individual projects. I used to be editor of my college paper."

"That sounds fine," Walker said casually, "I have a little favor I want to ask of you. I want you to write me your autobiography."

"What?" Tom asked in astonishment.

"Nothing very long," Walker said. "Just as much as you can manage to type out in an hour. One of my girls will give you a room with a typewriter."

"Is there anything in particular you want me to tell you about?"

"Yourself," Walker said, looking hugely pleased. "Explain yourself to me. Tell me what kind of person you are. Explain why we should hire you."

"I'll try," Tom said weakly.

"You'll have precisely an hour," Walker said. "You see, this is a device I use in employing people—I find it most helpful. For this particular job, I have twenty or thirty applicants. It's hard to tell from a brief interview whom to choose, so I ask them all to write about themselves for an hour. You'd be surprised how revealing the results are. . . ."

He paused, still smiling. Tom said nothing.

"Just a few hints," Walker continued. "Write anything you want, but at the end of your last page, I'd like you to finish this sentence: 'The most significant fact about me is . . .' "

"The most significant fact about me is . . ." Tom repeated idiotically.

"The results, of course, will be entirely confidential." Walked lifted a bulky arm and inspected his wrist watch. "It's now five minutes to twelve," he concluded. "I'll expect your paper on my desk at precisely one o'clock."

Tom stood up, put on his coat, said, "Thank you," and went out of the room. The utilitarian secretary already had a stack of typewriting paper ready for him. She led him to a small room a few doors down the hall in which were a typewriter and a hard office chair. There was a large clock on the wall. The room had no windows. Across the ceiling was a glaring fluorescent light which made the bare white plaster walls look yellow. The secretary walked out without a word, shutting the door silently behind her.

Tom sat down in the chair, which had been designed for a stenographer and was far too small for him. Son of a bitch, he thought—I guess the laws about cruel and unusual punishment don't apply to personnel men. He tried to think of something to write, but all he could remember was Betsy and the drab little house and the need to buy a new washing machine, and the time he had thrown a vase that cost forty dollars against the wall. "The most significant fact about me is that I once threw a vase costing forty dollars against a wall." That would be as sensible as anything else he could think of, but he doubted whether it would get him the job. He thought of Janey saying, "It isn't *fair!*" and the worn linoleum on the kitchen floor. "The most significant fact about me is . . ." It was a stupid sentence to ask a man to finish.

I have children, he thought—that's probably the most significant fact about me, the only one that will have much importance for long. Anything about a man can be summed up in numbers. Thomas R. Rath, thirty-three years old, making seven thousand dollars a year, owner of a 1939 Ford, a six-room house, and ten thousand dollars' worth of G.I. Life Insurance which, in case of his death, would pay his widow about forty dollars a month. Six feet one and a half inches tall; weight, 198 pounds. He served four and a half years in the Army, most of it in Europe and the rest in the South Pacific.

Another statistical fact came to him then, a fact which he knew would be ridiculously melodramatic to put into an application for a job at the United Broadcasting Corporation, or to think about at all. He hadn't thought about this for a long while. It wasn't a thing he had deliberately tried to forget—he simply hadn't thought about it for quite a few years. It was the unreal-sounding, probably irrelevant, but quite accurate fact that he had killed seventeen men.

It had been during the war, of course. He had been a paratrooper. Lots of other people had killed more men than he had. Lots of bomber crews and artillerymen had, but, of course, they never really knew it. Lots of infantrymen and lots of paratroopers had, and most of them knew it. Plenty of men had been dropped behind the enemy lines, as Tom had been on five different occasions, and they had had to do some of their killing silently, with blackjacks and knives. They had known what they were doing, and most of them were healthy enough not to be morbid about it, and not to be proud of it, and not to be ashamed of it. Such things were merely part of the war, the war before the Korean one. It was no longer fashionable to talk about the war, and certainly it had never been fashionable to talk about the number of men one had killed. Tom couldn't forget the number, "seventeen," but it didn't seem real any more; it was just a small, isolated statistic that nobody wanted. His mind went blank. Suddenly the word "Maria" flashed into it.

"The most significant fact about me is that I . . ."

Nonsense, he thought, and brought himself back to the present with a jerk. Only masochists can get along without editing their own memories. Maria was a girl he had known in Italy during the war, a long time ago, and he never thought about her any more, just as he never thought about the seventeen men he had killed. It wasn't always easy to forget, but it was certainly necessary to try.

"The most significant fact about me is that for four and a half years my profession was jumping out of airplanes with a gun, and now I want to go into public relations."

That probably wouldn't get him the job, Tom thought. "The most significant fact about me is that I detest the United Broadcasting Corporation, with all its soap operas, commercials, and yammering studio audiences, and the only reason I'm willing to spend my life in such a ridiculous enterprise is that I want to buy a more expensive house and a better brand of gin."

That certainly wouldn't get him the job.

"The most significant fact about me is that I've become a cheap cynic."

That would not be apt to get him the job.

"The most significant fact about me is that as a young man in college, I played the mandolin incessantly. I, champion mandolin player, am applying to you for a position in the public-relations department!"

That would not be likely to get him far. Impatiently he sat down at the typewriter and glanced at his wrist watch. It was a big loud ticking wrist watch with a black face, luminous figures, and a red sweep hand that rapidly ticked off the seconds. He had bought it years ago at an Army post exchange and had worn it all through the war. The watch was the closest thing to a good-luck charm he had ever had, although he never thought of it as such. Now it was more reassuring to look at than the big impersonal clock on the wall, though both said it was almost twelve-thirty. So far he had written nothing. What the hell, he thought. I was a damn fool to think I wanted to work here anyway. Then he thought of Betsy asking, as she would be sure to, "Did you get the job? How did it go?" And he decided to try.

"Anybody's life can be summed up in a paragraph," he wrote. "I was born on November 20, 1920, in my grandmother's house in South Bay, Connecticut. I was graduated from Covington Academy in 1937, and from Harvard College in 1941. I spent four and a half years in the Army, reaching the rank of captain. Since 1946, I have been employed as an assistant to the director of the Schanenhauser Foundation. I live in Westport, Connecticut, with my wife and three children. From the point of view of the United Broadcasting Corporation, the most significant fact about me is that I am applying for a position in its public-relations department, and after an initial period of learning, I probably would do a good job. I will be glad to answer any questions which seem relevant, but after considerable thought, I have decided that I do not wish to attempt an autobiography as part of an application for a job."

He typed this paragraph neatly in the precise center of a clean piece of paper, added his name and address, and carried to into Walker's office. It was only quarter to one, and Walker was obviously surprised to see him. "You've still got fifteen minutes!" he said.

"I've written all I think is necessary," Tom replied, and handed him the almost empty page.

Walker read it slowly, his big pale face expressionless. When he had finished it, he dropped it into a drawer. "We'll let you know our decision in a week or so," he said.

36

Launching the Montgomery Bus Boycott
Jo Ann Gibson Robinson

In March 1954, two months before the U.S. Supreme Court in Oliver Brown v. Board of Education of Topeka, Kansas, *declared segregated schools to be unconstitutional, the Women's Political Council of Montgomery, Alabama (WPC) remonstrated with the City Commission to end abusive practices against African Americans on the city's buses. Shortly after, this organization of African American women, modeled after the League of Women Voters (whose Montgomery chapter had refused them membership), threatened to join with other African American community organizations to boycott the buses citywide. On December 5, 1955, four days after Mrs. Rosa Parks was arrested for refusing to surrender her bus seat, the WPC did just that.*

Robinson's careful narrative explains the role of her organization in beginning the boycott as well as her own part in writing, mimeographing, and distributing over fifty thousand flyers urging the African American community to boycott the buses on December 5. Their plan for a one-day boycott grew wondrously into nearly a year of walking, carpooling, and facing down all the intimidation that Jim Crow (codes of segregation) could devise until a Supreme Court decision brought them victory. This long-neglected story of the WPC is a major part of the first significant victory of the civil rights movement and the emergence of its greatest leader, Mrs. Robinson's minister at the Dexter Avenue Baptist Church, the Reverend Martin Luther King, Jr.

BEFORE YOU READ

1. What was the Women's Political Council and why was it able to respond so rapidly to the crisis provoked by Mrs. Parks's arrest?

2. What pressures did the crisis impose on Dr. Trenholm, president of Alabama State College?

3. Why was the leadership of black ministers so important to the boycott?

In the afternoon of Thursday, December 1, a prominent black woman named Mrs. Rosa Parks was arrested for refusing to vacate her seat for a white man. Mrs. Parks was a medium-sized, cultured mulatto woman; a civic and religious worker; quiet, unassuming, and pleasant in manner and appearance; dignified and reserved; of high morals and a strong character. She was—and still is, for she lives to tell the story—respected in all black circles. By trade she was a seamstress, adept and competent in her work.

Tired from work, Mrs. Parks boarded a bus. The "reserved seats" were partially filled, but the seats just behind the reserved section were vacant, and Mrs. Parks sat down in one. It was during the busy evening rush hour. More black and white passengers boarded the bus, and soon all the reserved seats were occupied. The driver demanded that Mrs. Parks get up and surrender her seat to a white man, but she was tired from her work. Besides, she was a woman, and the person waiting was a man. She remained seated. In a few minutes, police summoned by the driver appeared, placed Mrs. Parks under arrest, and took her to jail.

It was the first time the soft-spoken, middle-aged woman had been arrested. She maintained decorum and poise, and the word of her arrest spread. Mr. E. D. Nixon, a longtime stalwart of our NAACP branch, along with liberal white attorney Clifford Durr and his wife Virginia, went to the jail and obtained Mrs. Parks's release on bond. Her trial was scheduled for Monday, December 5, 1955.

The news traveled like wildfire into every black home. Telephones jangled; people congregated on street corners and in homes and talked. But nothing was done. A numbing helplessness seemed to paralyze everyone. Very few stayed off the buses the rest of that day or the next. There was fear, discontent, and uncertainty. Everyone seemed to wait for someone to *do* something, but nobody made a move. For that day and a half, black Americans rode the buses as before, as if nothing had happened. They were sullen and uncommunicative, but they rode the buses. There was a silent, tension-filled waiting. For blacks were not talking loudly in public places—they were quiet, sullen, waiting. Just waiting!

Thursday evening came and went. Thursday night was far spent, when, at about 11:30 P.M., I sat alone in my peaceful single-family dwelling on a quiet street. I was thinking about the situation. Lost in thought, I was startled by the telephone's ring. Black attorney Fred Gray, who had been out of town all day, had just gotten back and was returning the phone message I had left for him about Mrs. Parks's arrest. Attorney Gray, though a very young man, had been one of my most active colleagues in our previous meetings with bus company officials and Commissioner Birmingham. A Montgomery native who had attended Alabama State and been one of my students, Fred Gray had gone on to law school in Ohio before returning to his home town to open a practice with the only other black lawyer in Montgomery, Charles Langford.

Fred Gray and his wife Bernice were good friends of mine, and we talked often. In addition to being a lawyer, Gray was a trained, ordained minister of the gospel, actively serving as assistant pastor of Holt Street Church of Christ.

Tonight his voice on the phone was very short and to the point. Fred was shocked by the news of Mrs. Parks's arrest. I informed him that I already was thinking that the WPC should distribute thousands of notices calling for all bus riders to stay off the buses on Monday, the day of Mrs. Parks's trial. "Are you ready?" he asked. Without hesitation, I assured him that we were. With that he hung up, and I went to work.

I made some notes on the back of an envelope: "The Women's Political Council will not wait for Mrs. Parks's consent to call for a boycott of city buses. On Friday, December 2, 1955, the women of Montgomery will call for a boycott to take place on Monday, December 5."

Some of the WPC officers previously had discussed plans for distributing thousands of notices announcing a bus boycott. Now the time had come for me to write just such a notice. I sat down and quickly drafted a message and then called a good friend and colleague, John Cannon, chairman of the business department at the college, who had access to the college's mimeograph equipment. When I told him that the WPC was staging a boycott and needed to run off the notices, he told me that he too had suffered embarrassment on the city buses. Like myself, he had been hurt and angry. He said that he would happily assist me. Along with two of my most trusted senior students, we quickly agreed to meet almost immediately, in the middle of the night, at the college's duplicating room. We were able to get three messages to a page, greatly reducing the number of pages that had to be mimeographed in order to produce the tens of thousands of leaflets we knew would be needed. By 4 A.M. Friday, the sheets had been duplicated, cut in thirds, and bundled. Each leaflet read:

> Another Negro woman has been arrested and thrown in jail because she re-
> fused to get up out of her seat on the bus for a white person to sit down. It is the
> second time since the Claudette Colvin case that a Negro woman has been ar-
> rested for the same thing. This has to be stopped. Negroes have rights, too, for
> if Negroes did not ride the buses, they could not operate. Three-fourths of the
> riders are Negroes, yet we are arrested, or have to stand over empty seats. If we
> do not do something to stop these arrests, they will continue. The next time it
> may be you, or your daughter, or mother. This woman's case will come up on
> Monday. We are, therefore, asking every Negro to stay off the buses Monday in
> protest of the arrest and trial. Don't ride the buses to work, to town, to school,
> or anywhere on Monday. You can afford to stay out of school for one day if you
> have no other way to go except by bus. You can also afford to stay out of town
> for one day. If you work, take a cab, or walk. But please, children and grown-ups,
> don't ride the bus at all on Monday. Please stay off of all buses Monday.

Between 4 and 7 A.M., the two students and I mapped out distribution routes for the notices. Some of the WPC officers previously had discussed how and where to deliver thousands of leaflets announcing a boycott, and those plans now stood me in good stead. We outlined our routes, arranged the bundles in sequences, stacked them in our cars, and arrived at my 8 A.M. class, in which both young men were enrolled, with several minutes to spare. We weren't even tired or hungry. Just like me, the two students felt a tremendous sense of satisfaction at being able to contribute to the cause of justice.

After class my two students and I quickly finalized our plans for distribut-ing the thousands of leaflets so that one would reach every black home in Montgomery. I took out the WPC membership roster and called the former president, Dr. Mary Fair Burks, then the Pierces, the Glasses, Mrs. Mary Cross, Mrs. Elizabeth Arrington, Mrs. Josie Lawrence, Mrs. Geraldine Nes-bitt, Mrs. H. Councill Trenholm, Mrs. Catherine N. Johnson, and a dozen or more others. I alerted all of them to the forthcoming distribution of the leaflets, and enlisted their aid in speeding and organizing the distribution net-work. Each would have one person waiting at a certain place to take a package of notices as soon as my car stopped and the young men could hand them a bundle of leaflets.

Then I and my two student helpers set out. Throughout the late morning and early afternoon hours we dropped off tens of thousands of leaflets. Some of our bundles were dropped off at schools, where both students and staff members helped distribute them further and spread the word for people to read the notices and then pass them on to neighbors. Leaflets were also dropped off at business places, storefronts, beauty parlors, beer halls, factories, barber shops, and every other available place. Workers would pass along notices both to other employees as well as to customers.

During those hours of crucial work, nothing went wrong. Suspicion was never raised. The action of all involved was so casual, so unconcerned, so nonchalant, that suspicion was never raised, and neither the city nor its people ever suspected a thing! We never missed a spot. And no one missed a class, a job, or a normal routine. Everything was done by the plan, with perfect timing. By 2 o'clock, thousands of the mimeographed handbills had changed hands many times. Practically every black man, woman, and child in Montgomery knew the plan and was passing the word along. No one knew where the notices had come from or who had arranged for their circulation, and no one cared. Those who passed them on did so efficiently, quietly, and without comment. But deep within the heart of every black person was a joy he or she dared not reveal.

Meanwhile, at the college, one of the women teachers who was not a member of the Women's Political Council, nor even a resident of Montgomery (she lived in Mobile), took a leaflet as I and my two seniors got into my car to leave the campus on our delivery route. She carried that leaflet straight to the office of the president of Alabama State College, Dr. H. Councill Trenholm.

Dr. Trenholm was president of Alabama State College [ASC] for a total of thirty-eight years. . . .

He was a diligent worker, a stickler for perfection—a "work ox," somebody labeled him. The institution was a junior college when he first took over, with a few students, limited grounds, and even fewer teachers. He immediately began to go out, meet people, introduce himself, and give scholarships to the very poor and deserving students who wanted to go on but had no money to matriculate. Being a young, ambitious man, he began visiting the immediate communities and talking with parents and young people who were hoping for a college education. In a very short time, he had a large number of students matriculating. He was in a tough position because state funds for "black" college students were limited, and in some places there was no appropriation at all for black students. However, Dr. Trenholm talked with state officials, plus local financiers, and things began to change. Enrollments increased; parents became involved. The junior college became a senior college, and seniors graduated. The state purchased more land, added more space, and the student body grew.

During the depression, when funds were limited, Dr. Trenholm had helped fund the institution with money from his own savings and from money-raising projects. He gave his youth, his intellect, his *all* to ASC. In so doing, he built an institution that was an intellectual light to the city of Montgomery and the state of Alabama. Thousands of graduates are rendering service to mankind all over the United States and even in other parts of the globe.

When I returned to the campus that Friday for my two o'clock class, after delivering the notices, I found a message from Dr. Trenholm, asking me to come to his office immediately. Very angry and visibly shaken, the president showed me the leaflet and demanded to know what the movement was about and what *my* role was. I informed Dr. Trenholm of the arrest of Mrs. Rosa Parks and of how in the past others had been arrested for the same thing, for refusing to give up their seats to white people.

"Were there other seats?" he asked. I assured him there were not. I informed him that there were many adults who had been arrested for the same thing, and that because the college had no direct connection with the persons, college personnel often had no way of knowing about it. I stressed the fact that black people, innocent black people young and old, were suffering, and that they could not help themselves.

"What are they being arrested for?" he asked. And I did not hesitate to inform him. For all of a sudden, I remembered that time when I was made to get up from a seat in the fifth row from the front of a bus, when there were only three people riding the entire bus.

In this powerful man's presence I felt fear for the first time, a fear that penetrated my entire being. He had a frown on his face; his voice revealed impatience. For the first time I felt that he might fire me. But at that moment, I did not care if he did! I breathed a silent prayer for guidance and felt a wave of peace inundate me. I knew then that if he fired me, I would stay right there until the right was won.

I described the frequent repetition of these outrages, how many children, men, and women, old and middle-aged people, had been humiliated and made to relinquish their seats to white people. I told him of Claudette Colvin and of Mrs. Rosa Parks, both of whom had been jailed. He stopped me several times to ask questions; then I would proceed.

As I talked, I could see the anger slowly receding from his face and heard his tone of voice softening. Concern began to show in his expression, as he settled in his chair. I relaxed a bit. Then I told him of the three hundred black women who had organized the WPC to fight any inhumane impositions upon black people. I assured him that the WPC would never involve the college, that ASC had not been mentioned nor would it ever be. I convinced him also that if some intelligent, organized group did not take the initiative and seek improvements from the city hall power structure, angry hot-heads would resort to other means. We would choose to fight not with weapons, but with reason. When I told him that somebody, or some organization, had to fight this assault on blacks' rights, and that the WPC was prepared to do it, I felt that I had said enough. I sat with my eyes cast downward breathing a prayer while I waited for his response. His anger gone, deep sympathetic concern spread over his face; his eyes seemed to penetrate the walls of his office; he sat for a moment, pondering, lost in thought. He seemed to have aged years in the brief span of our conversation, and he leaned on his desk as he talked to me. He seemed so tired.

Then he said: "Your group must continue to press for civil rights." He cautioned me, however, to be careful, to work behind the scenes, not to involve the college, and not to neglect my responsibilities as a member of the faculty of Alabama State College. Then he stood up to indicate the discussion was ended.

But before the door closed completely, he called me back.

"Jo Ann," he said, smiling now.

"Yes, Dr. Trenholm?" I responded hesitatingly, realizing he had not yet finished.

"I called Mr. John Cannon's office after receiving this notice of the boycott. Mr. Cannon confirmed my suspicion that you ran off these boycott notices on school paper."

"Yes, sir, that is correct," I admitted. "Let me see, sir. We used thirty-five reams of paper at 500 sheets per ream. That made 17,500 sheets, cut into thirds, for a total of 52,500 leaflets distributed. So by my count, sir, the Women's Political Council owes Mr. Cannon's office for thirty-five reams of paper. We will find out the cost from Mr. Cannon and pay that bill immediately, sir." Actually, the WPC *had no treasury!* I paid that bill out of my own pocket.

As we will see, once the battle was begun, the bus company and city officials would request Dr. Trenholm to sit on a board with them to help arrive at a satisfactory conclusion of the boycott.

Dr. Trenholm did not participate personally in the boycott. But he was mentally and spiritually involved—and deeply so! He was financially involved, too, and often contributed to the collections for people who were suffering because of the loss of their jobs. He never went onto the housetop and screamed of what his contributions had been, but his actions, his constant advice, his donations, and his guidance amounted to much more than dollars and cents.

. . . Many times I went to him for advice for the WPC, and he never sent me away without submitting workable solutions to almost insoluble problems. Each answer he gave took consideration of the students, the college, and the masses who walked the streets daily for a better way of life, for he loved them all. His answers were in line with those of the ministers, for all we were demanding was justice on the buses. The Trenholms' concern reached out to the entire body of teachers, students, workers, and all that touched the college family. They were involved!

Thus I worked on the boycott with Dr. Trenholm's approval. Even so, I never missed a class! Or if I did, I made up the time. It wasn't easy. I had ten minutes' break to change classes, a thirty-minute morning break, forty-five minutes for lunch, and then back to class for the rest of the day. All crucial meetings pertaining to the boycott were scheduled during my off periods, evenings, and Saturdays. Nobody complained. But if I had to leave a class, I gave the students work to do, for I never, in thirty years of teaching, went to a class without a lesson plan. I worked and got paid for my service, both in terms of finance and students' gratitude. Students knew that I was asked to serve, and they were proud, for they would have an opportunity to speak their opinion, and they had excellent ideas. I taught white and black students and never saw color. I was pleased that I had such support for my involvement in the planning and subsequent day-to-day activities of the Montgomery Bus Boycott.

THE BOYCOTT BEGINS

On Friday morning, December 2, 1955, a goodly number of Montgomery's black clergymen happened to be meeting at the Hilliard Chapel A.M.E. Zion Church on Highland Avenue. When the Women's Political Council officers learned that the ministers were assembled in that meeting, we felt that God was on our side. It was easy for my two students and me to leave a handful of our circulars at the church, and those disciples of God could not truthfully have told where the notices came from if their very lives had depended on it. Many of the ministers received their notices of the boycott at the same time, in the same place. They all felt equal, included, appreciated, needed. It seemed predestined that this should be so.

One minister read the circular, inquired about the announcements, and found that all the city's black congregations were quite intelligent on the matter and were planning to support the one-day boycott with or without their ministers' leadership. It was then that the ministers decided that it was time for them, the leaders, to catch up with the masses. If the people were really determined to stage this one-day protest, then they would need moral support and Christian leadership. The churches could serve as channels of communication, as well as altars where people could come for prayer and spiritual guidance. Since the ministers were servants of the people and of God, and believed in the gospel of social justice, and since the churches were institutions supported by the people, the clerics could serve as channels through which all the necessary benefits could flow. Thus, for the first time in the history of Montgomery, black ministers united to lead action for civic improvement. There was no thought of denomination. Baptists, Presbyterians, Episcopalians, Lutherans, Congregationalists, and others joined together and became one band of ministerial brothers, offering their leadership to the masses. Had they not done so, they might have alienated themselves from their congregations and indeed lost members, for the masses were ready, and they were united!

The black ministers and their churches made the Montgomery Bus Boycott of 1955–1956 the success that it was. Had it not been for the ministers and the support they received from their wonderful congregations, the outcome of the boycott might have been different. The ministers gave themselves, their time, their contributions, their minds, their prayers, and their leadership, all of which set examples for the laymen to follow. They gave us confidence, faith in ourselves, faith in them and their leadership, that helped the congregations to support the movement every foot of the way.

Under the aegis of the Interdenominational Ministerial Alliance a meeting was called for that Friday evening at the Dexter Avenue Baptist Church, of which the Reverend Dr. Martin Luther King, Jr., was pastor. To this meeting were invited all the ministers, all club presidents and officers, all church organization heads, and any interested persons.

In the meantime, domestic workers who worked late into the day toyed with the slips of paper carrying the important information of the protest. Most of them destroyed the evidence, buried the information in their memories, and went merrily on their way to work. However, one lone black woman, a domestic loyal to her "white lady," in spite of her concern over the plight of her black peers and without any sense of obligation to her people, carried the handbill to her job and did not stop until the precious paper was safe in her "white lady's" hands. It was only a matter of minutes before the bus company, the City Commission, the chief of police, and the press knew its contents. The *Alabama Journal*, Montgomery's afternoon newspaper, ran a story on Saturday. Another article appeared in the *Montgomery Advertiser* on Sunday. The two local television stations and the four radio stations completed the coverage. The secret was out.

In recalling this particular incident later, the leaders of the boycott wondered if that woman's action had been providential, part of a divine plan to make the boycott succeed. If this was the case, she was not disloyal to her people, but rather was following the dictates of a higher authority!

The original intention had been that the whole affair would come as a complete surprise to whites. Then if all the darker set did not cooperate, no one would be the wiser. But now the news was out, and some misgivings and fear among blacks followed. Southern blacks, who had never been known to stick together as a group, to follow leadership, or to keep their mouths shut from exposing secrets, were on the spot!

One good thing, however, came from the revelation: the few black citizens in remote corners of the city who might not have gotten the news of the boycott, knew it now. The news that circulated through the newspapers, radio, television, and other channels of communication covered every possible isolated place not reached by the leaflets.

Publicity given the Monday boycott probably accounted, too, for the very large attendance which turned out for the Friday night meeting at Dexter Avenue Baptist Church. More than one hundred leaders were present.

There the organization of the boycott began. Special committees were set up. The main one focused on transportation. To help the walking public, volunteer cars had to be pooled, taxis had to be contacted, and donations had to be determined through cooperative means. Routes had to be mapped out to get workers to all parts of the city. Regular bus routes had to be followed so that workers who "walked along" the streets could be picked up. This committee, headed by Alfonso Campbell and staffed by volunteer workers, worked all night Friday to complete this phase of the program. The pickup system was so effectively planned that many writers described it as comparable in precision to a military operation.

What the ministers failed to do at that meeting was to select one person who would head the boycott. Those present discussed it, pointing out the leadership preparation of various individuals, but no definite decision was made. That had to wait until Monday afternoon, when the ministers realized that the one-day boycott was going to be successful. Then they met again, and Dr. Martin Luther King, Jr., agreed to accept the leadership post.

Lieutenant William Calley at the time of his trial for the massacre of Vietnamese at the village of My Lai. Sentenced to life imprisonment for killing "at least" twenty-two people, Calley won public support and was paroled in 1974.

PART SIX

New Boundaries

Discontent and Yearning for Security

Americans in the first half of the twentieth century built a new kind of nation. In the second half of that century, they have lived uneasily in it. They have a national culture that dominates all regions of the nation and much of the world, a national consumer-driven market, mass media that shape our most personal aspirations, active governments that provide services and regulations both greatly wanted and deeply suspect, and an international role of superpower that has made for a massive national security state.

The African American struggle for equality, the unrest among young people, the rise of a greatly enlarged and mobile middle class, and the reawakening of vocal political movements on both the political right and the left were products of the new era. The idealism of the 1960s found expression in the "Port Huron Statement" by the influential Students for a Democratic Society. Both the idealism and the heartbreak of that decade are reflected in letters sent home by civil rights workers in Mississippi. The fight for civil liberties continued past the 1960s, most notably in the women's movement, whose roots in the postwar years are visible in the letters written to Betty Friedan after publication of her seminal book, *The Feminine Mystique*, in 1963.

Overshadowing all American lives, however, was the Vietnam War, the nation's longest and strangest war. The incident at My Lai, untypical as it was in most ways, became a potent symbol of what the war—and, many feared, the nation—had become. The stalemated war contributed to a major change in national mood as a sizable segment of society began calling for order, consolidation, and traditional values.

Yet much of the American future continues to reflect the strengths of the past. A new generation of immigrants, represented by José and Rosa in the excerpt from their interview with Al Santoli, like generations of immigrants before them, left political and economic instability in their homelands to come to a new land in renewal of the American dream of prosperity and good fortune. And as in previous times, Americans of longer ancestry in this country were disturbed by the presence of the newcomers. And Ronald Reagan's presidency, intertwining American hopes and memories in a way that no popular critic could disentangle, ushered in a new conservative era. Attacks on active government made welfare a target for reformers jeopardizing the way of life of women like Odessa Williams. Mark Helprin's rethinking of his stance toward the war in Vietnam is representative of the struggle within many Americans to understand and define the nation we have become. And, just as a character in the 1967 film *The Graduate* whispered to the young hero the magic word *plastics*, so a new generation hears the vocabulary of computers as they make themselves at home in the newest new frontier of cyberspace.

Points of View: The My Lai Incident (1968–70)

37

Disbelief and Corroboration

Ronald L. Ridenhour et al.

Throughout the twentieth century, guerrilla wars have led to atrocities, and Vietnam was no exception. Guerrillas do not obey the international rules of warfare and often control areas through deliberate terror. When the Vietcong (Vietnamese communists) captured the ancient city of Hué during the Tet Offensive, they murdered hundreds, perhaps thousands, some of whom were buried alive. The attempt to eradicate guerrillas from among a population, any member of which might be a friend, an enemy, or simply a poor peasant who wants to be left alone, inevitably produces episodes of indiscriminate killing of civilians. One U.S. "pacification" effort in a Mekong Delta province in 1969, for example, produced an official body count of eleven thousand Vietcong killed. That only 748 weapons were captured makes it likely that very many of those dead were noncombatants.

The massacre at My Lai on March 16, 1968 was the most notorious atrocity on the part of the American forces in Vietnam, causing many around the world to forget the discipline and restraint of countless other American troops since the beginning of the intervention. Company C (Charlie) of Task Force Barker, part of the Americal Division, after a particularly forceful briefing in which the men were reminded of previous casualties they had suffered at the hands of the VC, attacked the village of My Lai, known to be a VC stronghold. Finding no enemy forces there, they nevertheless opened fire on the old men, women, and children who remained in the ham-

let, killing somewhere between two and four hundred. Rapes preceded several of the killings.

However awful the war in Vietnam and however frequent atrocities on all sides, the men of Charlie Company and those who heard about My Lai knew that they had done something far out of the ordinary. Neither they nor their superiors wanted to talk about what happened. The standard press release, although written by an eyewitness, made no reference to atrocities. A cover-up had begun that lasted until a year later when Ronald Ridenhour, a former infantryman, wrote a letter to Congress, forcing an investigation that made available the documents you will read.

BEFORE YOU READ

1. Why did Ridenhour write his letter? Does the letter convincingly present the need for an investigation?

2. Are there any indications in the documents that military personnel during the raid objected to what was happening?

3. What did the author of the press release intend to convey? Why do you think he did this? Do you think he was ordered to do so?

LETTER TO CONGRESS FROM RON RIDENHOUR

Mr. Ron Ridenhour
1416 East Thomas Road #104
Phoenix, Arizona

March 29, 1969

Gentlemen:

It was late in April, 1968 that I first heard of "Pinkville"[1] and what allegedly happened there. I received that first report with some skepticism, but in the following months I was to hear similar stories from such a wide variety of people that it became impossible for me to disbelieve that something rather dark and bloody did indeed occur sometime in March, 1968 in a village called "Pinkville" in the Republic of Viet Nam.

The circumstances that led to my having access to the reports I'm about to relate need explanation. I was inducted in March, 1967 into the U. S. Army. After receiving various training I was assigned to the 70th Infantry Detachment (LRP), 11th Light Infantry Brigade at Schofield Barracks, Hawaii, in early October, 1967. That unit, the 70th Infantry Detachment (LRP), was disbanded a week before the 11th Brigade shipped out for Viet Nam on the 5th of December, 1967. All of the men from whom I later heard reports of the "Pinkville" incident were reassigned to "C" Company, 1st Battalion, 20th Infantry, 11th Light Infantry Brigade. I was reassigned to the aviation section of

Peers Report, vol. 1, pp. 1–7 to 1–11.

    1. **"Pinkville":** army slang for the vicinity around My Lai.

Headquarters Company 11th LIB. After we had been in Viet Nam for 3 to 4 months many of the men from the 70th Inf. Det. (LRP) began to transfer into the same unit, "E" Company, 51st Infantry (LRP).

In late April, 1968 I was awaiting orders for a transfer from HHC, 11th Brigade to Company "E," 51st Inf. (LRP), when I happened to run into Pfc "Butch" Gruver, whom I had known in Hawaii. Gruver told me he had been assigned to "C" Company 1st of the 20th until April 1st when he transferred to the unit that I was headed for. During the course of our conversation he told me the first of many reports I was to hear of "Pinkville."

"Charlie" Company 1/20 had been assigned to Task Force Barker in late February, 1968 to help conduct "search and destroy" operations on the Batangan Peninsula, Barker's area of operation. The task force was operating out of L. F. Dottie, located five or six miles north of Quang Nhai city on Viet Namese National Highway 1. Gruver said that Charlie Company had sustained casualties; primarily from mines and booby traps, almost everyday from the first day they arrived on the peninsula. One village area was particularly troublesome and seemed to be infested with booby traps and enemy soldiers. It was located about six miles northeast of Quang Nhai city at approximate coordinates B.S. 728795. It was a notorious area and the men of Task Force Barker had a special name for it: they called it "Pinkville." One morning in the latter part of March, Task Force Barker moved out from its firebase headed for "Pinkville." Its mission: destroy the trouble spot and all of its inhabitants.

When "Butch" told me this I didn't quite believe that what he was telling me was true, but he assured me that it was and went on to describe what had happened. The other two companies that made up the task force cordoned off the village so that "Charlie" Company could move through to destroy the structures and kill the inhabitants. Any villagers who ran from Charlie Company were stopped by the encircling companies. I asked "Butch" several times if all the people were killed. He said that he thought they were, men, women and children. He recalled seeing a small boy, about three or four years old, standing by the trail with a gunshot wound in one arm. The boy was clutching his wounded arm with his other hand, while blood trickled between his fingers. He was staring around himself in shock and disbelief at what he saw. "He just stood there with big eyes staring around like he didn't understand; he didn't believe what was happening. Then the captain's RTO (radio operator) put a burst of 16 (M-16 rifle) fire into him." It was so bad, Gruver said, that one of the men in his squad shot himself in the foot in order to be medivac-ed out of the area so that he would not have to participate in the slaughter. Although he had not seen it, Gruver had been told by people he considered trustworthy that one of the company's officers, 2nd Lieutenant Kally (this spelling may be incorrect) had rounded up several groups of villagers (each group consisting of a minimum of 20 persons of both sexes and all ages). According to the story, Kally then machine-gunned each group. Gruver estimated that the population of the village had been 300 to 400 people and that very few, if any, escaped.

After hearing this account I couldn't quite accept it. Somehow I just couldn't believe that not only had so many young American men participated in such an act of barbarism, but that their officers had ordered it. There were other men in the unit I was soon to be assigned to, "E" Company, 51st Infantry (LRP), who had been in Charlie Company at the time that Gruver alleged the incident at "Pinkville" had occurred. I became determined to ask them about "Pinkville" so that I might compare their accounts with Pfc Gruver's.

When I arrived at "Echo" Company, 51st Infantry (LRP) the first men I looked for were Pfc's Michael Terry, and William Doherty. Both were veterans of "Charlie" Company, 1/20 and "Pinkville." Instead of contradicting "Butch" Gruver's story they corroborated it, adding some tasty tidbits of information of their own. Terry and Doherty had been in the same squad and their platoon was the third platoon of "C" Company to pass through the village. Most of the people they came to were already dead. Those that weren't were sought out and shot. The platoon left nothing alive, neither livestock nor people. Around noon the two soldiers' squad stopped to eat. "Billy and I started to get out our chow," Terry said, "but close to us was a bunch of Vietnamese in a heap, and some of them were moaning. Kally (2nd Lt. Kally) had been through before us and all of them had been shot, but many weren't dead. It was obvious that they weren't going to get any medical attention so Billy and I got up and went over to where they were. I guess we sort of finished them off." Terry went on to say that he and Doherty then returned to where their packs were and ate lunch. He estimated the size of the village to be 200 to 300 people. Doherty thought that the population of "Pinkville" had been 400 people.

If Terry, Doherty and Gruver could be believed, then not only had "Charlie" Company received orders to slaughter all the inhabitants of the village, but those orders had come from the commanding officer of Task Force Barker, or possibly even higher in the chain of command. Pfc Terry stated that when Captain Medina (Charlie Company's commanding officer Captain Ernest Medina) issued the order for the destruction of "Pinkville" he had been hesitant, as if it were something he didn't want to do but had to. Others I spoke to concurred with Terry on this.

It was June before I spoke to anyone who had something of significance to add to what I had already been told of the "Pinkville" incident. It was the end of June, 1968 when I ran into Sargent Larry La Croix at the USO in Chu Lai. La Croix had been in 2nd Lt. Kally's platoon on the day Task Force Barker swept through "Pinkville." What he told me verified the stories of the others, but he also had something new to add. He had been a witness to Kally's gunning down of at least three separate groups of villagers. "It was terrible. They were slaughtering the villagers like so many sheep." Kally's men were dragging people out of bunkers and hootches and putting them together in a group. The people in the group were men, women and children of all ages. As soon as he felt that the group was big enough, Kally ordered an M-60 (machine-gun) set up and the people killed. La Croix said that he bore witness to this procedure at least three times. The three groups were of different sizes, one of about twenty people, one of about thirty people, and one of about forty people. When the first group was put together Kally ordered Pfc Torres to man the machine-gun and open fire on the villagers that had been grouped together. This Torres did, but before everyone in the group was down he ceased fire and refused to fire again. After ordering Torres to recommence firing several times, Lieutenant Kally took over the M-60 and finished shooting the remaining villagers in that first group himself. Sargent La Croix told me that Kally didn't bother to order anyone to take the machine-gun when the other two groups of villagers were formed. He simply manned it himself and shot down all villagers in both groups.

This account of Sargent La Croix's confirmed the rumors that Gruver, Terry and Doherty had previously told me about Lieutenant Kally. It also convinced me that there was a very substantial amount of truth to the stories that all of these men had told. If I needed more convincing, I was to receive it.

It was in the middle of November, 1968 just a few weeks before I was to return to the United States for separation from the army that I talked to Pfc Michael Bernhardt. Bernhardt had served his entire year in Viet Nam in "Charlie" Company 1/20 and he too was about to go home. "Bernie" substantiated the tales told by the other men I had talked to in vivid, bloody detail and added this. "Bernie" had absolutely refused to take part in the massacre of the villagers of "Pinkville" that morning and he thought that it was rather strange that the officers of the company had not made an issue of it. But that evening "Medina (Captain Ernest Medina) came up to me ("Bernie") and told me not to do anything stupid like write my congressman" about what had happened that day. Bernhardt assured Captain Medina that he had no such thing in mind. He had nine months left in Viet Nam and felt that it was dangerous enough just fighting the acknowledged enemy.

Exactly what did, in fact, occur in the village of "Pinkville" in March, 1968 I do not know for *certain*, but I am convinced that it was something very black indeed. I remain irrevocably persuaded that if you and I do truly believe in the principles, of justice and the equality of every man, however humble, before the law, that form the very backbone that this country is founded on, then we must press forward a widespread and public investigation of this matter with all our combined efforts. I think that it was Winston Churchill who once said "A country without a conscience is a country without a soul, and a country without a soul is a country that cannot survive." I feel that I must take some positive action on this matter. I hope that you will launch an investigation immediately and keep me informed of your progress. If you cannot, then I don't know what other course of action to take.

I have considered sending this to newspapers, magazines, and broadcasting companies, but I somehow feel that investigation and action by the Congress of the United States is the appropriate procedure, and as a conscientious citizen I have no desire to further besmirch the image of the American serviceman in the eyes of the world. I feel that this action, while probably it would promote attention, would not bring about the constructive actions that the direct actions of the Congress of the United States would.

Sincerely,

/s/ Ron Ridenhour

TESTIMONY OF ROBERT T'SOUVAS

Q: Have you ever heard of Pinkville?

A: Yes. As far as I remember Pinkville consisted of My Lai (4), My Lai (5), and My Lai (6), and maybe some other Hamlets. The Pinkville area was mostly our area of operation, to my knowledge.

Q: Is there one operation in the Pinkville area that stands out in your mind?

A: Yes. In March 1968 we went on an operation to My Lai (4) which is in the Pinkville area. This area stands out in my mind because there was so many women, children, and men killed.

I do not remember the name of my Platoon Leader or my Platoon Sergeant. After we got out of the helicopters, we organized. As soon as I got out the helicopter threw a smoke bomb and I and my Squad were told to look for the Viet Cong in the vicinity where the helicopter had dropped the smoke bomb. Names are hard to remember and I do not know at this time who the soldiers were that accompanied me. We searched for the Viet Cong, but we could not find them until the helicopter radioed and hovered at a certain spot right over the Viet Cong. Personnel in our Company went to the busy area and found a weapon. I do not know if they found the Viet Cong. I was there with my machine gun. After this my Platoon moved into the Hamlet and we just had to search and destroy mission. I seen people shot that didn't have weapons. I've seen the hootches burn, animals killed—just like saying going to Seoul and start burning hootches and shooting—a massacre wherein innocent people were being killed, hootches being burned, everything destroyed. They had no weapons and we were told that they were VC sympathizers. To come right to the point, we carried out our orders to the very point—Search and Destroy. In my mind, that covered the whole situation.

Q: How many people do you think was shot by C Company in My Lai (4)?

A: This is hard to say—from my personal observation I would say 80 that I have seen myself.

Q: What did the people that you saw shot consist of?

A: Women, men, children and animals.

Q: Did you at anytime receive hostile fire?

A: I was told that we were fired upon, but I myself did not receive direct fire.

My Lai File, Army Crimes Records Center, Fort Belvoir, Virginia.

Q: Were there still any people living in the Hamlet when you came through?

A: When we got there there was still people alive in the Hamlet and the Company was shooting them, however, when we left the Hamlet there was still some people alive.

Q: Did you see a trail in the village with a pile of dead women and children?

A: I seen dead women, children and men in groups and scattered on the trails and the rice paddies. I seen people running and just innocently being shot.

Q: Did you shoot 2 wounded children laying on the trail outside of My Lai (4)?

A: I opened up on people that were running. I do not remember that I shot at 2 children that were laying down on the trail. However, I do remember I did shoot a girl that was sitting there amongst 5 or more people, sitting there completely torn apart. She was screaming. I felt just as if it was my mother dying. I shot her to get her out of her misery. She was around 15. This happened inside the hamlet. However, I do not remember about the 2 children laying on the trail. I also shot 5 wounded villagers because they did not give them medical aid. They refused to give them medical aid. . . .

Q: Was the combat assault on My Lai (4) different than any of the others you were on?

A: Yes, I never heard anything so stupid as to search and destroy and to kill all those people.

Q: Is there anything else you would like to say?

A: I wanted to talk about this for a long time—and am glad now that it is off my chest—it is wrong. Even before it was investigated, I wanted to write about it to my Senator, but I didn't know how to go about it. This is all that I know about the incident. It is such a long time ago and it is hard to remember the exact sequence of events and I am not too good map reader and I will not be able to draw a sketch of the Hamlet and show how we went through the Hamlet.

JOURNAL OF THOMAS R. PARTSCH

Mar. 16 Sat.

Got up at 5:30 left at 7:15 we had 9 choppers. 2 lifts first landed had mortar team with us. We started to move slowly through the village shooting everything in sight children men and women and animals. Some was sickening. There legs were shot off and they were still moving it was just hanging there. I think there bodies were made of rubber. I didn't fire a round yet and didn't kill anybody not even a chicken I couldn't. We are know suppose to push through 2 more it is about 10 A.M. and we are taken a rest before going in. We also got 2 weapons M1 and a carbine our final destination is the Pinkville suppose to be cement bunkers we killed about 100 people after a while they said not to kill women and children. Stopped for chow about 1 P.M. we didn't do much after that. . . .

Mar. 17 Sun.

Got up at 6:30 foggy out. We didn't go to Pinkville went to My Lai 2, 3, and 4 no one was there we burned as we pushed. We got 4 VC and a nurse. . . .

Mar. 18 Mon.

We got with company and CA out to Dottie [their base] there is a lot of fuss on what happened at the village a Gen was asking questions. There is going to be an investigation on MEDINA. We are not supposed to say anything. I didn't think it was right but we did it at least I can say I didn't kill anybody. I think I wanted to but in another way I didn't.

CAPTAIN BRIAN LIVINGSTON'S LETTER
TO HIS WIFE

Saturday 16 March 68

Dear Betz,

Well its been a long day, saw some nasty sights. I saw the insertion of infantrymen and were they animals. The[y] preped the area first, then a lot of women and kids left the village. Then a gun team from the shark[s], a notorious killer of civilians, used their minny guns, people falling dead on the road. I've never seen so many people dead in one spot. Ninety-five percent were women and kids. We told the grunts on the ground of some injured kids. They helped them al[l-]right. A captain walked up to this little girl, he turned away took five steps, and fired a volly of shots into her. This Negro sergeant started shooting people in the head. Finally our OH23 saw some wounded kids, so we acted like medivacs[mede-vacs]. Another kid whom the grunts were going to "take care of" was next on our list. The OH23 took him to Quang Nai [Ngai] hospital. We had to do this while *we* held machine guns on our own troops— American troops. I'll tell you something it sure makes one wonder why we are here. I can also see why they hate helicopter pilots. If I ever [hear] a shark open his big mouth I'm going to shove my fist into his mouth.

We're trying to get the captain and sergeant afore mentioned reprimanded. I don't know if we will be successful, but we're trying. Enough for that.

Brian

Peers Report, vol. 4, exhibit M–21, p. 111.

38

Cover-Up and Outcome

General Westmoreland, President Nixon et al.

The revelation of the massacre at My Lai completed the thorough shaking of American confidence that events since its occurrence had initiated. Between March 1968 when the incident occurred and December 1969 when the New York Times and Life magazine broke the story, Martin Luther King, Jr., and Robert Kennedy were both assassinated; ghettoes all over the country erupted in riots; the Democratic National Convention degenerated into violence; George Wallace conducted his divisive presidential campaign; antiwar demonstrations escalated enormously; and despite a strategy of "disengagement" (that was being renamed "Vietnamization") American casualties were greater in 1969 than in any previous year.

With so much wrong it became difficult to assign responsibility for the massacre. A thorough and careful investigation, directed by the highly respected General William R. Peers, recommended charges against fourteen officers: two generals, two colonels, two lieutenant colonels, four majors, two captains, and two first lieutenants. In the end only Lieutenant William Calley was found guilty of killing. He was convicted of the deaths of "at least" twenty-two people and sentenced to life in prison. Several higher officers suffered administrative penalties: demotions, lost decorations, and letters of censure placed in their files for covering up the incident, although according to military law they could have been held responsible for criminal acts of which they should have been aware. The documents you will read present evidence of the cover-up and some of the reasons why it occurred.

Calley's conviction stirred massive controversy. Some regarded him a scapegoat for higher-ranking officers; others argued that amidst the confusion over who was a friend and who was an enemy in Vietnam, his acts could not be considered criminal. Jimmy Carter, then governor of Georgia, thought it unfair to single out Calley for punishment. President Nixon reduced his sentence, and in March 1974 he was paroled. When hearing of Calley's parole, General Peers told reporters: "To think that out of all those men, only one, Lieutenant William Calley, was brought to justice. And now, he's practically a hero. It's a tragedy." And in My Lai, Nyugen Bat, a hamlet chief who was not a Vietcong before the massacre, recalled, "After the shooting, all the villagers became Communists."

BEFORE YOU READ

1. Why did the Barker report and the Henderson investigation cover up the events at My Lai? What light does the Vietcong document throw on this question?

2. How does the testimony of Herbert L. Carter help you to understand why participants and observers at My Lai did not reveal what had happened?

3. How does General Westmoreland explain the My Lai incident? How persuasive is his explanation?

4. Why did President Nixon reduce Calley's sentence? Was this the right thing to do?

SERGEANT JAY ROBERTS, PRESS RELEASE ON MY LAI

CHU LAI, Vietnam—For the third time in recent weeks, the Americal Division's 11th Brigade infantrymen from Task Force Barker raided a Viet Cong stronghold known as "Pinkville" six miles northeast of Quang Ngai, killing 128 enemy in a running battle.

The action occurred in the coastal town of My Lai where, three weeks earlier, another company of the brigade's Task Force Barker fought its way out of a VC ambush, leaving 80 enemy dead.

The action began as units of the task force conducted a combat assault into a known Viet Cong stronghold. "Shark" gunships of the 174th Aviation Company escorted the troops into the area and killed four enemy during the assault. Other choppers from the 123d Aviation Battalion killed two enemy.

"The combat assault went like clockwork," commented LTC Frank Barker, New Haven, Conn., the task force commander. "We had two entire companies on the ground in less than an hour."

A company led by CPT Ernest Medina, Schofield Barracks, Hawaii, killed 14 VC minutes after landing. They recovered two M1 rifles, a carbine, a short-wave radio and enemy documents.

CAPTAIN BRIAN LIVINGSTON'S
LETTER TO HIS WIFE

19 March 68

Dear Betz,

. . . You remember I told you about the massacre I witnessed, well I read a follow-up story in the paper. The article said I quote "The American troops were in heavy combat with an unknown number of V. C. Two Americans were killed, seven wounded, and 128 V. C. killed." Thats a bunch of bull. I saw four V. C., that is, those with weapons, and the amazing thing about that, is two of them got away. It made me sick to watch it.

Brian

LIEUTENANT COLONEL FRANK A. BARKER, JR.,
"COMBAT ACTION REPORT" ON MY LAI

28 March 1968

8. *Intelligence:* Enemy forces in the area of operation were estimated to be one local force battalion located in the vicinity of My Lai, BS 728795 as shown in

Peers Report, vol. 4, p. 245.
Peers Report, vol. 4, Exhibit M–22, p. 113.
Peers Report, vol. 4, pp. 401–05.

Inclosure 1. This information was based upon previous combat operations in this area, visual reconnaissance, and PW and agent reports. During the operation it was estimated that only two local force companies supported by two to three local guerrilla platoons opposed the friendly forces. The area of operation consisted of six hamlets to varying degree of ruin, each separated by rice paddies which were bounded by a series of hedge rows and tree lines. The area was also honeycombed with tunnels and bunkers. . . .

9. *Mission:* To destroy enemy forces and fortifications in a VC base camp and to capture enemy personnel, weapons and supplies.

10. *Concept of Operation:* Task Force Barker conducts a helicopter assault on 160730 Mar 68 on a VC base camp vicinity BS 728795 with Company C, 1st Battalion, 20th Infantry landing to the west and Company B, 4th Battalion, 3d Infantry landing to the southeast of the VC base camp. Company A, 3d Battalion, 1st Infantry moves by foot to blocking positions north of the base camp prior to the helicopter assault. . . .

11. *Execution:* The order was issued on 14 March 1968. Coordination with supporting arms reconnaissance and positioning of forces was conducted on 15 Mar 68. On 160726 Mar 68 a three minute artillery preparation began on the first landing zone and at 0730 hours the first lift for Co C touched down while helicopter gunships provided suppressive fires. At 0747 hours the last lift of Co C was completed. The initial preparation resulted in 68 VC KIA's in the enemy's combat outpost positions. Co C then immediately attacked to the east receiving enemy small arms fire as they pressed forward. At 0809H a three minute artillery preparation on the second landing zone began and the first lift for Co B touched down at 0815 hours. At 0827 the last lift of Co B was completed and Co B moved to the north and east receiving only light enemy resistance initially. As Co B approached the area of the VC base camp, enemy defensive fires increased. One platoon from Co B flanked the enemy positions and engaged one enemy platoon resulting in 30 enemy KIA. Throughout the day Co B and Co C received sporadic sniper fire and encountered numerous enemy booby traps. . . . At 1715 hours Co C linked-up with Co B and both units went into a perimeter defense for the night in preparation for conducting search and destroy operations the next day. With the establishment of the night defensive position at 161800 March 1968 the operation was terminated.

12. *Results:*

A. Enemy losses:
   (1) Personnel:
      128 KIA
       11 VCS CIA
   (2) Equipment captured:
       1 M-1 rifle
       2 M-1 carbines
      10 Chicom hand grenades

     8 US M-26 hand grenades
  410 rounds small arms ammo
     4 US steel helmets with liners
     5 US canteens with covers
     7 US pistol belts
     9 sets US web equipment
     2 short wave transistor radios
     3 boxes of medical supplies

 (3) Equipment and facilities destroyed:

    16 booby traps
     1 large tunnel complex
    14 small tunnel complexes
     8 bunkers
       numerous sets of web equipment

B. Friendly losses:

     2 US KHA
   11 US WHA

15. *Commander Analysis:* This operation was well planned, well executed and successful. Friendly casualties were light and the enemy suffered heavily. On this operation the civilian population supporting the VC in the area numbered approximately 200. This created a problem in population control and medical care of those civilians caught in fires of the opposing forces. However, the infantry unit on the ground and helicopters were able to assist civilians in leaving the area and in caring for and/or evacuating the wounded.

A VIETCONG LEAFLET ON MY LAI

Since the Americans heavy loss in the spring they have become like wounded animals that are crazy and cruel. They bomb places where many people live, places which are not good choices for bombings, such as the cities within the provinces, especially in Hue, Saigon, and Ben Tre. In Hue the US newspapers reported that 70% of the homes were destroyed and 10,000 people killed or left homeless. The newspapers and radios of Europe also tell of the killing of the South Vietnamese people by the Americans. The English tell of the action where the Americans are bombing the cities of South Vietnam. The Americans will be sentenced first by the Public in Saigon. It is there where the people will lose sentiment for them because they bomb the people and all people will soon be against them. The world public objects to this bombing including the American public and that of its Allies. The American often shuts his eye and closes his ear and continues his crime.

In the operation of 15 March 1968 in Son Tinh District the American enemies went crazy. They used machine guns and every other kind of weapon to

Peers Report, vol. 4, pp. 264–65.

kill 500 people who had empty hands, in Tinh Khe (Son My) Village (Son Tinh District, Quang Ngai Province). There were many pregnant women some of which were only a few days from childbirth. The Americans would shoot everybody they say. They killed people and cows, burned homes. There were some families in which all members were killed.

When the red evil Americans remove their prayer shirts they appear as barbaric men.

When the American wolves remove their sheepskin their sharp meat-eating teeth show. They drink our peoples blood with animal sentimentalities.

Our people must choose one way to beat them until they are dead, and stop wriggling.

COLONEL FRANK HENDERSON, REPORT OF INVESTIGATION OF MY LAI INCIDENT

24 April 1968

Commanding General
Americal Division
APO SF 96374

1. (U) An investigation has been conducted of the allegations cited in Inclosure 1. The following are the results of this investigations.

2. (C) On the day in question, 16 March 1968, Co C 1st Bn 20th Inf and Co B 4th Bn 3rd Inf as part of Task Force Barker, 11th Inf Bde, conducted a combat air assault in the vicinity of My Lai Hamlet (Son My Village) in eastern Son Tinh District. This area has long been an enemy strong hold, and Task Force Barker had met heavy enemy opposition in this area on 12 and 23 February 1968. All persons living in this area are considered to be VC or VC sympathizers by the District Chief. Artillery and gunship preparatory fire were placed on the landing zones used by the two companies. Upon landing and during their advance on the enemy positions, the attacking forces were supported by gunships from the 174th Avn Co and Co B, 23rd Avn Bn. By 1500 hours all enemy resistance had ceased and the remaining enemy forces had withdrawn. The results of this operation were 128 VC soldiers KIA. During preparatory fires and the ground action by the attacking companies 20 noncombatants caught in the battle area were killed. US Forces suffered 2 KHA and 10 WHA by booby traps and 1 man slightly wounded in the foot by small arms fire. No US soldier was killed by sniper fire as was the alleged reson for killing the civilians. Interviews with LTC Frank A. Barker, TF Commander; Maj Charles C. Calhoun, TF S3; CPT Ernest L. Medina, Co Co C, 1–20 and CPT Earl Michles, Co Co B, 4–3 revealed that at no time were any civilians gathered together and killed by US soldiers. The civilian habitants in the area

Peers Report, vol. 3, pp. 261–62.

began withdrawing to the southwest as soon as the operation began and within the first hour and a half all visible civilians had cleared the area of operations.

3. (C) The Son Tinh District Chief does not give the allegations any importance and he pointed out that the two hamlets where the incidents is alleged to have happened are in an area controlled by the VC since 1964. CC Toen, Cmdr 2d Arvn Div reported that the making of such allegations against US Forces is a common technique of the VC propaganda machine. Inclosure 2 is a translation of an actual VC propaganda message targeted at the ARVN soldier and urging him to shoot Americans. This message was given to this headquarters by the CO, 2d ARVN Division o/a 17 April 1968 as matter of information. It makes the same allegations as made by the Son My Village Chief in addition to other claims of atrocities by American soldiers.

4. (C) It is concluded that 20 non-combatants were inadvertently killed when caught in the area of preparatory fires and in the cross fires of the US and VC forces on 16 March 1968. It is further concluded that no civilians were gathered together and shot by US soldiers. The allegation that US Forces shot and killed 450–500 civilians is obviously a Viet Cong propaganda move to discredit the United States in the eyes of the Vietnamese people in general and the ARVN soldier in particular.

5. (C) It is recommended that a counter-propaganda campaign be waged against the VC in eastern Son Tinh District.

TESTIMONY OF HERBERT L. CARTER

Q: Did you ever hear anything about an investigation into the My Lai incident?

A: Yes.

Q: What did you hear?

A: I heard that they said if anybody asks around or any questions about what happened at My Lai, to tell them that we were fired upon and say that a sniper round had come in or something.

Q: Whom did you hear this from?

A: I was in the hospital at this time at Qui Nhon, and a couple of guys from the company came over. I'm not bragging, but most of the guys in that company liked me. I didn't bother nobody. I did my job and they did their job. We drank together.

Q: They came to see you in the hospital?

A: Yes. A lot of guys came over. You know, when they came back through, they would come over.

Q: Captain MEDINA told us that soon after this operation he got the company together and told them that there was an investigation and it would be better if nobody talked about it while the investigation was underway. Did your friends say anything about this?

Peers Report, vol. 2, bk. 24, pp. 44–50.

A: No. The way they ran it down to me was like somebody was trying to cover something up or something, which I knew they were. They had to cover up something like that.

Q: I think you know that it took a long time for the story of My Lai to get out. What is your opinion as to why this wasn't reported right at the time? You did mention about some of your friends coming and telling you to keep quiet. Do you know anything else?

A: Like a lot of people wondered how come I didn't say something. Now, who would believe me. I go up to you with a story like that and you would call me a nut. You would tell me I am a nut and that there was nothing like this going on. You would think that nothing like this goes on in the United States. Just like I was in a bar a couple of weeks ago, and there was a drunk in there. He was standing there reading a paper and he was asking me if I believed that things like that actually went on, and I said, "I wouldn't know, pal." It was kind of weird. This happened three different times. One time I was sitting up there with a friend of mine, and my partner told me to be quiet about the whole mess. Some people want to talk that talk all day long, and they just don't know this and that about what they are talking about.

Q: Did you or the other members of the company ever think about these killings as a war crime?

A: Not at that time. No. I didn't want to think about anything at the time.

Q: In your statement to Mr. CASH you spoke of it as murder?

A: Yes.

Q: You looked at it as being murder, but you didn't think about it as being a war crime?

A: That's right. I thought it was just the poor misfortunes of war.

GENERAL WILLIAM C. WESTMORELAND

In the criminal cases, acquittal resulted in all but that of a platoon leader, First Lieutenant William L. Calley, Jr. Charged with the murder of more than a hundred civilians, he was convicted on March 29, 1971, of the murder of "at least" twenty-two. He was sentenced to dismissal from the service and con-finement at hard labor for life, but the latter was reduced by judicial review to twenty years and further reduced after my retirement by Secretary of the Army Howard Callaway to ten years, an action that President Nixon sustained. The case was subsequently and for a long time under judicial appeal in the federal courts.

Lieutenant Calley was legally judged by a jury whose members all were fa-miliar with the nature of combat in Vietnam and well aware that even the kind of war waged in Vietnam is no license for murder. The vast majority of Amer-icans in Vietnam did their best to protect civilian lives and property, often at their own peril. That some civilians, even many, died by accident or inevitably

William C. Westmoreland, *A Soldier Reports* (New York: Doubleday, 1976), pp. 377–78.

in the course of essential military operations dictated by the enemy's presence among the people was no justification or rationale for the conscious massacre of defenseless babies, children, mothers, and old men in a kind of diabolical slow-motion nightmare that went on for the better part of a day, with a cold-blooded break for lunch. I said at the time of the revelation: "It could not have happened—but it did."

Although I can in no way condone Lieutenant Calley's acts—or those of any of his colleagues who may have participated but went unpunished—I must have compassion for him. Judging from the events at My Lai, being an officer in the United States Army exceeded Lieutenant Calley's abilities. Had it not been for educational draft deferments, which prevented the Army from drawing upon the intellectual segment of society for its junior officers, Calley probably never would have been an officer. Denied that usual reservoir of talent, the Army had to lower its standards. Although some who became officers under those conditions performed well, others, such as Calley, failed.

An army has a corps of officers to insure leadership: to see that orders are given and carried out and that the men conduct themselves properly. Setting aside the crime involved, Lieutenant Calley's obvious lack of supervision and failure to set a proper example himself were contrary to orders and policy, and the supervision he exercised fell far short.

In reducing standards for officers, both the United States Army and the House Armed Services Committee, which originated the policy of deferments for college students, must bear the blame. It would have been better to have gone short of officers than to have accepted applicants whose credentials left a question as to their potential as leaders.

PRESIDENT RICHARD M. NIXON

On March 29, 1971, just days after the withdrawal of ARVN troops from Laos, First Lieutenant William Calley, Jr., was found guilty by an Army court-martial of the premeditated murder of twenty-two South Vietnamese civilians. The public furore over Lam Son had just begun to settle down, and now we were faced with still another Vietnam-related controversy. This one had been simmering since the fall of 1969, when the murders were first revealed.

It was in March 1968, ten months before I became President, that Calley led his platoon into My Lai, a small hamlet about 100 miles northeast of Saigon. The village had been a Vietcong stronghold, and our forces had suffered many casualties trying to clear it out. Calley had his men round up the villagers and then ordered that they be shot; many were left sprawled lifeless in a drainage ditch.

Calley's crime was inexcusable. But I felt that many of the commentators and congressmen who professed outrage about My Lai were not really as interested in the moral questions raised by the Calley case as they were interested

Richard M. Nixon, *RN: The Memoirs of Richard Nixon* (New York: Grossett, 1978), pp. 449–50.

in using it to make political attacks against the Vietnam War. For one thing, they had been noticeably uncritical of North Vietnamese atrocities. In fact, the calculated and continual role that terror, murder, and massacre played in the Vietcong strategy was one of the most underreported aspects of the entire Vietnam war. Much to the discredit of the media and the antiwar activists, this side of the story was only rarely included in descriptions of Vietcong policy and practices.

On March 31 the court-martial sentenced Calley to life in prison at hard labor. Public reaction to this announcement was emotional and sharply divided. More than 5,000 telegrams arrived at the White House, running 100 to 1 in favor of clemency.

John Connally and Jerry Ford recommended in strong terms that I use my powers as Commander in Chief to reduce Calley's prison time. Connally said that justice had been served by the sentence, and that now the reality of maintaining public support for the armed services and for the war had to be given primary consideration. I talked to Carl Albert and other congressional leaders. All of them agreed that emotions in Congress were running high in favor of presidential intervention.

I called Admiral Moorer on April 1 and ordered that, pending Calley's appeal, he should be released from the stockade and confined instead to his quarters on the base. When this was announced to the House of Representatives, there was a spontaneous round of applause on the floor. Reaction was particularly strong and positive in the South. George Wallace, after a visit with Calley, said that I had done the right thing. Governor Jimmy Carter of Georgia said that I had made a wise decision. Two days later I had Ehrlichman announce that I would personally review the Calley case before any final sentence was carried out.

By April 1974, Calley's sentence had been reduced to ten years, with eligibility for parole as early as the end of that year. I reviewed the case as I had said I would but decided not to intervene. Three months after I resigned, the Secretary of the Army decided to parole Calley.

I think most Americans understood that the My Lai massacre was not representative of our people, of the war we were fighting, or of our men who were fighting it; but from the time it first became public the whole tragic episode was used by the media and the antiwar forces to chip away at our efforts to build public support for our Vietnam objectives and policies.

FOR CRITICAL THINKING

1. Why did the My Lai massacre occur? Does the response to it, including both the cover-up and the outcome, suggest why it could occur?

2. Did higher-ranking officers bear any of the responsibility for the massacre? What policies encouraged such an occurrence?

3. Should Calley have been required to serve a larger part of his sentence, or were the actions of President Nixon and other officials the right ones to take?

39

Agenda for a Generation

Students for a Democratic Society

In the course of the 1960s, hundreds of thousands of college students engaged in protests against nuclear weapons, in support of the civil rights movement, in protest against college and university policies, and, especially, against the Vietnam War. Student radicalism was generally a local phenomenon, as specific campuses reacted to local or national events. But campus radicals did reach out for some limited coordination and inspiration. Much of it came from Students for a Democratic Society (SDS).

While SDS had its origins in a youth movement connected with the anticommunist socialist group, the League for Industrial Democracy, it assumed the role of spokesperson for politically left students when two activists at the University of Michigan, Al Haber and Tom Hayden, coordinated groups at numerous campuses and organized a national meeting in 1962. This meeting, held at the United Auto Workers center in Port Huron, Michigan, approved the following manifesto, which was drafted by Hayden. The Port Huron Statement *touched on most of the themes of 1960s radicalism, offering an "agenda for a generation," an agenda which that generation eventually took into the streets.*

BEFORE YOU READ

1. What is the tone of *The Port Huron Statement?* Why might it have appealed particularly to college students?

2. What are its main criticisms of American society? Its main hopes for the future? Does it emphasize cultural and moral issues or political and economic ones?

3. Do you think the authors of this statement expected the protests and demonstrations that college students were later to engage in?

INTRODUCTION: AGENDA
FOR A GENERATION

We are people of this generation, bred in at least modest comfort, housed now in universities, looking uncomfortably to the world we inherit.

When we were kids the United States was the wealthiest and strongest country in the world; the only one with the atom bomb, the least scarred by modern war, an initiator of the United Nations that we thought would distribute Western influence throughout the world. Freedom and equality for each individual, government of, by, and for the people—these American values we found good, principles by which we could live as men. Many of us began maturing in complacency.

As we grew, however, our comfort was penetrated by events too troubling to dismiss. First, the permeating and victimizing fact of human degradation, symbolized by the Southern struggle against racial bigotry, compelled most of us from silence to activism. Second, the enclosing fact of the Cold War, symbolized by the presence of the Bomb, brought awareness that we ourselves, and our friends, and millions of abstract "others" we knew more directly because of our common peril, might die at any time. We might deliberately ignore, or avoid, or fail to feel all other human problems, but not these two, for these were too immediate and crushing in their impact, too challenging in the demand that we as individuals take the responsibility for encounter and resolution.

While these and other problems either directly oppressed us or rankled our consciences and became our own subjective concerns, we began to see complicated and disturbing paradoxes in our surrounding America. The declaration "all men are created equal . . ." rang hollow before the facts of Negro life in the South and the big cities of the North. The proclaimed peaceful intentions of the United States contradicted its economic and military investments in the Cold War status quo.

We witnessed, and continue to witness, other paradoxes. With nuclear energy whole cities can easily be powered, yet the dominant nation-states seem more likely to unleash destruction greater than that incurred in all wars of human history. Although our own technology is destroying old and creating new forms of social organization, men still tolerate meaningless work and idleness. While two-thirds of mankind suffers undernourishment, our own upper classes revel amidst superfluous abundance. Although world population is expected to double in forty years, the nations still tolerate anarchy as a major principle of international conduct and uncontrolled exploitation governs the mapping of the earth's physical resources. Although mankind desperately needs revolutionary leadership, America rests in national stalemate, its goals ambiguous and tradition-bound instead of informed and clear, its democratic system apathetic and manipulated rather than "of, by, and for the people."

Not only did tarnish appear on our image of American virtue, not only did disillusion occur when the hypocrisy of American ideals was discovered, but we began to sense that what we had originally seen as the American Golden Age was actually the decline of an era. The worldwide outbreak of revolution against colonialism and imperialism, the entrenchment of totalitarian states, the menace of war, overpopulation, international disorder, supertechnology— these trends were testing the tenacity of our own commitment to democracy and freedom and our abilities to visualize their application to a world in upheaval.

Some would have us believe that Americans feel contentment amidst prosperity—but might it not better be called a glaze above deeply felt anxieties about their role in the new world? And if these anxieties produce a developed indifference to human affairs, do they not as well produce a yearning to believe there *is* an alternative to the present, that something *can* be done to change circumstances in the school, the workplaces, the bureaucracies, the government? It is to this latter yearning, at once the spark and engine of change, that we direct our present appeal. The search for truly democratic alternatives to the present, and a commitment to social experimentation with them, is a worthy and fulfilling human enterprise, one which moves us and, we hope, others today. On such a basis do we offer this document of our convictions and analysis: as an effort in understanding and changing the conditions of humanity in the late twentieth century, an effort rooted in the ancient, still unfulfilled conception of man attaining determining influence over his circumstances of life.

VALUES

Making values explicit—an initial task in establishing alternatives—is an activity that has been devalued and corrupted. The conventional moral terms of the age, the politician moralities—"free world," "people's democracies"—reflect realities poorly, if at all, and seem to function more as ruling myths than as descriptive principles. But neither has our experience in the universities brought us moral enlightenment. Our professors and administrators sacrifice controversy to public relations; their curriculums change more slowly than the living events of the world; their skills and silence are purchased by investors in the arms race; passion is called unscholastic. The questions we might want raised—what is really important? can we live in a different and better way? if we wanted to change society, how would we do it?—are not thought to be questions of a "fruitful, empirical nature," and thus are brushed aside.

Men have unrealized potential for self-cultivation, self-direction, self-understanding, and creativity. It is this potential that we regard as crucial and to which we appeal, not to the human potentiality for violence, unreason, and submission to authority. The goal of man and society should be human independence: a concern not with image of popularity but with finding a meaning in life that is personally authentic; a quality of mind not compulsively driven by a sense of powerlessness, nor one which unthinkingly adopts status values, nor one which represses all threats to its habits, but one which has full, spontaneous access to present and past experiences, one which easily unites the fragmented parts of personal history, one which openly faces problems which are troubling and unresolved; one with an intuitive awareness of possibilities, an active sense of curiosity, an ability and willingness to learn.

This kind of independence does not mean egotistic individualism—the object is not to have one's way so much as it is to have a way that is one's own. Nor do we deify man—we merely have faith in his potential.

Human relationships should involve fraternity and honesty. Human interdependence is contemporary fact; human brotherhood must be willed, however, as a condition of future survival and as the most appropriate form of social relations. Personal links between man and man are needed, especially to go beyond the partial and fragmentary bonds of function that bind men only as worker to worker, employer to employee, teacher to student, American to Russian.

Loneliness, estrangement, isolation describe the vast distance between man and man today. These dominant tendencies cannot be overcome by better personnel management, nor by improved gadgets, but only when a love of man overcomes the idolatrous worship of things by man. As the individualism we affirm is not egoism, the selflessness we affirm is not self-elimination. On the contrary, we believe in generosity of a kind that imprints one's unique individual qualities in the relation to other men, and to all human activity. Further, to dislike isolation is not to favor the abolition of privacy; the latter differs from isolation in that it occurs or is abolished according to individual will.

We would replace power rooted in possession, privilege, or circumstance by power and uniqueness rooted in love, reflectiveness, reason, and creativity. As a *social system* we seek the establishment of a democracy of individual participation, governed by two central aims: that the individual share in those social decisions determining the quality and direction of his life; that society be organized to encourage independence in men and provide the media for their common participation. . . .

THE STUDENTS

In the last few years, thousands of American students demonstrated that they at least felt the urgency of the times. They moved actively and directly against racial injustices, the threat of war, violations of individual rights of conscience and, less frequently, against economic manipulation. They succeeded in restoring a small measure of controversy to the campuses after the stillness of the McCarthy period. They succeeded, too, in gaining some concessions from the people and institutions they opposed, especially in the fight against racial bigotry.

The significance of these scattered movements lies not in their success or failure in gaining objectives—at least not yet. Nor does the significance lie in the intellectual "competence" or "maturity" of the students involved—as some pedantic elders allege. The significance is in the fact the students are breaking the crust of apathy and overcoming the inner alienation that remain the defining characteristics of American college life.

If student movements for change are still rarities on the campus scene, what is commonplace there? The real campus, the familiar campus, is a place of private people, engaged in their notorious "inner emigration." It is a place of commitment to business-as-usual, getting ahead, playing it cool. It is a place of mass affirmation of the Twist, but mass reluctance toward the controversial public stance. Rules are accepted as "inevitable," bureaucracy as "just circumstances," irrelevance as "scholarship," selflessness as "martyrdom," politics as "just another way to make people do what you want, and an unprofitable one, too."

Almost no students value activity as citizens. Passive in public, they are hardly more idealistic in arranging their private lives: Gallup concludes they will settle for "low success, and won't risk high failure." There is not much willingness to take risks (not even in business), no setting of dangerous goals, no real conception of personal identity except one manufactured in the image of others, no real urge for personal fulfillment except to be almost as successful as the very successful people. Attention is being paid to social status (the quality of shirt collars, meeting people, getting wives or husbands, making solid contacts for later on); much, too, is paid to academic status (grades, honors, the med school rat race). But neglected generally is real intellectual status, the personal cultivation of the mind.

"Students don't even give a damn about the apathy," one has said. Apathy toward apathy begets a privately constructed universe, a place of systematic study schedules, two nights each week for beer, a girl or two, and early marriage; a framework infused with personality, warmth, and under control, no matter how unsatisfying otherwise. . . .

The academic life contains reinforcing counterparts to the way in which extracurricular life is organized. The academic world is founded on a teacher-student relation analogous to the parent-child relation which characterizes *in loco parentis*. Further, academia includes a radical separation of the student from the material of study. That which is studied, the social reality, is "objectified" to sterility, dividing the student from life—just as he is restrained in active involvement by the deans controlling student government. The specialization of function and knowledge, admittedly necessary to our complex technological and social structure, has produced an exaggerated compartmentalization of study and understanding. This has contributed to an overly parochial view, by faculty, of the role of its research and scholarship, to a discontinuous and truncated understanding, by students, of the surrounding social order; and to a loss of personal attachment, by nearly all, to the worth of study as a humanistic enterprise.

There is, finally, the cumbersome academic bureaucracy extending throughout the academic as well as the extracurricular structures, contributing to the sense of outer complexity and inner powerlessness that transforms the honest searching of many students to a ratification of convention and, worse, to a numbness to present and future catastrophes. The size and financing systems of the university enhance the permanent trusteeship of the administrative bureaucracy, their power leading to a shift within the university toward the value standards of business and the administrative mentality. Huge foundations and other private financial interests shape the under-financed colleges and universities, not only making them more commercial, but less disposed to diagnose society critically, less open to dissent. Many social and physical scientists, neglecting the liberating heritage of higher learning, develop "human relations" or "morale-producing" techniques for the corporate economy, while others exercise their intellectual skills to accelerate the arms race.

40

Letters to Betty Friedan

Anonymous

The end of World War II brought a modernized version of older public attitudes about the role of women in American society. Women were told to use newly acquired managerial skills to organize their households, arrange car pools, run the local PTA, and otherwise make a full-time commitment to maintaining their family's mental and physical well-being. The Feminine Mystique, *the title of Betty Friedan's book published in 1963, gave this domestic ideology a name.*

In one vital way, women's behavior was already in sharp conflict with this ideology. The number of female wage earners was higher than before the war, and it continued to rise steadily. Most women worked in what were considered "female" occupations—clerical jobs, domestic service, elementary school teaching. Women were acquiring a smaller proportion of college and professional degrees than they had forty years before. Still, by 1960 the number of women working at other than domestic tasks was almost equal to that of men.

Criticizing the "feminine mystique," Friedan urged women to find meaningful work or public roles, to return to school, and to develop their own personalities and identities. Her message found many willing listeners. Still, as these letters to her attest, the issue was by no means simple. Among these letters from the Friedan Manuscript Collection at Radcliffe College are many shades of opinion about the prospects and appropriate roles of women.

BEFORE YOU READ

1. What is the "feminine mystique"? Is it an ideal, or does it describe a reality in the lives of some of these women?

2. How did these correspondents perceive the past role of women and how different or similar did they think present roles should be?

3. These letters were written before the new women's movement had emerged in the late 1960s. What arguments about that movement do you see foreshadowed in these letters?

14 May 1963
Brookline, Mass.

My life spans the two eras—the ebb tide of feminism and the rise of the "mystique." My parents were products of the early twentieth century Liberalism and believed firmly that everyone—poor, Negroes, and women too—had a

The Friedan Manuscript Collection, Schlesinger Library Manuscript Collections, Radcliffe College, Cambridge, Massachusetts. Quoted in Elaine Tyler May, *Homeward Bound: American Families in the Cold War Era* (New York: Basic Books, 1988), pp. 52, 209–17.

right to have a "rendezvous with Destiny." . . . My feeling of betrayal is not directed against society so much as at the women who beat the drums for the "passionate journey" into darkness. . . . My undiluted wrath is expended on those of us who were educated, and therefore privileged, who put on our black organza nightgowns and went willingly, joyful, without so much as a backward look at the hard-won freedoms handed down to us by the feminists (men and women). The men, in my experience, were interested by-standers, bewildered, amused, and maybe a bit joyful at having two mommies at home — one for the children and one for themselves. . . . My children grew up in the mystique jungle but somehow escaped it.

13 March 1963
Ridgewood, N.J.

. . . [I am] the mother of five and the wife of a successful partner in an investment banking firm. In seeking that something "more" out of life, I have tried large doses of everything from alcohol to religion, from a frenzy of sports activities to PTA . . . to every phase of church work. . . . Each served its purpose at the time, but I suddenly realized that none had any real future. Our children are all in school except for the baby. . . . However, I felt that if I waited until she's in school I'll be too close to forty to learn any new tricks. I've seen too many women say they would "do something" when the last child went to school. The something has usually been bridge, bowling, or drinking.

24 August, 1963
Pittsburgh, PA

. . . I entered graduate school at Yale, met a man, left school, and married in 1951. I have since then moved thirteen times, lived in eight states, had four miscarriages, and produced two children. . . . Finally, when I fill out the income tax now, it is occupation: Painter, not housewife. . . . My one advantage over the rest of my generation is, I suppose, the fact that I was raised in a family of feminists. . . . I still tend, belatedly and belligerently, to champion women's rights. The cloying and sentimental public effort of the last decade to raise the prestige of the home and represent it as demanding all that we have to give has more than once precipitated me into incoherent outrage. . . .

21 January 1963
New York City

. . . Since scientific findings reveal the strong effect of the child's environment upon the child, the poor mother has been made to replace God in her omnipotence. It is the terror of this misinterpreted omnipotence that in many cases is keeping women home. I still remember the tear-stained face of a brilliant young woman economist who had earned a Ph.D. in her field when she had to give up a newly discovered exciting job because her pediatrician convinced her that her six- and three-year-old children would become social menaces without her presence 24 hours a day. . . . [*Quoting a school official:*] "Show me a delinquent child and I'll show you a working mother."

Rockaway, New York

. . . What is wrong with the women trapped in the Feminine Mystique is what's wrong with men trapped in the Rat Race. . . . Isn't it true that one of the problems, the biggest really, of our present day society is that there isn't enough meaningful creative work for *anyone* these days? Isn't that one of the reasons fathers are taking their parental role with the seriousness of a career?

23 April 1963
Leicester, Mass.

For the last few years, I have been on the "old housekeeping merry-go-round." . . . I cleaned and I cleaned . . . and then I cleaned some more! All day—every day. My mother had returned to teaching school when I was twelve, and I had resented it, and consequently vowed that when I married and had children I would make it my vocation. I was quite convinced that I was very happy with my role in life as we had our own home and my husband is a good husband and father and a very sufficient provider. However, one night last November, all Hell broke loose in my psyche. I was sitting calmly reading when I became overwhelmed with waves of anxiety. I couldn't imagine what was happening. . . . I visited my family doctor. He put me on tranquilizers and diagnosed it as a mild state of anxiety. However there was no explanation. . . . I see now. . . . I chose security over everything else. . . . I felt I had something more to offer the world and wanted to do something about it. . . . I now have a goal and no longer feel like a vegetable.

23 October 1963
Queens Village, N.Y.

[*Written by a woman recalling the realities and perspectives of her emigrant family in the 1930s.*]

. . . The emigrant mother often had to work not only in her home, but outside as well, under the most harrowing conditions. . . . For the son, it was important and necessary to obtain an education, so he could escape the sweatshop labor of his father. For the daughter, however, the most precious legacy was an escape from the hard work and drudgery of her mother and the attainment of leisure—the very leisure this emigrant mother never knew herself, and which she so desperately needed. . . . To this emigrant mother, education was only necessary for her son to get a better job, and the daughter, with nothing else besides her femininity, would, with luck, marry well and thereby achieve the leisure her mother never knew.

4 August 1964
Glen Ridge, N.J.

Most of us would be delighted to chuck the wage earning back in our husbands' laps and devote ourselves exclusively to homemaking and community projects.

We worry about the children while we're at work. We don't really like to throw the last load of clothes in the washer at 11:30 P.M., and set the alarm for 6:00 so we can iron a blouse for a school age daughter, fix breakfast and school lunches all at the same time, do as much housework as possible before bolting for the office, and face the rest of it, and the grocery shopping and preparing dinner when we get home. This isn't our idea of fulfillment. It doesn't make us more interesting people or more stimulating companions for our husbands. It just makes us very, very tired.

29 May, 1964
Folcroft, Pa.

Believe me, a modern woman of today would have to be *four* women to be everything that is expected of her. . . . My husband wants me to work not for the satisfaction I might get out of working, but for the extra money *he* will have for himself. . . . *But,* how about the extra burden it would put on me? I would go out to work if possible, but I cannot do that and come home to a house full of screaming kids, dishes piled in the sink, and mountains of laundry to do. It is no fun to come home and see the sweet, dear, lazy bum asleep on the couch after being on my feet all day. He still likes his home-made pies, cakes, and appetizing meals. . . . I have worked in stores; the post-office; given dinners for a pot and pan outfit; minded children; and sold things door-to-door. At present, I take in sewing and ironing. . . . If I work, then my housework suffers and I get told about that. I would like nothing better than to just do my own work, have some time to myself once in a while so I could just go downtown once in while without having someone else's work staring at me. I get very tired of reading about women working outside the home. . . . I cannot divide myself into more than one person. . . . I have plenty to occupy my time and I happen to enjoy being a house-wife. . . . My husband . . . thinks it's great for women to work, but until men get some of their Victorian ideas out of their heads then I am staying home. Unless he would be willing to help with the housework then I cannot go to work. He thinks he would lose some of his masculinity if anyone saw him hanging out the wash, or washing dishes. And if he had to give up any of his fishing or hunting or running around visiting his buddies to keep an eye on the kids, well, I'm not killing myself for the almighty dollar.

41

Mississippi Summer Freedom Project
Student Workers

In the summer of 1964, after nearly a decade of civil rights demonstrations, more than a thousand people, most of them white northern college students, volunteered to go to Mississippi to help African Americans register to vote and to teach African American children their own history in "freedom schools." The Mississippi Summer Freedom Project was a high point and nearly the end of the integrated, nonviolent civil rights movement of the 1950s and 1960s. It was a hard summer. Consider this macabre score: at least one African American and two white civil rights workers were killed, not including an uncertain number of African American Mississippians who died mysteriously; more than eighty were wounded; more than a thousand were arrested; thirty-five African American churches were burned; and thirty homes and other buildings were bombed. Twelve hundred new African American voters registered in the state.

But another score can be calculated. Mississippi Summer contributed to the success of the voting rights bill of 1965 that quickly secured for millions of southern blacks the right to vote. And the murders of James Chaney, Michael Schwerner, and Andrew Goodman forced federal authorities to infiltrate and destroy the Ku Klux Klan in Mississippi.

National attention fixed on the murders in Philadelphia, Mississippi, of the three young volunteers. These letters home from participants in the project (some supplied without attribution) testify to the intensity of the volunteers' experiences that summer.

BEFORE YOU READ

1. Why did these young men and women go to Mississippi in 1964?
2. What were the difficulties and the rewards of their being there?
3. Had you been a college student in 1964, would you have gone to Mississippi?

Mileston, August 18

Dear folks,

One can't move onto a plantation cold; or canvas a plantation in the same manner as the Negro ghetto in town. It's far too dangerous. Many plantations—homes included—are posted, meaning that no trespassing is permitted, and the owner feels that he has the prerogative to shoot us on sight when we are in the house of one of *his* Negroes.

Before we canvas a plantation, our preparation includes finding out whether the houses are posted, driving through or around the plantation without stopping, meanwhile making a detailed map of the plantation.

We're especially concerned with the number of roads in and out of the plantation. For instance, some houses could be too dangerous to canvas because of their location near the boss man's house and on a dead end road.

In addition to mapping, we attempt to talk to some of the tenants when they are off the plantation, and ask them about conditions. The kids often have contacts, and can get on the plantation unnoticed by the boss man, with the pretense of just visiting friends.

Our canvassing includes not only voter registration, but also extensive reports on conditions — wages, treatment by the boss man, condition of the houses, number of acres of cotton, etc. Much more such work needs to be done. The plantation system is crucial in Delta politics and economics, and the plantation system must be brought to an end if democracy is to be brought to the Delta. . . .

Love,
Joel

July 18

. . . Four of us went to distribute flyers announcing the meeting. I talked to a woman who had been down to register a week before. She was afraid. Her husband had lost his job. Even before we got there a couple of her sons had been man-handled by the police. She was now full of wild rumors about shootings and beatings, etc. I checked out two of them later. They were groundless. This sort of rumorspreading is quite prevalent when people get really scared. . . .

At 6 P.M. we returned to Drew for the meeting, to be held in front of a church (they wouldn't let us meet inside, but hadn't told us not to meet outside). A number of kids collected and stood around in a circle with about 15 of us to sing freedom songs. Across the street perhaps 100 adults stood watching. Since this was the first meeting in town, we passed out mimeoed song sheets. Fred Miller, Negro from Mobile, stepped out to the edge of the street to give somebody a sheet. The cops nabbed him. I was about to follow suit so he wouldn't be alone, but Mac's policy [Charles McLaurin, SNCC — a civil rights group — project director] was to ignore the arrest. We sang on mightily "Ain't going to let no jailing turn me around." A group of girls was sort of leaning against the cars on the periphery of the meeting. Mac went over to encourage them to join us. I gave a couple of song sheets to the girls. A cop rushed across the street and told me to come along. I guess I was sort of aware that my actions would get me arrested, but felt that we had to show these girls that we were not afraid. I was also concerned with what might happen to Fred if he was the only one.

. . . The cop at the station was quite scrupulous about letting me make a phone call. I was then driven to a little concrete structure which looked like a power house. I could hear Fred's courageous, off-key rendition of a freedom song from inside and joined him as we approached. He was very happy to see me. Not long thereafter, four more of our group were driven up to make their calls. . . .

Holly Springs

Dear Mom and Dad:

The atmosphere in class is unbelievable. It is what every teacher dreams about — real, honest enthusiasm and desire to learn anything and everything. The girls come to class of their own free will. They respond to everything that is said. They are excited about learning. They drain me of everything that I have to offer so that I go home at night completely exhausted but very happy. . . .

I start out at 10:30 teaching what we call the Core Curriculum, which is Negro History and the History and Philosophy of the Movement, to about fifteen girls ranging from 15 to 25 years of age. I have one girl who is married with four children, another who is 23 and a graduate from a white college in Tennessee, also very poorly educated. The majority go to a Roman Catholic High School in Holly Springs and have therefore received a fairly decent education by Mississippi standards. They can, for the most part, express themselves on paper but their skills in no way compare to juniors and seniors in northern suburban schools.

In one of my first classes, I gave a talk on Haiti and the slave revolt which took place at the end of the eighteenth century. I told them how the French government (during the French Revolution) abolished slavery all over the French Empire. And then I told them that the English decided to invade the island and take it over for a colony of their own. I watched faces fall all around me. They knew that a small island, run by former slaves, could not defeat England. And then I told them that the people of Haiti succeeded in keeping the English out. I watched a smile spread slowly over a girl's face. And I felt the girls sit up and look at me intently. Then I told them that Napoleon came to power, reinstated slavery, and sent an expedition to reconquer Haiti. Their faces began to fall again. They waited for me to tell them that France defeated the former slaves, hoping against hope that I would say that they didn't. But when I told them that the French generals tricked the Haitian leader Toussaint to come aboard their ship, captured him and sent him back to France to die, they knew that there was no hope. They waited for me to spell out the defeat. And when I told them that Haiti did succeed in keeping out the European powers and was recognized finally as an independent republic, they just looked at me and smiled. The room stirred with a gladness and a pride that this could have happened. And I felt so happy and so humble that I could have told them this little story and it could have meant so much.

We have also talked about what it means to be a Southern white who wants to stand up but who is alone, rejected by other whites and not fully accepted by the Negroes. We have talked about their feelings about Southern whites. One day three little white girls came to our school and I asked them to understand how the three girls felt by remembering how it feels when they are around a lot of whites. We agreed that we would not stare at the girls but try to make them feel as normal as possible.

Along with my Core class I teach a religion class at one every afternoon and a class on non-violence at four-fifteen. All my classes are approximately an hour. Both these classes are made up of four to six girls from my morning class and about four boys of the same age group. In religion they are being confronted for the first time with people whom they respect who do not believe in God and with people who believe in God but do not take the Bible literally. It's a challenging class because I have no desire to destroy their belief, whether Roman Catholic or Baptist, but I want them to learn to look at all things critically and to learn to separate fact from interpretation and myth in all areas, not just religion.

Every class is beautiful. The girls respond, respond, respond. And they disagree among themselves. I have no doubt that soon they will be disagreeing with me. At least this one thing that I am working towards. They are a sharp group. But they are under-educated and starved for knowledge. They know that they have been cheated and they want anything and everything that we can give them.

I have a great deal of faith in these students. They are very mature and very concerned about other people. I really think that they will be able to carry on without us. At least this is my dream. . . .

Love,
Pam

Biloxi, Aug. 16

In the Freedom School one day during poetry writing, a 12-year-old girl handed in this poem to her teacher:

What Is Wrong?

What is wrong with me everywhere I go
   No one seems to look at me.
Sometimes I cry.

I walk through woods and sit on a stone.
   I look at the stars and I sometimes wish.

Probably if my wish ever comes true,
   Everyone will look at me.

Then she broke down crying in her sister's arms. The Freedom School here had given this girl the opportunity of meeting someone she felt she could express her problems to. . . .

Ruleville

To my brother,

Last night, I was a long time before sleeping, although I was extremely tired. Every shadow, every noise—the bark of a dog, the sound of a car—in my fear and exhaustion was turned into a terrorist's approach. And I believed that I heard the back door open and a Klansman walk in, until he was close by the bed. Almost paralyzed by the fear, silent, I finally shone my flashlight on the spot where I thought he was standing. . . . I tried consciously to overcome this fear. To relax, I began to breathe deep, think the words of a song, pull the sheet up close to my neck . . . still the tension. Then I rethought why I was here, rethought what could be gained in view of what could be lost. All this was in rather personal terms, and then in larger scope of the whole Project. I remembered Bob Moses saying he had felt justified in asking hundreds of students to go to Mississippi because he was not asking anyone to do something that he would not do. . . . I became aware of the uselessness of fear that immobilizes an individual. Then I began to relax.

"We are not afraid. Oh Lord, deep in my heart, I do believe. We Shall Overcome Someday" and then I think I began to truly understand what the words meant. Anyone who comes down here and is not afraid I think must be crazy as well as dangerous to this project where security is quite important. But the type of fear that they mean when they, when we, sing "we are not afraid" is the type that immobilizes. . . . The songs help to dissipate the fear. Some of the words in the songs do not hold real meaning on their own, others become rather monotonous—but when they are sung in unison, or sung silently by oneself, they take on new meaning beyond words or rhythm. . . . There is almost a religious quality about some of these songs, having little to do with the usual concept of a god. It has to do with the miracle that youth has organized to fight hatred and ignorance. It has to do with the holiness of the dignity of man. The god that makes such miracles is the god I do believe in when we sing "God is on our side." I know I am on that god's side. And I do hope he is on ours.

Jon, please be considerate to Mom and Dad. The fear I just expressed, I am sure they feel much more intensely without the relief of being here to know exactly how things are. Please don't go defending me or attacking them if they are critical of the Project. . . .

They said over the phone "Did you know how much it takes to make a child?" and I thought of how much it took to make a Herbert Lee (or many others whose names I do not know). . . . I thought of how much it took to be a Negro in Mississippi twelve months a year for a lifetime. How can such a thing as a life be weighed? . . .

With constant love,
Heather

Tchula, July 16

Yesterday while the Mississippi River was being dragged looking for the three missing civil rights workers, two bodies of Negroes were found———one cut in half and one without a head. Mississippi is the only state where you can drag a river any time and find bodies you were not expecting. Things are really much better for rabbits—there's a closed season on rabbits.

Meridian, August 4

Last night Pete Seeger was giving a concert in Meridian. We sang a lot of freedom songs, and every time a verse like "No more lynchings" was sung, or "before I'd be a slave I'd be buried in my grave," I had the flash of understanding that sometimes comes when you suddenly think about the meaning of a familiar song. . . . I wanted to stand up and shout to them, "Think about what you are singing—people really have died to keep us all from being slaves." Most of the people there still did not know that the bodies had been found. Finally just before the singing of "We Shall Overcome," Pete Seeger made the announcement. "We must sing 'We Shall Overcome' now," said Seeger. "The three boys would not have wanted us to weep now, but to sing and understand this song." That seems to me the best way to explain the greatness of this project—that death can have this meaning. Dying is not an everpresent possibility in Meridian, the way some reports may suggest. Nor do any of us want to die. Yet in a moment like last night, we can feel that anyone who did die for the Project would wish to be remembered not by tributes or grief but by understanding and continuation of what he was doing. . . .

As we left the church, we heard on the radio the end of President Johnson's speech announcing the air attacks on Vietnam. . . . I could only think "This must not be the beginning of a war. There is still a freedom fight, and we are winning. We must have time to live and help Mississippi to be alive." Half an hour before, I had understood death in a new way. Now I realized that Mississippi, in spite of itself, has given real meaning to life. In Mississippi you never ask, "What is the meaning of life?" or "Is there any point to it all?" but only that we may have enough life to do all that there is to be done. . . .

Meridian, August 5

At the Freedom school and at the community center, many of the kids had known Mickey and almost all knew Jimmy Chaney. Today we asked the kids to describe Mickey and Jimmy because we had never known them.

"Mickey was a big guy. He wore blue jeans all the time." . . . I asked the kids, "What did his eyes look like?" and they told me they were "friendly eyes" "nice eyes" ("nice" is a lovely word in a Mississippi accent). "Mickey was a man who was at home everywhere and with anybody," said the 17-year-old girl I stay with. The littlest kids, the 6, 7, 8 years olds, tell about how he played "Frankenstein" with them or took them for drives or talked with them about Freedom. Many of the teen-age boys were delinquents until Mickey went down to the bars and jails and showed them that one person at least would respect them if they began to fight for something important. . . . And the grownups too, trusted him. The lady I stay with tells with pride of how Mickey and Rita came to supper at their house, and police cars circled around the house all during the meal. But Mickey could make them feel glad to take the risk.

People talk less about James Chaney here, but feel more. The kids describe a boy who played with them—whom everyone respected but who never had to join in fights to maintain this respect—a quiet boy but very sharp and very understanding when he did speak. Mostly we know James through his sisters and especially his 12-year-old brother, Ben. Today Ben was in the Freedom School. At lunchtime the kids have a jazz band (piano, washtub bass, cardboard boxes and bongos as drums) and tiny Ben was there leading all even with his broken arm, with so much energy and rhythm that even Senator Eastland would have had to stop and listen if he'd been walking by. . . .

Meridian, August 11

. . . In the line I was in, there were about 150 people—white and Negro— walking solemnly, quietly, and without incident for about a mile and half through white and Negro neighborhoods (segregation is like a checkerboard here). The police held up traffic at the stoplights, and of all the white people watching only one girl heckled. I dislike remembering the service—the photographers with their television cameras were omnipresent, it was really bad. And cameras when people are crying . . . and bright lights. Someone said it was on television later. I suppose it was.

Dave Dennis spoke—it was as if he was realizing his anger and feeling only as he spoke. As if the deepest emotion—the bitterness, then hatred—came as he expressed it, and could not have been planned or forethought. . . .

Laurel, August 11

Dear Folks,

. . . The memorial service began around 7:30 with over 120 people filling the small, wooden-pew lined church. David Dennis of CORE [a civil rights group], the Assistant Director for the Mississippi Summer Project, spoke for COFO [an amalgam of civil rights organizations]. He talked to the Negro people of Meridian—it was a speech to move people, to end the lethargy, to make people stand up. It went something like this:

"I am not here to memorialize James Chaney, I am not here to pay tribute— I am too sick and tired. Do YOU hear me, I am S-I-C-K and T-I-R-E-D. I have attended too many memorials, too many funerals. This has got to stop. Mack Parker, Medgar Evers, Herbert Lee, Lewis Allen, Emmett Till, four little girls in Birmingham, a 13-year-old boy in Birmingham, and the list goes on and on. I have attended these funerals and memorials and I am SICK and TIRED. But the trouble is that YOU are NOT sick and tired and for that reason YOU, yes YOU, are to blame. Everyone of your damn souls. And if you are going to let this continue now then you are to blame, yes YOU. Just as much as the monsters of hate who pulled the trigger or brought down the club; just as much to blame as the sheriff and the chief of police, as the governor in Jackson who said that he 'did not have time' for Mrs. Schwerner when she went to see him, and just as much to blame as the President and Attorney General in Washington who wouldn't provide protection for Chaney, Goodman and

Schwerner when we told them that protection was necessary in Neshoba County. . . . Yes, I am angry, I AM. And it's high time that you got angry too, angry enough to go up to the courthouse Monday and register—everyone of you. Angry enough to take five and then other people with you. Then and only then can these brutal killings be stopped. Remember it is your sons and your daughters who have been killed all these years and you have done nothing about it, and if you don't do nothing NOW baby, I say God Damn Your Souls." . . .

Mileston, August 9

Dear Blake,

. . . Dave finally broke down and couldn't finish and the Chaney family was moaning and much of the audience and I were also crying. It's such an impossible thing to describe but suddenly again, as I'd first realized when I heard the three men were missing when we were still training up at Oxford [Ohio], I felt the sacrifice the Negroes have been making for so long. How the Negro people are able to accept all the abuses of the whites—all the insults and injustices which make me ashamed to be white—and then turn around and say they want to love us, is beyond me. There are Negroes who want to kill whites and many Negroes have much bitterness but still the majority seem to have the quality of being able to look for a future in which whites will love the Negroes. Our kids talk very critically of all the whites around here and still they have a dream of freedom in which both races understand and accept each other. There is such an overpowering task ahead of these kids that sometimes I can't do anything but cry for them. I hope they are up to the task, I'm not sure I would be if I were a Mississippi Negro. As a white northerner I can get involved whenever I feel like it and run home whenever I get bored or frustrated or scared. I hate the attitude and position of the Northern whites and despise myself when I think that way. Lately I've been feeling homesick and longing for pleasant old Westport and sailing and swimming and my friends. I don't quite know what to do because I can't ignore my desire to go home and yet I feel I am a much weaker person than I like to think I am because I do have these emotions. I've always tried to avoid situations which aren't so nice, like arguments and dirty houses and now maybe Mississippi. I asked my father if I could stay down here for a whole year and I was almost glad when he said "no" that we couldn't afford it because it would mean supporting me this year in addition to three more years of college. I have a desire to go home and to read a lot and go to Quaker meetings and be by myself so I can think about all this rather than being in the middle of it all the time. But I know if my emotions run like they have in the past, that I can only take that pacific sort of life for a little while and then I get the desire to be active again and get involved with knowing other people. I guess this all sounds crazy and I seem to always think out my problems as I write to you. I am angry because I have a choice as to whether or not to work in the Movement and I am playing upon that choice and leaving here. I wish I could talk with you 'cause I'd like to know if you ever felt this way about anything. I mean have you ever despised yourself for your weak conviction or something. And what is making it worse is that all those damn northerners are thinking of me as a brave hero. . . .

Martha

42

Crossing the Rio Grande
Al Santoli

Throughout American history waves of immigration have shaped the nation's life. Only in the period from 1924 to 1965, when federal law set racial and ethnic quotas, did migration become somewhat less influential. Since the mid-1960s the historic American pattern has reasserted itself, with migrants—particularly from Asia, the Caribbean, and Latin America—strongly affecting American social, economic, and cultural life.

The new Americans are at least as varied as the old: Mexican, Central American, Filipino, Korean, Indian, Iranian, Jamaican, Taiwanese, Vietnamese, and others fill the stream of legal immigrants. In addition, a large number of illegal aliens from Mexico and elsewhere in Latin America have swelled the populations of Florida, Texas, Arizona, New Mexico, and southern California. All have different stories, motives, and prospects in the society they enter. Some have been viewed as essential labor; others as potential welfare cases; and still others as entrepreneurs who will fuel a rebirth of economic growth. The U.S. government has recognized the value of this new immigration by granting citizenship to those who have resided in this country for a number of years—the "amnesty" José Luis mentions in his interview. The interviews collected in Al Santoli's New Americans: An Oral History, *published in 1988, suggest that we are still a nation of immigrants.*

BEFORE YOU READ

1. What goals do Rosa and José pursue? How do these goals compare with those of people born in the United States?

2. What kind of work do Rosa and José do? Are they competing for jobs with citizens?

3. What is the role of the *migra?*

4. What arguments can you think of for and against allowing Rosa and José to become citizens of the United States?

Rosa María Urbina, age thirty-five, crossed the muddy Rio Grande in 1984 with the hope that she could earn enough money as a housecleaner in El Paso to take her three children out of an orphanage. A widow, she had to place her children in an institution because the $14 a week she earned on a factory assembly line in Juárez was not enough to feed them.

Each morning she joined hundreds of other young to middle-aged women from the hillside *colonias,* who walked down to the concrete riverbank and paid men called *burros* to ferry them across the river on their shoulders—and back to the squalor of Juárez in the evening. On one of these excursions, she met a handsome farm worker, José Luis, age twenty-six, with dark mestizo features. It was fate, they believe. Within months, Rosa's children joined them in a two-room apartment on the American side of the river.

I was introduced to José and Rosa during a tour of overcrowded tenement buildings in South El Paso that house many of the city's fifty thousand illegal residents. In Mexican slang, they are called *mojados*, or "wets," the river people.

My guide, Julie Padilla, a public-health nurse from the Centro de Salud Familiar La Fe clinic, visits the Urbinas to give their two-month-old baby, José Luis, Jr., a post-natal checkup. We walked up a dark stairwell to a dimly lit landing decorated with a colorful gold-framed mural of Our Lady of Guadalupe, the religious patron of all Mexican Catholics. There are sixteen apartments with ripped screen doors along a narrow graffiti-covered corridor. On the back fire-escape is a closet-sized communal toilet. Julie said, "There used to be one bathtub that every family on the corridor shared. But in the past year, that's been taken out. I don't know where they bathe now."

Rosa María, José, and the children have the luxury apartment. Half of the 12-foot-square room is taken up by a bed covered by a magenta Woolworth blanket. On the wall, above a calendar of the Good Shepherd, is a portrait of Pope John Paul II. A Winnie the Pooh blanket serves as a makeshift closet door. On a miniature two-tiered nightstand, alongside baby bottles and a green plant, are metal-framed elementary-school photos of the children. Their seven-year-old daughter's Honor Roll certificate is proudly displayed on a mirror above an all-purpose foldout table.

During winter months, José Luis is out of farm work. The baby is Rosa's full-time chore. They survive on $58 a month in food stamps earmarked for the baby, who is an American citizen by virtue of his birth in El Paso. And WICC, the Women, Infant and Children Care program, provides a bag of groceries each week. Although the children attend public school, José and Rosa seldom leave the apartment. They fear that border patrolmen will send them back across the river to the squalor of Juárez.

José: The majority of the people in our apartment building have the same problem as my family. All of us are in El Paso without legal papers. I have been living here since 1981.

Rosa: I came in 1984, to find work. After José and I were married and we found a place to live, I brought my children from a previous marriage. We lived across the river, in Juárez. But I was born further south, in Zacatecas.

José: My hometown is Juárez. Since I was nine years old, I've been coming to El Paso to work. At first I did gardening in people's yards, but I have stayed in El Paso constantly since 1981, going out to the fields to do farm work. I used to go to Juárez to visit my relatives at least one day each month. But in the last year, I haven't gone, because of the immigration law. To visit Juárez I have to swim across the river. I can't cross the bridge or the *"migra"* [Border Patrol officers] can catch me right there.

During the past few months, the river has been very high and fast. That's one reason why not so many people have been crossing lately. I am not working now, because it isn't the growing or harvesting season on the big farms. On February 15, we usually begin to plant onions. That is when the main agricultural season begins. But during a three-month period between planting and harvesting, there is no work.

We haven't paid our rent since December. If we're lucky, I can find some part-time work to pay for food. Our baby, José Luis, is two months old. Because he was born in El Paso, he is an American citizen. We can only get food assistance for him. Once in a while, I find a job as a construction laborer, house painter, whatever is available. We use the money to buy food for the baby and the other three children first.

Rosa: I haven't been able to work lately, because the baby is so small. My other children are all in school. Lorenzo is twelve years old, José Rubén is ten, and Miriam is seven. From the time I came to El Paso, I have worked as a housekeeper and minding homes for people. I am not used to staying in the apartment every day, but I have no other choice, because of my small baby.

I have known many changes in my life. I moved to Juárez from a farm in Zacatecas when I was seven years old. My mother and father were split up. After mother re-married, my stepfather took us to Juárez. We lived in an adobe house in the *colonias* [ramshackle housing projects] up in the hills.

When I was a teenager, I worked as a hairdresser in a beauty salon, cutting hair. My first husband was a mechanic, fixing cars. We made a good living. But my husband spent the money he made drinking in the *cantinas*. And after a while, he wouldn't let me work, because I had young children to take care of. When he died in 1984, he left me nothing at all. He drank too much and died from cirrhosis of his liver. I had no money . . . nothing. My children were nine, seven, and three years old. I had to find a way to pay rent and feed them.

At that time, the economy in Mexico had become horrible. Inflation was going crazy. The peso jumped to 500 per dollar. Today it is still climbing at 1,000 per dollar. I found a job working on an assembly line at a factory. We produced rubber gloves for hospitals and medical supplies like little caps for syringes. I would go into work at 4:30 in the afternoon and stay until 2:00 A.M. I was paid only 7,000 pesos [$14] each week. That was not enough to feed my kids. And I didn't have any relatives or friends to watch the kids while I worked. So I had no other choice but to put them in a special institution, like an orphanage, for children without parents. This upset me very much. But with my husband dead, and no other form of support, there was nothing I could do.

My only hope was to cross the river to the United States. If I could find a job that paid enough money, my children could join me. I wanted them to have an education and a proper life . . . to be someone.

After I made up my mind to cross the river, I met José Luis. It was like fate—we just found each other. You could say it was love at first sight. [Laughs] I had two young boys who needed a good man to learn from. When he asked me to live with him, I said yes.

José: Before I met Rosa, I lived with my grandmother in Juárez. I would go back and forth across the river to work in El Paso or the farms in New Mexico. After Rosa and I fell in love, we decided to rent this apartment in El Paso and live together.

Rosa: Before I met José, I crossed back and forth across the river five days each week to my housekeeping jobs in El Paso. On weekends, I took my children out of the orphanage. Then I had to reluctantly return them to the orphanage on Sunday evenings and prepare to go back across the river.

For a while, I traveled alone, which can be dangerous. But after I met José Luis, we crossed together. There are men who carry people across the river on their shoulders. The water is kind of rough, but that's what these men do to make a living. They charge passengers 1,500 to 2,000 pesos [$1.50 to $2.50]. The water is up to their chests, but they manage to hold us up on their shoulders so we can get to work dry.

José: Crossing the river can be very dangerous, especially if you cross alone. There are fast water currents, and sometimes the water is quite high. If you don't know how to swim, the undercurrents can pull you right down. And in places the bottom of the river is like quicksand that can trap you. The water turns into kind of a funnel that can drag you down. Some friends of mine have died.

Rosa: I don't know how to swim. I relied on José Luis, who is a good swimmer. We were both very lucky. I can clearly remember an incident where we almost drowned. It began on a Sunday evening, which is a customary time for crossing. At the time, a man was running loose who was raping and killing women who crossed alone. So there were a lot of American border patrolmen and Mexican police along both banks.

After the sun went down and it became quite dark, José and I waited for a while near the riverbank, but it seemed hopeless to try to cross the river undetected. We waited until the next morning to try again.

When the sun came up, we saw that the men who carried people across on their shoulders weren't working, because of all the police. When we noticed that the border patrolmen had left the area, we decided to try to cross by ourselves. That was a big mistake. The current was very fast that day. In the middle of the river, we lost our balance and began to be dragged downstream. I felt helpless and began to panic. Fortunately, another man who was a strong swimmer came to our rescue. He pulled us to the shore.

After José and I began living together in El Paso, I decided to bring my children across the river. The water was too high and swift to risk men carrying them on their shoulders. So I had the children taxied across on a rubber raft.

José: Another danger for people who cross the river is crime. Packs of men hang around the riverbank like wolves. They try to steal people's knapsacks or purses. Sometimes they demand that you give your wallet or wristwatch. If you don't obey them, they will knife you.

Were we ever caught by the *migra* when we crossed the river together? Oh, yes. [Laughs] Lots of times. But the patrolmen are really okay people. They arrest you, ask the usual questions. If you get rough, they will get rough, too. Otherwise they are fine. It all depends on the person who arrests you. If he has a mean personality, he will treat you rudely, whether you are impolite or not. But most of the time, it is a routine procedure.

When the *migra* catch us, they just put us in their truck and take us to their station. They ask our name, address, where we were born. They keep us in a cell maybe three or four hours. Then they put us in a bus and drive us back to Juárez. They drop the women off very near the main bridge. The men are taken a little further away from town.

Our favorite place to cross the river is close to the Black Bridge, which is not far from downtown El Paso. Many of us would stand on the Juárez riverbank and wait for the change of Border Patrol shifts. Each morning, the shift changes between seven-thirty and eight-thirty, sometimes nine-thirty. We learn by observing over long periods of time. And all of our friends have been held in the immigration station. We observed certain patrolmen coming in to work and others checking out after their shifts.

Experienced river crossers pass this information to new people who are just learning the daily routines. Over a period of time, we learn the shift changes by recognizing different officers' faces. Some Mexican people even know the *migra* by name.

Rosa: Suppose I am caught by the patrolmen at seven-thirty in the morning. They will take me to the station and hold me for a few hours, then bus me back to Juárez. I would walk back to a crossing point and try once again. It is like a game. I think the most times I was ever caught by the *migra* was six times in one day. No matter how many times they catch me, I keep coming back.

The majority of the people in the *colonia* where I lived in Juárez worked in El Paso, mostly as housekeepers, construction workers, or helpers in the fields. In the United States there is a lot of work, but in Mexico we have nothing.

José: The men, like myself, who work in the fields come across the river at around 2:30 A.M. to meet the buses that take us to the fields from El Paso. The transportation is owned by the *padrone* of the farms, or by the labor-crew chiefs who hire and pay the workers. In the evenings, we ride the buses back to the river. Sometimes I work twelve hours in a day and earn $20. I've learned to check around to see which farms pay the best. Some pay up to $35 a day.

Farm-labor jobs are not very steady. We just grab whatever is open at the moment. I accept anything, any time, as long as it is work. But suppose I take a job that only pays me $12 a day. It would only be enough to cover my transportation and meals in the field. I must find jobs that pay enough to feed my family.

In order to make $25, I must pick seventy-two buckets of chili peppers. That could take me four or five hours; it depends on how fast my hands are. The total amount of buckets we pick depends upon the amount contracted by the big companies in California. For a big contract, we work as long as necessary to complete the order. But the most I can earn in a day is $35.

During the summer, it gets very hot in the fields, up to 110 degrees. We work for eight hours with a half-hour break for lunch. To save money, I bring my lunch from home. The companies usually provide us with a thermos bottle of cold water. The farthest we travel from El Paso is to Lordsburg, New Mexico. That is around three and a half hours by bus. We leave El Paso at 3:00 A.M. For Las Cruces we leave at 5:00 or 5:30 A.M.

Rosa: To my housekeeping jobs I can take a regular El Paso city bus at 7:00 or 8:00 A.M. I usually come home around 3:30 or 4:00 P.M. each day. For a long while, I worked at one house—a Mexican-American family. They started me at $20 a day. Eventually they increased my wages to $25. They live near a large shopping center in the eastern part of town. The job was a little bit easier than working in the factory in Juárez, and paid much better.

In the factory, a whistle blows to let us know when to start, when to stop, when to eat dinner, and when to resume work. Doing housecleaning, I can rest a little when I need to take a short break.

To compare our apartment in El Paso with where I lived in Juárez, I prefer it a little better over there, because in the *colonia* I had a place to hang my clothes after I washed them. The bathroom was outside of the house. But we don't have a bathroom in our apartment here, either. All of the apartments in this part of the building share a toilet on the back stairwell. But in this apartment we have electric appliances, which makes life better than my previous home.

José: The landlord who owns this building is very generous. He lets us owe him rent for the months that I am not working. He understands how tough our life is. We pay whatever we can, even if it's only $50. And he knows that, if the day comes where we are raided by immigration officers, we will run.

The rent for this apartment is $125 a month plus electricity. We all live and sleep in this one room. The two boys sleep on the couch. Our daughter, Miriam, sleeps with us on the bed. And the baby sleeps in a crib next to our bed. Fortunately, we have a kitchen, and a closet in this room. Living conditions in Juárez were better, but there was no work at all.

If it is possible, Rosa and I would like to become American citizens. I would have my documents, and the government wouldn't be after us. All we want is to be able to work in peace.

Our dream is to be able to give our children the best of everything. We know that, for them to have a better future and purpose in life, they need a good education. Of the three children in school now, Miriam is the fastest learner. She received an award for being an honor student, the best in her classroom.

We hope the children can finish high school and have the career of their choice. We are going to sacrifice for them, so that they can have the profession that they desire.

I was only allowed to finish grammar school. I am the oldest in my family, of five sisters and two boys. I had to stop going to school when I was twelve, to work with my father to support the family. I would have liked to finish school, but my parents needed me to work. They chose my sisters to study. So I gave up my studies to support my sisters.

At first, I liked working better than going to school. But after a while, I wanted to attend junior high school. But my mother told me that the family couldn't afford for me to go, and she said my sisters seemed to like the books better than I did. So I continued working. My father had a fruit-and-vegetable business. We sold from a pushcart in downtown Juárez, and I came across the river to do some gardening.

Even though I've come to work in Texas and New Mexico for many years, I've never learned to speak much English. I would like to learn, but I've never had the chance to study. I have a lot of responsibility now to provide for the children. It is more important that they have school, so I must work.

The dreams that Rosa Maria and I had of living in the U.S. and reality are not the same. We hoped to find a job and live comfortably. Now that we are here, our main purpose is to survive.

I worry about our status under the new immigration law. In the previous place where I lived, I paid the rent all the time, but the landlord threw away all of the receipts. So we have no proof that we have been living here enough years to qualify for amnesty.

On the farms where I worked, my employers or crew bosses didn't keep pay records, because I only worked temporarily at each place. And, besides, I was illegal. So what was the use? If the police showed up, we would be in trouble whether or not the employer had a record. And the employers wanted to protect themselves. They didn't pay us with checks; it was always cash.

Fortunately, the last farmer I worked for took taxes and Social Security out of our wages. He is sending me a W-2 form as proof. I am waiting for it now. But things are getting worse, because the immigration police are putting pressure on people who hire undocumented workers. If the police catch illegals on a job site, the boss can be arrested under the new law. So most places have stopped hiring illegals. For example, my last job in El Paso, I was fired because the *migra* would raid the construction site every day. We would have to stop working and run.

When the planting season begins on the farms, I hope the immigration police don't show up. They raid a farm with a truck and four or five police cars. They position themselves outside the entrance to the farm and wait for us to walk by. They ask us for identification. If we cannot show proof that we are legal, we've had it. They'll take us away.

On the farms where I work, some people are legal and others aren't. If you drive your own car, the police usually won't question you. But if you come to work in the employer's bus, they'll take you away.

Rosa: In town, we don't feel comfortable walking on the street. If the immigration officers see us, they will grab us. We are not afraid for ourselves, because we are accustomed to it. But I worry about the children. They have just begun studying in school here in El Paso. They like it very much. My sons are in the sixth and fifth grades, and Miriam is in second grade. They are learning English very quickly. My oldest boy, Lorenzo, likes social studies and mathematics; he would like to be a doctor. My other son likes the army a lot. He could probably be a good soldier.

José: If we become citizens and the United States government asks them to spend time in the army, we would be honored if they are chosen to serve. We would be very proud of our children for doing their duty for their country.

Rosa: My daughter, Miriam, received a certificate from her teacher. You can ask her what she would like to do when she finishes school.

Miriam: [Big grin] I like to study English and mathematics. Some day I would like to be a teacher.

Rosa: In the buildings on this block, the majority of the people are families. In each apartment there are three or four children. This is the only area we found where the landlords don't mind renting to families with kids. The kids play outside, in the alley behind our building. Not many cars pass on this street at night, so it is pretty quiet. But other neighborhoods are more active and there is more crime on the streets.

We would like to have an ordinary life, but our problems with the *migra* are nothing new. If they catch me again and send me back to Juárez, I will just come back across the river.

43

A Welfare Great Grandmother
David Zucchino

The Welfare Reform Act, which became law in August, 1996, ended the federal gov-
ernment's guarantee of financial support for low-income families with dependent chil-
dren. Among the thirteen million people affected by the new law (eight million of
them children) was Odessa Williams, who had been on and off welfare several times
in her adult life and continuously dependent on welfare, disability, and food stamps
since the mid-1980s. A welfare mother, grandmother, and great grandmother, she
lived in a poor, mostly black neighborhood in North Philadelphia, where she slept
every night with a tiny loaded pistol under her pillow.

David Zucchino, a Pulitzer Prize–winning journalist with The Philadelphia
Inquirer, *realized that, like most of the senators and representatives who voted on wel-*
fare bills, he had never had a conversation with a person on welfare and had no idea
what any of them did with their time or the checks they received from the government.
So he spent nearly a year-and-a-half following the lives of several unmarried welfare
mothers in the period before the passage of the Personal Responsibility and Work Op-
portunity Reconciliation Act (the actual title of the welfare reform act). "I wanted to
know," he writes, "how they spent their checks, how they managed their finances, how
they fed and clothed their children, how they obtained medical care, and whether they
had realistic possibilities of finding jobs."

One of the women David Zucchino followed was Odessa Williams, who lived at 714
Allegheny Avenue with four grandchildren and two great grandchildren. He accom-
panied her on the various errands of her life, including her favorite, described below:
trash picking in better white neighborhoods to furnish her house and clothe her grand-
children and great grandchildren. On this particular outing she "hit the jackpot": three
boxes of clean, neatly folded clothing.

BEFORE YOU READ

1. How does Odessa Williams manage to take care of her family? What is her income and on what does she spend it?
2. How did she come to be on welfare?
3. Do you think she has "realistic possibilities" of finding and holding a job?

Odessa [Williams] was a woman who tried to see the best in everything and
everybody. She could drive down Allegheny Avenue, through some of the
worst slums in North America, get to thinking about her recovering drug ad-

David Zucchino, *Myth of the Welfare Queen: A Pulitzer Prize-Winning Journalist's Portrait of Women
on the Line* (New York: Scribner, 1997), pp. 16–18, 21–22, 24–31, 34–35.

dict son in prison, and still laugh out loud. She found humor in many things, including her own meager circumstances. She was on welfare. She lived off food stamps. She had four grandchildren and two great-grandchildren to feed and clothe. She lived in a tumbledown row house so crammed with relatives that every morning she had to step over the sleeping forms of her grandsons spread out like corpses on her living room floor. She joked about squashing them like little bugs.

She had to laugh at herself. Otherwise she might dissolve into tears at the futility that sometimes nearly suffocated her. She owed $3,250 to the gas company, which had cut off her service, leaving her dependent in winter on foul-smelling and dangerous kerosene heaters. She was several months behind on her electric bill. Her phone service was about to be cut off. There was a gaping hole in her dining room ceiling because she had lost her temper and ripped out the ceiling tiles while searching for the source of the leak that sent water dripping onto her dining room table. She could not afford to have the hole repaired because she barely survived from welfare check to welfare check every two weeks. There were many times when she was literally down to her last dollar and she had to spend it on an eight-pack of bony chicken backs that she boiled into a pasty stew over rice. And the next day her grandchildren would have to go off to school without their snack money.

Odessa did not complain. She was beyond that. She was fifty-six years old, with a lifetime spent making do. That was what her mother had taught her: you make do with what you have. When there was a problem in the family, or even in the neighborhood, Odessa did what she could to solve it. She had raised eight children of her own. But she also had raised two of her grandchildren when her own daughters failed as parents because they were mere children themselves. Sometimes she felt like a mother to the world.

In addition to caring for the children of her own children, Odessa had taken in three children from the neighborhood whose parents had beaten and starved them. Those children, too, she raised as her own. One of them was a little white boy named Michael, who was now a grown man who called her "Mama" whenever he telephoned from his army post, in Georgia. For three years Odessa had cared for four children of crack-addicted mothers because she could not bear the thought of them being taken away by the child welfare people and raised by strangers. And now, when Odessa should have been a grandmother who spoiled and coddled her grandchildren on weekend visits, she was a seven-day-a-week mother to her daughter's children and to her granddaughter's children. She was raising four of her thirty-two grandchildren and helping to raise two of her seven great-grandchildren. Their own mothers had failed them, so Odessa did as her own mother had done. She made do.

She did not believe in waiting for things to come to her. She waited on God and no one else. That is why she was driving her Caprice Classic down Allegheny Avenue one sweltering August evening in the summer of 1995. . . . On many evenings, especially in summer, she climbed behind the wheel and drove out to Northeast Philadelphia for a long, leisurely night of trash picking at suburban curbsides. She always looked forward to rummaging through other people's trash, especially white people's trash, because white people threw away the damnedest things. She once found an entire set of china still in its original packing box. She had found perfectly usable TV sets, VCRs, vacuum cleaners, suitcases. In fact, she had furnished her entire house via this method. Trash picking had clothed her grandchildren and helped stretch her meager welfare check by enabling her to apply it solely to the sort of essentials that you couldn't trash-pick, such as food.

Sometimes sifting through other people's throwaways so relaxed her that she could almost feel her blood pressure dropping. She cherished each new treasure she dragged home: a bed, a sofa, a cabinet, a child's snowsuit, a bouquet of plastic flowers. But she cherished even more the hours she spent away from home—as Odessa the woman, not Grandma the caretaker. She called it her trash therapy. It gave her time to reflect on her life, away from the clatter of children and the demands of squalling babies and meals uncooked and clothes unwashed. And each long drive on Allegheny Avenue was like a journey through her past, for she saw at each passing block a reminder of a family member or some long-ago event that either filled her heart with gladness or pierced it with a pain that felt like it would never go away. . . .

Odessa prided herself on the quality of her trash picking. She had a discerning eye. She did not bring home junk. And for her there was no stigma attached to the base origins of these objects. Each item she dragged home represented to her a form of independence. She might be on welfare, but she wasn't dependent, and she certainly wasn't helpless. She did not expect anyone to give her anything, but she saw no reason not to take advantage of what was available. Just as she qualified for welfare, she was also entitled to root through people's trash cans and seize for herself those things that others lacked the common sense or initiative to put to good use. When people visited her home, Odessa would point out her latest find and describe in detail how she had unearthed it and extracted it and cleaned it and hauled it home. Often she would cock her head and admire the new item and ask, "What kind of fool threw *that* in the trash?"

In a way, the very house that held her trash-picked treasures was itself trash-picked. Odessa had noticed the place while driving down Allegheny one day in 1986. It was a wreck. Junkies had been shooting up inside, and the downstairs was smeared with filth and crammed with trash, but the house remained strong and solid. Odessa knew her sons could help her fix it up. She went down to city hall and looked up the the name of the owner, who agreed to rent her the place for $185 a month.

It took three pickup truck loads to haul off all the trash inside, but in a mere matter of weeks Odessa and her grown sons had made the house habitable. They put up drywall, fixed the roof, laid in a new bathroom, replaced broken pipes, updated the kitchen. The owner dropped by one day to check on the place and was so impressed, according to Odessa, that he asked her: "You want this house? It's yours." . . .

In the nine years since then, Odessa had grown as comfortable and secure in the old row house as in anyplace she had ever lived, and it was the only home she had ever owned. It was also the only true home her grandchildren had ever known, except perhaps for Jim, who was still trying to bury the painful memories of the cold and filthy row houses in which he had spent his first five years. The children felt safe and special in their grandmother's house. It always smelled of rich food—pancakes and syrup in the mornings, grilled cheese sandwiches for lunch, and in the evenings, fried pork chops or pigs' feet with turnip greens and rice and pink beans. In summer the house had the close, pungent odor of mildew and wood rot. In the winter it was cozy and warm, and the kerosene heater gave off a slick, oily scent that seemed to calm the children the minute they rushed in from the frigid air and tossed off their coats.

It did not bother the children that their grandmother was an indifferent housekeeper. Odessa tried to clean up every day, but the demands of the children often overwhelmed her. She had neither the time nor the energy to wipe down the greasy kitchen walls or to clean what remained of the grimy and tattered linoleum squares on the dining room floor. Sometimes scraps of food fell from the table and remained on the floor for days, turning hard and sticking to the bare wood beneath the torn linoleum. On some days cockroaches feasted in the corners of the kitchen and did not bother to scurry away when people passed by, and in the late afternoons they could be observed marching single file up and down the living room walls. In the summertime the flies gave off a steady hum, like a small generator, and sometimes they sought out the moisture of the children's eyes and noses. Odessa hung fly strips from the ceiling, but they quickly filled up, and still the flies came. The children scarcely noticed, for this was home, and for the most part they were safe and happy at Grandma's. . . .

Odessa walked across the sidewalk to the curb and bent low to pick up two plastic trash barrels that someone had knocked over, then fished out the car keys from her purse and unlocked the Chevrolet. The car was a thirdhand piece of junk, but it was in many ways her most valued possession. Without the car, she would be trapped at home, certainly not free to trash-pick; she laughed at the thought of trying to lug home some bulky cabinet or bed frame on a city bus. She would not be able to drive to the thrift stores and discount outlets and dollar stores and butcher shops to find the best bargains on food and clothing. Without a car, in fact, she would have no means to make the most important trip she took every fortnight: the one to pick up her welfare check.

The Caprice had been a gift from Odessa's second-oldest daughter, Bertha, who had bought a minivan to replace the Chevrolet, which she had bought used from the owner of the Chinese store up the street. Odessa was proud of

Bertha. She regarded her daughter as a person of substance—what people on the street called "thorough." Bertha had graduated from high school and had worked her entire adult life. Bertha was, in fact, the only one of Odessa's four daughters who had not relied at some point on welfare. Unlike the other daughters, Bertha was married to the father of her children, who worked as a counselor at a school for troubled boys. Bertha lived in a fine house in West Philadelphia and worked as a medical assistant. She was a stabilizing influence on the entire family. Odessa did not mention it to other family members, but secretly she favored Bert—that was the special nickname Odessa had given her—for another reason. She was the one daughter who looked just like Odessa. . . .

In the rearview mirror Odessa could see the white front door of the row house occupied by her eldest daughter, Joyce. Joyce lived a block west on the same side of Allegheny Avenue as her mother, in a battered row house a few steps up the street from the cacophony of the corner drug market. Odessa watched Joyce's front door fly open and slam shut as Joyce's boy Elliott— nicknamed Geedy—ran inside. She was relieved to see him safely home, for some of the drug dealers were already arriving for the busy evening shift. Odessa was relieved, too, that Joyce had set down for her children the same rules Odessa laid down for her grandchildren: everybody home by dark.

Odessa admired Joyce's obstinate ways. She was serious and determined, and so single-minded that she had decided while still in high school to become a successful career woman. Joyce had always worked, despite raising four children on her own and then getting swept up in the neighborhood crack epidemic of the late 1980s. She had managed to overcome her addiction and to rid herself of the crack-addicted man who had fathered one of her children and nearly dragged her life down to the low, desperate level of his own. Joyce had an entrepreneurial spirit, and for a time she had run a small restaurant at Sixth and Allegheny. After that she worked for ten years as a nurse's aide, but had to quit after wrenching her back lifting a heavy patient, after which she was no longer able to meet the physical demands of the job.

After her injury, for the first time in her life Joyce had had to fall back on welfare. It was an unpleasant experience, and her self-image suffered. She did not think of herself as a dependent person, and despised people who could not or would not rely on themselves. And she knew more than a few welfare recipients who could have found work but preferred to lie around and collect "aid," or "fixed income," or "the check," or "DPW" (for Department of Public Welfare), as welfare was variously known in North Philadelphia. Yet now Joyce was taking her own easy money. She tried to justify it because of her bad back and the responsibility of feeding and clothing her children, but still it ate away at her.

By early summer, Joyce had decided she wanted off welfare. She went to see her caseworker, who helped her enroll in a business administration course in Northeast Philadelphia, near the very neighborhoods where Odessa did some of her most productive trash picking. Soon Joyce was learning all the latest computer programs, even Windows 95, which wasn't commercially available yet. Odessa was pleased. She knew how much Joyce hated to take charity—that's really all welfare was, she thought—and she knew Joyce would blossom once she was supporting herself again. Her heart went out to her daughter every time she saw her thrust out her jaw and declare, "I'm a person who *needs* to work."

Even if Joyce did one day return to work, it would not end her troubles. The tensions Joyce felt between work and welfare extended to her entire family, and she was especially dismayed by the reluctance of her own daughter, Iesha, to take charge of her life and end her passive reliance on welfare. Iesha was just eighteen, but already she had given birth to three children. There were the twins, Danielle and Darryl, who turned two years old that August, and the baby, Khalil, almost a year old.

Iesha had dropped out of high school and immediately applied for welfare. Now her check and her food stamps seemed to insulate her from responsibility. Joyce despised the politicians in Washington, who seemed to be on the news every night that summer, suggesting that people on welfare were lazy and shiftless. Most people she knew on welfare were, like herself, using it as a springboard to a better life. She regarded welfare as a temporary crutch to feed and clothe her children, not a permanent means of support. Even so, Joyce had to acknowledge that her own daughter fit the politicians' stereotype—welfare was becoming a way of life for Iesha. And though it pained her to admit it, Joyce herself was contributing to Iesha's sloth. She gave her daughter a place to live and paid the house bills, so the $248 in cash Iesha received every two weeks and the $288 in food stamps she picked up every month were sufficient to sustain her. All summer, Joyce and Odessa had been carping at Iesha to register for classes for the high school year beginning in September. Iesha did speak vaguely of going back to school, but Joyce had doubts about her sincerity. It didn't help that Iesha was overweight and that she spent many afternoons that summer on her front porch, eating potato chips. "I hate to say this about my own daughter," Joyce said one day, "but she's just plain lazy." . . .

Brenda had been Odessa's sweetest and most respectful child. She was such a dutiful little girl, so helpful and trusting, that Odessa had longed for her to grow up and have children of her own. But just after Brenda turned thirteen, her personality abruptly changed. She got cheeky and talked back, and started staying out late at night, in defiance of Odessa's strict curfew. She threatened to run away from home. "Brenda went bad," Odessa often said, "and she stayed there."

Odessa blamed her ex-husband, Willie, who had been no help with Brenda. He had refused to discipline her. The very first time Brenda, at thirteen, stayed out all night, Odessa had whipped her with a belt. Brenda promptly telephoned her father—Willie and Odessa had split up in 1967—and told him she did not want to live with her mother anymore. The next day she packed up and moved in with her father, and it was then that Odessa knew that she had lost her. The way Odessa tells it, Willie let Brenda do whatever she wanted, and soon she was smoking marijuana. When crack hit the streets of North Philadelphia, in the mid-1980s, Brenda tried it and liked it. She became hopelessly addicted. To raise money, she began to prostitute herself. At the same time, she began having sex with a series of drug-addicted boyfriends. One of them fathered Jim, Kevin, and Delena. Another fathered Brian.

Odessa tried to keep up with her grandchildren, trailing Brenda from one filthy crack house to the next. She would take the children for a few days, feed them, bathe them, give them clean clothes. Then Brenda would beg to get them back, promise to clean herself up, and Odessa would relent. Brenda would enroll in a drug rehab program for a time, then drop out and sign up for another. Each time she ended up back where she had begun, smoking crack and pulling tricks under the elevated train tracks along Frankford Avenue. She spent her welfare checks on drugs, sold her food stamps for cash or crack.

By 1987, when Jim was five, Brenda had taken Jim, Kevin, and Delena to live in a shabby row house a few miles from Odessa's home on Allegheny Avenue. Odessa was repulsed at the filth that surrounded her grandchildren. Brenda tried to keep her mother away from the place, but Odessa often barged in and cleaned it up. One day, as Odessa rested at her own home, worrying about Brenda and the children, the phone rang. It was Jim.

"Grandma," he said, "we hungry. We been here all day but we haven't ate nothing. Mama said she be back in a jiffy, but she ain't back."

It was 3 P.M. Jim told Odessa that he had managed to open two cans of green beans to feed Kevin and Delena, but everybody was still hungry.

"Stay right there, baby," Odessa said. "Grandma's coming right over."

Odessa did not have a car in those days, so she caught a bus on Allegheny and reached Brenda's row house a half hour later. On the bus, she prayed that Jim was exaggerating, that Brenda had just stepped out for a few minutes. But when she got inside she was staggered by what she saw. The children were smeared with filth. Kevin and Delena wore soiled, soggy diapers. The house reeked of urine. The floor was carpeted with trash. Odessa tried not to cry. She cleaned up the children, gave them some food she had brought along, and sat down to wait for Brenda.

At 8 P.M., Brenda walked through the front door, high on crack. Odessa wanted to smack her. She screamed at her. Brenda screamed back. Odessa told her she was taking the children away—for good this time. Brenda said nobody, not even her mother, was taking her kids away from her. They were her kids, and she would raise them anyway she damn well pleased. Odessa began to gather up the children. "You just try and stop me," she said.

Brenda said, "I'm gonna call the police on you," and she ran to the phone and dialed 911.

Two officers arrived. Brenda told them Odessa was trying to kidnap her children. Odessa told them to ask Jim what had happened. The cops questioned Jim, who told them about being left alone all day with no food. The officers listened intently and looked around the house. Finally they told Brenda she had two choices: the child welfare people or Grandma.

And that is how Odessa, at age forty-eight, became a mother all over again. It is also how she ended up back on welfare long after she had thought she was through with welfare forever. After she went to court and obtained legal custody of her four grandchildren—Brian was born during that process—Odessa took over Brenda's welfare benefits. Now she received $201.50 every two weeks, plus $87 per month in food stamps, to support the four children. She also received $490 a month in Supplemental Security Income under a federal program for the disabled; she qualified because of her stroke.

Through Brian, Odessa received a second SSI check for $490 a month. In the eyes of the Social Security Administration, which administers SSI, Brian was disabled. He was what came to be called, during the great crack cocaine epidemic that devastated America's inner cities in the 1980s, a crack baby. Health care people preferred the term "crack-affected baby" because it shifted the onus for crack use away from the child. But whatever the term, Brian was indeed a child of cocaine. . . .

For all of Brian's problems, his SSI check was a godsend. Without it, the family simply would not have been able to survive. But even with it, Odessa's monthly income was just $1,382, not counting food stamps. That came to $16,584 a year, or about $1,000 short of the federal poverty line of $17,449 for a family of five. Odessa laughed at the notion of a poverty line. She did not need a number from the government to tell her she was poor, nor did it surprise her to learn that fully half the families in her neighborhood were, according to the 1990 census, officially living in poverty. In fact, she would have guessed that the number was even higher. It seemed to her that just about everyone she knew was on the check.

As the big Chevy lurched up the hill where Allegheny crests at Sixth Street, Odessa passed the row house of her youngest daughter, Elaine, at the opposite end of the block from her own. Elaine was a big, open-faced, good-natured woman who walked slowly and deliberately and seemed to take life as it came, with few complaints and little comment.

Like Joyce, Elaine was on welfare but wanted off. She had enrolled twice in job training courses, but each time some emergency with her children or some calamity at home caused her to drop out just before graduation. She found it hard to properly care for her children while away in class all day, even when the welfare department paid for her child care. She needed to be there for them. They didn't need a baby-sitter, she thought. They needed their mother.

But after Joyce signed on at the business school, Elaine felt pressure from the family to keep abreast of her sister. She went to see her welfare caseworker, who helped her enroll in yet another job training class at another trade school, in Northeast Philadelphia. She signed up to study hotel management and food services. She would begin the six-week course in October. By New Year's, she hoped, she would be working in a motel or restaurant somewhere.

Elaine was only thirty, but already she had six children. Her first child was born when Elaine was just twelve. She had been raped by the seventeen-year-old brother of one of her playmates, an episode so traumatic that no one in the family ever spoke of it. By the time a doctor at a public health clinic had diagnosed Elaine's upset stomach as pregnancy, it was too late for an abortion—not that Odessa would have gone through with it anyway. The child was born and they named him Raysonno, and Odessa had raised him as her own. His face was so round that Odessa nicknamed him "Pie Face," later shortened to "Pie." Raysonno was followed by four more children born to Elaine, who all lived in a weather-beaten row house that Odessa could see out of her passenger window each time she drove out to go to trash picking. All five children were being raised by Elaine without benefit of their biological fathers.

Sometimes Elaine got so overwhelmed that she let the house fall into disrepair. She had bought it for $11,000 five years earlier and was still paying off the mortgage. The house was in woeful condition. Several months earlier one of the neighbors—Elaine never found out which one—had telephoned the city Department of Human Services and said Elaine's children were living in an unclean and unsafe environment. A woman from DHS had inspected the home and subsequently declared it unfit for raising children. She gave Elaine twenty-four hours to clean up the place or risk having her children remanded to the custody of DHS.

Elaine went immediately to Odessa, who got on the phone and called everyone in the family. The next day more than a dozen family members marched into the place and went to work putting up new drywall, patching the holes in the ceiling and walls, repairing the plumbing in the bathroom. They washed down the kitchen, deep-cleaned the living room and bedrooms, replaced broken windowpanes, and painted all the walls. When the DHS woman returned to inspect the house, she was speechless. "That poor lady just broke down and cried. She kept bawling and wiping her eyes and saying she'd never seen a family come together like that," Odessa remembered. Elaine kept her children. . . .

Now, as Odessa drove down Allegheny Avenue past Howard Street, she thought about how little welfare had increased in the twenty-eight years since she'd first gone on public assistance. To support her four grandchildren, she now received just $51 more every two weeks than she'd once received to raise eight children. She told herself that she was not complaining, but merely observing. The paltry amounts that welfare provided made it clear to her that it was not designed to support anyone. It was meant only to supplement the various means that families in North Philadelphia utilized to scrape up money—from family members and friends, from part-time jobs that never got reported, from odd jobs performed for neighbors, from dealing drugs, and from letting drug dealers hide their stashes in their homes. She was proud that she had never done anything seriously illegal, that she had never touched alcohol or drugs, that no one in her immediate family sold drugs, that she never sold her food stamps for fifty cents on the dollar as some people did.

44

Reconsidering Draft Dodging

Mark Helprin

Mark Helprin's address to the 1992 graduating class of the United States Military Academy at West Point raised afresh the question of why so many young American men deliberately avoided military service during the Vietnam War. Not that this was entirely new in American history. In some previous wars there had been no enforced draft at all, and in the Civil War anyone who could afford to might buy his freedom from the draft for $300 to pay for a "substitute." Neither was public opposition to war a new phenomenon. It had been important during the American Revolution, the War of 1812, the Mexican War, the Civil War, the American subjugation of the Philippines, and World War I. Helprin gives his own reasons for his actions and then explains with impressive honesty why they came to feel wrong to him.

Helprin is a leading publicist for conservatism as well as a widely praised author of novels and short stories. He has served as a contributing editor to the conservative Wall Street Journal *(in which this speech first appeared in print) and wrote several important speeches for Bob Dole in 1996 before disagreements with other speechwriters and political managers led him to withdraw from the Dole presidential campaign.*

BEFORE YOU READ

1. Why did Helprin dodge the draft? To your knowledge, were his reasons similar to the reasons others have given?

2. Why did he change his mind about his actions?

3. While you cannot question his feelings about what he did, do you agree with his argument against avoiding the draft?

4. Can you offer arguments to support the refusal to serve in a war you consider unjust? Can you imagine circumstances under which you might refuse to serve in the military? Would you have served in Vietnam?

I am frequently asked how it is that I, an American, served in the Israeli Army and Air Force, and not in the military of my own country.

The first part of the question is easy to answer. I point out the long tradition of Americans serving in the armed forces of allies—the Lafayette Escadrille, Faulkner in the Canadian Royal Air Force, e.e. cummings and John Dos Passos in the Norton-Harjes Ambulance Corps, the Eagle Squadron, the Flying Tigers. I mention that before I served under another flag I reported to the Department of State and formally swore an oath of loyalty to the United States and to defend the Constitution. And I remind my questioners that Is-

Mark Helprin, "I Dodged the Draft, and I Was Wrong," *Backward and Upward: The New Conservative Writing,* ed. David Brooks (New York: Vintage Books, 1996), pp. 235–39.

rael fought not only armies trained and equipped by the Soviet Union, but, sometimes, Soviet soldiers themselves. In that period, the United States and Israel worked very closely together.

To the second part of the question, I reply that though the men in my family have served, since our arrival in this country, with Pershing in Mexico, in the First World War, and so many in the Second World War that the welcome home had to be held in a hotel, that despite this tradition in which I was certain I would have a place, I did not serve.

If you think that it is easy to stand here in front of thousands of officers and future officers of the United States Army and explain this, think again. But just as the heart of your profession is your willingness to give your lives in defense of your country, even, as the case has been, as you are mocked, reviled, and dismissed by those for whom you will die, the heart of my profession is to convey the truth.

Let me try to convey, then, what I have come to believe is the truth of a time that was over before many of you were born. I do so not to gain approval or to attain an end, but in service of illumination and memory.

My conduct in the Vietnam era can be expressed by stating that although in the Israeli Army I later had, but for corrective lenses, a perfect physical rating for combat, here I was officially, legally, and properly 4-F. If I were Bill Clinton, I would take ten thousand words to explain this and say nothing, but I'm not Bill Clinton, and I can get to the heart of it in eight: What I did was called dodging the draft.

I thought Vietnam was so much the wrong place to fight and that the conduct of the war was so destructive in human terms and of American power, prestige, and purpose that I was justified in staying out. What the existence of the reeducation camps and the boat people, and the triumph of containment have taught me is that my political assessment was not all that I thought it was. I have also come to believe that, even if it had been, I still would not have been released from honoring the compact under which I had lived until that moment, and which I then broke. I did not want to participate in a war the conduct of which was often morally ambiguous. Now I understand that this was precisely my obligation.

So you can imagine what I felt when I came to a passage in David McCullough's *Truman*, explaining how Truman had volunteered in the First World War:

> He turned thirty-three the spring of 1917, which was two years beyond the age limit set by the new Selective Service Act. He had been out of the National Guard for nearly six years. His eyes were far below the standard requirements for any of the armed services. And he was the sole supporter of his mother and sister. As a farmer, furthermore, he was supposed to remain on the farm. . . . So Harry might have stayed where he was for any of several reasons. That he chose to go . . . was his own doing entirely.

Truman had five unimpeachable reasons not to serve, and he tossed them to the wind. Had he tossed them at my class at Harvard, I assure you, they would have been fought over like five flawless versions of the Hope Diamond.

His actions were all the more impressive when it is remembered that the First World War was far more brutal than the war in Vietnam, far more costly, and far more senseless. At least the war in Vietnam was fought in the context of a policy of containment that later was to triumph. Even were Vietnam not the best place to make a stand, it was the fact that a stand was made that mattered.

In contrast, the First World War was fought almost entirely for nothing. Though it is true that the country was more enthusiastic about it, that just drives home the fact, as did Vietnam, that you simply cannot know how things will turn out, and that a war may be right or wrong, opportune or inopportune, the proper time and place to make a stand, or it may not be, but that this is something to be determined in national debate and not in the private legislatures of each person with a draft card.

I am absolutely certain that in not serving I was wrong. I began to realize this in 1967, when I served briefly in the British Merchant Navy. In the Atlantic we saw a lot of American warships, and every time we did I felt both affection and pride. One of the other sailors, a seaman named Roberts, was a partisan of the Royal Navy and maintained that it was more powerful than our own. As I was a regular reader of the Proceedings of the United States Naval Institute, and had almost memorized *Jane's Fighting Ships*, I quickly, let us say, blew his arguments out of the water.

And then, in riposte, he asked why I was not in uniform. I answered with the full force of the rationalizations so painstakingly developed by the American intellectual elite. Still, he kept coming at me. Although he was not an educated man, and although I thought I had him in a lock, the last thing he said broke the lock. I remember his words exactly. He said: "But they're your mates."

That was the essence of it. Although I did not modify my position until it was too late, I began to know then that I was wrong. I thought, mistakenly, perhaps just for the sake of holding my own in an argument, that he was saying, "My country, right or wrong," but it was not what he was saying at all. Only my sophistry converted the many virtues of his simple words from something I would not fully understand until much later.

Neither a man nor his country can always pick the ideal quarrel, and not every war can be fought with moral surety or immediacy of effect. It would be nice if that were so, but it isn't. Any great struggle, while it remains undecided and sometimes even afterward, unfolds not in certainties but in doubts. It cannot be any other way. It never has been.

In the Cambridge Cemetery are several rows of graves in which rest the remains of those who were killed in Vietnam. On one of the many days of that long war, I was passing by as a family was burying their son. I stopped, in respect. I could not move. And they looked at me, not in anger, as I might have expected, but with love. You see, they had had a son.

Soon thereafter, not understanding fully why, I was on my way to the Middle East, in a fury to put myself on the line. And though I did, it can never make up for what I did not do. For the truth is that each and every one of the Vietnam memorials in that cemetery and in every other—those that are full, those that are empty, and those that are still waiting—belongs to a man who may have died in my place. And that is something I can never put behind me.

I want you to know this so that perhaps you may use it. For someday you may find yourself in a terrible place, about to die from a wound that is too big for a pressure bandage, or you may find yourself in an enemy prison, facing years of torture, or you may find yourself, more likely, as I did, in a freezing rain-soaked trench, at four o'clock in the morning, listening to your heart beat like thunder as you stare into the hallucinatory darkness of a field sown with mines. You may speak to yourself out loud, asking, why am I here? I could have been someplace else. I could have done it another way. I could have been home.

If that should happen to you, your first comfort will be your God, and then you will have—believe me—the undying image of your family, and then duty, honor, country. These will carry you through.

But if, after you have run through them again and again, you have time and thought left, then perhaps you will think of me, and this day at the beginning of your careers. I hope it will be encouragement. For that I was not with you, in my time, at Khe Sanh, and Da Nang, and Hue, and all the other places, is for me now, looking back, a great surprise, an even greater disappointment, and a regret that I will carry to my grave.

45

Life and Death on the Internet
Katie Argyle

The Internet is a worldwide nexus of many smaller networks of computers tied together by a set of specialized router computers. It uses a unique software to disassemble all transmissions into tiny data packets and then reassemble them at their destination. If a route is damaged, the software automatically reroutes the data another way. A return acknowledgement — or its absence — ensures that no packet is ever lost.

These features reflect the Internet's short but dramatic history. The Department of Defense sponsored it in the 1960s and 1970s as a means of securing transmission of military data in the event of a nuclear attack. The department wisely decided that making the original software and network, called ARPANET, available to researchers would speed its evolution. In 1983, when the military began linking its computers via ARPANET, the entire network served fewer than six hundred computers. Then, in 1986, the National Science Foundation (NSF), the federal agency that supports basic research, began to develop a network to join all researchers in computer science. The two networks quickly merged.

Continued technical improvements encouraged the Internet's growing use. The number of connected computers nearly doubled every ten months, rising above two million by 1993. Realizing that government could no longer afford to pay for the network, in 1991 the NSF sponsored the creation of a nonprofit corporation to enlarge it and take ownership of the existing lines and computers. From a communication link mainly used by scientists, engineers, and government and military agencies, the Internet had grown in a decade into a worldwide common ground that promises — or threatens — to change radically the way the world thinks, feels, and does business.

Katie Argyle's account of experiencing death on the Internet will probably speak more directly to younger students than to older faculty — productively, we hope, reversing some classroom roles. Yet the emotions of mourning she and members of her computer community experienced over Michael Current's death indicate ways in which a virtual community nevertheless remains a community of a more traditional sort.

BEFORE YOU READ

1. What did Katie Argyle mean by "carnivalesque" and in what ways is the Internet carnivalesque?

2. Why was she at first not sure whether Michael Current had really died?

3. What do "meat" and "fleshmeet" mean? What is their significance to Katie and her virtual friends?

4. Are we asking the right questions? What do you think?

Rose Shields, ed., *Cultures of Internet* (Thousand Oaks: Sage Publications, 1996), pp. 133–41.

Every day the mailbox in my computer account fills up. E-mail continuously flows to my "home" address from four mailing lists that I subscribe to. Every day I am challenged by the volume of mail these lists generate. If I don't attend to them, they are soon unmanageable, multiplying to masses of 400 and 500 messages awaiting my attention.

Soon all the message headers become familiar, because topics are constantly recirculated within the lists as "threads." It all becomes boring and tedious. What I forget is that I *feel* bored by the incoming e-mail, and I *feel* tired at the thought of constantly cleaning out the mailbox. But I am still *feeling* something; I am connected to the lists, to the topics and the mail in my mailbox sent there by others who are on the Net with me.

"Cybermind" is the mailing list I subscribe to which is the primary source of all this mail. In over a year of membership of Cybermind, there is a single event which haunts me. It occurred in July 1994, quietly appearing amidst all the usual postings of cybervamps, unsubscribe messages, and banter about threads of discussion that had been ongoing over several days. Postings and exchanges began to appear about the death of Michael Current. It sometimes happened that Michael Current was a focal point for discussion on Cybermind, but this was talk *of* Michael, not talk *from* Michael. As one of the administrators, Michael Current was extremely active on Cybermind.[1] Every day there were two or three messages written by him as he reached out over the wires to address questions posed to him, or to express his point of view. I was accustomed to seeing letters from him on the list.

Amongst the routine chatter of messages competing for my attention there was a series addressed to the group as death, net death, and various "goodbye Michael" combinations. Had he "really" died, I wondered? I was suspicious that this was an esoteric and metaphorical use of the word *death* — the kind of semantic wordplay that the Net is filled with. Never assume that anything is as it first appears on the Net.[2] But in this case, it was: Michael had died.

I have never encountered this situation before or since. In over five years of online activity this was the first time someone whom I had never met in the flesh, but who was very familiar to me in textual form, had died and would post no more. I thought it wasn't real. I thought it was a hoax, and so did others.

1. As an administrator of the Cybermind list, Michael was responsible, along with Alan Sondheim, for the smooth functioning of this mailing list, and for moderating the talk on the list in order to stay within topics that are related to cyberspace activities and theories. [This and following notes are Argyle's.]

2. All the quoted messages were taken from the Cybermind mailing list over the following days: 23 to 25 July 1994. I have noted the names of the participants quoted, and in brackets I have included the names that appeared as signatures if they were different. The date of their messages follows their names.

Problems of authenticity abound on the Net. These two methods of identification still do not guarantee the authenticity of the text. Pseudonyms are frequently encountered in cyberspace, as is the borrowing of accounts amongst friends or acquaintances. Therefore, what is sent under the name of one person could actually have been written by someone totally different. For the purposes of this text I have quoted the works as they appeared to me, in my home mailbox: kargyle@ccs.carleton.ca. My current home address is aa992@freenet.carleton.ca.

pardon my lack of knowledge, who was (is) Michael Current? Is he dead?

I'm sure, like many, the first notice that came through I thought, "How cruel, this isn't funny. Michael's on this list and I am sure he doesn't need to read forged postings about his death." And then the reality sinks in a little and I realise how cruel it really is.[3]

And perhaps if I had only read the messages that questioned his death, and maybe one death notice, I would have dismissed it as just talk. I would have assumed that Michael Current just wanted off the Net.

A few times on BBSs in the past, I have witnessed the furious deletion of messages by someone who wants to remove all traces of their existence and past participation. In one case, I was online and logged into a newsgroup when a member known as Quiet erased all writings they had posted. Threads of conversations now referred to someone who did not exist. On every level I was disturbed by this action he was taking. I watched my screen as messages disappeared before my eyes.

I paged Quiet over the system.[4] Did he know he was changing the landscape, rewriting the history of what had been? Yes. He was committing suicide. As a protest gesture, he was killing the persona of Quiet. The deletions were a loss; I wondered at the psychological state of the man-who-was-Quiet. Was the man the next suicide? At other times, I had witnessed the growing boredom, the growing disenchantment with the Net, and the need for users, myself included, to take a break from Net activity.

This was not the same situation on the Cybermind list. There was to be no life after Net death here. I became more convinced as the messages piled up. Each one filled with grief. Each one filled with the process of mourning, and the need to stop and adjust to the event. Each one trying to understand what this meant to them. I did not write then. I feel self-conscious writing about it now. This is private: for those not on the Net, who "weren't there," I can only explain that I am transgressing. Off-line, net.death is a taboo subject. I am speaking about something that is so personal (yet collective), so private (yet public), and so emotionally painful (yet technologized), that it is better left alone. I am digging and disturbing the ground that's been laid to rest, for my own purposes. I am going against the group, and speaking out of turn. The time has passed for this. I had my chance, I missed it. I—and many other recipients with even no sense of membership or loyalty at all—chose to be silent.

3. Michael Maranda, 23 July 1994.
4. Paging is a method that many communication systems, such as BBSs or bulletin board services, offer their patrons. A "page" will be sent directly to a designated user which will interrupt whatever activity they are involved in. It opens up a direct chat line between users where they exchange words (text) from different areas of a BBS. In this example, I paged Quiet from a newsgroup while he was erasing his messages in his mailbox. Intrigued by his actions, we arranged to have a conversation over the telephone about what he had done as I was concerned about his actions. He confirmed that he was "committing suicide" re: the persona Quiet and that all traces of Quiet's existence would be removed from the BBS.

It is odd that I feel so personally about the death messages. I didn't *know* Michael Current, yet I will never forget him. His death, rather than an ending, is an event which haunts me. The emotional force of the postings, the emotional impact on Cybermind members, and the willingness to grieve in public, is very striking. For, as concerned as I am about upsetting those who wrote the messages I quote from and dissect, the messages were placed in an extremely public forum. Anyone could have copied them, and they were indeed distributed throughout alt. groups and lists on the Net. There were no guarantees that these private lamentations would stay amongst the grievers. I am sure they are archived with the rest of the material Cybermind generates, waiting for someone to read them, when they will again appear in exactly the same format on a screen, as fresh as when they were first composed.

The events of that day in July brought into focus how tied I am to the list, the extent to which participants rely on each other for support, even as nonposting list-members, or as silent lurkers, and how willing they are to express this. Western society tells us to grieve quietly. Be brave and stoic in public despite your loss. Don't risk appearing foolish or weak. Cybermind transgressed those rules.

> Oh Alan. Everybody. I am so sad. I watch these letters inch by, worm by, and spurt packets of tears. Words don't come.[5]

I felt exactly the same. What was going on with me? Why was I so upset? Why did I have to read all of these messages? Why do I still think about it now? I am sure that part of the reason is a basic curiosity and a fascination with my involvement in a situation that I have never encountered before. Also it is the privilege of witnessing raw emotions, of sharing in something with a larger group. A feeling of belonging. I always knew that *I* was this involved with the Net; what I didn't realize was that so many others felt the same way. It was good to know that I was *normal* and my feelings were similar to others who read the announcements and responded without self-censoring their messages. It made me grateful that these ties of sociability were there. Members turned to each other to help them through this crisis:

> Yes, yes to all of it.
> Thanks, thank you all who are never thanked enough,
> or hugged or kissed or silently embraced.
> For everything, forever.
> There is always time for memory.[6]

> Can anyone still doubt that we are a
> community?[7]

What I have since concluded is that we were all involved in a process of growth and transformation. The list grieved as one, strengthening the bonds between its members whether they were active "posters" or not. Others saw this too:

5. Michael Sweet (Quiet) July 1993, via Technical Magic BBS, Ottawa, Ontario, Canada. Sadly, this great board no longer exists.
6. Judith Frederika Rodenbeck, 23 July 1994 (fido).
7. a.h.s. boy, 24 July 1994 (spud).

as i sat here last night, watching in horror as
cybermind grieved its loss, watching the postings pop up
one by one, knowing that others sat there with
me—somewhere.[8]

There is a void where Michael's electricity was, where his
energy took up this space, made things happen. The quiet of
the __list__ is eery. What does it mean that we're here, to and
for each other; doesn't the presence of even the least of us
make some difference to the rest of us. Or not![9]

For me the ritual has already begun in the cycling of
messages repeated and repeated from list to list and I leaf
through five, six, seven copies of the same awkward anguish,
one copy for each place we haunted together, one current copy,
and one copy bouncing off to mcurrent@picard.[10]

The talk of ritual, of voids, of spaces, has caused me to think of the Net as a
unique place that allows for the transgression of cultural rules, the breaking of
taboos, the freedom to express what you need to, when you need to. Often
members discuss the subject of a threat to these freedoms through the imposition of outside legislation or authority upon the Net and, therefore, upon the
freedom of its users.

This Internet space, of which Cybermind is but one representative piece,
has a special character that cannot be found in "real life." In many aspects it
displays signs of the carnivalesque as described by Mikhail Bakhtin in his books
Rabelais and his World (1984) and *Speech Genres and Other Late Essays* (1986).[11]

During carnival, all codes of conduct, all rules of behaviour are abandoned.
Carnival "discloses the potentiality of an entirely different world, of another
order, another way of life"[12] When we are in another type of world, where the
rules of behaviour are not familiar to us, there is an opportunity to turn such
rules upside down . . . in the carnivalesque. As an illustration I think of the
"myth" of the 14-year-old hacker who can take a corporation down with his
ability to break into their security systems. In real life, he's just another "troubled youth" who cannot wield power over corporation heads were he to step
into their offices. In cyberspace, the hacker is king.

The potential for the subversion, and the inversion of our societal rules, can
cause confusion amongst participants who seek to act "correctly" but may not
know exactly what that is on the Net.

I'm bothered I guess, by the fact that there are no rituals of loss, mourning, passage . . .[13]

8. Jerry Everard, 25 July 1994.
9. Brian Chambers, 24 July 1994.
10. mcurrent@picard was the home Internet address of Michael Current. Jane Hudson, 25
July 1994.
11. Previously, Laurie Cubbinson had initiated a discussion of Bakhtin on Cybermind but
carnival was not mentioned. This confirmed my application of Bakhtin to Internet groups.
12. Michael Gardiner, *The Dialogics of Critique* (London: Routledge, 1992), p. 58.
13. Judith Frederika Rodenbeck, 24 July 1994 (fido).

I think some sort of ritual is called for what exactly its form would take I'm not sure . . .[14]

Never having lost an e-mail friend, I don't know the protocol for this . . .[15]

The default method for coping on the Net then lies in the choice between writing or lurking. Lurking is participation by watching without revealing your presence to the group. The catch is, others may not know you are there, but you know you are, and so you are as involved as they are. You are still part of the group.

Carnival, in short, "is 'the only feast the people offer themselves,' and there is no barrier between actors or performers and those who witness it."[16] Send your mail, follow your own feelings, and see what others do in response.

The act of writing was the choice many made in the crisis created by Michael Current's death. Others, myself included, participated by reading, and experiencing other users' words. As with quoting,[17] which uses the texts of others to speak for us, something that is rampant on the Net and Cybermind, I and others allowed the group to voice our pain.

This voicing, this continuous dialogue amongst members, whether it goes on in the written text or in the minds of those reading the text, is an indicator of heteroglossia. Bakhtin noted that during the carnivalesque there would be many voices, many forms of speech. One form would not supersede the other. All voices are allowed to speak, and so a mixing of voices shares the same space.

ping, dammit, ping, ping, ping. Not in so many words.
ping.[18]

The desert crying, Carry the Net in your head!
The desert crying, Your body is imaginary!
And the desert crying, Your are ghosts!
And the desert crying, Ghosts, ghosts!
And the desert crying, All of you are ghosts!
(Crying, the desert to itself. Crying, the flat plate
of the sky.)[19]

Or. . . . . Would the memory of the Michael whose shadow I have traced through your grief be better served by a vigorous examination of the concept of Mortality?[20]

14. Mike Gurstein, 24 July 1994 (Mikeg).
15. LMLESLIE@ucs.indiana.edu, 23 July 1994 (Ishmael).
16. Gardiner, p. 52.
17. Remember that communication programs often allow users to reply to the messages that they have just read. Users may choose to post only their opinions on the topic at hand, (this is also called continuing a "thread"), or they may choose to include the text of the previous post. The system will prompt them to answer yes or no as to whether they want the text "quoted" in their own letter. Often communication packages will allow the user to choose what specific parts of the previous text they would like to quote, giving the user editing tools that they can apply to their own textual productions.
18. Heath Michael R., 24 July 1994 (Free agent? Rez).
19. Alan Sondheim, 25 July 1994.
20. Rose Mulvale, 25 July 1994.

These "voices" of the Net express human needs and feelings. They are evidence that humanity is alive on the Net. Here there is room for voices that are neither those of work, or the workplace, nor that of leisure, though both of these can be found. This is a further example of the heteroglossia of the Net which cannot be limited to one style of textual expression, one topic, or one area of the Internet. . . .

Mike Gurstein posted a message on Cybermind that contained no text written by him. He quoted a message written by "tommyc." Tommyc's message originated on another mailing list called Future Culture. Tommyc in turn had quoted a message that he saw in a Usenet group called soc.motss.[21] This message contained the news of Michael's death, the circumstances of his death, and a personal reaction to this death.

This particular Cybermind poster did not reveal his own feelings directly to the group.[22] However, by appropriating the words of others, he used them to speak for him. . . . Text, and its accompanying expressiveness, can be copied and deposited where it can inform any group the user decides to post it in. Outside authorities cannot prevent these acts except by blocking reception of entire groups on their institutions' computers. . . .

Even in these situations, users may choose to log into other, geographically, remote systems until they can access the offending groups—not just through long-distance telephone link to some foreign bulletin board, but through a local connection to the Internet itself using programs such as telnet to log on to a foreign computer via Internet connections. Authority extends only so far into the Net. If need be, a user may have their account killed by authorities, but this doesn't preclude them from getting an account with Net access from somewhere else in their community. It is difficult to completely ban an individual from the Net. This leaves individual behaviour on the Net governed entirely by the judgement of the users themselves.[23]

. . . Free agent? rez . . . in his letter entitled 'Michael current and the meat' . . . writes,

this is visceral. words words words words meat.[24]

It is visceral. He tells us Michael's death is felt in his body. In his blood and guts; in the viscera. So much for leaving our bodies out of this.

The body is often referred to as the "meat" in cyberspace. Meat is a collective term for flesh. It does not categorize or differentiate between types of meat. It is just all meat. And the body, meat, is vulgar. This collective, lowest

---

21. Thus a group on social issues concerning "members of the same sex" (motss).
22. Mike Gurstein, 23 July 1994 (Mikeg).
23. Like the grotesque body, text on the Net expands beyond our control or direction. We, as individuals, cannot contain or restrict this growth. The products of the Net belong to anyone who can get them. There will always be those who will not participate in these acts (software piracy, for example) but there are an equal number who see this as legitimate activity. It is the nature of the net and the nature of carnivalesque to be able to exercise the freedom to choose your own actions.
24. Heath Michael R., 24 July 1994 (Free agent? Rez).

common denominator type of body is exactly what Bakhtin had in mind with his term "grotesque body"—not beautiful or idealized but above all alive, sensate, feeling and interacting.

One term, one flesh, one group. What is felt in the words is also felt in bodies. Michael Current has died, but his presence remains in Net postings, and in us: he has entered the realm of the meat. His physical death has been transformed from that of an individual dying, to a representation of this in text, and finally to a feeling in the body of other human beings. Another user, fido, echoes this:

> Michael has finessed the fleshmeet question with, as usual, a devastatingly simple gesture.[25]

"Fleshmeet" is a reference to a gathering of individuals in person, or in "real life," not on the Net. They are meeting in the flesh. Fido observes that the death of Michael, his gesture, elegantly brought the group together, even though Michael can now never participate in a fleshmeet. But the reference shows that this gathering is not restricted to the Net, and therefore to the text on the Net, but extends to the flesh, the physical body. In this rare case, uncannily, even though online, we feel we meet in the flesh. Or is this so rare?

I too felt queasy, watching the text about Michael's death, feeling the anguish of the others scroll by on my screen. The raw emotion contained in those texts, the undisguised pain, was passed from the writer to the reader, to me. Michael Current's death had to be understood by my mind, and absorbed by my body. The pain of the others touched the pain held within myself. Personal experiences of loss, memories of funerals and the sorrow of those left behind all flooded me. It was not just a bunch of letters from strangers about a guy I didn't know, but real people, feeling real things, deeply, and openly. I grieved with them, for myself and my losses, and for theirs. I knew I could not stay in this high emotional state, and that I would have to find ways to cope with the feelings that had been generated, and with the fact of Michael Current's death.

There can be no final word, no endpoint during the carnivalesque. The grotesque body absorbs events and moves on. Mike Gurstein notices that

> the personal statements of some is being followed with no evident break or closure by the noise of more or less inane net chatter.[26]

Alan Sondheim replies:

> I think whatever rituals there are in regards to Michael are private, personal; perhaps one of the things we can learn from the Net is that there *is* no closure. . . .[27]

Michael Current died, but his presence lives on, in those who came into contact with him, and who pass this on, through their texts, through Michael's own

25. Judith Frederika Rodenbeck, 24 July 1994 (fido).
26. Mike Gurstein, 24 July 1994 (Mikeg).
27. Alan Sondheim, 24 July 1994.

texts, and through their changed perception of themselves due to their involvement in this event. . . . The Cybermind list, and the other parts of the Net
where Michael Current travelled, shared in the sadness of his loss. The Internet community displayed itself as a place where the individual is not alone. The
individual is part of a larger group that spreads further than the single user can
imagine. Everywhere we rub shoulders with each other. Everywhere users present themselves to each other, freely saying and doing what they choose. This
freedom is the cornerstone of the carnivalesque, and where there is carnivalesque, there is transformation. It is inevitable that this will happen, . . . and it
is inevitable that it will continue to happen. There can be no end to this.

> good bye, michael. thank you for enriching me.
> rest peacefully. even i, someone you didn't even know,
> will miss you too.[28]

28. Brian Chambers, 24 July 1994.

(Acknowledgments continued from page iv)

[6] "Teacher of the Freedmen" from Wayne E. Reilly, ed., *Sarah Jane Foster, Teacher of the Freedmen: A Diary and Letters*, pp. 59–60, 66–68, 87–88, 95–96, and 103–107. Reprinted by permission of The University Press of Virginia.

[8] "Anti-Lynching Campaign in Tennessee" from Alfreda M. Duster, ed., *Crusade for Justice: The Autobiography of Ida B. Wells*. Copyright © 1980 by The University of Chicago. Reprinted with the permission of The University of Chicago Press.

[14] "A Prairie Populist" from Jane Taylor Nelsen, ed., *A Prairie Populist: The Memoirs of Luna Kellie*, pp. 6–14, 21–4, 33–4, and 63–4. Copyright © 1992 by the University of Iowa Press. Reprinted with the permission of the publishers.

[19] "Part of the Working Class" from Herbert Shapiro and David L. Sterling, eds., *I Belong to the Working Class: The Unfinished Autobiography of Rose Pastor Stokes*, pp. 42–53, 55–60, 63–64, 67–69, 79–81, and 83–86. Copyright © 1992 by The University of Georgia Press. Reprinted with the permission of the publishers.

[20] "A Bintel Brief" from Isaac Metzker, *A Bintel Brief: Sixty Years of Letters from the Lower East Side to the* Jewish Daily Forward (New York: Doubleday, 1971), pp. 42–44, 49–51, 54–55, 58–59, 63 61, 68–70, 109–10, and 117–18. Copyright © 1971 by Isaac Metzker. Reprinted with the permission of Isaac Metzker and *Jewish Daily Forward*.

[24] "Letters from the Great Migration" from Emmett J. Scott, "Letters of Negro Migrants of 1916–1918" from *Journal of Negro History:* 177–80. Copyright © by Association for the Study of Afro-American Life and History. Reprinted with the permission of the publishers.

[25] "Life in the Trenches—France" from Louis Felix Ranlett, *Let's Go!: The Story of A.S. No. 2448602*, pp. 94–107. Copyright 1927 by Louis Felix Ranlett. Reprinted with the permission of Houghton Mifflin Company. All rights reserved.

[26] "Memories of College Days" by Zora Neale Hurston. Reprinted with the permission of Lucy Hurston.

[27] "My Fight for Birth Control" from Margaret Sanger, *My Fight for Birth Control* (New York: Farrar-Rinehart, 1931), pp. 46–56 and 152–60. Copyright 1931 by Margaret Sanger. Reprinted with the permission of Sanger Resources and Management, Inc.

[28] "Down and Out in the Great Depression" from Robert S. McElvaine, *Down and Out in the Great Depression: Letter from the Forgotten Man*. Copyright © 1983 The University of North Carolina Press. Reprinted with the permission of the publishers.

[29] "Letter from Los Alamos" from Phyllis Fisher, *The Los Alamos Experience* (Tokyo: Japan Publications, 1985), pp. 24–27, 29–30, 32, 46–50, 115–17, 121, 122, and 145. Copyright © 1985 by Phyllis Fisher. Reprinted with the permission of the author.

[31] "Rosie the Riveter: Fanny Christina Hill" from Sherna Berger Gluck, *Rosie the Riveter Revisited* (Boston: Twayne Publishers, 1987), pp. 28–33, 35–38, 40–45, and 48–49. Copyright © 1987 by Sherna Berger Gluck. Reprinted with the permission of Twayne Publishers, an imprint of Simon & Schuster Macmillan, and the Elaine Markson Literary Agency.

[32] "Memories of the Internment Camp" from Archie Satterfield, *The Home Front: An Oral History of the War Years in America* (New York: Playboy Press, 1981), pp. 330–38. Copyright © 1981 by Archie Satterfield. Reprinted with the permission of the Dominick Abel Literary Agency, Inc.

[33] "The Bataan Death March" from Donald Knox, *Death March: The Survivors of Bataan*, pp. 122–39 *passim*. Copyright © 1981 by Donald Knox. Reprinted with the permission of Harcourt Brace and Company.

[34] "The Post-World War II 'Red Scare' " (originally titled "Mark Goodson") from Griffin Fariello, *Red Scare: Memories of the American Inquisition, An Oral History*, pp. 320–26. Copyright © 1995 by Griffin Fariello. Reprinted with the permission of W. W. Norton & Company, Inc. and the Sandra Dijkstra Literary Agency.

[35] "Life in Gray Flannel" from Sloan Wilson, *The Man in the Gray Flannel Suit*, pp. 3–17. Copyright © 1955 and renewed 1983 by Sloan Wilson. Reprinted with the permission of the author and Simon & Schuster, Inc.

[36] "Launching the Montgomery Bus Boycott" from David J. Garrow, *The Montgomery Bus Boycott and the Women Who Started It: The Memoir of Jo Ann Gibson Robinson*, pp. 43–46. Copyright © 1987 by The University of Tennessee Press. Reprinted by permission of the publisher.

[38a] "The My Lai Incident" from William C. Westmoreland, *A Soldier Reports* (New York: Doubleday, 1976), pp. 377–78. Copyright © 1976 by William C. Westmoreland. Reprinted with the permission of the author.

[38b] "Cover Up and Outcome" from *RN: The Memoirs of Richard Nixon*, pp. 449–50. Copyright © 1978 by Richard Nixon. Reprinted with the permission of Grossett & Dunlap Publishers, Inc.

[40] "Letters to Betty Friedan" from The Friedan Manuscript Collection, Schlesinger Library Manuscript Collections, Radcliffe College, Cambridge, Massachusetts. Reprinted by permission.

[41] "Mississippi Summer Freedom Project" from Elizabeth Sutherland, *Letters from Mississippi*. Copyright © 1965 by the McGraw-Hill Publishing Company. Reprinted with the permission of the publishers.

[42] "Mojoados (Wetbacks)" from Al Santoli, *New Americans: An Oral History*, pp. 266–74. Copyright © 1988 by Al Santoli. Used by permission of Viking Penguin, a division of Penguin Books USA, Inc. and the author c/o Janklow & Nesbitt Associates.

[43] "A Welfare Great Grandmother" from David Zucchino, *Myth of the Welfare Queen: A Pulitzer Prize Winning Journalist's Portrait of Women on the Line*, pp. 16–18, 21–22, 24–31, and 34–35. Copyright © 1997 by David Zucchino. Reprinted with the permission of Scribners, a division of Simon & Schuster, Inc. and Sterling Lord Literistic, Inc.

[44] "Reconsidering Draft Dodging" from Mark Helprin, "I Dodged the Draft, and I Was Wrong" in David Brooks, ed., *Backward and Upward: The New Conservative Writing* (New York: Vintage Books, 1996), pp. 235–39. Reprinted with the permission of the author.

[45] "Life and Death on the Internet" from Katie Argyle, "Life After Death" in Rose Shields, ed., *Cultures of Internet: Virtual Spaces, Real Histories, Living Bodies*, pp. 133–41. Copyright © 1996. Reprinted with the permission of Sage Publications, Ltd.

NOUVELLE HISTOIRE
DE LA FRANCE

10559167

DU MÊME AUTEUR

La Banque, l'argent et leur histoire, Paris, Nathan, Monde en poche junior, 1989.

Empire colonial et capitalisme français : histoire d'un divorce, Paris, Seuil, Points Histoire, 1989.

Puissance et faiblesse de la France industrielle : XIXᵉ-XXᵉ siècle, Paris, Seuil, Points Histoire, 1997.

collection tempus

JACQUES MARSEILLE

NOUVELLE HISTOIRE DE LA FRANCE

*

De la Préhistoire à la fin de l'Ancien Régime

Perrin

www.editions-perrin.fr

© Dimanche, Le Nouvel... les Éditions Perrin, 1999
et 2002 pour... cette... édition.

tempus est une collection... des Éditions Perrin.

© Dictionnaires Le Robert pour les Éditions Perrin, 1999
et 2002 pour la présente édition.
ISBN : 978-2-262-01966-2
tempus est une collection des éditions Perrin.

SOMMAIRE

II LA CONSTRUCTION D'UN ÉTAT (de la guerre de Cent Ans aux Lumières)

PREMIÈRE PARTIE

LA CONSTRUCTION DE LA FRANCE

Peut-on admettre que la situation géographique et le climat d'un pays influencent fortement son histoire, que l'environnement exerce à tout moment une action directe sur les hommes ?

Pour les auteurs anciens, la réponse à cette question ne faisait aucun doute. L'histoire d'un peuple leur semblait inséparable de la contrée qu'il habite. De même qu'on ne pouvait imaginer l'histoire des Grecs ailleurs qu'autour de la mer Méditerranée, celle des Égyptiens ailleurs qu'aux bords du Nil, celle des Anglais ailleurs que dans leur île et celle des Américains ailleurs que dans les vastes plaines de l'Ouest, on ne pouvait imaginer l'histoire de France sans faire appel à l'être géographique que semble constituer le territoire français.

Dès l'Antiquité, l'attention des géographes avait été attirée par la forme particulière de ce territoire qui, engagé dans le continent, mais situé à une sorte de goulet d'étranglement, se trouve au point de jonction des deux systèmes maritimes du Nord et du Sud. Strabon, qui vivait à l'époque de Jésus-Christ, admirait dans ce pays dont il vantait « la correspondance qui s'y montre sous le rapport des fleuves et de la mer, de la mer intérieure et de l'Océan » ce qu'il appelait une « prévision intelligente », un véritable cadeau des dieux.

Quand les vieux manuels de géographie apprenaient aux jeunes écoliers que la France avait la forme d'un hexagone divisé en deux parties égales par le méridien de Paris, qu'elle avait un contour harmonieux d'une régularité presque géométrique, que la nature l'avait comblée en lui accordant un aspect avenant et une situation privilégiée, qu'elle était à égale distance du pôle et de l'équateur, que les montagnes d'altitude moyenne prédominaient dans la configuration du sol, que les diverses régions n'étaient nulle part séparées par des obstacles naturels, qu'elle était le jardin du monde, qu'elle contenait toutes les beautés de la terre, les bois d'orangers et les plantations de cyprès de la côte méditerranéenne, la lande désertique et les falaises du Nord, les cimes neigeuses des Alpes, les volcans d'Auvergne et la grâce royale de Paris, ils n'avaient pas tout à fait tort.

Quand Ronsard chantait ses louanges en écrivant :

... sans voguer ailleurs, toutes commodités
Se produisent ici, blés, vins forêts et prées :
Ainsi le trop de chaud n'offense nos contrées,
Ni le trop de froideur, ni le vent ruineux,
Ni le trac écaillé des dragons venimeux,
Ni rochers infertis, ni sablons inutiles,

il reconnaissait l'élégante répartition des terres d'une puissance douée de raison.

À la veille de la Première Guerre mondiale, le grand géographe, Vidal de La Blache inaugurait l'*Histoire de la France* réalisée sous la direction d'Ernest Lavisse par un « Tableau de la géographie de la France ». Il s'interrogeait sur les moyens employés pour réaliser et maintenir dans le long terme l'harmonie entre un territoire diversifié et les aventures d'une nation aux sources multiples. Il émettait l'hypothèse que l'atmosphère du pays, son agréable climat et sa richesse relative – même durant les époques autrement plus dures que la nôtre – avaient contribué à la naissance d'un genre particulier de sociabilité. « La France, observait-il, est une terre qui semble faite pour absorber en grande partie sa propre émigration. Une multitude d'impulsions locales, nées de différences juxtaposées de sol, y ont agi de façon à mettre les hommes à même de se fréquenter et de se connaître, dans un horizon toutefois restreint. »

Pointant les deux portes naturelles qui ouvrent le pays aux influences extérieures, la route maritime de la Méditerranée et l'artère qui l'associe aux palpitations venues du bassin du Danube, des ouvertures « naturelles » qui ont attiré les migrants et fait la richesse et l'originalité du pays, il écrivait : « Les rapports entre le sol et l'homme sont empreints, en France, d'un caractère original d'ancienneté, de continuité. De bonne heure les établissements humains paraissent y avoir acquis de la fixité ; l'homme s'y est arrêté parce qu'il a trouvé, avec les moyens de subsistance, les matériaux de ses constructions et de ses industries. Pendant de longs siècles, il a mené une vie locale, qui s'est imprégnée lentement des sucs de la terre. Une adaptation s'est opérée, grâce à des habitudes transmises et entretenues sur les lieux où elles avaient pris naissance. Il y a un fait que l'on a souvent l'occasion de remarquer en notre pays, c'est que les habitants se sont succédé de temps immémorial aux mêmes endroits. Les niveaux de sources, les roches calcaires propices à la construction et à la défense, ont été dès l'origine des nids d'attraction qui n'ont guère été abandonnés dans la suite... L'homme a été chez nous le disciple longtemps fidèle du sol. »

À Soleilhac, en Haute-Loire, voilà environ un million d'années, des hommes ébauchaient déjà l'aménagement d'un espace en levant des blocs au bord de la plage d'un ancien lac. Il y a 700 000 ans, près de Nice et dans la basse vallée de la Durance, ils maîtrisaient le feu et organisaient autour du foyer les premiers usages d'une vie sociale. Il y a 50 000 ans, ils enterraient leurs morts, disposaient des offrandes auprès des corps et prenaient soin des infirmes qui ne pouvaient concourir à la quête de nourriture pour le groupe. Il y a 30 000 ans, ils devenaient métaphysiciens, poètes et artistes et dessinaient des œuvres pleines de force et de vie dont la qualité esthétique nous stupéfie.

Ainsi, la néolithisation qui était autrefois présentée comme la grande révolution de l'histoire humaine, le passage décisif de la cueillette et de la chasse à l'agriculture et à l'élevage, le « grand-bond-en-avant » qui aurait permis à l'homme d'être mieux nourri, de croître et de se multiplier, n'éclate pas franchement comme un éclair dans un ciel serein.

À partir de 6 000 ans avant notre ère et tout au long du cinquième millénaire, trois « France » semblent se partager l'espace géographique dessiné par l'hexagone.

Au sud, tandis que se diffuse l'élevage des chèvres et des moutons et que se développe, à partir des côtes méditerranéennes, une agriculture modeste, chasse, pêche et cueillette rythment encore la vie des hommes qui n'ont pas si facilement renoncé au mode de vie antérieur, adapté au milieu naturel.

Au nord, par contre, au fond des vallées de l'Aisne, de la Marne, de la Seine, de l'Oise et le long du Rhin, des colons venus d'Europe centrale édifient de vastes et solides maisons collectives, défrichent les bonnes terres du Bassin parisien et font paître bœufs et porcs à proximité de leurs ancêtres sauvages, les aurochs et les sangliers.

À l'ouest, enfin, où l'on ne s'aventure guère encore, des communautés fort mystérieuses manient d'énormes pierres pour édifier dolmens et cromlech's, dresser des menhirs et bâtir un nouvel ordre social.

Cela n'empêche pas les contacts. Certes, ils demeurent épisodiques, mais les similitudes observées dans les décors de poteries en font foi. Ces relations, que l'on imagine alternativement pacifiques et violentes inaugurent la lente et patiente construction de notre unité nationale.

Les premiers « Français »

Vieux de 400 000 ans, le crâne découvert en 1971 à Tautavel, dans une grotte des Pyrénées, la caune de l'Arago, est le plus ancien crâne de Français connu. Cependant des galets de quartz taillés, datés d'il y a 2 millions d'années, mêlés à des ossements brisés d'animaux, dont certains portent les marques faites par l'outil qui a servi à détacher la chair de l'os, ont été retrouvés dans le Massif central. Ces galets relancent ainsi la question de savoir à quelle date un « homme » a foulé pour la première fois le sol du pays qu'on appelle aujourd'hui la France. Nous ne le saurons jamais avec exactitude. Reste que c'est probablement la France qui, après l'Afrique, a vu se multiplier les premières traces d'activité humaine.

Quelques galets taillés pour traces

Dans la partie du Massif central où les volcans furent en activité entre 2,5 millions d'années et 600 000 ou 500 000 ans avant notre ère, les coulées basaltiques ont piégé les traces les plus anciennes d'une activité humaine en Europe. L'âge de ces traces, qui fait l'objet d'un débat parmi la communauté scientifique, est aujourd'hui estimé par certains chercheurs à 2 millions d'années, peut-être même plus.

Pour mesurer le vertige du préhistorien devant ces découvertes, il suffit de dire que les fouilles entreprises depuis une vingtaine d'années ont fait reculer de plus de 500 000 ans l'estimation de la première apparition de l'Homme en France ! Ces découvertes, si elles se multipliaient, pourraient ainsi bouleverser le schéma de l'évolution humaine qui admettait comme acquis le fait que l'Afrique constituait la souche de tout le peuplement humain terrestre !

Deux millions d'années, deux mille millénaires, vingt mille siècles, telle serait donc la fantastique durée de notre histoire !

Mais d'où venaient ces hommes qui, à Rochelambert, à Blassac, à Saint-Eble, à Perrier-les-Etouaires, à Nolhac, à Senèze ou à Chilhac, ont brisé, comme en Éthiopie à la même époque, des galets pour en rendre les arêtes plus tranchantes ? S'étaient-ils vraiment évadés du berceau africain pour partir à la conquête de la planète ? Ces *Homo erectus*, aussi grands que les hommes actuels, mais plus robustes, menaient-ils une vie misérable, condamnés à la même errance que les bandes de gorilles, ou étaient-ils assez ingénieux pour s'aménager quelque abri ?

Il faut effectuer un bond d'un million d'années pour relever des traces plus nombreuses, au moment où se prolonge un refroidissement marqué du climat. La grotte dite du Trou des Renards, au long du Vallonnet, un petit torrent de la commune de Roquebrune, dans les Alpes-Maritimes, est le plus vieil habitat actuellement connu en Europe. Ouverte vers le nord, elle est constituée par un étroit couloir qui débouche, à 5 mètres de l'entrée, dans une salle exiguë. Les galets aménagés et les éclats de taille ont été abandonnés au centre de la petite salle.

Les grands ossements de mammifères, en revanche, avaient généralement été rejetés contre les parois. Ces hommes, qui ne connaissaient pas le feu, avaient traîné dans leur habitat une forte proportion d'animaux âgés, vraisemblablement des bêtes mortes ou malades.

Ils y avaient aussi amené des fragments de carcasse d'une baleine, probablement échouée sur une plage proche et en voie de décomposition.

À cette même date, à Soleilhac, près du Puy, sur les rives d'un ancien lac de montagne, d'autres hommes taillaient le quartz, chassaient les éléphants qui s'enlisaient au bord du lac et alignaient des blocs de basalte et de granite de 6 mètres de long et de 1,50 m de large.

Mais, faute de squelette fossile, nous ne pouvons toujours pas dessiner les contours et les caractéristiques physiques de cet *Homo* mystérieux qui, pourtant, au fil des millénaires et des glaciations successives, améliore sa technique de taille et diversifie son outillage.

La maîtrise du feu

Vers 700 000 ans, dans la grotte de l'Escale, dans la basse vallée de la Durance, on soupçonne la présence de grands feux au milieu des restes d'un ancêtre des loups, d'un félin de la taille d'un lion et d'un cerf à ramures palmées. Même si les traces d'un feu intentionnel sont mises en doute par de nombreux chercheurs, les couches de cendre, qui atteignent plus de 10 centimètres d'épaisseur et sont constituées de résidus de branches d'arbres, semblent bien attester le fait que ces foyers sont d'origine humaine. Ce seraient les plus anciens témoignages au monde de la maîtrise du feu !

Après quoi, toutefois, les traces disparaissent pour longtemps. Elles se font plus nombreuses et plus précises vers les 500 000 ans, au cours d'une période interglaciaire qui voit la température augmenter en moyenne de 2 à 3 °C. Près de trois cents sites recensés font de cette période décisive un véritable « tournant » de notre histoire, où le feu est réellement maîtrisé. Parmi les plus vieux foyers, celui de la grotte du Mas des Caves, à Lunel-Viel, entre Nîmes et Montpellier, révèle l'aménagement d'une véritable cuisine ! L'un des « fourneaux » est aménagé en forme de cuvette en partie entourée de grosses pierres disposées en cercle. Une ouverture avait été laissée, peut-être pour faciliter le tirage. Autour du foyer, le sol est piétiné par endroits et pavé de galets. Un bloc-siège a même été identifié. Dans de légères cavités, l'argile a conservé des empreintes de rameaux de feuilles et de faisceaux d'herbes, probablement des litières qui couvraient à peu près 2 mètres carrés. Ailleurs, des fosses ont gardé des empreintes de graines et de coquilles.

À proximité du vieux port de Nice, les foyers retrouvés dans les dunes fossiles de Terra Amata, datés de 380 000 ans, étaient placés au centre de campements temporaires. La fouille a révélé que les chasseurs fréquentaient l'endroit régulièrement mais n'y faisaient que de courtes étapes, au cours de déplacements saisonniers, abandonnant à leur départ outils, éclats et même... excréments dont on a retrouvé les restes. Leur étude a aussi permis de déterminer, par les pollens qu'ils contenaient, que les séjours avaient lieu durant l'été.

Ces hommes qui chassaient à profusion lapins, cerfs, sangliers, mais aussi ours, rhinocéros et petits éléphants, faisaient également leur ordinaire de coquillages marins. Les dunes ont aussi conservé fidèlement les traces de vingt et un emplacements de huttes ayant chacune de 9 à 16 mètres de long sur 4 à 7 mètres de large. Le feu était entretenu sur un dallage de galets ou dans une cuvette creusée dans le sable. Une murette coupe-vent protégeait la combustion.

À Plouhinec enfin, dans le sud du Finistère, on a découvert en 1995 dans une ancienne grotte effondrée les traces d'un feu datées de 465 000 ans avant notre ère. Les ossements trouvés à proximité montrent qu'il a été utilisé pour cuire de la viande de rhinocéros et de grands bovidés.

De telles dispositions laissent donc deviner une réelle maîtrise du feu, le « foyer », comme on dit aujourd'hui, étant bien intégré dans un espace habité dont il constituait le centre d'attraction. On ne peut qu'être lyrique devant un tel « progrès » qu'aucun animal ne maîtrisa jamais et qui semble indissociable du développement de l'humanité.

Tout d'abord, la cuisson de la viande, la rendant plus digeste, facilita sa consommation. Il en résulta l'absorption d'une plus grande quantité de calories. En l'attendrissant, elle allait aussi provoquer une réduction du temps de mastication qui se traduisit par une diminution des muscles de la face et contribua au raccourcissement des maxillaires.

Le feu facilita également la conservation de la chair du gibier abattu et des poissons capturés. Tout en gardant l'essentiel de leurs qualités alimentaires, ces aliments fumés pouvaient être consommés longtemps après l'abattage.

De plus, outre la chaleur qu'il procure, le feu apportait une source d'éclairage artificiel favorisant l'occupation de grottes profondes et encourageant la communication entre individus qui purent prolonger autour de lui les activités de la vie quotidienne. Enfin, le feu constituait une arme de défense efficace permettant de tenir à distance les animaux rôdeurs en quête de quelque quartier de viande.

Autant de « progrès » qui invitent à penser que le fait d'avoir un jour osé s'emparer à main nue du feu pour s'en approprier la puissance a pu être considéré comme la deuxième naissance de l'humanité. Après avoir créé l'outil, prolongement de son être physique, l'homme devenait, avec le feu, maître d'un élément naturel qu'il transformait en instrument de sa volonté.

Mais comment, alors, ne pas multiplier les interrogations sur les conditions dans lesquelles est apparu ce fantastique « progrès » ? Pourquoi l'homme a-t-il attendu si longtemps avant de domestiquer le feu alors que son utilisation apporte de tels avantages ?

C'est que non seulement le feu ne pouvait être maîtrisé sans un minimum d'aptitudes intellectuelles mais que surtout son utilisation entraînait d'évidentes transformations sociales.

La maîtrise du feu oblige en effet à passer un temps important à récolter du combustible, autant de temps que l'on ne pourra consacrer à l'acquisition d'aliments, surtout si le feu doit être entretenu en permanence.

Cela suppose aussi des notions d'organisation et de prévision qui nous paraissent évidentes mais l'étaient peut-être moins pour nos lointains ancêtres. En outre, la prise en commun des repas qu'impose en partie la consommation de viande grillée entraîne une division du temps, exige un horaire qui n'est plus individuel mais collectif. À partir du moment où la cuisson intervient, elle réunit le groupe en un lieu et un temps donnés et le repas devient bien un élément majeur d'intégration du groupe familial ou social. L'acte alimentaire prend alors la valeur symbolique qu'il gardera jusqu'à aujourd'hui.

Enfin, avec l'introduction du « foyer », c'en est aussi fini de l'anarchie des premiers habitats. Désormais il devient le pôle privilégié autour duquel s'organisent l'espace et les activités. C'est alors qu'on voit se différencier les zones de travail de la pierre, les zones de préparation alimentaire et les zones de rejet des déchets domestiques.

C'est probablement aussi au sein du groupe que se partagent les activités, la surveillance constante des braises faisant émerger une division des tâches selon les individus, le sexe ou l'âge.

Ainsi, si la maîtrise du feu est apparue si tard dans l'histoire de l'humanité, ce n'est sans doute pas en raison d'une quelconque incapacité technique à le produire, les systèmes traditionnels de production étant finalement très simples, mais parce qu'elle nécessitait un changement fondamental de comportement à mettre sur le compte d'un progrès plus psychique que technique.

Les premiers industriels

L'époque qui voit apparaître les premiers foyers correspond aussi, ce qui n'est d'ailleurs pas un hasard, à des innovations majeures dans les industries de la pierre taillée.

À partir de 400 000 ans, en effet, le geste simple qui impliquait de frapper à 90 degrés le bord d'un galet pour en faire naître un tranchant se transforme au fil du temps en un véritable « coup de main » nécessitant l'acquisition d'une série de gestes supplémentaires aussi précis qu'effectués dans un ordre strict.

En effet, en vue d'obtenir un outil (lame, pointe, etc.), on ne se contente pas de dégrossir le bloc de pierre mais l'on cherche au contraire, par une succession de petits enlèvements, à en ôter un éclat de forme prédéterminée qui deviendra l'outil, le reste du bloc, appelé nucléus (le noyau), devenant ainsi inutile. C'est la technique Levallois, du nom de la commune de la banlieue de Paris où ont été faites les premières découvertes.

Comme pour la maîtrise du feu, il y a bien, là aussi, intention et prévision puisque, et c'est capital, la forme que prendra l'outil doit préexister dans l'esprit de l'artisan.

Cette technique constitue ce que l'humanité a créé de plus élaboré pour la fabrication des outils de silex. L'existence de vastes ateliers où les hommes sont venus, génération après génération, débiter leur matière première permet, sur des dizaines de milliers d'éclats, de nucléus épuisés, de ratés de fabrication, de se représenter le haut degré de technicité auquel ils étaient parvenus.

Ainsi, avec une quantité moindre de matière première, l'artisan peut fabriquer des outils plus efficaces et moins pesants. Alors qu'il obtenait 10 centimètres de tranchant pour 1 kilogramme de galets aménagés il y a 2 millions d'années, il obtient 40 centimètres pour 1 kilogramme de bifaces il y a 500 000 ans, 2 mètres de tranchant il y a 50 000 ans et 10 mètres il y a 35 000 ans.

Et c'est probablement parce que la France regorgeait de silex, cette matière première plus dure que l'acier, que l'évolution de l'homme y a été précocement favorisée.

L'Homme, enfin...

Si la présence multipliée d'outils taillés permet d'affirmer l'existence de l'Homme en France, seule une dent de lait d'un enfant de quatre à cinq ans, trouvée au milieu de gros animaux piégés à Vergranne, dans le Doubs, permet de traquer enfin le premier Français, il y a 400 000 ans. Avec un fragment de molaire recueilli à Prvezletice, en République tchèque, une mandibule découverte à Mauer, en Allemagne, et une autre à Montmaurin, dans la Haute-Garonne, elle représente le plus ancien et le seul témoin osseux connu en Europe.

Sur le site de Terra Amata, une empreinte de pied humain de 24 centimètres de longueur paraît correspondre à un individu pouvant mesurer un peu moins de 1,60 m.

Surtout, une grotte des Pyrénées nous donne, pour la première fois, un aperçu de la personne qui, entre 400 000 et 350 000 ans, taillait aussi ingénieusement les éclats. En juillet 1971 en effet, à Tautavel, une commune située à 19 kilomètres au nord-ouest de Perpignan, la caune de l'Arago nous livrait, gisant au milieu d'outils et

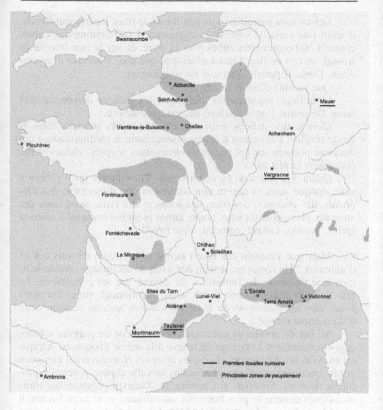

Les sites du Paléolithique inférieur
(– 2 000 000 à – 135 000 ans).

d'ossements animaux, un crâne, les dents tournés vers le ciel. Deux autres mâchoires, des dents isolées, des fragments de pariétaux, une rotule et des phalanges nous permettent de nous faire une idée de ce plus vieux des « Français ».

D'après diverses indications, telles une molaire peu usée et une suture frontale pas tout à fait ossifiée, il s'agissait d'un jeune homme d'une vingtaine d'années dont l'épaisseur des os et la puissance des insertions musculaires suggèrent une robustesse et une force certaines. C'était un rude gaillard.

Les arcades sourcilières un peu fortes, le front légèrement fuyant, il avait une capacité cérébrale de presque 1 100 centimètres cubes, contre 1 500 centimètres cubes pour la nôtre, et, sur la face interne du frontal, un cap de Broca aussi développé que chez l'homme d'aujour-d'hui. Donc, il parlait, quel que fût son langage.

Que raconte d'autre ce rescapé ?

L'outillage apparaît très archaïque, les bifaces demeurant très rares. De même l'on n'a relevé aucune trace de feu.

L'étude des pollens ainsi que des sédiments présents dans la grotte révèlent l'existence d'arbres essentiellement méditerranéens qui devaient pousser sur les pentes environnantes (cyprès, chênes verts, pistachiers et platanes).

Quant aux restes de faune retrouvés, ils indiquent qu'il y avait à cette époque dans la région non seulement des rhinocéros, des élé-phants, des chevaux, des ours, des loups et des lynx, mais aussi des animaux plus petits (belette, taupe, lapin) et un bel éventail d'oiseaux (grive, perdrix, canard, corbeau, aigle royal).

Mais que faisaient ces restes humains au milieu de tous ces os d'animaux ? Un fémur présentant des stries de découpage semble indi-quer que l'homme de Tautavel a été dévoré par ses congénères. Le bris de la boîte crânienne paraît aussi intentionnel, suggérant ainsi l'idée que les ossements de notre plus ancien ancêtre seraient ceux d'un homme mangé !

Si, par de nombreux caractères, les restes de ce premier « Fran-çais » ressemblent à ceux qu'on trouve à la même époque en Afrique ou en Asie, les différences physiques entre cet *Homo erectus* européen et les spécimens asiatiques et africains de cette espèce posent un pro-blème de fond. En effet, si l'homme de Tautavel présente des traits archaïques comme le gros bourrelet sus-orbitaire et le front fuyant, il possède également des caractères de type *sapiens* tels que l'augmenta-tion de la capacité crânienne ou l'aplatissement des os de la nuque.

Qui étaient donc ces 2 000 ou 3 000 « Français » qui, selon les estimations, peuplaient alors la France ?

CHAPITRE **2**

La naissance de la mort

Enraciné pendant près de 100 000 années dans le sol français, l'homme de Néandertal s'affirme ouvrier plus qu'habile et se présente comme le premier à avoir offert une tombe à ses morts. En témoigne le squelette d'un Néandertalien retrouvé, en compagnie de sept autres (dont plusieurs enfants), à La Ferrassie, en Dordogne. Les jambes repliées sous les cuisses, le bras gauche le long du corps, le bras droit plié et la tête tournée vers la gauche, il révèle l'existence de pratiques funéraires et fait de ce site l'une des plus anciennes sépultures de l'histoire de l'humanité.

Un homme doté d'un certain charme

C'est au lendemain d'une longue période glaciaire qui s'étend sur près de mille siècles, de 235 000 à 135 000 ans avant notre ère, que se produit une nouvelle évolution décisive. À cette date, apparaissent ceux qui, réellement *sapiens*, allaient devenir nos plus proches ancêtres.

Des ancêtres qui n'ont pourtant pas bonne presse. En effet, lorsqu'en 1856 on découvrit dans une grotte de la vallée du Neander, près de Düsseldorf, en Allemagne, les restes de celui qu'on allait baptiser l'homme de Néandertal, on eut du mal à admettre que le crâne qu'on venait d'exhumer ait pu appartenir à un ancêtre direct de l'homme moderne.

Des savants anatomistes allemands, Rudolf Virchow et Robert von Mayer, attribuèrent ce crâne à un homme récent mais dégénéré, rachitique et d'origine mongoloïde. D'autres, estimant que les fémurs courbés trahissaient la pratique de l'équitation, y virent le squelette d'un cosaque déserteur de l'armée russe au temps des guerres napoléoniennes. Seul l'Anglais Thomas Huxley soupçonna qu'il pouvait s'agir d'un précurseur de l'homme moderne et, devant les sarcasmes d'un confrère, répliqua qu'il préférait avoir pour ancêtre un singe réussi qu'un Adam dégénéré.

En 1920 encore, Marcellin Boule, professeur au Muséum d'histoire naturelle, décrivait en ces termes l'homme qu'il avait découvert en 1912 à La Chapelle-aux-Saints, en Corrèze : « L'absence probable de toute trace de préoccupation d'ordre esthétique ou d'ordre moral [s'accorde] bien avec l'aspect brutal de ce corps vigoureux et lourd, de cette tête osseuse aux mâchoires robustes et où s'affirme encore la prédominance des fonctions purement végétatives ou bestiales sur les fonctions cérébrales. »

Or cet homme souffrait en réalité, on le sait maintenant, d'arthrose de la hanche, de l'épaule et du cou, ce qui devait rendre ses mouvements et ses déplacements particulièrement douloureux.

Le discrédit dont fut ainsi victime l'homme de Néandertal donna lieu à de nombreuses représentations soulignant son caractère grossier et lourd, dont la plus célèbre demeure la statue dite de l'Homme primitif, devant le musée de la Préhistoire des Eyzies-de-Tayac-Sireuil, qui résume, selon le mot d'André Leroi-Gourhan, « la somme des traditions erronées d'un siècle et demi de lutte scientifique ».

Peu perceptibles si l'on se contente d'un examen superficiel, les caractères « modernes » de notre homme deviennent manifestes dès lors qu'on compare son cerveau, sa posture, son mode de locomotion ou son appareil masticateur à ceux de ses prédécesseurs. Comme l'écrit Jean-Paul Demoule, « dans la rue, coiffé d'un chapeau, nous ne le remarquerions même pas », car son crâne est simplement moins haut et plus allongé vers l'arrière que le nôtre.

Les Néandertaliens mesuraient entre 1,55 et 1,78 m, en moyenne 1,65 m. Ils étaient plus robustes, avec une forte charpente osseuse, et leur poids était élevé par rapport à leur taille. La musculature de leurs bras était beaucoup plus développée que la nôtre. La morphologie de l'omoplate montre en particulier l'énorme développement des muscles qui maintiennent l'articulation de l'épaule et permettent la rotation du bras.

Sur l'humérus, les insertions du grand pectoral et des muscles du dos, qui servent à escalader, à frapper ou à lancer, étaient beaucoup plus larges que chez nos meilleurs culturistes. C'est également le cas des muscles de la main. Les doigts larges et épais étaient terminés par des pulpes épaisses qui augmentaient encore la puissance de la préhension.

Enfin, bien que le pouce des Néandertaliens soit de même taille que le nôtre, ses deux phalanges étaient presque d'égale longueur alors que notre première phalange est plus longue d'un tiers. Cette particularité anatomique donnait une force extrême à la main, la préhension s'effectuant par le milieu du pouce et non pas, comme chez nous, par l'extrémité.

Robustesse et endurance, telles étaient les qualités premières de ces hommes qui devaient se déplacer sans cesse en quête de nourriture pour le groupe.

Leur visage présentait une configuration unique, avec une projection vers l'avant des mâchoires et du nez, tandis que les pommettes étaient inclinées vers l'arrière, au contraire des nôtres. Or ce qui a longtemps passé pour un caractère primitif est apparu récemment au travers de recherches nouvelles comme la conséquence d'une habitude culturelle, l'utilisation des canines et des incisives comme d'une troisième main.

Car si la denture de ces hommes est la même que la nôtre, prémolaires et molaires variant dans des proportions identiques, canines et incisives, en revanche, sont nettement plus grandes et devaient donc s'user plus lentement. Or les squelettes néandertaliens présentent des incisives et des canines usées jusqu'à la racine dès l'âge de trente-cinq ou quarante ans, ce qui laisse penser qu'elles étaient utilisées pour maintenir des objets tout autant que pour les déchiqueter.

Enfin l'espérance de vie néandertalienne était faible, les plus âgés n'atteignant pas cinquante ans et la plupart mourant avant quarante ans. Ces décès précoces peuvent aussi s'expliquer par un taux élevé de blessures liées aux risques de la chasse.

L'ébauche de régions

L'énergie dont les Néandertaliens ont dû faire preuve dans leur quête de nourriture ou la maîtrise de leur environnement se retrouve aussi dans les objets qu'ils façonnent, nommés « moustériens » du nom de l'abri-sous-roche du Moustier, dans la vallée de la Vézère, quelques kilomètres avant sa confluence avec la Dordogne, un abri qui a livré en abondance des silex et des cailloux calcaires brûlés.

C'est l'homme de Néandertal, en particulier, qui va porter à la perfection la taille des éclats Levallois, remplaçant le biface par les pointes triangulaires produites à partir de petits éclats de 4 à 7 centimètres de longueur. Burins, racloirs, grattoirs, couteaux, outils à encoches pour travailler le bois complètent l'industrie « moustérienne ». Des outils mieux définis et mieux appropriés à leurs fonctions. Surtout, ces outils montrent, par leur différence d'origine géologique, que les Néandertaliens effectuaient des parcours et des choix complexes pour rechercher leur matière première. Ainsi, nombre des silex trouvés dans toute la vallée du Tarn provenaient du Verdier, au nord de Gaillac, où les gens de la région venaient s'approvisionner en apportant avec eux leurs outils de débitage. Certains silex du Périgord pouvaient avoir été transportés sur plus de 80 kilomètres.

Rationnels, les hommes de Néandertal utilisaient aussi la matière première locale pour l'outillage courant, réservant les matières plus rares et plus lointaines aux outils les plus délicats comme les pointes, qui faisaient l'objet d'une réalisation plus soignée.

Enfin, des sortes de « frontières » commencent même à se dessiner. Au nord des vallées du Tarn et de son affluent l'Agout, on fabriquait des bifaces ; au sud, il n'y en avait aucune trace. Cela suggère un territoire, une certaine unité régionale qui peut aussi avoir été culturelle, même si, avec peut-être 4 000 habitants sur le sol de France, l'encombrement était pour le moins réduit. Autant d'interrogations qui rendent encore bien mystérieuse cette civilisation « moustérienne ».

Une civilisation d'hommes qui donnent le sentiment de parcourir de long en large cette « France » qui est leur territoire, d'en connaître par le menu les gués et les rivières, les pistes et les sites et, surtout, les bons gisements de silex. Car la pierre, ils savent l'utiliser. Pour en faire des murets ou des pavages comme celui de La Ferrassie, en Dordogne. Pour en faire aussi des murailles comme celle qui, épaisse de 3 mètres à la base et plus haute qu'un homme, fermait l'abri de Roc-en-Pail, à Chalonnes-sur-Loire, en Maine-et-Loire.

Car, au cours des périodes froides de ces longs millénaires, il a bien fallu se protéger, même si la légende de l'homme de Néandertal se terrant dans les cavernes est absurde. En fait, le mode de vie de ces chasseurs-cueilleurs impliquait une multiplicité de « résidences » dont on retrouve les traces, les sites d'habitat variant en fonction de plusieurs impératifs.

Les installations de plein air correspondaient à des stations brèves pour des chasseurs à la traque. À Achenheim, en Alsace, on trouve des aires de dépeçage du gibier où, sur plus de 200 mètres carrés, gisent en abondance carcasses et mandibules de chevaux et de rhinocéros, alors que peu d'outils les accompagnent. Ces outils, on les retrouve en revanche avec les nucléus, abandonnés dans ce qui devait être des ateliers de taille.

Cannibalisme et « humanité »

Un des hauts lieux de l'habitat néandertalien est la grotte de l'Hortus, à 20 kilomètres au nord de Montpellier. Elle s'ouvre sur un escarpement rocheux au pied d'une paroi abrupte de 100 mètres mais surplombe la vallée de 200 mètres. Le massif, le plateau calcaire, la vallée constituaient autant de zones de chasse offrant en abondance un gibier varié, surtout du bouquetin dont ces hommes semblaient friands. Ils se succédèrent dans cette grotte pendant des millénaires, sans s'installer de façon permanente mais en l'utilisant comme gîte temporaire de chasse, à l'abri d'un porche d'entrée, sur une grande dalle rocheuse. En arrière de cette dalle, une faille étroite, profonde de quelques mètres, recevait les déchets. Or, parmi ces déchets, se trouvaient les restes d'une trentaine d'individus, brisés et dispersés au milieu des ossements d'animaux consommés.

Selon Henri de Lumley, qui a dirigé les fouilles, ce pourrait être le témoignage d'un cannibalisme rituel. Cette hypothèse semble confirmée par les débris humains que l'on a trouvés dans les mêmes conditions dans le site de La Quina, en Charente, mais surtout dans celui de Krapina, en Croatie. Là, en effet, les « os à moelle » sont pilés alors que les autres sont intacts. La présomption est aussi forte pour le crâne du mont Circé, en Italie. Il reposait au pied d'une grotte, isolé au milieu d'un cercle de pierres, et le trou occipital avait été agrandi comme pour faciliter l'extraction du cerveau. Mais, pour d'autres préhistoriens, le crâne aurait aussi pu être perforé par les dents d'un carnassier comme la hyène.

Si cannibalisme il y eut, et c'est fort probable, les motivations nous échappent.

En effet, le cannibalisme répond exceptionnellement à des besoins alimentaires qui peuvent se manifester lors de terribles famines. Plus souvent, il témoigne d'autres préoccupations, comme la possibilité d'acquérir, par la consommation des parties nobles, cerveau, foie ou phallus, les vertus du mort.

Aussi incongru que cela puisse paraître, le cannibalisme peut aussi être considéré comme une forme de sépulture. Comme l'écrit

L.V. Thomas, un anthropologue qui a multiplié les études sur les pratiques funéraires, « l'incorporation cannibalique est un procédé simple, quoique paradoxal, qui évite la corruption de la chair tout en conservant, incorporée socialement, une parcelle de l'être disparu ». Un vieux Diola, au Sénégal, ne lui fit-il pas cet aveu : « Quelle meilleure demeure pour le mort que la terre du ventre de ceux qui le mangent ? »

En fait, ces pratiques témoigneraient d'une « sensibilité » plus complexe qu'on ne pourrait le penser de prime abord, de pratiques très codifiées bien difficiles à interpréter pour cette époque.

Ainsi, le préhistorien suisse Emil Bächler avait, en 1920, avancé l'hypothèse d'un culte rendu aux ours. Dans la grotte de Drachenluch, il avait remarqué une accumulation d'ossements tout à fait particuliers : sept crânes, la gueule orientée vers l'entrée, entourés de plaquettes de pierre dessinant une sorte de caisson cubique d'un mètre de côté et coiffé d'une dalle massive. L'idée a été abandonnée mais une découverte spectaculaire dans la grotte du Régourdou, en Dordogne, a reposé la question.

Dans cette tombe recouverte d'un tertre protecteur, on a mis au jour, en effet, un ensemble de structures faites de fosses et de coffrages de pierres amassées et contenant des ossements d'ours.

À proximité d'une fosse recouverte d'une dalle de plus de 800 kilos, qui contenait un squelette d'ours brun, gisait un squelette humain accompagné de quelques outils et d'un bois de cerf.

Dans la mesure où les ossements de l'ours étaient complets et soigneusement disposés, même s'ils n'occupaient pas leur position anatomique, l'ensevelissement revêt bien un caractère intentionnel même si sa motivation reste, là encore, mystérieuse.

Les premières sépultures humaines

La mort est désormais devenue une des préoccupations de l'homme, à tel point qu'on peut souscrire à l'affirmation de l'historien Pierre Chaunu : « L'histoire commence vraiment avec la tombe. » Car c'est bien l'attitude nouvelle des hommes de Néandertal face à la mort qui en fait de véritables hommes « modernes », voici plus de 100 000 ans.

Ce furent eux, en effet, qui creusèrent les plus anciennes tombes, dont la première fut découverte en 1908 par trois abbés, les pères L. Bardon et J. et A. Bouyssonie, dans la grotte corrézienne de La Chapelle-aux-Saints.

C'était une fosse rectangulaire de 1,50 m sur 1 mètre, profonde de 30 centimètres et creusée dans un sol de marne blanche. D'après la description des abbés, le corps était couché sur le dos, la tête à l'ouest et calée par quelques pierres, le bras gauche étendu et le droit plié, la main vers la tête, les jambes repliées et renversées vers la droite. Près de la tête, se trouvait l'extrémité d'une patte postérieure de bovidé dont les os en connexion donnaient, selon les abbés, « la preuve évidente que la patte avait été posée là avec sa chair, peut-être pour la nourriture du mort ».

À la même époque, Denis Peyrony commençait à La Ferrassie une série de découvertes qui allaient s'échelonner jusqu'en 1920. Ce fut d'abord les squelettes de deux adultes, un homme et une femme, gisant côte à côte, en position fléchie. À quelques mètres, deux petites fosses contenaient des restes d'enfants, l'une d'un enfant d'une dizaine d'années, l'autre de deux nouveau-nés.

En 1920, il découvrit, dans une autre fosse fermée par une dalle calcaire, le squelette d'un enfant de trois ans. Le crâne, sans mandibule, se trouvait à 1,50 m du corps, hors de la fosse. À cela, il faut ajouter les débris d'un fœtus humain dans une petite dépression.

Ce type de sépulture, repéré de l'Ouzbékistan à l'Italie et jusqu'en Israël, témoigne bien d'une inhumation volontaire. Non seulement les hommes de Néandertal se préoccupaient de donner une sépulture à leurs morts mais ils semblaient aussi entretenir avec eux des relations faites de respect et, pourquoi pas, d'amour. Peut-on dire pour autant qu'ils avaient une religion et pensaient à l'avenir du disparu ? Difficile, en l'état actuel de nos connaissances, d'en comprendre les possibles rituels.

Nous pouvons seulement constater que, dans la mesure où les sépultures concernaient hommes, femmes et enfants, il n'y avait pas de discrimination en fonction du sexe ou de l'âge. En revanche, si la disposition du corps des enfants semble « désordonnée », les adultes étaient couchés sur le dos ou sur le côté, en chien de fusil.

L'autre interrogation concerne les dépôts d'« offrandes » accompagnant le squelette. À La Ferrassie, trois racloirs disposés au-dessus du squelette invitent à penser que ces « offrandes » n'étaient pas seulement alimentaires. Dans le gisement du Régourdou, l'homme reposait sur un lit de pierres plates, recouvert par d'autres blocs parmi lesquels avaient été aussi disposés des éclats, des racloirs et des nucléus.

De même, dans la grotte de Shanidar, en Irak, l'inhumation aurait donné lieu, selon l'analyse des pollens menée par Arlette Leroi-Gourhan, au dépôt du corps sur une litière de tiges d'éphédra garnie de fleurs jaunes de séneçon et de fleurs bleues d'une liliacée.

Toutes ces découvertes dissipent le cliché d'un homme de Néandertal brutal et fruste. Premier à enterrer ses morts, il a été aussi le premier à prendre soin des infirmes qui ne pouvaient concourir à la quête de nourriture pour le groupe comme cet homme retrouvé à Shanidar, en Irak, qui a survécu plusieurs années avec de graves handicaps : il était borgne, avait un bras atrophié et souffrait d'arthrose de la jambe.

Solidaire, l'homme de Néandertal est également curieux, ce que semble indiquer l'ébauche d'activités désintéressées comme le ramassage et le transport d'objets sans utilité pratique, morceaux de cristaux, pyrites ou fossiles.

Comment faut-il aussi interpréter le fait que beaucoup de sépultures révèlent des traces d'ocre rouge, cette matière colorante qui connaîtra une telle importance dans le développement ultérieur de l'art ?

Reste le mystère du langage. Cette question, objet de nombreux débats, a été relancée par la découverte, dans une sépulture du site de Kébara, en Israël, d'un os hyoïde vieux de 60 000 ans, semblable par la forme et la taille à celui d'un homme moderne.

Ce petit os, en forme de U, localisé au-dessus du larynx, entre la mandibule et la colonne vertébrale, est le point de repère en ce qui concerne la position anatomique de l'appareil vocal, simplement parce que l'épiglotte, le cartilage le plus haut placé du larynx, et les cordes vocales sont toujours situées sous l'os hyoïde.

Si l'acquisition du langage articulé était démontrée, ce serait une autre preuve d'un comportement culturel « avancé ».

Bien sûr, le fait que ces hommes possédaient les bases anatomiques du langage articulé ne signifie pas qu'ils aient réellement utilisé le langage.

Reste que l'hypothèse soulevée par les données provenant du fossile de Kébara confirmerait le niveau de développement culturel relativement élevé atteint par l'homme de Néandertal, que ce soit dans l'évolution des outillages, dans les stratégies de chasse, dans le choix des grottes pour l'habitat de longue durée et, surtout, dans la manifestation de pratiques funéraires.

Autant de preuves indirectes de la capacité de ces hommes à communiquer au moyen du langage, même sur des sujets aussi abstraits que la tradition et la mort.

Pourquoi l'homme de Néandertal a-t-il disparu ?

Les Néandertaliens ont disparu pratiquement sans descendance, très peu, sinon aucun, de leurs caractères génétiques ayant été transmis aux hommes « modernes » qui allaient progressivement les remplacer sur le sol de France.

Mais cette disparition, mal expliquée, est aujourd'hui interprétée en termes nouveaux.

Selon l'explication traditionnelle, l'homme de Néandertal se serait éteint entre 40 000 et 35 000 ans pour être remplacé par l'*Homo sapiens sapiens*, un homme identique à nous-mêmes, biologiquement et intellectuellement supérieur à son prédécesseur.

Les plus anciens spécimens de ces hommes modernes apparaissent en Afrique, il y a peut-être 200 000 ans. On les retrouve au Proche-Orient il y a 100 000 ans, en Australie il y a 50 000 ans, dans les Balkans il y a 40 000 ans. Ils prennent possession de la France vers 35 000 ans avant notre ère.

Le plus ancien de ces hommes semble bien être celui qui a été identifié au lieu dit Cro-Magnon, dans le sud-ouest de la France, où plusieurs tombes ont été découvertes en 1868 près du village des Eyzies-de-Tayac. L'étude des ossements, confiée alors à un médecin célèbre, Paul Broca, servit de référence pour décrire ces hommes « nouveaux ». Leur taille était supérieure à 1,75 m. Le crâne, de forte capacité, était allongé d'avant en arrière et doté d'arcades sourcilières assez moyennes. Le nez était étroit et le menton saillant. Tous les os des membres indiquaient une assez grande robustesse.

Dans la mesure où cette nouvelle « race » semblait apporter une civilisation supérieure, on imagina que les hommes de Cro-Magnon avaient éliminé, à la suite d'un véritable massacre, les Néandertaliens, incapables de rivaliser avec ces « envahisseurs ».

Cependant, la découverte, en 1979, d'un squelette néandertalien à Saint-Césaire, près de Saintes, en Charente-Maritime, a mis à mal cette hypothèse. Cet homme, on ne peut plus néandertalien, a en effet été trouvé là où on ne l'attendait pas, dans un niveau dont la date peut être estimée à 32 000 ans, accompagné d'objets qui témoignent d'une nette évolution vers la « modernité », comme des pointes fines, des lames à dos ou des grattoirs. Cela signifie tout simplement que l'homme de Néandertal a cohabité avec l'homme de Cro-Magnon pendant peut-être 8 000 ans.

Ainsi, ces hommes auraient évolué parallèlement et subi les mêmes contraintes d'un environnement écologique en pleine mutation. Quelle catastrophe a donc atteint les seuls Néandertaliens ? Même étalée sur un ou deux millénaires, cette disparition est rapide à l'échelle zoologique. Or il n'y a aucune trace de « génocide » ou de dégénérescence.

Récemment, on a avancé l'idée que les nouveaux arrivants, porteurs, sinon de la grippe, du moins des germes de la sphère pharyngée, auraient fait des ravages chez les Néandertaliens, dont les sinus, très vastes, n'auraient pas supporté ces infections.

Il suffisait, par exemple, d'un léger désavantage démographique, de l'ordre de 1 à 2 % de taux de mortalité supplémentaire pour qu'en trente générations, c'est-à-dire en 1 000 ans, l'homme de Néandertal disparaisse complètement.

De l'étude comparative des dents de l'une et l'autre population, on a aussi observé que trois Néandertaliens sur quatre souffraient d'un amincissement de l'émail dû à une carence alimentaire alors que les hommes de Cro-Magnon n'étaient que 30 % à souffrir des mêmes maux, ce qui révélerait une meilleure nutrition et, sans doute, des techniques de chasse plus efficaces. Certes, les Néandertaliens étaient capables de faire évoluer leurs techniques mais ils n'auraient pas tenu la distance !

En fait, il y a tout lieu de penser que les deux « races » ont coexisté pendant une très longue période, la plus ancienne se fondant lentement dans la nouvelle. Ce serait la première et véritable époque d'assimilation qu'auraient vécue les habitants de la France.

CHAPITRE 3

La découverte de la femme

Sculptée dans l'ivoire entre 29 000 et 22 000 ans avant notre ère, la « Dame à la capuche », découverte en 1894 à Brassempouy, dans les Landes, est une œuvre rare dans la mesure où, contrairement aux autres statuettes de la même époque, les traits du visage sont esquissés. Quant à la masse quadrillée qui entoure la tête, il s'agit peut-être moins d'un couvre-chef que d'une disposition élaborée de la chevelure. Constituant l'une des premières représentations du visage humain, elle s'impose comme la manifestation spectaculaire d'un art dont l'invention caractérise les brillantes civilisations des hommes de Cro-Magnon, qui physiquement sont déjà très proches de nous.

Les hommes du froid

Vers 35 000 ans avant notre ère, les Néandertaliens cèdent donc la place aux hommes de Cro-Magnon.

À cet égard, les possibilités qu'offre aujourd'hui la biologie moléculaire, en particulier les études sur l'A.D.N., le support de l'hérédité, ou sur les groupes sanguins, révèlent de manière stupéfiante la profonde homogénéité de l'humanité actuelle, c'est-à-dire son origine commune vraisemblable.

Les « races » que nous définissons aujourd'hui selon la couleur, les Noirs, les Jaunes ou les Blancs, n'ont en fait aucune justification génétique. Elles résultent simplement de l'action des rayons ultraviolets sur la peau et de l'implantation géographique de nos ancêtres communs ces 20 000 dernières années. Une misère à l'échelle du temps historique.

Autant dire aussi que les Français d'aujourd'hui conservent dans leurs « gènes » les sensibilités de ces hommes de Cro-Magnon.

Même si le climat changea bien souvent au cours de cet « âge d'or » long de vingt-cinq millénaires, de 35 000 à 10 000 ans avant notre ère, l'homme de Cro-Magnon est avant tout un homme du froid qui a vécu une des périodes les plus rudes de l'histoire cyclique du climat terrestre.

La carte de la France, et plus généralement de l'Europe, se divisait alors en trois grandes zones. La première était constituée d'une calotte de glace, non salée, à l'opposé de la banquise, qui couvrait la terre ferme jusqu'à une limite fluctuant autour d'un axe Berlin-sud de l'Angleterre. Un mur blanc bordait ainsi la France au nord de ses limites actuelles. La Manche n'existait pas, le niveau de la mer étant 110 mètres plus bas qu'aujourd'hui.

En fait, les rivages de la côte « française » avançaient de plusieurs dizaines de kilomètres vers l'ouest, sur l'actuel plateau continental. Ainsi la Loire se jetait dans l'Océan à plus de 150 kilomètres au sud-ouest de Saint-Nazaire tandis que de nombreuses îles actuelles se trouvaient rattachées au continent, telles Oléron, Noirmoutier, Ré ou bien encore Ouessant, qui se trouvait à 50 kilomètres du littoral.

Au sud de cette muraille de glace s'étendait, jusqu'au milieu de la France, un désert périglaciaire abritant peu d'animaux, encore moins d'hommes. Recouvertes totalement de glace pendant le long hiver, certaines parties pouvaient dégeler en été. Pendant quelques semaines, il y poussait alors une végétation éphémère proche de celle du nord du Canada. Les températures variaient de + 5 °C à − 50 °C, voire − 70 °C.

Domaine de la steppe ou de la toundra, le sol était balayé par des vents chargés de poussière. En se déposant sur des mètres d'épaisseur, celle-ci formait des sables et des limons très fins qu'on appelle lœss et qui couvraient des centaines de kilomètres carrés de la Bretagne à l'Alsace. L'arbre et les herbes y étaient rares : quelques pins sylvestres et des pissenlits. En fait, notre « France du Midi » était la zone la plus hospitalière. Certes, comme le reste de l'Europe, elle était soumise aux influences glaciaires, mais le dégel régulier durait plusieurs mois et assurait le développement d'une végétation permettant aux hommes de côtoyer mammouths, rhinocéros laineux et rennes.

La température y était d'environ 15 °C en été. Cette zone recouvrait toutefois des régions ayant des différences assez nettes.

Dans les Alpes, la mer de Glace n'existait pas puisque, épais peut-être de deux bons kilomètres supplémentaires, un vaste plateau glaciaire, dont le mont Blanc ne devait constituer que le principal renflement, recouvrait l'ensemble des massifs montagneux.

En Corse, comme dans le Massif central, les glaciers descendaient jusque vers 900 mètres. La vallée du Rhône était ouverte aux grands vents et au froid arctique.

Le Sud méditerranéen était donc le plus favorisé même si, là encore, de nombreuses variations climatiques pouvaient se faire sentir, affectant notamment la végétation. Ainsi dans les périodes froides, la Côte d'Azur, qui présentait alors une couverture végétale pratiquement identique à celle des Vosges, se couvrait d'armoises et d'éphédras, auxquels succédaient, lors des réchauffements, des chênes verts, des pins d'Alep et des oliviers.

Avec une température des eaux, en été, inférieure à 5 °C dans le golfe de Gascogne, la présence d'icebergs en juillet jusqu'au nord des côtes de l'Espagne était plus que probable.

Au bord de la Vézère, dans un paysage de toundra enneigée, on pouvait voir des troupeaux de rennes voisinant avec de jeunes mammouths.

Concentrés sur un grand quart sud-ouest de la France, les hommes étaient donc soumis à l'alternance de tempêtes glacées et de courts redoux, au cours desquels nos fleuves d'aujourd'hui ressemblaient à de véritables mers roulant furieusement de terribles remous sur toute la largeur de leur vallée.

Pourtant (est-ce une manifestation du miracle géographique français ?), tous les sites de cette période ont fourni des pollens d'arbres. Bien qu'en faible quantité, ils subsistaient à peu près partout, même dans les régions les plus rudes. Et c'est au cours des étés que se développait une faune exubérante qui jamais par la suite n'atteindra une telle diversité.

Aussi, les préhistoriens considèrent que nos ancêtres vivaient finalement « heureux » dans cet environnement qu'ils maîtrisaient comme le font les Esquimaux actuels, bien protégés, bien adaptés et habitués au froid.

Chasseurs de rennes

On comptait un peu plus de 10 000 hommes sur le territoire actuel de la France, répartis en trois cents campements environ. Leur densité était très forte en Guyenne, dans les Charentes, autour de la

35

Vienne, de la Creuse et du bas Rhône mais plus clairsemée dans le Midi méditerranéen, le Bassin parisien au sens large, le bassin inférieur de la Loire et sur les côtes de Bretagne. En basse Normandie et dans le Nord, si proche de la calotte glaciaire, les populations étaient fort rares.

Même s'il faut se garder de généraliser, à partir de fouilles isolées mais exemplaires, le mode de vie de ces populations qui ont vécu plus de deux cents bons siècles sur un espace où les différences géographiques étaient sensibles, les recherches menées par André Leroi-Gourhan au lieu dit Pincevent, près de Montereau, en Seine-et-Marne, puis les fouilles d'Étiolles, dans l'Essonne, et de Verberie, dans l'Oise, permettent d'entrer dans le quotidien de ces nomades chasseurs qui ont campé là, voilà 15 000 ans, à l'époque qu'on appelle magdalénienne.

En effet, grâce à de nouvelles méthodes de fouilles qui ne concernent plus seulement l'étude des ossements des animaux ou la datation des outils, mais également la reconstitution des surfaces d'habitat, l'analyse des déchets et des objets, de leur répartition spatiale, de leur degré d'usure, ou bien encore d'indices moins directement identifiables, comme la présence de poussière d'ocre rouge, on peut restituer de manière incroyablement précise la vie de ces hommes et de ces femmes qui, près de la Seine, sur les plages de limon, avaient monté deux ou trois tentes pour y venir durant la bonne saison chasser et manger surtout du renne.

Ainsi, à partir de l'examen des dents des animaux, qui permet de déterminer leur âge (les animaux naissant toujours au printemps), on a pu préciser la date de leur mort (pour la plupart en été ou au printemps), ainsi que le nombre minimal de rennes consommés durant le séjour estival à Pincevent, à savoir douze ou quatorze, dont sept jeunes.

La chasse est une activité organisée qui mobilise la communauté. Cachés depuis la rive opposée, les chasseurs qui guettaient les troupeaux traversant la Seine à cet endroit étaient armés de sagaies et de harpons en bois de renne fichés dans une hampe en bois. Ils utilisaient aussi, pour améliorer la justesse du tir et la force de pénétration du projectile, un propulseur, souvent admirablement décoré. Pour approcher les animaux, ils devaient employer la ruse et, par exemple, imiter le brame du mâle pendant la période du rut. Ou, comme les Amérindiens pour la chasse au bison, ils pouvaient, recouverts d'une peau de bête, ramper à contre-courant et sous le vent vers le troupeau et, arrivés à bonne distance, lancer leur arme. Cette ruse, ils l'ont d'ailleurs gravée sur un bois de renne découvert à Laugerie-Basse, en Dordogne.

Mais nos hommes, pour nourrir une population qui pouvait bien dépasser trente personnes par foyer, ne négligeaient pas le petit gibier, perdrix des neiges, pigeons ou lièvres, ni les œufs dont on a retrouvé les coquilles. En Dordogne, les poissons, surtout le saumon, étaient une proie de choix, lorsqu'ils remontaient le courant pour frayer. Il suffisait de surveiller les barrages naturels pour les voir sauter au-dessus de l'obstacle. Leur capture nécessitait donc de l'habileté manuelle plutôt qu'un outillage sophistiqué. Les fourchettes en bois de renne dont les dents traversaient la proie et l'immobilisaient devaient faire l'affaire. C'est du moins ce que nous pouvons imaginer. De même, les « hameçons » courbés ou droits laissent supposer l'utilisation de lignes pour la pêche, bien qu'aucune preuve ne puisse être avancée.

C'est aussi toute une société avec ses usages et ses fonctions que dessinent les fouilles. Comme aucun trou de poteau n'apparaît autour des quelque trente-cinq foyers dégagés par la suite à Pincevent, ni le moindre blocage de pierre, on devait construire léger. Chaque famille taillait quelques longues perches qu'on dressait et liait en cône ; on y tendait les peaux pour former une tente de 3 mètres de diamètre, et on pense aujourd'hui que les ouvertures se faisaient face, délimitant un grand espace commun.

Le foyer principal constituait bien le centre de l'activité domestique. Il était composé de pierres soigneusement agencées et régulièrement changées lorsqu'elles éclatent sous l'effet du feu. Certaines ont dû servir à caler des moyens de cuisson ou même constituer des plaques de cuisson pour des quartiers de viande. D'autres, plongées dans des récipients en cuir, ont chauffé efficacement un liquide.

L'arbre étant rare, on entretenait une combustion économique en choisissant des bois qui brûlent lentement et laissent peu de cendres. Et pour renforcer la lumière que la flamme offre aux membres de l'habitation, on brûlait de la graisse dans un bloc de pierre creusé en forme de coupe.

Autour du foyer principal qui servait à de multiples usages – on y chauffait le silex pour mieux le débiter, on exposait les sagaies à la chaleur pour redresser la courbure du bois de renne dans lequel elles étaient taillées – se répartissaient des zones concentriques à usage spécialisé. On peut ainsi distinguer le côté « cuisine » du côté « atelier » d'un foyer. C'est dans ce dernier qu'on fabriquait armes et outils, qu'on travaillait l'os et le cuir et qu'on bavardait en organisant la prochaine battue.

Les « aires de repos », probablement recouvertes de peaux, se signalent par une propreté exemplaire, tous les déchets de cuisine et les éclats de taille en ayant été expulsés. D'autres zones, jonchées d'éclats de pierre malhabiles, signalent des aires de « jeu » ou plutôt d'apprentissage où devaient s'exercer nos jeunes Magdaléniens.

Dans des zones « abattoirs », le travail de boucherie est lisible sur le sol. À Verberie, un campement au bord de l'Oise, des segments de colonnes vertébrales et des extrémités de pattes caractérisent ces zones de découpage analogues à celles que l'on connaît dans les campements d'Esquimaux de l'Amérique du Nord. De plus l'existence, à Verberie, de plusieurs zones vides, à la périphérie des foyers, autour desquelles on a retrouvé des restes d'ossements de rennes, suggère l'idée que l'on pratiquait le dépeçage des bêtes, en vue de conserver et sécher la viande débarrassée de ses os. On pouvait ainsi la transporter et la consommer pendant l'hiver.

Les traces laissées sur différents types de grattoirs et de perçoirs et la présence de quelques poinçons et aiguilles confirment aussi que les peaux étaient traitées et cousues sur place et qu'elles étaient utilisées pour la confection des vêtements et des tentes. Dans ces tentes, on installait des litières de branchages ou de peaux et on y serrait les objets précieux. Sur le sol, de la poudre d'ocre, qui servait probablement aussi dans les procédés de tannage, dessinait le contour de la zone de couchage.

Mais quels liens unissaient les différentes familles qui cohabitaient sur le site ? À cette question, il est difficile d'apporter une réponse précise. On peut seulement souligner qu'elles vivaient en bonne entente, comme l'atteste le partage de la viande d'un même animal.

On peut surtout reconstituer leurs pratiques alimentaires. La moelle des os longs, très nutritive, était fort appréciée. On préparait aussi des bouillons clairs, en portant à ébullition de l'eau contenue dans un seau en peau ou un baquet de bois et en mélangeant un peu de viande attachée à des os fracassés de moins de 5 centimètres de longueur.

On concassait aussi ces ossements pour que, bouillis, ils dégagent un jus gras ; la neige qui était alors jetée dans le récipient figeait la graisse.

Ce plat de base était complété par des baies comme les myrtilles, des noisettes ou des œufs. Ces hommes du froid ne souffraient donc pas de carences alimentaires comme l'atteste l'état de leurs dents et de leurs squelettes, qui ne présentent jamais de traces de rachitisme.

Mais l'actinomycose, cette maladie provoquée par le contact avec des graminées parasitées par des champignons, les guettait.

Les médecins, chargés d'ausculter leurs squelettes, relèvent aussi plusieurs cas de spondylose, dont un de cervicarthrose, qui témoignent d'une vie relativement sédentaire et d'une fréquente position assise.

On ne note qu'une seule séquelle de traumatisme : une entorse. L'un a eu des ennuis rachidiens, avec vertèbres soudées, sacrum asymétrique et légère scoliose de compensation. L'autre présente une déformation du talon, séquelle d'une fracture de la malléole interne.

Une jeune femme, enfin, portant deux petites dents surnuméraires à la mâchoire supérieure, avait un abcès grave, avec ostéite, de la racine de la première molaire droite qui a pu être à l'origine d'une septicémie mortelle.

La perfection technique

Peu avant 18 000 avant ère apparaît en France, pour disparaître 2 500 ans plus tard, une des industries de la pierre les plus mystérieuses qu'ait connues la préhistoire. En effet, jusqu'alors, et ce depuis des centaines de milliers d'années, la fabrication d'outils ne répondait qu'au seul critère fonctionnel. Il s'agissait de produire des racloirs ou des burins aussi efficaces que solides, et tout le savoir-faire accumulé au fil des millénaires par nos tailleurs de pierre ne concourait qu'à ce but. Aussi la question se pose de savoir pourquoi, tout d'un coup, de l'Aquitaine à la Bourgogne, ils se mettent à réaliser des outils dont l'utilité pratique non seulement n'apparaît guère mais encore semble céder le pas à une certaine gratuité, voire à une motivation d'ordre esthétique.

La technique utilisée se caractérise principalement par l'emploi de nombreuses retouches qui recouvrent plus ou moins largement la plupart des pointes et des lames retrouvées. Ces retouches sont obtenues non plus par pression directe comme auparavant, mais par percussion à l'aide d'un percuteur tendre, tel le bois de renne, parfois après chauffage de la pierre.

Cette industrie, appelée solutréenne, du nom du site de Solutré qui en marque la frontière nord, a suscité l'éclosion des fascinantes « feuilles de laurier », minces, retouchées sur les deux faces et particulièrement esthétiques. Mais pourquoi avoir couvert tant de pièces de ces retouches plates, légères et régulières, en languettes aux bords si souvent presque parallèles ?

D'un point de vue pratique, cette intervention était tout à fait inutile et, surtout, fort peu économe. La plupart des lames et des pointes solutréennes trouvées dans les sites sont en effet cassées, non seulement parce qu'elles devaient se briser à l'usage mais aussi parce que la taille nécessitait un tel doigté qu'il fallait souvent interrompre le travail et jeter le silex qu'une infime erreur avait gâché. Pourquoi donc avoir pris tant de peine pour sculpter des « œuvres » qui, pour les préhistoriens, sont l'équivalent de la Joconde ? À quoi pouvaient servir ces « feuilles de laurier » ? À mieux pénétrer la chair des animaux chassés ? Rien n'est moins sûr. À mieux couper ? À cet égard, les lames plus classiques, obtenues sans débitage, s'avèrent plus utiles. Force est alors d'imaginer que la taille solutréenne a été un phénomène culturel, que l'émotion artistique, en dehors de toute utilité pratique, présidait à la fabrication de ces « feuilles de laurier ».

Comment expliquer aussi le fait que le Solutréen soit typiquement français et qu'il faille rechercher les origines de cette mystérieuse industrie uniquement en Périgord ou en Ardèche, même si la technique a traversé les Pyrénées pour s'imposer en Espagne ou au Portugal alors qu'en France elle ne franchit pas le Rhône et la Loire et ignore la Provence ? Pour quelles raisons, là et pas ailleurs, certains hommes se sont-ils mis ainsi à travailler de manière aussi raffinée ?

Et pourquoi enfin, ces faiseurs de chefs-d'œuvre se sont-ils « brusquement » évanouis tout comme leurs « feuilles de laurier » ? Autant de questions sans réponse et qui laissent entier le mystère.

Ce sont les mêmes qui ont inventé l'un des instruments les plus utiles, l'aiguille à chas qui permet véritablement la couture des vêtements.

C'est à l'époque magdalénienne, celle des chasseurs de Pincevent, que le travail de l'os atteint son apogée avec les sagaies de l'épaisseur d'un crayon, longues de 30 centimètres, et les harpons à barbelures. Ces outils en os et ces objets en ivoire accomplissent d'étonnants voyages qui démontrent le prix qu'on leur accordait et dessinent une sorte de géographie des échanges. On s'aperçoit ainsi de certaines relations privilégiées qui unissent notamment les zones côtières avec l'intérieur, comme en témoignent ces colliers de coquillages retrouvés dans le Périgord et provenant des rivages de l'Atlantique.

Comment ont-ils voyagé ? Est-on allé les chercher ou les a-t-on échangés à des « tribus » de passage ? Quelle est aussi l'origine de ce besoin de coquillage symbole ? Et quelle est la signification des pendeloques aux décors complexes ? Témoignent-ils de l'existence de foyers culturels, d'hommes plus créatifs qui ont marqué de leur talent les orientations d'un groupe ?

Et que signifient ces « bâtons percés » ? Ces os allongés en tubes comptant plusieurs trous ? Sont-ils, comme on le croyait autrefois, des bâtons de commandement appartenant à des chefs ou bien des outils ayant servi à redresser à chaud les hampes de flèche en bois de renne ou à assouplir des lanières de cuir ? Et pourquoi sont-ils souvent ornés de signes abstraits ?

Encore des questions qui montrent notre ignorance mais aussi les multiples sentiers qui ont façonné, depuis très longtemps, la mosaïque culturelle française.

Le corps et l'esprit de la femme

Même si la quête de nourriture nécessitait une attention de tous les instants, les chasseurs de rennes avaient réussi à dégager assez de temps libre pour construire la première société de loisirs. C'est la raison pour laquelle ils se mettent à sculpter le corps des femmes.

La plus ancienne statuette, découverte à Laugerie-Basse en 1864, a été baptisée la « Vénus impudique ». Haute de 8 centimètres, sculptée dans l'ivoire, dépourvue de tête, les seins absents, le ventre plat, elle est d'une remarquable maigreur. Depuis cette date, plus d'une vingtaine de sites ont livré des figures de femme, à Brassempouy, dans les Landes, ou dans les grottes de Grimaldi, près de Menton.

Et certaines, cette fois, montrent que les sculpteurs avaient une vision plus nette, sinon plus réaliste, du corps féminin.

Beaucoup de ces statuettes présentent en effet des formes hypertrophiées, notamment les seins, les hanches et le ventre, comme celle, célèbre, de Lespugue, sans que l'on puisse un instant songer que les compagnes de nos chasseurs de rennes avaient de telles rondeurs. Quelle est donc la signification de ces statuettes, que les préhistoriens désignent sous le terme de « Vénus » (sans qu'il y ait toutefois de rapport avec la divinité latine) ? Culte de la fécondité représentant des femmes enceintes ? Mais pourquoi les avoir taillées si petites ? Est-ce la traduction de l'idée qu'ils se faisaient de la femme, exagérant de façon irréelle ce qui est simplement féminin ?

Pour quelle raison aussi la Vénus de Laussel, sculptée en bas-relief, tient-elle une corne de bison dans laquelle, dirait-on, elle s'apprête à boire ? Quelle était aussi la symbolique sexuelle de ce bâton percé provenant des abris de Bruniquel qui s'ouvrent dans la vallée de l'Aveyron ? L'extrémité du manche a été sculptée et incisée pour figurer avec une précision anatomique indiscutable le gland d'un pénis. Et celui découvert dans l'abri de La Madeleine ? Là, sur une baguette, on voit une tête d'ours, la gueule légèrement entrouverte. Un phallus humain turgescent frôle les naseaux de l'ours, et la base de ce phallus est incisée dans un motif double qui représente avec une certaine vraisemblance les testicules.

Nul doute que ces hommes ont exprimé leur sexualité, leurs pulsions et leurs sentiments, mais en des termes qui sont pour nous peu intelligibles.

Ces femmes qu'ils ont représentées, ils les ont aussi plus soigneusement encore ensevelies, comme cette jeune fille, âgée de vingt à vingt-cinq ans, découverte en 1935, dans l'abri de Saint-Germain-la-Rivière, en Gironde. Saupoudrée d'ocre rouge, elle reposait sous deux dalles de pierre. La parure accompagnant la défunte était constituée de soixante-dix canines de cerf, dont certaines portaient des signes géométriques, et de coquillages, sans doute autrefois cousus sur les vêtements.

Preuve de l'éveil d'une spiritualité chez les Néandertaliens lors de la période précédente, la sépulture comme le sexe paraissent devenir les pivots essentiels d'un nouvel imaginaire dont on a peine à discerner la cohérence, d'un nouvel art de vivre dont nous devinons mal les signes.

CHAPITRE **4**

L'invention de l'art

Découverte en 1940, la grotte de Lascaux a été surnommée la « chapelle Sixtine de la préhistoire ». Les chasseurs de rennes qui travaillaient les pierres et sculptaient l'ivoire nous ont laissé des « œuvres d'art » qui nous font comprendre à quel point ils étaient proches de nous et, comme nous, sensibles à la beauté. En revanche, la signification de leur production artistique, essentiellement composée de représentations animalières, demeure encore pour nous, par bien des aspects, mystérieuse.

Une reconnaissance difficile

En 1875, un jeune aristocrate espagnol, le marquis de Sautuola, visitait une grotte qui venait d'être ouverte à Altamira, près de Santillana del Mar, dans la province de Santander.

Sans prêter attention aux signes abstraits de la galerie principale, il recueillit quelques ossements et silex taillés. Trois ans plus tard, il se rendit à l'Exposition universelle de Paris et y découvrit les collections d'objets préhistoriques.

Enthousiasmé par les perspectives de cette préhistoire naissante, il retourna en 1878 à Altamira et reprit ses recherches, accompagné de sa fille, Maria, âgée de cinq ans. Celle-ci, désignant du doigt les grandes taches d'ocre qui couvraient le plafond de la grotte, s'écria soudain : « *Toros ! Toros !* »

Dans le mémoire que Sautuola publia en 1880, le marquis écrivit : « Il est évident, d'après certaines découvertes qu'on ne peut mettre en doute, comme celle qui nous intéresse, que l'homme, même quand il n'avait d'autres logis que les grottes, reproduisait sur des cornes et des défenses d'éléphants, non seulement sa propre figure mais encore celle des animaux qu'il voyait. Il n'est donc point aventureux d'admettre, puisque à cette époque appartiennent d'aussi parfaites reproductions réalisées sur des corps durs, que les peintures dont il s'agit aient une aussi lointaine origine... Il est difficile de concevoir qu'à une date récente il y ait eu quelqu'un d'assez capricieux pour s'enfermer dans cet endroit et y peindre des animaux inconnus dans cette région et à cette époque. »

Cette intuition, remarquable de prudence et de sagesse, se heurta évidemment à l'opposition acharnée des préhistoriens, surtout français, qui tournèrent le marquis en ridicule et prétendirent que ces peintures étaient une supercherie d'un peintre moderne.

Il fallut les découvertes de La Mouthe en 1895, puis des Combarelles et de Font-de-Gaume en 1901, pour que les adversaires du marquis se rendent à la raison. Le 14 août 1902, un aréopage de préhistoriens visita la région des Eyzies à la fin d'un congrès. Ce fut selon l'abbé Breuil, le premier « pape » de la préhistoire, « le jour de la reconnaissance officielle par le monde scientifique de l'art pariétal des cavernes de l'Âge du Renne ».

Émile Cartailhac, qui avait traité le malheureux Sautuola d'imposteur, fit amende honorable en publiant en 1902 *Mea culpa d'un sceptique*. Avec la découverte de Lascaux, le 12 septembre 1940, il devenait enfin acquis que l'homme « primitif » avait bien écrit, il y a environ 20 000 ans, dans ce qui est aujourd'hui la France, la première page de l'histoire universelle de l'art. Reste que la raison d'être de cet art continue à tourmenter les spécialistes, qui n'ont toujours pas réussi à comprendre le langage de ces artistes et à traduire leurs intentions.

Au plus profond des cavernes

Comment expliquer tout d'abord le fait que la terre de France ait été le lieu privilégié de l'art pariétal ?

Jusqu'à maintenant, en effet, on n'en a trouvé pour cette époque aucune trace ni en Amérique, ni en Afrique, ni en Asie. Il semble concentré dans une aire géographique qui s'étend sur les Charentes, le Périgord, le Quercy, les Landes, les Pyrénées pour la partie française, le Guipúzcoa, la Biscaye, la Cantabrie et les Asturies pour la partie espagnole. Dans ce foyer de 300 kilomètres de rayon, on trouve cent quatre-vingts grottes au moins qui abritent des peintures, tandis qu'une dizaine seulement ont été découvertes en Italie et une seule en Europe de l'Est, à Kapova, dans les montagnes de l'Oural.

Cette disproportion ne doit rien au hasard de la géographie ou des fouilles. En effet, on connaît dans les Carpates, les Alpes ou l'Oural des grottes topographiquement comparables. En outre, ces dernières années, les spéléologues ont exploré et répertorié la plupart des cavernes d'Europe.

Enfin, la vaste région périglaciaire qui, à cette époque, s'étendait de la France à l'Oural comprenait de nombreux sites de peuplement qui ont livré en quantités considérables les statuettes féminines, les « bâtons de commandement », les outils travaillés ou les objets en ivoire. Autant de faits qui rendent étonnante cette concentration de l'« art des cavernes » dans une région aussi délimitée.

Est-ce parce qu'à cette époque les rivières du Sud-Ouest regorgeaient de saumons et que les habitants avaient moins à se déplacer pour chercher leur nourriture ? Si le travail de l'os et de l'ivoire était le domaine de chasseurs nomades, l'art des cavernes aurait été le fait de populations plus sédentaires bénéficiant de moyens de subsistance plus variés et plus assurés.

Pendant plus de 8 000 ans, les hommes ont donc pénétré le plus loin qu'ils ont pu sous la terre pour peindre des animaux et tracer des signes. Mais il faut aussi souligner, et c'est fascinant, que nous sommes plus proches d'eux qu'ils ne l'étaient eux-mêmes de leurs ancêtres qui sculptaient les premières « Vénus », 15 000 ans avant eux !

Ces grottes étaient parfois d'un accès extrêmement difficile. Ainsi les artistes de la grotte basque d'Etxeberriko Kharbea ont dû ramper dans des boyaux, franchir des cheminées, longer des à-pic, traverser des lacs et des rivières aux eaux tumultueuses. Plus d'une heure de progression difficile est nécessaire pour atteindre les sites peints. Est-ce parce que l'émotion provoquée par le danger faisait partie du rituel ?

Ces artistes, nous pouvons d'ailleurs les suivre pas à pas, dans certaines grottes comme Niaux, Aldène ou Fontanet, dont le sol argileux a conservé la trace des empreintes de ces hommes et de ces enfants ayant, par mégarde, par jeu ou peut-être en vertu d'une cérémonie initiatique, marché dans les flaques boueuses. Parfois ces empreintes témoignent d'un unique passage et révèlent ainsi qu'une fois les œuvres peintes au fond de la grotte ni l'artiste ni personne d'autre n'est revenu sur les lieux. D'autres galeries, moins profondes,

Lascaux par exemple, avaient fait l'objet de nombreuses occupations, comme si, à travers le temps, la « tribu » avait émigré dans des territoires plus éloignés pour revenir ensuite se réinstaller dans les environs et fréquenter de nouveau le sanctuaire dont le groupe gardait le souvenir.

Les centaines d'images inscrites sur les parois de la grotte relèvent d'un même « style » et montrent une grande homogénéité dans l'exécution, comme si les générations successives d'artistes faisaient partie d'une véritable « école » dont les représentants auraient reproduit les enseignements.

Ces traces montrent enfin que les artistes ont souvent réalisé leurs œuvres sur des surfaces difficilement accessibles. Nombreuses sont les œuvres placées tellement haut qu'elles n'ont pu être exécutées depuis le sol. Le choix de ces parties élevées peut s'expliquer par le désir de travailler sur des panneaux de roche saine, les zones les plus basses étant plus attaquées par l'érosion. L'accès à ces parois a donc nécessité tout un matériel : des échafaudages, des échelles probablement composées de troncs d'arbres dont les branches servaient de barreaux. Dans la grotte de Lascaux, on a découvert, enrobé dans l'argile, un vestige de corde végétale tressée de 30 centimètres de long sur 8 millimètres de diamètre, âgé d'au moins 15 000 ans. C'est le plus vieux cordage connu au monde.

Il fallait surtout que ces peintres des cavernes s'éclairent. Rien qu'à Lascaux, le nombre des objets qui ont pu servir de lampes s'élève à cent trente. Si la plupart sont de simples plaques de calcaire présentant une cuvette naturelle peu profonde, d'autres ont été aménagées. L'une d'entre elles, unique, est entièrement façonnée dans du grès rose, avec un long manche décoré d'incisions et un cuilleron très régulier. On y faisait brûler des corps gras provenant de grands mammifères, suif de bœuf ou de veau, graisse de cheval ou moelle osseuse. Des expériences ont montré que chacune de ces lampes pouvait fournir l'éclairage d'une ou plusieurs bougies. Pour l'allumage, les lichens prélevés sur les branches d'arbres ou d'arbustes faisaient parfaitement l'affaire.

Enfin, les artistes ont laissé les traces du confort dont ils s'étaient dotés, des peaux pour se reposer, des coussins d'herbe pour d'asseoir et, évidemment, les restes des jeunes rennes qui leur avaient servi de nourriture.

Un art animalier

Grâce aux microscopes électroniques à balayage, on a identifié les « recettes de peinture » des artistes de la préhistoire. Ils utilisaient des colorants naturels, oxydes de fer (ocres jaunes et rouges) et oxydes de manganèse. Les rouges sombres étaient obtenus, par exemple, par une fine argile brûlée de Pithiviers. Ils avaient également recours à du charbon de bois finement broyé. La peinture résultait du mélange de ces pigments broyés avec la « charge » qui assure un meilleur pouvoir couvrant sur les parois. Deux types de charges étaient utilisés, le feldspath potassique, d'une part, et un mélange de feldspath potassique et de biotite, correspondant à du granite, d'autre part, ces deux minéraux étant disponibles aussi bien à l'intérieur qu'à l'extérieur des grottes. Le liant, indispensable pour accrocher le pigment à la surface, était l'eau de la grotte elle-même, fortement chargée en calcium, l'urine aussi et probablement une huile d'origine animale.

Pour peindre, ces créateurs disposaient d'instruments variés. Pour tracer certains traits, ils utilisaient simplement leurs doigts. Ils avaient aussi recours à des pinceaux en poil de blaireau, en bambou écrasé et en plume qui dessinaient les traits les plus réguliers. Ils se servaient également de souffleurs, des tubes qui dispersaient la couleur sur la pierre. Des lissoirs en pierre permettaient ensuite de polir ou de régulariser le trait.

Quand l'œuvre était presque terminée, ils accentuaient les contours en gravant quelques détails particuliers, comme les yeux, les cornes, le mufle et les sabots. Parfois, les peintures étaient lavées et frottées par endroits pour adoucir les contours et obtenir des effets de couleur plus tendres.

Pour sculpter des bas- ou des hauts-reliefs, ils taillaient dans le plan ou dans un bloc rocheux. Les bas-reliefs étaient obtenus par des évidements aboutissant à faire légèrement ressortir les figures de leur support, comme le cheval gravé de la grotte de Commarque, en Dordogne. Enfin, ils modelaient aussi l'argile pour créer, par exemple, les bisons d'argile du Tuc-d'Audoubert, en Ariège.

Restent les œuvres elles-mêmes. Un premier constat s'impose. L'art des cavernes est surtout un vaste bestiaire, la grande majorité des peintures, des gravures et des reliefs représentant en effet du gros gibier. L'animal le plus fréquemment figuré est le cheval. Il est présent sur près d'un tiers des dessins et ne manque dans presque aucune composition. Les chevaux de ce temps étaient plus petits que ceux d'aujourd'hui ; ils avaient un ventre rebondi d'une couleur plus claire que le reste du corps, des jambes courtes mais sveltes et une crinière dressée. Le sexe n'est jamais représenté, même si certains dessins montrent des positions préliminaires à la copulation.

Les bisons et les aurochs abondent. Les premiers se distinguent du bison moderne par des cornes tournées vers le haut, légèrement incurvées en S, et par un profil de tête uni à la bosse en une courbe presque continue. Les aurochs sont des animaux plus sveltes, aux grandes cornes courbées vers l'avant et vers l'extérieur.

Les autres animaux apparaissent moins, même si cerfs, éléphants et chèvres sont abondamment représentés. Dans la grotte Cosquer, découverte au mois de septembre 1991, au large du cap Morgiou, près de Marseille, on voit aussi des phoques, plusieurs méduses et trois grands pingouins *Alca impennis*, une espèce apparentée au petit pingouin qui a aujourd'hui disparu et qu'on ne trouve nulle part ailleurs. Dans la grotte de la Combe d'Arc, découverte dans la vallée de l'Ardèche le 18 décembre 1994 par Jean-Marie Chauvet, on trouve aussi la seule panthère tachetée représentée dans l'art préhistorique et des ours, alors que ces animaux figurent très rarement dans les autres cavernes. En outre, la présence d'un crâne d'ours sur une pierre qui pourrait évoquer un autel relance le débat sur le culte des ours. On y trouve aussi le seul hibou connu de l'art pariétal.

Les représentations diffèrent donc d'une région à l'autre. Là, comme à Rouffignac, dominent mammouths et rhinocéros laineux. Ailleurs, comme à Niaux ou à Lascaux, chevaux, aurochs et bisons l'emportent.

L'art des cavernes est bien avant tout un art animalier, l'expression d'une union esthétique de chasseurs avec les animaux sauvages qui sont les compagnons désirés et redoutés de leur destinée et qui hantent les rêves de peuples quotidiennement soumis à la faim.

Bien moins fréquentes que les figures animales, les représentations humaines suscitent beaucoup d'interrogations. On trouve en effet des silhouettes féminines réalistes ou stylisées, des organes génitaux, des visages ou des portraits en pied, des personnages masqués ou blessés, des êtres fantomatiques, des mains aux doigts mutilés.

On voit aussi, énigmatiques, des êtres cornus, mi-hommes mi-animaux comme le sorcier de la grotte des Trois-Frères, peint à 4 mètres de haut, sur la voûte, dominant un fouillis d'animaux et qui est apparu à l'abbé Breuil comme « l'Esprit régissant la multiplication du gibier et les expéditions de chasse ». À ces êtres s'ajoutent quelques contours imprécis qui semblent relever de la caricature humoristique.

Encore plus énigmatiques, de multiples signes géométriques accompagnent çà et là les animaux des peintures rupestres. Selon Leroi-Gourhan, ils seraient les manifestations les plus impressionnantes de l'art paléolithique sur le plan intellectuel. Ces signes montrent des motifs extrêmement divers, des plus simples (points, lignes) aux plus complexes : bâtonnets ; triangles (généralement divisés par une ligne verticale) ; rectangles (avec une ou plusieurs lignes verticales à l'intérieur, en forme de peigne ou complètement vides) ; figures rayées aux traits obliques entrecroisés ; en forme de toit (inspirés de la structure des huttes) ; ovales, en forme de barque (avec un ou deux ovales l'un dans l'autre, ou avec un ovale coupé d'une ligne longitudinale), claviformes ; parfois avec des appendices, en forme d'oiseau, de coupe...

À la rencontre du surnaturel

Si, aujourd'hui, la lumière infrarouge permet de reconstituer le processus de création, de décomposer les gestes, de banaliser en quelque sorte le métier du peintre, il faut se rappeler que les grottes n'étaient pas des galeries d'art ouvertes à la curiosité des chalands mais de véritables sanctuaires, des sortes de cathédrales qui devaient inspirer aux « fidèles » s'enfonçant dans le noir à la faible lueur des torches des émotions particulièrement fortes, des émotions leur faisant rencontrer un « surnaturel » dont nous cherchons désespérément les voies.

À la fin du XIXᵉ siècle, lorsqu'on découvrit les premières grottes, les motifs qui recouvraient les parois semblaient si proches des goûts des contemporains qu'on formula l'idée que les hommes avaient simplement voulu s'entourer de beauté, sans autre but que la satisfaction artistique. On imaginait que, bénéficiant de conditions de vie plus favorables, ils avaient pu dégager assez de temps libre pour décorer les cavernes qu'ils habitaient et les objets qu'ils utilisaient. L'art pour l'art, en somme.

On n'accordait alors aucune importance au fait que les représentations se situaient quasiment toutes au plus profond des grottes et presque jamais dans les campements.

Dans un deuxième temps, à mesure que les explorateurs européens découvraient d'autres cultures, celle des aborigènes d'Australie en particulier, on prit conscience que ces peintures avaient une autre fonction que celle de « faire beau ». On développa l'idée que les chasseurs représentaient les animaux convoités et, par des pratiques magiques d'envoûtement sur leurs images, assuraient le succès de leur chasse.

L'abbé Breuil fut l'un des premiers à noter la présence de signes, ressemblant à des flèches, qui transperçaient les flancs des bisons et des chevaux de Lascaux ou de Niaux. Parfois même, l'animal représenté est presque entièrement détruit par des coups de sagaie ou des jets de pierres. Ainsi à Montespan, un ours sculpté et un cheval peint ont subi les assauts des habitants de la grotte, comme s'ils s'étaient livrés à une véritable cérémonie propitiatoire avant de partir à la chasse.

Mais qui dit pratiques magiques, dit sorcier. On a ainsi cru en repérer quelques figures, comme sur le bâton perforé de Teyjat, où ils apparaissent coiffés d'une tête de chamois leur descendant sur les épaules. Mais une telle représentation suggère au moins autant la ruse d'un chasseur caché sous une peau d'animal pour s'approcher du reste du troupeau que l'habit rituel du chaman ou du sorcier.

Séduisant, ce lien entre l'art et la magie posait toutefois de nombreux problèmes. Tout d'abord, les représentations incontestablement liées à une activité de chasse, comme pourrait l'être une scène figurant des hommes armés de sagaies poursuivant des animaux, sont extrêmement rares.

Surtout, le décalage, d'abord souligné par André Leroi-Gourhan puis quantifié par de nombreux chercheurs, entre la fréquence des espèces animales les plus chassées et celle des animaux les plus souvent dessinés est manifeste. En effet, bien que le cerf et le renne constituent l'essentiel de l'alimentation carnée dans l'espace franco-cantabrique, le bison et le cheval dominent dans les représentations artistiques. Si les peintures avaient été essentiellement inspirées par la magie et destinées à s'assurer une bonne chasse, il est surprenant que le gibier le plus rentable ne soit pas omniprésent dans l'art pariétal. Par ailleurs, l'hypothèse de la magie ne permet pas d'expliquer pourquoi cet art est si limité géographiquement, alors que les chasseurs du Paléolithique ont chassé le gros gibier dans de nombreuses régions d'Europe où les traces d'art sont fort rares.

Au début des années 1960, s'appuyant sur des études de terrain minutieuses et le comptage systématique des signes et des espèces représentés dans chaque grotte, André Leroi-Gourhan proposa une explication radicalement différente, en montrant qu'il existait une structure cohérente dans l'ornementation. À ses yeux, cette structure symbolique était de nature sexuelle. Se fondant sur les premières gravures représentant des sexes féminins et sur les « Vénus » des époques antérieures, il démontra que la plupart des signes, des plus simplifiés, comme le triangle fendu ou le trait garni de barbelures, aux plus complexes, comme les lignes de barbelés, étaient dérivés des premières représentations d'organes génitaux.

En outre, observait-il, ces signes ne se rencontrent pas n'importe où dans une grotte et ne sont pas associés à n'importe quel animal. Reconstituant l'organisation spatiale de la caverne de Lascaux et observant la fréquence et l'emplacement de certains animaux, il constata que si les cerfs se trouvent, dans 75 % des cas, à l'entrée ou au fond des sanctuaires, si le bison, le cheval, le mammouth et le bœuf occupent, à 90 %, le cœur des grands panneaux, les félins, l'ours et l'homme, c'est-à-dire les carnivores, se situent dans 75 % des cas aux tréfonds du site.

Ainsi, dans la théorie élaborée par le célèbre préhistorien, un triangle sur un bison, par exemple à Lascaux, ne signifie pas que l'animal a été blessé par une flèche mais que l'espèce bison est assimilée au principe féminin, comme l'aurochs et le mammouth, alors que le cheval est un symbole mâle. Et il en veut pour preuve l'extraordinaire séquence représentée au plafond du Pech-Merle où, en cinq gravures successives, l'artiste a transformé la silhouette d'un grand ruminant en un profil de femme.

Ainsi, nos lointains ancêtres auraient fondé leur cosmogonie sur l'équilibre de deux grands principes complémentaires, le principe mâle et le principe femelle, le yin et le yang en quelque sorte. Le respect de cet équilibre fondamental aurait entretenu la fécondité du groupe et l'aurait en même temps rassuré sur la bonne marche du monde.

Des découvertes récentes ont pourtant commencé à nuancer la parole du maître de la préhistoire moderne. Dans de nombreux petits sanctuaires de l'Ardèche, on ne trouve plus de couple bison-cheval mais une profusion inexplicable de mammouths. De même, au fond de la grotte de Niaux, l'animal vedette est... une petite belette, seule au milieu d'une large paroi. En fait, la vision d'ensemble proposée par André Leroi-Gourhan est trop systématique pour s'appliquer, sans variations, sur une période de 25 000 ans ! En outre, si les représentations des bisons étaient uniquement symboliques, comment expliquer le fait que ces animaux peuvent être aujourd'hui identifiés par des éthologues avec une précision extrême sur leur sexe, leur âge ou leur état (blessé, mort, gravide...) ? Si chaque animal est ainsi individualisé, comment peut-il être en même temps un stéréotype interchangeable ?

D'autre part, nous savons aujourd'hui que l'art a été particulièrement florissant au moment même où les conditions climatiques se détérioraient, au plus fort de la fin de l'ère glaciaire et immédiatement après. Les sites de cette époque témoignent de ce que la chasse au renne et au cerf est alors devenue intensive. Au fur et à mesure que les glaciers recouvraient l'Europe septentrionale et que de vastes espaces devenaient inhospitaliers, les plantes, les animaux mais aussi les hommes ont pu se réfugier dans le sud-ouest de l'Europe.

Cet accroissement de la population semble être la cause principale des changements observés dans le mode de subsistance entre 20 000 et 10 000 avant notre ère. Auparavant, on chassait sans doute le renne et le cerf en attaquant de petits groupes ou en poursuivant des animaux isolés. À partir de ce moment, d'immenses battues sont organisées sur le passage des troupeaux. Pour nourrir une population plus nombreuse, les chasseurs ont dû chercher à améliorer le rendement de la chasse, en préférant les espèces fournissant le plus de viande, comme les bisons et les chevaux. Ainsi a-t-on avancé l'idée que les représentations, plus réalistes que symboliques, seraient une sorte d'« aide-mémoire » destiné à faciliter la tâche du chasseur en lui fournissant toutes les informations utiles. Si les animaux sont souvent figurés de profil, c'est que cette perspective permet au chasseur d'estimer la quantité de viande de la bête. Si la dimension de ces quartiers de chair est parfois exagérée, ce serait pour mettre en valeur cette partie de l'anatomie.

Cette observation vaut aussi pour le profil des ramures, dont la dimension permettrait de définir, comme à Lascaux, la taille des cerfs au cours des différentes saisons. Et si l'on peut voir des représentations de bouquetins lâchant d'énormes crottes, finement sculptées à l'extrémité des propulseurs provenant des Pyrénées, c'est que les excréments sont, pour les chasseurs, une véritable mine d'informations.

Tous ces indices auraient ainsi facilité la reconnaissance des traces, pistes et autres signes gardés en mémoire.

Une autre explication, due à David Lewis Williams, un chercheur sud-africain qui a beaucoup étudié les Bochimans du Kalahari, met en avant le chamanisme. Il part du principe que ces hommes ayant le même système nerveux que le nôtre pouvaient comme nous, par diverses méthodes (absorption de drogues, jeûne, musique...), parvenir à un état de transe pour avoir des visions et pénétrer dans un monde parallèle. Là, ils rencontraient des esprits qui allaient les aider. Par exemple, lorsque le gibier se faisait rare, le chaman se serait lancé à la recherche de l'esprit tutélaire des animaux pour le persuader de cesser de les retenir.

En fait, l'« évangile » de ces chasseurs est loin de pouvoir être lu. Nous pouvons seulement affirmer, et ce n'est pas si mal, que ces grottes étaient bien des sanctuaires, que l'art était bien une manière de s'adapter aux exigences de plus en plus complexes d'une vie collective, que ces communautés avaient conçu des formes de culte, qu'il y avait des maîtres parmi ces premiers peintres et que, surtout, si ces œuvres restent éloignées de notre compréhension, elles parlent toujours à notre sensibilité.

Les premiers paysans

V ers 8000 avant notre ère disparaissent de l'actuel territoire de la France les grands troupeaux sur l'exploitation desquels étaient fondées la nourriture et la civilisation des chasseurs. Tout est alors en place pour que s'effectue une mutation fondamentale. Deux mille ans plus tard apparaissent dans les grottes du Midi les premières poteries, telles celles retrouvées à Oullins, dans les gorges de l'Ardèche. Ce sont les premiers témoignages de l'agriculture en France. Autrefois nomade, l'homme s'enracine alors dans un espace restreint. Désormais son horizon se fige.

Le temps du redoux

Le temps, le temps qu'il fait, est évidemment pour beaucoup dans le bouleversement des modes de vie des chasseurs de la fin du Paléolithique. L'avènement d'un climat tempéré, tout à fait comparable à notre climat actuel, a eu, en effet, des répercussions considérables sur l'environnement écologique des hommes. Partout ruissellent les eaux libérées par la fonte des glaciers tandis que les mers recouvrent désormais les zones côtières.

Ainsi, vers 10 000 avant J.-C., la ligne de rivage de la Méditerranée était située à 60 mètres au-dessous de son niveau actuel au large du Petit Rhône. Quatre mille ans plus tard, elle n'est plus qu'à − 20 mètres. Sur la côte picarde on était également à − 60 mètres vers 9700 avant J.-C., et vers 5000 avant J.-C. le niveau de la « Manche » avait remonté et se trouvait à − 25 mètres au Havre.

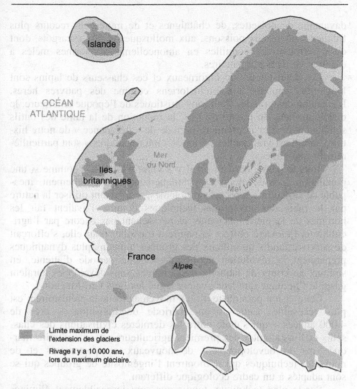

Carte de l'Europe pendant la dernière glaciation, il y a 10 000 ans.

Partout aussi, la steppe recule au profit d'une forêt dense de chênes et de hêtres dont la croissance est favorisée par le renforcement de l'humidité.

De telles perturbations ont affecté la faune. Tandis que le renne ou le bœuf musqué migrent en Europe du Nord, le mammouth et le rhinocéros laineux s'éteignent bientôt au profit des espèces favorisées par le climat tempéré et le développement des forêts : l'aurochs, le cerf, le sanglier et le lapin.

Insensiblement, au fil du temps, les hommes ont dû s'adapter à cet environnement différent. Les nourritures changent : beaucoup moins de gros gibiers, davantage de petits animaux faciles à piéger, davantage de noisettes, de châtaignes et de mûres, un recours plus fréquent encore aux poissons, aux mollusques et aux escargots, dont on a retrouvé les coquilles en amoncellements énormes mêlés à d'autres vestiges alimentaires.

Ces dégustateurs de bigorneaux et ces chasseurs de lapins sont longtemps apparus aux préhistoriens comme des pauvres hères. L'abandon des grandes traditions artistiques de l'époque antérieure, le développement du travail de l'os, la réduction de la taille des outils semblaient révéler la première période de « décadence » de notre histoire, tant il est vrai que les périodes « intermédiaires » sont particulièrement mal-aimées.

Tout se passe, écrivait-on il y a vingt-cinq ans, « comme si une population sous-développée, techniquement et culturellement, incapable de résoudre ses propres problèmes, ne pouvant utiliser la nature par le biais des inventions techniques comme l'avaient fait les hommes de la pierre ancienne, et ne sachant pas encore par l'agriculture et l'élevage obliger la nature à travailler pour elle, s'efforçait de survivre tandis qu'ailleurs des groupes humains plus dynamiques préparaient la révolution néolithique ». Une période d'attente, en somme, au cours de laquelle des hommes sous-développés auraient gaspillé l'héritage que leur avaient légué les fiers Cro-Magnon !

Cette vision pessimiste d'un « moyen âge » de la préhistoire n'est plus recevable. Cette longue période de transition – près de 4 000 années – qui s'étale entre les dernières civilisations des chasseurs et l'installation des premiers agriculteurs est au contraire marquée par le développement de nouveaux comportements et de nouvelles techniques qui démontrent l'ingéniosité de groupes qui se sont adaptés à un cadre écologique différent.

Sur le plan technique, tandis que sont insensiblement éliminés les harpons et les pointes en os, de tout petits outils en silex, les microlithes, font leur apparition. Longs de quelques centimètres et pesant parfois moins d'un gramme, de forme souvent géométrique, pointes, triangles, segments, trapèzes en viennent à former l'essentiel de l'outillage.

Si cette miniaturisation extrême marque bien le terme d'une évolution technique amorcée dès le début de l'industrie de la pierre et visant à réduire le poids et la dimension de l'outillage, elle montre l'habileté extrême de ces hommes qui ont taillé et retouché certaines pièces comme jamais on ne l'avait fait avant eux.

En fait, ces microlithes n'étaient pas des outils mais des éléments d'outils qui devaient être pour la plupart emmanchés et faire partie d'instruments en bois ou en os, la fixation des armatures étant assurée par des matières végétales servant de colle. Dans les zones tempérées et froides, les résines de bouleau et de conifères faisaient parfaitement l'affaire. Mais on utilisait aussi une glu obtenue par la cuisson de l'écorce interne du houx ou des tiges de gui.

Le règne des archers

Les microlithes nous mettent surtout sur la piste de l'arc, dont c'est la grande époque, un préhistorien affirmant même que l'invention de l'arc et de la flèche a eu autant d'importance pour l'homme de cette époque que celle de l'arme nucléaire pour l'homme moderne.

Sans céder à l'exagération, il faut toutefois admettre que l'arc a bien constitué un progrès technique considérable permettant d'accroître l'efficacité de la chasse, bien plus que ne l'avait fait le propulseur pour les chasseurs de rennes.

Jusque-là, en effet, on cherchait surtout à augmenter la masse du projectile, dans les limites compatibles avec la force du bras, et à approcher le plus près possible de la bête. Mais comme le mouvement de lancer ne pouvait passer inaperçu, la proie commençait à s'enfuir avant d'avoir été touchée. L'impact en perdait donc en précision et en puissance. D'où l'utilité de rabatteurs amenant de face l'animal, dont la charge pouvait cependant être mortelle pour le chasseur.

Avec l'arc, le problème est tout autre puisque désormais la vitesse du projectile est plus importante que sa masse. Les expériences ont montré que nos ancêtres avaient empiriquement calculé que l'optimum de l'efficacité était atteint par des flèches de 90 centimètres à 1 mètre de long, de 1 centimètre de diamètre, dont le fût pesait de 20 à 30 grammes et qui étaient armées d'une pointe de 0,5 à 1 gramme. À 50 mètres, ces flèches pénétraient plus que les plombs de chasse de calibre 14 et traversaient le gibier de part en part. Un grizzly de 450 kilos attaqué de face à 54 mètres est pénétré jusqu'à la face postérieure du corps, avec section de la veine cave.

Ainsi, la vitesse permet de tirer de plus loin, donc de sélectionner les bêtes et de réduire les risques de la chasse pour les archers. Désormais deux ou trois hommes peuvent remplacer la communauté. Pour la première fois sans doute dans l'histoire, la cellule sociale fondamentale devient un couple et ses enfants. Cette profonde transformation sociale, attestée par les nouvelles dimensions des sites, qui ne rassemblent plus que de 10 à 20 personnes, et par une forte augmentation de la population sur l'ensemble du territoire, s'accompagne d'une modification des rapports avec un animal moins redouté et moins présent.

Ainsi, en inventant l'arc, l'homme inaugurait une nouvelle civilisation qui rendait périmés vingt millénaires de tradition.

C'est à peu près à la même époque qu'il semble aussi bénéficier des services de celui qui est son plus vieil ami, le chien. Les plus anciens ossements attribuables à cet animal sont ceux du gisement du Pont d'Ambon, en Dordogne, datés d'environ 9500 avant notre ère, mais les étapes de sa domestication nous demeurent encore mystérieuses. Certainement attiré par la présence de nourriture dans les campements, le chien a dû rôder de plus en plus fréquemment autour de ces sites, s'habituant du même coup à la présence humaine. Il est également probable que les hommes apprécièrent cet animal qui les débarrassaient des déchets alimentaires, tandis que les enfants trouvaient dans les jeunes chiots des compagnons de jeu idéaux. Cette relation de complémentarité a dû également se manifester dans la chasse, les chiens et les hommes s'aidant mutuellement dans la traque des proies.

Probablement mieux nourris par une chasse plus efficace, nos archers ont aussi montré du goût pour les nourritures accessoires que sont les escargots, les mollusques ou les grenouilles. Les sites connus montrent une telle accumulation de coquilles qu'on avait autrefois dépeint ces hommes comme des êtres faméliques réduits à fonder leur alimentation sur la chair des escargots. En fait, on estime aujourd'hui que ramasser des escargots ou attraper des grenouilles est plutôt le signe d'une vie faste qui laisse assez de loisirs.

On a en effet calculé que ces mangeurs de grenouilles bénéficiaient en moyenne de 2 500 calories par jour et par personne y compris les enfants, et que les rations minimales de protéines nécessaires à un homme adulte étaient toujours largement dépassées.

C'est la raison pour laquelle la population de la France triple au cours de cette période pour atteindre environ 50 000 habitants, répartis à peu près également sur tout le territoire. Pour la première fois de notre histoire, tout le terrain est occupé simultanément, à l'échelle des cantons et même des communes actuelles. Cette augmentation considérable de la population a ainsi contribué à la multiplication d'esprits inventifs, d'autant plus que la vie facile de nos archers laissait à l'imagination tout le temps de se développer.

Reste toutefois à se poser la question de savoir pour quelles raisons l'art animalier a totalement disparu. Est-ce parce que l'homme a cessé de fréquenter les grottes à la suite du réchauffement climatique ?

Est-ce parce que, la chasse devenant plus facile, il n'aurait plus eu besoin de recourir à la magie ou à la mémoire pour assurer son succès ? Toujours est-il que seul subsiste alors un art abstrait dont le caractère schématique suscite de nombreuses interrogations. Ainsi, si la disposition des traits et des points peints sur les galets plats retrouvés en abondance ne paraît pas livrée au seul hasard, quelle signification doit-on lui accorder ? Des combinaisons ont pu être repérées, qui semblent suggérer une véritable syntaxe. Selon certains préhistoriens, il pourrait s'agir d'un système de computation, peut-être en relation avec les lunaisons.

La naissance de l'agriculture

La grande rupture que représente la diffusion de l'agriculture et de l'élevage ne s'est pas faite sans de longs préliminaires. Si le terme de « révolution » a pu être employé pour désigner cette grande mutation, cela ne signifie nullement qu'elle a été brutale.

Ces hommes qui connaissaient les moindres ressources des forêts, les herbes et les racines, les fruits et les graines, en savaient largement assez pour envisager un jour de nouvelles relations avec la nature. Bien avant de cultiver les plantes, on devait savoir comment les domestiquer, tout en continuant à tirer de la chasse et de la cueillette l'essentiel de la nourriture. D'ailleurs, les plus anciens témoignages d'agriculture ont été découverts dans des régions où poussaient déjà à l'état sauvage les ancêtres de nos céréales actuelles.

Ainsi, dans les fouilles récentes entreprises dans l'Hérault, le Gard, le Var (la grotte de Fontbrégoua) et l'Aude, on trouve, datés du VIIe millénaire avant notre ère, de nombreux vestiges végétaux carbonisés qui non seulement entraient dans l'alimentation mais encore étaient stockés dans les habitations. Ce sont des noisettes, des pépins de raisin et, surtout, des lentilles et des pois chiches.

L'étude des dernières communautés de chasseurs-collecteurs nous aide à mieux cerner le mode de vie des hommes de la préhistoire. Ainsi, dans les vallées du Sacramento et du San Joaquin, en Californie, les Indiens chasseurs sont capables, en stockant, après les avoir séchés, des glands de plusieurs espèces de chênes, d'assurer la nourriture de 40 personnes sur 100 kilomètres carrés, soit une densité supérieure à celle des Indiens agriculteurs de l'est des États-Unis. Une observation qui montre à quel point la naissance de l'agriculture ne peut plus être considérée comme une rupture « révolutionnaire », brusque et sans transition, dans l'histoire de l'humanité.

Nos premiers « Français » avaient-ils donc commencé à produire leur nourriture avant que la culture du blé et de l'orge soit importée d'Orient ? Des indices, tels les larges couteaux en silex retrouvés à Rouffignac, en Dordogne, qui portent sur la lame un lustré habituellement présent sur les faucilles, peuvent peut-être le laisser supposer.

La question de l'existence, dès cette époque, de l'élevage, se pose également. Les preuves semblent là plus convaincantes, notamment à Châteauneuf-lès-Martigues, où, dès le VIᵉ millénaire, la présence du mouton, probablement domestique, est attestée. Dès lors, cet animal va bientôt prospérer à un tel point qu'il transformera le paysage de manière irréversible.

Toujours à cette même époque, la Méditerranée n'est plus une barrière, l'homme sachant fabriquer des embarcations sommaires taillées dans des troncs d'arbres et naviguer le long des côtes. Jusqu'alors interdite, la mer permet désormais de nombreux échanges tant culturels que techniques entre les différents peuples.

À ce moment s'amorce réellement la « néolithisation » de la France, c'est-à-dire un changement au moins aussi important pour notre histoire que celui qui vit au XIXᵉ siècle la naissance et le développement de l'industrie.

Le développement de l'agriculture entraîna en effet un bouleversement essentiel à la fois du mode de vie et des mentalités, donnant en particulier naissance à une notion nouvelle, promise à un bel avenir, le rendement. Comme l'explique G. Camps, « l'homme apprit qu'en défrichant, qu'en semant et qu'en sarclant, son effort du jour serait récompensé dans une saison future par un apport alimentaire très largement supérieur à celui qu'il avait confié au sol ». Du même coup, il dut calculer, spéculer et analyser les causes des calamités afin d'y porter remède.

Avec le passage d'une économie de prédation telle que la connaissaient les chasseurs-cueilleurs à une économie de production, l'homme dut s'habituer à toute une série d'opérations jusqu'alors étrangères à son univers mental. Afin de prévoir et d'assurer la récolte suivante, il dut aussi apprendre à soustraire et à garder suffisamment de grains pour les prochaines semences, à additionner et à multiplier pour prévoir le rendement et enfin à diviser pour distribuer à chacun sa part. Pour la première fois, il sut ce qu'était gagner son pain à la sueur de son front.

On ne sait aujourd'hui qui est à l'origine de l'introduction de l'agriculture en France. S'est-elle développée à la suite d'une migration de population la pratiquant déjà ? Ou bien est-elle simplement liée à l'évolution des pratiques de la population indigène ?

Seul est assuré le fait que les premiers paysans ont fait leur apparition dès 10 000 avant notre ère en Turquie, en Palestine, en Irak et en Iran.

Autre certitude, l'introduction de l'agriculture en France s'est faite suivant deux axes qui joueront tout au long de notre histoire un rôle essentiel : au sud par la Méditerranée, et à l'est par le Danube, depuis une voie qui, partie du nord des Balkans, gagne l'Europe centrale avant d'atteindre le Bassin parisien. Deux « portes naturelles » par lesquelles, tout au long de notre histoire, pénétreront les influences étrangères.

Gens du Nord, gens du Midi

C'est dans la France du Midi que, pour la première fois, l'homme a poli la pierre, édifié des villages, pratiqué l'agriculture et fabriqué des poteries décorées avec des motifs imprimés exécutés à l'aide du rebord d'un coquillage, le cardium. D'où l'adjectif « cardial » qui a servi à désigner l'ensemble culturel qui a recouvert la Méditerranée occidentale.

On a retrouvé en effet des poteries étonnamment voisines en Toscane, en Ligurie, en Corse et dans le bas Languedoc. De même, certains vases du midi de la France ont été fidèlement copiés jusqu'en Espagne, dans la région de Valence.

Réalisée par impressions, sur la pâte fraîche, de cardium, de coups d'ongle ou de dents de peigne, la décoration de ces poteries présente un aspect assez varié et se limite le plus souvent à la partie supérieure : points, lignes horizontales, verticales, en zigzag ou en croix, formant des sillons ou des bourrelets.

Cette civilisation du Cardial se caractérise aussi par plusieurs autres innovations, notamment la fabrication de haches de pierre polie et le polissage de bracelets.

C'est bien un autre mode de vie qui se diffuse lentement à partir de 5000 avant notre ère dans les basses Alpes, en Ardèche, dans les Cévennes occidentales, dans la Montagne Noire. L'extension à l'intérieur des terres oscille entre 50 et 100 kilomètres, ce qui est peu.

Ces gens, probablement venus par la Méditerranée, que les archers ont vus s'établir et auxquels ils ont fait volontiers de la place, n'avaient d'ailleurs rien de « révolutionnaires ». S'ils pratiquent massivement l'élevage du mouton, développent celui du bœuf et du porc et cultivent les terrains les plus favorables, la chasse continue à jouer un rôle capital, ainsi que la pêche que l'on pratique même en haute mer, comme en témoignent les restes d'un espadon retrouvés dans un village aujourd'hui englouti sous les eaux de l'étang de Leucate (Aude).

Et si les premiers villages font leur apparition, la majorité des sites d'habitat restent des grottes ou des abris-sous-roche.

Le premier village connu en France est celui de Courthézon, dans le Vaucluse, daté de 4650 avant notre ère. Les sols de deux cabanes, empierrés de gros galets de quartzite, y ont été dégagés ; l'une d'elles, de forme ovale, mesure 4,80 m sur 4,40 m. La superstructure devait être en matériaux légers.

Meules et lames attestent avec certitude la culture de céréales.

Ainsi, cette « néolithisation » des provinces méridionales nous offre le tableau de très petits groupes humains qui, par contacts maritimes épisodiques avec les régions méditerranéennes plus lointaines, ont eu connaissance de techniques nouvelles dont ils ont assimilé un certain nombre avec succès, mais sans véritable rupture avec le passé. L'exemple de l'abri Jean Cros, dans les Corbières occidentales, est une bonne illustration de cette combinaison d'activités anciennes et modernes.

Situé sur un plateau recouvert de bois et d'étendues herbeuses, cet abri servait deux fois l'an, au printemps et à l'automne, de gîte-étape pour les bergers.

À la sortie de l'hiver, la communauté confiait à un petit nombre d'hommes la tâche de conduire le troupeau vers les hautes terres riches en herbe. Une fois le camp de base quitté et les premiers contreforts des Corbières atteints, ces hommes, tout en veillant sur les moutons, retrouvaient leurs habitudes de cueilleurs et de chasseurs, collectant les végétaux, traquant le sanglier et, plus rarement, le cerf.

Avec les premiers mauvais jours, les bergers, qui avaient poussé les bêtes plus haut pour atteindre l'estive, revenaient au camp de base, effectuant le chemin en sens inverse.

Ainsi, dans ces premières communautés de paysans, élevage et cueillette tenaient encore une large place même si certains individus pouvaient se voir assigner des tâches plus précises.

Si les gens du Midi ont procédé lentement, ceux du Nord ont été plus rapides. Venus d'Europe centrale, de la moyenne vallée du Danube, ils se sont introduits en France par les grands axes de circulation et surtout par les rivières, laissant les archers continuer leur vie de chasse dans les grandes forêts vierges de chênes et de tilleuls.

En effet, ces « colons » qui se répandent de proche en proche n'occupent pas tout le territoire mais recherchent de façon sélective les terroirs qui conviennent le mieux à la culture des céréales, en particulier les zones à sol léger et très fertile que sont les régions couvertes de lœss, ce dépôt qui s'était formé en abondance en Europe centrale au cours de la dernière glaciation.

C'est sur ces terres qu'ils cultivent le blé et l'orge, les pois et les lentilles. À la différence des gens du Midi, la viande qu'ils consomment est fournie à plus de 80 % par l'élevage, la part de la chasse étant très faible.

Et leurs poteries sont fréquemment décorées d'incisions en spirale, en méandre ou en volute gravées sur l'argile fraîche. D'où le nom de « civilisation rubanée » donnée à cette société du nord de la France.

Surtout, contrairement à ce qui se passe dans le Midi, l'installation de villages accompagne automatiquement l'annexion des meilleures terres. Vers 4500 avant notre ère, on voit les « colons » construire leurs longues maisons. C'est dans la vallée de l'Aisne, à Cuiry-lès-Chaudardes, qu'a été mis au jour le premier village « danubien ». Les fouilles ont permis de dégager de nombreuses maisons, longues de 10 à 40 mètres, larges de 6 à 8 mètres, qui sont parmi les plus grandes de la préhistoire européenne.

La reconstitution d'une de ces maisons, qui ressemblent aux fermes traditionnelles telles qu'on devait encore en bâtir jusqu'à la fin du XIXe siècle, permet de se faire une idée précise de leur habitat.

Sa construction, qui avait nécessité l'abattage de six cents arbres, s'était effectuée en tenant probablement compte de l'orientation des vents, la porte se trouvant du côté opposé aux vents les plus violents. Le toit à double pente, constitué de chaume ou de roseaux cousus par bottes sur plusieurs épaisseurs, reposait sur une série de poteaux internes tandis que les murs étaient soutenus par des poteaux externes.

Ces demeures des premiers paysans français abritaient nécessairement plusieurs familles, ce qui implique une population oscillant entre 50 et 170 habitants par village. Lorsque la communauté, en raison de l'accroissement démographique, dépassait un certain seuil, plusieurs familles s'en détachaient pour fonder un nouveau village sur des terres vierges.

Ils pratiquaient une agriculture temporaire sur brûlis, qui consistait très certainement à brûler les bois avant d'ensemencer la terre, jusqu'à épuisement du sol, ce qui entraînait le départ de la communauté. Toutefois le site ancien pouvait, une fois sa régénérescence assurée par le rétablissement de la forêt, être réexploité par un nouveau groupe qui, à son tour, brûlait, ensemençait, etc.

De nombreuses hypothèses ont été émises au sujet de la répartition des tâches et du rôle social joué par chacun au sein de la communauté danubienne. Les femmes semblent avoir tenu une place importante parmi ces gens du Nord. En témoignent les riches sépultures auxquelles certaines ont droit, comme celle de cette jeune femme, enterrée à Vert-la-Gravelle, dans la Marne, et parée de perles et de coquillages.

Ainsi, l'implantation de l'agriculture sur notre territoire distingue déjà deux France, la France cardiale du Midi et la France rubanée du Nord, qui se sont développées indépendamment l'une de l'autre. Reste à se poser la question de savoir ce que ces gens ont « gagné » en devenant paysans, en se gardant d'interpréter l'histoire de l'humanité comme une marche irréversible vers le « progrès ». Pourquoi les chasseurs-cueilleurs n'ont-ils guère éprouvé le besoin de se convertir à ce nouveau mode de vie ? C'est qu'en fait, à court terme – mais l'homme vit-il jamais autrement qu'à court terme ? –, l'agriculture imposait un surcroît de travail que rien ne semblait justifier. On a ainsi calculé qu'ils devaient consacrer entre trois et cinq heures par jour à la quête de leur nourriture, ce qui fait dire à un anthropologue américain qu'il s'agit d'un emploi du temps de banquiers !

Avec l'agriculture, l'homme était conduit à travailler davantage. Piégé par le développement technique, il se condamnait aux travaux forcés à perpétuité. Ainsi s'enclenchait il y a 7 000 ans en France un processus continu d'enracinement dans un espace limité par un horizon qui allait se figer. Au vaste territoire parcouru par les chasseurs succédait le terroir restreint des communautés villageoises.

CHAPITRE **6**

Les premiers architectes

*Vers 4 000 ans avant notre ère, à l'ouest, dans ce cul-de-sac du conti-
nent européen qu'est la Bretagne, à peine fréquenté par quelques
pionniers danubiens et quelques aventuriers méditerranéens, une autre
facette de la riche mosaïque française se développe pendant près de vingt
siècles. Parmi les témoignages que nous ont laissés les premiers « Bretons », les plus spectaculaires sont les impressionnants monuments mégalithiques, édifiés près de 2 000 années avant les premières pyramides
d'Égypte, comme à Gavr'inis, dans le Morbihan, un ensemble hors du
commun où tout semble démesuré et dont les signes gravés nous restent
toujours indéchiffrables.*

L'art des mégalithes

Les ancêtres des Bretons sont bien les premiers grands architectes
du monde connus. Vers 4000 avant notre ère, comme sortis du néant,
se dressent alors sur la façade atlantique de l'Europe dolmens, menhirs
et cromlechs.

« Tables de pierre », les dolmens sont de grandes tombes collectives comportant une chambre funéraire faite de grosses pierres à
laquelle on accède par une allée ou un couloir. Ces ensembles monu-
mentaux étaient recouverts de pierres ou de terre, de sorte qu'à
l'époque de leur utilisation ils devaient se présenter comme de grosses
buttes dans lesquelles on pénétrait par un trou sombre.

« Pierres longues », les menhirs sont des blocs rocheux uniques fichés verticalement dans la terre. Plusieurs paraissent associés à des sépultures, mais on ignore si l'érection des menhirs et celle des dolmens se sont faites à la même époque. Leur répartition sur le territoire ne recoupe pas non plus celle des dolmens.

Enfin, les cromlechs, cercles de pierres dressées de taille variable, rassemblant, comme à Carnac, plusieurs centaines de menhirs, gardent toujours leur mystère.

Jusqu'à cette explosion architecturale, les premiers « Bretons » étaient des chasseurs-cueilleurs comme les autres, qui poursuivaient le sanglier, le cerf et le chevreuil mais aussi le goéland et le canard, dépeçaient les cétacés et les phoques échoués sur les plages, consommaient en quantité impressionnante moules, coques, huîtres et bigorneaux et enterraient leurs morts en position fléchie, saupoudrés d'ocre rouge et parés de coquillages, des bois de cerf entourant le corps et formant une sorte de cage autour de la tête.

Pourtant, quelques siècles seulement plus tard, les descendants des ramasseurs de coquillages élèvent, sur des promontoires dont les eaux montantes vont parfois faire des îles, d'imposantes pyramides de pierre. L'une des constructions les plus anciennes est celle de Barnenez, qui s'élève sur la rive droite de la baie de Morlaix, près du village de Plouézoch. Mesurant 70 mètres de long et 25 mètres de large, l'ensemble contient onze chambres funéraires aux voûtes encorbellées, de 2 à 3 mètres de diamètre environ, auxquelles on accédait par des couloirs parallèles, tous orientés sud-nord, et pouvant atteindre jusqu'à 12 mètres de longueur. Les murs en gradins, la plupart des chambres, ainsi que tout le remplissage du monument, sont en pierres sèches, pour l'essentiel en dolérite verdâtre trouvée alentour ou en granite clair, transporté sur 2 kilomètres au moins.

D'autres ensembles postérieurs atteignent des dimensions encore plus grandes. Dans la région de Carnac, le tumulus Saint-Michel mesure 125 mètres de long sur 60 mètres de large. À Locmariaquer, le cairn de Mané-er-Hroeck est étalé sur 100 mètres de long. En face, sur l'autre côté du goulet du golfe du Morbihan, le tumulus de Tumiac dresse son imposante butte de terre. Mais on trouve aussi ces constructions ailleurs qu'en Bretagne, à Dissignac, en Loire-Atlantique, ou à Bougon, dans les Deux-Sèvres, où un bel ensemble mégalithique contenant des centaines de squelettes révèle que cette sépulture collective a été utilisée sur un millénaire.

La construction de telles bâtisses est un phénomène qui nous laisse encore songeurs. Longtemps, les préhistoriens ont refusé d'attribuer ces ensembles grandioses aux « barbares » qui ramassaient les moules sur les plages de Bretagne. Selon eux, ces pyramides de pierre avaient été probablement édifiées par des gens venus d'ailleurs, des navigateurs expérimentés, peut-être originaires de Crète, qui auraient diffusé leur religion et leurs techniques le long des côtes de l'Atlantique, en commençant par l'Espagne vers 2500 avant notre ère.

Mais les datations au radiocarbone ont anéanti toutes ces hypothèses. Ces dolmens sont antérieurs à toutes les autres constructions de pierre de la Méditerranée occidentale, et c'est vers 4500 ou 4000 avant notre ère qu'est apparue cette civilisation nouvelle, dans des sociétés indigènes où s'édifie précocement un nouvel ordre social.

Comment expliquer alors le fait que ces populations aient pu ainsi, de leur propre chef, arracher aux montagnes alentour ces énormes blocs de pierre pour bâtir de telles sépultures ? Comment expliquer surtout que des communautés composées au plus de quelques centaines d'individus aient consacré autant de temps (probablement plusieurs mois par an, répartis sur des années) à de tels travaux, au détriment d'activités productrices aussi importantes que l'agriculture ou l'élevage ?

Cela laisse supposer une société en pleine mutation comprenant, au moins au stade embryonnaire, une certaine organisation, une certaine hiérarchie. En effet si, comme les expérimentations l'ont confirmé, la taille et l'extraction des blocs ne réclamaient pas de révolution technique et pouvaient s'effectuer avec des pics de roche dure de 1 à 2 kilos et des coins de bois enfoncés au percuteur lourd et arrosés d'eau pour les faire gonfler et disjoindre les blocs, leur transport nécessitait non seulement une main-d'œuvre importante, volontaire ou résignée, mais aussi des chefs politiques et religieux ainsi que des architectes, des ingénieurs et des chefs de chantier. Pour tracter la dalle du dolmen de Bougon, qui pesait 32 tonnes, sur un chemin de roulement constitué de rouleaux de bois se déplaçant sur deux rails de troncs de chêne équarris, une expérience récente a montré qu'il fallait rassembler au moins 200 hommes, dont une vingtaine, munis de leviers individuels placés à l'arrière, aidaient au démarrage. Il était donc nécessaire que soient réunies la compétence et la diplomatie et, surtout, que se manifeste une volonté politique pour réaliser une telle opération. À moins que la force d'un sentiment sacré, lié sans doute au culte des ancêtres inhumés dans ces nécropoles, suffise à mobiliser les énergies.

Cela supposait aussi l'existence d'artistes, l'ornementation des premiers mégalithes démontrant un art consommé dont Gavr'inis est une sorte de fleuron. Là, sur les vingt-neuf pierres qui constituent les parois du monument, vingt-trois sont en totalité décorées de gravures, réalisées par un lent et patient piquetage du granite, au moyen de percuteurs en quartz. Composant une sorte de répertoire des thèmes et figurations de l'art des dolmens, les motifs représentés sont variés : arceaux emboîtés et présents sur chaque dalle, spirales, signes en U, que l'on a parfois assimilés à des bateaux, écussons, crosses, mais aussi haches polies, arcs et serpents.

Surtout, de nouvelles fouilles, entreprises de 1979 à 1984, ont révélé l'existence de gravures au dos de plusieurs de ces piliers et de la dalle de couverture, donc sur leur face non visible.

D'un style différent et plus ancien, ces gravures, qui représentent des haches, des bœufs et une « hache-charrue », témoignaient ainsi du réemploi de ces dalles pour la construction d'un nouveau monument. Ce démembrement des anciens mégalithes pouvait également s'accompagner d'un débitage des grandes dalles. On a ainsi pu établir que les dessins de la table qui constituait le plafond de la chambre funéraire du dolmen de Gavr'inis se raccordaient avec ceux des dalles d'ouverture de deux autres dolmens de Locmariaquer : celui de la table des Marchand et celui d'Er Vinglé.

C'était donc un gigantesque bloc de 4 mètres de largeur à sa base et de 14 mètres de haut que l'on avait ainsi brisé comme un vulgaire matériau de construction, sans respect pour les imposantes représentations qui y avaient été gravées. Cette idole de pierre a-t-elle été abattue, comme on l'a supposé, à la suite d'une révolution des idées et des pratiques religieuses ?

Ces gravures et ces signes dont le sens symbolique est encore mystérieux se retrouvent sur les monuments mégalithiques du Portugal, de Galice, d'Irlande et du pays de Galles mais sont absents des autres régions de l'Europe. Ils suggèrent donc l'existence dans cette zone atlantique d'une certaine communauté culturelle.

Ces signes supposent enfin un ensemble de croyances. Les images de la hache polie, de la crosse et de l'arc représenteraient les symboles du pouvoir terrestre, sans doute masculin. Doit-on aussi associer à la force virile l'image du bovidé aux grandes cornes représenté sur le bloc de couverture de Gavr'inis ? Et la figure de l'« écusson » n'est-elle pas une représentation schématique d'une déesse, tour à tour gardienne des morts, mère ancêtre d'une nombreuse descendance et divinité agraire garantissant la germination dans des sociétés devenues sédentaires ?

Comment interpréter enfin les alignements spectaculaires de menhirs comme celui de Carnac, où près de trois mille « pierres longues » s'échelonnent en une dizaine de files sur environ 8 kilomètres ? Sont-ils de complexes repères astronomiques alignés en fonction des levers et des couchers du soleil aux solstices d'hiver et d'été ? Sont-ils des observatoires permettant de prédire les éclipses ? Sont-ils des unités de mesure particulières ou des systèmes géométriques ? Célèbrent-ils les grandes étapes de la vie agricole, labours, semailles et récoltes ? Chacune de ces « pierres longues » représente-t-elle un ancêtre disparu ?

Autant d'interrogations auxquelles malheureusement l'absence de renseignements sur les milieux où vivaient ces architectes et ces bâtisseurs ne nous permet pas de répondre. Tout au plus la forte concentration entre la baie de Quiberon et le golfe du Morbihan des mégalithes les plus imposants, tant par leur dimension que par leur richesse artistique, suggère fortement l'existence dans cette région de communautés organisées ayant à leur tête des chefs politiques et religieux au pouvoir suffisamment puissant pour imposer et diriger la construction de tels monuments. Toujours est-il qu'à partir de 2800 avant notre ère plus aucun monument de pierre n'a été construit en Europe. La période de gloire de la mystérieuse « religion mégalithique » était terminée.

La première unité française

Tandis que les paysans de l'Ouest affirment avec éclat leur originalité, ceux du Midi partent résolument à la conquête de la France. À partir de 3700 avant notre ère, ceux qu'on appelle les Chasséens – du nom d'un de leurs campements situé à Chassey, en Saône-et-Loire – occupent progressivement le territoire de l'Hexagone et marquent profondément de leur empreinte les populations auxquelles ils vont se mêler.

Alors que, jusque-là, les cultures régionales avaient été largement influencées par des mouvements venus du Danube ou de l'Orient méditerranéen, avec les Chasséens, ce sont bien des autochtones qui, après avoir affûté leurs techniques, échafaudent en moins de deux siècles la première « unité française ». Après s'être ouvert les portes du Bassin parisien, ces colons défrichent toutes les terres cultivables et repoussent les Danubiens au nord d'une ligne courant de Dunkerque à Belfort. Comment expliquer une telle vitalité ?

Avec leur belle poterie au lissé soigné et à la cuisson parfaite, avec leur outillage perfectionné qui compte en forte proportion lames tranchantes et couteaux, faucilles et haches polies, pilons et mortiers, les Chasséens offrent tout d'abord une impression d'abondance. Les formes de vases se multiplient, suggérant le développement d'une cuisine longuement mijotée, soupes de céréales et bouillons de viande se substituant aux primitives grillades. D'importantes transformations, tant dans les modes de vie que dans l'alimentation, se font jour. L'agriculture connaît un important essor de sa production, imposant ainsi sa marque aux villages chasséens, où l'on a retrouvé la trace de puits profonds de plusieurs mètres, ainsi que celle de grands silos à grains creusés à même le sol.

Cette plus grande maîtrise des sources de nourriture est également visible dans le déclin du rôle de la chasse, qui devient une activité de plus en plus marginale, la viande provenant principalement de l'élevage. Parmi les espèces domestiquées, le bœuf occupe désormais la première place devant le porc, la chèvre et le mouton.

Autour du bassin moyen du Rhône, dans la région toulousaine, le long des principaux cours d'eau, les Chasséens ont édifié d'imposants villages, dont les principaux couvraient une trentaine d'hectares. À Saint-Michel-du-Touch, le village occupait une butte dominant la confluence du Touch et de la Garonne. À Villeneuve-Tolosane, on a aussi découvert un des plus anciens puits d'Europe. De 1,50 m de diamètre, il atteignait 7 mètres de profondeur. Autant d'aménagements qui témoignent d'une forte vitalité démographique et annoncent l'expansion future. Ainsi, en un millénaire, la population de la France décuple et passe peut-être de 100 000 habitants en 3700 avant J.-C. à 1 million en 2700 avant J.-C. ! En même temps, les Chasséens semblent avoir pratiqué avec profit le commerce. Ainsi les haches polies fabriquées dans les ateliers spécialisés de Plussulien, dans les Côtes-d'Armor, sont « exportées » sur le Rhin, dans les Alpes, les Pyrénées et même en Angleterre.

Ces changements économiques se sont aussi accompagnés d'une profonde transformation des modes de pensée. En un temps où l'agriculture est devenue la principale source de richesse, se multiplient les petites figurines, généralement modelées dans l'argile comme celle, haute de 9 centimètres, découverte à Noyen-sur-Seine. Elle représente une femme aux petits seins modelés, aux bras collés au corps et sans mains. Autant de divinités de la fertilité qu'on devait implorer pour permettre chaque année d'abondantes récoltes.

Plus énigmatiques encore, se multiplient en Provence, dans le Languedoc, en Corse, en terre chasséenne donc, des statues-menhirs. Elles ne sont pas taillées en forme de silhouette humaine, mais une face, rarement les deux, est sculptée ou gravée d'une représentation

schématique de personnage féminin ou asexué. La bouche est systématiquement absente. Est-ce pour évoquer la difficulté de communication avec le monde divin qu'éprouvaient les hommes ? Seuls les yeux
et le nez traduisent le visage, tandis que le tronc porte les bras en
faible relief, parfois deux petits seins et souvent un objet mystérieux
en forme de crosse. Les vêtements sont rares. En revanche, les ceintures sont relativement fréquentes.

Mystérieuse enfin, se dresse à Capdenac-le-Haut, dans le Lot, en
bordure d'un habitat chasséen, la plus ancienne statue préhistorique
de France. Haute de 27 centimètres et large de 17 centimètres pour
une profondeur de 25 centimètres, cette pièce a été sculptée dans une
arkose (grès feldspathique) vraisemblablement locale. La tête, sans
cou, à peine séparée du corps, porte un long nez, deux yeux en pastille
et une bouche lippue. Représentés par deux disques symétriques aux
contours nets, les seins, démarrant sous la tête, surplombent trois gros
doigts figurant les mains reposées sur le ventre. Étrange personnage
que cette statue, pour l'instant unique en France.

Ces témoignages n'expliquent pas pourquoi cette première unifi-
cation française s'est faite au profit des Chasséens et non des gens
du Nord, qui avaient pourtant organisé de puissantes communautés
paysannes. Le Nord a-t-il été « colonisé » par le Midi parce que les
gens du Rubané se sont « endormis » sur les vastes plaines de lœss du
Bassin parisien alors que les Chasséens, dans la verdeur de leur jeunesse, ont mis à profit la diversité de leur terroir d'origine pour mieux
s'adapter aux conditions nouvelles qu'ils découvraient au cours de
leur expansion ? Toujours est-il que dominant, dynamique, conquérant, le Chasséen impose pour longtemps dans l'Hexagone le primat
culturel méditerranéen.

Le sens de la propriété

Parce que les espaces libres tendent partout à se restreindre, les
hommes prennent aussi pied sur les plateaux du Jura et les contreforts
alpins, installant leurs villages sur les hautes terres incertaines ou inha-
bitables qu'avaient boudées les chasseurs de rennes.

Tandis que les coteaux bien exposés se couronnent de remparts
et de fossés, les lacs voient partout s'établir sur des presqu'îles favorables les premiers villages « sur pilotis ».

Ces « cités lacustres » ont longtemps alimenté une mythologie
romantique, à l'origine de bien des représentations erronées. Succédant, en un tableau tout en ombre et lumière, à la vision d'une longue

nuit préhistorique symbolisée par l'homme de Néandertal, vivant dans des cavernes et vêtu de peaux de bêtes, de telles représentations s'attachaient à dépeindre le spectacle bucolique de paysans regagnant en barque, sur les eaux calmes des lacs, leurs habitations sur « pilotis », après s'être adonnés aux travaux des champs près des rives. En effet, lorsqu'en 1854 la baisse considérable du niveau du lac de Zurich, due à un hiver particulièrement rigoureux et sec, permit la mise au jour du premier de ces villages par le savant Ferdinand Keller, ce dernier fit immédiatement le rapprochement avec les villages sur pilotis habités du Bénin ou de Nouvelle-Guinée, que les explorateurs faisaient alors découvrir à la même époque.

Une telle explication fut cependant progressivement combattue et des fouilles minutieuses, entreprises à partir de 1940, vinrent mettre un terme au mythe des « cités lacustres ». La preuve fut ainsi faite que la plupart de ces villages avaient été bâtis sur la terre ferme, des plages parfois marécageuses ou des buttes émergées, une remontée postérieure du niveau des lacs expliquant le fait qu'ils se trouvaient désormais sous l'eau. À Charavines, par exemple, vers 2740 avant notre ère, dans les collines du bas Dauphiné, des hommes de type « caucasien » se sont installés au bord du lac de Paladru, édifiant sur la plage de craie six maisons montées en pieux de sapin pouvant abriter une cinquantaine d'habitants.

Conservés intacts par l'humidité de l'eau et dégagés de la boue des lacs, planches et poteaux en bois, paniers, filets et nasses, bobines de bois avec leur fil, peignes en buis, perches de porteur d'eau, pilons, poignards de silex à la poignée recouverte d'osier, tissus brodés et sandales en cuir, récipients d'écorce, cuillères et louches en bois, mais aussi litières du bétail contenant encore les larves des mouches, miettes de galettes de blé, crottes de chien et jusqu'à la trace des pieds des hommes ou des sabots du bétail enfoncés dans la vase à proximité des maisons livrent des renseignements spectaculaires qu'aucune fouille de terre ferme n'a jamais pu fournir.

Ils nous permettent par exemple de savoir que la ration de viande moyenne atteignait 280 grammes par semaine et par personne (enfants compris), ce qui est tout à fait satisfaisant, que, pour mieux être conservées, les pommes étaient coupées en deux et probablement séchées, que la famille de la maison 2 consommait sept fois plus de noisettes que celle de la maison 3, que les pignes étaient une friandise particulièrement appréciée, que chaque famille avait une « vaisselle » très personnelle, l'une préférant les bols tronconiques, l'autre, les blocs globuleux, que les gens de Charavines cultivaient le pavot, dont les graines écrasées donnaient l'huile d'œillette mais servaient aussi à confectionner des galettes, et qu'on ne mangeait pas avec les doigts mais avec une cuillère !

Ces modestes villages révèlent aussi la nécessité inquiète de se protéger à une époque où semblent apparaître les tensions entre communautés et individus. Parmi les squelettes, certains portent parfois des lames ou des pointes de flèches en silex encore fichées dans les vertèbres. Ce sont les premières traces de violence que laisse aussi pressentir l'édification de puissants remparts à Noyen-sur-Seine, dans la vallée de la Seine, à Vitteaux, dans la Côte-d'Or, à Peu-Richard, en Charente-Maritime, ou à Nieul-sur-l'Autise, en Vendée. Là, on a élevé un rempart qui devait atteindre 5 mètres de hauteur et creusé des fossés qui totalisaient 1,5 km de développement, pour une largeur moyenne de 5 mètres et une profondeur de 2,50 m. Des « marqueurs territoriaux » manifestent, vis-à-vis également des autres communautés, un ancrage dans le sol bien plus fort qu'auparavant et un sens de la propriété appelé à un bel avenir.

Progressivement, le paysan allait aussi devoir apprendre à se faire guerrier.

CHAPITRE 7

Les premiers forgerons

*A vec la croissance démographique, la découverte du métal, l'émer-
gence de hiérarchies importantes au sein de communautés dominées
par des princes et l'exaltation des armes qui deviennent l'emblème d'un
certain prestige social, la guerre fait son apparition et prend dans notre
société une place déterminante, qu'elle n'a plus perdue. En témoigne l'inquiétant personnage barbu, les bras levés, brandissant deux poignards,
surnommé « le Sorcier », qui a été gravé, vers 1800 avant notre ère, sur
les roches de la vallée des Merveilles, près du col de Tende, à la frontière
franco-italienne.*

Le premier « marché commun »

Danube et Méditerranée sont, une fois encore, les deux voies de
pénétration du métal en France. Comme la poterie, la métallurgie fut
le résultat d'un long apprentissage technique. Il fallut tout d'abord
reconnaître et recueillir le métal. Le premier à être exploité fut certainement l'or qu'on trouvait en paillettes dans le lit des cours d'eau ou
en pépites dans certains filons à l'air libre ; puis le cuivre que les
hommes broyaient depuis longtemps pour produire une poudre vert et
bleu utilisée pour les colorants ou les fards ; enfin le bronze, un alliage
de cuivre et d'étain, moins cassant et plus résistant que le cuivre.

Après avoir martelé le métal pour préparer des objets de parure,
on apprit à le fondre quand les fours à poterie, de mieux en mieux

conçus, finirent par atteindre la température de 1 100 °C qu'exige la fusion du cuivre. Liquide, le métal était alors coulé dans des moules en pierre ou en sable. Pour la première fois de son histoire, l'homme put alors reproduire à l'identique des objets fabriqués.

Inventée vers 7 000 ans avant notre ère en Mésopotamie, en Iran et en Turquie, puis développée autour de la mer Noire et dans toute l'Europe des Balkans, la métallurgie du cuivre apparaît en France entre 3 000 et 2 500 ans avant notre ère, en Corse et dans la région cévenole. Là, des creusets avec des restes de scories ne laissent aucun doute sur l'existence de forgerons indigènes. Ailleurs, des objets en métal importés d'Orient accompagnent dans leurs tombes les nouveaux puissants. De même, la pendeloque sculptée sur la poitrine de la statue-menhir de Collorgues, dans le Gard, qui n'est pas sans rappeler les colliers d'Europe balkanique, témoigne de ces échanges et de ces influences.

C'est aussi dans les tombes que l'on voit apparaître, à la même époque, des vases d'un type nouveau nommés « campaniformes » parce que leur forme évoque celle d'une cloche renversée. Présentant le plus souvent des décorations très particulières de type géométrique (lignes brisées, hachures, triangles...) en bandes horizontales sur toute la surface, ils sont d'une facture soignée. Mais, phénomène jusque-là sans précédent, ces vases connaissent une diffusion extrêmement rapide. En un seul siècle, ils se trouvent aux quatre coins de l'Europe, du Danemark jusqu'au Portugal, des îles Britanniques jusqu'à la Hongrie, de l'Écosse à la Sicile et même en Afrique du Nord.

Autre fait pour le moins mystérieux, les archéologues ont remarqué que l'on découvre dans les tombes, associés à ces vases, des vestiges caractéristiques : pointes de flèches, poignards en cuivre de forme triangulaire, boutons en os, pendeloques en pierre ou en ambre et surtout plaquettes perforées, le plus souvent en os, parfois en pierre, qui servaient probablement à protéger le poignet lors du retour de la corde de l'arc, lorsque la flèche est tirée. Une telle association répétée d'objets suggère une communauté de culture ainsi qu'une diffusion homogène, mais pose la question de savoir qui étaient donc ces hommes du Campaniforme.

Plusieurs hypothèses ont été avancées à leur sujet. Certains ont ainsi cru deviner des forgerons au savoir-faire aussi habile que novateur, parcourant l'Europe, tels des Tziganes, faisant le commerce d'une production métallique standardisée comme leurs poignards en cuivre si particuliers. On a aussi soupçonné des envahisseurs dont l'origine reste toutefois problématique. Pays-Bas, Europe centrale ou embouchure du Tage ? Les plus audacieux, enfin, reconnaissant dans certains squelettes un type anthropologique original, caractérisé par des sujets de grande taille, à tête ronde, avec un occiput aplati, ont même avancé l'hypothèse d'une « race » campaniforme.

Dans ce cas, le « creuset » français aurait alors déjà remarquablement bien fonctionné. Nulle part, en effet, sur notre territoire, ces mystérieuses peuplades n'ont formé des groupes homogènes capables d'« absorber » les autochtones. C'est plutôt le contraire qui se vérifie, leurs vestiges se retrouvant mêlés dans les tombes collectives à ceux des populations locales. Enfin, la fouille des habitats de l'Âge du cuivre ne montre qu'assez rarement des villages appartenant en propre aux hommes du Campaniforme. La plupart du temps, ils composent avec les premiers habitants.

Quoi qu'il en soit, ils ont bien fait preuve d'un dynamisme exceptionnel, aucune civilisation antérieure n'ayant possédé une telle capacité d'extension. Auraient-ils même été les premiers diffuseurs, en Occident, des langues indo-européennes ? C'est vraisemblable. Quatre millénaires avant le nôtre, ils avaient constitué en quelque sorte, selon l'expression de Jean Guilaine, un « marché commun » et façonné par les transferts de technologie et le brassage des idées une certaine unité européenne.

Morts au combat

Tandis que se multiplient les échanges, la guerre fait une apparition remarquée dans notre pays. Jusqu'alors, les hommes étaient toujours parvenus à surmonter les périodes de crise. Tant en raison de la faible densité de population que des possibilités offertes par la chasse, la pêche et la cueillette, ils avaient ainsi réussi à s'adapter aussi bien aux variations climatiques qu'à l'appauvrissement des sols lié à l'agriculture sur brûlis. Il suffisait le plus souvent de se déplacer vers d'autres terres ou que quelques familles quittent la communauté pour que les choses rentrent dans l'ordre. Mais l'importante poussée démographique qui se produisit à cette époque rendit les problèmes à la fois plus nombreux et plus complexes. Alors que la France comptait peut-être 1 million d'habitants vers 2700 avant notre ère, elle en abrite probablement 4 millions 1 000 ans plus tard, dont les préhistoriens connaissent de mieux en mieux les maladies, les souffrances et les infirmités.

Ces hommes plus nombreux ont donc dû produire davantage et convoiter les meilleures terres, celles, évidemment, du voisin. Ce n'est d'ailleurs pas un hasard si les tensions les plus vives apparaissent précocement dans les espaces restreints que sont les îles comme la Corse, où les villages semblent déjà en compétition permanente.

À cette époque, en effet, l'île se couvre de fortifications spectaculaires, les *castelli*, construites par les indigènes pour se protéger des pillards que la mer amenait sur les côtes. Ces véritables citadelles se composaient d'un donjon circulaire ceint de longues murailles en pierres sèches dont l'épaisseur pouvait atteindre jusqu'à 10 mètres, comme au *castellu* d'Araghiu, au nord-ouest de Porto-Vecchio, où l'on peut également observer un chemin de ronde, des tours ainsi que des casemates. En même temps, les statues-menhirs à l'étrange visage de granite représentent des guerriers, certains casqués, parfois peut-être même cuirassés, portant gravés sur leur poitrine ou sur le côté des épées, des poignards et des baudriers.

Dans les tombes aussi, fouillées par les archéologues, on trouve en plus grand nombre des membres de la tribu morts au combat. À Roaix, dans le Vaucluse, plusieurs dizaines de squelettes portant des traces de flèches gisaient pêle-mêle dans le vaste ossuaire collectif, comme jetés là à la hâte après un massacre. Dans celui du Capitaine, également dans le Vaucluse, des pointes de flèches tranchantes étaient fichées dans les vertèbres d'un individu. Il faut croire que si les tirs de flèches étaient fréquents, les combats pouvaient aussi se faire au corps à corps, comme l'attestent les lames de silex plantées dans la colonne vertébrale de plusieurs hommes de la vallée du Petit-Morin, dans la Marne.

C'est peut-être aussi la montée de l'insécurité qui pousse certains à enterrer provisoirement leur fortune dans des cachettes où s'entassent armes, outils de la vie quotidienne et parures.

Derrière la perfection artistique des objets, on peut aussi entendre la brutalité clinquante d'un nouvel art de tuer, les artisans du métal commençant à forger pour des siècles la garde-robe du guerrier. Tandis que les armes offensives, comme l'épée, se font plus longues et plus robustes pour mieux s'enfoncer dans le corps, casques, cuirasses et jambières ont pour mission de le protéger.

Le culte des chefs

Le métal est encore trop précieux pour armer l'ensemble des combattants. Ainsi, les nouvelles armes demeurent un signe de richesse, y compris dans l'au-delà comme en témoigne leur présence dans les seules tombes des personnages les plus riches.

Car les hiérarchies sociales ont aussi été bouleversées par la diffusion de la métallurgie. Les mutations économiques qui s'amorcent, les nouvelles routes commerciales qui se dessinent, la recherche avide de l'étain, les bénéfices de l'exportation des produits finis, la propagation de belles poteries sont autant de signes qui laissent deviner l'émergence d'une aristocratie et la constitution de petites communautés dominées par de nouveaux princes.

Bien que les villes soient encore absentes du territoire, le commerce est assez important pour procurer aux chefs qui règnent sur les lieux de production ou les carrefours de distribution une richesse et une puissance auparavant insoupçonnées. Poignards, fortes haches, perles, bracelets, épingles ornementales, alênes et aiguilles sont activement colportés. Le Rhône, le long duquel se développe une civilisation originale et dynamique, assume alors pleinement son rôle d'intermédiaire entre les terres d'Allemagne et les rives de la Méditerranée. On retrouve ainsi en Bourgogne, en Languedoc-Roussillon, dans le Massif central et en Aquitaine les belles productions des forgerons rhodaniens, qui font alors l'objet d'un vaste commerce.

Toujours à la même époque s'allument aussi sur le littoral atlantique de nouveaux foyers de métallurgie, chaque centre de production se spécialisant dans un type de hache, de poignard, de lance ou d'épée. Et là encore, la société devient de plus en plus hiérarchisée comme le suggère le développement de nouveaux types de sépultures. Les caveaux collectifs de l'époque mégalithique cèdent désormais la place à de belles tombes individuelles dans lesquelles les dépouilles, baignant dans le luxe, font l'objet d'un singulier respect.

Mesurant 40 mètres de diamètre et 6 mètres de haut, le tumulus de Kernonen, à Plouvorn, dans le Finistère, contenait, sous une énorme dalle de 7 tonnes, un caveau de forme rectangulaire dont le sol avait été pavé puis couvert d'un plancher. À côté du squelette, on avait déposé trois coffres en chêne. Le premier contenait des pointes de flèches en silex, d'une grande finesse de taille, ainsi que des épingles et trois poignards en bronze, dont les manches en bois étaient rehaussés de plusieurs milliers de microscopiques clous d'or. Le deuxième renfermait quatre haches en bronze. Enfin, dans le dernier coffre, on a retrouvé une quarantaine d'autres pointes de flèches, un poignard avec un pommeau en os et un pendentif en ambre. Plusieurs autres plaquettes d'ambre ont été également découvertes dans cette tombe. La présence de tels bijoux témoigne de l'existence d'échanges commerciaux avec la Baltique, principal centre d'extraction de l'ambre et dont les productions étaient particulièrement appréciées à l'époque, notamment en Europe du Nord.

Vases et gobelets en or et en argent, bracelets en argent, chaînes, lunules et torques en or se trouvent aussi dans de nombreuses sépultures de la région, notamment à Saint-Adrien, à La Motte et à Ploumilliau, dans les Côtes-d'Armor, à Saint-Fiacre, dans le Morbihan, ou bien encore à Carnoët, dans le Finistère, comme, à la même époque, de l'autre côté de la Manche, où s'épanouit dans le Wessex, au sud de l'Angleterre, une civilisation tout à fait comparable à celle de la Bretagne.

À côté des tombes de guerriers, les tombes de femmes et d'enfants de « haut rang » sont aussi honorées. Ainsi, la richesse exceptionnelle de la parure accompagnant le corps d'une fillette âgée de sept ou huit ans, enterrée, vers 1500 avant notre ère, à Lastours, dans l'Aude, laisse penser qu'il s'agit probablement d'une princesse. On a en effet retrouvé des perles en verre bleu, blanc ou vert et en ambre, des bracelets de bronze et surtout une pendeloque en ambre de la Baltique, décorée d'un œil, d'inspiration orientale.

C'est aussi le verre, probablement d'origine mycénienne, qui fait son apparition dans la panoplie des parures sophistiquées, en Aquitaine, en Loir-et-Cher, en Alsace ou en Bretagne.

Autant de « signes extérieurs » de richesse qui soulignent l'émergence de sociétés moins égalitaires.

Le prestige du héros se reconnaît aussi au culte de nouveaux dieux qui rejettent dans l'ombre les déesses-mères chargées autrefois d'assurer la fécondité du groupe. Elles sont désormais moins vénérées que ces mâles guerriers dont les effigies sont dotées d'armes, tels des poignards et des épées, comme les statues-menhirs de Corse. Au val Lunigiana, au nord-ouest de la Toscane, on a même masculinisé une ancienne statue féminine en pratiquant l'ablation des seins et en rajoutant une épée !

Et tandis que le soleil fait l'objet d'une vénération particulière, on semble craindre et respecter un étrange personnage qui manie le feu à sa guise et qui rend les roches liquides avant de les transformer en glaives, haches, pointes de lances et bijoux précieux.

L'exaltation des armes

Manifestant l'émergence d'un nouvel ordre social, l'exaltation des armes qui accompagne le culte des héros et des dieux guerriers se retrouve dans les représentations artistiques, comme en témoignent celles, d'une importance exceptionnelle, du grand sanctuaire à ciel ouvert de la vallée des Merveilles, à plus de 2 000 mètres d'altitude, sur les pentes du mont Bego, près du col de Tende, dans les Alpes-Maritimes.

Vers 1800 avant notre ère, sur les surfaces à peu près planes des schistes gris-vert, parfois patinés de rose, les hommes ont réalisé par piquetage plus de cent mille gravures. Toutefois, malgré leur nombre, leur variété est réduite et peut se résumer à quatre grandes catégories.

Pour plus de la moitié, ces gravures représentent des bœufs, dessinés le plus souvent sous la forme d'un rectangle, assorti de deux larges cornes. Ils sont fréquemment regroupés par paires ou par quatre, certains attelés à un araire, figuré par un long manche, parfois flanqués d'un petit personnage. La forte présence et la stylisation des bovidés laissent supposer que les hommes du mont Bego, suivant en cela de nombreuses civilisations du bassin méditerranéen à la même époque, vouaient un culte au taureau.

On distingue également un certain nombre de figures géométriques, droites, cercles, ovales, carrés, rectangles simples ou quadrillés comme des grilles, dont l'interprétation demeure incertaine : s'agit-il de parcs à bestiaux, de parcelles de champs ou bien encore d'une sorte de cadastre ?

Un troisième type de motifs représentés est constitué par les armes. Poignards à lames triangulaires et pointues et « hallebardes » emmanchées comme des haches au bout d'une longue hampe sont en effet très fréquents.

Enfin, dernière catégorie, les figurations humaines schématisées sont les plus rares. L'une des plus célèbres est le « Sorcier », inquiétante face barbue aux deux bras levés brandissant des poignards. Une autre, le « Chef de tribu », représente un homme debout, reconnaissable à son sexe, qui porte sur la poitrine une sorte de pectoral représentant une tête de bœuf. Un autre personnage, sans jambes, les bras ondulant le long du corps, qui émerge d'un quadrillage, a une hache comme fichée dans la tête, ronde et sans visage. Enfin, une autre silhouette, bras et jambes écartés, semble exécuter un pas de danse, à caractère peut-être initiatique comme le suggère le cercle de points autour de son torse.

Ces signes gravés sont autant d'archives sur les transformations qui affectent la future France au temps des premiers forgerons. Ce n'est pas un hasard si, aussitôt inventées, les armes deviennent un thème privilégié de représentation et si les femmes aux formes sexuelles marquées que sculptaient les chasseurs de rennes font maintenant place à des hommes armés. C'est bien à cette époque, en effet, que la guerre et l'exaltation de la guerre prennent une importance qu'elles n'ont plus perdue depuis lors.

Nous voici donc à l'aube d'une société où le culte de la force et l'esprit de domination mènent le jeu. L'histoire des riches, des héros et des puissants peut alors commencer.

Le temps des migrateurs

*V*ers 1 200 avant notre ère, du Rhin aux Pyrénées, de grands bouleversements marquent pour des siècles l'histoire de la France. Des
peuplades apparaissent, assez dynamiques pour imposer leur empreinte
aux populations qui les avaient précédées sur notre sol, favorisant l'émergence d'une nouvelle société. Avec l'usage du fer qui se généralise à partir du IXe siècle, de véritables « princes » règnent désormais sur des
résidences fortifiées et font étalage d'un luxe jusqu'alors inconnu. Ainsi
le célèbre cratère de Vix, découvert dans la tombe d'une princesse, témoigne de la richesse de cette aristocratie dont la fortune et le pouvoir reposent sur les échanges commerciaux avec la Grèce et l'Italie.

Le peuple des champs d'urnes

Nous connaissons mal les origines et le mode d'expansion des
peuplades qui apparaissent dans notre pays à cette époque. Le mouvement de migration n'est d'ailleurs pas limité à la France. Il affecte
en effet l'Europe et le Proche-Orient. En Grèce, ces nouveaux venus
détruisent l'opulente Mycènes. En Asie Mineure, ils abattent l'Empire
hittite et pénètrent en Égypte. En Europe centrale, les civilisations du
bronze disparaissent devant ces « étrangers » qui, après avoir franchi
le Rhin, étendent leur influence jusqu'à l'Espagne.

Ces hommes se distinguent surtout par leur rituel funéraire. Au lieu d'inhumer leurs morts selon le rituel courant, ils les incinèrent. Après avoir brûlé le défunt sur un bûcher, parfois avec ses armes ou ses bijoux, ils recueillent les restes dans une urne funéraire qu'ils disposent dans une fosse creusée à même le sol. De sorte que les cimetières de cette époque se présentent comme de vastes champs d'urnes, enterrées les unes à côté des autres.

Certes, les vieilles coutumes ne sont pas totalement supprimées. Ici, comme à Veuxhaulles-sur-Aube, en Côte-d'Or, ou à La Colombine, dans l'Yonne, on enterre encore parfois le défunt. Là, comme à Pougues-les-Eaux, dans la Nièvre, un cimetière compte autant d'urnes que de tombes. Mais rapidement, les trois quarts de la France se convertissent à cette « civilisation des champs d'urnes », seul l'ouest du pays résistant obstinément à l'influence des peuples incinérateurs.

L'adoption massive de l'incinération s'accompagne aussi d'un renouvellement marqué de la céramique : on affectionne désormais les poteries à pâte noire et brillante, ornées de petites bosses ou de cannelures. Enfin, la multiplication des villages et leur proximité suggèrent un peuplement plus dense. Jusque-là, en effet, la terre ne semblait pas avoir fait défaut. Ce n'est désormais plus le cas, et les fortifications, sous forme de levées de terre, qui entourent fréquemment les habitats témoignent de l'intensité des tensions entre les communautés. À Merri, dans l'Orne, trois enceintes, dont l'une haute de 6 mètres, protègent un village vaste de 4 hectares. À Aslonnes, dans la Vienne, un site d'éperon de 2 hectares est flanqué d'un rempart en arc de cercle de 250 mètres.

La quête du pain quotidien accompagne alors cette large poussée de la vie qu'excite peut-être une immigration plus intense. Tandis que la culture des céréales ne cesse de s'étendre, que l'orge prend une part grandissante tout au long de la période, que l'on récolte aussi l'avoine, le millet, les fèves, les pommes, les glands et les noisettes, les défrichements de nouveaux espaces et de terres moins fertiles s'accentuent. L'abondance de haches mieux emmanchées, l'apparition de faucilles en métal, l'usage de l'araire illustrent le souci de se doter de meilleurs outils.

Surtout, le cheval, domestiqué, semble désormais jouer un rôle déterminant. Encore chassé vers 2 500 ans avant notre ère, il devient l'un des plus dévoués collaborateurs de l'homme sans qu'on puisse dater précisément le moment où il est devenu un animal de trait. Seules la multiplication des pièces de harnachement dans les cachettes d'objets métalliques comme les figurations schématiques de chevaux ornant les poteries nous permettent de deviner qu'entre 1200 et 1000 l'homme a bien achevé la plus noble de ses conquêtes.

Ces fortes innovations qui se diffusent largement sur le territoire sont-elles liées à l'irruption de ces dynamiques « envahisseurs » ?

Cette question fait aujourd'hui l'objet de nombreuses discussions, certains avançant l'idée que l'incinération des morts peut s'exporter progressivement, au prix d'une nouvelle spiritualité, sans qu'un « peuple » en armes soit derrière. En outre, l'apparition de cette nouvelle pratique funéraire, simultanément, en différents points de l'Europe occidentale ne suggère pas qu'elle ait été diffusée à partir d'un berceau d'origine d'où seraient partis ces peuples conquérants. Pourquoi n'y aurait-il pas eu simple acculturation, c'est-à-dire initiation progressive des populations en place par des groupuscules dynamiques ou des marchands ambulants ?

Reste qu'il est troublant de constater que certains carrefours stratégiques ont bien été, au cours de cette période, une terre d'« enjeu » entre deux cultures, sinon entre deux populations. Ainsi, la région de Paris devient une zone d'âpre concurrence entre deux grands courants. Tandis qu'à l'ouest prédominent les influences atlantiques et que se développe une métallurgie inspirée par des modèles normands, au sud-est, en Seine-et-Marne et dans l'Essonne, les rites de l'incinération triomphent comme les armes d'inspiration centro-européenne, les deux tendances semblant camper pendant deux siècles, de 900 à 700, sur leurs positions.

Concurrence des produits, des styles et des cultures, tel semble bien être le trait dominant de cette période de transition où les contacts multipliés entre des hommes plus nombreux soulignent que l'existence de petits groupes isolés dans de vastes espaces appartient désormais au passé.

Les cavaliers du fer

Vers 900 ans avant notre ère, de nouveaux types de tombes nous révèlent des migrations de plus grande ampleur. Ces tombes, sous tumulus, concentrées en France à l'est et au sud d'une ligne qui irait de la Lorraine et de la Champagne jusqu'à l'embouchure de la Loire mais qui s'étendent en Europe centrale jusqu'au Danube et à la Morava, tranchent sur l'aspect relativement égalitaire des sépultures antérieures.

À côté de la vaisselle en terre cuite, sont déposées dans les tombes masculines des épées en bronze puis en fer ainsi que des pièces de harnachement. La richesse de ces ensembles comme le volume des matériaux nécessités pour leur construction prouvent à l'évidence que nous avons désormais affaire à de véritables « princes ».

Dans la nécropole de Chavéria, dans le Jura, les offrandes dont les défunts étaient gratifiés se composaient de poteries, d'épées, d'un couteau, de bracelets, d'anneaux, de deux mors de cheval en bronze, d'une gourmette de soixante-dix éléments en os, d'une perle en ambre et d'un plat en tôle de bronze d'influence étrusque. À Saint-Romain-de-Jalionas, dans l'Isère, le défunt portait un torque, un bracelet et une épingle en or. Il était accompagné d'un jeune bœuf, d'un couteau en fer, d'une longue épée, de trois récipients en bronze et d'un service à boisson.

Dans la nécropole de Hallstatt, près de Salzbourg, en Autriche, qui a donné son nom à cette première civilisation du fer, les tombes féminines offrent de nombreuses parures cliquetantes et des fibules volumineuses qui témoignent du goût exubérant de l'époque.

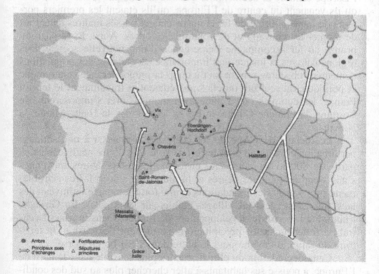

Aire d'expansion de la civilisation de Hallstatt.

Dans celle d'Eberdingen-Hochdorf, en Allemagne, le défunt, âgé de quarante à cinquante ans et de taille élevée (1,87 m), était étendu sur une banquette de bronze rembourrée de tissus et de fourrures. Il portait un collier, deux fibules et une ceinture en or, un poignard et un brassard incrustés d'or. Ses chaussures, en forme de poulaines, étaient elles aussi couvertes de feuilles d'or, alors qu'un couvre-chef conique, posé près de la tête, était façonné en écorce de bouleau décorée de motifs estampés. Dans l'angle de la chambre funéraire qui avait la taille d'un carré de 7 mètres de côté, était placé un grand chaudron en bronze qui était plein d'hydromel au moment de la fermeture de la tombe. Le service à boire était composé de neuf cornes ornées de feuilles d'or et suspendues par des pitons de fer aux parois de bois du caveau, que recouvraient des tentures multicolores. Le long d'une paroi avait été disposé un char à quatre roues, long de 4,50 m et fait de bois orné d'appliques de fer. Dans la caisse de ce véhicule reposaient un joug, le harnachement de deux chevaux, des assiettes et des coupes en bronze, une hache et un couteau en fer.

De ces « aristocrates » dont les familles couvrent l'essentiel de l'Europe centrale et occidentale, nous ne savons pas grand-chose sauf qu'ils venaient du centre de l'Europe, qu'ils étaient les premiers porteurs de la métallurgie du fer et qu'ils étaient passés maîtres dans l'art de monter les chevaux et de conduire les chars. Ainsi, le passage du bronze au fer accompagne l'émergence d'une nouvelle société. Des régions pauvres et jusque-là d'importance secondaire, des populations demeurées obscures prirent tout à coup la prépondérance économique et politique, du seul fait qu'elles possédaient et travaillaient le fer. En France, les contrées où la mine avoisinait la forêt s'imposèrent : la Lorraine, la Franche-Comté, le Berry, le Morvan, la Haute-Marne, la Nièvre.

Les débuts de l'Âge du fer correspondent aussi à une sérieuse perturbation climatique dont les effets sont loin d'être négligeables. À partir de 800 avant notre ère, en effet, les températures moyennes s'abaissent de quelques degrés et la pluviosité s'accroît très sensiblement, provoquant des inondations et une forte remontée du niveau des lacs, qui submergent les villages établis sur leurs côtes. En Gironde, l'humidité favorise le développement de l'aulne. Dans le Massif central, la fraîcheur et les précipitations permettent l'extension du territoire du sapin, de même pour le hêtre dans l'Est ou en Corse.

Cette dégradation du climat, encore plus sensible dans le nord de l'Europe, a poussé ses habitants à aller chercher plus au sud des conditions de vie plus favorables. Ainsi s'amorce une période de remue-ménage qui voit se répandre des populations qui peuvent s'appuyer sur l'efficacité de nouvelles armes de fer et sur les facilités de déplacement offertes par la domestication du cheval et la généralisation du chariot attelé. L'Âge du fer est donc une période de multiples migrations qui ont contribué à accroître encore la densité du peuplement de la France.

En même temps, se multiplient les sites fortifiés qui matérialisent le pouvoir de cette aristocratie princière. Ces sites, assez régulièrement distribués, entourés de villages ouverts, font songer aux « capitales » de territoires d'une cinquantaine de kilomètres de rayon. Mais la situation géographique et topographique de ces forteresses, les nombreux objets importés qu'elles recèlent montrent aussi qu'elles étaient destinées à contrôler d'importantes voies de passage terrestre ou fluvial, par lesquelles transitaient les convois.

En France, le plus célèbre de ces sites fortifiés est celui du mont Lassois, en Bourgogne, une butte majestueuse qui domine le bocage bourguignon au nord de Châtillon-sur-Seine. Parmi les sépultures princières dressées près de l'agglomération, la « tombe de Vix » évoque de manière spectaculaire l'importance de ces courants d'échanges comme le faste de ceux qui en étaient les intermédiaires obligés.

La dame de Vix

Découverte dans la plaine de Vix en 1953 par René Joffroy, sous un tumulus rasé pour les besoins de l'agriculture au IIe siècle après J.-C. et qui atteignait primitivement 42 mètres de diamètre, la « tombe de Vix » se composait d'une chambre funéraire en bois d'environ 3 mètres de côté. Les murs et le toit avaient été coffrés en bois.

Une femme, âgée d'une trentaine d'années, gisait allongée sur la caisse d'un petit char dont les quatre roues, cerclées de fer, avaient été démontées.

Le crâne était enserré par une sorte de diadème d'or de 480 grammes ; sur la poitrine, on trouva les éléments d'un collier fait de perles d'ambre, de diorite, de serpentine et ceux d'un grand torque tubulaire en bronze ; à chaque poignet, trois bracelets de schiste et un bracelet de perles d'ambre ; chaque cheville portait un anneau tubulaire ; huit fibules maintenaient les vêtements, six en bronze parmi lesquelles cinq étaient ornées de corail et d'ambre, l'une en fer avec cabochon d'or et de corail.

Contre la paroi ouest, on avait disposé trois bassins de bronze d'origine étrusque. Enfin, dans l'angle nord-ouest se trouvait le célèbre cratère de Vix, le plus grand vase en bronze jamais fabriqué dans l'Antiquité. Haut de 1,64 m, cet énorme cratère de 208 kilos et de 1 100 litres de capacité était coiffé d'un couvercle surmonté d'une statuette, perforé comme une passoire pour laisser passer le vin et l'eau. Le col s'ornait d'une frise représentant des guerriers et des chars tirés par des chevaux, guidés par des auriges. Il était pourvu d'anses à volutes décorées du buste d'une grimaçante Gorgone, que terminaient des serpents appuyés au sommet de sa panse. Posée sur le bord du vase, une coupe attique servait à la dégustation.

Cette tombe, qui constitue l'une des plus importantes découvertes archéologiques de notre histoire ancienne, suscite encore bien des discussions. Si les nombreux objets déposés permettent une datation précise de l'inhumation (entre 510 et 490 avant notre ère), demeure la question de l'origine même de ces pièces. Si les coupes à figures noires sont attiques, si les plats et l'œnochoé (vase à verser le vin) de bronze viennent à peu près certainement d'Étrurie, d'où peut venir le prestigieux cratère ? De Corinthe, de l'Italie du Sud colonisée par les Grecs ou de Phocée, en Asie Mineure ? Nous l'ignorons. Nous savons seulement, par les lettres grecques qui permirent l'assemblage, qu'il a été livré en pièces détachées. Quant au diadème d'or qui ornait la tête de la défunte, certains auteurs estiment qu'une telle pièce a son origine dans la péninsule Ibérique, où existait une forte tradition d'orfèvrerie, d'autres songeant à un centre de production situé sur les bords de la mer Noire.

Surtout, le cratère de Vix nous dessine les routes commerciales qui s'étaient alors nouées entre les sociétés raffinées de la Grèce et de l'Italie et les « royaumes barbares » qui s'étaient édifiés en Europe centrale et occidentale. Par la vallée du Rhône, les précieuses céramiques étrusques ou grecques remontaient pour s'échanger contre l'étain, le bois, le cuir, le minerai de fer, l'ambre de la Baltique, les salaisons, voire des esclaves. Un texte tardif de l'historien grec Diodore, mort vers 20 avant J.-C., nous précise les conditions probables de ce trafic : « En Bretagne, près du promontoire qu'on appelle Bélérion [cap Land's End], les indigènes sont particulièrement amis des étrangers et civilisés par leur fréquentation des commerçants du dehors. Ils produisent de l'étain qu'ils extraient des roches dans lesquelles ils pratiquent des galeries ; ils le fondent et en font des lingots qu'ils portent dans une île, en avant de la Bretagne, et qu'on nomme Ictis [Wight]. La marée découvre l'espace situé entre la Bretagne et cette île, de sorte que c'est par chariot qu'on y apporte de grandes quantités d'étain. Là, des marchands viennent l'acheter et le transportent en Gaule. Ils mettent trente jours pour l'apporter à dos de cheval jusqu'à l'embouchure du Rhône. » Cette information s'applique certainement pour la période où la princesse de Vix régnait sur un site dominant justement une des routes commerciales qui permettaient de passer du bassin de la Seine, au point où le fleuve cesse d'être navigable, vers le Sillon rhodanien ou qui gagnaient l'Italie du Nord par les cols alpins.

Dès cette époque, en effet, les principautés de la Bourgogne aux régions du Danube sont inondées par des objets d'origine grecque et, surtout, par les amphores pour transporter ou conserver le vin, une boisson qui semble avoir été particulièrement prisée. En raison de sa position géographique, la France était bien un excellent marché à conquérir.

La fondation de Marseille

Vers 650 avant notre ère, les rouliers de la Méditerranée que sont les Phéniciens, les Grecs et les Étrusques engagent la bataille commerciale pour installer des comptoirs le long de ses côtes. Les Étrusques et les Phéniciens semblent avoir été les premiers à reconnaître celles de la Provence, du Languedoc et du Roussillon. Plusieurs épaves chargées d'amphores à vin et de vaisselle fine étrusque ont été retrouvées au large des côtes de Provence. Ces marchandises étaient apportées dans de petits bateaux de 12 à 15 mètres de long qui ne pouvaient contenir plus de deux cents amphores.

Puis les marchandises grecques arrivent à leur tour. On retrouve dans les nécropoles languedociennes de Mailhac et d'Agde et dans quelques habitats bas rhodaniens comme Sanilhac, dans la vallée du Gardon, et Saint-Blaise, à l'ouest de Marseille, ces coupes à vin qui révèlent le caractère hautement symbolique du vase à boire dans ces premiers échanges avec les chefs locaux. Mais, à la différence de leurs concurrents, les Grecs ne se contentent pas de ce simple commerce. C'est le temps où, la terre manquant aux cités mères surpeuplées, les plus aventureux de leurs fils vont chercher fortune ailleurs. La création vers 600 de Massalia, la future Marseille, par des colons originaires de Phocée, en Asie Mineure, constitue, à cet égard, un événement capital dans l'histoire de notre pays.

La légende qui entoure cette fondation mérite d'être rappelée. D'après les historiens grecs, des commerçants de Phocée auraient abordé dans une calanque au moment même où Nannos, le roi de la population locale, les Ségobriges, était en train de célébrer le mariage de sa fille Gyptis. Le chef de l'expédition phocéenne, Protis, fut invité à la fête. À la fin du banquet, la fille du roi devait désigner son futur époux en lui offrant une coupe d'eau ou de vin. Elle désigna le jeune et beau Grec, qui obtint du roi Nannos un territoire autour d'une calanque profonde, le Lacydon – le Vieux-Port actuel.

Ce récit légendaire démontre en fait que, dans des territoires encore peu peuplés et où la mer n'occupait qu'une faible place dans l'économie, la cession de quelques arpents côtiers à des étrangers dépourvus d'intentions belliqueuses mais pourvus d'objets séduisants ne pouvait présenter que des avantages.

À cet égard, le choix de Massalia ne pouvait être meilleur. Site privilégié, à la fois ouvert sur la mer et facile à protéger, ce port était de plus situé à proximité de la grande artère rhodanienne, au débouché du trafic qui assura la fortune de la princesse de Vix. Il était d'autre part un indispensable relais entre les terres grecques et les marchés tant convoités du monde occidental. Au départ, d'ailleurs, la ville reste fort exiguë et l'essentiel de son activité repose sur quelque chose qu'on appellerait de nos jours « l'import-export ».

Les échanges se développent alors à une grande échelle. Ils s'accompagnent de la fondation de nouveaux comptoirs comme Emporium (Ampurias) sur la côte catalane espagnole, Antipolis (Antibes), Nikaia (Nice), Taurœis (Le Brusc), Agathè (Agde). Le golfe du Lion tend à devenir un « lac phocéen », et cette prospérité est attestée par les petites monnaies d'argent frappées par la cité phocéenne, dès 525 avant notre ère, et qui constituent les premières monnaies d'Extrême-Occident. La concurrence devient âpre avec les Carthaginois et les Étrusques qui, en 537 avant notre ère, infligent aux Grecs de lourdes pertes à la bataille navale d'Alalia (Aléria, en Corse).

Les Phocéens n'en restent pas moins maîtres du trafic méditerranéen. Plus subtilement, c'est l'hellénisation de l'arrière-pays qui s'amorce. Le signe le plus sensible en est la diminution parfois spectaculaire de la part des céramiques modelées indigènes : à Bessan, leur part dans les vestiges exhumés devient minime alors qu'elle atteignait les quatre cinquièmes un siècle auparavant. À la variété des productions locales répond désormais la grande uniformité des amphores à pâte micacée et de la vaisselle commune originaire de Marseille que l'on rencontre en série sur tous les sites du Languedoc et de la Provence.

C'est aussi au cours de cette période qu'apparaissent les premières maisons de pierre, d'abord dans les localités les plus proches de Marseille, autour de l'étang de Berre. Ces nouvelles constructions adoptent d'emblée un plan quadrangulaire, alors que les maisons de l'époque antérieure avaient un plan circulaire ou arrondi. Plus propice à l'utilisation de la pierre, le plan quadrangulaire permet surtout d'accoler beaucoup plus facilement des pièces supplémentaires ou des annexes et de transformer ainsi à volonté l'espace intérieur. Outre la pierre, la technique de la brique crue apparaît, comme à Mailhac, pour construire les murs sur des soubassements de pierre ou des remparts.

À Gailhan, dans le Gard, on a reconnu une maison qui couvrait 36 mètres carrés et possédait deux pièces. La première, qui servait à la cuisine, contenait huit jarres de stockage, une série de récipients rangés (écuelles, cruches, pots) et une zone de préparation des aliments avec deux pierres plates enfoncées dans le sol. La pièce du fond était consacrée à la vie collective et au repos de la famille, avec une banquette en pierre le long des murs et un foyer décoré au centre.

Enfin, l'apparition de rues sur les sites indigènes témoigne d'une nouvelle organisation de l'espace et de la fusion des cultures qui s'échafaude à travers et grâce au commerce. Mais si, en quelques décennies, les « barbares » ont pu apprendre les usages d'une vie plus raffinée, c'est que la distance culturelle entre les migrants méditerranéens et les populations indigènes était moins grande qu'on ne l'a autrefois supposée.

Le temps des Gaulois

*C*inq siècles avant notre ère, une autre rupture majeure affecte la quasi-totalité de l'Hexagone alors envahi par de nouveaux migrants qui, partis d'Europe centrale, ravagent Rome en 390, Delphes en 279, avant de s'établir en Espagne, en Grande-Bretagne, en Irlande et en Anatolie, où ils fondent le royaume des Galates. Avec ceux que nous appelons Gaulois, que les Romains appelaient Galli et qui se nommaient eux-mêmes « Celtes » dans leur langue, se réalise, pour la première fois, l'union intime de la terre qui est aujourd'hui celle de la France et d'hommes qui nous ont légué les noms de la plupart de nos fleuves, de nos montagnes et de nos villes.

Des guerriers intrépides

Les auteurs de l'Antiquité dépeignent les Gaulois comme de redoutables combattants animés par une véritable fureur guerrière. Tout en eux épouvante, « l'horrible harmonie de leurs chants sauvages et de leurs clameurs bizarres », « leur stature gigantesque et le bruit de leurs armes frappées l'une contre l'autre », « leurs boucliers qui résonnent », « les injures ou les menaces que leur jactance lance contre l'adversaire », la « belle mort » qu'ils recherchent au combat pour accéder au paradis des héros, le fait aussi que, parfois, ils combattent nus, couverts seulement par un grand bouclier.

« C'était un spectacle frappant que l'apparition et les mouvements de ces hommes nus, pleins de jeunesse et de belle stature, écrit le Grec Polybe dans ses *Histoires*. Tous ceux du premier rang portaient des colliers et des bracelets d'or... Dans l'action, leur nudité leur était un grand désavantage, le bouclier gaulois ne pouvant couvrir l'homme tout entier, la partie du corps qui dépassait était particulièrement exposée aux traits. »

Difficile d'imaginer le vacarme qui accompagnait la foule de ces guerriers en mouvement, le fracas des chariots, le son rauque des longues trompes dont le pavillon, dressé au-dessus de la troupe, figurait la gueule de quelque animal fantastique.

Ce sont aussi les chars de combat que les Romains découvrent pour la première fois avec ces Gaulois. Véhicule très léger, presque tout entier en bois ou en osier, ce char était conduit par un cocher qui n'hésitait pas à se livrer à de multiples acrobaties pour défiler à toute vitesse devant l'ennemi tandis qu'à ses côtés le guerrier lançait ses javelots puis sautait à terre pour combattre à pied.

C'est enfin la coutume des têtes-trophées que Grecs et Romains trouvent particulièrement répugnante : « Ils tranchent la tête des ennemis tombés et les attachent à l'encolure de leurs chevaux. Ils confient les crânes ensanglantés à leurs valets et les emportent comme butin, en clamant le péan et en chantant un chant de triomphe. Ils clouent ces dépouilles à leurs maisons comme le font, dans certaines chasses, ceux qui ont terrassé des bêtes sauvages. Ils embaument dans de l'huile de cèdre les têtes des ennemis les plus illustres et les conservent soigneusement dans un coffre. Ils les montrent aux étrangers en se vantant d'avoir, eux-mêmes ou leurs pères, refusé de grandes sommes qu'on leur offrait de telle ou telle tête. On dit que certains se flattent d'avoir refusé un poids d'or égal à celui de la tête, faisant montre ainsi d'une sorte de grandeur barbare » (Diodore de Sicile, vers 50-20 avant J.-C.).

Ces pratiques, en grande partie confirmées par l'archéologie, montrent à quel point la civilisation qui se met en mouvement à partir de 500 est une civilisation guerrière où les hommes qui ont le pouvoir sont en même temps ceux qui portent les armes. Dans la région champenoise, qu'ils colonisent massivement, la fouille de centaines de nécropoles et de milliers de sépultures permet d'approcher les modes de vie et d'expansion de cette nouvelle aristocratie dirigeante.

Leurs tombes, qui n'ont plus le caractère fastueux de celles des princesses et des princes de Hallstatt, sont surtout des tombes de guerriers. Les chars funéraires à quatre roues des sépultures princières sont remplacés par des chars de guerre à deux roues de bois, cerclées de fer, reposant en position verticale dans des logements symétriques. Habillé et paré, les pieds dirigés vers le joug, le défunt, muni de ses armes et de son casque, était étendu dans la caisse du char.

La répartition générale de ces tombes, une en moyenne dans chaque nécropole, confirme bien le statut aristocratique de celui qui y était inhumé. Les armes, plus nombreuses que dans les autres sépultures de guerriers, y sont plus belles. Le défunt est aussi le seul à posséder des parures en or et des objets d'importation. Par ailleurs, la densité des nécropoles qui se distribuent dans le paysage, à raison d'une à quatre pour le territoire d'un village actuel, suggère l'existence de nombreuses petites communautés militarisées organisées selon une stricte hiérarchie sociale, les guerriers plus modestes n'emportant qu'une seule arme dans leur tombe.

Le philosophe stoïcien Posidonius d'Apamée, l'un des premiers à avoir visité ces régions gauloises, vers 100 avant notre ère, nous montre les coutumes de ces guerriers : « Les Celtes, parfois pendant leurs repas, organisent des vrais duels. Toujours armés dans leurs réunions, ils se livrent à des combats simulés et luttent entre eux du bout des mains ; mais parfois aussi, ils vont jusqu'aux blessures ; ils en viennent à se tuer. » Poursuivant son récit, il décrit les banquets où la place de chacun est assignée : « Quand les convives sont nombreux, ils s'asseyent en cercle et la place du milieu est au plus grand personnage qui est comme le coryphée du chœur : c'est lui qui se distingue entre tous par son habileté à la guerre, par sa naissance ou ses richesses. Près de lui, s'assied celui qui reçoit, et, successivement, de chaque côté, tous les autres, selon leur rang plus ou moins élevé. Les servants d'armes – ceux qui tiennent le bouclier – sont derrière et, en face, les doryphores ou porte-lances, assis en cercle comme les maîtres, mangent en même temps. Ceux qui servent font circuler la boisson dans des vases qui ressemblent à nos ambiques et sont de terre ou d'argent. »

Cette description, conforme aux représentations que l'on peut observer sur des objets dès le VIe siècle avant notre ère, est bien celle d'une société guerrière courant les chemins et les routes d'Europe à la recherche de nouvelles terres.

L'expansion des Celtes

C'est à partir d'une forte zone d'implantation entre Rhin et Marne qu'aux alentours de 400 avant notre ère les Celtes se mettent en mouvement. Parmi les forces qui ont déclenché cette expansion, la pression démographique d'une population féconde a pu avoir son rôle. C'est du moins l'explication qu'en donne l'historien romain Tite-Live quand il écrit : « La Celtique, une des trois provinces de la Gaule, obéissait aux Bituriges [les Gaulois de Bourges] qui lui donnaient un roi. Celui-ci était alors Ambigat, tout-puissant tant par son propre mérite que par la prospérité de son peuple. Sous son commandement, la Gaule était si féconde en moissons et en hommes que leur multitude surabondante devenait difficile à gouverner. Déjà avancé en âge, le roi voulut débarrasser le pays de ce trop-plein qui l'étouffait. Il avait deux neveux, Bellovèse et Sigovèse, les fils de sa sœur, jeunes gens pleins d'ardeur ; il annonça l'intention de les envoyer vers les terres que les dieux indiqueraient par leurs augures ; ils pourraient prendre avec eux autant de monde qu'ils voudraient, de façon qu'aucun peuple ne puisse leur résister. À Sigovèse, le sort assigna la direction de la forêt Hercynienne [les territoires danubiens] ; Bellovèse fut conduit par les dieux vers une contrée plus séduisante, l'Italie [...]. Il partit avec des forces innombrables de fantassins et de cavaliers vers la vallée du Rhône et les Alpes. »

Au-delà de son caractère légendaire, cette histoire met bien l'accent sur ces phénomènes de trop-plein démographique que l'archéologie semble en partie confirmer.

L'obligation de virginité jusqu'à vingt ans passés que César observe chez les Germains pourrait en être un autre témoignage, car le retard de l'âge au mariage a toujours été, avec l'infanticide, un des moyens couramment utilisés par les sociétés anciennes pour limiter les naissances. « Plus on a gardé longtemps sa virginité, écrit-il, plus on est estimé par son entourage : les uns pensent qu'on devient ainsi plus grand, les autres plus fort et plus nerveux. De fait, connaître la femme avant l'âge de vingt ans est à leurs yeux une honte des plus grandes ; on ne fait pourtant point mystère de ces choses-là, car hommes et femmes se baignent ensemble dans les rivières, et d'ailleurs, ils n'ont d'autres vêtements que des peaux ou de courts rénons [gilets faits d'une fourrure d'animal] qui laissent la plus grande part du corps à nu. »

En Italie, ce sont bien des dizaines de milliers d'hommes et de femmes guidés par les Sénons qui, après avoir franchi les Alpes, écrasent les Romains à la bataille de l'Allia, détruisent Rome vers 390 avant J.-C., se gorgent de butin et s'installent massivement dans le nord de la péninsule, formant ce que les Romains appelleront la Gaule cisalpine. Une terrible humiliation dont se souviendront longtemps les habitants de la Ville éternelle.

Au sud-est de l'Europe, après avoir, en 335 avant J.-C., rencontré Alexandre le Grand et lui avoir affirmé qu'ils ne craignaient rien, si ce n'est que le ciel leur tombe sur la tête, les Celtes pénètrent en Grèce et pillent le sanctuaire sacré de Delphes en 279 avant J.-C. En Asie Mineure, ils fondent le royaume des Galates qui, bataillant sans relâche contre ses voisins de Pergame, gardera jusqu'à la fin de la domination romaine ses traditions.

Au-delà de ces raids spectaculaires et de ces aventures sans lendemain qui ont tant impressionné les auteurs grecs et latins, leur progressive et lente implantation sur le territoire de la France actuelle est bien moins connue. Tout laisse pourtant penser qu'il s'est agi ici d'infiltration plus que d'invasion, d'acculturation plus que d'occupation massive, comme en témoignent l'extension des tombes à char jusqu'au seuil du Poitou, l'apparition de fibules celtiques au cœur des Pyrénées ou les décors des poteries bretonnes fortement influencés par les productions italo-celtiques.

À l'apogée de leur expansion, de 350 à 250 avant notre ère, les peuples celtiques occupent ainsi un très vaste territoire qui s'étend des îles Britanniques et de l'Irlande à l'embouchure du Danube et de la grande plaine septentrionale allemande et polonaise jusqu'aux Apennins. Et c'est dans l'actuelle France que leur influence culturelle sera particulièrement marquée.

Une religion mystérieuse

Une des manifestations essentielles de la culture des peuples celtiques est la force du sentiment religieux, entretenue par un clergé dont l'influence sur la vie politique et sociale apparaît considérable. Les druides, dont le nom signifie « ceux qui savent » en celtique ancien, dictaient le dogme et la morale, réglaient la liturgie des cérémonies religieuses, observaient les mouvements des astres afin d'établir le calendrier nécessaire à la tenue des grandes fêtes annuelles, pansaient les blessures, réduisaient les fractures, pratiquaient la magie et transmettaient au cœur des forêts leur enseignement aux jeunes aristocrates de moins de vingt ans.

Exemptés de toute fonction militaire et d'impôts, conseillers privilégiés des rois, qui ne pouvaient apparemment rien décider sans eux, ces druides obéissaient à un chef unique qui, à sa mort, était remplacé par un autre chef désigné par élection. Spirituels, ils nous auraient légué le goût de l'éloquence et du beau parler qui semble avoir constitué, selon les Romains, le signe distinctif de la société celtique. Une fois l'an, ils se réunissaient aux environs de Chartres, dans un lieu qui passait pour occuper le centre de la Gaule, pour tenir des assises solennelles concernant aussi bien les litiges privés que les affaires concernant l'ensemble du peuple gaulois.

Leur enseignement exclusivement oral, la transcription écrite étant interdite peut-être pour tisser cette chaîne d'influences secrètes qui va de la pensée du maître à la pensée du disciple, était fondé sur la croyance à l'immortalité de l'âme, symbolisée par le gui qui reste vert lorsque tombent les feuilles du chêne sur lequel il fructifie.

« Le point essentiel de leur enseignement, écrit César, c'est que les âmes ne périssent pas, mais qu'après la mort elles passent d'un corps dans un autre ; ils pensent que cette croyance est le meilleur stimulant du courage, parce qu'on n'a plus peur de la mort. »

Cette croyance explique peut-être que les Gaulois n'hésitaient pas à se prêter entre eux des sommes remboursables dans l'autre monde et qu'ils imaginaient, au-delà de la tombe, une existence assez semblable à celle du monde dans lequel ils vivaient.

Pour eux, le « paradis » devait être ce séjour heureux où des ruisseaux d'hydromel et de vin coulaient au pied d'arbres chargés de fruits merveilleux, où la pluie était de bière et où les porcs qui paissaient dans la plaine renaissaient, sitôt mangés, pour de nouveaux festins. Un paradis matériel où la vie continuait sans fin, apportant au mort tout ce qu'il avait aimé ou désiré de son vivant. La communication entre le monde des vivants et le monde des morts se fêtait dans la nuit du 1er novembre, une nuit où les hommes offraient aux esprits menaçants les offrandes prélevées sur les fruits de la saison chaude et féconde qui s'achevait.

Alors que les religions grecque et romaine étaient organisées autour d'un panthéon hiérarchisé où chaque divinité, conçue à l'image de l'homme, avait ses attributions bien définies, la religion gauloise, même si on lui connaît plus de quatre mille dieux et déesses, semble structurée de manière assez souple autour de quelques grandes figures divines possédant de multiples attributions.

« Le dieu qu'ils honorent le plus, écrit toujours César, est Mercure : ses statues sont les plus nombreuses, ils le considèrent comme l'inventeur de tous les arts, il est pour eux le dieu qui indique la route à suivre, qui guide le voyageur, il est celui qui est le plus capable de faire gagner de l'argent et de protéger le commerce. »

Ce dieu, dont nous ne connaissons pas le nom en langue gauloise, semble l'équivalent irlandais de Lug Samildanach, le « polytechnicien », fêté le 1er août, et dont le nom Lug est à l'origine des noms de

Lyon, Laon, et Lons-le-Saunier en France. Il est à la fois charpentier, forgeron et poète, capable d'exécuter n'importe quel ouvrage.

Dieu à la ramure de cerf, Cernunnos, représenté sur un bas-relief de Reims, assis les jambes croisées sur un trône bas, un flot de monnaies s'échappant d'un grand sac qu'il tient sur ses genoux, est un dieu de l'outre-tombe en même temps que de la fécondité.

Dis Pater serait une sorte de Jupiter, la divinité paternelle des Gaulois, un dieu infernal, maître de la mort mais en même temps de la vie, époux de la Terre-Mère et père de la race des hommes.

Mais l'assimilation des dieux gaulois aux dieux romains est artificielle dans la mesure où la religion celtique semble échapper à la rationalité désespérément recherchée par les auteurs anciens, chaque dieu prenant des formes différentes selon les régions, chaque peuple ayant ses animaux divins, ses héros protecteurs, ses arbres, ses fleuves, ses eaux chaudes et ses sources sacrés. Le Gaulois, pilleur du temple de Delphes, aurait, dit-on, éclaté de rire à l'idée que les Grecs croyaient que les dieux avaient une forme humaine. Rien dans la religion gauloise ne ressemble au rituel minutieux dont usaient les Romains envers leurs dieux, à cette sorte de marchandage qu'ils établissaient chaque fois qu'ils voulaient en obtenir un service précis.

Si Taranis, le « dieu à la roue », souvent représenté par la suite sous la forme d'un cavalier écrasant un monstre à queue de serpent, est largement honoré sur l'ensemble du territoire, Epona, la « déesse au cheval », très connue à l'est du pays, est largement ignorée au sud de la Seine. Si Belisama est ici une sorte de déesse du foyer et aussi des industries du feu, de la forge, de la poterie et de l'émail, là, elle apparaît comme une divinité guerrière, une déesse féroce de la bataille et du carnage, volant comme un oiseau au-dessus des combattants et jetant la panique chez l'ennemi. Si Teutatès apparaît pour les uns comme le dieu cruel de la guerre auquel on sacrifiait des victimes en les étouffant dans un tonneau rempli d'eau, il est pour d'autres un dieu paisible et protecteur de la tribu. Si Esus semble l'inventeur de tous les arts, le maître des chemins et des voyages, le défricheur des forêts et le constructeur de péniches, il est aussi le dieu sanguinaire auquel on offrait des victimes pendues dans les arbres avant d'être mises en pièces.

Mentionnés par les auteurs anciens, ces sacrifices humains ont suscité des interprétations contradictoires et alimenté des polémiques dont la violence est à la mesure de l'attachement que nous portons à ceux que nous considérons comme nos plus proches ancêtres. Pour certains historiens, loin d'être de doux poètes grimpant dans les chênes au mois de décembre pour y couper le gui avec une faucille d'or, les druides auraient été les grands prêtres de la mort, serviteurs de divinités assoiffées de chair humaine. Alors que les paysans romains, habitués à régler leurs conflits de bornage par des arbitrages, avaient mis la violence au rang de la sauvagerie, les Gaulois, ayant pour seuls biens leurs troupeaux et leurs femmes, ne pouvaient survivre qu'en tuant. C'est la raison pour laquelle les druides auraient cultivé l'art de rendre le désir homicide conscient et recherché.

D'autres historiens se gardent de prendre au pied de la lettre des auteurs étrangers au monde gaulois qui répètent à satiété des clichés complaisants. En fait, mieux vaut faire confiance à l'archéologie, qui, sur ce terrain, apporte des informations plus précises. Ayant découvert et fouillé des sanctuaires gaulois, à Gournay-sur-Aronde, dans l'Oise, et à Ribemont-sur-Ancre, dans la Somme, Jean-Louis Brunaux montre à quel point les sacrifices humains sont une pratique exceptionnelle fondée sur une conception profondément religieuse du monde. Un tel acte, qu'il ne faut surtout pas juger avec les critères mentaux d'aujourd'hui, apparaît comme une transgression toujours clairement perçue par ceux qui y recouraient. On est fort loin des « barbares »...

Le sanctuaire de Gournay-sur-Aronde, daté d'environ 100 avant notre ère, se présente comme un ensemble quadrangulaire, d'une cinquantaine de mètres de côté, délimité par un fossé et un talus surmonté d'une palissade. Au centre, se trouvait une grande fosse, bordée par neuf fosses plus petites. Deux types de sacrifices y étaient pratiqués. Le premier consistait en une sorte de boucherie, des moutons, des porcs et même des chiens étaient mis à mort puis consommés sur place. Le second était le « privilège » du bœuf : l'animal était abattu d'un coup de hache sur la nuque avant d'être égorgé. Déposée dans la grande fosse du sanctuaire où elle séjournait plusieurs mois, sa dépouille était offerte au dieu souterrain qui se nourrissait du produit de la putréfaction. Le crâne était alors récupéré pour être exposé sur la clôture du sanctuaire au milieu de crânes humains suspendus tandis que la carcasse était jetée dans le fossé, où gisaient aussi des armes prises à l'ennemi et des os longs humains portant des traces de coups ou de découpe.

À Ribemont-sur-Ancre, un spectaculaire ossuaire contenait des milliers de trophées qui, au lieu d'être seulement faits d'armes, comme dans le monde grec et romain, incluaient aussi les corps des guerriers ficelés à des poteaux pour être conservés et exposés. Placé en bordure extérieure, un trophée collectif comprenait environ 60 personnes qui, rangées, semble-t-il, en rang d'oignons, formaient une sorte de bataillon funèbre, placé environ à la hauteur d'un étage, dans un bâtiment couvert. Compte tenu de la quasi-absence des crânes, on peut admettre qu'il s'agit de guerriers vaincus et décapités. Les sujets sont en effet presque toujours masculins, jeunes et, chez beaucoup, la puissance des insertions musculaires semble confirmer qu'il s'agit d'une population entraînée au combat. Le fait que les armes, de très bonne qualité, soient restées très longtemps suspendues, certainement cinquante ou soixante ans avant d'être rongées par les intempéries, confirmerait l'hypothèse de trophées. En outre, si les rites de dépeçage des corps ne font aucun doute, les conditions de la mort, au combat ou par sacrifice, restent mystérieuses.

Un pays de cocagne

Loin d'être de féroces éleveurs de troupeaux habitant dans de misérables huttes au milieu des forêts, les Gaulois apparaissent comme les acteurs éclairés d'une économie en plein développement. Richesse et fécondité, tels sont les mots qui reviennent sans cesse dans les descriptions que font de la Gaule les voyageurs anciens. « Pour le quart d'une obole, s'émerveille Polybe, l'hôtelier vous fournit un repas qui ne laisse rien à désirer et la vie est si facile que l'on compte par tête, globalement, au lieu de faire un prix de détail. »

Pline l'Ancien énumère les techniques de marnage qui font le blé abondant et moins cher que partout ailleurs. « Il y a une méthode que la Gaule et la [Grande-] Bretagne ont inventée et qui consiste à engraisser la terre par la terre ; celle-ci se nomme « marne ». Elle passe pour renfermer nombre de principes féconds. C'est une espèce de graisse terrestre comparable aux glandes dans le corps et qui se condense en noyaux [...] Il convient de parler avec soin de cette marne qui enrichit la Gaule et la [Grande-] Bretagne. On n'en connaissait que deux espèces, mais récemment l'usage de plusieurs espèces a été introduit par les progrès de l'agriculture. »

Il décrit aussi une curiosité qui a été considérée comme la première machine à moissonner : « Dans les vastes domaines de la Gaule, une grande caisse dont le bord est armé de dents et que portent deux roues est conduite dans le champ de blé par un bœuf qui la pousse devant lui ; les épis arrachés par les dents tombent dans la caisse. »

Si, bien avant leur arrivée, les campagnes étaient déjà largement défrichées et produisaient en abondance blé, orge et millet, les Celtes ont mis au point la plupart des outils de fer qui allaient, jusqu'au XIX⁰ siècle, constituer l'outillage de base de toute exploitation rurale : les grandes faux qui permettent de couper l'herbe haute, les serpettes, les haches, les bêches, les houes, les faucilles et les forces pour tondre les moutons. Surtout, grâce à la charrue à coutre de fer qui remplace avantageusement l'araire, ils ont considérablement amélioré le labour et pu mettre en culture les terres les plus lourdes.

Cette efficacité de l'agriculture a permis une expansion démographique sans précédent, à tel point que la Gaule compte peut-être 8 millions d'habitants à la veille des conquêtes de Jules César, des habitants qui exportent leurs produits et se régalent de salaisons, de jambons, d'oies, de fromage et même de foies gras, et dont les porcs, remarque Strabon, acquièrent ici « une vigueur et une vitesse si grandes qu'il y a danger à s'en approcher quand on n'en est pas connu et qu'un loup lui-même courrait de grands risques à le faire ».

Cet enrichissement global d'une population croissante explique aussi le formidable développement de l'artisanat et du commerce. Les Gaulois étaient un peuple de techniciens, avec une ingéniosité et un esprit ouvert qu'ils ont peut-être légués aux Français d'aujourd'hui.

Incomparables dans le travail du fer, les Gaulois sont aussi des charpentiers, des potiers, des mouleurs, des ciseleurs et des verriers réputés. C'est à eux que l'on doit le pas de vis, qui ouvrait de nombreuses possibilités à la mécanique et à la construction. Dès cette époque, à l'est du pays, apparaît une technique de pointe : de minces lames de fer, tressées ensemble, puis martelées, donnent les premières épées damasquinées. Bronziers habiles, ils laminent le métal pour en faire des vases ou le fondent pour en faire des fibules, des bracelets et des torques qui sont comme l'insigne de la nationalité gauloise. Ils argentent la vaisselle ou les tôles de bronze qui garnissent les chars et fabriquent des émaux remarquables. Ils produisent aussi en série le verre plat utilisé pour les fenêtres, les vases à boire, les bouteilles trapues, les gobelets, les coupes et les vases à parfum.

Sans rivaux pour le travail du bois, ils ont inventé le tonneau, qui remplace avantageusement l'amphore. Et tous les chariots utilisés à Rome étaient soit achetés en Gaule soit copiés sur des modèles gaulois, à tel point que tous les noms de véhicules, en latin, sont des mots gaulois. Premiers en Europe à fabriquer du savon, bons cordonniers (les *gallicae* sont de grosses galoches à semelles épaisses) ils manifestent enfin leur fantaisie dans le domaine de l'habillement en confectionnant des chemises ouvertes, des braies et des manteaux en étoffes de couleur vive, décorées de bandes verticales ou de carreaux alternés qui étonnent les Romains habitués à l'uniformité des pièces de toile écrue.

Agriculture, élevage et artisanat alimentent un commerce de grande ampleur qu'illustrent les épaves chargées de vin italien retrouvées près des côtes méditerranéennes. On estime que de cinq cent mille à un million d'amphores arrivaient tous les ans en Gaule afin de s'échanger contre l'étain, le cuir, les salaisons, le bétail et, surtout, les esclaves, dont la livraison implique des guerres permanentes entre peuples voisins pour fournir cette précieuse marchandise humaine. Le vin, en effet, écrit Diodore de Sicile, « inspire aux Gaulois une véritable passion ; ils absorbent pur celui qu'introduisent chez eux les marchands et leur gourmandise les portant à en boire largement, ils s'enivrent jusqu'au sommeil ou à l'égarement. C'est pourquoi de nombreux commerçants italiens, poussés par leur habituelle cupidité, font de ce penchant des Gaulois pour le vin une source de profits. Par bateaux, sur les fleuves navigables, ou bien par voie de terre et par chariots, ils importent du vin et reçoivent en échange de la boisson l'esclave qui l'a servie ».

Les monnaies témoignent aussi de cette activité commerciale intense. Imitant à l'origine les statères d'or de Philippe de Macédoine, frappés entre 359 et 336 avant notre ère, les peuples du centre de la Gaule finissent par adopter la monnaie d'argent sur laquelle ils gravent des sangliers, des chevaux à tête humaine, des personnages dansants ou des génies volants. En outre, l'apparition d'un étalon aligné sur le demi-denier d'argent romain et la drachme de Marseille suppose l'émergence d'une sorte de zone économique avec des monnaies interchangeables et des hommes d'affaires capables de négocier les termes de l'échange.

L'or, exploité activement dans le Limousin mais aussi dans les Pyrénées, excitait aussi l'imagination des étrangers, qui voyaient dans la Gaule un véritable Eldorado. Dans ce pays, explique Diodore de Sicile, les fleuves, « en érodant le flanc des montagnes, amoncellent des alluvions et des sables pleins d'or. Les indigènes qui ne sont pas occupés à d'autres travaux recueillent ce sable et le criblent. C'est ainsi que les Gaulois ramassent de grandes quantités d'or dont ils font des ornements non seulement pour les femmes mais pour les hommes qui portent des bracelets, des colliers et même des cuirasses d'or ».

Enfin, accompagnant et contrôlant le progrès économique, naissent les premières villes que César appelle *oppida*. Généralement situées à proximité des voies de communication et des grandes zones agricoles, protégées par un fossé profond et un mur d'environ 4 mètres d'épaisseur qui marque physiquement la séparation entre « ville » et « campagne », elles sont prêtes à accueillir des foules les jours de foire, de fêtes religieuses ou à servir de refuge contre des envahisseurs et des pillards. Mais çà et là, des monuments exceptionnels, des quartiers spécialisés annoncent un premier urbanisme. Ainsi, les fouilles de Bibracte, la capitale des Éduens, sur le mont Beuvray, près d'Autun, ont révélé un espace réellement aménagé, avec une fontaine publique qui a pu être datée de 126 avant notre ère et dont les techniques de construction rappellent celles utilisées à la même époque en Italie, ainsi qu'un bassin monumental de granite rose qui évoque une coque de navire et constituerait le « nombril » de la cité, le point sacré à partir duquel elle aurait été fondée et organisée, des voies, des maisons de riches et des maisons de pauvres, des auberges et des ateliers de production de fibules travaillant pour toute une région.

Si les fouilles de Bibracte révèlent la naissance d'une ville enrichie par le commerce et l'industrie, on se demande ce que pouvaient être Avaricum (Bourges), « la plus belle presque des villes de la Gaule », selon César, Lutèce, Cabillonum (Chalon-sur-Saône), Cenabum (Orléans), Rotomagus (Rouen) qui constituent la première trame d'un réseau urbain.

Toutes ces découvertes comme celle, récente, d'une maison de Vaize, près de Lyon, qui porte des enduits peints du même style que ceux retrouvés à Pompéi montrent l'intensité des relations tissées entre la Gaule et l'ensemble du monde antique. Si, pour les Romains, les Gaulois apparaissaient comme des êtres féroces et inquiétants, la Gaule était toujours vantée comme un pays de cocagne où les ressources agricoles étaient considérables, les réserves d'or abondantes et les possibles esclaves nombreux. Danger potentiel, péril permanent, la Gaule était aussi le plus désirable des marchés à prendre.

10

La guerre des Gaules

*L*a guerre des Gaules ne commence pas avec les premières campagnes
de Jules César en 58 avant J.-C., mais en 390 avant J.-C., quand les
Gaulois, déferlant sur l'Italie, sont devenus l'ennemi « héréditaire » qu'il
fallait réduire. La reconquête de l'Italie du Nord achevée, la province de
la Gaule narbonnaise fondée, Rome peut se lancer à l'assaut d'une Gaule
divisée et menacée au nord par les Germains. L'échec, en 52 avant J.-C.,
de la révolte menée par Vercingétorix, vaincu à Alésia par des Romains
passés maîtres dans l'art des sièges, marque la fin de la Gaule indépendante.

Les Gaulois pris en tenailles

Le pillage de Rome par les Gaulois en - 390 et le massacre des
patriciens ont été pour les Romains une terrible humiliation. Il faut
relire le récit qu'en a fait l'historien romain Tite-Live pour mesurer la
honte ressentie par son peuple : « Alors le Sénat se réunit et chargea
les tribuns militaires de traiter avec l'ennemi. Il y eut une entrevue du
tribun militaire Quintus Sulpicius et du chef des Gaulois Brennus. Un
accord fut conclu et on estima à mille livres d'or la rançon d'un peuple
appelé à devenir bientôt le maître du monde. À cette honte vint s'ajouter un outrage : les Gaulois avaient apporté des poids et, comme le
tribun les refusait, l'insolent ennemi y ajouta son épée et fit entendre
ces paroles intolérables pour les Romains : « Malheur aux vaincus ! »

Ce « malheur aux vaincus » a résonné longtemps dans la cité du Latium. Rome avait une revanche à prendre contre ces Gaulois féroces et sacrilèges, pillards et perfides, instables et batailleurs et dont la monstrueuse religion exigeait des sacrifices humains.

Il fallut tout d'abord plus d'un siècle pour s'affranchir de la menace que faisaient peser les Celtes installés en Italie du Nord où ils développaient une civilisation brillante au contact des Grecs et des Étrusques. Après avoir soumis les Sénons en 283 avant J.-C. et s'être emparée de leur territoire, qui s'étendait d'Ancône à Rimini, Rome s'ouvrait la route du Nord. Après la prise de Milan en 222 avant J.-C., la Gaule cisalpine qui l'avait tant narguée était subjuguée.

Toutefois l'aide que les Gaulois offrirent au Carthaginois Hannibal pour franchir les cols des Alpes et renforcer son armée démontrait que le péril n'était toujours pas exorcisé. Le sort de la Gaule indépendante, celle qui s'étendait au-delà des Alpes, allait être désormais lié à la stratégie de Rome en Méditerranée occidentale. Quand l'Espagne fut définitivement conquise, en 133 avant J.-C., le contrôle des territoires de la côte, entre les Alpes et les Pyrénées, ne semblait plus qu'une question de temps, surtout quand Marseille, la fidèle alliée des Romains, fit appel à eux pour assurer sa sécurité.

En 181, Rome était intervenue une première fois pour la débarrasser des pirates qui attaquaient ses bateaux sur la côte ligure, entre Gênes et Nice. En 154, elle envoya pour la première fois des troupes pour écraser deux peuplades qui assiégeaient les comptoirs d'Antibes et de Nice. En 125 enfin, Marseille ayant une nouvelle fois appelé au secours contre les Salyens qui ravageaient son territoire, Rome décida de s'installer dans la région que la cité alliée semblait impuissante à contrôler. En 124, le consul C. Sextius Calvinus s'empara de l'imposant oppidum d'Entremont et installa, au carrefour des routes d'Italie, de Marseille et de la Gaule, un poste fortifié en un lieu où jaillissaient des sources chaudes. Ces eaux, *aquae*, associées à son nom Sextius, donnèrent *Aquae Sextiae*, la future ville thermale d'Aix-en-Provence.

Les Allobroges, installés sur la rive gauche du Rhône, et les Arvernes, qui étaient parmi les peuples les plus puissants de la Gaule, étant intervenus, une autre armée romaine infligea, au confluent de l'Isère et du Rhône, une cuisante défaite au roi arverne Bituit (ou Bituitos) qui, selon les auteurs anciens, s'avançait sur son char garni d'argent, entouré des chiens de sa meute. « S'ils viennent comme ambassadeurs, aurait-il dit des Romains, ils sont bien nombreux ; si c'est pour se battre, il y a là à peine pour la curée de mes chiens. »

Après cette victoire, Rome put affirmer son emprise et fonder, en 118 avant J.-C., sa première colonie en Gaule, Narbonne, qui porta le nom du dieu de la guerre, Mars (*Narbo Martius*), et devint ensuite la capitale d'une nouvelle province, la Gaule narbonnaise, appelée également transalpine. Cette même année commença la construction de la route qui allait réaliser la liaison terrestre entre l'Espagne et l'Italie, la *via Domitia*, du nom du consul Domitius Ahénobarbus, resté sur place pour organiser la nouvelle conquête qui s'étendait d'Antibes à Toulouse et du lac Léman au delta du Rhône. Pour les Gaulois, la route de la Méditerranée était désormais fermée.

Refoulés du Sud par les Romains, les Gaulois étaient menacés au nord par de nouveaux peuples migrateurs, les Germains, qui n'avaient pas encore été amollis par les raffinements de la civilisation. « Il fut un temps, écrit Jules César, où les Gaulois surpassaient les Germains en bravoure, portaient la guerre chez eux, envoyaient des colonies au-delà du Rhin parce qu'ils étaient trop nombreux et n'avaient pas assez de terres [...]. Mais aujourd'hui, tandis que les Germains continuent de mener une vie de pauvreté et de privations patiemment supportées, qu'ils n'ont rien changé à leur alimentation ni à leur vêtement, les Gaulois, au contraire, grâce au voisinage de nos provinces et au commerce maritime, ont appris à connaître la vie large et à en jouir : peu à peu, ils se sont accoutumés à être les plus faibles et, maintes fois vaincus, ils renoncent eux-mêmes à se comparer aux Germains pour la valeur militaire. »

En deux vagues, au IIIe puis au IIe siècle avant notre ère, les Belges, qui se disaient Germains malgré la racine celtique de leur nom, traversent le Rhin et occupent le nord de la France actuelle. Rèmes (autour de Reims), Atrébates (en Artois), Ambiens (autour d'Amiens), Bellovaques (dans la région de Beauvais) puis, dans un second temps Morins, Ménapes, Nerviens, Éburons, Atuatuques (entre Pas-de-Calais et Pays-Bas actuels) refoulent au sud de la Seine et de la Marne et à l'est de la Meuse les peuples qui occupaient autrefois ces territoires. Tandis que les Séquanes de la Seine se déplacent vers la Franche-Comté, d'autres choisissent d'aller s'établir outre-Manche. Les tombes à char disparaissent alors de Champagne, le foyer ancestral à partir duquel les Celtes s'étaient répandus en Gaule, pour apparaître au même moment en Angleterre.

Vers 120 avant J.-C., quittant les rives de la mer du Nord et le Jutland, Cimbres et Teutons, deux autres peuples germaniques, amorcent leur marche vers le sud pour s'installer en Europe centrale. Envoyée à leur rencontre, une armée romaine est écrasée à Noreia, dans le Norique. Remontant alors vers le nord-est, ils passent le Rhin, envahissent la Gaule, dont les habitants se retranchent dans les *oppida*, battent une nouvelle armée romaine puis se détournent vers l'Aquitaine. En 105 avant J.-C., ils se lancent à l'attaque de la Transalpine et écrasent à nouveau près d'Orange une armée de 80 000 hommes. La route de l'Italie est ouverte mais ils ne l'empruntent pas encore, poursuivant leurs razzias et leurs raids meurtriers en Gaule et en Espagne. En 103, enfin, comme autrefois les Gaulois, ils semblent vouloir prendre le chemin de l'Italie, mais ils sont définitivement arrêtés par le consul Marius près d'Aix-en-Provence, en 102, et en Italie du Nord, en 101.

Cette folle équipée, qui avait réveillé chez les Romains le cauchemar des incursions gauloises, allait avoir des conséquences importantes. Elle leur révélait en effet que ces Gaulois qu'ils avaient tant redoutés n'étaient plus assez vaillants pour s'opposer à ces nouveaux Barbares venus du nord et que la Gaule était militairement trop faible pour constituer un rempart efficace. Pris en tenailles entre la pression des Germains au nord et les intérêts stratégiques des Romains au sud, les Celtes de Gaule pouvaient craindre pour leur indépendance et pour leur liberté.

Une proie facile

Il fallut près de soixante années, deux générations, pour que la menace romaine devienne réalité. Pour consolider le « glacis » qui la séparait des Germains, Rome n'envisagea pas, en effet, la conquête immédiate de la Gaule. Une politique d'alliance avec des peuples « amis » lui semblait suffisante. Tenant solidement en main la riche Transalpine, Rome préféra s'appuyer sur des élites indigènes qui avaient plus d'appétit pour se faire « acheter » que pour résister aux charmes du mode de vie romain.

Accorder la citoyenneté romaine, attirer les enfants des notables dans la Ville éternelle pour les éduquer, livrer des parts substantielles de butin aux soldats qui accompagnaient les légions romaines à titre d'auxiliaires, faire couler à flots le vin tant prisé, tels étaient les meilleurs moyens de « romaniser » des élites plus sensibles aux signes de la réussite sociale qu'aux vertus d'un patriotisme gaulois dont les manifestations sont fort difficiles à repérer. Il suffit pour s'en convaincre de voir avec quel empressement certains princes gaulois romanisent leur nom et s'empressent de porter les insignes de leur nouveau statut.

En fait, si les Gaulois avaient la même langue et les mêmes traditions, les mêmes rendez-vous religieux et les mêmes prêtres, la Gaule était une mosaïque de peuples indépendants, sans cesse en conflit, qui se présentait comme une proie facile à quiconque voulait la prendre.

Si la Gaule fut incapable de réagir à la poussée des Germains, c'est que peuples et familles étaient sans cesse déchirés par des rivalités internes. Un peu partout, le pouvoir appartenait à des ambitieux que César appelle les equites, les « chevaliers », dont l'influence reposait sur leur capacité à grouper autour d'eux le maximum de « clients ». « En Gaule, écrit toujours César qui a su diviser pour régner, non seulement toutes les cités, tous les cantons et fractions de cantons, mais même, peut-on dire, toutes les familles sont divisées en partis rivaux ; à la tête de ces partis sont les hommes à qui l'on accorde le plus de crédit ; c'est à ceux-là qu'il appartient de juger en dernier ressort pour toutes les affaires à régler, pour toutes les décisions à prendre. »

Chez les Éduens, et probablement chez bon nombre d'autres peuples, le pouvoir exécutif revenait à un magistrat qui portait le titre de vergobret. C'était un juge souverain qui avait droit de vie et de mort sur tous. Mais de nombreuses précautions étaient prises pour limiter une puissance qui pouvait se révéler dangereuse. Sa magistrature ne durait qu'un an ; il ne pouvait franchir les frontières de la cité et ne paraissait pas à la tête des armées, si ce n'est après être sorti de charge. Il lui était donc malaisé de devenir conquérant ou usurpateur.

Les lois éduennes, en particulier, avaient multiplié les règlements de prudence destinés à freiner l'ardeur des ambitieux. Il ne devait pas y avoir, dans la cité, deux chefs appartenant à la même famille et le « sénat » qui rassemblait les chefs de tribu ou les chefs de famille ne pouvait non plus renfermer deux parents. Mais ces règles n'empêchaient pas le désordre qu'engendrait le clientélisme.

Dépourvus de toute influence politique, écrasés par le poids des dettes et des impôts, les gens du peuple n'avaient comme ressource que de se donner à ceux qui avaient les moyens de les protéger. Ces puissants se partageaient en fait en deux grands « partis », les proromains et les autres, qui redoutaient la perte de leur indépendance et d'une certaine « identité » gauloise. Ainsi, chez les Éduens, qui étaient à la fois l'un des peuples les plus puissants de la Gaule et les alliés fidèles de Rome, Diviciac, un druide que l'on pourrait considérer comme défenseur des valeurs traditionnelles, était venu à Rome, où il s'était ménagé des amitiés, celle de Cicéron notamment, qui parle de lui comme d'un homme distingué, tandis que son frère Dumnorix, qui s'était considérablement enrichi, appelait son peuple à défendre sa liberté. Ces rivalités expliquent sans doute que la Gaule, qui avait apparemment tout pour résister, la richesse et le nombre d'habitants, ait été conquise en six ans seulement alors que Rome avait mis deux siècles à maîtriser l'Espagne.

La Gaule conquise

La faiblesse de la Gaule, ouverte aux influences romaines, divisée en cités rivales, impuissante à faire face à la menace des Germains, apparaît de plus en plus évidente en ce Ier siècle avant J.-C. et semble ouvrir la voie à une possible conquête.

Encore fallait-il que l'occasion se présente et qu'un homme de génie ait l'habileté de l'exploiter. C'est le hasard qui en décida. En mars de l'année 58 avant J.-C., on apprit à Rome qu'un peuple de la Gaule indépendante, les Helvètes, qui occupait le territoire de la Suisse actuelle, se préparait à gagner le territoire des Santons, dans l'actuelle Saintonge. Une migration pacifique décidée deux ans plus tôt, avec probablement l'accord des peuples concernés. Toutes les mesures avaient en effet été prises. Ils avaient établi la liste des émigrants, rassemblé du blé pour trois mois, construit les chariots, brûlé leurs fermes et leurs villages et s'étaient rassemblés sur les bords du Rhône, à sa sortie du lac Léman. Il revenait au gouverneur de la Gaule transalpine de prendre toutes les mesures nécessaires pour surveiller cette opération.

Or, depuis le 1er janvier 58, ce gouverneur se nommait Caius Julius Caesar, désigné dans des circonstances exceptionnelles qui méritent d'être soulignées. Cet homme qui, à quarante-trois ans, selon une anecdote probablement fausse, avait pleuré devant une statue d'Alexandre le Grand en s'accusant de n'avoir encore rien fait à un âge où Alexandre avait déjà soumis l'univers, et qui se flattait d'avoir pour lointaine ancêtre la déesse Vénus, rêvait de jouer un rôle politique à la mesure de ses ambitions. Or, face aux deux « grands » de l'époque, Pompée, auréolé de ses victoires en Orient, et Crassus, l'homme le plus riche de Rome, César n'avait à son actif que quelques maigres succès remportés en Espagne. Pour surpasser ses rivaux et réaliser sa formidable ambition, il lui fallait remporter de grandes victoires et amasser une solide fortune.

Élu consul en 59 avant J.-C., César devait, selon la loi, se voir confier à sa sortie de charge le gouvernement d'une province. Le Sénat, qui se méfiait de son ambition, avait décidé que ces provinces seraient deux misérables districts de l'Italie méridionale tout juste bonnes à faire paître quelques chèvres. Il fallut l'intervention d'un tribun dévoué à sa cause pour faire passer devant le peuple un plébiscite lui confiant pour une durée exceptionnelle de cinq ans la Gaule cisalpine et l'Illyricum (les régions côtières de l'ex-Yougoslavie). César ne put réprimer sa joie. Au nord de ces deux provinces, en effet, coulait un fleuve mythique et gigantesque, le Danube, au-delà duquel s'étendaient de vastes et riches plaines habitées par des peuples mystérieux et inquiétants qui pouvaient fondre à tout moment sur l'Italie. Comme Alexandre, César pouvait rêver d'atteindre un fleuve légendaire, de conquérir un nouveau monde, de l'ouvrir au commerce et de livrer de glorieux combats. Le hasard en décida autrement. Le proconsul de la Gaule transalpine étant mort subitement dans des conditions mystérieuses, le Sénat ajouta le midi de la France au gouvernement confié à César. C'était donc à lui de régler la question helvète.

Aux ambassadeurs qui lui demandèrent de traverser le nord de la province romaine en l'assurant qu'ils ne commettraient aucun dégât, il opposa un ferme refus. Et quand les Helvètes décidèrent d'emprunter un autre itinéraire, plus au nord, il décida, de sa propre initiative, de les attaquer en grossissant, dans ses rapports envoyés au Sénat, la menace que représentait cette pacifique migration. Ainsi s'ouvrait la conquête de la Gaule.

Ayant taillé en pièces les Helvètes et ordonné aux survivants de retourner d'où ils venaient, César s'installa chez ses « amis » éduens qui lui offrirent l'hospitalité dans leur oppidum de Bibracte. C'est là qu'il reçut les représentants de presque tous les peuples de la Gaule, qui non seulement le félicitèrent d'avoir délivré le pays de l'« invasion » mais surtout le prièrent de les débarrasser du péril que faisait peser sur eux le Germain Arioviste, une supplique qui montrait à quel point les Gaulois avaient capitulé devant les périls extérieurs.

« À moins qu'ils ne trouvent une aide auprès de César et du peuple romain, expliquèrent-ils, tous les Gaulois seront dans la nécessité de faire ce qu'ont fait les Helvètes, d'émigrer, de chercher d'autres toits, d'autres terres, loin des Germains, de tenter enfin la fortune, quelle qu'elle puisse être [...]. Mais César, par son prestige personnel et celui de son armée, grâce à sa récente victoire, grâce au respect qu'inspire le nom romain, peut empêcher qu'un plus grand nombre de Germains ne franchisse le Rhin et protéger toute la Gaule contre les violences d'Arioviste. »

Promu par les Gaulois eux-mêmes « sauveur » et bouclier de la Gaule, César voyait s'ouvrir devant lui des horizons inespérés. S'il n'avait probablement pas envisagé la conquête au moment où il avait pris ses fonctions, l'occasion qui lui était offerte était trop belle pour qu'il la laisse passer. Après avoir tenté de négocier avec le Germain,

La conquête de la Gaule par César.

César le mit en déroute au sud des Vosges et l'obligea à repasser le Rhin. En un seul été, et par deux succès éclatants, il venait de régler pour un long temps le destin de la Gaule en posant comme principe que le Rhin était la frontière « naturelle » qui devait désormais séparer le monde « barbare » du monde « civilisé ». C'est lui qui, en fait, crée de toutes pièces deux « pays » quand il décrète et écrit que le Rhin est la grande frontière entre *Gallia* et *Germania* alors que la civilisation « celtique » ou « gauloise » chevauchait largement cette limite. Encore fallait-il imposer sa loi à ceux qui, trop éloignés de Rome et de ses marchands, interdisaient absolument l'importation du vin et de tout autre produit de luxe susceptible d'amollir leur volonté et d'affaiblir leur courage.

C'est la raison pour laquelle, en 57 avant J.-C., César fonça sur la Belgique, sachant qu'une victoire sur ces redoutables guerriers lui vaudrait un prestige considérable. Ayant obtenu la précieuse collaboration du premier des peuples belges qu'il aborda, les Rèmes, il battit facilement Bellovaques, Nerviens et Atuatuques. Dans le même temps, son lieutenant Publius Crassus obtenait la soumission des peuples de l'Armorique. Ces victoires, obtenues sur des terres pratiquement inconnues des Romains et sur lesquelles, pensaient-ils, régnait l'hiver un froid cruel qui glaçait les cours d'eau, produisirent l'effet escompté. Le Sénat ordonna quinze jours d'actions de grâce envers les dieux, un « honneur » jamais célébré auparavant à pareille échelle.

César consacra les années suivantes à de folles entreprises qui ne peuvent se comprendre que par la volonté de frapper les imaginations en réalisant des exploits que personne avant lui n'avait accomplis. Franchir le Rhin et pénétrer dans des contrées inhospitalières, construire en quelques mois une flotte et détruire les deux cents navires que les Vénètes avaient rassemblés dans le golfe du Morbihan, leur enlever les clés des relations commerciales avec la Bretagne (nous dirions la Grande-Bretagne), traverser la Manche où, selon les auteurs anciens, la grisaille générale empêchait de distinguer la mer du rivage et dont l'apparence pouvait, selon Pythéas le Massaliote qui l'avait explorée vers 330 avant J.-C., se comparer à une méduse transparente, étaient des opérations de propagande qu'un discours flagorneur de Cicéron sur les provinces consulaires, prononcé en juin 56, nous permet d'apprécier : « Quoi de plus âpre, s'exclamait le célèbre orateur, que ces terres, de plus mal policé que ces villes, de plus sauvage que ces peuplades, mais aussi de plus admirable que toutes ces victoires, de plus lointain que l'Océan ?... César a remporté des succès complets dans des engagements très importants sur les peuplades les plus belliqueuses et les plus puissantes des Germains et des Helvètes ; toutes les autres, il a réussi à les effrayer, les repousser, les dompter, les habituer à obéir à l'autorité du peuple romain, si bien que des contrées et des nations que ni la littérature, ni la tradition orale, ni la légende ne nous avaient fait connaître déjà ont été parcourues par notre général, par notre armée et par les armes du peuple romain. »

La Gaule insurgée

Les victoires remportées par César, on a eu l'occasion de le souligner, ne peuvent se comprendre que par l'appui actif que les Gaulois eux-mêmes lui ont assuré. Ce sont les Séquanes, les Éduens, les Rèmes, les Lingons (de la région de Langres) et même les Arvernes qui, n'ayant dans un premier temps pas bougé, lui ont permis de vaincre les Helvètes et les Belges et de contrôler un territoire de près de 500 000 kilomètres carrés avec une armée qui n'a jamais dépassé 50 000 hommes. Comment expliquer alors la grande révolte qui, en 52 avant J.-C., va rassembler derrière Vercingétorix la quasi-totalité des peuples gaulois insurgés pour défendre leur liberté et leur « patrie » ?

Certainement par le fait que César a multiplié les maladresses, réalisant l'exploit d'unir ceux qui avaient toujours été divisés ! Se comportant tout d'abord en maître absolu, il a indisposé ses plus fidèles alliés, en détrônant là un roi ou un magistrat pour le remplacer par un homme à lui, en renversant à sa guise les pouvoirs établis, en ne comprenant pas la complexité des relations entre des peuples dont les Romains ignoraient les coutumes, en trahissant sa parole, faisant mettre à mort des chefs révoltés auxquels il avait pourtant promis le pardon. L'une de ses plaisanteries en dit long sur le mépris qu'il a pu afficher au cours de son commandement : « Envoie-moi qui tu veux, écrit-il à Cicéron, j'en ferai un roi en Gaule ! »

Peut-être aussi a-t-il sous-estimé l'indignation que ses campagnes « terroristes » ont pu soulever. Outre les 600 000 ou 700 000 tués, ce qui constitue peut-être le total des pertes gauloises, soit le dixième de la population que comptait alors la Gaule indépendante, le demi-million de prisonniers vendus comme esclaves, la dévastation systématique des campagnes, César s'est livré à de véritables opérations d'extermination, comme celles dont furent victimes, en 53, les Éburons. Ces derniers s'étant révoltés, César voulut, écrit-il lui-même, « anéantir leur race et leur nom même » : une définition anticipée de ce qu'on nomme un génocide.

Toujours est-il qu'à l'automne de l'année 53, dans la forêt sacrée des Carnutes, alors que César est retenu en Italie et que les critiques se multiplient contre son action, les druides semblent appeler le pays à la guerre sainte pour l'indépendance. « Mieux vaut mourir en combattant que de ne pas recouvrer l'antique honneur militaire et la liberté que les aïeux ont légués », telles sont les nobles paroles que

César prête aux insurgés. À la date prévue du soulèvement, en janvier 52, des citoyens et des négociants romains établis à Cenabum (Orléans) sont égorgés. Le signal étant ainsi donné, la nouvelle est transmise à toutes les cités par un système de relais vocaux dont l'efficacité semble remarquable, puisque le jour même la nouvelle est reçue chez les Arvernes, à 250 kilomètres à vol d'oiseau de Cenabum.

C'est alors qu'apparaît pour la première fois un personnage appelé à jouer un rôle capital dans l'histoire mythologique de la France, Vercingétorix, dont le nom signifie « le roi suprême de ceux qui marchent à l'ennemi ». Âgé de moins de trente ans, fils de Celtillos, qui avait été mis à mort par ses compatriotes pour avoir voulu rétablir la royauté, Vercingétorix connaît bien les Romains. Il a chevauché avec les contingents gaulois plus ou moins volontaires enrôlés en gage de fidélité. Il a même reçu le titre d'« ami du chef romain ». Banni par son oncle qui dirigeait le parti proromain, il s'empare bientôt du pouvoir en recrutant ceux que César appelle les miséreux et la canaille. C'est probablement le passé prestigieux du peuple arverne qui lui vaut d'être promu à l'unanimité au commandement des peuples qui, les uns après les autres, se rangent dans le camp de l'insurrection.

César ayant pu regagner son armée et reprendre l'initiative des opérations en châtiant les Carnutes, Vercingétorix réussit à imposer une nouvelle tactique peu conforme aux traditions gauloises : la tactique de la terre brûlée. Plutôt que d'affronter l'armée romaine, il faut l'affamer en détruisant sur son chemin tous les points possibles de ravitaillement, les fermes, les granges, les bourgs et même les villes. Il suffira alors d'exterminer les détachements que César sera bien contraint d'envoyer au loin pour se procurer le blé et le fourrage. Si les Gaulois trouvent ces mesures dures et cruelles, plaide Vercingétorix pour les convaincre, « ils doivent trouver bien plus dur encore que leurs enfants et leurs femmes soient emmenés en esclavage et qu'eux-mêmes soient égorgés : car c'est là le sort qui fatalement attend les vaincus ».

Aussitôt, les incendies s'allument de tous les côtés. Le jeune Arverne cède toutefois aux Bituriges. Ceux-ci le supplient d'épargner leur capitale Avaricum (Bourges), « la plus belle de toute la Gaule » et qui, défendue naturellement par des cours d'eau et des marais, semblait imprenable.

Avaricum tomba pourtant, au terme d'un siège difficile de vingt-cinq jours qui démontra la science des légionnaires en matière de technique de siège. Seuls 800 habitants sur 40 000 échappèrent à un carnage qui n'a rien de commun avec les pratiques habituelles des Romains et témoigne d'une sorte de folie meurtrière. Alors que la ville renfermait une population de qualité exceptionnelle, des artisans de pointe, des métallurgistes de talent qui auraient été facilement vendus en Espagne, des femmes et des filles de familles nobles qui constituaient un gibier de choix pour le personnel des grandes maisons romaines ou les bordels de Rome et de la Campanie, les légionnaires de César ont préféré exterminer ce formidable butin humain.

Ce grave échec qui livrait aux Romains des vivres en quantité considérable ne fit pourtant que consolider l'autorité de Vercingétorix. N'avait-il pas eu raison de préconiser l'incendie de la ville ? « Ce n'est point par leur valeur et en bataille rangée que les Romains ont triomphé, déclara-t-il pour encourager les siens au lendemain de la défaite, mais grâce à une technique, à un art des sièges qui ont surpris l'ignorance des Gaulois. On se trompe, si l'on s'attend, dans la guerre, à n'avoir que des succès. Pour lui, il n'a jamais été d'avis de défendre Avaricum, eux-mêmes en sont témoins ; le malheur est dû au manque de sagesse des Bituriges et à l'excessive complaisance des autres. N'importe, il aura vite fait de le réparer par de plus importants succès. »

La victoire qu'il remporta sur le chef romain à Gergovie eut, à cet égard, un énorme retentissement. Voulant frapper le cœur de la rébellion en pays arverne et anéantir la révolte gauloise grâce à une victoire décisive, César suit Vercingétorix, qui se dirige vers son oppidum de Gergovie, près de Clermont-Ferrand. Établissant son camp principal dans la plaine, il cherche l'occasion propice pour prendre d'assaut une colline particulièrement difficile d'accès.

Ayant observé qu'un secteur du mur d'enceinte était peu protégé, il tente une attaque surprise qui est repoussée. Même si les pertes romaines sont limitées à 700 hommes, cette victoire fouetta le moral des insurgés et rallia les indécis. Ainsi, les Éduens, les plus anciens alliés des Romains, abandonnèrent César et prirent la cité de *Noviodunum* (peut-être Nevers) où il avait fait entasser armes, argent et ravitaillement pour la poursuite de la campagne. En juillet 52, réunis à Bibracte, tous les peuples de la Gaule, à l'exception des Rèmes et des Lingons, confirment Vercingétorix dans son commandement.

Dérouté, César décide alors de se replier avec ses armées exténuées vers le Rhône et la province romaine de Transalpine en espérant ne pas avoir à livrer bataille sur son chemin. Ayant recruté des cavaliers germains pour assurer sa retraite face aux 15 000 cavaliers gaulois, il est même obligé de leur attribuer les derniers chevaux qui restaient à l'armée romaine. C'est alors que Vercingétorix commet l'erreur qui fait basculer le destin. Renonçant à la tactique attentiste qui lui avait réussi, fort d'une cavalerie nettement supérieure, sans doute pressé par l'impatience de ceux qui voyaient se dessiner la victoire, certainement persuadé que l'occasion était bonne de dégoûter à jamais les Romains de remettre les pieds en Gaule indépendante, il décide de livrer un assaut décisif, sous-estimant les possibilités de réaction de l'adversaire.

Au lieu de se contenter d'accomplir sobrement leur mission, les cavaliers gaulois jurent en effet de ne pas rentrer sous leur toit sans avoir traversé deux fois les rangs ennemis. Une fanfaronnade qui se retourne contre eux. Surpris par l'intervention des cavaliers germains dont ils ignoraient probablement la présence, les Gaulois sont mis en déroute. Vercingétorix commet alors sa seconde erreur en s'enfermant dans l'oppidum d'Alésia (Alise-Sainte-Reine), sur le mont Auxois, avec trente jours de vivres. Mais pouvait-il l'imaginer, alors que, plus vaste et avec des vues plus étendues que celui de Gergovie, le site d'Alésia semblait interdire toute attaque surprise ? Tandis qu'un général romain « ordinaire » se serait hâté de regagner ses bases à marches forcées, profitant du répit que sa victoire lui aurait assuré, César eut une intuition fulgurante : il comprit que le chef gaulois s'était lui-même pris dans un piège qu'il fallait s'empresser de refermer. Le destin qui semblait l'avoir abandonné lui accordait une nouvelle fois sa chance.

Alésia

La stratégie de Vercingétorix paraissait logique et consistait à fixer l'ennemi, puis à le prendre à revers entre cette forteresse naturelle et l'armée de secours que l'extension de la révolte allait lever. Du premier coup d'œil, César s'était d'ailleurs rendu compte que l'oppidum des Mandubiens interdisait toute possibilité d'assaut. La place d'Alésia proprement dite, écrit-il, « était au sommet d'une colline, à une grande altitude, en sorte qu'on voyait bien qu'il était impossible de la prendre autrement que par un siège en règle. Le pied de la colline était de deux côtés baigné par des cours d'eau. En avant de la ville une plaine s'étendait sur une longueur d'environ trois milles [4,5 km] ; de tous les autres côtés la colline était entourée à peu de distance de hauteurs dont l'altitude égalaient la sienne ».

À la différence de Gergovie, Alésia était ceinturée par des plateaux au nord, nord-est, est, sud-est et sud. Au sud-ouest et à l'ouest, s'étendait la vaste plaine des Laumes.

Aussi César fit-il installer une défense linéaire continue de 15 kilomètres de long, composée de trois fossés successifs, la « contrevallation » qui devait interdire toute sortie aux assiégés. Comme la nappe phréatique était souvent proche et qu'il était donc impossible de creuser profondément, César multiplia les obstacles en largeur.

En avant des fossés, il fit placer trois séries de pièges destinées à ralentir les sorties probables des Gaulois : tout d'abord, on coupa des arbres ou des branches robustes en conservant leurs rameaux ; on les écorça, on les tailla en pointe et on les fixa au fond de cinq long fossés parallèles, profonds de 1,50 m en les attachant entre eux pour que personne ne puisse les arracher. En avant de ces obstacles appelés *cippi*, on fixa dans des trous profonds de 90 centimètres de gros pieux pointus, durcis au feu, dissimulés sous des branchages et des broussailles. En raison de leur forme, on les appela les « lys » ou *lilia*. Enfin, tout en avant, on enfonça dans le sol des pointes de fer pratiquement invisibles, que les soldats appelèrent *stimuli* (« aiguillons »). Quand ces travaux gigantesques furent terminés, César entreprit de protéger ses arrières en installant une autre ligne de défense linéaire, la « circonvallation ». Mesurant 20,7 km de tour et comportant des fortifications, elle devait briser les assauts de l'armée de secours.

« C'était, écrit Camille Jullian, comme une forteresse en couronne qui s'était bâtie autour de la montagne, fermant la plaine, barrant les rivières et les vallées, escaladant les pentes, dominant la crête des collines, et défiant d'un côté Vercingétorix et de l'autre la Gaule entière. »

Dans ces conditions, l'issue du siège ne pouvait guère faire de doute. Avec une cruauté sans nom, le conseil des chefs expulsa d'abord les non-combattants, les femmes, les enfants et les vieillards.

Descendant de la montagne jusqu'aux fortifications des Romains, ces malheureux s'offrirent comme captifs si on voulait seulement les nourrir. Mais César donna l'ordre de les repousser et leurs cadavres jonchèrent bientôt les flancs de la montagne.

Puis l'armée gauloise appelée en renfort arriva, encadrée par des chefs prestigieux, l'Atrébate Commios et l'Arverne Vercassivellaunos. Elle comptait 250 000 fantassins et 8 000 cavaliers. Une première attaque de cavalerie fut brisée par l'intervention des Germains. Puis une sortie de Vercingétorix se brisa sur la « contrevallation ». Enfin, les Gaulois du dehors tentèrent un nouvel assaut, après avoir passé vingt-quatre heures à fabriquer des échelles, des crocs et des clayonnages. Mais, repoussés, ils prirent la fuite, chaque contingent regagnant sa cité. Vercingétorix comprit alors que tout était perdu et décida de se livrer au vainqueur. La scène de cette reddition, qui a suscité les images les plus romantiques, est sobrement décrite par César qui écrit : « Vercingétorix convoque l'assemblée : il déclare que cette guerre n'a pas été entreprise par lui à des fins personnelles, mais pour conquérir la liberté de tous ; puisqu'il faut céder à la fortune, il s'offre à eux, ils peuvent, à leur choix, apaiser les Romains par sa mort ou le livrer vivant. On envoie à ce sujet une députation à César. Il ordonne qu'on lui remette les armes, qu'on lui amène les chefs des cités [...]. On lui livre Vercingétorix, on jette les armes à ses pieds. » Le jeune chef arverne devait rester prisonnier pendant six ans avant de figurer dans le triomphe de César en septembre 46 et être, selon la coutume, étranglé.

Livrée à Alésia, la grande bataille de l'indépendance avait été perdue. Même si, dans les mois qui suivirent, César dut mater quelques « patriotes » obstinés comme ceux qui, à Uxellodunum (dans la région de Cahors), eurent la main droite tranchée pour avoir bravé pendant deux mois ses armées, la guerre des Gaules était terminée.

La Gaule romanisée

*A*près avoir fait trembler pendant des siècles les peuples de l'Antiquité, les Gaulois succombèrent sans grande résistance, à tel point
que la Gaule connut seulement deux mouvements de révolte, en 21 et en
68 après J.-C., au cours des deux siècles qui suivirent sa conquête. Hormis
ces deux sursauts d'orgueil limités, les Gaulois s'appliquèrent plus à imiter leurs vainqueurs qu'à cultiver leur originalité. Ce ralliement favorisa
la tâche de Rome qui, en quelques décennies, dota le pays de nouvelles
structures politiques et administratives, transforma les villes comme les
campagnes, multiplia les réalisations spectaculaires tel le pont du Gard,
et marqua ainsi la Gaule d'une empreinte profonde.

La Gaule séduite

Aussi habile dans l'art de séduire que cruel dans le châtiment,
César sut tout d'abord ménager la susceptibilité des vaincus. Ainsi
libéra-t-il au lendemain d'Alésia 20 000 prisonniers arvernes et éduens
qu'il rendit à leurs cités. De plus, le tribut de 40 millions de sesterces,
exigé annuellement de la nouvelle conquête, n'était pas exorbitant
puisqu'il représentait environ 10 francs actuels par habitant et par an.
Surtout, pour renforcer son armée lors de la guerre civile qui l'opposa
à Pompée, il fit largement appel à l'élite des guerriers qui multiplia
les actes de dévouement à son égard. À Alexandrie, ils le protégèrent

contre une multitude d'ennemis. À Thurium, près de Tarente, une garnison de Gaulois massacra même le Romain qui voulait trahir !

Bénéficiant de la citoyenneté romaine dès leur retour de l'armée, nombreux furent ceux qui accolèrent le « gentilice » Julius et le prénom Caius à leur nom gaulois. Certains d'entre eux furent même promus sénateurs par ses soins à tel point qu'on disait à Rome dans les milieux hostiles à ces barbares mal dégrossis : « César va conduisant les Gaulois à son triomphe ; les Gaulois, eux, vont déposer leurs braies à la curie, et y revêtent le laticlave [la toge des sénateurs]. » C'est un fait que la Gaule conquise ne résista guère aux charmes de son vainqueur.

Un vainqueur qui créa avec elle une sorte de lien personnel que les successeurs de César surent cultiver. Auguste, son héritier, fit quatre séjours en Gaule, organisant administrativement le territoire auquel il portait un intérêt particulier, peut-être par fidélité à l'égard de son père adoptif. Tandis que la florissante Transalpine devenait la Narbonnaise, l'ancienne Gaule indépendante fut divisée en trois provinces, l'Aquitaine, la Lyonnaise et la Belgique. Cette division, qui séparait déjà la France en un Midi largement ouvert aux influences romaines et un Nord dont l'importance économique fut accrue par la conquête de la Grande-Bretagne et la présence d'importantes armées sur la nouvelle frontière du Rhin, avait aussi pour mission de séparer les peuples qui avaient autrefois joué un rôle important, tels les Arvernes et les Éduens, et de limiter leur influence en détachant ceux qui faisaient partie de leur clientèle. Puisant sur son énorme fortune ou sur les trésors qu'il avait enlevés à Cléopâtre, Auguste multiplia aussi les grands travaux destinés à embellir les villes nouvelles dont beaucoup portèrent son nom ou celui de César, associé à un radical gaulois, *dunum* ou *durum* (« forteresse »), *magus* (« marché ») ou *nemetum* (« lieu sacré ») : Augustonemetum (Clermont-Ferrand), Augustodunum (Autun), Caesarodunum (Tours), Juliomagus (Angers), Augustodurum (Bayeux), Juliobona (Lillebonne), Augustobona (Troyes), Augustomagus (Senlis)... C'est ainsi qu'on lui doit la Maison carrée de Nîmes, le viaduc du pont du Gard, les théâtres d'Orange, d'Arles, de Vienne et de Lyon.

Cette ville, fondée en 43 avant J.-C. par un lieutenant de César, Munatius Plancus, devint rapidement le carrefour et la capitale de la nouvelle Gaule romaine, et c'est au-dessus du confluent du Rhône et de la Saône, au lieu dit Condate, que fut inauguré le 1er août de l'an 12 avant J.-C. le sanctuaire fédéral des Trois Gaules destiné à célébrer leur union religieuse et politique avec l'Empire romain. Administré par les représentants des cités qui, chaque année, élisaient le prêtre chargé de célébrer le culte « de Rome et d'Auguste », ce sanctuaire, situé à l'emplacement actuel de la Croix-Rousse, se présentait comme une vaste terrasse sur laquelle s'élevait un autel monumental portant le nom des soixante cités gauloises, représentées aussi par des statues. De chaque côté de l'autel, deux colonnes soutenaient deux grandes victoires ailées en bronze.

Assuré à Lyon par les notables les plus influents des cités gauloises qui se flattaient de cette prestigieuse promotion, le culte de l'empereur fut aussi un puissant facteur de promotion sociale dans les cités gauloises où des sévirs augustaux pouvaient accéder à la notabilité en acceptant la charge onéreuse d'offrir, au nom de leurs concitoyens, des offrandes au « génie » d'Auguste et de distribuer l'encens et le vin à tous les habitants. Un honneur et une charge qui leur valaient aussi des places de choix aux jeux et le droit de porter la toge prétexte ! Ainsi s'affirmait la réconciliation des Gaulois avec leur conquérant.

Mais c'est surtout Claude dont le règne marque une étape essentielle dans la romanisation de la Gaule. Né à Lyon le 1ᵉʳ août de l'an 10 avant J.-C., le jour même où se réunissait l'assemblée des Trois Gaules, il fut l'empereur qui fit le plus pour l'intégration des Gaulois dans l'Empire, en leur distribuant généreusement le droit de cité romain mais surtout en leur offrant, en 48 après J.-C., la possibilité de devenir sénateurs et d'être affectés à des fonctions administratives de premier plan dans l'Empire. « Il voulait voir tout le monde en toge, Grecs, Gaulois, Espagnols, Bretons, laissera-t-il seulement un étranger pour la graine ? », se moquait Sénèque qui, par mépris, surnomma Claude l'empereur gaulois.

Cette initiative libérale provoqua en effet une rude opposition dans les milieux conservateurs dont les arguments sont ainsi repris par l'historien romain Tacite : « L'Italie n'était pas à ce point malade, qu'elle ne pût fournir un sénat à sa Ville (Rome). Jadis, au temps de la République, les seuls Romains et les peuples consanguins y auraient suffi... N'était-ce pas suffisant d'avoir vu dans la Curie l'irruption des Vénètes et des Insubres sans qu'une tourbe d'étrangers y introduise, en quelque sorte, des prisonniers de guerre !... Ils allaient boucher toutes les carrières, ces richards dont les aïeux, chefs des nations ennemies, avaient massacré nos légions, assiégé le divin César près d'Alésia. Et ce n'étaient là que des faits récents. Allait-on oublier le souvenir de ceux qui étaient morts en foule, au Capitole, à la citadelle de Rome, sous les coups des mêmes Gaulois ? » Comme quoi, quatre siècles après le sac de Rome par Brennus, le péril gaulois constituait toujours un argument de poids.

Passant outre, Claude répondit à ces critiques par un discours fameux, dont le texte, en partie conservé par Tacite, fut gravé sur des tables de bronze retrouvées à Lyon. Exprimant l'idée qu'en appelant les anciens vaincus à participer aux décisions générales Rome ferait d'eux les membres solidaires d'un même corps, il rappelait avec justesse que, de toutes les guerres que Rome avait menées, celle des Gaules avait été la plus brève. Depuis lors, observait-il, régnait une paix constante et fidèle. « Désormais mêlés aux nôtres par les mœurs, les métiers, les alliances, qu'ils nous infusent leur or et leurs richesses au lieu de les posséder séparément ! »

Si les Éduens furent les premiers à obtenir le droit de siéger au sénat, en raison de leur ancienne amitié avec Rome, les nobles des autres cités suivirent bientôt. À cet égard, la destinée d'une famille de Saintes illustre à quel point l'aristocratie gauloise a assimilé rapidement les trajectoires de la romanisation. L'arrière-grand-père se nommait Epotsorovidos. Son fils, fait citoyen romain par César, se fait nommer Caius Julius Gedomo, seul le troisième nom restant gaulois. Son petit-fils, Caius Julius Otuaneunos, possède encore un surnom gaulois qu'abandonne définitivement l'arrière-petit-fils. Entièrement assimilé, ce dernier, Caius Julius Rufus, est, en 19 après J.-C., grand prêtre à l'autel fédéral des Trois Gaules.

Assister à l'inauguration de sa propre statue, tel pouvait être aussi le couronnement d'une carrière de romanisé comme celle de Titus Sennius Sollemnis, l'un des principaux magistrats de la cité des Viducasses, Vieux, à une trentaine de kilomètres de Caen, qui, après avoir parcouru toute la gamme des honneurs, put, le 16 décembre 238 après J.-C., lire sur le marbre qu'en raison de tous les services qu'il avait rendus aux personnages influents de Rome, il était « le premier auquel les trois provinces de Gaule ont jamais élevé un monument dans sa propre cité ».

Les gens du peuple bénéficièrent aussi des avantages de la romanisation en s'enrôlant comme auxiliaires dans les légions romaines. Au terme de vingt-cinq années de service au cours desquelles ils avaient bénéficié d'une solde confortable, les vétérans pouvaient être installés par l'État dans une colonie comme Trèves, Autun ou Die. Le vétéran, ayant reçu une portion de terrain dont la dimension variait selon les régions, finissait alors paisiblement ses jours au milieu de sa famille tout en exhibant les titres qu'il avait reçus et les parures d'honneur qui ornaient sa poitrine.

Après sa mort, une pierre tombale sculptée conservait son portrait. Nombreux furent aussi les esclaves affranchis qui, par leur travail ou leur astuce, purent bénéficier d'une ascension sociale autrefois refusée à la plèbe gauloise.

Rome n'a donc pas eu besoin de coloniser la Gaule pour la romaniser. Peu nombreux furent les Romains qui vinrent habiter la Gaule de manière définitive. On a évalué à une centaine de mille le nombre de colons établis avec leurs familles dans le Midi, à Fréjus, Béziers, Arles, Orange, Vienne et Valence notamment. « Gallo-romain » est une appellation moderne qui pourrait faire croire à une fusion de populations mais qui traduit mal la réalité du temps. Ce fut en fait la force de Rome d'avoir latinisé un pays comme la Gaule avec une poignée d'occupants, quelques fonctionnaires de passage, une infime minorité de colons ou de marchands noyés dans une population qui ne donna guère de soucis à son vainqueur, quoi qu'en disent certains historiens visiblement agacés par les défaillances patriotiques de nos ancêtres.

La seule révolte d'envergure exprime d'ailleurs plus la fidélité à Rome que la résistance à son occupation. Elle éclate en 68 sous le règne de Néron, quand Julius Vindex, fils d'un noble gaulois admis au sénat romain sous Claude et lui-même gouverneur de la Lyonnaise, appelle ses administrés à la révolte contre un empereur dont la personnalité et la conduite lui semblaient déshonorer le nom de la dynastie impériale qui avait tant fait pour la Gaule. On prête d'ailleurs à Vindex ce mot d'ordre fort peu nationaliste : « Soulevez-vous maintenant, et, en veillant à votre propre salut, secourez aussi les Romains, libérez l'Univers. »

Les révoltes qui éclatent alors dans plusieurs points de la Gaule sont souvent menées par des notables qui, jusque-là, avaient loyalement servi Rome. Mais quand l'armée du Rhin marche en 69 sur la Gaule, qu'un Batave, Caius Julius Civilis, se met à la tête des légions débandées et offre aux Gaulois de recouvrer leur liberté, l'assemblée des peuples gaulois, conviée à Reims par les Rèmes, inquiète devant ce qu'elle interprète comme une nouvelle menace germanique, affirme sa fidélité à Rome et, en 70, enjoint aux révoltés d'abandonner la lutte et avoue préférer la paix à l'indépendance. Cet épisode sans conséquence, qui constitua en fait le meilleur test de la romanisation, marquait aussi le triomphe d'une aristocratie assimilée pour laquelle la paix était la condition indispensable de la prospérité économique.

Le grenier de l'Empire

Enfin protégée des migrations dévastatrices par une forte armée qui tint solidement la frontière du Rhin pendant près de trois siècles, enfin débarrassée des guerres intestines qui avaient tant distrait son énergie au temps de l'indépendance, la Gaule connut une formidable réussite économique liée à la constitution d'un réseau d'échanges international centré, au sud, sur la Méditerranée, et fécondé, au nord, par le commerce outre-Rhin et le trafic transmanche assuré par l'intégration de l'archipel britannique dans l'Empire.

Les armées stationnées aux frontières du Rhin et en Grande-Bretagne ont fait en partie la fortune de la Gaule et largement effacé le réel traumatisme que fut pour elle la conquête de César. On a ainsi calculé que la nourriture de base des 50 000 hommes présents sur le Rhin au IIe siècle nécessitait entre 50 et 70 tonnes de blé par jour, auxquelles il faut ajouter les animaux pour la viande et pour les peaux, les chevaux et le fourrage, les vêtements, les armes, l'huile, le vin, les matériaux de construction...

Tandis que la Gaule régale les gourmets romains avec son blé, ses charcuteries en provenance du Jura, ses oies de la région de Boulogne et ses vins dont la production se développe au cours du Ier siècle après J.-C., d'abord sur les bords de la Méditerranée, puis en Bourgogne, en Champagne, dans la vallée du Rhin et dans le Bordelais, elle exporte aussi à grande échelle les vaisselles en bronze et en verre, les fibules émaillées et, surtout, la céramique sigillée, à pâte fine et vernissée, dont la mode avait pénétré la Gaule par l'intermédiaire des légions. À Lezoux, en Auvergne, à la Graufesenque, près de Millau, certains fours permettaient la cuisson simultanée de plusieurs dizaines de milliers de pièces commercialisées dans tout l'Occident et jusqu'en Afrique. Une caisse de bols et de lampes, fabriqués pour l'essentiel à la Graufesenque, a ainsi été trouvée, encore fermée, sous la lave de Pompéi.

En contrepartie, la Gaule importe l'huile des olives d'Andalousie, l'étain et le cuivre d'Espagne, le fer des Asturies, le plomb de Bretagne, les marbres de Grèce et d'Asie, les porphyres d'Égypte qui ornent les somptueuses demeures de l'aristocratie. Les monuments funéraires nous montrent que ce grand commerce était pratiqué par de riches négociants qui tenaient le haut du pavé et parmi lesquels, à Narbonne ou à Lyon, on comptait beaucoup d'étrangers, des Syriens, des Carthaginois et de nombreux Grecs. Dans les grands ports, Marseille – conquise par César en 49 avant J.-C. pour avoir pris le parti de Pompée –, Narbonne, Arles – reliée directement à la mer par un canal –, Bordeaux, régnait ainsi une animation fébrile. Les dockers embarquaient et débarquaient des milliers d'amphores. Les métreurs vérifiaient le poids et la valeur de la cargaison. Dans les entrepôts, les comptables enregistraient méticuleusement le mouvement des marchandises tandis que le personnel administratif évaluait le montant de l'impôt qui s'élevait au quarantième de la valeur de tout chargement entrant en Gaule. Près du quai, un patron recrutait des marins tandis qu'un peu plus loin, des calfats étanchaient les joints d'un bateau avec de l'étoupe de chanvre.

On circule aussi en tous sens en Gaule romaine grâce à un réseau routier remarquable qui permettait de parcourir en moyenne 45 kilomètres par jour avant de trouver le gîte et le couvert dans ces tavernes dont les enseignes étaient autant d'invites mais qui avaient une fort mauvaise réputation : « Les Trois Tavernes » qui ont donné le nom actuel de Saverne, en Alsace, l'« Auberge de Mercure et d'Apollon » à Lyon, « Au Coq de Basse-Cour » à Narbonne, « Au Poulet Noir », « Aux Dix Pays », « À l'Arbre Fruitier ». À Antibes, une plaque de pierre portait l'invitation suivante : « Voyageur, écoute ! Entre, s'il te plaît, tu trouveras une tablette de bronze qui te donnera tous renseignements. »

Mis en place par Agrippa, le gendre d'Auguste, ce réseau routier était balisé tous les milles (environ 1 480 mètres) par une borne routière en pierre, haute de deux mètres, qui portait le nom et les titres de l'empereur régnant et l'indication de distance, avec parfois celle par rapport à Rome. Complétant heureusement les grandes routes héritées de la Gaule indépendante, il ouvrait surtout deux grands axes, l'axe Méditerranée-Rhône-Lyon-Boulogne qui assurait l'important trafic transmanche, et l'axe Méditerranée-Rhône-Saône-Moselle-Rhin qui approvisionnait l'armée stationnée aux frontières de l'Empire. C'est ainsi que Boulogne, petit port de pêche des Morins, et Amiens, simple relais d'étape, devinrent de grands centres de commerce et d'entrepôt.

Plus appréciée des Gaulois qui l'utilisaient de préférence à la route, la navigation fluviale offrait le charme et la lenteur de déplacements plus paisibles et moins risqués. « Monte en hâte sur un bateau, conseille le poète gaulois Ausone à un ami venu le retrouver dans sa demeure bordelaise, déroule le lin replié de ta voile. Le souffle du vent du Médoc t'emportera, étalé sous des draperies, allongé sur un lit, pour que toute secousse soit épargnée à ta forte personne. » Sur les grands fleuves, le Rhône, la Saône, la Seine, la Loire, mais aussi sur des cours d'eau plus modestes s'affairaient mariniers, conducteurs de radeaux, haleurs et flotteurs de bois, bateliers des rivières et des lacs, qui transportaient cinq à dix fois moins cher que par la route les multiples marchandises nécessaires à la construction et à l'alimentation des villes.

Car, plus que le grand commerce international, ce qui a assuré l'essentiel de cette réussite économique, ce sont les modestes échanges entre villes et campagnes, les fructueuses activités du commerce de détail, le patient labeur des boutiquiers de toutes sortes, tailleurs

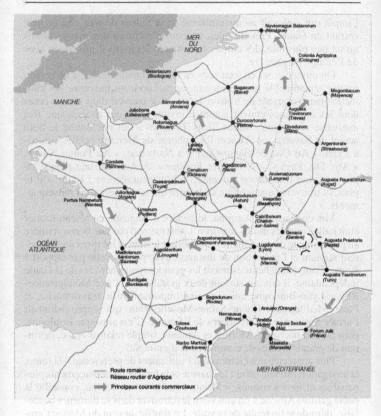

Routes et courants commerciaux.

d'habits et marchands de légumes secs, charcutiers et marchands d'huile, marchands de vin et de cervoise, marchandes de fleurs qui annoncent ne vendre leurs couronnes qu'aux seuls amants.

Les premières pierres de la France urbaine

« Quand le bâtiment va, tout va », ce populaire baromètre de la conjoncture économique s'applique à merveille à la Gaule romanisée. Si, partout dans ses provinces, Rome a fondé et transformé des villes,

126

nulle part elle ne l'a fait de manière aussi spectaculaire qu'en Gaule. Rare fut dans l'histoire de France une aussi profonde mutation que celle qui affecta alors notre pays.

« Une végétation de murailles en pierre, en brique, en ciment, poussa de partout, écrivait l'historien Camille Jullian, qui ajoutait : On eût dit que la vie humaine, au-delà même de la mort, ne pouvait plus s'agiter que dans un cadre de pierre. »

Construites et mises en scène pour affirmer la puissance de Rome et de sa civilisation, jamais villes ne furent aussi encombrées de chantiers que celles des Gaules aux deux premiers siècles de notre ère. On éleva des remparts aux murs énormes flanqués de tours nombreuses et des portes monumentales pour impressionner le visiteur ; on traça des chaussées rectilignes de quatre à six mètres de largeur, bordées de trottoirs et de maisons, formant un réseau de chemins coupés à angles droits ; on aménagea des forums aux contours réguliers entourés de portiques à colonnades et ornés de statues ; on édifia des temples pour le culte des dieux, des basiliques pour les séances des magistrats et des curies pour les décurions chargés de la gestion municipale ; des arcs de triomphe pour glorifier l'histoire ; des marchés pour échanger les marchandises et les nouvelles ; des cirques, des théâtres et des amphithéâtres pour l'amusement des citadins et des thermes pour leur bien-être ; on creusa un système d'égouts qui les débarrassaient des matières usées et un système de canaux qui leur amena, en un conduit souterrain ou sur les arcades d'un aqueduc, les eaux pures des sources lointaines.

Ces aqueducs qui, aujourd'hui, nous impressionnent tant, comme celui du pont du Gard, étaient en fait, on l'a découvert récemment, un luxe inutile qui avait pour seule fonction d'affirmer l'excellence et la supériorité de la technique romaine. Il faut savoir en effet que les villes gallo-romaines recevaient des quantités d'eau largement supérieures à celles d'une ville moyenne actuelle alors que leur nombre d'habitants, leur activité industrielle et leurs besoins réels étaient très largement inférieurs. Ces aqueducs, souvent affectés de nombreuses malfaçons, étaient en fait des constructions « gratuites », qui n'avaient pas pour principale mission d'améliorer le confort des individus, resté fort précaire, mais seulement d'affirmer le prestige de la romanité.

C'est aussi la raison pour laquelle il est impossible de réduire les établissements thermaux à des bâtiments fonctionnels ouverts à ceux qui voulaient uniquement se laver. Comment expliquer alors le fait que des villes modestes en possédaient plusieurs et que la piscine des thermes de Sainte-Barbe à Trèves était plus longue et plus large qu'une piscine olympique moderne ? Simplement par le fait que ces établissements qui s'adressaient à l'esprit comme au corps étaient les vitrines d'un modèle culturel diffusé à grand prix.

La floraison exceptionnelle des monuments du spectacle en est une autre illustration puisque, pour une population inférieure à 10 millions d'habitants, la Gaule comptait en moyenne trois à quatre fois plus de places de spectacle que la France aujourd'hui ! Non seulement les villes de Gaule ont édifié des monuments qui comptent parmi les plus imposants du monde, les amphithéâtres d'Autun ou de Poitiers approchant les dimensions du Colisée de Rome, mais encore, sur cent cinquante monuments aujourd'hui recensés sur notre territoire, près de la moitié se situent dans des agglomérations secondaires ou même en rase campagne, accompagnés de forums, de basiliques, de temples et de thermes sans aucune commune mesure avec la densité de la population environnante. Ainsi, le forum des Tours-Mirandes, dans la Vienne, est aussi vaste que celui de Trajan à Rome ! C'est que ces bâtiments avaient eux aussi pour principale mission de romaniser les campagnes qui rassemblaient toujours 90 % de la population totale des Gaules.

Si, au premier siècle de notre ère, Rome accueillait plus de 700 000 habitants, Alexandrie, Antioche et Carthage, plus de 200 000, les villes les plus vastes de Gaule – Trèves, Lyon, Reims, Autun, Narbonne et Nîmes – ne comptaient guère plus de 20 000 habitants et la plupart des chefs-lieux de cité en rassemblaient probablement moins de 5 000, ce qui en faisait des bourgades où les faits et gestes de chacun étaient commentés. Plus que des centres d'activité nécessaires, les villes gallo-romaines apparaissent surtout comme des lieux de représentation au sein desquels les nouvelles élites peuvent afficher leur romanité.

La romanisation des campagnes

Les nouvelles élites gauloises ralliées à Rome, qui ressentent l'ardente obligation de dépenser pour paraître et d'embellir leurs cités pour affirmer leur statut, tirent l'essentiel de leurs ressources des campagnes qui, en deçà de la parade urbaine, restent bien le tissu nourricier de la Gaule, l'activité qui emploie le plus de bras, le grenier dans lequel le conquérant a largement puisé.

Un grenier dont le nouveau statut juridique devint le signe le plus criant de la dépendance. En droit, en effet, les terres des pays conquis avaient été confisquées en faveur du peuple romain qui, par bon vouloir, pouvait en abandonner la jouissance aux vaincus. On distinguait ainsi les terres des citoyens romains, propriétaires de plein droit et exonérés de l'impôt, et celles des non-citoyens, frappées de l'impôt foncier, symbole manifeste de la sujétion.

Pour recenser l'ensemble des terres et établir l'assiette de l'impôt, Auguste ordonna une énorme opération cadastrale dont se chargea son gendre Agrippa et qui traduit une volonté systématique d'appropriation et d'organisation du pays qu'aucune autre période de notre histoire n'a connue.

Après la confiscation, l'*agrimensor* romain (l'arpenteur) procédait au découpage des terres en lots de superficie égale, appelés « centuries ». Formant le plus souvent un carré de 2 400 pieds, soit 710 mètres de côté, elles mesuraient 50,512 hectares. Pour quadriller le terrain qu'il traitait comme une table rase où tout était permis, l'arpenteur déterminait avec un outil simple, la *groma*, deux axes principaux se coupant à angle droit : le *decumanus maximus* d'est en ouest et le *cardo maximus* du nord au sud. À partir de ce tracé, il menait des lignes parallèles (*limites*) qui formaient la trame du quadrillage et qui étaient matérialisées au sol par des chemins souvent bordés de fossés. Ces *limites*, qui apparaissent encore sur les cartes et les photographies aériennes, sont restées jusqu'aux remembrements récents imprimées dans le paysage rural de nombreuses régions. Ainsi, la limite entre les départements du Vaucluse et de la Drôme suit, dans la traversée du Rhône, le tracé d'un *decumanus* tandis que tel supermarché, après de multiples études techniques, s'est implanté dans les limites exactes d'une centurie antique.

Le cadastre le plus spectaculaire, unique dans tout le monde romain, est celui d'Orange, connu par 415 fragments de marbre retrouvés de 1852 à 1960. Il distinguait cinq catégories de terres. Les premières – les meilleures –, confisquées aux indigènes et exemptes de l'impôt foncier, avaient été attribuées aux vétérans de la IIe légion Gallica. Les deuxièmes – le plus souvent des friches ou des pâtures –, étaient confiées à des locataires moyennant une contribution annuelle insignifiante. Les troisièmes se composaient de terrains vagues ou incultes non attribués. Les quatrièmes étaient les terres – bien évidemment les plus médiocres – rendues à la peuplade indigène des Tricastins. La cinquième enfin concernait les terres non cadastrées.

Probablement affichées dans la basilique judiciaire ou la curie d'Orange, sans doute en 77 après J.-C., ces plaques mentionnaient pour chaque centurie la surface des lots assignés aux vétérans, les terres publiques avec le tarif des redevances et le nom des adjudicataires. Hors de la Narbonnaise toutefois, la cadastration des terres est restée limitée. On en retrouve pourtant certains vestiges autour de

Lyon, en Bretagne, en Picardie, au sud d'Amiens, en Alsace, autour de Reims, dans le Jura, en Côte-d'Or, dans le Berry, en Auvergne et en Normandie.

Découvertes par l'archéologie aérienne qui a révélé des milliers de plans d'établissements ruraux disséminés dans les campagnes, les *villae* constituent l'autre empreinte de la romanisation des campagnes. Construites en pierre et luxueusement décorées par de grands propriétaires qui avaient aussi leur maison en ville, elles font pénétrer dans les terres les plus reculées le mode de vie romain.

De taille et de plan extrêmement divers, ces *villae* – qui peuvent se définir comme un ensemble architectural regroupant une maison d'habitation et des bâtiments d'exploitation agricole – présentent toutefois une étonnante similitude dans leur conception. Au centre d'un domaine rural qui compte des champs cultivés, des prairies, des forêts, des vignes dans le Midi, mais aussi des tuileries, des forges, des ateliers pour la poterie, le tissage, le travail du cuir, elles comportent deux groupes de construction établis autour de deux cours fermées ; la *pars urbana*, la partie résidentielle, et la *pars agraria* ou *rustica*, comprenant les bâtiments d'exploitation et l'habitation du régisseur chargé d'exploiter le domaine.

Par le luxe qu'elle déploie fréquemment, la demeure du maître transpire la romanité. Les thermes et le système de chauffage par le sol en sont les manifestations les plus spectaculaires. Les mosaïques, les salles d'apparat, les fontaines d'agrément, les peintures murales recherchées, les corniches et les frises en stuc moulé, les marbres, les sculptures traduisent la volonté de « faire romain ».

Implantée au milieu du Iᵉʳ siècle après J.-C. en pays de Comminges, sur la rive gauche de la Save, la *villa* de Montmaurin est l'exemple caricatural de ces somptueuses demeures. L'habitation du « maître », qui vivait dans un raffinement que ne connaîtra pas Louis XIV à Versailles, comprenait une cinquantaine de pièces aux murs revêtus de marbres polychromes et dont au moins une douzaine étaient chauffées. Dans la *villa* de Chiragan, sur la rive gauche de la Garonne, qui possédait comme les demeures de Pompéi un atrium et deux péristyles, près de trois cents statues d'empereurs romains ou des membres de leurs familles ont été recensées. À 25 kilomètres au nord de Lyon, près d'Anse, la *villa* de la Grange-du-Bief déployait 175 mètres de façade dont la galerie couverte débouchait, à chacune des extrémités, sur des pièces ornées de mosaïques.

On avance aujourd'hui le chiffre stupéfiant de cinq cent mille *villae*, soit une pour 100 hectares en moyenne, des *villae* qui ont bien été des vitrines destinées à affirmer l'excellence du modèle romain.

CHAPITRE 12

La romanisation des âmes

S'étonnant que ses livres fussent vendus dans la capitale des Trois Gaules, Pline le Jeune écrivait : « Je ne pensais pas qu'il y eût des libraires à Lyon ! » Cette méprisante boutade donne la mesure de la romanisation. Il ne suffit pas en effet de reconstituer les cadres de la vie publique ou de recenser les vestiges de l'architecture romaine pour apprécier la diffusion de ce qu'on appellerait aujourd'hui le « Roman way of life ». Si les élites ont adopté le modèle culturel romain, si le latin, enseigné aux enfants des milieux favorisés, est devenu la langue de l'administration, qu'en est-il du paysan gaulois qui porte, comme au temps de Vercingétorix, les pantalons et les cheveux longs ?

Les jeux du cirque

S'il fallait mesurer la romanisation des âmes à l'aune des spectacles populaires, nul doute que Rome a gagné la partie, imposant les types de monuments et de distractions qui portaient sa marque. « De Rome, écrivait l'historien Camille Jullian, les Gaulois empruntèrent les jeux, les plaisirs et les vices : tableaux vivants, mystères mythologiques, mimes et pantomimes sur les théâtres innombrables des villes et des lieux de foire, combats de gladiateurs ou exécutions judiciaires dans les amphithéâtres des capitales de cités, courses de chars dans les cirques des métropoles de province, et partout, baignades en commun, promenades et jeux d'oisifs dans les thermes, on s'amusa à Paris à l'instar de Rome, et à Paris comme à Rome, rien ne délecta plus la plèbe ou les riches que les prouesses sanglantes de la gladiature. »

Certes, ajoutait-il, les combats de gladiateurs n'étaient pas plus barbares que les sacrifices humains si chers aux Gaulois, mais les spectateurs de ces sacrifices n'en faisaient pas un motif de distraction. La Gaule aurait pu demander à ses maîtres romains autre chose que d'exiger la mort dans les arènes pour distraire ses loisirs.

Pour se convaincre de l'engouement des Gaulois pour ces spectacles, il suffit de rappeler le nombre des « théâtres-amphithéâtres », ces établissements pouvant accueillir plusieurs types de spectacles, qui se montent à une trentaine dans la seule province de Lyonnaise, la plupart d'entre eux se trouvant dans des campagnes isolées où ils recevraient, comme à Sanxay, dans la Vienne, 6 600 spectateurs sur des gradins de bois, ce qui suppose que s'y réunissaient les paysans de la région.

Il suffit aussi de voir les fortunes que dépensaient les notables pour organiser les spectacles : Titus Sennius Sollemnis, par exemple, engloutit 332 000 sesterces (près de 700 000 de nos francs) pour organiser durant quatre jours trente-deux combats de gladiateurs à Lyon.

C'est que les Gaulois disposant de plus de cent trente jours fériés par an, la principale préoccupation des décurions était d'assurer l'emploi de ces journées libres et d'améliorer la qualité des fêtes qui les accompagnaient, le « bon peuple » appréciant les innovations, comptant le nombre des gladiateurs, des léopards et des victimes.

Ce n'étaient pas en effet les grandes œuvres du théâtre antique qui assuraient la romanisation des esprits, mais les statues qui ornaient les murs de scène, les multiples Victoires, Centaures, Silènes et Ménades, les combats d'Amazones, les Vénus et les Cariatides qui étaient autant d'illustrations de la mythologie gréco-latine.

Il est probable que ces légendes qui, en Italie, fournissaient prétexte à des œuvres dramatiques, étaient aussi des sujets de pièces à grand spectacle où le geste avait plus de place que la parole, des scènes mimées évoquant par exemple les aspects les plus osés des légendes mythologiques.

Mais ce furent surtout les combats de gladiateurs ou les combats d'animaux qui connurent le plus vif succès, la Gaule comptant le quart des amphithéâtres connus dans tout l'Empire, l'Italie ne la dépassant que d'une vingtaine. Il faut d'ailleurs souligner que si les intellectuels condamnaient de tels spectacles, affectant, comme Cicéron à Rome, de bouder ces jours de fête pour écrire leurs livres, la plupart, comme lui aussi, s'empressaient de partager avec la plèbe ces sensations fortes et morbides. Il semble bien d'ailleurs qu'en la matière, la Gaule

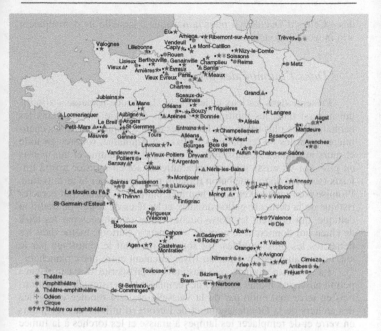

Monuments de spectacle connus (par fouilles, repérages ou inscriptions).

apporta sa contribution au spectacle, Autun, ville universitaire et capitale de l'esprit, étant aussi fameuse par son école de gladiateurs.

Et si l'on observe un silence pudique sur certaines exécutions publiques, les martyres des premiers chrétiens, suppliciés dans l'amphithéâtre de Lyon en 177, nous donnent la mesure de la cruauté du peuple qui assistait en masse à ce spectacle. « Ils furent encore passés par les verges, comme c'est la coutume du lieu, écrivit un témoin, traînés par les bêtes, soumis à tout ce qu'un peuple en délire ordonnait de tous côtés par ses clameurs ; enfin on les fit asseoir sur la chaise de fer, où l'odeur de graisse dégagée par leur chair brûlée les suffoquait. Mais le peuple n'était pas calmé et sa fureur ne cessait de grandir : on voulait vaincre la constance des martyrs... Pendant toute cette journée, ils avaient été en spectacle au monde et avaient tenu lieu de toute la variété qu'on trouve aux luttes de gladiateurs. »

Sans doute faut-il aussi rappeler que les Lyonnais étaient très friands des spectacles de l'odéon, un auteur ancien soulignant le goût des « Celtes d'Occident » pour la musique à laquelle ils demandaient « le moyen d'adoucir les cœurs » !

Dans l'intimité des foyers

Présente dans les jeux et les loisirs, la « mode romaine » s'introduisit aussi dans les multiples interstices de la vie privée. Dans les habitations les plus modestes, les huttes de la Campine belge, les chaumières picardes ou les pauvres maisons d'Aquitaine, toitures en tuile et murs maçonnés se substituèrent aux toits de chaume et aux parois en pisé. On vit aussi souvent apparaître un sol en mortier rose à tuileaux (souvent dénommé béton romain) pour remplacer la terre battue. Promise à un grand avenir, la cheminée murale devint un trait caractéristique de la demeure gallo-romaine, et les têtes de bélier, de tradition celtique, qui ornaient les porte-bûches furent remplacées par les têtes de chien qui donnèrent le nom de « chenets ». Surtout, même dans les demeures les plus humbles, fut souvent introduit le chauffage par le sol, l'air chaud dispensé par un foyer circulant entre deux planchers.

La modeste aisance que suscitait la prospérité des campagnes permit aussi aux moins pauvres de remplacer leurs ustensiles traditionnels en terre mal cuite par de la vaisselle en terre moulée et sigillée des ateliers de la Graufesenque et de Lezoux, d'utiliser des récipients en verre et de remplacer les lampes à graisse et les torches à la fumée malodorante par des lampes à huile bon marché. On a retrouvé des lampes-réclames portant la mention « Achetez les lampes à un as », ornées de scènes de la vie quotidienne ou de motifs érotiques.

De même, si les paysans gaulois restèrent fidèles à leurs traditions alimentaires, ils se mirent à consommer, au lieu de la bouillie de froment ou d'orge séchée au four et des viandes bouillies ou rôties en brochettes, de gros pains ronds plus raffinés, des viandes assaisonnées, des fromages, des poissons et des fruits de mer qui semblent avoir bénéficié d'une grande faveur. Les fouilles ont ainsi livré dans tous les points de la Gaule des quantités considérables d'écailles d'huîtres qui semblent avoir voyagé sans dommage. Ausone toujours, notre épicurien bordelais, en détaille les variétés : « À mon avis, les meilleures de toutes, nourrissons de l'Océan médocain, ont porté le nom de Bordeaux, grâce à leurs admirateurs, sur la table des Césars, qui les a rendues aussi fameuses que notre vin [...] Elles ont la chair grasse et blanche, un jus doux et délicat, où une légère saveur de sel se mêle à celle de l'eau marine. Derrière elles, mais très loin, viennent celles de Marseille [...] Il y a aussi des amateurs pour les huîtres de la mer armoricaine, pour celles que ramasse l'habitant de la côte des Pictons [en Vendée] [...] » Nous livrant aussi le plaisir qu'il a éprouvé en dégustant des moules à son premier déjeuner, il précise que ce mets délicieux « coûte peu au foyer des pauvres » qui avaient aussi, selon les auteurs anciens, l'art de multiplier les espèces de boissons capables d'engendrer l'ébriété. « Remplis, patron, verse ! », « J'ai encore soif ! », « Plus tu seras malheureux, moins tu boiras ; plus tu seras heureux, plus tu boiras », telles sont parmi tant d'autres les inscriptions des vases à boire dont les habitants de la Gaule semblent avoir fait grand usage.

De même, si les braies, ces pantalons longs qui étaient la pièce maîtresse du costume national, ont survécu et si la *caracalla*, le manteau sans manches, fut même porté par les empereurs, les femmes adoptèrent la mode romaine des longues robes plissées et du drapé pour « s'habiller ». Les coiffures des femmes de haut rang trahissent en particulier les caprices de la mode romaine. Au début du Ier siècle, les cheveux sont simplement disposés en deux bandeaux séparés par une raie et terminés en chignon sur la nuque. Ce type de coiffure, que l'on voit à la même époque sur les portraits de Julie, la fille d'Auguste, est parfois agrémenté de boucles frisées tombant sur chaque épaule. Dans la seconde moitié du Ier siècle, toujours à l'instar de Rome, cette inflation de boucles trouve son épanouissement avec la coiffure dite en « nid d'abeilles », arborée par la riche Nîmoise Cintia Honorata, la raie médiane étant remplacée par un volumineux et continu étagement de boucles formant comme un énorme diadème. Puis, au IIe siècle, vient la mode des enroulements de nattes qui, à la manière d'un turban, occupent tout le sommet du crâne. Avec l'impératrice Sabine, la femme d'Hadrien, on retrouve la simplicité des cheveux partagés par une raie médiane mais, cette fois, avec des cheveux plus ondulés et plus hauts... Quant aux hommes, surtout dans le Midi, après s'être rasés de près à la mode romaine, ils reviennent au IIe siècle à la barbe, la moustache, les cheveux plus longs et bouclés popularisés par l'empereur Hadrien qui voulait, dit-on, cacher une mauvaise cicatrice. Et le torque gaulois, si caractéristique de l'art celtique, n'orna plus que le cou des divinités.

On peut aussi se demander si les femmes gauloises, connues au temps de l'indépendance pour leur extrême fécondité, n'ont pas, comme les Romaines, cherché à limiter leur progéniture. À Vienne, un pointage opéré sur 117 unions des trois premiers siècles de notre ère montre que 27 semblent avoir été frappées de stérilité, 63 ont donné naissance à un enfant, 19 à deux, 7 à trois et une seule à six.

En revanche, on ne trouve aucune trace en Gaule de la décadence de l'esprit de famille qui, à la même époque, gangrenait Rome. S'il faut interpréter avec précaution les inscriptions funéraires qui donnent aux veufs l'occasion de vanter à l'envi les vertus conjugales de leurs femmes – l'un déclarant que son épouse était « la chose la plus précieuse du monde », l'autre qu'il a vécu avec elle « sans la moindre querelle », le plus pauvre déclarant qu'il avait honoré « la mémoire de son épouse pieuse et pure, du mieux que le lui permettait sa pauvreté » –, le faible nombre de divorces, si fréquents dans la haute société romaine, témoignerait de la solidité des familles.

Plus sincères sans doute sont les formules funéraires que portent les tombes des enfants trop tôt disparus. « Ô sort indigne, s'écrie une mère, ici repose ma fille, si belle ! Cela est plus que de la douleur : on m'a ravi ma fille jolie... ! Ô heureux père, qui n'a pas vu une telle douleur ! C'est dans le cœur de sa mère qu'est la blessure... » Ces enfants qu'on surnomme Homullus, « Petit Homme », Pullus, « Poulet », Ursulus, « Ourson », Pupa, « Poupée », Filiolus, « Fiston », Carilla, « Petite Chérie » et qui vouaient une grande affection à leurs *pappos aviasque trementes*, « les grands-papas et les grands-mamans tout tremblotants », sont là pour nous donner l'image d'heureuses familles au sein desquelles les femmes ont joué un rôle moins négligeable que pourrait le faire croire l'infériorité de leur statut juridique. Soulignons qu'après la mort de leur mari, elles jouissaient d'une disposition particulièrement favorable : outre la dot, qui leur revenait, elles touchaient une somme égale à cette dot et, de plus, les « fruits » de cette mise de fonds commune, ce qui devait assurer leur sécurité matérielle.

Les résistances de l'identité

En perdant leur langue, les Gaulois ont perdu leur identité. Encore est-il fort malaisé de repérer les étapes de cet effacement. À la fin du IIᵉ siècle, plus de deux cents ans après la conquête, Irénée, l'évêque de Lyon, se plaignait de devoir apprendre le dialecte « barbare » qu'on parlait autour de lui. Au IVᵉ siècle encore, le père d'Ausone, médecin réputé et fin lettré, confessait qu'il n'était jamais parvenu à parler facilement le latin et, à la même époque, saint Jérôme signalait que les Galates d'Asie Mineure parlaient presque exactement la même langue que les habitants de la région de Trèves. Souvent, en fait, comme l'atteste une inscription du IIIᵉ siècle, on devait parler une sorte de dialecte où la langue latine empruntait au gaulois des mots qu'elle habillait tandis que le gaulois s'enrichissait de mots latins qu'il déformait. On y lit en effet *nata vimpi curmi da*, où *nata* (« la fille ») et *da* (« donne-moi ») sont latins, et *vimpi* (« jolie ? ») et *curmi* (« de la bière ») sont gaulois. Et lorsque les potiers écrivent dans leur comptabilité les noms latins des vases, nouveaux pour eux, ils transforment *acetabula* (« vinaigriers ») en *acitabli*, *atramentaria* (« encriers ») en *atramitaria*, et *vinaria* (« vases à vin ») en *vinareus*. Latin défiguré et gaulois parlé ont dû constituer le langage courant des Gallo-Romains, même si la langue du conquérant avait tout pour imposer sa loi.

Elle était la langue de l'armée où de nombreux Gaulois furent enrôlés ; des commerçants qui s'arrêtaient dans le moindre bourg ; de l'administration, aucun document public n'étant rédigé en gaulois ; des monnaies qui passaient de main en main ; des bornes milliaires que le voyageur rencontrait au bord de la route ; des inscriptions placées au fronton des monuments ; des pantomimes qu'on jouait dans les théâtres ruraux ; des déclarations sentimentales gravées sur les vases à boire ou sur les bagues.

Surtout, les druides ayant disparu, frappés d'interdiction par l'empereur Claude, la langue latine est devenue la langue unique d'un enseignement chargé d'alimenter les carrières de l'administration publique. Apprendre à écrire l'alphabet latin de vingt-trois lettres avec un stylet en bronze ou en fer sur des tablettes de bois dont la surface évidée était enduite de cire, subir le fouet en cas d'erreur, apprendre par cœur, à partir de onze ans, les textes des poètes classiques, les règles de la grammaire, commenter les termes géographiques, historiques et mythologiques, acquérir enfin l'art oratoire dans les écoles réputées d'Autun, de Marseille ou de Bordeaux, tel était le parcours des brillants écoliers qui surent devenir des orateurs remarquables, l'apprentissage de la rhétorique latine ayant dû être un délice pour ces jeunes Gaulois si sensibles, selon les auteurs anciens, au plaisir de se mettre en valeur par de belles formules et de déprécier les autres par quelque trait d'esprit.

S'il y a une preuve de la résistance de l'identité gauloise à l'insolence du vainqueur, c'est bien dans la persistance des divinités et des rites hérités du passé. Les dieux du panthéon gréco-romain se sont apparemment imposés parce qu'ils ont été contraints de se celtiser. Mercure, le dieu gréco-romain du commerce et l'« inventeur de tous les arts », apparaît comme le dieu le plus vénéré de toute la Gaule romaine, car les Gaulois l'ont assimilé à Lug, l'une de leurs grandes divinités. Si les croyances et les pratiques des occupants ont été adoptées, c'est qu'elles correspondaient à des traditions profondes du passé gaulois. Ainsi, lorsqu'un Gallo-Romain fait graver une dédicace à Jupiter ou à Apollon, le plus souvent, il s'agit d'un dieu gaulois assimilé nominalement à Jupiter ou Apollon.

Pour démontrer que les dieux gallo-romains sont plus gaulois que romains, il suffit d'ailleurs de regarder les lieux où se dressent les sanctuaires et d'observer tel détail de leur représentation. Les divinités animales, les cultes des montagnes, des arbres, des forêts, des sources, suscitent les mêmes rites aux mêmes lieux et souvent sous les mêmes noms. Et ce n'est pas un hasard si la fête d'Auguste et de Rome fut placée à Lyon, le 1er août, jour de la fête de Lug.

Peut-être même, comme le suggère la spectaculaire découverte du calendrier gaulois de Coligny, dans l'Ain, rédigé en langue gauloise au IIe siècle, en pleine époque romaine, les Gaulois ont-ils résisté au rythme du temps romain, préférant commencer la journée, non pas comme à Rome avec le milieu ou la fin de la nuit, mais au début de la nuit, divisant les mois en deux quinzaines et comptant les jours selon leur place après la nouvelle ou la pleine lune. Ainsi résistaient, à travers un océan de romanité, les infimes ruisseaux de l'identité gauloise.

13

Le temps des malheurs

*E*n *162, alors qu'en Arménie les Parthes envahissent l'Empire romain, les Chattes, un peuple germanique, s'infiltrent dans le nord de la Belgique. En 166, deux siècles après que Jules César eut rejeté Ario- viste au-delà du Rhin, des Quades et des Marcomans franchissent le Danube, traversent les Alpes et se montrent en Italie du Nord, comme au temps des Cimbres et des Teutons. En 172, d'autres pénètrent en Alsace. Avec ces premières brèches dans la ligne de défense édifiée depuis deux siècles pour endiguer la menace germanique, les mauvais temps s'annon- cent en Gaule romaine, comme si une « crise de société » minait le bel édifice construit par Rome et désespérait des hommes saisis de lassitude.*

La frontière transpercée

Aux menaces qui surgissent de l'extérieur s'ajoutent des troubles internes dont les premiers signes se manifestent après la mort de l'em- pereur Marc Aurèle, emporté en 180 par l'épidémie de peste qui sévis- sait alors, comme si ce terrible fléau annonçait aussi que l'âge d'or de la paix romaine avait épuisé son temps. En 186, un soldat du rang, Maternus, rassemble une troupe de déserteurs et se transforme en roi des brigands, courant les campagnes et rançonnant les villes. En 196, la Gaule devient le théâtre de la lutte entre deux généraux proclamés empereurs par leurs troupes, Septime Sévère et Claudius Albinus, sou- tenu par les élites romanisées. Le choc entre les deux prétendants eut lieu sous les murs de Lyon le 19 février 197 et Septime, vainqueur, laissa ses troupes piller la ville et y mettre le feu. Un désastre qui laissa des traces durables dans la capitale des Gaules.

Surtout, à partir de 235 et pendant près d'un demi-siècle, tandis que des pirates infestent les côtes de la Manche, la frontière du Rhin est régulièrement transpercée par des peuples qui ne se contentent plus de simples razzias mais apparaissent décidés à fuir le lugubre horizon des plaines du Nord pour se tailler une place au soleil en terre romaine. En 233 et 234, ce sont les Alamans qui ouvrent le bal, franchissant le *limes* et détruisant Strasbourg. En 253 et 254, les Alamans s'aventurèrent une nouvelle fois en Suisse, en Bourgogne et même en Auvergne, les plus hardis s'approchant de Milan, alors que les Francs franchissent à leur tour le Rhin et descendent par Metz qui est détruite, Reims et Paris. En 259 et 260, des troupes de Germains parviennent même jusqu'en Espagne et en Afrique après avoir sillonné les routes de Gaule. Et en 260, l'empereur Valérien est fait prisonnier par le roi de Perse Chahpour qui se serait servi de son captif comme marchepied pour monter à cheval. Jamais, depuis qu'on obéissait à ceux qui étaient honorés comme des divinités, l'Empire n'avait connu une telle humiliation.

L'insécurité, qu'attestent les multiples trésors monétaires enfouis par des populations apeurées, est telle, le sentiment d'être abandonné par Rome est si grand qu'un officier gaulois, Postumus, responsable du commandement sur le front rhénan, est proclamé empereur par ses troupes. Il ne s'agissait pas, bien sûr, pour les « rebelles », de faire « sécession » et de signifier que la Gaule ne voulait plus être romaine mais, tout au contraire, de se donner des moyens plus efficaces pour le rester.

Salué comme le « restaurateur des Gaules », doué d'une forte intelligence politique et de solides qualités militaires, Postumus s'appliqua à réparer les routes, à restaurer la monnaie et à repousser les Barbares qui, pendant les huit années de son règne, ne purent réussir à franchir le Rhin. Hélas ! en 268, il fut assassiné par ses troupes auxquelles il avait refusé le pillage de la ville de Mayence. L'empire des Gaules ne lui survécut guère. Après Marius et Victorinus, Tetricus, un notable de Bordeaux, fut désigné malgré lui pour lui succéder et se rallia finalement à Aurélien en 274.

À la mort de ce dernier, en 275, les invasions reprirent de plus belle. Ce fut, selon les chroniqueurs du temps, la grande curée, des milliers de Francs et d'Alamans déferlant sur les cités sans murailles, incendiant les édifices publics, dépouillant les temples de leurs trésors, profanant les tombeaux et pillant les riches *villae*. À Paris, les édifices qui s'élevaient sur la montagne Sainte-Geneviève furent éventrés, tandis que soixante ou soixante-dix villes étaient mises à sac. Comme l'écrivit le biographe de l'empereur Probus, qui tenta de colmater les brèches ouvertes par les « Barbares », « les Gaules étaient comme tombées au pouvoir des Germains ».

La Gaule retranchée

Frappée du dehors, la Gaule semble aussi minée du dedans. Déjà, on avait observé que l'empereur Antonin, né à Nîmes, n'avait fait construire aucun monument dans sa ville natale, que les grandes firmes industrielles, comme les poteries de Lezoux, voyaient leur production décliner, que les routes ne semblaient plus être aussi soigneusement entretenues, que les fonctions municipales étaient moins recherchées, les charges devenant trop lourdes pour des particuliers dont les fortunes commençaient à s'étioler, à la mesure d'une inflation qui, tout au long du IIIe siècle, avait rongé la monnaie. En 215, l'*antoninianus* valant deux deniers pesait 5,11 g ; en 269, il pesait 3 grammes seulement. De plus, alors qu'il y avait encore 50 % d'argent dans la pièce de 215, celle de 269 n'en contenait plus que 1 %. Autant dire que cette monnaie « saucée » de cuivre et de plomb ne valait pratiquement rien. Il faut ajouter que, véritable maîtresse de l'Empire qui ne pouvait survivre sans elle, l'armée dévorait les finances d'un État dont la seule ressource était d'augmenter les impôts.

À en croire les contemporains, l'aspect des villes était lugubre, les édifices élevés à la gloire de Rome servant d'asile de nuit aux vagabonds. Visitant Besançon au milieu du IVe siècle après J.-C., l'empereur Julien observait que la ville était ramassée sur elle-même alors qu'autrefois, « elle était grande et ornée de sanctuaires luxueux ». Même si, aujourd'hui, les historiens nuancent ce trop sombre tableau, reste qu'il faut bien observer que les villes encore ouvertes s'enferment dans des fortifications élevées avec les ruines des monuments détruits par les invasions. Ce fut le cas à Lutèce, Sens, Tours ou Périgueux. Autun qui, sous Auguste, avait une enceinte de 6 kilomètres et une superficie de 200 hectares, se voit réduite à 11 hectares frileusement protégés par un rempart qui ne mesure plus que 1 300 mètres. Saintes se réduit de 168 à 18 hectares, Amiens de 100 à 10. À Nîmes, les fortifications n'englobent plus que 32 hectares au lieu des 220 que comptait la cité avant les invasions. Et si Bourges, Poitiers, Sens ou surtout Narbonne manifestent encore quelques splendeurs, Senlis,

Soissons, Auxerre, Évreux, Rennes, Le Mans, Nantes, Périgueux et Limoges font piètre figure.

Tandis que dans certaines villes le pavé et les trottoirs disparaissaient sous un amoncellement de décombres où se mêlaient les vestiges de la vie d'autrefois, les campagnes devenaient la proie de véritables jacqueries. Cultivateurs spoliés, soldats déserteurs, esclaves en cavale, petit peuple des villes que l'absence de grands travaux laissait sans travail alimentaient des troupes de pillards qui se désignaient elles-mêmes sous le nom de bagaudes (*baga* étant un mot celte qui signifie « combat »).

Et, alors que les temples ruraux n'étaient plus que des masses de décombres, que les drainages n'étaient plus entretenus, que les paysans réoccupaient les oppidums perchés, abandonnés par leurs ancêtres après la conquête romaine, les riches aristocrates, fuyant les villes où se dissolvaient les plaisirs et les liens que la romanisation avait tissés, ajoutaient à leurs *villae* des tours de défense qui annonçaient les châteaux forts. Surtout, profitant des malheurs du temps pour accaparer les terres des petits propriétaires ruinés, ils se taillaient des domaines qui devenaient des sortes d'usines champêtres. Le propriétaire de la *villa* de Montmaurin agrandit ainsi son ancienne demeure pour édifier un château de deux cents pièces juxtaposées sur plus de 4 hectares.

En même temps, à mesure que se rétracte l'économie de marché que ne lubrifie plus le commerce sur des routes incertaines, ces immenses propriétés tentent de se replier sur elles-mêmes et de vivre en une économie fermée où chacun aspire à pourvoir à ses besoins. Ausone, notre poète-professeur bordelais, s'en félicite : « Salut, petit héritage, royaume de mes ancêtres, que mon bisaïeul, mon grand-père, mon père ont cultivé et que celui-ci m'a laissé déjà vieux, lors de sa mort prématurée... Je cultive 200 jugères de champs, 100 jugères de vignobles et la moitié de prairies ; les bois s'étendent sur plus du double des prés, vignes et terres labourables. Mes cultivateurs ne sont pas trop nombreux et ne manquent pas non plus. Auprès, une source, un petit puits et le fleuve aux eaux pures, navigable, soumis aux pulsations de la marée qui m'amène et me remporte. J'engrange toujours les récoltes pour deux années, car qui n'a pas de grandes réserves est voué rapidement à la famine. Ma terre n'est située ni loin de la ville, ni près de la ville ; ainsi j'échappe aux foules et je profite de mes biens. »

Les invasions ont également charrié une transformation appelée à un grand avenir. Acceptés par les autorités, des Germains faits prisonniers, qu'on appelle des lètes, s'installent dans les campagnes, surtout dans l'est et le centre de la Gaule. « Ici, nous dit-on, les Barbares de Batavie se rendent avec femmes, parents et biens et passent en des régions depuis longtemps désertées afin de rendre en culture des terres qu'eux-mêmes avaient un jour dévastées au cours de leurs déprédations. » Un autre peut dire avec orgueil : « C'est pour moi que labourent à cette heure le Chamave ou le Frison, que ce vagabond, ce pillard peine à travailler sans relâche mes terres en friche, peuple mon marché du bétail qu'il vient y vendre, et que le laboureur barbare fait baisser le prix des denrées. » Un dernier, prononçant en 297 l'éloge du futur empereur Constance, déclare : « Sous les portiques de toutes les cités, les Barbares prisonniers sont assis à la file [...] tous, répartis entre les provinciaux pour servir chez eux, attendant d'être conduits sur les terres désolées dont ils doivent assurer la culture. »

Certes, cette colonisation a permis de résoudre les problèmes de main-d'œuvre et de dépopulation, mais elle a aussi introduit en terre gauloise un élément germanique qui a probablement ralenti les progrès de la romanisation. Est-ce pour cette raison que, dans la religion comme dans l'art, resurgit le vieux fonds indigène que la vague romaine semblait avoir submergé ? Toujours est-il que les dieux gaulois déguisés sous l'habit gréco-romain reprennent désormais les formes spontanées et primitives qu'ils avaient autrefois. C'est aussi la lieue gauloise de 2 222 mètres qui prend sur les bornes milliaires la place du mille romain de 1 480 mètres. Sur les pièces frappées dans les provinces, on retrouve certains motifs et certains symboles du répertoire indigène d'avant la conquête. Le bois et les matériaux légers supplantent la pierre. Le souvenir des anciens peuples de la Gaule resurgit enfin, leur nom s'imposant pour désigner les capitales des nouvelles cités. Ainsi Avaricum prend le nom des Bituriges qui deviendra Bourges, Lutèce celui des Parisii. Et c'est pour cette raison que nos plus vieilles villes de France portent aujourd'hui non pas le nom romain qui leur avait été donné au moment de la conquête mais celui des anciens peuples de la Gaule, les Bellovaques à Beauvais, les Rèmes à Reims, les Lémovices à Limoges, les Carnutes à Chartres, les Pictons à Poitiers.

Des religions mystères aux premiers chrétiens

Les malheurs des temps expliquent la vogue des religions orientales qui font davantage appel à la valeur personnelle et aux actes de la vie pour assurer la survie après la mort.

Il en va ainsi des hommages rendus à Cybèle, la Grande Mère phrygienne, à laquelle on sacrifie des taureaux à Lyon en décembre de l'année 160. À Marseille, à Nîmes, à Arles et à Lyon, est aussi célébré le culte de la déesse égyptienne Isis. Puis celui du dieu perse Mithra, honoré dans des temples semi-enterrés où l'on pratiquait le sacrifice du taureau dont le sang purifiait les fidèles, laisse des traces nombreuses dans les vallées du Rhône et de la Saône, et surtout parmi les soldats campés à la frontière du Rhin. Enfin, les premiers chrétiens font leur apparition à Vienne, à Autun, et surtout à Lyon, dans les communautés orientales de marchands convertis par des missionnaires venus d'Asie.

Tout ce que nous savons sur la première Église de Lyon nous est connu par une lettre que les chrétiens de cette ville envoyèrent en 177 à leurs frères d'Asie, au lendemain de la sanglante persécution qui venait de les frapper. À cette date, l'Église de Lyon avait pour évêque Pothin, un vieillard d'origine orientale qui avait plus de quatre-vingt-dix ans et aurait pu connaître, dans sa prime jeunesse, l'apôtre Jean. Le récit des souffrances endurées par les premières victimes des persécutions permet de mesurer l'hostilité suscitée par une religion qui, se voulant universelle et exclusive, faisait apparaître ses fidèles comme des dissidents au sein de la cité romaine, comme une secte illégale hostile à l'État. « Non seulement, peut-on lire, on nous interdisait les maisons, les bains, le forum, mais encore, d'une manière générale, on défendait à chacun de nous de paraître en quelque lieu que ce fût. »

Puis, on les accusa, surtout dans les milieux populaires, d'adorer un personnage à tête d'âne et, dans leurs réunions, d'égorger les enfants, de dévorer leur chair et de se livrer à d'abominables débauches. Dans l'amphithéâtre où ils furent martyrisés, Attale, un de leurs membres, fait allusion à ces accusations en s'écriant : « Ce n'est pas nous qui mangeons la chair humaine ; nous ne faisons rien de mal. » Vers la fin du règne de Marc Aurèle, ces haines s'exaspèrent, peut-être excitées par les adorateurs de Cybèle.

Arrêtés puis jugés, ils participent aux spectacles offerts au début du mois d'août à la foule qui se pressait près de l'autel des Trois Gaules dédié à Rome et à Auguste. Il est même probable que celui qui fut alors élu comme grand prêtre ait trouvé judicieux de limiter les dépenses qu'entraînait le recrutement de gladiateurs et habile d'offrir ce nouveau divertissement à des spectateurs toujours avides de « nouveautés ».

Le déchaînement de fureur que la foule manifesta lors du supplice de Blandine, une jeune esclave réservée pour le dernier jour des combats, montre à quel point l'attitude du gouvernement impérial à l'égard des premiers chrétiens est largement déterminée par la crainte de voir l'ordre public menacé par des fanatiques dont l'intolérance lui faisait peur.

Toujours selon le rédacteur de la lettre, après leur mort, on exposa pendant six jours ce qui restait des membres déchirés par les bêtes ou dévorés par le feu. « Ensuite, on les brûla, on les réduisit en cendres et les pervers les jetèrent dans le Rhône qui coule près de là, afin qu'il ne parût plus aucun vestige d'eux sur la terre. Ils faisaient cela comme s'ils pouvaient vaincre Dieu et priver leurs victimes de la nouvelle naissance, afin, disaient-ils, qu'ils n'aient plus l'espoir d'une résurrection en la foi de laquelle ils introduisent chez nous un culte étranger et nouveau et méprisent les supplices, prêts à aller joyeusement à la mort. Maintenant voyons s'ils ressusciteront et si leur Dieu pourra les secourir et les arracher de nos mains. »

Après ces tragiques événements et l'épiscopat d'Irénée qui succéda à Pothin, l'Église de Lyon disparaît pendant tout le IIIᵉ siècle et nous ignorons presque tout des autres communautés fondées en Gaule. À Autun, l'existence de chrétiens est toutefois attestée par une inscription trouvée dans cette ville, gravée en grec par un habitant nommé Pektorios et empreinte du symbolisme mystique qui voyait dans l'image du poisson l'image même du Christ : « Race divine du Poisson céleste, peut-on lire, fortifie ton cœur, toi qui as reçu la vie immortelle parmi les mortels. Dans les eaux divines, réjouis ton âme, mon ami, par les flots éternels de la sagesse qui donne les trésors [...] Poisson qui nourris les poissons, maître et sauveur, lumière des morts, je t'en conjure, que ma mère repose en paix. Aschandios, père bien-aimé de mon cœur, avec ma tendre mère et mes frères [...], souviens-toi de Pektorios. »

Fondée sur des images simples où le Christ apparaissait comme un protecteur doux et familier sous les traits du Bon Pasteur, où la mort n'était qu'un sommeil transitoire et le Paradis un beau jardin plein de lumière et de parfums, nul doute que cette religion nouvelle ne pouvait que séduire des âmes troublées par les malheurs du temps.

L'évêque et le barbare

« D es peuples innombrables et sauvages occupent la Gaule. Des Alpes à l'Océan, des Pyrénées au Rhin, on voit les Quades, les Vandales, les Sarmates, les Alains, les Gépides, les Hérules, les Saxons, les Burgondes et les Alamans dévaster villes et villages. [...] Reims est en ruine. Amiens, Arras, l'extrême terre des Morins, Tournai, Spire et Strasbourg sont passées à la Germanie. L'Aquitaine est ravagée. » Ce pitoyable tableau que dresse de la Gaule saint Jérôme en 410 montre assez que les hommes de ce temps ont bien eu conscience de vivre la « fin d'un monde ». En réponse à ce désarroi se développe une nouvelle religion dont témoignent les multiples représentations du Christ, et s'affirme un nouveau pouvoir, l'Église, qui paraît seul capable de tenir tête aux Barbares.

Le « melting pot » gaulois

Depuis le IIIe siècle, par infiltrations progressives plus que par invasions massives, les « Barbares » ont investi la Gaule. C'est qu'entre la terre qui manquait de bras et l'armée qui en réclamait sans cesse, on se disputait les hommes.

Certes, les empereurs Dioclétien (284-305) puis Constantin (306-337) ont bien tenté de réformer l'État. Mais ils ont eu beau mettre en place la tétrarchie, un gouvernement simultané de l'Empire par quatre chefs, deux Augustes, l'un à l'ouest et l'autre à l'est, épaulés par deux Césars appelés à leur succéder, regrouper en deux diocèses les dix-sept provinces de la Gaule, renforcer la défense du *limes* par la constitution d'une armée mobile d'intervention, contenir l'inflation par un sévère contrôle des prix, émettre une monnaie plus saine, le *solidus*, le futur sou, et revoir l'assiette de l'impôt pour en soulager le fardeau, l'utilisation croissante de Barbares au sein de l'armée comme la multiplication de colons dans les campagnes ont progressivement « barbarisé » la Gaule, tant il est vrai que les minorités fécondes sont souvent le levain des sociétés.

Même s'il est particulièrement difficile de dresser la courbe de la population gallo-romaine, force est de constater l'émoi des empereurs et de leurs fonctionnaires devant ce qu'ils perçoivent bien comme une baisse dramatique de la fécondité des couples. Il suffit d'observer l'arbre généalogique du notable et poète aquitain Ausone pour en prendre la mesure. Le grand-père maternel d'Ausone a eu quatre enfants et son grand-père paternel cinq. Le père d'Ausone en a eu quatre et son beau-père trois, comme Ausone lui-même. Mais, parmi ses descendants, on note deux ménages avec un seul enfant et un ménage sans enfants. Et dans les familles encore plus fortunées, les plus instruites et les plus sensibles aux conseils des médecins qui ont mis à leur disposition un éventail de recettes et de produits, le taux de fécondité est largement descendu en dessous du seuil de remplacement des générations. Peut-être faut-il y voir aussi l'influence de l'Église chrétienne qui place la virginité au premier rang des valeurs humaines, multiplie les périodes de continence sexuelle et exhorte les veuves à ne pas se remarier ?

Même s'il ne faut pas exagérer l'influence de cette nouvelle morale sexuelle, cette « dépression » démographique sensible a bien aspiré l'immigration de Barbares devenus si nombreux et si visibles qu'un historien oriental n'a pas hésité à les qualifier de nouveau « peuple de Gaule ». Dans le nord du pays, en particulier, leur pourcentage atteint peut-être 12 à 21 % de la population totale, ce qui est considérable. Des toponymes comme Gueux (de Goths) ou Villers-Franqueux (de Francs) autour de Reims, Sermoise (de Sarmates) près de Nevers, Allainville (d'Alains), sur la route d'Orléans, Allonnes (toujours d'Alains) près du Mans, Gandalou ou Gandaille dans le Toulousain ou dans l'Albigeois (de Vandales), gardent la trace de leurs établissements.

Et après avoir occupé très tôt la région de Calais et de Boulogne, les Saxons occupent ensuite le Bessin tandis que des Bretons sont appelés pour tenir garnison en Armorique. Les fouilles de Saint-Urnel à Plomeur, dans le Finistère, ont ainsi démontré que dans la seconde moitié du IVᵉ siècle, les caractères anthropologiques des cadavres inhumés étaient totalement différents de ceux de la population indigène mais identiques, en revanche, à ceux des habitants de l'ouest des îles Britanniques.

L'armée, surtout, assure la montée en puissance des chefs barbares. Après avoir été enrôlés par engagement personnel ou sous forme de troupes auxiliaires, on les retrouve bientôt dans le haut commandement. Des Francs sous l'empereur Constantin, des Goths sous Théodose ont désormais la responsabilité d'opérations militaires. À cet égard, l'histoire de l'aventurier Charietto est exemplaire. Après avoir abandonné son pays et s'être établi à Trèves, l'idée lui vient de défendre les villes de la Gaule contre ses frères barbares. Un jour, il va surprendre dans les forêts des bandes de Germains, alors qu'ils sont plongés dans l'ivresse et le sommeil, coupe les têtes de ceux qu'il a tués et revient les montrer aux habitants de Trèves. Bientôt, il est le chef d'une troupe qu'il met au service de l'empereur. Quelques années plus tard, on le retrouve investi d'un commandement militaire important.

Si, au siècle précédent, l'empereur Probus avait dissimulé les 16 000 Barbares qu'il avait enrôlés en les disséminant dans diverses provinces dans la mesure où, disait-il, « il ne faut pas qu'on voie ce que Rome doit aux auxiliaires barbares », Constantin les autorise à porter leur emblème sur leurs boucliers, à garder leurs casques et leurs vêtements et à chanter leur cri de guerre qu'ils introduisent finalement dans l'armée romaine. Et, en 360, Julien est proclamé Auguste par ses troupes à Paris en étant élevé sur le pavois, selon la coutume franque. En 372, enfin, l'empereur Valentinien confie le commandement en chef de l'armée au Franc Mérobaud qui, en 377, devient consul !

Éprouvant un vif sentiment de lassitude et de désespoir, se trouvant mêlés à des « immigrés » dont ils supportaient mal l'odeur et les usages, constatant la déliquescence de l'administration, se plaignant que le latin s'abâtardissait et que le grec n'était plus enseigné, les hommes de ce temps ont ainsi eu la conviction que la *Romania*, leur patrie commune, se dérobait sous leurs pieds. En 397, 399 et 416, des lois peuvent bien interdire à Rome le port des cheveux longs, des bottes et des braies qui tendaient à devenir la mode et que des empereurs avaient adoptés, la barbarisation était si avancée que la Ville éternelle apparaissait captive avant d'être prise, même si un panégyriste du temps pouvait encore écrire de la *Romania* : « C'est elle qui seule a reçu dans son sein ceux qu'elle avait vaincus, et, se conduisant en mère, non en reine, a donné un même nom à tout le genre humain ; de ceux qu'elle a domptés, elle a fait des citoyens, elle a réuni par des liens sacrés les peuples éloignés. C'est grâce à sa politique pacifique que partout nous retrouvons une patrie, que nous ne formons tous qu'une nation. Jamais il n'y aura de terme à la domination romaine ! »

Un ouragan sur la Gaule

Si l'intégration progressive de Barbares aux plus hautes fonctions militaires et politiques peut apparaître comme la preuve d'une assimilation maîtrisée, l'invasion qui se déclenche le 31 décembre 406 frappe cette fois la Gaule comme un véritable ouragan. Ce jour-là, en effet, franchissant le Rhin gelé près de Mayence avec femmes, enfants, vieillards et troupeaux, deux peuples germaniques, les Vandales et les Suèves, et une peuplade d'origine orientale, les Alains, se déversent en masse en terre gauloise.

Fuyant devant la pression des redoutables Huns qui, après avoir traversé le Don en 375, ont poussé devant eux des tribus entières vers l'ouest, ils balaient les Francs rhénans qui tentent de les repousser et, empruntant les confortables voies romaines, traversent la Gaule de long en large, dévastant les riches plaines céréalières du Nord avant de ravager l'Aquitaine et de franchir les Pyrénées en octobre 409.

« Vois avec quelle soudaineté la mort a pesé sur le monde entier, écrit alors Orens, l'évêque d'Auch, combien la violence de la guerre a frappé de peuples. Ni le sol raboteux des bois épais ou des hautes montagnes, ni le courant des rivières aux tourbillons rapides, ni l'abri que constituent pour les châteaux leur site, pour les villes leurs remparts, ni même les cavernes que surplombent de sombres rochers, n'ont pu échapper aux mains des Barbares [...] Dans les bourgs, les domaines, les campagnes, aux carrefours, dans tous les districts, çà et là, tout le long des routes, c'est la mort, la souffrance, la destruction, l'incendie, le deuil. Toute la Gaule, en un seul bûcher, est partie en fumée. »

Pour accroître la confusion et désespérer tous ceux qui respectaient encore le pouvoir impérial, Rome fut mise à sac en 410 par les Wisigoths qui s'acheminèrent alors vers la Gaule en emmenant dans leurs bagages Galla Placidia, la sœur de l'empereur, qu'épousa le 1er janvier 414 à Narbonne le roi Athaulf. À cette occasion, le Barbare, vêtu d'une toge romaine, témoigna d'une grande déférence à l'égard de son épouse, lui cédant l'honneur de conduire la procession.

Ce mariage entre la princesse du Sud et le Barbare du Nord traduisait bien en fait la réalité des temps. Rome était désormais incapable de colmater les brèches et de s'opposer aux peuples qui avaient la compréhensible ambition de profiter des circonstances pour s'installer, cette fois-ci, de façon durable en concluant avec l'empereur un *foedus*, ou traité.

Les Wisigoths furent précisément les premiers à en bénéficier.

En 418, ils reçurent l'autorisation de s'établir de manière permanente en opulente Aquitaine pour défendre les rivages occidentaux de la Gaule contre les écumeurs des mers et l'intérieur des terres contre toute bagaude. En contrepartie, pour subvenir à leurs besoins, ils reçurent les deux tiers des terres laissées vacantes par leurs propriétaires ou appartenant à l'État. D'abord centré sur Toulouse, la capitale, le royaume des Goths ne cessa de s'étendre au fil du siècle, grâce au ralliement d'une partie de l'aristocratie romaine pour qui ces « Barbares », au demeurant fort prévenants, apparaissaient parfois comme les instruments de la vengeance de Dieu contre une société corrompue. « Les Romains souhaitent de n'être plus jamais contraints à redevenir sujets de Rome, écrit au milieu du siècle Salvien, prêtre à Marseille, ils prient le ciel de les laisser vivre comme ils vivent avec les Barbares », tandis qu'un autre avoue, « les Barbares, exécrant leurs glaives, se tournent vers la charrue, ils traitent en alliés, en amis les Romains qui préfèrent vivre au milieu des Barbares, pauvres mais libres, qu'écrasés d'impôts sous la protection des fonctionnaires romains ».

Après la Novempopulanie (Gascogne), le Berry est atteint en 469, la Provence annexée en 470-472, la Septimanie en 472, l'Auvergne en 474-475 et l'Espagne est à son tour gagnée, de sorte qu'à son apogée, le royaume des Goths comptait sans doute pas loin de 10 millions d'habitants et s'étendait sur quelque 750 000 kilomètres carrés.

Amoureux des arts, des lettres et du droit, les rois de Toulouse surent respecter les biens de ceux dont ils avaient pillé les maisons et séduire les grands esprits de leur temps à tel point qu'une bonne partie de l'« opinion » régionale leur fut bien vite acquise. Seul obstacle, mais de taille, à leur intégration totale, les Goths avaient épousé l'arianisme, une forme du christianisme qui niait l'unité de la Trinité et établissait une différence entre Dieu, le Père et le Fils, une hérésie qui allait bientôt mobiliser contre eux la hiérarchie ecclésiastique.

À l'est, ce sont les Burgondes qui, d'abord installés en *Sapaudia* (la Suisse romande et le sud du Jura français actuels), s'étendent dans les années 457-485 jusqu'à Dijon et Langres, mettant au passage la main sur Lyon. Flatté de recevoir de l'empereur romain des titres aussi

prestigieux que « patrice » ou « maître de la milice », le roi Gondebaud, dont l'évêque de Vienne vante l'esprit philosophique et l'éloquence, sut pratiquer une politique de tolérance religieuse, une partie
de la famille royale dont Clotilde, la future épouse de Clovis, se
convertissant même au catholicisme. Cultivant les terres qui leur
avaient été attribuées, ils surent aussi respecter la propriété d'autrui,
les vols étant sévèrement punis, parfois de mort.

Contrairement aux Wisigoths, aux Burgondes ou aux Alamans
qui profitent aussi de l'invasion de 406 pour s'établir en Alsace et
dans le Palatinat, les Francs ne sont pas des nouveaux venus en Gaule.
Originaires de la rive droite du bas Rhin, ceux qu'on appelait
« Francs », soit parce qu'ils s'étaient « libérés » du joug romain (ce
serait le premier sens du mot « franc »), soit parce qu'ils étaient considérés comme particulièrement « hardis » (ce serait l'autre sens du mot
« franc »), avaient mis leurs qualités militaires au service de l'armée
romaine. Parmi cet ensemble de tribus, deux s'étaient progressivement
affirmées. À l'est, ceux qu'on appelait Rhénans étaient placés sous
l'autorité d'un roi installé à Cologne et s'étaient implantés à l'ouest
du fleuve, sur une profondeur de 50 à 100 kilomètres. Au nord, ceux
qu'on appelait Saliens, peut-être parce qu'ils étaient placés sous l'autorité d'une famille originaire du Salland, dans les Pays-Bas actuels,
paraissaient divisés en plusieurs chefferies associées entre elles par
des mariages. Leur implantation dans la moitié nord de la Belgique et
dans l'extrême nord de la France était tellement forte qu'ils avaient
fini par y imposer l'usage, définitif dans la plupart de ces régions, de
leur langue comme l'atteste la fréquence des noms de lieux terminés
en *hem*, *ghem*, *ghien*, *ain*, *sala*, *seele*, *zele*, qui indiquent la demeure.

C'est dans la région de Tournai que s'observent les premiers
signes de leur ascension. En 448, un chef militaire salien nommé Clo-
dion avait étendu son influence en direction d'Arras et de Cambrai.
Dans les années 460-470, un de leurs rois, Childéric, avait conduit ses
guerriers jusqu'aux bords de la Loire où il s'était heurté aux Wisigoths
qui voulaient franchir le fleuve et aux Saxons qui voulaient le
remonter.

Mais c'est alliés au généralissime romain Aetius qu'en 451 Wisigoths, Alains, Burgondes, Bretons d'Armorique, Saxons et Francs
repoussent près de Troyes, à la bataille des champs Catalauniques, le
Hun Attila qui avait pénétré dans une Gaule que ces « Barbares »
défendaient désormais comme leur « terre promise ».

Les défricheurs d'âmes

Tandis que la Gaule romaine se désintégrait sous la pression des Barbares, un mouvement de portée considérable se déroulait dans les villes et les campagnes et amorçait la naissance d'un *nouveau monde*, vivifié par la patiente progression du christianisme.

Depuis qu'en 313, l'empereur Constantin, converti à la nouvelle religion, avait établi dans tout l'Empire la pleine liberté de conscience, l'Église pouvait désormais compter sur le soutien de l'État pour conquérir les esprits et défricher les âmes. Dès 314, au concile d'Arles qui réunit les évêques d'Occident, seize cités gauloises sont représentées, dont Vienne, Lyon, Vaison, Marseille, Bordeaux, Autun, Rouen et Reims. Trente ans plus tard, au concile de Cologne, on en compte soixante-dix, Langres, Sens, Auxerre, Troyes, Orléans, Paris, Metz, Verdun, Amiens, Strasbourg, Besançon apparaissant pour la première fois. À la fin du siècle, quand l'empereur Théodose interdit le paganisme, chaque cité a désormais son évêque.

Deux fortes personnalités furent les incontestables « patrons » de ces premiers chrétiens. Né à Poitiers, vers 315, Hilaire y acquiert une solide formation littéraire avant de comprendre que les biens terrestres, « quoiqu'ils rassemblent en eux-mêmes les plus grands et les meilleurs agréments de la vie, ne semblent pas différer beaucoup de ceux où se complaisent les animaux ». Élu évêque de sa ville en 350, peu de temps après son baptême, il combat vigoureusement l'arianisme, qui progressait dans les cercles gouvernementaux, et s'affirme comme le farouche défenseur d'une orthodoxie encore fragile. Exilé par l'empereur Constance, il écrit son traité *Sur la Trinité*, première production théologique conservée d'une Gaule qui échappera, grâce à lui, aux tourments provoqués en Orient par l'hérésie. « La malignité des hérétiques, disait-il, nous force à faire des choses illicites, à gravir des cimes inaccessibles, à parler de sujets ineffables, à oser aborder des questions interdites. Il devrait suffire d'accomplir par la foi seule ce qui est prescrit, c'est-à-dire d'adorer le Père, de vénérer avec lui le Fils et de nous remplir du Saint-Esprit. Mais nous sommes contraints d'appliquer notre humble parole aux mystères les plus inénarrables. La faute d'autrui nous jette nous-mêmes dans cette faute d'exposer aux risques du langage humain ce qu'il aurait fallu tenir renfermé dans la religion de nos âmes. »

C'est toutefois avec saint Martin, évêque de Tours de 371 à sa mort en 397, que la Gaule allait avoir, faute de martyr, un grand saint populaire à vénérer, à tel point que le vocable d'église Saint-Martin et le nom de village Saint-Martin sont aujourd'hui les plus répandus en France. Sa vie, écrite avant même sa mort par l'Aquitain Sulpice Sévère qui le rencontra à plusieurs reprises, connut un énorme succès et nous permet, au-delà du merveilleux, de pénétrer l'intimité de ces défricheurs d'âmes.

Martin naît en 316 à Sabaria en Pannonie, non loin de la frontière du Danube. Ayant embrassé, comme son père, la carrière militaire, on le retrouve aux environs de sa dix-huitième année en garnison à Amiens où il reçoit probablement le baptême. C'est là que le récit de Sulpice Sévère place le geste de charité qui l'a rendu célèbre, partageant son manteau d'un coup d'épée pour en donner la moitié à un pauvre.

Après avoir quitté l'armée en 356, être allé trouver Hilaire à Poitiers et avoir tenté en vain de convertir sa famille au christianisme, il installe à Ligugé une communauté de moines qui pratiquent l'ascèse et le soin aux pauvres. En 371, « enlevé » par les habitants qui l'arrachent à sa cellule, il est élu évêque de Tours contre l'avis des évêques présents qui déclarent « indigne de l'épiscopat un homme de si piteuse mine, mal vêtu, mal peigné ».

À partir du monastère de Marmoutier dans lequel il occupe une cellule en bois, il parcourt les campagnes pour s'attaquer aux centres de cultes païens encore vivaces, y substituer des églises et des monastères et y ordonner des prêtres. Il meurt à Candes, non loin de Tours, en novembre 397. Ses funérailles furent l'occasion d'une cérémonie exceptionnelle, et la première chapelle qui surmonta son tombeau attira bientôt les pèlerins qui s'y pressaient dans l'attente d'une guérison miraculeuse. Tours était bien alors devenue la capitale religieuse de la Gaule.

Dans cette Gaule livrée à elle-même, l'image de l'évêque Martin s'imposait aussi comme celle du « veilleur », gardien des fidèles et bâtisseur, protecteur des faibles contre les puissants.

Dans une société où se délitaient les pouvoirs publics, l'évêque, élu par le suffrage des fidèles, apparaît en effet comme le seul pouvoir susceptible de tenir tête aux Barbares et de servir d'intermédiaire entre les nouveaux maîtres et les anciennes populations. Selon une législation dont l'origine remonte peut-être à l'empereur Constantin, il suffisait que, dans un procès, l'une des parties veuille déférer l'affaire à un évêque pour que les tribunaux laïques en soient dessaisis.

Aussi, administrateur de biens que la générosité des nouveaux convertis lui a légués, l'évêque devient bâtisseur, élevant des hospices et des lieux de culte et entretenant dans son diocèse la tradition architecturale qui avait fait la gloire de la Gaule romaine. En témoigne le poème que Sidoine Apollinaire consacre, vers 470, à décrire l'église construite à Lyon à l'initiative de l'évêque Patiens. « Le temple élevé brille [...] À l'intérieur, la lumière scintille et le soleil est à ce point attiré par le plafond doré que ses reflets empruntent la couleur au métal fauve. Du marbre orné de teintes variées règne sur la voûte, le sol, les fenêtres et, en des dessins chatoyants, sur fond d'herbe printanière, des incrustations font serpenter leurs petites pierres de saphir sur une surface de verre [...] D'un côté, le bruit de la route, de l'autre, la Saône font écho. D'un côté le voyageur à pied ou à cheval et le conducteur de chariots grinçants qui prennent le tournant, de l'autre le chœur des haleurs courbés en deux qui élèvent vers le Christ le chant rythmé des bateliers, tandis que les rives répondent en écho Alléluia. »

Reste à mesurer l'attrait qu'a exercé la nouvelle religion sur le batelier de la Saône. S'il est difficile d'évaluer la pénétration de l'Église dans l'âme des Gaulois, il semble bien toutefois que les populations aient trouvé dans les nouvelles croyances des compensations aux malheurs des temps. La fréquence de certaines formules gravées sur les sarcophages indique à quel point se diffuse une spiritualité exigeante où humilité, chasteté, ascèse deviennent des valeurs recherchées.

Renoncer aux biens terrestres, partir vers l'Égypte afin de voir comment la vie chrétienne y fleurit, tel devient le rêve des jeunes de bonne famille désireux de fuir le siècle. « La malpropreté de tes vêtements sera l'indice de la netteté de ton âme, la tunique grossière sera la preuve que tu méprises le monde », écrit Jérôme au jeune Gaulois Rusticus, envoyé à Rome par sa mère pour parfaire son éducation.

C'est Honorat, issu d'une puissante famille, qui, au retour d'un pèlerinage en Orient, s'établit dans l'île de Lérins et y organise un « camp de Dieu » destiné à recevoir dans son « sein charitable, écrit un de ses disciples, ceux qui sont échappés au naufrage du monde orageux et les recueille avec sollicitude, tous agités encore par la tempête du siècle, afin qu'ils reprennent le souffle sous l'ombre intime de Dieu ».

C'est Cassien qui, après avoir visité les couvents orientaux, fonde à Marseille deux monastères, l'un d'hommes, celui de Saint-Victor, l'autre de femmes, où il propose de « repasser en silence pendant les heures de la nuit les textes qu'on n'avait pas compris de prime abord ».

C'est Germain, l'évêque d'Auxerre, qui mène comme Martin une vie de solitude et continue de vivre comme un ermite. C'est Geneviève, la fille d'une famille de hauts dignitaires romains, vierge consacrée, qui prédit aux Parisiens que leur ville sera épargnée par Attila s'ils jeûnent trois jours, sans manger ni boire jusqu'au coucher du soleil.

Faut-il pour autant accuser l'Église, comme on le faisait autrefois, d'avoir rendu les populations de la Gaule trop indifférentes à leurs malheurs et trop résignées aux occupations des « bandes » barbares ? Ce serait confondre lâcheté et recherche d'une nouvelle spiritualité, patriotisme et aspiration à la sainteté.

CHAPITRE 15

Clovis, le premier roi chrétien

« C hildericus *étant mort*, Chlodovechus, *son fils, fut appelé à lui succéder.* » *C'est en ces termes fort peu bavards que Grégoire de Tours
évoque, dans l'*Histoire des Francs, *la prise de pouvoir de Clovis dont le
règne est de la plus haute importance pour les destinées de la France. Sa
conversion au catholicisme scelle en effet l'union des rois et de l'Église,
union que cette dernière contribua à rappeler et à magnifier. Ainsi, le diptyque d'ivoire consacré à la vie de saint Remi, postérieur de quatre siècles
au baptême de Clovis, nous en offre la première représentation. La mise en
scène, qui insiste sur l'aspect quasi divin de l'événement, tente de le faire
apparaître comme l'acte fondateur de la monarchie française.*

La promesse d'alliance

Né en 466, Clovis est âgé de quinze ans lorsqu'il succède à son
père Childéric. La tombe de ce dernier – découverte par hasard à
Tournai le 27 mai 1653 par un maçon sourd-muet, Adrien Quinquin,
à l'occasion des travaux de reconstruction de l'hospice Saint-Brice –
permet de mesurer l'ascension des Francs Saliens et le degré de
romanisation auquel ils étaient parvenus.

Childéric avait été revêtu d'habits de soie brochée d'or, et drapé
dans les larges plis d'un manteau de pourpre semé d'abeilles d'or. À
son ceinturon, garni de clous de même métal, on avait suspendu une
bourse contenant plus de trois cents monnaies d'or et d'argent aux

effigies des empereurs romains. On lui avait mis au cou un collier formé de médailles, au bras un bracelet, au doigt sa bague nuptiale et son anneau sigillaire, dont le chaton était orné de son image gravée en creux, avec cette légende : *Childirici Regis*.

Ses armes avaient pris place à côté de lui : d'une part, la framée ou lance royale, qui était comme le sceptre du roi germanique ; de l'autre, sa grande épée et la francisque, la redoutable hache d'armes des Francs.

À l'occasion des funérailles, plusieurs dizaines de jeunes étalons avaient été sacrifiés et enterrés dans des fosses disposées de façon rayonnante à une vingtaine de mètres de la tombe royale, une tombe de grande importance archéologique pour un roi d'assez modeste envergure.

La question qui mérite donc d'être posée est de savoir comment son fils a pu, en une vingtaine d'années, plier sous son autorité les puissants Barbares qui s'étaient partagé les dépouilles de la Gaule romaine, étendre les frontières de son royaume des rives du Rhin jusqu'aux Pyrénées et devenir le seul grand souverain d'Occident aux côtés de l'empereur de Byzance.

Une lettre signée par Remi, l'évêque de Reims, et adressée à Clovis au lendemain de sa prise de pouvoir souligne l'influence de l'Église dans cette fascinante destinée.

« Au seigneur insigne, magnifique par ses actions, le roi Clovis, Remi, évêque.

Une rumeur importante est parvenue jusqu'à nous : vous avez pris l'administration de la Belgique seconde. Il n'y a là rien de bien nouveau, tu deviens ce que tes parents ont toujours été.

Pour que le jugement du Seigneur ne t'abandonne pas, puisque tu es parvenu au faîte des honneurs, tu dois accomplir des actes méritoires car ce sont les actes qui témoignent en faveur de l'homme.

Tu dois t'attacher des conseillers qui seront l'ornement de ta renommée. Ta bonté doit s'exercer de manière chaste et honnête. Tu dois être rempli de respect pour les prêtres et recourir toujours à leurs conseils. Si tu t'accordes bien avec eux, ta province en sera renforcée. Aide les habitants des cités, relève les affligés, soutiens les veuves, nourris les orphelins et que tous t'aiment et te craignent à la fois.

Que la justice s'exprime par ta bouche, impartialement, sans attendre de dons des pauvres et des pérégrins. Que ton prétoire soit accessible à tous et que personne n'en soit chassé. Tu possèdes les richesses de ton père ; alors tu peux libérer les captifs et les absoudre du joug de la servitude. Si quelqu'un se présente devant toi, fais en sorte qu'il ne se sente pas étranger.

Amuse-toi avec les jeunes, discute avec les vieux, et, si tu veux régner, juge noblement. »

Chef spirituel de la Belgique seconde, Remi trace en fait pour le fils de Childéric un programme chrétien de gouvernement. Qu'il rende la justice, assure la paix et la liberté, protège les veuves et les orphelins, libère les opprimés et écoute les conseils des prêtres, et l'appui de l'Église lui sera acquis. Toute l'histoire des Francs est en germe dans cette promesse d'alliance qui révèle à quel point un roi pourtant païen présentait aux yeux des autorités religieuses de singuliers attraits.

En 481, pourtant, de tous les peuples barbares qui occupaient la Gaule, ce n'étaient pas les Francs Saliens qui tenaient le haut du pavé mais les Wisigoths qui, déjà maîtres de la moitié du pays, semblaient bien capables d'en conquérir le reste. Mais l'arianisme militant du roi Euric, qui avait multiplié les vexations à l'égard des catholiques, confisquant des églises pour les remettre au culte arien, interdisant les mariages mixtes et les pèlerinages à Saint-Sernin de Toulouse, lui avait aliéné le corps épiscopal et les populations catholiques, en particulier dans la région de Tours et en Auvergne où Sidoine Apollinaire, l'évêque de Clermont, animait la résistance.

La mort d'Euric en 484 et la minorité de son fils Alaric allaient donner à Clovis l'occasion favorable d'amorcer sa marche vers le Sud et de tester les promesses de l'épiscopat.

Pour ce faire, le jeune roi devait d'abord en découdre avec Syagrius, qui s'intitulait toujours « roi des Romains » et cherchait à maintenir, au centre du pays, entre Loire, Somme et Meuse, l'illusion de l'Empire. Ayant échappé non seulement à la grande invasion barbare de 406 mais aussi à celle d'Attila en 451, sa capitale, Soissons, apparaissait alors comme l'ultime bastion de la romanité dans une Gaule du Nord largement barbarisée.

Après avoir assuré ses arrières en contractant alliance avec les Francs Saliens de Cambrai et les Francs rhénans de Cologne, Clovis ouvrit les hostilités en 486, en sommant Syagrius de lui fixer le jour et le lieu du combat. Il se conformait en cela à l'usage germanique qui voulait qu'on n'attaque pas un ennemi sans l'avoir au préalable défié.

Vaincu, Syagrius s'enfuit à Toulouse auprès du roi des Wisigoths qui, au mépris des lois de l'hospitalité, le livra par la suite à Clovis. Ce dernier, selon Grégoire de Tours, le fit égorger en secret après avoir pris possession de son royaume qui lui assurait la maîtrise de toute la Gaule du Nord jusqu'à la Loire et aux confins de l'Armorique.

Désormais installé dans le palais de Syagrius, il put s'approprier le produit de l'impôt, tirer profit de la frappe des monnaies et installer ses troupes dans les riches domaines de la Gaule septentrionale.

En même temps, ce succès montrait à quel point les espérances de l'évêque de Reims n'étaient pas vaines, comme l'atteste le célèbre et légendaire épisode du vase de Soissons. En effet, selon la tradition, les soldats francs avaient mis au pillage les régions que la victoire venait de leur livrer, et en particulier les églises qui recelaient de précieux vases sacrés. Toujours selon la coutume, ce butin devait être équitablement partagé entre les guerriers, chacun tirant sa part au sort.

Or, parmi ce butin, se trouvait un vase en argent auquel l'évêque du diocèse tenait particulièrement. Il pria donc Clovis de lui faire rendre cet objet d'art. En préférant satisfaire la revendication de l'évêque plutôt que de respecter la loi de son armée – le vase, selon la légende, ayant été brisé par un guerrier furieux –, Clovis montrait clairement qu'il avait choisi le parti des évêques, au risque de se couper de son propre peuple.

Si l'anecdote est révélatrice de la politique de Clovis à l'égard du clergé catholique, elle est aussi instructive sur le tempérament du jeune roi. L'année suivante, passant ses troupes en revue au commencement d'une nouvelle campagne militaire, il retrouva l'homme au vase et lui reprocha l'état de ses armes. « Nul, dit-il, n'est aussi mal équipé que toi ; ta framée, ton épée, ta hache, rien ne vaut. » Lui arrachant cette dernière arme des mains, il la jeta à terre. Comme le soldat se baissait pour la ramasser, Clovis lui abattit sa francisque sur la tête en disant : « C'est ce que tu as fait au vase de Soissons. »

Rancune et dissimulation, tels sont aussi les défauts d'un roi ambitieux qui n'hésite pas à faire massacrer ses proches parents pour prendre possession de leurs royaumes, sans parler de ceux qu'il se contente de faire tondre pour leur enlever cette force que symbolisaient alors les cheveux longs.

Le baptême de Clovis

Clovis sait utiliser sa patience à des fins diplomatiques quand il s'allie à Théodoric, le puissant roi italien des Ostrogoths, en lui accordant la main de sa sœur Alboflède. Diplomatie surtout quand il décide, vers 493, de signer un pacte de non-agression avec l'influent roi des Burgondes, Gondebaud, en épousant sa nièce Clotilde, une princesse de Genève dont ses ambassadeurs lui avaient plus d'une fois vanté les charmes. Selon l'usage, une ambassade solennelle alla chercher la jeune fiancée et la ramena à son époux, qui était venu à sa rencontre à Villery, près de Troyes, aux limites des deux royaumes. À en croire les apparences, l'union fut heureuse et Clovis s'attacha d'un cœur sincère à son épouse, laissant Clotilde apporter le souffle de l'Évangile dans son nouveau foyer.

Convertir Clovis, telle fut en effet la lourde mission que se fixa Clotilde, une mission qu'un drame faillit pourtant compromettre.

En effet, le roi avait accepté que leur premier enfant, Ingomer, soit baptisé et Clotilde avait pu mesurer dans cette concession l'ascendant qu'elle avait déjà acquis sur son époux. Mais l'enfant n'avait pas encore déposé la robe blanche du baptême qu'il était emporté par la mort. La douleur de Clovis se traduisit par des paroles pleines d'amertume : « C'est votre baptême qui est la cause de sa mort ; si je l'avais consacré à nos dieux, il serait encore vivant. » Ce à quoi Clotilde répondit en remerciant Dieu d'accueillir Ingomer dans son royaume : « Je rends grâce, dit-elle, au Dieu tout-puissant et créateur de toutes choses, qui ne m'a pas trouvée indigne d'être la mère d'un enfant admis dans son céleste royaume. La douleur de sa perte ne trouble pas mon âme ; sorti de ce monde avec la robe blanche de son innocence, il se nourrira de la vue de Dieu pendant toute l'éternité. »

L'année suivante, un autre fils, Clodomir, fut également baptisé et, là encore, commença à dépérir après son baptême. « Pouvait-il lui arriver autre chose qu'à son frère ? constata Clovis. Il a été baptisé au nom de votre Christ, il faut donc bien qu'il meure. »

Heureusement pour le destin religieux du royaume, cette sombre prédiction ne se réalisa pas.

Au-delà de l'anecdote, ces détails de la vie domestique, enjolivés par Grégoire de Tours, veulent simplement témoigner du fait que la conversion du roi ne se fit pas sans mal, Clovis hésitant devant un engagement qui risquait de troubler son peuple, un peuple persuadé qu'il tirait sa force de la protection des dieux ancestraux. Le catholicisme, professé par les populations soumises, ne pouvait-il pas être considéré comme une religion de vaincus ?

Ne fallait-il pas alors un « miracle » pour convaincre Clovis ? Ce « miracle », selon la tradition, aurait eu lieu vers 496, au cours de la bataille de Tolbiac (Zülpich, à 35 kilomètres au sud-ouest de Cologne) contre les Alamans qui, venus de haute Rhénanie, menaçaient les positions acquises par les Francs à l'est du royaume.

Alors que l'armée des Francs commençait à fléchir devant la furia alémanique, Clovis, abandonné de ses dieux, se serait écrié : « Jésus-Christ, que Clotilde proclame être le fils du Dieu vivant, toi qui, dit-on, viens au secours de ceux qui peinent, et donnes la victoire à ceux qui espèrent en toi, je sollicite ta glorieuse assistance. Si tu m'accordes de l'emporter sur ces ennemis et si j'éprouve les effets de cette puissance dont le peuple qui t'appartient prétend avoir fait l'expérience, je croirai en toi et me ferai baptiser en ton nom. »

Le combat ayant brusquement changé d'âme et la victoire étant acquise, il ne restait plus à Clovis qu'à respecter sa promesse. Ce vœu de conversion rappelle trop le précédent de l'empereur romain Constantin se convertissant au christianisme lors de la bataille de Milvius en 312, pour être pris au pied de la lettre. L'histoire a beau être suspecte, c'est bien à partir de cette bataille que s'accélèrent les préparatifs du baptême.

Encore fallait-il que cet homme fort prudent, « *astutissimus* » écrit Grégoire, s'assure de l'exactitude des récits colportés sur les miracles opérés par l'intercession des saints sur le lieu de leur sépulture. C'est peut-être le sens du pèlerinage que Clovis effectua à Tours sur le tombeau de saint Martin, le sanctuaire prestigieux du saint le plus vénéré en Gaule.

Ses proches guerriers gagnés à la cause, la cérémonie du baptême put être fixée, probablement le jour de Noël 498. Tout avait été préparé pour faire de cet événement un acte de propagande politique, comme en témoignent les invitations lancées aux prélats de la Gaule du Sud, sujets des rois wisigoth ou burgonde, comme Avit, l'évêque de Vienne, qui regretta de ne pouvoir s'y rendre et envoya à Clovis une lettre de félicitations.

De riches tapis ornaient la façade des maisons ; de grands voiles brodés, tendus à travers les rues, y faisaient régner un demi-jour solennel ; les églises resplendissaient de tous leurs trésors et le baptistère était décoré avec luxe, des cierges innombrables brillant à travers les nuages de l'encens qui fumait dans les encensoirs.

En tête du cortège qui amenait Clovis du palais de la porte Basée, où il résidait, jusqu'à la cathédrale Notre-Dame, venait la croix, suivie des livres sacrés portés par des clercs ; puis, selon Grégoire, s'avançait le roi, dont l'évêque tenait la main comme pour lui servir de guide vers la maison de Dieu. Derrière lui marchait Clotilde, la grande triomphatrice de cette journée ; elle était accompagnée de Thierry, le fils aîné de Clovis qu'il avait eu d'une première compagne, et de ses sœurs Aboflède et Lanthilde. Trois mille guerriers suivaient le roi pour être, comme lui, baptisés.

Arrivé sur le seuil du baptistère, où les évêques réunis pour la cérémonie étaient venus à la rencontre du cortège, Clovis prit, le premier, la parole et demanda que Remi lui confère le baptême.

« *Depona colla, Sigamber* ! » aurait alors lancé l'évêque, ce qui ne veut pas dire « Baisse la tête, fier Sicambre », comme a voulu le faire croire la tradition, mais tout simplement « Dépose tes colliers », c'est-à-dire, abandonne les amulettes et autres porte-bonheur que portent les païens.

Il ne manquait que l'onction divine pour consacrer cette alliance du Ciel et de la Terre. Ce fut chose faite avec la légende, diffusée à la fin du IXe siècle par Hincmar, un successeur de Remi à l'évêché de Reims. Dans la *Vie de saint Remi* qu'il écrivit entre 877 et 882, il raconte qu'au moment de verser l'eau sur la tête de Clovis, Remi s'aperçut que le chrême qui devait être, selon les prescriptions liturgiques, versé dans l'eau aussitôt après la bénédiction de celle-ci faisait défaut, parce que le prêtre chargé de l'apporter n'avait pu se frayer un passage à travers la foule qui se pressait aux abords du baptistère. Alors, il aurait levé les yeux au ciel dans une supplication émue et une colombe, tenant dans son bec une ampoule remplie du précieux onguent, serait descendue jusqu'à lui et l'aurait laissée tomber dans ses mains avant de disparaître.

Cette confusion délibérée entre le baptême et le prétendu sacre de Clovis avait pour mission d'exalter le fondateur de la royauté franque, de légitimer Reims comme lieu du sacre et d'asseoir fermement l'alliance entre l'Église et la royauté. Car si le baptême de Clovis affirmait le prestige et la prééminence du catholicisme en Gaule, il permettait aussi à Clovis de présenter ses conquêtes futures comme autant d'entreprises de libération des Gallo-Romains contre leurs oppresseurs ariens.

Le « libérateur » des Gaules

Quand les Francs poursuivirent leur marche vers le Sud, l'expédition militaire prit l'allure d'une véritable croisade. « Tous désiraient d'un amour ardent qu'ils règnent », écrit Grégoire de Tours, qui ajoute : « Beaucoup déjà en Gaule désiraient très ardemment avoir des Francs pour maîtres. » Avit, l'évêque de Vienne, sous domination burgonde, n'hésitant pas à faire de Clovis l'égal de l'empereur de Byzance, n'écrit-il pas dans sa lettre de félicitations, « votre foi c'est notre victoire » ?

Après avoir, par un édit royal publié avant l'entrée en campagne, prescrit un respect absolu des personnes et des choses, interdisant à quiconque de s'emparer de quoi que ce soit, « sinon de l'herbe et de l'eau », Clovis prit soin d'associer saint Martin à sa cause en ouvrant sa campagne par une nouvelle visite au sanctuaire de Tours et en déclarant qu'il voulait libérer le pays de la souillure des hérétiques.

Au moment où ses envoyés entraient dans la basilique pour prier le saint d'accorder une issue favorable à la campagne, le moine qui dirigeait les chants du chœur fit exécuter l'antienne suivante, extraite du psaume XVII : « Seigneur, vous m'avez armé de courage pour les combats, vous avez renversé à mes pieds ceux qui se dressaient contre moi, vous m'avez livré les dos de mes ennemis, et vous avez dispersé ceux qui me poursuivent de leur haine. » On ne pouvait rêver meilleur présage ! Plus loin, quand Clovis arrive aux bords de la Vienne grossie par les pluies, une biche lui indique un gué tandis qu'au-dessus de la basilique de Saint-Hilaire, à Poitiers, brille un globe de feu qui éclaire sa marche.

C'est à Vouillé, en 507, à une quinzaine de kilomètres au nord de Poitiers, qu'eut lieu le choc décisif entre Clovis et Alaric. La défaite des Wisigoths fut totale et Alaric tué dans le combat. Quelques mois plus tard, Clovis s'était emparé de la majeure partie de l'Aquitaine mais ne put mettre la main sur les rivages de la Méditerranée, les Ostrogoths étant intervenus pour s'emparer de la Provence et sauver les débris du royaume des Wisigoths.

Une déception atténuée par l'hommage que lui adressa Anastase, l'empereur de Byzance, en lui conférant les insignes du consulat qui faisaient du roi barbare l'héritier d'une tradition séculaire et, surtout, lui permettaient d'asseoir encore sa légitimité aux yeux des populations que ses conquêtes venaient de lui livrer.

Du coup, revenu dans la cité de Tours, Clovis célébra son triomphe à la manière d'un général romain. À cheval, vêtu d'une tunique de pourpre, d'une chlamyde (manteau militaire) et d'un diadème d'or, il jeta à pleines mains les pièces d'or et d'argent au peuple qui se pressait sur le parcours et l'acclamait aux cris de « consul » et même d'« Auguste ».

Après avoir liquidé – souvent par assassinat – les autres rois francs du Nord et du Nord-Est, Clovis régnait désormais sur un gigantesque royaume. Seuls lui échappaient le delta du Rhin, tenu par les Frisons, l'Armorique, aux mains de royautés celtiques, les Pyrénées occidentales, sous le pouvoir des montagnards basques, le Languedoc méditerranéen, toujours wisigothique, la Provence, tombée sous le joug des Ostrogoths, et le royaume burgonde.

C'est alors que Clovis prit la décision, capitale pour l'avenir de la France, de fixer sa résidence à Paris, qui jouissait d'une situation exceptionnelle – une île renforcée par les fortifications du Bas-Empire, à la croisée d'une voie fluviale est-ouest et des grandes voies nord-sud, à mi-chemin de ses terres du Nord et de ses récentes conquêtes du Sud. Il s'installa dans le palais de la Cité, qui avait été un lieu de séjour apprécié des empereurs Julien (entre 357 et 360) et Valentinien Iᵉʳ (en 365-366), et voulut apporter sa contribution à l'héritage antique en faisant édifier, sur le tombeau de sainte Geneviève, décédée vers 502, une basilique dédiée aux saints apôtres Pierre et Paul. Son corps ainsi que celui de Clotilde devaient y être déposés. On ne retrouva jamais sa sépulture.

Quelques mois avant sa mort qui survint le 27 novembre 511, il réunit à Orléans un concile regroupant trente-deux évêques, soit la moitié des évêques du royaume. Il y fut décidé en particulier qu'aucun laïc ne pourrait devenir clerc sans l'autorisation du roi, ce qui était une manière de contrôler l'élection de ces hommes puissants auxquels il devait largement ses succès.

Toutefois, en dédiant les canons du concile à leur « seigneur, le *rex gloriosissimus* Clovis, fils de la sainte Église », les prélats acceptaient de bonne grâce l'autorité de celui qui, avec un art consommé de la propagande – une propagande qu'ils avaient largement inspirée –, s'était posé comme l'héritier de Rome et du Christ.

Les temps mérovingiens

*B*rutes sanguinaires ou rois « fainéants », les descendants de Clovis
n'ont pas bonne presse. Entre le glorieux règne du roi des Francs,
qui inaugure l'alliance avec l'Église, et le couronnement de Charlemagne, qui marque la renaissance de l'empire en Occident, les temps
mérovingiens, que sauve pour un temps le gouvernement de Dagobert,
font partie de ces périodes « mal aimées » de l'Histoire.
En fait, les temps mérovingiens ne méritent pas le mépris qui les a
relégués dans les « bas-fonds » de notre mémoire. Les contemporains
semblent d'ailleurs avoir été plus lucides, à l'instar d'Agathias, qui écrivait à l'époque de l'empereur Justinien : « Ce que j'admire chez eux, c'est
leur droiture et leur union. »

L'expansion du royaume des Francs

À la mort de Clovis, en 511, si ses quatre fils, Thierry, l'aîné, né
d'une concubine rhénane avant le mariage avec Clotilde, Clodomir,
Childebert et Clotaire, semblent se partager le royaume comme un
vulgaire butin, ce partage ne les a pas empêchés de poursuivre avec
succès l'expansion amorcée par leur père.

En 534, ils mettent la main sur le royaume des Burgondes, après
avoir défait le roi Gondemar II. En 537, les Ostrogoths leur abandonnent la Provence pour se ménager leur soutien contre l'empereur de

Byzance, Justinien, qui s'apprêtait à reconquérir l'Italie. Objet de toutes les convoitises, la Méditerranée est enfin atteinte, et Théodebert, le fils de Thierry, peut organiser des courses à l'antique dans le cirque de la ville d'Arles et frapper une monnaie d'or à son effigie, ce qui scandalise les Byzantins. Entre 534 et 548, ils soumettent les Alamans, les Thuringiens et les Bavarois, qui occupaient la Germanie méridionale. Seules échappaient alors à leur pouvoir les bouches du Rhin, occupées par les Frisons, la Septimanie, aux mains des Wisigoths, les Pyrénées occidentales, bastion des Vascons, ou Basques, et l'Armorique, que peuplait une vigoureuse immigration venue d'outre-Manche.

Au milieu du VIᵉ siècle, le royaume des Francs formait ainsi l'ensemble territorial le plus puissant de l'Europe occidentale et, avec Byzance, le principal héritier de l'Empire romain. Non seulement les fils de Clovis avaient atteint les limites que César assignait à la Gaule, les Pyrénées, les Alpes et le Rhin, mais en outre, pour la première fois, ils avaient réussi à fondre dans un cadre politique commun Gaule et Germanie.

Certes, ces territoires passés sous autorité franque ont été rarement réunis entre les mains d'un seul roi, sous Clotaire Iᵉʳ, le dernier survivant des fils de Clovis entre 558 et 561, sous Clotaire II et son fils Dagobert, de 613 à 639, mais les partages répétés n'ont pas été aussi anarchiques qu'on l'a souvent cru.

Il faut tout d'abord observer que, s'il y eut pratiquement toujours plusieurs rois, il n'y eut toujours aussi qu'un seul *regnum Francorum*. Aucun des rois n'avait de suprématie sur les autres. Tous avaient les mêmes droits. Chacun d'eux s'intitulait roi des Francs, sans jamais désigner la région qu'il gouvernait. Ce que l'on partageait en fait, ce n'était pas la royauté mais l'exercice de la royauté.

Il faut aussi souligner que les capitales choisies par les quatre fils de Clovis, Reims et non Cologne par Thierry, Soissons et non Tournai par Clotaire, Orléans et non Tours par Clodomir, et Paris par Childebert, étaient assez proches les unes des autres, comme si cette proximité avait été voulue, pour faciliter les relations entre les différents palais et administrer efficacement un royaume dont l'étendue était considérable.

Certes, haines, intrigues et meurtres emplissent de leur fureur les temps mérovingiens. C'est que la coutume germanique de la vengeance privée, la *faida*, obligeait le groupe familial à laver l'affront quand l'un de ses membres s'était trouvé atteint dans son honneur ou dans son sang. Clotilde elle-même, la pieuse épouse de Clovis, appelle ses fils à venger le meurtre de ses parents burgondes en leur disant :

« Que je n'aie point à me repentir, mes fils, de vous avoir nourris avec tendresse, que votre indignation ressente mon injure, mettez un zèle ardent à venger la mort de mon père et de ma mère. » Le roi Gontran, après l'assassinat de son frère Chilpéric Ier, s'écrie : « Nous ne devons pas nous considérer comme des hommes si nous ne sommes pas capables de venger cette mort cette année. » Le moindre conflit devient ainsi le premier maillon d'une chaîne sans fin de vendettas, l'injure appelant l'injure, le meurtre exigeant le meurtre.

De grands personnages gallo-romains, « savants et versés dans les lettres », suivent le même code d'honneur et vident leurs querelles dans le sang, comme Secundinus et Asteriolus, deux familiers de la cour de Théodebert. « Secundinus, écrit Grégoire de Tours, tua Asteriolus. Celui-ci, en mourant, laissa un fils qui, grandissant et parvenu à l'âge d'homme, commença à vouloir venger l'injure de son père. Secundinus, frappé de terreur, se sauva devant lui d'une terre dans une autre et, se voyant pressé par son ennemi, il s'empoisonna, dit-on, pour ne pas tomber dans ses mains. »

La sanglante rivalité qui opposa, dans le dernier tiers du VIe siècle, Brunehaut et Frédégonde, épouses respectives de Sigebert Ier et de Chilpéric Ier, en est une autre illustration. Quand Sigebert Ier fut assassiné, en 575, par des émissaires de son frère Chilpéric Ier, Brunehaut n'eut de cesse de le venger. Ce fut le début d'une guerre civile qui épuisa la Gaule pendant près de trente ans et s'acheva en 613, quand Clotaire II, le fils de Frédégonde, fit exécuter l'ennemie de sa mère, alors âgée de soixante-dix ans. Elle fut d'abord assise sur un chameau et promenée à travers les rangs de l'armée. Puis, on l'attacha par les cheveux, un bras et un pied à la queue d'un cheval sauvage qui l'entraîna dans une course où son corps fut disloqué.

Certains ont voulu voir dans ce jugement un véritable meurtre rituel destiné à rallier tous les sujets. Brunehaut aurait été mise à mort deux fois : la première fois attachée sur le dos d'un chameau, la tête tournée vers la queue, car c'était là le châtiment des usurpateurs à Rome. La seconde fois, le corps brisé par le cheval au galop, car telle était la mise à mort des usurpateurs chez les Germaniques. Son supplice, pour être cruel, aurait eu pour fonction symbolique de satisfaire les deux populations de la Gaule mérovingienne.

Si de telles mœurs choquent notre sensibilité, il faut toutefois noter que ces crimes étaient monnaie courante dans les cours policées de l'Empire romain. On oublie aussi que ces meurtres dont parle Grégoire de Tours s'espacent sur près d'un siècle et que la plupart d'entre eux sont liés à des faits de guerre, de telle sorte qu'on peut estimer que les Mérovingiens ne sont pas plus sanguinaires que les hommes qui leur ont succédé. Enfin, ces mœurs « barbares » n'ont pas empêché le maintien de l'administration et de la diplomatie. La correspondance échangée par les rois francs avec les empereurs de Byzance ou avec le pape montrent que les usages de l'administration romaine s'associent aux coutumes germaniques pour imposer la notion d'État à des royautés jusque-là essentiellement guerrières. C'est parce qu'ont disparu les innombrables actes écrits imposés par la vie courante que nous avons eu tendance à faire des rois mérovingiens des rois « fainéants ».

Le pouvoir royal

À l'origine, le roi mérovingien était un chef de guerre dont le prestige magique, le *mund*, était attesté par l'éblouissante chevelure qu'il portait. Tondre un chef mérovingien était ainsi le plus sûr moyen de le dégrader et de le rendre incapable de régner. Ce prestige magique, transmis par le sang, était également partagé entre tous les descendants de Clovis. C'est aussi pour cette raison qu'il était impossible de faire un choix entre eux lors des successions. Dans une large mesure, le pouvoir royal était fondé sur les liens de fidélité personnels, tous les hommes libres prêtant un serment de fidélité au roi à son avènement au trône. Ce pouvoir absolu était en fait limité par une série de bornes difficilement franchissables. Un roi absolu a le droit de tout ordonner, mais encore faut-il qu'il puisse réaliser sa volonté et faire exécuter ses décisions. Son autorité était surtout tempérée par la propension des grands à répondre à la force par la force, à se révolter, à trahir et assassiner, si bien qu'on a pu dire du gouvernement des Mérovingiens qu'il était « un despotisme tempéré par l'assassinat ».

Aussi, pour assurer leur protection, les rois multiplièrent auprès d'eux des fidèles, appelés antrustions. Leur nom vient du latin *trustis*, qui signifie à l'origine « aide ». Ces fidèles constituaient une suite de gardes du corps qui s'engageaient à ne pas leur nuire et à les suivre au combat, charge aux rois de les entretenir sous forme de gratifications ou de terres. La formule de l'engagement nous est connue grâce à un formulaire du VIIᵉ siècle :

« Parce que notre fidèle, avec l'aide de Dieu, est venu ici dans notre palais, avec son arme, et qu'on l'a vu jurer dans notre main truste et fidélité, à cause de cela, par le présent précepte, nous décrétons et ordonnons qu'il soit désormais compté au nombre de nos antrustions. »

Pour entretenir cette troupe de fidèles, les rois doivent donc avoir un trésor important qu'ils exhibent avec fierté. Ainsi, le roi Chilpéric Ier montre à ses invités un grand bassin qu'il a fait fabriquer d'or et de pierres précieuses et qui pèse cinquante livres en disant : « J'ai fait cela pour ennoblir et faire "briller" la nation des Francs. » Lorsque, en 584, Rigunthe, sa fille, part épouser le prince wisigoth Recarède, son père lui remet une dot considérable, « cinquante chars, écrit Grégoire de Tours, étant remplis d'un amoncellement d'or, d'argent et d'objets précieux ».

Le destin de ce trésor donne aussi la mesure de la fragilité des ressources royales. Au premier arrêt en dehors de Paris, une partie de l'escorte de la princesse disparaît en emportant tout ce qu'elle peut voler. À Toulouse, le duc Didier, commandant l'Aquitaine pour Chilpéric Ier, ayant appris l'assassinat du roi, s'empare du reste et renvoie la princesse complètement dépouillée à sa mère Frédégonde !

Ces trésors étaient alimentés par les revenus des biens de l'état romain et de tous les biens vacants au moment de la conquête, par le produit des amendes et des confiscations prononcées par les tribunaux, par les impôts indirects pesant sur les marchandises transportées et vendues sur les marchés et, surtout, par les prises de guerre et les tributs imposés aux peuples vaincus. Car il fut pratiquement impossible d'imposer au peuple la perception des impôts établis en Gaule par Rome. En 548, Parthenius fut lynché par la foule à Trèves parce qu'il avait alourdi les impôts. En 584, en Neustrie, Audon échappa à un sort identique en se réfugiant dans une église. Effrayé par les malheurs qui le frappaient coup sur coup, et dans lesquels il voyait une punition du ciel pour les exactions dont il avait accablé son peuple, Chilpéric Ier suivit ainsi les conseils de Frédégonde, qui lui aurait dit : « Nous avons perdu des enfants, et voici que les larmes des pauvres, les gémissements des veuves, les soupirs des orphelins vont encore causer la mort de ceux-ci. Pourquoi donc nos caves regorgent-elles de vin ? Pourquoi nos greniers plient-ils sous le poids du froment ? Nous thésaurisons et nous ne savons pour qui. Brûlons tous ces rôles d'impôts », et il fit jeter au feu les livres de l'impôt !

Héritage de Rome et coutumes germaniques se lisent aussi dans l'organisation du palais, qui désigne rarement une demeure royale mais le plus souvent l'entourage du roi, rassemblant un personnel nombreux et fort dévoué, dans la mesure où le palais est la source de toutes les faveurs et la clé de toutes les fortunes.

Certains fonctionnaires ont une vocation à la fois publique et privée. Ainsi, le camérier sert le roi dans sa chambre mais est chargé en même temps de garder le trésor du roi, placé dans sa chambre, à charge pour lui d'en contrôler les flux d'entrée et de sortie. Le maréchal veille, lui, sur les chevaux du roi et, en tant que militaire, peut diriger la cavalerie. Le sénéchal, doyen des serviteurs, est chargé du ravitaillement mais siège aussi au tribunal du roi.

On trouve également des officiers attachés aux tâches domestiques, comme le chef des échansons, qui surveille la cuisine, le *mapparius*, qui, à table, présente au roi l'essuie-mains, le *spatarius*, qui porte l'épée devant lui.

D'autres ont des noms et des fonctions empruntés à l'administration impériale : c'est le cas du référendaire, qui établit par écrit les diplômes royaux et veille, lors de leur délivrance, à y apposer le sceau du roi. C'est aussi le cas des comtes du palais, qui dirigent les débats judiciaires, attestent que toutes les formalités de la procédure ont été observées, rédigent le rapport d'après lequel la sentence est rendue, puis veillent à son exécution.

Un de ces officiers, le *major domus*, le maire du palais, allait prendre au cours du temps une importance grandissante. Chargé de la discipline du palais, il a juridiction sur l'ensemble des personnes qui s'y trouvent réunies. Outre cette prérogative essentielle, il est chargé de superviser la gestion des domaines royaux et d'ordonner le paiement de toute dépense décidée par le roi. Si ce dernier est mineur, c'est lui qui dirige son éducation, en qualité de gouverneur. Du fait des nombreuses minorités royales provoquées par les guerres civiles et les assassinats, il allait devenir le seul agent permanent du gouvernement et le chef de toute la hiérarchie sociale qui se mettait en place dans le royaume.

Enfin, la cour jouait le rôle d'école de cadres pour un grand nombre de jeunes aristocrates qui y faisaient leur apprentissage politique et qui, adultes, regrettaient, comme l'évêque Didier de Cahors, le temps « où nous avions coutume de nous délasser en échangeant des propos sans importance ». Contrairement à l'image qui en a été transmise, l'entourage des rois mérovingiens n'était pas si sinistre. Sa réputation avait même franchi les frontières de la Gaule, puisque la veuve du roi Edwin de Northumbrie y envoya ses deux fils pour qu'ils y soient éduqués.

Les correspondances échangées entre les rois mérovingiens et les principales puissances du temps mesurent également la persistance des usages de l'administration romaine comme le rayonnement international du royaume franc. Quand l'empereur de Byzance s'adresse à lui, il le qualifie de *vir gloriosus*, d'*eminentia*, et ajoute de sa propre main à la correspondance qu'il lui destine « parent très chrétien et très aimé ». Une formule qui n'était pas seulement une flatterie lorsqu'on

LES MÉROVINGIENS

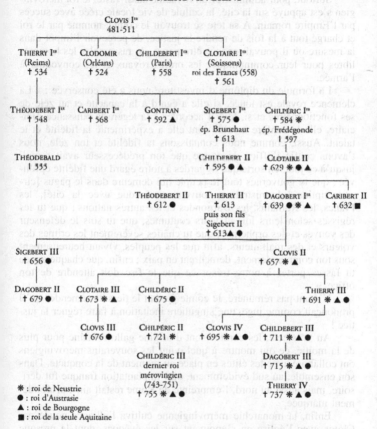

CLOVIS Iᵉʳ
481-511

THIERRY Iᵉʳ (Reims) † 534	CLODOMIR (Orléans) † 524	CHILDEBERT Iᵉʳ (Paris) † 558	CLOTAIRE Iᵉʳ (Soissons) roi des Francs (558) † 561	

THÉODEBERT Iᵉʳ † 548 — CARIBERT Iᵉʳ † 568 — GONTRAN † 592 ▲ — SIGEBERT Iᵉʳ † 575 ● ép. Brunehaut † 613 — CHILPÉRIC Iᵉʳ † 584 ✳ ép. Frédégonde † 597

THÉODEBALD † 555

CHILDEBERT II † 595 ● ▲

CLOTAIRE II † 629 ✳ ● ▲

THÉODEBERT II † 612 ● — THIERRY II † 613 puis son fils Sigebert II † 613 ▲ ● — DAGOBERT Iᵉʳ † 639 ● ✳ ▲ — CARIBERT II † 632 ■

SIGEBERT III † 656 ●

CLOVIS II † 657 ✳ ▲

DAGOBERT II † 679 ● — CLOTAIRE III † 673 ✳ ▲ — CHILDÉRIC II † 675 ● — THIERRY III † 691 ✳ ▲ ●

CLOVIS III † 676 ● — CHILPÉRIC II † 721 ✳ — CLOVIS IV † 695 ✳ ▲ ● — CHILDEBERT III † 711 ✳ ▲ ●

CHILDÉRIC III dernier roi mérovingien (743-751) † 755 ✳ ▲ ●

DAGOBERT III † 715 ✳ ▲ ●

THIERRY IV † 737 ✳ ▲ ●

✳ : roi de Neustrie
● : roi d'Austrasie
▲ : roi de Bourgogne
■ : roi de la seule Aquitaine

sait que l'empereur Maurice offrit, en 584, cinquante mille sous d'or, une somme considérable, au roi d'Austrasie Childebert II pour qu'il chasse les Lombards de la péninsule italienne. Finalement, ces derniers offrirent aussi de l'argent, et le roi franc, ayant touché des deux côtés, se retira de la vallée du Pô, qu'il avait cruellement ravagée. L'empereur eut beau réclamer les sommes versées, Childebert II, « confiant en sa puissance, dit la chronique, ne daigna même pas répondre ».

Surtout, pour administrer un royaume aussi vaste, le roi mérovingien s'est appuyé sur la cité, la cellule de vie locale créée avec succès par l'Empire romain. À sa tête se trouvait le comte, nommé par le roi et chargé tout à la fois de rendre la justice, de percevoir l'impôt dans la mesure où il pouvait encore être perçu, de rassembler les hommes libres pour leur communiquer les ordres royaux et les convoquer à l'armée.

La formule du diplôme d'investiture nous a été conservée : « La clémence royale est louée, si elle a égard à la capacité et au zèle de ses fonctionnaires et si, loin d'accorder à la légère la puissance judiciaire, elle la confère à celui dont elle a expérimenté la fidélité et le talent. Aussi, comme nous connaissons ta fidélité et ton zèle, nous t'avons confié l'office de comte que ton prédécesseur avait rempli jusqu'à ce jour, en sorte que tu gardes à notre égard une fidélité éprouvée ; que tu gouvernes tout le peuple qui demeure dans le pagus [circonscription administrative souvent confondue avec la cité], les Francs, les Romains, les Burgondes et les autres nations ; que tu les régisses selon leurs lois et leurs coutumes, que tu sois le défenseur des veuves et des orphelins ; que tu châties sévèrement les crimes des voleurs et des malfaiteurs, afin que les peuples, vivant heureusement sous ton commandement, demeurent en paix ; enfin, que chaque année tu fasses porter à notre trésor ce que le fisc doit attendre de ton office. »

N'étant pas rémunéré, le comte gardait le tiers des amendes qu'il prononçait comme juge, une singulière incitation à faire régner la justice !

Au VIe siècle, les comtes sont d'origine gallo-romaine pour plus de la moitié, ce qui montre à quel point les souverains mérovingiens ont collaboré avec les élites en place au moment de la conquête. Dans son ensemble, au sud évidemment, où l'implantation franque fut dérisoire, mais aussi au nord, l'empreinte de Rome restait ainsi profondément marquée.

Enfin, la monarchie mérovingienne cultiva l'alliance nouée par Clovis avec l'église en s'appuyant sur les évêques, dont la presque totalité a été recrutée, elle aussi, dans l'aristocratie gallo-romaine. Devenus, dans les derniers temps de l'Empire romain, défenseurs des pauvres, souvent amenés à s'opposer au comte quand ce dernier multipliait les amendes, les évêques sont les premiers personnages de la cité. « C'est grâce à vous, proclame en 585 le roi Gontran, que l'ordre public et le salut des peuples peuvent être assurés. » Ce sont eux qui restaurent ou bâtissent, aménagent les ports et créent des moulins, organisent l'enseignement et les hospices, visitent les prisons et font respecter le droit d'asile. Églises, oratoires, baptistères, monastères se multiplient à l'intérieur des remparts urbains. Jamais, peut-être, on n'en a bâti autant. Metz compte alors 40 églises, Paris 29, Reims 22, Lyon 18 et Bordeaux 12. Enrichies par les offrandes des pèlerins et les legs de riches donateurs, ces églises deviennent les lieux de vie et d'échanges qui maintiennent timidement la tradition urbaine.

Mais en même temps, dans la mesure où, au concile réuni par Clovis à Orléans en 511, il avait été décidé qu'aucun laïc ne pourrait devenir clerc sans l'autorisation royale, l'évêque risquait d'apparaître comme un agent de l'administration royale. Ce qui paraît certain, c'est que, au fil du temps, beaucoup de laïcs n'ont embrassé la carrière épiscopale que pour jouir des biens de l'église.

Sauvegarder la paix publique et la famille

Faire bonne justice au peuple, tel était le principal conseil que Remi avait adressé au jeune Clovis. Ce dernier, comme ses successeurs, s'y attacha, en s'appliquant à limiter le cycle de la vengeance privée. Et là, comme pour tous les éléments de la civilisation mérovingienne, la rédaction des lois et l'organisation de la justice apparaissent comme une synthèse entre la tradition romaine, les coutumes germaniques et les idéaux chrétiens qui imprégnaient peu à peu la société.

En Aquitaine, Clovis bénéficia de l'œuvre du roi wisigoth Alaric II, dont le Bréviaire, destiné aux Gallo-Romains vivant dans son royaume, donnait pleine satisfaction. Étendue à ceux du Nord, cette compilation rendit de précieux services dans la mesure où le droit romain régissait de nombreux domaines dans lesquels les lois germaniques n'avaient rien décidé.

Pour les Francs, Clovis fit mettre par écrit, entre 507 et 511, les coutumes d'un peuple jusque-là essentiellement guerrier, après les avoir passées au filtre de sa nouvelle foi chrétienne. Se voulant l'égal des lois romaines, le *Pactus Legis Salicae*, ou loi salique, fait apparaître un conquérant singulièrement adouci, attaché à sauvegarder la paix publique.

C'est bien le sens de la compensation financière appelée *wergeld* (« le prix de l'homme »), somme que devait verser à la victime ou à sa famille l'auteur d'un délit ou d'un crime. Cette amende, ou « composition », était tarifée selon un barème qui révèle avec une extrême précision les hiérarchies de la société franque. Un homme libre ayant tué un esclave, bon ouvrier tel un orfèvre, sera condamné à verser 75 sous d'or. Le meurtre d'un Romain libre coûtera 100 sous, celui d'un Franc libre 200 sous, celui d'un antrustion 600 sous, celui d'un garçon de moins de douze ans, encore incapable de se défendre, 600 sous également, comme celui d'une femme enceinte.

La composition est aussi minutieusement tarifée selon la nature et la gravité du délit. Quelqu'un ayant tenté de donner la mort à un autre sans y parvenir est condamné à payer 62 sous et demi. Quiconque aura blessé un autre à la tête de telle sorte que le sang ait coulé jusqu'à terre sera condamné à payer 15 sous ; s'il est sorti trois esquilles, 30 sous ; si le cerveau a été mis à découvert, 45 sous ; si la blessure a été faite au milieu des côtes et qu'elle a pénétré à l'intérieur du corps, 30 sous ; si la gangrène s'empare de la blessure, 62 sous et demi, outre les frais de maladie, évalués à 9 sous.

Pour tous les crimes, un tiers du *wergeld* était versé au roi, comme indemnité de l'offense faite à la paix publique. De ce tiers, le comte gardait un tiers et reversait le reste au trésor royal. L'autre partie de l'amende était partagée entre les membres de la famille, en proportions inégales, selon le degré de parenté.

Si le meurtrier était incapable de payer, il pouvait faire appel à une famille élargie aux cousins, jusqu'au sixième degré, selon un curieux rituel appelé *chenecruda* et qui avait pour mission de préserver jusqu'aux dernières limites ses chances de survie. Après avoir juré qu'il n'avait pas de quoi payer la composition, il devait entrer dans sa maison, y ramasser de la terre et la jeter par-dessus son épaule sur ses parents les plus proches. Enfin, vêtu d'une chemise, sans ceinture et déchaussé, il devait sauter par-dessus la haie de son enclos, pour signifier aux membres de sa famille qu'il leur cédait sa maison.

La solidarité familiale semble bien avoir été la force de la société franque, l'individu se trouvant enserré dans un système très rigoureux de dépendances. Ainsi, à sa mort, ses biens revenaient automatiquement à ses enfants. S'il n'en laissait pas, l'ordre d'héritage était le suivant : les père et mère, puis les frères et sœurs, ensuite les sœurs de la mère puis celles du père. Enfin, s'il n'y avait aucun survivant, les plus proches parents du côté paternel.

Il existait aussi des procédures permettant à un père de déshériter ses enfants s'ils s'étaient rendus coupables d'un quelconque manquement à la moralité ou au loyalisme. Pour échapper au poids de ces contraintes, il n'y avait qu'une solution, réglée par un autre rituel : « Quiconque voudra briser les liens civils qui l'unissent à sa famille se présentera à l'audience du tribunal... Là, il brisera au-dessus de sa tête quatre branches d'aulne et en jettera les morceaux aux quatre coins de la salle en présence de tout le monde. Puis il dira qu'il entend renoncer au droit d'hérédité et à tous les rapports qui l'unissent civilement à sa famille. » Il perdait alors tout droit à la succession et au *wergeld*.

Tous ces gestes rituels, une branche ou une motte de terre remise de la main à la main pour échanger un terrain, une tuile ou une corde de cloche pour une maison, un gant pour la remise d'une dot, traduisent la force de coutumes orales qui s'infiltrent dans la législation écrite.

Ils nous font aussi apparaître des hommes proches de la nature, attachés à leur terre, à leur troupeau et à leur maison. Même si la famille est large, le Franc vit dans une maison individuelle bien construite, entourée d'un enclos limité par des haies ou des palissades. Du Bassin Parisien à l'Alsace, de l'Aquitaine au Pas-de-Calais, les fouilles archéologiques révèlent des grandes maisons qui mesurent en moyenne 10 mètres de long sur 5 de large ; des maisons solidement accrochées au sol par des poteaux et dont les solides charpentes lui assurent longue vie ; des maisons qui n'ont en général qu'une porte et qui sont assez vastes pour permettre la conservation des aliments, la fabrication de vêtements et une petite activité métallurgique ; des maisons où la place de la femme n'est pas non plus si mineure.

Ainsi, un long édit, composé, vers 573, par Chilpéric Ier, favorise la succession de la terre dans une même famille, préférant qu'elle échoie aux femmes plutôt qu'aux voisins, dont on devine à la lecture du texte la convoitise : « Agissant avec nos très magnifiques grands, nos antrustions et tout notre peuple, nous décidons [...] que si un homme meurt, qui a des voisins, des fils et des filles en vie, que les fils aient la terre leur vie durant, selon la loi salique. Si les fils meurent rapidement, que les filles reçoivent la terre, puis les fils de celles-ci si elles en ont. Si un homme meurt, qui ne laisse qu'un frère en vie, que le frère reçoive la terre et non les voisins. Si un homme meurt qui n'a pas de frère pour héritier, alors que la sœur, s'il en a, reçoive la terre et la possède. »

Même si le fonctionnement de la justice peut aussi apparaître naïf ou « barbare », à y regarder de plus près et, surtout, à prendre en compte la foi intense qui anime ces hommes mérovingiens, on peut deviner un instrument, certes, rude, mais moins irrationnel qu'il ne semble de prime abord.

Lorsqu'un suspect était amené devant le *mallus*, le tribunal composé du comte et de notables locaux appelés rachimbourgs, auxquels revenait le soin de lire la loi applicable et de délivrer le jugement, il disposait de deux sortes de recours. Soit il affirmait son innocence en prononçant un serment avec la garantie de ses voisins ou d'amis prêts, eux aussi, à jurer qu'il n'était pas coupable. Soit il avait recours à l'ordalie, s'il n'avait pas réussi à trouver des témoins prêts à le défendre. Par l'épreuve de l'eau simple préalablement bénie par un prêtre, si la personne, jetée à l'eau, s'enfonçait, on la tenait pour innocente ; si elle flottait, c'est que l'eau, qui ne pouvait recevoir un objet impur, la rejetait, et, donc, qu'elle était coupable. Si la main touchée par un fer rouge ou plongée dans l'eau bouillante était intacte, c'était l'innocence ; de même, si l'accusé pouvait choisir, les yeux bandés, un morceau de bois marqué parmi d'autres.

Grégoire de Tours fait allusion à un diacre catholique qui s'était mesuré à un prêtre arien « afin de prouver la vérité de sa religion face au schisme arien. Il plongea son bras dans un chaudron d'eau bouillante pour en retirer un petit anneau et ne fut pas brûlé, tandis que la peau du prêtre arien se détachait de l'os ».

Serment et ordalie relèvent en fait de la même croyance en la justice divine. Lorsqu'on se sait coupable, c'est courir à l'échec que de se soumettre à l'ordalie. Par sa foi, le coupable sait que Dieu le démasquera. Dès lors, au moment de l'épreuve, il renonce et avoue publiquement sa culpabilité. De même, parjurer et faire parjurer tous ceux qui acceptent de défendre l'accusé est singulièrement risqué à une époque où tout serment implique que celui qui le prête touche de la main, au moment où il jure, des reliques de saints ou une bible.

En outre, lors du procès, il était fréquent que les juges choisissent le mode de preuve répondant à la présomption qu'ils se faisaient de la culpabilité ou de l'innocence de l'accusé. S'ils l'estimaient innocent, ils choisissaient l'ordalie de l'eau chaude, dont on pouvait se tirer sans trop de difficulté. En revanche, s'ils l'estimaient probablement coupable, ils avaient recours à l'ordalie du fer rouge, de laquelle il était difficile de sortir indemne. Ainsi la justice mérovingienne n'était-elle pas dépourvue de sagesse ni de rationalité.

Le bon roi Dagobert

Le règne de Dagobert, pourtant de courte durée, semble alors marquer l'apogée des temps mérovingiens. Les territoires sur lesquels s'exerce son autorité sont immenses. Pendant les sept années où il dirige seul le *regnum Francorum*, de 632 à 639, il intervient sur tous les fronts, ne dormant presque pas, mangeant à peine, mais, « enflammé de sales désirs », se livrant, selon la chronique, « plus qu'il ne convient à l'amour des femmes ». En Aquitaine, il dépêche, en 635, une armée qui écrase les Basques et contraint leur roi à venir à sa cour implorer son pardon et lui jurer fidélité. Puis c'est au tour de

Judicaël, le roi des Bretons, de rendre visite à Dagobert pour faire sa soumission et conclure la paix. En Espagne, il intervient pour substituer un roi wisigoth à un autre et se faire payer deux cent mille sous d'or pour prix de son soutien. Dans la basse vallée du Rhin, il enlève Utrecht et Dorestad aux Frisons. Sur la frontière orientale du royaume, il dicte sa loi aux Alamans et aux Bavarois, installe en Thuringe un duc franc, Radulf, chargé de tenir les Slaves en respect, et massacre en Bavière des réfugiés bulgares à la recherche de terres et de protection. Enfin, en 630 ou 631, il conclut avec l'empereur de Byzance Héraclius une promesse de « paix perpétuelle ». Sa domination s'étendait alors sur un domaine qui allait des Pyrénées au Rhin, de la Bretagne à la Weser, voire à l'Elbe. Dagobert est bien le dernier roi mérovingien à avoir tenu toute la Gaule sous son autorité, à s'être fait respecter au-dehors et craint au-dedans.

Surtout, il a fait de son palais un véritable creuset où les élites du Nord ont fréquenté celles du Midi et nourri une complicité qui en ont fait des collaborateurs de talent. Dadon, le futur saint Ouen, devient le chef de la chancellerie avec le titre de référendaire. Desiderius, le futur saint Didier, est trésorier du roi. Éloi, un orfèvre réputé, est une sorte de ministre des Finances. Ainsi, ce roi polygame, qui répudia sa femme Gomatrude pour épouser une jeune fille de « basse naissance », traita deux autres femmes en reines et eut d'innombrables concubines, sut s'entourer de saints qui bâtirent sa légende et en firent un nouveau Salomon. L'éclat du règne de Dagobert tient pour une bonne part à la qualité de ces hommes qui deviendront tous, pour finir, évêques et saints, missionnaires actifs autant que véritables agents de l'autorité royale, concentrant entre leurs mains la tradition chrétienne et le passé romain.

Enfin, en multipliant les donations en faveur de la basilique de Saint-Denis, magnifiquement décorée par Éloi, il allait faire de la région parisienne le centre de gravité de la future France. Par un privilège exorbitant accordé en 634-635, les religieux de cette ville étaient autorisés à organiser chaque année, à partir du 9 octobre, fête de saint Denis, une foire à proximité de la basilique et à percevoir tous les tonlieux et les revenus dans la limite du comté de Paris pendant la durée de la manifestation. Essentiellement foire aux vins, elle allait attirer les peuples du Nord, gros demandeurs, et animer la vie économique du bassin de Paris.

Sentant sa fin proche, Dagobert prit soin de s'y faire transporter pour y mourir, le 19 janvier 639, et être enterré à droite du tombeau des saints. Écrite quelque vingt ans après sa mort par un clerc qui prenait ainsi la suite de l'*Histoire des Francs* de Grégoire de Tours, la chronique dite de Frédégaire relate ses derniers instants : « La seizième année de son règne (en 638), Dagobert tomba malade d'un flux de ventre dans sa maison d'Épinay, sur les bords de la Seine, non loin de Paris ; de là, les siens le transportèrent dans la basilique de Saint-Denis. Quelques jours après, se voyant en danger de la vie, il fit venir en toute hâte Aega, maire du palais de Neustrie, et lui recommanda la reine Nanthilde et son fils Clovis. Il se sentait près de mourir et, estimant la sagesse d'Aega, pensait que par lui le royaume serait bien gouverné. Cela fait, peu de jours après, Dagobert rendit l'âme et fut enseveli dans l'église de Saint-Denis, qu'il avait magnifiquement ornée d'or, de pierreries et d'objets précieux, et dont il avait fait construire l'enceinte, désirant la précieuse protection de ce saint. Il donna à l'église tant de richesses, de domaines et de possessions, situés en divers lieux, que beaucoup de gens s'en étonnèrent. » Dagobert espérait assurer ainsi le salut de son âme. Il allait surtout assurer le succès de sa légende.

L'ascension des maires du palais

Si Rome et la Méditerranée avaient, au VIᵉ siècle encore, constitué le modèle politique et culturel de l'aristocratie franque, au VIIᵉ siècle, ce sont incontestablement les terres brumeuses du Nord et les épaisses forêts austrasiennes qui enfantent un monde nouveau. Un monde dont la vitalité est telle que certains ont pu écrire que la Gaule avait alors connu un véritable « âge d'or ».

Les monastères, comme celui de Jouarre, deviennent les laboratoires d'une nouvelle sensibilité religieuse et esthétique, tandis que dans les moindres villages les populations viennent enterrer leurs morts près des églises paroissiales ; comme si la cité des morts ne pouvait plus être séparée de celle des vivants.

Une modeste aisance

Les épidémies et les famines qui avaient périodiquement décimé les populations semblent désormais vouloir les épargner. Jusqu'à l'extrême fin du VIᵉ siècle, en effet, la Gaule a souffert d'une conjoncture météorologique particulièrement maussade. En 580, écrit Grégoire de Tours, « de grands déluges s'abattirent sur l'Auvergne au point que, pendant douze jours, il ne cessa de pleuvoir et la Limagne fut noyée sous une telle inondation que cela empêcha beaucoup de gens de faire des semailles ». Après la sécheresse de 584, l'année suivante, « il y eut de fréquentes pluies et les fleuves grossirent au point que de fréquents naufrages se produisirent. Ces fleuves, en débordant, endommagèrent gravement les maisons voisines et les prés qu'ils inondaient, et les mois de printemps et d'été furent si humides qu'on s'imaginait que c'était l'hiver plutôt que l'été ». En 586 et 587, « au printemps, il y eut de fortes pluies et alors que les arbres et les vignes s'étaient déjà couverts de feuilles, la neige tomba qui couvrit tout. Puis une gelée étant ensuite survenue, les pousses de vigne comme les autres bourgeons qui se montraient furent grillés et la vigueur du froid fut telle que les hirondelles qui étaient venues des régions étrangères périrent aussi par suite de la violence de ce froid ». En 591, une « sécheresse intense anéantit le fourrage d'où il résulta une grave maladie parmi le bétail et les juments [...]. En effet, non seulement les bêtes domestiques furent atteintes par cette peste, mais aussi toute espèce de bêtes sauvages. On découvrit en des lieux loin de toute route une multitude de cerfs et autres animaux prostrés à terre ». Même s'il faut se méfier des chroniqueurs du temps, qui avaient tendance à exagérer ces calamités pour les attribuer à la colère divine, les données fournies par la glaciologie, l'examen des pollens conservés dans les tourbières ou celui des cercles concentriques annuels des troncs d'arbres laissent penser que l'Europe occidentale a bien connu, entre le début du Ve siècle et le VIIe siècle, un « temps pourri ». Fièvre typhoïde, dysenterie, variole et peste bubonique sont alors le lourd tribut payé par les hommes à cette oppression persistante d'un climat défavorable qui, en année de grande disette, les contraint à mêler avec un peu de farine des racines de fougères séchées et réduites en poudre pour en faire du pain.

Dans la seconde moitié du VIe siècle, on ne dénombre pas moins d'une dizaine d'épidémies. En 543-546, une épidémie de peste se répand à travers l'Italie et l'Espagne, envahit une grande partie de la Gaule et pousse jusqu'aux rives du Rhin, attaquant surtout les enfants promis à une mort immédiate. Dans tel cimetière mérovingien, sur vingt-sept squelettes, douze sont ceux d'enfants, dont neuf âgés de moins de dix ans. En 571, écrit Grégoire de Tours, « la mortalité fut si grande parmi le peuple de tout le pays qu'on ne saurait compter combien de légions y périrent. Un dimanche, on compta dans la basilique Saint-Pierre trois cents cadavres [...] ». En 580-582, « une maladie dysentérique envahit presque toutes les Gaules. Ceux qui en souffraient avaient une forte fièvre avec vomissements, une grande douleur de reins, de la pesanteur dans la tête et dans le cou. Les matières qu'ils rendaient par la bouche étaient jaunes ou même vertes.

Il y en avait beaucoup qui assuraient que c'était un poison secret ». Entre 587 et 618, la peste règne toujours en Italie et en Provence.

Or, après cette date, cette sinistre litanie disparaît des chroniques. Dans la lutte que les hommes doivent mener quotidiennement contre une nature encore sauvage, le VIIe siècle apparaît bien comme une période relativement « idyllique ». Ainsi, la *Vie de saint Didier*, évêque de Cahors, nous apprend que, durant son épiscopat (630-655), « l'abondance des fruits, la richesse des vendanges et des moissons, augmenta, foisonna et déborda tellement à cette époque que de mémoire d'homme personne n'en avait vu pareille ni autrefois ni après lui. En effet, il n'y avait presque pas de gens dans le besoin, personne n'avait de difficulté à trouver ce qu'il recherchait, il ne manqua jamais nourriture ou vêtement, car tout était plein, tout débordait » Certes, il faut toujours se garder de ces témoignages hagiographiques, mais, là encore, tout porte à croire qu'une hausse infime des moyennes thermiques annuelles, de l'ordre, peut-être, de 1 °C, variation qui correspond à peu près à la différence observée, dans la France actuelle, entre le climat de Dunkerque et celui de Rennes, ou entre le climat de Belfort et celui de Lyon, permit d'améliorer de manière sensible la production céréalière, d'autant plus que l'été et l'automne étaient devenus plus secs.

Les cimetières donnent la mesure de cet accroissement de la population. Frénouville, dans le Calvados, qui ne comptait que 250 habitants à l'époque gallo-romaine, atteint les 1 400 au VIIe siècle. En Picardie, les habitants reconstruisent leurs habitations en pierre, un usage qui s'était perdu depuis la fin du IIIe siècle. Dans les vallées du sud de l'Aquitaine et dans le Massif central, des terres cultivées à l'époque gallo-romaine et retournées à la friche depuis les invasions barbares sont remises en culture.

Ce sont surtout les régions septentrionales qui semblent avoir le plus bénéficié de cette amélioration. Dans la zone méditerranéenne, par contre, le surcroît d'aridité rendit sans doute le sol plus fragile et plus vulnérable aux effets destructeurs des défrichements. Ce sont même les traditions alimentaires qui subissent une lente modification. On se rappelle le dégoût qu'inspirait à Sidoine Apollinaire la cuisine des Burgondes, à base de beurre et d'oignon. Or, au VIIe siècle, dans toute la Gaule, l'usage du lard et de la graisse tend à se substituer à celui de l'huile, tandis que les rations journalières des artisans qui travaillent sur les chantiers font désormais une large place à la viande de porc. Dans les lourdes ripailles dont se délectent longuement ceux qu'on appelle encore des « sénateurs », les viandes baignent dans « une sauce extrêmement grasse » et l'on apprécie les « écuelles de verre chargées de poulets bouillis », les quartiers de bœuf ou de porc « dressés en forme de montagne », mais surtout les cailles, les faisans, les lapereaux et le gros gibier, biche, cerf, sanglier, buffle, le tout fortement épicé.

Il faut y voir aussi le déplacement prononcé des routes commerciales. Même si la Méditerranée n'est pas tout à fait désertée, même si l'on trouve toujours à Marseille et à Fos du vin de Gaza, du garum, un condiment à base de poisson pimenté, fortement apprécié, du riz, des dattes, des figues, du poivre, du cumin, des clous de girofle et de la cannelle, du papyrus d'Égypte, des grenats d'Asie mineure et des laines de Syrie, c'est vers le Nord encore qu'il faut regarder pour voir s'établir des itinéraires marchands plus actifs. Dans les années 670-680, la chancellerie des rois mérovingiens abandonne le papyrus au bénéfice du parchemin pour la rédaction des diplômes.

Contrôlé par les Frisons, qui naviguent hardiment le long des côtes de la mer du Nord et de la Baltique jusqu'au débouché des fleuves russes, ce nouveau trafic offre à la Gaule du Nord peaux et fourrures, laine et draps, ambre et ivoire, pierres précieuses et esclaves. En liaison avec ces échanges se développent, à partir des environs de 600, les ports de Dorestad, sur le Rhin, et de Quentovic, sur la Canche. Irrigués par cette « Méditerranée nordique », Rhin, Escaut et Meuse deviennent les voies de pénétration dans lesquelles s'engouffrent les marchands. En même temps, c'est la monnaie d'or léguée par Rome et toujours en vigueur à Byzance qui est balayée par la monnaie d'argent frappée par les Frisons. Mieux adaptés aux nouvelles données commerciales, ces deniers d'argent d'un poids approximatif de 1,10 g et au graphisme barbare marquent le début d'une nouvelle époque. Le centre de gravité de la Gaule s'est bien déplacé du Sud vers le Nord. Dans ces conditions, il n'est pas surprenant que les moines de Saint-Denis aient voulu, en 694, troquer la rente de cent sous qui leur avait été accordée sur les revenus de la douane de Marseille contre l'acquisition d'un domaine agricole dans le Berry. Ils savaient que l'avenir était au Nord.

Des moines conquérants

Laboratoire de nouveaux circuits comme de nouvelles idées, le Nord devient aussi, au VIIe siècle, le foyer d'une nouvelle sensibilité religieuse initiée par des moines qui traversent eux aussi la mer du Nord pour « pérégriner » au service de Dieu. Grâce à ces moines peu conformistes, au prosélytisme dévastateur, et à leurs disciples, le clergé gaulois redécouvre alors une vocation spirituelle qu'avaient altérée le goût pour les choses administratives et le peu d'intérêt pour la théologie et l'exégèse.

Si on lisait certainement la Bible dans l'Église mérovingienne, on considérait surtout le texte sacré comme un classique parmi d'autres dont il fallait nourrir la mémoire plus que l'esprit et le cœur. Lorsque Grégoire de Tours fait l'éloge de l'évêque Maurille d'Angers, il écrit ainsi : « Il fut remarquablement nourri des Écritures, si bien qu'il récitait par cœur la série des diverses générations qui sont exposées dans l'Ancien Testament, ce qui est difficile à retenir. ». Présenter la vérité chrétienne sous une forme agréable était le plus grand souci d'évêques pétris de culture antique qui aimaient surtout faire étalage de leur érudition et de leurs talents oratoires.

Autant dire que certains d'entre eux furent scandalisés par l'austérité exigeante et l'indépendance d'esprit de ces Irlandais qui furent les agents actifs de l'évangélisation d'une Gaule du Nord encore bien peu christianisée. Comme l'attestent les nombreuses mises en garde des conciles mérovingiens, le paganisme y gardait de beaux restes, ce dont témoigne la *Vie de saint Éloi*, évêque de Noyon de 641 à 660, qui nous en fournit une illustration. Alors que, le jour de la Saint-Pierre, le prédicateur vilipendait « les jeux diaboliques, les danses perverses et autres superstitions », les notables de la ville décidèrent de tuer ce trouble-fête. Averti de leur intention, le saint accepta le martyre et continua ses exhortations. Le porte-parole des notables s'adressa alors à lui en ces termes : « Romain que vous êtes, bien que vous nous tracassiez sans cesse, nous n'abandonnerons jamais nos coutumes et, comme nous l'avons toujours fait, nous continuerons à célébrer nos rites, encore et toujours. Il n'existera jamais aucun homme capable de nous contraindre à arrêter nos fêtes et nos jeux favoris. »

Colomban, venu de Bangor, au nord-est de l'Irlande, sut relever ce défi. Alors que les premiers moines (du grec *monachos*, « celui qui vit seul ») étaient des êtres d'exception qui recherchaient dans la vie solitaire le moyen le plus sûr de parvenir au salut de l'âme, à l'exemple de leurs prédécesseurs qui, en Égypte, s'étaient retirés à la limite du désert pour rompre tout lien avec le monde, les moines irlandais qui débarquent en Gaule à la fin du VIᵉ siècle se veulent surtout des prédicateurs itinérants parcourant en tous sens le pays pour y implanter des monastères et en faire les bases logistiques de l'évangélisation des campagnes.

Le monastère de Luxeuil, fondé en Bourgogne par Colomban en 591, devient rapidement un modèle. Prière personnelle ou collective, travaux manuels, mortifications, tel est le programme assigné à des moines dont la formation religieuse ne doit pas s'encombrer du culte des belles lettres. Si l'audience de Colomban est à peu près nulle auprès des autorités religieuses, qui adoptent à son égard une attitude hostile, il a un immense succès auprès des élites aristocratiques, particulièrement séduites par la rigueur de cette ascèse.

Ainsi, de nombreux Aquitains quittent pour la première fois les limites de leur « patrie » pour adopter les pratiques itinérantes des Irlandais et venir évangéliser les pays austrasiens et germaniques. Valéry, un ancien berger originaire d'Auvergne, après être passé par Luxeuil, part évangéliser les païens du Vimeu et meurt, vers 620, dans le monastère qu'il a fondé et auquel son nom fut donné : Saint-Valéry-sur-Somme.

Amand, né en Herbauge, dans le bas Poitou, fait d'abord un séjour dans le monastère de l'île d'Yeu, probablement irlandais. Après deux voyages à Rome, pour aller chercher des reliques, il part évangéliser le pays de Gand, où il rachète des esclaves pour les instruire et les baptiser. En 639, il fonde un monastère sur les bords de l'Elnone (aujourd'hui Saint-Amand-les-Eaux). Nommé, en 647, évêque de Tongres-Maastricht, il ne tient pas en place et reprend ses pérégrinations chez les Slovènes, puis en Thuringe, enfin chez les Vascons. Comme il le dit lui-même dans son testament : « Nous avons couru en longueur et en largeur. »

Remacle, Aquitain aussi, peut-être originaire du Berry, fonde, en 645, le monastère de Cugnon, sur la Semois, puis, au beau milieu de la forêt d'Ardenne, aux confins des diocèses de Tongres et de Cologne, « en des lieux d'horreur et de vastes solitudes où pullulent des troupes de bêtes sauvages », deux abbayes, à Stavelot et Malmédy, qui forment un couvent double à la manière irlandaise (un couvent d'hommes, un couvent de femmes).

En accord avec Amand, Rictrude, femme noble d'origine toulousaine, crée, vers 647, Marchiennes. La reine Bathilde une esclave anglo-saxonne rachetée qui avait épousé le roi Clovis II, fait don, vers 654, de la terre initiale à l'Aquitain Philibert, un ancien de Luxeuil, lui aussi, pour lui permettre de fonder l'abbaye de Jumièges. Puis, vers 659, devenue veuve, elle installe, avec l'accord de son fils Clotaire III, un autre monastère luxovien dans la région de Corbie, avant de fonder à Chelles un monastère de moniales dans lequel elle se retire.

Ainsi, alors qu'au VIᵉ siècle les monastères importants étaient situés en Provence, en Bourgogne ou en Aquitaine, au siècle suivant, c'est dans le Nord et l'Est que sont surtout implantés les quelque deux cents monastères fondés en Gaule entre la fin du VIᵉ siècle et le début du VIIIe siècle, quarante l'ayant été dans les seuls diocèses de Thérouanne, Tournai, Cambrai et Liège entre 625 et 700.

Et, par une superbe contradiction avec l'intention de leurs fondateurs, ces monastères, qui se voulaient nichés au cœur d'une nature hostile, allaient devenir de véritables puissances foncières et économiques, le prestige des moines auprès de l'aristocratie étant tel qu'ils allaient bénéficier de donations considérables. Ce sont 10 000 hectares de terre qui sont donnés à Amand pour fonder Elnone. Ce sont 20 000 hectares que Bathilde lègue à Corbie. Tout le versant occidental des Vosges est entre les mains des cinq grandes abbayes de Senones, Étival, Moyenmoutier, Saint-Dié et Remiremont. C'est aussi le travail de défrichement, la mise en valeur des alentours immédiats du monastère et l'aménagement de routes qui finissent par mettre ces lieux de retraite en communication avec le monde. Peu à peu, la communauté monastique rayonne sur la région environnante, attire fidèles, malades et pécheurs, le *Pénitentiel* de Colomban prévoyant, pour punir des crimes majeurs comme le parjure, la fornication ou l'adultère, de longs séjours dans les monastères. Vers la fin du VIIe siècle, un passage de la *Vie de saint Philibert* nous permet d'imaginer les bâtiments qui ont remplacé les huttes primitives des premiers ermites : « C'est là que la prévoyance des moines aboutit à la construction, sur un plan carré, de murailles flanquées de tours et, pour les hôtes, d'admirables cloîtres [...]. À l'intérieur resplendit une paisible demeure digne des moines. À l'est s'élève l'église, bâtie en forme de croix ; au nord, une petite église dédiée au bienheureux martyr Denis et à Germain, confesseur ; à droite, une église dédiée à saint Pierre ; à côté, un oratoire dédié à saint Martin ; orientée au sud se trouve la cellule de Philibert. Le bâtiment des moines élève ses deux étages du côté de l'est. Sur chaque texte, la lumière irradie ses rayons, secondant la vue du lecteur. »

C'est que, points de passage obligés entre les îles Britanniques et l'Italie, les monastères de la Gaule du Nord sont devenus par la force des choses des centres de vie culturelle et artistique. Ils enrichissent leurs bibliothèques des manuscrits d'auteurs classiques ramenés d'Italie, et dans les *scriptoria* de Corbie, de Laon, de Saint-Denis, de Luxeuil, de Fleury, de Saint-Martin de Tours, de Jumièges ou de Fontenelle, les scribes inventent bientôt un nouveau type d'écriture où s'associent des éléments anglo-saxons et romains. S'inspirant des broderies des tissus orientaux et des motifs de l'art copte, les peintres ornent les initiales d'entrelacs, d'éléments géométriques ou zoomorphes (oiseaux, poissons), et par le choix des couleurs franches, le vert, le rouge, le jaune, donnent aux manuscrits une gaieté légère et pleine de charme. Ainsi s'humanise, à la fin du VIIe siècle, la culture ascétique des premiers moines colombaniens.

Les sarcophages de Théodechilde, première abbesse du monastère de Jouarre, et de son frère Agilbert sont les plus beaux exemples d'un art « mérovingien » profondément imprégné d'espérance chrétienne. Sur les deux longues faces du sarcophage de Théodechilde était gravée cette épitaphe : « Ce sépulcre recouvre les derniers restes de la bienheureuse Théodechilde. Vierge sans tache, de noble race, étincelante de mérites, zélée dans ses mœurs, elle brûlait pour le dogme vivifiant. Mère de ce monastère, elle apprit à ses filles consacrées au Seigneur à courir vers le Christ leur époux, comme les vierges sages, avec leurs lampes garnies d'huile. Morte, elle exulte finalement dans le triomphe du paradis. » Sur le panneau du sarcophage d'Agilbert, on pouvait voir la félicité des élus, le jour du Jugement dernier, acclamant, bras levés, le Christ auréolé.

Toujours plus au nord, toujours vers les terres où résident les nouveaux puissants, tel semble être l'axe missionnaire des moines conquérants. Quatre régions les ont particulièrement attirés, la Champagne avec Troyes, Châlons-en-Champagne et la campagne rémoise, les pays rhénans et les terres mosanes et, sur les confins picardo-flamands, une zone limitée par le quadrilatère Thérouanne-Amiens-Noyon-Bavay. Tel était le principal résultat du déplacement du centre de gravité du Midi vers le Nord. Celui-ci pouvait désormais s'appuyer sur des forces matérielles et spirituelles jeunes pour accentuer sa pression politique sur un Midi d'où se retirait un héritage romain vieillissant.

Le pouvoir de l'aristocratie

Théodechilde et Agilbert illustrent l'ascension d'une aristocratie qui a su accaparer les dividendes de la croissance et reprendre à son compte l'élan missionnaire initié par les moines irlandais.

C'est elle qui, après la mort de Dagobert, devient la seule force capable de remplir les fonctions assignées par l'Église à Clovis, aider les habitants du royaume, relever les affligés, soutenir les veuves et nourrir les orphelins. Patiemment, elle annexe les pouvoirs de justice, de fiscalité et de gouvernement qui avaient été ceux des empereurs romains, puis des rois francs.

Fruit du mariage entre les vieilles familles sénatoriales gallo-romaines et les chefs de guerre « barbares », cette aristocratie était formée de tous ceux qui, vivant à la cour du roi ou exerçant des fonctions publiques en son nom, bénéficiaient de ses largesses. Tout au long du VIIᵉ siècle, elle a su profiter de la faiblesse grandissante du pouvoir royal pour arracher de nouveaux avantages.

Après sa victoire sur Brunehaut, Clotaire II avait été obligé de faire aux grands une concession importante. En octobre 614, lors d'un concile les rassemblant à Paris, il avait publié un édit dont l'article 12 stipulait : « Aucun comte originaire d'autres provinces ou régions ne sera nommé en d'autres lieux (que son pays d'origine), afin que, s'il commet quelques maux lors de l'exercice de sa charge, il soit obligé de restituer, selon la loi, sur ses propres biens, ce qu'il aura enlevé à tort. »

Une telle mesure avait pour but évident de réprimer les excès de pouvoir et les « insolences des méchants », mais, en même temps, elle impliquait le risque de voir les intérêts de l'aristocratie l'emporter sur ceux du service public. Les grands étaient désormais bien placés pour arrondir leurs propriétés et garder pour eux les terres du fisc qui leur servaient d'émoluments. Dagobert avait bien perçu le danger lorsqu'il confisqua tous les biens de ceux qui se révoltaient, mais, après sa mort, l'enracinement des grandes familles dans leur région d'origine allait amener la constitution progressive de véritables dynasties et la dislocation du royaume en régions de plus en plus autonomes.

Une poignée de grands propriétaires terriens étend ainsi son emprise sur le pays, prenant sous sa « protection » une masse de plus en plus grande de « clients », de nombreuses familles recherchant alors le patronage d'un puissant qui puisse les protéger, les aider à résister à la pression d'un chef local ou simplement les nourrir. Un formulaire daté du début du VIIIᵉ siècle nous donne les clauses du contrat qui établissait les relations de dépendance entre deux personnes d'inégale fortune et nous éclaire sur les conditions dans lesquelles des hommes libres étaient amenés à aliéner leur liberté : « Au seigneur magnifique (un tel), moi (un tel), attendu qu'il est parfaitement connu de tous que je n'ai pas de quoi me nourrir ni me vêtir, j'ai demandé à votre pitié – et votre bonne volonté me l'a accordé – de pouvoir me livrer ou me recommander en votre maimbour [protection]. Ce que j'ai fait aux conditions suivantes. Vous devrez m'aider et me soutenir, pour la nourriture autant que pour le vêtement, dans la mesure où je pourrai vous servir et bien mériter de vous. Aussi longtemps que je vivrai, je vous devrai le service et l'obéissance qu'on peut attendre d'un homme libre, et je n'aurai pas le pouvoir de me soustraire à votre puissance ou maimbour, mais je devrai au contraire rester tous les jours de ma vie sous votre puissance et protection. »

Parfois, c'était aussi le souci de s'assurer le salut dans l'au-delà qui poussait certains à abandonner leur indépendance et à devenir « clients » d'un établissement religieux. Celui qui se commandait à un maître (*dominus*) ou à un seigneur (du latin *senior*, « l'ancien ») devenait son « homme » – on dira bientôt son vassal (*vassus*).

En même temps, l'insécurité grandissante amenait les paysans à se jeter dans les bras des puissants et à leur céder leur lopin de terre, à condition d'en conserver la jouissance. Cela d'autant plus qu'églises et puissants obtenaient de plus en plus du roi le privilège d'immunité qui avait pour effet de soustraire leurs domaines à l'action des fonctionnaires royaux et d'en faire des enclaves qui échappaient en grande partie à l'autorité publique. Désormais, ces grands propriétaires tenaient vis-à-vis de leurs protégés la place des fonctionnaires royaux qui ne pouvaient plus pénétrer dans leurs domaines pour y rendre la justice ou percevoir l'impôt.

Continuant et développant un usage introduit dès l'époque romaine, ils ont aussi, au moment où les sources traditionnelles de l'esclavage étaient en train de se tarir, organisé l'exploitation de leur domaine de manière à exiger de leurs dépendants divers services qu'accomplissaient autrefois les esclaves. Ainsi se répand, au VIIe siècle, un système d'exploitation du sol lourd d'avenir. D'un côté, on trouve la terre réservée au maître, la réserve ; de l'autre, de petites exploitations concédées aux « dépendants », les manses, dont les propriétaires devaient, à l'occasion des moissons ou des vendanges, un certain nombre de « corvées » en échange de la protection qui leur était accordée.

Émanations de cette aristocratie dont ils défendent les intérêts, les maires du palais de Neustrie, de Bourgogne et d'Austrasie partent alors à la conquête du pouvoir. Du désordre qui naît de ces luttes « autonomistes » allait progressivement triompher une famille qui possédait d'immenses domaines en Austrasie, dans la région qui devenait l'un des axes importants de la vie économique et le foyer actif d'un christianisme conquérant.

Charles Martel, le « presque-roi »

Parmi les grands qui ont aidé Clotaire II à venir à bout de Brunehaut figuraient deux aristocrates austrasiens, Arnoul, de Metz, et Pépin de Landen, dont le parcours illustre le pouvoir croissant de ces grands. Né vers 580, Arnoul possède d'immenses domaines dans le pays de

LES PIPPINIDES ET LES PREMIERS CAROLINGIENS

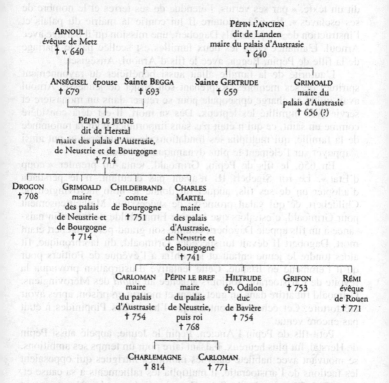

ARNOUL
évêque de Metz
† v. 640

PÉPIN L'ANCIEN
dit de Landen
maire du palais d'Austrasie
† 640

ANSÉGISEL épouse Sainte BEGGA
† 679   † 693

Sainte GERTRUDE
† 659

GRIMOALD
maire du
palais d'Austrasie
† 656 (?)

PÉPIN LE JEUNE
dit de Herstal
maire des palais d'Austrasie,
de Neustrie et de Bourgogne
† 714

DROGON
† 708

GRIMOALD
maire
des palais
de Neustrie et
de Bourgogne
† 714

CHILDEBRAND
comte
de Bourgogne
† 751

CHARLES
MARTEL
maire
des palais
d'Austrasie,
de Neustrie et
de Bourgogne
† 741

CARLOMAN
maire
du palais
d'Austrasie
† 754

PÉPIN LE BREF
maire
du palais
de Neustrie,
puis roi
† 768

HILTRUDE
ép. Odilon
duc
de Bavière
† 754

GRIFON
† 753

RÉMI
évêque
de Rouen
† 771

CHARLEMAGNE
† 814

CARLOMAN
† 771

Woëvre, entre la Moselle et la Meuse, mais également dans la région de Worms. Entré, comme beaucoup de jeunes fils de grande famille, à la cour du roi, il se fait remarquer par ses qualités militaires et devient intendant des domaines royaux. Mais, séduit par l'ascétisme prêché par Colomban, il songe à fuir le monde et à rejoindre les moines irlandais. Toutefois, sous la pression de ses parents, qui désirent agrandir leurs possessions, il accepte d'épouser une jeune fille d'illustre famille. En 614, il est nommé évêque de Metz, une charge importante puisque cette ville est capitale du royaume d'Austrasie.

Pépin l'Ancien, plus connu sous le nom de Pépin de Landen, est issu d'une famille qui, elle aussi, possède d'immenses domaines dans le Brabant, la Hesbaye et le Namurois. Il a épousé Itta, célèbre, nous dit un texte, « par ses vertus, l'étendue de ses terres et le nombre de ses esclaves ». En 623, Clotaire II lui confie la mairie du palais et l'instruction de son jeune fils Dagobert, une mission qu'il partage avec Arnoul. L'alliance entre les deux familles est scellée par le mariage de la fille de Pépin, Begga, avec le fils d'Arnoul, Anségisel.

L'autorité de la famille allait aussi bénéficier du rayonnement spirituel de ses membres. Reprenant son projet de jeunesse, Arnoul avait quitté sa charge épiscopale pour se retirer dans un monastère et servir avec humilité les lépreux. Dès sa mort, il est déjà considéré comme un saint, ce qui n'était pas sans importance pour la renommée de la famille, qui multiplia les fondations de monastères et put ainsi s'appuyer sur l'élément le plus dynamique de l'Église.

En 656, le fils de Pépin, Grimoald, tenta un premier « coup d'État ». Le roi Sigebert III n'ayant pas d'enfant, il le persuada d'adopter un de ses fils, auquel fut donné le nom mérovingien de Childebert, ce qui valait promesse de succession. Malheureusement pour Grimoald, c'est alors que la reine Emnechilde donna enfin naissance à un fils appelé Dagobert, comme son grand-père. Sigebert étant mort, Dagobert II devait lui succéder. Grimoald, dit la chronique, fit alors tondre le jeune enfant et le confia à l'évêque de Poitiers pour qu'il l'emmène en Irlande. Cette tentative d'usurpation provoqua la révolte de l'aristocratie, toujours attachée au *mund* des Mérovingiens. Grimoald fut attiré dans un guet-apens et mourut en prison, après avoir été torturé. Cet échec démontrait que l'heure des Pippinides n'était pas encore venue.

Petit-fils de Pépin l'Ancien, Pépin le Jeune, appelé aussi Pépin de Herstal, fut plus heureux. Faisant taire pour un temps ses ambitions, se mouvant avec habileté dans les multiples intrigues qui opposaient les factions de l'aristocratie, il multiplia les ralliements à sa cause et, en 687, à Tertry, près de Saint-Quentin, il écrasa les Neustriens et s'empara du roi Thierry III et de son trésor.

Toutefois, plutôt que d'adopter une politique brutale de conquête, il préféra ménager les susceptibilités. Réinstallant dans ses domaines un roi dont la signature apparaît toujours au bas des diplômes, il se fit désigner par lui comme le seul maire du palais du *regnum Francorum*. Un texte écrit au IXe siècle, les *Annales de Metz*, illustre la façon dont s'associent encore le respect envers les descendants de Clovis et la réalité du pouvoir.

« Tous les ans aux calendes de mars, le maire du palais Pépin II tenait une assemblée générale avec tous les Francs, selon la coutume des Anciens. À cause de la révérence due au titre de roi, il y faisait présider le roi jusqu'à ce qu'il ait reçu de tous les grands parmi les Francs les dons annuels, qu'il eût fait une harangue pour la paix et la protection des églises de Dieu, des orphelins, des veuves, qu'il eût interdit fermement le rapt des femmes, le crime de l'incendiaire, qu'il eût ordonné à l'armée d'être préparée pour le jour annoncé pour partir. Alors, Pépin renvoya le roi à sa villa royale de Mamaccas (Montmacq-sur-Oise) pour y être gardé avec honneur et vénération, tandis que lui-même gouvernait le royaume des Francs. »

Jusqu'en 714, date de sa mort, tout en déléguant à son fils Grimoald les deux palais de Neustrie et de Bourgogne, Pépin le Jeune gouverne en fait seul et peut apparaître comme le restaurateur de l'unité franque. Ce sont les moines de son entourage qui forgent alors de toutes pièces la légende des « rois fainéants », une caricature qui vise à discréditer les Mérovingiens en les présentant comme des rois paresseux, incapables de se tenir à cheval et réduits à se faire traîner comme des femmes dans un char à bœufs.

À la mort de Pépin le Jeune, précédée par celle de son fils aîné Drogon, en 708, et l'assassinat de son fils cadet Grimoald, en 714, la patiente construction échafaudée par le maire du palais austrasien semble toutefois bien menacée. Les petits-fils légitimes de Pépin sont des enfants, mais, d'une épouse de second rang, il avait eu un autre fils, auquel il avait donné le nom de Karl (Charles), un nom jamais encore porté dans la famille et qui devait signifier « brave », « valeureux ».

Dès la mort de Pépin le Jeune, sa veuve Plectrude jette le « bâtard » en prison et tente de gouverner seule le royaume au nom de ses petits-fils. C'est le signal de la révolte de tous ceux qui n'avaient pas supporté l'emprise de Pépin. Les grands de Neustrie portent un des leurs, Ragenfred, à la mairie du palais, battent les hommes de Plectrude dans la forêt de Compiègne et font alliance avec les Frisons et les Saxons pour régler leur compte aux Austrasiens.

Dans la confusion générale, Charles s'échappe alors de prison, réunit des partisans et triomphe de tous ses ennemis l'un après l'autre.

À Amblève, près de Malmédy, en 716, et à Vincy, près de Cambrai, en 717, il bat les Neustriens. Puis il contraint Plectrude, réfugiée à Cologne, à lui remettre le trésor de Pépin. En 719, il pourchasse les Saxons et les Frisons, rétablit son autorité sur la rive gauche du bas-Rhin et, la même année, met en fuite Eudes, le duc d'Aquitaine, qui s'était porté au nord de la Loire avec des contingents basques pour soutenir les Neustriens. Même si Charles apparaît alors sans rival, son emprise sur le royaume franc reste précaire. Au sud, l'Aquitaine demeurait pratiquement indépendante. En Bourgogne, les évêques d'Auxerre et de Lyon régnaient en maîtres sur leur région. Enfin, Bavière, Alémanie échappaient au contrôle du maire de palais austrasien, tandis que les Frisons étaient prêts à reprendre l'offensive.

Pour assurer sa domination, Charles va s'attacher à rassembler autour de lui des fidèles. Pratiquant systématiquement une politique de dépouilles, sécularisant une grande partie des biens de l'Église, pour les confier à des hommes sûrs, il s'est donné les moyens de mettre au pas ses rivaux. Utilisant sur une grande échelle les liens de « recommandation », il rémunère ses « vassaux » en leur distribuant des terres qui leur permettent d'équiper et d'entretenir un cheval, ce qui était fort coûteux (le prix de dix-huit à vingt vaches au temps de Dagobert). Alors que l'infanterie avait été jusque-là la force principale des Francs, la cavalerie devient l'arme mobile d'une armée sans cesse sollicitée dans des campagnes aussi rapides que répétées.

Charles peut alors multiplier les équipées, intervenir à l'Est et réduire les Bavarois et les Alamans à l'obéissance, tenir en respect les Saxons, soumettre les Frisons en étant capable de mener à bien une expédition navale, puis saisir l'occasion qu'offrait l'invasion de troupes musulmanes en Aquitaine pour devenir le champion de la chrétienté et le « martel » de Dieu.

Après avoir, depuis 711, conquis une grande partie de l'Espagne, les Arabes musulmans et les Berbères convertis à l'Islam ont franchi les Pyrénées, occupé Narbonne, Carcassonne, Nîmes et lancé un raid le long de l'axe Rhône-Saône jusqu'à Autun, qui a été saccagée. En 732, le *wali*, ou gouverneur d'Espagne, Abd al-Rahmān lance une nouvelle offensive. Il pénètre en Aquitaine par le Pays Basque, pille et dévaste les faubourgs de Bordeaux, s'élance vers Poitiers et cherche à gagner la basilique Saint-Martin de Tours, aux richesses si tentantes.

Appelé au secours par le duc d'Aquitaine, Eudes, Charles accourt et, à Moussais, sur la voie romaine de Poitiers à Tours, le 25 octobre 732, il bat les troupes arabes, Abd al-Rahmān étant parmi les morts. Attendant de pied ferme la charge furieuse des cavaliers arabes, dont la tactique est d'effrayer l'ennemi et d'émietter ses rangs, les Francs, en rangs serrés, « immobiles comme un mur » selon un contemporain, lancent leurs redoutables francisques, qui s'en vont fracasser les crânes et les corps des assaillants.

Même si la bataille de Poitiers n'a pas été le coup d'arrêt décisif porté à l'expansion de l'Islam, elle eut un grand retentissement dans tout l'Occident. Elle marque bien la victoire des gens du Nord, les Austrasiens, sur ceux du Midi. Profitant de son succès, Charles impose en effet sa souveraineté à l'Aquitaine, à la Bourgogne et à la Provence, soumettant les aristocraties locales qui, depuis longtemps, s'étaient rendues indépendantes. Le maire du palais est désormais le personnage le plus en vue, non seulement du royaume mérovingien, mais de tout l'Occident.

D'ailleurs, c'est à lui que, en 739, le pape Grégoire III écrit pour demander aide contre les Lombards, qui, en Italie, menacent « la sainte Église de Dieu et le patrimoine du bienheureux Pierre, prince des Apôtres ». Avec ses lettres, il lui envoie de riches présents, en particulier un reliquaire contenant un peu de limaille des chaînes de saint Pierre incorporées dans une clé, et le nomme *subregulus* et *princeps Francorum*, « presque-roi » et « prince des Francs ». Toutefois, si Charles reçut avec les honneurs l'ambassade romaine, il déclina l'invitation, refusant de se mêler des affaires d'Italie. En fait, la coopération entre la papauté et la famille des Pippinides n'était que partie remise.

Avant de mourir, le 22 octobre 741, Charles a réglé sa succession comme un roi, partageant le royaume entre ses fils, « après avoir pris l'avis de ses grands ». L'aîné, Carloman, reçoit l'Austrasie, l'Alémanie et la Thuringe. Pépin, le cadet, la Neustrie, la Bourgogne et la Provence. Quant à Grifon, un fils qu'il avait eu d'une épouse de second rang, il bénéficia de quelques territoires dispersés dans le royaume. Quand il fut enterré à l'abbaye de Saint-Denis, comme Dagobert, l'abbé d'Echternach écrivit dans le *Calendrier*, où étaient notés les grands événements : « Octobre 741, mort du roi Charles. »

Charlemagne, empereur d'Occident

*Le royaume dont héritent, en 741, les fils de Charles Martel restait un
ensemble fragile toujours soumis à des révoltes que seule la poigne
de Charles avait réussi à « marteler ». Le « coup d'État » mené à bien dix
ans plus tard par Pépin, qui, avec l'appui du pape, se fait sacrer roi, et
l'inlassable énergie déployée par Charlemagne, « couronné par Dieu,
grand et pacifique empereur », jettent les bases d'un vaste empire,
conquis par le fer des cavaliers francs, restant en grande partie l'Empire
romain d'Occident et administré selon le modèle de la Cité de Dieu décrit
par saint Augustin.*

Le sacre de Pépin

Dès la mort de Charles Martel, une série de soulèvements mettent
en péril ses descendants, les « presque-rois » Carloman et Pépin. Grifon, leur demi-frère, mécontent du partage, exige de prendre possession de ses biens. Odilon, le duc de Bavière, qui avait épousé contre
son gré leur sœur Hiltrude, fait alliance avec Hunald, le duc d'Aquitaine, et Théodebald, celui des Alamans, pour secouer la tutelle de
ceux dont il conteste la légitimité.

Carloman et Pépin doivent alors, comme le « Martel », multiplier
les interventions du sud à l'est du royaume, mater leur demi-frère,
qu'ils enferment dans le château de Chèvremont, près de Liège, placer
sa mère sous la surveillance des religieuses de Chelles, prendre

Bourges, raser la forteresse de Loches, écraser dans un bain de sang les Alamans, défaire Odilon sur le Lech et l'obliger à reconnaître leur supériorité.

Avaient-ils le sentiment que cette révolte des princes soulignait leur absence de légitimité ? Toujours est-il que, en 743, ils éprouvent le besoin d'aller chercher dans un monastère un jeune prince mérovingien et de le rétablir sur le trône demeuré vacant depuis 737. Certes, ce rétablissement était purement formel. Pour s'en convaincre, il suffit de lire les actes officiels signés par le nouveau roi Childéric III : « Childéric, roi des Francs, à l'éminent Carloman, maire du palais, qui nous a établi sur le trône [...]. » Il témoignait toutefois que le changement de dynastie posait bien des problèmes, malgré la propagande qui avait tout fait pour déconsidérer les « rois fainéants ».

Si les aristocrates alamans, aquitains et bavarois s'étaient soulevés, c'est bien parce qu'ils se considéraient à égalité avec les Pippinides. De plus, à une époque où le paganisme était loin d'avoir disparu, le fait que les Mérovingiens étaient rattachés à des ancêtres mythiques et que le sang de Clovis coulait dans leurs veines n'était pas sans importance. En rétablissant Childéric III, ceux qui n'étaient que « princes des Francs » avaient sans doute le sentiment de faire provisoirement une concession aux grands du royaume.

La retraite de Carloman, qui, en 747, décida d'abandonner les affaires du monde et de se retirer dans le couvent italien du Mont-Cassin, hâta peut-être la décision de Pépin de franchir le pas décisif et de prendre officiellement la place du roi mérovingien.

Ce « coup d'État » fut organisé avec soin. On rappela tout d'abord les mérites de la famille, la sainteté d'Arnoul, le glorieux ancêtre, et la victoire de Charles Martel sur les Infidèles ; on prépara ensuite l'« opinion » en démontrant qu'un roi qui ne faisait rien n'était pas digne de régner. Déjà, dans un acte du mois d'août 750, Pépin rend publiquement la justice au palais mérovingien d'Attigny, qu'il appelle « son palais » ; il déclare y siéger « entouré de ses grands » et y exercer le pouvoir « qui lui a été confié par Dieu ».

Puis, Pépin envoya à Rome Fulrad, abbé de Saint-Denis, et Burchard, évêque de Würzburg, pour interroger le pape Zacharie « au sujet des rois qui étaient en France sans exercer le pouvoir » et lui demander « si cela était bon ou mauvais ». À cette question, le pape aurait répondu qu'« il valait mieux appeler roi celui qui avait, plutôt que celui qui n'avait pas le pouvoir royal. Et, continue l'auteur des *Annales du royaume des Francs*, notre seule source sur cette négociation, il aurait ordonné que Pépin fût fait roi, « afin que l'ordre ne fût point troublé ».

De quel ordre s'agissait-il ? En prenant parti contre le sang de Clovis, le pape s'appuyait en fait sur la tradition des Pères de l'Église, qui, comme saint Augustin, concevaient la Cité terrestre comme un monde harmonieux au sein duquel chacun devait occuper le rang que Dieu lui avait assigné pour ne pas troubler l'« ordre » providentiel. C'est en fonction de cette tradition que, en Espagne wisigothique, quelques rois incapables avaient été déposés et que, dans la loi des Alamans, il était écrit que « le duc incapable d'aller à l'armée, de monter à cheval, de manier les armes peut être déposé ». Surtout, en diplomate habile, Zacharie pensait sans doute obtenir de Pépin ce qu'avait refusé Charles Martel, l'intervention des Francs en Italie contre les Lombards qui menaçaient Rome.

Fort de l'appui du pape, Pépin put réunir les grands à Soissons, en novembre 751, et se faire élire roi des Francs. Childéric III, le dernier mérovingien, fut tonsuré et renvoyé au monastère de Saint-Bertin, où il mourut en 755.

Enfin, inaugurant une cérémonie jusque-là inédite en Gaule, Pépin se fit sacrer avec l'huile sainte par les évêques, sans doute conduits par Boniface. Ce missionnaire anglo-saxon, primitivement appelé Wynfrid, avait, avec l'appui de Charles Martel, évangélisé la Germanie. Puis, avec celui de Carloman, il avait entrepris une grande réforme de l'Église franque, éliminant de la hiérarchie les évêques ignares, ivrognes, batailleurs ou particulièrement débauchés et dressant une longue liste de superstitions qu'il fallait pourchasser, comme les banquets auprès des églises et des tombes, les sacrifices dans les forêts près des fontaines et des pierres, le culte de Mercure et de Jupiter, qui connaissait un certain renouveau...

Vieil « ami » de la famille des Pippinides, sans le patronage duquel, avait-il écrit, « je ne peux ni gouverner les fidèles de l'Église, ni défendre les prêtres et les clercs », ni « empêcher les rites païens et la pratique de l'idôlatrie », il avait préparé la collaboration entre Pépin et la papauté.

Parmi les modèles qui ont pu amener Pépin à recevoir l'onction sainte, nul doute que la lecture de l'Ancien Testament a probablement inspiré ses conseillers. Le prophète Samuel avait oint de l'huile sainte d'abord Saül, puis David, pour marquer l'alliance du peuple hébreu avec son Dieu. En étant sacré, le roi des Francs était donc élevé au rang des rois de l'Ancien Testament. Ainsi, il devenait l'élu de Dieu chargé de conduire les siens vers le salut. Il ne se privera pas de le rappeler, écrivant dans ses diplômes : « La divine Providence nous ayant oint pour le trône royal », ou : « Avec l'aide du Seigneur qui nous a placé sur le trône », ou encore : « Notre élévation au trône ayant été faite entièrement avec l'aide du Seigneur. »

Surtout, en 754, profitant de l'appel au secours du nouveau pape Étienne II, venu lui-même en Gaule le supplier d'intervenir en Italie, il se fit sacrer une nouvelle fois par le souverain pontife au terme d'un cérémonial qui montre à quel point la liaison d'intérêts était étroite entre la nouvelle royauté franque et la papauté.

Après avoir traversé, en plein hiver, les cols des Alpes, Étienne II, d'abord accueilli par Fulrad, puis par le jeune prince Charles (le futur Charlemagne), âgé de sept ans, arriva au palais royal de Ponthion, non loin de l'actuel Vitry-le-François, le 6 janvier 754. Là, à trois milles du palais, Pépin prit lui-même les brides du cheval et le guida pour la dernière partie du chemin, accomplissant le geste de respect dont avaient usé les derniers empereurs romains à l'égard des évêques de Rome.

Après avoir persuadé Pépin d'intervenir en Italie, le pape sacra de nouveau Pépin à Saint-Denis et conféra aussi l'onction à ses deux fils, Charles et Carloman, ainsi qu'à la reine Bertrade (Berthe). Le moine de Saint-Denis qui fait le récit fleuri de cet événement en souligne en même temps la portée historique : « Par la main du pontife, Étienne, dans l'église des bienheureux martyrs Denis, Rustique et Éleuthère, où l'on sait que le vénérable Fulrad est archiprêtre et abbé, Pépin a été oint et béni au nom de la sainte Trinité comme roi et patrice, ainsi que ses fils Charles et Carloman.

Dans la même église, le même jour, le même vénérable pontife a béni par la grâce de l'Esprit la très noble, très pieuse et très dévote envers les saints martyrs, Berthe, épouse du très florissant roi, revêtue de la robe royale à traîne.

De même, il confirma par la grâce du Saint-Esprit les princes des Francs et les engagea, sous peine d'interdit et d'excommunication, à ne jamais tenter à l'avenir d'élire un roi qui ne serait pas né de ceux-là mêmes que la divine piété a jugé bon d'élever et, avec l'aide des saints apôtres, de confirmer et de consacrer, par la main du vicaire, le bienheureux pontife. »

Ainsi naissait en France la royauté de droit divin. Celui qui, dix ans auparavant, pouvait encore apparaître comme un usurpateur devenait, lui et ses descendants, l'élu de Dieu et le « patrice des Romains », c'est-à-dire le protecteur désigné de Rome et de sa population. Non seulement le pape fondait ainsi la nouvelle dynastie des Carolingiens ; bien plus, il s'engageait à la soutenir, s'il le fallait, par l'excommunication.

Restait à Pépin à tenir ses promesses, ce qui impliquait pour cet homme du Nord un changement fondamental de stratégie. Intervenir en Italie voulait dire, en effet, s'attaquer aux Lombards, qui étaient puissants, et braver l'empereur byzantin, qui, même lointain, demeurait le souverain légitime de Rome.

Il est possible que, au cours des entretiens de Ponthion, le pape ait évoqué la fausse donation de Constantin. En vertu de ce faux, le plus célèbre de l'Histoire, rédigé par la chancellerie du Latran, l'empereur Constantin, après sa conversion au christianisme et avant la fondation de sa nouvelle capitale, à Constantinople, en 330, aurait concédé au pape Sylvestre Ier non seulement la ville de Rome, mais encore l'Italie et tout l'Occident. S'il est maintenant presque certain que cette fausse donation a été composée dans la seconde moitié du VIIIe siècle, il est probable qu'Étienne II en connaissait déjà la teneur et qu'il s'en est probablement servi pour faire impression sur le prince franc. Comment expliquer autrement le fait que Pépin ait promis de s'employer par tous les moyens à restituer au pape les territoires occupés par les Lombards ?

Quoi qu'il en soit, après avoir convaincu une aristocratie toujours réticente à entreprendre cette aventure, Pépin intervint à deux reprises en Italie, pendant l'été 754 et en 756, pour « restituer » officiellement au pape vingt-deux villes d'Italie centrale dont les clés furent solennellement déposées sur l'autel de saint Pierre, dans la basilique romaine du Vatican. Ainsi était créé, grâce au roi des Francs, un État pontifical qui ne disparut qu'en 1870.

Après ses deux expéditions italiennes, Pépin s'employa à consolider sa domination sur le midi de la Gaule. En 759, il s'empara de la Septimanie, après avoir massacré la garnison arabe de Narbonne. Puis, de 760 à 768, il fit tous les ans campagne en Aquitaine, prenant ville après ville et ravageant systématiquement une région qui sortit complètement meurtrie d'une guerre atroce qui marquait le triomphe du Nord sur le vieux Midi romain.

À la veille de sa mort, son prestige était immense. L'empereur byzantin envisageait un mariage entre son fils et Gisèle, la fille de Pépin, des émissaires chargés de présents faisant le déplacement à Compiègne. En 767, dans le palais royal de Gentilly, des théologiens grecs et francs discutent les problèmes concernant la Sainte-Trinité et le culte des images. Dans l'hiver 768, des envoyés du calife al-Mansur de Bagdad passent tout un hiver à Metz.

Quand Pépin meurt, à Saint-Denis, le 24 septembre 768, celui que les historiens ont appelé le « Bref », en raison sans doute de sa petite taille, apparaît bien, aux yeux des chrétiens de son temps, comme un nouveau David. « Comment te nommerais-je autrement que nouveau Moïse, comment te qualifierais-je autrement que resplendissant David ? » lui a déclaré le pape. La *Cité de Dieu* de saint Augustin, le livre préféré de son fils Charlemagne, semblait une réalisation possible sur terre.

L'Europe de Charlemagne

La succession de Pépin ne répondit pas totalement au modèle d'harmonie rêvé par les hommes d'Église. Comme l'avaient fait les Mérovingiens avant lui, le « Bref », avant de mourir, partagea en effet son royaume entre ses deux fils, qui ne s'entendaient guère, malgré les efforts que leur mère Bertrade avait prodigués pour les rapprocher. Par « chance » pour la dynastie carolingienne, la mort prématurée de Carloman laissa, en 771, Charles seul maître de la Gaule.

Âgé alors de vingt-quatre ans, ce géant de 1,90 m, à la voix fluette et à l'épaisse moustache, était un chasseur émérite, un nageur hors pair, un père jaloux et un amoureux ardent qui eut quatre épouses et de nombreuses concubines jusqu'à un âge avancé. Infatigable soldat, il occupa la plus grande partie de son règne à des guerres de conquête, payant de sa personne pendant plus de trente ans.

À sa mort, en 814, son empire avait une superficie de plus d'un million de kilomètres carrés, ce qui représentait une grande partie de l'ancien Occident romain. Résumant les conquêtes de Charles et voulant mesurer la *dilatatio regni*, cette extension spectaculaire du royaume, Éginhard, son biographe, écrivait : « Telles sont les guerres que ce roi tout-puissant, au cours des quarante-sept années de son règne, fit dans les diverses parties du monde avec autant de prudence que de bonheur. Aussi le royaume des Francs que son père Pépin lui avait transmis déjà vaste et fort sortit-il de ses mains glorieuses accru de près du double. Avant lui, en effet, ce royaume, abstraction faite du pays des Alamans et de celui des Bavarois, qui en formaient une dépendance, comprenait seulement la partie de la Gaule sise entre le Rhin, la Loire, l'Océan et la mer Baléare et la partie de la Germanie habitée par les Francs dits orientaux entre la Saxe, le Danube, le Rhin et la Saale, qui sépare le pays des Thuringiens de celui des Sorabes. À la suite des guerres que nous venons de rappeler, il y annexa l'Aquitaine, la Gascogne, toute la chaîne des Pyrénées et le pays jusqu'à l'Èbre [...]. Il y ajouta toute l'Italie, qui, d'Aoste jusqu'à la Calabre inférieure, où se trouve la frontière entre les Grecs et les Bénéventins, s'étend sur une longueur de près d'un million de pas. Il y joignit encore les deux Pannonie, la Dacie, l'Istrie, la Liburnie, la Dalmatie [...]. Enfin, entre le Rhin, l'Océan, la Vistule et le Danube, il dompta et soumis au tribut tous les peuples barbares et sauvages de Germanie [...]. »

Même si les conquêtes de Charlemagne se sont faites sans plan préétabli, elles répondent toutefois à quelques principes directeurs. Charles veut d'abord unifier le royaume que lui a légué Pépin, puis le protéger contre les attaques des païens et des infidèles, les Arabes au Sud, les Slaves et les Avars à l'Est. Patrice des Romains, comme l'était son père, il veut aussi s'imposer en Italie.

C'est là qu'il entame sa politique conquérante. Répondant à l'appel du pape Adrien Ier, de nouveau menacé par les Lombards, il franchit les cols des Alpes, enferme le roi Didier dans sa capitale de Pavie, prend le temps d'aller, en avril 774, célébrer Pâques à Rome – c'est la première fois qu'un roi franc vient dans la Ville de saint Pierre –, confirme la promesse de donation faite par Pépin et se pare, en juin, du titre de roi des Lombards, après avoir fait tondre Didier et l'avoir envoyé dans le monastère picard de Corbie.

Dès 772 aussi, il s'attaque aux Saxons en détruisant, lors d'une première campagne, l'*Irminsul*, un tronc en forme de colonne censé soutenir la voûte céleste et auprès duquel les Saxons enterraient des trésors d'or et d'argent et se livraient à des sacrifices sanglants. Plus de trente années de combats acharnés, de baptêmes forcés, de prises d'otages, d'exécutions sommaires seront cependant nécessaires pour venir à bout de ces redoutables païens, farouchement attachés à leur indépendance. Ainsi Charles n'hésite-t-il pas, à la suite de l'insurrection de Widukind, à se faire livrer en représailles quatre mille cinq cents Saxons et à les faire décapiter. À l'Est, ce sont aussi les Bavarois et les Frisons dont les territoires sont incorporés au royaume franc.

Charles eut moins de succès avec les Arabes. Invité à intervenir en Espagne par le gouverneur de Saragosse, révolté contre l'émir de Cordoue, il eut l'imprudence d'accepter, rêvant peut-être de renouveler les exploits de Charles Martel et de reprendre l'Espagne aux Infidèles. En 778, il franchit les Pyrénées, rase Pampelune, mais échoue devant Saragosse. C'est au retour que son arrière-garde, commandée par le comte Roland, est massacrée à Roncevaux par des Basques. Charles en ressentit, dit la chronique, une profonde « douleur » qui « voila dans son cœur une grande partie des succès obtenus en Espagne ». Renonçant aux projets de grande envergure qu'il avait pu nourrir en 778, Charles se limita à prendre pied dans la zone comprise entre les Pyrénées et l'Èbre et à constituer une « marche » dont Barcelone serait la capitale. Cette « marche » avait pour mission de protéger l'Aquitaine et la Septimanie aussi bien contre les Arabes que contre les Basques. Au XIe siècle encore, on appellera *los Francos* les habitants de ce pays qui recevra au XIIe siècle son nom de Catalogne.

Charles ne réussit pas non plus à soumettre les Bretons, un peuple qui avait toujours échappé à la domination des Francs. Les considérant comme des « brutti », dont ils faisaient venir le nom de Bretons, les Carolingiens écrivaient : « Cette nation perfide et insolente a toujours été rebelle et dénuée de bons sentiments. Traîtresse à sa foi, elle n'est plus chrétienne que de nom, car d'œuvres, de culte, de religion, plus de traces. Nul égard pour les enfants, ni pour les veuves ni pour les églises. Le frère et la sœur partagent le même lit. Le frère prend l'épouse du frère. Tous vivent dans l'inceste et le crime. Ils habitent les bois et installent leurs couches dans les fourrés. Ils vivent de rapts, semblables à des bêtes sauvages. »

Charles eut beau multiplier les campagnes, il ne réussit jamais à dompter ces redoutables Celtes d'Armorique. Le seul résultat fut, là aussi, le renforcement d'une « marche » chargée de les contenir et de préparer une pénétration méthodique du pays breton.

Charles fut, en revanche, plus heureux avec les Avars, qui, venus du cœur de l'Asie, campaient au centre de la vallée danubienne et multipliaient les courses de pillage dans les Balkans et en Europe occidentale. En 795 et en 796, il réussit à s'emparer de leur *Ring*, un camp fortifié circulaire dans lequel ils accumulaient leurs trésors.

« Pas une guerre, de mémoire d'homme, écrit Éginhard, ne rapporta aux Francs un pareil butin et un pareil accroissement de richesses. Ceux qui jusque-là pouvaient presque passer pour pauvres trouvèrent dans le palais du Khagan tant d'or et tant d'argent, tant de dépouilles précieuses conquises par la force des armes qu'on ne se tromperait guère en disant que ce fut une juste reprise de ce que les Huns avaient injustement enlevé aux autres peuples. » Ce butin, ramené par quinze chars tirés chacun par quatre bœufs, fut distribué en partie aux églises, Saint-Pierre de Rome en tête, et permit à Charles de récompenser ses fidèles.

Ces victoires reposent sur une armée dont l'organisation rappelle, dans une certaine mesure, le modèle romain, tous les hommes libres devant le service militaire, le service de l'ost. Tous les ans, le roi les convoquait au mois de mai ou de juin, à une époque où le foin pouvait être coupé pour nourrir les chevaux. « Sache, écrit Charles à l'abbé de Saint-Quentin, que nous avons convoqué notre plaid [assemblée] général cette année en Saxe orientale, sur le fleuve de Bode, au lieudit appelé Strassfurt. Nous t'enjoignons de t'y rendre le 15 des calendes de juillet (17 juin), avec tous tes hommes, bien armés et équipés avec armes et bagages et tout le fourniment de guerre, en vivres et vêtements. Que chaque cavalier ait un bouclier, une lance, une épée longue, une épée courte, un arc et un carquois garni de flèches. Qu'il y ait dans vos chariots des outils de tout genre et aussi des vivres pour trois mois à partir de ce lieu de rassemblement [...]. » Il ne s'agit pas d'arriver en retard, tout homme qui n'arrive pas à temps étant privé de viande et de vin pour autant de jours qu'il aura eu de retard.

Dans la mesure, toutefois, où l'armement et l'équipement coûtaient cher et où les hommes de troupe avaient hâte de revenir chez eux pour la moisson et les vendanges, Charlemagne répartit la charge militaire selon la richesse de chacun en terres, les plus pauvres pouvant se grouper pour fournir un homme à frais communs. Surtout, pour assurer la rapidité de la mobilisation, il convoquait le nombre de guerriers nécessaires dans les régions voisines des opérations.

En fait, la guerre devenait au fil du temps le privilège et le passe-temps favori des aristocrates dont l'éducation sportive était entièrement destinée au métier des armes et dont le cheval était le compagnon qu'ils n'abandonnaient à aucun prix : « Fais périr ma mère, je n'en ai cure, s'écrie un aristocrate aquitain à un Sarrasin, le cheval que tu me demandes, jamais je ne te le livrerai. » Parmi ces cavaliers se distinguaient les guerriers d'élite, des « hommes de fer » redoutables, portant la brogne, une chemise de cuir recouverte d'écailles de métal qui, à elle seule, coûtait autant que six vaches. Recrutés parmi les jeunes du palais, sans astreinte de calendrier, ils pouvaient intervenir partout et mener rapidement l'offensive là où le danger était le plus pressant.

Stratège de talent, Charles fut aussi un homme implacable, convaincu de son bon droit, qui mania la terreur pour châtier les « ennemis de Dieu », prescrivant la mort pour les délits les plus anodins, coupant les mains, crevant les yeux, exécutant les otages et déportant les populations. C'est grâce à de tels moyens qu'il put contrôler pendant près d'un demi-siècle un empire aussi vaste avec une armée qui ne devait pas dépasser cinquante mille hommes. Même si son empire fut une construction éphémère, une coquille vide où personne ne comprenait la langue de l'autre et où chaque *regnum* formait un monde à part qui gardait ses lois et ses traditions, il apparaît bien comme la première ébauche de l'Europe. Les contemporains en avaient d'ailleurs conscience qui célébraient en Charles « le phare de l'Europe qui rayonne d'une lumière plus resplendissante que le soleil ».

Le couronnement de Charlemagne

Tout naturellement, dans le milieu des clercs lettrés qui entourent Charles germe l'idée d'une restauration de l'Empire romain, disparu en 476. Alcuin, grammairien et théologien anglo-saxon que Charles a débauché pour en faire son maître, prend l'habitude, dès 795, d'appeler Charles David, précisant que c'est « sous ce même nom, animé de la même vertu et de la même foi, que règne maintenant notre chef et notre guide, un roi à l'ombre duquel le peuple chrétien repose dans la paix et qui de toutes parts inspire la terreur aux nations païennes »...
À la cour, un poète anonyme exalte le roi Charles, « tête du monde et sommet de l'Europe, le nouvel Auguste qui règne dans la nouvelle Rome », c'est-à-dire Aix-la-Chapelle, le palais installé en 794 dans la station thermale déjà appréciée des Celtes et des Romains. Charles lui-même prend conscience de sa mission, n'hésitant pas à s'en prendre à l'impératrice byzantine Irène dont « la faiblesse de son sexe et la versatilité de son cœur féminin, écrit-il, ne (lui) permettent pas d'exercer l'autorité suprême en matière de foi et de rang ».

C'est également la papauté qui encourage l'idée d'une restauration impériale. À partir de 775, les papes ne demandent plus à l'empereur byzantin la ratification de leur élection au siège de saint Pierre. Entre 798 et 800, une mosaïque placée dans la salle de réception du palais du Latran offre aux visiteurs cette image : à gauche d'une scène principale figurant le Christ demandant à ses apôtres d'évangéliser le monde, le pape Sylvestre Ier et Constantin reçoivent du Christ les clés et l'étendard du royaume céleste ; à droite, dans une symétrie parfaite, saint Pierre agit de même en faveur de Léon III (pape depuis 795) et du roi Charles. Une comparaison sans équivoque.

Deux événements vont précipiter la restauration de l'empire. Depuis son élection, Léon III, d'origine modeste, doit subir le mépris de l'aristocratie romaine. Accusé d'actes « criminels et scélérats », notamment d'adultère et de parjure, il est victime, le 25 avril 799, d'un attentat et ne doit son salut qu'à l'intervention de deux émissaires de Charles.

Le second événement est une révolution de palais à Constantinople. En 797, l'impératrice Irène fait crever les yeux de son jeune fils Constantin VI et prend le pouvoir. Dans une lettre de juin 799, Alcuin, faisant allusion à ces deux événements, écrit alors à Charlemagne : « Jusqu'alors trois personnes ont été au sommet de la hiérarchie dans le monde :

1° Le représentant de la sublimité apostolique, vicaire du bien-heureux Pierre, prince des Apôtres, dont il occupe le siège. Ce qui est advenu au détenteur actuel de ce siège, [l'attentat d'avril] votre bonté a pris soin de me le faire savoir.

2° Vient ensuite le titulaire de la dignité impériale, qui exerce la puissance séculière dans la seconde Rome. De quelle façon impie le chef de cet empire a été déposé, non par des étrangers, mais par les siens [sa mère Irène] et par ses concitoyens, la nouvelle s'en est répandue.

3° Vient en troisième lieu la dignité royale, que notre Seigneur Jésus-Christ vous a réservée pour que vous gouverniez le peuple chrétien. Elle l'emporte sur les deux autres dignités, les éclipse en sagesse et les surpasse.

C'est maintenant sur toi seul que s'appuient les Églises du Christ, de toi seul qu'elles attendent le salut : de toi, vengeur des crimes, guide de ceux qui errent, consolateur des affligés, soutien des bons. » On ne saurait délivrer un message plus clair.

À l'automne 800, une année qui, selon certaines prédictions, devait marquer la fin du monde, Charles se rend à Rome pour présider l'assemblée qui doit examiner les plaintes portées contre le pape et recevoir le serment par lequel il se déclare innocent. Cette cérémonie fort humiliante a lieu le 23 décembre. Le même jour, cette même assemblée prend toutefois une autre décision, que nous rapporte le rédacteur bien informé des *Annales de Lorsch* : « Comme dans le pays des Grecs il n'y avait plus d'empereur et qu'ils étaient tous sous l'emprise d'une femme, il parut au pape Léon et à tous les pères qui siégeaient à l'assemblée, ainsi qu'à tout le peuple chrétien, qu'ils devaient donner le nom d'empereur au roi des Francs, Charles, qui occupait Rome où toujours les Césars avaient eu l'habitude de résider, et aussi l'Italie, la Gaule et la Germanie. Dieu tout-puissant ayant consenti à placer ces pays sous son autorité, il serait juste, conformé-ment à la demande de tout le peuple chrétien, qu'il portât lui aussi le titre impérial. »

La cérémonie du couronnement eut lieu le jour de Noël 800, selon le rituel utilisé à Byzance. Mais alors que, à Byzance, le couron-nement comportait trois étapes : acclamations de la foule et de l'ar-mée, couronnement, puis adoration du nouvel empereur par le patriarche pour montrer que le pouvoir venait du peuple et des vic-toires de l'empereur, Léon décida d'inverser l'ordre. Pour avoir le premier rôle, laver l'humiliation qu'il avait subie et signifier que tout pouvoir venait de Dieu, il impose d'abord la couronne, puis invite l'assemblée à acclamer trois fois. « Charles, auguste, couronné par

Dieu grand et pacifique empereur ». À en croire Éginhard, Charles n'apprécia guère cette initiative : « Il affirmait qu'il aurait renoncé à entrer dans l'église ce jour-là, bien que ce fût jour de grande fête, s'il avait pu connaître d'avance le dessein du pontife. » Ainsi commençaient les difficiles rapports entre l'empire et la papauté.

Le nouvel empereur prit toutefois les choses au sérieux. Dès le 29 mai 801, il s'intitule dans ses diplômes « Charles, sérénissime Auguste, couronné par Dieu, grand et pacifique empereur gouvernant l'Empire romain, et par la grâce de Dieu roi des Francs et des Lombards ». Sur les monnaies, il se fait représenter, comme autrefois Constantin, couronné de lauriers et vêtu du *paludamentum*, le manteau des généraux romains, et scelle certains de ses actes d'une bulle portant au revers les portes de Rome avec la légende *Renovatio Romani Imperii*.

Toutefois, cet empire apparaît bien fragile. Alors que l'idée de *res publica* faisait de l'empereur romain l'exécuteur de la volonté collective d'un peuple de citoyens, Charles, comme ses prédécesseurs, préféra asseoir son autorité sur les liens de fidélité personnels, les aristocraties n'ayant nullement conscience du « bien commun » qui faisait la force de la romanité. C'est ainsi que, en 802, Charles voulut que tous les hommes libres âgés de plus de douze ans prêtent sur les reliques ce serment : « À mon seigneur Charles, le très pieux empereur, fils du roi Pépin et de Berthe, je suis fidèle comme un homme par droit doit l'être à son seigneur pour le bien de son royaume et de son droit. Et ce serment que j'ai juré, je le garderai et je veux le garder dans la mesure de ce que je sais et comprends, dorénavant à dater de ce jour, si m'aide Dieu qui créa le ciel et la terre et ces reliques des saints. »

Charles eut surtout le souci d'améliorer le fonctionnement de l'administration et de moraliser son action. Rompant avec la tradition remontant à l'édit de Clotaire de 614, il envoya les comtes dans les cités où ils n'avaient pas d'intérêts personnels. De plus, il les fit surveiller par ses envoyés personnels, les *missi dominici*, dont l'institution se développe après 800. Associant un laïc et un évêque, ils vont, munis d'instructions très précises, surveiller tous les fonctionnaires de l'empire, entendre les plaintes, régler les cas litigieux et veiller à ce que les décisions prises par les assemblées générales des grands et formulées en une série d'articles appelés chapitres (*capitula*) soient appliquées.

Charles tenta enfin de réorganiser le système monétaire en faisant frapper une seule monnaie, le denier d'argent, à raison de douze deniers par sou et de vingt sous par livre d'un peu plus de 400 grammes.

Le roi anglo-saxon Offa de Mercie ayant adopté cette réforme, l'Angleterre restera fidèle à ce système jusqu'en 1970 !

Siège de cette administration, le palais d'Aix-la-Chapelle, qui devient résidence permanente, et donc véritable capitale de l'empire à partir de 807, apparaît bien comme la nouvelle Rome en terre austrasienne. Assistant aux offices religieux dans la célèbre chapelle octogonale entourée d'un déambulatoire à seize pans voûtés d'arêtes et surmontée de tribunes, Charles pouvait voir, en face de son trône, l'autel du Sauveur et, juste au-dessous, l'autel de la Vierge, autour duquel se regroupaient les serviteurs. Il pouvait aussi admirer les colonnes de marbre provenant de Rome et de Ravenne, les balustrades de bronze massif, la mosaïque de la coupole qui représentait le Christ en majesté acclamé par les vingt-quatre vieillards de l'Apocalypse. La vision symbolique d'un empire chrétien.

CHAPITRE **19**

La renaissance carolingienne

*L*ecteur assidu de La Cité de Dieu, *écrit par saint Augustin de 413 à*
426, Charles voulait faire régner dans la cité terrestre l'« ordre » qui
avait valu à son père d'être sacré roi. Il voulait que chacun soit à la place
que Dieu lui avait assignée, que les « moines se conforment à leur règle
de vie », que chacun s'efforce de respecter ses engagements « parce que
le dominus imperator *n'est pas en mesure d'exercer sa surveillance et sa*
discipline sur tous et sur chacun [...] ». Cette mise en « ordre » de la
société inspire la « renaissance » carolingienne, une renaissance qui
puise dans l'héritage antique le modèle d'un renouveau culturel, symbo-
lisé par le palais, qui, à Aix-la-Chapelle, se veut une troisième Rome.

L'ordre dans les campagnes

La « renaissance » voulue par le nouvel empereur n'est pas seulement spirituelle. Elle est aussi matérielle. Charles, qui déteste les
« oisifs », qui a horreur de la paresse, qui demande de ne pas faire
l'aumône aux mendiants valides ne travaillant pas, qui règle avec
minutie le repos dominical et veut donner aux mois de l'année des
noms nouveaux caractérisés par une activité agricole précise, le « mois
des jachères » pour juin, le « mois des foins » pour juillet, le « mois
des épis » pour août, le « mois des bois » pour septembre, le « mois
des vendanges » pour octobre, veut aussi que l'ordre règne dans ses
domaines.

Si les campagnes ont alors connu une réelle prospérité, elles le doivent en partie à la volonté obsessionnelle de Charlemagne de multiplier les règlements pour que les équilibres naturels entre labours et forêts soient scrupuleusement respectés. Dans le capitulaire *De villis* consacré à l'administration des domaines royaux, on peut ainsi lire : « Que nos bois et nos forêts soient bien surveillés ; et là où il y a une place à défricher, que nos intendants la fassent défricher et qu'ils ne permettent pas aux champs de gagner sur les bois ; et où il doit y avoir des bois, qu'ils ne permettent pas de trop les couper. »

Ce que montre surtout cet extraordinaire document, c'est le désir manifeste de proposer des modèles d'exploitation, de rationaliser la gestion pour que chaque domaine trouve sa place dans les circuits commerciaux locaux, mais aussi internationaux.

Les intendants qui en ont la charge doivent établir, chaque année, les revenus de chaque parcelle, réserver les grains pour les semailles de l'année suivante, gérer les stocks pour amortir les mauvaises années, organiser la rotation des cultures, entretenir le jardin potager et le poulailler, établir la liste des ustensiles et des outils agricoles, du cheptel et de la volaille. Ils doivent aussi fixer la date des semailles, des labours et des moissons, veiller au bon état des pressoirs, à la reproduction des chevaux, prévoir avec soin le travail des artisans, dresser la liste des redevances dues par les paysans. Ces redevances, au demeurant légères, leur laissent de longs moments pour effectuer les cultures sur leurs propres terres et leur permettent, lors des bonnes saisons, de vendre sur les marchés ruraux le surplus de leur récolte et même, assez loin, leur vin ou leur blé.

À un prix que, là encore, Charlemagne cherche à contrôler, pour éviter la spéculation. En 806, il donne ainsi la mesure du « juste prix » en écrivant : « Tous ceux qui, au temps de la moisson ou de la vendange, acquièrent du blé et du vin sans nécessité mais avec une arrière-pensée de cupidité, par exemple en achetant un muid pour deux deniers et en le conservant jusqu'à ce qu'ils puissent le revendre à six deniers ou même davantage, commettent un gain malhonnête. Si, au contraire, ils l'achètent par nécessité, afin de le garder pour eux-mêmes ou de le revendre dans un délai normal, nous appelons cela un acte de commerce. »

Est-ce aussi pour assurer l'ordre « naturel » des choses que Charlemagne condamna les pratiques contraceptives et rappela que la procréation devait être la finalité du mariage chrétien ? Toujours est-il que tout comportement sexuel non procréatif, comme le coït interrompu ou la position retro de l'homme couché sous la femme, fut interdit. Le seul moyen autorisé pour limiter les naissances fut la continence périodique, mais lorsqu'on sait que l'Église interdisait les rapports entre époux quarante jours avant Noël, quarante jours avant Pâques et huit jours après, huit jours après la Pentecôte, la veille des grandes fêtes, les dimanches, mais aussi les mercredis et les vendredis, pendant la grossesse de la femme jusqu'au quatrième jour après la naissance, si c'est une fille, et au trentième jour si c'est un garçon, pendant la période menstruelle, cinq jours avant la communion... on constate que les jours de plaisir n'étaient pas si nombreux...

L'ordre dans les églises

Pour préparer le salut des chrétiens qui lui ont été confiés, Charles voulut que l'Église soit réformée, que l'ordre règne du haut en bas de la hiérarchie et que soit proposée aux hommes d'Église une définition claire de leur mission et de leur statut. Qu'il s'agisse de discipline ecclésiastique, de la vie intérieure des monastères, de la formation et du recrutement du clergé, de l'instruction religieuse des fidèles, de leur assiduité aux offices et à la communion, de l'observation du repos dominical et des fêtes religieuses, de la liturgie et des sacrements, qu'il s'agisse même du dogme, rien n'a échappé à la vigilance de Charlemagne.

Il rétablit les provinces métropolitaines qui ont chacune à leur tête un archevêque. En 814, on en compte vingt et une : Rome, Ravenne, Milan, Cividale-en-Frioul, Grado, Cologne, Mayence, Salzbourg, Trèves, Sens, Besançon, Lyon, Rouen, Reims, Arles, Vienne, Moutiers-en-Tarentaise, Embrun, Bordeaux, Tours et Bourges.

Il nomme les évêques parmi les clercs de son entourage ou dans les familles aristocratiques qui lui sont fidèles.

Il veille à ce que les conciles soient périodiquement réunis, les préside, trace le programme des débats et prend souvent part aux délibérations. Dans l'affaire du culte des images évoquée au concile de Francfort, en 794, c'est sous son impulsion qu'est formulée la doctrine officielle de l'Occident opposée à celle des Byzantins, sans même qu'un accord préalable ait été recherché avec le pape, qui laisse Charles et ses théologiens trancher en une matière aussi délicate. Réprouvant l'adoration des images, dans laquelle il voit une cause d'idolâtrie païenne, Charles déclare sacrilège d'appeler sainte une image ou de l'encenser, car, dit plaisamment Alcuin qui relate les débats de ce concile, si on encense un tableau représentant la fuite en Égypte, encensera-t-on la Vierge ou l'âne qui la porte ? En 809, le capitulaire d'Aix décrète, encore contre Byzance, que le Saint-Esprit procède non « du Père par le Fils », mais « du Père et du Fils », et Charlemagne s'obstine, malgré le veto de Léon III, à faire chanter en sa chapelle la formule selon laquelle le Saint-Esprit procède aussi bien de Dieu le Fils que de Dieu le Père.

Dans un autre concile, tenu en 802, on le voit intervenir pour rappeler les clercs au respect des canons de l'Église et leur faire distribuer un recueil, soigneusement mis à jour. En 811, il envoie à tous les évêques métropolitains un questionnaire sur la façon dont les prêtres baptisent et expliquent la cérémonie aux fidèles. On ne peut imaginer Église plus soumise. Dans la lettre d'envoi qu'ils joignent à l'énoncé de leurs vœux, les Pères du concile de Mayence déclarent remercier Dieu d'avoir « donné à l'Église un chef – c'est de Charlemagne qu'il s'agit – aussi pieux, aussi dévoué au service de Dieu et qui, faisant jaillir la source de la sagesse sacrée, dispense avec une telle constance la sainte nourriture aux brebis du Christ ».

Se méfiant par ailleurs des moines « gyrovagues », particulièrement des moines anglo-saxons qui échappaient à toute autorité, il rappela aussi continuellement les principes du monachisme, observance des vœux, chasteté, pauvreté, interdiction de toute activité extérieure, intervention des évêques dans les monastères, et mena une action vigoureuse pour imposer partout la règle de saint Benoît, qui lui paraissait excellente. Witiza, fils d'un aristocrate wisigoth formé au palais, connu sous le nom de Benoît, l'aida dans cette entreprise. À partir du monastère qu'il fonda sur ses propres terres à Aniane, dans le midi languedocien, le « second Benoît » réforma de nombreuses abbayes d'Aquitaine, de Septimanie et de Provence.

Au nord, Saint-Riquier, près de l'estuaire de la Somme, allait devenir l'autre laboratoire du monachisme carolingien. Le nombre des autels des trois édifices du monastère s'élevait à trente, multiple de trois, en l'honneur de la Trinité ; les moines étaient aussi au nombre de trois cents, et l'on répartissait les quatre-vingt-dix-neuf élèves de la *Schola cantorum* en trois groupes de trente-trois. Là, les moines s'employaient à prier jour et nuit et à chanter Dieu non seulement par la beauté du texte, mais encore par la douceur des sons, dont, là encore, l'harmonie fut ordonnée : « Pas de voix trop élevées, ni désordonnées ni déréglées, mais des voix égales et arrondies, pour que l'esprit de ceux qui chantent se nourrisse de la douce pensée des Psaumes, en même temps que l'âme des auditeurs de leur suave modulation. »

Les nombreux autels qui occupaient les nefs latérales de l'église principale constituaient autant de stations d'un système liturgique dont nous pouvons suivre le déroulement grâce à la méticuleuse *Institution des Offices divins* établie par Angilbert, l'abbé de Saint-Riquier. Ainsi, le dimanche de Pâques, en tête de la grande procession, venaient sept diacres, sept sous-diacres, sept acolytes, sept exorcistes, sept lecteurs, sept portiers, puis les moines sept par sept, la *Schola cantorum*, puis les croix des sept villages voisins. Une division septenaire en l'honneur des sept dons du Saint-Esprit. C'est ce monachisme réformé, ouvert à l'hospitalité et à l'aumône, aux pauvres et aux malades, à l'étude et à l'art, qui allait devenir l'institution la plus durable de l'Empire carolingien.

« Heureuse, écrit, vers 795, Alcuin, la nation dont Dieu est le Seigneur ; heureux le peuple exalté par un chef et soutenu par un prédicateur de la foi dont la main droite brandit le glaive des triomphes et dont la bouche fait retentir la trompette de la Vérité catholique. C'est ainsi que jadis David, choisi par Dieu comme roi du peuple, qui était alors son peuple élu [...], soumit à Israël par son glaive victorieux les nations d'alentour et prêcha parmi les siens la loi divine. De la noble descendance d'Israël est sortie, pour le salut du monde, la « fleur des champs et des vallées », le Christ, à qui de nos jours le [nouveau] peuple doit un autre roi David. Sous le même nom, animé de la même vertu et de la même foi, celui-ci est maintenant notre chef et notre guide : un chef « à l'ombre duquel » le peuple chrétien repose dans la paix et qui de toutes parts inspire la terreur aux nations païennes ; un guide dont la dévotion ne cesse, par sa fermeté évangélique, de fortifier la foi catholique contre les sectateurs de l'hérésie, veillant à ce que rien de contraire à la doctrine des Apôtres ne vienne se glisser en quelque endroit et s'employant à faire resplendir partout cette foi catholique à la lumière de la grâce céleste. »

Un hommage appuyé dont on aurait sans doute tort de nier la sincérité.

L'ordre dans les écoles

Gestionnaire avisé, « docteur » en théologie, Charles eut aussi le mérite de capter les premiers signes du réveil culturel de l'Occident pour multiplier les écoles, harmoniser leur enseignement, donner aux savants les moyens de leurs ambitions et créer les conditions d'une véritable renaissance artistique.

Animateur d'un mouvement dont il percevait le sens et appréciait la valeur, il fit venir à sa cour les meilleurs esprits de son temps, les chrétiens d'Espagne fuyant l'occupation arabe comme Théodulf, les grammairiens italiens comme Pierre de Pise, les Lombards comme Paul Diacre ou Paulin, les Anglo-Saxons comme Alcuin, grand artisan de la renaissance carolingienne, les Irlandais passionnés pour la cosmographie et dont les audaces intellectuelles suscitaient les jalousies.

Tous, effectivement, se jalousent, s'égratignent d'épigrammes, s'accusent de déviations doctrinales tout en partageant avec Charles les loisirs de la baignade dans la piscine d'Aix-la-Chapelle, où il arrivait, écrit Éginhard, « qu'il y eût dans l'eau avec lui jusqu'à cent personnes et même davantage ». Prodigues de bons mots, ils décrivent avec humour les cuisines du palais et, connaissant leur Ancien Testament, rappellent que c'est le maître cuisinier du roi de Babylone, Nabuchodonosor, qui assiégea et pilla Jérusalem. Ces repas sont pour les poètes l'occasion de descriptions « à l'antique », tous prenant des noms littéraires ou bibliques pour effacer les exigences du protocole, tous étant aussi sensibles aux « colombes couronnées qui volent dans les chambres du palais » comme les filles de Charles, qui, faute de pouvoir se marier, se laissent volontiers courtiser par les grands.

Charles, lui-même, montre l'exemple. À en croire Éginhard, « il cultiva passionnément les arts libéraux et, plein de vénération pour ceux qui les enseignaient, il les combla d'honneurs. Pour l'étude de la grammaire, il suivit les leçons du diacre Pierre de Pise, alors dans sa vieillesse ; pour les autres disciplines, son maître Alcuin [...], l'homme le plus savant qui fût alors. Il consacra beaucoup de temps et de labeur à apprendre auprès de lui la rhétorique, la dialectique et surtout l'astronomie. Il apprit le calcul et s'appliqua avec attention et sagacité à étudier le cours des astres. Il s'essaya aussi à écrire et il avait l'habitude de placer sous les coussins de son lit des tablettes et des feuilles de parchemin, afin de profiter de ses instants de loisir pour s'exercer à tracer des lettres ; mais il s'y prit trop tard et le résultat fut fort médiocre ».

Convaincu qu'il fallait relever le niveau intellectuel de la société pour mieux prier Dieu, il voulut que le clergé ait une instruction suffisante pour instruire à son tour le peuple dont il avait la charge. En 789, dans l'*Admonitio generalis*, qui se présente comme une véritable loi-cadre, il écrit : « Nous voulons que des écoles soient créées pour apprendre à lire aux enfants. Dans tous les monastères et les évêchés, enseignez les psaumes, les notes, le chant, le *comput*, la grammaire et corrigez soigneusement les livres religieux. Car souvent, alors que certains désirent bien prier Dieu, ils y arrivent mal à cause de l'imperfection et des fautes des livres. Ne permettez pas que vos élèves les détournent de leur sens, soit en les lisant, soit en les écrivant. »

Apprendre à lire, à écrire et à compter, tel a été de tout temps le programme scolaire minimal qu'ont toujours souhaité voir assurer les responsables de l'« éducation nationale ». Dans une enquête de 803, Charles rappelle d'ailleurs que les parents doivent envoyer leurs enfants à l'école et, bien conscient de la difficulté de faire appliquer partout cette exigence, encourage les évêques à créer des écoles rurales dans les villages et les bourgades.

Quelques manuscrits qui paraissent être des cahiers nous livrent les exercices qui rythmaient la vie quotidienne de l'écolier. Il lisait les *Proverbes* de Salomon, les fables de Phèdre, les distiques de Caton. Il apprenait à faire de courtes phrases en utilisant le vocabulaire usuel. Il disposait de glossaires lui donnant les noms des bêtes, des ustensiles, des pièces de la maison. Il apprenait par cœur des poèmes ou des déclinaisons. Il répondait à de petits problèmes d'arithmétique posés sous la forme de devinettes. Par exemple : Trois frères ont chacun une sœur, les six voyageurs arrivent à une rivière, mais un seul bateau ne peut contenir que deux personnes. La morale demande que chaque sœur passe avec son frère. Comment vont-ils faire ? Ou bien : Six ouvriers sont engagés pour bâtir une maison. Cinq ont de l'expérience, l'un est apprenti. Les cinq hommes divisent entre eux un salaire de vingt-cinq deniers par jour, moins le paiement de l'apprenti, qui représente la moitié du salaire que reçoit chacun des maîtres. Combien chacun recevra-t-il ?

Instrument privilégié de la culture, le livre est l'objet de tous les soins. Dans les *scriptoria* des grands monastères apparaît, vers 780, une nouvelle écriture qu'on appellera « caroline » en l'honneur de Charlemagne. De petit module, régulière, séparant les espaces entre les mots, elle s'imposera dans tout l'Occident et sera adoptée par les premiers imprimeurs de la Renaissance. Elle a donné le « bas-de-casse » de notre typographie actuelle.

D'un bout à l'autre de l'empire, des milliers de copistes recopient alors les œuvres des Pères de l'Église, des grammairiens et des poètes latins, dont près de huit mille manuscrits nous sont parvenus. Entourés de leur matériel, leurs feuilles de parchemin posées sur un pupitre ou sur leurs genoux, leurs cornets à encre, leurs plumes et leurs grattoirs, assis sur un banc, les pieds sur un escabeau, ils écrivent sous la dictée du lecteur. Parfois, ils notent en marge du texte qu'ils copient des réflexions personnelles comme « il fait froid aujourd'hui », « la lampe éclaire mal », « c'est maintenant l'heure du déjeuner » !

En général, comme l'explique l'historien Pierre Riché, il faut deux ou trois mois pour copier un manuscrit de dimension moyenne, même si certains se vantent d'avoir transcrit la loi salique en deux jours. Le chef de l'atelier revoit le manuscrit, rectifie la ponctuation ou l'orthographe, souligne d'une série de points un mot incompréhensible et donne le mot convenable en marge. Puis, lorsqu'il s'agit d'un psautier de luxe, d'un évangéliaire ou d'un sacramentaire commandé par un évêque ou un prince, d'un ouvrage littéraire ou scientifique antique, le peintre succède au scribe pour décorer les initiales et illustrer les pages avec des trompettes, des rouleaux, des entrelacs, des branches légères gouachées en blanc sur fond sombre, des cornets disposés tête-bêche, des chapiteaux violets, rouges et verts, selon le style de l'« école » qui l'a formé, Tours, Reims ou Metz. Le manuscrit est ensuite confié à des orfèvres ou à des artistes, qui le protègent en confectionnant des reliures ornées à profusion d'ivoire, de pierres et d'or.

La renaissance carolingienne qui se prolongera tout au long du Xᵉ siècle, se lit enfin dans l'extraordinaire floraison d'une architecture essentiellement religieuse qui puise ses modèles dans les traités d'architecture antique, tel celui de Vitruve, et prend parfois ses matériaux dans les monuments anciens. Entre 768 et 814, on construisit au total 27 cathédrales, 232 monastères et 65 ensembles palatiaux ! Se voulant antique, cet art fait alterner les marbres de couleur, la pierre blanche taillée en cube avec la brique longue. L'intérieur des églises est décoré avec des mosaïques inspirées de modèles romains, comme celle qui a subsisté à Germigny-des-Prés, dans l'oratoire que Théodulf fit édifier non loin de son siège épiscopal d'Orléans. Rappelant les palais byzantins, le Saint-Sépulcre de Jérusalem et le baptistère de Saint-Jean-de-Latran à Rome, la chapelle du palais d'Aix-la-Chapelle est le chef-d'œuvre de cette architecture qui jette les bases de l'art occidental, sens de la ligne et du volume, jeu des couleurs, refus de l'art pour l'art, affirmation d'une grandeur humaine et divine. En architecture, le secret de la grandeur est d'associer de grands espaces et des formes simples.

C'est dans cette chapelle que Charlemagne fut enterré, le jour même de sa mort, le 28 janvier 814. Éginhard nous a rapporté le texte de son épitaphe : « Sous cette pierre repose le corps de Charles, grand et orthodoxe empereur, qui noblement accrut le royaume des Francs et pendant XLVII années le gouverna heureusement, mort septuagénaire l'an du Seigneur DCCCXIV, indiction VII, le V des calendes de février. »

La naissance de la France

D e la mort de Charlemagne en 814 à celle de Charles le Chauve, son petit-fils, en 877, le mythe impérial tourne court. Les querelles entre les fils de Louis le Pieux, le choc de nouvelles invasions, la pression des Grands provoquent la dislocation de l'empire. En vain, les clercs cherchent à sauver la cause de l'unité, convaincus que le démembrement de l'empire risque de provoquer le déclin de l'Église. En vain, ils imaginent des solutions pour limiter les inconvénients des partages. Mais la revanche du réel comme les rivalités des hommes dessinent bientôt les frontières de nouveaux royaumes et préparent les inimitiés des futures nations. C'est à Verdun, en 843, que naît, pour la première fois, une Francia occidentalis *dont les limites ne varieront plus guère.*

Pieux ou Débonnaire ?

Le hasard a, une nouvelle fois, bien fait les choses. Pépin étant mort en 810 et Charles en 811, Louis, le benjamin, devient le seul héritier du royaume de son père. En 813, Charlemagne, après lui avoir exposé les devoirs de sa charge, lui remet à Aix-la-Chapelle la couronne impériale, cette fois sans l'intervention du pape. Après la messe, les deux empereurs quittent la chapelle, le père appuyé sur le fils.

En 814, quand Louis entre en possession de l'empire, il est âgé de trente-six ans. Il a les yeux grands et clairs, le nez long et droit, la poitrine large, les bras puissants et la voix forte. Son plaisir favori est la chasse et nul ne sait aussi bien que lui tendre un arc ou lancer un javelot. Mais Louis sait aussi lire le grec et le latin. Particulièrement dévot, il pleure en priant et courbe son front jusqu'à toucher le pavé de l'église, d'où le surnom de « pieux » que ses contemporains lui ont donné. Dès son avènement, il justifie cette réputation en chassant les nombreuses prostituées du palais d'Aix-la-Chapelle, en renvoyant ses sœurs dans les monastères qu'elles avaient reçus en héritage et en écartant leurs nombreux amants.

Un peu faible toutefois, manquant souvent de fermeté, écoutant facilement le dernier venu, il reçut aussi le surnom péjoratif de « débonnaire » qui traduit surtout le fait que c'est désormais l'église qui dicte sa loi à un empereur trop obsédé par la pensée de ses péchés pour diriger d'une main ferme les rênes de l'État.

Ainsi, bien qu'il eût été couronné par son père, il se fait une nouvelle fois couronner à Reims par le pape Étienne IV en octobre 816 après s'être avancé à un mille de la ville, pied à terre, et avoir servi d'écuyer au pontife. C'est manifester que Dieu seul est la source de tout pouvoir et gommer les efforts de Charlemagne pour limiter l'influence de la papauté. Dès son avènement, Louis renonce aussi aux titres de roi des Francs et des Lombards auxquels tenait son père et s'intitule : « Par la Providence divine, empereur auguste ».

Se présentant comme chargé d'un ministère divin, comme il le faisait graver sur ses monnaies (*munus divinum*), il se soumet à la théorie du pouvoir formulée par les évêques dont l'essentiel repose sur l'idée que le pouvoir ne vient pas des hommes mais de Dieu. Si, entre Dieu et Charlemagne, il n'y avait pas eu d'intermédiaire, entre Dieu et Louis le Pieux se trouve désormais l'épiscopat qui, au nom de l'unité de la foi, prétend effacer la diversité des peuples : « Plus de Gentils, ni de Juifs, de Barbares, de Scythes, d'Aquitains, ni de Lombards, de Burgondes et d'Alamans ! » proclame Agobard, l'archevêque de Lyon. « Si Dieu a souffert pour qu'il rapprochât dans son sang ceux qui étaient éloignés [...] est-ce qu'à ce travail divin de l'unité ne s'oppose pas cette incroyable diversité des lois, qui règne non seulement dans chaque région ou chaque cité ? »

Vouloir faire disparaître les différentes nationalités et gommer les diversités, n'était-ce pas pure idéologie ?

Préparer sa succession trois ans seulement après son accession au pouvoir, n'est-ce pas non plus laisser envisager sa prochaine disparition ? La décision de régler son héritage semble avoir été prise à la suite d'un événement qui pouvait apparaître comme un avertissement divin. Le jeudi saint 9 avril 817, une partie du portique en bois qui reliait le palais

LA DYNASTIE CAROLINGIENNE

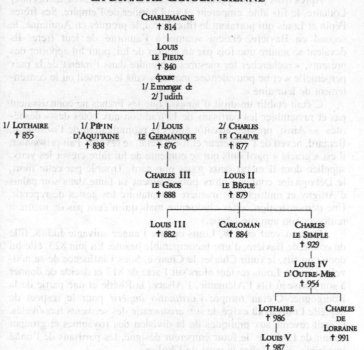

CHARLEMAGNE
† 814

LOUIS
LE PIEUX
† 840
épouse
1/ Ermengar de
2/ Judith

1/ LOTHAIRE
† 855

1/ PÉPIN
D'AQUITAINE
† 838

1/ LOUIS
LE GERMANIQUE
† 876

2/ CHARLES
LE CHAUVE
† 877

CHARLES III
LE GROS
† 888

LOUIS II
LE BÈGUE
† 879

LOUIS III
† 882

CARLOMAN
† 884

CHARLES
LE SIMPLE
† 929

LOUIS IV
D'OUTRE-MER
† 954

LOTHAIRE
† 986

CHARLES
DE
LORRAINE
† 991

LOUIS V
† 987

et la chapelle d'Aix-la-Chapelle s'effondra au moment où l'empereur le franchissait avec sa suite. Il y eut une vingtaine de blessés dont Louis.

Écartant les pratiques des partages précédents, contre l'avis des anciens conseillers de Charlemagne, Louis manifesta clairement sa volonté d'imposer un nouvel « ordre » dans le préambule de l'*ordinatio imperii* élaborée en juillet 817 : « Quoique cette requête ait été présentée avec dévouement et fidélité, il ne nous apparut point, ni à nous, ni à ceux qui jugent sainement » – on mesure bien ici l'influence du milieu épiscopal – « qu'il fût possible par amour pour nos fils de laisser rompre en procédant à un partage l'unité d'un empire que Dieu a maintenu à notre profit. Nous n'avons pas voulu courir le risque de déchaîner ainsi un scandale dans la sainte Église et d'offenser ceux en la puissance de qui reposent les droits de tous les royaumes. »

Après trois jours de jeûne et de prière, il décida donc de déclarer Lothaire, le fils aîné, empereur et seul héritier de l'empire. Ses frères Pépin et Louis qui portaient le titre de roi, le premier en Aquitaine, le second en Bavière, étaient soumis à l'autorité de leur frère. Ils devaient se rendre une fois par an auprès de lui, pour lui apporter des présents, « rechercher les mesures à prendre dans l'intérêt de la paix perpétuelle » et ne pouvaient se marier « sans le conseil ou le consentement de leur aîné ».

C'était établir un droit d'aînesse que les Francs ne connaissaient pas et rassembler les partisans de la tradition aux côtés des « déshérités ». Ainsi, presque aussitôt après la promulgation de l'*ordinatio*, Bernard, neveu de l'empereur et roi d'Italie, se révolte. Fait prisonnier, il est « gracié » par Louis qui se contente de lui faire crever les yeux, supplice dont il meurt deux jours plus tard. Troublé par cette mort, le Débonnaire confesse alors publiquement sa faute dans son palais d'Attigny et multiplie de manière ostentatoire les gestes de repentir. Une démonstration certes chrétienne mais qui n'était pas de nature à renforcer son autorité laïque.

Devenu veuf en 818, Louis épouse l'année suivante Judith, fille du comte de Bavière, d'une incomparable beauté. En juin 823, elle lui donne un fils, le futur Charles le Chauve. Sous l'influence de sa nouvelle femme, Louis revient alors sur l'acte de 817 et décide de donner à son nouveau fils l'Alémanie, l'Alsace, la Rhétie et une partie de la Bourgogne. C'était rompre l'*ordinatio imperii* pour le respect de laquelle Louis avait exigé de son aristocratie des serments renouvelés. C'était revenir aux pratiques de la division des royaumes et grouper autour de Lothaire, le futur empereur désigné, les partisans de l'unité impériale, c'est-à-dire le parti de l'Église.

La fin du règne est alors marquée par une série de crises qui mettent non seulement aux prises les fils de Louis entre eux mais, en même temps, les fils ligués contre leur père qui meurt, le 20 juin 840, alors qu'il était à la poursuite de son fils Louis le Germanique.

L'empire se trouvait alors disloqué et la fidélité des Grands sérieusement mise à l'épreuve par les partages successifs et les serments rompus. Le mercredi 5 mai 840, en plein jour, le ciel s'était si totalement obscurci que les clercs y avaient vu l'horrible présage de la fin d'un monde. C'était seulement la fin de la fragile construction carolingienne.

Le partage de Verdun

Dès la mort de leur père, Louis le Pieux, qui ne leur cause pas grande douleur, s'engage la guerre des trois frères. Lothaire envoie des messagers partout, annonçant qu'il va venir prendre possession de l'empire qui lui a jadis été confié. Charles, alors âgé de dix-sept ans, veut l'ouest de l'empire qu'un partage lui avait promis en 839. Louis en revendique la partie orientale.

C'est à qui débauchera les fidèles de ses frères et leur fera renier leurs serments.

Le 25 juin 841, à Fontenoy-en-Puisaye, au sud d'Auxerre, les armées de Louis et de Charles affrontent celle de Lothaire. Ce fut l'une des batailles les plus meurtrières de l'époque carolingienne. Le poète Angilbert, qui prit part à l'action, nous en a laissé l'écho : « Que ni la rosée, ni l'averse, ni la pluie ne tombent jamais sur les prés où les guerriers les plus exercés au combat ont péri [...] Les vêtements des guerriers francs blanchissaient la plaine, comme les oiseaux ont coutume de le faire en automne. Cette bataille n'est pas digne d'être célébrée dans un chant mélodieux. Que l'est, le sud, l'ouest et le nord pleurent tous ceux qui ont été tués ainsi. »

Battu, Lothaire revient à la charge. Ses deux frères échangent alors à Strasbourg, le 14 février 842, un serment qui est le plus ancien texte connu en langue « française ». En effet, tandis que Charles s'exprimait en langue germanique pour être compris des soldats de Louis, ce dernier parla en langue « romane » pour être compris des fidèles de Charles. « Pour l'amour de Dieu, jura Louis, et pour le peuple chrétien et notre salut commun (*Pro Deo amur et pro christian poblo et nostro commun salvament*...), à partir de ce jour, dans la mesure où Dieu me donnera savoir et pouvoir, je secourrai ce mien frère Charles par mon aide et en chacune chose, ainsi qu'on doit selon le droit secourir son frère, pourvu qu'il en fasse autant pour moi ; et, avec Lothaire, je ne tiendrai jamais aucun plaid qui, de ma volonté, soit dommageable à ce mien frère Charles. »

En juin 842, les trois frères se rencontrent près de Mâcon et acceptent le principe d'un partage de l'empire de Charlemagne en trois lots aussi « égaux que possible ». Une commission de 120 experts travaille pendant plus d'un an pour en définir les limites. Signé à Verdun en août 843, le traité peut être considéré comme l'acte de naissance de la France.

Louis reçut les territoires à l'est du Rhin et au nord des Alpes. Lothaire, qui gardait le titre d'empereur, avait un royaume qui s'étendait de la mer du Nord au sud de l'Italie et réunissait les deux capitales de l'empire, Aix-la-Chapelle et Rome. À Charles, échut la partie occidentale de l'empire, les limites de son royaume suivant approximativement l'Escaut, la Meuse, la Saône et le Rhône. Même s'il est difficile de percer les intentions des « experts », il semble bien que le partage de Verdun ait eu pour but d'équilibrer les parts de chacun des héritiers de Louis le Pieux afin de leur composer un territoire produisant à la fois des céréales, des fourrages pour les bestiaux, de l'herbe pour les moutons, des olives pour la fabrication de l'huile et toutes sortes de fruits. Ainsi, la part de Louis, concentrée à l'est du Rhin, le franchissait en certaines parties pour lui fournir les vignobles dont il était privé dans le Midi. Chacun recevait aussi sa part des résidences royales, entre Liège et Aix pour Lothaire, de Francfort à Worms pour Louis, entre Laon et Paris pour Charles.

Surtout, on a tenu compte des liens de fidélité qui étaient devenus l'assise de toute autorité. C'est ainsi que Lothaire se plaint « du sort des fidèles qui l'avaient suivi en prétendant que, dans la part qu'on lui offrait, il n'avait pas de quoi pouvoir les dédommager de ce qu'ils perdaient ». À l'occasion du partage de Verdun se sont ainsi produits des transferts de fidélité, certains grands possessionnés en Germanie préférant passer au service de Charles.

Certes, il n'y avait chez les « experts » aucune intention de respecter les sentiments « nationaux ». Cependant, force est de constater que la *Francia occidentalis*, de près de 400 000 kilomètres carrés, est bien la première ébauche de la France d'aujourd'hui et que les frontières tracées à Verdun se sont maintenues pendant des siècles. Ainsi, dans la forêt de l'Argonne, l'insignifiant cours d'eau qu'était la Biesme séparait le royaume de Charles de celui de Lothaire. Or, en 1288 encore, près de 450 années après le traité de Verdun, les habitants du pays, interrogés, savaient très bien distinguer « ces qui sont par desai le dit ru, qui sont de l'empire, et ces qui sont par delai le dit ru, qui sont dou roiaulme de France » (« ceux qui étaient en deçà du ruisseau et qui habitaient l'empire, et ceux qui étaient au-delà du ruisseau et qui étaient du royaume de France »). Aujourd'hui encore, la Biesme sépare le département de la Meuse de celui de la Marne. Et il y a à peine cent ans, les bateliers du Rhône conservaient l'usage d'appeler « riau » (abréviation de « riaume », c'est-à-dire royaume) la rive occidentale du fleuve, et « empi » (abréviation d'empire) la rive opposée.

Pour les clercs, comme le poète Florus de Lyon, ce partage signifiait la fin du grand rêve unitaire : « Le nom et la gloire de l'empire sont également perdus. Les royaumes, jusqu'alors unis, ont été déchirés en trois parts. Au lieu d'un roi, un roitelet ; au lieu d'un royaume, des fragments de royaume. » Le partage de Verdun marquait en fait la constitution de royaumes sur des bases réalistes. « *Gallia*, ma patrie », écrit en 844 l'abbé Loup de Ferrières, un homme de l'ouest. À cet égard, Charles le Chauve peut bien apparaître comme le premier roi de « France ».

De nouveaux envahisseurs

À partir de la mort de Charlemagne, on a le sentiment que les Carolingiens n'ont plus les moyens d'assurer l'ordre dans un aussi vaste empire. De tous les horizons surgissent de nouveaux envahisseurs dont les plus dangereux arrivent par mer.

Dès la fin du VIIIe siècle, ceux qu'on appelle « hommes du Nord », c'est-à-dire Normands ou encore Vikings, les « hommes qui fréquentent les baies », abordent les côtes anglaises sur des vaisseaux de guerre qui pouvaient contenir 60 à 70 hommes. De haute stature, ces hardis marins devenaient, une fois débarqués, de redoutables guerriers connaissant à fond toutes les ruses de guerre.

Avec ses fleuves débouchant dans la mer par de larges estuaires et coulant au pied de riches abbayes, la *Francia occidentalis* était une proie tentante, un eldorado fascinant. Apparus dans la Manche aux environs de 800, les Normands doublent le Finistère avant 819. En 811, pour renforcer les défenses maritimes, Charlemagne avait lui-même inspecté les flottilles de Gand et de Boulogne et fait restaurer dans cette dernière ville le phare romain abandonné depuis longtemps.

Profitant des crises politiques qui marquent la fin du règne de Louis le Pieux, les Normands multiplient leurs raids à partir de 834. Quentovic et Dorestad, sur les débouchés commerciaux de l'Escaut, de la Meuse et du Rhin, sont régulièrement pillés.

Le 12 mai 841, Rouen est attaqué. Le 24 juin 843, les Normands arrivent à Nantes. Les habitants se réfugient dans l'église de Saint-Pierre et Saint-Paul dont ils barricadent les portes. Mais les Vikings brisent les clôtures et massacrent l'évêque dont le sang se répand sur l'autel. En mars 845, le dimanche de Pâques, Paris, abandonné par ses habitants, est pillé et ses églises incendiées. Saint-Martin de Tours subit le même sort en 853. À partir de 856, Paris, à nouveau, Chartres, Évreux, Bayeux, Beauvais, Angers, Tours, Noyon, Amiens, Melun, Meaux, Orléans, Périgueux, Limoges sont la proie de ceux qui se rient de Dieu et vendent les chrétiens comme esclaves. Alors commence le pitoyable exode des moines qui, pendant deux générations, vont courir les routes pour tenter de sauver les reliques des saints dont ils assurent la garde. L'exemple le plus connu est la longue errance des reliques de saint Philibert, parties de Noirmoutier en 836 pour s'installer définitivement à Tournus, en Bourgogne, après de longues étapes dans le Poitou, puis en Velay.

Comment l'Église n'interpréterait-elle pas ces malheurs comme le produit de la vengeance divine ? Au concile de Meaux, en 845, les évêques le disent bien : « Comme ses ordres divins n'étaient pas exécutés, Dieu permit comme châtiment l'apparition des persécuteurs des chrétiens, les Normands, qui s'avancèrent jusqu'à Paris. » C'est souligner le fait que les dirigeants de la cité terrestre n'étaient plus capables d'assurer la sécurité de la Cité de Dieu, l'idée de défendre la collectivité ne venant pas à l'esprit de Grands plus soucieux de profiter des circonstances que de protéger les églises sans défense. « Dans leur engourdissement, au milieu de leurs rivalités réciproques, écrit Ermentaire de Noirmoutier, ils rachètent au prix de tributs ce qu'ils auraient dû défendre, les armes à la main, et ils laissent sombrer le royaume des Chrétiens. »

En 845, Charles le Chauve convoque ses fidèles pour défendre Saint-Denis, joyau des abbayes royales mais, constate le rédacteur des *Annales*, « beaucoup vinrent, mais pas tous ». Mieux, ceux qui viennent refusent l'affrontement et conseillent au roi de payer les 7 000 livres qu'exige le chef normand Ragnar. En 858, alors que Charles le Chauve s'apprête à prendre d'assaut le camp viking d'Oscelle, près de Mantes, ses fidèles l'abandonnent pour soutenir son frère Louis le Germanique, affirmant « qu'ils ne pouvaient supporter plus longtemps la tyrannie de Charles ».

Puis, comme les autres envahisseurs avant eux, les Normands songent à remplacer la razzia par le commerce et à s'installer sur le sol de France, nombre d'entre eux étant partis, poussés par le désir de s'établir sur des terres plus hospitalières. Des communautés se fixent à Bayonne, à Nantes et sur la basse Seine. En 873, les Normands installés sur la Loire reçoivent l'autorisation royale de créer un marché dans l'île où ils étaient établis, les esclaves constituant l'essentiel du trafic.

Et, en 911, alors que les Normands conduits par le Norvégien Rollon subissent pourtant une lourde défaite devant Chartres, le roi Charles le Simple, encouragé par les archevêques de Reims et de Rouen, a l'idée de leur proposer la défense des cités de Rouen, d'Évreux et de Lisieux en échange du baptême et d'un serment de fidélité. Pendant l'été 911, le roi carolingien rencontre à Saint-Clair-sur-Epte Rollon, qui s'engage à cesser toute attaque et à embrasser le christianisme.

Le succès de cet « État » normand allait être considérable, en partie grâce à la christianisation rapide de ces païens qui déployèrent pour leur nouvelle religion un zèle de néophytes. Tandis que d'importantes abbayes étaient fondées ou se relevaient de leurs ruines comme Jumièges, Saint-Wandrille, Fécamp, les villages étaient rebâtis, un grand nombre d'entre eux recevant des noms scandinaves comme tous ceux qui se terminent en *beuf*, de la racine *bud*, qui veut dire « demeure » (Quillebeuf, Elbeuf, Criquebeuf, Daubeuf), ou en *fleur*, venant du norois *flodh* qui veut dire « baie » (Barfleur, Harfleur, Honfleur). Ces envahisseurs qui avaient mis la France à feu et à sang allaient aussi devenir les agents les plus actifs du rayonnement de leur nouvelle « patrie ». Singulière et nouvelle démonstration des capacités de la France à assimiler les « immigrés ».

Au sud du pays, le danger vient d'autres pirates, les Sarrasins, qui, après avoir enlevé la Sicile aux Byzantins, attaquent les Baléares, la Corse et la Sardaigne. En Provence, ils établissent aux environs de 890 une tête de pont à Fraxinetum (près de Saint-Tropez) dans le massif des Maures et, de là, lancent des raids à travers les vallées des Alpes pour se livrer à la chasse aux esclaves qu'ils vendent sur les marchés espagnols. Ils ne seront délogés qu'en 972-973.

Enfin, les Hongrois qui, pour les Occidentaux, rappellent les Huns pénètrent au début du Xe siècle en Alsace, en Lorraine, en Bourgogne et en Languedoc avant de se fixer vers 955 dans la plaine du Danube central.

« Quoi d'étonnant si les païens et les peuples étrangers s'imposent à nous et nous prennent nos biens temporels, peut-on lire dans un capitulaire de 884, puisque chacun ôte à son voisin le plus proche ce dont il doit tirer sa vie ? » Impuissance, règne du chacun pour soi, tel est le sentiment qui anime ceux qui réfléchissent à la cause de ces tourments. La Germanie s'est désintéressée du danger normand qui ne la concernait pas tandis que la France ne s'est préoccupée des menaces hongroises que lorsqu'elle a été directement visée. De plus en plus, les grandes unités territoriales nées de la dislocation de l'empire de Charlemagne sont devenues étrangères les unes aux autres.

L'affirmation des régions

Les invasions normandes, sarrasines et hongroises ont révélé de fortes personnalités et accéléré la mise en place de nouveaux pouvoirs. Rassemblée chaque printemps pour se lancer dans des équipées cavalières de la Frise au Frioul ou de l'Espagne à la Saxe et en ramener de copieux butins, l'armée impériale, faite pour la guerre offensive, lente à se rassembler et à se mouvoir, s'est montrée incapable de

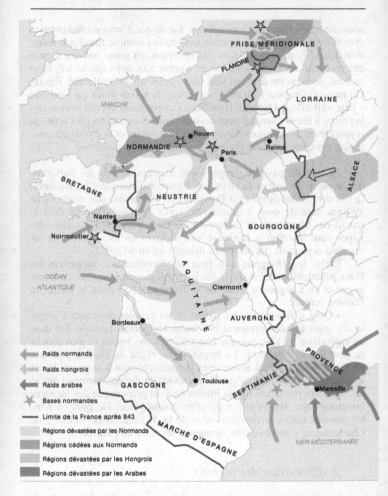

Les invasions en France aux IXᵉ et Xᵉ siècles.

repousser les envahisseurs et de prévenir leurs incursions fondées sur la surprise et la rapidité d'exécution.

Au quotidien, les seuls chefs de guerre susceptibles de repousser ces attaques imprévisibles et de rassembler rapidement tous les hommes valides ont été ceux qui, placés à la tête des comtés pour exécuter les ordres de l'empereur, sont devenus les vrais héros de la résistance. Ainsi, en 886, quand les Normands ont mis le siège devant Paris, c'est le comte Eudes qui a tenu en respect les assaillants alors qu'appelé à la rescousse, l'empereur Charles le Gros n'a pas osé engager la bataille, préférant acheter leur départ moyennant sept cents livres et leur laisser la Bourgogne à piller pendant l'hiver. Bientôt, dans les assemblées de guerriers, on chantera en longues mélopées des cantilènes qui tournent en dérision l'impuissance des souverains et exaltent les exploits des seigneurs.

Dans tout le royaume, les hommes qui, autrefois, avaient pour mission de rassembler les contingents de guerriers et de les mener à l'ost se détachent de plus en plus d'une famille royale dont les rivalités ont affaibli le prestige et qui, faute de nouvelles conquêtes, n'a plus de récompenses à distribuer. Pourquoi les grands affronteraient-ils les fatigues et les dangers de chevauchées interminables pour plaire à un souverain qui ne leur donne plus rien ?

Déjà, en novembre 843, au cours de l'assemblée générale des grands, tenue à Coulaines, près du Mans, Charles le Chauve, qui n'a pas encore réellement pris possession du royaume que lui a attribué le partage de Verdun, a signé un acte essentiel qui va définir pour longtemps les rapports entre la royauté et l'aristocratie. Afin de rendre « stable et durable », la jeune *Francia occidentalis*, l'« ordre vénérable des clercs » et les « nobles laïcs » se sont engagés à travailler « au bien et à la paix de chacun et de tout le peuple », à prendre des décisions « unanimes et raisonnables », à apporter au roi « conseil et aide », à assurer entre eux « paix, concorde et amitié ».

De son côté, Charles, répudiant les erreurs qu'il attribue à sa jeunesse et à son ignorance, renonçant « aux mesures qu'il a prises par inexpérience [...] sous l'empire de la nécessité ou sous une influence trompeuse », demande aux grands de les oublier et de l'aider dans son gouvernement. Surtout, il promet de « conserver à chacun, quel que soit son ordre ou sa dignité, sa loi propre », telle que « l'ont connue ses ancêtres », disant clairement qu'il ne peut révoquer par pur caprice ceux qui sont en place. C'est là le point essentiel du pacte de Coulaines qui établissait clairement les droits et les devoirs des uns et des autres. Les grands devaient service et obéissance au roi qui, en échange, ne pouvait les priver de leur « honneur », c'est-à-dire de la charge qu'ils occupaient et des droits qui y étaient attachés.

Le 14 juin 877, à Quierzy, Charles ira plus loin. Si un comte meurt, le capitulaire prévoit que son fils gérera la circonscription. Si un vassal meurt, sa veuve et ses enfants disposeront provisoirement de ses bénéfices. Certes, ces mesures étaient exceptionnelles, Charles étant obligé de régler le problème de la vacance des charges publiques avant son départ pour l'Italie. Reste qu'il était amené à constater le fait que l'hérédité des charges publiques était devenue la norme courante, la tendance naturelle des pères étant de survivre en leurs fils. Après être passé de l'empereur aux rois, le pouvoir descendait du roi aux puissants.

Cet affaiblissement du pouvoir central au profit des pouvoirs locaux, souvent compris comme un aveu d'impuissance, voire comme un signe de désordre, peut aussi être interprété comme un facteur d'équilibre lié aux simples réalités de l'histoire des provinces dont la diversité fait la richesse de la France. Phénomène ancien, apparu dès la préhistoire et confirmé au temps des Gaulois, l'apparition de régions se manifeste nettement pendant les années qui suivent le partage de Verdun.

Tandis que les descendants de Charlemagne poursuivent leurs chimères, comtes et ducs, enracinés dans leurs régions, font reconnaître leurs traditions et leurs coutumes. Au cœur des périls, l'union des habitants autour de leurs protecteurs naturels, seuls capables d'apaiser des foules inquiètes, est bien l'amorce d'une prise de conscience régionale sans laquelle la France ne serait pas la France.

Au cœur de la *Francia occidentalis*, naissent ou renaissent ainsi, des années 890 aux années 920, des principautés sans réelle existence institutionnelle mais qui constituent des unités fortement individualisées, cumulant plusieurs comtés ou *pagi*. Voici la Bourgogne dont Richard le Justicier, mort en 921, fut le prince fondateur. Voici l'Aquitaine dont trois lignages se disputent le titre ducal, ceux de Toulouse, d'Auvergne puis de Poitiers. Voici la Gascogne qu'avec le titre de « comte et marquis », Garsie Sanche (886-920) a soustrait totalement à l'autorité royale. Avec son petit-fils, Guillaume Sanche, la Gascogne englobe alors Bigorre, Agen et Bordeaux tandis que les textes du temps nous donnent l'image d'un prince infatigable, présent sur tous les fronts, levant des contingents pour détruire les installations landaises des Normands et repousser les musulmans en Espagne. Du monastère de Saint-Sever qu'il a restauré, il inaugure l'histoire d'un peuple et d'une région.

Voici, bien sûr, la Bretagne, jamais soumise, dont le duc Alain dit le Grand, s'intitule « roi des Bretons par la grâce de Dieu ». Voici la Catalogne dont tous les comtes se recrutent et se succèdent à l'intérieur d'une même famille au sein de laquelle s'illustre Guifred surnommé *Pilosus*, le Poilu. Dans le Nord, un comte de Flandre, Baudouin dit « Bras de Fer », profite, lui aussi, des invasions normandes pour créer sa principauté, après avoir enlevé et épousé Judith, la fille de Charles le Chauve. Entre Seine et Loire, la famille de Robert le Fort exerce au cœur du royaume un commandement particulier qui vaudra à Eudes, l'héroïque défenseur de Paris, d'être élu roi par les Grands en 888, au détriment de l'héritier carolingien, le jeune Charles, fils de Louis le Bègue.

Robert le Fort, Richard le Justicier, Alain le Grand, Alain Barbe-Torte, Guillaume Tête d'Étoupe, Guillaume Longue Épée, Baudouin Bras de Fer, Guillaume Fièrebrace, telles sont les impressionnantes figures de proue d'une génération dont les sobriquets traduisent les fortes personnalités de ceux qui en arrivent à inscrire sur les monnaies dont ils contrôlent la frappe leur nom en lieu et place de celui du souverain.

Ces nouveaux pouvoirs s'inscrivent aussi dans le paysage. C'est à partir de 860 qu'apparaissent près des villages ou à l'angle des bourgs les châteaux en bois construits sur de grosses mottes de terre rondes, des châteaux dont les tours dessinent la carte des nouveaux lieux de pouvoir. En vingt-quatre ans de règne, Charles le Simple aura émis 122 diplômes, soit en moyenne 5 par an. En dix-huit ans de règne, Louis IV d'Outre-Mer en a émis 53, soit 3 par an. En trente-deux ans de règne, Lothaire en a émis 56, moins de 2 par an. Signe incontestable du ralentissement de l'action du pouvoir central. Il en est un autre. Si l'on totalise, dans les diplômes royaux, les mentions de grands qualifiés de *fideles regis* par rapport à ceux qui ne le sont pas, on trouve, sous Charles le Simple, 70 *fideles* contre 90, soit près de la moitié de l'ensemble ; sous Louis IV d'Outre-Mer, 22 contre 55 ; sous Lothaire et Louis V, 14 contre 40, soit un quart.

Aux approches de l'an mille, l'hérédité a changé de camp. Ce ne sont plus les rois, mais les princes qui se succèdent de père en fils. La province est bien devenue l'horizon politique d'une France qui a appris, depuis beau temps, à vivre hors de l'autorité centrale.

21

Les premiers Capétiens

En mars 986, meurt Lothaire, l'arrière-arrière-petit-fils de Charles le Chauve. Le 22 mai 987, Louis V, qui avait succédé à son père, meurt sans héritier des suites d'un accident de chasse. Certes, il restait un Carolingien, son oncle Charles de Lorraine, mais les Grands lui faisaient grief d'être au service d'un roi « étranger » et de s'être mal marié en épousant la fille d'un modeste chevalier. Le 1er juin 987, ils élisent roi Hugues Capet qui est sacré le dimanche 3 juillet, probablement à Noyon. Ainsi disparaissaient du pouvoir les Carolingiens, trois siècles après la victoire de Tertry (687) qui avait permis à Pépin le Jeune d'unir les mairies du palais d'Austrasie et de Neustrie. Ainsi naissait dans l'indifférence une dynastie qui allait gouverner la France pendant huit siècles.

L'avènement d'Hugues Capet

En 750, Pépin le Bref avait interrogé le pape Zacharie « au sujet des rois qui étaient en France sans exercer le pouvoir » et lui avait demandé « si cela était bon ou mauvais ». Au nom de l'« ordre » social, le pape avait légitimé l'« usurpation » en lui répondant qu'il valait « mieux appeler roi celui qui avait, plutôt que celui qui n'avait pas le pouvoir royal ». En 987, selon les chroniqueurs du temps, Hugues se serait tourné vers Adalbéron, l'archevêque de Reims, « pour demander à l'éminent prélat de donner son avis sur ce qui était bien pour le royaume, parce qu'il excellait dans la connaissance des choses divines et humaines et qu'il pouvait exprimer son avis efficacement ».

Faisant valoir qu'en l'absence d'héritier direct, le trône devait revenir par élection au prince qui était le plus capable, Adalbéron aurait déclaré devant l'assemblée des Grands réunis à Senlis : « Le trône ne s'acquiert pas par droit héréditaire, et l'on ne doit mettre à la tête du royaume que celui qui se distingue non seulement par la noblesse corporelle mais encore par des qualités d'esprit. »

Puis, désignant Hugues Capet dont la famille avait déjà compté trois rois, son grand-oncle Eudes entre 888 et 898, son grand-père Robert entre 922 et 923 et son oncle Raoul entre 923 et 936, il aurait ajouté : « Vous trouverez en lui un défenseur non seulement pour l'État, mais encore pour vos intérêts privés. Grâce à son dévouement, vous aurez en lui un père. »

Des arguments que l'archevêque aurait pu tenir deux siècles plus tôt lorsque Pépin avait déposé le dernier roi mérovingien. Face aux Carolingiens qui dénoncèrent ce qu'ils estimaient être une usurpation et se groupèrent derrière Charles de Lorraine pour tenter de reprendre la couronne, Hugues détenait la véritable autorité. Il devait être roi. Déjà, en 985, Gerbert d'Aurillac, le plus grand savant de son temps, le futur pape de l'an mille, constatait : « Lothaire est roi de France de nom, Hugues l'est de fait. »

En votant de manière unanime en sa faveur, alors qu'Hugues n'avait rien à donner à des princes qui étaient déjà à la tête de puissantes principautés, les Grands manifestaient la force des liens de fidélité qui faisaient de la royauté un corps mystique dont les membres étaient les grands et la tête le roi : « Qui serait assez fou pour se couper la tête de sa propre main ? » interrogeait l'abbé de Fleury, Abbon, à la fin du siècle.

Patron des comtes installés sur les bords de Seine et autour de Paris, abbé de Saint-Martin de Tours, le saint protecteur des Francs dont la célèbre relique, le manteau (la *capa*), a sans doute valu à Hugues le surnom de « Capet », contrôlant l'important monastère de Saint-Denis, ayant pour frère le duc de Bourgogne et pour beaux-frères les ducs de Normandie et d'Aquitaine, Hugues apparaissait bien comme le plus apte à exercer la royauté.

Surtout, oint du Seigneur, chef sacré, même dans les régions où il n'exerçait aucun pouvoir réel, le roi était devenu, avec la pieuse complicité des hommes d'Église, celui qui « par la grâce divine l'emporte sur les autres mortels ». Soucieux d'asseoir le prestige de son siège épiscopal et d'assurer la promotion de saint Remi qui faisait pâle figure par rapport à saint Martin et à saint Denis, Hincmar, archevêque de Reims de 845 à 882, avait écrit vers 880 une vie de Remi où était développée la légende selon laquelle, lors du baptême de Clovis, une colombe, dans laquelle on reconnut vite le Saint-Esprit, avait apporté du ciel dans une ampoule l'huile d'onction miraculeuse. Au milieu du Xe siècle, Flodoard, un chanoine, toujours rémois, avait enrichi cette légende. Remi, « saisi de l'esprit prophétique », aurait prédit à Clovis et ses descendants qu'ils étendraient « glorieusement les limites du royaume » et triompheraient « des nations étrangères » s'ils restaient vertueux et obéissants à Dieu. Autant de légendes de nature à assurer à Reims le monopole du sacre, ce qui sera chose faite à partir du règne d'Henri Ier, à la seule exception de Louis VI sacré en 1108 à Orléans.

Les rites de la cérémonie, mis en place depuis Hincmar, traduisent clairement la volonté d'assimiler la fonction royale à la fonction épiscopale, de faire du roi un personnage à part, doté, comme les hommes d'Église, d'un ministère particulier. S'adressant d'abord aux évêques, le roi leur dit : « Je vous promets de conserver à vous et à vos églises les privilèges canoniques, la loi et la justice qui vous sont dus. Autant qu'il sera en mon pouvoir, et avec l'aide de Dieu, j'assurerai par droit la défense, comme le roi en son royaume doit l'assurer, à chacun des évêques, à chacune des églises qui leur sont soumises. » Puis, se tournant vers le peuple, il déclare : « Ces trois choses, je les promets au nom du Christ au peuple chrétien qui m'est soumis. Premièrement, que tout chrétien en tout temps tiendra l'église de Dieu, moi arbitre, en vraie paix. Deuxièmement, que je m'opposerai à toute rapacité et iniquité. Troisièmement, que je prescrirai en tout jugement l'équité et la miséricorde. »

Représentant de Dieu, l'archevêque « élisait » alors le roi puis enduisait son corps avec l'huile miraculeuse qui, écrivait Hincmar, « se répand sur la tête du roi, descend dans son intérieur et pénètre le fond de son cœur ». Suivait alors la remise des insignes, le sceptre, homologue de la crosse épiscopale, l'anneau, homologue de celui qui unissait l'évêque au peuple de son diocèse.

Ne tenant son ministère que de Dieu, le roi est bien la clé de voûte du système politique. Même si l'avènement d'Hugues Capet n'est pas en soi un événement, la royauté, elle, demeure d'une extrême importance puisque le sacre assure à l'« élu » de Dieu une force surnaturelle qui en fait le garant de la fécondité du royaume et du bon « ordre » des choses.

Parce qu'il lui manquait sans doute le caractère et l'esprit d'entreprise, Hugues Capet le comprit. Tout de suite après son avènement, il associa son fils Robert au trône avec l'assentiment des Grands et le fit sacrer le jour de Noël 987, six mois après lui. Tous ses successeurs l'imitèrent. Ainsi s'établit la coutume selon laquelle, sans cesser d'être élective, la couronne se transmettait de manière héréditaire au sein de la famille royale. La grande chance des Capétiens fut d'avoir, pendant trois siècles, des fils pour leur succéder ! Point n'était besoin d'être génial pour gouverner, il suffisait dans un premier temps de durer.

Des rois « imbéciles »

Les premiers rois de la nouvelle dynastie capétienne n'ont pas bonne réputation. D'Hugues Capet, on ne sait pratiquement rien. Robert le Pieux semble inactif. Henri Ier paraît bien pâle malgré son mariage avec Anne de Kiev qui devait donner à leur fils aîné un nom tiré de la tradition byzantine, Philippe. Ce dernier, devenu Philippe Ier, dont le règne est l'un des plus longs de l'histoire de France (1060-1108), aurait été un roi avachi, « alourdi par la masse de la chair et plus préoccupé de manger et de dormir que de combattre ». Il paraissait dominé par Bertrade de Montfort, une compagne digne de lui, astucieuse et cynique, qui aurait trouvé moyen, au cours d'un bon dîner, de réconcilier Foulques d'Anjou, son premier mari, et Philippe qui l'avait arrachée à lui. « Une véritable virago, écrivait l'abbé antiféministe de Saint-Denis, Suger, mais séductrice, rompue à la pratique de ces artifices qui sont un don étonnant chez les femmes, et par lesquelles elles ont coutume, en leur audace, de mettre sous leurs pieds leurs maris après les avoir harcelés d'injustice. »

Un dialogue fameux inventé vers l'an 1030 par un chroniqueur aquitain, Adémar de Chabannes, donne la mesure du rétrécissement du pouvoir royal. « Qui t'a fait comte ? » auraient déclaré Hugues Capet et son fils Robert au comte Audebert de Périgord. « Qui vous a fait rois ? » aurait répliqué ce dernier.

Même inventé, ce dialogue pouvait apparaître vraisemblable tant le pouvoir matériel de la royauté semblait se réduire en peau de chagrin. Alors qu'en dix ans de règne, Hugues Capet a signé une douzaine de diplômes, son contemporain Otton III d'Allemagne, en moins de vingt années de règne, en a signé plus de quatre cents. En outre, la carte d'implantation géographique de ces diplômes révèle d'importantes absences. Au sud de la Loire, tout le pays échappe à l'action du roi. L'année même de son élection, appelé au secours par le comte Borrell de Barcelone que menace al-Mansur, Hugues Capet n'intervient pas. Désormais, les princes de cette région s'orienteront vers d'autres appuis.

Les Grands désertent aussi la cour du roi qui perd le caractère solennel des plaids carolingiens. Parmi les vassaux, dont les souscriptions au bas des diplômes royaux certifient leur présence, on ne rencontre pas une seule fois, de 987 à 1108, le comte de Gascogne, le comte de Toulouse, le duc de Gothie, le comte de la Marche d'Espagne. Le duc d'Aquitaine n'y paraît que fort rarement, le comte d'Auvergne, à titre tout à fait exceptionnel. Pénétrant en Gascogne vers l'an mille pour aller visiter le prieuré de La Réole, Abbon de Fleury dit en plaisantant aux moines qui l'accompagnent : « Me voici plus puissant en ce pays que le roi de France, car ici personne ne craint sa domination. »

Surtout, jusqu'en 987, les diplômes royaux étaient l'objet d'une souscription de chancellerie qui, jointe à l'apposition du seing royal, donnait à ces actes la valeur d'actes publics dont l'autorité royale était l'unique fondement. Passée cette date, se substituent à la signature des évêques et des princes les noms des personnes de sa parenté qui entourent le roi au moment où les actes sont expédiés, les vassaux issus de la petite aristocratie, les chefs de service qui veillent au bon ordre des banquets, comme le sénéchal ou le bouteiller, responsable des caves. Faire confirmer l'authenticité d'un acte par ces « domestiques » est le signe le plus manifeste de la dégradation de la puissance publique et de l'impuissance du roi à rassembler autour de lui ceux qui l'ont pourtant acclamé lors de la cérémonie du sacre.

Bientôt une expression courra : *Imbecillitas regis*, faiblesse du roi, incapacité à agir. Dans son *Poème au roi Robert* rédigé entre 1027 et 1031, le vieil évêque Adalbéron de Laon se fait l'écho de ces plaintes en écrivant : « L'État est entraîné à sa ruine, les lois sont abolies », puis, sarcastique : « Une place de prélat se trouve-t-elle vacante ? Vite, qu'on y consacre un pâtre, un marinier, le premier venu, qu'importe ? ».

Au sacre de Philippe Ier en 1059, si les princes, tous présents sauf le duc des Normands, ont encore manifesté par les cris poussés dans la cathédrale de Reims leur volonté de porter « aide et conseil » au souverain, un demi-siècle plus tard, les ducs de Normandie, d'Aquitaine et de Bourgogne refusent de rendre hommage à son successeur, Louis VI, oint à Orléans par l'archevêque de Sens avec une huile qui ne venait pas de la sainte ampoule.

En outre, les cartes dressées du domaine royal donnent l'image d'un territoire fort étriqué, de Compiègne au nord à Orléans au sud, sans aucune commune mesure avec les ensembles aquitains ou bourguignons. Les cités de Paris, Orléans et Senlis, quelques forteresses majeures comme Dreux, Poissy, Étampes, Melun et celle, plus excentrique, de

LES ROBERTIENS ET
LES PREMIERS CAPÉTIENS

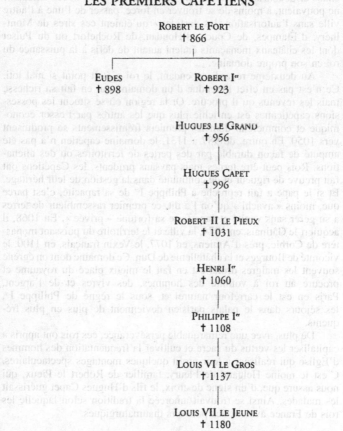

ROBERT LE FORT
† 866

EUDES
† 898

ROBERT Ier
† 923

HUGUES LE GRAND
† 956

HUGUES CAPET
† 996

ROBERT II LE PIEUX
† 1031

HENRI Ier
† 1060

PHILIPPE Ier
† 1108

LOUIS VI LE GROS
† 1137

LOUIS VII LE JEUNE
† 1180

Montreuil-sur-Mer en constituent l'armature. Dans ce domaine, le roi aurait été absorbé par sa lutte contre les accaparements de la petite noblesse et les intrigues des domestiques de sa cour. Un roi incapable en 1079 de prendre le château du Puiset, en Orléanais, et qui aurait avoué à son fils, peu avant de mourir, que la tour de Montlhéry, dont le sire bloquait le chemin de Paris à Orléans, l'avait fait « vieillir avant l'âge » ! Entre Paris et Orléans, écrira plus tard l'abbé Suger, « le chaos et la confusion étaient tels que ni les Parisiens ni les Orléanais ne pouvaient, à moins de se trouver en force, passer de l'une à l'autre ville sans l'autorisation des perfides » qu'étaient ces sires de Montlhéry, d'Étampes, de Coucy, d'Houdan, de Rochefort ou du Puiset dont les châteaux menaçants étaient autant de défis à la puissance du roi en son propre domaine.

Au deuxième regard, cependant, le roi n'était point si mal loti. Ce n'est pas en effet l'étendue d'un domaine qui en fait sa richesse mais les revenus qu'il procure. Or la région où se situent les possessions capétiennes est enrichie plus que les autres par l'essor économique et commercial dont les premiers frémissements se produisent vers 1050. En outre, de 987 à 1131, le domaine capétien n'a pas été amputé de façon durable par des pertes de territoires ou des aliénations. Rois peut-être ternes mais paysans prudents, les Capétiens ont fait preuve de rigueur et de continuité dans la gestion de leur héritage. Et si le pape a fait reproche à Philippe Ier de sa rapacité, c'est parce que, moins « avachi » qu'on l'a dit, ce premier rassembleur de terres a su gérer sans vanité et sans faste sa fortune « privée ». En 1068, il acquiert le Gâtinais, en 1074, la ville et le territoire du puissant monastère de Corbie, près d'Amiens, en 1077, le Vexin français, en 1100, le vicomté de Bourges et la châtellenie de Dun. Ce domaine dont on égrène souvent les maigres droits est en fait le mieux placé du royaume et procure au roi à volonté des hommes, des vivres et de l'argent. Paris en est le carrefour naturel et, sous le règne de Philippe Ier, les séjours dans le palais parisien deviennent de plus en plus fréquents.

De plus, avec une remarquable persévérance, ces rois ont appris à capitaliser les vertus du sacre et cultiver la fréquentation des hommes d'Église qui réalisent à leur profit quelques montages spectaculaires. C'est le moine Helgaud de Fleury, familier de Robert le Pieux, qui nous assure que, d'un signe de croix, le fils d'Hugues Capet guérissait les malades. Ainsi se trouvait amorcée la tradition selon laquelle les rois de France avaient des pouvoirs thaumaturgiques.

La gloire des princes

Au premier regard, pourtant, face aux besogneux rassembleurs de terre que sont les premiers rois capétiens, ce sont les princes de la France profonde, ceux des marches et des zones frontières, qui manifestent le plus de grandeur et de prestige. Dans leur palais de Poitiers, les ducs d'Aquitaine sont des presque-rois auxquels il ne manque que le sacre. Les épithètes qui les désignent, « très pieux », « princes sérénissimes », sont autant d'emprunts au vocabulaire impérial et royal. Celui de l'an mille, surnommé Guillaume le Grand, ce qui n'est pas rien, entreprend tous les ans de lointains pèlerinages, vers Rome ou Saint-Jacques de Compostelle, entretient des relations directes et échange des cadeaux avec Alphonse de Castille, Sanche de Navarre, Canut le Grand du Danemark et d'Angleterre et l'empereur germanique Henri II, songeant un moment à accepter la couronne d'Italie. Et quand Robert le Pieux vient en Aquitaine, c'est en visiteur chargé de présents, d'un lourd plat d'or et d'étoffes précieuses. Eudes II, le comte de Blois et de Chartres, véritable tête brûlée, s'empare de la Champagne et rêve de la couronne impériale. Foulques Nerra, comte d'Anjou, fortifie une principauté que son fils, Geoffroy Martel, étend à la Touraine et au Maine.

Au nord, le comte de Flandre essaie hardiment de se créer un royaume aux Pays-Bas, nargue les empereurs, établit des liaisons avec l'Angleterre et stimule le développement économique de Lille, Gand et Bruges.

À l'extrême sud, Henri, petit-fils du duc Robert de Bourgogne, après avoir joué un rôle capital dans la première « reconquête » de l'Espagne sur les musulmans, épouse une princesse castillane et, en 1097, devient le premier comte de Portugal. Son fils en sera le roi.

Dès le début du XIᵉ siècle, Robert Guiscard, un Normand, fils de Tancrède de Hauteville, s'empare de la Campanie, se fait reconnaître en 1059 par le pape duc des Pouilles et de la Calabre, prend la Sicile aux musulmans et chasse les Byzantins d'Italie. Ainsi est fondé le royaume normand de Sicile, une des créations politiques les plus originales du Moyen Âge, dont la capitale, Palerme, devient un port animé et une ville cosmopolite où le latin, le grec et l'arabe sont les trois langues officielles de la chancellerie royale et au sein de laquelle les magnifiques églises combinent en des synthèses originales les solutions chrétiennes et les traditions byzantines et musulmanes.

Normand toujours, mais tenu désormais pour un « Franc » tant son peuple s'est rapidement intégré à la civilisation « française », Guillaume le Bâtard, fort d'une clientèle de vassaux solidement tenus en main et dont le dynamisme est à la mesure de la rapacité, revendique en 1066 la couronne d'Angleterre que lui aurait promise son cousin Édouard le Confesseur. Celui qui a su favoriser sur ses terres le développement d'une brillante civilisation monastique, détruire les châteaux élevés sans sa permission et canaliser en une puissante cavalerie la fougue des anciens pirates, débarque en Angleterre le 29 septembre 1066 et, le 14 octobre, à Hastings, triomphe de son rival Harold qui meurt au cours du combat. Le jour de Noël, Guillaume, devenu « le Conquérant », se fait sacrer roi d'Angleterre à Westminster. Administrateurs et juristes de talent, comme en témoignent les institutions originales nées en Normandie – l'échiquier, cour chargée de contrôler toute l'administration du domaine, le système du jury et le recours à l'enquête par témoins en matière de procédure judiciaire –, les Normands dressent alors le *Domesday Book*. Cette sorte de cadastre recense les titres de propriété des nouveaux maîtres en Angleterre. Quatre personnes, Guillaume, la reine Mathilde et les deux demi-frères, s'appropriaient près de 25 % de ces terres. Quinze autres aristocrates normands reçurent des fiefs représentant 30 % de l'ensemble de la richesse terrienne anglaise. Ensemble, dix-neuf personnes contrôlaient ainsi plus de la moitié de l'Angleterre, le reste étant en grande partie dévolu aux églises et aux abbayes dont tous les titulaires étaient normands. Cette conquête, qui accroissait de manière considérable la richesse et le prestige du duc de Normandie, était un rude défi pour le roi de France.

Le retour du roi

Entourés par des « familiers » fiers de leurs fonctions, devenus maîtres de l'Île-de-France, servis par des hommes d'Église de talent aptes à inventer de belles légendes pour conforter leur fonction, Louis VI (1108-1137) puis Louis VII (1137-1180) relèvent le défi que représente la redoutable concurrence du Normand et étendent patiemment leur emprise sur le royaume.

Ils ont su, tout d'abord, affirmer leur autorité « chez eux », en soumettant les sires qui les avaient jusque-là tourmentés.

Philippe Ier, à la fin de son long règne, puis Louis VI ont tout d'abord doté la justice royale d'une efficacité qu'elle n'avait jamais eue, annonçant l'image du roi-justicier qu'incarnera saint Louis. Au début de son règne, Louis VI fait condamner par sa cour Bouchard IV, seigneur de Montmorency, qui persécute l'abbaye de Saint-Denis, et ravage ses terres pour le forcer à respecter ce jugement. Dans les années suivantes, ce sont les comtes de Montfort et de Beaumont, les sires de Rochefort, du Puiset et de La Ferté-Alais qui sont mis à la raison. À la fin du règne de Louis VII, ces impertinents châtelains ont été « domestiqués ». Passés au service du roi, ils lui fournissent les agents dont il a besoin pour faire exécuter sa volonté. Il suffit, pour en prendre la mesure, de compter les actes émanant de la chancellerie royale : 171 pendant le règne de Philippe Ier, 359 sous Louis VI, 800 au moins sous Louis VII.

Chargés d'encadrer les populations, de rendre la justice, de collecter les revenus réguliers du domaine, les prévôts, généralement recrutés dans les milieux modestes, sont une vingtaine en 1137, une quarantaine en 1180. Ils traduisent en revenus divers la volonté du roi de gérer attentivement ses biens, de favoriser l'activité des métiers, de contrôler les flux de navigation et de tirer parti du renouveau commercial. Certes, avec peut-être un revenu de 19 000 livres parisis par mois, Louis VII est assurément moins riche que le duc de Normandie. On connaît le témoignage contemporain de Gautier Map, un familier du roi d'Angleterre à qui Louis VII aurait lancé un jour : « Ton seigneur le roi d'Angleterre ne manque de rien : hommes, chevaux, or, soie, diamants, gibier, fruits, il a tout en abondance. Nous, en France, nous n'avons que du pain, du vin et de la gaieté ! » Une boutade qui forçait à plaisir le trait. Car si le roi d'Angleterre dut fréquemment recourir à des taxes extraordinaires pour faire face à ses dépenses, le roi de France, apparemment, ne connut aucune difficulté de trésorerie.

En outre, dès les débuts du règne de Louis VI le Gros, la géographie des interventions royales s'élargit. En 1108 ou 1109, le roi est sollicité de juger un différend entre le seigneur Aimon de Bourbon et son neveu, ce qui accroît son prestige en Berry. Vers 1122-1126, c'est en Aquitaine qu'il agit, forçant le comte Guillaume d'Auvergne à plier. Après plus d'un siècle d'absence, la royauté réapparaissait en ces régions. En 1132, le roi « approuve le jugement » intervenu entre l'évêque d'Arras et un seigneur du comté de Flandre et déclare en adopter désormais la solution « partout en son royaume vis-à-vis de toutes les églises ». C'est donner à la justice royale valeur universelle et faire céder les particularismes locaux.

Signe éclatant du renouveau monarchique, les ducs d'Aquitaine, de Bourgogne et de Normandie qui, en 1108, avaient refusé de prêter hommage à Louis VI au moment de son couronnement, finissent par se rendre à la raison et reconnaître que leur principauté est partie intégrante du royaume. « Si le comte d'Auvergne a commis quelque faute, c'est à moi de le présenter à votre cour sur votre ordre parce qu'il tient de moi l'Auvergne que moi je tiens de vous », aurait déclaré au roi Louis VI le duc d'Aquitaine lors de l'expédition d'Auvergne de 1123, traduisant en ces termes la mutation fondamentale en cours tout au long du XIIe siècle. « Ce n'est plus seulement la Francie qui est votre royaume, bien que le titre royal la désigne particulièrement.

La Bourgogne est aussi vôtre », écrit à Louis VII, en 1166, Eudes, l'abbé de Cluny.

Cette mutation se manifeste aussi avec éclat en 1124 lorsque l'empereur Henri V, ulcéré par le soutien que Louis VI apporte au pape avec lequel il est en conflit, annonce qu'il va envahir le royaume de France et détruire Reims, ville symbole ô combien. Louis VI se présente alors devant saint Denis, dont les reliques ont été sorties de leur châsse, prend sur l'autel l'oriflamme de Saint-Denis, que l'on disait être miraculeusement conservée, la bannière même de Charlemagne, et convoque les nobles de France contre les « Teutons ».

« Passons hardiment chez eux, disaient les plus enflammés d'entre eux, de crainte que, s'ils s'en retournent, l'orgueilleuse présomption avec laquelle ils se sont jetés sur la France ne demeure impunie. Il faut qu'ils sentent ce que leur présomption leur a mérité, non sur notre terre, mais sur la leur, laquelle, conformément au droit royal des Français, se trouve soumise aux Français pour avoir été souvent domptée par eux. »

Se présentent ainsi contre l'« envahisseur » le duc de Bourgogne, le comte de Nevers, le comte de Flandre et celui du Vermandois, les comtes de Champagne et de Blois tandis qu'accourent aussi, sans avoir eu bien le temps de mobiliser leurs contingents, le duc d'Aquitaine et les comtes de Bretagne et d'Anjou. Toute une France rassemblée derrière son roi. Impressionné sans doute par une telle mobilisation, l'empereur, prétextant des troubles dans la ville de Worms, ne vint pas.

Moine d'obscure naissance, compagnon d'étude du futur Louis VI, abbé de Saint-Denis en 1122, tuteur du roi Louis VII, habile administrateur, homme rompu à l'art du politique mais aussi homme d'action capable au cours des trois années 1123, 1124 et 1125 de parcourir environ 2 000 lieues, soit 8 000 kilomètres, Suger fut la cheville ouvrière du renouveau monarchique. C'est lui qui consolida l'idéologie royale en suggérant que la couronne était un principe abstrait, distinct de la personne physique du roi, l'image d'un cercle rassemblant toutes les églises et toutes les seigneuries du royaume, chacun de ses fleurons représentant un fief. C'est à lui que fut confiée la régence du royaume quand Louis VII décida en 1147 de prendre la croix pour secourir la chrétienté menacée en Orient.

Cette seconde croisade contribua pour beaucoup au prestige du Capétien. Certes, les armées franques subirent de graves échecs en Orient, certes, Aliénor, l'épouse de Louis VII, semble avoir éprouvé, au cours de ce voyage, une certaine lassitude envers un époux trop austère et quelque peu éteint, les ragots colportés par les gens d'Église allant même jusqu'à lui prêter une idylle avec Saladin, le prince des Infidèles. Toujours est-il que l'époux trompé y gagna la réputation d'un saint laïque qui fit oublier sa part de responsabilité dans l'échec humiliant que venait de subir « sa » croisade. Les Grands, qui ont passé deux ans sous ses ordres, tisseront avec lui des liens qui ne se relâcheront pas. Quand, en juin 1155, il les réunira à Soissons pour instaurer une paix générale dans le royaume et « contenir la violence de ceux qui pillent », ils seront tous là, acceptant par leur présence le principe d'une collaboration entre eux et le roi en vue de promouvoir la paix.

MAISONS DE NORMANDIE, D'ANJOU ET DE BLOIS-CHAMPAGNE MARIAGES ET ALLIANCES

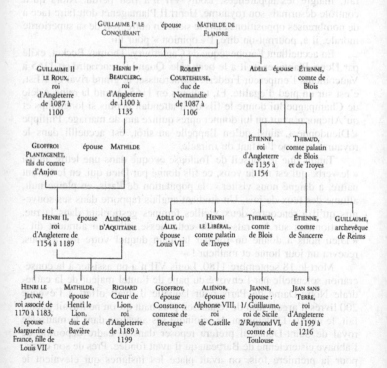

239

Mieux, son divorce avec Aliénor le grandit. Aux yeux de ses contemporains, il s'en trouva purifié. Pourtant, le remariage d'Aliénor avec Henri II Plantagenêt, comte d'Anjou, deux mois après avoir été répudiée, semblait faire peser une grave menace sur le royaume capétien. La famille d'Anjou connaissait en effet une ascension spectaculaire. Le père d'Henri, Geoffroi, marié à la fille unique de Henri Ier Beauclerc, duc de Normandie et roi d'Angleterre (fils de Guillaume le Conquérant), avait obtenu non sans mal la possession du duché de Normandie. Un an après son remariage, Henri se faisait reconnaître roi d'Angleterre. Aliénor lui apportait l'Aquitaine, le Poitou, l'Aunis, la Saintonge, l'Angoumois, le Périgord et une grande partie de l'Auvergne. Il se trouvait désormais à la tête d'un « empire » qui couvrait à la fois l'Angleterre et près de la moitié du royaume de France. En fait, malgré les apparences, Louis VII n'a rien perdu. Alors qu'il contrôle désormais son royaume, Henri II Plantagenêt doit faire face à de nombreuses oppositions dans le sien. En outre, fort de sa supériorité morale, il a, pourrait-on dire, l'« opinion » pour lui.

En accueillant l'archevêque de Canterbury, Thomas Becket, exilé par Henri Plantagenêt, il a le beau rôle. Quand il rencontre en 1165 à Vaucouleurs l'empereur Frédéric Barberousse, le grand rival de l'Est, c'est sur un pied d'égalité. Et, toujours en 1165, quand la reine Adèle de Champagne lui donne le fils qu'il attendait depuis si longtemps et qu'Aliénor n'avait pu lui donner après quinze ans de mariage, Philippe « Dieudonné », ainsi qu'on l'appelle aussitôt, est accueilli dans le royaume comme l'enfant du miracle.

Tandis que le conseil de Toulouse évoque dans une lettre au roi « le verbe qui est né de vous, ce fils donné par Dieu qui, en le faisant naître, a daigné nous visiter », la population de Paris, en pleine nuit, allume des feux de joie. Un étudiant anglais rapporte dans ses souvenirs qu'il a rencontré deux vieilles femmes gesticulant dans la rue. Questionnées sur les raisons de cette liesse, elles lui auraient dit : « Dieu nous a donné un roi par la main duquel votre roi, à vous, recevra un jour honte et malheur ! »

Mort le 18 septembre 1180, Louis VII n'a pu assister à la consécration solennelle par l'envoyé du pape de l'autel majeur de la cathédrale Notre-Dame de Paris pour laquelle il avait offert à l'évêque 200 livres d'argent afin de rehausser, plus haut qu'on ne l'avait jamais fait, le chœur. Dédaignant de rejoindre ses ancêtres dans le mausolée royal de Saint-Denis, il préféra reposer dans le cadre dépouillé de l'abbaye cistercienne de Barbeau qu'il avait fondée. Près de son corps, pour la première fois, on avait placé les insignes qui élevaient le souverain au-dessus des mortels, le sceptre et le sceau. Sur la tombe était gravée cette épitaphe :

« *Celui à qui tu survis, tu lui survis successeur de sa dignité ;*
Tu manques à ta lignée si tu manques à sa renommée. »

22

Le temps de l'embellie

*T*andis qu'approchait la troisième année qui suivit le millénaire
« *[...], le monde secouant sa poussière pour rejeter sa vétusté, parut
se revêtir partout d'un blanc manteau d'églises.* » Ainsi s'exprime Raoul
dit Glaber, un moine bourguignon qui écrivit avant 1048 cinq livres
d'Histoires qui sont une histoire du monde depuis le début du Xᵉ siècle.
Témoignage précieux que celui de cet homme d'Église qui aurait dû être
sensible, plus que d'autres, à la prophétie de l'apôtre saint Jean selon
laquelle « Satan sera déchaîné après mille ans accomplis ». Pourtant,
moine bavard et crédule, Raoul Glaber est surtout sensible à l'embellie
qui ouvre le IIᵉ millénaire, à l'élan de vie qui, partout, peuple les chaumières, ouvre les clairières et anime les villes.

Les terreurs de l'an mille

An mille. Ces deux mots semblent évoquer un temps de
désordres, d'angoisses, de terreurs collectives. Dans une superbe
envolée romantique, Jules Michelet écrivait en 1833 : « Cette fin d'un
monde si triste était tout ensemble l'espoir et l'effroi du Moyen Âge.
Voyez ces vieilles statues dans les cathédrales des Xᵉ et XIᵉ siècles,
maigres, muettes et grimaçantes dans leur roideur contractée, l'air
souffrant comme la vie, et laides comme la mort. Voyez comme elles
imploraient, les mains jointes, ce moment souhaité et terrible, cette

seconde mort de la résurrection, qui doit les faire sortir de leurs ineffables tristesses, et les faire passer du néant à l'être, du tombeau en Dieu. C'est l'image de ce pauvre monde sans espoir après tant de ruines... Le captif attendait dans le noir donjon ; le serf attendait sur son sillon, à l'ombre de l'odieuse tour ; le moine attendait dans les abstinences du cloître, dans les tumultes solitaires du cœur, au milieu des tentations et des chutes, des remords et des visions étranges, misérable jouet du diable, qui folâtrait cruellement autour de lui, et qui, le soir, tirant sa couverture, lui disait gaiement à l'oreille : « Tu es damné ! »

En fait, les terreurs de l'an mille n'ont jamais existé. Aucun document contemporain ne fait état de vagues d'épouvante, les hommes de ce temps ne sachant d'ailleurs pas qu'ils étaient arrivés à la millième année de l'incarnation !

Certes, certains ecclésiastiques, qui savaient calculer les dates, ont pu éprouver une certaine angoisse devant un certain nombre de catastrophes ou de signes énigmatiques, une éclipse de soleil, une lune couleur de sang, le passage d'une comète, une sécheresse inhabituelle, des pluies diluviennes, une famine exceptionnelle. Certes, Abbon, abbé de Fleury-sur-Loire, né vers 940, rapporte que, dans sa jeunesse, il entendit « prêcher au peuple dans une église à Paris que l'Antéchrist viendrait à la fin de l'an mille et que le Jugement général suivrait de peu ». Certes, en 997, Adémar de Chabannes voit sévir en Limousin un « mal des ardents », un « feu caché » en fait provoqué par des carences alimentaires qui, après s'en être pris à un membre, consume le corps entier en une nuit. Certes, on a le sentiment que les générations qui ont vécu de part et d'autre de l'an mille ont connu un lot inhabituel de misère et d'effrois. Rien toutefois ne permet d'imaginer des terreurs collectives, le début du second millénaire semblant au contraire marqué par la fin d'une longue série noire et l'amorce d'un intense renouveau.

Des hommes de plus en plus nombreux

Si la France s'est revêtue à partir de l'an mille d'un « blanc manteau d'églises », c'est que les hommes sont devenus de plus en plus nombreux et qu'il a fallu permettre au peuple chrétien de tenir tout entier dans les édifices religieux. Même s'il est malaisé de les compter, de multiples signes traduisent l'ampleur d'une puissante lame de fond qui, amorcée vers 950, va probablement porter la population de la France de 5 millions d'habitants vers l'an mille à 9,2 millions d'habitants en 1200. Un quasi-doublement en deux cents ans.

Des calculs plus précis effectués en Picardie font apparaître que les parents nés vers l'an mille auraient eu par ménage « fécond » 3,5 enfants ; les parents nés vers 1075, 5 ou 6 enfants. Des généalogies reconstituées pour la noblesse du pays de Chartres entre 1050 et 1250 donnent près de cinq enfants par couple. En Charente, le pourcentage des familles de trois garçons et plus atteint presque 50 % vers 1025-1050 et 1125-1150. En Mâconnais, entre 980 et 1050, les familles qui affichent cinq ou six fils ayant survécu à la mortalité de la première enfance ne sont pas rares.

Certes, périodiquement encore, des famines viennent briser la vague, en 1032-1033, en 1123-1125, en 1195-1197, mais on a bien le sentiment qu'elles sont à la fois moins nombreuses et moins meurtrières qu'auparavant. Passé l'an mille, les squelettes retrouvés dans les cimetières témoignent d'une longévité plus grande, notamment chez les femmes, d'une meilleure qualité de l'ossature et d'une denture plus solide.

Il est difficile de répondre à la troublante question que pose toujours la démographie, pourquoi ? Sans doute doit-on tenir compte du fait que les invasions normandes, sarrasines et hongroises sont les dernières que la France ait connues. Peut-être faut-il faire la part d'une phase de réchauffement climatique plus favorable aux être vivants. Entre 900 et 1300, les températures moyennes se seraient en effet élevées d'un à deux degrés tandis qu'une moindre humidité aurait favorisé les cultures céréalières. Sans doute aussi, la valorisation de la femme a fait reculer les infanticides de fillettes qui semblent avoir été importants jusque-là. Peut-être enfin qu'en confiant plus souvent leurs nouveau-nés à des nourrices, beaucoup de femmes se sont trouvées en état d'être fécondées sans le long intervalle qu'entraînait un allaitement poussé parfois jusqu'à 18 mois.

Cette lame de fond démographique, nous en percevons surtout les conséquences. Mauvaises et peu sûres, routes et pistes apparaissent pourtant animées par l'intense va-et-vient des hommes. S'y croisent aussi bien les « mauvais moines » qui « vagabondent en rond », les chercheurs d'aventures, mi-soldats, mi-bandits, les paysans avides d'une existence meilleure espérant trouver loin de leur première patrie quelques champs à défricher, des pèlerins en marche, des étudiants en route vers leurs écoles, des princes qui, pour tenir leur pays, n'ont d'autre moyen que de chevaucher sans trêve et en tous sens.

Entre le milieu du XIe siècle et la fin du XIIe siècle, les Bretons se retrouvent ainsi partout entre Loire et Seine, y compris à Paris où leur

présence se renforce. En Aragon et en Castille, on note la présence
nombreuse de « surnoms » d'origine française. Et les villes semblent
attirer « étrangers », « aubains », « forains », c'est-à-dire simplement
ceux qui sont venus d'ailleurs. Ainsi s'élargissent les horizons et
s'échangent les idées.

La faim de terres

Après avoir discrètement desserré l'étreinte de la nature, élargi
progressivement les clairières en faisant reculer les taillis et les broussailles qui encerclaient les villages, creusé clandestinement de nouveaux sillons en bordure des anciens champs pour échapper aux taxes
des maîtres du sol, des paysans plus hardis se lancent à la conquête
de nouvelles terres, s'attaquent à de grandes forêts ou à des marécages,
endiguent les polders et créent des villages neufs. C'est le grand
« bond en avant » des campagnes françaises, « le plus grand accroissement de la surface culturale dont notre sol ait été le théâtre depuis les
temps préhistoriques », écrivait Marc Bloch, le grand historien qui, au
début des années 1930, décrivait *Les Caractères originaux de l'histoire rurale française*.

Affamés de terres, pourvus d'outils plus résistants et plus perfec-
tionnés où le fer supplante désormais le bois, haches, scies, serpes,
pics, fourches, cognées et, surtout, charrues, l'arme principale du
laboureur, des équipes de défricheurs ou « sartiers » élargissent l'espace cultivé. En Île-de-France, les forêts de Rambouillet, de Saint-
Germain-en-Laye, de Marly, de Fontainebleau et d'Orléans sont rudement attaquées. Dans le Bordelais, les innombrables lieux-dits
« sarts », « essarts » ou « artigues » témoignent de l'ampleur du mouvement de défrichement. En Picardie, on a calculé que les terres nouvelles gagnées sur les friches représentaient entre 14 et 19 % des sols.

La conquête des marais de Dol, de Guérande, du Marais breton,
du Marais poitevin, des paluds du bas Languedoc frappe l'imagination. Dès le temps du comte Baudouin V (1036-1067), la transformation des marais flamands infertiles en prairies suscite l'admiration des
contemporains. Et que dire du titanesque effort de mise en valeur des
pentes ravinées des collines méditerranéennes où il fallut assembler
les pierres et hisser la terre à la hotte ?

C'est aussi le désir nouveau d'être son maître, d'avoir le sentiment d'être indépendant dans une société fort collective qui a poussé
certains à s'isoler de leurs villages et à s'installer à l'écart des « autres ». Ainsi, entre 1025 et 1150, des ermites un tantinet marginaux

ont joué un rôle important dans le grignotage de la forêt à tel point qu'au début du XIIe siècle, le seigneur de Fougères craignait une destruction complète de ses bois. Dans la Bretagne méridionale ou le Poitou maritime, les toponymes en -ière, -ère, -erie comme la Villardière, la Rogère, la Caillaudrie, la Berenerie, rappellent le nom du pionnier fondateur. En Angoumois, dans une partie du Sud-Ouest, les noms de lieux précédés de Chez (de *casa*, « demeure ») tels Chez Garnier, Chez Guillaume, Chez Trappe traduisent aussi la volonté de marquer son territoire et d'enclore ses conquêtes.

Enfin, mieux connue, l'extension des terroirs cultivés s'est manifestée par la fondation de villages neufs. Dans la plupart des cas, ces « villeneuves » eurent pour origine la décision d'un seigneur laïque ou ecclésiastique d'attirer des « hôtes » sur ses terres, soit pour renforcer la sécurité d'une route en peuplant les forêts qu'elle traversait, population serrée disant brigandage moins aisé, soit pour accroître le nombre de ses sujets afin de créer des centres supplémentaires de perception de droits de marché ou d'amendes de justice, soit pour implanter, afin de mieux tenir leur territoire, des communautés qui pourraient fournir des soldats.

Pour attirer les « hôtes » sur des terres réputées hostiles, il fallait toutefois leur promettre des avantages, les nourrir pendant les premiers mois, céder la jouissance d'un terrain et d'une maison, fournir les outils ou les semences, prendre en charge les travaux collectifs. Les « villeneuves » de l'Île-de-France, les « bourgs » de Normandie et du Poitou, souvent proches des châteaux, voire établis au pied même des forteresses, les « castelnaux » de Guyenne et de Gascogne, les noms de lieux contenant « motte », « fossat », « roque », « garde », « isle », « castel » traduisaient la volonté des maîtres du sol de canaliser la fièvre des campagnes et d'en tirer le meilleur parti. Toujours dans le Midi, en particulier dans le Médoc, les « sauvetés », souvent fondées par des maisons religieuses, étaient des territoires délimités par des croix dans lesquels les violences étaient interdites et la sécurité renforcée. La plus ancienne doit être celle de Macau dans le Bordelais. Les villages fondés près des abbayes qui disposaient de reliques jouissaient d'un prestige considérable. À en croire les chroniques du temps, il suffisait au XIe siècle que les ennemis voient à l'horizon le clocher d'un monastère pour qu'ils n'osent pousser plus avant.

Les rois capétiens et l'abbé Suger ont été en ce domaine des initiateurs particulièrement avisés. La charte de franchises que Louis VI accorda aux habitants de Lorris-en-Gâtinais (1108 et 1137) fut copiée dans les pays de Loire et en Bourgogne. L'organisation en 1145 de la villeneuve de Vaucresson par Suger est aussi exemplaire. L'abbé de

Saint-Denis accorde à chaque hôte un arpent et quart, soit environ un demi-hectare, moyennant un cens modique de 12 deniers et, pour chaque arpent supplémentaire conquis sur la forêt, 4 autres deniers. D'autre part, les amendes sont plafonnées à 10 deniers et le service militaire ne sera dû que sur ordre et en présence de l'abbé. Ce lieu, écrit-il, était « comme une caverne de voleurs, étant désert sur plus de deux lieues et d'aucun rapport pour notre abbaye. En raison de la proximité des bois, il convenait aux voleurs et à leurs suppôts... Aussi avons-nous décidé que nos frères y serviraient Dieu, afin que les retraites habitées jadis par les dragons voient grandir le roseau et le jonc ».

Plus optimistes, plus inventifs, plus entreprenants, les hommes ont pu améliorer l'ordinaire, égayer leurs menus et arrondir leurs revenus. Même s'il apparaît peu de techniques nouvelles, l'usage plus fréquent de la charrue, la multiplication de labours plus profonds, une utilisation moins parcimonieuse des engrais, l'emploi intensif de la main-d'œuvre pour arracher les mauvaises herbes, bêcher et sarcler haussent légèrement les rendements. La construction des moulins dans les campagnes comme dans les villes en est la manifestation la plus spectaculaire. À Troyes, on en construit onze entre 1157 et 1191. Dans un quartier de Rouen, il existait deux moulins sur un ruisseau au Xe siècle. Au même endroit, on en construisit cinq nouveaux au XIIe siècle. Bientôt apparaissent en Normandie puis en Flandre les moulins à vent qui, en libérant du temps, ont en même temps libéré des bras pour les grands travaux et les défrichements. Enfin, le grand essor de la vigne, dans le Sud comme dans le Nord, à proximité des zones de forte consommation, a largement contribué à absorber la croissance démographique. Elle a donné du travail aux paysans les plus modestes, diffusé le salariat et contribué au désenclavement des campagnes. Moments forts de la vie rurale, les vendanges qui mobilisaient une main-d'œuvre importante tant pour ramasser les grappes que pour les transporter jusqu'à la cuve à fouler, étaient impatiemment attendues. Occasion de gagner quelques pièces d'argent, elles étaient aussi prétexte à de copieuses ripailles où harengs et fromages côtoyaient quartiers de bœuf et de porc.

La renaissance des villes

Peu avant l'an mille, on assiste à la renaissance des villes qui, à la suite des invasions normandes, s'étaient repliées et assoupies derrière leurs murailles. Concurrencées dans leur rôle militaire par les châteaux ruraux et dans leur rôle religieux par les monastères, elles avaient vu aussi s'étioler leur activité économique, les échanges devenant limités au commerce de produits de luxe réservés à une infime minorité de puissants.

Dès le milieu du Xᵉ siècle, alimenté par les surplus de l'embellie agricole, l'élan reprend en Flandre et dans l'Ouest. Un siècle plus tard, la renaissance urbaine est générale, étroitement greffée sur l'essor des campagnes qui fournissent clients et vendeurs pour le marché, matières premières et main-d'œuvre pour l'artisanat.

Car c'est moins le grand commerce international, dont la reprise est animée par les cités maritimes italiennes, Venise, Amalfi, Pise et Gênes, qui irrigue les villes que les livraisons d'avoine, de céréales et de vin livrés aux granges urbaines par chariots, hottes, sacs et brancards.

La naissance de la cité d'Ardres, près de Calais, est une illustration de ces modestes connexions entre croissance démographique, initiative seigneuriale et animation commerciale. « Quant au lieu où se presse actuellement la population d'Ardres, peut-on lire dans l'*Histoire des comtes de Guînes et des seigneurs d'Ardres*, il était alors à l'usage de pâture et presque désert ; seulement le long de la route qui le traversait, vers l'emplacement du marché actuel, demeurait un brasseur de bière, chez qui les gens de la campagne s'assemblaient pour boire ou jouer à la paume, à cause du grand espace qu'il y avait là. Tout le reste, [...] tenu à l'état de terre vague, était appelé « la pâture », c'est-à-dire « arde » dans le langage du pays [...]. Plus tard, des gens d'autres régions vinrent y demeurer et, par l'accroissement de la population, il se forma un village [...]. Arnoul Iᵉʳ, voyant la fortune lui sourire, construisit dans le marais une écluse située à environ un jet de pierre d'un moulin, ainsi qu'une seconde écluse. Entre ces écluses, au milieu des marais, presque au pied de la hauteur qui les borde, il aménagea, en signe de sa puissance militaire et en terre rapportée une motte très élevée, ou donjon, qui fut amoncelée entre la hauteur et la digue. Dans une cachette très secrète de cette terre amassée, ils placèrent, en signe d'un présage heureux, une petite pierre fixée sur une très belle monture d'or qui devait rester enterrée à perpétuité. Il entoura d'un très puissant fossé le terrain compris dans l'enceinte extérieure, à l'intérieur de laquelle fut inclus le moulin. »

Peu après l'an mille, partout, les mentions de ponts se multiplient. Sur la Meuse, six ponts sont édifiés dans le courant du XIᵉ siècle. À Paris, le Grand-Pont, tout en bois, avait remplacé le pont romain situé un peu en amont dès la fin du IXᵉ siècle. Sur la Loire, le pont d'Amboise date peut-être de 1015, celui d'Angers, reconstruit en pierre, de 1028, celui de Tours des années 1034-1037. À Albi, un pont est entrepris sur le Tarn en 1035. Sur la Saône, le premier pont de

Lyon fut achevé entre 1052 et 1077. À Grenoble, le pont romain sur l'Isère est rebâti vers 1100.

« Route qui marche », la voie d'eau transporte tous les produits de base, vin, grains, sel, laine. La multiplication des péages sur les fleuves fait la fortune de Rouen et de Paris. Dès 1121, Louis VI fait remise aux marchands parisiens des 60 sous que le roi percevait sur chaque bateau abordant au port de Paris à l'époque des vendanges. En 1171, Louis VII confirme les privilèges des « marchands de l'eau » en interdisant à d'autres qu'eux d'acheminer des marchandises entre les ponts de Paris et celui de Mantes. Quant aux marchands de Rouen, ils reçoivent en 1150 le monopole du commerce des vins français exportés par la Seine et celui de l'importation dans le royaume de toute denrée d'origine anglaise.

Points de convergence des routes, des produits et des monnaies bonnes et mauvaises qu'évaluent des changeurs, les foires aussi se multiplient, rendez-vous périodiques où des marchands itinérants se rencontrent pour traiter d'affaires en gros. Certaines prennent la suite de rassemblements pré-chrétiens, comme celle du Mont-Dol en Bretagne. D'autres naissent à un carrefour ou à un point de rupture de charge. Celles de Champagne, qui deviennent au XIIe siècle l'étape intermédiaire entre les Flandres et l'Italie, doivent leur succès à l'action intelligente des comtes de Champagne qui accordent aux marchands des « conduits » assurant leur protection et qui favorisent la venue des étrangers en construisant des logements où se regroupent, sous la direction d'un consul, les marchands de même origine.

À partir de 1150, toute l'Europe marchande se retrouve à Lagny, Bar-sur-Aube, Provins et Troyes dont les six foires forment un cycle couvrant presque toute l'année. Les Flamands y vendent draps et toiles, les Italiens, soieries, épices et produits de luxe, les gens du Midi français des cuirs, les Allemands des fourrures et des cuirs.

Ainsi s'épanouit le phénomène urbain, particulièrement précoce là où se conjuguent riches terroirs agricoles et itinéraires commerciaux majeurs. En Flandre, en particulier, alimentées par les fournitures massives de laine indigène, poussent, à Lille, Ypres, Bruges et Gand, des villes-champignons où l'on tisse, foule et teint des draps qui se vendent jusqu'à Novgorod, le grand emporium situé aux portes de la Russie. Arras, Saint-Omer et les villes de la Somme profitent de ce rayonnement flamand. Laon, où les vignerons des coteaux voisins viennent acheter leur nourriture, est déjà considéré par l'abbé Guibert de Nogent comme un lieu de perdition. Les vieilles cités épiscopales, Reims, Châlons, Soissons, Noyon, Tours, Lyon, Vienne, Narbonne, et Bourges sortent de leur assoupissement et se couvrent d'églises nouvelles. À Vienne, au Puy, à Saintes, à Sens, à Albi, à Limoges, à Valenciennes, à Nîmes, une nouvelle ville se crée face à l'ancienne. À Poitiers, la *rua fabroria*, mentionnée vers 970, est sans doute le premier nom de rue connu en France. À Paris, entre Saint-Merry et Saint-Germain, le long de la Seine, se développe un quartier nouveau animé par les mariniers, les bouchers et les poissonniers pendant que les changeurs s'installent sur le Grand-Pont.

Au début du XIᵉ siècle, apparaît alors un nom nouveau pour désigner ces nouveaux citadins : les bourgeois. On le trouve pour la première fois dans un texte de 1007 évoquant les *burgenses* qui résident dans le bourg de Beaulieu-lès-Loches en Touraine. Le terme est bientôt employé à Poitiers, en Normandie, à Albi au moment de la construction du pont, à Saint-Omer en 1056. Dans un diplôme émis par le roi Louis VII en 1141, le rédacteur évoque « les clercs, les chevaliers et les bourgeois ». À l'origine, habitant du bourg, le bourgeois en vient à désigner l'ensemble des habitants d'une ville qui n'appartiennent ni au clergé ni à l'aristocratie. Il exprime surtout la solidarité de ceux qui, marchands et artisans, commencent à prendre conscience d'un intérêt commun.

Engagés dans une vie de relations aux horizons plus larges, en contact fréquent avec des gens venus d'ailleurs, mieux informés et plus innovateurs, n'hésitant pas au marché à abuser de la naïveté des ruraux, actifs et souvent turbulents, ils ont rapidement constitué des associations mêlant religion, aide mutuelle, banquets et beuveries solennelles qui occupent une bonne place dans les règlements des ghildes flamandes comme celles de Valenciennes ou de Saint-Omer. Bientôt, secouant le joug de ceux qui voulaient confisquer les profits de l'embellie, ils cherchent à devenir leurs propres maîtres.

En butte aux seigneurs qui imposent de lourds péages aux portes et aux ports des villes et qui monnayent cher leur « protection », au Mans, pour la première fois en 1070, à Noyon en 1108, à Laon en 1112, ils forment une « conspiration » appelée « commune » pour arracher leur autonomie en matière d'administration et de justice et obtenir des détenteurs du pouvoir la reconnaissance de « franchises » qui suppriment les entraves au commerce. À Laon, armés d'épées, de haches, d'arcs et de cognées, ils prennent d'assaut le palais épiscopal et lynchent l'évêque Gaudri qu'ils découvrent blotti dans un tonneau.

Violent dans le Nord, plus pacifique dans le Sud où des « consulats » apparaissent à Narbonne, à Béziers, à Nîmes et à Toulouse, ce mouvement communal, « nom nouveau et détestable », s'écrie l'abbé Guibert de Nogent au début du XIIᵉ siècle, met en place de nouvelles formes institutionnelles, diffuse de nouvelles manières de penser et ébranle l'ordre féodal.

CHAPITRE 23

L'ordre féodal

A *ux environs de l'an mille, tandis que s'amorce le temps de l'embellie, que de hardis pionniers apprennent à mieux tirer parti du sol, qu'apparaissent des centaines de villes neuves, que le goût du risque et la recherche du profit travaillent une société jusque-là immobile, les hommes d'Église inventent le modèle d'une société idéale qui connaît aussitôt un vif succès. Vers 1020, l'évêque Adalbéron de Laon explique que « la maison de Dieu que l'on croit une, est divisée en trois : les uns prient, les autres combattent, les autres, enfin, travaillent ». Cette définition de l'« ordre féodal », ce rêve d'une société harmonieuse, où chacun devait se tenir à sa place et dans laquelle la sécurité de tous serait assurée par la multiplication des serments de fidélité, allait se heurter aux âpres réalités des ambitions personnelles et des luttes sociales.*

Les trois ordres

Alors qu'une mutation économique généralisée affecte toutes les couches de la société, l'idée même de croissance demeure totalement étrangère aux conceptions d'une époque où vouloir produire plus qu'il n'est nécessaire est considéré comme un péché capital. Dans cette société hostile au désir d'ascension, chaque homme doit rester à sa place et ne pas troubler l'harmonie voulue par Dieu.

Dans le poème adressé au roi Robert le Pieux, Adalbéron a donné la définition la plus élaborée de cette société féodale dont la représentation persistera jusqu'à la réunion des trois « ordres » à Versailles en 1789. « La société des fidèles ne forme qu'un corps ; mais l'État en comprend trois. Car l'autre loi, la loi humaine, distingue deux autres classes : nobles et serfs, en effet, ne sont pas régis par le même statut [...] Ceux-ci sont les guerriers, protecteurs des églises, ils sont les défenseurs du peuple [...] L'autre classe est celle des serfs : cette malheureuse engeance ne possède rien qu'au prix de sa peine [...] Argent, vêtement, nourriture, les serfs fournissent tout à tout le monde ; pas un homme libre ne pourrait subsister sans les serfs [...] Le maître est nourri par le serf, lui qui prétend le nourrir. La maison de Dieu, que l'on croit une, est donc divisée en trois : les uns prient, les autres combattent, les autres, enfin, travaillent. Ces trois parties qui coexistent ne souffrent pas d'être disjointes ; les services rendus par l'une sont la condition des œuvres des deux autres. Ainsi, cet assemblage triple n'en est pas moins uni, et c'est ainsi que la loi a pu triompher, et le monde jouir de la paix. »

Ce texte qui soumet les paysans aux guerriers et les guerriers au clergé, les *laboratores* aux *bellatores* et les *bellatores* aux *oratores*, est capital dans la mesure où il définit aussi une société où les clivages entre exploiteurs et exploités, maîtres et serviteurs semblent correspondre à des catégories génétiques. Le sang qui coule dans les veines des *bellatores*, d'où vient leur valeur militaire et leur beauté, ne peut être celui des *laboratores* qui, à la sueur de leur front, doivent préparer la nourriture des autres. Quiconque voudrait annuler ces différences et quitter sa condition, c'est-à-dire son « ordre », commettrait le sacrilège de mettre en péril la maison de Dieu.

Une fable enseignée à la même époque par Eadmer de Canterbury est une autre illustration de cet ordre tripartite qui renvoie au mystère de la Sainte Trinité : « La raison des moutons, c'est de fournir du lait et de la laine ; celle des bœufs de travailler la terre ; celle des chiens de défendre des loups les moutons et les bœufs. Si chaque espèce de ces animaux remplit son office, Dieu les protège [...] Ainsi fait-il des ordres qu'il a établis en vue des divers offices à remplir dans ce monde. Il a établi les uns – les clercs et les moines – pour qu'ils prient pour les autres et que, pleins de douceur, comme les moutons, ils les abreuvent du lait de la prédication et leur inspirent par la laine du bon exemple un fervent amour de Dieu. Il a établi les paysans pour qu'ils fassent vivre – comme les bœufs par leur travail – et eux-mêmes et les autres. D'autres enfin – les guerriers – il les a établis pour qu'ils manifestent dans la mesure du nécessaire la force et qu'ils défendent ceux qui prient et ceux qui cultivent la terre des ennemis comme des loups. »

Ce modèle d'organisation où les tâches sont parfaitement réparties traduit aussi la réalité d'une époque où les besoins de sécurité ont amené les hommes à devenir les « hommes » d'autres hommes, une alliance de mots qui scande le vocabulaire féodal et définit un système de relations où les faibles éprouvent le besoin de se mettre sous la protection des forts.

« Voulez-vous être mon homme ? » « Je le veux. » Tout au long du Moyen Âge, ces formules rituelles ont marqué l'entrée en dépendance. Ainsi s'est édifiée une société où les serfs étaient les « hommes » de leurs seigneurs tandis que les seigneurs étaient les « hommes » des princes, eux-mêmes « hommes » du roi.

En multipliant les « dévoués » qui les avaient aidés à s'emparer du trône, en exigeant le serment de fidélité de tous les hommes libres, en espérant renforcer l'État par un réseau de subordinations dont il tiendrait les fils, les souverains ont en fait, sans s'en rendre compte, fini par faire du neuf en s'efforçant d'adapter le vieux. En voulant faire régner dans leur royaume l'ordre et la paix, ils ont multiplié des rapports de protection qui, à la suite des invasions du IXe siècle, ont cessé de s'opérer à leur profit, la fidélité à un souverain lointain étant plus lâche que la dépendance à l'égard d'un seigneur proche. Est née alors ce qu'on appelle la féodalité, c'est-à-dire un système qui repose sur l'existence de « fiefs » ou « bienfaits » concédés par des seigneurs à des vassaux en échange de services. Dans l'état d'insécurité permanente où désormais vit le royaume, les hommes cherchent des chefs qui les protègent et les nourrissent, les chefs cherchent des hommes pour sauvegarder ou accroître leur puissance. L'un promet de protéger et d'entretenir. L'autre promet d'obéir et d'aider. Vassal et seigneur, ces deux termes sont en fait issus du vocabulaire familial, vassal désignant le gars, le valet, c'est-à-dire le jeune, seigneur venant de senior, c'est-à-dire le vieux, le père qui accueille ses vassaux dans sa maison comme ses propres enfants.

Comme l'écrit Georges Duby, ce « fractionnement de l'autorité en multiples cellules autonomes » doit se comprendre comme « la parfaite adaptation des relations politiques et sociales à la réalité concrète d'une civilisation primitive et toute rurale où l'espace était immense et coupé d'innombrables obstacles, où les hommes étaient rares, séparés par des distances mal franchissables et d'une culture intellectuelle si fruste que leur conscience se montrait impuissante à percevoir les notions abstraites d'autorité : un chef ne pouvait obtenir obéissance s'il ne se montrait pas en personne et s'il ne manifestait pas physiquement sa présence ».

Alors que Rome avait établi son autorité par la ville, la route et la monnaie, dans une société devenue toute paysanne, la puissance ne pouvait s'exercer que sur un territoire restreint englobant au plus une vingtaine de paroisses.

Vers l'an mille, rites, droits et devoirs de chacun sont désormais fixés. Ils ne varieront plus guère jusqu'à la Révolution. Deux hommes sont face à face : le vassal qui veut servir ; le seigneur qui accepte d'être chef. Le premier se présente tête nue, sans armes, s'agenouille et place ses mains dans les mains du second pour déclarer sa volonté de devenir son « homme » car la dépendance du vassal, contrairement à celle de l'esclave, est librement consentie. Puis le seigneur relève le vassal et le baise parfois sur la bouche, symbole d'accord et d'amitié. Ce rite de l'hommage, sans doute d'origine germanique, était accompagné d'un serment prêté sur des livres saints ou sur une châsse contenant des reliques afin que la promesse du vassal soit sous la protection de Dieu. Le nœud ainsi formé durait, en principe, autant que les deux vies qu'il joignait et ne pouvait être rompu que par la mort de l'un ou de l'autre.

Une lettre de l'évêque Fulbert de Chartres au duc Guillaume d'Aquitaine, écrite vers 1020, nous donne une idée des engagements pris par le vassal. Bien sûr, le serment de fidélité impliquait qu'il s'abstienne de tout acte préjudiciable à la personne ou aux biens de son seigneur. Mais être vassal, c'était surtout aider militairement son seigneur, charge très lourde exigeant un équipement complet et un entraînement de tous les instants. C'était aussi former sa cour, l'aider à rendre la justice, participer financièrement aux dépenses exceptionnelles qu'étaient l'armement du fils aîné, le mariage de la fille aînée, la rançon à payer en cas de capture ou le départ pour la croisade. Aide et conseil, amour et loyauté, telles étaient les règles d'un ordre politique fondé sur des solidarités volontaires et quasi charnelles.

Mais pour que le vassal entré dans la dépendance d'un seigneur puisse accomplir son service, se nourrir, lui et sa famille, acheter et entretenir son armement, le cheval de bataille, la forte épée, la lance, le casque, la cuirasse et le bouclier, le seigneur devait se montrer généreux. C'est pourquoi, dans une société où la monnaie était rare, il lui concédait un « bienfait », un « fief », une terre offerte pour rémunérer l'aide et le conseil. Au cours de l'investiture qui suivait la cérémonie de l'hommage, il lui remettait une motte de terre, un étendard, un sceptre, une bannière ou un simple bâton qui symbolisait, devant témoins, le bien concédé. Il le « chasait », disait-on dans les pays de langue française, c'est-à-dire qu'il le dotait d'une maison (*casa*).

Certes, à l'origine, ce fief n'était pas la « propriété » du vassal, mais un droit assimilable à l'usufruit d'une nue-propriété. Certes, contre le vassal infidèle, le « félon », le seigneur pouvait confisquer le fief, reste qu'au fil du temps triompha l'hérédité, pièce essentielle de l'ordre féodal. Comment pouvait-il en être autrement dans une société où les liens du sang avaient une telle force ? Pour le fils du vassal défunt, refuser l'hommage, c'était du même coup perdre une part considérable du patrimoine paternel. Pour le seigneur, où recruter ses « hommes » mieux que parmi la postérité de ceux qui l'avaient déjà servi ? Plus grave encore, refuser à un fils le fief paternel aurait consisté à mécontenter les autres vassaux et risquer de décourager de nouvelles fidélités. Vassaux et seigneurs en viennent ainsi à constituer la caste de ceux qui combattent, menant le même genre de vie, renforçant les liens du sang par des mariages entre lignages, partageant les mêmes privilèges et exerçant les mêmes pouvoirs à l'égard des non-nobles, des « ignobles » chargés de les nourrir.

Guerriers et paysans

À l'ombre des châteaux, des églises et des gibets, guerriers et paysans, chevaliers et vilains – c'est-à-dire tout bonnement ceux qui habitent le village – vivent ainsi en mutuelle dépendance. Tandis que certains prient pour leur salut et que d'autres sont chargés en principe de les défendre, les paysans doivent livrer une partie de leur production et verser un certain nombre de taxes à ceux qui détiennent la terre et exercent dans leur seigneurie le droit de « ban », c'est-à-dire le pouvoir de justice usurpé à l'État.

On aurait tort toutefois d'imaginer la vie des « manants », mot qui vient simplement de *manere* (avoir une *mansio*, une « maison »), comme un long chemin de croix. Certes, on n'en finirait pas d'énumérer les charges dues par les *laboratores*, les corvées, les cens, les dîmes, les tailles, les amendes, les justices, les aides diverses, les banalités exigées pour l'utilisation obligatoire du moulin ou du pressoir banal, les gerbes prélevées pour nourrir les montures, ce que les manants appelaient « exaction » qui signifie simplement « levée », « prise » ou « coutume », reste qu'on a pu calculer que l'ensemble de ces prélèvements représentait peut-être un tiers de leur revenu, soit une « contribution » moins forte que celle aujourd'hui prélevée par l'État français sur le revenu national (plus de 45 %) ! L'anachronisme serait d'oublier qu'en retour de leurs contributions, les paysans recevaient des bénéfices semblables à ceux qu'on attend de l'État moderne, semblables mais peut-être plus concrets.

Enfin, la tutelle d'un seigneur qui est du village, le quitte rarement, veille à son troupeau, parcourt ses vignes et demeure d'accès facile pour des paysans dont il connaît les besoins n'a jamais été insupportable. Les corvées pour transporter le vin, curer le bief du moulin, élever une motte, entretenir les voies sont dans l'intérêt commun. De plus, ces « corvées » étaient souvent source de convivialité comme celle qui imposait aux habitants de Lorris-en-Gâtinais de transporter dans leurs charrettes, une fois l'an, le vin du roi à Orléans. Bonne occasion pour eux d'un joyeux déplacement à la ville voisine. D'ailleurs, on ne voit pas que les paysans aient contesté le principe de ces « contributions » tant que le seigneur faisait son « métier » qui était de juger et de défendre. Quant aux banalités, elles ne constituaient en aucune façon une charge humiliante. Moudre sa farine au moulin banal, cuire son pain au four banal, porter le fruit de sa vigne au pressoir banal étaient une nécessité en contrepartie de laquelle il était légitime que le seigneur exige une redevance.

Ce qu'ils n'aimaient pas, en revanche, c'était la dîme, car ils pensaient, non sans raison, que l'Église était bien assez riche pour pouvoir se passer de cet impôt qui, pesant sur le blé comme le vin, la laine comme le sel, les agneaux comme les œufs, n'était guère marchandable. À cet égard, même si l'Église a proclamé qu'on vivait mieux dans les seigneuries ecclésiastiques, dans la dépendance de l'évêque ou de l'abbé, rien n'est moins sûr. Moins brutaux mais meilleurs comptables, les hommes d'Église ont su, comme le prouve l'excellente tenue de leurs comptes et de leurs registres, exiger tout leur dû.

Certes, on trouvait dans les villages de nombreux serfs, c'est-à-dire des paysans non libres que le seigneur pouvait poursuivre et ramener de force s'il leur arrivait de s'enfuir et qui devaient s'acquitter de certaines taxes symbolisant leur soumission, le chevage, le droit de formariage s'ils épousaient un conjoint étranger à la seigneurie et celui de mainmorte payé par leurs héritiers ; mais ces serfs n'ont représenté qu'une minorité amenuisée au fur et à mesure que les défrichements amenaient de nombreux seigneurs à promettre la liberté à ceux qui devenaient leurs hôtes. Même si les maîtres éprouvaient du mépris pour ceux que les sources littéraires dépeignaient comme des « brutes noires comme du charbon », ils n'étaient pas assez stupides pour décourager le travail de ceux qui assuraient leur nourriture et l'essentiel de leur revenu ! Les paysans avaient besoin du château comme le château avait besoin des paysans.

En fait aussi, et de manière pragmatique, les paysans ont su faire jouer les solidarités villageoises pour résister au château et défendre les « bonnes » coutumes contre les « mauvaises », c'est-à-dire les nouvelles que les maîtres s'acharnaient à vouloir lever. Eux récitaient périodiquement devant le prévôt la liste de leurs devoirs et de leurs droits, oubliant les premiers pour rappeler les seconds, et la « coutume » qui se trouvait en dépôt dans leur mémoire s'imposait aux maîtres, si puissants soient-ils. « Franchises », « libertés », « communes », tels sont les mots qui scandent aussi le vocabulaire féodal, des mots qui montrent que, forts de leur nombre, les paysans n'ont jamais été « taillables et corvéables à merci ».

Et si les châteaux que l'on croit toujours « forts » hérissent tant d'éperons et ornent tant de campagnes, c'est que le premier devoir du seigneur est de protéger et qu'il faut donc donner quelque allure à son logis. Car ces châteaux qui se sont multipliés à partir du milieu du XIe siècle sont d'abord destinés à sauvegarder ceux dont les corvées ont assuré l'édification. À tel point que, lorsqu'ils accordent des chartes de franchise ou créent des villes neuves, seigneurs ou abbés promettent expressément de faire élever un château, s'il n'existe pas, ou de bien entretenir celui qui existe. Un texte du XVe siècle, écrit à une époque où la guerre franco-anglaise faisait régner l'insécurité dans les campagnes, en est une tardive mais probable illustration : « Tout ce qu'on pouvait cultiver dans ce temps-là en ces parages, c'était seulement autour et à l'intérieur des places ou châteaux assez près pour que, du haut de la tour ou de l'échauguette, l'œil du guetteur pût apercevoir les brigands en train de courir sus. Alors, à son de cloche ou de trompe ou de tout autre instrument, ils donnaient à tous ceux qui travaillaient aux champs ou aux vignes le signal de se replier sur le point fortifié. C'était la chose commune et fréquente presque partout : à ce point que les bœufs et les chevaux de labour, une fois détachés de la charrue, quand ils entendaient le signal du guetteur, aussitôt et sans guides, instruits par une longue habitude, regagnaient au galop, affolés, le refuge où ils se sentaient en sûreté. Brebis et porcs avaient pris la même habitude. »

Si le maître du château protège sa demeure qu'on appelle ordinairement tour, plus rarement donjon, par un fossé, une palissade et une motte artificielle faite de terre et de caillasse, il doit aussi clore l'enceinte, la basse-cour ou *baile*, où se réfugieront les villageois et leur troupeau et où logeront les guerriers à sa solde.

Cœur et âme du château, le donjon, qui domine toutes les constructions voisines et peut atteindre, comme à Loches, 40 mètres de hauteur, est essentiellement conçu pour servir d'habitation au seigneur, à sa famille et aux jeunes vassaux qu'il héberge. Au centre, la salle « à tout faire » où le maître rend la justice, reçoit ses dépendants, regarde les jongleurs, mange sur la table « dressée » sur des tréteaux, devise et même dort avec ses hommes. Le mobilier est composé de bancs, couverts de tissu ou de tapisserie, de sièges pliants, de bancs mobiles à dossier ou sans dossier appelés « dois », de coffres, parfois d'armoires ou de bahuts aménagés dans l'épaisseur du mur.

Le sol est jonché de joncs, de fleurs, d'herbes odorantes pour chasser les odeurs fortes exhalées par les mets. Les murs sont tendus de drap, de tapisseries représentant les épisodes les plus célèbres des légendes du temps, parfois recouverts de fourrures ou enduits et peints de scènes de chasse et de guerre. On y distingue des arbres généalogiques qui rappellent les origines et les armes du seigneur et les lignages sur la loyauté desquels il peut compter, les « amis charnels », précise-t-on parfois dans les textes, tant les liens du sang semblent primer sur tous les autres.

À côté de cette salle, la chambre du maître est occupée sur tout un côté par une immense cheminée souvent placée entre deux baies et peinte comme le reste de la chambre en tons assez vifs où l'ocre et le jaune dominent. C'est là qu'on se réunit après le souper, groupés autour du feu, un fauteuil étant réservé pour le seigneur dont les pieds reposent sur un escabeau qu'un mouvement de colère peut projeter au bout de la pièce. Le lit où se reproduit le lignage est large et majestueux, entouré de courtines suspendues à des traverses qui dissimulent entièrement les dormeurs. Au-dessus, les dortoirs de la famille du maître, clos pour les filles, ouverts pour les garçons.

Principaux bénéficiaires de la croissance économique, les seigneurs en sont aussi le principal moteur, la dépense aristocratique excitant le travail du textile, l'industrie du fer et le bâtiment. Mourant, Guillaume le Maréchal, un chevalier dont Georges Duby nous a livré une biographie exemplaire, lance à ceux qui lui conseillent de vendre sa précieuse garde-robe et d'en faire don aux communautés religieuses pour acheter sa rédemption : « Taisez-vous, mauvais. J'en ai par-dessus la tête de tels conseils. C'est bientôt la Pentecôte, la saison où les chevaliers de ma maison doivent recevoir leurs nouveaux atours. Je le sais bien, jamais plus je ne pourrai les leur distribuer. Et c'est maintenant que vous venez m'entortiller. Approchez, Jean d'Early [son vieil ami]. Par cette foi que vous devez à Dieu et à moi, je vous mande de faire pour moi le partage de toutes ces robes. Et s'il n'y en a pas assez pour tout le monde, envoyez encore à Londres acheter ce qui manque. Que nul de mes gens n'ait à se plaindre de moi. » Être noble, en effet, c'est avoir table ouverte et bien garnie, organiser des fêtes brillantes et somptueuses, se distinguer par le costume et le bijou, se vêtir de fines étoffes et rechercher de fiers destriers. Exercer le pouvoir, c'est prélever mais aussi redistribuer. Et surtout combattre. Pour ces hommes turbulents et brutaux, la guerre est en effet un véritable sport qui dicte leur comportement, peuple leurs rêves et fonde leur morale. « C'est joyeuse chose que la guerre », nous disent les chroniques, c'est l'activité par excellence des chevaliers, l'occasion de montrer leur vaillance, de souder les alliances, de ramasser du butin. Aussi est-ce avec impatience qu'est attendu le printemps, la saison où commencent les opérations, celle où les mâles saisissent le moindre prétexte, prêts à rejoindre au loin tel prince dont on raconte qu'il prépare une expédition tentante.

Vengeances privées, luttes contre des villes pour écraser des « conspirations », luttes entre seigneurs pour grappiller de nouveaux territoires, toutes les occasions sont bonnes pour ceux que les textes appellent « milites » (chevaliers) de venir en « stage » – c'est le mot de l'époque –, à l'intérieur d'un château, y loger pour un temps, bénéficier des largesses du maître, nourrir les camaraderies, bien boire, entreprendre les pucelles, exciter le « vieux », le senior, à combattre, un « vieux » pour qui la présence de ces « petits gars » était symbole de force et de gloire.

Chasse, tournois et exercices militaires étaient les principales distractions de ces « chevaliers ». On chasse tous les jours quand il fait beau, pour le plaisir mais aussi pour protéger les vilains des bêtes fauves et sauver les récoltes. La plus belle et la plus captivante est la chasse au faucon ou au gerfaut, un art difficile accessible aux femmes. Point de château sans fauconnerie, point de château non plus sans chenil, les lévriers étant symboles de constance et de fidélité.

Mais c'étaient les tournois qui figuraient à la première place des plaisirs du seigneur. Il suffisait que se répande l'« esclandre », c'est-à-dire le bruit qu'un tournoi se prépare, pour qu'en deux semaines, de Flandre et de Bourgogne, de Normandie et de Bretagne, de Touraine et d'Anjou, accourent les champions, principalement les « bacheliers », c'est-à-dire les chevaliers sans fief courant le cachet ou venant là, comme à la guerre, pour ravir des armes, des harnais ou des destriers. Un plaisir qui était aussi dépense et procurait du travail aux selliers et maréchaux-ferrants qui soignaient les chevaux, aux fournisseurs d'armes, aux menuisiers qui préparaient les lices, aux charpentiers, aux maçons, aux peintres qui décoraient d'armoiries les écus, aux boulangers, aux bouchers et aux paysans qui fournissaient les victuailles pour les assistants, aux couturières, aux fourreurs et aux lingères qui travaillaient pour que les dames puissent exhiber leurs plus beaux atours. Il fallait qu'un chevalier ait vu son sang couler, pensait-on à l'époque, que ses dents aient craqué sous les coups de poing, que, jeté à terre, il y ait senti le poids du corps de son adversaire et, vingt fois désarçonné, que vingt fois il se soit relevé de sa chute, plus ardent que jamais au combat, pour devenir un vrai guerrier.

Dans cet univers de mâles, l'adoubement était, pour les garçons, le plus important des rites sociaux qui se déroulait lorsqu'on avait atteint l'âge de dix-huit ou vingt ans, un jour dont chaque chevalier se souvenait comme du plus beau de son existence. Au postulant, un chevalier plus ancien remettait d'abord les armes de son futur état, notamment l'épée. Puis, du plat de la main, ce « parrain » assenait un grand coup sur la nuque ou la joue du « petit gars », la seule gifle, observe un chroniqueur qu'un chevalier devait jamais recevoir sans la rendre. Enfin, le nouveau chevalier s'élançait à cheval et allait, d'un coup de lance, transpercer ou abattre une panoplie fixée à un pieu, la « quintaine ». Un rituel laïque qui, par ses origines et sa nature, se rattache aux cérémonies d'initiation qui, dans les sociétés antiques, avaient pour objet de faire passer le jeune garçon au rang de membre parfait du groupe dont, jusque-là, son âge l'avait exclu.

La paix de Dieu

« Non militia, sed malitia. » Cette formule, qu'on pourrait traduire par « chevalerie égale méchanceté », traduit le mépris de l'Église pour ces hommes de proie dont elle a cherché à vaincre la superbe. Aux approches de l'an mille, des conciles décident de lancer le mouvement de la paix de Dieu pour contenir la brutalité émanant des châteaux. Alors qu'aux premiers temps de l'âge féodal, on se disait le chevalier de quelqu'un parce qu'on tenait de lui un fief, il faudra désormais une sorte de « consécration » pour mériter ce nom et faire partie du deuxième « ordre » établi par Dieu.

Dès avant 1100, on ne « fait » plus seulement un chevalier, on l'« ordonne ». Bientôt, la cérémonie de l'adoubement comporte la bénédiction de l'épée puis celle du futur chevalier lui-même. Enfin, avant qu'il ne reprenne son épée sur l'autel, un serment lui est demandé qui précise ses obligations. « Je n'assaillirai pas l'église, ni son enclos, ni les dépôts qu'il abrite, ni les clercs, ni les moines, ni leur escorte, s'ils ne sont pas armés », doit jurer après 1020 le chevalier.

Avec le glaive que nul ne songe à lui interdire de tirer, il doit protéger la veuve, le pauvre et l'orphelin, punir les méchants et poursuivre les malfaiteurs. Il doit jurer de ne pas brûler les maisons, de ne pas saisir le bétail, le paysan ou la paysanne pour en tirer rançon, de ne pas couper les vignes, de ne pas vider les moulins, de ne pas s'emparer dans les pâturages, entre le carême et la Toussaint, des mulets, des chevaux, des juments et des poulains. Sous peine d'excommunication, il ne peut, du mercredi soir à l'aube du lundi suivant, « oser prendre par la force quoi que ce fût à quiconque ».

« Seigneur très saint, Père tout-puissant... toi qui as permis, sur terre, l'emploi du glaive pour réprimer la malice des méchants et défendre la justice ; qui, pour la protection du peuple, as voulu instituer l'ordre de chevalerie... fais, en disposant son cœur au bien, que ton serviteur que voici n'use jamais de ce glaive ou d'un autre pour léser injustement personne ; mais qu'il s'en serve toujours pour défendre le Juste et le Droit ». Telle était la prière qui, en assignant à la chevalerie une tâche idéale, légitimait un « ordre » habilité en même temps à « tirer son bien-être » des choses que lui procuraient « la fatigue et la peine » de ses hommes.

CHAPITRE 24

La foi conquérante

*D*ans une société brutale où pillages, homicides et guerres privées sont devenus l'activité principale des féodaux, l'Église s'est efforcée de faire respecter la paix, de multiplier l'usage des serments et de menacer les parjures des pires châtiments. Mais, en même temps, l'Église a offert des rêves et proposé une raison d'espérer à tous ceux qui étaient écrasés par la dureté des temps. En faisant l'apologie de la pauvreté, en aidant les pèlerins à trouver leur chemin, en apaisant les inquiétudes des pécheurs, « ceux qui prient » ont permis aux hommes de mériter leur salut. Si les tympans, comme celui de Moissac, qui représentent le Jugement dernier, sculptent les mains du diable prenant possession des damnés, ils montrent aussi qu'il y a davantage de monde au ciel qu'en enfer.

Le monastère, cité de Dieu

« Je viens d'être ordonné évêque par mon archevêque ; j'ai donné cent sous pour qu'il me conférât l'épiscopat. » Cette plainte d'un clerc traduit assez l'emprise de la féodalité sur des hommes d'Église qui en sont venus à considérer leur charge comme des « bienfaits » et la crosse et l'anneau comme les insignes de leur « fief ». Recrutés presque totalement dans le monde des seigneurs, cadets de bonne famille, amis auxquels on a voulu rendre service, filles que l'on n'a pas pu marier, évêques, abbés et chanoinesses pouvaient difficilement prétendre incarner le plus noble des ordres. Souillé par le sexe et l'argent, vendant les sacrements, extorquant les dons, vivant dans des palais, versant le sang à la guerre, entouré d'épouses ou de concubines, festoyant et ripaillant sans cesse, à Noël, à Pâques et à la Pentecôte, mais aussi à la Saint-Jean-Baptiste, à la Saint-Pierre et la Saint-Martin, le monde des clercs était largement pénétré, dans son corps comme dans son esprit, par la société féodale dont il était issu. À la fin de l'époque carolingienne, on a pu calculer que les rations alimentaires par jour de fête, dont le nombre a pu grimper jusqu'à 156 par an, oscillaient entre 5 000 et 9 000 calories. Au Mans, par exemple, chaque convive disposait de 1,660 kg de pain, d'une ration de viande dépassant un kilo et d'un morceau de fromage de plus de 250 grammes !

Raoul Glaber, toujours lui, dénonçait cet amour des richesses qui rendait imminents des temps périlleux pour les âmes. « Cette peste, écrivait-il, a sévi en long et en large parmi tous les prélats des églises disséminées par le monde. Le don gratuit et vénérable du Christ seigneur tout-puissant, ils l'ont converti, comme pour rendre plus sûre leur propre damnation, en un trafic de cupidité. De tels prélats paraissent d'autant moins capables d'accomplir l'œuvre divine qu'on sait bien qu'ils n'ont point accédé à leurs fonctions en passant par la porte principale... Même les rois, qui devraient être les juges de la capacité des candidats aux emplois sacrés, corrompus par les présents qui leur sont prodigués, préfèrent, pour gouverner les églises et les âmes, celui dont ils espèrent recevoir les plus riches cadeaux. » De l'église aux reliques, en effet, tout se vend. On verra même, en 1053, le roi de France mettre aux enchères publiques l'évêché du Puy. On s'endette pour acheter un évêché. On se rembourse en vendant le baptême. Quant aux paroisses rurales, elles sont devenues de véritables fiefs dont les titulaires doivent prêter serment de fidélité aux grands propriétaires qui les ont désignés.

Comment l'homme de l'an mille aurait-il pu mettre sa confiance dans ce clergé dont l'abaissement était le symptôme le plus manifeste des troubles qui ébranlaient la chrétienté ?

Dans un monde où, pour apaiser la colère de Dieu, on avait le sentiment qu'il fallait renoncer aux quatre convoitises par lesquelles Satan tenait ses esclaves prisonniers, la viande, la guerre, l'or et la femme, l'aspiration au renouveau ne pouvait venir que de ceux qui sauraient renoncer aux richesses, déposer les armes, vivre dans la chasteté et jeûner, c'est-à-dire les moines. Les monastères allaient ainsi devenir, à côté et en face des châteaux, des lieux d'asile et d'espoir, des forteresses dont les défenses sauraient repousser les armées du Diable. Établis à la campagne, mieux adaptés aux exigences et aux structures d'une société essentiellement rurale, abritant des reliques nanties de pouvoirs formidables, élevés sur le tombeau de martyrs qui étaient autant de héros des luttes contre le mal, ils allaient devenir les intermédiaires obligés capables de capter le pardon divin et de racheter une communauté de fidèles qui se considéraient comme trop ignares pour se sauver eux-mêmes. « Dans les villages, les châteaux, les villes et les forteresses, et même dans les champs et les bois, on vit s'activer de véritables essaims de moines », se rappelle vers 1115 l'abbé Guibert de Nogent, « en sorte que des tanières de fauves, des repaires de brigands se changèrent en lieux saints. »

La fondation, en 910, de l'abbaye de Cluny par Guillaume le Pieux, duc d'Aquitaine, inaugure le renouveau de l'institution monastique. D'après la charte de fondation établie par un prince qui avait voulu paradoxalement soustraire le monastère à toute ingérence laïque, l'abbé de Cluny, élu par les moines, ne dépendait que du pape. L'exemple deviendrait vite un modèle. À une société dominée par des seigneurs aux mœurs brutales, les abbayes réformées opposaient l'image d'une société de seigneurs vivant dans la prière et l'obéissance. À la fin du XIe siècle, le premier ordre monastique de l'histoire de l'Occident regroupait, sous la direction de l'abbé de Cluny, plus de 1 100 établissements dont 800 en France, à l'intérieur desquels des moines accumulaient « sans interruption depuis la première heure du jour jusqu'à l'heure du repos » prières liturgiques, oraisons et chants dont la qualité préfigurait les fastes de la vie éternelle. Cluny ne cherchait pas à démontrer la foi. Il visait à communiquer avec l'invisible par la psalmodie. Les dimensions de la somptueuse église de la maison mère, dont le pape vint en 1095 consacrer le chœur, excédaient celles des basiliques élevées sur le tombeau de saint Pierre et de saint Paul à Rome, et sa nef s'étirait comme un long chemin conduisant au séjour des anges. Les « tons » de la musique, représentés sur les chapiteaux du chœur, fournissaient la clef de l'harmonie universelle. Une chronique de l'époque décrit cette basilique comme « si grande et si belle qu'il est difficile de juger si c'est par sa taille qu'elle suscite autant d'admiration ou si elle est plus admirable encore par son art. Elle est d'une beauté et d'une splendeur telles que l'on peut dire qu'elle est le promenoir des anges ».

Une nouvelle milice chrétienne aux ordres de Rome était née, prête à satisfaire le besoin de renouveau et capable d'intervenir dans le monde pour exercer son influence. Cette réussite a tenu à la qualité exceptionnelle des cinq abbés qui, pendant deux siècles, ont assumé successivement la direction de l'ordre et à la parfaite adaptation d'une institution religieuse aux fonctions qu'un monde tourmenté attendait d'elle. « Sache, écrivait Raoul Glaber, que ce couvent n'a pas son pareil [...] pour délivrer les âmes qui sont tombées sous la seigneurie du démon. On y consomme si fréquemment le sacrifice vivifiant qu'il ne se passe presque pas de jour sans que cette incessante relation permette d'arracher quelque âme au pouvoir des démons malins. » Ce furent les abbés cluniens qui affirmèrent que l'âme en peine pouvait se libérer plus tôt des tourments de l'enfer si on ordonnait à son intention des prières et inventèrent la commémoration de tous les défunts le 2 novembre. Ce fut enfin Cluny qui défricha le terrain pour Rome et permit au pape Grégoire VII (1073-1085) d'interdire aux évêques de recevoir leurs charges des mains d'un laïc, de contraindre les prêtres au célibat et d'affirmer qu'il était au-dessus de tous les princes qu'il pouvait déposer s'ils ne respectaient pas les droits de Dieu et de l'Église. Excommunié pour bigamie et inceste, mais surtout pour avoir pratiqué la simonie, le roi de France Philippe Ier, « dont l'adultère, disaient les agents du pape, souillait le royaume de France », fut une des victimes de la réforme grégorienne.

« Rome est à la tête du monde », proclama en 1139 le deuxième concile du Latran. Rénovée, l'Église était juchée en position dominante dans la hiérarchie des pouvoirs terrestres.

Intervenir dans les affaires du monde risquait toutefois de faire perdre de vue l'idéal monastique. Chanter si longtemps la gloire de Dieu nécessitait l'abandon du travail manuel. Forts de toutes les richesses que des domaines bien gérés produisaient chaque jour en plus grande abondance et des dons que la dévotion des fidèles faisaient affluer sur l'abbaye, les monastères cluniens s'appliquèrent à posséder des églises somptueuses, à recouvrir les autels d'orfèvrerie, à adapter les décors aux fastes quotidiens de la liturgie.

Aussi voit-on bientôt partout des hommes chercher d'autres voies et d'autres formes de spiritualité. Préférant la pauvreté à la croissance, l'égalité aux hiérarchies de l'ordre féodal, le retrait du monde à l'engagement dans le siècle, ils souhaitent revenir à la vocation primitive du monachisme qui est austérité, pauvreté, silence et méditation. En 1084, Bruno s'établit au cœur des Alpes pour jeter dans un « désert » les fondements de la Grande-Chartreuse. En 1101, Robert d'Arbrissel réunit à Fontevrault, en Anjou, des pécheresses repenties. En 1098, Robert de Molesme s'établit avec quelques moines à Cîteaux, en Bourgogne, pour vivre intégralement la règle de saint Benoît qu'il accuse Cluny d'avoir défigurée. Dans le vêtement grossier de laine écrue, dans la nourriture réduite au minimum, dans la nudité des églises dépouillées de toute ornementation, dans le travail manuel, ils affirment une religion d'amour dépouillée des monstres et des chimères et se défient de l'intelligence qui veut tout expliquer. Dans cette nouvelle spiritualité, le culte de la Vierge devient l'un des piliers du christianisme occidental.

Sous l'influence de saint Bernard, entré à Cîteaux en 1112 avant de fonder l'abbaye de Clairvaux en 1115, les moines blancs connaissent un succès fulgurant. Bientôt, l'ordre regroupe plus de 500 maisons réparties de l'Espagne à l'Irlande et à la Pologne. Bientôt aussi, ils supplantent les moines noirs de Cluny auprès des rois et des princes qui les écoutent et leur font des dons. Bientôt enfin, leurs granges mises en valeur par des frères « convers », fils de paysans, produisent en quantité la laine et le cuir, les fromages et la viande que réclame une population urbaine en forte croissance. Une trajectoire qui souligne la situation paradoxale des moines en ces temps féodaux. Leur rayonnement spirituel leur vaut la fortune qui affaiblit à la fin leur vocation première.

La passion de bâtir

Manifestant le renouveau de la foi et l'éclosion d'une nouvelle spiritualité, les progrès du savoir alliés à la passion de bâtir conduisent à donner aux édifices religieux une harmonie et un éclat qui proclament la puissance de Dieu et livrent aux manants un commentaire imagé des grandes vérités de la foi. Jumièges, Cluny, Saint-Sernin, Tournus, Vézelay, autant de noms qui traduisent l'apogée d'un art qui marie les connaissances empiriques des hommes de métier, les carriers, les tailleurs de pierre et les maçons, et la vision d'ensemble d'un prélat constructeur qui impose ses préférences esthétiques.

Art roman, ce mot forgé au XIXᵉ siècle rappelle les traditions romaines avec lesquelles renouent les créateurs des XIᵉ et XIIᵉ siècles. Puisant dans le folklore européen et en Orient la vision de ces animaux étranges qui envahissent la statuaire, empruntant à l'Antiquité le mur romain, les colonnes supportant des entablements, les frontons triangulaires, à Byzance la construction des coupoles, l'art roman n'en est pas moins une création originale dont les variantes sont inspirées par les influences locales. La sécheresse des édifices normands s'oppose à l'exubérance des églises bourguignonnes ou languedociennes.

À partir des années 1050, tandis que la voûte amorce une conquête décisive et que les proportions des édifices se développent, les images d'un Dieu-juge, la représentation des travaux et des jours, la laideur grotesque des péchés capitaux et des monstres s'étalent sur les façades et les chapiteaux, développant une pédagogie par l'image à destination du peuple qui distingue fort bien l'Enfer et le Paradis des Jugements derniers qui ornent les tympans sculptés.

Puis, à partir de 1140, au moment où s'achève la construction de la basilique de Vézelay et où est consacré à Saint-Denis le chœur construit par Suger, s'affirme un nouveau style qui marque le triomphe de la lumière et traduit un élan irrésistible vers le ciel qui commande toute l'ordonnance intérieure. Ce « gothique » naissant se présente comme un compromis entre l'art de Cîteaux et les conceptions esthétiques de l'abbé de Saint-Denis. Tandis que saint Bernard ne peut concevoir que la maison de Dieu exhibe avec ostentation des richesses qui ne sont que les fruits de la vanité humaine et estime que les somptueuses décorations détournent sur elles l'attention des fidèles et diminuent leur recueillement, Suger écrit : « Ceux qui nous critiquent objectent que pour la célébration [de l'Eucharistie] doivent suffire une âme sainte, un esprit pur, une intention fidèle et, nous l'admettons, c'est cela qui importe avant tout. Mais nous affirmons aussi que l'on doit servir Dieu par des ornements extérieurs, en toute pureté intérieure, mais aussi avec magnificence. »

Alors que les figures terrifiantes sont reléguées à l'arrière-plan, la mère du Seigneur qui, dans l'art roman, n'était souvent qu'une idole lointaine, trônant dans une posture hiératique, devient la Vierge Mère faisant fuir les démons et les songes impurs. Au moment où le culte de la Vierge, environnée d'une escorte de saintes, s'introduit dans la piété du XIIe siècle, dans les cours chevaleresques des pays de Loire et du Poitou, les chevaliers commencent à exalter les femmes dont tous les jeunes s'essayent à gagner le cœur. La France de ce temps découvre l'amour courtois en même temps que l'amour de Marie.

Les marcheurs de Dieu

« Dieu le veut ! »... C'est par ce cri que, le 27 novembre 1095, les chevaliers répondent avec enthousiasme à l'appel que lance le pape Urbain II. Au dixième jour du concile de Clermont réuni pour affirmer solennellement la paix de Dieu, le pape, issu d'une famille de chevaliers champenois, ancien grand prieur de Cluny, s'adresse aux gens de guerre présents, leur demande de ne plus se livrer bataille et de retourner leurs armes contre les ennemis de Dieu qui se sont emparés de la ville sacrée de Jérusalem. « Qu'ils aillent donc au combat contre les infidèles, ceux-là qui jusqu'ici s'adonnaient à des guerres privées et abusives au grand dam des fidèles, lance le pontife. Qu'ils soient désormais les chevaliers du Christ, ceux-là qui n'étaient que des brigands ! Qu'ils luttent maintenant, à bon droit, contre les barbares, ceux-là qui se battaient contre leurs frères et leurs parents ! Ce sont les récompenses éternelles qu'ils vont gagner, ceux qui se faisaient mercenaires pour quelques misérables sous. Ils travailleront pour un double honneur, ceux-là qui se fatiguaient au détriment de leur corps et de leur âme. Ils étaient ici tristes et pauvres : ils seront là-bas joyeux et riches. Ici, ils étaient les ennemis du Seigneur ; là-bas, ils seront ses amis. »

Cet appel à la guerre sainte offrait un exutoire à la violence mal contenue des chevaliers. Pour émouvoir un auditoire de jeunes guerriers turbulents, rien de mieux que de les enrôler dans une milice sacrée et de brandir la croix comme un étendard. Quand les fresques romanes montrent des christs farouches tenant entre leurs dents serrées le glaive de la justice et de la victoire, quand le Royaume de Dieu est représenté comme une citadelle assiégée par les puissances malignes, quand saint Michel et le Démon s'affrontent, comme les champions d'une joute chevaleresque, se faire les fidèles vassaux d'un Dieu vengeur pour délivrer le tombeau de Jésus était un exaltant défi.

Si la croisade répond aux attentes d'une chevalerie qui aspire au salut sans vouloir renoncer à son mode de vie guerrier, elle prolonge aussi le pèlerinage qui était aussi une promesse de salut offerte à ceux que tracassait le poids de leurs péchés. Sortir du groupe familial, s'en aller pour des mois, affronter l'insécurité mais aussi le plaisir du voyage, prendre le chemin du Saint-Sépulcre pour mériter la Jérusalem céleste était une forme d'ascèse qui connut une vogue considérable peu avant l'an mille, l'Église imposant souvent le pèlerinage en pénitence pour des crimes graves. Tous les chrétiens qui cherchaient, par le pèlerinage, à s'assurer de la clémence divine rêvaient de prier un jour devant trois tombeaux, celui de saint Pierre à Rome, celui de saint Jacques à Compostelle et surtout celui du Christ à Jérusalem. « En l'année 1033, écrit Raoul Glaber, une foule innombrable se mit à converger du monde entier vers le sépulcre du Sauveur. Ce furent d'abord les gens des classes inférieures, puis ceux du moyen peuple, puis tous les plus grands, rois, comtes, marquis, prélats ; enfin, ce qui ne s'était jamais vu, beaucoup de femmes, les plus nobles avec les plus pauvres, se rendirent là-bas. La plupart avaient le désir d'y mourir. » On comprend mieux l'émotion des chevaliers lorsque le pape leur annonça – ce qui était faux ou du moins très exagéré – que, par la faute des Turcs musulmans, le pèlerinage au Saint-Sépulcre était désormais impossible.

En appelant les chevaliers à devenir des « soldats du Christ », en proposant un pèlerinage en armes, en promettant l'indulgence totale de leurs péchés à tous ceux qui partiraient en croisade, en demandant aux croisés de risquer leur vie pour celui qui avait accepté de mourir pour racheter leurs fautes, Urbain II offrait une nouvelle perspective de salut en même temps qu'il définissait les conditions d'une guerre « juste ».

Traduisant à merveille les tensions et les aspirations du temps, l'appel de Clermont eut un retentissement considérable. Avant même que s'ébranle du Puy, le 15 août 1096, la croisade des princes qui ont cousu la croix sur leur vêtement, des milliers de pèlerins, entraînés par des ermites plus ou moins « inspirés », après avoir, tout au long de leur chemin, massacré les juifs qui refusaient de se convertir, ont été exterminés par les Turcs près de Nicée. Mais, le vendredi 15 juillet 1099, à l'heure même, disait-on, où le Christ était mort sur la croix, Jérusalem était prise et ses habitants massacrés par les chevaliers conduits par Raymond de Saint-Gilles, comte de Toulouse, Tancrède de Hauteville et Godefroy de Bouillon qui refusa le titre de roi pour celui d'« avoué (c'est-à-dire protecteur) du Saint-Sépulcre ». Après avoir accompli leur sanglant pèlerinage, les croisés s'en retournèrent, laissant derrière eux, à Antioche, Édesse, Tripoli et Jérusalem des États francs d'Orient bien isolés.

Quand, en 1146, à Vézelay, saint Bernard prêcha une seconde croisade pour soutenir ces chrétiens menacés par la poussée musulmane, on évalue à près de 200 000 personnes le nombre de ceux qui partirent, toujours dans l'espoir d'obtenir la rémission pleine et entière de leurs péchés. Saint Bernard décrivit ainsi l'effet de sa prédication : « J'ai ouvert la bouche, j'ai parlé et aussitôt les croisés se sont multipliés à l'infini. Les villages et les bourgs sont déserts. Vous trouverez difficilement un homme entre sept femmes. On ne voit partout que des veuves dont les maris sont encore vivants. »

Un témoignage emphatique de la formidable vitalité qui animait alors les hommes de France.

Philippe Auguste, le roi chanceux

*L*e 18 septembre 1180, un garçon de quinze ans mal peigné inaugurait
l'un des règnes les plus longs de l'histoire de France. En quarante-
trois ans, de 1180 à 1223, Philippe II, qui reçut de son vivant l'épithète
d'« Auguste », allait quadrupler l'étendue du domaine royal, briser la
résistance des grands féodaux, créer les rouages d'une administration
« moderne », imposer l'empreinte de son sceau, faire de Paris la capitale
du royaume et remporter, en 1214 à Bouvines, une victoire éclatante dont
le retentissement populaire fut considérable. Roi chanceux, fortunatissi-
mus, disait-on de son temps même, il a su saisir toutes les occasions pour
assurer à la dynastie capétienne la suprématie sur l'Europe occidentale
et se poser en successeur de Charlemagne.

Un jeune homme volontaire et impulsif

Quel type d'homme était Philippe Auguste ? C'est chose difficile
que de percer l'intimité de ce roi dont le règne fut pourtant un « moment » décisif de l'histoire de la France. Payen Gastinel, un chanoine
tourangeau, qui semble l'avoir bien connu, en a brossé rapidement le
portrait : « Beau et bien bâti, écrit-il, il était chauve ; d'un visage
respirant la joie de vivre, le teint rubicond, il aimait le vin et la bonne
chère et il était porté sur les femmes. Généreux envers ses amis, il
convoitait les biens de ses adversaires et il était très expert dans l'art

de l'intrigue. Religieux, de sage conseil, il se tenait rapidement à ce qu'il avait dit, et portait des jugements rapides et très droits. Favorisé par la victoire, il craignait pour sa vie et s'emportait aussi facilement qu'il se calmait. Il réprimait la malignité des grands du royaume et provoquait leurs discordes, mais il ne mit jamais à mort nul qui fut en prison. Recourant au conseil des humbles, il n'éprouvait de haine pour personne sinon un court moment et se montra le dompteur des superbes, le défenseur de l'Église et le nourrisseur des pauvres. »

Ce panégyrique doit être nuancé par un jugement plus critique porté par Gille de Paris, le précepteur de son fils Louis VIII : « Oui, sans doute, personne, à moins d'être un méchant et un ennemi, ne peut nier que, pour notre temps, Philippe ne soit un bon prince. Il est certain que, sous sa domination, le royaume s'est fortifié et que la puissance royale a fait de grands progrès. Seulement, s'il avait puisé à la source de la mansuétude divine un peu plus de modération, s'il s'était formé à la douceur paternelle, s'il était aussi abordable, aussi patient qu'il se montre intolérant et emporté, s'il était aussi calme qu'actif, aussi prudent et circonspect qu'empressé à satisfaire ses convoitises, le royaume n'en serait qu'en meilleur état. »

Rapidité de jugement mais nervosité extrême, justesse de raisonnement mais goût de l'intrigue, bravoure mais paralysie au moment de prendre les décisions les plus graves, pieux mais sans scrupule, tels seraient les vertus et les vices d'un roi dont les cheveux ébouriffés et hérissés lui avaient valu dans sa jeunesse le surnom de malpeigné. Conviction profonde de sa mission, volonté d'affermir la foi chrétienne et de travailler pour le bien de son peuple, tels seraient aussi les traits dominants d'un fils unique qui savait, dès sa naissance, que l'avenir de la dynastie reposait sur lui. Dans une lettre, Thomas Becket rapporte une anecdote que, manifestement, il n'a pu inventer. En 1169, lors d'une rencontre entre Louis VII et Henri II Plantagenêt, Philippe, âgé de cinq ans, aurait interpellé le roi d'Angleterre pour l'adjurer d'aimer son père, la France et lui-même s'il voulait obtenir la grâce de Dieu.

Avant même son avènement, Philippe démontre qu'il n'est pas de caractère à se laisser dominer par les clans qui espèrent le manœuvrer. Pour secouer la tutelle étouffante de sa mère Adèle et de ses oncles de Champagne, il épouse en avril 1180 Isabelle de Hainaut, la nièce du puissant comte de Flandre qui lui apporte en dot la région qui prendra plus tard le nom d'Artois et comprend les riches villes d'Arras, de Bapaume, de Saint-Omer et d'Aire-sur-la-Lys. Et pour offenser encore plus le « parti » champenois, il viole le droit exclusif qu'avait l'archevêque de Reims de célébrer les sacres et se fait couronner avec la reine à Saint-Denis par l'archevêque de Sens, assisté par les évêques de Paris et d'Orléans.

Puis, à la suite de multiples rebondissements qui soulignent son talent précoce pour nouer des intrigues, il s'en prend en 1184 au « parti flamand ». Prétextant que le mariage n'a pas été consommé, il annonce son intention de se séparer de la reine. Isabelle, vêtue en pauvresse, ameute alors le peuple en demandant publiquement miséricorde dans les rues de Senlis, geste spectaculaire qui fait renoncer Philippe au divorce. Le 5 septembre 1187, elle lui donne un fils, le prince Louis, qui lui permet d'assurer sa lignée.

C'est alors qu'il se retourne contre le vieux roi d'Angleterre Henri Plantagenêt, qui l'avait pourtant soutenu sans réserve pendant les premières années de son règne, en excitant ses fils contre lui. Les combats qui se déroulent aux frontières des deux royaumes sont ponctués de nombreuses entrevues entre les belligérants au cours desquelles Philippe est parfois pris de crises de fureur imprévisibles. Ainsi, à Gisors, en août 1188, le parti d'Henri bénéficie de l'ombre d'un orme, tandis que celui de Philippe rôtit au soleil. Les pourparlers n'ayant pas abouti, Philippe fait abattre l'arbre vénérable à coups de hache.

Dès son plus jeune âge, ce roi impulsif a aussi compris l'intérêt qu'il avait à s'appuyer sur l'Église. Sa première campagne, en 1180, l'a conduit en Mâconnais pour châtier les seigneurs qui ne respectaient pas l'œuvre de paix engagée par son père. Cette même année, à l'opposé de la politique de son père accusé de les avoir trop protégés, il fait arrêter tous les juifs dans leurs synagogues le jour du sabbat, met la main sur leurs biens, abolit toutes les dettes des chrétiens envers eux, et leur extorque avant de les relâcher 31 000 livres parisis, une fois et demie ce que rapportait mensuellement le domaine royal.

Débordant de zèle religieux mais toujours calculateur, Philippe sait également tirer profit de la troisième croisade qu'il entreprend en 1190. Avant de partir en compagnie de Richard Cœur de Lion, le nouveau roi d'Angleterre, il rédige un *Testament* célèbre qui est une ordonnance organisant le pouvoir en son absence et prévoyant sa succession au cas où il trouverait la mort en Terre Sainte.

La régence était confiée à la reine mère Adèle de Champagne et à l'archevêque de Reims, mais toutes les précautions étaient prises pour les empêcher d'abuser de ce pouvoir. Les régents n'avaient pas le droit de prélever des impôts et ne pouvaient disposer du trésor royal confié aux Templiers. Les clefs de ce trésor étaient aux mains de six bourgeois de Paris assistés de frère Bernard. Des « baillis » rendaient la justice en son nom et ne pouvaient être destitués par les régents sauf en cas de crime grave. Tous devaient lui rendre des comptes régulièrement, le progrès des liaisons maritimes permettant l'acheminement rapide des messages à l'armée en croisade. Chaque année, à la Saint-Remi, à la Chandeleur et à l'Ascension, « tous ses revenus, redevances et recettes extraordinaires seraient portés à Paris », une ville qu'il ordonne d'enfermer dans de fortes murailles en prévision de possibles désordres. Chaque ligne du *Testament* montre ainsi chez son auteur la volonté de continuer à administrer la France du fond de l'Orient. N'emporte-t-il pas avec lui le sceau de majesté qui scelle les actes décisifs pour le royaume ? Texte institutionnel fondamental, l'ordonnance de 1190 inaugure aussi la naissance d'un véritable État détaché de la constellation des Grands qui se voient privés de leurs pouvoirs au profit des hommes que le roi a choisis pour leur compétence et leur dévouement.

Au cours de la croisade, le contraste entre l'attitude des deux rois est flagrant. Tandis que Richard Cœur de Lion recherche la prouesse et multiplie les gestes de magnificence, Philippe s'économise. Après avoir repris la ville de Saint-Jean-d'Acre aux Infidèles, quitte à paraître couard et à être accusé de trahir son vœu de croisé, il annonce le 22 juillet 1191 son intention de regagner la France. Invoquant la maladie de son fils dont la nouvelle vient de lui parvenir de Paris, la sienne qui a provoqué la chute de ses ongles et de ses cheveux, une fièvre aujourd'hui considérée par les cliniciens comme une manifestation précoce de la suette, une variante de la typhoïde, il confie le commandement des forces françaises au duc de Bourgogne et revient à Paris le 27 décembre 1191. À vrai dire, la mort du comte de Flandre Philippe d'Alsace devant Saint-Jean-d'Acre le 1er juillet a sans doute précipité sa décision, la prise de possession de son important héritage flamand lui paraissant sans doute plus capitale que la délivrance de Jérusalem tombée aux mains de Saladin. La lettre qu'il envoya d'Acre aux nobles de Péronne en témoigne. Leur annonçant la mort du comte de Flandre, il leur ordonne de prêter serment de fidélité aux régents.

L'hécatombe des féodaux lors de la croisade fut aussi une chance pour Philippe. Des grands qui l'avaient accompagné, les plus importants vassaux du royaume, presque tous étaient morts devant Saint-Jean-d'Acre. Décapités, les lignages allaient offrir une moindre résistance à un roi qui, placé au sommet de la pyramide des hommages, sut utiliser tous les moyens pour intervenir dans ces principautés qui avaient perdu les hommes physiquement capables de manier l'épée.

Enfin, Philippe profite de la chance que lui offrent la capture de Richard par le duc d'Autriche, humilié par « le Lion » devant Acre, et sa captivité pendant deux années pour traiter avec son jeune frère, Jean sans Terre, envahir la Normandie et saisir l'importante forteresse de Gisors ainsi que les principaux châteaux de la frontière de l'Epte. À l'âge de dix ans, rapporte une autre anecdote, il avait accompagné son père dans ce château du roi d'Angleterre et, comme chacun s'émerveillait devant sa puissance et sa richesse, il se serait fâché, disant qu'il voulait qu'il fût encore plus fort et plus riche d'or, d'argent et de diamants. Comme on lui demandait pourquoi, il répondit : « Plus les matériaux de ce château seront précieux, plus j'aurai de joie plus tard à le posséder quand il sera tombé entre mes mains. »

À vingt-cinq ans, ce jeune homme qui avait du caractère était prêt à tirer tous les avantages de son heureuse « fortune ». Encore fallait-il assurer l'avenir de la dynastie, la reine Isabelle étant morte et le jeune roi Louis, un enfant de quatre ans, venant d'être mis en danger par une grave maladie.

Les vicissitudes déroutantes du second mariage de Philippe sont peut-être dues à la maladie contractée à la croisade. Le 15 août 1193, au lendemain de ses noces avec Ingeburge, sœur du roi de Danemark, Philippe, par un de ces coups de folie qui lui ont été familiers, annonce son intention de faire annuler le mariage et exige en vain que l'ambassade qui l'avait escortée la ramène à son père. « Empêché par un maléfice », explique le moine Rigord, son biographe, il aurait eu les « aiguillettes nouées » et n'aurait pu la déflorer. Le 5 novembre, une assemblée se réunit à Compiègne sous la présidence de l'archevêque de Reims. Quinze témoins viennent jurer que le roi était cousin au quatrième degré d'Ingeburge, ce qui était faux, mais permit aux prélats d'annuler le mariage pour cause de consanguinité et à Philippe de contracter une nouvelle union avec Agnès de Méranie. Le pape Innocent III eut beau, en 1198, condamner le roi de France pour bigamie et lancer l'interdit sur le royaume, une sanction redoutable qui menaçait de suspendre l'activité religieuse dans tout le pays, Philippe tint bon, s'appuyant sur le haut clergé de France qui refusa de publier la sentence. C'était faire preuve de l'opiniâtreté qui, souvent, vint corriger les maladresses dues à son impulsivité.

Les hommes du roi

En 1194, une fois sa liberté rachetée par une phénoménale rançon de 100 000 marcs d'argent, Richard Cœur de Lion regagne l'Angleterre et se hâte de retourner en Normandie pour forcer Philippe Auguste à battre en retraite. Pendant cinq ans, de 1194 à 1199, il inflige défaite sur défaite au roi de France et à ses chevaliers. La plus fameuse et, paradoxalement, la plus bénéfique pour la France fut certainement celle de Fréteval, dans le Vendômois, le 3 juillet 1194. Contraint d'abandonner sur le champ de bataille un de ses trésors, le sceau royal et ses archives jusque-là itinérantes au gré des déplacements, Philippe décide dorénavant de les abriter à demeure dans son palais de Paris où elles forment le noyau des futures Archives de France.

En fait, les revers de la guerre, qui ne sont que chevauchées saisonnières sans conséquence, n'entament pas le pouvoir et le prestige d'un roi qui, patiemment et sans éclat, en homme de cabinet plus que d'action, construit les fondements d'un État moderne dont il allait bientôt recueillir les bénéfices.

S'appuyant sur un petit groupe d'hommes en qui il a une totale confiance, écartant les féodaux et les prélats de haut rang qui continuent à siéger à la Cour mais sans réel pouvoir politique, Philippe a su capter les forces neuves de la bourgeoisie et du clergé formés à l'école du droit pour gérer au mieux la justice et les finances, resserrer le filet où les grandes seigneuries du royaume se trouvaient captives et mettre en place un système administratif qui allait devenir une machine de guerre bien plus redoutable que les lances et les épées de son fougueux rival au cœur de lion.

Passant inaperçus des chroniqueurs en raison de leur jeunesse et de leur condition modeste, ces hommes du roi, entièrement tributaires de sa faveur, vont se montrer des collaborateurs autrement plus dévoués et efficaces que les anciens barons. Les archives nous font ainsi connaître Gautier le Chambellan, Barthélemy de Roye, frère Haimard, un Templier, et, surtout, frère Guérin dont on retrouve la main partout. Sans autre titre officiel que « conseiller spécial » du roi, il « traitait les affaires du royaume, nous dit un témoin, comme le second après le roi ».

Pratiquement inconnus avant le règne de Philippe Auguste, les baillis assurent la présence du roi à travers un royaume qui découvre avec eux ce que pouvoir central veut dire. Entrés relativement jeunes dans leur fonction, véritables fonctionnaires nommés et bien salariés, ayant servi la monarchie pendant au moins dix ans et, pour la moitié d'entre eux, pendant au moins quinze ans, ces nouveaux hommes du roi vont avoir pour principale mission de juger et de percevoir les revenus de la couronne. Trois fois par an, ils doivent aller rendre leurs comptes à Paris et tenir régulièrement des assises judiciaires dans les localités de leur ressort, des « préfets » avant la lettre.

L'anecdote suivante, une rumeur manifestement colportée par la propagande royale, laisse entendre que Philippe, comme plus tard Saint Louis, veillait à réprimer leurs abus. Un bailli du roi avait grande envie d'une terre que possédait un chevalier, son voisin, mais il ne put le décider à la vendre. Le propriétaire meurt, laissant une veuve qui, elle aussi, refuse de se dessaisir de son bien. Le bailli va chercher deux portefaix sur la place publique, les habille convenablement, leur promet de l'argent et, la nuit suivante, les mène au cimetière où le chevalier est enterré. Avec l'aide des deux hommes, il ouvre la tombe, met le mort sur ses pieds et l'adjure, devant ses deux témoins, de lui vendre le domaine en question. « Qui ne dit mot consent », dit l'un des témoins, le marché est conclu. On met de l'argent dans la main du cadavre ; la tombe est refermée, et, le lendemain, le bailli envoie ses ouvriers travailler sur la terre comme si elle lui appartenait. La veuve réclame : il affirme que la vente a eu lieu. L'affaire est portée devant Philippe Auguste. Le bailli produit ses deux témoins qui attestent la vente. Le roi s'avise d'un stratagème. Il prend l'un des témoins à part, dans un coin, et lui dit : « Sais-tu le *Pater noster* ? Récite-le. » Et pendant que l'homme murmure son oraison, Philippe s'écrie de temps à autre, de façon à être entendu de la galerie : « C'est bien cela, tu dis la vérité. » La récitation faite : « Tu ne m'as pas menti, dit le roi : tu peux compter sur ta grâce », puis il le fait enfermer dans une chambre. Alors il se retourne vers le second témoin : « Voyons, ne mens pas non plus ; ton ami m'a révélé tout ce qui s'était passé, aussi vrai que s'il avait récité le *Pater noster*. » L'autre, croyant que tout est découvert, finit par avouer le stratagème. Le bailli se jette aux pieds du roi : Philippe le condamne au bannissement perpétuel et donne à la pauvre veuve la maison et les domaines du coupable. « Ce jugement, conclut le chroniqueur, vaut bien celui de Salomon. »

Ainsi s'installe l'ordre capétien, un ordre qui traduit aussi la percée du calcul et du registre dans l'administration française.

En 1223, un dignitaire de l'église de Lausanne se trouvait à Paris au moment de la mort de Philippe Auguste. On lui assura que, tandis que Louis VII n'avait eu que 19 000 livres à dépenser par mois, Philippe laissait à son fils un revenu *quotidien* de 1 200 livres. Grand amasseur de trésors, Philippe sut faire rentrer l'argent nécessaire aux dépenses croissantes d'une royauté sans cesse en état de guerre et dont la diplomatie s'activait dans toute l'Europe. Il transforma tout d'abord une grande partie des prestations et des corvées dues par les vilains du domaine royal en taxes financières, ce qui facilitait et régularisait leur perception. Il développa, d'autre part, certains revenus extraordinaires qui, sous les règnes précédents, produisaient peu ou ne produisaient rien.

Ainsi, jusqu'à lui, les Capétiens n'avaient pas bénéficié du droit de « relief » prélevé par un seigneur sur toute terre vassale quand elle changeait de propriétaire. En vertu du droit de suzeraineté suprême que la théorie élaborée par les hommes d'Église a su mettre en place, Philippe Auguste assujettit pour la première fois les grands féodaux au relief. En 1181, un an après son avènement, le comte de Nevers et d'Auxerre meurt. Il n'a qu'une fille. Pendant trois ans, le roi, gardien de l'héritière, rafle tous les revenus de la seigneurie, puis donne la jeune fille en mariage à son cousin de Courtenay. Devenue veuve, il reprend sa tutelle et la donne à Hervé de Donzy, en prélevant le relief, et réserve la fille issue de ce second mariage à son propre petit-fils, faisant promettre à Hervé de ne jamais disposer d'elle sans son consentement. Les reliefs d'une grande baronnie comme la Flandre ou la Normandie peuvent fournir un quart ou un tiers du revenu annuel ordinaire ! Quoique occasionnels, ces droits, pour la première fois perçus, vont représenter une part importante des finances royales et permettre de dégager des excédents confortables, Philippe ne dépensant en moyenne que 70 % de ses recettes.

En 1189, à la mort d'Henri II Plantagenêt, Richard Cœur de Lion, qui lui succède à la tête du duché de Normandie, promet de verser plus de 43 000 livres au titre du relief. Même si cette somme n'a pas été payée, la promesse de Richard montre à quel point les experts qui entouraient le roi ont su convaincre les féodaux que, parce qu'il était roi, le Capétien, ne devant prêter hommage à personne, pouvait considérer chaque principauté comme une simple tenure.

Sous les règnes précédents, les grands féodaux réglaient leurs rapports avec les hommes de leur principauté sans demander au roi la confirmation de leurs actes. Sous Philippe, ils demandent ou subissent la sanction du sceau royal pour ces accords. Ils en arrivent ainsi à accepter ses décisions et à leur donner force de loi dans leurs domaines.

L'exemple de la Champagne montre à quel point un grand fief a pu ainsi perdre son indépendance sous les armes des légistes qui n'ont fait qu'appliquer toutes les potentialités de l'ordre féodal. En 1201, Thibaut III, comte de Champagne, meurt, laissant une fille jeune et une veuve, Blanche de Navarre, sur le point d'accoucher. Philippe impose immédiatement un traité à la comtesse. Acceptant de recevoir son hommage, il lui fait jurer de ne pas se remarier sans son consentement et de lui confier sa fille et l'enfant dont elle est enceinte. En gage de cet accord, qui liait les principaux barons champenois, le roi recevait aussi les deux forteresses de Bray et de Montereau. Peu après, Blanche met au monde un fils, Thibaut, mais doit convenir avec Philippe qu'il restera en minorité jusqu'à l'âge de vingt et un ans. Dès que l'enfant atteint sa douzième année, Philippe conclut avec la mère un nouveau traité qui aggrave le premier. Blanche et Thibaut jurent de servir fidèlement le roi de France et s'interdisent, avant la majorité du comte, de fortifier Meaux, Lagny, Provins et Coulommiers sous peine d'une amende de 20 000 livres.

En 1215, le roi annonce à la comtesse, comme à l'un de ses baillis, qu'il a modifié la législation relative au duel judiciaire : « Sachez, lui fait-il écrire, que sur le conseil d'hommes sages et dans l'intérêt général, nous avons décidé qu'à l'avenir, les champions devront combattre avec des bâtons dont la longueur ne dépassera pas trois pieds. Nous vous mandons par la loi que vous nous devez, et vous requérons de faire publier et observer cette ordonnance dans toute l'étendue de votre État. » En 1216, elle doit demander au roi l'autorisation de reconstruire un mur du château de Provins, qui lui interdit toutefois d'y mettre des tourelles. En 1222, Thibaut est devenu majeur. Le premier acte du comte est un engagement de servir fidèlement le roi de France. Et quand, en décembre de cette même année, les officiers du comte veulent saisir, suivant la coutume, les biens de l'évêque de Meaux décédé, Philippe Auguste écrit directement aux agents de son vassal, comme à ses propres agents, leur interdisant d'occuper les domaines épiscopaux. C'était changer progressivement les bases du système féodal et préparer l'unité monarchique. C'était, par infiltration pacifique et rédaction des lois, élargir la zone d'intervention du roi. Alors que nous conservons 798 actes écrits sous le règne de Louis VII, ce sont 2 500 actes qui ont été rédigés sous le règne de Philippe Auguste. Mandements, hommages consignés dans des chartes, statistiques, inventaires et enquêtes, relevés de services et de taxes, coutumes et sentences, autant d'actes écrits dont la courbe ascendante marque l'irrésistible percée de l'administration et, chez les hommes du roi, un sens de l'organisation peu commun.

La conquête de la Normandie

De solides finances, une armée mieux équipée, des forteresses solidement établies aux limites du domaine, l'exploitation méthodique des coutumes féodales, une chancellerie collectant systématiquement par écrit les hommages et les serments de fidélité de ses vassaux, telles furent les armes d'un roi bien conseillé qui, à la suite de ce grand mouvement de réforme, put s'en prendre, les armes et les coutumes à la main, à l'« empire » des Plantagenêts.

Le 8 mai 1199, « Dieu visita le royaume de France », écrivit Guillaume le Breton, le chapelain du roi. Ce jour-là, en effet, au cours du siège du château de Châlus, Richard Cœur de Lion, le grand rival, était blessé grièvement par un carreau d'arbalète. Quelques jours plus tard, il mourait sans fils légitime. Une chance pour Philippe qui allait utiliser avec une terrible efficacité le droit féodal pour conquérir la Normandie.

À la succession de Richard se présentent en effet deux prétendants, Jean, son frère, qui se fait couronner à Canterbury dès le 27 mai 1199, et son neveu, Arthur de Bretagne, âgé de douze ans, qui, selon les coutumes angevines, réclamait à bon droit l'Anjou, le Maine et la Touraine dont son père disparu aurait dû hériter à la mort d'un « Lion » trop imprévoyant pour avoir réglé sa succession.

Philippe profite de cette aubaine, prend Arthur sous sa protection, l'emmène à Paris et s'en sert comme carte dans la partie serrée qu'il allait mener contre le roi d'Angleterre dont un chroniqueur remarquait que, « par un jugement secret de la Providence, (il) se faisait toujours des ennemis de ses propres amis et rassemblait lui-même les verges dont il devait être battu ». En 1200, en effet, Jean commet une lourde faute en enlevant et épousant de force Isabelle d'Angoulême promise à l'un de ses principaux vassaux, Hugues, comte de la Marche et sire de Lusignan. Les barons poitevins, scandalisés par cette « félonie », réclament alors justice au seigneur des seigneurs, le roi de France, qui ne manque pas l'occasion d'accueillir cette plainte et convoque Jean à sa cour à Paris. En l'absence du « félon » qui se dérobe, la cour prononce la « commise », c'est-à-dire la confiscation de tous les fiefs qu'il tient du roi de France. Une sanction que prévoyait certes le droit féodal mais qui n'avait jamais été portée sur une principauté. Il fallait bien que se soit produit une « révolution » juridique pour que Philippe se sente la force de rendre un tel jugement et le fasse exécuter par ses barons.

En juin 1202, Philippe envahit la Normandie tandis que Jean se déconsidère encore plus en faisant assassiner son neveu Arthur fait prisonnier. Le 6 mars 1204, au prix d'un siège de huit mois, la formidable forteresse de Château-Gaillard, qui verrouillait la vallée de la Seine face aux Andelys, est enlevée. Après avoir barré le cours de la Seine à l'aide de nombreux bateaux plats reliés les uns aux autres entre les deux rives, Philippe Auguste entreprend la construction d'un chemin couvert destiné à protéger les mineurs, ou taupins, qui creusent galeries et sapes dans les fondations afin de provoquer des éboulements. La prise de Château-Gaillard ouvre les portes de la Normandie. Le 24 juin 1204, les bourgeois de Rouen, assurés par le roi du maintien de leurs privilèges commerciaux, livrent leur ville. La Normandie, conquise par le droit, faisait désormais partie du domaine royal ainsi devenu une grande puissance maritime. Fleuron des fiefs continentaux du roi d'Angleterre, riche et dotée d'une solide administration, la Normandie était bien la plus importante annexion jamais faite par les Capétiens. L'année suivante, l'Anjou et la Touraine étaient occupés sans coup férir.

Le dimanche de Bouvines

Avec son gouvernement qui prétend imposer partout l'autorité royale, Philippe Auguste sème le trouble dans une Europe qui refuse de s'incliner devant son prestige. Selon les mots du pape Innocent III, « de notoriété publique, le roi de France ne reconnaît au temporel aucune autorité supérieure à la sienne » et ses vertus sont exaltées par tout un groupe d'écrivains politiques qui en font un nouvel « empereur magne » dont les lys héraldiques font reculer les léopards et les lions. La coalition qui se noue contre Philippe rassemble ainsi tous ceux qui s'inquiètent de cette formidable avancée capétienne ; en tout premier lieu, Jean sans Terre, bien résolu à recouvrer ses fiefs perdus, mais aussi Otton de Brunswick, offensé de l'opposition de Philippe à son élection au trône impérial et du soutien qu'il apporte à son rival Frédéric de Hohenstaufen, Renaud de Dammartin, le comte de Boulogne, qui complote de longue date contre Philippe, et Ferrand, le comte de Flandre, qui hésite longtemps à trahir l'hommage rendu à son suzerain. En 1214, les coalisés décident de prendre Philippe dans une tenaille. Otton et Ferrand attaqueront par le Nord tandis qu'au Sud, Jean entreprendra la reconquête de son héritage et marchera sur Paris.

En février, Jean débarque à La Rochelle, franchit la Loire, occupe Angers et vient mettre le siège devant la forteresse de La Roche-aux-Moines qui tient la route de Nantes. Mais, le 2 juillet 1214, à la seule approche du prince Louis, le fils de Philippe, il abandonne ses machines de guerre et s'enfuit sans combattre. Le dimanche 27 du même mois, Philippe remporte à Bouvines une victoire éclatante qui allait s'inscrire comme un fait majeur de l'histoire de France. Un rapport écrit sur le champ de bataille par Guillaume le Breton, qui prend des notes en même temps qu'il prie et chante les *Psaumes* de David, nous permet de prendre la mesure de ce qui fut une vraie bataille, un gigantesque tournoi, un duel à mort où se rangent face à face, aux deux extrémités d'un terrain choisi pour les charges de la cavalerie, deux rois, celui de France avec l'oriflamme et la bannière rouge semée de fleurs de lys, celui d'Allemagne, avec sa terrifiante enseigne représentant un aigle surmontant un dragon. D'un côté, très unies, les troupes « françaises », uniquement « françaises », soudées les unes aux autres par l'amitié de leurs chefs ; de l'autre, un ensemble disparate de conjurés travaillés par les intrigues et pervertis par les 40 000 marcs d'argent généreusement distribués par le roi d'Angleterre. Bouvines apparaît bien aux contemporains comme un formidable pari sur une victoire ou une défaite totale, une sorte de jugement de Dieu livré un dimanche, jour où il est interdit aux chrétiens de combattre.

Persuadés que les coalisés ne combattront pas ce jour sacré, les conseillers militaires traditionnels de Philippe le dissuadent de lancer une attaque immédiate. Mais frère Guérin, qui a compris le danger et pressenti la manœuvre en cours des coalisés, demande que l'on engage l'action sur-le-champ. La décison cruciale est prise à midi, près du pont de Bouvines où Philippe, accablé par la canicule, avait enlevé son armure et mangeait une soupe au vin à l'ombre d'un frêne. Après avoir pénétré dans la chapelle Saint-Pierre, proche de l'endroit où il avait pris sa collation, et récité une brève prière, Philippe déclare adopter l'avis de frère Guérin, rappelle ses troupes qui avaient déjà franchi le pont de Bouvines en direction de Lille et décide de livrer combat sur le terrain choisi par son « conseiller spécial ». Les Impériaux possédaient l'avantage de se trouver au sommet du plateau mais avaient le grand inconvénient de supporter le lourd soleil de ce mois de juillet en plein devant les yeux.

D'un côté, Philippe dispose de 1 200 chevaliers, peut-être d'autant de sergents à cheval et de 4 500 à 5 000 fantassins tandis que, de l'autre, les coalisés alignent 1 500 chevaliers et 7 500 sergents à pied. Au moment où le combat va s'engager entre les deux armées, distantes d'un jet de flèches, le silence est tel « qu'on n'entend pas une seule voix ». Philippe, qui approche de la cinquantaine, un âge où les seigneurs se retiraient du jeu militaire, respectant le rituel d'une cérémonie quasi religieuse, harangue ses troupes puis, élevant ses mains, implore pour elles la bénédiction divine. « Dieu est tout notre espoir, aurait-il dit, toute notre confiance. Le roi Otton et son armée ont été excommuniés par le Pape, car ils sont les ennemis, les persécuteurs de la sainte Église. L'argent qui sert à les solder est le produit des larmes des pauvres, du pillage des terres appartenant à Dieu et au Clergé. Nous, nous sommes chrétiens, en paix et en communion avec la sainte Église. Tout pécheurs que nous soyons, nous sommes en bon accord avec les serviteurs de Dieu et défendons, dans la mesure de nos forces, les libertés des clercs. Nous pouvons donc compter sur la miséricorde divine. Dieu nous donnera le moyen de triompher de nos ennemis, qui sont les siens. » D'un côté, les suppôts du Diable, de l'autre, des chevaliers loyaux et le peuple valeureux des milices communales auquel a été confiée la garde de l'oriflamme. Une nation soudée contre un royaume pourri. Par chance ou par calcul, Philippe était en effet en paix avec l'Église. En avril 1213, il avait rappelé auprès de lui Ingeburge, dont il était séparé depuis près de vingt ans et, Agnès de Méranie étant morte, le pape avait légitimé les deux enfants qu'elle lui avait donnés. Un compromis particulièrement bien venu !

Vue par Guillaume le Breton depuis sa position centrale privilégiée, la bataille qui s'engage alors apparaît comme une chorégraphie se déroulant sur trois scènes. Sur la droite, Guérin lance à l'assaut les 150 sergents à cheval de Soissons contre les chevaliers flamands du comte Ferrand qui considèrent comme une insulte cette attaque de cavaliers roturiers. Désorganisés par des charges répétées, les rangs flamands finissent par s'amenuiser et, après trois heures de combat, Ferrand, gravement blessé, doit se rendre.

Sur la scène centrale, Philippe Auguste est confronté à l'empereur qui a juré de combattre jusqu'à la mort du roi. Tandis que la mêlée de la cavalerie occupe entièrement les chevaliers français, les sergents impériaux parviennent à désarçonner Philippe grâce à de longs crocs et essayent de trouver le défaut de son haubert pour lui porter un coup de dague. Mais sa lourde armure et le secours de ses chevaliers qui se mettent au-devant des coups sauvent la vie du roi. C'est au tour d'Otton d'être mis en danger. Blessé à l'œil, son cheval s'enfuit et l'empereur « montre alors son dos à ses adversaires ». On avance un autre destrier à Otton qui, à peine remonté en selle, s'enfuit et rejoint Valenciennes à bride abattue pour se mettre à l'abri. Malmené, l'étendard impérial est triomphalement présenté au roi.

À l'aile gauche, Renaud de Dammartin surprend ses adversaires en plaçant une double rangée de sergents à pied, serrés à la manière d'une roue et armés de piques sur lesquelles viennent se blesser les destriers qui s'efforcent de rompre ce « hérisson » au milieu duquel Renaud vient reprendre haleine et se rafraîchir. Un sergent français, Pierre de Tournelle, finit cependant par le faire tomber de son cheval et à le blesser. S'ensuit alors une chaude dispute entre les chevaliers français pour savoir qui aura l'honneur de capturer le traître qui préfère se rendre entre les mains de Guérin auquel ses victoires sur l'aile droite ont permis de passer à l'aile gauche. La nuit approchant, les troupes françaises regagnent leur camp au son des trompes tandis que 700 mercenaires brabançons, des piétons restés hagards sur le plateau, sont massacrés par le sire de Saint-Valéry qui, avec ses chevaliers et ses fantassins, achève de nettoyer le champ de bataille.

Bouvines est bien une spectaculaire victoire. Les prisonniers sont à la fois nombreux, on en compte 130, et considérables, la valeur de ce butin faisant aussi de cette bataille une prodigieuse « affaire » pour les finances royales. Il y a parmi eux trois chefs de la coalition, le comte de Boulogne, le comte de Salisbury, demi-frère du roi d'Angleterre, et Ferrand, le comte de Flandre, enchaîné et logé dans une cage de fer placée sur un chariot qui l'amène en captivité à Paris au milieu d'une foule qui accourt sur le bord du chemin pour acclamer son roi, danser et chanter de bonheur. À Paris, les écoliers, le clergé et le peuple vont au-devant de l'armée victorieuse et la fête dure une semaine, jour et nuit, flambeaux et lanternes illuminant la ville. C'était l'éveil d'une conscience nationale, une gigantesque fête populaire qui célébrait les noces d'un peuple et de son roi et tranchait en faveur du Capétien le nœud des rivalités qui travaillaient l'Occident.

De ce dimanche qui a « fait la France », Georges Duby peut écrire : « Bouvines est bien d'abord un duel entre jaloux, qui sont venus là pour le plaisir d'en découdre. Il est permis cependant de parler en ce lieu de politique... Les tumultes qui, chaque printemps, font jaillir de chaque château, sous prétexte d'honneur, un petit essaim de cavaliers pillards, à l'affût de toute occasion de rapine, commencent d'être quelque peu contenus par la main d'un comte, d'un duc ou d'un roi. Ce chef a le moyen désormais de faire respecter la morale de la vassalité et les obligations du fief, de mieux attacher à sa personne les moindres seigneurs, de rassembler pour le bien commun toute la chevalerie d'un pays, d'imposer ses arbitrages, de punir les félons, de commander de loin par intermédiaires gagés, et, parce qu'il donne davantage, parce qu'il peut payer des soldats, de se faire obéir. L'horizon de cet homme est ainsi beaucoup moins borné que jadis. »

Quand Philippe meurt, le 14 juillet 1223, il laisse à ses héritiers un triple héritage : une administration capable d'imposer le droit, des réserves financières pour alimenter leur prestige, enfin et peut-être surtout, une « religion royale » qui a fait du vainqueur de Bouvines un véritable « auguste » considéré par tous ses contemporains comme le successeur direct de Charlemagne. En juin 1204, au moment d'entrer dans Rouen, Philippe s'est intitulé pour la première fois « roi de France » (*rex Franciae*) et non plus « roi des Francs » (*rex Francorum*). C'est bien à ce moment, au début du XIIIᵉ siècle, que s'épanouit la sensibilité des Français à la France.

Le règne de l'argent

*I*l y eut en France un usurier dont le serviteur s'appelait Enfer et la
« *I* servante Mort. Mort subitement, il n'eut pour fossoyeurs qu'Enfer
et Mort. » Ce destin de l'usurier présenté dans un sermon par Eudes de
Sully, évêque de Paris de 1196 à 1208, résume laconiquement les inquiétudes qui tourmentent l'Église devant l'invasion de l'argent, l'ascension
de nouveaux groupes professionnels et la diffusion du crédit. Le marchand ne peut pas ou difficilement plaire à Dieu, tel est aussi l'enseignement que livrent les chapiteaux des églises. La mort du mauvais riche qui
refuse à Lazare sa pitance traduit aussi l'éthique d'une société pour
laquelle un « amant de l'argent » ne peut être que « l'esclave du vice ».

Les circuits de l'argent

Les uns vont en Angleterre
Laines et cuirs et bacons quérir ;
Les autres revont en Espagne,
Et tels en a qui vont en Bretagne
Bœufs et porcs, vaches acheter
[...] Et reviennent de tous pays
Les bons marchands à Paris
Pour la mercerie acheter.
[...] Il y a marchands de drap,
Et de toile et de canevas,

De basane et de cordouan,
De cire, d'alun, de safran,
De draps d'or et de cendal...

L'auteur de ces vers extraits du *Dit des Marchands* ne parvient pas, malgré son talent, à épuiser la liste des articles qui éveillent les tentations de ses contemporains. Dans l'histoire du commerce au long cours, le XIIIᵉ siècle est bien un âge d'or dont se nourrissent des artisans boutiquiers à l'honnête aisance, des marchands de grande envergure, des capitaines d'industrie ou des financiers-négociants qui, à l'exemple des Italiens, importent le vin et exportent le drap, prennent à ferme les recettes royales et prêtent aux grands et aux souverains. La révolution économique amorcée à la fin du XIᵉ siècle produit maintenant tous ses effets. C'est parce qu'il a su habilement capter les richesses nées de cette croissance que Philippe Auguste a pu aussi élargir ses capacités d'intervention dans le monde qui était le sien.

Heureusement placée au carrefour des grandes routes qui relient les mondes nordiques et les mondes méditerranéens, la France est largement irriguée par les voies essentielles du grand commerce international. À leur apogée, entre 1150 et 1250, les foires de Champagne sont le carrefour où ces divers courants se rejoignent, le grand rendez-vous des marchands, le géographe arabe Edusi citant Troyes comme une ville où l'on peut se procurer toutes choses.

Tandis que les marchands des cités italiennes, Venise et Gênes surtout, enrichis par les profits des croisades et le partage des dépouilles de l'Empire byzantin fournissent à l'Occident les produits importés d'Orient, l'alun d'Asie Mineure, le coton du Proche-Orient, la laine d'Afrique du Nord, les blés de Crimée, les vins des îles grecques, le sel des Baléares, le sucre de canne de Mésopotamie et de Chypre, les épices, dont le manuel du Florentin Pegolotti énumère plus de trois cents types, les mousselines et damas et les fourrures venues des terres russes par la mer Noire, les marchands de la « Méditerranée du Nord », pour désigner l'espace nordique qui s'étend de la côte orientale de l'Angleterre jusqu'au fond de la Baltique, sont les grands pourvoyeurs de matières premières et de produits alimentaires, grains de Rhénanie, harengs de Scandinavie, sel de Lüneburg, bois d'Allemagne, de Scandinavie et de Russie, poix de Russie, laine surtout, indispensable matière première de l'industrie textile dont l'Angleterre fournit annuellement 3 000 à 4 000 tonnes.

Rythmant ces activités marchandes et mettant en relation ces deux pôles majeurs de développement, les foires de Champagne qui bénéficient, à partir de 1209, de la sauvegarde du roi de France, se déroulent en trois séquences, la « montre », autrement dit l'étalage des marchandises, la vente, où celles-ci changent de mains, et les paiements, au cours desquels interviennent les opérations de change. À cette occasion, se développent, sous l'impulsion des gens de Sienne, de Plaisance et de Florence, de nouvelles techniques de crédit, reconnaissances de dettes négociables, créances payables sur une autre place, les Génois recevant à Gênes des deniers génois contre lesquels ils s'engagent à remettre aux foires des deniers de Provins, virements de compte à compte, autant de contrats qui permettent de dissimuler dans le taux de change l'intérêt d'un argent sur l'argent, faire enfanter de l'argent à l'argent étant un crime contre nature dénoncé par l'Église. « *Nummus non parit nummos* », « l'argent ne se reproduit pas », écrit saint Thomas d'Aquin qui affirme : « La monnaie [...] a été principalement inventée pour les échanges, ainsi son usage propre et premier est d'être consommée, dépensée dans les échanges. Par suite, il est injuste en soi de recevoir un prix pour l'usage de l'argent prêté ; c'est en cela que consiste l'usure. »

Pourtant, à l'occasion des croisades, la confrérie des « pauvres chevaliers du Christ », fondée en 1118 par le chevalier champenois Hugues de Payns, est devenue une véritable banque de dépôts pouvant, par un simple jeu d'écritures, se faire payer à Paris d'une créance consentie à Londres ou en Orient. Assurant les transferts d'hommes et de fonds de l'Occident vers les lieux de combat en Terre sainte, l'ordre du Temple pouvait en effet procurer à un voyageur des fonds équivalents à ceux qu'il avait déposés dans un établissement de son pays d'origine et lui éviter de transporter de fortes sommes avec le risque de se les faire voler. Gérant par ailleurs avec rigueur les fonds provenant des revenus de leurs propriétés ou des dons des fidèles, les Templiers sont devenus des hommes d'affaires appréciés en même temps que détestés par tous ceux qu'indisposait cette invasion de l'argent. C'est sous leur garde que Philippe Auguste a conservé, durant tout son règne, son Trésor à Paris, frère Haimard se chargeant de recevoir les surplus des revenus royaux trois fois par an et de verser les sommes pour les opérations du gouvernement et pour la guerre.

Malgré leur importance, les foires de Champagne n'ont toutefois pas monopolisé les circuits du commerce et de l'argent. C'est aussi la façade atlantique qui s'éveille à partir de deux produits clés, aux destins entremêlés, le sel poitevin exporté en Angleterre et à Hambourg, les vins d'Aunis et du Poitou dont le principal débouché est l'Angleterre puis, après la prise de La Rochelle par le roi de France en 1224, la Flandre. Dès ce moment, La Rochelle est le grand port français de l'Atlantique, le mouvement des bateaux y dépassant sans doute le millier par an. Juifs, Cahorsins, Lombards et Génois s'y installent en grand nombre, Marco Polo parlant même de la « mer de La Rochelle ».

La fortune de Bordeaux et des vins de Gascogne doit aussi beaucoup au rattachement de La Rochelle au domaine royal. L'Angleterre devient alors un débouché particulièrement « enivrant », les vallées de la Garonne et de ses affluents drainant « un véritable fleuve de vin », 850 000 hectolitres environ étant exportés par an au début du XIVe siècle.

Dans le Sud, les croisades ont donné une grande impulsion au commerce de Marseille qui devient l'un des principaux ports de transit des draps de la France septentrionale et de ses marges. Ceux d'Arras, Lille, Saint-Quentin, Ypres, Douai, Cambrai sont enregistrés. On y voit aussi ceux de Chartres, de Louviers, de Rouen et de Paris. Les filés d'or en provenance de Montpellier et de Gênes, les draps d'or venant de Lucques et les toiles de Champagne y sont négociées. Grand centre de transit et de redistribution, Marseille est aussi devenue un chantier actif de constructions navales. Sur ces navires dont les principaux départs se font en avril et mai, il faut vingt jours pour gagner l'Égypte et quarante jours pour atteindre Saint-Jean-d'Acre et les ports syriens. En partant en avril, on pouvait espérer être revenu au 30 novembre. Les Marseillais connaissent aussi l'usage de la lettre de change pour camoufler un prêt à intérêt. Ainsi, en 1248, une lettre de change établie à Marseille stipule que 270 livres de monnaie mêlée doivent être payées à Provins 200 livres tournois. Or le taux de change montre que sur cette place, 270 livres de monnaie mêlée valent seulement 157 livres tournois. Le profit est donc de 43 livres tournois, soit un intérêt d'environ 25 %. Tandis que les théologiens commentent à l'envi les textes de la Bible où il est dit « Tu ne prêteras pas à intérêt à ton frère, qu'il s'agisse d'un prêt d'argent ou de vivres, ou de quoi que ce soit dont on exige l'intérêt » (Deutéronome, XXIII, 20), les hommes d'affaires inventent empiriquement les moyens de grossir leur bourse, au risque de perdre dans l'au-delà les bénéfices de la vie éternelle.

Les voies de la fortune

Aubergistes, bouchers, jongleurs, alchimistes, médecins, chirurgiens, souteneurs, prostituées, notaires, marchands mais aussi foulons, tisserands, bourreliers, teinturiers, pâtissiers, cordonniers, jardiniers, peintres, pêcheurs, barbiers, douaniers, changeurs, tailleurs, parfumeurs, tripiers, meuniers, tels sont les métiers les plus souvent dénoncés par les hommes d'Église et qui semblent déplaire à Dieu. Tabou du sang qui joue contre les bouchers, les chirurgiens et les médecins. Tabou de l'impureté qui repousse les foulons, les teinturiers, les cuisiniers et même, pour saint Thomas d'Aquin, les laveurs de vaisselle ! Tabou de l'argent qui exclut les prostituées, les marchands, les changeurs et, surtout, les usuriers, écrit Jacques Le Goff dans *La Bourse et la vie*.

Jacques de Vitry, prédicateur vedette, mort peu avant 1240, en a fait la cible privilégiée des *exempla* qu'il a prononcés, des récits brefs, présentés comme véridiques et destinés à s'insérer dans un sermon pour impressionner l'auditoire et lui indiquer les voies du salut. « Un prédicateur qui voulait montrer à tous que le métier d'usurier était si honteux que nul n'osait l'avouer, dit dans son sermon : « Je veux vous donner l'absolution selon vos activités professionnelles et vos métiers. Debout, les forgerons ! » Et ils se levèrent. Après leur avoir donné l'absolution, il dit : « Debout, les fourreurs » et ils se levèrent, et ainsi de suite au fur et à mesure qu'il nommait les différents artisans, ils se levaient. Enfin, il s'écria : « Debout les usuriers pour recevoir l'absolution. » Les usuriers étaient plus nombreux que les gens des autres métiers mais par vergogne ils se cachaient. Sous les rires et les railleries, ils se retirèrent, pleins de confusion. »

Partageant avec les jongleurs et les prostituées le sort funeste de se voir refuser la sépulture chrétienne, les hommes qui s'enrichissent en dormant, en vendant seulement le temps qui s'écoule entre le moment du prêt et celui du remboursement, illustrent à la caricature la schizophrénie d'une société qui courtise et adule ceux qui réussissent en même temps qu'elle les craint et les méprise. Autant dire qu'au XIIIe siècle, les enrichis avaient intérêt à quitter l'église pendant le sermon pour la taverne, sa grande concurrente.

Car c'est bien à ce moment que l'élan des affaires et les opportunités de l'échange mettent en scène le riche et le pauvre, le gros et le menu, et imposent de choisir entre la richesse et le paradis, l'argent et l'enfer. Dans chaque ordre, en fait, s'accroissent les écarts de fortune entre les extrêmes : entre le paysan bien pourvu de terres et celui qui n'a que ses bras, entre le seigneur qui n'a que ses droits fonciers et celui qui bat monnaie et protège les foires ; entre le bourgeois des villes qui détient tous les leviers de commande et le modeste salarié des métiers. Pénétrant partout, dans les chaumières comme dans les seigneuries, l'argent bouleverse les hiérarchies en place et reclasse les individus en fonction de leur talent ou de leur chance.

Dans les campagnes, la hausse générale des prix, qu'ont stimulée la poursuite de la croissance démographique et le ravitaillement des villes, a enrichi tous ceux qui avaient quelque chose à vendre. En Normandie, le cours des bœufs double de 1190 à 1255, celui des moutons est multiplié par quatre de 1203 à 1255. À Coutances, le boisseau de froment qui valait 2 sous en 1255 grimpe à 4 sous en 1272. Pour développer leur production, s'insérer dans les circuits commerciaux, planter quelques arpents de vigne pour satisfaire une demande toujours croissante, se faire octroyer des chartes de franchise ou d'affranchissement que le seigneur à court d'argent monnaie au prix fort, se procurer des outils ou du cheptel, les paysans empruntent à des juifs ou des Lombards, à des marchands ou à des abbayes. Déjà en usage vers 1200, l'usage de la rente constituée connaît un vif succès après 1250. Il consiste pour l'emprunteur à asseoir sur la tenure qu'il possède une rente annuelle perpétuelle en argent ou en grains qu'il acquitte au prêteur et qui représente, en général, de 4 % à 8 % de la somme empruntée. Ces créances rurales qui se multiplient témoignent davantage de l'expansion économique que d'une situation de détresse.

Exploitant la gêne des sires et tirant parti d'une inflation qui fait baisser la valeur réelle des redevances en argent dont le réajustement se heurte à la force de la coutume, les vilains ont pu au cours du siècle s'affranchir du poids des contraintes qui pesaient sur leurs parcelles. Vers 1300, les 30 sous qu'un chevalier bourguignon retirait de ses soixante-deux tenures ne lui auraient permis de payer qu'à peine le tiers du salaire dû à un valet en complément de sa nourriture ! À la même époque, le tenancier d'un manse mâconnais versait à son seigneur 10 sous pour une terre rapportant une vingtaine de livres, conservant ainsi pour lui 98 % des profits. En moins de trente ans, dans la région parisienne, là où l'histoire allait plus vite parce que le pays, résidence royale, était le plus riche du royaume, le servage avait disparu et le paysan pouvait vendre, acheter et tester en toute liberté. Le bon temps des cathédrales est aussi celui de l'inflation.

Une inflation qui édifie toutefois une pyramide à la base élargie et au sommet étroit. Ainsi, à Molesmes, au début du XIVe siècle, sur 522 censitaires recensés par les cisterciens, seigneurs du lieu, une trentaine semble émerger du commun, tels dame Rose et son fils Ferri, qui ont 4 maisons, 2 vignes, 2 granges et de nombreux champs alors que sa fille Guillemette possède une terre, 2 prés et 5 vignes tandis que l'autre de ses deux fils, Jean, tient 9 vignes, 2 prés et 3 journaux de terre. Dans le Cambrésis, à la même époque, on a pu déceler 12 % d'individus en marge de la société, mendiants, miséreux ayant dressé leurs cabanes en dehors du village et louant leurs bras lors de la fenaison ou de la moisson, et 19 % de « riches » qui dominent tous les autres, des forts en gueule entreprenants, hauts en couleur et qui, en relations fréquentes avec le château, entendent bien faire anoblir leur opulence.

Car les frontières ne sont pas toujours étanches entre chevaliers et manants. Autour de Bar-sur-Seine, sur la soixantaine de familles nobles qui possédaient des seigneuries vers 1200, il n'en subsiste plus que vingt-cinq en 1300. Plusieurs se sont éteintes mais la plupart des autres se sont fondues dans la paysannerie. En Picardie, des 100 lignages que l'on peut suivre après 115, 40 sont encore visibles au milieu du XIIe siècle et 12 seulement vers 1300. C'est que bien des seigneurs besogneux se trouvent démunis, l'inflation et le goût de la parade, stimulé par les marchands ou les bailleurs de fonds, ayant laminé leur patrimoine. Sur les 38 fiefs de la châtellenie de Bar-sur-Seine, dont la valeur est connue au début du XIVe siècle, 24 avaient un revenu inférieur à 10 livres parisis, leurs détenteurs ne pouvant vivre de ce maigre revenu. En Île-de-France, on trouve des hobereaux qui ne semblent même pas avoir de demeure à eux et qui doivent prendre à rente une chaumière de vilain. À Tremblay, Jacquin du Mont ne possède ainsi que « granche, estable à chevaulx, cuisine, chambre derrière la cuisine et cour ». Sur le plateau lyonnais, les patrimoines nobiliaires sont devenus insignifiants. À l'opposé, au sommet de la pyramide féodale, une minorité de seigneurs peuvent compter leur fortune par dizaines de milliers de livres et accroître leur puissance en acceptant les achats qui leur sont proposés par des seigneurs aux abois. Ainsi, vers 1200, les comtes de Forez contrôlaient deux fois plus de forteresses qu'en 1150.

Contestés par les coqs de village enrichis auxquels ils sont parfois acculés d'accorder leur fille en mariage, les féodaux tentent alors d'affirmer la qualité de leur sang et de se distinguer des rustres en insistant plus qu'auparavant sur les préséances, les titres et les hiérarchies. Les armoiries que l'on fait peindre sur la porte et sur le bouclier, les tours qu'aucune menace n'explique mais qui signalent à tous la demeure du noble, l'usage de mots nouveaux comme « écuyer » ou « damoiseau » pour désigner des chevaliers trop pauvres pour se faire adouber sont des réactions de défense dont la littérature transmet l'écho.

« Ne faites pas un évêque du fils de votre berger. Prenez un fils de roi, de duc, de comte, ou encore le fils d'une pauvre vavasseur. Si vous trouvez un de ceux-là, vous auriez grand tort d'en chercher un meilleur... Ne faites pas de votre serf votre maître. Laissez le vilain à son sillon, car le vilain n'a que faire d'un fief et sa nature finit toujours par reprendre le dessus », peut-on lire dans la *Chanson d'Aspremont*, écrite vers 1195. Dans les fabliaux du XIIIe siècle, le vilain parvenu qui épouse sans dot la fille d'un seigneur ruiné est un thème familier. Invité à la table seigneuriale, il s'empiffre et tente même de dérober du lard qu'il cache sous son bonnet, et que la chaleur fait fondre. Armé chevalier, il veut faire croire qu'il a vaillamment combattu alors qu'il est allé dans la forêt cabosser ses armes en les frappant contre les troncs d'arbre. Le tromper est presque un devoir, et si un jeune et beau chevalier lui ravit sa jeune femme, il doit s'estimer heureux de s'en tirer à si bon compte :

Au travail me convient retourner,
Dit le vilain sans plus attendre,
Et gagner nouvel avoir.
Bien sais que je ne fus pas sage
Quand me pris à si haut parage.

Dureté des temps, hypocrisie des clercs, égoïsme des possédants, telle est la subtile satire d'un *Roman de Renart* où l'auteur peut s'abriter derrière la fiction animale. Un monde à l'envers remis à l'endroit, le vilain à sa charrue et la fille du chevalier restant dans son milieu, telle est l'illusion des nobles que flattent les poètes. La réalité est bien différente. Si, à partir de 1250, seuls les fils des chevaliers du Temple peuvent accéder à l'ordre, à la cour du roi, les fils de marchands qui savent tenir les comptes sont trop compétents pour être mis à l'écart.

L'orgueil des villes

« La dame Hersent au large ventre et son mari sont tous deux natifs de Bourgogne. Quand ils vinrent à Orléans, la grande ville, ils n'avaient pas cinq sous vaillants. Ils étaient chétifs, mendiants, dolents, morts de faim. Mais ils firent tant par l'usure qu'en cinq ans ils ont amassé une fortune. Ils tiennent en gage les deux tiers de la ville ; partout ils achètent fours et moulins, et déshéritent tous les francs hommes. »

Les poètes et les jongleurs ont beau tourner le bourgeois en ridicule et le présenter comme un ivrogne et un voleur, ils ne peuvent s'opposer à la marée montante de ceux qui, épousant la vague de l'intelligence, du risque, du progrès et de la modernité, fournissent à un État quelque peu lourdaud leur irremplaçable vivacité.

Même si la population des villes représente peut-être moins de 10 % de la population totale, elle marque de son empreinte créatrice la France du XIIIe siècle et en accélère le cours de l'Histoire. Faisant circuler au coude à coude dans ses rues le savetier et le financier, le bailli du roi et le porteur d'eau, l'étudiant en théologie et le marchand d'épices, le chanoine et la prostituée, elle précipite les échanges, brasse sans fin la vie des hommes et, connaissant, au moins de vue, ceux qui tiennent en mains le pouvoir, fait l'« opinion » en les acclamant ou les brocardant.

Les chroniques du temps, en particulier la *Philippide* de Guillaume le Breton, abondent en descriptions de villes. En Flandre, c'est Gand, « fière de ses maisons ornées de tours, de ses trésors et de sa population nombreuse ; Ypres, renommée pour la teinture, les laines ; Arras, l'antique ville remplie de richesses et avide de grain ; Lille, qui se pare de ses marchands élégants, fait briller dans les royaumes étrangers les draps qu'elle a teints et en rapporte des fortunes dont elle s'enorgueillit. » En Normandie, c'est Rouen, c'est Caen, la cité opulente « tellement pleine d'églises, de maisons et d'habitants qu'elle se reconnaît à peine inférieure à Paris » ; dans la vallée de la Loire, Tours « assise entre deux fleuves, agréable par les eaux qui l'avoisinent, riche en arbres fruitiers et en grains, Angers, ville riche, autour de laquelle s'étendent des champs chargés de vignes, qui fournissent à boire aux Normands et aux Bretons ; Nantes qu'enrichit la Loire poissonneuse et qui fait, avec les pays lointains, un commerce de saumons et de lamproies. »

Même si, dans ces éloges de villes, il faut faire la part des exagérations de l'écrivain, reste que, dans la période précédente, nul ne se serait avisé d'adresser de telles louanges à une population de vilains. Séparée le plus souvent de l'extérieur par une muraille ambitieuse dont l'entretien est le ciment des solidarités, affirmant sa prospérité et son dynamisme par des points de repère emblématiques, la cathédrale, le couvent des ordres mendiants, le château, le beffroi, la halle, la ville prend progressivement conscience d'elle-même.

Faute de pouvoir évaluer précisément l'accroissement de la population urbaine, l'augmentation du périmètre des murailles, la multiplication des paroisses, des couvents et des maisons donnent la mesure de l'« explosion » qui se concentre sur la période 1160-1210. Avec une population dont les estimations varient de 80 000 à 200 000 habitants, Paris est peut-être la ville la plus peuplée d'Occident. Rouen et Montpellier comptent environ 40 000 habitants, Toulouse, 35 000, Tours, 30 000, Orléans, Strasbourg et Narbonne, 25 000, Amiens, Bordeaux, Lille et Metz, 20 000 habitants recrutés pour l'essentiel dans leur environnement proche, l'essentiel des immigrants provenant d'un rayon de moins de 30 kilomètres.

Face à l'idéal aristocratique fondé sur l'oisiveté et la largesse, la ville, dont l'activité repose sur la circulation de l'argent, impose un autre idéal où travail et calcul sont vertus cardinales. Alors que dans les villages, les hommes partis aux champs sont absents une grande partie de la journée, dans le dédale des rues où s'alignent les échoppes des artisans, les hommes sont là à toute heure, travaillant en public. Avec près de trois cents métiers à la fin du XIIᵉ siècle contre cent trente vers 1260, Paris constitue avec la zone flamande la deuxième zone « industrielle » du royaume, un lieu privilégié de l'industrie du luxe et des métiers d'art, où s'échangent vêtements de soie et aumônières brodées, chapeaux de plume et bibelots d'ivoire, tapis et objets de piété, livres d'heures et statuettes. L'argent y afflue de partout, des revenus que le roi tire de son domaine, des dépenses qu'y font les seigneurs de sa suite, les évêques, les abbés, les ambassadeurs, les étudiants et les visiteurs de tous rangs.

Consommateurs et travailleurs y forment une foule tellement nombreuse que la zone d'achalandage de la ville s'élargit de la Bourgogne à l'Oise, des ports de la Manche à la Champagne. De tous les circuits commerciaux qui alimentent la cité, le marché au poisson de mer est le mieux organisé de tous, et aussi le mieux connu grâce au *Livre des métiers* rédigé en 1268 par le prévôt du roi, Étienne Boileau, à des fins de contrôle et de surveillance. Les « marchands étrangers », plus tard appelés « chasse-marée », conduisent les charrettes des ports de mer, de Calais ou de Honfleur, grâce à des relais de chevaux aménagés sur le trajet. Le poisson, pêché et ramené au port l'après-midi, part le soir même, voyage toute la nuit et arrive aux halles de Paris au petit matin. Il leur est interdit de vendre du poisson en route, sous peine d'une amende de 5 sous parisis. Enfin, pour que le contrôle et la vente soient facilités, le poisson doit être présenté dans des paniers de format réglementaire et remplis jusqu'en haut d'une seule sorte de poisson. Quatre jurés qui prêtent serment au prévôt visitent ces paniers pour vérifier la fraîcheur du poisson, pris alors en charge par des vendeurs qui doivent, avant leur entrée en fonction, déposer caution entre les mains des jurés. Leur rôle consiste à vendre la marchandise au meilleur prix possible, les « chasse-marée » ne pouvant vendre eux-mêmes le poisson qu'ils ont apporté. Leur rémunération est fixe et ils doivent remettre dès le lendemain l'argent qu'ils ont retiré de la vente. Les autres intermédiaires, revendeurs des halles ou regrattiers chez qui les particuliers viennent s'approvisionner doivent, eux aussi, acheter leur métier au roi et se soumettre à des règlements très stricts qui leur interdisent, par exemple, de mélanger le poisson de deux marées.

Avec des prud'hommes pour les diriger et des gardes pour en faire respecter minutieusement les règlements, les métiers groupent ainsi les artisans ou les marchands d'une même profession. Fixant les règles de la concurrence, ils protègent le client, limitent les possibilités de fraude mais, une fois acquis, les privilèges qui leur assurent une place honorable dans la société se transforment en monopoles cherchant à limiter l'accès à la profession.

À elle seule, Paris résume en fait l'orgueil des villes médiévales, son dynamisme se manifestant dans la topographie de ses quartiers. La rive droite, au débouché du Grand Pont, devient le foyer du commerce et de l'industrie et gagne tout l'espace compris entre la place de Grève et les Champeaux. En 1183, Philippe Auguste avait acheté aux lépreux les terrains qu'ils y possédaient pour y faire construire deux grands bâtiments que l'on nomma les Halles. Une enceinte de murs, percée de plusieurs portes que l'on fermait le soir, permettait aux marchands de mettre, la nuit, leurs marchandises à l'abri du vol. Aux alentours, se massaient artisans et marchands groupés par métiers qui donnaient leur nom aux rues qu'ils occupaient : la Ferronnerie et la Charronnerie, la Courroierie et la Cordonnerie, la Savonnerie et la Tannerie, la Draperie et la Tisseranderie, la Poterie et la Verrerie. Et l'on voyait dans ce quartier d'Outre-Grand-Pont, les maisons des banquiers lombards et celles des usuriers juifs, dans le quartier de Beaubourg, du Bourg-Thibout et de la basse rue du Temple.

Sur la rive gauche, autrefois couverte de prés et de vignes, l'ancien quartier de calmes monastères est envahi par un peuple de gens d'étude, maîtres et écoliers qui s'établissent sur les pentes de la montagne Sainte-Geneviève. L'industrie du livre, caractéristique du quartier, était ramassée auprès de Saint-Séverin, les écrivains occupant presque toute la rue aux Écrivains.

Au centre, l'île de la Cité est le siège du gouvernement et du pouvoir religieux. Tandis que le Palais devient la résidence quasi permanente du roi, la cathédrale Notre-Dame, dont l'essentiel est achevé en 1240, manifeste l'union entre l'Église et la royauté. Sur la façade, les statues des rois de Juda, sculptées dans ses pierres massives, manifestaient la puissance nouvelle de la monarchie.

Même s'il fallut attendre la première moitié du XIVe siècle pour voir apparaître dans les textes l'appellation *caput regni*, « chef du royaume », Paris est bien devenue à partir de Philippe Auguste la « capitale » de fait, admirée et louangée dans le royaume et à l'étranger.

Ces villes orgueilleuses sont aussi des « nouveaux mondes » où les ascensions sociales restent possibles, des pays de cocagne où l'on peut espérer trouver par terre des bourses remplies de deniers. À Paris,

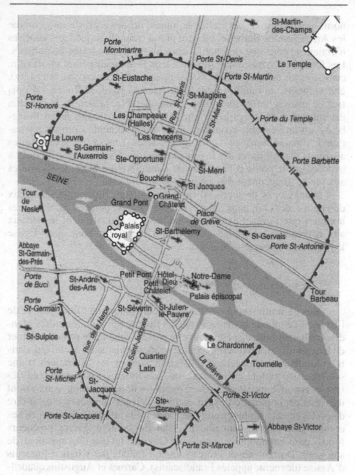

Paris sous Philippe Auguste.

les rues Bertin-Poirée, la rue des Bourdonnais qu'habitaient les Bour-
don, la rue du Bourg-Tibourg, ainsi nommée de Tibout-le-Riche, la
rue Grenier-sur-l'Eau, ainsi nommée par déformation du nom de Garnier dessus l'Eau, la rue Simon-Le-Franc, du nom de Simon Franque,
la rue Guérin-Boisseau, du nom de Guérin Boucel, gardent, par leur

nom, le souvenir de ces riches hommes, de ces « gros » qui, comme les Arrode ou les Barbette, mènent grand train alors que leurs ancêtres n'étaient encore que de chétifs artisans ou de modestes colporteurs. Les Crespin d'Arras ont commencé leur fortune en gérant un moulin, cent ans plus tard, ce sont de riches banquiers. À Besançon, vers 1300, une vingtaine de familles tiennent le haut du pavé. À Rouen, où l'office de maire confère une autorité considérable, la famille Val-Richin détient huit fois la mairie au XIIIe siècle. À Douai, sire Jehan Boinebroke est un véritable tyran qui, dans son testament, a promis réparation aux innombrables « menus qu'il a lésés dans sa vie, les locataires auxquels il a fait payer des loyers exorbitants, les petits artisans qu'il a trompés sur le poids et la qualité de la matière première, les ouvrières auxquelles il accordait des salaires de misère ».

Bienfaiteurs de leurs villes et exploiteurs du peuple, généreux donateurs des hôpitaux mais dilapidant les deniers publics, ces hommes que l'argent avait fait « nobles » et qui offraient les vitraux aux cathédrales en pleine construction méritaient bien que l'Église leur accorde quelque indulgence.

La naissance du Purgatoire

Nés du sentiment que leurs fondateurs eurent de l'inadaptation de l'Église à ce monde bouleversé par les flux de l'argent, les ordres Mendiants allaient faire de cette nouvelle société urbaine le principal gibier de leur apostolat. En réaction contre un monachisme en déclin qui, dans la solitude des campagnes, satisfaisait surtout les aspirations d'une société aristocratique et chevaleresque, ces moines « nouveaux » édifièrent leurs couvents dans les villes, parmi les hommes « nouveaux » dont ils voulaient combattre l'esprit de lucre. Vivant de quêtes, c'est-à-dire de prélèvements sur les circuits de l'argent, ils allaient offrir, aux riches comme aux pauvres, un nouvel idéal de sainteté. Frères prêcheurs fondés par l'Espagnol Dominique de Guzmán (et que l'on appellera, de son nom, Dominicains), Frères mineurs fondés par l'Italien François d'Assise (de même appelés Franciscains), Carmes et Augustins quadrillent les villes. Plus de 400 couvents ont été fondés entre le début des années 1210-1220 et 1275. En 1330, il y a en France 226 villes à couvents mendiants dont 28 avec 4 couvents et 24 avec 3 couvents.

Spécialistes du sermon dont ils font un grand spectacle populaire, auteurs des principaux manuels de confesseurs, à la suite de l'obligation fixée à tous les chrétiens par le concile du Latran en 1215 de se confesser au moins une fois l'an, offrant aux familles des notables bourgeois une sépulture dans leurs églises, ils allaient lever les obstacles qui allaient permettre aux hommes d'argent de concilier la bourse et la vie éternelle.

Comme l'a superbement montré Jacques Le Goff, la naissance du Purgatoire, antichambre assurée du Paradis, offre à ceux dont la vie n'avait pas été exemplaire l'espoir d'échapper à l'Enfer, au premier chef à l'usurier. L'histoire de l'usurier de Liège, composée vers 1220 par le cistercien Césaire de Heisterbach, sous forme d'un dialogue entre un moine et un novice, en est un parfait *exemplum*.

Le moine : « Un usurier de Liège mourut, à notre époque. L'évêque le fit expulser du cimetière. Sa femme se rendit auprès du siège apostolique pour implorer qu'il fût enterré en Terre sainte. Le pape refusa. Elle plaida alors pour son époux : « On m'a dit, Seigneur, qu'homme et femme ne font qu'un et que, selon l'Apôtre, l'homme infidèle peut être sauvé par la femme fidèle. Ce que mon mari a oublié de faire, moi, qui suis une partie de son corps, je le ferai volontiers à sa place. Je suis prête à me faire recluse pour lui et à racheter à Dieu ses péchés. » Cédant aux prières des cardinaux, le pape fit rendre le mort au cimetière. Sa femme élut domicile auprès de son tombeau, s'enferma comme recluse, et s'efforça jour et nuit d'apaiser Dieu pour le salut de son âme par des aumônes, des jeûnes, des prières et des veilles. Au bout de sept ans, son mari lui apparut, vêtu de noir, et la remercia : « Dieu te le rende, car grâce à tes épreuves, j'ai été retiré des profondeurs de l'Enfer et des plus terribles peines. Si tu me rends encore de tels services pendant sept ans, je serai complètement délivré. » Elle le fit. Il lui apparut de nouveau au bout de sept ans, mais, cette fois, vêtu de blanc et l'air heureux. « Merci à Dieu et à toi car j'ai été libéré aujourd'hui. »

Le novice : « Comment peut-il se dire libéré aujourd'hui de l'Enfer, endroit d'où il n'y a nul rachat possible ? »

Le moine : « Les profondeurs de l'Enfer, cela veut dire l'âpreté du Purgatoire. De même lorsque l'Église prie pour les défunts en disant : « Seigneur Jésus-Christ, Roi de Gloire, libère les âmes de tous les fidèles défunts de la main de l'Enfer et des profondeurs du gouffre », elle ne prie pas pour les damnés, mais pour ceux qu'on peut sauver. La main de l'Enfer, les profondeurs du gouffre, cela veut dire ici l'âpreté du Purgatoire. Quant à notre usurier, il n'aurait pas été libéré de ses peines, s'il n'avait pas exprimé une contrition finale. »

Pour les auditeurs de ce texte, et ce dut être une énorme surprise, l'usurier pouvait donc être sauvé par un repentir *in extremis* et par le dévouement d'une femme. En sauvant de l'Enfer des pécheurs qui n'avaient aucune chance d'y échapper auparavant, le Purgatoire levait les obstacles qui auraient pu contenir l'irrésistible ascension de l'argent.

Le temps
de « Monseigneur Saint Louis »

En 1267, avant de partir pour la seconde fois en croisade, Louis IX compose à l'intention de son fils aîné Philippe un testament. « Cher fils, s'il advient que tu deviennes roi, peut-on lire, prends soin d'avoir les qualités qui appartiennent aux rois, c'est-à-dire que tu sois si juste que, quoi qu'il arrive, tu ne t'écartes de la justice. Et s'il advient qu'il y ait querelle entre un pauvre et un riche, soutiens de préférence le pauvre contre le riche jusqu'à ce que tu saches la vérité, et quand tu la connaîtras, fais justice. » *Rendre bonne justice, telle a bien été l'image de ce roi dont la plupart des contemporains pressentaient qu'il serait saint. Porté par les conquêtes matérielles et spirituelles d'une longue période d'essor, il a été la figure emblématique de son siècle.*

La croisade contre les albigeois

Saint Louis est né le 25 avril 1214, quelques semaines avant la bataille de Bouvines. Il est le premier roi de France à avoir connu son grand-père, un grand-père dont la forte personnalité semble l'avoir marqué. En 1226, trois ans après la mort de Philippe Auguste, son père Louis VIII meurt de dysenterie en Auvergne, au retour d'une chevauchée contre les hérétiques du Midi. Voilà donc à la tête du royaume un enfant de douze ans, dont la mère, Blanche de Castille, est une « femme étrangère » n'ayant « ni parents ni amis dans le royaume de France », écrit Joinville, le biographe de Saint Louis. La minorité du jeune roi s'annonce donc difficile, les habitants du royaume, taraudés par l'inquiétude religieuse, se rappelant de l'imprécation de l'Ecclésiaste, « Malheur à la terre dont le roi est un enfant ».

Certes, Louis hérite d'un royaume élargi, riche, solidement tenu en main par les baillis et où le roi ne tient son pouvoir que de Dieu. Pourtant, au-delà de la Loire et sur les rives de la Méditerranée, dans le vieux pays des Goths, l'écho de Bouvines ne semble pas avoir été entendu. Pour les hommes du Nord, ce Midi reste un monde étrange dont ils ne comprennent pas la langue. Berceau d'Aliénor d'Aquitaine, de funeste mémoire, c'est aussi pour eux un monde sans foi ni loi, hypocrite et indécent à destination duquel les migrations sont rares. On migre beaucoup dans la France de Saint Louis, d'ouest en est, d'Aquitaine vers le Languedoc ou la Provence, rarement du sud vers le nord. Limousins et Auvergnats ignorent le Bassin parisien tandis que la présence des *Francigenae* est exceptionnelle en Midi.

Dans ces pays où la parole a toujours été libre, les troubadours insolents, la femme plus indépendante, le peuple accoutumé à la palabre, l'anticléricalisme est aussi beaucoup plus vivace, la corruption du clergé et l'ardeur de l'Église à exiger la dîme y étant pour beaucoup. Dans cette région de contraste qui juxtapose villes opulentes et terres ingrates, où les maisons agglutinées dans les *castra*, ces villages de hauteur, sont autant de réseaux de solidarité et de rébellion, l'hérésie qui fleurit un peu partout en Europe a trouvé son terreau. Des clercs critiques composent des textes satiriques très violents contre une hiérarchie souillée par l'argent. Le rituel des liturgies cesse de satisfaire des chevaliers et des marchands qui cherchent une nourriture plus spirituelle. Des prédicateurs itinérants prêchent la pénitence, récusent le pouvoir du pape et invitent hommes et femmes à « suivre nus le Christ nu ». C'est prôner le « mépris du monde » et vouloir revenir à la pureté originelle du christianisme.

Vers 1170, Pierre Valdo, un riche marchand de Lyon, découvre dans l'Évangile que sa richesse lui ferme à jamais l'entrée du Paradis, décide de tout quitter pour prêcher la pénitence et la pauvreté, et fonde la secte des pauvres de Lyon. Ses disciples, condamnés par le pape, s'établissent dans les Alpes, en Italie et en Provence et séduisent une population admirant ces « bonshommes ».

Mais de toutes les hérésies, la plus spectaculaire est celle que nous appelons aujourd'hui « catharisme » mais dont les adeptes étaient le plus souvent appelés « albigeois » par les contemporains. Dans un temps où le diable était partout, hantant les rêves des moines et faisant le siège des sculptures romanes, les cathares croient que Dieu, parfait et éternel, n'a pu créer le mal. Ils croient donc à l'existence de deux dieux qui se livrent une guerre sans merci, un Dieu bon, invisible, qui sauve les âmes, et un Dieu mauvais, le Dieu de colère de l'Ancien Testament, maître du monde visible, qui corrompt les corps et les âmes. Clef de voûte de leur enseignement : le monde matériel n'a jamais été créé par Dieu ; il est tout entier l'œuvre de Satan. Le Christ n'a-t-il pas dit, citation favorite des cathares : « Mon royaume n'est pas de ce monde ? »

Prince du monde terrestre, le Diable a su égarer les hommes, faisant de l'Église, assimilée à la Bête de l'Apocalypse, sa prostituée. Tout ce qui vient d'elle est néfaste : ses sacrements n'ont aucune valeur ; bien plus, ce sont des pièges dans la mesure où ils font croire aux hommes que des gestes purement mécaniques peuvent apporter le salut. L'hostie ne peut être le corps du Christ et la croix, instrument de l'humiliation de Jésus, doit faire horreur.

Ayant posé en principe la création du monde par l'esprit du mal, les cathares sont amenés à condamner toutes les manifestations de la vie terrestre et à respecter les commandements suivants : ne pas tuer, fût-ce un animal, ne pas juger, de pas invoquer le nom de Dieu, ne pas prononcer de serment, ne pas posséder de biens terrestres, ne pas manger de nourriture d'origine animale car, provenant de la procréation, elle est impure. Seul le poisson qui passe, au Moyen Âge, pour être asexué, peut être consommé. En outre, les prêtres cathares doivent s'abstenir de tout rapport sexuel dans la mesure où la procréation risque de causer la perdition de nouvelles âmes.

Pour être sauvé, c'est-à-dire réconcilié avec l'Esprit saint, il faut entrer dans l'Église cathare et recevoir l'imposition des mains d'un de ses ministres, un « parfait ». Ce baptême, le « consolament », est en même temps une absolution quand il est donné à un croyant à l'article de la mort. Lavant *in extremis* les fautes commises tout au long d'une vie « imparfaite », ce « consolament » était un formidable passeport pour l'au-delà. Avec ses deux dieux, le dualisme cathare permettait de résoudre en fait ce qui reste l'énigme majeure pour les chrétiens non versés en théologie : comment un Dieu bon et tout-puissant peut permettre tant de malheurs sur terre ?

Rejetant les dogmes essentiels du catholicisme comme ses symboles les plus sacrés, l'Eucharistie et l'Incarnation, convertissant les élites urbaines et rurales, la petite noblesse comme la bourgeoisie des villes, les autorités comme une partie du clergé, le catharisme était pour l'Église établie une formidable menace.

Contre lui, elle lança d'abord des missionnaires qui se jugeaient aussi « parfaits » que les parfaits, les moines cisterciens. Ils n'eurent aucun succès. À partir de 1206, imposant un nouveau style de prédication plus humble, organisant de grands débats publics avec les hérétiques, les frères prêcheurs de Dominique tentent de se montrer aussi ascétiques et fermes dans leur foi que leurs adversaires. Sans grand succès non plus.

Pour le nouveau pape, Innocent III, élu en 1198, la parole devait désormais céder la place à l'épée. En 1204, puis en 1205 et 1207, il sollicite l'intervention de Philippe Auguste qui se dérobe, les conseillers du roi répugnant à ces aventures trop lointaines. En janvier 1208, l'assassinat, à Saint-Gilles, du légat du pape, Pierre de Castelnau, par l'un des serviteurs du comte de Toulouse, soupçonné de complicité avec les hérétiques, est le prétexte qui permet de déclencher la croisade contre les « albigeois », la première croisade lancée par l'Église à l'intérieur même de la chrétienté. Philippe, qui ne peut plus se récuser, autorise ses chevaliers à partir.

En juin 1209, placée sous le commandement du comte Simon de Montfort-l'Amaury, une troupe de croisés, accompagnée par des mercenaires avides, part de Lyon, s'avance en pays hérétique et massacre la population de Béziers en juillet. C'est là que le légat du pape Arnaud Amaury aurait prononcé la fameuse phrase : « Tuez-les tous, Dieu reconnaîtra les siens ! » C'est le début d'une guerre sanglante où les prétextes religieux cachent mal les appétits territoriaux des hommes du Nord. En 1213, à Muret, Simon écrase le comte de Toulouse et le roi d'Aragon venu à son secours. En 1215, Philippe laisse enfin son fils Louis accomplir son vœu de croisade et montrer une armée royale dans le Midi. Devenu roi en 1223, Louis VIII prend une nouvelle fois la croix en 1226 et obtient aisément la soumission du Languedoc avant de mourir sur le chemin du retour. En 1229, au traité de Paris, le comte de Toulouse finit par s'accorder avec Blanche de Castille, veuve et régente, promet de céder ses fiefs à la couronne en mariant son unique héritière au frère du roi de France et se prête à une cérémonie d'expiation dans Notre-Dame de Paris. Et en 1244, alors que l'Inquisition, instituée par le pape Grégoire IX en 1233 et confiée aux dominicains, pourchasse méthodiquement les hérétiques, la forteresse de Montségur, dernier sanctuaire du catharisme, tombe après un siège de dix mois. Deux cents parfaits périssent sur le bûcher. Saint Louis a ainsi été le premier roi de France à faire brûler des hérétiques. « Quand on entend médire de la foi chrétienne, confiait-il à Joinville, il ne faut la défendre qu'avec l'épée, dont on doit donner dans le ventre autant qu'elle y peut entrer. » Et dans les *Enseignements* qu'il donne à son fils, il écrit : « Fais chasser les hérétiques et les mauvaises gens de ta terre autant que tu le pourras en requérant comme il le faut le sage conseil des bonnes gens afin que ta terre en soit purgée. » Le saint roi est aussi un roi persécuteur, en harmonie avec un siècle qui ressent comme une menace tout ce qui peut troubler son harmonie. C'est au nom de cette pureté qu'il pourchassera les prostituées fort nombreuses dans l'île de la Cité et qu'il croisait quand il allait entendre la messe à Notre-Dame, proscrira les jeux de hasard, punira le blasphème et ceux qui « osaient dire de vilaines paroles », fera brûler les exemplaires du Talmud et interdira aux juifs d'exercer l'usure.

Un saint laïc

Lors du procès de canonisation de 1297, l'un des témoins dit : « Non seulement, dans le gouvernement du royaume, il avait jour et nuit veillé à la protection des corps et des choses corporelles comme il sied à l'office royal [...] mais, préoccupé plus qu'on ne saurait croire du salut des âmes, il en avait un tel souci [...] qu'il avait exercé à la manière d'un roi le sacerdoce, à la manière d'un prêtre la royauté. » Saint Louis voulut en effet être *rex* et *sacerdos*, roi et prêtre à la fois, régir ses passions comme régir ses sujets avec la même mesure, devenir un saint laïc.

Dans le domaine particulièrement sensible de la sexualité, il a voulu être un parfait époux chrétien. Ainsi, marié en 1234 à Marguerite de Provence, il a respecté la recommandation que l'Église faisait à l'intention des jeunes mariés. Il a attendu trois nuits avant de s'unir charnellement à sa jeune épouse et les a consacrées à la prière, pour montrer que le mariage n'a pas pour seul but de satisfaire les besoins sexuels. Puis, tout au long de son mariage, il a scrupuleusement respecté les interdits issus du calendrier liturgique, y ajoutant des périodes supplémentaires de continence. Pourtant, « véritable tempérament », durant les périodes où les rapports étaient permis, le roi ne se contentait pas de retrouver Marguerite la nuit. Il aimait aussi « consommer » le jour, au grand désespoir de sa mère qui tentait de s'introduire dans leur chambre pour mettre fin à leurs ébats. Saint Louis est donc, et c'est une exception, un saint qui a eu des relations sexuelles mais qui, par totale maîtrise de lui-même, a respecté à la lettre la discipline chrétienne de la sexualité conjugale. Une manière d'épouser l'esprit d'un siècle qui, réhabilitant l'idée de nature, finissait par admettre tout ce qui était charnel. Une manière surtout d'incarner cette autre idée force de son temps, l'idée de mesure qui place le bon chrétien à égale distance entre l'ange et la bête.

Cette volonté de mesure, qui a fait dire à ses proches que l'on ne vit jamais un « homme plus harmonieux ni de plus grande perfection en tout ce qui peut être vu en un homme », s'est aussi exprimée à table où le roi a adopté le modèle alimentaire ascétique des ordres mendiants. « Son système alimentaire », écrit Jacques Le Goff dans la biographie exemplaire qu'il lui a consacrée, « consiste à manger ce qui est moins bon (par exemple les petits poissons plutôt que les gros), à déprécier ce qui est bon (par exemple mettre de l'eau froide dans les sauces, les soupes, le vin), à s'abstenir de ce qui est délicat (lamproies, fruits frais), à manger et boire modérément, manger et boire toujours la même quantité mesurément (par exemple pour le pain et le vin), pratiquer fréquemment le jeûne. Il corrige le caractère royal de la vaisselle – sa coupe d'or – par la médiocrité du contenu de nourriture ou de boisson. Par cette ascèse, il renonce aux plaisirs de la table auxquels il est naturellement porté et, inversement, s'oblige à consommer ce qui ne lui plaît pas, par exemple la bière. »

Saint Louis a voulu aussi être un saint guerrier, la mesure en la matière consistant à n'être jamais agresseur et à rechercher toujours la juste paix. « Cher fils », écrivait-il toujours dans son testament, « si l'on te fait tort, essaie plusieurs voies pour savoir si tu ne pourras trouver moyen de recouvrer ton droit avant de faire guerre. » Ainsi, malgré l'avis des gens de son conseil et quitte à apparaître faible, il préféra traiter avec le roi d'Angleterre. En 1259, le traité de Paris rétrocédait à Henri III d'Angleterre les droits que Philippe Auguste avait acquis en Limousin, en Périgord et en Quercy. En échange, le roi d'Angleterre renonçait définitivement à la Normandie, à l'Anjou, à la Touraine, au Maine et au Poitou et s'obligeait à prêter au Capétien l'hommage du vassal pour les fiefs qu'il tenait en France. Le 4 décembre 1259, dans le jardin du palais de la Cité, en présence de nombreux prélats et barons anglais et français et du peuple venu en foule, il mit genou en terre, ses mains dans celles de Louis. L'année précédente, le roi de France avait également renoncé à ses droits sur la marche d'Espagne tenue par le roi d'Aragon en échange du Languedoc.

Saint Louis fut surtout animé par une « jalousie de justice », voulant, comme le roi Salomon, faire partout régner l'équité. À cet effet, en 1247, il fit entreprendre une vaste enquête sur l'administration du royaume pour corriger les abus commis auparavant. En décembre 1254, surtout, prenant en compte les résultats de cette première enquête, une grande ordonnance dessine les voies d'une vaste réforme de l'État. Les hommes du roi doivent désormais « rendre la justice sans distinction des personnes » et n'accepter aucun cadeau. Ils ne peuvent acheter des immeubles sur le territoire où ils exercent leurs fonctions et doivent considérer que tout accusé non encore condamné est présumé innocent. Et quand ils quittent leur charge, ils doivent rester sur place quarante jours pour pouvoir répondre aux plaintes dont ils feraient l'objet. Nommé prévôt de Paris, Étienne Boileau est l'homme à poigne qui rétablit l'ordre dans une cité turbulente et fait rédiger *Le Livre des métiers*.

C'est à cette époque en effet que commence l'enregistrement des arrêts rendus par la Cour du roi lors de ses « Parlements », c'est-à-dire lors de ses sessions judiciaires. C'était accoutumer le peuple à faire appel à la justice royale et développer l'usage de la jurisprudence. En 1261, l'interdiction du duel judiciaire au profit de l'enquête et de la preuve par témoin sanctionne le recul d'une justice féodale et l'irrésistible ascension d'un État de droit.

L'ordonnance de 1262, qui interdit de contrefaire la monnaie royale et qui impose dans certaines limites le monopole de sa circulation dans le royaume en est une autre illustration. L'établissement d'une « bonne » monnaie contre une « mauvaise », la frappe de « purs » deniers (l'expression est dans les ordonnances) pour remplacer les deniers « pelés », usés, contrefaits ou de mauvais aloi sont, pour les théologiens du temps, autant d'actes de justice conformes au plan de Dieu. Bientôt, la contrefaçon de la monnaie royale sera considérée comme un crime de lèse-majesté.

Sur les écus d'or qu'il a fait frapper, après cinq siècles d'interruption, on voyait, au droit, le symbole capétien, un écu aux fleurs de lys, avec la légende : « Louis par la grâce de Dieu roi de France », et au revers une croix fleuronnée cantonnée de quatre fleurs de lys et la proclamation solennelle : « Le Christ triomphe, le Christ règne, le Christ domine ». Une inscription qui signifiait à quel point la monnaie était « sacrée ».

Mais le grand dessein du roi, qui a voulu être un modèle de roi chrétien, est resté la croisade, une croisade dont l'esprit s'effilochait au rythme des échecs répétés, une croisade qui le conduira à la captivité et à la mort. En 1244, au sortir d'une maladie très grave au cours de laquelle il aurait eu une vision, il décide de prendre la croix malgré la farouche opposition de sa mère et de l'évêque de Paris qui veulent le faire renoncer à son projet. Il ne la quittera plus. Le 12 juin 1248, à Saint-Denis, il prend l'oriflamme, le bâton et la besace des pèlerins, gagne Notre-Dame puis, pieds nus, accompagné d'une grande procession du peuple, se rend à l'abbaye royale de Saint-Antoine-des-Champs fondée par Foulques, le prédicateur de la première croisade. Le 28 août, il s'embarque à Aigues-Mortes, dans ce Midi qui faisait partie depuis peu du domaine royal. Sa femme et ses frères l'accompagnent. Il en reviendra six années plus tard, en 1254, après avoir vu son armée massacrée par les Sarrasins à Mansourah en février 1250, avoir été fait lui-même prisonnier, avoir payé une énorme rançon de 400 000 livres et être resté en Terre sainte pour en organiser la défense et tenter naïvement de convertir le grand Mongol en dépêchant chez ces « fils de l'Enfer » un moine franciscain, Guillaume de Rubrouck !

C'est parce qu'il fut accablé par l'échec de cette croisade et se demanda ce qu'il fallait faire pour plaire à Dieu que Louis se lança alors dans l'œuvre de justice dont la grande ordonnance de 1254 est le point d'orgue. Rejetant les ornements dont il aimait se parer dans sa jeunesse, ne quittant pratiquement plus les sévères vêtements qu'il avait pris en se croisant, s'attardant aux offices, entouré des Frères Mendiants, soignant les lépreux et distribuant largement les aumônes, il voulut étendre à son royaume le programme de pénitence et de purification qui ordonnait sa propre existence.

Les ordonnances qu'il publia à la veille de son départ pour une nouvelle croisade « pour péché abattre » en sont une nouvelle illustration. En 1269, on obligea les juifs à assister aux sermons des convertisseurs et à porter la rouelle de feutre ou de drap écarlate en matière de signe d'infamie. Et, le 25 juin 1270, une semaine avant de s'embarquer, il enverra d'Aigues-Mortes une lettre recommandant aux « lieutenants » à qui il avait confié le royaume de punir vigoureusement tous les pollueurs, blasphémateurs, prostituées, malfaiteurs et autres scélérats.

Le 1er juillet 1270, au plus fort de la canicule, le roi s'embarqua pour Tunis, pensant peut-être, avec l'illusion qui a caractérisé sa vision du monde, en convertir l'émir. De nouveau la dysenterie et le typhus déciment l'armée de 15 000 hommes qui a débarqué à La Goulette. Après la mort de son fils Jean, le 3 août, Saint Louis meurt à son tour le 25. Les funérailles du roi « martyr » auront lieu à Saint Denis, le 22 mai 1271, presque neuf mois après sa mort. Sur le chemin du retour, en Sicile et en Italie, ses ossements et ses entrailles, disputés entre son fils Philippe et son frère Charles d'Anjou après qu'on les eut fait bouillir dans du vin mélangé d'eau pour que les chairs se détachent des os, avaient déjà fait des miracles.

Le temps des cathédrales

Fers de lance du royaume très chrétien, les cathédrales, sur les chantiers desquelles on s'attardait depuis parfois près d'un siècle, sont achevées en moins d'une génération, comme s'il était devenu urgent de célébrer l'alliance entre le Capétien et l'Église et de diffuser à une société troublée par l'hérésie le message d'une foi rénovée. Chartres, Reims, Beauvais, Rouen, Bourges, Laon, Noyon, Soissons, Amiens, Notre-Dame de Paris, autant de chantiers que stimulent la prospérité des villes, l'afflux des aumônes, la science des « docteurs ès pierres », l'ardeur spirituelle des fidèles et la passion contagieuse de bâtir des évêques. Autant d'édifices qui affirment les nouveaux liens entre l'œuvre d'art et la fierté urbaine, à une époque où le premier critère de la beauté était celui de la grandeur. On sait ce qui arriva à Beauvais où, par orgueil, on voulut construire le chœur de la cathédrale à une hauteur de 48 mètres. La voûte s'effondra en 1284 !

Des textes célèbres traduisent l'émerveillement des contemporains au spectacle de ces chantiers immenses : des hommes et des femmes de haut rang courbant la nuque pour s'atteler, comme des animaux, aux chariots chargés des matériaux nécessaires à la construction ; pendant ces lourds transports, un silence et un ordre absolus ; aux haltes, les confessions et les prières ; des infirmes transportés dans l'espoir d'une guérison miraculeuse ; un prêtre auprès de chaque chariot, ordonnant les exercices de piété aux fidèles qui s'étendent sur la terre pour la baiser ; des enfants donnant l'exemple du zèle, la présentation des reliques, des corps dénudés jusqu'à la ceinture rampant vers les autels et l'appel d'une foule qui réclame la flagellation comme une grâce et bénit chacun des coups de verge tombant sur les épaules... Un travail de titans et de fourmis à la fois, accompli par des légions de bénévoles, poussés par la piété ou le désir de mortification et réunis pour édifier, au chant des cantiques, la maison de Dieu.

La réalité est souvent moins poétique, tout donnant à penser que, plus souvent que la foi, c'est la nécessité qui a attiré les armées de porteurs de hotte, de piqueurs et de bêcheurs. En outre, l'entente entre le peuple et les évêques n'a pas toujours été parfaite. C'est avec les pierres du chantier de la cathédrale que les habitants de Reims élevèrent en 1233 des barricades pour manifester contre leur archevêque. Si le chantier de la cathédrale Saint-Sauveur d'Aix-en-Provence n'avançait pas, c'est que les bourgeois montraient plus d'empressement à financer les couvents des Frères Mendiants. Les sépultures que l'Église autorisa à l'intérieur de la maison de Dieu sont bien des distinctions offertes aux puissants. Et les effigies des évêques établies sur les grandes verrières des cathédrales marquent bien la volonté des prélats de célébrer leur gloire.

Reste que, édifiées au moment où les Frères prêcheurs s'efforcent d'atteindre leur auditoire en employant la langue de tous les jours et en introduisant dans leurs sermons des anecdotes adaptées à la sensibilité de leur public, les cathédrales s'élèvent comme des sermons permanents adressés au peuple des villes, comme des Bibles illustrées où, rangés en bon ordre, les vertus et les vices fournissent aux prédicateurs les thèmes de leurs enseignements moraux. Le saint du XIIe siècle était un saint aristocratique, obsédé par la prouesse ascétique. Le saint du XIIIe siècle apparaît moins tendu, plus souriant, plus « urbain ». Alors que l'art roman était un hommage craintif à la gloire divine, les nouveaux édifices dont les flèches s'élèvent majestueusement au-dessus des cités ont pour mission de réhabiliter une nature dont les cathares avaient fait l'œuvre de Satan.

L'harmonie des cathédrales exprime cette nouvelle vision du monde. Ce n'est plus seulement la terre qui s'élève vers le ciel, mais le ciel qui descend sur la terre grâce à la lumière qui s'y déverse à travers les vastes verrières que la maîtrise technique et le génie géométrique ont permis d'ouvrir dans des parois libérées de la poussée des voûtes. Dieu est lumière, et sa maison doit préfigurer la Jérusalem céleste dont les murs, selon le texte de l'*Apocalypse*, sont construits de pierres précieuses. À Saint-Denis, Suger avait donné le ton ; à la Sainte-Chapelle, l'audacieux maître d'œuvre a quasiment fait disparaître les murs. Défiant les lois de la pesanteur mais de dimensions modestes, la chapelle du palais royal marie hardiesse et modestie, dévotion et ostentation, à l'image du saint roi qui en a fait son lieu de prière.

L'art gothique est une fête, et l'homme peut, comme saint François, composer des chansons d'amour et retrouver dans les créatures terrestres la bonté du Créateur. Combattant le fondement même du catharisme, l'art des cathédrales est un hymne à la Création et à la Nature. Il substitue au bestiaire monstrueux des chapiteaux romans et aux démons du Jugement dernier des fleurs réelles et des personnages humains qui montrent sur leur visage le sourire des anges et dont les yeux s'ouvrent sur les merveilles du monde. Ce sont des êtres sereins, lavés de tout péché et appelés à ressusciter, à l'image du roi saint dont les traits physiques, dessinés par un chroniqueur, font référence à la joie qui illuminait son visage : « Par sa stature, il dépassait tout le monde des épaules et au-dessus, la beauté de son corps tenait à l'harmonie de ses proportions, sa tête était ronde comme il convient au siège de la sagesse, son visage placide et serein avait extérieurement quelque chose d'angélique, ses yeux de colombe émettaient des rayons gracieux, sa face était à la fois blanche et brillante.... On était mû intérieurement vers la joie au seul aspect extérieur du roi. »

Le Dieu des cathédrales gothiques n'est pas un Éternel abstrait que symbolise l'éclat du buisson ardent, mais un Dieu vivant qui a pris le visage de l'homme, vécu et souffert comme lui. Et puisque les cathares font de l'hostie une matière impure qui ne saurait être un véhicule de l'Esprit, les statues de Reims distribuent la communion, ce sacrement majeur de la foi catholique.

En achetant pour 100 000 livres aux barons latins qui s'étaient emparés de Constantinople en 1204 la plus précieuse des reliques, la couronne d'épines que Jésus aurait portée pendant sa Passion, Saint Louis combat plus efficacement l'hérésie cathare que les croisés de Simon de Montfort. Couronne d'humilité, la couronne d'épines illustre bien en effet l'image du Christ nouveau qui s'impose au fronton des cathédrales, un Christ humilié qui, après avoir pris corps dans le ventre d'une femme, a souffert dans sa chair avant de mourir sur la croix, cette croix dont les parfaits avaient fait un insigne dérisoire.

En même temps, il réalisait un formidable « coup de maître » en faisant de la France la terre chérie de Dieu. « De même que notre Seigneur Jésus Christ a choisi la Terre de la promesse (la Terre sainte) pour y montrer les mystères de sa rédemption », proclame alors l'archevêque de Sens, Gautier Cornut, « de même il semble bien et l'on croit que pour vénérer plus pieusement le triomphe de sa Passion, il a choisi spécialement notre France... »

Possession privée du roi, la relique protégeait, à travers sa personne, le royaume et ses sujets.

La diffusion des « Lumières »

Un petit recueil de trente-trois feuillets de parchemin cousus sous une peau épaisse et couverts de dessins et de commentaires en dialecte picard nous fait pénétrer dans l'intimité de ces architectes le plus souvent anonymes qui ont édifié les cathédrales à l'aune de leur talent et de leur foi. On y lit au commencement : « Villard de Honnecourt vous salue et demande à tous ceux qui travailleront aux divers genres d'ouvrages contenus en ce livre de prier pour lui, car dans ce livre on peut trouver grand secours pour s'instruire des principes fondamentaux de la maçonnerie et de la construction en charpente. Vous y trouverez aussi la méthode pour dessiner au trait, selon que l'art de la géométrie le commande et enseigne. » C'est dans cet *Album* qu'apparaît pour la première fois le mot « *ogive* ».

Né à Honnecourt, un village au bord de l'Escaut, près de Cambrai, Villard a reçu sa première formation dans l'abbaye cistercienne voisine de Vauxcelles, où il réalisa ses premiers travaux. Puis il voyagea, visitant les chantiers des cathédrales de Chartres, de Meaux et surtout de Reims et de Laon. Vers 1235, il part en Hongrie, où il construit un grand nombre d'abbayes cisterciennes. En 1257, c'est probablement lui qui achève la construction de l'église collégiale de Saint-Quentin. En effet, les élévations intérieure et extérieure du chœur sont conformes à celles de la cathédrale de Reims, notées dans son *Album*, et le tracé incorrect de la rose de Chartres est reproduit dans l'une des chapelles de la collégiale. Même s'il n'a pas le génie géométrique d'un Hugues Libergier, qui a dirigé la construction de l'église Saint-Nicaise de Reims, d'un Jean d'Orbais, le premier architecte de Reims, ou d'un Pierre de Montreuil, le maître d'œuvre de Notre-Dame de Paris, Villard de Honnecourt est représentatif de l'homme cultivé de son temps.

Tout d'abord, tandis que jusque-là les intellectuels composaient en dictant, Villard écrit comme les producteurs de sermons et les légistes du roi. Une société de tradition orale s'habitue désormais à manier l'écrit comme elle fait l'apprentissage de l'argent dans la vie économique. Ensuite, il partage avec ses lecteurs un immense appétit de savoir, un goût pour l'encyclopédie, s'intéressant à la zoologie, à la manière de confectionner un herbier, aux recettes contre les blessures, fréquentes sur les chantiers, au fonctionnement des machines dont il trace le schéma, aux problèmes élémentaires de géométrie pratique, au calcul de la résistance des matériaux, aux représentations de la figure humaine et des animaux, à l'art de retrouver les poses, aux automates, telle cette colombe qui pouvait absorber une coupe d'eau.

Voilà bien aussi le type d'ouvrages qui plaisait au roi, non un ouvrage de savante théologie comme en produisaient les grands universitaires de son temps, Albert le Grand ou Thomas d'Aquin, mais une encyclopédie qui rassemble la masse des faits et des idées produits pendant les siècles précédents, à l'image du *Grand Miroir* composé par Vincent de Beauvais, un travail qui mobilisa toute une équipe de dominicains.

Le temps de Saint Louis est aussi celui d'un épanouissement intellectuel exceptionnel, Paris devenant la capitale culturelle de l'Occident. C'est ce que voulaient exprimer le cardinal Eudes de Châteauroux en disant que « la Gaule est le four où cuit le pain intellectuel du monde entier » et le pape Innocent III quand il écrivait que l'université parisienne était le « fleuve qui féconde la terre de l'Église universelle ». Communautés de maîtres et d'étudiants dont les privilèges sont garantis par les autorités du lieu et placées sous l'autorité directe du pape, les universités sont des foyers de bouillonnement intellectuel et des milieux particulièrement remuants, où se frottent des « escholiers » d'origines sociales diverses et de « nations » différentes, Français, Picards, Normands et Anglais élisant un chef commun.

En 1229, dans les premières années de la régence, le jeune roi de France doit ainsi gérer la grève de l'université de Paris, la première grande grève connue de l'Occident. Elle éclate à la suite d'une bagarre d'étudiants chez un cabaretier du faubourg Saint-Marcel. Pour rétablir l'ordre, les sergents royaux et leurs archers tuent et blessent quelques étudiants. Il faudra deux ans pour que le conflit s'apaise, Louis ayant fait les concessions nécessaires en payant une amende pour les violences subies par les étudiants. Véritable charte de l'université de Paris, la bulle papale *Parens scientiarum* d'avril 1231 lui assurait définitivement son autonomie et ses privilèges. À la même époque, Montpellier devient un centre d'études médicales et juridiques, Orléans se spécialise dans l'enseignement du droit romain et Toulouse est fondée pour combattre l'hérésie. Et comme beaucoup d'étudiants sont obligés de travailler pour payer leur nourriture et leurs livres, des mécènes fondent des collèges qui sont des hôtels meublés où ces jeunes gens désargentés trouvent le vivre et le couvert. Ainsi, en 1257, Robert de Sorbon, l'un des confesseurs de Saint Louis, fonde rue Coupe-Gueule un collège pour seize étudiants se destinant à la théologie et qui portera son nom.

Dans ce royaume très chrétien où s'agite ce petit monde des intellectuels, l'Arabe est à la mode, à tel point que l'un d'entre eux, Adélard de Bath, avouera malicieusement qu'il a attribué à des Arabes ses pensées personnelles pour mieux les faire admettre par ses lecteurs. En effet, depuis que l'Occident a redécouvert les œuvres jusqu'alors inconnues d'Aristote grâce aux traductions et aux commentaires des philosophes arabes comme Averroès, la majorité des lettrés s'est précipitée sur cette nourriture suspecte avec une avidité que la soif de savoir ne suffit pas à expliquer. L'autorité ecclésiastique tenta bien de la contenir, mais, en 1231, le pape dut accorder l'absolution aux maîtres et aux étudiants excommuniés pour avoir lu le philosophe grec et laisser ses admirateurs déclarer, modestement ironiques, que ce qui est vrai suivant la foi ne l'est pas toujours selon la raison.

Il appartenait aux dominicains, décidément au four et au moulin, de réaliser l'indispensable synthèse entre le savoir profane et la science sacrée pour que, rectifiée, la pensée fulgurante du païen puisse être adaptée au message du Christ. Ce fut l'œuvre d'Albert le Grand puis de son élève, Thomas d'Aquin, professeur à Paris, dont la *Somme théologique* représente un gigantesque effort pour assimiler la pensée antique et ne pas troubler l'harmonie du monde chrétien.

Ce n'est peut-être pas l'œuvre la plus caractéristique du siècle de Saint Louis. Si Aristote séduisait l'université et Lancelot le public des châteaux, le *Roman de la Rose*, commencé sous la régence de Blanche de Castille par Guillaume de Lorris et repris, vers 1270, par Jean de Meung, traduit, mieux que tout, la marche du temps. Propagateur dévôt de l'amour courtois, Guillaume de Lorris avait composé un art d'aimer d'une inégalable délicatesse où Amour avait pour ennemi Male-Bouche, la médisante, qui, lorsqu'elle veille aux créneaux où la Rose est recluse, s'épuise à chanter contre les femmes. Dans les vers de Guillaume, Raison, voulant détourner l'Amant du service d'Amour, s'efforce en vain de lui démontrer combien, à aimer, il y a peu de joie pour tant de peines. Dans la suite de Jean de Meung, Raison tient un autre discours.

« Aimez, dit-elle maintenant, mais fuyez cet amour insensé où s'égare la rêverie, fuyez ce pays de convention que vous peuplez de chimères, où la femme est idole, où la volupté multiplie ses raffinements corrupteurs. Aimez ; mais aimez comme il faut aimer : en cédant, sans le compliquer, à l'instinct qui doit assurer la perpétuité des espèces. »

Une manière brutale de rejeter Idéal pour peindre la vie. Une manière de célébrer dame Nature et de penser hardiment que Faux-Semblant, le fils de Tromperie et de Mensonge, était en train de faire le siège du royaume de France. Le temps de « Monseigneur Saint Louis » ne fut peut-être qu'un éphémère âge d'or.

France, fin de siècle

Q *uand, en 1285, Philippe le Bel devient roi de France, le royaume semble alors à son apogée. La France est de loin l'État le plus peuplé d'Europe et depuis qu'en 1261, le fils d'un artisan de Troyes est devenu pape, le monde chrétien semble vivre à l'heure française. Le 29 novembre 1314, quand il meurt, le temps de « Monseigneur Saint Louis » apparaît déjà comme celui d'une « Belle Époque » révolue. Cette même année, en effet, on découvre que, se laissant prendre aux délices de l'amour courtois, les brus de Philippe ont livré leur corps à des amants. Au-delà du fait divers, la révélation du scandale montrait que le péché avait souillé une dynastie dont la sainteté avait fait la force. En cette fin de siècle, le prince du mal semble avoir pris de nouveau possession du royaume.*

L'exaltation de l'État

En 1180, quand Philippe Auguste était devenu roi de France, Noyon, Paris, Sens et Bourges bornaient les limites de son domaine. Un siècle plus tard, le Capétien est seigneur sur les rives de la Manche, de l'Atlantique et de la Méditerranée. En 1271, à la suite de la mort sans enfants d'Alphonse de Poitiers et de sa femme Jeanne de Toulouse, leur héritage est tombé dans l'escarcelle du roi, comme le prévoyait le traité de Paris de 1229. En 1284, le mariage du futur Philippe le Bel avec Jeanne, l'héritière du royaume de Navarre et du comté de Champagne et de Brie, prépare leur réunion au domaine. Et même si quatre grands fiefs échappent encore au roi, la Bretagne, la Bourgogne, la Guyenne et la Flandre, le petit-fils de Saint Louis, fort conscient d'une légitimité que le martyre de son grand-père a consacrée, a le sentiment que ses vassaux, fussent-ils grands, comptent pour bien peu de chose.

En 1294, 1295 et 1296, des expéditions rondement menées en Guyenne ont ôté au roi d'Angleterre le goût d'intervenir sur le continent. En Flandre, en revanche, les armées royales se heurtent à la résistance d'un peuple rebelle à la fleur de lys. En 1302, à Courtrai, les arbalétriers flamands infligent aux chevaliers français, empêtrés dans leurs lourdes armures, une sanglante défaite et peuvent tapisser Notre-Dame de Courtrai avec les éperons d'or ramassés sur le champ de bataille. Mais en 1304, à Mons-en-Pévèle, le roi lui-même, impressionnant par sa grande taille et maniant hardiment la hache au premier rang, venge cet affront et impose à la Flandre une indemnité de guerre considérable, 400 000 livres à payer en quatre ans, l'équivalent du revenu annuel du royaume !

Au sein de l'Occident, aucun État ne jouit d'un tel prestige et ne présente une telle solidité. Personne d'ailleurs, parmi les contemporains, ne semble douter de la supériorité d'un royaume à nul autre pareil. En Italie, depuis que les héritiers de Charles d'Anjou, frère de Saint Louis, gouvernent à Naples, s'affirment les ambitions brouillonnes des cadets de la famille royale. En terre d'Empire, Philippe achète patiemment et souvent « bon marché » la vassalité des princes qui règnent en Brabant, en Hainaut, en Barrois, en Luxembourg, en Franche-Comté, à Lyon, en Dauphiné et en Savoie, au-delà donc des « frontières » fixées par le traité de Verdun. Et quand le pape Clément V, l'archevêque de Bordeaux, s'établit à Avignon en 1309, c'est rappeler l'influence du Capétien sur le Saint-Siège. En 1312, Philippe le Bel peut écrire à l'empereur Henri VII : « Il est enseigné par tous et partout que, depuis le temps du Christ, le royaume de France n'a obéi qu'à son roi seul [...], ne reconnaissant ou ne subissant aucun pouvoir temporel supérieur, quel que soit l'empereur régnant. »

Du fond de sa Normandie où, à Coutances, il exerce la profession d'avocat, Pierre du Bois se fait l'écho de l'opinion publique quand il affirme que l'univers doit être soumis aux Français. La France, écrit-il dans sa *Summaria doctrina*, est un pays favorisé entre tous, l'expérience ayant prouvé que les astres s'y présentent sous un meilleur aspect et y exercent une influence plus favorable que dans les autres royaumes. Soutenant que la France doit affirmer ses prétentions en

Italie, en Aragon, en Angleterre, en Castille et en Hongrie, dans l'empire d'Orient et en Allemagne, il ajoute à l'adresse du roi : « Vous possédez, sire, un trésor inépuisable d'hommes qui suffirait à toutes les guerres qui peuvent se présenter. Si Votre Majesté connaissait les ressources de son peuple, elle aborderait, sans hésitation et sans crainte, les grandes entreprises dont je parle. » Ensuite, Philippe pourrait, à l'exemple des empereurs romains ou du khan des Tatars, rester chez lui, sous la bienfaisante influence des constellations, « pour vaquer à la procréation des enfants et à la formation des armées, ordonnateur et dispensateur de tout ce qui se fera en deçà de la mer méridionale ».

Présomption ? Folle vanité patriotique ? Certes, mais quand Marco Polo, de retour de Chine, veut diffuser le récit de son aventure, c'est la langue française qu'il choisit.

Le vieux palais de la Cité, agrandi et refondu, devient désormais le siège d'une administration qui, au prestige du sacre, ajoute l'efficacité d'un droit désormais enseigné aux universités de Toulouse et de Montpellier. Venus de ces provinces méridionales récemment annexées au royaume, des « légistes », saisis par la passion de l'État, affirment systématiquement la souveraineté de la loi.

Si les frères du roi et les princes siègent encore à son Conseil, ce sont ces « légistes » qui déterminent en fait les grandes décisions politiques, une vingtaine de personnes aux compétences très larges qui, après avoir gravi l'échelle des responsabilités, prennent la place de la vieille noblesse. On y trouve Pierre Flotte et Pons d'Aumelas, Gilles Aycelin et Philippe de Villepreux, Pierre de Châlon et Pierre de Latilly, Biche et Mouche, Enguerrand de Marigny et Guillaume de Nogaret surtout, des hommes d'Église et des bourgeois, des Italiens et des Normands, des juifs convertis et des fils de serfs, des banquiers et des professeurs de droit qui, en servant le roi, n'oublient pas de faire fortune en accumulant rentes et pensions. « Serfs, vilains, avocassiers sont devenus empereurs », écrit en 1314 Geoffroy de Paris, exprimant l'amertume des anciens barons qui s'estiment trahis par ces « chevaliers de cuisine ».

L'ancienne Cour du roi qui rassemblait la « famille » des vassaux se transforme ainsi en une série d'administrations « spécialisées » à la mesure d'un royaume dont la taille s'est considérablement dilatée et dont le roi, en l'absence de cartes, est incapable de se représenter les limites. Depuis 1278, le « parlement », où le roi n'apparaît plus physiquement, comporte plusieurs sections chargées d'instruire et de juger en permanence toutes les affaires que les appels interjetés contre les officiers et les seigneurs locaux amènent au Palais, des appels

qu'encouragent aussi les baillis proches des grandes principautés territoriales pour y faire entrer la justice du roi. Il y eut bientôt une
Chambre des requêtes, chargée d'examiner les affaires portées devant
le roi et de juger sommairement de leur recevabilité, une Chambre des
enquêtes, chargée de comprendre et de débrouiller les appels, et une
Grand-Chambre, où les plaidoiries et les arrêts étaient prononcés. Pour
recevoir la foule des plaideurs, des avocats, des témoins et des
curieux, loger un personnel qui a doublé en nombre et abriter la quantité énorme de registres où s'inscrivent les sentences rendues, il fallut
aménager dans le Palais de la Cité de très vastes locaux. Édifiée parallèlement à la Seine, la grande salle à deux nefs, longue de 70 mètres
et large de 29, entourée des statues des rois de France, passait pour la
plus belle du royaume.

En 1303, s'installe également au Palais une « Chambre des
comptes » où s'activent ceux que l'on appelle bientôt les « gens des
Comptes », des gens « sérieux » qui veillent sur les revenus du
Domaine royal, surveillent tous les comptables, s'occupent de la gestion des forêts et des douanes, lèvent des impôts qui n'ont plus rien
d'exceptionnel et font la politique monétaire. Deux fois par an, baillis
et sénéchaux, receveurs et collecteurs devaient venir à Paris rendre
compte de leur gestion financière et exhiber les mandements royaux
en vertu desquels ils avaient effectué paiements et assignations. Bientôt, on verra ces maîtres des comptes refuser d'entériner les largesses
du roi qui leur sembleront excessives. C'est bien la raison d'État qui
s'introduit subrepticement dans un royaume de moins en moins féodal.
À la fin du règne, cette administration centrale compte ainsi près de
1 000 personnes, ce qui, avec leurs familles et leurs nombreux domestiques, représente peut-être une population de près de 5 000 personnes.
« En France, a tout plein d'avocats », écrit encore Geoffroy de Paris.

La fin de l'embellie

La modernisation de l'État coûte évidemment fort cher, d'autant
plus que le roi vit sur un grand pied, entretenant par exemple 44 personnes à la seule vénerie pour satisfaire à sa passion de la chasse, à
laquelle il consacre plusieurs mois par an. Des chambellans aux sau-
ciers, des barbiers aux lavandières, des fauconniers aux souffleurs
chargés du feu de la cuisine, ce sont près de 500 « domestiques » qui
s'affairent autour du roi et de son entourage et composent son « Hôtel ».
Car le petit-fils de Saint Louis aime le luxe et la fête, comme celle
qui, en 1313, marque l'inauguration du nouveau palais de la Cité. En

deux jours, on jette entre l'île de la Cité et l'île Notre-Dame un pont de bois large de 40 pieds et long de 160 pour que le peuple puisse prendre part à la fête.

La guerre et la diplomatie coûtent cependant bien plus. Alors que les revenus du Domaine procurent au Trésor un peu plus de 400 000 livres par an, Philippe achète pour 200 000 livres, en 1293, l'alliance de son cousin, Charles II d'Anjou, roi de Naples ! La guerre de Gascogne engloutit, entre 1293 et 1297, 2 à 3 millions de livres et la moindre garnison d'un château frontalier coûte bien, en temps de paix, 500 livres par an.

Certes, pour couvrir ces dépenses de moins en moins occasionnelles, on pouvait, comme auparavant, rançonner les juifs ou les « Lombards », tous ces changeurs et marchands italiens qui, fort peu populaires, connaissaient les risques du métier, susciter les « dons » forcés des bourgeois, décider que les biens ecclésiastiques devaient supporter leur part de frais « pour la défense du royaume » et en prélever le « décime » (un dixième des revenus), mais de tels expédients ne suffisaient plus. Force fut donc d'innover, d'imaginer des « novelletés », ce qui n'est guère populaire.

Idée fort prometteuse mais encore prématurée, on tente d'instituer un impôt permanent. On se contente d'abord de contraindre ceux qui devaient « aide » au roi, les vassaux qui, selon le droit féodal, devaient conduire leurs hommes d'armes à l'ost royal, participer financièrement aux frais de chevalerie du fils aîné du roi et à ceux des mariages. On peut surtout exiger de l'ensemble des habitants qu'ils rachètent le service armé, chaque paiement obligeant toutefois les collecteurs de l'impôt à négocier, les gens du Midi prétendant qu'ils ont payé plus que leur part pour les campagnes de Guyenne et estimant que c'est aux gens du Nord d'assumer la charge des campagnes de Flandre. L'instruction secrète alors adressée aux receveurs de l'impôt montre à quel point les pouvoirs du roi sont en la matière limités.

« Vous devez être avisés de parler au peuple par douces paroles et de montrer les grandes désobéissances, rébellions et dommages que nos sujets de Flandre ont faits à nous et à notre royaume, ceci afin de le rendre attentif à notre intention.

Vous devez faire ces levées au moindre esclandre que vous pourrez et à la moindre commotion du menu peuple.

Et soyez encore avisés de mettre des sergents débonnaires et traitables pour faire vos exécutions [...].

En toutes matières, montrez-leur comment, par cette voie de payer, ils sont hors des périls de leur corps, des grands coûts des chevaux et de leurs dépens, et comment ils pourront ainsi vaquer à leur marchandise et administrer les biens de leur terre. »

Cette campagne de persuasion dut être efficace puisque l'impôt prélevé en 1304, 735 000 livres, permit de payer l'armée qui, le 13 août, écrasera les Flamands à Mons-en-Pévèle !

On eut aussi l'idée d'un impôt sur les exportations, le devoir du roi étant de veiller à ce que l'on n'emporte pas hors du royaume ce qui est nécessaire à la vie de ses sujets. On expérimenta un impôt sur la fortune fixé à 2 % du capital et un impôt de 20 % sur les revenus, le « vingtième », mais pour restaurer l'idée d'État et de l'intérêt « commun » à une société que des siècles de féodalité avaient atomisée, le chemin était encore long.

Riche d'avenir aussi fut l'idée de « manipuler » la monnaie et de pratiquer ce que nous appelons aujourd'hui la dévaluation. Philippe le Bel inaugure ainsi une réputation de « faux-monnayeur », largement imméritée dans la mesure où, pour ceux qui, dès le temps de Saint Louis, avaient relu Aristote, « la monnaie n'existe que par la Loi », le prince pouvant en changer la valeur en fonction du « bien commun ». En ces temps où il faut distinguer la « monnaie réelle », celle qui circule sous forme de pièces sur lesquelles aucune valeur n'est inscrite, rares écus d'or, deniers d'argent et piécettes d'appoint, et la « monnaie de compte », qui détermine les rapports d'échange entre ces pièces en en fixant la valeur en livres, sous et deniers, il était fort tentant, sans modifier le poids ni le titre des pièces sonnantes et trébuchantes, de changer seulement leur valeur d'échange.

En outre, à une époque où était établi un rapport légal entre la valeur de l'or et celle de l'argent, il suffisait que le rapport commercial entre ces deux métaux précieux évolue sous l'influence du marché international pour provoquer des troubles monétaires graves sans que le pouvoir royal y soit pour quelque chose. Ainsi, le rapport commercial de l'or à l'argent est de 1 à 12 au début du règne de Philippe le Bel, de 1 à 16 en 1309, de 1 à 19,6 puis de 1 à 15,3 en 1311. Sur le marché, le cours des pièces métalliques peut ainsi varier de jour en jour, perturbant les utilisateurs enclins à voir dans ces fluctuations la main des spéculateurs, des « Lombards » ou des juifs.

En 1295, Philippe inaugure sa « politique monétaire » en faisant passer la valeur du « gros » tournoi d'argent pur, émis en 1266 par Saint Louis, de 12 à 15 deniers, sans changer ni sa forme ni son poids. Dans le même temps, il émet une nouvelle pièce, un « double », dont la teneur en argent fin est supérieure de 50 % à celle du denier mais dont la valeur légale est fixée au double. Une monnaie qui vaut

« réellement » un denier et demi et « légalement », en monnaie de compte, 2 deniers.

En 1303 surtout, alors que les besoins financiers de l'État deviennent pressants, des pièces d'or qui, au taux du « bon » écu de Saint Louis, auraient dû valoir en monnaie de compte 258 deniers sont échangées contre 750 deniers, tandis que la valeur légale du « gros » tournoi d'argent s'élève désormais à 26 deniers.

C'était favoriser les débiteurs et frapper les créanciers puisque le créancier d'une livre tournoi qui aurait reçu en paiement 20 « gros » tournois d'argent en 1295 n'en recevait plus en 1303 que moins de 10. « J'ai vu chaque année mon revenu diminuer de 500 livres tournois », écrit alors Pierre du Bois, pourtant peu suspect d'hostilité à l'égard de la monarchie, « depuis que l'on a commencé à altérer les monnaies, et je crois, tout bien considéré, que le roi a perdu et perd encore par cette altération plus qu'il ne gagnera jamais. Il faut que le roi le sache, car l'ignorance n'excuse point. Je ne crois pas qu'un homme sain d'esprit puisse ou doive penser que le roi aurait ainsi détérioré sa monnaie s'il avait su que de tels malheurs en résulteraient. [...] Les auteurs de ces mesures chercheraient le moyen de réparer des pertes si grandes et si générales, s'ils pensaient qu'ils doivent mourir. »

En juin 1306, le retour à une « bonne » monnaie du poids, de l'aloi et de la valeur légale du temps de Saint Louis fut pourtant le pire des remèdes, la frappe d'une monnaie « forte » après dix ans de monnaie « faible » amenant les créanciers à vouloir prendre leur revanche sur les débiteurs. À Paris, les bourgeois ayant voulu percevoir les loyers dans cette nouvelle monnaie « forte », une émeute rassemblant épiciers, foulons, tisserands et taverniers saccagea la maison d'Étienne Barbette, qui passait pour avoir conseillé cette mesure, et se dirigea vers le Temple où le roi était avec ses conseillers « afin que personne ne puisse le ravitailler ». Le lendemain, on pendit 28 manifestants aux quatre ormes des quatre entrées de la ville, pour l'exemple.

En fait, ce que le roi ne pouvait dire ou imaginer, c'est qu'au moment où le Palais devait traiter une masse croissante d'affaires, solder et encadrer des armées, gager des masses d'officiers et d'agents et multiplier les artifices pour accroître ses recettes, l'embellie matérielle qui avait soutenu le temps des cathédrales montrait ses premiers signes de défaillance sans que les hommes y soient, évidemment, pour grand-chose. Est-ce l'influence d'un climat moins favorable, aux hivers plus froids et aux étés pluvieux, toujours est-il que, dès la fin du règne de Saint Louis, se manifestent les premiers grippages de la croissance.

En Forez, la disette, qui avait disparu, se manifeste en 1277, 1285, 1298, 1302, 1310. En Normandie, les terres perdent beaucoup de valeur entre 1260 et 1313. En Île-de-France, la hausse du prix des céréales qui avait entretenu la prospérité des campagnes s'interrompt dans les dernières années du siècle. En 1305, à la demande des bourgeois de Paris qui s'inquiètent du ravitaillement de leur cité, des commissaires royaux sont dépêchés jusqu'à Amiens, Vitry-sur-Marne et Tours pour élargir l'aire d'approvisionnement de la capitale. En 1308, le chapitre général des cisterciens déclare que « l'ordre glisse vers une profonde misère ». Le spectre de la faim, conjuré depuis plus d'un siècle, se dessine de nouveau à l'horizon.

C'est aussi le négoce qui est affecté par le retournement de la conjoncture et la redistribution des courants d'échanges internationaux. L'ouverture à la navigation régulière de la voie maritime qui, par Gibraltar, relie Gênes à Bruges et Londres, détourne une partie du trafic des voies terrestres qui irriguaient le royaume. Le premier navire génois atteint Bruges en 1277, Londres en 1280. Pour quelles raisons, alors, faudrait-il se déplacer en Champagne alors que l'on peut aller faire directement son marché à moindre coût dans les foires flamandes ? De 1296 à 1320, le volume des affaires traitées à la foire de Troyes diminue de moitié ! Et comment les monnayeurs n'auraient-ils pas la tête tournée quand, sous l'effet des bouleversements qui affectent l'Afrique ou l'Asie, le rapport de l'or à l'argent oscille de 1 pour 11 à 1 pour 18,8 entre 1289 et 1305 ?

Les émeutes qui se multiplient aux alentours de 1300, la haine des « menus » contre les « gros », ne sont que la traduction sociale d'une conjoncture qui se déprime et rend insupportables les initiatives du roi en matière fiscale ou monétaire. À Arras, en 1285, Jean Cabos mène à l'assaut des maisons riches la foule rassemblée pour la procession de la Pentecôte. À Rouen, en 1292, la maison du receveur royal est mise à sac. Philippe le Bel serait-il le premier des rois « maudits » ?

Le temps des « affaires »

Ce n'est peut-être pas un hasard si, se greffant sur le pesant malaise ressenti depuis les années 1280, les « affaires » qui troublent l'harmonie du monde chrétien deviennent, aux yeux des contemporains, les signes d'un temps qui se défait. Il y a bien « quelque chose de pourri » dans le royaume de France.

En 1296, le pape Boniface VIII, que l'âge rend irascible, rappelle au roi que la levée des décimes sur les revenus de l'Église de France est subordonnée à son consentement. Philippe riposte en interdisant l'exportation de l'or et de l'argent hors du royaume, mettant ainsi l'embargo sur les sommes que les banquiers italiens devaient transférer à Rome. Le 20 septembre 1296, la lettre *Ineffabilis* ouvre les hostilités. Non seulement Boniface rappelle au roi qu'il a perdu le « cœur de ses sujets », mais encore il menace de l'excommunier. « Les sujets du roi, peut-on lire, ne peuvent que souffrir de ces rigueurs, écrasés qu'ils sont par des charges si diverses que leur obéissance et leur dévouement ordinaires se refroidissent et se refroidiront à mesure qu'ils seront plus accablés. Ce n'est pas une médiocre perte que celle du cœur de ses sujets. »

Puis, affirmant des prétentions difficilement supportables, il lance de vives accusations contre la politique royale, ajoutant : « Cherche, très cher fils, quel est le roi, quel est le prince, qui attaque ton royaume sans avoir été d'abord attaqué ou offensé par toi ! Le roi des Romains ne se plaint-il pas de ce que tes prédécesseurs et toi ayez occupé des cités, des pays et des terres appartenant à l'Empire, en particulier le comté de Bourgogne, qui est notoirement un fief d'Empire et qui doit être tenu de lui ? Notre cher fils d'Angleterre ne porte-t-il pas les mêmes accusations au sujet de certaines terres de Gascogne ? [...] Récusent-ils le jugement et la décision du Siège apostolique, qui a autorité sur tous les chrétiens ? Du moment qu'ils t'accusent de t'être rendu coupable envers eux de péché, c'est à ce juge qu'appartient évidemment le jugement. »

C'était mettre en cause la souveraineté même du roi de France en son royaume et en faire le justiciable du Saint-Siège. C'était défier maladroitement le patriotisme naissant des Français. Dès la fin de l'année 1296, *Le Dialogue du clerc et du chevalier*, rédigé par un pamphlétaire anonyme probablement inspiré par les « légistes », rappelait l'avertissement de l'apôtre saint Paul dans sa lettre à Timothée : « Que nul de ceux qui se consacrent au service de Dieu ne se mêle aux affaires du siècle ! », tandis que Pierre Flotte, un des proches conseillers de Philippe, rappelait que le Seigneur avait dit aux prêtres du Temple : « Rendez à César ce qui est à César, et à Dieu ce qui est à Dieu. »

Après une trêve marquée par la canonisation, en 1297, de Saint Louis, le conflit reprend de plus belle peu après Noël 1301, à la suite de l'arrestation de l'évêque de Pamiers, Bernard Saisset, qui, dans son

Languedoc, se livrait à des écarts de langage peu canoniques, prétendant que Philippe était un bâtard et un faux-monnayeur. La bulle *Ausculta fili* était aussi peu diplomatique que les propos de l'évêque de
Pamiers : « Nous prions et exhortons Ta Grandeur, t'ordonnant par
ces lettres apostoliques de laisser cet évêque, que nous voulons avoir
près de nous, libre de s'en aller, de lui permettre de venir en notre
présence en toute sécurité, de lui faire restituer ses biens qui sont
occupés, saisis et détenus par toi et les tiens, de le dédommager pour
ceux qui auraient disparu et de ne jamais étendre ainsi à l'avenir tes
mains cupides, mais de te comporter toujours de telle manière que
la divine Majesté ou la dignité du Siège apostolique n'en soient pas
offensés. »

En avril 1302, une assemblée extraordinaire, réunissant à Notre-
Dame de Paris un millier de barons et de prélats, de docteurs et de
bourgeois, dénonce la « perverse volonté » du pape et approuve la
politique de Philippe le Bel. En novembre, la bulle *Unam sanctam*
affirme, comme on ne l'avait jamais fait, l'autorité suprême d'un pontife qui se pose en maître absolu de la société chrétienne : « Les deux
glaives, écrivait-il, sont au pouvoir de l'Église : le spirituel et le temporel. Celui-ci doit être tiré pour l'Église, celui-là par l'Église. L'un
par la main du prêtre, l'autre par celle des rois et des chevaliers, mais
sur l'ordre et avec la permission du prêtre. Il faut en effet que l'un
des glaives soit sous l'autre, et que l'autorité temporelle soit soumise
au spirituel. »

L'« affaire » devait mal tourner. En juin 1303, une nouvelle
assemblée, réunie au Louvre, met en cause les bonnes mœurs de Boniface, l'accusant d'hérésie, de « bougrerie », de simonie et de sodomie,
et réclame sa déposition par un concile. Dans la nuit du 6 au 7 septembre, agissant avant que le pape ne lance l'excommunication contre
le roi, Guillaume de Nogaret, acompagné d'une bande armée, force
les portes d'Anagni, où Boniface résidait pendant l'été, et le cite à
comparaître. Très affecté par cette humiliation, le pape meurt le
11 octobre sans avoir tenté de réagir. En 1311, par la bulle *Rex gloriae*
datée d'Avignon, le pape Clément V annulait tous les actes qui avaient
mis en cause le roi de France, affirmant que, « mû par un juste zèle »,
ce dernier n'avait agi que pour le bien de l'Église. Philippe le Bel
était bien devenu « empereur en son royaume ».

Le 13 octobre 1307, avec l'arrestation des Templiers, commence
la deuxième grande « affaire » du règne. S'il est certain que la fortune
de l'ordre et ses fonctions bancaires ont excité les convoitises des
conseillers du roi et attisé les fantasmes d'une population malmenée

par la conjoncture, il est plus probable que Philippe, homme d'une piété farouche, a cru sincèrement les accusations portées contre eux et estimé que son devoir était d'extirper l'hérésie. C'est la raison pour laquelle, au lendemain de l'arrestation de ceux que l'on accuse d'être secrètement affiliés à l'islam, de cracher sur la Croix et de pratiquer des rites secrets obscènes – baisers sur l'anus ou les parties génitales –, Philippe écrit aux autres souverains européens pour les presser d'imiter son exemple. En 1312, une bulle pontificale supprimait l'ordre dont les biens en France, étaient dévolus aux Hospitaliers. Préparé par une propagande intense qui diffusait sur-le-champ à l'opinion les aveux extorqués aux Frères par la torture, le supplice du grand maître de l'ordre Jacques de Molay, brûlé vif le 19 mars 1314, traduisait les troubles d'une génération qui, après la prise de Saint-Jean-d'Acre par les musulmans en 1291, voyait sonner le glas de la présence chrétienne en Terre sainte et s'évanouir le rêve de croisade.

En mai 1314, quelques semaines après le supplice de Jacques de Molay, on apprit que les belles-filles du roi, Marguerite et Blanche, étaient devenues les maîtresses de deux chevaliers de l'Hôtel, Gautier et Philippe d'Aunay. Sans participer aux ébats, Jeanne, la sœur de Blanche, était au courant de tout. Tandis que les princesses étaient emprisonnées, les frères d'Aunay furent jugés pour lèse-majesté et exécutés sur-le-champ : on les écorcha vifs, on les mutila et on donna leur sexe aux chiens.

Décidément, bien des ombres planaient sur une cour dont l'austérité avait fait la force. Quand Philippe meurt brusquement le 29 novembre 1314 d'une maladie étrange, c'est pour beaucoup le signe que Dieu veut châtier les rois qui pressurent leurs sujets au lieu de les défendre.

CONCLUSION

Dans sa *Chronique*, écrite au début du Xe siècle, l'abbé Reginon de Prüm raconte qu'en 746, Carloman, frère de Pépin le Bref, se rend au monastère du mont Cassin, près de Rome, pour y devenir moine. En l'accueillant, le père abbé lui demande « de quelle patrie et de quelle race il est ». Carloman répond qu'il est un « Francus » et qu'il vient de « Francia ». Est-il possible qu'à une époque où la langue maternelle des premiers Carolingiens était incontestablement le germanique, ceux qui régnaient sur l'ensemble territorial que nous appelons aujourd'hui la France se soient ainsi considérés comme « Français de France » ?

Si le doute est permis, en ce qui concerne Charlemagne, la naissance d'un sentiment « national » apparaît bien dans les années qui suivent la mort de l'empereur. Le partage de l'Empire en 843, à Verdun, qui donne naissance à la *Francia occidentalis* a beau être un accord de circonstance conclu entre les trois petits-fils de Charlemagne, il avait la géographie pour lui. Nul ne pouvait alors prévoir ce qu'il adviendrait de cette *Francia occidentalis*, royaume jamais constitué jusqu'alors sous cette forme, ses limites n'épousant aucune limite naturelle ou ethnique manifeste. Reste que cette Francie romane, confiée à Charles le Chauve, allait connaître une étonnante longévité.

Nul doute, en effet, que cette communauté de langue suscitait déjà un réel sentiment de solidarité. L'anecdote racontée par Richer de Reims à la fin du Xe siècle en est une autre illustration : « En 920, écrit-il, lors d'un séjour que fit dans la région de Worms le roi Charles le Simple auprès de Henri l'Oiseleur, roi de Germanie (vers 876-936), de jeunes Germains et de jeunes Gaulois, que la différence de langue avait l'habitude d'exciter les uns contre les autres, commencèrent à s'injurier avec une grande animosité. »

Et quand Eudes, comte de Paris et ancêtre des premiers Capétiens, est élu roi en 888, après avoir défendu vaillamment Paris contre les Normands, Reginon de Prüm, toujours lui, écrit : « Les Peuples des Gaules tirèrent un roi de leurs propres entrailles. » Certes, le royaume des Francs était évidemment loin de constituer déjà une nation. La France s'est toutefois bien esquissée, à ce moment-là, entre 840 et l'an mille.

Dès la fin du XIᵉ siècle, et plus nettement encore au XIIᵉ siècle, un réel « chauvinisme » français que les croisades ont alimenté se manifeste.

Affectant de mépriser les Teutons, le chroniqueur Guibert de Nogent (1053-vers 1130), affirme que la nation des Français « demeurera toujours distinguée et sera toujours au milieu de toutes les autres une nation noble, sage, belliqueuse et parfaitement pure... Le nom du roi et du royaume de France, ajoute-t-il, s'élève majestueusement au-dessus des noms de tous les autres royaumes ». Dans le *Couronnement de Louis*, une chanson de geste du XIIᵉ siècle, on lit que Dieu, lorsqu'il créa les quatre-vingt-dix-neuf royaumes, réserva le meilleur pour la « douce France ».

C'est que les premiers rois capétiens qui régnaient sur cette « douce France » étaient bien moins faibles qu'on le pensait autrefois. En dépit de la faiblesse apparente de leurs moyens, ils jouissaient d'un prestige et d'un pouvoir sans commune mesure avec ceux que détenaient les princes les plus puissants. Pour tous les habitants du royaume, le roi demeurait l'oint du Seigneur, le vicaire de Dieu, celui dont les prières pouvaient attirer les bénédictions du ciel sur son peuple. Tout au long du XIIᵉ siècle, soutenus par l'Église et par des serviteurs zélés, les rois ont su capitaliser le prestige du sacre et asseoir leur emprise sur le pays. Installé à Paris, là où se pressaient les grands vassaux du royaume le plus riche et le plus peuplé d'Occident, l'une des capitales intellectuelles et religieuses de la chrétienté, le roi a pu, pour la première fois en 1155, oser établir la paix pour dix ans dans « tout le royaume ». Cette paix pour les églises, les paysans et les marchands, promulguée par « parole de roi » et jurée par les barons présents, affirme l'autorité croissante du souverain sur les turbulents chevaliers de la société féodale, à une époque où les cathédrales qui s'élèvent dans son domaine imposent une nouvelle manière de construire les édifices sacrés, l'*opus francigenum*, l'« ouvrage d'origine française ».

Dans ce domaine, celui qu'on appelle le « roi des Francs », un roi qui ne doit d'hommage à personne, détient de solides atouts. Dans un monde féodal où la loyauté est le pilier de la morale, il peut compter sur le soutien de ses vassaux. Même si ces derniers n'entendent pas que le roi s'immisce dans leurs affaires, ils savent que le sacre et le couronnement le placent au-dessus d'eux.

Surtout, arme capitale, le roi bénéficie de l'entier dévouement d'une Église qui en a fait son champion contre les Infidèles, les mauvais princes ou les hérétiques. Reste la valeur des hommes. Celle des souverains qui se sont succédé de Philippe Auguste à Philippe le Bel n'était pas mince. Quand, en 1302, la bulle de Boniface VIII, *Ausculta fili*, qui affirme la supériorité de la tiare pontificale sur la couronne royale, est lue et commentée devant un millier de « représentants » du royaume convoqués à Notre-Dame de Paris « pour délibérer sur certaines affaires qui intéressent au plus haut point le roi, le royaume, tous et chacun », nobles, clercs et prud'hommes envoyés par les bonnes villes lancent cet avertissement au souverain pontife : « Que le pape ne détruise pas cette ancienne union qui est entre l'Église, le roi et le royaume. »

Certes, ces assemblées n'étaient pas des lieux de discussion mais des sortes de plébiscites destinés à faire accepter des décisions délicates. Certes, en France, le royaume restait le roi. Reste que dans un temps où l'État veut se dégager des contraintes de la féodalité pour devenir plus « moderne », il lui faut gagner la confiance, s'expliquer avec la « nation ». En devenant « moderne », la France capétienne devenait ainsi, bien timidement encore, « constitutionnelle ». En excitant l'activité politique dans le pays par des consultations répétées, en en appelant à l'« opinion » pour faire accepter les « novelletés », les conseillers de Philippe le Bel inauguraient des habitudes qui ne seront plus oubliées.

DEUXIÈME PARTIE

LA CONSTRUCTION D'UN ÉTAT

*Temps de douleur et de tentation
Âge de pleur, d'envie et de tourment,
Temps de langueur et de damnation,
Âge mineur, près du définement.*

Ces vers, écrits par le poète Eustache Deschamps, né vers 1346, expriment la mélancolie d'une génération qui, le temps d'une vie, aura connu les charniers de la peste, les ravages de la guerre, les révoltes des Jacques et du petit peuple des villes, les divisions de l'Église affaiblie par le grand schisme et la folie d'un roi. Certes, ayant vu sa maison de Vertus, en Champagne, brûlée par les Anglais, et sa femme morte de bonne heure, Eustache Deschamps n'a cessé de gémir jusqu'à sa mort, son humeur s'aigrissant avec l'âge. Pourtant sa complainte traduit bien le désenchantement des Français qui ont bien eu conscience de vivre un temps de malheurs et d'incertitudes.

Guerre, peste et famine, tels sont bien les trois fléaux qui ont douloureusement assombri l'horizon des Français à partir des années 1340. Dès le début du XIVe siècle, ils regrettaient déjà « le bon temps de monseigneur Saint Louis ». Un siècle plus tard, réduits peut-être de moitié, ils accumulaient fébrilement les messes et les prières pour échapper à un enfer qui, sur les fresques et les retables, se mettait à ressembler à une véritable chambre de torture.

Au XIIIe siècle, les puissantes structures des cathédrales gothiques figuraient la structure même de l'univers, ordonné et lumineux, géométrique et majestueux. En 1400, c'est l'infinie subtilité des choses que traduisent les arabesques « flamboyantes » des nervures et l'exubérance des feuillages de pierre. Les décors des théâtres, les jeux de scène, les gesticulations des prédicateurs, les pompes funèbres ne s'adressent plus à l'intelligence mais à la sensibilité d'hommes remués par la peur, mais qui, en même temps, saisissent mieux le sens des souffrances du Christ.

C'est pourtant au cœur de cette sombre période que s'affirme l'État, comme si l'État puisait du temps des épreuves les moyens de son affirmation. En 1483, à la mort de Louis XI, celui que Jean Molinot, un clerc hostile, avait dépeint comme l'« universelle araigne », la reconstruction de la France, amorcée dans les années 1440-1445 par Charles VII, le « Bien servi », est chose faite.

À cette date, le royaume s'étend désormais sur environ 450 000 km² et le domaine en couvre 340 000 contre 220 000 en 1461. La seule principauté importante reste le duché de Bretagne et les princes qui prétendaient défendre le « Bien public » ont dû se soumettre à la justice du roi. Doté d'une armée efficace que les épreuves de la guerre ont forgée et de finances permanentes qu'aucun autre souverain ne peut rassembler, le roi peut imposer la « raison d'État » à ceux qui, quelques décennies plus tôt, pouvaient encore affirmer qu'il se souciait autant de lui que d'« un étron de chien ».

Songeant à faire de la France le centre d'un vaste trafic international où les marchands de toutes les nations, « tant chrétiennes qu'infidèles », viendraient décharger leurs marchandises, rêvant de « mettre une grande police [c'est-à-dire une autorité centrale] en ce royaume », visant à unifier les lois, les règlements et les coutumes dans un « beau livre » écrit en français, Louis XI est à deux doigts de fonder la religion du Prince qui marque la fin du Moyen Âge et l'aube des Temps modernes.

En 1483, libéré de la menace d'une Lotharingie bourguignonne et de l'hypothèque anglaise, il est surtout le premier prince de la chrétienté. Réunis à Tours le 5 janvier 1484, les états qualifiés pour la première fois de « généraux » peuvent faire leurs habituelles allusions au despotisme ruineux du dernier roi et regretter qu'il n'ait pas appliqué les sages ordonnances de ses prédécesseurs, ils s'en remettent toutefois pour l'essentiel « au bon plaisir » d'Anne de Beaujeu, fille de Louis Xi et régente du royaume. Affermie par le consentement tacite de l'« opinion publique », la royauté pouvait espérer s'occuper activement des « affaires de ses voisins ».

« Il y a des pays plus fertiles et plus riches ; il y en a de plus grands et de plus puissants [...] mais nul n'est aussi uni, aussi facile à manier que la France. Voilà sa force à mon sens : unité et obéissance. Aussi les Français, qui se sentent peu faits pour se gouverner eux-mêmes, ont-ils entièrement remis leur liberté et leur volonté aux mains de leur roi. Il lui suffit de dire : "Je veux telle ou telle somme, j'ordonne, je consens", et l'exécution est aussi prompte que si c'était la nation entière qui eût décidé de son propre mouvement. »

Sous la plume de l'ambassadeur vénitien, Marino Cavalli, cet éloge de la France de 1500 illustre l'admiration des observateurs étrangers devant la puissance de la monarchie française. Mosaïque complexe de cultures, de coutumes et de pratiques, cette France de 40 000 paroisses et de 80 000 seigneuries, cette France, où chaque pays, chaque ville, chaque village, chaque métier, chaque groupe social possède son statut et ses privilèges, qu'il tient à garantir contre toute « novelleté », est toutefois une même « nation » dont le ciment est le roi qui a su jouer de cette diversité pour faire admettre sa légitimité et, comme disaient souvent les textes de cette époque, « gagner le cœur de ses sujets ».

Même si, dans les mois qui suivent la mort de Louis XI, en 1483, les barons se révoltent une nouvelle fois contre le gouvernement d'Anne de Beaujeu, régente d'un royaume que son frère Charles VIII n'est pas encore en âge de diriger, le patriotisme fortifié par la guerre de Cent Ans est cependant trop vif pour que les ambitions aristocratiques puissent réellement menacer une monarchie capable de résister aux assauts de ses ennemis extérieurs, aux frondes des princes, aux révoltes des nu-pieds, ainsi qu'au tumulte des guerres de Religion.

29

La marche à la guerre

À la Toussaint de 1337, Henri Burgersh, évêque de Lincoln, arrive à Paris et remet à Philippe VI de Valois, « qui se dit roi de France », les lettres de défi du roi d'Angleterre. Ainsi débute officiellement la guerre dite de Cent Ans. Cette guerre avait en fait commencé en 1154 quand Henri Plantagenêt, comte d'Anjou et duc de Normandie, était devenu roi d'Angleterre et, par son mariage avec Aliénor, maître de l'Aquitaine. Certes, les Capétiens avaient peu à peu rogné les possessions de leur orgueilleux vassal. Certes, en 1259, Saint Louis avait voulu « mettre amour entre ses enfants et les siens qui sont cousins germains ». Pourtant entre un roi de France qui se disait « empereur en son royaume » et un roi d'Angleterre qui ne pouvait renoncer à son héritage, entre des « nations » en gestation, la guerre était inévitable.

La fin du « miracle » capétien

Le 1er février 1328 mourait Charles IV, le troisième et dernier fils de Philippe le Bel. Il avait été marié trois fois. Sa première femme, Blanche de Bourgogne, prise en flagrant délit d'adultère, avait été enfermée dix ans à Château-Gaillard, avant de mourir religieuse. La deuxième, Marie de Luxembourg, avait eu un fils, mort-né. La troisième, Jeanne d'Évreux, n'avait encore donné le jour qu'à des filles, mais elle était enceinte à la mort du roi. De nouveau, se posait la question de savoir qui allait être roi. Si l'enfant attendu était un fils, il suffirait de désigner un régent. Si c'était une fille, ferait-on jouer, comme en 1316, la clause de masculinité ?

À cette date, en effet, quand Louis X, le fils aîné de Philippe le Bel, était mort sans laisser d'héritier mâle, cette situation, entièrement nouvelle, avait ému l'entourage royal et excité l'imagination des légistes. Du premier mariage de Louis avec Marguerite de Bourgogne était née en 1311 une fille, Jeanne. Mais un doute s'était immédiatement élevé sur la légitimité de cette naissance, Marguerite ayant été convaincue d'un adultère qui durait depuis plusieurs années. En juillet 1315, Louis X s'était remarié avec Clémence de Hongrie, qui était enceinte à sa mort. En novembre 1316, elle mit au monde un fils, Jean, qui mourut quelques jours après.

Qui appeler alors à la succession ? Personne n'imagina de confier la couronne à Jeanne, la fille aînée et suspecte du roi défunt. Exploitant à son profit cette situation incertaine, Philippe, le deuxième fils de Philippe le Bel, prit le titre de roi dans le courant du mois de décembre et se fit sacrer à Reims le 9 janvier 1317. Puis, pour couper court à toute opposition, il réunit en février à Paris une assemblée composée de barons, de prélats et de bourgeois qui déclara solennellement que « femme ne succède pas à la couronne de France ».

Acceptée par tous, cette règle ne fut pas contestée en janvier 1322, à la mort de Philippe V, qui laissait quatre filles. La couronne passa, sans la moindre difficulté, au frère du roi défunt, Charles de la Marche, troisième fils de Philippe le Bel. À la mort du roi Charles IV, on pouvait donc penser que joueraient une nouvelle fois les règles fixées en 1316 et en 1322. Pourtant, pour la première fois depuis douze générations successives, depuis que Hugues Capet était devenu roi de France en 987, il n'y avait plus de fils direct ni de frère pour succéder à la couronne. Ainsi s'achevait le « miracle » capétien.

Car la situation de 1328 ne ressemblait plus à celle de 1316. Trois candidats pouvaient faire entendre leur voix. Le plus proche parent du roi défunt était son neveu Édouard III, roi d'Angleterre, petit-fils de Philippe le Bel par sa mère Isabelle. Les deux autres, Philippe de Valois et Philippe d'Évreux, époux de Jeanne de Navarre, n'étaient que les cousins germains du roi défunt et les neveux de Philippe le Bel. À ne prendre en considération que les degrés de parenté, le roi d'Angleterre était bien le mieux placé, mais le sentiment « national » était trop puissant pour que l'on accepte que la couronne de France passe en des mains étrangères. Ainsi ne furent pas écoutés ceux qui soutenaient que si les femmes ne pouvaient recueillir la couronne, du

LA FIN DES CAPÉTIENS

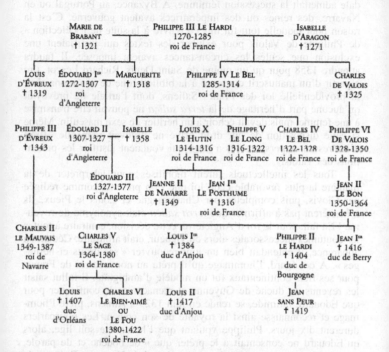

moins pouvaient-elles « faire pont et planche », c'est-à-dire transmettre à leurs héritiers mâles les droits que leur sexe leur refusait.

Finalement, comme en 1316, une assemblée de barons, d'évêques et de représentants des villes déclara que « femme, ni par conséquent son fils ne pouvait succéder au royaume de France ». Philippe de Valois fut établi régent puis roi, après la naissance de la fille posthume de Charles IV le 1er avril 1328. Le roi d'Angleterre, qui parlait le français mieux que l'anglais, eut beau protester : pour l'« opinion publique », « il n'avait jamais été vu ni su que le royaume de France eût été soumis au gouvernement du roi d'Angleterre ». Même si cela n'était pas clairement exprimé, la préférence « nationale » paraissait désormais acquise.

Pourtant, quand vint le moment de les exclure, bien des arguments juridiques militaient en faveur des femmes. En Aquitaine, en

Toulousain, en Champagne, en Flandre ou en Artois, la coutume féodale admettait la succession féminine. À Byzance, au Portugal ou en Navarre, des reines ou des impératrices avaient gouverné. C'est la raison pour laquelle tout fut mis en œuvre à la suite de l'« élection » de Philippe de Valois pour exhiber des textes qui justifiaient une exclusion que seules les circonstances avaient imposée. Il faudra attendre 1358 pour qu'un moine de Saint-Denis, Richard Lescot, tire à partir d'un manuscrit conservé à la bibliothèque de son monastère, la providentielle loi des Francs Saliens, dont l'article 62 prévoyait qu'aucune part d'héritage de la *terra salica* ne pouvait être transmise à une femme, mais devait échoir à un héritier de sexe masculin. Même si cette disposition de pur droit privé ne prouvait rien, elle offrait d'intéressantes perspectives à ceux qui voulaient justifier les prétentions des Valois.

Tous les intellectuels furent mobilisés pour interpréter de la manière la plus favorable cette loi que l'on présenta comme rédigée par Clovis, puis complétée par Charlemagne et Louis le Pieux. Ils n'hésitèrent pas à affirmer que *terra salica* était synonyme de royaume ! En fait, pour le roi d'Angleterre, cette décision, contraire à toutes les coutumes successorales alors en vigueur, était arbitraire. Cédant en apparence, il entendait bien un jour recouvrer « ses droits et héritages ». À cet égard, l'hommage qu'il prêta au nouveau roi de France pour ses fiefs continentaux fut un modèle d'ambiguïté. Il fallut saisir les revenus du duché de Guyenne et menacer de le confisquer pour que Édouard, intimidé, se rende en juin 1329 à Amiens, prête l'hommage et reconnaisse ainsi la royauté de son cousin. Les pourparlers durèrent dix jours, Philippe voulant que l'hommage soit lige, alors qu'Édouard ne consentait à le prêter que « de bouche et de parole, sans les mains mettre entre les mains du roi de France ». Il demanda même à retourner en Angleterre pour examiner « les privilèges de jadis qui devaient éclaircir le dit hommage ». Ce fut seulement le 30 mars 1331 que des lettres patentes, munies du grand sceau d'Angleterre, confirmèrent que l'hommage prêté à Amiens devait bien être tenu pour lige.

L'éclat des Valois

On peut se poser la question de savoir si la rupture de la continuité dynastique n'a pas transformé le style du gouvernement et les mœurs de la cour. Fils de Charles de Valois, éternel prétendant, surnommé par dérision Charles sans Terre tant ses ambitions brouillonnes avaient ridiculisé un prince qui, brillant capitaine, s'était avéré médiocre politique, Philippe n'a pas été élevé, comme Philippe le Bel, Saint Louis ou Philippe Auguste dans le culte du « commun profit » du royaume, dans l'esprit que le port de la couronne crée des devoirs plus que des droits.

Aimant le faste et la fête, il n'est pas l'héritier d'une tradition qui a compté avec un soin jaloux les revenus du Domaine. Comblant son fils aîné de rentes et de domaines, il lui a donné en apanage la Normandie, l'Anjou et le Maine ! Quand celui-ci est malade, le roi prévient lui même les gens des Comptes « que notre très chère compagne la reine a fait faire de notre commandement un pot d'or, du poids de quatre marcs onze esterlins pour la nécessité de la maladie de Jean notre fils ».

Sa cour est devenue le rendez-vous d'une chevalerie pour laquelle il multiplie les fêtes. Froissart décrit la large vie que l'on y menait : « Et tenait trois rois en son hôtel et ducs et comtes et barons sans nombre ; et n'y avait onques mais eu roi en France, dont il souvint qu'il eut tenu l'état pareil au dit roi Philippe. Et faisait faire fêtes, joutes, tournois et ébattements, et lui même les devisait et ordonnait. »

En portant à la couronne l'un des leurs, les grands princes ont en fait pris leur revanche sur les rois capétiens qui les avait privés du pouvoir pour mettre à leur place ces légistes, baillis et sénéchaux qui s'étaient permis de leur donner des ordres alors qu'ils étaient venus de rien. En 1314, dans les derniers mois du règne de Philippe le Bel, puis en 1316, ils s'étaient ligués pour qu'on les laisse « guerroyer les uns aux autres, chevaucher, aller, venir et porter les armes, sans être contraints de donner trêves » et que l'on rétablisse « les bonnes coutumes anciennes ». En avril 1315, c'est le père du futur roi, Charles de Valois, qui avait obtenu la pendaison d'Enguerrand de Marigny, ce chevalier pauvre devenu le bras droit de Philippe le Bel.

De leur point de vue, le règne de Philippe VI de Valois commence par un coup d'éclat. Appelé à l'aide par le comte de Flandre pour mater les vilains qui, à Bruges, Ypres et Cassel, s'étaient révoltés contre les collecteurs d'impôts et les Leliaerts, les nobles alliés du roi de France, Philippe offre aux chevaliers français l'occasion de venger de manière spectaculaire l'affront subi à Courtrai en 1302. À Nicolas Zannequin, le chef des insurgés, qui, retranché sur les hauteurs du mont Cassel, envoie des messagers au roi pour fixer, selon la coutume chevaleresque, « jour de bataille », on répond qu'ils sont « gens sans chef » et qu'on les rossera. Le 23 août 1328, surpris par les Flamands qui attaquent à l'improviste le camp royal au moment de la sieste, Philippe, revêtant à la hâte une cotte aux armes de France et un bassinet de cuir blanc, se fait hisser sur son cheval et montre à ses barons son mépris du danger. Pas un des Flamands n'échappe au massacre. Cette victoire de Cassel apparaît comme un « jugement de Dieu » confirmant la nouvelle dynastie. Philippe est bien le successeur légitime de celui qui avait déjà maté la piétaille à Mons-en-Pévèle.

Fort de cette victoire, Philippe peut nourrir de grands desseins. Il peut rêver de croisade malgré les réticences d'un pape qui l'invite lui-même à différer son départ pour ne pas mettre en péril son royaume. Il peut préparer l'acquisition de Montpellier et du Dauphiné et s'ouvrir ainsi les portes de la riche Italie. Ses officiers peuvent harceler l'Anglais sur les frontières de Guyenne et trouver toutes les occasions de blesser l'amour-propre du duc-roi. Philippe peut soutenir les Écossais en lutte pour leur indépendance et menacer l'Angleterre d'une invasion. Il ne fait rien pour empêcher la course que livrent les marins de Dieppe et de Rouen à ceux de Southampton. Le 24 mai 1337, enfin, accusant de félonie Édouard III qui prépare ouvertement la guerre et multiplie les ambassades en Europe pour obtenir l'alliance du duc de Brabant et de l'empereur Louis de Bavière, il prononce la saisie du duché de Guyenne. À la Toussaint, l'évêque de Lincoln apporte alors à Philippe les lettres de défi de celui qui avait déjà passé commande d'une couronne fleurdelisée.

Ainsi commençait un conflit féodal, une guerre traditionnelle qui, pour les contemporains, allait mettre aux prises, comme dans le passé, des seigneurs qui se défiaient pour des histoires d'héritages, de fiefs, d'empiétements du suzerain sur les droits du vassal et de manquements du vassal au serment de l'hommage. Personne n'avait encore le sentiment que s'ouvrait un conflit entre la France et l'Angleterre, entre deux États « modernes », entre deux « nations » aux usages identiques mais que divisait l'éveil d'un sentiment national.

Et pourtant ! Tandis qu'en France, on opposait la douceur du lys à la cruauté des léopards anglais, « car le léopard ne va qu'orgueil signifiant, et la fleur de lys est humilité manant », en Angleterre, circulait une anecdote édifiante. Un chroniqueur du temps racontait que Marguerite de France, seconde femme d'Édouard Ier, avait une nourrice française pour son fils. Mais celui-ci ne cessait de pleurer, de vomir le lait, jusqu'au moment où la funeste nourrice française fut remplacée par une bonne nourrice anglaise. Tout alors s'arrangea et l'enfant put enfin profiter du lait « national » !

La déroute de la chevalerie française

À première vue, le défi que lance le roi d'Angleterre au roi de France ressemble à celui qu'avait jeté David à Goliath. Même agrandi du pays de Galles, dont Édouard Ier avait achevé la conquête, le royaume d'Angleterre est un petit royaume en comparaison du royaume de France. Trois millions d'habitants d'un côté, plus de quinze millions de l'autre. D'un côté, un pays de grosses bourgades, essentiellement agricole, de l'autre, un pays urbanisé et industrieux dominé par une capitale à côté de laquelle Londres fait pâle figure. Pourtant, l'essentiel n'est pas là. Si, le plus souvent, les armées françaises sont deux ou trois fois plus nombreuses que les forces anglaises, ces dernières, aguerries au cours des campagnes sévères menées contre les Gallois et les Écossais, vont rapidement démontrer une supériorité que personne ne soupçonnait.

Si les chevaliers français ne craignent personne en matière de bravoure, la différence essentielle entre les deux armées se situe au niveau des gens de pied. Tandis que le roi de France ne peut compter que sur des « sergents » médiocrement entraînés, désignés par les villages et par les villes au moment des moissons et des vendanges, c'est-à-dire au moment où l'on préfère garder les plus robustes et envoyer à la guerre les moins indispensables, l'infanterie anglaise est recrutée parmi tous les hommes libres du royaume astreints au service de seize à soixante ans.

Parmi eux sont choisis les plus valides, les plus courageux, les plus endurcis à la fatigue et, surtout, les plus exercés au tir à l'arc, l'archerie étant devenue un sport national dont la pratique est vigoureusement encouragée par les autorités. Fait en bois d'if, d'environ 1,60 m de hauteur, le grand arc gallois, adopté par les Anglais au cours du XIIIe siècle, est une arme redoutable pour celui qui sait le manier, un archer pouvant tirer trois flèches dans le temps où un arbalétrier ne peut tirer qu'un seul carreau. Édouard III dispose aussi des terribles coutilliers capables d'introduire dans les interstices des armures de longs couteaux effilés, emmanchés sur des piques en bois.

Sur le continent, le roi d'Angleterre peut compter sur le soutien des Flamands, pour lesquels la laine anglaise est la matière première vitale de l'activité. Après avoir prohibé la sortie des laines de son royaume et contraint au chômage les artisans des villes drapières, Édouard III encourage l'agitation qui gronde à Ypres, Bruges et Gand. Placé à la tête de l'insurrection, Jacques Van Artevelde, grand marchand gantois, réussit à unir ces cités traditionnellement rivales et à contraindre le comte de Flandre à se réfugier à Paris. En décembre 1339, les Flamands reconnaissent Édouard comme roi de France en échange d'un traité qui leur garantit le marché de la laine et leur promet la restitution des villes de Lille, Douai et Orchies dès qu'Édouard aura pris possession de son nouveau royaume. Pour la première fois, Édouard III prend alors le titre de roi de France et d'Angleterre, change ses armes en un écartelé de France aux fleurs de lys et d'Angleterre aux trois léopards et date ses chartes de la première année de son règne en France.

À cette date, commencent vraiment les hostilités. Le 24 juin 1340, mal commandée par deux marins improvisés, Hugues Quiéret et Nicolas Béhuchet, la flotte du roi de France qui avait pris position à L'Écluse, l'avant-port de Bruges, est prise d'assaut par les Anglais, commandés par Édouard III en personne, dont le navire porte bannière aux armes de France et d'Angleterre. Entassés bords à bords, voiles abattues, pour dresser une sorte de barrage d'une rive à l'autre du Zwin, les navires français sont pris à l'abordage sous le tir nourri des onze mille archers anglais. Si les pertes anglaises sont lourdes, chez les Français, c'est le désastre, trente navires sur deux cents seulement réussissant à s'échapper. C'en est fini des espoirs de débarquement outre-Manche. La maîtrise de la mer est désormais anglaise.

En 1341, la succession du duché de Bretagne offre au roi d'Angleterre une nouvelle tête de pont sur le continent. Le duc Jean III étant mort le 30 avril 1341 sans enfant légitime, sa succession, qui pose une nouvelle fois le problème de la capacité des femmes à hériter, est disputée entre sa nièce, Jeanne de Penthièvre, mariée à Charles de Blois, neveu du roi de France, et l'oncle de Jeanne, Jean de Montfort, qui reçoit le soutien d'Édouard III estimant, écrit Froissart, « que sa guerre au roi de France en serait grandement embellie et qu'il ne pouvait avoir plus belle entrée au royaume ni plus profitable que par la Bretagne ». En hiver 1342, les deux rois se trouvent face à face aux environs de Vannes, mais deux cardinaux, envoyés par le pape, imposent une trêve de trois ans signée à Malestroit le 19 janvier 1343.

Elle ne fut guère favorable à un roi de France qui, empêtré dans les difficultés financières, tente, dans une conjoncture encore plus défavorable, de suivre l'exemple de Philippe le Bel. En mars 1343, il décide d'établir un impôt de 1,7 % sur les transactions et organise la gabelle du sel, c'est-à-dire le contrôle royal sur le commerce d'une denrée de première nécessité. Il lève des décimes sur les revenus de l'Église pour financer une croisade qui ne se fera pas. Il suspend pour un an les gages des officiers de l'Hôtel. Il diminue de 20 % le nombre des membres du Parlement et de la Chambre des comptes. Et alors que la livre tournois s'est effondrée de 1336 à 1342, passant de 82 g d'argent fin à 16,6 g, il tente d'« acheter » l'impôt à ses riches sujets en leur offrant une politique de monnaie « forte » qui revalorise leurs créances. Le 26 octobre 1343, le gros d'argent fin, qui valait soixante deniers en monnaie de compte, est mis à quinze deniers. Quand la guerre reprend activement au début de l'année 1346, les états de langue d'oïl, réunis à Paris, parlent de réforme, refusent de nouvelles impositions et décident qu'ils retourneront en leur pays afin que, « par bon avis de ceux à qui ils s'en conseilleraient, ils pussent faire meilleure et plus certaine réponse ».

Peu de temps après, le 12 juillet 1346, Édouard III débarque à Saint-Vaast-la-Hougue, sur la côte orientale du Cotentin, pour une chevauchée dévastatrice qui commence par une aimable promenade. Ayant pris et pillé Caen le 20 juillet, Édouard passe la Seine à Poissy puis, après avoir fait craindre le pire à la population de Paris, se dirige vers les ports du Nord, chargé d'un copieux butin. Philippe, jusqu'alors étrangement « dolent et angoisseux », concentre son armée à Saint-Denis et part à marches forcées à la poursuite de son cousin qui l'a tant nargué. Le 25 août, il pense le tenir, Édouard étant acculé à un combat qu'il redoute, tant ses troupes sont fatiguées.

Le seul avantage dont dispose le roi d'Angleterre est le terrain, une série de légères hauteurs entre les deux villages de Crécy et de Wadicourt, près d'Abbeville, dans le Ponthieu. Il a déployé son armée en ligne, en trois unités, ou « batailles », sur une longueur de 2 kilomètres, ce qui paraît dangereux, dans la mesure où il ne dispose que de onze à douze mille combattants. À droite, il place son avant-garde, sa force principale, sous le commandement de son fils, le prince de Galles, le futur Prince Noir, alors âgé de seize ans. À gauche, se range son arrière-garde, tandis que lui-même, à la tête de la troisième unité, se tient en réserve, un peu en arrière. En fait, il n'aura même pas à combattre.

La première originalité du dispositif anglais vient du fait que tout le monde est à pied. Chevaux, bagages et serviteurs ont été regroupés à l'arrière, dans un camp retranché protégé par des chariots. C'est un inconvénient dans la mesure où l'absence de chevaux interdit de charger l'ennemi au moment le plus favorable ou de fuir en cas de danger. Par contre, ce dispositif offre l'avantage d'opposer une masse compacte aux assauts de la cavalerie adverse.

La deuxième originalité tient dans le rôle confié aux archers, qui vont demeurer tout au long de la bataille au premier rang. On imagine le courage qu'il allait falloir pour affronter une véritable muraille de cavaliers lourdement armés, lancés au galop. Chacun a dans son carquois une douzaine de flèches qu'il devra tirer quand la cavalerie ennemie se trouvera à quelque 100 ou 150 mètres. Une dizaine de secondes les sépareront alors du choc direct des chevaux. Ce sera le laps de temps pendant lequel, avec une ou deux flèches, il faudra briser leur élan et provoquer la bousculade en mettant à profit l'affolement des chevaux jetés à terre sous l'effet des blessures.

Le matin du samedi 26 août, pendant que le roi de France, après avoir entendu la messe, quitte Abbeville pour franchir les 18 kilomètres qui le séparent des Anglais, on vient l'avertir du dispositif mis en place par l'ennemi. Les éclaireurs, ayant constaté que les Anglais étaient frais et dispos, conseillent de faire halte, de choisir une tactique et d'attendre le lendemain pour livrer combat. Mais, débordé par l'élan de ses troupes qui veulent en découdre enfin et ne respectent pas l'ordre qui a été donné de s'arrêter, le roi perd son sang-froid et se trouve contraint de livrer bataille alors que la journée est déjà avancée, que les chevaux et les cavaliers sont fatigués et que l'orage éclate en cette fin d'après-midi étouffante.

Pour faire pièce aux archers anglais, Philippe fait passer au premier rang les arbalétriers génois embauchés à l'improviste et qui, portant leur lourde arbalète depuis le matin, protestent qu'ils sont épuisés. En outre, l'orage a détendu les cordes de leurs armes, tandis que, pendant l'averse, les archers anglais ont mis les leurs à l'abri dans leurs bonnets.

Dès le début du combat, se dessine le désastre, annoncé à ces hommes superstitieux par le passage entre les deux armées d'une grande et épaisse volée de corbeaux. Sous la grêle de traits qui s'abat sur eux comme neige et la panique provoquée par les quelques boulets tirés par les Anglais pour expérimenter la nouvelle artillerie, les arbalétriers refluent en désordre, taillés en pièces par les chevaliers français, qui s'emportent contre cette « ribaudaille » qui leur encombre le chemin.

La suite est si confuse que les chroniqueurs Jean le Bel et Froissart avouent leur impuissance à raconter la fin de la journée. Répartis en huit ou neuf « batailles », fortes chacune d'un millier d'hommes, les chevaliers français chargent à une quinzaine de reprises, bien au-delà de la nuit tombée, sans résultat. Mais, comme l'honneur l'exige, on se fait massacrer plutôt que de renoncer. Fidèle allié du roi de France, Jean de Luxembourg, roi de Bohême, pourtant aveugle, se fait conduire par ses compagnons au cœur de la mêlée et s'écroule après avoir donné quelques coups d'épée. Légèrement blessé, Philippe quitte le champ de bataille alors que la lutte dure encore. Escorté de quelques chevaliers et d'une cinquantaine d'hommes, il se réfugie quelques heures au château de Labroye, puis galope vers Amiens, où, le lendemain, il apprend la déroute de la chevalerie française. Parmi les morts, on compte Louis de Nevers, le comte de Flandre et Charles, le propre frère du roi. De leur côté, les Anglais n'ont laissé sur le terrain que quelques chevaliers et quelques dizaines d'archers. Manifestement, Crécy marque le triomphe des coutilliers, des coupe-jarrets, des archers, des haches et des massues. Bientôt, armures, lances et chevaux iront peupler le musée de l'éthique chevaleresque. Édouard III n'était pas un lâche, mais, ne pouvant s'offrir le luxe d'une bataille selon les règles, il a simplement fait preuve d'habileté tactique et manifesté sa capacité à s'adapter.

Pour l'instant, par petites étapes, brûlant villes et villages, il marche sur Calais, qui capitule le 4 août 1347 après un siège de onze mois et des appels désespérés au roi de France, qui, après avoir rassemblé une armée de secours et gagné Sangatte, en vue de la ville assiégée, préfère se retirer. Calais, dont les bourgeois sont sauvés par les prières de la reine d'Angleterre, Philippa de Hainaut, devient une ville anglaise, ses habitants étant remplacés par des marchands et des artisans amenés des principales villes d'Angleterre.

Réunis en novembre 1347, les états généraux sont sévères pour le roi de France, le contribuable n'appréciant pas d'avoir payé fort cher une armée qui s'est fait battre et une autre qui n'a pas combattu. « Vous êtes allé en ces lieux honoré, et à grand compagnie, à grands coûts et à grands frais. On vous y a tenu honteusement et ramené vilainement. On vous a toujours fait donner des trêves, bien que les ennemis fussent en votre royaume [...]. Par de tels conseils, vous avez été déshonoré. »

À Crécy, ce roi « déshonoré » avait même perdu l'oriflamme, signe de sa mission divine. Dieu semblait bien avoir choisi son camp.

30

Le temps de l'apocalypse

*L*e 1ᵉʳ *novembre 1347, jour de la Toussaint, des galères génoises, venues de Crimée, arrivent à Marseille. Selon la rumeur qui les avait précédées, elles transportaient avec leurs marchandises un mal épouvantable qui avait fait des milliers de morts à Constantinople et Messine, leurs précédentes escales. Quelques jours plus tard, la peste a gagné la ville. En 1348, l'épidémie se répand dans le pays en empruntant les voies commerciales. La bataille de Crécy avait fait quelques centaines de morts. La peste allait faucher un bon tiers de la population du royaume. Une complainte bourguignonne traduit la stupéfaction de ceux qui voyaient en elle l'un des cavaliers destructeurs annoncés par l'Apocalypse :*

« En mil trois cent quarante-huit
À Nuits de cent restèrent huit.
En mil trois cent quarante-neuf
À Beaune de cent restèrent neuf. »

Un monde trop plein

Si la peste, qui ne s'était plus manifestée en Occident depuis sept siècles, a fait tant de ravages, c'est qu'elle attaquait un monde trop plein que peinait à nourrir une agriculture aux rendements décroissants. Prélude à la grande désolation, la fin de l'embellie multiplie, dans les trente premières années du XIVᵉ siècle, les pauvres et les mal-nourris. Une première disette s'était déjà produite au printemps de 1305. De 1315 à 1317, la famine montre désormais le bout du nez. Du 1er mai au 1er novembre 1316, elle envoie au cimetière un habitant d'Ypres sur dix. Pluies torrentielles et printemps pourris suffisent à rompre un équilibre que près de deux siècles de modeste aisance avaient réussi à imposer, à désorganiser un système de production parvenu aux limites de ses possibilités. La loi établie par le pasteur Malthus à la fin du XVIIIe siècle semble trouver son champ d'application. Alors que le nombre de bouches à nourrir suit une progression géométrique, celui de la terre cultivée suit une progression arithmétique. La maladie qui emporte les plus fragiles est alors le seul moyen de rétablir momentanément l'équilibre.

À Montaillou, ce petit village occitan dont Emmanuel Le Roy Ladurie a ressuscité la vie quotidienne grâce aux archives de l'inquisiteur Jacques Fournier, évêque de Pamiers, les ponctions d'hommes, effectuées par l'émigration, ne suffisent plus à soulager la misère des affamés. Conscients de vivre dans un monde que surcharge leur haute fécondité, ces paysans se demandent : « Où donc pourrait-on mettre ces âmes tellement nombreuses de tous les hommes qui sont morts et de ceux qui sont encore vivants. À ce compte, le monde serait plein d'âmes ! Tout l'espace compris entre la ville de Toulouse et le col de Mérens ne parviendrait pas à contenir celles-ci. »

Établi en 1328 par le roi pour recenser et donc imposer de manière plus systématique la population du royaume, l'État des paroisses et des feux mesure cette inflation des hommes. 23 671 paroisses et 2 469 987 feux couvrent alors les 320 000 kilomètres carrés que compte le domaine royal, les apanages (27 000 kilomètres carrés) et les grands fiefs (83 000 kilomètres carrés) n'ayant pas été dénombrés. En adoptant un coefficient moyen de 4,5 habitants par feu, le domaine royal aurait compté près de 15 millions d'habitants et la France, dans ses frontières actuelles, près de 20 millions. Un chiffre considérable qui fait du royaume un « monde plein comme un œuf » écrit le chroniqueur Jean Froissart. La région parisienne compte de 120 à 150 habitants au kilomètre carré. La Flandre rurale connaît une densité de près de 70 habitants au kilomètre carré ; la Provence abriterait 400 000 habitants ; le Dauphiné 300 000 et bien des villages sont plus peuplés qu'au milieu du XIXe siècle.

À ce jeu, la majeure partie des tenures paysannes ne suffit plus à entretenir ceux qui les exploitent. En Picardie, elles se sont contractées comme peau de chagrin tout au long du XIIIe siècle. En Lorraine, leur superficie serait quatre fois moins vaste qu'à l'époque carolingienne. Dans le Bassin parisien, les deux tiers des exploitations n'atteignent pas la taille de 5 à 6 hectares nécessaire pour faire vivre un couple et trois enfants.

Si l'on mange encore relativement à sa faim dans cette France de 1328, l'avenir n'est plus assuré. Les défrichements intempestifs ont livré à la culture des terres marginales, trop vite épuisées. Dans les plaines, la culture des céréales, qui procure à l'homme l'essentiel de ses calories, prive les troupeaux de pacages et limite ainsi le fumier, le principal engrais utilisé par les paysans.

Alertés aussi par la dégradation du patrimoine forestier, les seigneurs avisés ont voulu ménager les arbres et protéger leurs forêts. Dans cette période où la consommation croissante des villes renchérit le prix du bois, ils espacent les coupes et emploient des gardes forestiers plus vigilants. Ressource majeure du roi, les forêts de Saint-Germain-en-Laye, de Montargis et d'Orléans sont désormais bien arpentées. Dans la Flandre surpeuplée, mais aussi dans le haut Var, le Cantal, l'Oisans ou le Briançonnais, on ne compte plus les conflits entre seigneurs et communautés paysannes à la recherche de pacages. C'est aussi le droit de chasse des « manants » qui est limité, l'alimentation des « gros » exigeant un gibier de plus en plus abondant.

Paradoxalement, on survit mieux dans les régions « pauvres » que dans les « riches » plaines céréalières, où a été mis en culture tout ce qui pouvait l'être. À Montaillou, si des crises de subsistance sont signalées en 1310 et en 1323, le lait offert par un parent, le fromage produit par les bergers dans les montagnes ariégeoises, la soupe mêlant lard, pain, verdure de choux et poireaux cultivés en abondance dans les jardins, les truites des torrents, les escargots et les faisans fournissent le nécessaire. Hier comme aujourd'hui, mieux vaut « vivre du sien » que de devoir acheter le pain quotidien. Ailleurs, par contre, dans les régions surpeuplées d'Île-de-France et de Flandre, on vit finalement moins bien. Là, dans ces paysages de plaine ouverte, l'État peut plus facilement débusquer le numéraire et les vilains n'échappent ni aux taxes, ni à la dîme, ni à l'impôt, qui prélèvent la moitié de ce qu'ils gagnent. À Montaillou, là où la montagne est grande et la monnaie rare, les gens peuvent se glisser sans trop de mal entre les mailles du filet. « C'est en fin de compte dans les régions d'agriculture les plus commercialement actives [...], écrit Emmanuel Le Roy Ladurie, que se produit ou se produira le clash entre une noblesse pourvue d'argent par les marchés qui rentabilisent ses domaines et les paysans qui voudraient bien, eux, avoir davantage que les miettes du gâteau à se partager. » C'est en Beauvaisis et non en Ariège qu'éclateront un peu plus tard les jacqueries.

Dans les villes aussi, encombrées par les ruraux avides de ressources d'appoint ou simplement d'aumônes, on murmure contre les malheurs du temps. Exposées de plein fouet aux « novelletés » fiscales et aux « remuements » de la monnaie, engourdies par les réglementations excessives et l'aveuglement conservateur des maîtres, qui veulent fabriquer des draps aux couleurs immuables, elles résistent mal aux transformations de la mode. Au beau drap de laine de tradition, aux lourdes robes de naguère, on préfère les vêtements plus légers et mieux ajustés, le drap de soie importé de Toscane, le pourpoint qui met en valeur la finesse de la taille et les chausses de drap fin qui moulent joliment les jambes. Née parmi les jeunes élégants de la cour du Valois, cette mode « new look » représente pour les gens âgés un véritable attentat à la pudeur qui témoigne de la dégénérescence de la noblesse française. Coup dur pour Bruges, Ypres, Gand, Douai, Saint-Omer, Rouen ou Paris, qui voient péricliter leur draperie. Les Flamands qui se révoltent en 1328 sont aussi les victimes de la mode.

Comme chaque fois que la vie devient plus difficile, qu'un âge s'achève alors qu'un autre, meilleur, tarde à venir, nombreux sont ceux qui cherchent des boucs émissaires à des fléaux qui ne peuvent avoir été envoyés que par Dieu pour châtier les péchés des hommes. Déjà, en 1251, à l'époque où Saint Louis était à la croisade, le mouvement des pastoureaux (les bergers) avait révélé la facilité avec laquelle des meneurs charismatiques pouvaient entraîner les simples gens, « comme l'aimant attire le fer », écrit Guillaume de Nangis, abasourdi par ce « prodige stupéfiant et inouï ». Traversant la Flandre et la Picardie, rassemblant les bergers et les populations flottantes auxquels ils distribuaient des croix et donnaient l'absolution, ils s'en étaient pris, à Orléans et à Bourges, aux synagogues pour brûler les livres des Juifs et les dépouiller de leurs biens.

En mai 1320, dans le Bassin parisien et en Normandie, munis d'une besace et d'un bâton, de nouveaux pastoureaux, des bergers victimes des humeurs de la conjoncture, déploient des bannières représentant la crucifixion, prétendent combattre les Infidèles et, faute de partir en Terre sainte, s'en prennent à ceux qu'ils ont sous la main, les Juifs, une nouvelle fois, qu'ils massacrent en Aquitaine avec la complicité de la foule qui coopère mollement avec les autorités pour les arrêter.

En 1321, née dans le Poitou, la rumeur se répand que les lépreux auraient empoisonné les puits et les fontaines en y versant une poudre confectionnée par les Juifs, mélange de sang humain et d'urine séchée additionné de trois herbes mystérieuses. Un lépreux aurait même été surpris alors qu'il transportait un breuvage noirâtre où nageaient une tête de serpent, des pattes de crapaud et des cheveux de femme. En lançant l'ordre d'arrêter tous les lépreux du royaume et de les interroger, le roi Philippe V amplifie la rumeur. Un peu partout, des bûchers s'allument.

Si le royaume tient encore au moment où Édouard III revendique la couronne de France, l'édifice se lézarde sous l'effet conjugué des assauts qu'il subit. Quand les navires génois entrent dans le port de Marseille en novembre 1347, les corps affaiblis et les esprits tourmentés n'ont guère de défenses pour résister au bacille de Yersin.

La peste noire

Parti du Turkestan, dans la zone des steppes du lac Balkhach, le bacille de Yersin (du nom de Yersin, qui le découvrit en 1894), après avoir suivi la route de la soie, commence à se manifester en 1347 à Caffa, un comptoir génois de Crimée. Les Tartares, contaminés, auraient alors inventé la guerre bactériologique en catapultant dans la ville assiégée les cadavres des pestiférés. Véhiculée par la puce *Xenopsylla cheopis*, qui loge sur les rongeurs, en particulier le rat, la peste peut se propager sous deux formes. Pulmonaire, elle se transmet en hiver par les gouttelettes très fines rejetées lorsque l'on parle ou que l'on tousse. La période d'incubation est très courte, deux à trois jours, et la mort emporte la totalité de ceux qui sont contaminés. Bubonique, elle se transmet en été par piqûre de la puce. Elle provoque une forte température et la formation d'un bubon dur et douloureux, à l'aine, à l'aisselle ou au cou. La mort intervient dans 80 à 85 % des cas.

En novembre 1347, elle débarque donc à Marseille, dont les habitants, affolés, fuient de tous côtés, emportant le mal avec eux. En décembre, elle ravage la Corse et Aix-en-Provence. Au début du mois de janvier, elle atteint Arles et Avignon, où, les anciens cimetières étant saturés, on doit en ouvrir un nouveau pour ensevelir les onze mille morts qu'elle fait en un mois et demi. En février, elle frappe aux portes de Montpellier, de Béziers et de Narbonne. En mars, elle est à Carcassonne et Perpignan. À partir du mois d'avril, la peste pulmonaire qui avait prospéré dans cet hiver froid et humide est relayée par la bubonique.

Après avoir ravagé Toulon, Lyon, Toulouse et Montauban, elle pénètre en Auvergne. En mai, elle envahit le comté de Nice, le Dauphiné, le Lyonnais et l'Aquitaine. Fin juin, elle est à Bordeaux, d'où elle s'embarque pour l'Angleterre et Rouen, qu'elle aborde le 25 juillet. Le 20 août, elle pénètre dans Paris. Le 28, elle est en Bourgogne et, en décembre, les Anglais de Londres l'exportent à Calais.

Après avoir été ralentie par les froids vifs de l'hiver 1348-1349, elle resurgit dès le mois d'avril 1349 et marche vers le Nord et l'Est. En juillet, elle frappe Strasbourg ; en décembre, elle parvient à Metz. Puis, après quelques brèves réapparitions en 1350 et 1351, elle disparaît en 1352, laissant derrière elle une population hébétée.

Consultés par le roi sur les origines de l'épidémie et les moyens de la combattre, les maîtres de la Sorbonne déclarent que « [...] Aristote et Albert le Grand sont d'avis que les conjonctions d'astres errants peuvent engendrer un air malsain ; c'est pour cela que l'année a été chaude et humide, ce qui dispose à la putridité de l'air ». Jean de Venette, le prieur des Carmes de la place Maubert, a vu en août 1348, exploser une étoile formidable. « On la vit vers l'ouest, grande et brillante, écrit-il, après l'heure de Vêpres, alors que le soleil encore brillant descendait sur l'horizon. Elle n'était pas, comme sont les autres, très lointaine au-dessus de notre hémisphère. Elle paraissait au contraire assez proche. Le soleil se couchait, et la nuit venait. Il nous sembla, à mes frères et à moi, qu'elle ne bougeait pas. À la nuit tombante, cette grosse étoile se dispersa en plusieurs rayons. Nous l'avons vue, et bien des gens s'en émerveillèrent avec nous. Projetant ses rayons au-dessus de Paris et vers l'Orient, elle disparut totalement, annulée en son intégralité. Était-ce une comète ou une autre, ou quelque formation d'exhalaisons, soudain dissoute en vapeurs ? Je laisse aux astronomes le soin d'en juger. Il est cependant possible que ce fût le présage de la peste. » Pour Guy de Chauliac, médecin du pape Clément VI, c'est la conjonction dans le quatorzième degré du Verseau de Saturne, Jupiter et Mars, le 24 mars 1345, qui « émeut l'air comme l'aimant attire le fer ; puis la Nature, remise peu à peu, provoque alors bubons et autres apothèmes ». Pour échapper à la mort, la Faculté recommande un mode de vie sain, l'abstinence sexuelle, le recours au vinaigre et aux parfums, les légumes cuits, les poudres et les sirops, les pilules de safran, de myrrhe et d'aloès, la sérénité morale et, surtout... la fuite, qui, générale, assure en fait une diffusion plus large et plus rapide du mal.

Les historiens retiennent aujourd'hui l'estimation que Froissart faisait à chaud : « Bien la tierce partie du monde mourut. » En deux ou trois ans, la mort envoya en effet au cimetière un homme sur trois, une proportion six fois supérieure à celles des victimes des guerres mondiales du XXe siècle ! Le registre paroissial du village bourguignon de Givry, document unique, nous indique que les décès, qui en temps normal s'élevaient à 20 ou 25 par an, atteignent le chiffre de 622 entre le 22 juillet et le 19 novembre 1348. Dans le val de Rians, au nord-est d'Aix, l'enquêteur chargé de recenser les feux n'en trouve plus que 264 en 1359 contre 432 en 1346, soit une baisse de l'ordre de 39 %. Apt et Forcalquier perdent 46 et 48 % de leurs habitants. Moutiers et Riez sont réduites des deux tiers. À Castres et à Albi, une famille sur deux a disparu. Des 140 frères prêcheurs de Montpellier, 7 seulement ont survécu. À Marseille, les 150 frères cordeliers sont tous morts comme tous les augustins d'Avignon. À Perpignan, sur les 10 notaires et les 8 médecins de la ville, 2 seulement échappent au fléau. Seules la Flandre au nord de Lille, certaines vallées des hautes Pyrénées, une partie du Hainaut et du Brabant, le Rouergue et le Béarn semblent avoir été épargnés.

Sévissant désormais de façon endémique, avec de fortes poussées en 1360-1362, 1369, 1374-1375, 1399-1402 et 1418-1420, la peste et la famine, sa compagne, vont peser de manière tragique sur le destin des hommes. La seule estimation précise concerne l'Angleterre. À la veille du premier assaut de l'épidémie, elle compte 3 125 000 habitants. En 1377, elle n'en a plus que 2 250 000 et moins de 2 millions au début du XVᵉ siècle. Montpellier passe de 40 000 habitants avant 1348 à 18 000 en 1367 et 11 400 en 1448-1449. Périgueux compte 1 224 feux en 1345, 719 en 1455 ; Reims rassemble 16 000 à 18 000 habitants en 1328, 10 000 au milieu du XVᵉ siècle. Le doyenné de Montmorency, au nord de Paris, passe d'une densité de 19 feux au kilomètre carré en 1328 à une densité de 5,25 en 1470. En un siècle, de 1347 à 1450, la France, dans ses frontières de 1328, serait passée de 16 à 8 millions d'habitants, avec des régions particulièrement dévastées, comme la Normandie orientale, une bonne partie du Bassin parisien, dont la Champagne, de larges secteurs de l'Aunis et de la Saintonge.

On peut imaginer sans peine les bouleversements provoqués par cette catastrophe, l'avancée des landes et des maquis, le pullulement des bêtes sauvages, en particulier des loups, le recul massif de la production céréalière, l'absence d'entretien des canaux de drainage et des digues. Pour les survivants, en revanche, qui dans les familles aisées accumulent les héritages inespérés et dans les couches modestes bénéficient de la forte hausse des salaires que les employeurs ont dû consentir pour les retenir, le temps de l'Apocalypse a été une véritable aubaine. Le patron qui ne veut pas fermer boutique ou le propriétaire du sol qui cherche un fermier pour l'exploiter n'ont pas le choix, même si le gouvernement tente d'enrayer la flambée des salaires en ordonnant que « nul maître de métier, quel qu'il soit, n'enchérisse sur l'autre maître des valets du métier, sous peine d'amende arbitraire ».

À Paris, le salaire du maçon quadruple dans les dix années qui suivent le passage du fléau. En Normandie orientale, l'ouvrier qualifié touche deux sous par jour en 1320-1340, puis quatre sous de 1340 à 1405. Deux fois moins nombreux, les vilains vont désormais manger de la viande, boire du vin, porter du drap et du linge et bâtir en pierre ce qu'ils construisaient en torchis. Mais, en 1348, celui qui est entouré de cadavres ne peut savoir qu'il va connaître un âge d'or. Seulement étonné d'en avoir réchappé, il prie saint Sébastien ou saint Roch et cherche des coupables.

La danse macabre

« Rêvons, transposons dans notre époque anxieuse afin de mieux nous représenter ce que put être le choc, imaginons, écrit Georges Duby : quatre, cinq millions de personnes dans la seule région parisienne, mourant en quelques heures durant un seul été et d'un mal que nul ne savait guérir. Désarroi. Que faire d'abord de ce monceau de cadavres ? Et puis les questions pressantes : quelle faute collective méritait cette punition ? Comment, par quelle pénitence, se soustraire aux coups du fléau ? Furent ébranlées jusque dans leur fondement toutes les idées que l'on se faisait de l'univers, des rapports de l'homme avec la surnature. » Le bouleversement des esprits est bien plus sensible que celui de l'économie.

À Toulon, dans la nuit du 13 au 14 avril 1348, 40 Juifs sont massacrés et leurs maisons pillées. Tour à tour, la Provence, le Languedoc, la Savoie et le Dauphiné sont touchés par le mouvement. Au pont de Beauvoisin, plusieurs Juifs sont précipités dans un puits qu'on les accuse d'avoir empoisonné. À Strasbourg, sur 1 884 Juifs qui habitaient alors la ville, près de 900 sont brûlés vifs le 14 février 1349, malgré l'opposition des autorités.

À Strasbourg toujours, en juillet 1349, arrive un groupe de 200 flagellants qui, sur le parvis de la cathédrale, devant une foule immense, se lacèrent mutuellement le corps en psalmodiant d'étranges prières. Né en Italie, le mouvement des flagellants se présente comme une secte mystique au charisme ravageur dans la mesure où ils affirment qu'ils sont certains d'échapper à la mort. Recrutés essentiellement parmi les gens du peuple, les flagellants s'engagent pour trente-trois jours et demi (en souvenir des trente-trois ans et demi de vie terrestre du Christ) à suivre un pèlerinage. Un capuchon baissé sur les yeux, portant une croix rouge sur la poitrine, faisant des prières en commun, ils se fondent sur une prétendue « lettre tombée du Ciel » et s'infligent, deux fois par jour, sur la place publique des villes et des villages, un véritable supplice à l'aide d'un fouet à triple lanière terminé par des pointes de fer, assimilant le sang qui coule de leurs blessures au sang versé par le Christ lors de sa Passion.

Après avoir parcouru l'Alsace, ils se répandent dans le nord de la France, à Maubeuge, Lille, Douai, Valenciennes, Béthune, Saint-Omer, Arras puis, en septembre, gagnent Avignon pour faire approuver leurs statuts par le pape. Condamnant ce mouvement qui met en danger une hiérarchie ecclésiastique décimée et trouble les esprits, le pape condamne le recours à la flagellation et charge l'Inquisition de mettre les obstinés à la raison. En fait, les flagellants disparaîtront avec la peste comme ils étaient venus avec elle.

Plus durablement, la peste inaugure une nouvelle vision de la mort, une mort qui n'est plus la mort sereine permettant au défunt de « reposer en paix », mais une mort horrible qui prend le visage d'un cadavre décharné. Danses macabres et gisants squelettiques traduisent le découragement d'une société qui demande comme une grâce d'avoir le temps de se préparer à une mort subite qui laisse dans la rue tous les cadavres que nul fossoyeur ne peut ensevelir, frappe aussi bien l'évêque, le chevalier ou le pauvre laboureur et sécrète l'angoisse de se retrouver seul, face à Dieu, sans avoir reçu les derniers sacrements.

« Le père ne visite pas son fils, ni la mère sa fille, ni le frère son frère, ni le fils son père, ni l'ami son ami, ni un voisin un voisin, ni un allié un allié à moins de vouloir mourir immédiatement avec lui. » Ce témoignage d'un chanoine brugeois écrivant d'Avignon en 1348 exprime les troubles d'une génération travaillée par l'inhumaine réalité d'un mal qui brise les naturelles solidarités.

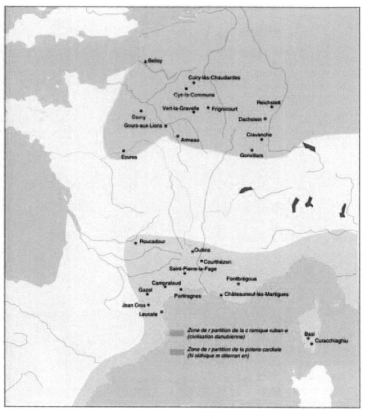

*Principaux sites du Rubané et du Cardial, en France, au Néolithique
(du VIe au IVe millénaire).*

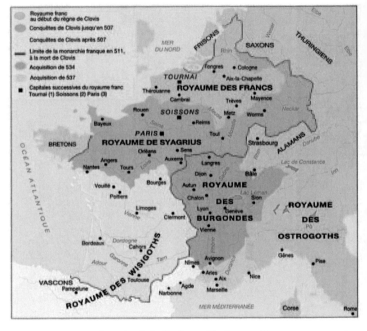

Conquête de la Gaule par Clovis et ses fils.

Le partage de Verdun en 843.

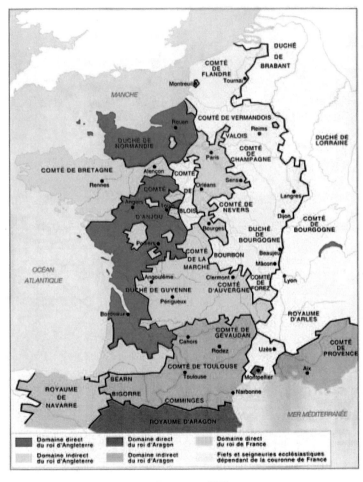

La France vers 1180.

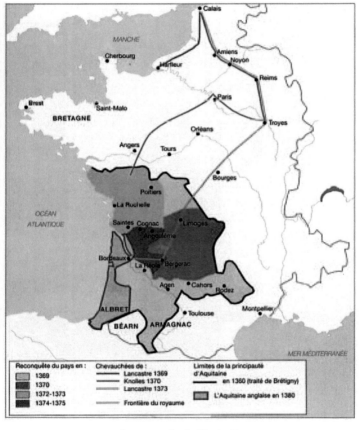

La reconquête de Charles V.

L'État bourguignon sous Charles le Téméraire.

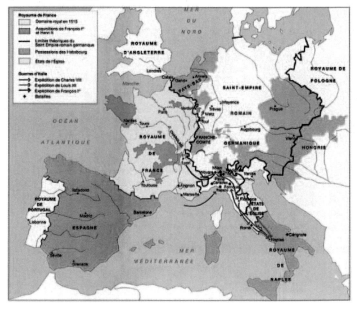

L'Europe au milieu du XVIᵉ siècle.

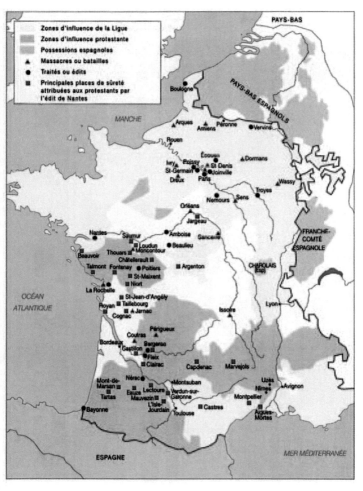

Les guerres de Religion.

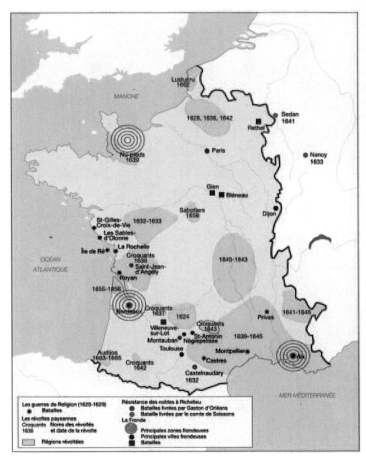

Frondes et révoltes au XVIIᵉ siècle.

La grande misère
du royaume de France

*U*n roi de France fait prisonnier, un dauphin malingre et sans expérience, des impôts qui ne financent que des défaites, des partis aristocratiques qui multiplient les intrigues au gré de leurs convoitises, les bourgeois de Paris qui se révoltent et envahissent le palais royal, des paysans qui font rôtir un chevalier et obligent sa femme à consommer les morceaux, un roi d'Angleterre qui veut se faire sacrer à Reims, un traité de paix qui cède en toute souveraineté aux Anglais la Guyenne, le Poitou, la Saintonge, l'Agenais, le Périgord, le Limousin, le Quercy, Tarbes, le comté de Bigorre, l'Angoumois, le Rouergue, le Ponthieu et Calais : telles furent les grandes misères du royaume de France sous le règne d'un roi qui a été surnommé « le Bon ». En ces temps de malheurs, la France apparaît bien comme une noble dame en haillons.*

Poitiers

Le roi qui se fait sacrer à Reims le 26 septembre 1350, « lent à informer et dur à ôter d'une opinion », selon la chronique, était certainement moins incapable et moins superficiel qu'on l'a dit. Homme de cœur sensible aux misères de son temps, il avait du goût pour les lettres, les arts et la musique. Pétrarque, venu à Paris en 1361, dont l'indépendance d'esprit est prouvée, le trouvait « très bon et très bienveillant ». Certes, comme tous les Valois, il aimait les riches habits, les belles pièces d'orfèvrerie, les meubles d'apparat, les banquets, les fêtes et les tournois. Fort généreux à l'égard de ses fidèles et aimant régaler ses amis, il fut surnommé « le Bon », ce qui n'est pas tout à fait un compliment. Médiocre politique et piètre tacticien, Jean le Bon est surtout dépressif, coléreux et impulsif, sujet à de brusques accès de violence, multipliant les vexations et aiguisant à plaisir les mécontentements. Obsédé par la trahison, il inaugure son règne en faisant décapiter sans jugement son connétable Raoul de Brienne, comte d'Eu et de Guînes, un baron lié aux plus grandes familles du royaume, ce qui scandalise la noblesse, trouble l'opinion, suscite les rumeurs et engendre la méfiance. Surtout quand il nomme pour le remplacer Charles d'Espagne, un prince castillan qui passait pour son mignon.

C'est peut-être parce qu'il se sent environné de traîtres qu'il crée en 1351 l'ordre de l'Étoile, pendant de l'ordre de la Jarretière fondé par le roi d'Angleterre en 1348. Désignés par le roi pour défendre la dynastie, cinq cents chevaliers, « les plus suffisants du royaume », devaient faire preuve d'une loyauté à toute épreuve et devenir l'élite d'une chevalerie rénovée. Placés sous le patronage des Rois Mages, les chevaliers arboraient le costume blanc et rouge, les chausses noires et les souliers dorés et s'engageaient par serment à ne jamais « fuir en bataille », quitte à être tués. Ainsi, en 1353, dans une simple embuscade, en Bretagne, un grand nombre d'entre eux se firent massacrer pour ne pas trahir leur serment. Jean le Bon restait bien un homme du passé qui, n'ayant pas tiré les leçons de Crécy, confondait bravoure et stratégie et rêvait de reconstituer les fidélités que les hommages du droit féodal n'assuraient plus.

Pour gouverner un royaume que la peste noire avait totalement désorganisé et régenter des esprits bouleversés par les malheurs du temps, il aurait fallu avoir des nerfs d'acier. Jean ne les avait pas. Quand il se voit entouré de traîtres, il ne se trompe pourtant pas. Son principal ennemi, il le trouve dans la famille royale. Personnage ambitieux, rusé, charmeur, fourbe et irrésolu, Charles de Navarre, qu'un chroniqueur espagnol surnommera « el Malo » (le Mauvais) en 1571 est, par sa mère Jeanne, petit-fils du roi Louis X le Hutin, arrière-petit-fils de Philippe le Bel et première victime de l'exclusion des femmes. Contre les Valois, il répète que, lui, est issu « de la droite lignée royale de France » et qu'il peut revendiquer la couronne. Il faut dire que s'il était né quelques années plus tôt — il vient au monde en 1332 — ses droits auraient, en 1328, primé ceux du roi d'Angleterre. Certes, ses parents avaient abandonné toute prétention à la couronne en « élisant » le Valois, mais Charles considérait qu'ils n'avaient pu légitimement renoncer, avant sa naissance, à un droit qui n'appartenait qu'à lui seul. En fait, Charles sait bien que l'on ne reviendra pas sur le choix de 1328. Il veut simplement accroître sa puissance et monnayer son soutien. Ayant hérité de sa mère le petit royaume pyrénéen de Navarre et de son père Philippe d'Évreux des terres en Normandie, du Cotentin à Pontoise, il est en même temps le gendre du roi Jean. Quand ce dernier fait connétable Charles d'Espagne, il s'estime, non sans raison, volé.

Captant le mécontentement d'une partie de la noblesse attachée à son indépendance, trouvant des partisans parmi les clercs, en particulier l'ambitieux évêque de Laon, Robert Le Coq, et les bourgeois qu'il séduit en disant s'opposer à la monnaie « faible » et à la levée des impôts, il marque son entrée dans l'intrigue politique en faisant assassiner, le 8 janvier 1354, Charles d'Espagne, le favori du roi et en se vantant de cet acte accompli, prétend-il, pour le bien du royaume. Puis il complote avec le roi d'Angleterre, auquel il promet d'ouvrir la Normandie, et cherche enfin à dresser contre son père le fils aîné de Jean le Bon, le dauphin Charles. Dans l'un de ces mouvements de colère qui lui étaient familiers, Jean le Bon, en armes, fait irruption le 5 avril 1356 à Rouen, au moment où le dauphin donnait un grand banquet en l'honneur du Navarrais, viole les lois de l'hospitalité, fait décapiter sur le champ quatre nobles normands, dont le prestigieux comte d'Harcourt, et jette en prison Charles de Navarre, dont il fait saisir les biens. En juin 1356, assurés de l'appui du « parti » navarrais, les Anglais débarquent en Normandie.

Affaibli par ces intrigues qui divisent sa noblesse, le roi doit aussi faire face à l'opposition des états, qui entendent contrôler le financement de la guerre et monnayer leur consentement à l'impôt. C'est qu'il n'était plus possible de dévaluer la monnaie. Quatre-vingt-un actes avaient modifié sa valeur depuis 1350. En novembre 1355, la pièce d'argent, que l'on appelait le blanc pour la distinguer des pièces « noires » à faible teneur de métal, ne valait plus que 10 % de sa valeur cinq ans auparavant. La monnaie était devenue à l'époque de Jean le Bon un sujet qui excitait l'opinion publique et sur lequel chacun avait un avis, les abus du pouvoir ayant permis le tour de force de réunir des mécontentements divergents et de rassembler des intérêts diamétralement opposés. Réunis à Paris le 2 décembre 1355, les états que l'on appelle désormais généraux, à la différence de ceux qui les avaient précédés, soumettent le vote d'un nouvel impôt à de sévères conditions. Dans chaque diocèse, des personnes « bonnes et honnêtes », désignées par les états, établiront l'assiette de l'impôt et en surveilleront la levée. Au-dessus d'eux, neuf « généraux » également désignés à raison de trois par état, formeront une juridiction qui tranchera les litiges. De l'argent, rien n'ira au roi ni à ses agents, tout étant destiné à l'entretien, pendant un an d'une armée de trente mille hommes. Ce sont enfin les délégués des états qui organiseront les troupes royales, les passeront en revue, ou « montres », pour vérifier l'état des armes et des effectifs et payeront eux-mêmes les hommes d'armes. Au printemps 1356, réunis à Toulouse, les états de Languedoc imposent les mêmes exigences. C'était la première tentative de monarchie contrôlée, le premier programme d'une « réformacion du royaume », formulé au moment où reprennent les hostilités.

En octobre 1355, en effet, le prince de Galles, surnommé le Prince Noir à cause de la couleur de son armure, lance, avec le soutien des pauvres gascons des Landes, une chevauchée qui dévaste le Languedoc, une terre « moult riche et plantureuse », brûle les faubourgs de Toulouse, Carcassonne et Narbonne et accumule un butin dont il se vante auprès de son père Édouard III dès son retour à Bordeaux. Cette nouvelle tactique vise un double but : sur le plan matériel, détruire les biens de l'adversaire, villages, récoltes, bétail, moulins, pressoirs ; sur le plan psychologique, démontrer la puissance du roi d'Angleterre et la faiblesse du roi de France.

Après l'arrestation de Charles le Mauvais, des troupes commandées par le duc de Lancastre débarquent en Normandie et pillent Pont-Audemer, Verneuil et Argentan. Pendant ce temps, le Prince Noir lance une nouvelle chevauchée vers le « pays d'Auvergne, si gras et si rempli de tous biens que c'était merveille à voir », puis marche vers la Loire pour opérer la jonction avec l'armée anglaise campée au nord du fleuve. Mais l'arrivée des troupes de Jean le Bon le contraint à se retirer. Après une semaine de poursuites, la bataille décisive a lieu à Poitiers, le 19 septembre 1356, une bataille qui ressemble étrangement à celle qui s'était déroulée à Crécy dix ans auparavant.

Comme à Crécy, le Prince Noir, contraint à la défensive devant un ennemi largement supérieur en nombre, a choisi son terrain : un plateau ondulé, défendu sur les côtés par des pentes douces, coupées de haies et de vignes, et, en arrière, par la rivière du Miosson. Comme à Crécy, Jean engage la bataille alors que son maréchal lui recommande de cerner et d'affamer les Anglais au lieu de courir au massacre. Comme à Crécy, la chevalerie française refuse cette tactique qui serait « œuvre de couardise ». Comme à Crécy, elle se fait massacrer par l'archerie anglaise plutôt que de reculer. Mais, contrairement à son père Philippe VI, Jean le Bon ne fuira pas. Pire : en vaillant chevalier, il se bat jusqu'au bout et est fait prisonnier. Trop heureux, le Prince Noir comble son cousin de politesses chevaleresques et reprend le chemin de Bordeaux à petites journées pour exhiber sa prestigieuse capture. En avril 1357, le prisonnier doré s'embarque pour Londres, où sa table est garnie des épices les plus rares. Lisant des romans de chevalerie, consultant son astrologue, se faisant égayer par un fou, entretenant des ménestrels, faisant venir du vin de France, achetant une harpe et une horloge portative, il attend le versement de la rançon.

Étienne Marcel

Le dauphin Charles qui prend, à dix-huit ans, la direction du royaume au lendemain de la « déconfiture » de Poitiers — c'est ainsi que les contemporains appelèrent cette défaite —, semblait bien fragile pour assumer une telle responsabilité. Sorti par son père de la bataille en plein cœur du combat pour protéger l'avenir de la dynastie, il apparaît s'être dérobé, sinon manquer de courage. Seul, il ne pouvait compter que sur le soutien de ses deux frères, Jean, qui allait sur ses seize ans, et Louis, qui en avait dix-sept. La noblesse, qui depuis trois siècles incarnait dans ses châteaux l'ordre féodal, était discréditée. Si le roi avait sauvé son honneur et fait son devoir en se battant jusqu'au bout, qu'avaient fait ses chevaliers de parade, que leur passion pour les femmes et les beaux costumes avait rendus inaptes au combat ? Comment pouvaient-ils encore prétendre jouir de leurs privilèges alors que leur défaillance morale avait attiré la colère divine sur le royaume et conduit le roi en captivité ? « De tels gens, déclare une complainte écrite à chaud, ne peut être dite bonne chanson [...]. France est à tous temps par eux déshonorée. »

Aux états généraux de langue d'oïl réunis à Paris le 17 octobre 1356, l'opposition se déchaîne, animée par l'évêque de Laon, Robert Le Coq, membre du « parti » navarrais qu'excite l'absence du roi Jean le Bon, et Étienne Marcel, le prévôt des marchands de Paris. Ce dernier, marchand drapier, membre de l'une des plus puissantes familles de bourgeois de Paris, est le porte-parole des idées forces du moment : éviction des « mauvais » conseillers du roi et égalité des sacrifices dus par chacun pour défendre le royaume. Dans la capitale, il se pose aussi en chef de guerre, organisant la milice parisienne, entreprenant de grands travaux de fortification et rassemblant des armes et des munitions.

N'ayant rien obtenu du dauphin, les députés des états se réunissent à nouveau en février 1357 et arrachent la promulgation, le 3 mars, d'une ordonnance qui met véritablement la monarchie sous contrôle. Affirmant en préambule que la France a été jusque-là « gouvernée par des gens avaricieux, convoiteux ou négligents » et qu'il faut les remplacer par des « prud'hommes sages, véritables, diligents et loyaux », l'ordonnance décide la déchéance de vingt-deux conseillers du roi. Elle déclare la suspension provisoire de tous les officiers royaux en attendant que soient nommés ceux qui, désignés par des « réformateurs généraux » issus des états, seront chargés de continuer leur service. Elle ordonne au souverain et aux princes de restreindre leurs dépenses et aux fonctionnaires de commencer leur travail « à l'heure du soleil levant » sans « muser et s'en aller sans rien faire ». Elle prévoit qu'il sera fait une nouvelle monnaie d'or et d'argent que l'on ne modifiera pas avant un an. Elle donne aux états la possibilité de se réunir sans attendre la convocation ou la bonne volonté du souverain. Et, une fois de plus, elle décide que les états contrôleront eux-mêmes la perception de l'impôt. Ce que veulent en fait les états, c'est mettre la main sur le Conseil du roi, prendre le contrôle de l'administration et de l'impôt, assurer la périodicité de leurs réunions, bref, prendre le pouvoir dans une situation que l'évasion, le 9 novembre 1357, de Charles de Navarre rend encore plus confuse.

D'un côté, dans les difficultés, la personnalité du dauphin s'affirme. Le 11 janvier 1358, il n'hésite pas, accompagné seulement de huit personnes, à haranguer les Parisiens vers neuf heures du matin aux Halles. Attaquant sans ménagement « ceux qui avaient pris le gouvernement et n'y mettaient nul remède », se demandant où était passé l'argent qu'avaient collecté les délégués des états, lui-même n'en ayant reçu « ni denier ni obole », il annonce son intention « de gouverner dès lors en avant » et de demander des comptes à ceux qui avaient pris « le gouvernement et la finance ».

Charles de Navarre, quant à lui, se pose en roi et, à la manière des prédicateurs populaires, « prêche au peuple » pendant des heures, lui arrachant des larmes au récit de ses malheurs. Le 10 janvier 1358, les corps des victimes décapitées à Rouen par le roi Jean le Bon font l'objet d'un hommage funèbre, une longue procession à travers la ville réhabilitant la mémoire de ceux que le Mauvais qualifie de « vrais martyrs ».

Étienne Marcel, lui, compte ses fidèles et organise son « parti », invitant les « bonnes gens » de Paris à se coiffer de chaperons rouge et bleu, les couleurs de la ville, et à s'engager « à bonne fin », telle est sa devise, de mener jusqu'à son terme la lutte pour la réforme du royaume. Le samedi 27 janvier 1358, on peut voir dans Paris un spectacle qui montre à quel point la capitale est déchirée. D'un côté, conduit par Étienne Marcel, s'ébranle le cortège funèbre de Perrin Marc, un changeur pendu pour avoir au cours d'une dispute tué Jean

Baillet, le trésorier du dauphin. De l'autre, au même moment, le dauphin en personne préside les obsèques solennelles de Jean Baillet.

Le 22 février 1358, sentant que la situation est en train de lui échapper, Étienne Marcel organise une manifestation qui dégénère. Trois mille gens de métier armés envahissent le palais royal, pénètrent dans la chambre du dauphin terrorisé, assassinent sous ses yeux deux de ses conseillers, Jean de Conflans, maréchal de Champagne, et Robert de Clermont, maréchal de Normandie tandis qu'Étienne Marcel coiffe le prince de son chaperon bleu et rouge et se coiffe du chapeau de Charles pour montrer ou faire croire qu'ils ne forment qu'une seule tête. Comme l'écrit le rédacteur de la chronique des quatres premiers Valois du règne en conclusion du récit de cette journée « insurrectionnelle » : « Et alors les gouverneurs des trois états pensèrent avoir paisiblement le royaume de France. » Pourtant, loin d'être résigné, Charles annonce sa décision de porter désormais le titre de régent et réussit à quitter Paris pour engager, avec l'appui de la « province », la lutte contre le prévôt des marchands. L'occupation et la mise en défense de Meaux et de Montereau sont les premiers actes de guerre du régent.

La Jacquerie

Menacé de voir Paris assiégé, Étienne Marcel croit trouver le salut en s'alliant avec les Jacques. Aux portes de Paris, en effet, dans les sages campagnes d'Île-de-France et de Picardie, explose en mai 1358 une révolte d'une rare violence, dont les récits et témoignages montrent assez l'effroi qu'elle a suscité.

Le 28 mai 1358, à Saint-Leu-d'Esserent, près de Chantilly, une rixe oppose les paysans à des gentilshommes probablement venus là pour mettre garnison dans la région. Quatre chevaliers et cinq écuyers restent sur le terrain, égorgés. Un fait divers, somme toute banal, qui traduit un mouvement spontané de résistance face aux bandes de soldats qui, mal payés pendant la guerre et sans solde pendant les trêves, vivaient sur le pays. « Dans cette année 1358, écrit Jean de Venette, beaucoup de villages dépourvus de fortifications, se firent de vraies citadelles de leurs églises, en creusant autour d'elles des fossés et en garnissant leurs tours et leurs clochers de machines de guerre, de pierriers et de balistes, afin de se défendre, si les brigands venaient les attaquer, ce qui arrivait, à ce qu'il paraît, fort souvent. » En l'absence des protecteurs traditionnels, vaincus à Poitiers, les Jacques, surnom alors donné aux vilains, tissent des solidarités qui traduisent aussi la vivacité du sentiment national. Ainsi, vers 1358-1359, un paysan qui avait le nom de Grand Ferré, se dresse contre l'« Anglais » et, se battant comme un chevalier, fait régner dans sa région l'ordre que n'assure plus une noblesse inutile.

La rixe de Saint-Leu révèle donc des haines que l'avalanche des calamités a accumulées. En moins d'une semaine, plusieurs foyers de révolte naissent en Beauvaisis, dans le Vexin, aux confins de la Normandie, en Picardie et en Auxerrois. Armés de faux, de gourdins, de couteaux, les Jacques, dont les bannières s'ornent de fleurs de lys et qui adoptent « Montjoie » comme cri de guerre, s'en prennent uniquement aux châteaux, qu'ils pillent et incendient. De temps à autre, ils violent et ils tuent. Froissart les accuse même d'avoir fait rôtir à la broche un seigneur sous les yeux de sa famille qu'ils veulent contraindre à en manger.

Si Guillaume Carle, qui connaissait le métier des armes, dirige les insurgés en Beauvaisis, le soulèvement est presque partout spontané. C'est la réaction de paysans assez aisés, touchés par les malheurs du temps et qui se dressent contre les forteresses d'une noblesse que la « déconfiture » de Poitiers a déconsidérée. Si les gens de la campagne ont pris les armes contre les nobles, écrit encore Jean de Venette qui les connaissait bien, c'est « qu'ils voyaient les maux et les oppressions qui leur étaient portés de toute part et qu'ils n'étaient pas protégés par leurs nobles, mais qu'au contraire ceux-ci, se conduisant comme des ennemis, les opprimaient plus gravement encore ».

Ne mesurant pas que les Jacques allaient pousser cette noblesse, jusqu'alors fort active dans le parti des réformes, dans les bras d'un régent désormais garant de l'ordre social, Étienne Marcel mène des actions communes avec eux jusqu'au moment où Charles le Mauvais, qui reste avant tout un prince, écrase les insurgés à Mello le 10 juin, après s'être emparé de Guillaume Carle, qu'il attire dans un piège peu chevaleresque en le conviant à venir parlementer. Ensuite, c'est le massacre des Jacques, les nobles, revenus de leur grande peur, assouvissant leur vengeance dans un bain de sang.

Déconsidéré par les excès des Jacques qu'il a encouragés, de plus en plus isolé, Étienne Marcel achève de se rendre impopulaire en livrant la capitale au roi de Navarre et aux mercenaires anglais que ce dernier a embauchés pour maintenir l'ordre. Les bourgeois de Paris abandonnent alors leur prévôt, qui est assassiné le 31 juillet 1358 à la suite d'un vif incident devant la porte Saint-Antoine. Le 2 août, le régent entre dans la capitale et signe, le 10, des lettres de rémission donnant aux Parisiens un pardon général. Paradoxalement, la crise, trop violente, a renforcé la royauté. De l'œuvre accomplie par les états de langue d'oïl, il ne reste presque rien, les intérêts de Paris et de sa région n'étant pas ceux de la France.

La France de Brétigny

Profitant des troubles qui, vus de l'extérieur, affaiblissent la couronne, Édouard III pense pouvoir imposer un traité de paix particulièrement humiliant. En mars 1359, il obtient de son prisonnier Jean le Bon l'acceptation d'un accord qui fixe une rançon énorme de quatre millions d'écus d'or et cède, en toute souveraineté, au roi d'Angleterre la Guyenne élargie et le Poitou, le Limousin et le Périgord, l'Agenais et le comté de Bigorre, la Touraine, l'Anjou, le Maine, la Normandie, le comté de Ponthieu, le vicomté de Montreuil, les comtés de Boulogne et de Guînes, ainsi que la souveraineté sur la Bretagne ! C'était reconstituer l'ancien empire Plantagenêt, interdire au royaume de France l'accès aux rivages de l'océan Atlantique, de la Manche et de la mer du Nord et le réduire de moitié ! Comment Jean le Bon et ses conseillers de Londres ont-ils pu accepter une telle humiliation et écrire que ces cessions étaient « choses bien légères à faire » ? Inconscience ou solution d'attente ?

En fait, Édouard III avait sous-estimé l'assurance nouvelle du régent. Décidé à refuser ce que son père avait accepté, il réunit une assemblée des états qui, en mai 1359, déclare que ce traité est « moult déplaisant à tout le peuple de France », ni « passable ni faisable » et, pour cette raison, ordonne de « faire bonne guerre aux Anglais ». En 1359, l'amour de la « patrie » qui avait saisi le Grand Ferré poussait les Français à refuser que « le noble royaume fût ainsi amoindri ».

Édouard III décide alors d'intervenir militairement. Le 28 octobre 1359, son armée débarque à Calais, avec un matériel considérable, jusqu'à des moulins à bras, des fours de campagne, des canots en cuir bouilli pour pêcher dans les étangs en temps de carême et une vénerie de trente fauconniers à cheval. Par un mauvais automne, chemins détrempés, rivières en crue, à travers un pays épuisé, il se met en route vers Reims dans l'espoir de s'y faire sacrer et couronner. Mais après un siège de quarante jours devant la ville, il doit abandonner. En mars 1360, il tente le tout pour le tout en se dirigeant sur Paris, mais le régent, qui a décidé de pratiquer « la grève du combat », donne l'ordre de garder son sang-froid et de ne pas répondre aux provocations. Le dimanche 12 avril, les Anglais lèvent une nouvelle fois le camp et prennent la route de Chartres. Le lundi, un terrible orage s'abat sur une armée transie par le froid qui, faute de charrois, doit brûler une partie des bagages. Édouard III, ridicule victime des giboulées, craignant que la chevauchée ne s'achève en désastre, entame alors de nouvelles négociations qui, le 8 mai 1360, aboutissent aux préliminaires de paix de Brétigny, un hameau proche de Chartres.

La rançon était ramenée à trois millions d'écus payables par tranches annuelles et garantis par l'envoi d'otages à Londres. Édouard recevait en toute souveraineté la grande Aquitaine d'Aliénor, Calais, le Ponthieu et le comté de Guînes. En échange, il renonçait à ses droits sur la couronne de France. Ces conditions furent ratifiées par les deux rois à Calais, le 24 octobre 1360. Mais on apporta au traité une modification dont les négociateurs n'avaient peut être pas mesuré les conséquences. Par la fameuse clause des « renonciations », il était prévu que le roi de France renoncerait à sa souveraineté sur l'Aquitaine et le roi d'Angleterre à la couronne de France quand l'ensemble des terres cédées seraient remises aux Anglais, avec, comme dernier délai le 30 novembre 1361. Or cette date ne fut jamais respectée, les procédures pour constituer les dossiers de cession, faire l'inventaire des biens, recevoir les hommages des vassaux et les serments des bourgeois étant fort longues. On en verra plus tard l'usage qu'en fera le futur Charles V.

Pendant ce temps, les otages s'ennuyaient. En septembre 1363, n'y tenant plus, Louis d'Anjou, le deuxième fils de Jean le Bon, faisant fi des manières chevaleresques, s'évade de Calais pour rejoindre son épouse, avec laquelle il n'avait vécu que quelques mois. Pour sauver l'honneur de son lignage et reprendre les négociations compromises par cette évasion, Jean le Bon se substitue alors à son fils et retourne en Angleterre. Il y meurt le 8 avril 1364.

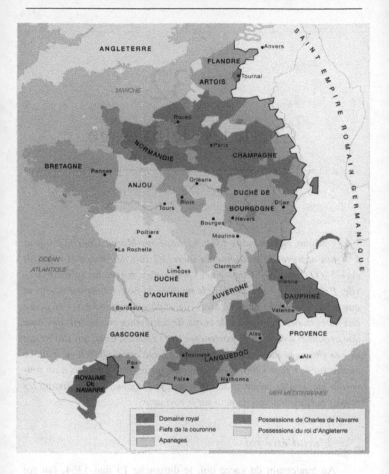

La France de Brétigny.

Charles V, le roi sage

Agonisant, en septembre 1380, à Beauté-sur-Marne, Charles V aurait fait apporter la couronne du sacre des rois de France et se serait écrié : « Ô couronne ! Comme tu es précieuse ; mais en même temps très vile. Précieuse si l'on considère le mystère de justice que tu contiens et que tu portes vigoureusement. Mais vile, et plus vile que tout, si l'on pense aux labeurs, peines de cœur, de corps, de conscience et les périls de l'âme que tu donnes à ceux qui te portent sur leurs épaules. Celui qui s'aviserait de ces choses te laisserait plutôt dans la boue que de te relever pour te mettre sur sa tête. » Charles aurait ainsi exprimé les tourments d'un souverain qui, le jour même de sa mort, signait l'ordonnance abolissant les impôts qui pesaient lourdement sur le royaume.

L'art d'être roi

Au lendemain du sacre qui, le dimanche 19 mai 1364, fait roi celui qui avait jusque-là vécu dans l'ombre de son père, Charles aurait changé de manière spectaculaire. Selon la femme de lettres Christine de Pisan, qui en fit son modèle, il aurait ouvert les yeux, regardé son peuple et son royaume « battu et désolé » et, délaissant les mœurs de la jeunesse, se serait converti à la sagesse. Ce témoignage, confirmé par d'autres contemporains, montre en effet Charles renonçant aux habits « jolis, vagues et curieux » des jeunes gens à la mode pour ne plus porter désormais que la robe longue des clercs, des hommes de loi et des professeurs, s'entourant de « bonnes et sages » personnes et réglant sa vie au rythme des horloges mécaniques pour lesquelles il s'enthousiasmait.

« L'heure de son découcher à matin, raconte Christine de Pisan, était réglementé de six à sept heures. » Tout de suite, il faisait le signe de la croix et, tout en se vêtant, « truffait » ses chambellans de « paroles joyeuses et honnêtes », leur montrant un aimable visage. Une fois peigné et vêtu, on lui apportait son bréviaire qu'il disait avec son chapelain. Vers huit heures, il allait à la messe et, vers huit heures et demie recevait et écoutait avec bienveillance tous ceux qui, « gens riches et pauvres, dames ou damoiselles, femmes veuves ou autres », avaient des requêtes à lui présenter. Aux jours fixés pour les séances, il se rendait à son Conseil, qu'il présidait avec solennité. Puis, vers dix heures, il se mettait à table, ne se chargeant pas de viandes et buvant un « vin clair et sain, sans grand fumet ». À la fin du repas, vers onze heures, il écoutait volontiers « instruments bas pour réjouir les esprits » et recevait les chevaliers et les ambassadeurs des pays étrangers. Puis, pendant deux heures, il travaillait avec ses conseillers privés, signant des lettres, accordant grâces et dons « raisonnables » et attribuant les offices vacants. Après quoi, il allait se reposer pendant une heure.

Puis, après vêpres, la fin de l'après-midi était consacrée soit aux « ébattements de choses agréables », aux conversations avec la reine et avec les femmes auxquelles il demandait des nouvelles de leurs enfants, aux marchands qui « venaient apporter velours, drap d'or et tout autres manières de belles choses étranges », soit à la lecture et au commentaire des « belles histoires de la Sainte Écriture ou des faits des Romains ou moralités des philosophes et d'autres sciences » jusqu'à l'heure du souper.

S'il vivait avec cette majestueuse régularité, remarque Christine de Pisan, c'était pour « garder, maintenir et donner exemple à ses successeurs à venir que par solennel ordre se doit tenir et mener le très digne degré de la haute couronne de France ».

Aucun roi de France n'a cultivé avec autant de méthode l'art d'être roi. Aucun roi n'a voulu autant se conformer à l'image du prince idéal dessinée par le philosophe grec Aristote. Atteint probablement d'une terrible goutte, infirme de la main droite, marqué par la souffrance physique tout au long de sa courte vie, Charles a voulu substituer aux vertus guerrières des rois chevaliers, batailleurs et emportés, l'image d'un roi calme, patient, maître de soi, puisant dans les livres et la fréquentation des savants les idées et les méthodes d'un bon gouvernement.

Parmi les très nombreux portraits qui le représentent, une miniature illustrant la traduction française de l'*Éthique* d'Aristote nous livre l'image qu'il se faisait du pouvoir et qu'une habile propagande a diffusée jusqu'à nos jours, l'image d'un roi « écolier » suivant attentivement les leçons du professeur. L'inventaire du mobilier royal nous apprend aussi que Charles possédait quatre paires de « besicles », dont l'une « environnée de corne noire ». Jamais roi ne fut plus « intellectuel ».

Installée dans l'une des tours du Louvre, la « librairie » (bibliothèque) du roi, amorcée sous le règne de Jean le Bon, comptait, en 1380, neuf cent dix-sept volumes, selon un inventaire tenu régulièrement à jour. La Sorbonne, à l'époque, n'en avait guère plus. Les murs du premier étage avaient été recouverts avec du bois d'Irlande et le plafond garni de bois de cyprès. L'entrée de chaque pièce était fermée par une porte haute et épaisse et toutes les fenêtres étaient garnies de treillis pour protéger les livres « des oiseaux et autres bêtes ». Trente chandeliers dans des niches et une lampe d'argent assuraient l'éclairage. Cette « librairie » comportait les textes sacrés en latin et en français, des traductions des principaux traités d'Aristote, le *Timée* de Platon, la *Cité de Dieu* de saint Augustin, le *Polycraticus* de Jean de Salisbury, des compilations encyclopédiques, une immense collection de livres astronomiques et astrologiques, trente volumes sur la géromancie, dix bestiaires, une série complète d'ouvrages scientifiques traduits de l'arabe, un *Atlas* catalan, cinq exemplaires de *Marco Polo*, le *Roman de Renart* et *le Roman de la rose*, des grammaires élémentaires et des dictionnaires, une véritable bibliothèque sur les croisades et le Songe du vergier, un traité de science politique composé par un proche du roi. « Tant que sapience [sagesse] sera honorée en ce royaume, disait Charles V, il continuera en prospérité, mais quand elle en sera déboutée, il tombera en déchéance. »

Instruit par la dure expérience des années 1356-1358, Charles a surtout voulu consolider le prestige d'une couronne durement mise à mal pendant ces années de grande misère. C'est sous son règne qu'est confirmée l'exclusion des femmes au droit de faire « le pont et la planche » et qu'est fixée la majorité des rois de France à l'entrée dans leur quatorzième année. En 1365, il fait rédiger un nouvel « ordo » du sacre, qui prend une solennité nouvelle. L'entrée à Reims, toujours plus fastueuse, marque désormais le temps fort d'une cérémonie tout au long de laquelle le spectacle de la rue prend le pas sur l'office religieux. C'est que Charles aime se montrer « en représentation », ses déplacements, en fait peu nombreux, devenant l'occasion de prolonger les bénéfices du sacre. Le rituel des « entrées royales » enrichit la panoplie des instruments de propagande, le contact avec les populations des « bonnes villes » étant un moment fort du dialogue que le prince entretient avec le pays. La foule est bruyante, les enfants agitent des bannières et jettent des fleurs dans un aimable désordre qu'encouragent les agents du roi pour symboliser la liesse populaire.

Quand l'empereur germanique Charles IV se rend à Paris en janvier 1378 pour discuter avec son neveu de la situation internationale, le détail des réjouissances et du protocole est minutieusement réglé pour affirmer la totale souveraineté du roi de France. À l'entrée de Paris, le roi monté sur un cheval blanc, vient au-devant de son oncle, à qui il a fait donner un cheval noir parce que, dans les coutumes impériales, les empereurs entraient dans leurs villes sur un cheval blanc et qu'il était donc impossible de le faire entrer dans Paris sur une monture dont la couleur aurait pu être un signe de souveraineté. Au grand banquet dans la grande salle du palais, les invités prennent les places désignées et la mise en scène est à la hauteur des richesses étalées. L'emprise du service d'ordre est telle qu'aucun gobelet d'argent ne disparaît, malgré la présence de huit cents chevaliers.

Charles fut aussi très attentif à la symbolique des objets et insignes de la « religion » royale. Le sceptre du sacre de 1364 porte au sommet une fleur de lys sur laquelle trône Charlemagne brandissant un sceptre et un globe, manière de « récupérer » le grand empereur. L'oriflamme, le drapeau de couleur rouge que le roi lève à Saint-Denis quand il part à la guerre ou en croisade, malmené à Crécy et à Poitiers, fait l'objet d'une véritable liturgie. Les lys, toujours représentés de couleur or — couleur du soleil et des vêtements des rois — sur fond d'azur — couleur du ciel —, suggèrent en permanence le rapport entre le souverain et Dieu. C'est aussi sous Charles le Sage qu'a été enrichie la légende de la Sainte Ampoule assurant aux rois de France un pouvoir sacré et thaumaturgique à nul autre pareil.

Le « bon gouvernement »

Roi « sage » qui mobilisa les ressources de la propagande et rechercha les conseils des « intellectuels », Philippe de Mézières, Nicolas Oresme ou Raoul de Presles, Charles sut aussi s'entourer de collaborateurs compétents et dévoués, soucieux d'assurer au royaume « bon gouvernement ». « Quand les œuvres du prince ne tendent pas au profit commun du peuple, peut-on lire dans *Le Songe du vergier*, mais à son propre et singulier profit, il doit être appelé tyran et ne seigneurie pas justement. » Telle fut l'opinion de Guillaume de Melun, Jean et Guillaume de Dormans, Jean de la Grange, Pierre d'Orgemont, le rude prévôt de Paris Hugues Aubriot, Bureau de la Rivière, le confident des dernières années, sans parler des collaborateurs militaires, Jean de Vienne, qui redonna à la France une marine de guerre et le connétable Bertrand du Guesclin. Formant une famille spirituelle qu'unissait une réelle fraternité, ces hommes que Charles souhaita voir enterrés avec lui à Saint-Denis vont faire souffler un esprit nouveau sur les rouages de l'État.

Les préambules des actes les plus importants rappellent ce souci. « De tant comme les grands faits et les grandes besognes sont faites par conseil de plusieurs sages hommes, peut-on lire, de tant sont-elles plus sûres et plus certaines ; et aussi nous et nos prédécesseurs nous sommes toujours gouvernés et nous gouvernons en tous nos faits par conseil de grand nombre de sages hommes, clercs et laïcs. »

Pour éviter l'arbitraire et garantir aux officiers de la couronne une certaine indépendance, Charles applique l'enseignement d'Aristote, qui voulait que toute magistrature soit élective. C'est le Grand Conseil qui élit Bertrand du Guesclin connétable en 1370 et, en 1373, quand il faut désigner un nouveau chancelier, cent trente personnes sont réunies pour élire Pierre d'Orgemont. Après que le greffier eut décompté les voix, le roi nomma celui qui avait obtenu le « trop plus grand nombre ».

Dans le domaine sensible des finances, on fait désormais la distinction entre les dépenses de la couronne et les dépenses de l'État, entre l'impôt dont l'affectation est contrôlée par le collège des « généraux conseillers » et les revenus du Domaine. Ainsi se met en place l'un des principes fondamentaux de l'État moderne, un État qui compte et se méfie des éternels quémandeurs. Bien souvent, le roi doit ajouter un mot de sa main pour que les contrôleurs et les payeurs sachent bien que « cela vient de sa conscience ».

Une conscience qui a été toutefois troublée par la pression fiscale que les nécessités de la guerre ont fait peser sur les sujets. Ainsi, en Languedoc, les fouages, impôts directs prélevés sur les villes et les campagnes, ont doublé de 1366 à 1378, passant de cinq francs par feu à douze francs. C'est Philippe de Mézières qui rapporte au roi les mécomptes d'une malheureuse famille : « Pour dix sous qu'ils devaient de taille, de fouage ou de gabelle que véritablement ils n'avaient pas de quoi payer, ils étaient si malmenés qu'on leur ôtait la couette sous la pauvre femme gisant d'enfant et la seule bassine qui lui était restée pour baigner son enfant. » Une discussion à chaud, rapportée dans *Le Songe du vergier*, montre les débats animés qui divisent les proches conseillers du roi. Un trésor en or et en argent, lui fait-on remarquer, ne vaut pas le plus précieux des trésors : l'amour de ses sujets.

« Il n'est pas sire de son pays
Qui de ses hommes est haï. »

Impôt lourd et franc fort, telle fut pourtant, imposée par les circonstances, la politique financière du roi sage ! C'est parce que ses conseillers estimaient que la monnaie devait être protégée contre les caprices de la personne royale que Charles renonça aux mutations qu'avaient tant pratiquées ses prédécesseurs. Dans son court *Traité des monnaies*, Nicolas Oresme, protestant contre la théorie souvent exprimée selon laquelle la monnaie était le fait du Prince, disait au contraire qu'elle était le bien du peuple dont elle représentait le travail et appartenait à la « communauté », au bénéfice de laquelle elle devait être « forgée ». Il est certain, écrivait-il, « que le cours et le prix des monnaies doivent être au royaume comme une loi et une ferme ordonnance, qui nullement ne se doit muer ni changer ».

Né le 5 décembre 1360 au moment du retour de captivité de Jean le Bon, le franc, nouvelle monnaie contenant 3,88 g d'or fin et valant, en monnaie de compte vingt sous tournois, c'est-à-dire une livre, maintiendra sa parité pendant vingt-cinq ans. Pourquoi avoir appelé franc cette nouvelle monnaie ? Pour rappeler la légende, développée à l'époque, selon laquelle les Francs descendaient du Troyen Francus. Pour dire aux sujets du roi qu'ils étaient « francs », c'est à dire « libres ». Pour servir la propagande du roi, Charles ne s'étant pas fait représenter, comme son père, à cheval et armé d'une épée, mais debout sous un dais avec le sceptre et la main de justice. Une monnaie sage pour un roi sage.

La reconquête du royaume

Associée au nom de Bertrand du Guesclin, le bon connétable, la reconquête du royaume amoindri par le traité de Brétigny fut une œuvre de longue haleine, âpre et dure, qui demanda en fait plus de patience et de subtilité que de prouesses et de vaillance. Christine de Pisan l'a bien souligné quand elle écrivait : « Ce roi, par son sens, sa magnanimité, sa force, sa clémence et sa libéralité, désencombra son pays de ses ennemis tant qu'ils n'y firent plus leurs chevauchées. Et lui, sans se mouvoir de ses palais et sièges royaux, reconquit, refit et augmenta son royaume qui, auparavant, avait été désolé, perdu et dépris par ses devanciers portant les armes et très chevalereux. Et la chevalerie de France qui était devenue comme tout amortie par l'épouvantement des mauvaises fortunes passées, fut par lui réveillée. »

En 1360, au sortir des terribles épreuves qu'il avait traversées, le royaume était anémié, livré aux bandes de gens d'armes que la paix avait réduits au « chômage ». « Cassées aux gages », c'est-à-dire licenciées sur place, les épaves des armées anglaises, navarraises ou françaises se réunissent en « grandes compagnies », « sociétés » ou « routes » et sous la direction de capitaines, simples aventuriers ou cadets de bonne noblesse, le Wallon Eustache d'Auberchicourt, le Navarrais Enriquez de Pampelune, l'Anglais Robert Knolles, le Gascon Jean de Ségur, le Breton Crocquart, le Périgourdin Arnaud de Cervole, dit l'Archiprêtre, pillent les granges et les églises, violent les femmes, qu'ils enlèvent et traînent dans leurs bagages, volent les enfants pour en faire des pages, s'emparent de forteresses, dont ils font le siège de leur puissance, rançonnent les marchands et les villes ou cherchent à s'employer en Allemagne ou en Espagne, partout où se présentent des occasions de profit. Le 6 avril 1362, une armée royale est taillée en pièces à Brignais, au sud de Lyon, par les routiers qui dévalent les collines en poussant leur cri de guerre : « Aye Dieu ! Aye aux compagnies ! »

Mais, ne sachant que faire de leur victoire, les bandes se dispersent à travers la vallée du Rhône, le Languedoc et le Massif central, faisant régner une insécurité finalement plus dommageable que la guerre elle-même. Au moins doit-on mettre à leur crédit le fait que les habitants du royaume ont mieux accepté l'impôt que le roi prélevait pour les débarrasser de ce véritable fléau et bouter les Anglais hors du royaume.

Charles, en effet, n'a jamais accepté la « déshonorable paix » de Brétigny, signée contre sa volonté. Si pendant les premières années de son règne, il en exécuta les clauses, versant encore six cent mille écus sur les deux millions qui restaient à payer pour la rançon d'un roi décédé, il prépara surtout la revanche en remettant en état le système défensif et en nouant de fructueuses alliances. Il y eut bientôt une véritable inspection militaire du royaume, chargée de détruire les murailles et les châteaux mal tenus, de renforcer les défenses des places fortes stratégiques, de payer régulièrement une armée mieux encadrée et mieux surveillée, de la pourvoir d'une artillerie efficace et de reconstituer une marine de guerre. À Paris, une nouvelle enceinte fut édifiée sur la rive droite, défendue par une imposante forteresse, la « bastide Saint-Antoine », que l'on appellera bientôt « la Bastille ».

Et à Vincennes, le grand chantier du règne, le château dressait ses tours neuves et son donjon au décor peint et sculpté.

Habile négociateur, Charles sut aussi trouver des alliés. En cédant au comte de Flandre les villes de Douai, Lille et Orchies enlevées au temps de Philippe le Bel, il gagne pour son frère Philippe, déjà duc de Bourgogne, la main de Marguerite de Flandre que son père avait voulu marier à un fils du roi d'Angleterre. En échange d'avantages commerciaux consentis dans les ports français, les Castillans mettent à sa disposition des navires de guerre qui, en 1372 aident la nouvelle flotte française à détruire la flotte anglaise au large de La Rochelle. Enfin, Charles pouvait compter sur la sympathie de son oncle, l'empereur germanique.

Après avoir pour un temps écarté la menace que faisaient toujours peser les partisans de Charles de Navarre, neutralisé la Bretagne en obtenant du nouveau duc Jean de Montfort, le candidat anglais, qu'il accepte sa suzeraineté, et purgé une partie du royaume des bandes de routiers, Charles peut alors exploiter les subtilités juridiques du traité de Calais.

L'occasion se présente en 1368 quand le comte d'Armagnac et d'autres seigneurs gascons refusent au Prince Noir, qui gouverne la Guyenne, de lever un impôt sur leurs terres. Suite à une démarche infructueuse à Londres, ils font appel au roi de France. Après avoir consulté des juristes de Bologne, de Toulouse et de Montpellier, le roi, à l'issue d'une décision prise en Conseil, accepte de recevoir cet appel adressé par les Gascons à celui qui reste leur suzerain. Dans la mesure, en effet, où les renonciations prévues par le traité de Calais n'avaient pas été échangées, le roi de France gardait, en droit, la souveraineté des territoires cédés. En quelques semaines, huit cents villes et bourgades s'engouffrent dans cette brèche juridique et font appel à leur tour. Au duc de Lancastre qui déclare : « Notre adversaire n'est pas un sage prince, ce n'est qu'un avocat », Charles répond : « Si nous sommes avocats, nous leur bâtirons tel plaid que la sentence les ennuiera ». En janvier 1369, le roi de France fait porter au Prince Noir une citation à comparaître devant le Parlement de Paris et en novembre, alors qu'Édouard III a repris son titre de roi de France, prononce la confiscation de la Guyenne.

Alors que les Anglais, fidèles à la stratégie qui leur avait jusquelà réussi, lancent une chevauchée, Charles impose à ses chefs de guerre, qui « bouillaient d'ardeur agressive », une nouvelle tactique qui consiste à éviter la bataille rangée, à abriter dans les villes fortifiées et les châteaux renforcés les habitants du plat pays, et à se contenter de harceler l'ennemi pour grignoter patiemment ses possessions. Élu connétable le 2 octobre 1370, Bertrand du Guesclin était l'homme qu'il fallait pour mener cette stratégie. Aux belles rencontres hasardeuses, ce Breton issu d'une famille de moyenne noblesse, carré et moustachu, musclé et batailleur, têtu et méfiant, mais très économe du sang de ses hommes, préférait la guerre de surprises et de sièges, dans laquelle les Bretons excellaient. Il était assez proche en fait des chefs de compagnies qu'il eut pour mission de conduire en Espagne au service d'un prétendant à la couronne de Castille. Sa force fut surtout de mettre ses rudes talents au service d'une guerre « sale », celle qu'il fallait faire pour gagner la paix.

Au terme de sept années de guerre, de chevauchées anglaises aussi vaines militairement que ruineuses pour les campagnes, Brétigny était effacé, les Anglais ne conservant plus que Calais, Brest, quelques places bretonnes, Bordeaux, Bayonne et une Guyenne réduite à la portion congrue. Le Prince Noir était mort en 1376, Édouard III en 1377, et en 1378, Charles de Navarre, au terme d'une ultime intrigue, avait été obligé de traiter. Ruiné, dépouillé de ses domaines en France, son royaume de Navarre livré aux créanciers, il mourut en 1387, misérable et déshonoré.

Il était dit, pourtant, que Charles ne finirait pas ses jours en paix. Le 6 février 1378, meurt en couches la reine Jeanne de Bourbon, l'épouse qu'il semble avoir passionnément aimée. Sa fille Isabelle, qui avait cinq ans, meurt peu après. En 1378, encore, au Puy et à Nîmes, on grogne et se révolte contre les « lourds impôts ». En 1378, enfin, commence le Grand Schisme qui va diviser la chrétienté d'Occident pendant près d'un demi-siècle. En mars 1378, meurt le pape Grégoire XI, qui a quitté Avignon pour Rome quinze mois plus tôt. Effrayés par les manières brutales et autoritaires du pape italien Urbain VI qu'ils ont élu en avril sous la pression du peuple romain, les cardinaux se réunissent de nouveau en conclave et élisent à l'unanimité moins l'abstention de trois Italiens, le cardinal de Genève, qui prend le nom de Clément VII. En se prononçant immédiatement pour lui, Charles V amène alors la chrétienté à se diviser en deux. L'Empire, l'Angleterre, l'Italie, la Hongrie, le Portugal rallient le pape de Rome. La France, l'Écosse, la Castille, l'Aragon, la Navarre, le Luxembourg et l'Autriche soutiennent Clément VII, qui reste à Avignon.

En juillet 1380, Charles, la conscience troublée, apprend la mort de Du Guesclin. Le 16 septembre, le jour même de sa mort, roi jusqu'à son dernier souffle, il achève son règne en prenant trois mesures. Il déclare tout d'abord que, s'il s'est trompé en pensant que Clément VII était le vrai pape, il demande pardon à Dieu et s'en remet au concile, qui pourra mettre fin au schisme. Il donne ensuite l'ordre à ses exécuteurs testamentaires de prendre deux cent mille francs, déposés dans la tour de Vincennes, pour payer ses dettes et accomplir son testament. Il abolit enfin les fouages qui avaient tant pesé sur ses sujets. Après avoir baisé la croix qui contenait la Sainte Épine, il aurait alors dit : « Dieu, mon sauveur et rédempteur, toi qui m'as fait ton vicaire pour gouverner le royaume de France, malgré mon indignité, pardonne-moi mes péchés ! »

Le temps de la folie

*L*e 5 août 1392, dans la forêt du Mans, Charles VI, lourdement vêtu de
velours noir et accablé par la chaleur, est pris d'un brutal accès de
folie. Se croyant encerclé d'ennemis, il tire son épée, charge pendant une
heure les membres de son entourage, menace son frère Louis d'Orléans,
qui est obligé de s'enfuir, et tue quatre hommes avant d'être maîtrisé.
Pour les hommes du temps, la maladie qui a frappé le roi de France et lui
a fait perdre la raison est bien le signe d'un châtiment divin. « À Paris, à
Rouen, écrit le chroniqueur du règne, on fit des processions, le peuple tout
nu pieds. Et l'on fit chanter des messes pour prier pour le roi. » Le temps
de la folie est aussi celui de la pénitence.

La folie des princes

En 1380, au lendemain des funérailles de Charles V, le roi
« sage » qui avait tant fait pour consolider la monarchie et pris tant
de dispositions pour protéger la couronne des rivalités et des convoitises des princes, ses frères se hâtent d'écarter les conseillers du défunt
et de confisquer à leur profit les bénéfices du pouvoir. Déjà, lors du
banquet qui suit la cérémonie du sacre, une querelle s'élève pour une
question de place entre Philippe de Bourgogne et Louis d'Anjou, qui
a mis à profit les quelques semaines de sa courte régence pour rafler
les fonds déposés à Vincennes par Charles V afin de payer ses legs et
honorer ses dettes.

Adopté comme héritier par la reine Jeanne de Naples, comtesse de Provence, le seul souci de Louis d'Anjou est de recueillir son héritage et de financer son aventure italienne. Philippe le Hardi, duc de Bourgogne, est occupé avant tout de la grandeur de sa maison. Beau-fils du comte de Flandre, il peut espérer rassembler Flandre, Bourgogne et Franche-Comté et puiser dans le trésor du royaume pour alimenter ses fortes ambitions vers les Pays-Bas et les terres d'Empire. Jean de Berry, le troisième oncle de Charles VI, ne poursuit pas de grands desseins politiques, mais la vie fastueuse qu'il mène exige du numéraire, dont il est sans cesse à court.

Il est toutefois difficile de prélever l'argent sur des sujets qui ont entendu, jusque dans les moindres bourgs, les lettres de Charles V supprimant les fouages. Dans Paris excité, Charles VI publie même le 16 novembre 1380 l'ordonnance abolissant tous les impôts levés depuis le temps de Philippe le Bel ! Quand, en 1382, les oncles sont amenés à rétablir les impôts indirects sur le vin et le sel, des troubles éclatent dans le royaume à Rouen, à Caen, à Orléans, à Reims, à Amiens, à Laon, à Paris.

À Rouen, les émeutiers prennent possession de la ville pendant trois jours, se donnent pour roi de carnaval un riche drapier, Jean Le Gras, réputé pour sa bêtise et son embonpoint, lui dressent un trône au marché et lui demandent d'abolir les impôts. Puis, la « merdaille » ouvre les portes des prisons, pille les maisons des anciens maires, boit le vin entreposé dans les celliers, massacre quelques Juifs et prêteurs sur gages et oblige les chanoines de la cathédrale à abandonner quatre cents livres de rente qu'ils percevaient sur les halles de la ville.

Le mercredi 26 février, troisième jour de l'émeute, les bourgeois tirent du trésor de la cathédrale la « Charte aux Normands », qui date de 1315, la font lire à haute voix et jurer à toutes les autorités de respecter cet acte qui garantit les privilèges des états de Normandie. Après quoi, l'émeute s'apaise et toutes les cloches recommencent à sonner.

À Paris, le 1er mars, un percepteur qui voulait contraindre une vieille marchande de cresson à payer la taxe, est entouré, saisi et massacré. Une troupe de plusieurs milliers de personnes qui suit un étendard formé d'un morceau de toile blanche, marche vers la place de Grève, envahit les magasins de l'Hôtel de Ville et s'empare des maillets de plomb qui y étaient entreposés. Les Maillotins se répandent alors dans la ville, s'en prennent aux fermiers des impôts, mettent le feu aux registres, boivent et distribuent le vin trouvé dans les caves des agents du roi, massacrent seize Juifs du quartier du Temple, tendent des chaînes en travers des rues et ferment les portes de la ville.

Dans le Languedoc livré à l'administration du duc de Berry, lieutenant du roi, se multiplient les Tuchins, des maquisards dont la première action est d'occuper Pont-Saint-Esprit pour faire cesser la perception de la gabelle.

En Flandre, les tisserands se soulèvent une nouvelle fois contre le comte Louis de Male, portent à leur tête Philippe Van Artevelde, le fils de celui qui avait conduit la révolte de 1337, pillent en mai 1382 la ville de Bruges, que le comte doit fuir sous un déguisement, et négocient avec le roi d'Angleterre.

Les princes allaient alors frapper fort. Le 27 novembre 1382, à Roosebeke, les Flamands sont écrasés par les armées du roi. En janvier et février 1383, c'est au tour de Paris de payer le prix de sa rébellion. La prévôté des marchands est abolie, les privilèges des Parisiens supprimés, les impôts alourdis et quarante exécutions ordonnées. Rouen, taxée d'une amende de soixante mille francs est ruinée pour longtemps. Et le Languedoc doit payer huit cent mille francs pour racheter son « crime de lèse-majesté ». Et comme le peuple aimait les cérémonies théâtrales, en Flandre, on pendit le cadavre d'Artevelde tué pendant le combat ; à Paris, on dressa un échafaud sur le bel escalier de marbre de la cour du palais et à Rouen, les têtes des six Rouennais décapités se balancèrent au-dessus de la porte de la ville.

Ainsi s'éteint en France la flambée de révolte qui agite alors toute l'Europe. En 1378, à Florence, les boutiquiers forcent les prisons et brûlent les registres des impôts. En 1381, en Angleterre, la levée d'un impôt de un shilling par tête, la valeur de douze journées de travail pour un feu, provoque le soulèvement des paysans. Conduits par Wat Tyler, ils entrent dans la capitale, piquent à l'entrée du pont de Londres les têtes de l'archevêque de Canterbury et du trésorier d'Angleterre et font rédiger des chartes d'affranchissement scellées du sceau royal. À la même époque, le sang juif coule dans toute l'Espagne. Partout, le *popolo minuto*, le petit peuple, exprime son indignation et son désarroi en détruisant les signes de la richesse et en faisant disparaître les traces écrites de son oppression.

La folie du roi

Le 3 novembre 1388, jour anniversaire de son sacre, Charles VI, qui allait avoir vingt ans, préside une grande assemblée du Conseil qu'il a convoquée à Reims. Le doyen des conseillers, Pierre Aycelin de Montaigu, cardinal de Laon, ouvre la séance et provoque un véritable coup de théâtre en posant la question de savoir si le roi n'est pas en âge de gouverner seul. L'archevêque de Reims et les chefs de guerre répondent que oui. Pour clore la séance, Charles VI prend la parole, remercie ses oncles « des peines et travaux qu'ils avaient eus de sa personne et des affaires du royaume », leur donne congé malgré leurs protestations et met immédiatement en place une nouvelle équipe où se retrouvent les anciens conseillers de son père écartés par les princes. Surnommés par dérision Marmousets, nom donné aux figures grotesques et grimaçantes qui servaient alors d'ornement architectural, ils s'engagent, par un « pacte d'alliance et d'amitié », « à se soutenir mutuellement de tout leur pouvoir et à n'avoir, tant dans la prospérité que dans l'adversité, qu'un même esprit, une même volonté, un même but ».

Sachant où ils vont et pourquoi, ils veulent montrer aux Français qu'à « nouveau roi », « nouvelle loi » et « nouvelle joie ». En quelques semaines, paraissent une série d'ordonnances qui montrent à quel point le roi a appris que pour avoir « bon gouvernement », il faut d'abord savoir gagner les cœurs. L'ordonnance du 5 février 1389 précise le principe de l'élection à tous les offices de justice. La haute administration est renouvelée au bénéfice d'un personnel plus jeune et plus dévoué. La taille, un impôt direct créé par les oncles en 1384, est abandonnée. Et lors du voyage qu'il fait en Languedoc, de septembre 1389 à février 1390, le roi examine les plaintes, révise les procès, fait vérifier par ses enquêteurs les comptes de Jean de Berry et envoie au bûcher Bétisac, le bras droit de l'oncle prodigue.

En mai 1389, à l'abbaye de Saint-Denis, un service funèbre en l'honneur de Du Guesclin est l'occasion de mettre en scène et d'exalter les services que le connétable avait rendus à l'État. Et Louis de Bourbon, l'oncle maternel du roi, qui a toujours soutenu la monarchie, même dans les pires moments, devient le modèle du « bon duc » qui ne fait pas de politique et se contente de servir. En prenant pour emblème le cerf-volant blanc ailé, Charles rend hommage à la maison de son oncle, qui avait depuis longtemps le cerf pour devise.

C'est pour faire respecter la majesté de la couronne que Charles VI chevauche, le 5 août 1392, sur la route du Mans, contre le duc de Bretagne qui le narguait en donnant asile à un baron breton, Pierre de Craon, auteur d'un guet-apens contre Olivier de Clisson, le connétable de France. Comme la troupe chemine, écrasée par la chaleur de midi, un vieillard de mauvaise mine, « vêtu d'une pauvre cotte de bure blanche », se jette devant le roi en criant : « Roi ne chevauche plus avant, mais retourne, car tu es trahi ! »

Peu après, l'un des jeunes pages qui suit le roi s'endort et laisse tomber sa lance sur le casque d'acier d'un soldat. Alors le roi

« tressaille tout soudainement » et hurle : « Je suis livré à mes enne-mis. » Dégainant son épée, il charge son entourage une heure durant, menace son frère Louis d'Orléans, qui s'enfuit, tue quatre hommes avant que son cheval s'épuise et que sa fureur tombe. Maîtrisé par un seigneur de sa suite, ses yeux roulant dans l'orbite, il est installé sur un chariot qui reprend la route du Mans.

Crises et rémissions allaient se succéder pendant trente ans. En crise, le roi ne reconnaît pas ses proches, oublie qui il est, hurle « comme s'il était piqué de mille pointes de fer », déchire avec son couteau les tapisseries brodées de fleurs de lys, jette les coussins au feu et danse de façon obscène, prétendant qu'il s'appelle Georges et que ses armoiries sont un lion traversé d'une épée. Pendant les périodes de rémission, il reprend avec lucidité son métier de roi et reçoit les ambassadeurs en n'oubliant pas un geste du protocole.

En fait, si la maladie a lourdement handicapé les affaires poli-tiques du royaume, elle n'a altéré en rien l'affection que les Français portaient à leur roi. Pour eux, Charles n'a jamais été le « roi fou » des historiens, mais Charles « le Bien-Aimé ». Pris d'angoisse, ils tentent d'apaiser la colère divine. Qu'avait donc fait le royaume pour s'attirer ce châtiment de Dieu ? Quel malheur allait encore survenir ? À Paris et à Rouen, les villes qui s'étaient révoltées dix ans plus tôt, on fait des processions en grande dévotion et on chante des messes pour le roi. Au lendemain du bal des Ardents, le peuple gronde contre les princes. Le mardi 28 janvier 1393, lors d'une fête donnée à la cour pour célébrer les noces d'une dame d'honneur de la reine, six sau-vages, vêtus de costumes collants enduits de poix et recouverts d'une toison d'étoupe, font irruption dans la grande salle de l'hôtel Saint-Paul en sautant et en hurlant comme des loups. Louis d'Orléans, le frère du roi, se saisit d'une torche et s'approche de l'un d'entre eux pour le reconnaître. Le feu prend aussitôt, brûlant atrocement les mal-heureux. Charles, qui faisait partie des seigneurs déguisés, est sauvé par la duchesse de Berry qui, sans le reconnaître, le roule dans le drap épais de sa longue robe. Pour calmer le peuple, scandalisé par cette mascarade, les princes, dès le lendemain, doivent traverser en proces-sion, nu pieds, le quartier des Halles et se rendre à Notre-Dame où est chantée la messe. Peu après, Louis d'Orléans, accusé de ce « grand meschef », doit faire bâtir, dans l'église des Célestins de Paris, une chapelle expiatoire.

Pour plaire à Dieu et guérir le roi, on interdit le blasphème, la prostitution et les jeux d'argent. À Paris, la porte d'Enfer, dont le nom, disait-on, provenait d'une belle courtisane qui n'était autre que le diable, est « exorcisée » et désormais appelée la porte Saint-Michel.

Et le 17 septembre 1394, une ordonnance expulse tous les Juifs du royaume pour apaiser cette « angoisse diffuse » qui « dictait à la reine, aux princes, aux sujets, divers gestes destinés à apaiser la colère de Dieu ». Comme les processions et les pèlerinages qui se multiplient alors, l'expulsion des Juifs est un rite de purification qui vise à faire du royaume de France une Terre sainte « où la foi est illuminée » et « où n'habite ni Juif ni païen ».

Le temps de la pénitence

Si les Français semblent avoir été si sensibles au drame personnel de leur roi, c'est qu'eux-mêmes se posaient des questions angoissantes sur le mal et la souffrance, le sens de la vie et la mort. En cette fin du XIVe siècle, apparaissent de nouvelles formes de piété qui expriment la mélancolie d'un peuple troublé par les malheurs du temps et la peur de l'au-delà.

En créant, en 1378, deux lignées de papes, ceux de Rome et ceux d'Avignon, le Grand Schisme a bouleversé en profondeur les consciences. Et si la folie du roi était la punition que Dieu infligeait aux Français pour expier le crime de Charles V, coupable d'avoir soutenu le pape d'Avignon ? « Il fut dit en secret au roi par ceux qui l'aimaient et désiraient sa guérison, écrit Froissart, que l'opinion commune du royaume de France était qu'il n'aurait jamais santé tant que l'Église serait en tel état. »

En janvier 1394, c'est avec l'autorisation du roi que l'Université organise un véritable référendum auprès de ses membres et propose la « voie de cession », c'est-à-dire la démission volontaire des deux papes. Mais l'opposition entre les ducs de Berry et de Bourgogne, favorables à cette solution réaliste, et le duc d'Orléans, qui continue à soutenir le pape d'Avignon dans l'espoir, peut-être, de faire proclamer la déchéance du roi fou afin de prendre la place de son frère, affaiblit la position de la France.

Au-delà du récit extraordinairement complexe des événements, le schisme marque surtout la fin d'un certain ordre, la fin du temps où le pape imposait son magistère moral à la chrétienté. Mettant en question ou prenant simplement leurs distances envers une hiérarchie complètement désorganisée, les fidèles se multiplient en dévotions et découvrent les affres de la solitude.

Les confréries qui organisent l'entraide et prévoient minutieusement les obsèques de leurs membres nouent des solidarités nouvelles entre des familles disloquées par la peste et les migrations. En

Normandie ou en Forez, chaque village en compte bientôt une, deux ou trois. Nés à la fin du XIIᵉ siècle en Flandre ou dans la vallée du Rhin, les béguinages, qui rassemblent des femmes se groupant pour prier ensemble et vivre dans l'austérité, se multiplient et inquiètent les autorités ecclésiastiques, troublées par le mysticisme démonstratif de ces femmes qui n'ont pas prêté les vœux perpétuels.

Processions, pèlerinages et représentations théâtrales traduisent aussi les mutations d'une piété exubérante. Le Mont-Saint-Michel devient un haut lieu de dévotion populaire et c'est en l'honneur de l'archange que la reine Isabeau de Bavière appelle sa fille Michelle, un prénom qui n'avait jamais été porté dans la famille royale. C'est par milliers que les Bretons parcourent chaque année les 525 kilomètres qui relient les sept sanctuaires de Dol, Saint-Malo, Saint-Brieuc, Tréguier, Saint-Pol, Quimper et Vannes. À Paris, nu pieds et une torche à la main, les Parisiens défilent de Sainte-Geneviève à Saint-Denis et de Boulogne à Vincennes pendant des journées entières. Et quand sur les parvis des églises, des mises en scène spectaculaires racontent pendant plusieurs jours l'histoire du Salut, les interventions miraculeuses de la Vierge ou la Passion, des milliers de citadins et de ruraux cessent le travail pour assister à ces représentations qui les transportent près de Dieu et des saints.

Surtout, apparues dans les testaments vers 1340-1360, les demandes de messes destinées à économiser les années de purgatoire prennent une ampleur considérable. 14 % des Lyonnais en exigent entre 1300 et 1348 ; ils sont 65 % vers 1400. À Paris, en 1394, Pierre du Châtel prévoit 1 000 messes le jour et le lendemain de ses obsèques. En 1399, Arnaud de Corbie en exige 4 550. Aux confins du Dauphiné et de la Provence, le seigneur de Grignan demande dans son testament 1 565 messes réparties sur sept ans, 365 la première année, 200 les six années suivantes. Cette accumulation fébrile qui amène les fidèles à courir les pardons, à réciter des rosaires entiers et à brûler des milliers de cierges est bien le symptôme d'une nouvelle relation à ce drame qu'est la mort, une mort dont l'image sinistre orne les livres d'heures, les murs des cimetières et des églises.

Hantés par la décomposition, la charogne et les vers, poètes et artistes évoquent ou sculptent alors des corps décharnés qui invitent à méditer sur la fragilité de la vie. Dans son testament, rédigé en 1392, Philippe de Mézières en vient à demander que l'on traîne son cadavre nu, sur une claie, dans le chœur de l'église et qu'on le jette ensuite dans la fosse. En cette fin de siècle, il est urgent de cultiver les anges gardiens pour se constituer des intercesseurs, d'honorer la Vierge et de convoquer les membres des confréries pour se faire entendre de

Dieu et échapper à un enfer qui, sur les fresques, les retables et les miniatures, ressemble désormais à une salle de torture où s'activent les démons chargés d'administrer les supplices. Cette nouvelle religiosité ne traduit pas seulement l'angoisse ou la panique. Elle exprime aussi la prise en charge par les simples fidèles de leur salut personnel. N'ayant plus qu'une confiance limitée à l'égard des intermédiaires traditionnels, ils préfèrent préparer eux-mêmes le redoutable voyage dans l'au-delà.

L'amour de la vie

Comme l'angoisse de la mort n'exclut nullement l'amour de la vie, le temps de la pénitence fut aussi celui de la fête. La prodigalité des princes fait de Paris, mais aussi de l'Anjou, du Berry et de la Bourgogne des foyers de culture et des lieux de création où se forment les goûts. Pour les gentilshommes qui inventent les modes et les bourgeois enrichis qui s'efforcent de les imiter, l'argent doit flamber et se consumer dans la fête. Dans ces temps de malheurs et d'angoisses, le noble doit affirmer sa puissance et marquer sa différence en gaspillant ostensiblement les biens qui asservissent ceux qui, par le travail, ne songent qu'à les amasser.

« La fête, écrit Georges Duby, est en effet d'abord, par essence, une cérémonie rituelle d'ostentation : le seigneur se montre dans sa puissance et dans sa gloire, revêtu de toutes les bijouteries de son trésor. Il a distribué des robes neuves à tous ceux qui ont répondu à son invite ; il les a revêtus de son propre éclat. Mais par essence également, la fête est cérémonie rituelle de destruction, offrande au plaisir de vivre, holocauste. C'est un sacrifice où l'on voit les maîtres anéantir d'un geste les biens, lentement, péniblement produits par le labeur des pauvres. Les ripailles des grands renient la misère des serfs. »

À la cour d'un roi qui en 1388 a vingt ans et d'une reine qui en a dix-sept, c'est un tourbillon d'amusements qui excite des jeunesses travaillées par les élans du cœur et les charmes des corps. Dans un traité de chirurgie composé au début du XIVe siècle, Henri de Mondeville reconnaît que la demande d'artifices capables de rehausser la séduction est fort vive et avoue que la beauté personnelle est devenue un atout décisif dans la compétition mondaine. Dans un Paris peu fou, les fêtes perverses organisées pour distraire le malheureux Charles de sa mélancolie sont autant d'occasions de triompher des morosités quotidiennes. Est-ce pour cette raison que joyeux lurons et dames hardies prennent tant de plaisir aux bals masqués et aux travestissements ?

En août 1389, Paris est transformé en théâtre pour fêter le couronnement de la reine Isabeau de Bavière et le mariage de Louis d'Orléans, alors âgé de dix-sept ans, avec Valentine Visconti, la fille du seigneur de Milan. Au milieu de la foule, se trouve le roi, déguisé en badaud et ravi des coups qu'il reçoit des sergents chargés du service d'ordre. Les bourgeois, saisissant l'occasion de présenter aux princes les pièces d'orfèvrerie exécutées par les artistes parisiens, se déguisent aussi en sauvages pour produire un effet de contraste avec le raffinement des présents.

La prolifération des ornements du gothique flamboyant, les débordements de l'orfèvrerie, la préciosité des matériaux, la virtuosité des artisans, les « verdures » des tapisseries, la souplesse des arabesques, la verve des poètes, la combinaison savante des rimes, les redondances des rhétoriqueurs, traduisent les goûts d'une génération que flattent l'objet d'art ou le livre enluminé.

Tandis que le duc de Berry traque l'argent de ses administrés pour faire travailler toute une armée d'artistes, transformer somptueusement ses résidences, collectionner les pierres précieuses, les tapisseries, les horloges extraordinaires et richement décorer ses manuscrits, que Louis d'Orléans veut faire de son château de Pierrefonds une merveille, Claus Sluter entreprend pour le duc de Bourgogne des œuvres maîtresses qui en font un artiste fortement novateur. Les plis tumultueux des vêtements des prophètes qui décorent la base du Puits de Moïse, les manteaux et les capuchons des pleurants qui entourent le tombeau de Philippe le Hardi, signent un style qui va se répandre dans toute l'Europe. Rien moins qu'anonymes, ces œuvres qui exaltent au portail des églises ou sur les marbres des tombeaux la réussite sociale des princes, leur goût du faste et de la parade, illustrent les transformations d'une société qui découvre les plaisirs et les angoisses du « moi », d'un « moi » qui veut fixer ses traits dans la pierre pour le mettre à l'abri des ravages du temps.

Le temps des désastres

*L*e 10 novembre 1422, Charles VI, le roi de France « bien-aimé », mort le 21 octobre, est porté en terre à Saint-Denis. En l'absence de tous les princes des fleurs de lys, l'Anglais Jean de Bedford conduit seul le deuil, portant devant lui l'épée nue du roi de France. Après avoir demandé à Dieu d'avoir pitié de l'âme du défunt, le héraut s'écrie : « Dieu donne bonne vie à Henri, par la grâce de Dieu, roi de France et d'Angleterre, notre souverain seigneur ! » Nul doute que, pour beaucoup de Français, ces tristes funérailles marquaient en même temps les funérailles de la France.

Bourgogne et Orléans

En août 1392, la folie qui a frappé Charles VI dans la forêt du Mans a été fatale à ceux que l'on avait surnommés les marmousets. Écartés du pouvoir en 1388, les princes se hâtent de renvoyer ceux qu'ils accusent d'avoir mal conseillé le roi et s'emploient à confisquer à leur profit les instruments du pouvoir, puisant à pleines mains dans le Trésor pour financer leurs ambitions personnelles, multiplier les prodigalités et amonceler les œuvres d'art.

Le Conseil devient alors un champ clos où s'affrontent deux clans animés par Philippe le Hardi et Louis d'Orléans.

Philippe, puissant duc de Bourgogne, comte de Flandre et d'Artois, fin politique, a du jugement et de l'expérience. Ménageant les intérêts des villes drapantes, il souhaite établir de bonnes relations

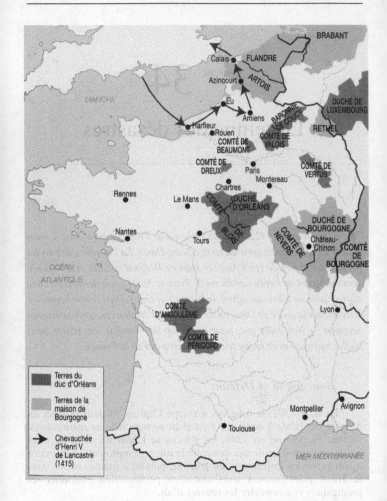

Les principales possessions de Bourgogne et d'Orléans.

avec l'Angleterre. Possédant de nombreuses terres dans l'Empire, il sait à quel point les populations qui y vivent sont attachées au pape de Rome et souhaite mettre fin au schisme qui divise la chrétienté.

Frère unique du roi, né en 1372, Louis d'Orléans est un prince fougueux et instruit, à l'esprit brillant et mordant. Toujours accompagné de ses lévriers, de ses fous et de ses ménestrels, il est amateur de parfums et de sucreries, de mets recherchés et de costumes étranges. Pieux et dévot, il reste longtemps à la messe, multiplie les dons aux églises et fait la fortune des Célestins, chez lesquels il a sa cellule. Volage et superficiel, il joue aux dés, aux tables et aux cartes qui font fureur à Paris et se vante de ses succès féminins. Pour les clercs qui déplorent sa lubricité, c'est un « putier » qui hennit comme un étalon après toutes les belles femmes. La reine Isabeau de Bavière aimait trop s'amuser en sa compagnie pour ne pas faire jaser.

Son domaine ne lui permettant pas de « vivre du sien », il ne peut se passer des dons et pensions du roi qui lui permettent de se constituer une clientèle, de racheter des seigneuries et de tenter de construire une principauté aussi prestigieuse que celle de son oncle, quadrillant le royaume pour mieux le contrôler.

Tant que vécut Philippe le Hardi, qui en imposait à son neveu, le conflit ne dégénéra pas, même si, à partir de 1401, pas une année ne se passa sans incidents, chaque prince tentant de placer ses hommes de confiance aux postes clefs. Mais après la mort du duc de Bourgogne, en avril 1404, la situation s'aggrava. Jean sans Peur, son fils, qui n'est plus que le cousin du roi, n'a plus les moyens de tenir tête au duc d'Orléans. Sans finesse ni grâce, il lui faut s'affirmer, malgré le prestige qu'il a acquis en conduisant en 1396 une croisade pourtant désastreuse contre les Turcs.

Il le fait en se posant en réformateur soucieux du bien public. Aussi habile à la ville qu'emprunté à la Cour, Jean sans Peur promet aux bourgeois une meilleure justice et des impôts moins lourds, ce qui n'engage à rien mais séduit beaucoup. Tandis que Louis d'Orléans veut construire un État fort sur des sujets obéissants, Jean sollicite leur aide et leur conseil pour l'« aider à conduire » les affaires, ne négligeant pas, par ailleurs, de faire circuler les rumeurs sur les coupables liaisons entre la reine et son rival.

Chaque jour, la haine grandit entre les deux cousins. Tandis que Louis, par provocation, choisit la devise « Je l'ennuie » et l'emblème du bâton noueux, Jean réplique en adoptant le rabot et la devise en flamand « Ich oud », « Je tiens ».

Bientôt exclu des affaires du royaume et privé de l'argent du roi dont il ne reçoit plus aides et pensions, Jean confie à Raoul d'Auquetonville le soin d'éliminer son rival. Le 23 novembre 1407, alors qu'il revient de l'hôtel Barbette, où logeait la reine qui relevait de couches, Louis est assassiné par une dizaine d'hommes qui lui fracassent le crâne et le criblent de coups de poignard. Pour toute oraison funèbre, les Parisiens qui n'aimaient guère Orléans se disent : « Le bâton noueux est plané ! »

Rondement menée, l'enquête conduit à Jean sans Peur qui reconnaît avoir, « poussé par le diable », ordonné le meurtre. Rejeté du Conseil par le duc de Berry qui lui en refuse l'entrée, celui qui a fait tuer son cousin germain par des tueurs à gages, sans le défier et sans lui permettre de préparer sa mort, quitte Paris. Ce meurtre, somme toute banal, était cependant assez détestable pour que les Français y voient la source des désastres dont ils allaient bientôt être accablés.

Armagnacs et Bourguignons

Tandis que Valentine Visconti, la veuve de Louis d'Orléans, réclame justice sans succès auprès de princes plus soucieux de leurs intérêts que de vengeance, Jean sans Peur s'emploie à récolter les fruits du meurtre. En janvier 1408, il annonce d'Amiens qu'il revient se justifier. Le 28 février, à Paris, jour de Mardi gras, il est acclamé par la foule qui, aux carrefours, crie « Noël » à haute voix, un cri réservé aux entrées royales. Le 8 mars, devant un Conseil élargi, Jean Petit, un théologien de renom acquis à la cause bourguignonne, prononce pendant quatre heures, de dix heures à deux heures, un discours qui est une justification de l'assassinat.

Modèle du genre universitaire, ce discours connu sous le nom d'« apologie du tyrannicide » démontre qu'il est licite de tuer un tyran pour la bonne cause. Traître poussé par la convoitise et l'ambition, sorcier responsable de la folie de son frère, coupable d'entretenir le schisme, Louis d'Orléans méritait d'être mis à mort. Donc le duc de Bourgogne avait fait œuvre méritoire et salutaire en faisant tuer son cousin. Pour ce crime, il devait être félicité et récompensé. Tel était l'étrange syllogisme qui, justifiant l'attentat politique, fut encore entendu deux siècles plus tard, au moment de l'assassinat d'Henri IV.

Muni dès le 9 mars des lettres de pardon signées de la main d'un roi redevenu momentanément lucide, Jean sans Peur triomphait même si, le 11 septembre 1408, Valentine Visconti et son fils Charles d'Orléans obtenaient, devant une assemblée aussi solennelle que celle du 8 mars, de faire réfuter par l'abbé de Cerisy la « justification » de Jean Petit.

Le 28 novembre, après avoir vaincu à la bataille d'Othée les Liégeois révoltés contre l'expansion bourguignonne et gagné son surnom de « sans Peur », Jean fait une nouvelle entrée triomphale à Paris. En 1409, il passe à l'offensive. Le 7 octobre, Jean de Montaigu, un « marmouset » maître des finances royales et proche des Orléans, est arrêté puis exécuté après avoir été accusé des mêmes crimes que son protecteur. C'est le début d'un vaste mouvement d'épuration qui permet de placer les partisans du Bourguignon dans l'appareil d'État. Enfin, le 31 décembre 1409, Jean se voit confier la garde du dauphin Louis de Guyenne, qui approche de ses treize ans.

Autour du duc de Bourgogne s'organise un véritable « parti » avec ses militants et ses fidèles, son programme et ses alliés. Moins de fonctionnaires et des fonctionnaires plus honnêtes, moins ou plus du tout d'impôts, une justice meilleure et plus rapide, paix à l'intérieur comme à l'extérieur du royaume, tel est le programme de « réforme » — le mot revient sans cesse dans les lettres de « propagande » que Jean sans Peur adresse aux « bonnes villes » —, qui plaît aux bourgeois des villes commerçantes, à l'Université de Paris et au « commun », le peuple de la capitale qui, sous la direction de la puissante corporation des bouchers, apparaît comme un nouvel acteur de la vie politique.

Paris, où s'entasse une masse d'« exclus », paysans refoulés des campagnes, artisans ruinés, sans abri et sans travail, familles disloquées par la guerre et l'épidémie, est bourguignon. Et l'on peut voir partout, même sur les statues des églises, le chaperon vert et la croix de Saint-André qui sont les insignes du « parti ». Et l'on peut boire partout les vins de Bourgogne qui, venus d'Auxerre, de Tonnerre, de Joigny et de Dijon, abreuvent les hôtels princiers et achètent des « partisans ».

Un État fort, appuyé sur des serviteurs efficaces et compétents, qui refuse de dialoguer avec les représentants de la « nation » et veut imposer une fiscalité sans consentement, tel est le programme fort peu démagogique de ceux que l'on commence à appeler « armagnacs », du nom de ces redoutables mercenaires gascons, cadets ou bâtards de petite noblesse que peut rassembler le comte d'Armagnac, beau-père du jeune duc Charles d'Orléans. Si le « parti » armagnac peut compter sur le soutien des vieux ducs de Berry et de Bourbon, des nobles du Midi, des manieurs d'or et d'argent parisiens qu'inquiètent le programme bourguignon et que ravissent les commandes du duc de Berry en pièces d'orfèvrerie et en joyaux, il lui manque un véritable chef, capable de faire pièce au populaire Jean de Bourgogne, dont le prénom est de plus en plus donné aux enfants que mettent au monde les Parisiens.

D'un côté, la finance et tous ceux dont les carrières sont brisées ou bloquées par l'afflux des Bourguignons, de l'autre, le grand commerce et les bouchers. Entre les deux camps, un « tiers parti » qui, sous la houlette du dauphin, tente le pari vain d'établir la concorde et de concilier les extrêmes. Enjeux des « partis », le roi, dont la souffrance mobilise toujours autant les prières des Français, la reine et le dauphin, qui incarnent la légitimité et les grands corps de l'État qu'il s'agit de noyauter. Et quand, faute d'argent, les troupes manquent aux Armagnacs et aux Bourguignons, on n'hésite pas à faire appel à des mercenaires anglais.

De 1409 à 1413, la mainmise des Bourguignons est totale. Copieusement arrosés de vins de Beaune, les bouchers, dont la fortune n'a cessé de croître au fur et à mesure qu'enflait la consommation de viande, sont maîtres de la capitale. Manipulant de fortes sommes d'argent, faisant aussi le commerce de la graisse, du suif, du grain et du bois, ces nouveaux riches que sont Garnier de Saint-Yon ou Guillaume Haussecul, maîtres de la Grande Boucherie de Paris, sentent toutefois trop la tripe pour rivaliser avec les marchands d'étoffes précieuses ou les orfèvres. Exclus de la « bonne » société et de l'administration municipale, ils trouvent leur intérêt à soutenir celui qui épure les grands corps de l'État pour placer des hommes nouveaux. Ouvrier des abattoirs chargé d'écorcher les bêtes, Simon le Coutelier, dit Caboche, qui s'y connaissait en couteaux, est leur homme de main, capable de rassembler écorcheurs et tripiers, couteliers et tanneurs, autant de « méchantes gens » capables, dit avec dédain Jouvenel des Ursins, qui rapporte les souvenirs de son père, armagnac modéré, de faire « de très inhumaines, détestables et déshonnêtes besognes ».

En 1413, alors que des états généraux sont réunis à Paris, pour la première fois depuis 1382, les manifestations du « commun » se multiplient, de plus en plus violentes. Le 28 avril, l'hôtel de Guyenne, rue Saint-Antoine, où habitait le dauphin, est envahi et des officiers royaux sont arrêtés. Au passage, quelques innocents sont massacrés. En mai, Paris se soulève encore, adoptant comme signe de ralliement le chaperon blanc, naguère porté par les Flamands révoltés contre leur comte. Le 22 mai, les cabochiens forcent l'hôtel Saint-Pol et conspuent la reine « étrangère ». Les 26 et 27 mai, au cours d'un lit de justice tenu par le roi au Parlement, est lue puis enregistrée une ordonnance en 258 articles. Dite « cabochienne », cette ordonnance, préparée par une commission de réforme inspirée par le « programme » bourguignon, est une nouvelle défense d'un « âge d'or » passé contre les avancées de l'État moderne. Réformer des choses qui vont de mal en pis, c'est chasser les mauvaises gens, réduire le nombre des fonctionnaires et rétablir l'ordre « ancien ». Une nostalgie qui plaît à la fois aux écorcheurs et aux universitaires troublés par les bouleversements de la société.

Pendant deux mois encore, les bouchers font la loi. Tandis que des têtes tombent, les cabochiens imposent un emprunt forcé aux riches bourgeois, ce qui est une faute politique. Une nuit, ils entrent dans l'hôtel du dauphin, lui reprochent ses danses et ses dépenses, et jettent l'effroi au milieu du bal. C'est trop imposer la « dictature des abattoirs ». Jean Jouvenel, avocat du roi, organise alors la résistance et rallie ceux que menacent les excès tandis que le vieux duc de Berry multiplie les contacts avec les princes armagnacs.

Le vendredi 4 août, le dauphin, escorté de bourgeois en armes, peut parcourir triomphalement les rues de Paris. Le 23, après avoir en vain tenté d'enlever le roi, Jean sans Peur doit quitter la capitale. Le 31, les princes armagnacs font leur entrée dans Paris et le 5 septembre, l'énorme ordonnance « cabochienne » est solennellement déchirée, page à page, par un greffier, devant le roi et les princes. À tous les postes, les Armagnacs remplacent les Bourguignons et à la violence des cabochiens succède celle aussi terrible des Gascons.

Le temps des massacres

Le 20 mars 1413, Henri V de Lancastre devient roi d'Angleterre. Après vingt années de troubles provoqués par l'opposition des barons au pouvoir royal, l'abdication de Richard II et l'avènement de la dynastie des Lancastre, la situation du royaume semble de nouveau se prêter aux ambitions d'un jeune souverain qui rêve de dominer la chrétienté et de reprendre Jérusalem aux Infidèles. L'aristocratie qui le soutient est résolue à reprendre la guerre contre une France qui, divisée, s'offre comme une proie particulièrement tentante. En mai 1414, au Parlement qui vote les crédits indispensables aux opérations militaires sur le continent, le duc d'Exeter se plaît à rappeler combien la France est « un pays fertile, plaisant et plein de ressources, avec de riches cités, de magnifiques villes, d'innombrables châteaux, vingt-quatre duchés puissants, plus de quatre-vingts provinces abondamment peuplées, cent trois évêchés fameux, plus de mille gras monastères et quatre-vingt-dix mille paroisses ».

À cette date, Jean sans Peur, comme avant lui Charles d'Orléans, cherche l'alliance anglaise et promet à Henri V de l'aider à conquérir les fiefs des princes armagnacs tout en voulant maintenir sa foi à l'égard du roi et du dauphin. Mais le roi d'Angleterre n'a que faire de ces propositions qui le confortent dans sa volonté de reconquérir l'« héritage » de ses ancêtres. En février 1415, à Paris, ses ambassadeurs exigent la couronne de France, la main de Catherine, la fille de Charles VI, avec une dot exorbitante de deux millions de francs, l'achèvement du paiement de la rançon du roi Jean le Bon et la cession en toute souveraineté de l'ancien empire Plantagenêt, de la Flandre et de l'Artois et même d'une partie de la Provence qui ne faisait pas partie du royaume de France !

Le 30 juin 1415, Henri V proclame la rupture aux diplomates français qui sont venus à Winchester apporter la réponse de Charles VI et, dans la nuit du 13 au 14 août, il débarque au Chef-de-Caux, en Normandie, à la tête d'une armée comprenant plus de 10 000 hommes. Après un mois de siège, Harfleur, soumise au pilonnage de l'artillerie anglaise, capitule et ses habitants sont expulsés. Puis, l'automne arrivant et les provisions s'épuisant, l'armée anglaise reprend la route autrefois suivie par Édouard III et se retire vers Calais afin de rembarquer.

Comme autrefois aussi, la fine fleur de la chevalerie française, commandée par le connétable Charles d'Albret et de jeunes princes inexpérimentés, part à la guerre comme à la fête et coupe la route des Anglais au nord de la Somme. Le 25 octobre, à Azincourt, les cavaliers français, éblouis par le soleil, trop nombreux pour se déployer sur un plateau étroit, sont une nouvelle fois criblés de flèches et massacrés par les archers anglais, qui tirent protégés par les pieux effilés plantés devant eux dans la terre molle. Au terme du combat, craignant un retour offensif des Français, Henri V décide alors de mettre à mort tous les prisonniers de moindre rang. De sang froid, les archers se chargent de la besogne et égorgent tous les captifs.

Parmi les milliers de morts dépouillés par les Anglais puis par les paysans du lieu qui les laissent nus dans la boue, on compte sept princes du sang, le connétable Charles d'Albret, la quasi-totalité des baillis de la France du Nord et la plus grande partie des serviteurs de la monarchie. Une véritable hécatombe.

Et tandis que Charles VI pleure en apprenant le désastre, Henri V annonce que son succès doit être interprété comme un jugement de Dieu. Consolant Charles d'Orléans, emmené prisonnier, il lui dit : « Beau cousin, faites bonne chère. Je connais que Dieu m'a donné la grâce d'avoir eu la victoire sur les Français, non pas que je la vaille ; mais je crois certainement que Dieu les a voulu punir, et, s'il est vrai ce que j'en ai ouï dire, ceci n'est merveille, car on dit que oncques plus grand desroi [*désordre*], ni désordonnance de volupté, de péchés et de mauvais vices ne furent vus, que règnent en France aujourd'hui. »

En France, les hommes du temps pensent en effet comme Henri de Lancastre que le royaume est en péril de mort, atteint par le même mal que celui qui frappe le roi. Si Charles VI est encore capable d'exécuter de façon mécanique les gestes du métier de roi, de recevoir des visiteurs, de rendre les saluts et de donner des baisers de paix, hébété, il est devenu totalement « absent », indifférent à ce qui se passe autour de lui. « Chacun qui de lui avait connaissance pouvait bien savoir l'état pitoyable et lamentable où il se trouvait pour lors », écrit le chroniqueur Pierre de Fénin.

Le dauphin Louis de Guyenne est mort le 18 décembre 1415. Le nouveau dauphin, Jean, duc de Touraine, meurt à son tour le 5 avril 1417, à l'âge de dix-neuf ans. Le vieux duc de Berry disparaît le 15 juin 1416. Dans Paris, assiégée par les Bourguignons et menacée par la famine, Bernard d'Armagnac, nommé connétable, fait régner la terreur, multiplie les impôts et des emprunts forcés, surveille les fêtes de famille et les cortèges de noces, interdit aux habitants de garder des armes, d'avoir à leurs fenêtres le moindre pot ou « bouteilles à vinaigre » et de se baigner dans la Seine, pour prévenir la fuite des suspects. Puis, prétextant les débauches de la cour, il fait exiler la reine Isabeau qui s'allie au duc de Bourgogne et met sur pied, à Troyes, un gouvernement rival avec un sceau, un Parlement et une chancellerie, se disant « par la grâce de Dieu reine de France, ayant, pour l'occupation de Monseigneur le roi, le gouvernement et administration de ce royaume ».

Dans la nuit du 28 au 29 mai 1418, les Bourguignons qui encerclaient la capitale entrent dans Paris grâce à la complicité d'une population excédée par les Armagnacs. De nouveau, le « commun » se déchaîne. Le 12 juin, Bernard d'Armagnac et la plupart de ceux qui avaient gouverné ou fait affaire avec lui sont horriblement massacrés. Le 14 juillet, Jean sans Peur et Isabeau font leur entrée dans Paris au milieu d'un foule qui jette des bouquets de fleurs sur le chariot de la reine. Le dimanche 21 août, commandés par le bourreau Capeluche qui a pris le relais de Caboche, désormais devenu un personnage officiel, les émeutiers se livrent à nouveau à une « grande tuerie ». Faute de Juifs, ce sont tous les « étrangers », Bretons ou Gascons, Lombards ou Génois, Catalans ou Castillans, qui font les frais du carnage. Dépouillés, mutilés, profanés, empalés, les corps sont jetés en tas comme des porcs au milieu de la rue tandis que, pour fêter saint André, patron de la Bourgogne, les Parisiens arborent un chapeau de roses vermeilles, boivent et mangent plus que de raison dans les rues où s'entassent les cadavres.

Capeluche, transgressant les bornes, éventre même une femme prête à accoucher, un crime qui le perd. Arrêté dans un cabaret des Halles sur l'ordre de Jean sans Peur, qu'il appelait « beau frère » en lui touchant la main, il est mené à l'échafaud et donne lui-même des conseils au nouveau bourreau, préparant avec soin les instruments de son supplice. À la même époque, une terrible épidémie de variole fait quelques dizaines de milliers de morts et met un point d'orgue aux massacres.

La France anglaise

Pendant ce temps, sans hâte et sans opposition, les Anglais conquièrent méthodiquement la Normandie. La destruction de la flotte française au Chef-de-Caux, le 29 juin 1417, leur assure la maîtrise de la Manche. Le 1er août, une forte armée débarque à Touques. Successivement, Caen, Argentan, Cherbourg, Alençon, Évreux, tombent aux mains du roi d'Angleterre, qui ménage les habitants et flatte le particularisme des Normands en leur confirmant la charte de 1315. Le 29 juillet 1418, tandis que l'on se massacre à Paris, Rouen, qui ne peut espérer aucun secours, est assiégée et cède le 19 janvier 1419, vaincue par la famine et le froid. Le 9 décembre 1419, faute de corde pour tirer l'eau du puits, Château-Gaillard se rend. Seul le Mont-Saint-Michel restait français.

Pour le roi d'Angleterre, l'heure était venue de négocier une « bonne paix ». Mais avec qui ? Qui pouvait être l'interlocuteur légitime ? Le duc de Bourgogne et la reine Isabeau ou le nouveau dauphin Charles qui, jeune homme de seize ans, incarne, sur les terres du duc de Berry où il a installé son gouvernement, une légitimité certaine ? Jean sans Peur a les Parisiens et la force pour lui. Fils unique et héritier du roi, Charles a pour lui le droit.

En juillet 1419, alors que les Anglais s'emparent de Mantes puis de Pontoise et menacent directement Paris dont la route est ouverte, les deux adversaires se rencontrent pour négocier, sans succès. Le dimanche 10 septembre de la même année, une nouvelle entrevue est organisée à Montereau, sur un pont au milieu de la Seine. Sans que l'on sache exactement comment s'est déroulée la scène, on entend des cris : « Tuez ! Tuez ! » puis, quelques minutes après, le duc de Bourgogne tombe, le crâne ouvert, frappé à coups d'épée et de hache par les serviteurs du dauphin. Une vengeance préméditée par les anciens compagnons de Louis d'Orléans et de Bernard d'Armagnac, au vu et au su du dauphin, telle est aujourd'hui la version des historiens, qui rejettent le récit répandu par les Armagnacs, un récit qui mettait Charles hors de cause et faisait reposer le meurtre sur le compte d'une malencontreuse bagarre déclenchée par les compagnons de la victime.

Meurtre fortuit ou vengeance préméditée, le crime de Montereau a pour effet immédiat de mettre un terme à toute tentative de réconciliation entre les Armagnacs qui entourent le dauphin et les Bourguignons. Sans enthousiasme mais sans autre choix possible, le nouveau duc de Bourgogne Philippe le Bon, qui veut venger son père, accepte les offres de paix d'Henri V et conclut avec lui une alliance, complétée par le mariage du duc de Bedford, frère du roi d'Angleterre, avec Anne, sœur de Philippe. Le 17 janvier 1420, une ordonnance du roi Charles VI déclare le dauphin indigne de la succession royale parce qu'il s'est « rendu parricide, criminel de lèse-majesté, détruiseur et ennemi de la chose publique »...

Le 21 mai, enfin, est signé en présence d'Henri V le traité de Troyes qui, en trente et un articles, fonde « la double monarchie » et lègue la couronne de France au roi d'Angleterre. Par son mariage avec Catherine, la fille du roi de France, le roi Henri, dit l'article premier, « est devenu notre fils et celui de notre très chère et très aimée compagne la reine ». Le « soi-disant dauphin » Charles étant déshérité, c'est lui qui devient l'héritier du royaume et prendra la couronne à la mort de Charles VI. Dès à présent, en raison de l'« empêchement » du roi, il exercera la régence et le gouvernement du royaume. Comme régent et plus tard comme roi, Henri V maintiendra les lois et coutumes des deux monarchies, les deux pays restant séparés sans que l'un puisse être soumis à l'autre.

Tandis que le mariage entre Henri V et Catherine de France était célébré, le 2 juin, par l'archevêque de Sens, les Parisiens approuvaient un traité qui semblait devoir ramener la paix et les gens de l'Université, qui avaient pris soin de faire garantir leurs avantages, n'y voyaient rien à redire, seulement préoccupés de réclamer au nouveau régent de nouvelles exemptions d'impôt. En 1420, écrit un témoin du temps, beaucoup de Français étaient prêts à crier « Vive n'importe qui pourvu qu'il nous donne la paix ».

Mort en France, au château de Vincennes, le 31 août 1422, à l'âge de trente-quatre ans, après avoir fêté la Pentecôte avec les Parisiens, Henri V fut enterré à Westminster le 12 novembre, quelques heures après que Charles VI eut été mis en terre à Saint-Denis. Henri VI, un enfant de onze mois né le 6 décembre 1421 au château de Windsor, devenait roi de France et d'Angleterre.

35

Le temps de la Pucelle

*C*lément de Fauquemberge, consciencieux greffier du Parlement de *Paris, qui avait l'habitude de noter sur son registre les événements du jour, écrit à la date du 30 mai 1431 : « Le trentième jour de mai 1431, par procès de l'Église, Jeanne qui se faisait appeler la Pucelle, qui avait été prise à une sortie de la ville de Compiègne par les gens de messire Jean de Luxembourg a été arse et brûlée en la ville de Rouen et prononça la sentence messire Pierre Cauchon évêque de Beauvais. » Ainsi était sobrement consignée la fin d'une aventure qui, au-delà de la légende, demeure aux yeux des historiens totalement extraordinaire.*

La France écartelée

Le 19 novembre 1422, neuf jours après la mise en terre de Charles VI, le duc Jean de Bedford, régent du royaume, préside une séance du Parlement de Paris au cours de laquelle il se déclare prêt à gouverner la France « en bonne justice, en bonne paix et tranquillité ». Tous les assistants jurent alors sur les Évangiles d'observer fidèlement le traité de Troyes et prêtent serment sans hésitation ni murmure à celui qui rédige des ordonnances au nom de « Henry, par la grâce de Dieu, roi de France et d'Angleterre ».

À cette date, Charles, le « soi-disant dauphin », est à son château de Mehun-sur-Yèvre, aux environs de Bourges, d'où sa chancellerie expédie des ordonnances au nom de « Charles, par la grâce de Dieu, roi de France ».

La France « anglaise » avait pour elle le Parlement et l'Université de Paris, les plus hautes autorités morales du pays. La France du « soidisant dauphin » avait pour elle la vivacité d'un sentiment national qu'exprimaient ici et là ceux qu'animait la haine de l'« étranger ». La France bourguignonne, celle du grand duc, est un enjeu capital. Sans son alliance, les Anglais ne peuvent espérer conquérir « leur » royaume. Mais Philippe le Bon est assez habile pour comprendre que l'alliance anglaise risque de lui faire perdre l'appui d'une « opinion » nationale de plus en plus hostile à l'« occupant ».

Exténués par les haines des partis et les ravages de la guerre, la plupart des Français réclamaient surtout un peu de sécurité et des impôts moins lourds. Entre les « collaborateurs » et les « résistants », les « attentistes » étaient sans doute les plus nombreux.

À vrai dire, pour bien des gens, la paix anglaise n'était pas dépourvue de charmes. Administrateur habile et homme politique de talent, le duc de Bedford gouverne avec intelligence la partie du royaume que contrôlent les Anglais, c'est-à-dire, outre la Guyenne et Calais, la Normandie, l'Île-de-France, une partie de la Picardie et de la Champagne. Respectant les clauses du traité, il a pour ambition d'établir solidement la dynastie des Lancastre en s'appuyant sur une administration qu'il laisse aux mains des Français. Dans le Grand Conseil de la régence, qui comprend seize membres, on ne compte que deux Anglais, l'évêque de Chichester et le célèbre capitaine de guerre John Falstolf. En Normandie, Bedford crée une université à Caen, confirme les privilèges et les franchises des villes et des corporations, installe à Rouen un Échiquier, une Chambre des comptes à Caen et punit sévèrement les méfaits des soldats anglais. Certes, nul n'était vraiment favorable à l'Anglais mais la renaissance du commerce sur l'axe de la Seine et la frappe d'une « bonne » monnaie nourrissaient une prospérité plus propice à l'accommodement qu'à la résistance.

Dans la partie qui lui était fidèle, celui que l'on appelait par dérision « le roi de Bourges » apparaissait alors bien faible. Jeune homme sans grande envergure, Charles ne semblait pas en mesure de peser sur les événements. Peu servi par un physique disgracieux, troublé par la propagande anglo-bourguignonne qui en faisait le bâtard d'une reine frivole, trop enclin à suivre l'avis du dernier qui avait parlé, ce roi peu belliqueux régnait sur une cour qui était un véritable « panier de crabes » et où les favoris se succédaient pour mener une politique sans grande cohérence. Enfin, constituée de bandes brutales commandées par des chefs de guerre indisciplinés, son armée ne semblait guère en mesure de « bouter les Anglais hors du royaume ». En

1424, renforcée par des contingents écossais, elle avait été massacrée sous les murs de Verneuil par les archers de Bedford, une lourde défaite comparable à celle d'Azincourt.

Pourtant, malgré ses réelles faiblesses, la France du dauphin disposait d'atouts certains. Charles avait d'abord pour lui tous les pays du sud de la Loire, des pays qui disposaient de ressources plus fortes que celles de la France « anglaise ». Au nord de la Loire, des troupes fidèles tenaient encore quelques places en Picardie et en Champagne. Bravement défendu, le Mont-Saint-Michel, assiégé en règle par terre et par mer, défiait les Anglais. À Bourges et à Poitiers, des hommes efficaces et compétents, chassés de Paris par l'épuration bourguignonne, faisaient tourner au ralenti une administration prête à prendre la relève.

Surtout, en France « occupée », naissait un mouvement de résistance appuyé sur le sentiment que le traité de Troyes n'avait aucune légitimité. Outre le fait que la maladie de Charles VI était de nature à enlever toute valeur à sa signature, la couronne de France était un bien inaliénable qui, en vertu de la Loi salique, devait revenir au fils aîné du roi.

Écrit après la publication du traité, un opuscule, la *Réponse d'un bon et loyal Français au peuple de France de tous États* affirmait qu'un roi ne pouvait disposer à sa guise du royaume et déshériter son fils et toute sa lignée. En 1422, Alain Chartier composait un *Quadrilogue invectif* où il apercevait, dans un rêve, « Dame France » dont les beaux vêtements étaient froissés et déchirés et qui, devant un riche palais en ruine, invectivait durement ses trois enfants, Noblesse, Clergé et Tiers État, auxquels elle demandait d'imiter les abeilles qui « mettent leur vie pour garder la seigneurie de leur Roy ». En Normandie, des « partisans » s'en prenaient aux « Français reniés » qui avaient accepté les faveurs de l'Anglais. En Bourgogne même, des grandes familles condamnaient l'alliance anglaise et, après plusieurs décennies de troubles au long desquelles les hommes qui gouvernaient le royaume s'étaient montrés incapables de remédier aux maux dont il était affligé, les âmes simples étaient prêtes à reporter leurs espérances sur une « pastourelle » appelée par le Ciel pour transmettre au vrai roi des avertissements et des signes.

En 1384, Constance, une veuve de Rabastens, en Albigeois, qui se qualifiait d'« épouse du Christ », avait assigné à Gaston Phébus, comte de Foix, la mission de sauver la France au bord de l'abîme. Quelques années plus tard, Jeanne-Marie de Maillé, une dame issue de la noblesse des pays de Loire, annonça à son entourage « beaucoup de choses qui allaient arriver dans le royaume de France » et fut reçue à Paris par Isabeau de Bavière à qui elle reprocha ses « poulaines » à la mode et son inconduite. En 1398, une simple paysanne, Marie Robine ou Marie la Gasconne, originaire d'Héchac, dans le diocèse d'Auch, prétend avoir des visions et dicte les révélations que Dieu lui transmet. Montrant la France ravagée par l'Antéchrist, elle n'hésite pas à prédire un soulèvement populaire qui détruirait la monarchie et Paris qu'elle voit noyé dans de grands fleuves de sang. Elle aurait même déclaré : « Quantités d'armes me sont apparues ; j'ai eu peur un instant d'être obligée de les porter moi-même. Il me fut dit de ne rien craindre, qu'elles ne m'étaient pas destinées, mais bien à une pucelle qui viendrait après moi et délivrerait le royaume. » Si, en 1429, une pucelle put être admise auprès du « roi de Bourges », c'est bien parce que d'autres prophétesses l'avaient précédée, ce qui rendait sa requête moins insolite. Dans l'atmosphère religieuse du temps, marquée par les défaillances des papes et des hommes d'Église, les femmes semblaient avoir reçu de Dieu des missions particulières.

Jeanne d'Arc

Jeannette, c'est ainsi qu'on l'appelait dans son pays, est née vers 1412, à Domrémy, un village situé aux confins de la Lorraine, de la Champagne et du Barrois, un des rares villages restés fidèles au « roi de Bourges » dans l'est du royaume. Son père, Jacques d'Arc, ou Dart, était un cultivateur aisé, fort influent dans la paroisse. Sa mère, Isabelle Romée, surnom qui lui venait d'un pèlerinage, a fait son instruction religieuse, complétée par les sermons des Frères mendiants dont la prédication se répandait dans les campagnes. Pas plus bergère que les autres filles du village qui conduisaient, chacune à leur tour, le troupeau commun, elle manifeste, en revanche, une piété qui sort de l'ordinaire et lui vaut la réputation de « béguine ». Elle portait une vénération particulière à sainte Catherine, vierge et martyre qui avait, à dix-huit ans, confondu les philosophes païens les plus renommés, et à sainte Marguerite, dont on racontait qu'elle s'était échappée de la maison paternelle en habit d'homme pour ne pas être livrée à un époux.

En 1425, l'année où les Bourguignons attaquent le village et enlèvent le bétail, mais l'année aussi où la nouvelle se répand que les défenseurs du Mont-Saint-Michel ont réussi à s'emparer de la flotte anglaise, elle entend des voix qui l'exhortent à venir au secours du roi de France. C'est elle, lui annonce l'archange Michel, que Dieu a désignée pour sauver un royaume qui était en grande « pitié ». Jeanne fait alors vœu de virginité et se fait par la suite appeler « la Pucelle ».

En février 1429, alors que les Anglais assiègent Orléans pour forcer le passage de la Loire et établir une liaison avec la Guyenne et Bordeaux, elle demande à Robert de Baudricourt, capitaine de la forteresse de Vaucouleurs, qui l'avait éconduite quelques mois plus tôt, un équipement et une escorte pour aller trouver le dauphin à Chinon. « N'avez-vous pas entendu dire qu'il a été prophétisé que la France serait perdue par une femme et restaurée par une vierge des marches de Lorraine ? » dit-elle au capitaine qui, vaincu par l'obstination de la Pucelle et gagné par la foi des habitants qui se cotisent pour offrir à Jeanne un équipement et un cheval, lui fournit un sauf-conduit et une escorte de six hommes.

Le 6 mars 1429, elle est reçue à Chinon par le roi qu'elle reconnaît parmi les courtisans et lui délivre son message : « Gentil (ce qui veut dire bien né) dauphin, j'ai nom Jeanne la Pucelle, et vous mande le roi des cieux par moi que vous serez sacré et couronné dans la ville de Reims et vous serez lieutenant du roi des cieux qui est roi de France. » Puis cette jeune fille en armes, habillée en homme et aux cheveux coupés court, affirme à ce jeune homme de vingt-six ans, troublé par sa possible bâtardise : « Je te dis, de la part de Messire, que tu es vrai héritier de France, et fils de Roi, et Il m'a envoyé à toi, pour te conduire à Reims, pour que tu reçoives ton couronnement et ta consécration si tu le veux. » Les témoins notent l'expression « radieuse » du roi après l'entretien personnel qu'il a quelques instants avec Jeanne.

Interrogée pendant trois semaines par les théologiens de Paris repliés à Poitiers et examinée par les matrones qui s'assurent de sa virginité, la Pucelle impressionne les sceptiques, qui ne trouvent en elle que « bien, humilité, virginité, dévotion, honnêteté, simplicité ». « Espérant en Dieu, car douter de la Pucelle eût été répugné au Saint-Esprit et se rendre indigne de l'aide de Dieu », Charles décide alors de tenter l'expérience et institue Jeanne « chef de la guerre », lui faisant faire une armure à ses mesures. Elle-même fait faire une bannière selon ses instructions, représentant le Christ en croix, et un étendard qui portait l'image de Dieu bénissant les fleurs de lys, avec la devise « Jésus Maria ». Le 22 mars, elle somme par lettre le roi d'Angleterre et le soi-disant régent du royaume de France de « faire raison au roi du Ciel » et de rendre les « clefs de toutes les villes qu'ils avaient prises et violées en France », ce qui n'impressionna guère les Anglais.

Le 29 avril, avec une poignée de chevaliers, elle réussit à entrer dans Orléans, accueillie par Jean, fils bâtard de Louis d'Orléans, qui défendait la ville assiégée depuis sept mois. Impatiente de combattre, elle galvanise les habitants qui lui font fête « comme s'ils avaient vu Dieu descendre parmi eux ». Le 8 mai, à la suite d'une série de combats victorieux au cours desquels Jeanne est blessée par une flèche, les Anglais lèvent le siège. C'est le « signe » que tous attendaient.

Au lendemain de la délivrance d'Orléans, le combat semble en effet avoir changé d'âme. Ce qui semblait perdu paraît désormais possible. Menée par le duc d'Alençon et par Jeanne, l'armée royale reprend Jargeau, Meung et Beaugency. Le 18 juin, les Anglais sont mis en déroute près de Patay. Du côté français, il y avait eu trois morts ; du côté anglais, les chroniqueurs bourguignons évaluent les pertes à 2 000 hommes. En quelques semaines, Bedford a perdu ses meilleurs capitaines, Talbot, Salisbury, Suffolk, Falstolf, tués ou prisonniers.

Contre l'avis des chefs militaires qui voudraient alors marcher sur Paris ou la Normandie, Jeanne obtient, le 29 juin, que l'armée traverse la France anglo-bourguignonne pour faire sacrer à Reims le « gentil dauphin ». Troyes, Châlons-sur-Marne et Reims se soumettent sans combat et, le 17 juillet 1429, Charles est sacré dans la cathédrale de Reims, en présence de Jeanne et de ses parents venus de Domrémy. Le 21 juillet, Charles se rend à Corbeny, prieuré dépendant de Saint-Remi de Reims où reposent les reliques de saint Marcoul, pour y toucher les écrouelles. En accomplissant pour la première fois le « miracle royal », il démontrait ainsi qu'il était devenu le « vrai » roi. « Ores est exécuté le plaisir de Dieu qui voulait que vinssiez à Reims recevoir votre digne sacre, en montrant que vous estes vrai roi et celui auquel le royaume doit appartenir », exulte alors la Pucelle.

Le sacre inattendu de Reims a ébranlé les consciences d'un peuple troublé par ce nouveau « signe ». L'émotion est extraordinaire, non seulement dans le royaume mais aussi à l'étranger. Tandis qu'un magistrat de Toulouse conseille de demander à Jeanne son avis sur les mutations des monnaies, que les foules se précipitent pour la voir et la toucher, que Bonne de Visconti la prie de l'aider à recouvrer le duché de Milan, que le comte d'Armagnac lui écrit pour lui demander qui est le vrai pape, que des légendes courent sur sa naissance et sa jeunesse, qu'on l'a fait venir à Lagny pour ressusciter un enfant, Christine de Pisan, retirée au couvent de Poissy, reprend la plume et écrit :

« L'an mil quatre cent vingt et neuf
Reprit à luire le soleil. »

Pourtant, quelques mois après l'apothéose de Reims, l'astre de Jeanne pâlit. Le 8 septembre, elle échoue devant Paris. À la cour de Charles VII, on pense que la reprise d'une action militaire énergique passe par la réconciliation avec le duc de Bourgogne, avec qui une trêve a été signée le 28 août. Dans cette optique, l'ardeur guerrière de Jeanne gêne un roi qui entend désormais mener lui-même sa propre politique. Pendant l'hiver 1429-1430, on lui confie des opérations secondaires dont on sait qu'elles lui rapporteront peu de gloire si elles réussissent, et nuiront à un prestige devenu encombrant si elles échouent. Le 23 mai 1430, elle est faite prisonnière devant Compiègne assiégée par les Bourguignons et livrée par Jean de Luxembourg aux Anglais pour 10 000 livres tournois.

Tandis que Charles VII se désintéresse du sort de Jeanne, l'Université de Paris est la première à exiger qu'elle soit jugée pour « crime sentant l'hérésie ». Pour tous les adversaires de celui qui avait été sacré à Reims, il était indispensable en effet de démontrer que Jeanne était une sorcière possédée par le diable. Annuler l'effet produit par le sacre, prouver que Charles avait été ensorcelé, châtier une « béguine » qui refusait de se soumettre à l'institution ecclésiastique, en appelait directement à Dieu et traduisait de manière spectaculaire la vigueur d'une religion populaire, tels étaient les enjeux du procès d'inquisition qui s'ouvrit le 9 janvier 1431 à Rouen.

Présidé par Pierre Cauchon, l'évêque de Beauvais dans le diocèse duquel Jeanne avait été capturée, le tribunal, composé de théologiens et d'universitaires, fit le procès politique dont les Anglais, qui en assumaient tous les frais, avaient besoin. Entre un Pierre Cauchon qui avait été le négociateur du traité de Troyes, des clercs « bourguignons » effrayés par la parole du peuple et les manifestations du diable et des Anglais qui voulaient la mort de celle à qui ils attribuaient leurs revers, la cause était entendue, même si les juges, voulant éviter tout reproche, firent tout pour que la procédure soit régulière.

Mais en même temps, ce procès politique est aussi celui de l'institution ecclésiastique au lendemain d'un Grand Schisme dont l'Église se remettait à peine. Affirmant que ses révélations venaient directement de Dieu et des saints du Ciel, sans l'intermédiaire des gens d'Église, Jeanne posait, de façon insupportable pour les hommes de la hiérarchie qui la jugeaient, la question du pouvoir de l'institution sur les fidèles. En répondant à ceux qui lui demandaient ce qu'elle ferait si l'« autorité » lui disait que ses révélations étaient choses diaboliques : « De cela, je m'en rapporterai toujours à Dieu dont j'ai toujours fait le commandement, et je sais bien que ce qui est contenu au procès vient par le commandement de Dieu, et ce que j'affirme dans ce procès avoir fait par commandement de Dieu, il m'eût été impossible d'en faire le contraire », elle signait son arrêt de mort, plus sûrement que par tout autre aveu.

L'affaire des vêtements d'homme que Jeanne refuse d'abandonner et qui prend une importance considérable au cours du procès en est le symbole. En ne croyant pas avoir le droit d'abandonner l'habit que les voix lui avaient conseillé de porter, Jeanne refusait de se soumettre à ceux qui prétendaient détenir de Dieu le pouvoir « infaillible » — le mot fut employé à deux reprises au cours du procès — de « connaître et juger des actes des fidèles ».

Le 24 mai 1431, dans le cimetière Saint-Ouen où la sentence allait être prononcée, Jeanne, qui voit le bûcher qu'on dresse ostensiblement non loin de là, a un moment de faiblesse et abjure ses fautes, promettant de ne plus porter ni habit d'homme ni cheveux rasés. L'aveu valant absolution, elle allait alors être simplement condamnée à la prison perpétuelle.

Mais en ne trouvant plus en prison les vêtements de femme que les Anglais furieux lui ont enlevés, Jeanne se ressaisit, reprend ses habits d'homme et révoque son abjuration, sachant ce qui l'attendait. Le 30 mai, elle meurt sur le bûcher dressé sur la place du Vieux-Marché, en implorant jusqu'à la fin l'aide des saints et des saintes du paradis.

Le traité d'Arras

Aussitôt après le supplice qui a bouleversé tous ceux qui y ont assisté, les Lancastre s'emploient à tirer les « bénéfices » du procès. Alors que Pierre Cauchon, dès le 7 juin, fait comparaître des témoins qui affirment que, le matin même de l'exécution, Jeanne a renié ses Voix et reconnu qu'elle avait été trompée et qu'elle avait trompé le peuple, le 8 juin, le régent du roi d'Angleterre adresse une lettre à l'empereur, aux souverains et aux princes de la chrétienté leur annonçant que « la trompeuse divinatrice qui s'était élevée dans [son] royaume de France [...] avait confessé sans ambiguïté », à l'approche de la mort, que « ces esprits, dont elle affirmait maintes fois qu'ils lui étaient apparus visiblement, étaient mauvais et menteurs » et qu'« elle avait été jouée ».

À Paris, le 4 juillet, l'inquisiteur de France fait une solennelle prédication dans laquelle il évoque la vie de Jeanne, « pleine de feu et de sang, de meurtre de chrétiens, jusqu'à ce qu'elle soit brûlée ». Et le 16 décembre 1431, pour tenter d'effacer Reims, le jeune

Henri VI, alors âgé de neuf ans, est couronné à Notre-Dame de Paris. Mais faute de sainte ampoule et de toucher d'écrouelles, l'effet est dérisoire. Le festin qui suivit fut, selon le Bourgeois de Paris, pourtant acquis à la cause anglaise, un fiasco : « Personne, écrit-il, n'eut à se louer du repas. La plupart des viandes, surtout celles qu'on destinait au commun, avaient été cuites le jeudi précédent, ce qui semblait très étrange aux Français. » Quant à la joute qui eut lieu le lendemain, le même témoin déclare que n'importe quel habitant de la cité eût engagé plus de frais pour marier sa fille que les Anglais n'en avaient fait pour couronner leur roi.

Dissipant la désespérance, le bref passage de la Pucelle avait déclenché un mouvement que rien ne semblait pouvoir arrêter. C'était désormais le « vrai » roi qui incarnait l'espoir des Français. En Normandie, les soulèvements sont de plus en plus fréquents. À Paris, les complots se multiplient. De son côté, Philippe le Bon, qui s'était abstenu d'assister au sacre d'Henri VI, se rapproche du « meurtrier » de son père. Après des premiers pourparlers à Nevers, en janvier 1435, se réunit au mois d'août, à Arras, une conférence de paix d'une importance inaccoutumée à laquelle participent des cardinaux représentant le pape, des délégations étrangères, des représentants de l'Université de Paris et de plusieurs grandes villes, le duc de Bourgogne et son conseiller Nicolas Rolin, une délégation anglaise menée par l'évêque de Winchester, le cardinal Beaufort, et au sein de laquelle figure Pierre Cauchon, et l'ambassade française conduite par l'archevêque de Reims Regnault de Chartres, Charles et Arthur de Richemont, beau-frère du duc de Bourgogne, qui dispose d'écus sonnants et trébuchants pour mieux faire comprendre ses arguments aux conseillers de Philippe le Bon.

Complètement irréalistes, les Anglais proposent à Charles VII d'abandonner sa couronne, de devenir Charles de Valois, un baron qui garderait les territoires qu'il occupe et se reconnaîtrait le vassal d'Henri VI, roi de France et d'Angleterre ! Le 6 septembre, n'ayant rien obtenu du « vrai » roi dont les troupes viennent de s'emparer de Saint-Denis, les Anglais, furieux, quittent Arras. Le 21 septembre, en revanche, les pourparlers franco-bourguignons se terminent par un accord dont Bedford a eu le temps d'apprendre la teneur avant de mourir, le 14 septembre, au château de Rouen.

Pour Charles VII, le prix à payer passait par la dénonciation du crime de Montereau. Faisant amende honorable, il désavouait le meurtre de Jean sans Peur, promettait de poursuivre et de punir les coupables, de dire des messes de requiem en l'église de Montereau et en l'église des Chartreux de Dijon, de construire et d'entretenir à ses frais un couvent de Chartreux à Montereau et d'édifier une belle croix sur le pont « au lieu où fut perpétré ledit mauvais cas ».

De plus, Charles VII cédait au duc de Bourgogne les comtés de Mâcon et d'Auxerre, les châtellenies de Bar-sur-Seine, Péronne, Montdidier et Roye et tous les territoires au nord de la Somme, avec toutefois la possibilité de les racheter moyennant 400 000 écus. Enfin, sa vie durant, Philippe le Bon était dispensé d'hommage pour ses possessions sises dans le royaume de France.

Le 21 septembre, les lettres notifiant le traité furent signées et lues dans l'église Saint-Vaast. Jean Tudert, le vieux conseiller de Charles VII, alla s'agenouiller aux pieds de Philippe le Bon, et récita la formule d'amende honorable contenue dans le traité. Le duc répondit qu'il ôtait de son cœur toute rancune, releva l'ambassadeur et l'embrassa. Puis il jura sur la croix de ne jamais rappeler la mort de son père et d'entretenir bonne paix et union avec le roi. Le légat du pape le déclara alors absous du serment qu'il avait fait aux Anglais et un *Te Deum* termina la cérémonie au milieu de l'allégresse générale.

Même si ses dispositions valurent aux négociateurs français de sérieuses critiques, le traité d'Arras annulait celui de Troyes, confirmait la légitimité de Charles et mettait les Anglais dans une situation difficile. Le 13 avril 1436, les troupes royales de Richemont et les troupes bourguignonnes de Villiers de L'Isle-Adam faisaient leur entrée dans Paris, dont la population, du haut des fenêtres, criblait les Anglais de pierres, de bûches et d'ustensiles de ménage. La garnison anglaise, réfugiée à la Bastille, et les Français « reniés » les plus compromis purent toutefois quitter la capitale sans représailles et s'embarquer pour Rouen sous les huées de la foule. Le 12 novembre 1437, Charles, qui ne pardonnait pas les épreuves qu'il avait connues en 1418, fit son entrée solennelle dans la capitale. Trois semaines après, il repartit pour ses résidences de la Loire.

Il fallut attendre le 15 février 1450 pour qu'il demande à son conseiller, le théologien Guillaume Bouillé, de faire une enquête sur le procès de Jeanne « et la manière selon laquelle il a été conduit et procédé ». La procédure, qui nécessitait l'accord du pape, fut mise en route en 1452 à la demande de la mère de Jeanne, qui vivait à Orléans, et de son frère. Elle aboutit le 7 juillet 1456 à la sentence qui annulait le procès de 1431 et déclarait que Jeanne devait être « déchargée et disculpée ». Une « réhabilitation » prononcée du bout des lèvres mais qu'exigeait la raison d'État. Charles VII ne pouvait devoir son trône à une sorcière.

Charles le « Bien servi »

Au lendemain de son entrée à Paris, le « gentil dauphin » semble avoir pris confiance en son destin. Certes, le roi de France reste ce personnage dégingandé aux genoux cagneux et aux traits ingrats. Mais celui qui a été sauvé par la Pucelle prend de l'assurance. Le jeune homme timide et indolent sort de sa torpeur, se transforme en guerrier courageux et en amant sensuel. Entouré de serviteurs fidèles passionnément dévoués à sa cause, il « boute » les Anglais hors de France et donne à la monarchie les instruments permanents de son autorité. Ces changements aussi brusques qu'inattendus ont vivement frappé les contemporains. Le « gentil dauphin » y gagne un nouveau surnom : Charles, le « Bien servi ».

La nouvelle armée du roi

Au lendemain du traité d'Arras, Charles VII semble inaugurer un nouveau règne comme si le doute sur sa légitimité qui l'avait taraudé jusque-là avait cessé de le torturer. Au siège de Montereau, en 1437, le roi stupéfie par la précision de ses ordres, son application à surveiller les moindres détails, son insouciance à risquer sa vie. Inquiets de sa témérité, ceux qui l'entourent lui prêchent la prudence. Il répond que « la guerre [est] à lui, non à un autre et qu'il [doit] prendre sa part de diligence ». C'est lui qui, le premier, gravit l'échelle appliquée contre la muraille et enjambe les créneaux. Le triste dauphin disgracié par la nature se transforme en souverain jaloux de son autorité. Le roi chaste et pieux organise des fêtes somptueuses et devient amoureux éperdu d'Agnès Sorel, « Mademoiselle de Beauté », qui devient la première favorite officielle d'un roi de France et lui donne quatre filles. À sa mort, le 9 février 1450, de suite de couches, le Bien servi prend pour nouvelle maîtresse Antoinette de Maignelais, la cousine d'Agnès, ce qui fait écrire à Camulio, l'ambassadeur milanais : « Le roi de France est entièrement livré aux femmes. »

En fait, ces escapades amoureuses n'ont pas nui à l'exercice des fonctions royales. Peut-être même ont-elles affermi le caractère d'un roi qui, sous l'influence de ses maîtresses, sut choisir ceux qui lui ont valu le surnom de « Bien servi », Pierre de Brézé, Dunois, Jean de Buell, Jean d'Estouteville, Guillaume Cousinot, Jacques Cœur, Jean et Guillaume Jouvenel des Ursins, les frères Bureau. De « petite lignée » pour la plupart, passionnément dévoués à la cause monarchique, ils ont préparé les ordonnances qui ont redonné au royaume un véritable gouvernement.

Dans un premier temps, il a fallu le « nettoyer » des écorcheurs qui y avaient établi leur siège. Ainsi nommés parce qu'ils dépouillaient jusqu'à la chemise tous ceux qu'ils rencontraient, ils couraient le pays, le saccageant et le rançonnant sans merci.

En 1444, comme l'avait fait autrefois du Guesclin avec les grandes compagnies, le dauphin Louis emmena ces « coupe-jarrets » en Alsace pour lutter contre les Suisses rebelles au duc d'Autriche, tandis que le roi dirigeait lui-même une expédition dans l'Est pour soutenir son beau-frère, René d'Anjou, duc de Lorraine, en lutte contre la ville de Metz. Louis accomplit sa tâche avec bonheur, réussissant à vaincre les redoutables montagnards helvètes tout en faisant massacrer quelques milliers d'écorcheurs au cours de rudes embuscades.

Surtout, pour arracher ces gens de guerre à leur vie d'errance et les transformer en soldats réguliers, l'ordonnance du 26 mai 1445, rendue au château de Louppy, jetait les fondements d'une armée permanente en temps de paix, libérant ainsi le roi de l'obligation de négocier avec les féodaux pour obtenir leur concours et avec les états pour le financement de campagnes aux durées incertaines. Quinze capitaines nommés par le roi et révocables à volonté furent désignés pour diriger quinze compagnies, dites « compagnies d'ordonnance » parce qu'elles étaient « ordonnées » par le roi et non formées au gré de tel ou tel capitaine. Chaque compagnie se composait de cent lances, à raison de six hommes par lance : un homme d'armes, qui tenait la lance et commandait son groupe, un coutilier et un page, deux archers et un valet de guerre, tous montés.

Les compagnies ainsi retenues, après un tri sévère qui ne conserva que les hommes les plus expérimentés et les mieux équipés, étaient cantonnées dans des villes déterminées et entretenues aux frais de la province, sous la responsabilité des officiers locaux chargés de faire régulièrement des « montres ». D'autre part, pour rompre la solidarité qui pouvait exister entre les écorcheurs, on décida d'accorder une amnistie générale pour les crimes et les délits commis. Tandis que, munis de leurs lettres de rémission, les soldats « licenciés », au moins la moitié, étaient reconduits, par petits détachements, dans leur pays, ceux qui furent enrôlés dans les compagnies d'ordonnance devinrent assez « sages » pour que les chroniqueurs, même hostiles à Charles VII, soulignent le succès d'une réforme qui n'était pas totalement nouvelle mais fut réellement appliquée.

Plus novatrice, l'ordonnance du 28 avril 1448 instituait une infanterie de francs-archers, ainsi nommés parce qu'ils étaient exemptés de la taille. Chaque paroisse devait fournir un archer ou un arbalétrier, dans la force de l'âge, robuste et adroit. Les hommes choisis étaient soumis à un entraînement régulier, le dimanche, à une inspection mensuelle et à une montre tous les deux ou trois ans.

Moins d'un mois plus tard, par ses lettres du 22 mai 1448, Charles VII entreprit de réorganiser le service des nobles en ordonnant à ses commissaires de consigner dans des registres les noms et surnoms des nobles ainsi que la nature et la valeur de leurs fiefs. Dans les six mois, tous ces nobles devaient s'engager à être prêts. Toutefois, s'ils étaient mobilisés, ils toucheraient des gages comparables à ceux versés aux gens de guerre de l'ordonnance : 15 livres tournois par mois pour un homme d'armes pourvu de trois chevaux, 7 livres 10 sous pour un archer monté.

Enfin, sous la direction de Jean et Gaspard Bureau et avec l'aide de techniciens étrangers, comme le Génois Louis Giribaut, l'artillerie fut à même de jouer un rôle décisif dans les dernières grandes batailles de la guerre de Cent Ans. Charles VII avait désormais les moyens de « bouter » les Anglais hors de France.

Les Anglais « boutés » hors de France

Le 24 mars 1449, François de Surienne, dit l'Aragonais, opérant pour le compte des Anglais, s'empare de la ville de Fougères, place forte du duc de Bretagne, revenu dans l'alliance du roi de France. Poussé par ses conseillers et se sentant assez fort, Charles VII décide de rompre la trêve et de reprendre les armes contre l'ennemi. La prise de Verneuil, le 21 juillet, amorce la reconquête de la Normandie, la population accueillant les troupes royales avec enthousiasme. Le 10 novembre 1449, le roi fait une entrée triomphale dans Rouen soulevée contre les troupes du duc de Somerset. Le 15 avril 1450, une armée de secours venue d'Angleterre, commandée par Thomas Kyriel, est écrasée à Formigny, à 16 kilomètres de Bayeux. Caen capitule le 1er juillet. Cherbourg, enfin, dernière place tenue par les Anglais, tombe le 12 août 1450. Ceux qui avaient brûlé Jeanne d'Arc étaient chassés de Normandie.

La reconquête de la Guyenne fut plus difficile, la population vivant largement des liens commerciaux avec l'Angleterre, l'unique débouché des vins bordelais. Au printemps de 1451, une armée de 6 000 hommes, commandée par Dunois, occupa une à une les places qui commandaient l'entrée du Bordelais. À la suite d'un traité conclu avec les représentants de la cité qui confirmait les privilèges et les institutions du duché et laissait aux habitants qui ne voudraient pas « se tourner Français » toute liberté d'émigrer dans les six mois, Bordeaux se rendit le 23 juin et Bayonne le 20 août.

Mais, en 1452, une conjuration se forma pour rappeler les Anglais et une armée commandée par le prestigieux John Talbot débarqua à Soulac en octobre et réoccupa Bordeaux le 23. Au printemps 1453 s'ouvre alors une nouvelle campagne de Guyenne. Le 17 juillet 1453, la bataille décisive a lieu à Castillon, près de Libourne. La charge de Talbot se brise sur les Français retranchés derrière des palissades et sur les trois cents canons de Giribault, qui fauchent les troupes anglaises et vengent les désastres de Crécy, de Poitiers et d'Azincourt. Talbot finit au milieu de cette défaite sa glorieuse vie. Les Bordelais, assiégés par terre et par mer, doivent capituler le 19 octobre et paient au prix fort leur volonté de résistance. Une amende collective de 100 000 écus, plus tard réduite à 30 000, fut imposée à la cité rebelle. De lourdes taxes frappèrent le commerce et la cour souveraine de justice fut supprimée, les plaignants devant désormais recourir en appel au Parlement de Paris et suivre sa procédure.

Cette rigueur détermina un grand mouvement d'émigration, quelque 2 000 Gascons préférant continuer leur activité en Angleterre. L'héritage d'Aliénor d'Aquitaine revenu dans le giron du royaume de France, il ne restait aux Anglais sur le continent que Calais et le comté de Guines. En fait, la guerre de Cent Ans était finie, même s'il n'y eut jamais de traité de paix. La « réduction » de la Normandie et la conquête de la Guyenne suscitèrent l'admiration durable des contemporains. Thomas Basin, homme d'Église et historien, exprimait certainement leur sentiment en écrivant : « Les Anglais tenaient depuis près de deux cent cinquante ans une grande partie de la Guyenne, et cependant ce vaillant roi Charles a chassé les Anglais de la Normandie et de la Guyenne et de presque tout le royaume avec seulement 1 500 lances payées à la solde ordinaire. Il a mis sur pied les francs-archers, mais ceux-ci restaient chacun chez soi, s'occupant à cultiver leurs champs ou à exercer leurs métiers, et ils ne recevaient aucune paye sauf s'ils étaient appelés à faire campagne hors de leur pays. C'est avec de telles forces qu'il a chassé les Anglais, qui pourtant avaient déjà pris racine tant en Guyenne qu'en Normandie et qu'il a forcé les Bourguignons à demander la paix. » Un miracle, en somme ! Sur la médaille commémorant l'expulsion des Anglais hors de France, on pouvait aussi lire : « Gloire et paix à toi, roi Charles, et louange perpétuelle. La rage des ennemis a été vaincue et ton énergie, grâce au conseil du Christ et au secours de la loi, refait le royaume qu'une crise si grave avait ébranlé. » La « reconstruction » du pays pouvait alors commencer.

La « reconstruction » du royaume

Le 15 avril 1454, moins d'un an après la bataille de Castillon, était publiée l'ordonnance de Montil-lès-Tours, un monument de procédure qui marquait la volonté de restaurer l'ordre dans l'État et dans le droit. Pour faire face à l'afflux des procès que la remise en état du pays suscitait, on scinda en deux la Chambre des enquêtes et on peupla le Parlement d'hommes « recommandables par leur loyauté, leur expérience juridique et leur haute moralité », écrit Thomas Basin. Recevant régulièrement leurs gages, les conseillers furent invités à refuser les « épices », et les « dons corrompables », faits avant le jugement, furent interdits.

Surtout, l'ordonnance de 1454 prescrivit la rédaction générale des coutumes des pays et des villes dans la partie du royaume où régnait le droit coutumier, le roi voulant donner à ses tribunaux le moyen de juger les sujets, d'où qu'ils viennent, selon les coutumes de leur pays, en pleine connaissance du droit. Cette rédaction, si elle fixa pour long-temps des particularismes locaux — il y eut plus de deux cent cin-quante coutumes —, facilita toutefois dans l'instant la tâche des juges et des avocats qui devaient faire face à des plaideurs produisant sou-vent des allégations difficiles à vérifier et brandissant des coutumes qui variaient « à leur appétit ».

Sur le plan fiscal, le règne de Charles VII se traduisit par une évolution lourde d'avenir. L'impôt, autrefois consenti par les « états », devint une contribution permanente « imposée » par le roi. Après 1436 pour les aides indirectes, et après 1439 pour l'impôt direct, on ne demanda plus leur avis aux états généraux de Languedoïl. Au moment où l'armée tendait à devenir permanente, la taille, dont le produit était affecté à la défense du royaume, évoluait dans le même sens.

En 1451, on supprima l'« aide pour la conduite de la guerre » mais on maintint la « taille des gens de guerre » destinée à entretenir les compagnies d'ordonnance. Puis on accoutuma les habitants du royaume à la payer tous les ans, sans préciser si elle servait ou non à l'entretien de l'armée. L'impôt permanent était né et, avec lui, l'État moderne. La dernière année du règne, les revenus de la couronne s'élevaient à 1 800 000 livres, les produits du domaine ne figurant plus que pour 50 000 livres.

Pourtant, on a pu dire que les dernières années du règne de Charles VII furent « l'âge d'or du contribuable ». Malgré les plaintes rituelles des sujets qui déploraient des impositions toujours trop élevées et rappelaient que le roi devait vivre du « sien », ces formules stéréotypées dont nous sommes encore coutumiers rappellent plutôt que la pression fiscale était devenue supportable et que les exigences royales ne provoquaient plus misère et désolation.

C'est que, de bonne foi, Charles VII pouvait rappeler à ses sujets que le péril anglais demeurait, l'ennemi n'étant qu'à six heures de voile, par bon vent, de la Normandie et que l'étendue du littoral à défendre était immense. Au sortir de la terrible épreuve, l'« opinion publique » était prête à accepter l'impôt qui permettait à la monarchie d'entretenir les compagnies d'ordonnance, de dissuader l'ennemi de débarquer et de maintenir l'ordre dans un pays que ne ravageaient plus les écorcheurs.

C'est que, aussi, pour mieux faire « passer » l'impôt permanent, le gouvernement avait supprimé les autres charges qui pesaient sur le peuple et réservé au roi seul le droit d'imposer. L'article 44 de l'ordonnance du 2 novembre 1439 disposait ainsi que les seigneurs ne pourraient plus, désormais, lever de taille sans l'autorisation du roi. On interdit aux états de lever des deniers sans la permission du roi. On contrôla et on réduisit le vote de taxes locales. Secondé par un nombreux personnel d'officiers, disposant d'une armée permanente et d'impôts permanents, le roi était désormais en mesure de réduire à l'obéissance l'Église et la noblesse.

En 1438, réunie à Bourges, une assemblée du clergé de France prend un certain nombre de décisions qui aboutissent à la publication, le 7 juillet 1438, de la « pragmatique sanction ». Le préambule prend la forme d'un réquisitoire contre les abus commis par un Saint-Siège sorti affaibli de l'épreuve du Grand Schisme. Le roi dénonçait les « usurpations très graves » dont étaient victimes les églises de France, se plaignait de voir les revenus de son clergé attirés « en des régions étrangères » et s'affligeait de constater que les études théologiques étaient abandonnées parce que la faveur seule, et non le mérite, décidait de la nomination des clercs aux bénéfices ecclésiastiques.

Émancipant fortement l'Église de France de l'autorité du pape, la pragmatique sanction donnait au gouvernement royal le pouvoir de recommander ses candidats aux élections d'évêques et d'abbés. Les bulles pontificales ne seraient plus publiées sans sa permission. Le pape ne jouirait plus de la possibilité de concéder un bénéfice avant qu'il ne soit vacant ni du droit d'en créer de nouveaux. Les annates, droits versés par un clerc lors de son installation dans un bénéfice mineur, étaient supprimées et les prélèvements du Saint-Siège sur le clergé de France étaient réduits au cinquième de ce qu'il percevait auparavant. Enfin le pape ne pouvait juger les procès en appel qu'une fois toutes les juridictions intermédiaires épuisées par les plaideurs.

En fait, autrefois présentée comme l'une des grandes victoires de l'État français contre l'Église de Rome, la pragmatique sanction ne marquait aucune volonté de rupture avec le Saint-Siège, Charles VII la considérant simplement comme une monnaie d'échange dans ses négociations avec le pape et comme un moyen de faire bénéficier ses protégés des riches prébendes. C'est ainsi qu'il prétendit imposer Pierre Bureau comme évêque d'Orléans et fit élire à l'archevêché de Bourges le fils de Jacques Cœur, âgé de vingt-cinq ans.

Surtout, évolution plus capitale, les fondements religieux du pouvoir royal, qui ne sont évidemment pas chose nouvelle, sont particulièrement exaltés en cette fin de Moyen Âge. On le mesure assez dans les entrées solennelles du roi qui prennent pour modèle l'entrée de Jésus à Jérusalem, dans les funérailles où la présence de l'effigie du monarque, revêtue de tous ses insignes, manifeste, malgré la mort, la perpétuation de la dignité royale, dans le culte de ces saints qui sont devenus les protecteurs particuliers d'une France transformée en véritable Terre promise, tous ces saints qui ont donné des victoires inattendues contre les Anglais, saint Martial à Limoges, saint Léonard à Noblat, saint Pierre au Dorat, sainte Radegonde à Poitiers, sainte Catherine à Fierbois mais aussi saint Denis, saint Louis, saint Michel enfin, devenu le gardien privilégié du roi et du royaume.

C'est aussi lors des messes dominicales qu'est exaltée la dignité royale. On y prie « pour nostre seigneur le Roy de France, pour toute sa lignée, pour tout le bon conseil et pour tous bons seigneurs qui ont terre à garder et gouverner ». Précisant dans un opuscule « comment on doit se tenir à la messe », le théologien Jean de Gerson écrit : « Quent on sonne la messe, on doit penser que ce sont les messages du Roy qui dient la nouvelle que le Roy vient... et doit on avoir grand joye de sa venue... Quand on commence la messe, vous devez savoir et penser que le Roy entre en la porte, et devez aler à l'encontre par désir et le devez saluer et dire : « Bien soiez vous venus beau sire Dieu » ; et devez penser comme il est grant, comme il est puissant, comme il est débonnaire et comme il est misercors. »

Plus que la pragmatique sanction, c'est cette assimilation entre Dieu et le roi qui montre la place considérable de la religion dans la réaffirmation du pouvoir royal au lendemain des épreuves de la guerre. Si Charles VII put si facilement déjouer les intrigues des princes, c'est bien parce que l'« opinion publique » était avec lui. En 1439, reprochant au roi de ne pas suivre leurs conseils et mécontents de l'ordonnance qui leur faisait perdre leur pouvoir militaire, les Princes se révoltent et gagnent à leur cause le dauphin Louis que son père avait chargé de faire appliquer la réforme en Poitou. Les ducs de Bourbon, d'Alençon et de Bretagne, le sire de La Trémoille et le vieux comte de Vendôme sont au cœur de cette révolte, de cette « Praguerie » appelée ainsi en souvenir de la guerre civile qui venait d'ensanglanter la Bohême.

En quelques mois de l'année 1440, le « Bien servi » mate les révoltés et les déloge des forteresses qu'ils occupaient, les villes ayant fermé leurs portes aux rebelles en leur déclarant qu'elles avaient déjà un roi.

Deux autres affaires montrent à quel point la noblesse est désormais sous contrôle. Jugé en 1458 pour avoir invité les Anglais à envahir le Cotentin et la Picardie, le duc Jean II d'Alençon est condamné par ses pairs à la peine capitale et gracié par le roi qui différa l'exécution « jusques à son bon plaisir ». Le rebelle fut enfermé au château de Loches et le duché d'Alençon annexé au domaine royal. En 1460, Jean V, le comte d'Armagnac, fut condamné au bannissement perpétuel et à la confiscation de ses biens pour avoir bravé l'autorité royale, avoir pris pour maîtresse sa sœur Isabelle et avoir eu d'elle trois enfants, au mépris de l'excommunication.

Peu de temps avant sa mort, Charles VII reçut à Bourges des envoyés de l'empereur de Trébizonde, du roi de Perse, du prince de Géorgie, du roi d'Arménie et du roi d'Abyssinie qui, réunis par un moine franciscain d'humeur entreprenante, voulaient combattre les Turcs qui, en 1453, avaient pris Constantinople et mis fin à l'histoire de l'Empire byzantin. Ils avaient d'abord visité le pape et le duc de Bourgogne mais recherchaient surtout le soutien de ce qu'ils appelaient « la première nacion ».

Au moment où l'Angleterre était en proie à la « guerre des Deux-Roses » qui, durant dix-huit ans, la plongea dans l'anarchie, la France avait retrouvé la place qui était la sienne avant la défaite de Crécy. L'« ange gardien » qui avait servi le « Bien servi » de bout en bout de son règne l'accompagna au moment de sa mort, en 1461, Charles connaissant la chance de disparaître à l'apogée de son succès. Tandis que les pays étrangers célébraient la mémoire du « second Auguste », du « nouveau César triomphant sur le monde », de l'« autre Charlemagne victorieux », l'« opinion publique » citait le prince mort comme un « exemple de haute perfection ».

> « Et quand Angloys furent dehors,
> Chacun se mit en ses efforts
> De bâtir et de marchander
> Et en biens superabonder. »

*C*es vers d'un notaire de Laval, composés au lendemain de la guerre
de Cent Ans, traduisent bien les sentiments de ceux qui ont vécu la
convalescence du royaume de France. Tandis que les campagnes rever-
dissent, que la fécondité des couples repeuple les berceaux, le renouveau
des affaires trace les voies de nouvelles aventures et enrichit ceux qui
savent saisir les opportunités de cette renaissance. Le goût de la vie saisit
alors tous ceux qui ont eu la bonne fortune de survivre au temps des
désastres.

La « copiosité du populaire »

Vers 1440, dans la plupart des régions françaises, s'amorce, après
le temps des malheurs, celui de la convalescence. Déprimée depuis le
milieu du XIVe siècle, la conjoncture tressaille, annonçant l'aube d'une
renaissance. À la base de cet élan, on trouve, comme souvent, la
fécondité des hommes, qui aboutit bientôt à une véritable explosion
des naissances. En 1519, au terme de ce mouvement, Claude de Seyssel écrit dans sa *Grande Monarchie de France* : « par les champs

aussi, on connaît bien évidemment la copiosité du populaire, parce que plusieurs lieux et grandes contrées qui souloient être incultes ou en friches ou en bois, à présent sont tous cultivés et habités de villages et de maisons ».

Nombreux sont en effet les villages qui ont vu leur population quintupler en l'espace d'un demi-siècle. Le Bos, en Normandie, comptait 22 habitants jouissant de droits de pâturage en 1444-1445, 77 en 1459-1460, 102 en 1495-1496. En Barrois, Colombey-lès-Choiseul abritait 35 familles en 1444, 104 en 1485. En région lyonnaise, vers 1410, le nombre moyen d'enfants par ménage s'élevait à 1,3. Entre 1470 et 1480, il atteint 5,1. À Figeac, les familles de laboureurs comptent en moyenne 4,8 enfants vivants. Dans le Quercy, certaines familles rurales atteignent 7 et 9 enfants.

Si les épidémies n'ont pas capitulé, leur pression se relâche. La peste, désormais, ne s'étend plus au royaume tout entier, limitant ses ravages à une ou deux provinces. À Cambrai, le nombre de sépultures creusées pour les pauvres ne dépasse qu'une fois la normale entre 1440 et 1470, contre quatre fois de 1410 à 1440. En Bretagne, de 1460 à 1520, deux années seulement, 1472 et 1483, enregistrent une poussée de la mortalité. Autre grande pourvoyeuse des cimetières, la guerre disparaît, les combats se déroulant désormais à l'extérieur du royaume. Presque partout aussi, les disettes cessent leurs funèbres fauchaisons. De 1465 à 1527, le pays nantais n'enregistre qu'une seule récolte déficitaire, en 1472. Le Cambrésis, entre 1439 et 1523, subit une seule disette sérieuse, en 1492. Sans disparaître, les obsessions relatives à la mort cessent d'occuper pour un temps les esprits.

Multipliées, les populations deviennent aussi remuantes, la France étant alors sillonnée de migrants à la recherche de terres prometteuses. Abandonnés à la suite des guerres anglaises, de nombreux villages de Gironde sont repeuplés par des familles de Saintongeais, d'Angoumois, de Poitevins, des *gabaïs*, ou gavaches, qui garderont longtemps leur originalité et implanteront la langue d'oïl en pays d'oc. Vers 1440, le village de Sépeaux, près de Sens, n'avait plus ni curé ni paroissiens. Cinquante ans plus tard, on y compte 80 ménages de Bretons, de Limousins et de Tourangeaux. À Marolles-en-Hurepoix, en 1475, un tiers au moins de la population était d'origine extérieure. En Poitou-Charentes, sur les terres du chapitre cathédral de Limoges, en 1476, 26 des 33 familles de 1402 avaient disparu au profit des nouveaux arrivants.

Dans une large mesure, les seigneurs du sol ont pris l'initiative de ces repeuplements. Dès 1408, le vicomte de Limoges fait proclamer que ceux qui viendront s'installer en pays d'Ans, au nord-est de Périgueux, seront exempts de tout impôt pendant quatre ans. À Bagneux, Athis-Mons et Sucy-en-Brie, les redevances en nature sont remplacées par un cens en argent moins élevé et plus précis. En 1447, 1450 et 1455, des ordonnances de Charles VII prescrivent la réfection du bornage des terres et accordent aux seigneurs le pouvoir de donner à bail à de nouveaux tenanciers les terres abandonnées par ceux qui ont « déguerpi ». On imagine mal en effet l'imbroglio juridique provoqué par les guerres, les épidémies, les départs précipités et les fuites devant l'impôt. Comment repeupler en ménageant les droits de ceux qui ont, provisoirement peut-être, disparu ? Sur les terres de l'abbé de Saint-Denis, si un an après quatre « criées » espacées d'une quinzaine de jours, l'ancien tenancier ne s'était pas manifesté, le seigneur pouvait concéder de nouveau les tenures non réclamées. On ne sait pas très bien comment a circulé l'information auprès des populations intéressées. Toujours est-il que cette « propagande » a bien fonctionné. En Provence, des « actes d'habitation » conclus entre les seigneurs et des groupes de « forains » permettent le repeuplement des sites abandonnés. La plupart du temps, moyennant la promesse d'y habiter « à perpétuité », les nouveaux venus obtiennent des garanties et des avantages financiers, des services agricoles et militaires réduits et le droit de s'organiser en communauté, avec syndic et conseillers. Sur l'ensemble de la France, vers 1480, les campagnes apparaissent alors aussi surpeuplées qu'elles l'avaient été au début du XIVe siècle et peuvent à nouveau envoyer des hommes vers les villes.

Vers 1440, en effet, les villes se plaignaient d'être « dépopulées ». À Paris, entre 1420 et 1440, sur le pont Notre-Dame, centre névralgique de la richesse marchande, une maison sur trois était abandonnée, un tiers de la superficie de l'île de la Cité était couvert de terrains vagues et la plupart des immeubles avaient vu leur valeur locative s'effondrer de 90 % ! À Amiens, vers 1410, on trouvait encore trace des destructions commises par les troupes navarraises en 1358. Un peu partout, la nature sauvage avait repris ses droits, les loups venant rôder jusqu'aux portes des cités.

Mais là comme dans les campagnes, s'amorce aux alentours de 1450 le temps de la convalescence. Annecy retrouve en 1475 sa population de 1339. À Dieppe, le nombre de contribuables double de 1452 à 1491. Périgueux connaît une ascension fulgurante sous la pression des familles nouvelles qui, en 1490, représentent 67 % de l'accroissement total de la population. À Arles, on compte, en 1438, 66 % de noms nouveaux par rapport au total de 1319. Une génération seulement après la fin de la guerre de Cent Ans, la France apparaissait de nouveau « pleine ». Effondrée au niveau de 10 millions d'habitants vers 1440, la population du royaume s'élançait alors vers les 20 millions atteints un siècle plus tard.

La restauration des campagnes

L'agriculture s'employa de son mieux pour nourrir les bouches nouvelles engendrées par la fécondité retrouvée du peuple de France. Vers 1450, toutes les campagnes enregistraient un fléchissement catastrophique de leur production. Au cœur de la guerre, la riche Île-de-France avait été frappée de plein fouet. Thomas Basin, l'auteur d'une *Histoire de Charles VII*, écrivait alors, en exagérant sans doute : « Nous-mêmes avons vu les vastes plaines de la Champagne, de la Beauce, de la Brie, du Gâtinais, du pays de Chartres, du pays de Dreux, du Maine, du Perche, du Vexin, tant français que normand, du Beauvaisis, du pays de Caux depuis la Seine jusque vers Amiens et Abbeville, du pays de Senlis, du Soissonnais et du Valois jusqu'à Laon, et au-delà du côté du Hainaut, absolument désertes, incultes, abandonnées, vides d'habitants, couvertes de broussailles et de ronces, ou bien dans la plupart des régions qui produisent les arbres les plus drus, ceux-ci pousser en épaisses forêts. »

Un demi-siècle plus tard, en revanche, différents indices suggèrent l'existence d'une paysannerie bien nourrie, pourvue de terres, mieux outillée et disposant d'un cheptel plus abondant. Même si le tableau ne doit pas être enjolivé, les cicatrices qu'avaient ouvertes les malheurs des temps semblent bien avoir été cicatrisées.

Pour ce faire, il a suffi, dans un premier temps, probablement sous l'aiguillon de la nécessité, de remettre en culture les terres qui avaient été abandonnées. À la ville comme à la campagne, le pain quotidien est ainsi mieux assuré et quand les récoltes sont mauvaises, elles n'entraînent au pire qu'une pénurie passagère et supportable. En l'espace de deux générations, la ration alimentaire se trouve bouleversée. À Carpentras, la consommation de viande par tête s'accroît de 30 % entre 1400 et 1473. À cette date, l'habitant de la cité absorbe 26 kilogrammes de viande de boucherie, salaisons exceptées, ce qui est supérieur aux chiffres du XIXe siècle.

Sous la pression aussi d'une demande urbaine excitée par le repeuplement, se développe le vignoble aux alentours des grands marchés de consommation et près des ports exportateurs. À Nantes, les exportations de la production régionale s'établissaient autour de 1 000 à 1 500 tonneaux par an vers 1350. Elles s'étaient effondrées à 300

tonneaux vers 1450. Elles atteignent entre 10 000 et 12 000 tonneaux
un siècle plus tard. Bordeaux, en contrepartie, trop lié au débouché
anglais, n'expédie plus que le cinquième des 80 000 tonneaux qu'il
expédiait pendant les années fastes du XIVᵉ siècle.

L'élevage, toutefois, que l'extension des friches avait développé,
est sacrifié au blé. Concurrent malchanceux de l'agriculture, il est
réduit à la portion congrue. Quelques règlements ont beau tenter de
garantir au bétail quelques étendues herbeuses, la plupart des troupeaux doivent se réfugier, faute de mieux, dans les bois et brouter
l'herbe des clairières. Ainsi manque le fumier, seul capable d'accroître
la productivité céréalière. C'est le cercle vicieux de l'agriculture
ancienne dont commencent à s'extraire, à la même époque, les Flamands ou les Anglais.

Dans les villages, les dividendes de la croissance retrouvée ont
été aussi mieux distribués. Dans l'ensemble, on vit plus à l'aise sur
des exploitations moins menues. Dans l'ensemble aussi, le servage,
quand il existait encore, est devenu un objet de musée. Si les seigneurs
sont encore puissants, ils ont dû lâcher du lest pour pouvoir encore
boire le vin de leurs vignes et vivre de leurs biens. Contraints et forcés,
ils ont allégé les charges pesant sur les tenures, réduit les cens, diminué les champarts, transformé les prélèvements sur les récoltes au
profit d'une redevance en argent, concédé des baux de longue durée,
parfois, comme en Sologne, sur deux ou trois vies. En Provence, à la
fin du règne de Charles VII, il est rare qu'un propriétaire obtienne de
son fermier le quart de la récolte en céréales. Quant au preneur d'un
troupeau de moutons, il réclame souvent plus de la moitié des produits
en laine et en fromages avec, au terme du bail, la pleine propriété de
la moitié du troupeau.

En Bourgogne, les microexploitations paysannes de 4 à 5 journaux (2 hectares) font place à des exploitations plus confortables de
10 à 20 journaux. En Languedoc, se multiplient des exploitations
moyennes qui peuvent devenir des « entreprises » plus productives.
Dans le Toulousain comme dans le Maine, se généralisent les « bordes » et les « métairies » dont l'étendue suffit pour nourrir honnêtement une famille. Et, du moins jusqu'aux années 1480, la main-
d'œuvre agricole est mieux rémunérée. En Languedoc, à cette date, le
moissonneur prélève plus que le décimateur. Pour obtenir un hectolitre
de froment, un faucheur d'avoine cambrésien doit travailler sur
2,65 ha de 1466 à 1476, au lieu de 2,85 de 1402 à 1406.

À l'époque où Fortescue, un voyageur anglais, voit « les gens du
peuple de France » vivre « dans une extrême misère » alors qu'ils
« habitent le plus fertile royaume du monde », Jean Vilain, tanneur de

Villepreux, près de Paris, peut, en 1483, doter sa fille d'« un lit garni de huit draps et une couverture, d'une demi-douzaine de couvre-chefs et de deux oreillers, de deux nappes, quatre serviettes et un coffre pour les mettre, de trois paires de robes, deux fourrées et une qui ne l'était point, deux chaperons et une ceinture ferrée d'argent et quarante livres tournois, avec le droit de demeurer toute sa vie dans une maison qu'il lui concède ».

La réalité, comme souvent, devait être à mi-chemin. S'il existait encore de nombreux miséreux dans la France convalescente que parcourait le visiteur anglais, la plupart des paysans vivaient à cette époque, sans le savoir, comme toujours, un petit « âge d'or ».

Le réveil du commerce

En partie nourri par la restauration des campagnes, le réveil du commerce est toutefois largement tributaire des nouveaux centres nerveux de l'économie européenne. Tandis que la Bretagne, le Forez et les villes du Languedoc méditerranéen entrent en stagnation, Nantes, Dieppe, Rouen, Poitiers, Tours, Bourges et surtout Lyon deviennent les têtes de pont de nouveaux espaces économiques.

Institué en 1420 par Charles VII pour faire pièce à Genève, allongé en 1444, le cycle des foires de Lyon est animé, à partir de 1460, par l'installation des banquiers italiens, en particulier des Médicis qui, en 1466, y transfèrent leur succursale de Genève.

La ville qui, entre le milieu et la fin du XVe siècle, a vu sa population doubler, attirait pour l'Épiphanie, à Pâques, à la mi-août et à la Toussaint des marchands qu'alimentaient les artisans d'un arrière-pays élargi, les tanneurs et les pelletiers des centres auvergnats, les chapeliers du Puy, les papetiers d'Ambert, de Vienne et du Comtat. Au carrefour des routes qui conduisaient aux régions motrices de l'économie européenne, les cités italiennes, les villes de l'Allemagne du sud et des Pays-Bas, Lyon devenait l'un des plus grands marchés de tissus européens et l'une des capitales financières de l'Europe.

En Normandie, après une longue période de stagnation, l'ancienne draperie urbaine connaît un nouvel essor et Rouen devient le plus grand centre bonnetier d'Europe. Entre 1460 et 1483, le nombre des orfèvres, souvent d'origine allemande, triple à Tours qui abrite aussi une cinquantaine d'ateliers d'armuriers. Au sud, Toulouse anime un riche marché agricole et à Bourges, un « homme sans littérature, mais très intelligent, d'un esprit ouvert et industrieux pour les affaires », prend une devise qui résume son esprit d'entreprise : « À vaillants cœurs rien impossible ».

Fils d'un pelletier aisé, né entre 1395 et 1400, Jacques Cœur est celui qui symbolise le mieux cette génération de marchands dont les vastes projets et les spéculations hasardeuses ont replacé le royaume dans les circuits du grand commerce international. Poursuivi puis gracié en 1429 pour avoir fabriqué à Bourges des pièces de mauvais aloi, il part, en 1432, acheter des épices au Levant sur un bateau affrété par des marchands narbonnais. Au retour, victime d'un naufrage au large des côtes de Calvi, il est dépouillé « jusqu'à la chemise » par les Corses. Malgré cette mésaventure, il entretient l'ambition de développer le commerce entre la France et l'Orient et s'emploie à concurrencer les Italiens sur leur terrain de prédilection.

Devenu en 1438 argentier du roi, il est chargé de veiller à l'entretien quotidien du souverain, de sa famille et de sa cour et tient, à Tours, un magasin d'étoffes, de bijoux, de meubles, de fourrures où ses riches clients viennent acquérir plumes d'autruche et armures de luxe. C'est le point de départ de la construction d'un empire qui va faire d'un modeste spéculateur un homme d'affaires international.

Installant des « facteurs » à Bruges, en Aragon, en Italie, à Genève, en Angleterre et dans toutes les villes du royaume, créant sa propre flotte, faisant de Montpellier puis de Marseille le centre de ses opérations maritimes, il exporte en Orient les denrées occidentales et en rapporte les étoffes précieuses, les tapis de la Perse, les parfums d'Arabie, les épices et les porcelaines de l'Extrême-Orient. Partant du Languedoc, ses galées, par Nice, Naples et Palerme, rejoignent l'île de Rhodes, pivot de son commerce au Levant. De là, elles gagnent Beyrouth, Damas et Alexandrie, têtes de ligne des caravanes orientales et relais vers le golfe Persique ou la mer Rouge. Par la Catalogne, Valence et les Baléares, ses capitaines atteignent le Maghreb. En même temps, ils assurent le transport de passagers chrétiens et musulmans et se livrent aussi à la traite des esclaves.

L'Argenterie ouvre aussi à Jacques Cœur la voie des grandes manœuvres financières. En 1441, il est chargé de négocier le montant de l'impôt avec les états du Languedoc et se fait verser des « épices », c'est-à-dire des pots-de-vin, pour que la région bénéficie de réductions d'impôts. Visiteur des gabelles, il fait voyager son sel en exemption de droits, le faisant passer pour celui du roi. La gabelle étant remboursée dans le cas de naufrage des bateaux, il se fait octroyer des indemnités pour des pertes imaginaires. Mais comment la monarchie pourrait-elle se passer d'un banquier qui procure des liquidités au

Trésor, finance la campagne de Normandie, avance 40 000 livres pour la prise de Cherbourg et 70 000 pour la campagne de Guyenne ?

Ayant compris l'importance de la circulation monétaire, il acquiert en Beaujolais et en Lyonnais des mines de plomb argentifère pour l'exploitation desquelles il fait appel à des spécialistes suisses et allemands. Homme de son temps, il est sensible aussi au prestige social que procure la terre et achète de nombreuses seigneuries rurales en Berry avec d'importants châteaux, en Bourbonnais et en Beaujolais. À Bourges, il fait construire un somptueux palais dans lequel il investit l'équivalent du salaire de quarante manœuvres pendant un siècle. Anobli en 1441, l'argentier obtient l'évêché de Luçon pour son frère et le siège archiépiscopal de Bourges pour son fils Jean.

Mais Jacques Cœur a fait trop d'envieux parmi ses débiteurs. Arrêté en 1451, il est accusé par le sire de Mortagne-sur-Gironde et sa femme, qui avaient dû lui abandonner deux seigneuries, d'avoir empoisonné celle qui était sa meilleure cliente, Agnès Sorel ! Même si cette calomnie ne peut être retenue, on trouve assez de chefs d'accusation pour le condamner en 1453 à la confiscation de ses biens, au bannissement perpétuel, à une restitution de 100 000 écus et à une amende de 300 000 pour avoir vendu des armes aux infidèles et détourné le produit des impôts pendant ses missions en Languedoc. Évadé à la fin de 1454 du château de Poitiers dans lequel il était en détention, il prend le commandement militaire d'une croisade contre les Turcs et meurt à Chio, le 25 novembre 1456, en combattant ceux avec lesquels il avait fait du commerce toute sa vie. Son principal adjoint, Guillaume de Varye, directeur de l'Argenterie sous Louis XI, saura toutefois faire vivre après sa mort les ambitions et les entreprises de son maître.

Le premier humanisme français

Homme hors du commun même s'il reste surtout homme de son temps, personnalité brillante, aventurier de l'argent, Jacques Cœur ressemble à ces marchands italiens ou allemands qui croient à l'organisation et à la méthode, au calcul et au raisonnement, et considèrent l'accroissement de la richesse comme le but de l'existence. Comme les condottieri qui gèrent les guerres comme des chefs d'entreprise et écrivent que « celui qui se glorifie des exploits de ses ancêtres s'enlève à lui-même mérite et honneur », il trace les voies d'une réussite individuelle qui place l'homme et son destin au centre du monde.

Ce n'est pas un hasard si, dans les villes où s'ancrent ces nouvelles fortunes, se multiplient alors les horloges qui permettent à chacun de mesurer le temps. Déjà, en 1393, les vignerons d'Auxerre refusaient de travailler du lever au coucher du soleil comme l'exigeaient leurs employeurs et débrayaient à l'heure de none sonnée par les cloches de la cathédrale, soit à trois heures de l'après-midi. À Saint-Nizier, en 1481, on réclame l'installation d'une horloge sur le clocher de l'église car, « si une telle horloge était faite, davantage de marchands viendraient aux foires, les citoyens seraient grandement consolés et joyeux et voudraient vivre d'une vie plus ordonnée ». Et si Rabelais fait dire à Gargantua que « jamais ne me suis assujetti à l'heure », c'est pour exprimer le refus des nouvelles contraintes imposées par les heures mécaniques de la nouvelle « civilisation » urbaine, une civilisation où les marchands tiennent la mesure du temps pour l'élément fondamental de la discipline et les palais qu'ils construisent pour l'affirmation ostentatoire de leur bonne fortune.

Le palais de Jacques Cœur, à Bourges, en est une exemplaire illustration. Si l'architecture évoque les châteaux princiers, en particulier ceux du duc de Berry, la disposition rationnelle et commode des pièces manifeste l'esprit pratique et le goût du confort de son propriétaire. Les miniatures et les tableaux des maîtres flamands nous font découvrir les signes de cette opulence, les parquets et les tapis, les meubles sculptés et les candélabres de fer, les plafonds peints et les bassins de cuivre, les coffres couverts de cuir et les murs lambrissés.

Parvenus mais aussi mécènes, les propriétaires de ces riches demeures veulent contribuer à l'embellissement de leurs cités. Au Puy, un marchand du Cantal, marié « pauvrettement », utilise sa fortune naissante à faire voûter l'église Saint-Hilaire. Dans les couvents des mendiants, les Frères succombent à la mode du temps et concèdent à ces mécènes impatients l'espace des chapelles pour qu'ils les ornent de verrières et de retables.

Ce goût nouveau pour le beau et l'antique qui se lit dans la mythologie des grandes tapisseries, du *Roman de Troie* aux Travaux d'Hercule, dessine les sentiers d'un humanisme français qui ne cherche pas ses modèles en Italie. En 1470, la première presse à imprimer, mise au point par Gutenberg, est installée dans la bibliothèque du collège de la Sorbonne par Guillaume Fichet, un Savoyard érudit, et Jean Heynlin, un Allemand. Très vite, la capitale possède un très grand nombre d'ateliers. Dès 1473, on imprime aussi à Lyon, puis, avant 1476, à Toulouse.

Dans une lettre qu'il écrit en 1472 à Robert Gaguin, général de l'ordre des Mathurins, Guillaume Fichet annonce cet humanisme naissant qui puise son inspiration dans la culture classique : « Je ressens la plus grande satisfaction, très érudit Robert, en voyant fleurir dans cette ville [Paris] qui les ignorait jadis, les compositions poétiques et toutes les parties de l'éloquence. Car lorsque je quittai pour la première fois le pays de Baux dans mes jeunes années, afin de venir à Paris étudier la science d'Aristote, je m'étonnais beaucoup de ne trouver que si rarement dans Paris tout entier un orateur ou un poète. Personne n'étudiait nuit et jour Cicéron, comme la plupart le font aujourd'hui, personne ne savait faire un vers correct, personne ne rajeunissait dans ses vers les fictions d'autrui, car l'école parisienne, déshabituée de la latinité, était à peine sortie de l'ignorance en tout discours. Mais de nos jours date une meilleure époque. »

À cette même époque, sous le pinceau de Jean Fouquet, perce aussi la Renaissance d'une peinture « à la française » qui emprunte au Nord et au Midi pour donner de l'homme une vision qui ne soit pas importée et développer un art de la mesure qui peut s'épanouir sans renier les traditions dans lesquelles il s'inscrit. Dans le *Diptyque de Melun* et le *Livre d'heures*, commandés par Étienne Chevalier, maître des comptes puis trésorier du roi, Jean Fouquet intègre les leçons de l'Italie et les procédés des maîtres flamands mais développe toutefois un art original capable d'influencer les autres. Il introduit ainsi en Italie, qui ne le connaissait pas, le portrait à mi-corps avec représentation du visage de trois quarts. Le temps de la convalescence précède de peu celui de la Renaissance.

38

L'« universelle araigne »

Aux environs du 25 juillet 1461, établi à Genappe, au sud de Bruxelles, le dauphin Louis apprend la nouvelle que son père Charles le « Bien servi » est mort le 22 juillet, convaincu que son fils l'a fait empoisonner. Louis le Onzième qui, selon les témoins, se « languissait en l'attente de l'heure promise », devenait enfin roi de France, à l'âge avancé de trente-huit ans. Ni beau, ni aimable, mais d'une intelligence exceptionnelle, il fut pour ses ennemis l'« universelle araigne » tendue vers un seul but, se faire obéir et fortifier son royaume. « Je suis la France », disait celui qui, contemporain de Machiavel, pensait certainement que le Prince devait « savoir bien user de la bête et de l'homme, être renard pour connaître les rets et lion pour effrayer les loups ».

Un personnage « ondoyant et divers »

À trente-huit ans — jamais depuis l'avènement d'Hugues Capet aucun roi de France n'était monté sur le trône à un âge aussi avancé —, Louis XI n'était pas un bel homme. Le poète breton Meschinot, qui le détestait, l'a dépeint en deux vers dans *Les Lunettes des princes* :

« Tu n'es pas tellement beau, agréable à voir, joli,
Ni par des joyaux tellement embelli. »

Thomas Basin nous assure qu'« avec ses cuisses et ses jambes fluettes, [il] n'avait de prime abord rien de beau ni d'agréable ».

421

Un dessin le représente alors, le nez à la courbure bossuée, les cheveux coupés à la mode monacale de la cour de Bourgogne, le visage pensif, les sourcils arqués, le regard aigu, l'expression un peu triste. La bouche, petite et bien dessinée, esquisse une légère moue. Le menton est rond et proéminent. Les joues, pleines mais ni rebondies ni tombantes, donnent au visage une apparence volontaire.

D'un aspect moins ingrat que son père, Louis XI manquait incontestablement de prestance. Contrairement aux Valois, il n'avait aucun goût du faste. Certes, à l'occasion, il savait s'habiller en roi, se vêtir de drap de damas blanc à gros boutons d'or, se faire couper par le tailleur du roi de Sicile un pourpoint dans une toile de coton à poil feutré, parfumer ses vêtements de poudre de violette et envoyer des cavaliers quérir des roses et des boutons à Provins mais, la plupart du temps, il s'habillait très simplement et se coiffait d'un mauvais chapeau de pèlerin, orné seulement d'une médaille sainte en plomb.

Grand voyageur et infatigable chasseur, le roi mettait sa coquetterie dans les soins de propreté et préférait pour leur commodité les « courts habits », pourpoint tombant à mi-cuisses, chausses et bottines. Comme il entrait à Abbeville, en compagnie du fastueux duc de Bourgogne, raconte Georges Chastellain, des simples gens qui n'avaient jamais vu le roi auraient dit tout haut :

« Benedicite ! Est-ce là un roy de France, le plus grand roy du monde ? Tout ne vaut pas vingt francs, cheval et habillement de son corps. »

Un état de santé précaire explique sans doute en partie cette apparence peu flatteuse. Peu de princes endurèrent en effet autant de maux. Très tôt, il souffrit d'hémorroïdes au point qu'il ne pouvait, en 1467, recevoir des ambassadeurs, ce qui l'amena à consulter le « spécialiste » Giammateo Ferrari de Grado, professeur à l'université de Pavie, qui lui prescrivit bains de siège et applications de pierres de jaspe. Troubles du foie et de la rate s'ajoutaient à une maladie de la peau, sans doute une dermatose, qu'il combattait par la consommation de fromages frais et de médicaments à base de pois. On soignait ses accidents hépatiques par l'emploi de la fumeterre, du houblon et de l'eau de rose tandis que, contre les douleurs gastriques, on faisait boulanger son pain avec du blé de Nîmes et de l'« eau hysope », une plante sensée guérir aussi bien les maux d'estomac que ceux du poumon, l'hydropisie que le mal de dents ! Louis suivait aussi toutes les prescriptions destinées à combattre l'épilepsie, une maladie alors considérée comme honteuse et dont il était peut-être atteint. Pour éviter « le mauvais air », il faisait placer dans ses appartements des roses, du « coq-menthe », sorte de chrysanthème, de la marjolaine et du romarin, des violettes et des églantines. Pour se « garder du sommeil », des bergers venus du Poitou lui jouaient dans le château qu'il se fit construire à Plessis-lès-Tours des airs mélodieux. Pour se préserver des refroidissements ou des insolations, il portait « toques doubles », longs bonnets et chapeaux à large bord tandis que, pour dormir la tête haute, il faisait placer derrière son lit un dossier de bois et remplaçait l'oreiller par « un gros coussin plein de coton ».

Cependant, note l'ambassadeur Panigarola, « sa personne est capable des plus durs travaux, qualité qui lui aide beaucoup ». Jamais roi ne voyagea autant. « Nul homme, écrivait Commynes, ne prêta jamais tant l'oreille aux gens, ni ne s'enquit de tant de choses. » Ses lettres, ses comptes, les chroniques, les dépêches nous le montrent en perpétuel voyage, les ambassadeurs étrangers ayant ordre de le voir devant quelquefois traverser la France entière avant d'obtenir un entretien.

On peut en prendre la mesure en le suivant au cours de l'année 1463. Selon Pierre-Roger Gaussin, le meilleur biographe de Louis XI, le 1er janvier, il est à Poitiers. Le 3, il visite le sanctuaire de la Vierge à Celles, à 50 kilomètres de Poitiers. Le 9, il vénère à Saintes les reliques de saint Eutrope. De là, il gagne le 11 janvier La Rochelle où il rencontre sa mère Marie d'Anjou, de retour de Compostelle. Il arrive le 16 à Soulac, après avoir traversé en barque l'estuaire de la Gironde, et fait ses dévotions dans l'abbaye bénédictine de Notre-Dame-de-la-Fin-des-Terres, un des grands pèlerinages de Guyenne. Le 19, il est à Castelnau-de-Médoc et y reçoit un envoyé du roi de Castille. À partir du 25 janvier, il séjourne un mois à Bordeaux. Le 23 février, il arrive à Tartas et le 28 à Dax, où il demeure trois semaines. Le 23 mars, il est à Bayonne et passe Pâques à Ustaritz, où il rencontre la reine d'Aragon. Le 28 avril, il a une entrevue peu cordiale avec le roi de Castille près d'Urtubie. Entre le 30 avril et le 11 mai, il séjourne à Saint-Jean-de-Luz d'où il s'occupe activement du rachat des villes de la Somme. Après Sorde-l'Abbaye, il s'arrête à Sauveterre-de-Béarn où Gaston comte de Foix le reçoit somptueusement. Par Lescar, Pau et Morlaas, le roi gagne alors Tarbes, arrive à Saint-Gaudens, puis à Saint-Martory, pour être à Muret le 23 mai, d'où il s'occupe d'affaires religieuses et commande des travaux pour son château d'Amboise. Le 26 mai, il fait une entrée solennelle à Toulouse, ravagée, quelques jours auparavant, par un gigantesque incendie. Louis XI y demeure trois semaines, participe, le 9 juin, à la procession de la Fête-Dieu et, sans doute ému par les malheurs de la cité, l'exempte de la taille pendant cent ans. Puis, après avoir convoqué les états du Languedoc à Montpellier pour le 30 juillet, il part pour Buzet et Gaillac, gagne le 20 juin Villefranche-de-Rouergue, puis Figeac où les habitants l'ac-clament bruyamment. De là, il se rend le 21 en pèlerinage à Rocama-dour pour honorer la Vierge noire. Quelques jours plus tard, le 27 juin, il fait son entrée à Brive-la-Gaillarde avant de gagner Uzerche.

Par Boisseuil, il arrive le 1er juillet à Limoges et y vénère les reliques de saint Martial. Le 3, il se trouve à Saint-Junien puis part pour Lussac-les-Châteaux. Il y fait halte puis arrive le 12 juillet à Amboise, où il demeure trois semaines, le temps de surveiller les tra-vaux poursuivis au château, de faire fortifier le donjon, de commencer l'édification de la chapelle Saint-Blaise et de l'aile dite des « sept Vertus » et... de faire un enfant à la reine Charlotte. Ce fut Jeanne de France, qui naquit en mai 1464.

Après avoir, le 2 août, reçu une ambassade catalane, il repart pour Alluyes, où il se trouve le 4 août. À Chartres, il passe une dizaine de jours, coupés d'une excursion à Meslay-le-Vidame. Puis, par Dour-dan et Montlhéry, il entre le 20 août à Paris et n'y demeure qu'une semaine. Le 31, il gagne le port de Chatou, puis Poissy, avant d'at-teindre Pontoise le 5 septembre. Sans doute se rend-il à l'église Notre-Dame-de-la-Santé dont le pèlerinage était le 8 septembre.

De Pontoise, il revient à Poissy puis part en direction du Vexin et du pays de Caux vers Gisors. Le 20, il prescrit à Gaillefontaine de procéder à la vérification des monnaies du Dauphiné, se trouve, le 21, à l'abbaye de Foucarmont, le 22 à Blangy et le 25 septembre à Eu. Le 27, il arrive à Abbeville, où les magistrats, les bourgeois en armes, les enfants et le clergé, avec la châsse de Saint-Vulfran, l'attendent à la porte de la ville. Les rues sont jonchées de feuillages et de fleurs, les façades des maisons tendues de tapisseries et, en plusieurs places et carrefours, on joue des mystères. Place Saint-Pierre, on lui offre trois bœufs gras, trois muids d'avoine, trois muids de vin de Beaune et un fromage du Marquenterre.

Puis il gagne Hesdin, en Artois, où le duc de Bourgogne lui offre une « hospitalité somptueuse ». Il y procède à la ratification de l'ac-cord de rachat de la Picardie et reçoit les ambassadeurs anglais, avec lesquels il signe une trêve. Le 22 octobre, il reprend la route, se rend à Rue où il va prier dans la chapelle du Saint-Esprit, devant le crucifix très vénéré qu'on disait avoir été découvert dans une barque vers 1100. Puis on le voit à Caours, près d'Abbeville, où il offre au sanctuaire de Notre-Dame de l'Orée un calice et un tableau qui le représente en prière devant la Vierge, et sur lequel on pouvait lire ces vers :

« Louis, par la grâce de Dieu,
Noble roi de tous les Français,

Vint visiter ce digne lieu
L'an mil quatre cent soixante trois. »

Entre le 26 et le 31 octobre, on le trouve à Neufchâtel-en-Bray. Le 6 novembre, il est à Dieppe, puis, par Eu, regagne Abbeville où, le 21 novembre, il reçoit les envoyés des cantons suisses venus le supplier de permettre à ses sujets de fréquenter les foires de Genève. Puis, le 4 décembre, il est au Crotoy, sur la baie de Somme, et à Eu de nouveau le 11. Le 18 décembre, il est à l'abbaye de Saint-Riquier, le 21 à Nouvion où il s'occupe des affaires de Gênes, invitant le duc de Milan, François Sforza, à occuper la ville. Le 25 décembre, il célèbre Noël à Abbeville où il se préoccupe d'abolir la pragmatique sanction.

Au cours de cette année 1463, qui fut marquée, selon la chronique, par un « hiver court sans être froid, un été long, une récolte de vin abondante et de qualité, des moissons sans grande abondance », compensées par une pêche maritime « fort fructueuse », Louis XI avait parcouru du Centre au Sud et du Midi au Nord, le plus souvent sur une mule, environ 2 800 kilomètres et avait été reçu et acclamé dans une cinquantaine de villes et de bourgades.

C'est que, aimant les « bains de foule », il se plaisait davantage avec les gens du peuple et les bourgeois qu'avec les seigneurs de la cour. D'une adresse remarquable, il ne participa pourtant jamais à un tournoi car il n'appréciait guère les exercices de parade. Tenu pour le plus grand veneur de son temps, il ne s'entourait à la chasse que de gens adroits et endurants, capables de le suivre pendant plusieurs jours, sans se soucier du gîte et de la nourriture. À sa cour, à laquelle il ne s'intéressait guère, les jeunes gens et les dames s'ennuyaient à mourir. Dans les villes où il passait, il logeait chez un bourgeois ou un fonctionnaire. Pour éviter les harangues et les réceptions, il arrivait à l'improviste par quelque petite ruelle et, s'il devait subir une « entrée » solennelle, demandait au moins à « n'estre pas reçu trop grandement ».

Aussi pieux que superstitieux, prodigue qu'avare, entreprenant que timide, clément que sévère, fidèle que parjure, novateur que traditionaliste, Louis XI fut en fait un personnage indescriptible, à l'image de cette maxime de Montaigne : « L'homme est un être ondoyant et divers. »

Une jeunesse rebelle

Quand il se précipite à Reims pour y être sacré, le 15 août 1461, Louis a déjà une solide expérience qu'une jeunesse solitaire a longuement forgée. Sa naissance, le 3 juillet 1423, dans le palais archiépiscopal de Bourges, fut un événement politique, Charles VII, alors âgé de vingt ans, n'étant pas sacré et sa légitimité étant contestée. Les lettres que le « gentil dauphin » envoya aux bonnes villes furent conservées soigneusement par les secrétaires de la chancellerie royale comme un modèle de faire-part. Apprenant la nouvelle, les bourgeois de Tournai firent allumer des feux de joie et les astrologues consultés, restés vagues dans leurs prédictions, affirmèrent prudemment que sa vieillesse serait plus heureuse que sa jeunesse !

L'enfant grandit, transplanté de résidence en résidence, privé de distractions, souvent séparé des « Grands » et de ses parents, la reine, toujours en couches, ayant mis au monde douze enfants, dont cinq seulement arrivèrent à l'âge adulte. À l'âge de dix ans, il apparaissait à Jean Jouvenel des Ursins, évêque de Beauvais, comme un enfant « sage et bien morigéné », capable de lire et d'écrire le latin, ce qui lui assura par la suite une réelle supériorité sur bien des princes. Ce fut Guillaume d'Avaugour, le bailli de Touraine, qui lui enseigna à monter à cheval, à tirer à l'arc, à manier l'épée et la lance. Le 23 juin 1436, on lui fit épouser Marguerite d'Écosse dont la main était sollicitée par Henri VI, le roi d'Angleterre. Elle mourra huit ans plus tard d'une maladie de langueur en murmurant : « Fi de la vie de ce monde, et ne m'en parlez plus, et plus qu'autre chose m'ennuie. »

À l'âge de seize ans, il fait ses débuts dans l'action politique en étant nommé lieutenant-général du Languedoc, avec pour mission de ramener la paix dans une région dévastée par les routiers et les seigneurs pillards. En 1439, il s'allie aux princes révoltés contre son père et participe à la Praguerie. Quand, le 15 juillet 1440, Charles VII lui déclare que les seigneurs rebelles et vaincus ne pourront plus reparaître à la cour, il s'écrie : « Monseigneur, il faut donc que je m'en retourne car ainsi je leur ai promis. » À quoi le roi répond : « Louis, les portes sont ouvertes. S'il vous plaît de vous en aller, allez-vous en, car au bon plaisir de Dieu, nous trouverons certains de notre sang qui nous aideront mieux que jamais vous ne l'avez fait jusqu'à présent. »

Réconcilié du bout des lèvres avec son père, il démontre ses capacités militaires en prenant d'assaut la ville de Dieppe en 1443 et en conduisant en Suisse une marée de milliers d'écorcheurs. Mais devenu tout à fait odieux, détestant Agnès Sorel et les conseillers qu'elle a placés auprès de son père, il est exilé en Dauphiné et quitte la cour le 1er janvier 1447.

De 1447 à 1456, « roi » en son Dauphiné, il fait de cette province jusqu'alors délaissée un État moderne, imposant l'hommage aux seigneurs et aux prélats, ordonnant en 1453 une révision générale des feux destinée à faire payer l'impôt à tous ceux qui en étaient exemptés, créant un Parlement à Grenoble et cinq compagnies d'ordonnance, surveillant l'exploitation des forêts soumises à des coupes déraisonnables, réglementant la chasse, instituant des foires à Valence, Montélimar, Gap et Briançon, concluant, en 1449, un accord de libre-échange avec la Savoie basé sur ce que « les deux peuples sont accoutumés d'aller commercer, vivre et communiquer l'un avec l'autre ».

En 1452, il crée une université à Valence agréable pour « les beautés de son territoire couvert de prairies et arrosé de fontaines sans nombre », pose les bases d'un service des postes en plaçant des chevaucheurs de ses écuries sur les principaux itinéraires, une innovation qu'il allait plus tard généraliser dans le royaume, et prend les banquiers juifs sous sa protection, en leur permettant de s'installer à Briançon, au grand dam des états du Dauphiné qui demandaient leur expulsion.

Et, sans se soucier des choix de son père dont il estime qu'il « gouverne aussi mal que possible », il mène une politique extérieure active en Italie, en Allemagne et aux Pays-Bas et, à vingt-sept ans, choisit lui-même comme épouse Charlotte de Savoie, âgée de onze ans, à la grande fureur de Charles VII qui entendait que son fils soit marié conformément « au bien et au profit de lui et du royaume ».

En 1456, pris de panique à l'annonce que Charles VII avait ordonné des préparatifs militaires et s'était mis en route à travers le Bourbonnais, il s'enfuit se réfugier chez le duc de Bourgogne.

Durant cinq années, dépourvu de ressources, il est accueilli à bras ouverts par son oncle Philippe le Bon qui l'installe au château de Genappe, au sud de Bruxelles, au cœur de la grande forêt des Soignes et lui verse une copieuse pension de 36 000 francs qui lui permet l'entretien de 40 personnes. C'est là que naît, le 15 juillet 1459, son premier fils, Joachim. C'est de là qu'il correspond par lettres avec son père, récriminant sans cesse contre les conseillers du « Bien servi ». Le 17 juillet 1461, prêt à foncer vers les routes de France, il convoque déjà le duc de Bourgogne en lui écrivant : « s'il advient que vous entendiez dire qu'il soit trépassé, nous vous prions de monter à cheval immédiatement et de venir, vous et vos gens, par devers nous, vers les marches de Reims ». Ce que fit le « bel oncle » en amenant cent quarante chariots remplis d'or monnayé, de vaisselle précieuse, de vins de Bourgogne et des troupeaux de bœufs et de moutons destinés aux banquets du sacre.

La fin de l'État bourguignon

Philippe le Bon, qui avait payé tous les frais du sacre et comblé les Parisiens de fêtes, de tournois et de cadeaux, dut trouver son neveu bien ingrat. Refusant poliment de donner des offices aux candidats que patronnait son « bel oncle », le nouveau roi démontra rapidement qu'il n'avait qu'un seul but, unifier son royaume, détruire les principautés et écarter les princes qui prétendaient détenir leurs titres « par la grâce de Dieu », à l'instar du duc de Bretagne qui allait jusqu'à porter couronne et utiliser un sceau de majesté.

Dès les débuts de son règne, l'« universelle araigne » révoque les officiers nommés par son père, nomme à leur place des gens à lui et suscite une nouvelle Praguerie, la Ligue du Bien public, qui rassemble tous ceux qui, une nouvelle fois, entendent protester contre les empiétements de la monarchie. Animée par Charles de Berry, le frère du roi, et par Charles le Téméraire, le fils du duc de Bourgogne, elle se heurte à l'hostilité des « bonnes villes », peu convaincues par leurs promesses de diminuer les impôts, et des milieux d'affaires, qui redoutent une nouvelle guerre civile. Si les Ligueurs mettent à mal l'armée royale, à Montlhéry, le 16 juillet 1465, et obligent le roi à acheter à prix d'or les services et les fidélités, Louis XI s'empresse ensuite de manœuvrer pour diviser les coalisés et regagner une partie de ce qu'il avait concédé.

Puis il s'emploie à tisser sa toile autour de Charles le Téméraire qui, en 1467, à la mort de son père Philippe le Bon, prend la direction de la maison de Bourgogne. À cette date, la puissance bourguignonne semble avoir atteint son apogée. Bénéficiant d'une bonne position géographique, regroupant de riches territoires dont les Flandres, l'une des régions les plus actives du continent, profitant de la faiblesse du Saint Empire romain germanique et des malheurs de la France durant la guerre de Cent Ans, Philippe le Bon, qui a régné de 1419 à 1467, a su faire de sa cour l'une des plus brillantes d'Europe.

Mécène attentif à l'évolution des arts, il a été le protecteur de Jan Van Eyck, nommé valet de chambre avec « honneurs, prérogatives, franchises, libertés, droits, profits et émoluments ».

L'ordre de la Toison d'or, créé en 1429, l'entoure d'une élite éprouvée. Nicolas Rolin a été un chancelier avisé. Les universités de Dole et de Louvain font de l'ombre au rayonnement de la Sorbonne. Les quatre Chambres des comptes de Dijon, Lille, Bruxelles et La Haye se partagent la gestion financière. Le « philippus » d'or, une monnaie « unique » créée en 1433 pour favoriser la reprise des affaires dans les diverses parties de la principauté, est une monnaie réputée. « Nulle autre maison de la chrétienté », écrivait Philippe de Commynes, ne pouvait être comparée à la maison de Bourgogne par ses « dépenses et habillements des hommes et des femmes », par ses « repas et banquets plus grands et dispendieux qu'en nul autre lieu », par les « bains et distractions » dont pouvaient profiter les fidèles du « grand duc d'Occident ».

Dispensé depuis le traité d'Arras de 1435 de prêter hommage au roi de France, Philippe le Bon a songé à construire un véritable État bourguignon, séparé de la France. Absorbant les biens de la branche du Brabant, de l'héritage de Jacqueline de Hainaut, mettant la main sur le Luxembourg, il double l'étendue de ses États et se trouve en passe de reconstituer l'ancienne Lotharingie, faisant écrire ou traduire des livres d'histoire qui raniment le souvenir d'une « nation » bourguignonne égale aux « nations » française et germanique et tentant d'obtenir la couronne impériale.

Mais, au regard de cette ambition, l'État bourguignon souffre de réelles faiblesses. Son revenu n'a jamais dépassé la moitié du revenu du roi de France et, tandis que dans le royaume l'impôt tendait à devenir permanent, le duc de Bourgogne devait constamment négocier avec les « états » pour obtenir le vote des aides. Militairement, si Charles a tenu tête à l'armée royale à Montlhéry, l'armée bourguignonne reste une armée « féodale », levée pour chaque campagne. Enfin, si l'exceptionnelle longévité de Philippe le Bon a donné quelque cohérence à la politique extérieure de la principauté, les susceptibilités de chacune des parties de l'ensemble, toujours prêtes à se révolter, fragilisaient la construction.

Si Philippe le Bon se considérait toujours comme « français » et fit normalement hommage à Louis XI le jour du sacre pour « tous les pays qu'il tenait de la couronne de France », Charles, qui se proclamait « portugais », ce qu'il était par sa mère Isabelle, ne se considérait plus comme un prince « des fleurs de lys ». Dans les lettres closes par lesquelles il fait part au roi de France de la mort de son père et de son accession au pouvoir, il appelle Louis XI « mon très redouté Seigneur » et non plus, comme l'y obligeait le traité d'Arras, « mon très redouté et souverain Seigneur ».

De dix ans le cadet de Louis XI, le Téméraire est un « tempérament ». Assez grand, large d'épaules, les bras longs, les cheveux noirs, le teint basané, les yeux bleus et clairs, la bouche pincée, c'est un sanguin qui dégage un air de sauvagerie s'accordant parfaitement avec ce goût pour la tempête et les mers houleuses que signalent en lui ses contemporains. Désireux d'être craint plutôt qu'aimé, autoritaire jusqu'à la violence, éloquent, sachant entraîner un auditoire, c'était aussi un travailleur acharné, ce qui lui valut aussi le surnom de « Traveillant ». Sa chasteté, surprenante pour l'époque, lui a même valu d'être soupçonné d'homosexualité.

Commynes disait de lui : « Nul homme ne le dépassait en générosité, car il aimait à entretenir beaucoup de familiers et leur fournir un train de vie large. Il était fort pompeux en habillement et en toutes autres choses et un peu trop. Il faisait grand honneur aux ambassadeurs et aux étrangers ; ils étaient fort bien festoyés et reçus chez lui. Il désirait grande gloire, c'était ce qui l'entraînait le plus dans des guerres et il eut bien voulu ressembler à ces anciens princes dont on a tant parlé après leur mort. »

Rêvant d'égaler Alexandre le Grand, mais trop pressé et autoritaire jusqu'à la violence, il veut forcer les choses et renforcer la cohésion de son « empire ». S'inspirant probablement du modèle français, il réforme la justice en établissant trois fois par semaine une audience publique au cours de laquelle il rend justice en personne. D'autre part, le Téméraire réussit à faire voter par ses états des aides considérables, levant en dix ans presque autant d'impôts que son père en quarante-cinq années. À partir de 1471, il constitue lui aussi des compagnies d'ordonnance bourguignonnes. En 1473, surtout, il crée à Malines un Parlement, véritable cour suprême de l'empire bourguignon, et y établit une Chambre des comptes qui remplace celles de Lille, Bruxelles et La Haye. En 1474, enfin, il interdit aux habitants du duché de Bourgogne de faire appel au Parlement de Paris, ce qui marque la volonté de faire de ses possessions un véritable État souverain, affranchi de la France.

Restait toutefois à unir cet ensemble territorial disparate. Il y parvient en acquérant successivement l'Alsace méridionale et une partie de la Forêt-Noire, le comté de Marle en Vermandois, la Gueldre puis la Lorraine. Mais en 1473, malgré ses avances à l'empereur Frédéric III, il n'obtient pas la couronne royale tant désirée. Les ambitions désordonnées du Téméraire avaient importuné trop de monde. Son étoile, déjà, déclinait.

Louis XI fut assez patient pour attendre son heure, opposant au fonceur qu'il avait pour ennemi et qu'il « haïssait de venin de mort », son art de reculer et de feindre. En octobre 1468, venu imprudemment chez son adversaire, à Péronne, muni d'un sauf-conduit, au moment même où ses ambassadeurs excitaient les habitants de Liège à se révolter contre le duc de Bourgogne, il boit la honte de l'humiliation, promet que les tribunaux de Gand, de Bruges et d'Ypres seront désormais exemptés de l'appel du Parlement de Paris, ce qui était abandonner la souveraineté française sur la Flandre et assiste à la répression du soulèvement des Liégeois. Le 30 octobre, il doit entrer dans la ville révoltée, la croix bourguignonne de Saint-André à son chapeau et crier « Vive Bourgoingne » devant les habitants qui ne pouvaient croire à sa trahison.

Mais, dès novembre 1470, Louis XI fait constater par une assemblée tenue à Tours la nullité des engagements qu'il a consentis sous l'effet de la violence et, en janvier 1471, envahit la Picardie. En 1472, ayant réorganisé son armée, le Téméraire reprend les hostilités en massacrant les habitants de la petite ville de Nesle mais échoue devant Beauvais, défendue par une fille du peuple, Jeanne Laisné, connue dans la légende sous le nom de Jeanne « Hachette ». Cet échec, confirmé en 1473 par la dérobade de l'empereur Frédéric III, marque bien les limites d'une puissance bourguignonne que Louis XI sape sans affronter. En 1474, l'échec du siège de Neuss, mené contre l'archevêque de Cologne, révèle la fragilité de l'armée du Téméraire. En 1475, le traité de Picquigny signé entre l'« universelle araigne » et Édouard IV incite le roi d'Angleterre à abandonner l'alliance qu'il avait nouée avec le duc de Bourgogne et à repasser la Manche avec les troupes qu'il avait débarquées, abandonnant contre 75 000 écus et la promesse d'une pension annuelle de 50 000 écus toute prétention de sa dynastie à la couronne de France. En 1476, un de leurs lugubres trompes, les « vachers » suisses détruisent l'armée bourguignonne à Grandson et à Morat, et c'est en assiégeant Nancy, capitale du duché de Lorraine, que Charles le Téméraire trouve la mort le 5 janvier 1477. On l'y retrouva deux jours plus tard, « nu, face contre terre, la peau collée au sol par le gel, un coup de hallebarde au milieu de la tête, de l'oreille jusqu'aux dents, un coup de pique au travers des cuisses et un autre coup de pique dans le fondement ».

Charles laissait une fille, Marie de Bourgogne, âgée de vingt ans, qui était sans aucun doute le plus beau parti de la chrétienté. Arguant du droit des apanages qui excluait les femmes de la succession, Louis XI fait occuper sur-le-champ les terres de sa filleule. Puis, après avoir montré peu d'enthousiasme pour un projet de mariage entre Marie et le dauphin, alors âgé de sept ans, il s'y rallie, mais trop tard. Marie, renonçant à une alliance qui avait pour seul objectif de dépecer son héritage, épouse en août 1477 Maximilien de Habsbourg, fils de l'empereur Frédéric III.

En 1479, la guerre dévaste l'Artois et la Picardie. Arras s'étant révolté contre le roi de France, Louis XI décide d'expulser ses habitants, de rebaptiser la ville Franchise et de la coloniser en y installant 3 000 ménages d'artisans et de boutiquiers venus des principales villes du royaume.

En 1482, Marie étant morte accidentellement des suites d'une chute de cheval, Maximilien, qui bataillait depuis cinq ans contre Louis XI, se résout à négocier. Au traité d'Arras, signé le 23 décembre, il renonce définitivement à la Bourgogne et à la Picardie que le roi de France occupait déjà, et assigne en dot la Franche-Comté, le Mâconnais, l'Auxerrois et l'Artois à sa fille Marguerite, fiancée à l'âge de deux ans au dauphin Charles et immédiatement confiée à Louis XI pour être élevée à la cour de France en attendant son mariage. Le démembrement de l'État bourguignon était accompli même si la maison d'Autriche, maintenant installée dans les Pays-Bas, présentait une réelle menace pour la monarchie française.

Si l'on ajoute à ces annexions, l'héritage angevin, acquis, par étapes, peu après, l'Anjou, le Maine, le Barrois, la Provence et le Roussillon, la moisson territoriale était impressionnante. La frontière traditionnelle du royaume, celle des « quatre rivières » du traité de Verdun, était dépassée.

Le premier « roi moderne » ?

Personnage « ondoyant et divers », Louis XI n'en finit pas de diviser les historiens, qui se posent toujours la question de savoir si son règne marque l'automne du Moyen Âge ou l'aube de la modernité.

Pour certains, son acharnement machiavélique à détruire les principautés, l'accroissement de la pression fiscale qui fit passer les recettes de 1 800 000 livres par an sous Charles VII à 4 600 000 en 1481, l'idée d'en appeler à l'« opinion publique » pour faire applaudir son action, les procès politiques qui se multiplièrent au cours du règne, l'enquête sur les vagabonds que le Parlement ordonna pour mieux sévir contre ces « parasites » seraient autant de signes de modernité. Louis XI n'aurait-il pas pu dire avant Machiavel : « Il faut que la patrie soit sauvée, avec gloire ou avec ignominie » ?

Pour d'autres, au contraire, ses impulsions brutales, sa dévotion superstitieuse, ses multiples pèlerinages, ses médailles au chapeau, ses marchandages avec l'au-delà, sa cruauté certaine, son goût de la vengeance en feraient un roi « médiéval ».

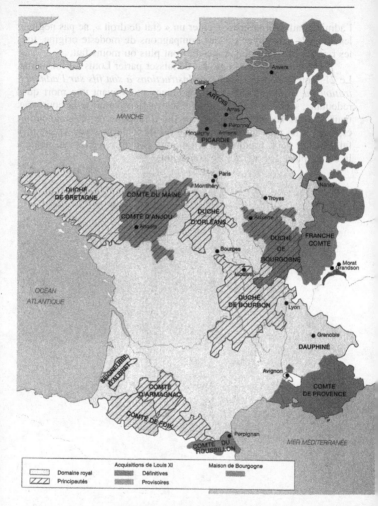

La France à la fin du règne de Louis XI.

Comme souvent, la réalité doit se situer au milieu. Accroître le domaine, en finir avec la superbe des princes, lutter contre les empiétements du Saint-Siège, accroître l'impôt et renforcer l'armée, réformer

433

l'administration et la justice, créer un « état de droit », ne pas négliger les conseils, s'appuyer sur des compagnons de modeste origine, tous les rois, depuis Philippe Auguste, l'ont plus ou moins fait.

Le mieux, en la matière, est de laisser parler Louis XI lui-même. Le 21 septembre 1482, dans ses *Instructions à son fils sur l'administration du royaume*, il écrivait, quelques mois avant une mort qu'il redoutait : « Grâce à Dieu, nous n'avons rien perdu de la couronne, mais l'avons augmentée et accrue de grandes terres et seigneuries, espérant d'ici peu, au plaisir et vouloir de Dieu notre dit créateur, y faire mettre paix, tranquillité et union ». C'était remettre lui-même à la bonne place les mérites de son action.

CHAPITRE **39**

Rêve d'Italie

*A près avoir fait rechercher dans les archives d'Aix-en-Provence la
bulle du pape Clément VII qui fondait les droits de la maison d'Anjou
sur la couronne de Naples, Charles VIII franchit les Alpes au Mont-
genèvre le 2 septembre 1494 à la tête d'une impressionnante armée de
30 000 combattants et dévale en Italie. Le 22 février 1495, il fait une
entrée triomphale à Naples, accueilli par le peuple en liesse. Aussitôt, il
dicte un bulletin de victoire sur lequel on peut lire : « Ce jour d'hui, je suis
entré en ma cité de Naples, en laquelle par les gentilhommes et citoyens
m'a été fait toute obéissance, serment et fidélité, comme mes bons et
loyaux sujets. » Pour plus d'un demi-siècle, à l'instar de ses rois, la
France allait rêver d'Italie.*

Le guêpier italien

En héritant des possessions du « bon roi » René en 1481,
Louis XI avait aussi hérité du royaume napolitain sur lequel les ducs
d'Anjou estimaient avoir des droits depuis le XIIIe siècle. En 1265, en
effet, Charles, duc d'Anjou et de Maine, comte de Provence et frère
de Saint Louis, avait été investi roi de Naples par le pape, qui voulait
évincer la dynastie allemande des Hohenstaufen, maîtresse du pays
qu'avaient conquis les aventuriers normands au siècle précédent. Mais,
au terme de péripéties mouvementées mettant aux prises Angevins et

Aragonais, régnait à Naples Ferrante d'Aragon, qui meurt le 25 janvier 1494.

Pour quelles raisons le jeune roi de France s'est-il écarté de la politique prudente de son père et a-t-il voulu reprendre à son compte les prétentions angevines ? Les historiens en discutent encore tant il est vrai que, de nos jours, les randonnées italiennes que vont mener les rois de France à la suite de Charles VIII ressemblent à un guêpier dans lequel ils vont s'enliser.

Sans doute faut-il tenir compte de la personnalité même de ce roi de vingt-quatre ans qui, sans être aussi « débile » que certains historiens l'ont prétendu, ne semble pas toutefois avoir été fort clairvoyant, un ambassadeur vénitien allant jusqu'à écrire : « Je tiens pour certain que, soit du corps, soit d'esprit, il vaut peu. »

Rêveur et mystique, optimiste impénitent, ce roi petit et laid — « plus petit qu'un pygmée », note un témoin de son temps —, a puisé dans les romans chevaleresques et les livres d'histoire qu'il dévore jusqu'à minuit ses rêves de croisade et d'épopée.

L'Histoire royale ou le *Livre des trois fils de roi*, un roman à succès de l'époque, semble l'avoir particulièrement marqué. On y voit un jeune roi de France, Philippe, délivrer le roi de Sicile, épouser sa fille et devenir empereur après avoir converti à la foi chrétienne le Grand Turc. Charles, qui a donné à son fils aîné le prénom de Charles-Orland, en souvenir de Charlemagne et du preux Roland, est aussi fort influencé par les prophéties diffusées dans le public au moyen de placards imprimés. L'une d'entre elles annonce que Charles VIII « sera de tous les roys de terre le souverain et dominateur sur tous les dominants et unique monarchie du monde ». L'autre qu'il chassera les Infidèles des Lieux saints, ceindra en Italie la deuxième couronne et ouvrira l'ère de paix de mille ans qui doit précéder le Jugement dernier.

En un temps où des prophètes annoncent comme tout proche le « millenium », en une fin de siècle où les devins musulmans se rencontrent avec les astrologues d'Occident pour prévoir de grands bouleversements, à une époque où, en Italie, des statues de saints se couvrent de sueur, nul doute que Charles VIII a bien eu le sentiment d'avoir la Justice pour épouse et le glaive de Dieu pour arme. Le règne de Charles a beau inaugurer les Temps « modernes », on n'en finit pas si facilement avec le Moyen Âge, avec les rêves de croisade et de chevalerie.

Sans doute aussi faut-il faire la part belle aux sirènes insistantes entendues d'Italie. À Florence, le prédicateur dominicain Savonarole annonce dans un prêche prononcé lors du carême de 1493 qu'il a « vu dans le ciel un glaive suspendu » et salue dans Charles l'élu de Dieu venu châtier la perversité de ses compatriotes et purifier la péninsule. À Milan, Ludovic Sforza, dit le More, fait sentir au roi de France les « fumées et gloires d'Italie, lui remontrant, écrit Philippe de Commynes, le droit qu'il avait en ce beau royaume de Naples ». À Venise, la Sérénissime République cherche son appui pour résister à l'empereur Maximilien d'Autriche, qui tient Trieste, Fiume et le Trentin. À Rome, le nouveau pape Alexandre Borgia déclare son hostilité à Ferrante. À la cour même, des barons napolitains exilés vantent les revenus du royaume italien et, apportant des cartes et « des plans au pinceau », démontrent que l'expédition militaire sera une aimable promenade. Autant d'appels qui tiennent Charles VIII en haleine et lui font penser que l'Italie l'attend comme un « messie ».

Sans doute, enfin, a joué l'ardeur belliqueuse d'une jeunesse au sang bleu qui s'ennuie et rêve de fortune. Devenue à la fin du règne de Louis XI ce que l'on appellerait aujourd'hui une « superpuissance », écrit Emmanuel Le Roy Ladurie, « on ne s'étonne pas que cet excès de force vive aille se répandre vers une zone de moindre résistance et de séduction maximale : l'Italie renaissante et divisée ». À l'heure où Ferdinand d'Aragon et Isabelle de Castille chassent les Infidèles de Grenade et que leurs caravelles découvrent l'Amérique, comment le roi de France pourrait-il ne pas écouter ceux qui, comme Étienne de Vesc, l'incitent à devenir le chef d'une nouvelle croisade qui, à partir de l'Italie, chassera les Turcs de Constantinople ? Lors d'une mission outre-Manche, Robert Gaguin, ambassadeur de Charles VIII, dit au roi d'Angleterre : « Le roi a l'intention de reprendre par les armes son royaume de Naples afin de s'en servir comme d'une base de départ de la croisade vers la Grèce. Il utilisera ses troupes uniquement pour renverser l'Empire ottoman. »

Ardemment désirée, l'« aventure » italienne a été soigneusement préparée. Le budget de l'expédition, près de 2 millions de livres, a été assuré par une augmentation de la taille de 800 000 livres et par des emprunts divers de 1 200 000 livres, les grands officiers du Parlement et de la Chambre des comptes ayant été « invités » à souscrire de manière quelque peu forcée. Cet énorme budget a permis de lever une armée de plus de 30 000 combattants, dont 3 000 mercenaires suisses, flanqués de 10 000 auxiliaires, valets et servants, équipés d'une invention toute récente, l'arquebuse. Huit mille chevaux doivent faire traverser les montagnes à l'artillerie, dont les canons de plus de 2 000 livres, les « double-courtault », qui assurent une force de feu impressionnante.

L'acquisition récente de la Bretagne et de la Provence et l'intense activité des chantiers navals ont aussi permis de rassembler à Gênes, dans l'été 1494, près de cent navires prêts à châtier la flotte napolitaine. Pierre d'Urfé, le grand écuyer, qui a organisé ce rassemblement, peut écrire au roi : « Sire, vous qui aimez la guerre, si vous voyiez votre armée de mer lorsqu'elle sera à la voile, quel grand triomphe à contempler ! Jamais homme qui vive n'aura vu en mer un triomphe semblable à celui que vous avez l'intention d'y mettre. »

Charles VIII a aussi mis le prix pour acheter la neutralité des trois grandes puissances susceptibles de prendre le royaume en tenailles. En 1492, le traité d'Étaples offre à Henri VII la somme coquette de 745 000 écus d'or en échange d'une paix « perpétuelle » entre la France et l'Angleterre. En 1493, le traité de Barcelone restitue à l'Espagne les comtés de Roussillon et de Cerdagne que lui avait enlevés Louis XI et y ajoute un convoi de cinquante mulets chargés de brocart d'or et de trente autres portant des ballots de draps de soie. En 1493, toujours, le traité de Senlis désarme l'adversaire le plus coriace, Maximilien d'Autriche, humilié par le renvoi de sa fille Marguerite, l'ancienne « fiancée » de Charles VIII qui a préféré épouser en décembre 1491 Anne de Bretagne, mariée par procuration à Maximilien en 1490 ! Comme signe d'accord, le futur empereur avait dépêché à Rennes un ambassadeur spécial qui avait glissé une jambe nue dans le lit pseudo-conjugal ou s'était étendue pour la forme la duchesse Anne. Mais le traité du Verger ayant en 1488 imposé au vieux duc François II de ne pas marier ses filles sans le consentement du roi de France, Charles VIII avait fait le siège de la Bretagne pour obliger Anne à rompre cette union si contraire à la raison d'État. Pour effacer ces péripéties conjugales, le traité de Senlis restitue à Maximilien la dot de sa fille, l'Artois, la Franche-Comté, le Charolais, Auxerre, Mâcon, Bar-sur-Seine et la seigneurie de Noyers. N'était-ce pas lâcher la proie pour l'ombre d'Italie ? Le rêve de gloire valait-il l'escapade napolitaine ?

L'entrée en Italie a pu le faire croire. En septembre 1494, à Rapallo, près de Gênes, pris entre les feux de la flotte et la *furia* des troupes françaises épaulées par les mercenaires suisses, les Napolitains sont contraints de s'enfuir. Le 14 octobre, Charles fait une entrée triomphale à Pavie. À Florence qui vient de chasser les Médicis, on suspend sur la façade du palais public un énorme écu de France et on abat une partie du mur de la ville pour que l'armée française puisse entrer sans encombre. Veillant, en compagnie de Savonarole, au chevet du lit où s'éteint le jeune philosophe Pic de la Mirandole, Charles écrit à son beau frère : « M'y a été fait autant d'honneur que j'eus jamais en ville de mon royaume. » Sienne lui ouvre ses portes le 2 décembre. Fin décembre, il entre à Rome, visite les innombrables églises de la ville, vénère les reliques qu'elles contiennent, distribue d'abondantes aumônes, fait pendre cinq soldats coupables de pillage, assiste à des jeux imités de l'ancienne Rome et touche les écrouelles de 500 malades venus voir s'exercer la vertu miraculeuse du roi de France. Puis, environ cinq mois après avoir mis pied en Italie, il entre à Naples où retentissent partout les cris de *Francia ! Francia !*

Se partageant les dépouilles des vaincus mais se préoccupant du sort des pauvres, consacrant les matinées à la messe et à l'administration et les après-midi au bon vin et aux charmes des Napolitaines, les Français goûtent avec volupté les fruits de la victoire et oublient le rêve de Terre sainte. Des fruits gâtés par une nouvelle maladie, la syphilis, peut-être importée par des marins revenus d'Amérique avec Christophe Colomb. Ce mal contagieux que les Français appelleront le mal *napolitain* et que les Italiens nommeront le mal *français* transforme le plaisir en cauchemar.

Surtout, signée le 1er avril dans la chambre du doge, une Ligue associe Venise, le pape, Milan, l'Espagne et le Saint Empire, pour s'opposer aux « agressions » de la France. Charles et son armée doivent alors prendre le chemin du retour, enfoncer le 6 juillet à Fornoue les forces de la Ligue et rentrer en France sans autre bénéfice que les battants de la porte de bronze sculptée du Château-Neuf, le grand vitrail de l'église de l'Annunziata, 130 tapisseries, 172 tapis, 1 140 volumes de la bibliothèque des rois d'Aragon et de multiples objets et tissus précieux sur lesquels veille le tapissier Nicolas Fagot, chargé de mener le butin à bon port.

Si les gains territoriaux sont nuls, la *furia francese* a impressionné et l'art nouveau a fait une entrée discrète à Amboise. Un bilan suffisamment « positif » pour encourager Louis XII à reprendre à son compte les rêves de Charles VIII, mort en 1498 après avoir heurté de front le linteau d'une porte basse du château d'Amboise !

Petit-fils de Valentine Visconti, fils du poète Charles d'Orléans et de Marie de Clèves, Louis XII ajoute aux prétentions napolitaines les droits de la maison d'Orléans sur le duché de Milan, les Visconti ayant été dépossédés du Milanais en 1450 par François Sforza, un *condottiere* dont le fils Ludovic, dit le More, est considéré comme un usurpateur par le nouveau roi de France.

Dès son avènement, il se proclame duc de Milan et, en 1499, après avoir fait annuler son mariage avec Jeanne, la pauvre fille infirme de Louis XI, et épousé Anne de Bretagne, la veuve de son neveu, Louis XII part à la conquête de son duché. Le 8 avril 1500,

Ludovic est défait à Novare et emmené prisonnier en France où il mourra après huit ans de captivité. Dans la foulée, Naples est reconquise en 1501 mais reperdue en 1503. Une nouvelle fois piégé par les méandres de la diplomatie italienne, Louis devient le « Barbare » qu'il faut chasser. En 1513, menacé par une nouvelle coalition que le pape a constituée, il doit évacuer le Milanais.

Devenu roi en 1515, François Ier rêve à son tour de descendre vers cette terre de soleil où sont rassemblées les splendeurs de l'Antiquité. Après avoir passé les Alpes à la tête d'une armée de 40 000 hommes, en faisant « couper les rocs pour faire chemin à passer les gens de cheval et l'artillerie », l'Hannibal français écrase les Suisses le 14 septembre 1515 à Marignan après avoir fêté, deux jours plus tôt, son vingt et unième anniversaire. Le soir même de sa victoire, il écrit à sa mère pour lui faire partager l'exaltation de cette belle prouesse.

> « Victoire, victoire, au noble Roy François,
> Victoire au gentil de Valois !
> Victoire au noble roy François ! »

Telles sont les paroles des chansons que font retentir dans les villes et les chaumières du royaume baladins, poètes et musiciens. Belle victoire militaire en effet, Marignan est aussi un succès diplomatique. Conclue à Fribourg le 29 novembre 1516, la Paix « perpétuelle » (elle le sera, en effet !) réserve le sang des Suisses à la France, ces redoutables soldats ne devant « consentir ni souffrir aller au service des princes [...] qui voudraient prétendre en dommages le dit Sieur Roi, en son royaume, en son duché de Milan ou ses appartenances ». Voilà assurée une partie de la frontière de l'est.

Signé le 18 août 1516 entre François Ier et le pape Léon X, le concordat de Bologne, qui restera en vigueur jusqu'en 1790, met l'Église de France dans la main du roi. Enfin, le traité de Cambrai, conclu le 11 mars 1517 entre François Ier, l'empereur Maximilien d'Autriche et son petit-fils Charles d'Espagne, garantit au roi de France le Milanais et prévoit, avec la bénédiction du pape, de lever une armée commune pour délivrer la Terre sainte... L'oriflamme reposée à Saint-Denis et les châsses du saint et de ses compagnons redescendues dans la crypte, l'Europe est en paix, pour longtemps, espère-t-elle.

Le roi et l'empereur

La paix dura en fait cinq ans. La mort de l'empereur Maximilien en 1519 excite en effet la rivalité entre le Valois et le Habsbourg et relance un conflit qui va tenir en haleine les cours européennes pendant près de quarante ans.

Rêvant de coiffer la couronne impériale pour devenir l'héritier de Charlemagne, François Ier multiplie les ambassades et dépense plus de 400 000 écus, soit environ une tonne et demie d'or, pour acheter les voix des sept électeurs, les archevêques-princes de Mayence, Trêves et Cologne, le roi de Bohême, le duc de Saxe, le margrave de Brandebourg et le comte palatin du Rhin, qui louvoient entre les compétiteurs au gré des sommes offertes.

Charles de Habsbourg, petit-fils de l'empereur défunt et roi d'Espagne depuis 1516, profite de l'immense crédit que lui offrent les Fugger et signe des traites à valoir après son élection pour un montant de 851 000 florins, l'équivalent de 2 tonnes d'or. Après avoir pris comptant l'or envoyé par François Ier, les Électeurs votent le 28 juin 1519 pour Charles afin que ses promesses d'« achat » soient honorées. Quand il apprend la nouvelle, le 3 juillet, le roi de France se retire à Fontainebleau et chasse furieusement pendant trois jours pour « mettre en oubli mélancolie », déclarant, paraît-il, que, somme toute, son échec valait mieux pour lui et son royaume.

François Ier se trouve pourtant face à un adversaire dont la puissance semble énorme. À l'âge de dix-neuf ans, le nouvel empereur, qui prend le nom de Charles Quint, est maître de l'Espagne, des Pays-Bas, de la Flandre, de l'Artois, de la Franche-Comté, de l'Autriche, du Tyrol, du royaume de Naples, de la Sicile et de la Sardaigne. De ses nouvelles colonies américaines conquises au détriment des Aztèques, des Incas et des Mayas, affluent bientôt l'or et l'argent. Même si cet ensemble manque d'unité, il menace bien d'encerclement le royaume de France.

Les hostilités commencent en mars 1521, après que Charles Quint s'est assuré de l'alliance anglaise, obtenue après la baroque entrevue du Camp du Drap d'or, au cours de laquelle le roi de France a jeté à terre le roi d'Angleterre au cours d'une joute improvisée pour le plaisir des dames. Tandis que Mézières, assiégée par les troupes impériales, est sauvée par l'intervention de Bayard, la défaite de La

Bicoque, à quelques lieues de Milan, contraint les Français à abandonner une nouvelle fois l'Italie.

Obsédé par la volonté de reprendre « son » Milanais, François franchit une nouvelle fois les Alpes en octobre 1524 mais est fait prisonnier à la bataille de Pavie le 25 février 1525.

Emmené en Espagne, le roi de France doit signer le 14 janvier 1526 le traité de Madrid par lequel il cède la Bourgogne à l'empereur et renonce à tous ses droits sur l'Italie. Libéré le 17 mars 1526 après avoir livré en otages ses deux fils, le Valois, qui n'est pas né à l'époque de Machiavel pour rien, s'emploie à dénoncer le traité qu'il a juré sans rire d'observer alors qu'il sait bien que le serment du sacre lui interdit d'aliéner une quelconque partie de son domaine.

Les hostilités reprennent en 1527 et s'apaisent en 1529 par la paix de Cambrai. Le roi de France garde la Bourgogne et les villes de Somme, renonce une nouvelle fois à l'Italie et s'engage à verser une énorme rançon de 2 millions d'écus (soit 7 tonnes d'or) pour la libération de ses jeunes fils. Enfin, le roi de France promet de devenir le beau-frère de son rival en épousant sa sœur Éléonore. Au soir du 1er juillet 1530, sur un ponton dressé au milieu de la Bidassoa, les barques échangent les pièces d'or méticuleusement contrôlées par les Espagnols contre une fiancée et deux enfants.

Après quelques années de paix, la guerre reprend en 1536 après que François Ier a osé conclure avec le sultan Soliman le Magnifique une alliance qui suscite l'indignation de toute la Chrétienté. Sous le couvert d'un accord commercial dont les clauses sont seules rédigées, les deux princes reconnaissent oralement leur commune hostilité à l'empereur. Après deux années de campagnes qui voient la Provence et la Picardie envahies, les deux « coqs », incapables de mener jusqu'au bout une lutte décisive, doivent conclure une trêve. Les deux beaux-frères se rencontrent à Aigues-Mortes, s'embrassent, se proclament unis comme frères et partagent la même chambre !

Mais toujours hanté par son rêve d'Italie, François Ier reprend la guerre en 1542. Si les Français remportent une brillante victoire à Cérisoles, dans le Piémont, les troupes de Charles Quint envahissent la Champagne, occupent Épernay et Château-Thierry tandis qu'Henri VIII, l'allié anglais, s'empare de Boulogne. Mais, faute d'argent, l'empereur doit signer une nouvelle paix le 18 septembre 1544, à Crépy-en-Laonnois.

La mort de François Ier, le 31 mars 1547, n'apaise pas les tensions entre le Valois et le Habsbourg. Souhaitée par Henri II, le nouveau roi de France, comme par son rival, la guerre reprend au printemps 1552. Tandis que les troupes françaises parviennent à s'emparer des trois évêchés de Metz, Toul et Verdun, Charles Quint lève 60 000 hommes, qui ne réussissent pas à reprendre Metz habilement défendue par François de Guise. En 1557, Philippe II, en faveur duquel Charles Quint a abdiqué, rassemble l'armée « la plus forte du siècle », massacre à Saint-Quentin les troupes commandées par le connétable de Montmorency mais, faute d'approvisionnements, se retire alors qu'il pouvait marcher sur Paris. Revenu d'Italie, toujours, où il bataillait pour reprendre Naples, le duc de Guise se porte au nord du royaume, s'empare de Guînes et, surtout, reprend Calais en janvier 1558.

Signé les 2 et 3 avril 1559 après cinq mois de négociations serrées, le traité de Cateau-Cambrésis clôt quarante années de luttes entre Valois et Habsbourg. Si la France gardait Calais pour huit ans ainsi que les Trois-Évêchés, elle renonçait définitivement à toutes ses ambitions italiennes et abandonnait la Savoie, la Bresse et le Bugey, occupés depuis un quart de siècle. Et comme il fallait sceller par des mariages tous ces arrangements, on décida qu'Élisabeth, la fille du roi de France, épouserait Philippe II, fraîchement veuf, tandis que Marguerite, la sœur d'Henri II, épouserait Emmanuel-Philibert de Savoie. « En une heure, et par un trait de plume, se lamentaient les militaires indignés, fallut tout rendre, et souiller et noircir toutes nos belles victoires passées, de trois ou quatre gouttes d'encre. »

Au terme de ces longues guerres, la France devait donc renoncer à ses rêves d'Italie pour gagner Metz, Toul et Verdun... Obsédée par ses mirages, elle avait concentré ses forces vers la Méditerranée au moment où de hardis navigateurs découvraient le nouveau monde et où des pêcheurs bretons et des marchands dieppois parvenaient à Terre-Neuve et au Brésil. Alors qu'Anvers, Lisbonne et Séville prenaient le relais de Gênes et de Venise, elle laissait Espagnols et Portugais se partager l'Amérique. Certes, en 1523-1524, Verrazzano, un Florentin, avait longé les côtes de l'Amérique du Nord pour le compte de François Ier et nommé « Nouvelle Angoulême » l'estuaire de l'Hudson. Certes, en 1535 et 1536, Jacques Cartier, un marin de Saint-Malo, a bien remonté le Saint-Laurent jusqu'au futur site de Montréal. Certes, entre 1540 et 1565, des Français ont bien tenté d'établir des « Nouvelles France » au Canada, au Brésil et en Floride, entreprises qui ont toutefois été menées sans esprit de suite. Certes, François Ier avait bien notifié en 1540 à Charles Quint « que le soleil chauffe pour lui comme pour les autres et qu'il désirait fort voir le testament d'Adam pour savoir comment celui-ci avait partagé le monde ». Certes, reçu par les notables de Rouen le 2 octobre 1550, Henri II a pu assister au spectacle singulier de cinquante Tupinambas se faisant face dans un décor simulant la forêt amazonienne, avec des arbres peints, des fruits multicolores, des perroquets et des guenons, le roi de France avait d'autres horizons que celui du Brésil vers lequel voulaient l'entraîner les négociants normands, même si, en 1555, le général des galères, Villegagnon, fondait dans la baie de Rio de Janeiro une Henryville dont il espérait faire la capitale de la « France antarctique ».

Le nerf de la guerre

Si les guerres extérieures ont purgé le royaume des « larrons, meurtriers, fainéants, vagabonds, mutins et voleurs », qui « gâtaient la simplicité des bons sujets » (Jean Bodin), si elles ont permis d'exporter l'ardeur belliqueuse des jeunes nobles, fourni un emploi de soldats ou de valets aux hommes les plus démunis et assuré, finalement, pendant plus d'un demi-siècle la paix intérieure à un royaume qui en avait bien besoin, elles ont aussi imposé au pays une charge financière accrue.

Sous le règne de François Ier, les frais militaires et diplomatiques ont représenté, à eux seuls, plus de la moitié des dépenses totales de la couronne, qui ne peut plus évidemment « vivre du sien », selon le vieil adage médiéval resté pourtant ancré dans la tête des contribuables. En 1515-1516, la seule campagne de Marignan coûte 7,5 millions de livres, alors que les recettes fiscales à la fin du règne de Louis XI s'élevait à 5,4 millions. De la déclaration de guerre de 1521 au désastre de Pavie en 1525, ce sont 20 millions de livres qui sont engloutis en cinquante mois. De 1542 à 1546, la dernière campagne de François Ier absorbe encore 30 millions de livres.

Si se battre coûte fort cher, à tel point qu'on évite souvent le contact dans l'espoir que, faute de vivres et d'argent, l'armée de l'adversaire finira par se dissoudre la première, négocier est aussi onéreux. À elle seule, l'inutile entrevue du Camp du Drap d'or a été « facturée » 400 000 livres, la libéralité et le faste d'un prince étant toujours considérés comme le signe de sa puissance. De 1516 à 1546, les pensions versées aux Suisses à la suite de la « Paix perpétuelle » conclue en 1516 se sont élevées à plus de 4 millions de livres. Quatre millions de livres, c'est aussi le prix payé pour acheter plutôt mal que bien l'incertaine alliance anglaise.

Quant au transfert des 7 tonnes d'or destinées à payer la rançon du roi François, il s'agit, de loin, du plus important transfert de fonds du temps. Selon les recherches méticuleuses menées par l'historien

Philippe Hamon, la monarchie aurait ainsi prélevé environ 200 millions de livres de 1515 à 1547, dont plus de la moitié consacrée au seul domaine de la guerre. Metz, Toul et Verdun auraient coûté fort cher ! Pour mesurer le poids de cette charge, il suffit de savoir que la construction et l'entretien des châteaux qui ont fait la gloire de la Renaissance française ont coûté, entre 1528 et 1550, moins de 2 millions de livres, soit cinquante fois moins que les dépenses de guerre.

Les dépenses anticipant toujours les recettes, les problèmes de trésorerie ont donc constitué le pain quotidien de ceux qui avaient pour tâche de remplir les caisses. Établie de façon permanente sous le règne de Charles VII, la taille est de loin la recette la plus importante. Sous le règne de François Ier, elle double par rapport au règne de Louis XII, le regretté « père du peuple », pour atteindre près de 5 millions de livres par an. Diversement perçue selon les provinces, la gabelle, qui taxe le sel, rapporte annuellement entre 300 000 et 400 000 livres.

Mais cela ne suffit pas. On met l'Église de France à contribution en lui demandant de verser périodiquement des « dons gratuits ». On impose aux « bien aizés » des villes des prêts qui ne sont jamais remboursés. Un vieux Parisien, Nicolas Versoris, manifeste son indignation en écrivant dans son livre de raison : « En ce temps [1521], le Roi fit une exaction indue sur les Parisiens, c'est à savoir tous les seigneurs et bourgeois de Paris, tant officiers que autres, furent contraints de payer, chacun selon sa qualité, en quantité de vaisselle d'argent [...] exaction indue et nouvellement créée ne peut plaire et agréer au peuple. »

Surtout, on emprunte, plus particulièrement sur la place de Lyon. En 1494, Charles VIII emprunte plus d'un million de livres pour financer sa première expédition italienne. En 1522, François Ier inaugure la dette publique en créant les rentes de l'Hôtel de Ville de Paris. La ville versait au souverain des capitaux dont les intérêts étaient gagés sur des recettes fiscales. En septembre 1522, le premier emprunt de 16 666 livres, au denier 12 (soit 8,33 % d'intérêt), était gagé sur les droits sur le vin et les moutons et brebis entrant dans la capitale. À la fin des années 1550, la dette de l'État atteignait quatre à cinq fois l'équivalent des recettes annuelles ! On comprend qu'en 1555 les banquiers aient eu l'idée de s'associer dans un « Grand Parti » pour limiter leurs risques.

Enfin, la monarchie utilise la fascination des notables pour la « fonction publique » en multipliant les offices de justice, de police et de finances et en les vendant aux acheteurs ravis d'accéder par l'argent à la noblesse de robe. Toujours prompt à donner son avis sur la politique intérieure de la France, un ambassadeur vénitien, Marino Cavalli, écrit en 1548 : « Les offices sont infinis et s'accroissent tous les jours. Avocats du roi dans chaque petite ville, receveurs de tailles, trésoriers, conseillers, présidents des comptes et de justice [...] et tant d'autres que la moitié suffirait. »

Afin de mieux contrôler cette inflation des dépenses comme des recettes, François Iᵉʳ créa en 1523 le Trésor de l'Épargne, dont le responsable assurait pour l'ensemble du royaume une comptabilité unique, établissait un état des recettes et des dépenses et signait tous les ordres de paiement... En 1542, seize recettes générales, Aix, Agen puis Bordeaux, Amiens, Bourges, Caen, Châlons, Dijon, Grenoble, Issoire puis Riom, Lyon, Montpellier, Paris, Poitiers, Rennes, Toulouse et Tours, avaient à leur tête un receveur général chargé de collecter tous les fonds de sa circonscription. Autant d'efforts déployés dans l'urgence pour combler des déficits chroniques et traquer la monnaie là où elle circulait.

Encore ne faut-il pas exagérer le poids du fardeau. Six à sept millions de livres prélevés par an sur quelque 19 millions de sujets, c'est moins que 20 millions de livres prélevés vers 1600, à l'époque du bon roi Henri IV ! La facilité avec laquelle a été rassemblée la rançon de François Iᵉʳ montre en fait que le royaume était assez riche pour pouvoir supporter l'accroissement de l'impôt et assez « patriote » pour exalter le roi dans ses victoires et le soutenir dans ses défaites.

La Renaissance française

En 1576, dans La République, *Jean Bodin, l'un des premiers théoriciens du pouvoir absolu, écrit :* « Décerner la guerre ou traiter la
paix est l'un des plus grands points de la majesté. » *Puisque le Ciel* « a
permis les guerres et inimitiés entre les peuples pour châtier les uns par
les autres et les tenir tous en crainte », *ajoute-t-il, le souverain reste
d'abord un* « roi de guerre » *dont les vertus militaires sont le premier fondement de la popularité.* « Dans ce pays-là, *observe encore en 1574 Jean
Michel, un ambassadeur vénitien,* « tout prince qui n'aime, qui ne cherche
point la guerre, n'est point estimé ». *C'est parce qu'il aimait* « la vie molle
et paisible » *et détestait les joutes et les tournois qu'Henri III aurait, selon
lui, beaucoup perdu* « dans l'opinion de son peuple ».

Le roi des bêtes

Dans la galerie des portraits des rois de France, François Ier
mérite certainement le titre de premier roi « absolu ». Maximilien, en
guise de boutade, aurait prétendu que si l'empereur n'était qu'un roi
des rois, celui de France était le roi des bêtes, « car en quelque chose
qu'il commande, il est obéi aussitôt comme l'homme l'est des bêtes ».
Si le trait est forcé, il n'en traduit pas moins le fait que celui que les
flatteurs appelaient l'« Hercule gaulois » a été le premier à être qualifié de Majesté et à employer, dès le septième jour de son règne, une

formule appelée à un grand avenir : « car tel est notre plaisir », ce qui veut dire « car telle est notre décision », et non « notre caprice ».

Poursuivant l'action entamée par les Capétiens, bénéficiant d'un territoire dont tous les contemporains soulignaient la configuration ramassée, servis par la diversité et l'abondance des productions, puisant dans le bas de laine d'une population importante des ressources fiscales sans commune mesure avec celles dont pouvaient disposer leurs rivaux, capitalisant le patriotisme qu'avait éveillé Jeanne d'Arc et qu'exaltera Ronsard, les Valois y ont ajouté le culte du « beau Prince » qui incarnait l'idéal nouveau des élites de la Renaissance.

Nul doute que la puissance physique de François Ier a contribué à forger l'image d'un roi dont le corps « parfait » était la représentation d'un royaume dont les poètes vantaient l'excellence. « Beau prince autant qu'il y en eust au monde », les chroniqueurs, les ambassadeurs, les contemporains le répètent à l'envi. Nouveau « César », nouvel « Auguste », nouveau « Constantin », François, qui mesure près de deux mètres, aime porter beau. Amateur de tournois, il a gardé de l'ancienne chevalerie le goût des conduites héroïques qui font tout perdre sauf l'honneur. Animé d'une extraordinaire joie de vivre, il sait plaire et séduire. Cultivant la beauté, les artistes et les femmes, il fait de la cour le miroir et l'instrument de sa puissance.

« Cour sans dames, printemps sans roses », affirme le sensuel François Ier tandis que, amer, l'évêque Jean de Monluc déplore : « Les dames peuvent tout ; elles tiennent les rois, leur font oublier les capitaines assiégés en Italie [...]. Peu sert de savoir les batailles et assauts, qui ne sait la cour et les dames. »

Si la cour remonte aux origines mêmes du pouvoir royal, elle connaît alors un développement spectaculaire, rassemblant de 15 000 à 18 000 personnes qui se déplacent au gré des envies et des besoins d'un monarque qui doit se montrer pour voir et entendre, inspecter et faire craindre, éblouir et accomplir des « miracles », en touchant les écrouelles des malades qui suivent son cortège. Dans la relation qu'il envoie au Sénat de Venise en 1535, l'ambassadeur vénitien, Marin Giustiniano, emporté malgré lui dans ce monde du voyage, décrit pour s'en plaindre cette course sans fin : « Mon ambassade dura quarante-cinq mois. J'ai été presque toujours en voyage. Peu de temps après mon arrivée à Paris, le roi partit pour Marseille : nous traversâmes, par des chaleurs excessives, le Bourbonnais, le Lyonnais, l'Auvergne et le Languedoc, et nous parvînmes en Provence [...]. De Marseille, nous allâmes par la Provence, le Dauphiné, le Lyonnais, la Bourgogne et la Champagne jusqu'en Lorraine, où le roi s'aboucha avec le landgrave de Hesse, et de là, nous retournâmes à Paris [...]. Le roi voulut partir ; je fus forcé d'acheter encore dix chevaux, et cela au moment où sa Majesté convoqua son arrière-ban, pour le passer en revue, à cheval et en armes, ce qui fit hausser de beaucoup le prix des chevaux. Et comme j'attendis en vain les subsides de Votre Sérénité, force fut de vendre une partie de mon argenterie. Jamais, du temps de mon ambassade, la cour ne s'arrêta dans le même endroit pendant quinze jours de suite. »

L'étude détaillée des déplacements de François Ier montre en effet que, en excluant les campagnes italiennes et la captivité à Madrid, il séjourne au cours de son règne dans 728 lieux différents, demeurant en moyenne dix jours dans chacun d'eux. Caravane de plein air, couchant souvent sous la tente ou dans les châteaux meublés à la hâte avec les tapisseries, les meubles, la vaisselle et le lit du roi transportés dans les charrettes, foule bruyante et pittoresque se déplaçant à cheval, en litière ou à pied, véritable ménagerie qui se compose de mules et de chiens de chasse, mais aussi d'ours, de lions et de chameaux, école d'élégance et de dépravation, camp « du Drap d'or » permanent, cette cour sans étiquette qui va de fête en fête, de banquet en ballet, de bal en concert, de tournoi en entrée royale, est aussi le théâtre où, à la manière des despotes orientaux, le souverain joue de sa faveur comme de sa disgrâce.

Traduit en français en 1537 par Jacques Colin, secrétaire du roi, l'ouvrage de Balthazar Castiglione, *Le Courtisan*, publié en 1528 à Venise, devient un « best-seller », le bréviaire du goût mondain et raffiné, le vade-mecum de ceux qui, croyant se séparer du commun des mortels, se moulent dans le modèle que le roi veut imposer pour les domestiques.

Un modèle que contribuent aussi à définir les humanistes pétris de références à l'Antiquité et qui concilient sans embarras l'idéal d'une monarchie sage et tempérée avec celui d'un pouvoir absolu. Dans sa *Grand' Monarchie de France*, publiée en 1519, l'évêque de Marseille, Claude de Seyssel exalte le « corps mystique » de la France dont le roi est la tête, le « chef », et dont les sujets sont les « membres ». Dans son *Institution du Prince* écrite pour François Ier en 1518-1519, mais publiée en 1547, Guillaume Budé émet l'idée assez neuve que, juge en dernier ressort, le roi peut, lorsque l'exige le « bien public », violer coutumes, traditions et lois existantes dans la mesure où *Princeps legibus solutus est*, il est au-dessus des lois. En 1576, dans les *Six Livres de la République*, Jean Bodin couronne cette évolution en écrivant que la souveraineté ne peut être partagée entre le roi et une quelconque assemblée. Dans un pamphlet anonyme intitulé *De l'obéissance due au Prince*, diffusé en 1590, au moment où l'autorité

du roi est contestée, une image est utilisée, promise à un bel avenir :
« Le Soleil fut fait roi de tous les astres ; ils le reconnaissent pour leur
prince, reçoivent de lui toute leur clarté, lui font honneur, vont au-
devant de lui, le saluent et l'assistent de leur conseil comme ses officiers et assesseurs. »

En 1527, François Ier sut faire briller de manière théâtrale la
lumière de cet astre naissant. Pour officialiser la confiscation des biens
du connétable de Bourbon, accusé de trahison, le roi présida, les 24,
26 et 27 juillet 1527, une séance du Parlement de Paris destinée à
faire enregistrer cette décision.

Usant d'une mise en scène grandiose, siégeant majestueusement
sur un trône dressé au-dessus du parquet, le roi tient un lit de justice
qui fera date. Furieux de voir sa souveraineté contestée par le président du Parlement, qui ose rappeler que le roi ne doit pas vouloir tout
ce qu'il peut sous peine de tomber dans l'arbitraire, François quitte
la grand-chambre et produit l'après-midi même un édit qui interdit
désormais aux magistrats de s'« entremettre » dans les affaires du gouvernement.

Les procès spectaculaires intentés contre les grands dignitaires de
l'État sont aussi l'occasion de rappeler que le roi peut du jour au
lendemain abaisser ceux qu'il a élevés. En 1527, après avoir fait
condamner le connétable de Bourbon, premier prince du sang, titulaire
d'un des plus grands offices de la couronne, pair de France, François Ier s'attaque à Jacques de Beaune, seigneur de Semblançay,
nommé en 1518 surintendant des finances. Accusé de malversations,
le vieil homme est conduit de la Bastille au gibet de Montfaucon et
pendu devant une foule immense. Nicolas Versoris, qui assiste au supplice, en tire la leçon en écrivant : « De cette histoire est bien connu
et entendu l'instabilité et mutation de fortune et aussi que service de
seigneur n'est pas héritage ni grâce éternelle. » C'est rappeler que la
disgrâce est devenue le moyen de démontrer que le dernier mot revient
toujours au roi et que personne ne peut concurrencer un pouvoir qu'il
veut « absolu », *absolutus* signifiant simplement « délié » en latin.
Signe manifeste de cette évolution, les états généraux ne furent plus
convoqués pendant près d'un demi-siècle.

Les instruments du pouvoir

Lieu privilégié où se prenaient la plupart des décisions concernant la marche des affaires, le Conseil du roi, où siégeaient les « conseillers nés », les princes du sang, les ducs et les pairs de France, et

les « conseillers faits », c'est-à-dire les grands officiers choisis pour leur compétence, tend à se restreindre, Louis XII puis François Ier prenant l'habitude de s'entourer de quelques confidents réunis chaque matin après leur lever et choisis, non pour leurs compétences particulières, mais pour leur fidélité. Tandis que le vieux Conseil issu de la *curia regis* capétienne perd de son importance politique et de ses attributions, ce nouveau conseil « restreint », appelé aussi « étroit », « secret » ou « Conseil des affaires », coiffe bientôt l'ensemble des institutions politiques. Ainsi, le célèbre arrêt sur la compétence du Parlement publié à la suite du spectaculaire lit de justice de 1527 est pris en présence de huit conseillers, deux princes du sang, le chancelier Duprat, trois officiers de la Maison du roi et l'archevêque de Bourges. En 1543, sur la quinzaine de membres que comptait le vieux Conseil, cinq seulement accèdent au conseil « étroit ». Jouant de la rivalité et des jalousies de ceux qu'il a choisis pour l'entourer, le roi entretient l'émulation et tient le rôle d'arbitre, rappelant à chaque occasion qu'il n'est pas tenu par leurs avis. Ainsi, en 1544, lors des opérations en Piémont, contre l'opinion de ses conseillers, il autorise les troupes françaises à livrer bataille aux Impériaux. « Or donc, rapporte l'amiral d'Annebaut, qui fait partie du Conseil, il n'en faut plus parler [...]. Si vous perdez, vous serez seul cause de la perte, et si vous gagnez, pareillement ; et tout seul en aurez le contentement, en ayant donné seul le congé [l'autorisation]. » Ce fut l'éclatante victoire de Cérisoles.

Appelés à connaître toutes les affaires, ce sont aussi les « notaires et secrétaires du roi » chargés, sous la responsabilité du chancelier, de mettre en forme les actes officiels qui prennent de l'importance. Quatre d'entre eux, les « secrétaires des finances », ont vu leurs compétences élargies, avec pour prérogatives de contresigner toutes les lettres royales, d'ouvrir les dépêches et d'examiner les rapports en provenance des provinces. Le 4 avril 1547, quelques semaines après la mort de François Ier, un règlement pris par Henri II établit un partage du royaume entre ces quatre secrétaires, chacun d'entre eux prenant en charge quelques provinces et les pays étrangers proches. Ainsi, le secrétaire qui traitait les dépêches provenant de Normandie et de Picardie recevait également celles d'Angleterre et d'Écosse. Le secrétaire pour la Champagne et la Bresse suivait aussi les affaires de l'Allemagne, de la Suisse et de la Savoie. En 1559, ils prennent le titre de secrétaires d'État, véritables ministres avant la lettre.

L'emprise du pouvoir central fut enfin mieux assurée par l'utilisation plus systématique des « maîtres de requêtes », qui furent plus d'une centaine sous le règne d'Henri III alors qu'ils n'étaient que six à l'époque de Louis XII. À partir de 1553, ils prirent l'habitude de faire des « chevauchées » dans tout le royaume avec pour missions de veiller à la collecte des impôts, d'enquêter sur le comportement des gens de guerre à l'égard des populations civiles, de recevoir les plaintes des populations et de régler tous les contentieux, en particulier sur le paiement de la taille. Ces ancêtres des futurs « intendants » allaient devenir les rouages indispensables de la machine monarchique.

Prendre des décisions est une chose. Les faire appliquer en est une autre. Selon la belle formule de Pierre Chaunu, « l'État, ce sont, d'abord, des hommes, une société d'hommes qui infléchit les vouloirs, qui s'impose comme le modèle d'un corps social ». Au début de son règne, François Ier disposait pour encadrer un royaume de 460 000 kilomètres carrés d'environ 4 000 officiers, ce qui donnait un officier pour 115 kilomètres carrés et, en incluant le « petit personnel », un officier pour 60 kilomètres carrés.

À la fin du siècle, le nombre de ceux que Rabelais appelait les « chats fourrés » avait peut-être doublé, les rois ayant par ailleurs multiplié les ventes d'offices pour se procurer les finances dont ils étaient toujours à court. Ainsi s'amorçait la ruée des élites françaises vers la « fonction publique » qui est l'un des traits les plus caractéristiques de notre histoire longue. Assurant une formidable promotion sociale aux notables des « bonnes villes », la « savonnette à vilain » fustigée par les aristocrates allait assurer à la monarchie une armature administrative assez efficace pour renforcer son emprise sur le territoire et assez servile pour assurer son contrôle sur les élites.

La construction d'un État plus pesant se traduit également par une activité réglementaire intense. On dénombre ainsi 32 000 actes pris sous le règne de François Ier, contre 2 500 à l'époque de Philippe Auguste. Plusieurs de ces textes constituent des monuments appelés à durer. L'ordonnance de janvier 1519 visant à punir les abus qui nuisent à la bonne conservation des forêts royales constitue le premier code pénal forestier. Celle de Villers-Cotterêts, datée d'août 1539, œuvre du chancelier Poyet, introduit, au milieu des 192 articles destinés à améliorer le fonctionnement de la justice et à unifier les procédures, les célèbres articles 50 à 54 qui sont à l'origine de notre état civil. Le roi demandait en effet que dans les paroisses de son royaume soient enregistrés tous les baptêmes, généralisant une pratique que certains évêques avaient introduite depuis le siècle précédent. Tenus par les curés, paraphés par un notaire, déposés tous les ans au greffe du bailliage, ces registres paroissiaux allaient permettre de mieux recenser l'évolution de la population. Surtout, l'ordonnance prescrit aux notaires de rédiger actes, contrats et arrêts en « langage maternel françois et non aultrement », imposant, pour la première fois, l'unité de la langue dans le royaume. En 1552, Henri II achève la réforme de la justice en créant soixante et un présidiaux de neuf juges chacun pour décharger les parlements des petites affaires et juger en appel les causes portées devant les tribunaux des bailliages et des sénéchaussées.

Enfin, le concordat de Bologne qui assure la mainmise de l'État sur l'Église de France permet au roi de tenir solidement la noblesse en lui faisant espérer des biens qui, contrairement aux offices, ne peuvent pas devenir héréditaires. « Il nomme, écrit l'ambassadeur vénitien Giustiniano, à 10 archevêchés, 82 évêchés, 527 abbayes, à une infinité de prieurés et canonicats. Ce droit de nomination lui procure une gran dissime servitude et obéissance des prélats et laïques, par le désir qu'ils ont des bénéfices [...]. Et de cette façon, il satisfait non seulement ses sujets de large façon, mais encore il se concilie une foule d'étrangers. »

Il faut toutefois souligner que roi « absolu » ne possédait pas tout pouvoir. Il devait respecter les « lois fondamentales du royaume » et ne pas transgresser les « bonnes coutumes » de son pays, intérioriser le message du Christ pour mieux l'appliquer à son royaume, apprendre à frapper le Mal pour effacer les ferments de discorde entre ses sujets. L'absolutisme n'a jamais été la tyrannie.

Le spectacle de la monarchie

Appelé par François Iᵉʳ pour décorer la grande galerie du nouveau palais de Fontainebleau, le peintre italien le Rosso imagine un programme qui illustre l'utilisation de ce nouveau « média » pour assurer la gloire du « beau Prince ». L'un des tableaux le montre entouré d'un marchand, d'un magistrat, d'un savant, d'un guerrier et d'un paysan. La grenade que le roi tient à la main, dont tous les grains sont contenus dans l'enveloppe du fruit, symbolise l'unité de l'État par-delà les diversités sociales. Un éléphant, symbole de force, de mémoire et de bonté, est revêtu d'un manteau couvert de fleurs de lys, orné d'un F, comme François. Sur un autre tableau, debout sur un nuage, couronné de lauriers, tel un guerrier romain, le roi brandit un long glaive de la main droite, porte un livre sous son bras gauche et franchit résolument la porte d'un temple sans être aveuglé par la fulgurante lumière qui en jaillit. Devant lui, dans la nuit, des enfants, des hommes, des femmes, aux yeux bandés, errent en tous sens, avec de grands gestes de désespoir.

Ainsi, écrit Joël Cornette, « la loi écrite [le livre] et la force armée [l'épée] seraient désignées par les peintres de Fontainebleau comme les deux attributs primordiaux et indissociables de la solitaire souveraineté du prince. Le roi apparaît seul capable de guider les hommes et les femmes aveugles, allégorie des sujets, seul capable aussi de voir et d'affronter l'éblouissante lumière émise par Jupiter, le roi des dieux, maître du monde et de la force ». À l'époque où les théoriciens posent les principes du pouvoir absolu, les artistes convoqués pour animer les chantiers de la Renaissance française conçoivent les symboles qui exaltent la puissance de celui qui est plus que jamais « empereur en son royaume » et inscrivent sur le papier, la toile et dans la pierre l'alphabet de son culte.

Les demeures royales étaient, en effet, n'étaient pas seulement des lieux de résidence, mais de véritables « musées » offerts aux regards du public. En 1543, François Ier fait lui-même visiter Fontainebleau à Wallop, l'ancien ambassadeur du roi d'Angleterre. Pour les personnages de moindre rang, un « concierge », l'ancêtre de nos conservateurs, guide le périple.

Tout contribue à la fièvre bâtisseuse qui saisit la France pendant les guerres d'Italie, le faste d'une noblesse plus argentée qui veut rénover les vieilles forteresses médiévales, le désir des « vilains savonnés » d'afficher leur réussite, la volonté du roi de manifester sa puissance et d'imprimer les canons de l'art nouveau importé d'Italie. Très souvent édifiés à la campagne, et tout particulièrement dans le Val de Loire, où les souverains avaient pris l'habitude de séjourner depuis le milieu du XVe siècle, les demeures et les châteaux constituent le pendant français des somptueuses villas italiennes. En 1498, Louis XII rénove son vieux château de Blois et fait placer dans le portique intérieur de l'aile d'entrée une statue équestre à son effigie. En 1515, François Ier y fait bâtir un corps de logis supplémentaire dans lequel on pénètre par un escalier à vis en forme de tourelle, inspiré des styles florentin et lombard. En 1519, il décide d'élever à Chambord, l'un de ses lieux de prédilection, un rendez-vous de chasse digne de sa gloire. Sur le plan traditionnel d'un château fort, avec son énorme donjon carré, les architectes distribuent les volumes pour donner à cet ensemble gigantesque un équilibre rigoureux.

En 1528, à son retour de captivité, François Ier, fait connaître au Bureau de la ville de Paris son désir de « dorénavant faire la plupart de notre demeure et séjour en notre bonne ville » et confie à Gilles Le Breton la construction d'un nouveau palais à Fontainebleau, dans la belle forêt giboyeuse de Bière, où se dressait déjà un vieux château habité par Saint Louis. C'est là qu'il allait conserver ses précieuses collections de peintures et d'objets qui ornent le « Cabinet des curiosités », un brûle-parfum dessiné par Raphaël, une salière créée sur sa demande, des marbres anciens. C'est là que le goût italianisant du souverain se manifeste avec le plus d'éclat. C'est là que sont rassemblés les œuvres de Raphaël offertes par Laurent le Magnifique et Léon X, la *Mona Lisa* de Léonard de Vinci, des Titien envoyés de Venise, la *Sainte Famille* d'Andrea del Sarto et de nombreux tableaux d'artistes florentins dont le style est fort prisé par le roi. Rassemblés dans les appartements des Bains qui restituaient le décor et le confort des thermes antiques, nombre d'entre eux furent abîmés par l'humidité. Sur les murs, des tapisseries, exécutées dans les ateliers de Bruxelles, reprennent des thèmes antiques et des scènes mythologiques.

Ainsi se forge l'école de Fontainebleau, qui est avant tout l'école des Italiens établis en France entre 1530 et 1570, des Italiens qui séduisent par leur brillant des aristocrates qui veulent tous avoir leur « galerie » à l'image de celle du roi. Partout, châteaux, hôtels, églises, fontaines et chapelles reproduisent ce nouveau langage esthétique, tandis que peintres et sculpteurs montrent à l'envi ces corps, nus bien souvent, qui traduisent cette redécouverte émerveillée de l'homme et cette recherche d'un plaisir sensuel fort teinté d'érotisme.

Dès 1502, Georges d'Amboise, cardinal de Rouen et vice-roi de Milan, fait venir des marbres de Carrare pour rénover son château de Gaillon. Philibert de l'Orme entreprend pour Diane de Poitiers la construction d'Anet. Pierre Chambiges rénove pour le connétable de Montmorency le manoir de Chantilly. Jean Goujon donne des dessins pour le château d'Écouen où les cheminées sont largement inspirées de l'art du Primatice. Le financier Gilles Berthelot élève Azay-le-Rideau. À Bury, une galerie bramantesque est directement inspirée des modèles italiens. Le plan carré de Chenonceau, possession de Thomas Bohier, receveur général des Finances, est une importation flagrante.

Dans la capitale, l'église Saint-Eustache, dont la première pierre est posée en 1532, s'inspire totalement de l'art nouveau. La fontaine des Innocents, à l'angle des rues Saint-Denis et aux Fers, sculptée par Jean Goujon et Pierre Lescot, exprime la volonté de mener une politique de l'eau destinée à assainir une ville qui est un véritable cloaque. En 1546, enfin, désireux d'aménager le sinistre palais du Louvre, dont la grosse tour s'était effondrée en 1528, François Ier désigne Pierre Lescot comme architecte. Lors de la visite de Charles Quint à Paris, en 1540, François Ier aurait, semble-t-il, ressenti avec humiliation le fait de ne pas posséder dans sa capitale une résidence digne de ce nom. Pierre Lescot dessine alors une nouvelle façade qui ne sera achevée que sous le règne d'Henri II et utilise pour les fenêtres tous les registres du répertoire antique, en insistant particulièrement sur les effets de symétrie. Le nouveau palais du Louvre, parfaitement équilibré, apparaît ainsi, malgré ses emprunts au répertoire italien, comme le premier édifice proprement français de la Renaissance, un modèle de purisme qui rejette les surcharges et exalte les valeurs classiques que sont l'horizontalité, la régularité et l'harmonie, ces « belles règles de nature, écrit alors Vitruve, qui concernent la commodité, l'usage et profit des habitants ».

L'exaltation de la langue française

Pétrie de culture antique, nourrie de latin et parfois de grec mais attachée à la « défense et illustration de la langue française », c'est aussi une nouvelle génération, avide de savoir, qui se lance à l'assaut des belles lettres et cultive tranquillement la chair et l'intelligence de l'homme. Comparant le présent au temps de sa jeunesse « encore ténébreux et sentant l'infélicité et calamité des Goths, qui avaient mis à destruction toute bonne littérature », le Gargantua de Rabelais s'enthousiasme : « Tout le monde est plein de gens savants, de précepteurs très doctes, de libraires très amples, et m'est avis que, ni au temps de Platon, ni de Cicéron, n'était telle commodité d'étude qu'on y voit maintenant [...]. Je vois les brigands, les bourreaux, les aventuriers, les palefreniers de maintenant, plus doctes que les docteurs et prêcheurs de mon temps [...]. »

Dans la plupart des bonnes villes, en effet, se multiplient les établissements ouverts aux jeunes gens de la boutique et du commerce. Dans le Forez, tout au long du XVIᵉ siècle, de petites écoles urbaines, souvent placées sous l'autorité de la municipalité, apprennent aux enfants des artisans et des marchands les rudiments de la lecture, de l'écriture et du calcul. Angoulême a son collège en 1516, Lyon en crée un en 1527, Dijon en 1531. Celui de Bordeaux, créé en 1532, accueille Michel de Montaigne qui y demeure sept ans. Convertis aux nouvelles modes pédagogiques importées d'Italie ou des Pays-Bas, les maîtres encouragent la lecture directe des œuvres, le travail et la réflexion personnelle de leurs élèves.

Aussi attentif aux choses de l'esprit qu'à celles de l'art, François Iᵉʳ subventionne, encourage et couronne le tout en créant en 1530, pour faire concurrence à la vieille et conservatrice Sorbonne, un Collège royal, notre Collège de France, chargé, hors du cadre universitaire, de donner des cours publics largement ouverts aux amateurs, des placards, affichés au Quartier latin, indiquant la date, l'heure et le lieu des cours.

Les premiers lecteurs royaux, payés par le Trésor, comptent parmi les plus grands érudits de leur temps. Dès la fin de 1530, Oronce Fine, né en 1494 à Briançon, y donne un enseignement de mathématiques, invente de curieuses machines, publie une trentaine d'ouvrages, dessine la première carte de France et fabrique, pour le cardinal de Lorraine, une pendule étonnante. Guillaume Postel, le premier titulaire de la chaire de langues orientales, prône la réconciliation entre l'islam et le christianisme. Agathio Guidacerio, d'origine calabraise, enseigne l'hébreu, Paul Paradis, juif vénitien, les langues hébraïques. L'Artésien Pierre Galland, qui professe l'éloquence, met son art en pratique en écrivant le discours funèbre de François Ier en 1547. C'est aussi l'essor de l'imprimerie qui favorise la propagation des idées nouvelles. En 1500, trente et une villes sont dotées d'une imprimerie, Paris et Lyon dominant l'ensemble. Et alors qu'en 1501 la production des classiques grecs, latins et humanistes ne représentait que 28 % de la production totale des ouvrages imprimés, en 1549 elle atteint 63 %. Rédigés pour être lus à haute voix ou transportés dans la hotte des colporteurs, des placards hâtivement imprimés et rehaussés de gravures racoleuses assouvissent enfin l'impétueux désir d'information de ce qui devient un public national.

Autant d'initiatives qui ont permis une alphabétisation plus large des Français mais, en même temps, creusé les écarts culturels. En 1574-1576, 72 % des laboureurs qui viennent à l'étude de maître Navarre, un notaire de Montpellier, ne savent pas signer, alors que les deux tiers des artisans de la ville sont capables de signer plus ou moins maladroitement leur nom. À Paris, entre 1551 et 1600, 86 % des hommes et 28 % des femmes pouvaient signer leur acte de mariage.

Au même moment, imposée dans les actes notariés par l'édit de Villers-Cotterêts, la langue française progresse de manière décisive. C'est en 1549 que paraît son plus éclatant manifeste, la *Défense et Illustration de la langue française*, rédigée par Joachim du Bellay, en étroite collaboration avec Pierre Ronsard. Manifeste d'une nouvelle génération contre les « gréciseurs » et les « latiniseurs », la « Défense » soutient que le génie français peut rivaliser avec celui des Italiens. « Je ne veux pas donner si haut les louanges à notre langue, pour ce qu'elle n'a point encore ses Cicérons et Virgiles, peut-on lire dans cette « Illustration », mais j'ose bien assurer que si les savants hommes de notre nation la daignaient autant estimer que les Romains faisaient la leur, elle pourrait quelquefois et bientôt se mettre au rang des plus fameuses. »

C'est bien la montée du sentiment national excité par les guerres étrangères qui explique, dans une large mesure, ce patriotisme linguistique. Tandis que les chansons du temps exaltent les victoires du « noble roy François », soutiennent Bayard et raillent le connétable de Bourbon, traître à son pays, Ronsard commence sa carrière poétique en faisant l'éloge d'une France épargnée par « la cruauté des vents malicieux » et où se plaît « Cérès la blonde », et Michel de Montaigne appelle de ses vœux une monarchie autoritaire capable de faire régner l'ordre nécessaire au repos de ses sujets.

Dans le même temps, le groupe de poètes qui prend en 1556 le nom de la Pléiade, soutenu par le mécénat royal, s'efforce de produire en langue nationale les genres nobles que sont la tragédie, la comédie, l'ode, l'épopée et le sonnet.

À l'heure où Luther traduit la Bible en un allemand accessible à tous, au moment où Calvin traduit en français *L'Institution de la religion chrétienne*, Rabelais, dont le *Gargantua* est publié en 1534, devient le meilleur représentant de cette Renaissance littéraire française, une Renaissance marquée par une immense curiosité intellectuelle, un rejet de l'intolérance sous toutes ses formes et l'affirmation de la primauté de l'homme et de sa féconde liberté.

CHAPITRE **41**

Le temps de l'inflation

*O*bservant en 1546 la situation du royaume de France, l'ambassadeur vénitien Marino Cavalli écrivait : « Le pays est si grand qu'il est naturel qu'il soit fort divers de paysages et de régions et qu'il produise des choses fort diverses. Ces produits sont d'une excellente qualité et tellement abondants qu'ils suffisent à l'usage des habitants et dépassent leurs besoins. » En 1568, Jean Bodin ajoutait : « Depuis cent ans, on a défriché un pays infini de forêts et de landes, bâti plusieurs villages, peuplé les villes [...]. » Après le « trou noir » des guerres de Cent Ans, c'était souligner une autre renaissance, celle des villes et des campagnes.

Le royaume le plus peuplé d'Europe

Amorcée vers 1450, dans les dernières années du règne de Charles VII, poursuivie sous le règne de l'« universelle araigne », la reprise démographique observée par Jean Bodin se poursuit jusque vers 1560, avec, sur un siècle, un taux annuel de croissance de 0,7 % (contre 0,4 % aujourd'hui). À cette date, avec 18 à 20 millions d'hommes et de femmes, la France est, dans ses frontières actuelles, le royaume le plus peuplé d'Europe. Vingt millions de Français, 40 habitants environ au kilomètre carré semblent d'ailleurs constituer un plafond qui ne sera pas dépassé avant le XVIIIᵉ siècle, comme si les conditions de production et de distribution ne permettaient pas de franchir ce seuil de peuplement. La France, en 1560 comme en 1320, était un monde « plein ».

Tout au long de cette période, dans les chaumières rustiques comme dans les logis urbains, on se marie plus jeune et on copule joyeusement, un moraliste pouvant évoquer les paysans qui « chantent tous les jours aux champs et ronflent la nuit dans leurs petites maisons ». Sous François Ier, les femmes se marient en moyenne à 20-21 ans, et comme près de la moitié des unions étaient contractées entre le 1er novembre et le 28 février, en une saison où le calendrier agricole laissait assez de loisirs pour préparer la fête, les premiers « fruits » du mariage voyaient souvent le jour à la fin des moissons et des vendanges ou, pour ceux qui avaient été conçus à l'éveil du printemps, au cœur de l'hiver.

Et comme l'arme de l'abstinence sexuelle semble avoir été fort émoussée, vingt années possibles de fécondité laissaient en moyenne 4 ou 5 enfants vivants par feu, les intervalles intergénésiques étant d'environ vingt-cinq mois.

Les familles nobles, en particulier, plus sensibles au modèle de virilité prolifique qu'aux austères recommandations du protestantisme naissant, semblent avoir, plus joyeusement que les autres, multiplié les enfants légitimes comme les bâtards. Dans la famille de Fontanges, par exemple, à Cropières, en haute Auvergne, on trouve, vers 1550, 24 bâtards pour trois mâles de deux générations. Antoine de Fontanges engendre 6 enfants illégitimes. Son frère Annet en a 10 et le fils légitime d'Annet au moins 8 ! L'idée que « le père est la plus forte cause de la génération » et que la mère n'est que le canal par où passe la noble semence explique le préjugé favorable dont jouissent en général ces bâtards. Joachim du Bellay va même jusqu'à prétendre que ces bâtards sont plus « généreux » que les fils légitimes « pour être au jeu d'amour l'homme plus vigoureux » avec une maîtresse qu'avec sa femme...

Des récoltes mieux assurées, un régime nutritif relativement bon, une meilleure évacuation des ordures, des mesures de quarantaine plus sévères, autant d'éléments qui ont desserré l'emprise de la mort. Certes, le paludisme, la mortalité infantile, le typhus introduit en Europe par des prisonniers turcs, la syphilis, probablement importée d'Amérique, écrèment toujours régulièrement les populations. Toutefois, le taux de mortalité générale, aux alentours de 30 ‰, est assez modestement remarquable, comme le sont aussi la victoire sur la lèpre et l'espacement des pestes.

Cette joyeuse croissance qui revitalise les campagnes « écorchées » par les soudards et les épidémies assure surtout le triomphe des villes, dont la population a doublé ou triplé dans les années 1470-1540. Paris, qui, selon l'état des feux de 1328, avait alors 200 000 habitants, en compte certainement 400 000 au milieu du XVIe siècle, ce qui en fait, avec Naples et Constantinople, la ville la plus peuplée

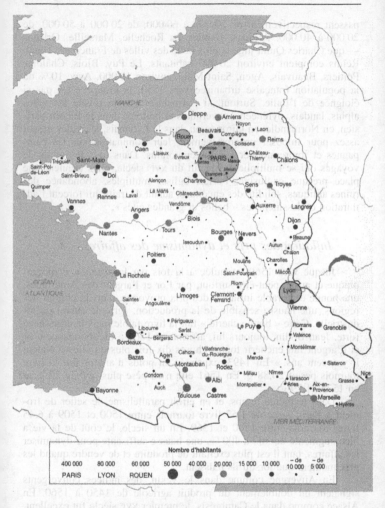

Le tissu urbain en France au temps de François Ier.

d'Europe. Lyon, « second œil de la France », selon le secrétaire de Marguerite d'Autriche, abrite vers 1550 quelque 80 000 habitants, contre 40 000 un demi-siècle plus tôt. Rouen, Bordeaux, Toulouse passent respectivement de 20 000 à 60 000, de 20 000 à 50 000, de 20 000 à 40 000. Amiens, Nantes, La Rochelle, Marseille, Orléans — que Charles Quint juge la plus belle des villes de France —, Tours, Reims comptent environ 20 000 habitants. Le Puy, Blois, Châlons, Poitiers, Beauvais, Agen, Saint-Malo, environ 10 000. Avec 10 % de la population française urbanisée vers 1550, la France n'est pas si éloignée de l'Italie. Surtout, si l'armature urbaine révèle les vides alpins, landais, pyrénéens, auvergnats et bretons, dans le Bassin parisien, en Normandie, en Gironde ou dans le Lyonnais, les villes pèsent assez pour imposer progressivement leur domination sur les campagnes et impressionner les contemporains. Dans tous les récits de voyages qui se multiplient à la fin du XVIᵉ siècle, elles tiennent une place presque exclusive. Portes, églises multiples, abondance des ruines antiques, solidité des enceintes, autant de traits qui forcent l'admiration et dessinent les « belles et grandes cités ».

Inflation des prix et dynamisme des affaires

Jusque vers 1560, stimulée à la fois par la pression démographique et aussi, peut-être surtout, par l'or et l'argent des Amériques, une bonne et durable inflation des prix provoque, dans la plupart des régions, une hausse sensible de la production, agricole autant qu'industrielle. Cette « bonne cherté » fait la livre faible mais la croissance forte. Jean Bodin, toujours lui, affirme en 1566 : « L'abondance d'or et d'argent fait enchérir toutes choses dix fois plus qu'elles n'étaient il y a cent ans. » En 1493, exprimée en poids d'argent fin, la livre tournois pesait 20,88 g. En 1561 elle n'en pèse plus que 14,27 g, et en 1575 11,79 g.

Dans le même temps, et en étroit parallélisme, le setier de froment à Paris passe de 1,57 livre tournois entre 1500 et 1509 à 6,45 livres tournois entre 1560 et 1569. En un siècle, le coût de la vie a bien augmenté de 300 à 400 %, une hausse suffisante pour dynamiser les affaires, tant il est plus excitant de produire et de vendre quand les prix montent que lorsqu'ils baissent.

En Auvergne comme dans le Vexin, des indices convergents signalent un doublement du produit agricole de 1450 à 1560. En Alsace comme dans le Cambrésis, le premier XVIᵉ siècle fut excellent. À elles seules, les livraisons de sel en provenance des marais salants de l'Atlantique, ce sel dont chaque Français consomme en moyenne 1,8 kg par an pour saler le cochon et donner du goût à la soupe, traduisent la joyeuse fébrilité de la conjoncture. Vers 1490, Nantes expédiait par la Loire de 8 à 10 000 muids de sel. Vers 1550, ce sont 16 000 muids qui partent vers un large arrière-pays. En 1567, près de 20 000 muids.

Comme pour les hommes, toutefois, les maxima de production atteints vers 1550-1560 semblent constituer un seuil difficile à franchir, quelques crise brutales venant souligner, dans les années 1520 comme dans les années 1530, les limites d'une agriculture à la productivité désespérément faible. Quatre grains récoltés pour un semé dans la France du Sud, cinq pour un sur les meilleures terres, sept pour un en cas de miracle, tels sont les rendements qui, jusqu'au XVIIIe siècle, dessinent un univers malthusien où la fécondité des hommes est constamment menacée par la faible productivité céréalière. Ainsi, l'obsession des blés, la nécessité d'assurer avant tout le pain quotidien, dont la consommation moyenne par habitant représente plus de 600 grammes par jour, limitent l'essor des autres productions. Si les jardins, amoureusement cultivés, livrent fruits et légumes, si l'Italie nous donne le melon et l'artichaut, légume préféré de l'aristocratie, si l'on cultive le maïs et le haricot importés d'Amérique, si le pastel fait un « tabac » en Aquitaine, seule la vigne prospère vraiment, tant l'eau, si souvent polluée, alimente avec raison la peur des buveurs de vin. Les muscadets aigrelets de la basse Loire font alors fureur. Paris, qui compte au moins 100 000 buveurs de solides « biberons », est fournie par les vignobles qui se multiplient aux portes de la capitale, à Chevilly ou à l'Haÿ-les-Roses. Entre 1515 et 1545, le nombre de tavernes à Lyon a été multiplié par cinq pour servir ce petit vin à 6 ou 8 deniers le litre alors qu'un manœuvre gagne une cinquantaine de deniers par jour.

Comme la vie semble meilleur marché en France que dans les pays voisins — c'est la remarque que fait Machiavel dans son *Tableau de France* en 1510 —, nombreux sont les étrangers qui viennent s'y établir pour faire du royaume un centre puissant de redistribution. En 1569, à Lyon, capitale des marchands italiens en France, les dix premiers totalisent 36,6 % de la valeur des importations ! Les Bonvisi, en particulier, qui brassent un chiffre d'affaires annuel de près d'un million de livres tournois, plus de 6 % des recettes royales, étendent leur empire dans toute l'Europe, négociant sur les épices, les vins et les soieries. Le Génois Promontorio assure à lui seul le quart des importations de velours de Gênes tandis que cinq ou six marchands allemands monopolisent les importations de cuivre rouge, de laiton et de feuilles de fer-blanc.

Donnant chair au rêve italien, Lyon a su saisir sa chance, devenant la plaque tournante des exportations françaises de biens courants :

toiles de Bresse et draps du Languedoc qui partent vers le Maghreb et les pays du Levant, quincaillerie, mais aussi livres imprimés qui s'exportent jusque dans le Nouveau Monde. Grâce à l'ancienne capitale des Gaules, la France s'ouvre à nouveau sur le monde des grandes affaires.

Annexée au domaine royal en 1481, à la mort de René d'Anjou, Marseille, mariée à Lyon pour le meilleur du commerce et de la finance, connaît une lente mais irrésistible ascension. La gabelle portuaire, qui en donne la mesure, s'établissait à 400 livres dans les dernières années du XVe siècle. Elle atteint 1 300 livres en 1519-1520, 3 000 en 1542 et 8 220 dans les années 1562-1570. La politique d'alliance avec Soliman le Magnifique menée par François Ier favorise l'activité au Levant et fait de Beyrouth et de Tripoli les comptoirs les plus actifs du commerce marseillais. Fondée en 1553 par le Corse Thomas Lenche, la grande Compagnie du Corail des mers de Bône pêche le corail entre le cap Matifou et le cap Nègre, noue des liens avec les marchands de Bougie, de Tunis et d'Oran et en vient à assurer 40 % du commerce français avec les États barbaresques. Marseille doit toutefois batailler ferme pour concurrencer Vénitiens, Génois et Florentins qui acceptent mal de lui entrebâiller les portes du profit méditerranéen.

À l'ouest, là où tout est nouveau, au moment où le vent des Amériques fait la fortune d'Anvers, de Lisbonne et de Séville, les havres français grappillent timidement les fruits des nouveaux négoces transocéaniques. Incorporés depuis 1491 au royaume, les navires bretons transportent le vin et le sel jusqu'aux Pays-Bas et en Angleterre. Mais ni Bordeaux, ni Nantes, ni Le Havre, fondé en 1517 pour servir de point de départ aux grandes aventures, ne peuvent rivaliser avec leurs concurrents flamands, espagnols ou portugais. Seuls les marchands de Rouen qui, dès 1508, se sont intéressés à Terre-Neuve et prospectent en Afrique, à Madagascar, à Sumatra et au Brésil sont à la hauteur du défi américain.

Cette expansion commerciale manifeste s'appuie d'abord, en fait, sur les marchés intérieurs que suscite une demande d'hommes plus nombreux qui se nourrissent mieux et veulent porter plus beau. Faut-il rappeler que naissent alors tous les ans près de 800 000 Français, soit plus qu'aujourd'hui (730 000) pour une population trois fois moins nombreuse ?

Ainsi, dans les campagnes, on cultive les plantes textiles dont l'exploitation sans grand labeur améliore l'ordinaire des familles rurales. Dans l'ouest du royaume, le chanvre, qui n'exige pas de bonnes terres mais de la main-d'œuvre qui surabonde, fait tourner les rouets et les métiers qui tissent les toiles de Bretagne. Autour de Rouen, de Beauvais, de Montdidier, de Reims, de Châlons, de Troyes, de Bourges, de Châtellerault, de Niort, de Lodève, de Béziers, de Carcassonne, de Limoux et de Montpellier, on tisse aussi des draps de qualité courante qui vont concurrencer les draps anglais en Italie, en Berbérie et dans les pays du Levant. Dans le Midi aquitain, le pastel fait la fortune des marchands de Toulouse qui vendent la précieuse teinture aux Espagnols.

Enfin, dans un monde où l'usage du fer se développe, pour les besoins de l'armement mais aussi pour ces multiples objets que sont épingles et clous, rasoirs d'acier et ciseaux, fourchettes ou plaques de cheminée, serrures et clefs, les forges partent à l'assaut des forêts qui, vers 1550, couvraient encore un tiers du territoire national. En 1543, François Iᵉʳ doit ordonner une réduction du nombre des forges à fer car, écrit-il, « il y a en ce royaume plus de quatre cent soixante forges. Il y en a plus de quatre cent érigées depuis cinquante ans ; par chacun an, il s'en érige vingt-cinq ou trente ». Et alors, poursuit-il, que les forgerons « sont les plus riches et opulents de ce royaume », ils ne paient « aucune aide ou subside » pour ce privilège. La région de Saint-Étienne et Saint-Chamond, où l'on expérimente l'usage du charbon de pierre, devient en particulier un grand centre de production d'armes, d'épées, de hallebardes et d'arquebuses.

Signe de cette première « mondialisation », la notion de « balance commerciale » devient alors clairement perçue. Dans les années 1550, un auteur anonyme a dressé pays par pays, groupe de marchandises par groupe de marchandises, le tableau des exportations et des importations. Seule cette dernière partie a été conservée, reprise en 1573 par Nicolas de Nicolaï, géographe du roi Charles IX. Elle nous montre le poids des héritages anciens, le monde méditerranéen assurant toujours près des deux tiers des importations. Elle nous montre aussi la part énorme des produits de luxe destinés à l'aristocratie.

Pourtant, grâce aux exportations de vins et de sel, de draps et de toiles de chanvre, de laine et de pastel, la balance semble positive pour la France. C'est ce que suggèrent les importations de métal précieux qui sont la contrepartie de cet excédent et permettent les frappes de pièces d'or et d'argent. Entre 1498 et 1502, on peut évaluer le total des frappes monétaires à 2,6 millions de livres, à 3,2 millions entre 1523 et 1527, à 5,9 millions entre 1548 et 1555, à 7 millions entre 1573 et 1577. Un signe, parmi d'autres, du dynamisme des affaires.

Le temps des « honnestes personnes »

Moins antisociale qu'on le dit trop souvent, l'inflation, dont les effets se sont fait sentir sur deux ou trois générations, a certainement fait plus d'heureux que de victimes, même si, comme toujours, des esprits chagrins ont été effrayés par l'esprit d'un siècle qu'ils jugeaient trop « pressé de vivre ».

Publiés en 1547, les *Propos rustiques* de Noël du Fail évoquent avec mélancolie la simplicité des mœurs d'autrefois, mettant ces paroles éternelles dans la bouche de vieux paysans bretons : « Ô temps heureux ! Ô siècles fortunés ! où nous avons vu nos prédécesseurs pères de famille se contentant, quant à l'accoutrement, d'une bonne robe de bureau, calfeutrée à la mode d'alors, celle pour les fêtes, et une autre pour les jours ouvriers, de bonne toile doublée de quelque vieux saye [...], chacun content de sa fortune et du métier duquel pouvait honnêtement vivre. »

Au village en effet, bénéficiaires d'une inflation qui a réduit à peu de chose les cens seigneuriaux exprimés, selon une coutume immémoriale, en monnaie fixe, tous ceux qui ont quelque chose à vendre ou qui exercent plusieurs métiers bénéficient de cette heureuse conjoncture. Dans les campagnes parisiennes, les droits seigneuriaux atteignent en moyenne 12 deniers parisis par arpent, ce qui équivaut à 12 litres de froment pour un hectare qui en rend facilement 1 500 ! Une « moyenne » paysannerie habile à saisir les opportunités se constitue alors en Hurepoix comme en Auvergne, ou en basse Bretagne où de nombreux paysans exploitent le sel dans les paluds et en assurent eux-mêmes l'exploitation en le transportant à dos de mule. À Belloy, en Île-de-France, les Chartier, qui n'avaient pas de capital, prennent à bail le domaine de Michel de La Grange et commencent ainsi une ascension qui les conduit au sommet de la société rurale. À Antony, près de Paris, la veuve Couet, propriétaire d'un peu plus de 1 hectare de vigne et de 1,20 ha de prairies, dégage tous les ans près de 60 livres de bénéfices tant les opportunités qu'offre la capitale pour la vente de ses produits sont exceptionnelles.

Certains laboureurs, plus opportunistes, plus entreprenants ou plus chanceux, insistent alors chez le notaire pour être appelés « honorables hommes » ou « honnestes personnes ». Et, à partir des années 1530, ils sont nombreux à remplacer les toits de chaume par des tuiles, à acheter des lits plus confortables, des matelas garnis de plumes, et à vouloir se faire inhumer dans l'église, sous une pierre tombale coûteuse qui les représente vêtus de leurs plus beaux atours, une longue houppelande et un pourpoint garni de boutons pour les hommes, un chaperon plat, à l'italienne, avec une robe garnie de velours pour les femmes. Au décès d'Antoine Bimont, qui labourait 160 hectares en 1588, le notaire chargé de dresser l'inventaire de ses biens trouva dans les coffres 32 draps, 20 nappes et 34 serviettes.

Certes, il n'est pas question de nier l'extrême précarité de l'existence pour la majorité des « laboureurs », toujours à la merci d'une mauvaise année, mais possédant vache, cochons et souvent cheval, cultivant quelques dizaines d'ares, en louant quelques dizaines d'autres à des prix raisonnables, disposant d'un coffre, d'une table, de lits, de linge et de vaisselle, ils sont plutôt mieux lotis que ne l'étaient leurs ancêtres. Ils représenteraient, dans l'Île-de-France minutieusement étudiée par Jean Jacquart, les deux tiers de la masse des paysans, formant le gros bataillon du monde rural. Comme toujours dans toute société, la frontière entre bénéficiaires et victimes de la conjoncture passait entre ceux qui laissaient filer l'argent et ceux qui parvenaient à le retenir, entre les « passoires et les éponges », écrit Emmanuel Le Roy Ladurie.

Cette très modeste aisance permet sans doute d'expliquer pourquoi les cahiers de doléances rédigés à l'occasion des états généraux de 1576 ne sont pas hostiles au système seigneurial, 2 % seulement des revendications portant sur les droits seigneuriaux et féodaux. En tête des doléances venaient en fait les désirs d'une réforme religieuse (20 %), d'une meilleure justice (15 %) et d'une taille moins lourde (15 %). Des paysans qui se préoccupent en premier de la qualité de leurs ecclésiastiques ne peuvent être que d'« honnestes personnes ».

À la ville, dans cette France du mouvement où se brassent les échanges et le crédit, émergent aussi du « menu peuple », des « gens vils et mécaniques », ceux qui « ont de quoi », les « opulents » et les « notables » qui ont « au soleil » le bien qui leur épargne la hantise du quotidien.

Aristocrates du vin et du pastel à Bordeaux et Toulouse, aristocrates de la marchandise et de la banque à Lyon, ils ajoutent au profit de leurs entreprises celui des prés et des vignes qu'ils donnent en location aux laboureurs de leur campagne. Une manière de ne pas mettre tous leurs œufs dans le même panier.

Ainsi en est-il de Guillaume Masenx, dont le « livre de raison », retrouvé par Emmanuel Le Roy Ladurie, nous trace de manière fort concrète l'itinéraire de ces « gens de bien » qui ont bénéficié du temps de l'inflation.

Né vers 1495 à Castelnau-de-Montmirail, dans le Languedoc, Guillaume Masenx, issu d'une famille de marchands, de prêtres et de simples paysans, doté d'une instruction minimale, ne sachant ni le français, ni le latin, épouse en 1516 la fille d'un fermier qui exploitait l'une des terres de la commanderie Saint-Pierre de Gaillac. En 1518, il en prend la direction, vendant le vin et le blé, percevant l'argent des rentes et des cens. En 1530 puis en 1535, il devient fermier d'un deuxième puis d'un troisième domaine. Prêteur de blé en mai et juin, avant la moisson, quand il est très cher, pratiquant l'usure, « de jour en jour et à sa volonté », précisent les contrats, il se fait rembourser en nature et en corvées diverses, tient aussi boutique, vendant de tout, bijoux et planches, couvertures et robes de mariée, tuiles et briques qu'il fabrique, cercles et futailles qui accompagnent les vins de Gaillac en Angleterre. « Pionnier capitaliste », rassembleur de terres, industriel et marchand, il organise aussi le 26 juillet 1537 la réception qui accueille plus ou moins clandestinement ceux qui viennent prêcher la Réforme protestante.

Cet exemple n'est pas unique. Toutes les villes ont des Masenx qui, grâce à de solides alliances, ont joui d'un mode de vie qui les apparentait à l'aristocratie. À Marseille, les fils des riches négociants portent volontiers l'épée au côté et se déplacent dans la ville en montant des chevaux de race pour afficher leur réussite. À Lyon, les marchands évincent les hommes de loi des leviers du pouvoir urbain, dix-sept familles, dont les Regnault, occupant sans relâche les charges consulaires. Mais si quelques magnats comme les Assezat à Toulouse ou les Gadagne à Lyon font construire de magnifiques hôtels, la plupart vivent dans des maisons relativement modestes, préférant investir dans les somptueuses maisons de plaisance qu'ils font édifier sur leurs terres, à une journée de cheval de la ville.

Surtout, par l'achat d'offices, de seigneuries ou d'épouses, il est toujours possible de franchir la stricte ordonnance des « états » et d'accéder à cette noblesse au « sang bleu » dont le pouvoir de la semence reste environné de mystère. Maurice Sauron, entré en 1547 comme apprenti chez un drapier marseillais, devient « marchand » trois ans plus tard, « noble écuyer », rang le plus bas de la noblesse, huit ans après et finit sa carrière en 1570 dans l'office prestigieux de consul français à Alger. Laboureur à Bouville, en Beauce, à la fin du XVᵉ siècle, Jean Lecoq arrondit ses propriétés à tel point que son arrière-petit-fils se fait appeler « sieur de Moisville » et, en 1595, marie sa fille unique à Jean de Serisy, écuyer, sieur de Congny, dont la noblesse est tout aussi fragile que la sienne. À cette date, en effet, seuls 21 % des seigneurs beaucerons sont nobles depuis plus d'un siècle, 25 % étant issus directement de la roture et 47 % étant nobles depuis moins de cent ans.

Au sommet de l'ordre « ancien » dont la « pureté » était définie avec acharnement et naïveté par ceux qui voyaient ainsi « souillée » leur « race », figurait la masse des gentilshommes qui avaient toujours pour eux le respect acquis et transmis, de 70 000 à 80 000 seigneurs qui quadrillaient le royaume et remplissaient assez leurs traditionnelles missions pour ne pas encourir les doléances de ceux qui, en droit sinon en fait, restaient leurs « sujets ».

Proches de leurs tenanciers, leur puissance n'était pas, contrairement à un schéma trop commode, forcément contestée, moins finalement par les paysans que par le roi. Solidement enraciné dans son Cotentin, Gilles de Gouberville, qui a écrit un *Journal* lu et commenté par Emmanuel Le Roy Ladurie, en est une belle illustration.

Propriétaire d'un vaste domaine au Mesnil-en-Val, à une heure de marche de Cherbourg, le sire de Gouberville, né vers 1517, esprit « éclairé », sait varier la semence et tester les engrais pour enrichir une terre médiocre et pleine de cailloux sur lesquels se brisent les charrues trop légères. Superstitieux toutefois, il achète en 1557 un livre de Nostradamus pour fixer la date des semailles, sans grand succès apparemment. Toujours assurées par des corvées qui semblent se faire dans la bonne humeur et se terminent par des fêtes ponctuées de danses, les moissons ne rapportent guère, le blé étant immédiatement distribué aux valets, aux parents, aux employés et aux pique-assiette.

Au premier rang des sources de revenus, se trouvent les porcs nourris par les glands des vastes forêts, tués en hiver et expédiés salés à Paris. Au second rang, le moulin banal, qui rapporte 331 boisseaux de froment par an, soit beaucoup plus que tous les autres revenus liés au statut de seigneur. Arme privilégiée de l'influence, les lapins, lièvres ou pâtés de cerf offerts aux dames qu'il veut séduire et aux juges qu'il s'agit de fléchir pour récupérer une rente de 100 sous par an alors que le procès lui a coûté 100 livres !

Céréalier médiocre et éleveur besogneux, Gouberville s'affirme en revanche fort innovateur en matière de pommes et de cidre qui, là encore, abreuve la famille et la main-d'œuvre de la seigneurie. Plantant et greffant du pommier à tout va, il sauve chaque année de la maladie ceux auxquels il offre l'occasion de ne plus boire d'eau. Toujours à court d'argent, il soupe dans l'étain et met ses pièces dans un mouchoir noué aux quatre coins qu'il perd souvent ou qu'on lui vole à plusieurs reprises. Aussi bien, imprégné de l'idéal autarcique, l'idée même de gagner de l'argent lui est totalement étrangère. Seules comptent à ses yeux les ripailles dont les menus conservés nous livrent témoignage. Recevant le 22 août 1553 le curé de Cherbourg, plus quatre hommes et l'épouse de l'un d'entre eux, ils dévorent :

Viande valant pour une livre tournois et 2 sous

Des poulets

Huit bécassines

Sucre, cannelle, clou de girofle, poivre, safran, gingembre, bref quantité d'épices pour faire « descendre » toute cette viande

Quatre pots de vin achetés à Valognes

Quatre pots de vin achetés à Cherbourg

Un pot d'hypocras ou vin épicé (le « pot » faisant environ deux litres).

Vieux garçon endurci, Gilles de Gouberville a pour nombreuse « famille » les bâtards et les bâtardes nés de son père, les siens propres qu'il a eus d'une maîtresse qu'il lui est interdit d'épouser, sous peine de mésalliance. Elle comprend aussi quatorze domestiques entretenus, logés et nourris, qu'il rosse parfois, sans que le destinataire y trouve à redire.

Plus manœuvrier que despote, il assure une justice de proximité, préside après la messe du dimanche l'assemblée des hommes du village qui se disputent la répartition de la taille ou adjugent aux enchères les pommes tombées dans le cimetière. Rebouteux à ses moments perdus, il perce les furoncles, remet les genoux déboîtés et, violemment hostile à la diète, administre aux patients des chevreaux et des pâtés, des potages de sa confection, à base de bette, de bourrache et d'épinards, assaisonnés de verjus, de jaune d'œuf et de beurre frais, du lait de chèvre, des feuilles de chou pour la goutte ou de l'eau d'aubépine pour la colique.

Gilles de Gouberville, enfin, ne semble pas obsédé par le « sang bleu » qui coule dans ses veines ni par les missions assignées à son « ordre ». Quand le ban le convoque à l'ost, il se comporte en « planqué » et prétexte un rhume ou une foulure pour ne pas rejoindre l'armée.

La noblesse, pour lui, est surtout le fait de ne pas avoir à payer l'impôt. D'ailleurs, en 1556, quand se produit dans le Cotentin une vérification générale des titres de noblesse, Gouberville fouille avec fébrilité dans ses paperasses pour recopier, « jusqu'à minuit », écrit-il, les preuves de noblesse de sa famille depuis 1400.

Certes, il est d'autres sires que des Gouberville dans le royaume de France, des aristocrates de cour qui bénéficient des largesses du Prince et s'accaparent de vastes domaines fonciers, des Anne de Montmorency ou des Guise capables de peser sur la politique royale par l'importance de leur clientèle, mais, dans le monde des privilégiés comme dans les autres, la frontière qui sépare les « exclus » de la croissance de ceux qui en tirent profit passe aussi entre les éponges et les passoires. Si, en basse Auvergne, les Estaing voient les revenus de leur seigneurie de Fernoël quadrupler entre 1500 et 1570, en Bretagne, le tiers des gentilshommes avaient des terres qui leur rapportaient moins de 15 livres, c'est-à-dire à peine le double de ce qu'il fallait pour assurer la subsistance d'une famille de cinq personnes.

D'où les nombreuses lamentations de nobles à qui leurs revenus, rognés par l'inflation, ne permettent pas de suivre une carrière militaire, encore moins de mener grand train. En 1587, François de La Noue plaint ces gentilshommes « déchus de cette ancienne richesse dont leurs maisons étaient ornées sous les règnes de nos bons rois Louis douzième et François premier », précisant que sur dix familles nobles, il s'en trouve huit « incommodées par les aliénations de quelque portion de leurs biens, engagements ou autres dettes ».

Rabaisser le vulgaire

L'inflation qui a accru le nombre de riches et fait les riches plus riches a aussi fait des victimes, tous ceux qui, finalement, ils étaient nombreux, n'avaient rien d'autre à vendre que leurs bras.

À la campagne, en particulier, le travailleur des champs, qui devait, à la mort de Louis XI, travailler soixante heures pour acheter un quintal de blé doit fournir cent heures pour le même prix à la mort de François Ier. Si le faucheur près de Paris a vu son salaire quotidien passer de 5 sous en 1495 à 12 sous en 1540, dans le même temps le prix du froment est passé de 15 sous le setier à 50 sous. Le faucheur y perd, mais pas trop. Il faut dire qu'en multipliant les bras la « copiosité du populaire » a excité la concurrence sur le marché du travail et laissé à ceux qui en détenaient les clefs la maîtrise des prix. Chez Gouberville, un garde-chèvres gagne 50 sous par an, plus une paire de chaussures. Un valet de ferme logé, responsable de la charrue, gagne 6 livres par an. Mais en Languedoc, nourri et logé, c'est 15 livres qu'il reçoit.

Ce sont aussi les petits exploitants qui, victimes de leur nombreuse progéniture, laissent à leurs descendants des propriétés morcelées par le diviseur successoral. Vers 1460, en Languedoc, le gros bataillon des propriétés couvrait 5 à 10 hectares, de quoi assurer une honnête autosuffisance. À la génération suivante, chaque descendant ne possède plus qu'une poignée d'hectares. Vers le milieu du xvıᵉ siècle, dans le Hurepoix, les tenanciers ne possèdent en moyenne que 1,3 ha par famille.

Une superficie insuffisante qui prépare l'endettement et bientôt l'aliénation pour dettes. En 1573, quand il meurt, Jean Pocquelin, marchand drapier et receveur de la ville de Beauvais, possédait 857 créances à l'encontre de débiteurs paysans disséminés dans 134 villages et hameaux. Autrefois soumises aux seigneurs qui bornaient souvent leurs efforts à regarder pousser les grandes forêts de leurs domaines, les campagnes ont subi l'arrivée massive de bourgeois autrement entreprenants, des notaires, des banquiers et des marchands. Dominants pour dominants.

À la ville, l'afflux de main-d'œuvre a aussi fait baisser les salaires. En 1450-1460 comme en 1545, un manœuvre parisien gagnait toujours 3 sous par jour, mais, dans le même temps, les produits de première nécessité avaient considérablement augmenté. Les prix du bois de chauffage, de la chandelle et de l'huile avaient été multipliés par cinq, celui du vin par six, celui des œufs par sept. Alors que sous Louis XII, le « père du peuple », le pain était bon marché, sous Henri II il est cher et se compose à moitié de seigle. Le bon pain de froment a disparu de la table des petites gens.

Autant d'évolutions qui expliquent la montée de la pauvreté et précipitent parfois les modestes artisans dans le « menu peuple ». Cette paupérisation latente provoque un peu partout des situations de grande tension. À Lyon, au printemps 1529, des « placards » signés « Le Povre » dénoncent la hausse des prix et accusent les spéculateurs. Le 25 avril, le couvent des cordeliers et des maisons de notables sont pillés et la maison de la ville est envahie par des petits charpentiers, des teinturiers, des menuisiers et aussi par des mendiants. C'est la « grande rebeine ». Dix ans plus tard, commencent les grèves — ou *trics* — des compagnons imprimeurs de Lyon et de Paris.

Surtout, cette poussée de misère, loin d'apitoyer les « honnestes personnes », modifie l'image du pauvre. Parce que « l'oisiveté est la mère de tous les vices », comme l'écrit Jean-Louis Vives en 1525, de nombreuses municipalités créent des organismes spécialisés pour mettre les pauvres à l'ouvrage. À Paris, à Lyon, à Rouen se créent en 1530, en 1531 et en 1534 des Aumônes générales où le travail est organisé. Dans le même temps, des mesures interdisent le vagabondage et la mendicité. En 1544, à Paris, est créé un « Bureau des Pauvres » pour les couper du reste de la population et rythmer leur emploi du temps par la prière, l'éducation et le travail.

À Lyon, en 1529, des témoins rapportent avoir vu des émeutiers briser les images de Jésus et des saints dans les demeures des « gens de bien ». Est-ce parce qu'ils savaient que l'Évangile, redécouvert par les humanistes, enseignait « l'égalité originelle de tous les hommes » ?

« Le nouveau visage de la pauvreté, écrit Richard Gascon, a transformé l'image que la société se faisait du pauvre et de la pauvreté. Cette pauvreté massive, présente en permanence au cœur de la cité et qui n'était plus représentée seulement par des infirmes de la naissance, de la maladie ou de l'âge, mais par des hommes capables de travailler, prenait un visage plus obsédant et plus inquiétant : elle tendait à substituer à l'image traditionnelle du Christ souffrant le visage inquiétant et hostile d'un être oisif, fainéant et sournois. Les textes et l'iconographie expriment cette transformation à laquelle peut-être les nouveaux idéaux de la Renaissance, la place donnée à la réussite, à la gloire, à l'exaltation de la beauté corporelle ne furent pas tellement étrangers. »

CHAPITRE 42

Le temps de la Réforme

*Le 24 août 1572, au lever du jour, une rumeur se répand dans Paris.
Une aubépine du cimetière des Saints-Innocents, desséchée depuis
plusieurs années, venait de refleurir. N'était-ce pas le signe envoyé par
Dieu pour inviter les Français à se débarrasser des « hérétiques » qui
souillaient le royaume ? Toujours est-il que, saisie d'une « fureur
incroyable », une masse fanatique, déjà excitée par la vie chère et la
disette, allait en quelques jours égorger sans doute 2 000 protestants rassemblés dans la capitale pour le mariage de Marguerite de Valois et
d'Henri de Navarre. Ce massacre de la Saint-Barthélemy, en aiguisant la
haine entre catholiques et partisans de la religion « réformée », compro-
mettait en même temps toutes les actions que la monarchie avait entreprises depuis un siècle pour mettre au pas les princes, assurer son pouvoir
absolu et prendre fermement la direction de l'État.*

Une piété plus exigeante

Dans le grand déchirement de la Chrétienté qu'annonce en 1517
l'affichage des 95 thèses de Luther, un moine allemand scandalisé par
les indulgences que le pape vendait aux fidèles pour leur permettre de
réduire les peines imposées au Purgatoire, le choix de la France pouvait être décisif. Tiraillé entre l'aspiration à la réforme qui saisissait
de nombreux chrétiens et la conviction que la force du royaume repo-

sait sur son unité spirituelle, le roi pouvait hésiter entre conciliation et répression, entre défense scrupuleuse de l'orthodoxie et désir de mieux écouter la Parole de Dieu.

Si les thèses de Luther rencontrèrent immédiatement un large écho, c'est qu'elles apportaient une réponse apaisante aux angoisses des fidèles et qu'elles rétablissaient un lien plus direct entre l'homme et le Christ. En affirmant que des « œuvres bonnes et justes ne font jamais un homme bon et juste » mais qu'« un homme bon et juste fait de bonnes œuvres », en soutenant que Dieu ne jugeait pas les hommes au moyen d'une balance pesant d'un côté leurs péchés et de l'autre leurs bonnes actions mais que le salut était justifié par la seule foi en sa miséricorde, Luther répondait aux attentes d'une piété plus exigeante, celle des élites alphabétisées qui accédaient par l'imprimé à l'Écriture sainte dont l'interprétation avait été jusque-là monopolisée par la hiérarchie ecclésiastique. Acquise grâce à l'imprimerie, cette intimité avec le sacré était une véritable révolution qui mettait en cause les fondements mêmes du catholicisme.

Nombreux étaient en effet les humanistes qui, critiquant le manque de rigueur de la hiérarchie ecclésiastique, l'ignorance du clergé et l'inutilité des moines, estimaient que le seul trésor de l'Église était l'Évangile et que Dieu seul, et non le pape, avait pouvoir de pardonner. Mettant l'accent sur la méditation et sur une piété plus désintéressée, ils critiquaient les formes de dévotion démonstratives dont le seul but était d'effacer périodiquement les « ardoises » du pécheur. « Tu pries Dieu pour que ne te surprenne pas une mort soudaine, écrivait en 1506 le Hollandais Érasme, infatigable propagateur de l'humanisme en Europe, et tu ne pries pas plutôt pour qu'il t'accorde un esprit meilleur [...]. Tu ne songes pas à changer de vie, et pourtant tu pries Dieu de ne pas mourir. Quel est donc ton but, quand tu fais cette prière ? Évidemment d'être en mesure de pécher le plus longtemps possible. » En 1516, il publie, à partir de l'original grec, un Nouveau Testament qui dévalorise auprès des gens « à la page » la Vulgate latine de saint Jérôme truffée d'erreurs, d'additions, de lacunes et d'extrapolations. Avant que Luther ne se soit fait connaître, il écrit encore : « Je voudrais que toutes les bonnes femmes lisent l'Évangile et les Épîtres de Paul. Qu'ils soient traduits dans toutes les langues ! Que le laboureur en chante des extraits en poussant sa charrue, que le tisserand en fredonne des airs à son métier [...]. » Ce sera chose faite quand Lefèvre d'Étaples publiera en 1523 la version française du Nouveau Testament, puis en 1530 la Bible complète.

Aux côtés de Lefèvre d'Étaples, un esprit curieux tourmenté par les problèmes religieux, on trouve tous ceux qui souhaitent définir les règles d'une vie intérieure plus exigeante et mieux adaptée à la culture renaissante. Ami de Marguerite d'Angoulême, sœur de François Ier et future reine de Navarre, Guillaume Briçonnet, évêque de Lodève puis de Meaux entre 1516 et 1534, prend la tête d'un mouvement qui souhaite rénover la prédication, introduire le français dans la liturgie, distribuer aux fidèles des traductions des Écritures, contraindre les moines à respecter les règles de leur ordre et les curés à résider auprès de leurs ouailles.

Certains de ces évangélistes, les « bibliens » de Meaux, comme on les appelait, hostiles aux superstitions qui entouraient le culte de la Vierge et des saints, en viennent à lacérer des images pieuses.

François d'Estaing, évêque de Rodez de 1501 à 1529, prescrit à son clergé « de porter des habits longs, fermés, d'avoir les cheveux courts et les oreilles découvertes, de s'interdire les auberges, les jeux, la compagnie des femmes ». À Langres, Nantes, Troyes, Paris, Chartres, des évêques restaurent la discipline et propagent la réforme jusque dans les paroisses profondes. Cluny, Cîteaux, et Prémontré ordonnent le retour au jeûne, au silence et à la vie commune.

Autant d'initiatives qui traduisent la volonté d'un retour aux sources mais qui ne sont en rien schismatiques. Pour les « évangélistes » qui veulent simplement allumer le « feu savoureux » qui purge les âmes et les illumine, c'est le roi qui doit prendre la tête de cette « rénovation » et mener son troupeau vers un nouvel âge d'or. À Rouen, le 5 août 1517, un spectacle donné à l'occasion de son entrée dans la ville le représentait sous les traits d'un jeune enfant descendant d'une étoile dont les rayons se répandaient partout pour signifier qu'une nouvelle clarté venait au monde. Sur l'écu que lui remettaient trois Grâces habillées de soie et d'or, on pouvait lire *prudentia servabit*, « la prudence sera ton salut ».

À partir de 1519, toutefois, la dévotion glisse vers l'hérésie quand les premières brochures de Luther, ficelées par colis de centaines d'exemplaires, arrivent à Paris. En condamnant en 1521 les erreurs de celui que le pape Léon X a excommunié et en faisant l'amalgame entre ses thèses et les idées réformatrices des « bibliens » de Meaux, la Sorbonne ferme les voies d'une possible réconciliation religieuse et ouvre la lutte entre deux conceptions de la vie et de la foi chrétienne.

En 1523, l'ermite normand Vallière est brûlé à Paris. C'est le premier martyr du protestantisme français. En 1525, Lefèvre d'Étaples s'exile à Strasbourg. En 1529, Louis de Berquin, qui avait longtemps bénéficié de la protection du roi, est étranglé et brûlé pour avoir traduit des ouvrages de Luther. Dans le même temps, les excès de réformés néophytes qui trouvent dans la provocation le moyen d'exprimer leurs nouvelles options religieuses forcent un roi plutôt conciliant à des choix qui n'étaient pas écrits d'avance. En 1528, la mutilation d'une statue de la Vierge à Paris provoque un premier scandale. Surtout, l'affaire des Placards force l'État à choisir son camp.

Dans la nuit du 17 au 18 octobre 1534, en plusieurs points de Paris, d'Orléans, de Blois et sur la porte même de la chambre à coucher de François Ier à Amboise, sont placardées des affichettes imprimées en lettres gothiques qui dépassent en virulence tout ce qui avait été écrit jusque-là, même par Luther. Rédigés par Antoine Marcourt, un pasteur d'origine lyonnaise, ces « Articles véritables sur les horribles, grands et importables [insupportables] abus de la Messe papale inventée directement contre la Sainte Cène de Jésus-Christ » qualifient de doctrine diabolique l'eucharistie, le noyau même de la doctrine catholique, ridiculisent le « Dieu de pâte », c'est-à-dire le pain de l'hostie, accusent le clergé romain d'exploiter « le pauvre peuple » et de vivre comme des « loups ravissants ».

Ne pouvant laisser bafouer aussi ostensiblement son autorité, le roi laisse éclater sa fureur. Tandis que des bûchers s'allument pour brûler les hérétiques, le roi, tête nue et un cierge à la main, participe dans Paris à une grande procession expiatoire pour laquelle on a sorti de la Sainte-Chapelle la couronne d'épines, la Vraie Croix, « la goutte du précieux sang de Notre Sauveur » et « la goutte de lait de la glorieuse Vierge Marie ».

En 1539, un édit est promulgué pour « extirper et déchasser du royaume les mauvaises erreurs ». Le 1er juin 1540, l'édit de Fontainebleau réduit les privilèges des cours ecclésiastiques, jugées trop lentes, charge les officiers royaux de la répression et invite tous les sujets à dénoncer les coupables pour « éteindre le feu public ». En 1545, les vaudois, assimilés aux protestants, sont massacrés. À Cabrières, femmes et enfants sont brûlés vifs dans l'église où ils s'étaient réfugiés. En 1546, l'éditeur Étienne Dolet est supplicié place Maubert. Autant de massacres annonciateurs de beaucoup d'autres et commis au nom de l'unité de la « nation françoise » qui, selon le roi, ne pouvait exister sans unité de Foi. Dans sa grande masse, en fait, la population française refusait de rompre avec le passé catholique.

Être protestant

Parmi ceux qui ont fui le royaume au lendemain de l'affaire des Placards, se trouvait Jean Calvin. Né à Noyon, en Picardie, en 1509, ce licencié en droit qui a fait ses études au sévère collège Montaigu à

Paris, puis aux universités d'Orléans et de Bourges, commence à afficher son « protestantisme » en 1533. En 1536, il publie à Bâle *L'Institution de la religion chrétienne,* un gros ouvrage en latin, dans lequel il veut livrer « une clef et ouverture pour donner accès à tous les enfants de Dieu à bien étroitement entendre l'Écriture sainte ». En 1541, il fait paraître la traduction française, précédée d'une adresse à François Ier dans laquelle on lit : « Tous ont honte de l'Évangile. Or c'est votre office, très gracieux roi, de ne détourner ni vos oreilles, ni votre courage, d'une si juste défense, principalement quand il est question de si grande chose : c'est à savoir comment la gloire de Dieu sera maintenue sur terre, comment le règne de Christ demeurera en son entier. Ô matière digne de vos oreilles, digne de votre juridiction, digne de votre trône royal. »

Soulignant, comme Luther et les évangélistes, que les Écritures sont le seul miroir que Dieu a donné aux hommes pour y découvrir la Révélation, il en tire toutefois une vision beaucoup plus sombre de l'humanité. Perverti par la faute originelle d'Adam, héréditairement « esclave du péché », l'homme est devenu inapte au bien et penche naturellement vers le mal. Ainsi, tout ce qui est fait par lui est « abomination » et « pollution ». Toutefois, dans son infinie bonté, le Christ a prévu d'accorder le salut à certains sans considération de leurs œuvres, alors que les autres sont voués à l'Enfer. Mais, contrairement aux apparences, cette prédestination n'est pas source d'angoisse pour les fidèles. L'homme qui persévère dans la foi et qui fait ce que Dieu lui commande et ordonne de faire peut espérer en sa miséricorde. Si ses desseins sont impénétrables, chaque croyant peut percevoir des indices de son élection dans l'action qu'il mène au service de Dieu. C'était rejeter plus fermement que Luther une grande partie des croyances et des institutions catholiques, le Purgatoire et les pèlerinages, les offrandes aux saints et à la Vierge, les processions et les mortifications. Personnage instruit, « de bonne vie et mœurs », le pasteur calviniste, « élu » par l'ensemble des fidèles, était un homme comme les autres, marié et chargé d'enfants, doué surtout « de la grâce singulière de prêcher ».

Avec Jean Calvin, la Réforme française avait trouvé son chef. De Genève transformée en cité gouvernée selon la parole de Dieu, des « missionnaires » suivent les grands axes de circulation et gagnent aux idées nouvelles les gens des villes. Des églises dites « plantées » se multiplient dans le royaume malgré les mesures répressives que multiplie Henri II. Vers 1560, la France compte sans doute un peu plus de 2 millions de protestants, soit environ 10 % de la population. La carte de leur implantation dessine fortement un croissant qui s'étend du

Poitou jusqu'à Lyon. Environ 700 églises sont « plantées » dans le sud du royaume, en Aunis et en Saintonge, en Guyenne et en Gascogne, en Béarn et dans les Cévennes, en Vivarais, dans le bas Languedoc et en Dauphiné, 500 seulement en domaine d'oïl, dans la plaine de Caen et dans les grandes villes que sont Rouen et Lyon, Paris et Orléans.

Si la foi protestante a peu touché la paysannerie, elle a largement mordu sur les élites et les gens des villes : artisans, juristes, médecins, négociants, universitaires, imprimeurs, mais aussi évêques, parlementaires et nobles séduits par cette religion du livre, de l'ascèse et de l'exigence morale. Jean, Abraham, Isaac, Pierre et Daniel, Marie, Judith, Sara, Susanne et Anne, autant de prénoms qui fleurent bon l'identité huguenote. Sobriété vestimentaire, pouvoir du père de famille, tempérance alimentaire, abstinence des jeux de hasard, de la danse et de la fête, autant de comportements qui dessinent une nouvelle manière de se gouverner soi-même. Ministre de La Rochelle, une des capitales du protestantisme, Pierre Merlin s'écrie : « Quelle honte est-ce de voir les hommes mener à la taverne les femmes et fils d'autrui ! Comment peut dans ces écoles de toute insolence, comme sont les tavernes, demeurer entières la chasteté et la pudicité, parmi la licence que chacun se donne entre le pot et le verre, vu qu'en ces lieux les plus saints, plusieurs osent jeter des regards peu chastes aux femmes et filles ? Et n'est-ce pas le comble du mal, quand après être échauffé de vin, on vient à la danse ? »

À partir des années 1550, avec la conversion de grandes familles aristocratiques, les Bourbons, les Condés ou les Châtillon, ce sont de nombreux « fidèles » démobilisés par la paix de Cateau-Cambrésis et appauvris qui suivent leurs « patrons », lorgnent sur les biens d'Église et tendent à former un véritable « parti » protestant d'une extraordinaire vigueur, capable de peser sur le fonctionnement de l'État et de « saboter » les mesures répressives prises contre les « réformés ».

En 1559, l'année même où Henri II signe le terrible édit d'Écouen qui ordonne le bûcher dans presque tous les cas jugés d'hérésie, se tient clandestinement à Paris le premier synode national, qui définit en quarante articles une « confession de foi » française, la *Confessio Gallica*, et met en place l'organisation générale de l'Église réformée. Dans chaque communauté locale, l'assemblée des chefs de famille était chargée de désigner les membres du « consistoire », une douzaine d'« anciens » chargés des relations avec Genève, de la gestion du patrimoine commun et du contrôle des mœurs des fidèles. Au sommet, le synode national arbitrait les questions doctrinales et définissait les grandes orientations politiques. Entre le consistoire et le synode national, un « colloque » régional et des synodes provinciaux débattaient de la doctrine, de la discipline, des écoles, de la nomination et de la déposition des ministres et des éventuels scandales.

Au moment où meurt accidentellement le roi Henri II, les huguenots se sentent assez forts pour s'attaquer à la « puante Ninive », à la « Grande Babylone » dont les dogmes et les rites ont travesti le message du Christ. N'hésitant plus à se montrer, à parler, voire à injurier les fidèles catholiques, ils ont le sentiment que la victoire est proche et s'attaquent aux tympans, aux gravures et aux statues. En 1560, ils tentent d'enlever le jeune roi François II pour le soustraire à l'influence des Guise qui sont les chefs de file des catholiques intransigeants. Pourtant, alors que les violences « papistes » comme huguenotes se multiplient, des esprits mesurés espèrent encore en un possible compromis.

Les guerres de religion

En septembre 1561, un colloque tenu à Poissy réunit les théologiens des deux confessions pour explorer les voies d'un rapprochement. Dans sa harangue d'ouverture, le chancelier Michel de L'Hospital invite les prélats catholiques à ne pas considérer comme « ennemis ceux qu'on dit de la nouvelle religion, et qui sont chrétiens comme eux, et baptisés » et à ne pas « leur fermer la porte, mais les recevoir en toute douceur, sans user contre eux d'aigreur et d'opiniâtreté ».

Mais Théodore de Bèze, lieutenant de Calvin à Genève, qui conduit la délégation protestante, compromet cette tentative de conciliation en déclarant, dès la séance d'ouverture, que le corps du Christ « est éloigné du pain et du vin autant que le plus haut ciel est éloigné de la terre ». Une déclaration sans compromis qui amène les traditionalistes catholiques à se déclarer hostiles à toute compromission avec les « chiens genevois ».

La publicité faite autour de ce colloque excite alors les tensions dans le royaume. Tandis que de nombreuses chansons et satires fusent du côté catholique comme du côté protestant, la tension iconoclaste est à son comble. À Montauban, s'arrêtant devant les maisons des catholiques auxquels ils lisent les passages de l'Écriture, les réformés brûlent les images de la plupart des sanctuaires de la ville. À Montpellier, la cathédrale est pillée de fond en comble. À Millau, des croix sont brisées. À Bressols, des huguenots se saisissent d'un prêtre qui chantait la messe, le forcent à monter sur un âne, le visage orienté vers la queue de la bête qu'il doit prendre dans la main, et le promènent dans la ville, une hostie collée sur le front. À l'église Saint-Médard, à Paris, des vitraux sont brisés.

Catherine de Médicis, régente du royaume depuis la mort de François II en décembre 1560, cherche toujours pourtant à apaiser les tensions. Le 17 janvier 1562, l'édit de Saint-Germain accorde la liberté de « leur religion » aux huguenots, à condition que cette liberté soit exercée à l'extérieur des murailles urbaines et en présence des officiers du roi. Dans les villes, le culte est autorisé dans les maisons privées. Nulle part ailleurs en Europe n'existait pareille reconnaissance légale.

Mais les catholiques, un moment débordés, prennent l'offensive. De leurs chaires, les prêtres les encouragent à réagir. À la cour, le duc de Guise, le connétable de Montmorency et le maréchal Saint-André jurent, lors d'une communion commune, de défendre la religion menacée. À Paris, des étudiants attaquent des protestants au Pré-aux-Clercs et assiègent la maison où ils ont trouvé refuge. Le 1er mars 1562, surtout, une escorte du duc de Guise massacre à Wassy, en Champagne, plusieurs dizaines de protestants réunis dans une grange aux cris de « Tue, tue, mort Dieu, ces huguenots ! ».

C'est alors le soulèvement général des forces protestantes, en fait préparé depuis 1560. Le 2 avril, le prince de Condé, qui est à leur tête, enlève Orléans. Poitiers, La Rochelle, Caen, Le Havre, Dieppe et Rouen sont à leur tour occupés. À Dreux, le 19 décembre 1562, une première bataille rangée met aux prises 29 000 combattants des deux camps. Les deux chefs ennemis, le connétable de Montmorency et Condé sont faits prisonniers. En février 1563, le duc de Guise, le héros catholique, est assassiné par un gentilhomme protestant devant Orléans. Ainsi s'ouvrent les guerres de religion qui, pendant plus de trente ans, vont ensanglanter le royaume.

Sièges et batailles rangées, atrocités et massacres, morts violentes des principaux chefs de parti, interventions des puissances étrangères, Anglais, Allemands et Hollandais au profit des protestants, Espagnols au profit des catholiques, inconsistance d'un gouvernement qui hésite et louvoie entre tolérance et répression, autant de troubles qui affaiblissent le pouvoir et altèrent le prestige du roi. Après son *Discours sur les misères de ce temps,* Ronsard écrit dans la *Continuation du discours des misères* :

« M'apparut tristement l'idole de la France
[...] Comme une pauvre femme atteinte de la mort.
Son sceptre lui pendait, et sa robe semée
De fleurs de lis était en cent lieux entamée ;
Son poil était hideux, son œil hâve et profond,
Et nulle majesté ne lui haussait le front. »

Ainsi s'achève une Renaissance fraîche et joyeuse, au moment même où s'épuise la croissance du « beau » XVIᵉ siècle et s'achève le temps de l'inflation. Même s'il ne faut pas céder au déterminisme matériel et expliquer les violences religieuses par le simple retournement de la conjoncture économique, force est de constater que le « mal des petits » a certainement constitué un terrain propice à l'exaspération des tensions.

À partir des années 1560, coïncidence des conjonctures, en même temps que la courbe des prix s'infléchit à la baisse, l'essor commercial se ralentit, la production agricole fait du surplace et la croissance démographique s'essouffle. Faut-il incriminer le climat ? Sans doute, dans la mesure où un petit « âge glaciaire » refroidit les hivers à partir de 1550 et fait avancer les glaciers. La réduction du nombre des moutons en Espagne après 1560 serait un autre indice de ce refroidissement.

La veuve Couet, qui récoltait 12 et même 15 muids de vin par an sur ses vignes d'Antony n'en récolte plus que 6 ou 7 dans les années 1570. Dans le Cambrésis, les dîmes, qui mesurent le niveau des récoltes, chutent de moitié. En Languedoc, le pastel toulousain inaugure sa décadence à partir de 1560. La viticulture charentaise s'effondre après 1572. À Lyon, les trois quarts des maisons bancaires cessent leurs activités dans les années 1580. Le commerce des épices, si actif, s'écroule après 1573. Dans la plupart des provinces, on observe un déficit marqué des naissances, une recrudescence des épidémies de peste, de typhus, de rougeole ou de coqueluche.

Ce mauvais « climat » dont se plaint en 1575 la municipalité de Paris excite les conflits. Dans les années 1560, le refus de payer les dîmes accompagne les progrès de la Réforme. En 1580, le Dauphiné connaît une jacquerie qui se manifeste avec éclat lors du carnaval de Romans, au mois de février. Tandis que les compagnons hostiles à l'oligarchie municipale s'habillent en rouge et bleu, des couleurs funéraires par lesquelles ils annoncent porter le deuil de leurs adversaires, les partisans de l'ordre se déguisent en rois, en archevêques, en chanceliers et en juges et prennent comme emblèmes l'aigle et le coq qui incarnent la force et le pouvoir, un pouvoir qu'ils font respecter en pourchassant et pendant les principaux chefs de la révolte.

La flambée de sorcellerie est un autre symptôme de la fièvre qui saisit le royaume dans les années 1570. Elle se nourrit de signes inquiétants que reproduisent à l'envi les feuilles volantes et les occasionnels souvent illustrés de gravures, apparition de monstres, comètes, éclipses. Elle se libère avec fureur lors du massacre de la Saint-Barthélemy.

Le lundi 18 août 1572, 1 000 gentilshommes huguenots sont venus à Paris, certains avec femmes et enfants, pour assister au mariage de Marguerite de France et d'Henri de Bourbon, roi de Navarre. Ce jeune homme, chef du parti protestant, refuse d'entrer dans la cathédrale Notre-Dame. Le mariage a lieu sur le parvis et seule Marguerite participe, à l'intérieur, à la messe du mariage que Catherine de Médicis a voulu pour souder les protestants à la monarchie et éviter une nouvelle guerre civile. Le vendredi 22 août, un attentat à l'arquebuse blesse l'amiral Gaspard de Coligny, un réformé qui s'est mis à jouer un rôle de premier plan auprès du roi Charles IX. Furieux, les huguenots menacent de se venger si justice n'est pas faite rapidement et accusent les Guise de ce meurtre raté. Dans la nuit du 23 au 24 août, un Conseil royal réuni à la hâte décide de supprimer une soixantaine de chefs protestants, désignés au prévôt des marchands, responsable de la milice bourgeoise.

Le dimanche 24 août, au petit matin, alors que le massacre « politique » s'ouvre par l'assassinat de l'amiral de Coligny, le massacre « populaire » que n'avaient pas prévu les ordonnateurs de l'exécution se transforme en pogrom hystérique dont la violence horrifie les témoins, même les catholiques les plus extrémistes. Le corps de l'amiral de Coligny, traîné dans la rue par des « petits enfants », est châtré, décapité, mutilé aux mains et aux pieds avant d'être tiré vers la Seine. Le roi aura beau, toute la journée du 24, faire crier à tous les coins de Paris des mandements ordonnant que la violence prenne fin, la foule, chauffée à blanc par les sermons des prêcheurs qui ont dénoncé l'« accouplement exécrable » entre Henri de Navarre et Marguerite de Valois, saisit l'occasion de débarrasser la France de la « pollution » protestante qui l'infecte et de mettre fin aux « novelletés » qui ont mis en péril un univers jusque-là cohérent.

Quand les cloches de toutes les églises se mettent à sonner pour annoncer qu'une aubépine a refleuri au cimetière des Saints-Innocents, les Parisiens y voient un signe de l'approbation divine et courent en criant « Miracle ! Miracle ! »

Au fur et à mesure que la nouvelle se répand en province, des massacres sont perpétrés à Orléans, Meaux, Bourges, Saumur, Angers, Lyon, Troyes, Rouen, Toulouse, Gaillac, Bordeaux, faisant peut-être 5 000 victimes, dont 2 000 au moins à Paris.

En annonçant, le mardi 26 août, devant le Parlement de Paris réuni pour un lit de justice solennel, que « ce qui est ainsi advenu a été son exprès commandement pour obvier et prévenir l'exécution d'une malheureuse conspiration faite par le dit Amiral et ses dits adhérents et complices », Charles IX prend officiellement la responsabilité du massacre et assume du même coup le fanatisme des tueurs au nom d'une obscure raison d'État.

La monarchie contestée

En endossant la responsabilité de la Saint-Barthélemy pour prévenir, semble-t-il, un embrasement général du royaume, Charles IX a en fait ruiné l'image du roi de justice élu par Dieu pour être le protecteur de *l'ensemble* de ses sujets. En promulguant dès le 11 juillet 1573 l'édit de Boulogne qui accorde aux huguenots la liberté de conscience et le plein exercice de leur culte dans les villes de La Rochelle, Nîmes puis Montauban, il se rend coupable, aux yeux des catholiques, de n'avoir pas su terminer la grande œuvre de purification commencée en 1572. Mais dans le camp protestant, il est devenu le symbole de la barbarie catholique à laquelle il est devenu légitime de résister.

En 1573, le *Franco-Gallia*, un livre publié par François Hotman, connaît un grand succès. Rappelant que, dans le passé, les chefs gaulois puis francs étaient désignés par l'« assemblée générale de toute la nation qu'on a appelé depuis l'assemblée des trois estats », l'auteur en tirait la leçon, comprise par tous ceux qui le lisaient, que les rois étaient rois « sous certaines lois et conditions [...] et non point comme tyrans avec une puissance absolue, excessive et infinie ». En 1575, Théodore de Bèze, le successeur de Calvin à Genève, va plus loin en développant dans *Du droit des magistrats sur leurs sujets* que ces derniers peuvent se rebeller contre leur prince si celui-ci ne respecte pas les obligations de sa charge et « les deux bornes que Dieu a lui-même plantées, assavoir Piété et Charité ». En 1579, le *Vindiciae contra tyrannos* attribué à Philippe Duplessis-Mornay, traduit en français sous le titre *De la puissance légitime du Prince sur le peuple et du peuple sur le Prince,* justifie le régicide en cas de « tyrannie ».

Ainsi la Saint-Barthélemy redonne-t-elle force au désir d'autonomie contre lequel la monarchie luttait depuis des siècles. Ainsi se développe la revendication d'un pouvoir local capable de faire barrage à l'autorité d'un roi contesté. Dans le Midi, les cités huguenotes multiplient les contacts entre elles et mettent en place à Millau, en décembre 1573, une organisation commune que les historiens ont appelée les « Provinces-Unies du Midi », un véritable contre-État avec ses chambres de justice, ses recettes fiscales et ses représentants élus, unis par un « serment d'union ». En 1576, Henri de Navarre, proclamé « protecteur de l'Union », partage le pouvoir exécutif avec un conseil permanent de dix membres et dispose de l'autorité d'un véritable souverain.

Dans le même temps, les catholiques, excédés par la faiblesse du pouvoir royal et les avantages obtenus par les huguenots, se regroupent dans des « ligues » pour rétablir « les droits, prééminences, franchises et libertés anciennes, telles qu'elles étaient au temps du roi Clovis, premier roi chrétien ». En juin 1584, la mort de François d'Anjou, le frère cadet du roi Henri III, aggrave la situation. En effet, dans la mesure où ce roi mal-aimé, dont les amitiés suspectes pour les mignons choquent ses contemporains, n'a pas d'enfant, la couronne doit revenir à son plus proche héritier qui n'est autre qu'Henri de Navarre, chef du parti protestant, pire, un relaps retourné à la Réforme après l'avoir abjurée au cours de la Saint-Barthélemy.

En septembre, se forme à Nancy une Ligue nobiliaire autour des ducs de Guise et de leur frère Mayenne qui signent un traité secret avec les envoyés du roi d'Espagne Philippe II. Moyennant un soutien financier de 50 000 écus par mois, le duc de Guise s'engageait, en cas de décès du roi, à favoriser le couronnement du cardinal de Bourbon, l'oncle d'Henri de Navarre. Sur le terrain, le clergé s'emploie par ailleurs à reconquérir le terrain perdu. Fort des résolutions adoptées par le concile de Trente, qui a réaffirmé avec vigueur tous les points de doctrine que les protestants avaient mis en cause, la nécessité des œuvres pour mériter le salut, l'existence du Purgatoire, la présence réelle du Christ dans le pain et le vin, le culte de la Vierge et des saints, des reliques et des images, les clercs, avec l'aide active des jésuites, ont pris en charge les âmes enfantines.

À Paris, le petit peuple, fanatisé par les sermons qui l'appellent à la croisade contre les protestants, dresse les premières barricades de son histoire et force le roi qui a voulu faire entrer des troupes dans la capitale à s'enfuir pour se réfugier à Chartres. En faisant assassiner Henri de Guise, Henri III, loin de briser l'élan de la Ligue, relance sa dynamique. De nombreuses villes comme Marseille adhèrent alors à l'Union dont Paris a pris la tête. Des processions de pénitents, à la piété fort démonstrative, rassemblent des milliers de participants qui font alterner actions de grâces et salves de mousquets.

Débordé par ces mouvements qui le présentent comme un suppôt de Satan, Henri III s'allie avec son cousin Henri et vient avec lui mettre le siège de la capitale, avec celui qui, deux ans auparavant, avait infligé, à Coutras, une terrible défaite à l'armée royale commandée par les chefs de la Ligue. Mais le 1er août 1589, il est assassiné par un jeune moine dominicain, Jacques Clément, convaincu d'avoir été désigné par Dieu pour tuer le « tyran » qui a osé s'allier à un hérétique. La France vit alors dans l'anarchie la plus totale. Dès le 4 août 1589, les Ligueurs ont reconnu comme souverain le cardinal de Bourbon sous le nom de Charles X. Henri de Navarre, devenu l'héritier légitime selon la Loi salique, cherche alors à mener une politique de conciliation, en s'engageant à garder le royaume dans sa confession catholique et à se faire instruire dans la religion romaine par « un bon, légitime et libre concile national ou général ». Surtout, son charisme, son intelligence politique, son habileté souriante, l'appui trop voyant du roi d'Espagne qui propose de mettre sa fille sur le trône... et ses largesses financières colossales lui valent bien des ralliements. Enfin, les victoires remportées à Arques et à Ivry nourrissent la propagande de celui qui a su faire briller son panache blanc. Ne restait plus, en somme, à Henri IV qu'à abjurer une nouvelle fois le protestantisme et à suivre l'avertissement que lui avait lancé Henri III avant de mourir : « Soyez certain, mon cher beau frère, que vous ne serez roi de France, si vous ne vous faites catholique. »

Un choix qui n'était pas si facile pour un roi qui ne pouvait compter que sur les forces réformées, à l'intérieur comme à l'extérieur, pour asseoir militairement son autorité.

43

Le meilleur roi du monde

« J e fais la guerre, je fais l'amour et je bâtis. » Les mots « historiques » sont souvent ceux qui forgent les légendes et traduisent l'esprit d'un temps. En les prononçant, Henri IV a su, de son vivant, brosser
le portrait du « bon roi », celui qui ramène la paix dans son royaume et,
telle la déesse Astrée, la fille de Zeus et de Thémis, offre à ses sujets la
corne d'abondance débordante de fleurs et de fruits. « Si Dieu me prête
encore de la vie, aurait aussi dit Henri, je ferai qu'il n'y aurait point de
laboureur en mon royaume qu'il n'ait le moyen d'avoir une poule dans
son pot. » Autant dire que le couteau de Ravaillac, en offrant au Béarnais
la couronne du martyre, a jeté les bases d'un mythe dont les images nourrissent toujours notre imaginaire.

Le triomphe d'un politique

À l'aube du 22 mars 1594, Henri IV entre dans Paris par la porte
Neuve, non loin des Tuileries. L'attendent le comte de Brissac, le
gouverneur de la capitale, et Jean Lhuillier, le prévôt des marchands,
jusqu'à ce jour deux des plus farouches adversaires du Béarnais.
Accompagnés d'une maigre troupe, les trois hommes descendent jusqu'à Notre-Dame, où les cloches sonnant le *Te Deum* annoncent aux
ligueurs que le roi de France est dans leur ville. Personne ne songe à
prendre les armes. Mieux, lorsque Henri se rend au Louvre, il est

entouré d'une foule compacte qui crie « Vive le roi », tandis que les clairons accompagnent cette marche triomphale. C'est bien l'ancien huguenot, le roi jadis honni de Paris, qui, en touchant de ses mains ointes du saint chrême des centaines de scrofuleux, s'inscrit dans la longue lignée des « rois thaumaturges ». Le soir même, Henri IV assiste, de la porte Saint-Denis, au départ piteux de la garnison espagnole, vaincue sans combat. La relation de cette journée, colportée dans tout le royaume, célébrée par de multiples gravures, assoit définitivement la légitimité du monarque. On parle de miracle. C'était en fait le couronnement d'une superbe manœuvre politique.

Depuis l'assassinat d'Henri III, le 1ᵉʳ août 1589, la France se trouvait en effet paralysée par une interminable querelle de succession, en même temps que déchirée par la guerre civile. Henri III avait beau avoir reconnu son cousin Henri de Navarre pour héritier légitime, ni les troupes catholiques, ni les parlements, ni même la majorité des Français ne l'avaient suivi. C'est le principe même d'autorité royale qui semblait s'être évanoui. Plus grave encore, la Loi salique, principe directeur de la succession royale, se trouvait mise en question par le roi d'Espagne Philippe II qui, en avril 1593, avait proposé la candidature de l'infante Isabelle, petite-fille d'Henri II. Entre un roi de droit héréditaire mais protestant et excommunié et une princesse catholique dont le handicap était plus d'être femme qu'étrangère, le choix n'était pas si tranché.

À cela s'ajoutait une situation totalement anarchique. Le nord et le sud du royaume se combattaient. Marseille cultivait avec soin son particularisme et croyait pouvoir devenir une « république », n'hésitant pas à ouvrir son port aux galères de Philippe II. Paris, surtout, quand elle ne vivait pas à l'heure espagnole, avait basculé dans la « révolution ». Dirigée par les Seize, un comité insurrectionnel constitué d'hommes de loi et de marchands, elle réclamait son autonomie de gouvernement contre le roi, quel qu'il soit.

Méridional et séducteur, homme de dialogue et de tolérance, fin manœuvrier mais ami qui sait être fidèle, bénéficiant du soutien de tous ceux qui détestent l'Espagne jésuitique, maniant avec habileté une propagande qui en fait un David huguenot triomphant du Goliath de la Ligue, bénéficiant du soutien de l'internationale protestante, de la reine d'Angleterre qui fournit la poudre et les canons aux princes allemands qui livrent des mercenaires, Henri a d'abord cherché à gagner du temps. En avril 1593, des pourparlers officieux ont débuté avec les « modérés », tandis qu'est diffusée la *Satire Ménippée*, un pamphlet qui ridiculise la Ligue et dénonce le machiavélisme de Philippe II qui, sous le couvert de la religion, masque son entreprise de domination politique.

Le Béarnais fait surtout courir le bruit de sa prochaine conversion au catholicisme, moyen habile de « tester » les sentiments réels des élites à son égard. Le résultat est convaincant. Le 28 juin 1593, le Parlement de Paris, dominé par les « bons Français », vote l'« Arrêt Le Maître » qui réaffirme les lois fondamentales du royaume, interdit de transférer la couronne « en main étrangère » et affirme la volonté de « pourvoir le plus promptement que faire se pourra au repos du peuple, pour l'extrême nécessité en laquelle il est réduit ».

Henri IV peut alors se livrer, selon sa propre expression, à un « saut périlleux ». Le dimanche 25 juillet 1593, en la basilique de Saint-Denis, il abjure le protestantisme en présence de l'archevêque de Bourges, qui lui donne l'absolution, devant une foule considérable venue acclamer les dévotions du roi au monastère de Montmartre. Ce même 25 juillet, Henri a fait parvenir une lettre aux huguenots pour justifier son acte et les rassurer sur la politique de tolérance qu'il entend mener. « Ce que j'en ai fait, écrit-il, n'ayant été qu'à fort bonne intention, et principalement pour la sûre assurance que j'ai d'y pouvoir faire mon salut, et pour n'être de ce point différent des rois mes prédécesseurs, qui ont heureusement et pacifiquement régné sur leurs sujets, espérant que Dieu me fera la même grâce, et que de ce moyen seraient ôtés non seulement les prétextes, mais aussi les causes des divisions et révoltes qui minent aujourd'hui cet État ; étant pour cela en mon intention qu'il ne soit fait aucune force ni violence aux consciences de mes sujets. »

Ayant éliminé le principal motif de la guerre religieuse, Henri peut désormais prendre l'initiative afin de restaurer la paix civile et le crédit de l'État. Pour ce faire, il doit être sacré, seule cérémonie susceptible de légitimer véritablement la transmission héréditaire. Cela supposait toutefois de trouver un lieu, puisque Reims était aux mains des ligueurs, et d'obtenir l'absolution du pape Clément VIII, puisque le roi avait été excommunié trois ans auparavant. Une fois encore, le Béarnais allait montrer son habileté politique. Pendant de longues semaines, il s'emploie à convaincre les moines de l'abbaye de Marmoutier de prêter la sainte ampoule conservée dans leur monastère. Les objets du sacre peuvent se copier et on fabrique pour la circonstance la couronne, le sceptre, la main de justice, le manteau royal et l'épée d'apparat. L'absolution papale, on s'en accommodera car l'urgence commande de ne pas laisser le royaume « vacant ». Enfin, à la place de Reims, on prendra Chartres, où le roi est sacré le 27 février 1594 par Nicolas de Thou, l'évêque du lieu.

Restait à séduire Paris. Certes, le sacre a fait naître des vocations tardives parmi les chefs de la Ligue. Dans la première quinzaine de mars 1594, des notables parisiens sont venus rencontrer le roi à Saint-

CAPÉTIENS-VALOIS

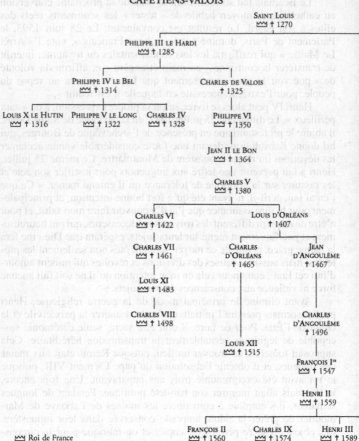

SAINT LOUIS
⚭ † 1270

PHILIPPE III LE HARDI
⚭ † 1285

PHILIPPE IV LE BEL
⚭ † 1314

CHARLES DE VALOIS
† 1325

LOUIS X LE HUTIN
⚭ † 1316

PHILIPPE V LE LONG
⚭ † 1322

CHARLES IV
⚭ † 1328

PHILIPPE VI
⚭ † 1350

JEAN II LE BON
⚭ † 1364

CHARLES V
⚭ † 1380

CHARLES VI
⚭ † 1422

LOUIS D'ORLÉANS
† 1407

CHARLES VII
⚭ † 1461

CHARLES D'ORLÉANS
† 1465

JEAN D'ANGOULÊME
† 1467

LOUIS XI
⚭ † 1483

CHARLES VIII
⚭ † 1498

CHARLES D'ANGOULÊME
† 1496

LOUIS XII
⚭ † 1515

FRANÇOIS Ier
⚭ † 1547

HENRI II
⚭ † 1559

⚭ Roi de France

FRANÇOIS II
⚭ † 1560

CHARLES IX
⚭ † 1574

HENRI III
⚭ † 1589

Denis. Le duc de Mayenne, son rival direct, qui a perçu le retournement, s'est replié avec armes et bagages à Soissons. Mais ces succès sont encore trop minces pour qu'Henri IV soit assuré de la capitale. Aussi use-t-il d'une stratégie qu'il applique avec constance depuis son accession au trône, acheter les puissants et garantir par écrit les privilèges des cités ralliées. Paris valait sûrement une messe et encore plus

BOURBONS

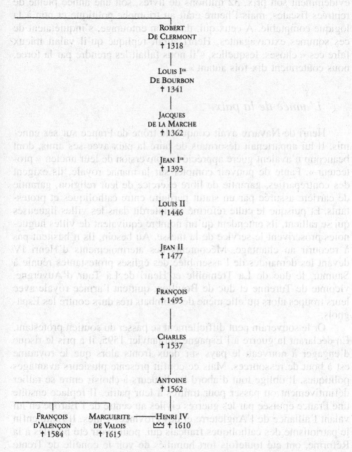

ROBERT
DE CLERMONT
† 1318

LOUIS Iᵉʳ
DE BOURBON
† 1341

JACQUES
DE LA MARCHE
† 1362

JEAN Iᵉʳ
† 1393

LOUIS II
† 1446

JEAN II
† 1477

FRANÇOIS
† 1495

CHARLES
† 1537

ANTOINE
† 1562

FRANÇOIS
D'ALENÇON
† 1584

MARGUERITE
DE VALOIS
† 1615

HENRI IV
† 1610

sûrement qu'Henri promette au comte de Brissac une charge de maréchal et 5 % des recettes fiscales d'une année ! Quant au sort de la ville, le roi précisait qu'il reconnaissait ses privilèges en matière de foires, d'impôts, de manufactures et, détail essentiel, les distinctions particulières dont bénéficiaient ses édiles. Paris pourrait jouir à nouveau des avantages d'une capitale, sans payer le prix de sa révolte, et cela valait bien qu'elle fît la paix avec le Béarnais. Tout cela avait évidemment son prix, 32 millions de livres, soit une année pleine de rentrées fiscales, mais l'heure était au triomphe politique et non à la logique comptable. À ceux qui, dans son entourage, s'inquiétaient de ces sommes extravagantes, Henri aurait répliqué qu'il valait mieux faire ces « choses, lesquelles, s'il nous fallait les prendre par la force, nous coûteraient dix fois autant ».

L'année de la paix

Henri de Navarre avait conquis le trône de France sur ses ennemis. Il lui appartenait désormais de faire la paix avec ses amis, dont beaucoup n'avaient guère apprécié la conversion de leur ancien « protecteur ». Faute de pouvoir compter sur la manne royale, ils exigent des contreparties, garantie de libre exercice de leur religion, garantie de carrière assurée par un statut paritaire entre catholiques et protestants. Et puisque le culte réformé est interdit dans les villes ligueuses qui se rallient, ils entendent qu'un nombre équivalent de villes huguenotes proscrivent le service de la messe. Au besoin, ils n'hésitent pas à recourir au chantage. Mécontents des atermoiements d'Henri IV devant les demandes de l'assemblée des églises protestantes réunie à Saumur, le duc de La Trémoille et Henri de La Tour d'Auvergne, vicomte de Turenne et duc de Bouillon, quittent l'armée royale avec leurs troupes alors qu'elle mène des combats très durs contre les Espagnols.

Or le souverain peut difficilement se passer du soutien protestant. En déclarant la guerre à l'Espagne, en janvier 1595, il a pris le risque d'engager à nouveau le pays sur deux fronts alors que le royaume est à bout de ressources. Mais ce conflit présente plusieurs avantages politiques. Il oblige tout d'abord les ligueurs à choisir entre se rallier définitivement ou passer pour traîtres à leur patrie. Il replace ensuite une France épuisée par les guerres civiles au centre de l'Europe en lui valant l'alliance de l'Angleterre et des Provinces-Unies. Il flatte enfin le patriotisme des catholiques français qui, pour avoir été hostiles à la Réforme, ont été toutefois fort humiliés de voir le concile de Trente affirmer la primauté de l'Espagne et de ce qui passait pour son bras armé, les jésuites.

La tentative d'assassinat dont Henri IV a été victime le 27 décembre 1594 a fourni un prétexte idéal. Jean Châtel, le coupable, était un ancien élève du collège jésuite de Clermont. Son maître, le père Jean Guignard, est soupçonné d'avoir incité son disciple au régicide. Pour faire bonne mesure, le jour où Jean Châtel est écartelé place de Grève, le Parlement bannit hors de France les « corrupteurs de jeunesse », les « perturbateurs du repos public », les « ennemis du roi et de l'État ».

Se battre contre l'Espagne, c'est bien cristalliser autour de la personne royale un sentiment « national » exaspéré par le soutien du pape à Madrid. C'est affirmer la supériorité des « Français, nation de tout temps héroïque et généreuse » sur les « glorieux et insolents Espagnols ». C'est exalter le patriotisme d'un peuple convaincu qu'il n'a pas de rival digne de lui. Dans *Le Secret des trésors de France*, on peut lire : « Le royaume est habité d'hommes qui, à vrai dire, représentent comme le chef-d'œuvre des plus excellentes perfections qui se puissent trouver sous la chape du ciel pour être comme ils sont doués de grâces singulières. »

Pourtant, la guerre tourne au profit des Espagnols, commandés par le comte de Fuentes, qui poussent leur avantage jusqu'à Cambrai et Calais et prennent Amiens le 11 mars 1597.

Il est temps pour Henri de rallier à sa cause tout ce qui peut l'être. Pour l'occasion, les enchères atteignent de tels sommets que l'ambassadeur de Venise se moquera des « satrapes » couverts d'or par un monarque démuni. Mayenne devient gouverneur de l'Île-de-France et obtient 2 640 000 livres. Henri de Joyeuse sort de son couvent des capucins pour empocher un million et demi de livres accompagnées d'un bâton de maréchal comme prix de la soumission du Languedoc. Le 25 septembre 1597, Mayenne le ligueur et Biron le huguenot reprennent Amiens. En janvier 1598, les pourparlers de paix sont engagés entre une Espagne résignée à sa défaite et une France à bout de souffle. Ce que confirme Henri IV lui-même dans une jolie formule datée du 1er mai 1598 : « La France et moi avons besoin de reprendre haleine. »

Encore fallait-il imposer cette pause à tous et faire sauter les ultimes verrous tenus par la Ligue. Marseille est tombée en 1596. En mars 1598, le duc de Mercœur, le dernier grand chef ligueur, remet au roi le gouvernement de Bretagne en échange du mariage de sa fille avec César de Vendôme, fils naturel d'Henri IV et de Gabrielle d'Estrées, et de coquettes pensions. Autant de succès qui mettent le roi en position de force et incitent les protestants à conclure la « paix de religion ».

L'édit « perpétuel et irrévocable », négocié depuis deux ans, est promulgué à Nantes le 13 avril 1598 et complété le 2 mai. Il comporte 92 articles de fond, 56 secrets et 2 « brevets ». Les protestants bénéficient tout d'abord de la liberté de culte, sauf à Paris, dans les villes épiscopales et dans une bonne moitié de la Bretagne. Jouissant de l'égalité civile, ils pourront être admis à tous les emplois publics et leurs enfants dans toutes les écoles. Pour leur assurer des juges non suspects, une chambre de l'Édit est créée à Paris, composée de dix magistrats catholiques et de six protestants. Une autre sera établie à Rouen en 1599. Enfin, les protestants peuvent demeurer un « parti » qui dispose de 150 lieux de « refuge », dont 51 places de « sûreté » défendues par une armée potentielle de 25 000 soldats.

En soi, ce texte n'est pas très neuf. Il reproduit presque intégralement certaines dispositions de l'édit de Poitiers de 1577. Mais, œuvre de circonstance entre les exigences protestantes et les haines catholiques, il exprime surtout la volonté d'en finir avec des guerres civiles qui s'éternisent depuis près de quarante ans.

Compromis inévitable, il permet aux deux confessions de vivre provisoirement ensemble. Toutefois, la tolérance accordée à « ceux qui font profession de la religion prétendue réformée » ne signifie pas que l'idéal d'unité religieuse a disparu, tant les esprits du temps sont convaincus que « la différence de religion défigure un État ».

En fait, ces dispositions, uniques en Europe occidentale, rencontrèrent au mieux la méfiance, le plus souvent l'hostilité générale. Réunis à la fin du mois de mai 1598 à Montpellier, les protestants ne prennent pas même la peine de remercier le roi de son intervention. Le pape s'indigne d'un édit qui permet « la liberté de conscience à tout un chacun, qui est la pire chose au monde ». Quant aux parlements, il fallut multiplier les exhortations et les pressions pour qu'ils enregistrent l'édit et le rendent effectif. Les Aixois et les Rennais y mirent plus d'un an. Les Rouennais, dix. Henri IV y gagna la réputation de « traître » à la cause de Dieu. Mais personne, à commencer par le pape, ne se risqua à condamner celui qui disposait d'un pouvoir assez fort pour le faire appliquer de façon loyale.

Cette volonté d'« ouverture » exceptionnelle a son versant diplomatique. À Vervins, le traité signé avec les Espagnols, le 2 mai 1598, reconduit les clauses de la paix du Cateau-Cambrésis. Cependant, brisant le grand rêve espagnol d'une monarchie universelle, Henri IV a réinstallé la France au cœur d'une diplomatie active qu'il entretient en cultivant l'amitié britannique, en soutenant financièrement les Hollandais contre l'Espagne et en annonçant son intention de défendre les « libertés germaniques ». « Vervins, écrit Emmanuel Le Roy Ladurie, demeure une date capitale. Cette fois, les guerres de Religion et les guerres civiles sont bien finies. Les premières refleuriront brièvement, mais dans le seul Midi au temps de Louis XIII. Les secondes connaîtront une courte et meurtrière flambée à l'heure de la Fronde. En gros, néanmoins, l'espace national, entre 1598 et 1789, n'expérimentera plus, même sous la Fronde pourtant si rude, de désordre ni de désastre intérieur qui se situerait au niveau des interminables catastrophes guerrières de la période 1560-1598. »

Du « cadavre de la France » à la « poule au pot »

Un désert peuplé de mendiants et d'affamés, des villes infestées de brigands et de pestiférés, des ateliers en panne et un État si endetté que le montant des arriérés à verser sur la dette publique excède deux bonnes années de rentrées fiscales. Un Français sorti d'un sommeil de quarante ans aurait eu le sentiment, à la fin des guerres de Religion, de contempler « non la France, mais un cadavre de France », selon la formule du parlementaire Étienne Pasquier.

Faute de travail, les villes embrigadent les mendiants pour leur faire reconstruire les murailles endommagées. S'installant par centaines dans les cimetières, ils détroussent les audacieux qui se hasardent dans les rues, « si bien, écrit le Suisse Thomas Platter, qu'il y a moins de risques à voyager dans une forêt vierge qu'à se trouver dans les rues de Paris, surtout lorsque les lanternes sont éteintes ».

Ces descriptions paraissent exagérées, mais elles sont si nombreuses qu'elles expriment sans doute l'intensité de l'effroi ressenti par les contemporains. Effroi de constater que le pays le plus peuplé du continent a vu mourir plus d'un sujet sur dix en l'espace de trente ans. Deux millions de victimes, sans doute, mortes plus souvent de faim que par l'épée. Effroi de constater, comme l'ambassadeur de Venise, que les Français ont pris goût au crime et au vol et que la misère, la vue du sang et la guerre les avaient rendus rusés, grossiers et sauvages. À Tours, un capitaine Sans-Crainte est reconnu coupable de cent vingt meurtres. Dans les forêts de Machecoul, le capitaine Guillery, un cadet de Bretagne, rançonne toute la Vendée avec ses 400 hommes. En 1594, des « croquants » du Limousin et du Périgord ont défilé au son du tambour pour dénoncer les officiers de finances, « qui se sont faits riches aux dépens du roi et du peuple ».

Le rétablissement de la paix, la modération de l'impôt, la protection du paysan et la chance qui voulut que le royaume connaisse onze années clémentes sur douze, tels furent les piliers de la restauration agricole.

En février 1597 et à nouveau en avril 1598, le roi interdit la chasse dans les blés et les vignes du printemps à l'automne, de même que la saisie des instruments et des bêtes des laboureurs, en cas de dette impayée. Dans un second temps, l'État modifie à la fois l'assiette et la répartition de la taille, éternel moyen de se concilier les faveurs du peuple en faisant, à court terme, baisser la pression fiscale dans de fortes proportions. Tandis que 40 000 « privilégiés » qui, à la faveur des troubles, s'étaient dispensés de la taille en se prétendant nobles sont de nouveau assujettis à l'impôt, le montant des tailles est réduit de 20 %. En même temps, l'abaissement du taux des rentes, de 8,33 % à 6,25 %, allège le poids des dettes qui, dans presque toutes les provinces, avaient fait fondre la part de la propriété paysanne.

Cette remise en ordre n'aurait toutefois pas suffi à installer la légende de la « poule au pot ». Il fallait qu'un homme incarne la prospérité et que les promoteurs d'idées nouvelles comme les tenants du bon sens se retrouvent dans son action. Ce fut le talent de Sully. Formé pour une carrière militaire, Maximilien de Béthune, né à Rosny-sur-Seine le 13 décembre 1559, protestant échappé au massacre de la Saint-Barthélemy, voue à Henri de Navarre une fidélité et un dévouement sans faille, même si, contrairement à une croyance tenace entretenue par ses soins, il ne lui servira jamais de mentor. S'il ignore tout de la comptabilité et des finances, ce baroudeur, qui a moins de goût pour l'administration que pour la guerre, a acquis une solide culture classique. L'inventaire de sa bibliothèque, établi à son décès, en décembre 1641, nous apprend qu'il était nourri d'histoire grecque et romaine. Xénophon, surtout, traduit par La Boétie, lui a fourni trois idées essentielles : en toutes choses, il y a un ordre qu'il faut préserver ; l'agriculture doit l'emporter sur l'artisanat qui « amollit » l'homme ; la gestion des affaires de la cité est identique à celle des intérêts privés.

Quand il parvient au Conseil des finances en 1595 puis devient surintendant en 1599, l'État est au bord de la banqueroute. Ses dettes sont évaluées à 200 millions de livres et il a fallu mettre en gage les joyaux de la couronne à Florence ! Le roi écrivait alors : « Je n'ai quasi pas un cheval sur lequel je puisse combattre, ni un harnais complet que je puisse endosser ; mes chemises sont toutes déchirées ; mes pourpoints troués au coude ; ma marmite est souvent renversée et depuis deux jours je dîne et soupe chez les uns et les autres, mes pourvoyeurs disant n'avoir plus moyen de rien fournir pour ma table, d'autant qu'il y a plus de six mois qu'ils n'ont reçu d'argent. »

« Se comportant en véritable baroudeur, écrit l'historienne Françoise Bayard, Sully pratique alors le vol et le racket pour faire entrer l'argent dans les caisses de l'État. »

Les créanciers de l'État sont les premières victimes, le surintendant des Finances estimant que les emprunts souscrits en temps de guerre ont été négociés sans que les monarques aient été en mesure d'en discuter les conditions. Ainsi quand le prince palatin réclame 473 210 écus 35 sols et 9 deniers, le Conseil des finances ramène cette dette à 286 134 écus 48 sols et 9 deniers ! Sully fait aussi traîner les versements jusqu'à ce que les créanciers se lassent. Malgré des manifestations de rentiers émus par la réduction des intérêts versés, il consolide et même annule une partie de la dette de l'État. Pour éviter d'être accusés de malversations, les officiers de finances versent une « composition » appelée aussi « prêt à jamais rendre »... Surtout, en décembre 1604, Sully exige de chaque officier désirant transmettre sa charge le versement d'un droit annuel. Ce sera la « paulette », du nom de Charles Paulet, le financier chargé de percevoir les revenus de l'affaire.

Moyennant le paiement d'une prime annuelle correspondant à 1,6 % de sa valeur d'achat, tout titulaire d'un office pourra transmettre sa charge à ses héritiers ou la revendre. On voit alors, écrit l'avocat au parlement de Paris, Charles Loyseau, « une grande troupe d'officiers se pressant et se poussant à qui le premier lui [à Paulet] baillerait son argent [...]. Puis, quand la nuit fit clore, le partisan ayant fermé son registre, j'ouïs un grand murmure de ceux qui étaient à dépêcher, faisant instance qu'on reçût leur argent, ne sachant, disaient-ils, s'ils ne mourraient point la nuit même ».

Enrichissement du Trésor et docilité des officiers vont désormais de pair. Mais dans le même temps, source de prestige et garantie de stabilité, l'office détourne durablement les profits du négoce et de l'industrie. Dans les trente années qui suivent l'instauration de la paulette, le prix moyen d'une charge de conseiller au Parlement de Paris passe de 10 000 à 120 000 livres ! Une plus-value qui mesure assez le prix que les élites accordent à la « fonction publique ».

La vraie mesure de la prospérité, dans la France de 1600, demeure pourtant la terre, celle qu'on possède et qu'on cultive. À cet égard, la baisse de la taille et des taux d'intérêt ont certainement excité une conjoncture dont la couronne a pu engranger les bénéfices. Publié en 1600, l'année même où Henri IV épouse en secondes noces Marie de Médicis, la fille de son banquier toscan qui apporte en dot l'équivalent d'un trimestre de déficit, le *Théâtre d'agriculture et mesnage des champs* connaît un succès inouï, huit éditions se succédant du vivant même de l'auteur, Olivier de Serres. Cet agronome protestant, pénétré de l'Ancien Testament, veut persuader le « bon père de famille » de se plaire sur sa terre et conseille aux gentilshommes qui ont abandonné la charrue pour l'épée de redécouvrir le bonheur en « la solitude de la campagne ». Henri IV, qui assura la promotion de l'ouvrage, ordonnait qu'on lui en fît lecture chaque soir. Citant le prophète Isaïe, « de leurs épées, ils forgeront des socs et de leurs lances des faucilles », Olivier de Serres, qui donne lui-même l'exemple sur ses terres du Pradel, définit ainsi un nouvel « art de vivre » noblement. Savoir choisir ses grains, augmenter ses rendements, engraisser ses terres, acclimater la betterave italienne, apprendre à cuisiner, telles doivent être désormais les vertus du gentilhomme transformé en bon gestionnaire de seigneurie.

D'autres mesures stimulent la reprise. Ponts, phares, canaux et routes, auxquels Sully, grand voyer de France, va jusqu'à consacrer 5 % des recettes annuelles de l'État, stimulent le commerce. Barthélemy de Laffemas, nommé « contrôleur général du commerce » en 1602, esquisse, quant à lui, un programme industriel dont la mission est de produire dans le royaume ce qui est importé de l'étranger. Des techniciens flamands viennent apprendre aux habitants de Senlis à faire de la dentelle. À Poitiers, La Rochelle et Nérac, des manufactures produisent des cuirs dorés qui concurrencent ceux de Cordoue. À Paris, des verreries de cristal et de miroirs imitent ceux de Venise. Pour les tapisseries, deux marchands flamands, Charles Coomans et François de La Planche, redonnent du « souffle » à l'ancienne maison des Gobelins. L'industrie de la soie se développe à Lyon. Pour les toiles fines, à la façon de Hollande, des manufactures sont ouvertes à Rouen et à Mantes. À Marseille, la gabelle du port mesure les profits de ce renouveau commercial. Après s'être accrue de 15 % des années 1590 aux années 1600, elle augmente de 81 % des années 1600 aux années 1610. À Lyon, les revenus du péage de Rochetaillée croissent de 18 % entre 1600 et 1607, puis de 45 % entre 1607 et 1621.

Toujours pour faire pencher du bon côté la balance du commerce, le roi suit avec sympathie les affaires canadiennes, contre l'avis de Sully qui affirme que de « telles conquêtes sont disproportionnées au naturel et à la cervelle des Français ». Suivant la piste des pêcheurs de morue, Samuel Champlain, navigateur catholique fils d'un marin protestant, fonde la ville de Québec le 3 juillet 1608 et ouvre, à partir du Saint-Laurent, deux grandes voies de pénétration, l'une vers l'Hudson, l'autre plus tardivement vers le lac Huron, par la rivière des Outaouais. Dans un mémorandum de 1615, il justifiera ce projet. Si nous ne nous y installons pas, prétendait-il, ce seront soit les Anglais, soit les Hollandais et c'en sera fini de la grande pêche à la morue avec ses quelque 600 à 700 navires. La première colonie française sera en fait une colonie « préventive ».

Malgré l'avènement d'un « petit âge glaciaire » qui fait avancer dans les Alpes les langues glaciaires et épouvante les habitants de

Chamonix qui, en 1601, signalent aux autorités savoyardes que « d'effroyables glaciers viennent, au cours d'une progression continue, de recouvrir deux de nos villages et d'en détruire un troisième », la conjoncture « henricienne » est bien celle de « la poule au pot ».

Henri le Grand

« Vous pouvez être sûr que je n'épargnerai aucun travail, ni ne craindrai aucun péril pour élever ma gloire et mon État en leur plus grande splendeur. » Henri de Navarre ne s'est pas encore rallié Paris que, déjà, il trace pour Sully son ambition, porter le prestige de la monarchie à son plus haut. En témoigne son intérêt pour un projet qui semble singulier au moment où il s'évertue à conquérir le pouvoir, construire à Cordouan, près de Royan, un phare qui doit « surpasser le phare d'Alexandrie » et qui, placé face à la mer domptée, symbolisera l'image d'un roi guidant son peuple au milieu des tempêtes.

Dans la capitale comme dans les villes, à des fins économiques ou militaires, les « grands travaux » exaltent le Bourbon. Partout Henri imprime sa marque. Sur les monnaies où il se transforme en Mars ou en Hercule vainqueur. Dans les portraits peints ou gravés qui diffusent l'image déjà légendaire de ce nez aquilin et ce sourire qui accrédite l'idée du « roi bon ». Au cœur des villes, à Charleville ou à Montauban, où les places portent l'empreinte de la personnalité du roi, un roi qui refuse le baroque et contribue à orienter les esprits vers un classicisme qui doit traduire, dans la ville, le même ordre que celui qui doit régner dans l'État.

Roi « parisien » par-dessus tout, installé au palais du Louvre qui redevient le temple de la monarchie, Henri IV, qui n'a pas l'humeur gyrovague des Valois, applique dans la capitale un véritable plan d'aménagement dont témoignent la place Royale et la place Dauphine. Intervenant dans le dessin des formes et des maisons, dans le choix des matériaux et la construction même, il veut inscrire dans la pierre l'autorité dont il est jaloux.

Mais cette installation en majesté aurait fait long feu si le Béarnais n'avait pas incarné les vertus que les Français aiment à se prêter et qu'Henri revendique pour parfaire sa réputation. La liberté dont se flattent ceux qui prétendent descendre tous des « Francs ». L'esprit de ceux qui se considèrent privilégiés par le climat. Et la galanterie empressée de ceux qui courtisent lestement le beau sexe. Autant de qualités ou de travers qui caractérisent la « bonne franquette », sorte de compromis entre la simplicité des mœurs et une pointe de trivialité que l'on oppose déjà à la « grossièreté » anglaise, la « stupidité » allemande ou la « duplicité » italienne.

Aidé de son équipe politique et littéraire, Henri IV organise de son vivant la représentation paternaliste, débonnaire et bon enfant qui a traversé les siècles. Une enfance verte et drue parmi les paysans béarnais. Une cordialité facile. Des mots crus employés dans les conversations qu'on lui prête. Un débraillé vestimentaire qui fait paraître différent. Un premier mariage raté mais un bon père de famille. Un ardent galant surtout qui put satisfaire pas moins de 56 maîtresses. Autant de traits « français » qui fleurent bon « la poule au pot » et expriment un vrai don de communication. *L'Astrée*, le roman d'Honoré d'Urfé dont la publication commence avec succès en 1607, est ainsi dédiée au « grand roi », dont la figure rappelle celle de cette déesse qui fit régner sur terre la paix, la justice et l'abondance avant que la méchanceté des hommes ne la contraigne à remonter au ciel.

Pour parfaire la vie du Béarnais, restait à en réussir le terme. Le 14 mai 1610, alors qu'Henri IV se prépare à une guerre contre les Habsbourg dont la charge financière aurait pu ternir son image auprès du peuple, un dénommé Ravaillac, un catholique dévot révolté par l'édit de Nantes, monte sur la roue du carrosse ralenti par les embarras de la circulation, rue de la Ferronnerie, et près d'une auberge *Au Cœur couronné percé d'une flèche*, porte deux coups de couteau au roi. Transporté au Louvre, Henri meurt quelques heures plus tard. À cet instant, dans la capitale, note Pierre de L'Estoile, « chacun crie, pleure, se lamente, grands et petits, jeunes et vieux ». La dix-huitième tentative d'assassinat sur « le meilleur roi du monde » avait réussi.

Le roi et le cardinal

Le 18 avril 1625, quelques mois après l'entrée du cardinal de Riche-lieu au Conseil d'en-haut, un ambassadeur italien écrit : « L'autorité du cardinal croît tous les jours et il sera difficile maintenant de le faire tomber. » En fait, les « grands hommes » ne surgissent jamais du néant. Entre un roi qui, à l'âge de neuf ans, déclarait déjà à son précepteur : « Réjouir le peuple, craindre Dieu, faire la justice, telle est la multiple fonction de Sa Majesté », et un cardinal qui n'avait d'autre ambition que le bien de la religion et de l'État, se nouait un « mariage de raison ». Un mariage qui, au terme de dix-huit années tumultueuses, aura permis de rabaisser l'orgueil des Grands et de relever le nom de la France dans le concert des nations.

Le temps des « malcontents »

Désignée le 14 mai 1610 par le Parlement de Paris pour devenir « régente en France, pour avoir l'administration des affaires du royaume pendant le bas âge de son fils, avec toute puissance et autori-té », Marie de Médicis, sacrée la veille de l'assassinat de son mari, n'a pas bonne presse. D'une intelligence médiocre, avide d'honneurs et de belles choses, elle n'a, semble-t-il, pour elle qu'un port majes-tueux et une belle santé. Henri IV, qui l'a beaucoup trompée, disait qu'elle avait un « naturel terriblement robuste et fort ». Sully admirait

« son beau port, sa bonne mine, sa belle taille, sa grâce, sa majestueuse présence et sa vénérable gravité, voire sa gentillesse, industrie et dextérité à gagner les cœurs et s'acquérir les volontés et affections des personnes ». Ne possédant toutefois aucun talent politique, Marie, qui s'épuise à suivre les traces de Catherine de Médicis, a besoin de conseils et accorde sa confiance à une amie d'enfance, Léonora Galigaï, et à son mari, l'aventurier Concini, dont l'ascension et l'enrichissement défraient bientôt la chronique. Conseiller d'État en juillet 1610, il acquiert le marquisat d'Ancre, en Picardie, en septembre puis le gouvernement de Roye, de Péronne et de Montdidier ainsi que la charge de premier gentilhomme de la chambre du roi. En février 1611, il est lieutenant général de Picardie et maréchal de France en 1613.

Il n'en faut pas plus pour ranimer l'esprit de rébellion qui, une fois encore, met en jeu la nature de l'État et l'autorité de la monarchie. Dans l'opposition, on retrouve les princes qui rêvent de revenir aux temps mythiques des rapports entre suzerains et vassaux et s'opposent à l'ascension des robins, ces acheteurs d'offices, les protestants qui veulent obtenir l'application pleine et entière de l'édit de Nantes et s'inquiètent des options proespagnoles de la régente, les catholiques « dévots » qui voudraient voir les articles du concile de Trente devenir lois du royaume et se félicitent du mariage conclu entre le jeune roi et Anne d'Autriche, fille aînée du roi d'Espagne.

Cette opposition se fait entendre en Bourgogne, en Dauphiné, en Provence, en Languedoc, en Bretagne, en Normandie, des provinces qui ont gardé leurs assemblées d'états au sein desquelles, chaque année, les trois ordres discutent des « affaires » et marchandent le montant de l'impôt. Elle s'exaspère sur la place publique à travers les conversations et les rumeurs, les pamphlets et les libelles qui pullulent, 1017 titres ayant été publiés pendant la régence de Marie de Médicis. « Dans ce pays, écrit en 1611 Scipione Ammirato, non seulement, il y a la liberté de conscience, mais encore celle de la langue et de la plume. » Une plume qui dépeint le plus souvent au vitriol le gouvernement des femmes, des reines et des étrangers.

Le 18 février 1614, Henri de Bourbon, prince de Condé, premier prince du sang, publie un manifeste dans lequel il expose les revendications des « malcontents » et s'en prend aux « mauvais conseillers » qui « profitent et rançonnent la minorité de notre jeune roi ». Animée par les ducs de Nevers et de Mayenne, le maréchal de Bouillon et les ducs de Longueville, de Luxembourg et de Vendôme, la grogne des princes obtient des pensions, des postes et la convocation des états généraux qui se réunissent à Paris le 27 octobre 1614.

Ces états, qui furent les derniers avant ceux de 1789, rassemblent au couvent des Grands Augustins 135 députés du clergé et 138 députés de la noblesse qui traitent de « valets » ou de « fils de savetiers et de cordonniers » les 187 députés du tiers état. « Après avoir perdu la possession des charges et dignités de l'Église, s'exclame un gentil-homme, nous avons aussi laissé partir de nos mains l'administration de la justice et ne sommes plus aujourd'hui que la proie de nos infé-rieurs, laissé élever deux monstres engendrés du tiers état qui nous ruinent et ruinent notre monarque et sa monarchie et qui nous ont déjà réduits en tels termes que nous n'avons plus aucune marque de différence entre eux et nous, ni par les charges, grades et qualités, ni par les armes et habits, si ce n'est qu'ils ont de toutes ces choses plus que nous. »

Tensions, querelles de préséance, âpres débats, autant d'aubaines pour le parti royal qui peut apparaître comme l'arbitre de groupes divisés et sort renforcé d'une épreuve que ses adversaires avaient voulu lui imposer.

Le 23 février 1615, lors de la séance de clôture, Armand du Ples-sis de Richelieu, évêque de Luçon et porte-parole du clergé, se fait remarquer en maniant à la fois la critique et l'encensoir. Critiquant la fiscalité excessive et l'éloignement des prélats des affaires publiques, il adresse en même temps un hommage appuyé à la régente en s'écriant : « Heureux le roi à qui Dieu donne une mère pleine d'amour envers sa personne, de zèle envers son État et d'expérience pour la conduite des affaires ! Entre une infinité de grâces que Votre Majesté a reçues du ciel, une des plus grandes dont vous lui soyez redevable est le don et la conservation d'une telle mère ; et entre toutes vos actions, la plus digne et la plus utile au rétablissement de votre État est celle que vous aurez faite en lui commettant la charge. »

Pour l'heure, Armand du Plessis se constitue un fort capital de relations et de fidélités, propose ses services à celle qu'il a flattée, fait l'expérience des cabales de cour et des changements de favoris et pâtit en 1617 de la chute de Concini. Avec l'autorisation de Louis, qui aura seize ans en septembre et manifeste « un désir extrême de prendre en main le gouvernail de son État », Concini est assassiné le 24 avril 1617 à l'entrée du Louvre et Léonora Galigaï, condamnée comme sorcière, est décapitée le 8 juillet avant que ses restes ne soient réduits en cendres.

L'acharnement avec lequel le peuple de Paris a déchiré le corps de « Conchine », déterré le 25 avril de l'église Saint-Germain-l'Auxerrois, traduit moins la fureur aveugle de la populace que le supplice exemplaire réservé à celui qui avait bravé le destin par la démesure de son orgueil. Dans cette société où l'honneur exigeait que la noblesse y sacrifiât sa vie, l'infamie devait nécessairement accompagner le châtiment.

« Décoyonné le coyon », c'est châtier le paillard qui a courtisé la reine mère et voulu usurper le pouvoir d'un roi père. Couper le nez, c'est défigurer le courtisan trop galant. Couper les mains, c'est punir le voleur pris la main dans le sac. Amputer les pieds, c'est interdire au poltron de fuir le danger. « Loué soit Dieu, me voilà roi », peut s'écrier Louis XIII qui congédie pour un temps sa mère et s'emploie à trouver sa personnalité.

Un mariage de raison

Né à Fontainebleau le 27 septembre 1601, le jeune Louis XIII a connu une rude enfance dont les tourments ont été méticuleusement notés par son médecin, Jean Héroard. Son précieux *Journal* consigne jour après jour les faits et gestes du royal patient. L'on sait ainsi presque tout de la couleur et de la consistance de ses selles, de ses peurs et de ses cauchemars, de ses haines et de ses amitiés, de ses distractions et de ses complexes, de ses crises dépressives et de son goût pour la vie militaire.

Pendant vingt-six ans, Héroard a été un observateur extraordinaire du quotidien. On apprend ainsi qu'entre 1608 et 1611, Louis a connu 17 dysfonctionnements intestinaux, 6 blessures par chute ou par coup, 4 maux de dents, 3 vomissements, 3 tuméfactions de l'aine et de la verge, 2 saignements de nez et 2 maux de gorge. On se pose toujours la question de savoir si le mariage avec Anne d'Autriche, en 1615, fut consommé, Héroard écrivant avec décence que le « guillery », c'est ainsi qu'il nommait le membre viril, « paraissait rouge », « paraissait » seulement. On perçoit surtout la psychologie complexe d'un jeune homme privé d'affection, souvent fouetté, timide et misanthrope, mal à l'aise avec les femmes, pénétré du stoïcisme chrétien du temps, pourfendeur du luxe et du libertinage, assez lucide pour connaître ses défauts et savoir qu'il avait besoin d'un collaborateur qui l'aide à exercer son métier de roi. Remarquables sont les quelques paroles qu'il prononce à la clôture des états généraux en février 1615 : « Messieurs, je ferai paraître le désir que j'ai de servir Dieu, soulager mon peuple, protéger un chacun, rendre la justice à tout un chacun et faire en sorte que vous soyez tous contents. »

Pierre Chevallier, biographe de Louis XIII, fait ainsi justice de la légende qui le peignait en roi-soliveau dominé par sa mère puis par ses favoris. Il révèle au contraire un roi opiniâtre qui fit son métier avec une solide conscience professionnelle, convaincu d'être responsable du bien-être public. « Dieu ne m'a fait roi que pour lui obéir et donner l'exemple », telle a été la clef de sa conduite.

Mais pour avoir voulu, entre 1617 et 1624, agir par lui-même sur toutes les affaires de son État, il a pris conscience qu'il ne peut parvenir seul au dessein qu'il s'est fixé. Attachant trop d'importance aux détails, assailli par les doutes et les regrets, il a l'intelligence de discerner la valeur de celui qui s'est compromis avec Concini et appelle en 1624 Richelieu à son Conseil.

Né en 1585 dans une famille poitevine de bonne noblesse, Armand Jean du Plessis de Richelieu est d'abord destiné à la carrière des armes. Son frère, Alphonse, nommé évêque de Luçon, ayant toutefois refusé cette charge pour entrer à la Grande Chartreuse, il est contraint de rentrer dans les ordres pour conserver à sa famille les revenus de cet évêché, « le plus crotté de France », écrit-il mélancoliquement le 21 décembre 1608.

Faisant cependant partie d'une génération qui entend remettre de l'ordre dans la pratique comme dans la morale religieuses, il se consacre avec ardeur à la réforme de son diocèse. À peine arrivé dans son évêché, il publie des règlements qui interdisent aux prêtres de fréquenter les foires, de boire et de jouer, sous peine de 10 livres d'amende par infraction. Il fait fermer les tavernes pendant les messes, inflige aux fidèles une leçon de catéchisme hebdomadaire avec récitation des dix commandements, surveille que les ouailles communient au moins aux grandes fêtes et, afin que nul n'ignore son zèle, écrit un traité, *L'Instruction du chrétien*, dont le titre montre à quel point il se veut à la pointe du combat religieux. Ce n'est donc pas un hasard si le pape Grégoire XV, en le faisant cardinal en septembre 1622, le compare à un « rempart de la religion catholique ».

Prélat d'une exemplaire dévotion, Richelieu est aussi un ambitieux, un homme de réseaux familiaux et amicaux qui sait flatter les personnages importants et manœuvrer avec autant d'habileté que de prudence. Homme de bureau, titulaire d'un doctorat en Sorbonne, dictant sans cesse les pièces qui deviendront son *Testament politique*, fondant en 1635 l'Académie française dont les membres ne tardent pas à composer des recueils de vers sur « le grand cardinal », il a aussi, comme tous les Grands de son temps, le goût du faste, dépensant somptueusement l'immense fortune qu'il accumule et comblant de largesses une foule de parents et d'amis. Émotif comme le roi, neurasthénique, d'une nervosité extrême, il est aussi constamment malade, souffrant de fièvre, de maux de tête continuels et d'hémorroïdes.

Redouté ou aimé, il sait à la fois briser par la violence les résistances à l'ordre royal et, en même temps, faire preuve d'indulgence et éprouver des affections profondes. « Je vous jure, écrivait Malherbe, qu'il y a dans cet homme quelque chose qui excède l'humanité. »

Entre un roi qui avait la plus haute idée de sa fonction et un cardinal qui avait pour ambition de servir passionnément la « personne sacrée » du roi en développant la puissance de l'État, se nouait un « mariage de raison » fondé sur la confiance réciproque, une confiance que méritera Richelieu en affrontant pendant six années une série d'orages particulièrement violents et en déjouant les intrigues d'une cour qui n'eut de cesse d'amener le roi à se débarrasser de son ministre. Le 11 novembre 1630, elle crut y parvenir quand la reine mère démit le cardinal de ses fonctions. Mais, alors que les courtisans se précipitaient au palais du Luxembourg pour féliciter Marie de Médicis de ce « coup de majesté », le roi, après bien des hésitations, trancha en faveur du cardinal qui put, au lendemain de cette journée des Dupes, appliquer sans réserve la politique qu'il a définie, mais après coup, dans son *Testament politique*.

En effet, il abusera bon nombre d'historiens en leur faisant croire qu'il avait, dès 1624, une claire conscience de l'action qu'il fallait mener. Il inaugurait ainsi un genre appelé à un grand avenir, les *Mémoires*, destinés à faire croire à la cohérence d'un programme rigoureusement établi. Dans le *Testament*, on peut lire en effet : « Lorsque Votre Majesté résolut de me donner en même temps l'entrée de ses conseils et grande part dans sa confiance pour la direction de ses affaires, je puis dire avec vérité que les huguenots partageaient l'État avec elle, que les Grands se conduisaient comme s'ils n'eussent pas été ses sujets, et les plus puissants gouverneurs des provinces comme s'ils eussent été souverains en leurs charges. [...]

Je puis dire encore que les alliances étrangères étaient méprisées, les intérêts particuliers préférés aux publics, en un mot, la dignité de la majesté royale tellement ravalée et si différente de ce qu'elle devait être [...] qu'il était presque impossible de la reconnaître.

Je lui promis d'employer toute mon industrie et toute l'autorité qu'il lui plaisait me donner pour ruiner le parti huguenot, rabaisser l'orgueil des Grands, réduire tous ses sujets en leurs devoirs et relever son nom dans les nations étrangères au point où il devait être. »

En fait, dans l'action qu'il entreprit à partir de son accession au Conseil, rien ne ressemble à ce plan. Remarquable opportuniste, Richelieu se plie aux circonstances et tente de démêler les problèmes qui se présentent tous à la fois, laissant à nouveau planer la menace de l'anarchie.

« *Ruiner le parti huguenot* »

Rudement grignotés par les offensives du renouveau catholique menées en particulier par l'armée des jésuites, les protestants qui, vers 1610, ne représentaient plus que 4 à 5 % de la population française et craignaient pour l'avenir de leur foi, avaient pris appui sur les deux cents places de sûreté qu'ils contrôlaient pour organiser la résistance.

Pouvant lever 25 000 hommes immédiatement, les partisans de la « Religion Prétendue Réformée » disposaient même d'effectifs supérieurs aux régiments permanents de la couronne. En mai 1611, au synode de Saumur, tandis que les fidèles du roi Henri avaient plaidé pour la conciliation, d'autres, emmenés par les grands seigneurs qu'étaient les ducs de Bouillon et de Rohan, se déclaraient prêts à reprendre les armes. En 1620, pour rétablir l'exercice du culte catholique en Béarn, conformément aux clauses de l'édit de Nantes, et restituer aux évêques les biens confisqués par les réformés, Louis XIII et son favori du moment, Luynes, ont montré leur présence dans la province et réuni le Béarn et la basse Navarre à la couronne.

Cette manifestation de force a provoqué de violents débats au cours de l'assemblée des protestants réunis en décembre 1620 à La Rochelle. Après avoir lancé un appel au roi d'Angleterre Jacques Ier Stuart, divisé le royaume en huit cercles militaires placés sous l'autorité d'un gouverneur et levé des taxes, ils décident de prendre les armes sous le commandement d'Henri, duc de Rohan. Dirigée par Louis XIII en personne, l'armée royale prend Saint-Jean-d'Angély, dont les remparts sont abattus et les privilèges abolis, mais échoue devant Montauban, victorieusement défendue par le sieur de La Force, et devant La Rochelle, où une flotte royale est repoussée. En octobre 1622, de guerre lasse, un traité conclu sous les murs de Montpellier renouvelle les principales dispositions de l'édit de Nantes mais exige que les protestants renoncent à tenir garnison dans quatre-vingts places. En dépit de la propagande royale qui multiplie les images du jeune souverain en roi de guerre, bravant les boulets, la paix de Montpellier n'avait pas décapité l'« État » protestant.

Forte de ses 28 000 habitants, de ses navires qui contrôlaient les rivages de l'Atlantique et de ses remparts qui défiaient l'assiégeant, la ville de La Rochelle pouvait même apparaître comme une Amsterdam en puissance, capable de prendre la tête d'un État dans l'État.

Pour en finir avec cette Babylone de l'hérésie, le roi et le cardinal décident d'en faire le siège auquel la construction d'une digue haute de 20 mètres et longue de 1 500 mètres donne sa dimension historique. Édifiée en trois mois sur les plans de l'ingénieur Métezeau, avec des gravats, des pieux et des débris de vaisseaux, la digue, qui ferme l'entrée du port à tout navire, devient la curiosité militaire du moment. Le Génois Spinola, considéré comme le plus grand homme de guerre de son temps, se déplace jusqu'à La Rochelle et convient que « c'était une chose qui lui eût semblé impossible, s'il n'en eût vu le commencement déjà avancé ». Le siège tient en haleine les cours d'Europe, convaincues d'assister à une nouvelle donne stratégique autant que diplomatique. Pour les Anglais, il s'agit de régler la question de la suprématie navale avec une France dont « le principal dessein, écrit le duc de Buckingham, est de nous déposséder de souveraineté en ces mers dont tous nos ancêtres ont joui de temps immémorial » et « d'étendre sa monarchie sur l'Océan ». Les Espagnols, alliés formels de la France, promettent le concours d'une flotte qui gagne les côtes bretonnes mais n'en bouge pas. Même les héros de l'affaire sont à la mesure de l'événement. Buckingham, le chef de la flotte anglaise de secours, est plus célèbre pour son charme que pour ses qualités d'amiral, tapissant, disait-il, sa cabine aux couleurs d'Anne d'Autriche à laquelle il avait osé faire la cour. Face à lui, Richelieu, grand maître de la flotte, inspecte les fortifications un exemplaire de l'historien latin Quinte-Curce à la main, l'épée au côté, la cotte de mailles et la pourpre cardinalice superposées, en faisant « l'Homme rouge » pour l'éternité. Le roi consacre plusieurs journées aux dévotions, comme si un long moment de prières était nécessaire pour combattre, en état de pureté, la cité de l'hérésie.

La seconde moitié de l'année 1628 se déroule au rythme des offensives anglaises pour percer le blocus de la ville et des duels d'artillerie sans équivalent dans l'histoire du temps, des témoins assurant avoir comptabilisé près de 5 000 boulets tirés par chaque camp. Le sort des assiégés, qui ne sont plus que 6 000 sur 28 000, devient un enjeu politique qui divise le Conseil. Une telle résistance était une outrecuidance qui appelait la vengeance, mais passer au fil de l'épée des gens si affaiblis par la faim qu'on avait vu « une mère dévorer sa fille morte et une sœur ronger les doigts de son frère », c'était prendre le risque de la guerre civile. Aussi les conditions imposées par Richelieu le 29 octobre prévoient l'amnistie des rebelles contre leur soumission au pouvoir monarchique. Les fortifications seront toutes démantelées, les privilèges de la ville abolis et l'acte de reddition sera signé par de subalternes maréchaux de camp, comme si le roi et le cardinal ne daignaient traiter d'égal à égal avec des insoumis.

Louis XIII y gagne le surnom de « Louis le Juste », qui punit et qui pardonne, comme le Dieu du Jugement et de la Miséricorde. Signée le 28 juin 1629, la paix d'Alès marquait la fin des guerres de Religion en France. Il confirmait les dispositions religieuses et juridiques de l'édit de Nantes mais supprimait toutes les places de sûreté et abolissait les privilèges politiques des huguenots, qui allaient désormais adopter un profil bas et faire preuve de prudence et de fidélité. « Autrefois, écrit Richelieu, le Roi faisait des traités avec ses sujets après qu'ils lui avaient fait la guerre ; maintenant, il leur accorde par grâce ce que bon lui semble. »

Grandeurs et misères de la guerre

Loin d'apaiser les esprits, la paix avec les huguenots aggrave le conflit entre deux politiques, donc entre deux « partis ». Pour le « parti » des « dévots », groupés derrière le cardinal de Bérulle, le chancelier Michel de Marillac, la reine mère, Anne d'Autriche, et Gaston d'Orléans, le brouillon frère du roi, toujours du côté des « malcontents », il convenait maintenant de révoquer l'édit de Nantes, d'abandonner toute attitude hostile à l'égard des Habsbourg et de s'entendre avec l'Espagne catholique et la papauté pour combattre l'hérésie, établir la paix chrétienne et la raison de Dieu.

Pour le « parti » des « bons Français », sur lequel s'appuie Richelieu, il ne faut pas confondre la raison d'État avec celle de la religion. Il est nécessaire, au contraire, de combattre les Habsbourg de Vienne comme de Madrid dont les possessions territoriales encerclent dangereusement le royaume. Dans un mémoire de janvier 1629, le cardinal avait exposé en détail les raisons d'une telle politique : « Maintenant que La Rochelle est prise [...] il faut avoir en dessein perpétuel d'arrêter le cours des progrès de l'Espagne, et, au lieu que cette nation a pour but d'augmenter sa domination et d'étendre ses limites, la France ne doit penser qu'à se fortifier en elle-même et s'ouvrir des portes pour entrer dans tous les États de ses voisins et les garantir des oppressions d'Espagne. »

Menée par le pieux cardinal, la politique des « bons Français » consiste donc à s'allier avec les protestants d'Allemagne, des Provinces-Unies ou de Scandinavie pour briser l'impérialisme des héritiers de Charles Quint. Un impérialisme qui n'est pas une chimère quand Philippe IV d'Espagne écrit lorsqu'il se rend avec une armée en Italie : « Quand j'aurai mené cette expédition, je ferai du monde, avec l'aide de Dieu, ce que je voudrai. » Le « bellicisme » des « bons Français » s'oppose ici au « pacifisme » des « dévots ».

À ceux qui pourraient l'accuser de machiavélisme pour ces alliances « hérétiques », Richelieu a répondu en écrivant en 1632 : « La chrétienté est travaillée par deux puissantes factions. L'une est celle des protestants, qui combattent la religion. L'autre est celle de la maison d'Autriche qui opprime la liberté et par la subversion de la justice et les moyens qu'elle tient pour parvenir à sa fin contraire à la religion chrétienne comme sont l'ambition, l'usurpation, le déguisement, l'art de semer les divisions entre les Grands, les révoltes parmi les peuples et les calomnies parmi les plus gens de bien qui ne suivent pas son parti, renversent avec le fondement de l'équité publique ceux de la piété qui sont conjoints inséparablement [...]. On peut dire que la France qui a réprimé en tous les siècles les excès de l'impiété et de l'injustice et de laquelle Dieu s'est servi pour maintenir l'Église et le repos commun contre les deux plus grands assauts de ces deux monstres est la seule qui soutienne ce travail avec tant de peine. »

Le cardinal ne se prive d'ailleurs pas de souligner qu'au moment où le roi était bloqué devant La Rochelle, la maison d'Autriche en profitait pour rallumer la guerre en Italie et s'emparer des villes de Casal et de Mantoue. C'est parce qu'ils se conduisent de manière non chrétienne que les Habsbourg doivent être combattus. Une argumentation parfois spécieuse violemment combattue par les pamphlétaires espagnols ou dévots. Paru dans l'été 1635, le *Mars gallicus* de Cornelius Jansen, évêque d'Ypres, accusait tous les rois de France d'être, depuis les Mérovingiens, des criminels, des usurpateurs, des hérétiques, alliés des musulmans et des protestants. Interdit en France mais approuvé silencieusement à Rome, ce pamphlet en latin, traduit en français et en espagnol, trois fois réédité, était un reproche argumenté à la raison d'État.

Sur le moment, prendre le parti de la guerre au moment où une épidémie de peste ravage le royaume est un choix particulièrement douloureux et impopulaire qui suppose de « quitter toute pensée de repos, d'épargne et de règlement du royaume ». « Mais l'aversion que les peuples ont de la guerre, affirme le cardinal, n'est pas un motif considérable pour porter à une telle paix, vu que souvent ils sentent et se plaignent aussi bien des maux nécessaires comme de ceux qu'on peut éviter ; qu'ils sont aussi ignorants de ce qui est utile à un État comme sensibles et prompts à se plaindre de maux qu'il faut souffrir pour en éviter de plus grands. »

Au lendemain de la journée des Dupes qui voit l'élimination du parti « dévot » et l'exil cette fois définitif de Marie de Médicis, qui ne reverra jamais plus son fils, Richelieu peut préparer le grand affrontement avec l'Espagne, qui dispose des trésors d'Amérique et de l'armée la plus redoutable d'Europe mais dont les possessions, dispersées sur le continent, constituent, face à une France compacte, la principale source de faiblesse.

« La séparation des États qui forment le corps de la monarchie espagnole, écrit toujours Richelieu, en rend la communication si mal aisée que pour leur donner quelque liaison, l'unique moyen que l'Espagne ait, est l'entretien d'un grand nombre de vaisseaux en l'Océan, de galères en la Méditerranée, qui, par leur trajet continuel, réunissent en quelque façon les membres à leur chef [...]. D'où il s'ensuit que, si on empêche la liberté de tels trajets, ces États, qui ne peuvent subsister d'eux-mêmes, ne sauraient éviter la confusion, la faiblesse et toutes les désolations dont Dieu menace un royaume divisé. Or, comme la côte de [Levant] de ce royaume sépare l'Espagne de tous les États possédés en Italie par leur roi, il semble que la providence de Dieu, qui veut tenir les choses en balance, a voulu que la situation de la France séparât les États d'Espagne pour les affaiblir en les divisant. »

La guerre de Trente Ans fournit au cardinal un terrain à sa mesure. L'enjeu de ce conflit, qui a commencé en 1618 à Prague par la défenestration de conseillers catholiques de l'empereur par une délégation protestante, est bien la prépondérance de la maison d'Autriche en Europe. Guerre allemande à l'origine, elle oppose un empereur catholique intransigeant dont l'ambition est d'éliminer l'hérésie de ses États à des princes protestants qui veulent défendre leur foi.

Guerre européenne au fur et à mesure de son déroulement, elle fait entrer dans la bataille tous ceux que menacent les ambitions des Habsbourg. Guerre totale, elle décime les populations et épuise les finances des États. Guerre nouvelle, elle révèle des *condottieri* de premier plan tels Albrecht von Wallenstein, Ambrogio Spinola ou Bernard de Saxe-Weimar et des chefs de guerre de génie comme le roi de Suède Gustave Adolphe. Le « roi des neiges » inaugure l'armée de conscription, constituée essentiellement de paysans luthériens, invente la cartouche et les canons légers, instaure l'ordre mince, des longues lignes groupant les hommes sur trois ou quatre rangs de profondeur seulement, et les charges de cavalerie pistolet au poing et non plus l'épée à la main.

Richelieu, qui n'est pas pressé de s'engager dans un conflit dont il pressent quel sera le prix, mène d'abord une guerre « couverte » en soutenant financièrement les princes protestants. Son principal souci est de trouver des soldats, et en masse, puisqu'il s'agit de quadrupler les effectifs et de les porter à 130 000 fantassins au moins, ce qui n'est pas rien lorsque l'on sait qu'un soldat coûtait en 1630 cinq fois plus qu'au siècle précédent. En 1635, toutefois, au lendemain de la défaite de l'armée suédoise devant les forces espagnoles et impériales à la bataille de Nördlingen, le cardinal est contraint de déclarer la guerre qu'il aurait souhaité pouvoir retarder encore.

Le 19 mai 1635, prétextant l'enlèvement par les Espagnols de l'Électeur de Trèves qui avait demandé la protection du roi de France, le cardinal exploite pour la dernière fois de l'histoire les formes rituelles du défi féodal. Un officier gascon nommé Jean Gratiollet, « héraut d'armes de France », franchit la frontière du royaume, accompagné d'un trompette, et se rend à Bruxelles porter en forme de défi la déclaration royale de la guerre au gouverneur des Pays-Bas et représentant du roi d'Espagne. Toute la journée du 19 mai, il multiplie en vain des demandes d'audience. Finalement, en désespoir de cause, à sept heures du soir, il se décide à jeter sur le sol de la place du Sablon, aux pieds de la foule assemblée, la déclaration de guerre et, à la frontière, au retour, attache la décision royale à un poteau au village de Bouilly, en présence de tous ceux du bourg. En évoquant ce rituel avec force détails dans ses *Mémoires*, Richelieu voulait affirmer que la France déclarait une guerre « juste » et « légitime » à ceux qui avaient bafoué « la dignité de l'Empire et le droit des gens ».

Dès les premières escarmouches, l'armée française montre toutefois qu'elle n'est pas à la hauteur du spectacle. La correspondance de Louis XIII, qui en a pris la tête, en porte témoignage.

En septembre, il écrit depuis Montceaux : « Je suis très fâché d'être contraint de vous écrire qu'il n'y a, à Saint-Dizier, ni trésorier ni munitionnaire et que toutes les troupes y sont sur le point de se débander s'il n'y est pourvu promptement. » Le 4 octobre, depuis le camp de Kœur : « Je suis bien fâché de vous dire qu'il ne faut faire nul état de notre noblesse volontaire, que pour faire perdre l'honneur à celui qui voudra entreprendre quelque chose de bon avec eux, où il y aura la moindre fatigue à faire ; quand on les veut envoyer seulement à trois heures d'ici [...], ils murmurent, jurent et disent tout haut qu'on les veut perdre et qu'ils s'en iront. Voyez à quoi est réduit celui qui commande une armée dont les principales forces sont composées de telles gens, comme la mienne à cette heure. »

En 1636, Espagnols et Impériaux passent à l'offensive sur tous les fronts. Porte de la Bourgogne, Saint-Jean-de-Losne est assiégée. Au sud-ouest, les Espagnols sont à Saint-Jean-de-Luz et ils occupent les îles de Lérins au sud-est. Au nord surtout, ils franchissent la

Somme le 4 août 1636, prennent Corbie le 15 août et font voir des éclaireurs à Pontoise. La panique s'empare de Paris où affluent les réfugiés. « Tout y fuyait et on ne voyait que carrosses, coches et chevaux sur les chemins d'Orléans et de Chartres qui sortaient de cette grande ville pour se mettre en sûreté, comme si déjà Paris eût été au pillage. » Richelieu, pris d'un accès de faiblesse, pense un moment fuir, lui aussi, la capitale mais le Père Joseph, son fidèle conseiller, l'incite à organiser la résistance. Le cardinal se rend alors sur le Pont-Neuf en carrosse, sans gardes et sans mousquetaires, et exhorte le peuple à la résistance. À Paris comme dans le royaume règne alors une atmosphère d'union « nationale » autour du roi. On mobilise la noblesse à cheval du côté de Saint Denis, on creuse des tranchées, la faculté de théologie de la Sorbonne décide d'équiper deux hommes et de les offrir pour la défense du royaume. À l'automne, Corbie est reprise et les Espagnols sont refoulés tandis que Saint-Jean-de-Losne résiste et gagne le surnom de Saint-Jean Belle-Défense. Le 17 novembre, un *Te Deum* puis un concert de canons célèbrent la victoire du roi.

Richelieu, aidé du secrétaire d'État à la Guerre François Sublet de Noyers, mobilise alors toutes les énergies pour renverser la balance des forces. En 1639, il peut aligner 167 000 hommes contre moins de 100 000 en 1636. La lutte contre l'absentéisme des chefs et les désertions des soldats est poursuivie sans relâche. On fait massivement appel aux mercenaires étrangers, qui représentent 31 % des effectifs en 1644 et 56 % en 1656. Domaine réservé du cardinal, la marine royale, forte en 1642 de 65 vaisseaux et de 22 galères, est devenue une force redoutable. À cette date, l'équilibre des forces a bien été modifié en faveur de la France et de ses alliés. Les régiments du roi se sont installés en Alsace et en Lorraine, ont occupé l'Artois et profité des révoltes des Portugais et des Catalans contre l'Espagne pour reconquérir le Roussillon et prendre Perpignan.

Quand Richelieu meurt, le 4 décembre 1642, quelques mois avant le roi, qui s'éteint à Saint-Germain-en-Laye le 14 mai 1643, on peut espérer qu'une paix victorieuse sera bientôt signée, surtout quand, le 19 mai 1643, le jeune duc d'Enghien, fils du prince de Condé, remporte à Rocroi une victoire totale qui enlève à l'Espagne toute possibilité d'envahir la France par le Nord.

Signés le 24 octobre 1648, les traités de Westphalie consacrent l'échec complet des Habsbourg de Vienne. Ils imposent en effet à l'empereur Ferdinand III le maintien de la division religieuse de l'Empire. Les « libertés germaniques », garanties par les rois de France et de Suède, assurent aux princes allemands une totale souveraineté.

Divisée en trois cent cinquante principautés et villes indépendantes, ruinée et dépeuplée par une guerre qui lui avait fait perdre la moitié de sa population, l'Allemagne n'était plus qu'un fantôme de puissance. La France, qui avait reçu la plus grande partie de l'Alsace, à l'exception de Strasbourg, avait mis fin au rêve de domination universelle des Habsbourg.

Restait toutefois l'Espagne qui, encouragée par le soulèvement des princes et d'une partie de la France contre Mazarin, le successeur de Richelieu, poursuivait le combat. Au terme de dix années de luttes où l'on put voir le vainqueur de Rocroi prendre la tête des troupes espagnoles et Dunkerque remise aux Anglais pour prix de leur alliance, le traité dit des Pyrénées, signé le 7 novembre 1659, abandonnait à la France le Roussillon et l'Artois (moins Aire-sur-la-Lys et Saint-Omer) et une série de places fortes de la Flandre au Luxembourg. Enfin, l'infante Marie-Thérèse était promise en mariage à Louis XIV. Une dot énorme de 500 000 écus d'or, à verser en trois termes, était le prix à payer pour que l'infante renonce à ses droits sur la couronne d'Espagne.

Les contemporains reconnaissaient dans ce traité la victoire de la France qui avait non seulement brisé le « chemin de ronde » qui l'encerclait mais avait en outre assuré sa prépondérance en Europe. Le jeune Louis XIV, déjà orgueilleux, pouvait écrire : « La paix était établie avec mes voisins, vraisemblablement pour aussi longtemps que je le voudrai moi-même. »

Il est vrai qu'en face d'une Espagne ruinée et d'une Allemagne ravagée et divisée, la France apparaissait bien comme la première parmi les puissances européennes. Rédigés en français, les traités de Westphalie avaient imposé la langue de Richelieu et de Louis XIII comme la langue de la diplomatie internationale.

Frondes et révoltes

En 1651, l'Anglais Thomas Hobbes publie le Léviathan, *en partie écrit en France au cours d'un exil de onze ans qui l'a vu assister aux révoltes et aux troubles qui ont secoué le royaume au cours des longues années de guerre. Constatant que « l'homme est un loup pour l'homme », incapable de contrôler les pulsions de sa nature, il pense que la « liberté naturelle » doit être abandonnée au bénéfice d'une autorité politique à laquelle tous les sujets seront contraints d'obéir, au profit d'un État absolu capable de tenir les hommes en respect et de leur permettre de vivre paisiblement entre eux. C'était vouloir mettre la violence légitime au service de l'État absolu et faire plier les Grands comme les nu-pieds.*

« La nécessité n'a point de loi »

« En matière de guerre, écrivait Richelieu à Louis XIII, on sait comment et quand elles commencent, mais nul ne peut prévoir le temps et la qualité de leur fin. » En choisissant, en 1630, le parti des « bons Français » contre celui des « dévots », en choisissant la guerre contre l'Espagne, l'empereur et la moitié des princes allemands, en choisissant en pleine offensive catholique de s'allier avec des États protestants pour se battre contre les puissances les plus ultramontaines d'Europe, le roi et le cardinal n'ont pas emprunté la voie la plus facile. En mobilisant toutes les ressources du royaume, en suivant la raison d'État plus que la raison, ils ont imposé une sorte de dictature de guerre et empêché l'avènement d'une monarchie tempérée.

À cet égard, écrit Pierre Goubert, la date de 1635 a déterminé tout le XVIIe siècle. Quand les mesures d'autorité prises dans l'urgence sont ensuite devenues des structures permanentes, elles ont modifié en profondeur la nature d'un régime qui n'avait pas encore trouvé sa voie. Au début du siècle, en effet, si le roi jouissait bien d'un pouvoir absolu, la royauté s'avérait finalement coutumière et bonhomme, respectueuse des conseils de ceux qui représentaient la « nation », les Grands, les états, les notables et les parlements. Publié en 1610, le *Traité des ordres et simples dignités* de Charles Loyseau définissait ce qu'auraient pu être les règles d'une monarchie « constitutionnelle » tempérée par les corps intermédiaires où le pouvoir aurait été mieux distribué, d'un État « bien réglé » où régnerait l'harmonie entre les trois ordres. Les circonstances en décidèrent autrement.

Dans un royaume en guerre, les frondes des Grands et les révoltes des petits devaient être châtiées sans pitié au nom de la raison d'État. Servir, obéir, payer, telle aurait pu être la maxime de celui qui faisait sienne la formule du conseiller d'État Cardin Le Bret : « La souveraineté est non plus divisible que le point en géométrie. » Publié en 1632, en pleine guerre « couverte », le *Traité de la souveraineté du Roi, de son domaine et de sa couronne* claque comme le manifeste d'un État qui se veut désormais absolu. « Il n'y a point de doute, écrit Cardin Le Bret, que le Roi peut user de sa puissance et changer les lois et ordonnances anciennes de son État [...] sans l'avis de son Conseil ni de ses cours souveraines. »

Cette même année, Philippe de Béthune écrit un traité général de « bon gouvernement » dans lequel on peut lire : le prince pourra « se dépêcher et faire mourir secrètement, et sans forme de Justice, ceux qui ne peuvent être punis sans trouble et sans danger de l'État. Rogner les ailes, et raccourcir les moyens de quelqu'un qui s'élève et se fortifie trop en l'État, et se rend redoutable, avant qu'il ait commodité d'entreprendre. Fouiller d'autorité en la bourse des plus riches en une grande nécessité et pauvreté de l'État. Révoquer les privilèges donnés à quelqu'un ou quelque communauté ou particuliers, au préjudice du souverain et de l'État. Se saisir d'une place voisine, de crainte qu'un autre l'occupant, il ne nous fasse la guerre et nous ruine. Toutes ces choses sont en soi injustes ; mais cette injustice est contrepesée par la nécessité et utilité publique. La nécessité, comme on dit, n'a point de loi ».

Pas encore tout à fait « solaire », le roi n'est décidément plus paternel. Les Grands furent les premiers à en prendre la mesure, perdant leur tête pour n'avoir pas compris la nature des enjeux. En 1626, le comte de Chalais, soupçonné d'avoir voulu assassiner Richelieu pour le compte de Gaston d'Orléans, avec peut-être la complicité d'Anne d'Autriche, est décapité cruellement à Nantes par un exécuteur improvisé qui s'y reprend à trente fois. C'est l'occasion pour le cardinal d'exploiter ce châtiment exemplaire et de définir à la noblesse la place qui doit être la sienne. « Que cette tranchée vous soit donc comme un miroir », clament les textes de sa propagande, « ne regardons autre pôle que celui de la royauté, vous y trouverez toujours avec le salut public votre bien particulier ». C'est aussi l'occasion de renforcer la protection du principal ministre, qui reçoit l'autorisation de disposer d'une garde personnelle, qui comportera plus de 300 hommes en 1634, dont un tiers de mousquetaires.

Le 22 juin 1627, François, comte de Montmorency-Bouteville et le comte Rosmadec des Chapelles sont exécutés en place de Grève pour n'avoir pas respecté l'édit royal interdisant le duel et avoir pris plaisir à braver l'autorité en se battant en pleine place Royale.

« J'avoue, écrira Richelieu, que mon esprit ne fut jamais plus combattu qu'en cette occasion où à peine pus-je m'empêcher de céder à la compassion universelle, que le malheur et la valeur de ces jeunes gentilshommes imprimaient au cœur de tout le monde, aux prières des personnes les plus qualifiées de la Cour et aux importunités de mes plus proches parents [...]. Mais les ruisseaux de sang de votre noblesse, qui ne pouvaient être arrêtés que par l'effusion du leur, me donnèrent la force de résister à moi-même et d'affermir Votre Majesté à faire exécuter, pour l'utilité de son État, tout ce qui était quasi contre le sens de tout le monde et contre mes sentiments particuliers. »

Au-delà du fait divers, cette exécution est le point d'orgue du dialogue fougueux entre les partisans de la raison d'État et les champions des valeurs nobiliaires traditionnelles. Interdire le duel, c'est interdire aux membres du second ordre de « faire acte de beste brutte » et les obliger à ne répandre leur sang que pour le service du roi. C'est interdire aussi aux aristocrates de se targuer d'un comportement qui les situerait à l'écart des autres ordres. Pour la haute noblesse qui tente d'empêcher l'exécution, défendre le duel c'est manifester au contraire « le désir de faire voir à un chacun la franchise de son courage », c'est rappeler, plaide alors Condé, la « coutume qui fait consister l'honneur en des actions périlleuses ».

Le 10 mai 1632, c'est le vieux maréchal de Marillac, grande figure du parti dévot, mais convaincu de malversations financières et de pots-de-vin, comme tant d'autres, qui est condamné à mort pour donner à réfléchir à ceux dont l'honnêteté pourrait être prise en défaut.

Le 30 octobre 1632, c'est le duc Henri de Montmorency, filleul d'Henri IV, maréchal de France et gouverneur du Languedoc, qui est décapité à Toulouse pour avoir tenté avec l'appui de Gaston d'Orléans de soulever sa province et avoir livré une bataille contre l'armée royale. Le 12 septembre 1642, c'est le jeune Henri Coiffier de Ruzé d'Effiat, marquis de Cinq-Mars, que le cardinal de Richelieu avait placé auprès du roi pour en faire son favori de cœur, qui meurt sur l'échafaud en compagnie de son ami le conseiller d'État François de Thou pour avoir comploté avec l'Espagne.

« Ton Prince et ton pays ont besoin de ton bras », peut-on entendre dans *Le Cid*, joué pour la première fois le 4 janvier 1637 au Marais, dans un jeu de paume transformé en théâtre, rue Vieille-du-Temple. Dans *Horace*, acceptant le sacrifice de sa vie pour sauver Rome, le héros proclame : « Contre qui que ce soit que mon pays m'emploie, J'accepte aveuglément cette gloire avec joie. »

Mieux que tout autre, sans doute, Pierre Corneille a exprimé les métamorphoses d'un ordre qui doit abdiquer une part de ses valeurs pour se mettre à la seule disposition d'un souverain qui cristallise, en sa personne, la volonté de l'État. Dramatique affrontement entre les exigences passionnelles et brouillonnes des libertés, de l'honneur et du rang et les logiques froides d'un pouvoir centralisateur et hiérarchique.

Un régime de guerre

Privilèges, exemptions et coutumes, qui étaient autant d'entraves et de contrepoids, sont remis en cause par un État « moderne » qui prétend unifier tous ses sujets sous sa loi. Les états généraux, « conférence paternelle, paisible, douce et aimable du roi avec ses sujets », suivant la définition qu'en proposait Robert Miron, représentant du Tiers aux états de 1614, ne seront plus convoqués avant 1789. En 1627 sont réunies pour la dernière fois avant 1787 les assemblées de notables dont la mission était de prendre, selon les mots mêmes de Louis XIII, « les résolutions convenables au bien de l'État ».

Les états provinciaux, qui, dans certaines provinces, disposaient de pouvoirs importants, sont mis au pas. Les états du Dauphiné ne seront plus réunis avant 1788. Les états du Languedoc perdent en 1632 le droit de discuter l'impôt. Les états de Normandie se réunissent pour la dernière fois en 1655.

Les parlements, qui étaient les défenseurs les plus vigoureux des « lois fondamentales » du royaume et pouvaient contester les arrêts contraires au « bien public », sont durement rappelés à l'ordre. Le

21 février 1641, au cours d'un lit de justice exceptionnel, le roi rappelle « les défauts qui se sont introduits en l'ordre de la justice par l'inexécution des ordonnances », souligne qu'il « ne peut souffrir qu'on mette la main au sceptre du souverain et qu'on partage son autorité » et réduit à deux les remontrances du Parlement avant l'enregistrement d'édits portant sur une question financière. Quant aux édits portant sur une « matière d'État », il interdit à « Messieurs du Parlement » de « mettre en dispute ni autrement délibérer sur les Édits et ordonnances qui leur seront envoyés ès choses qui appartiendront à l'État ». Refusant toute délibération, il privait en même temps les robes rouges des envolées oratoires, que prisaient fort ces magistrats lettrés épris de Cicéron.

En 1641, le premier ordre se voit aussi soumis à la raison d'État, des membres du clergé qui osaient affirmer l'immunité des biens d'Église étant exilés par lettres de cachet.

Apparus au début du règne d'Henri II, les « commissaires départis » ou « intendants de police, justice et finances », autrefois envoyés dans les provinces avec mission spéciale du roi pour résoudre une situation de crise, tendent à devenir à partir de 1635 des représentants permanents. Révocables à volonté, yeux et oreilles du pouvoir, ils deviennent le noyau d'une « classe politique » qui se sent vocation à gouverner le pays au lieu et place des officiers et de l'ancienne noblesse qui se voulait surtout d'épée. Ayant un sens aigu de la souveraineté de l'État, ils savent aussi, comme nos modernes énarques, que leur carrière est étroitement soumise à la volonté du prince et que leur docilité est la meilleure garantie de leur ascension.

Au sommet de la pyramide gouvernementale, le cardinal, « souverain confident » et « principal ministre », cumule titres et charges et, gentilhomme plutôt modeste dans les débuts, peut illustrer, aux yeux de tous ces « politiques », le parcours sans faute de celui qui a su marier la raison d'État et les voies de l'enrichissement personnel. Si l'État, en effet, ne se confond pas avec le roi, encore moins avec le « principal ministre », rien n'interdit toutefois de récompenser ceux qui le servent avec autant de dévouement que d'intérêt.

Richelieu fait de son frère Alphonse un cardinal-archevêque de Lyon et le grand aumônier de France. Son oncle, Amador de La Porte, est grand prieur de France et gouverneur de plusieurs places, dont La Rochelle. Son cousin, Charles de La Porte, devient grand maître de l'artillerie et maréchal de France. Son petit-neveu, général des galères. Son beau-frère, maréchal et son neveu, grand maître de la navigation. Le Conseil étroit, siège central du pouvoir, est peuplé de ses « créatures », dont la plus célèbre, le Père Joseph, devient ministre d'État en

1634. À sa mort, le serviteur de l'État laisse une succession estimée à la somme très confortable de 20 millions de livres, 25 % en terres, 20 % en espèces d'or et d'argent, le reste en offices publics, bénéfices ecclésiastiques meubles et immeubles, créances sur la couronne. La trésorerie du cardinal est à la mesure de celle du Prince. En 1575, les recettes de l'État s'élevaient à 15 millions de livres. Pour la seule année 1635, année « cardinale » entre toutes, elles s'élèvent à 208 millions de livres. Par la suite elles tournent autour de 100 millions de livres. Ce véritable « tour de vis » fiscal dont on n'avait pas connu l'équivalent depuis Louis XI pose de singuliers problèmes de trésorerie, la caisse royale pompant chaque année entre le tiers et la moitié de toute la circulation monétaire et peut-être 20 % de l'ensemble de la production de céréales du royaume. En 1617, l'impôt représentait 10 jours de travail, en 1640, 34. Force est alors, devant les difficultés de recouvrement, de faire appel à des « partisans » et des « traitants », des intermédiaires qui fournissent les sommes dont le roi a immédiatement besoin à des taux usuraires et se chargent ensuite de la récolte des contributions !

Avec le choix de la guerre, l'État absolu devient l'obligé des traitants, comme si le durcissement progressif de l'absolutisme accompagnait sa dépendance financière.

Croquants et nu-pieds

Le Prince serait bien avisé de « nous donner deux automnes, deux moissons et deux vendanges chaque année » s'il veut percevoir ses impôts, car « nous n'avons pas pu changer les pierres en pain, les fougères en argent, ni nos travaux continuels fournir à mille droits nouveaux inconnus de nos pères ». En 1637, les paysans d'Arques et ceux du Périgord trouvent les mêmes mots pour exprimer l'insupportable dureté des temps. Ils ne rêvent pas de révolution, mais ce monde « moderne » qui bouscule les traditions et exige des efforts inconnus de mémoire d'homme est trop agressif. Surtout lorsqu'il coïncide avec le retour de la peste et de la disette. Pire encore s'il s'accompagne de longues années de guerre. Comme toujours, les responsables sont tout trouvés : le roi, jamais, mais les ministres et leurs obligés qui saignent le pays, les « Parisiens » suspects de bénéficier des prébendes de la centralisation, les traitants et leurs commis. Comme souvent, on chante l'éternelle rengaine de l'âge d'or, celui du « bon roi Henri », celui de la décennie apaisée de la « poule au pot ».

Il faut dire que le monstrueux gonflement de la fiscalité royale est d'autant plus insupportable que la conjoncture, paisible depuis 1590, s'est nettement dégradée à la fin des années 1620, au moment même où le cardinal faisait le choix d'une guerre que ne voulaient pas les dévots. Le signe le plus inquiétant est le retour de « la maladie de la contagion », celle dont on n'ose plus dire le nom. Une nouvelle fois importé par les ports de la Méditerranée, le bacille prend logis chez les troupes de mendiants et de pauvres sans cesse à la recherche de nourriture et de travail. Il se délecte des concentrations de soldats qui assiègent La Rochelle ou Mantoue. Il court avec les hordes qui fuient les villages incendiés par les mercenaires. Les années les plus dures semblent se situer entre 1626 et 1631. Dans les pays de langue d'oc, un million de personnes et peut-être plus sont fauchées. Les officiers chargés de l'établissement de la taille nous fournissent des détails atroces, presque incroyables. Des villes comme Chambéry ou Digne voient disparaître 85 % de leurs habitants ; les terres perdues du causse du Larzac ne comptent plus que « 60 ou 80 communiants dans des villages où il y en avait 200 ». À Falcey, qui a perdu 38 ménages sur 40, les enquêteurs voient « au cimetière de ladite église la terre élevée en plus de quatre-vingts endroits, où ont été inhumés des corps morts depuis peu ».

L'épidémie prospère lorsque se greffent des récoltes médiocres. Au nord, des étés exécrables noient les blés et les font pourrir sur pied. Au sud, au contraire, des années de sécheresse échaudent les grains avant la moisson. Partout, les conséquences sont les mêmes : hausses vertigineuses des prix des grains et du pain, populations sous-alimentées, « mortalités » exceptionnelles.

Ce que les taillables supportent avec plus ou moins de fatalisme en temps normal devient odieux en période de difficultés économiques et de fiscalité accrue. Des années 1620 aux années 1660, il ne se passe guère d'année où l'on ne puisse, sur la carte du royaume, pointer un ou plusieurs soulèvements. Comme toujours, ce sont les provinces de l'Ouest et du Sud qui s'agitent le plus, celles qui avaient connu des états maîtres de la répartition et de la levée des impôts, celles où les privilèges et les libertés avaient été les mieux assurés.

En 1636, à Rennes, on entend les cris de « Vive le Roi sans la gabelle ! » À Blanzac, en Angoumois, au mois de juin, au moment de la grande foire annuelle, on voit défiler « environ quatre mille hommes armés d'arquebuses et de piques, distribués en douze ou quinze compagnies, conduites par leurs curés, tous marchant en bon ordre, au son de quelques fifres et violons par faute de tambours ». Dans l'atmosphère d'exaltation provoquée par la crue de la taille, un inconnu, accusé d'être à la fois agent du fisc et parisien, est promené, nu et sanguinolent, à travers le bourg, avant d'être mis à mort.

Au printemps 1637, ceux que l'opinion appelle les croquants se révoltent en Périgord, une province traversée par les troupes en marche vers le Pays basque et qui se trouve dans l'impossibilité de vendre ses châtaignes et son vin. Irrités par les tailles plus lourdes et les taxes accrues, ils hachent menu un commis du fisc et clouent sa chair sur les portes, se donnent comme chefs quelques forts en gueule, recrutent quelques officiers au rancart, fraternisent avec les gens des petites villes contre les « Parisiens » qui dévorent la substance du royaume, se donnent pour capitaine un noble local, La Mothe La Forêt, un vieux briscard qui prétend avoir eu des visions de la Vierge, et se font étriller à La Sauvetat-du-Dropt le 1er juin 1637.

Le 16 juillet 1639, à Avranches, se déclenche en Normandie la révolte de ceux qui se réclament d'un chef mystérieux, « Jean Nu-Pieds », qui passe pour avoir été prêtre. Sous la bannière de saint Jean-Baptiste et pour les mêmes raisons antifiscales, il enrôle un tiers des paroissiens d'Avranches et de Coutances, essentiellement des sauniers des plages voisines, qui marchent sans souliers ni sabots et craignent pour leurs privilèges, et trouve des émules en Haute-Normandi. Dans une province qui ignore la disette et la peste et ne voit pas passer les soldats, le soulèvement des miséreux s'en prend à un État accusé de ponctionner jusqu'à l'insupportable une région riche qui contribue pour un sixième à la taille nationale.

Comme l'écrit Emmanuel Le Roy Ladurie, la révolte des nu-pieds n'est pas seulement l'expression des classes paysannes ou du peuple des villes, elle est à sa manière une contre-société régionale qui s'oppose à la centralisation voulue et menée par Paris. Comme la société d'Ancien Régime, la révolte a « sa » noblesse plus riche de dettes que de terres, chargée de faire faire l'exercice aux « coquins » révoltés du Bocage, elle a ses curés sensibles aux malheurs de leurs ouailles et placés parmi les premiers à la tête du mouvement, elle a enfin son tiers état, avocats et petits robins pleins d'amertume à l'égard des gros requins de la gabelle et de la finance.

En octobre, le surintendant Bouthillier écrit à son fils : « La dépense du comptant monte à quarante millions au moins : les traitants nous abandonnent et les peuples ne veulent rien payer, ni les droits anciens, ni les nouveaux. Nous sommes maintenant au fond du pot, n'ayant plus les moyens de choisir entre les bons et les mauvais avis. Et je crains que notre guerre étrangère ne dégénère en guerre civile. Son Éminence, quand elle verra la réalité des affaires, y prendra quelque bon expédient, mais je vous confesse que je suis bien empêché et n'y vois aucun jour. » En fait, il suffit à Son Éminence de commander 4 000 hommes de pied et 1 200 cavaliers pour rétablir l'autorité. Si Richelieu a ordonné que la punition soit exemplaire, c'est qu'il craint la contagion séparatiste. Tandis que les pendaisons se multiplient, les parlementaires de Rouen sont démis de leurs fonctions, les officiers royaux qui n'ont fait aucun effort pour mater l'insurrection sanctionnés. Nu-pieds et croquants avaient beau avoir du bon sens et exprimer la haine toute neuve d'un État dont Paris devenait la pieuvre, le retour à l'âge d'or n'a jamais été un programme.

Le temps de la Fronde

La régence d'Anne d'Autriche, en 1643, la deuxième régence en une génération, ranime l'ardeur des « malcontents », des « croquants » aux « importants ». Déjà, la mort du roi a fait croire aux paysans que la perception de l'impôt allait être suspendue. Le 8 septembre 1643, l'intendant Denis de Heere écrit de Niort au chancelier Séguier : « Des difficultés sont survenues dans cette province à la levée des tailles depuis le décès du Roi [...]. Et j'ai essayé de détromper les peuples des faux bruits de remises des années précédentes et même de la meilleure partie de la courante. »

Le 18 mai, en faisant casser par le Parlement de Paris le testament de son mari et en se faisant doter de « l'administration libre, absolue et entière des affaires de son royaume » pendant la minorité du roi, Anne d'Autriche a réveillé les prétentions des cours souveraines. Dans une harangue à la régente, l'avocat général Omer Talon lui recommande « de nourrir et d'élever sans entraves Sa Majesté dans l'observation des lois fondamentales et dans le rétablissement de l'autorité que doit avoir cette compagnie, anéantie et comme dissipée depuis quelques années, sous le ministère du cardinal de Richelieu ».

Le soir du 18 mai, en annonçant à la surprise générale qu'elle nomme le cardinal Mazarin, parrain du roi, principal ministre et président du Conseil de régence, elle choisit pourtant celui qui, plus flexible et plus aimable que son prédécesseur, n'en continue pas moins la même politique. Ce Romain devenu français « par reconnaissance et par tempérament », ce diplomate-né qui brille au jeu de cartes et séduit les dames, cet homme profondément croyant mais avide d'argent veut poursuivre l'œuvre de celui qui l'a recommandé, avec autant d'énergie et de volonté. « Je puis bien dire qu'aux choses qui regardent le roi, écrit-il, je ne me contenterai pas d'y pourvoir ; je les soutiendrai avec plus de fermeté et de courage, quand il faudra venir là, que M. le Cardinal-duc l'a jamais fait. Je dissimule, je biaise, j'adoucis, j'accommode tout autant qu'il m'est possible ; mais, dans un besoin pressant, je ferai voir de quoi je suis capable. »

Ainsi, les tours de vis fiscaux sont maintenus et même renforcés. Au début du siècle, les dépenses de guerre avoisinaient 20 millions de francs par an. De 1635 à 1642, Richelieu les avait fait monter à près de 80 millions. Entre 1643 et 1647, Mazarin porte la charge à plus de 120 millions, usant d'innovations qui suscitent l'indignation des « assujettis ». En mars 1644, l'édit du toisé exhume un vieux texte de 1548 et taxe les propriétaires qui avaient fait bâtir de nouvelles maisons dans les faubourgs de Paris. Devant l'opposition du Parlement qui refuse de l'enregistrer, un autre édit tente en août 1644 de taxer les « aisés », mais cet emprunt forcé sur les fortunes est également retiré, car les « financiers » menaçaient de ne plus faire crédit au gouvernement.

Il ne restait donc qu'à accroître la taille, la gabelle et les octrois, à réduire les gages des officiers, à mettre en vente de nouveaux offices et à renforcer le pouvoir des intendants. Dans un royaume paralysé par la dépression économique et les ravages de la guerre, la boulimie fiscale de l'« Italien », dont la fortune a été évaluée à près de 40 millions de livres, soit la moitié du budget de la France en 1661, a de quoi exciter les haines.

En prenant le 13 mai 1648 l'initiative de convier les représentants des cours souveraines à travailler en commun à la réforme des abus de l'État, le Parlement de Paris ouvre le grand remue-ménage qui va mettre en branle pendant cinq ans tous ceux qui, « sous prétexte de bien public et de réformation, n'ont d'autres desseins que l'intérêt de leur grandeur particulière », mais aussi tous ceux qui, par leur fronde et leurs paroles, nous révèlent leurs frustrations, leurs rancunes et leurs désirs.

Le 2 juillet, une charte en 27 articles, aussitôt imprimée et diffusée dans le royaume, trace le programme d'une monarchie qu'on voudrait tempérée. Le premier article indique que les intendants de justice seront révoqués. Le deuxième demande « le rétablissement des officiers ordinaires dans l'exercice de leurs charges, et particulièrement les Trésoriers de France et les élus, afin d'empêcher que les tailles ne fussent mises désormais en parti ». Le troisième exige que « ne soient faites aucunes impositions et taxes, qu'en vertu d'édits et déclarations dûment vérifiés par les cours souveraines ». L'article 6 réclame l'abolition des lettres de cachet et demande « qu'aucun des sujets du roi, de quelque qualité et condition qu'il soit, ne puisse être détenu prisonnier passé vingt-quatre heures, sans être interrogé, suivant les ordonnances ». Abolition des instances administratives créées par la monarchie, consentement des cours souveraines à l'impôt, approbation de toutes les taxes nouvelles, ébauche d'un *habeas corpus*, autant d'exigences qui tracent les voies d'un État de droit qui se ferait pacifique et tempéré mais touchent la cour « à la prunelle de l'œil », comme l'écrit le cardinal de Retz.

Paris couvert de barricades, le roi et la reine en fuite, la moitié des provinces mutinées, les impôts refusés, les officiers en grève, les généraux en vue trahissant et s'alliant avec l'ennemi espagnol, les cinq années de Fronde peuvent apparaître comme une tragi-comédie. « La Fronde, écrit Michelet dans son *Histoire de France*, est réputée, non sans cause, pour l'une des périodes les plus amusantes de l'histoire de France, les plus divertissantes, celle où brille d'un inexprimable comique la vivacité légère et spirituelle du caractère national. » Si l'on essaie toutefois d'en comprendre le déroulement, rien de particulièrement « divertissant » dans cet événement qui est peut-être le meilleur révélateur des tensions sécrétées par les années « cardinales ».

Certes, dans une logique théâtrale, on pourrait la décomposer en trois actes ouverts par trois énormes bévues. L'arrestation du conseiller Broussel le 26 août 1648, le jour où l'on chante un *Te Deum* à Notre-Dame pour célébrer la victoire remportée à Lens par Condé sur les Espagnols, ouvre le premier acte. Comme en 1588, Paris se couvre en quelques heures de 1 260 barricades dressées par les patrons du négoce, de la boutique et de l'atelier. Mazarin, l'étranger haï, le « méchant conseiller », doit capituler, libérer Broussel, « le père du peuple », avec sa barbe blanche taillée à l'ancienne mode, limoger d'Émery, le surintendant des Finances, confirmer le programme du 2 juillet, réduire la taille de 20 % et accorder des remises sur les droits d'entrée de la viande, du sel et du pain dans Paris.

« Jamais triomphe de roi ou d'empereur romain n'a été plus grand que celui de ce pauvre petit homme qui n'avait rien de recommandable que d'être entêté de bien public et de la haine des impôts », écrit la femme de chambre d'Anne d'Autriche, Mme de Motteville, à propos de la libération de Broussel, l'incorruptible, qui habitait une modeste demeure sur le port Saint-Landry, en face de la place de Grève, et était toujours prompt à dénoncer le luxe des financiers, « ces corbeaux affamés ». La signature des traités de Westphalie, le 24 octobre, passe alors inaperçue.

La fuite de la cour vers le château glacial de Saint-Germain, dans la nuit du 5 au 6 janvier 1649, le jour où les Parisiens tirent les rois, ouvre le deuxième acte. Dans Paris assiégée mollement par les troupes insuffisantes de Condé, la rébellion rassemble une poignée de conjurateurs vieillissants, des précieuses qui entourent de leurs écharpes bleues les robes rouges des parlementaires et les bottes des militaires, les duchesses de Longueville, de Bouillon et de Chevreuse qui confondent intrigues amoureuses et révolution, le duc de Beaufort, pour qui les femmes des halles ont une dévotion particulière, le coadjuteur Paul de Gondi, le futur cardinal de Retz, qui écrit dans ses *Mémoires* : « Ce mélange d'écharpes bleues de dames, de cuirasses, de violons qui étaient dans la salle, de trompettes qui étaient dans la place, donnaient un spectacle qui se voit plus souvent dans les romans qu'ailleurs. »

Redoutant la « canaille » affamée par la hausse des prix et effrayé par la nouvelle de l'exécution du roi Charles Ier d'Angleterre, « le plus horrible et détestable parricide qui ait jamais été commis par les Chrétiens », le Parlement préfère toutefois mettre sa fronde en sourdine et signer la paix à Rueil le 11 mars 1649. Le roi accorde l'amnistie à tous ceux qui ont pris les armes et peut faire une entrée triomphale dans Paris le 18 août.

L'arrestation, le 18 janvier 1650, du prince de Condé, de son frère Conti et de son beau-frère Longueville, dont les grands airs et les exigences voraces en matière de gouvernements et de pensions irritaient le « couple » gouvernemental, ouvre le troisième et dernier acte. Dans une totale confusion baroque, l'arrestation des princes précipite dans l'opposition les chefs des grands lignages, les provinces qu'ils gouvernent, les parlementaires qui exigent le renvoi de Mazarin, les pamphlétaires qui inondent le royaume de « mazarinades » fort lestes, les nobles qui veulent défendre leur honneur blessé, les foules urbaines poussées par la misère, les parlementaires d'Aix et de Bordeaux qui se révoltent contre leurs gouverneurs, Gaston d'Orléans qui reverdit, et des curés qui se joignent sur le tard à la ronde pour s'en prendre aux évêques, aux jésuites et produire des libelles qui sentent le soufre.

En 1651, après que Condé a été libéré et que Mazarin fait mine de s'exiler, la farce se transforme en tragédie, les pillages des gens de guerre ravageant l'Île-de-France. « Les hommes mangent de la terre, des écorces et, ce que nous n'oserions dire si nous ne l'avions vu et qui fait horreur, ils se mangent les bras et les mains et meurent de désespoir. » Ce compte rendu des missionnaires de Vincent de Paul est confirmé par toutes les informations disponibles. Autour de Paris et jusqu'à Étampes, on laisse les cadavres pourrir dans les champs, mais la puanteur est telle que personne n'ose les cultiver ; les villes sont désertes et les habitants qui ont survécu doivent se débarrasser des loups. En certaines places, à Rouen, à Bagneux ou à Montmorency, le nombre des décès excède celui des naissances pendant plusieurs années. Les bois et les monastères redeviennent des lieux d'ultime refuge où s'entassent paysans, bêtes et blessés : « Nous avions les chevaux sous notre chambre et dans le chapitre, écrit mère Angélique Arnauld, abbesse de Port-Royal, et dans les caves, nous avions quelque quarante vaches à nous et aux pauvres gens [...]. L'église était pleine de blé, d'avoine, de pois, de fèves, de chaudrons, et de meubles. »

La supériorité des troupes royales commandées par le vicomte de Turenne, en retour de trahison, finit cependant par l'emporter. Le 21 octobre 1652, le roi et sa mère font leur entrée dans arls que Condé a été contraint de fuir pour se mettre au service de l'Espagne. En février 1653, c'est le retour du cardinal Mazarin lui-même, acclamé par une foule « qui ne veut plus entendre parler d'aucun remuement » et complimenté par le syndic des rentiers de l'Hôtel de Ville qui, en juin 1652, avait proclamé qu'il était « la plus grande ordure du siècle ». Le 3 août 1653, c'en est fini de l'Ormée de Bordeaux, cette fronde régionale qui tirait son nom d'un mail planté d'ormes où se retrouvaient régulièrement robins, artisans et marchands. Le 13 août 1653, enfin, Villeneuve-sur-Lot, le dernier bastion condéen, capitule.

Proclamé majeur le 7 septembre 1651, sacré à Reims le 7 juin 1654, Louis XIV, qui s'est éveillé à la vie politique au cours de cette Fronde qui n'avait rien d'une farce, n'oubliera jamais l'humiliation et l'insécurité de sa jeunesse, les désordres, les complots, les émeutes et les malheurs de cette guerre civile qu'il ne pouvait, comme ses contemporains, qu'attribuer à un désordre cosmique. Dans ses *Mémoires pour l'instruction du Dauphin*, évoquant la situation du royaume au lendemain de ce cataclysme, il écrira : « Il faut se représenter l'état des choses : des agitations terribles par tout le royaume avant et après ma majorité ; une guerre étrangère, où ces troubles domestiques avaient fait perdre à la France mille et mille avantages ; un prince de mon sang et d'un très grand nom à la tête des ennemis ; beaucoup de cabales dans l'État ; les Parlements en possession et en goût d'une autorité usurpée ; dans ma cour, très peu de fidélité sans intérêt, et par là mes sujets en apparence les plus soumis, autant à charge et autant à redouter pour moi que les plus rebelles ; un ministre rétabli malgré tant de factions, très habile, très adroit, qui m'aimait et que j'aimais, qui m'avait rendu de grands services, mais dont les pensées et les manières étaient naturellement très différentes des miennes, que je ne pouvais toutefois contredire ni lui ôter la moindre partie de son crédit sans exciter peut-être de nouveau contre lui, par cette image quoique fausse de disgrâce, les mêmes orages qu'on avait eu tant de peine à calmer ; moi-même, assez jeune encore, majeur à la vérité de la majorité des rois, que les lois de l'État ont avancée pour éviter de plus grands maux, mais non pas de celle où les simples particuliers commencent à gouverner librement leurs affaires ; qui ne connaissais entièrement que la grandeur du fardeau sans avoir pu jusques alors bien connaître mes propres forces ; préférant sans doute dans le cœur, à toutes choses et à la vie même, une haute réputation si je la pouvais acquérir, mais comprenant en même temps, que mes premières démarches ou en jetteraient les fondements, ou m'en feraient perdre pour jamais jusques à l'espérance, et qui me trouvais de cette sorte pressé et retardé presque également dans mon dessein par un seul et même désir de gloire. »

Autant de sentiments et de ressentiments qui annoncent l'irrésistible ascension d'un Roi-Soleil qui ne supportera plus les frondes.

La foi, la raison et les sorcières

Le 15 août 1638, à Abbeville, Louis XIII consacre solennellement le royaume à la Vierge et institue une procession annuelle. Enregistrée par le Parlement de Paris, une déclaration royale proclame que « prenunt la Très Sainte et Très Glorieuse Vierge pour protectrice spéciale de notre royaume, nous lui consacrons particulièrement notre personne, notre État, notre couronne et nos sujets, la suppliant de vouloir nous inspirer une si saine conduite et défendre avec tant de soins ce royaume contre l'effort de tous ses ennemis, que, soit qu'il souffre du fléau de la guerre ou jouisse des douceurs de la paix, nous demandons à Dieu de tout notre cœur qu'il ne sorte point des voies de la grâce qui conduisent à celle de la gloire ». Le 5 septembre, naît, après vingt-trois ans de mariage stérile, Louis Dieudonné, futur Louis XIV... Un premier miracle ?

Monsieur Vincent

Vincent de Paul est né à Pouy, dans les Landes, le 24 avril 1581. Fils de paysans pauvres, il voit tout d'abord dans l'Église un moyen d'acquérir des honneurs et de l'argent. Une anecdote révèle d'ailleurs son état d'esprit à l'époque où il étudiait à Dax : « Je me souviens qu'une fois au collège où j'étudiais, on vint me dire que mon père, qui était un pauvre paysan, me demandait. Je refusai de lui parler ; en quoi, je fis un grand péché. » Ordonné prêtre en 1600, il aspire alors sans succès à une cure du diocèse de Dax et continue ses études à Toulouse, en exerçant les fonctions de maître de pension. Après de mystérieuses aventures qui nous font perdre sa trace de 1605 à 1607, il « monte » à Paris et trouve les appuis efficaces qui lui procurent enfin les bénéfices qu'il espérait. Grâce au cardinal Pierre de Bérulle, la personnalité la plus remarquable du parti dévot, il obtient la cure de Clichy en 1612, devient précepteur du fils aîné de Philippe-Emmanuel de Gondi, général des galères, et, en 1617, est nommé à la cure de Châtillon-sur-Chalaronne, dans la Dombes, qu'il cumule avec celle de Clichy, ce qui est contraire aux prescriptions du concile de Trente.

C'est toutefois à cette date, alors qu'il est âgé de trente-six ans, qu'il se « convertit », en découvrant la misère spirituelle des paysans et le manque d'instruction du clergé. Sa « conversion » se traduit par un détachement de plus en plus grand des biens terrestres, un désir d'imiter la pauvreté évangélique et une ascèse du corps vécue comme un moyen de s'unir à la souffrance du Christ. « Coucher sur la dure, porter la haire, prendre la discipline et le reste de ce qui peut faire de la peine à notre corps, ce sont des choses que les chrétiens doivent faire, chacun selon son besoin », écrit-il.

En 1619, il est nommé aumônier général des galères et prêche une mission chez les forçats. Le 17 avril 1625, grâce aux 45 000 livres mises à sa disposition par les Gondi, il crée surtout la congrégation des Prêtres de la Mission pour aller de village en village « prêcher, instruire, exhorter et catéchiser les pauvres gens et les porter à faire tous une bonne confession générale ». À partir de 1632, il organise au prieuré Saint-Lazare des conférences qui, tous les mardis, « recyclent » le clergé parisien. De la Lorraine au Poitou, de la Pologne à l'Italie, de Madagascar à l'Afrique noire, les « lazaristes » multiplient les missions, prêchent la foi chrétienne et secourent les esclaves. Admis sous la régence d'Anne d'Autriche au Conseil de conscience chargé de procéder aux nominations ecclésiastiques, Vincent de Paul tente aussi d'exercer son influence pour réformer le haut clergé.

Mais dans un temps où la peste, la guerre et la famine ont repris possession du royaume, c'est au service des pauvres que Monsieur Vincent consacre désormais l'essentiel de son action. Pour assister les dames de la haute société qui visitaient les malades, il crée les Filles de la Charité, des filles du peuple non cloîtrées qui se voueront au secours de tous les misérables et continueront à porter le costume des paysannes. En 1638, elles prennent en charge l'œuvre des Enfants trouvés et sauvent 40 000 enfants en vingt ans, ces « petites créatures » qui sont l'image de Dieu incarné. Moïse et saint Jean n'étaient-ils pas des enfants trouvés ? Pressenti en 1656 pour prendre la direction de l'Hôpital général où devaient être enfermés « les pauvres mendiants valides ou invalides pour être employés aux ouvrages, manufactures et autres travaux », en fait un lieu de « renfermement » particulièrement ambigu, il préfère s'en « excuser », estimant que les lazaristes n'étaient « pas encore résolus de s'engager dans ces emplois pour ne pas assez connaître si le bon Dieu le veut ». Le 27 septembre 1660, il meurt à Saint-Lazare, perclus de douleurs, incapable de marcher depuis l'année précédente mais attentif jusqu'au bout aux multiples œuvres qu'il a fondées. De sa « conversion » à sa mort, Monsieur Vincent, canonisé en 1737, incarne l'esprit de ce siècle saisi de piété, l'élan de ferveur et de mysticisme qui, selon l'expression de l'historien Henri Brémond, en fait « le siècle des saints ».

Le siècle des saints

Bérulle, saint François de Sales, mère Angélique Arnauld, autant de figures qui illustrent le renouveau de l'Église de France au lendemain des guerres de Religion et marquent de leur empreinte un demi-siècle qui a vu 27 Françaises et Français canonisés ou béatifiés. De 1598 à 1643, un tiers des ouvrages imprimés à Paris traitent de sujets religieux et diffusent le message d'une spiritualité ragaillardie. Tandis que dans les salons de Mme Acarie, la femme d'un conseiller à la Chambre des comptes, on lit *Le Chemin de perfection* de Thérèse d'Avila et on commente l'*Introduction à la vie dévote* de François de Sales, les analphabètes des campagnes peuvent contempler les images d'anges adorant l'hostie ou les petits tableaux qui représentent le diable emportant en enfer la fille trop coquette.

En accordant en 1602 les lettres nécessaires à l'introduction des carmélites espagnoles en France, en nommant à Port-Royal-des-Champs Angélique Arnauld, une abbesse de onze ans, en appelant François de Sales à prêcher le carême au Louvre, en autorisant en 1603 la réouverture des collèges jésuites, et en prenant le père Coton comme confesseur, Henri IV, le huguenot converti, a sans doute été l'un des initiateurs les plus actifs de la Réforme catholique.

On peut être à la fois courtisan, homme du monde, guerrier et homme de Dieu. Tel est le modèle que proposent les réformateurs et qui séduit les dévots. Réconciliant les chrétiens avec leur siècle, les appelant à la sainteté sans les arracher à leur Prince, François de Sales ouvre ainsi aux laïcs qui s'y engouffrent les voies de la sainteté. « Jamais prédicateur ne m'a tant contenté que lui, avoue Henri IV, c'est le plus excellent que j'ai jamais ouï. »

L'oraison funèbre qu'il prononce le 27 avril 1602 pour les funérailles du duc de Mercœur, qui avait offert ses services à l'empereur pour lutter contre les Turcs en Hongrie, trace le modèle offert aux dévots : « Il n'employa jamais sa colère qu'en la guerre, ou pour maintenir le respect et l'honneur qui lui étaient nécessaires pour faire les grands services que le christianisme attendait de lui ; en quoi il imitait les abeilles qui font le miel pour les amis et piquent vivement leurs ennemis [...]. Bref, il rendait à l'Église beaucoup de révérence, au roi beaucoup d'honneur et d'obéissance, à son mariage beaucoup de fidélité, et aux princes une ouverte et agréable conversation, aux moindres une grande douceur et débonnaireté, à sa famille une grande affection, avec une paix et tranquillité admirable. »

Publiée à partir de 1609, l'*Introduction à la vie dévote* reprend ce thème pour ceux qui acceptent d'entreprendre le « chemin de perfection ». « Mon intention, écrit François de Sales, est d'instruire ceux qui vivent es villes, es ménages, à la cour, et qui par leur condition sont obligés de faire une vie commune à l'extérieur, lesquels bien souvent, sous le prétexte d'une prétendue impossibilité, ne veulent pas seulement penser à l'entreprise de la vie dévote. » Réédité quarante fois en dix ans, l'*Introduction*, sauvegardant les droits de la raison et de la liberté humaines sans pour autant nier ceux de la foi, inaugure également une école française de spiritualité où l'image et la métaphore sont les équivalents baroques des églises de la Contre-Réforme. « Vous voguez donc ainsi, sans aiguille, boussole et timon en l'océan des opinions humaines ; vous ne pouvez attendre autre chose qu'un misérable naufrage. Ah ! De grâce, pendant que ce jourd'hui dure, jetez-vous en l'esquif d'une sérieuse pénitence, et venez vous rendre en l'heureux navire, lequel à pleine voile va surgir au port de gloire. » Le temps de François de Sales est aussi celui des précieuses ridicules.

Autre figure du siècle, Pierre de Bérulle, fils d'un conseiller au Parlement de Paris, fonde en 1611 l'Oratoire de France pour mieux assurer la formation du clergé, auxquels il impose le port de la soutane et une rigoureuse discipline de vie. À sa mort, en 1629, les oratoriens ont déjà quarante-quatre maisons dont l'enseignement rivalise avec celui des jésuites et qui forment des prêtres convaincus d'être les médiateurs privilégiés entre les hommes et le Christ. Sous son influence, la procession de la Fête-Dieu, entièrement consacrée au « dieu de pâte » fustigé par les huguenots, devient l'une des principales armes de la reconquête catholique. C'est surtout en connaissant Jésus-Christ, en l'aimant et en se soumettant à ses volontés que le chrétien connaîtra et aimera Dieu, soutient le cardinal de Bérulle. Démarche fort téméraire qui surprend ses contemporains par son caractère novateur, alors que les chrétiens pensent aujourd'hui qu'elle a toujours existé.

La France se rue alors vers les couvents et les cloîtres, la religion devenant également pour les femmes un moyen de sortir de leur condition et d'affirmer leur place dans une société qui les avait jusque-là considérées comme mineures. Les carmélites essaiment dans tout le royaume. Les ursulines, établies à Paris en 1612 pour l'enseignement des filles, comptent près de quatre cents maisons à la fin du XVIIᵉ siècle. L'ordre de la Visitation, créé par Jeanne de Chantal en Savoie en 1610 à l'instigation de François de Sales, ouvre plus de cent maisons en un demi-siècle. En 1609, Angélique Arnauld, alors âgée de dix-huit ans, est bouleversée par le sermon d'un capucin et décide de réformer son abbaye cistercienne de Port-Royal en faisant respecter strictement la règle de la clôture et en fermant toute entrée à sa famille et au « monde ».

Les hommes ne sont pas en reste. Les collèges de jésuites, qui accueillent les fils de la bourgeoisie et de la noblesse, voient leur nombre multiplié par deux entre 1610 et 1650. Le plus célèbre est le collège de Clermont, fondé rue Saint-Jacques au début des années 1560. Moins sévères que les bérulliens peu indulgents à l'égard de la faiblesse humaine, les pères réussissent à concilier l'enseignement des humanités et la culture chrétienne, mettent les représentations théâtrales au service d'une pédagogie « moderne » et placent le ballet sur le même plan que l'équitation et les armes. Utilisant les images comme moyen d'exciter la méditation, convaincus que le « menu peuple est plutôt tiré par les sens que par l'esprit », ils ornent leurs églises de retables exubérants et introduisent un nouveau style de façade « à la romaine » qui fait l'originalité de l'église Saint-Paul-Saint-Louis et inspire la construction de l'église de la Sorbonne et du Val-de-Grâce. Grands prédicateurs et missionnaires intrépides, ils réussissent au Canada à fonder des paroisses indiennes qui assurent mieux que les rares colons la présence française.

Plus nombreux, mieux préparés à leur tâche, en vive compétition spirituelle, capucins, lazaristes, oratoriens et jésuites labourent aussi la France en tous sens pour y semer les germes d'un catholicisme sûr de lui et dominateur qui ne craint plus d'affronter les pasteurs de la « prétendue religion réformée ». Tandis que Jean Eudes parcourt la Normandie, le jésuite Julien Maunoir dirige, de 1640 à 1683, plus de quatre cents missions en Bretagne depuis Douarnenez, son port d'attache. On parlerait aujourd'hui de « sessions intensives », de dix à douze heures par jour, pendant au moins trois et souvent cinq semaines d'affilée. Avec Julien Maunoir, la mission devient en effet une entreprise systématique et parfaitement organisée. Le matin est consacré à une « conférence » de type question-réponse, l'après-midi à l'enseignement, le soir à une nouvelle « conférence ». La journée est scandée par des prières chantées et des sermons qui émeuvent tellement les fidèles qu'ils se ruent au confessionnal après avoir entendu Maunoir.

Tout est fait pour mettre de l'ordre dans les cérémonies. Dans les églises débarrassées des chiens et des mendiants, les sexes sont séparés, le silence est imposé et les laïcs sont exclus du chœur. Tout est fait aussi pour frapper les esprits, de la procession spectacle, où des fidèles méritants sont désignés pour jouer les scènes de la Passion et figurer les apôtres et les martyrs, aux tableaux peints montrant sous une forme allégorique les vices et les vertus ou bien encore aux têtes de mort utilisées pour appuyer le sermon.

Cette offensive a fini par travailler au cœur un peuple chrétien qui cède à son tour à la fièvre mystique et récite des *Ave Maria* sans relâche. Sainte-Anne d'Auray, Notre-Dame-des-Ardilliers de Saumur, Alise-Sainte-Reine, Notre-Dame de Liesse, Notre-Dame de Rocamadour, Notre-Dame du Puy, autant de pèlerinages qui attirent des dizaines de milliers de fidèles chaque année. Les miracles, évidemment, se multiplient au même rythme. À Notre-Dame de Verdelais, en Guyenne, on en compte plus d'une centaine en cinquante ans. À Auray, après que, le 7 mars 1625, un laboureur nommé Nicolazic découvre dans un champ une vieille statue de bois représentant sainte Anne, qui lui était apparue deux ans plus tôt, on comptabilise 1 267 miracles dans les soixante années qui suivent. Quarante mille bouteilles d'eau sainte d'Alise sont expédiées par charrettes chaque année, Anne d'Autriche lançant la mode en en faisant elle-même grande consommation.

La chasse aux sorcières

Le temps des miracles fut aussi le temps des sorcières. Des femmes qui, en signant un pacte avec Satan, contestaient, comme les croquants, les nu-pieds et autres rustres, la cohérence du monde que bâtissait l'autorité royale et que définissaient les juges et les saints. Si les procès de sorcellerie n'ont jamais été aussi nombreux en Europe des années 1560 aux années 1640, c'est bien que cette époque voyait, en France comme ailleurs, le difficile accouchement de l'homme « moderne », c'est-à-dire de l'homme « civilisé ».

Face à ce monde qui prétendait régir les esprits et les corps, vider les carnavals de leur substance, interdire le cabaret et la débauche, l'évasion diabolique était assurément une grande tentation même si les sorcières et leurs comparses savaient les risques qu'ils couraient lorsqu'une dénonciation ou une simple indiscrétion révélaient leurs agissements à un juge entreprenant. En 1609, Charles Le Brun de La Rochette, avocat à Villefranche, dans le Beaujolais, faisait paraître à Lyon *Le Procès civil et criminel*, contenant la méthodique liaison du droit et de la pratique judiciaire, civile et criminelle. Plusieurs fois réédité, ce gros traité définissait mieux que tout les impératifs de la nouvelle civilisation des mœurs. Oisiveté, pauvreté et luxure, telles étaient les trois armes utilisées par Satan pour pervertir les esprits faibles. Manifestation la plus éclatante de son pouvoir, la sorcellerie était bien dans l'esprit du magistrat l'expression d'un pacte antisocial destiné à subvertir une société qui devait promouvoir le travail et la retenue.

L'historien Robert Muchembled a d'ailleurs fait remarquer que les régions les plus touchées par les procès de sorcellerie étaient situées dans les zones frontières ou aux marges du royaume, dans des provinces qui partageaient la même volonté de résistance aux efforts de la monarchie pour imposer ses règles. À l'époque où le monarque décapitait les nobles qui bravaient ses interdits, il faisait brûler celles qui, éternelles tentatrices, se promenaient nues sur leur balai, offrant à tous leur corps impudique.

Ne sont-elles pas sorcières les femmes qui, écrit en 1619 le vicaire général de l'archevêque de Toulouse, « oublieuses de leur naturelle pudeur, se donnent la même licence des hommes et s'entretiennent bouche à bouche de discours profanes avec la jeunesse pendant les divins offices » ? Ne sont-elles pas sorcières ces femmes du Labourd dont la « coiffure semble témoigner leur désir », ces veuves qui « portent le morion sans crête pour marquer que le mâle leur fait défaut ». « En Labourd, écrit Pierre de Lancre, un juge bordelais chargé d'enquêter à Bayonne de juillet à novembre 1609, les femmes montrent leur derrière tellement que tout l'ornement de leurs cotillons plissés est derrière, et afin qu'il soit vu, elles retroussent leur robe et la mettent sur la tête et se couvrent jusqu'aux yeux. » N'est-il pas sorcier Urbain Grandier, le curé contestataire de la paroisse Saint-Pierre-du-Marché, à Loudun, accusé par les ursulines d'avoir introduit le démon dans leur couvent pour les envoûter ? C'est qu'il ne fait pas bon avoir l'esprit libre en ces temps fort pieux. Société plus ou moins secrète groupant des laïcs et des clercs, la compagnie du Saint-Sacrement, fondée en 1629, rassemble la fine fleur du parti dévot, de la noblesse de robe aux princes du sang, de la bourgeoisie marchande aux grandes dames de la société. Fer de lance de la Réforme catholique, les 4 000 confrères traquent les libertins et les prostituées, poursuivent les comédiens, assiègent les protestants dans leurs retranchements, font la police des mœurs et rêvent de faire de l'État royal une « cour sainte ».

En 1619, l'Italien Lucilio Vanini, qui soutenait que la religion était une invention des princes pour maintenir leur pouvoir, est brûlé sur ordre du parlement de Toulouse. En 1623, Théophile de Viau, accusé d'être le chef de file des « libertins », c'est-à-dire, accuse le père Garasse, des « ivrognets moucherons de tavernes, esprits insensibles à la piété, qui n'ont d'autre Dieu que leur ventre, qui sont enrôlés en cette maudite confrérie qui s'appellent la confrérie des bouteilles », est arrêté et doit à l'intervention de son protecteur, le duc de Montmorency, d'échapper aux flammes du bûcher. Rebelles au siècle des saints comme à la police des corps, les libertins faisaient hardiment profession de scepticisme et exprimaient l'idée que la religion n'était rien d'autre que ce que les hommes les plus habiles avaient inventé « pour expliquer les phénomènes des mœurs, des actions et des pensées des pauvres mortels, afin de leur donner certaines règles de vie exemptes, autant que faire se peut, de toute absurdité ».

Les vertiges du doute

Alors que le traité de démonologie, constamment republié, de Jean Bodin, le théoricien de la souveraineté royale, affirmait la réalité des vols nocturnes de celles qui prennent leur balai pour rejoindre Satan, d'autres hommes ouvraient des brèches dans le système de croyances et annonçaient une révolution intellectuelle d'une ampleur sans pareille.

Là où Jean Bodin invoquait Aristote pour chercher à expliquer de manière rationnelle les actions que les sorciers entretiennent « avec les démons et esprits malins », Galilée faisait paraître ses *Histoires et démonstrations sur les taches solaires* qui bouleversent les idées admises jusque-là. Mettant en doute le langage des signes qui, pour les hommes de son temps, étaient autant de manifestations de Dieu dans les affaires terrestres, il écrit en 1623 dans *L'Essayeur* : « La philosophie est écrite dans ce vaste livre constamment ouvert devant nos yeux (je veux dire l'univers), et on ne peut le comprendre si d'abord on n'apprend à connaître la langue et les caractères dans lesquels il est écrit. Or il est écrit en langage mathématique, et ses caractères sont le triangle et le cercle et autres figures géométriques sans lesquelles il est humainement impossible d'en comprendre un mot. »

Mais cette structure mathématique de l'univers telle que la présentait Galilée était-elle le reflet de la raison créatrice de Dieu, un être infini et tout-puissant aux desseins imprévisibles, ou une immense mécanique régie par des lois intangibles où le péché, le Christ et la rédemption n'avaient plus leur place ?

Interrogation redoutable où s'affrontaient d'un côté une Terre immobile, au centre de l'univers, exposée aux assauts des forces surnaturelles, et de l'autre une vaste machine fonctionnant de manière automatique. La foi aveugle contre le doute de la raison. En 1633, l'année même où Galilée était condamné par le tribunal de l'Inquisition, Jeanne des Anges, ursuline au couvent de Loudun, désignait les démons qui l'habitaient, Léviathan, logé au milieu du front, Aman, Isacaron, logé sous la dernière côte du côté droit, Balam, logé dans la seconde côte du côté droit, Asmodée, Béhémot...

En 1637, l'année où les croquants enflammaient le Périgord et où un jeune avocat célèbre, Antoine Le Maître, neveu d'Angélique Arnauld, décidait de se retirer du monde, près de l'abbaye de Port-Royal-des-Champs, pour s'abandonner complètement à Dieu, l'imprimeur Jean le Maire tirait à trois mille exemplaires, un chiffre très important pour l'époque, le *Discours de la méthode*, pour bien conduire sa raison et chercher la vérité dans les sciences. Plus la *Dioptrique*, les *Météores* et la *Géométrie* qui sont des essais de cette méthode.

L'auteur, René Descartes, fils d'un conseiller au parlement de Rennes, élevé au collège des jésuites de La Flèche, établi en Hollande, réputée pour sa tolérance, y livrait quatre « préceptes » pour prendre possession du monde. « Le premier était de ne recevoir jamais aucune chose pour vraie que je ne la connusse évidemment être telle [...]. Le second, de diviser chacune des difficultés que j'examinerais en autant de parcelles qu'il se pourrait et qu'il serait requis pour les mieux résoudre [...]. Le troisième, de conduire par ordre mes pensées, en commençant par les objets les plus simples et les plus aisés à connaître, pour monter peu à peu comme par degrés jusqu'à la connaissance des plus composés [...]. Et le dernier, de faire partout des dénombrements si entiers et des revues si générales que je fusse assuré de ne rien omettre. »

Mais pouvait-on être catholique et mathématicien ? Certes, Descartes affirmait qu'il fallait « obéir aux lois et coutumes de son pays » et retenir « constamment la religion dans laquelle Dieu vous avait fait naître », mais comment ne pas être déchiré entre l'optimisme de la raison et le pessimisme du péché, entre la misère et la grandeur de l'homme ? Dans le « perpétuel combat » qu'est la vie d'un chrétien

— l'expression est de Richelieu —, quelle place convenait-il de laisser à la raison ? Fallait-il l'installer, comme Descartes et le Cardinal, au cœur de l'esprit humain, lui faire confiance pour expliquer l'univers et distinguer les affaires de la foi et les données de la science ? Ou bien considérer, comme Pascal, que cette raison péchait par trop de défaillance dans le domaine des lois ou des mœurs ? Exiger, comme Cornelius Jansen, l'évêque d'Ypres, ou l'abbé de Saint-Cyran, le repentir complet dans l'espoir d'une grâce qui seule permettrait d'entendre le message divin ? Ou, comme Richelieu et les jésuites, condamner cet héroïsme de la perfection cultivé par les jansénistes, pardonner aux pécheurs et prôner l'attrition, c'est-à-dire la simple honte du péché ?

Blaise Pascal, une des intelligences les plus vives de son temps, aussi à l'aise en physique qu'en géométrie, mais qui ne pardonnait pas à Descartes d'avoir « voulu dans toute sa philosophie se passer de Dieu », y répondait, au lendemain du 23 novembre 1654, après sa « conversion », en jetant ses mots :

« Dieu d'Abraham, Dieu d'Isaac, Dieu de Jacob. Non des philosophes et des savants. Certitude. Sentiment. Joie. Paix.

Dieu de Jésus-Christ. »

47

Le métier de roi

*L*e 10 mars 1661, quelques heures après la mort de Mazarin, le roi *Louis XIV réunit son Conseil et, se tournant vers le chancelier Séguier, déclare : « Je vous ai fait assembler avec mes ministres et secré-taires d'État pour vous dire que jusqu'à présent, j'ai bien voulu laisser gouverner mes affaires par feu Monsieur le Cardinal ; il est temps que je les gouverne moi-même. » Puis, après avoir ordonné aux secrétaires d'État de ne rien signer sans son ordre et sans lui avoir rendu compte chaque jour des affaires, il ajoute : « La face du théâtre change [...]. Vous savez mes volontés ; c'est à vous maintenant, Messieurs, à les exécuter. » À vingt-deux ans, Louis XIV définissait ainsi les nouvelles règles du jeu. Prenant en charge les aspirations d'une « nation » excédée par les désordres de la Fronde, il affirmait qu'il ferait désormais seul son métier de roi.*

Un roi-soleil

Les 5 et 6 juin 1662, près de 15 000 Parisiens, provinciaux et étrangers, assemblés sur les gradins dressés face au palais des Tuile-ries, peuvent assister à un spectacle grandiose organisé en l'honneur du dauphin Louis, né le 1ᵉʳ novembre 1661. Un grand carrousel met en scène quatre quadrilles de Persans, Turcs, Indiens et Américains, respectivement commandés par Monsieur, le frère du roi, le prince de

Condé, le duc d'Enghien et le duc de Guise. Conduit par le roi lui-même, vêtu en *imperator*, d'un habit d'or et d'argent parsemé de pierreries, le cinquième quadrille, celui des Romains, est placé au centre de l'arène et reçoit la soumission des autres empires.

Pour devise, Louis a choisi *Nec pluribus impar*, qu'on peut traduire par : « Supérieur à tous », une devise dont il commente ainsi le sens dans ses *Mémoires* : « Ce fut là que je commençai à prendre [la devise] que j'ai toujours gardée depuis, et que vous voyez en tant de lieux. Je crus qu'elle devait représenter, en quelque sorte, les devoirs d'un prince, et m'exciter éternellement moi-même à les remplir. On choisit pour corps le soleil, qui, dans les règles de cet art, est le plus noble de tous, et qui, par la qualité d'unique, par l'éclat qui l'environne, par la lumière qu'il communique aux autres astres qui lui composent comme une espèce de cour, par le partage égal et juste qu'il fait de cette même lumière à tous les divers climats du monde, par le bien qu'il fait en tous lieux, produisant sans cesse de tous côtés la vie, la joie et l'action, par son mouvement sans relâche, où il paraît néanmoins toujours tranquille, par cette course constante et invariable, dont il ne s'écarte et ne se détourne jamais, est assurément la plus vive et la plus belle image d'un grand monarque. »

Les autres seigneurs n'ont pu que réfléchir la lumière de cet astre naissant. Le comte de Vivonne a choisi pour devise *Tua munera jacto*, « Je ne renvoie que ce que je reçois de vous ». Le duc de Noailles porte un aigle qui regarde fixement le soleil. Le comte de Lude prend un cadran exposé au soleil avec cette devise : *Te sine nomen iners*, « Sans toi, grande lumière, je ne suis rien au monde ».

Première fête d'un long règne, le carrousel de 1662 manifestait avec orgueil, démesure, enthousiasme juvénile, naïveté peut-être mais totale assurance la volonté de réduire à l'obéissance tous ceux qui avaient gâché la jeunesse du roi et compromis par leurs frondes le prestige de la monarchie.

Né le dimanche 5 septembre 1638, Louis Dieudonné peut afficher un horoscope prometteur. Venu spécialement d'Allemagne, un astronome-astrologue placé dans un cabinet, à côté de la chambre d'Anne d'Autriche, avait dressé ses machines dans l'attente du moment décisif. Alors il vit, dit-on, des choses ineffables qu'on eut beaucoup de peine à déchiffrer. *Diu*, *dure*, *feliciter*, tels furent les trois mots qui, selon lui, allaient caractériser le règne de ce nouveau-né, « longtemps », « durement », « heureusement ». Jean Racine, chargé d'écrire l'histoire du règne, inscrivit sur ses tablettes les prédictions d'un autre astrologue, Tommaso Campanella, alors en France : « Le Dauphin, comme le soleil, par sa chaleur et sa lumière, fera le bonheur de la

France et des amis de la France. Déjà il tète sa neuvième nourrice : elles le fuient toutes, parce qu'il maltraite leurs mamelles. »

Louis, devenu roi en 1643 à la mort de son père Louis XIII, peut surtout se flatter d'une prestigieuse ascendance qui marie la légitimité des Capétiens, la verdeur des Bourbons et la gloire des Habsbourg. Un généalogiste ayant eu la patience de retrouver 510 des 512 quartiers ascendants de Louis XIV compté 11 % d'ascendants germaniques, 7 % d'ascendants anglais et slaves, 28 % d'ascendants français, 26 % d'ascendants espagnols, 9 % d'ascendants portugais et 8 % d'ascendants italiens. Dans la galerie de ses aïeux apparaissent Charles Quint, Frédéric Barberousse, le poète Charles d'Orléans, le condottiere Jean de Médicis, Charles le Téméraire et même Riourik le Viking.

Ce roi à l'ego distendu et au sang mélangé était incontestablement beau. Des yeux bruns et un profil net dégageaient un charme qui séduisait et une majesté qui impressionnait, sa petite taille (1,67 m) étant compensée par un regard intimidant, plus tard par des talons et une haute perruque. L'ambassadeur de Venise écrivait : « Si la fortune ne l'avait pas fait naître un grand Roi, c'est chose certaine que la nature lui en a donné l'apparence. » Et ses contemporains applaudissaient Bérénice quand elle s'écriait :

En quelque obscurité que le sort l'eût fait naître
Le monde, en le voyant eût reconnu son maître.

D'une intelligence robuste et pragmatique, ayant la tête bien faite plutôt que bien pleine, il a fait du latin, appris le calcul, l'histoire, les langues, la guitare et le luth. Comme tous les jeunes souverains, il a surtout été rapidement initié aux règles de la guerre. Dès son plus jeune âge, il s'est « amusé » à la guerre, dans le jardin du Palais-Royal, attaquant un fortin avec des mousquets et de la vraie poudre. Pour l'endormir, le premier valet de chambre La Porte utilise la volumineuse *Histoire de France* de Mézeray, parue en 1643, qui cultive les actions guerrières de ses ancêtres. Quant à la géographie, définie comme la « science royale » par excellence, elle lui a permis, selon un traité d'éducation à l'usage des fils de roi, de connaître « la disposition des lieux où loger les troupes ou combattre » et, peut-être, lui a appris à modérer ses ambitions en limitant ses prétentions territoriales à de justes proportions. Comme l'écrivait le philosophe antique Sénèque, cité avec respect dans ce traité : « Que faites-vous, monarques ambitieux, quand vous répandez tant de sang, et que vous commettez tant de meurtres ? Vous entreprenez l'impossible, puisque vous voulez partager un point. Vous croyez avoir fait une conquête considérable quand vous avez ajouté une province à votre royaume, et vous ne considérez pas que cette province et votre royaume ne sont qu'une petite partie de la terre, et que la terre tout entière, comparée au ciel, n'est qu'un atome indivisible. » Grignoteur de terres, Louis XIV ne sera jamais, comme Napoléon, un conquérant de l'impossible, obsédé par le « toujours plus ».

Le jeune Louis a surtout été « dressé » au métier de roi par son tuteur, le cardinal Mazarin, et sa mère, Anne d'Autriche, à laquelle il voua une grande affection. Il en a en outre suivi la meilleure école, la rude école de la vie, celle qui lui a fait connaître les barricades parisiennes, l'humiliation de la fuite, les trahisons multiples de la famille et de l'entourage. De Mazarin, il a appris le goût du secret. De sa mère, celui de l'étiquette et de la parure. De son père, le culte des fleurs de lys. Le premier autographe que l'histoire a conservé de lui est une page d'écriture où il a recopié six fois la formule : « L'hommage est deub [dû] aux roys, ils font ce qu'il leur plaist. » Préoccupation du bonheur du peuple, fermeté d'âme, culte de l'ordre et du respect, telles sont depuis plusieurs siècles les valeurs que diffuse la culture absolutiste et qui s'épanouissent sous le règne d'un roi qu'une robuste santé fera vivre soixante-dix-sept ans. Dans une page préparée pour ses *Mémoires*, il a défini en ces termes les canons du roi absolu : « Tous les yeux sont attachés sur lui seul ; c'est à lui seul que s'adressent tous les vœux ; lui seul reçoit tous les respects, lui seul est l'objet de toutes les espérances ; on ne poursuit, on n'attend, on ne fait rien que par lui seul. On regarde ses bonnes grâces comme la seule source de tous les biens ; on ne croit s'élever qu'à mesure qu'on s'approche de sa personne ou de son estime ; tout le reste est stérile. »

Le baptême du « moi »

C'est le 10 mars 1661 que Louis, jeune homme dressé pour être roi, entre véritablement en scène en convoquant à sept heures du matin, au château de Vincennes, le Conseil, auquel il annonce que « la face du théâtre change ». Voulant frapper les esprits, ce roi qui a souvent avoué à ses proches n'avoir été, jusqu'alors, qu'un monarque en peinture, comprend qu'il faut effacer au plus vite l'ombre pesante du cardinal-ministre. Le maréchal de Gramont exprime la surprise des courtisans quand il écrit : « le lendemain [de la mort de Mazarin], [...] toutes les affaires changèrent de face à la cour ; le Roi, quoiqu'à la fleur de son âge et au milieu de ses plaisirs, prit seul le timon de l'État et se livra entièrement aux affaires [...]. La reine, sa mère, qui avait été régente si longtemps, n'eut plus de part aux affaires, non plus que les princes du sang et les plus grands seigneurs de France qui, jusques alors, avaient été admis dans les Conseils et fait une figure distinguée ». Louis-Henri Loménie de Brienne, secrétaire d'État, ajoute : « Le Roi avait fait assembler [...], dans la chambre de la Reine mère où les conseils se tenaient ci-devant [...] les princes, les ducs et les ministres d'État [...] pour leur faire entendre de sa propre bouche qu'il avait pris la résolution de commander lui-même son État sans s'en reposer que sur ses propres soins et les congédia bien honnêtement, en leur disant que, quand il aurait besoin de leurs bons avis, il les ferait appeler [...]. J'ai eu l'ordre d'écrire à tous les ministres étrangers la résolution que Sa Majesté avait prise de gouverner elle-même son État, afin qu'ils en donnassent part aux princes pour lesquels ils servent. »

En écartant de son Conseil l'aristocratie du sang, de l'épée et de la soutane et en annonçant sa décision de gouverner sans « principal ministre », Louis XIV a réalisé un fameux « coup de partie », comme disaient les joueurs de cartes du temps.

L'arrestation de Fouquet, le 5 septembre 1661, constitue le deuxième acte de cette pièce de théâtre composée par celui qui a décidé d'agir vite et fort. Préparée par Jean-Baptiste Colbert, devenu intendant des Finances en mars 1661, l'élimination de celui qui paraissait le plus en cour a été méticuleusement programmée. Devenu après la mort de Mazarin l'un des personnages les plus influents du régime, Nicolas Fouquet semble alors au faîte de sa puissance. Cet homme qui a l'oreille de la finance et du parti dévot est le bouc émissaire idéal auquel faire payer toutes les combinaisons frauduleuses échafaudées sous le règne de Mazarin. Ayant lui-même participé activement à l'exploitation financière de la monarchie, il peut devenir la victime expiatoire offerte à ceux qui souffrirent du « tour de vis » fiscal. La fête somptueuse qu'il a offerte au roi dans son château de Vaux-le-Vicomte n'a rien arrangé. Parc orné de statues antiques, jeux d'eau, musique de Lully, représentation des *Fâcheux* de Molière, dîner servi dans de la vaisselle en or, trop d'ostentation affichée pour l'amour-propre du jeune roi. Le 5 septembre, jour anniversaire de sa naissance, Louis fait arrêter le surintendant. Le 15 septembre, il annonce la suppression de la surintendance des Finances au profit d'un Conseil royal des finances composé de personnes de « capacité et de probité connues » et précise qu'il se réserve le contrôle absolu des dépenses. Louis, qui, le soir même de l'arrestation de Fouquet, a écrit à sa mère : « J'avais la plus grande impatience du monde que cela fût achevé », peut ainsi faire savoir à l'« opinion » que le temps des « maires du palais » est bien terminé. Jean-Baptiste Colbert, devenu ministre d'État, apparaît déjà comme le nouvel homme fort du gouvernement.

En 1661, toujours, apprenant que l'ambassadeur de France à Londres, le comte Godefroi d'Estrades, a dû céder le pas devant l'Espagnol Watteville lors d'une cérémonie protocolaire, Louis XIV rompt les relations diplomatiques avec son beau-père Philippe IV et obtient le 24 mars 1662 les excuses solennelles de l'Espagne devant les ambassadeurs de toute l'Europe rassemblés à Paris. En 1662, encore, à la suite d'une rixe qui, à Rome, a opposé des domestiques de l'ambassadeur de France et les gardes corses pontificaux, il rompt les relations diplomatiques avec le pape Alexandre VII et saisit le Comtat venaissin pour obtenir des excuses qui seront présentées à Fontainebleau, le 29 juillet 1664. Autre manifestation de prestige, il obtient que les Anglais saluent également le pavillon français sur les mers.

Au lendemain des « excuses » espagnoles, Louis XIV fait écrire dans ses *Mémoires* : « Je ne sais pas si depuis le commencement de la monarchie, il s'est jamais rien passé de plus glorieux pour elle, car les rois et les souverains que nos ancêtres ont vus quelquefois à leurs pieds leur rendre hommage, n'y étaient pas comme souverains et comme rois, mais comme seigneurs de quelque principauté moindre à laquelle ils pouvaient renoncer. Ici, c'est une espèce d'hommage véritablement d'une autre sorte, de roi à roi, de couronne à couronne, qui ne laisse plus douter à nos ennemis mêmes que la nôtre ne soit la première de la chrétienté. »

Les hommes du « moi »

Pour que l'État puisse refléter la volonté du « moi », il fallait d'abord structurer une administration faite de pièces historiques mal ajustées les unes aux autres. Épicentre de la décision, le Conseil d'État, appelé aussi Conseil étroit ou Conseil d'en-haut, examine les mercredi, jeudi et dimanche de chaque semaine, et un lundi sur deux, avant le dîner, qui était à une heure, les grandes affaires de politique intérieure et extérieure. Le roi siège dans son fauteuil, les conseillers sur des tabourets. Le fait d'y avoir été appelé, même une seule fois, vaut à l'élu le titre de ministre d'État. On en comptera seulement seize, à raison de trois ou quatre à la fois, de 1661 à 1715. Représentant du Brandebourg en France, Ezechiel Spanheim avance les raisons qui motivèrent Louis XIV à limiter considérablement le nombre de ses ministres : « En quoi, on peut juger que le Roi a eu trois ou quatre vues principales : l'une d'abaisser l'autorité des grands de son royaume, dont quelques-uns lui avaient fait la guerre et suscité de méchantes affaires durant sa minorité ; l'autre, de conserver et de ménager le secret dans la direction des affaires et des délibérations importantes de l'État, qui ne se trouvaient confiées qu'à deux ou trois personnes, ou quatre tout au plus, d'ailleurs d'une fidélité éprouvée ; la troisième, d'en paraître d'autant plus, et au-dedans et au-dehors du royaume, le maître des affaires [...] ; enfin, pour [éviter] de retomber sous le pouvoir d'un premier et absolu ministre, comme avait été le cardinal de Richelieu, sous le feu roi son père, et le cardinal de Mazarin durant et après sa minorité et jusques à la mort de ce cardinal. C'est-à-dire que l'amour-propre, les sentiments de la gloire, la défiance, la jalousie, l'esprit de vengeance, d'épargne et de précaution, se joignirent ensemble, ou eurent au moins leur part dans cette forme du gouvernement et du ministère qui s'établit. »

Ces ministres, disait Saint-Simon, « n'ont ni office, ni charge, ni patente, ni serment ; leur état est nul [...]. Cela est établi en l'air et n'a pas de véritable existence ». En fait, trois familles de « mandarins-bureaucrates », trois véritables clans se partagèrent la confiance de Louis XIV pendant ses cinquante-quatre années de règne personnel, le clan Colbert-Seignelay, le clan Le Tellier-Louvois et enfin, secondairement, le clan Phélypeaux-Pontchartrain dont les ascensions avaient exaspéré la jalousie de la vieille noblesse, une jalousie entretenue par le roi qui avouait : « Je crus qu'il n'était pas de mon intérêt de choisir des hommes de dignité plus éminente, parce qu'ayant besoin sur toutes choses d'établir ma propre réputation, il était important que le public connût, par le rang de ceux dont je me servais, que je n'étais pas en dessein de partager avec eux mon autorité, et qu'eux-mêmes sachant ce qu'ils étaient ne conçussent pas de plus hautes espérances que celles que je leur voudrais donner. »

Trois autres conseils de gouvernement assistent le roi. Le Conseil des dépêches, réuni une fois tous les quinze jours, rassemble le chancelier, les ministres et les quatre secrétaires d'État, qui se tiennent debout. Le dauphin y fera ses premières armes. Véritable « ministère de l'Intérieur », il examine « toutes les dépêches du dedans du royaume » et joue le rôle de tribunal administratif suprême.

Mis en place en septembre 1661, au lendemain de l'arrestation de Fouquet, le Conseil des finances, réuni en moyenne deux fois par semaine, le mardi et le samedi, contrôle le budget de l'État, établit le brevet de la taille, s'occupe des doléances des communautés, gère les offices et les revenus des domaines du roi.

Enfin, le Conseil privé, ou des parties, composé de techniciens du droit, examine les affaires que les plaideurs, c'est-à-dire les parties, portent en dernier ressort devant la justice du roi. Comprenant à l'origine 80 maîtres des requêtes et 30 conseillers d'État, il siège sans relâche, sauf quinze jours par an aux environs de Pâques. Le roi n'y paraissait que rarement mais sa présence était marquée par son fauteuil de velours rouge, bordé d'or et d'argent, qui demeurait vide au bout de la table, que recouvrait un tapis de velours violet à bordure d'or fleurdelisée.

De la tradition médiévale subsistait un rite. Les dimanches et jours de fête, deux maîtres des requêtes accompagnaient le roi à la messe et recevaient sur le chemin du retour les placets et les suppliques des sujets. Une façon de perpétuer l'image de saint Louis sous le chêne de Vincennes.

Amoureux du métier, professionnel de talent, Louis XIV ne fut sans doute pas un génie. Sachant s'entourer de « grands seconds », ces « tiercelets de ministres » que raillait Saint-Simon, contrôlant tout, assidu aux séances, travaillant en équipe, suivant d'ordinaire « la pluralité des suffrages » mais convaincu que c'était à lui seul de décider, s'astreignant lui-même à la tâche, multipliant les « je verrai » si commodes pour repousser les impatients, Louis XIV démontra toutefois comment un homme ordinaire peut, en épousant sa fonction, susciter admiration et obéissance.

La « maxime de l'ordre »

« Le désordre régnait partout. » Rien mieux que ce laconique commentaire n'illustre la volonté de Louis XIV d'en finir avec les rêves d'une monarchie contrôlée par les corps intermédiaires. C'est tout d'abord la noblesse qui est réduite au silence, avant d'être « domestiquée » à Versailles. Les gouverneurs qui considéraient autrefois leurs provinces comme de véritables fiefs ne sont plus nommés que pour trois ans et, après avoir fait une tournée initiale, sont tenus de résider à la cour. Désormais dans les provinces, 31 intendants exercent plus encore qu'avant l'essentiel des pouvoirs. Enquêteurs chevauchant d'une région à l'autre, à l'origine, ils se sont progressivement transformés en administrateurs attachés à une généralité, grignotant de toutes parts les attributions des officiers et des seigneurs locaux.

Devenus l'État présent dans les provinces, ces maîtres des requêtes issus de la noblesse de robe ont eu aussi pour mission de « mettre en carte » les nobles et, selon les instructions de Colbert, de vérifier de près l'authenticité de leurs titres. Jadis si remuants, les aristocrates, dont l'essence est désormais définie par le texte plus que par le sang, se transforment alors en conservateurs attentifs de leurs archives. « Les chênes deviennent des roseaux », selon la belle formule d'Emmanuel Le Roy Ladurie.

Le premier ordre est également réduit à l'obéissance. Le 10 mars 1661, peu après la séance mémorable du Conseil, Louis avait rencontré l'archevêque de Rouen Harlay de Champvallon, qui présidait l'assemblée du clergé.

« Votre Majesté m'avait ordonné de m'adresser à M. le cardinal pour toutes les affaires. Le voilà mort : à qui veut-Elle que je m'adresse ?

— À moi, Monsieur l'archevêque », avait répondu Louis.

« Roi-Très-Chrétien », estimant tenir son pouvoir de Dieu seul, Louis XIV se considère aussi comme responsable du salut de ses sujets. Il pense également, parce qu'il est encore jeune et avide de fêtes et de plaisirs, que les débordements mystiques doivent être ramenés à la raison. La compagnie du Saint-Sacrement, menacée de dissolution, mène jusqu'en 1665 une activité ralentie et ne peut empêcher la représentation de *Tartuffe* le 12 mai 1664 à Versailles. Par égard pour Anne d'Autriche, scandalisée, Louis fait interdire la pièce au public mais précise qu'il a pris un réel plaisir à entendre les vers que Molière a écrits :

Nous vivons sous un prince ennemi de la fraude,
Un prince dont les yeux se font jour dans les cœurs,
Et que ne peut tromper tout l'art des imposteurs.
D'un fin discernement sa grande âme pourvue
Sur les choses toujours jette une droite vue ;
Chez elle jamais rien ne surprend trop d'accès,
Et sa ferme raison ne tombe en nul excès.

Décidé à « exterminer entièrement le jansénisme » par « conscience », par « honneur » et « pour le bien de son État », il exige, en avril 1661, que tous les ecclésiastiques du royaume, séculiers comme réguliers, signent le formulaire condamnant les propositions que Cornelius Jansen, évêque d'Ypres, avait développées dans son livre l'*Augustinus* et qui faisaient figure de manifeste du mouvement janséniste.

Partie prenante du grand élan spirituel qui a traversé le « siècle des saints », le jansénisme avait surtout séduit les élites attirées par la rigueur d'une foi exigeante, le dépouillement de soi et la volonté de renouer avec la tradition de saint Augustin. En 1637, Antoine Le

Maître, un jeune avocat célèbre, neveu d'Angélique Arnauld et protégé du chancelier Séguier, avait inauguré le mouvement en se retirant, pour se vouer entièrement à Dieu, dans la vallée de Chevreuse, près de l'abbaye de Port-Royal-des-Champs, alors désertée par ses religieuses au profit de Port-Royal de Paris. La publication, en 1640, de l'*Augustinus*, qui affirmait que la grâce était un pur don de Dieu octroyé par lui à sa seule volonté, puis, en 1643, *De la fréquente communion*, dans laquelle l'auteur, Antoine Arnauld, condamnait l'usage immodéré que les hypocrites gens du monde faisaient de la « sainte viande », suscita l'engouement pour les disciples de Cornelius Jansen. Accourus à Port-Royal, où la mère Angélique Arnauld s'était de nouveau installée en 1648, les « solitaires » restauraient les bâtiments, assainissaient le vallon et créaient des « Petites Écoles » aux méthodes nouvelles, plus attentives à la personnalité de chaque enfant. Racine, qui fut leur élève, y acquit sa sensibilité. Évoquant Port-Royal, il écrivait : « Quelle paix ! Quel silence ! Quelle charité ! Quel amour pour la pauvreté et la mortification ! Un travail sans relâche, une prière continuelle, point d'ambition que pour les emplois les plus vils et les plus humiliants, aucune impatience dans les sœurs, nulle bizarrerie dans les Mères, l'obéissance toujours prompte, et le commandement toujours raisonnable. »

Si le jansénisme attire alors les sympathies et finit par constituer un réseau fort influent rassemblant tous les déçus du siècle, il irrite les jésuites, qui redoutent cette concurrence, et les autorités, qui n'ont jamais apprécié l'exaltation du libre examen. En 1653, cinq propositions de l'Augustinus sont déclarées hérétiques par le pape Innocent X. Malgré les *Provinciales* de Blaise Pascal, qui soutient ses amis de Port-Royal, le pape Alexandre VII renouvelle en 1656 la condamnation de Jansen. En mars 1657, l'Assemblée du clergé décide d'imposer à tous les ecclésiastiques la signature d'un formulaire ainsi rédigé : « Je soussigné me soumets à la constitution apostolique d'Innocent X, donnée le 31 mai 1653, et à celle d'Alexandre VII du 16 octobre 1656. Je rejette et condamne sincèrement les cinq propositions tirées du livre de Jansénius [Cornelius Jansen], intitulé *Augustinus*, dans le propre sens de l'auteur, comme le Saint-Siège les a condamnées par les mêmes constitutions. Je le jure ainsi. »

En 1664, les religieuses de Port-Royal ayant refusé de signer le formulaire, niant seulement le fait que les cinq propositions condamnées fussent dans Jansénius, l'archevêque de Paris, Hardouin de Péréfixe, traite la mère prieure de « petite pimbêche » et ordonne que les sœurs soient exilées dans d'autres couvents. Les solitaires sont contraints de se disperser et de fermer leurs écoles. Finalement, explique Saint-Simon, le roi s'était laissé persuader par les jésuites que toute autre école que la leur n'avait qu'un esprit « républicain ». Il avait estimé que ce « parti » si influent dans le monde de la robe était une forme de Fronde d'autant plus redoutable qu'elle était plus secrète. « Le Roi était prévenu, rapporte Racine, que les jansénistes n'étaient pas bien intentionnés pour sa personne et pour son État ; et ils avaient eux-mêmes, sans y penser, donné occasion de lui inspirer ces sentiments par leur facilité plus chrétienne que judicieuse à recevoir beaucoup de personnes, ou dégoûtées de la cour, ou tombées en disgrâce, qui venaient chez eux chercher des consolations. »

Ce sont également les bruits des parlements qui ne sont plus de saison. En avril 1655, Louis, seulement âgé de seize ans, avait déjà fait forte impression en pénétrant en tenue de chasse, un fouet à la main et en grosses bottes au Parlement de Paris pour déclarer : « Chacun sait combien vos assemblées ont excité de troubles dans mon État, et combien de dangereux effets elles ont produit. J'ai appris que vous prétendiez encore les continuer, sous prétexte de délibérer sur les édits qui ont été lus et publiés en ma présence. Je suis venu ici exprès pour vous en défendre la continuation... »

À partir de 1665, les cours souveraines ne sont plus dites que « supérieures ». En 1673, les parlementaires doivent enregistrer les édits sans délibération ni vote et ne peuvent présenter de « respectueuses remontrances » qu'après cet enregistrement. Si les états provinciaux subsistent en Bourgogne, en Languedoc et en Bretagne, leurs pouvoirs sont sérieusement réduits. Mme de Sévigné, qui assiste en août 1671 aux états de Bretagne, en porte témoignage : « Les états ne doivent pas être longs ; il n'y a qu'à demander ce que veut le roi ; on ne dit pas un mot : voila qui est fait [...]. Une infinité de présents, des pensions, des réparations des chemins et des villes, quinze ou vingt grandes tables, un jeu continuel, des bals éternels, des comédies trois fois la semaine, une grande « braverie » ; voilà les états. »

Ce sont aussi les villes, foyers d'agitation pendant la Fronde, qui sont mises à la raison. La punition de Marseille, qui avait fièrement inscrit le mot *Libertas* à l'entrée principale de la ville, fut spectaculaire. Louis ordonna de faire abattre la porte Royale, avec une partie des murailles, et entra solennellement le 2 mars 1660 par la brèche. Les magistrats municipaux perdaient leur titre prestigieux de consuls pour celui, plus modeste, d'échevins et se voyaient interdire d'y ajouter, comme le faisaient leurs prédécesseurs, celui de « gouverneurs et défenseurs des libertés, franchises et privilèges de la ville ».

À Paris, « qui doit servir d'exemple à toutes les autres villes de nostre Royaume », l'édit de mars 1667 crée un nouveau magistrat, le lieutenant général de police, aux multiples fonctions. Chargé de la sécurité, des subsistances, de l'hygiène, de la surveillance des mœurs et de la censure des livres, le premier titulaire de la charge, Gabriel Nicolas de La Reynie, s'avère l'oiseau rare dont Colbert avait tracé le portrait à Louis XIV : « Il faut que notre lieutenant de police soit un homme de simarre et d'épée, et si la savante hermine de docteur doit flotter sur ses épaules, il faut aussi qu'à son pied résonne le fort éperon de chevalier, qu'il soit impassible comme magistrat et comme soldat, intrépide, qu'il ne pâlisse pas devant les inondations du fleuve et la peste des hôpitaux, non plus que devant les rumeurs populaires et les menaces de vos courtisans. »

Ce magistrat limousin qui pensait avoir mieux à faire qu'à éplucher les dossiers du Conseil d'État déploiera pendant trente ans une incroyable activité, pavant et éclairant une ville dans laquelle on ne pouvait pas auparavant sortir la nuit sans risquer sa vie, prévenant l'incendie et l'inondation par des mesures qui évitèrent à la capitale le désastre qui ravagea Londres en 1666, inspectant halles et marchés pour traquer les fraudes et les tricheries, « écoutant » aussi « pour écumer et rapporter ce que chacun disait et pensait ».

Dans ses *Mémoires*, l'Italien Primi Visconti portait un témoignage sans doute exagéré sur les changements intervenus dans la capitale après la mise en place de la lieutenance générale de police : « C'était autrefois un nid de voleurs et d'assassins [...]. Il était impossible de se promener le jour, car les rues n'étaient pas pavées et le sol était gras comme celui des villages [...]. Le Roi a défendu le port de l'épée aux laquais sous peine de gibet [...]. Il a ensuite fait paver toute la ville, poser la nuit des lanternes dans chaque rue ; à tous les angles, il y a des sentinelles armées ; des cavaliers et des troupes sont postés par-ci par-là pour accourir au premier signal contre les malfaiteurs ; on peut ainsi circuler sûrement jusqu'à deux heures du matin. Il arrive néanmoins, de temps en temps, des vols, mais les coupables vont bien vite trébucher contre la roue ou le gibet ; les sentences contre les malfaiteurs sont rendues avec une célérité extraordinaire, à la mode française ; on prend le criminel aujourd'hui et on le pend demain, et tout cela se pratique avec la même exactitude dans tout le royaume : c'est pourquoi on voit sur les grands chemins tant d'expositions de chair humaine. »

C'est que le maintien de la tranquillité publique est devenu une tâche essentielle. Ainsi, siégeant à Clermont du 25 septembre 1665 au 30 janvier 1666, un tribunal extraordinaire composé d'officiers du

Parlement de Paris examine 1 360 affaires allant des meurtres, des rebellions et des viols aux faux monnayages et prononce 640 condamnations, dont 23 à mort. Ces Grands Jours d'Auvergne, en jugeant les seigneurs qui maltraitent leurs paysans comme les curés qui vendent les sacrements, montrent de manière spectaculaire aux Auvergnats qu'ils ont un roi capable de « purger la montagne d'une infinité de désordres ».

Mais quand le peuple se révolte, comme les Bonnets rouges, ces Bretons qui, en 1675, pillent les bureaux de vente du tabac et du papier timbré, ce sont les hommes de troupe qui sont envoyés sans ménagement chez l'habitant, un Rennais rapportant dans son journal, à la date du 13 décembre 1675, « qu'ils ont jeté leurs hôtes et hôtesses par les fenêtres après les avoir battus et excédés, ont violé des femmes, lié des enfants tout nus sur des broches pour les vouloir faire rôtir, rompu et brûlé les meubles, démoli les fenêtres et vitres des maisons, exigé grandes sommes de leurs hôtes et commis tant de crimes qu'ils égalent Rennes à la destruction de Jérusalem ».

Enfin, nouveau Justinien, Louis signe une série d'ordonnances préparées par Colbert qui tendent à « réduire tout le royaume sous une même loi, même mesure et même poids ». Le Code Louis qui vise à simplifier les justices civile (1667) et criminelle (1670), les ordonnances des eaux et forêts (1669), du commerce (1673) et de la marine (1681) énoncent des règlements dont certains continuent à nous régir, comme celui qui fait du rivage de la mer un domaine public ou de la forêt un patrimoine à préserver.

Ainsi commençait d'être appliqué ce que Colbert nommait « la maxime de l'ordre », un « ordre » dont il ne faudrait toutefois pas exagérer la pesée. Dans la France de Louis XIV, en effet, les mailles du « filet » restent bien lâches. En calculant au plus large, le nombre des « hommes du roi » ne dépassait pas 80 000 hommes pour une population d'environ 20 millions d'habitants. Et quand, en 1685, les protestants se virent interdire d'émigrer, 200 000 réussirent à sortir des « frontières » du royaume ! Preuve s'il en est que la monarchie « absolue » était bien « limitée ».

Les années Colbert

*I*l n'y a rien de plus nécessaire dans un État que le commerce ; c'est « *I* lui qui le rend florissant. » En travaillant avec acharnement pendant plus de vingt ans pour enrichir le royaume et servir la gloire de son roi, Jean-Baptiste Colbert, ministre à tout faire, a été le prêtre le plus zélé de la religion royale. Pourtant, quand il mourut, en 1683, regretté par personne, le roi ne manifesta guère d'émotion, écrivant à sa veuve : « Madame Colbert, je compatis à votre douleur d'autant plus que je sens par moi-même le sujet de votre affliction, puisque, si vous avez perdu un mari qui vous était cher, je regrette un fidèle ministre dont j'étais pleinement satisfait. » Des doléances fort convenues pour celui qui fut le plus grand de ses commis.

L'« homme de marbre »

En 1661, à la chute de Nicolas Fouquet, commence véritablement la carrière de celui que Gui Patin, doyen de la faculté de médecine de Paris, appelait l'« homme de marbre ». Contrairement à la légende qui en a fait un fils de marchand obscur grimpé aux sommets de l'État à la force du poignet, Colbert est le fruit éclos d'un arbre aux lointaines racines. Jean-Baptiste, né en 1619, est en fait issu d'une puissante lignée de marchands-banquiers qui tenait le haut du pavé à Reims depuis le milieu du xvie siècle et avait largement pénétré les sphères de la haute finance parisienne.

L'ancêtre du clan, Jehan Colbert, maçon à Reims, s'est enrichi à l'occasion de la reconstruction de la ville au lendemain de la guerre de Cent Ans. Son fils, Gérard, fait déjà figure de « parvenu », trafiquant en gros les articles de luxe, les tissus, les produits alimentaires, les matériaux de construction et les fournitures aux armées. Nicolas Colbert de Vandières (1590-1661), le père de Jean-Baptiste, est « partisan », receveur général des rentes de l'Hôtel de Ville de Paris, mêlé médiocrement aux affaires financières du royaume. L'oncle Oudard est le premier « millionnaire » du clan, menant grand train dans son château de Villacerf, sur les coteaux de la Seine. Son fils a épousé la sœur de Michel Le Tellier, secrétaire d'État à la Guerre.

Après avoir fait ses études au collège des jésuites de Reims, Jean-Baptiste fait son apprentissage chez un banquier lyonnais et chez un procureur au Châtelet parisien. Puis il est « lancé » par son oncle, qui le fait devenir commis au secrétariat d'État à la Guerre. En 1648, il consolide sa position en épousant une « damoiselle » Marie Charron de Menars, fille d'un fournisseur aux armées qui lui apporte 100 000 livres en dot, et en obtenant de Michel Le Tellier, premier témoin du mariage, un brevet de conseiller d'État.

En juin 1651, lors de la Fronde, il devient le gérant de l'immense fortune de Mazarin, exilé pour quelques mois en Allemagne. On le voit s'occuper de ses bois, de ses terres, de ses seigneuries et de ses abbayes, détourner l'argent de l'État pour le faire entrer dans les caisses du principal ministre, utiliser des prête-noms pour des combinaisons peu orthodoxes... faire préparer des confitures pour la famille royale, commander la garde-robe du cardinal, organiser les mariages de ses nièces et entretenir veaux, vaches et cochons, écrivant à Mazarin : « Nous avons trois veaux qui sont nourris par six vaches avec force œufs frais. Le premier serait excellent à présent. Nous avons six douzaines de poulets d'Inde, autant de poules et poulets qui sont fort bien nourris et qui seront excellents ; cent moutons ou brebis pour avoir des agneaux de bonne heure. La petite truie d'Inde a fait six cochons dont trois sont morts... Il y aura toute sorte de légumage. »

Canalisant l'immense clientèle de courtisans qui gravitent autour du parrain du roi, Colbert en profite pour placer sa « tribu », en particulier ses frères, prélever sa « quote-part » des rapines financières de Son Éminence, acquérir la noblesse en 1652 et acheter en 1657 la baronnie de Seignelay, la plus considérable du comté d'Auxerre. Véritable « drogué du travail », il écrivait à Mazarin : « Mon inclination est tellement au travail que je reconnais tous les jours en m'examinant en mon dedans, qu'il est impossible que mon esprit puisse soutenir l'oisiveté ou le travail modéré, en sorte que, du jour où ce malheur

m'arrivera dans le cours de ma vie, je n'aie pas six ans à vivre. »
Recommandé au roi par le cardinal, l'homme à la couleuvre, tel est
l'emblème de Colbert, s'emploie à charger l'homme à l'écureuil, l'animal agile que Fouquet a pris pour emblème. Jouant les modestes,
cachant l'ambition qui le dévore, flattant l'orgueil d'un roi qui ne s'y
entend guère en finances, Colbert s'applique à détourner l'attention
sur la fortune de Fouquet pour éviter de faire l'inventaire de celle de
Mazarin. Le surintendant mis à l'ombre, son procès orchestré pour en
faire le bouc émissaire offert sur l'autel de sa gloire, il ne reste plus
à Colbert qu'a prendre progressivement en main les rouages de l'État.
Ministre d'État depuis septembre 1661, il est surintendant des Bâtiments du roi en 1664, contrôleur général des Finances en 1665, secrétaire d'État à la Maison du roi en 1668, secrétaire d'État à la Marine
en 1669. En 1670, il acquiert encore la charge de grand maître des
Mines de France. Réduisant à presque rien les pouvoirs du chancelier,
il contrôle les Eaux-et-Forêts, les Monnaies, les Ponts-et-Chaussées,
la gestion des intendants, la lieutenance générale de police et même
une partie de la diplomatie lorsque son frère Charles, dit Colbert de
Croissy, accède aux Affaires étrangères, en 1679. « Il veut tout pour
lui, pour ses parents et pour son fils », notait l'ambassadeur de Savoie.
Seule la Guerre, chasse gardée du clan Le Tellier-Louvois, lui
échappe. Ministre à tout faire mais constamment demeuré sous le
contrôle du roi, il a su, par sa puissance de travail, élever des idées
banales au rang de « maximes d'ordre ». « Du "commis", écrit Pierre
Goubert, Colbert possède à la fois le caractère subordonné et très
général. Général, puisqu'il s'occupa pratiquement de tout, y compris
des maîtresses et des bâtards. Subordonné, car il ne fut rien sans le
roi, pourtant son complice... mais qui ne lui donna qu'au compte-
gouttes la plénitude de ses titres et de ses fonctions ; subordonné, car
le roi peut toujours ne pas l'écouter et même le contrarier, ce qu'il
fera surtout à partir du moment où il parut l'avoir comblé. »

L'« état au vrai »

Le principal mérite de Colbert, comme plus tard de Poincaré ou
d'Antoine Pinay, est d'avoir su émailler son « programme de réformation » de formules qui fleurent le « bon sens ». « Je crois, écrivait-il,
que l'on demeurera facilement d'accord sur ce principe qu'il n'y a
que l'abondance d'argent dans un État qui fasse la différence de sa
grandeur et de sa puissance [...]. Il n'y a qu'une même quantité d'argent qui roule dans toute l'Europe [...]. On ne peut augmenter l'argent

dans le royaume qu'en même temps que l'on en ôte la même quantité dans les États voisins [...]. Il faut augmenter l'argent dans le commerce public en l'attirant des pays où il vient, en le conservant au-dedans du royaume, empêchant qu'il n'en sorte, et en donnant des moyens aux hommes d'en tirer profit ; il n'y a que le commerce seul et tout ce qui en dépend qui peut produire ce grand effet [...]. Ce royaume a tout généralement en lui-même, si l'on excepte très peu de choses ; mais il n'en est pas de même des États qui lui confinent, et il faut de toute nécessité qu'ils aient recours à nous. »

Acheter peu et vendre beaucoup, dépenser moins et gagner plus, telles sont les bases d'un programme économique et financier dont l'originalité n'est pas le principal mérite. Comme la plupart des hommes de son temps, il pense que l'État, c'est-à-dire le roi, doit être fort ; que pour être fort, il doit être riche ; que la richesse, c'est l'or et l'argent ; que plus le royaume produira ce qu'il achète, plus il s'enrichira et que le grand moteur de l'enrichissement, c'est le travail. Le seul mérite de Colbert est, en fait, d'avoir voulu mettre en application ces principes fort banals, en s'informant beaucoup, en ne négligeant aucun détail et en bataillant contre un roi qui ne limita jamais ses ambitions au montant de ses recettes.

Profitant des années favorables qui ont suivi la paix des Pyrénées, Colbert réussit d'abord à remettre de l'ordre dans les finances publiques. Faisant légèrement baisser les tailles, à la grande satisfaction des paysans, il s'attaque aux dépenses moyennes annuelles qu'il réduit à 66 millions de livres, soit près de moitié moins que pendant les vingt-cinq années antérieures. Le budget est quasiment équilibré et l'intérêt versé aux financiers, qui atteignait 33 % et même 40 % à l'époque de Fouquet, est réduit à 16,6 % et ne dépassera plus 24,5 % pendant le règne de Louis XIV. Ce sont aussi 100 millions de livres qu'il récupère auprès de 4 000 financiers qu'il fait comparaître devant une chambre de justice chargée de rechercher les « abus et malversations commis depuis 1635 » et 8 millions de rentes qu'il annule.

Les nouvelles ressources, il les trouve en augmentant les impôts indirects, en créant le monopole fiscal du tabac, en « redressant » les faux nobles, en s'efforçant de passer avec les fermiers chargés de collecter l'impôt des baux mieux étudiés et en reconstituant les revenus du Domaine, qui passent ainsi de 1 160 000 francs en 1666 à 5 540 000 en 1681. Colbert établit enfin une présentation plus claire des comptes, ouvrant trois registres, l'un pour les prévisions de recettes, le deuxième pour les prévisions de dépenses et le troisième pour les ordonnances des dépenses engagées. Au début de chaque année, le bilan des douze mois précédents, « l'état au vrai », était présenté et soumis à l'examen de la Chambre des comptes et mis à la disposition du souverain, qui pouvait le porter dans sa poche !

En 1681, toutefois, au lendemain de la guerre de Hollande qui a ruiné ses efforts et mis le budget en déséquilibre en doublant les dépenses, il écrit, désabusé, au roi : « À l'égard de la dépense, quoique cela ne me regarde en rien, je supplie seulement Votre Majesté de me permettre de lui dire qu'en guerre et en paix, elle n'a jamais consulté ses finances pour résoudre ses dépenses, ce qui est si extraordinaire qu'assurément il n'y en a point d'exemple. Et si elle voulait bien se représenter et comparer les temps et les années passées depuis vingt ans que j'ai l'honneur de la servir, elle trouverait que, quoique les recettes aient beaucoup augmenté, les dépenses ont excédé de beaucoup les recettes, et peut-être que cela convierait Votre Majesté à modifier et retrancher les excessives, et mettre par ce moyen un peu plus de proportion entre les recettes et les dépenses. »

Le royaume en fiches

Malheureux en finances, Colbert a été plus heureux en statistiques. Héritier de ceux qui pensaient pouvoir écrire le monde en langage mathématique, soucieux de mieux répartir l'impôt, il a voulu mettre le royaume en fiches et encourager la « peuplade ». En septembre 1663, dans son Instruction pour les maîtres des requêtes, commissaires départis pour les provinces, il note que la répartition de la gabelle n'a presque plus de proportion avec le nombre d'habitants et prescrit de recenser méticuleusement la population « afin de pouvoir faire un nouveau régalement de l'impôt, plus juste et proportionné au nombre des habitants ».

Cette enquête aboutit à la confection d'un Atlas des gabelles comportant, pour chaque grenier, le nombre des paroisses, ceux des feux, des gabellants (personnes de plus de huit ans), des laboureurs, des nobles et des ecclésiastiques, avec les ventes de sel de l'année 1664. La plupart des intendants déposent alors de précieux mémoires qui deviennent les outils d'une science du gouvernement. À Paris, à partir de 1670, on dispose des statistiques mensuelles concernant les baptêmes, les mariages et les sépultures.

Améliorés après la mort de Colbert par le duc de Beauvillier, Fénelon et Vauban, qui propose en 1686 une Méthode générale et facile pour faire le dénombrement des peuples, « les nombres, qualités de chaque habitant, professions, caractères et richesses apparentes, état des terres, bois, prés, vignes, bestiaux, fertilité des unes et des autres, augmentation ou diminution des biens, améliorations des biens qu'on peut y faire, et tout cela par des états abrégés, clairs et intelligibles qui ne laissent rien de doute », ces premiers recensements systématiques qui doivent permettre au monarque de « pouvoir de son cabinet parcourir lui-même en une heure de temps l'état présent et passé d'un grand Royaume » aboutissent au total de 19 094 146 habitants en 1707 sur un peu moins de 500 000 kilomètres carrés, un dénombrement qui n'est pas fondamentalement critiqué par les historiens démographes d'aujourd'hui.

Persuadé que la population est une richesse que « plus le royaume est peuplé, plus il y a de contribuables, plus la consommation est grande et plus le roi tire d'argent », Colbert veut freiner le célibat, concéder des exemptions temporaires de tailles aux jeunes gens qui se marient avant vingt et un ans, réduire le nombre des ecclésiastiques et interdire l'émigration, qu'il considère comme une rupture du contrat que « les sujets contractent à leur naissance envers le souverain » et qui « ne peut être effacé que de son consentement ».

Toutefois, il encourage ou ordonne l'émigration au Canada en y envoyant les filles de l'Hôpital général de Paris, surtout des orphelines du roi, sans doute aussi quelques prostituées. Entre 1660 et 1669, 1 719 personnes débarquent ainsi en Nouvelle-France, originaires surtout de l'Ouest, du Perche en particulier, qui a fourni au moins 238 départs. Grâce à l'intendant Jean Talon, qui adresse à Colbert « un rôle exact de tous les habitants de la colonie », on sait ainsi que la population de la colonie s'élevait en 1685 à 12 373 habitants, dont 1 443 Indiens sédentarisés, qu'on comptait quelque 1 997 fusils pour 1 990 maisons, soit un fusil par famille, qu'il y avait un cheval pour 10 habitants, un bovin pour une personne, un porc pour 1,42 habitant et un mouton pour 3 habitants, qu'il y avait 112 ecclésiastiques et 83 religieuses, soit environ un prêtre pour 100 habitants !

Ces hommes qu'il veut plus nombreux et plus reproducteurs, Colbert les veut surtout moins oisifs. Traquant les « fainéants » et condamnant l'inactivité des rentiers, Colbert veut faire de tous les mendiants des ouvriers et oblige les administrateurs de l'Hôpital général « à faire travailler les gueux dans les savonneries ». Pensant qu'il n'y a rien qui entretienne plus la fainéantise que « ces aumônes publiques, qui se font presque sans cause et sans aucune connaissance de nécessité », il prie les moines de diviser ce qu'ils donnaient « moitié en pain et moitié en laine, à condition qu'ils la rapportent fabriquée en bas », pourchasse les faux pèlerins et tente d'attirer l'argent des rentiers vers les manufactures, persuadé que le développement de l'industrie était, plus que l'agriculture, la clef de la puissance.

Le « grand dessein »

Réglementer, protéger, produire, notamment les produits de luxe, exporter, si possible sur des navires français, telles sont les intentions du « grand dessein » de Colbert. Le bulletin de victoire qu'il dresse en 1669 apparaît spectaculaire : « État des manufactures — Serges de Londres, 120 métiers à Autun, Auxerre, Gournay, augmenteront et se perfectionneront tous les jours. Bas d'Angleterre, établis en plus de 30 villes ou bourgs, 6 000 métiers. Points de France, idem, 6 000 métiers. Draps, à Abbeville, Dieppe, Fécamp, Rouen, Sedan, Carcassonne. Cuivre jaune, à Bellecombre ou à la Ferté-Alais. Canons de fer, armes, fer-blanc et toutes sortes de manufactures de fer qui venait de Biscaye et de Suède, en Nivernais et Dauphiné. Salpêtres, poudres et mèches, partout. Toiles de Hollande, à Moret, Laval, Louviers et Le Bec. Toiles à voile, à Vienne. Grosses ancres, à Vienne et à Rochefort. Crics, en Nivernais [...]. Glaces de miroirs, à Paris, et Cherbourg, commencent à en envoyer dans les pays étrangers [...]. Recherches des mines, de toutes parts, en Languedoc, Rouergue, Foix, Roussillon, Auvergne, Normandie. Chanvres, achetés dans toutes les provinces au lieu de les prendre à Riga et en Prusse. Moulins à soie, établis dans les Pyrénées, Auvergne, Dauphiné et Provence. Fonderies de fonte, établies à Lyon, Toulon et Rochefort. Grands ateliers de la marine, établis à Toulon, Rochefort, Brest, Le Havre et Dunkerque. Sucreries établies à Bordeaux, La Rochelle, Nantes, Rouen, Dieppe et Dunkerque. Bâtiments — Eaux à Versailles, recherches. Eaux pour Saint-Germain, grande terrasse à achever, jardins, idem. Le Louvre, à continuer [...]. Arc de triomphe pour les conquêtes de terre. Observatoire pour les cieux. Grandeur et magnificence. »

Si l'action de Colbert s'inscrit dans une tradition qu'il prolonge et précise, nul doute qu'il donne en moins de dix ans une impulsion décisive dont les effets se poursuivront jusqu'en 1789. Quand Louis XIV visite les Gobelins, les ateliers de Beauvais, d'Abbeville, de Lille et les chantiers de Dunkerque, c'est bien pour manifester la volonté de l'État de prendre en main l'essor économique de la nation. Dans un pays où l'opinion se révèle peu favorable à l'industrie, dont les profits paraissent aléatoires aux « épargnants », le « lobby » industriel ne peut être dirigé que par l'État. Dénoncé aujourd'hui par la vague libérale comme la source du « mal » français, l'interventionnisme public était en fait justifié par le déficit de l'initiative privée. Évoquant les « capitalistes » lyonnais, Colbert écrivait : « Les habitants de cette ville feraient bien de considérer les faveurs dont leur industrie est l'objet comme des béquilles à l'aide desquelles ils devraient se mettre en mesure d'apprendre à marcher le plus tôt possible, et que mon intention est de leur retirer ensuite. »

Soutenir l'activité industrielle, c'est prendre en charge les frais de construction des bâtiments, passer des commandes, aider à la constitution de stocks, participer au capital, établir des tarifs protecteurs aux frontières, réglementer l'apprentissage et l'accès à la maîtrise pour améliorer la compétence des fabricants, encourager l'innovation technique, instaurer des droits de marque pour assurer la qualité indispensable en vue des exportations — comme le célèbre édit de 1669 sur la fabrication des draps qui, en pas moins de 317 articles, détermine la largeur, la longueur et la qualité des étoffes.

Avant-gardes des bataillons de l'industrie, les manufactures ont été l'objet de toutes les attentions. Les manufactures royales, des Gobelins ou la Savonnerie, considérées comme des établissements modèles, sont réorganisées. Employant 200 personnes, les Gobelins produisent bientôt la suite de tapisseries consacrées à « L'Histoire du roi » d'après des dessins et des cartons de Van der Meulen et de Charles Le Brun, son directeur. En août 1664, un édit crée la manufacture royale de tapisseries de Beauvais. Le 23 octobre 1665, le roi fait venir de Hollande Van Robais et 50 ouvriers qui établissent à Abbeville la manufacture de drap, « façon Hollande et Espagne ». En 1665, Nicolas Dunoyer, qui fait partie de la parenté de Colbert, bénéficie d'un privilège de vingt ans pour fonder la manufacture des glaces, futur Saint-Gobain, au bénéfice de laquelle sont débauchés des ouvriers vénitiens qui, fort sensibles au charme des Parisiennes, ne semblent plus pressés de ramener à Paris leurs femmes et leurs enfants.

Ces encouragements, qu'on peut évaluer à 16 millions de livres en vingt ans, n'ont pas été vains. La production lainière connaît une belle croissance des années 1660 aux années 1690. Les draps du Languedoc vont bientôt s'exporter dans tout le bassin méditerranéen. Nîmes voit décupler le nombre de ses moulins à soie entre 1661 et 1681, et les fabriques lyonnaises triplent leurs activités de 1661 à 1690, donnant de l'ouvrage de Saint-Chamond à Saint-Étienne et brisant le monopole italien, notamment de Milan.

Produire n'est pas tout ; il faut vendre. Rassemblant, le premier, des idées jusqu'alors diffuses, Colbert inaugure une véritable politique de communications. Du Levant au Ponant, il imagine un système unifié de relations par eaux qui prend corps avec le canal du Midi. C'est la « route royale » à destination des grands ports qui est entretenue. C'est la marine surtout qui est l'objet de toutes les sollicitudes. De 1664 à 1704, on double le nombre des navires de jauge supérieure à 100 tonneaux et Toulon, Marseille, Rochefort, Lorient, Brest, Le Havre et Dunkerque ne désarment pas. Surtout, pour stimuler les exportations, Colbert crée, en 1664, une compagnie des Indes orientales pour faire pièce aux compagnies hollandaises et anglaises. Installée à Lorient, cette compagnie au capital en partie souscrit par le roi se voit accorder pour cinquante ans le monopole de la navigation et du négoce « depuis le cap de Bonne-Espérance jusque dans toutes les Indes et mers orientales, et depuis le détroit de Magellan ou Le Maire dans toutes les mers du Sud ». Cette même année, la Compagnie des Indes occidentales reçoit le monopole du commerce avec les îles à sucre d'Amérique. En 1669, la Compagnie du Nord a pour vocation d'assurer le trafic dans la Baltique et, en 1670, la Compagnie du Levant est créée pour transporter aux Échelles les produits de nos manufactures.

En 1670 encore, entrevoyant les potentialités du commerce colonial, Colbert rattache les possessions outre-mer au secrétariat d'État à la Marine. En 1674, François Martin, un excellent négociateur, obtient d'un prince hindou la concession du futur Pondichéry. S'y ajouteront au cours du règne de Louis XIV Chandernagor et Calicut. En 1682, René Robert Cavelier de La Salle, ancien novice jésuite, avide de gloire et d'argent, prend possession de tout le territoire de la vallée du Mississippi, depuis les Grands Lacs jusqu'à l'embouchure, et baptise « Louisiane » ce territoire sur lequel se ruent les « coureux de bois ». La reprise en main des Antilles, occupées depuis 1635, relance l'économie sucrière. Vers 1664, 8 000 Blancs vivaient à la Martinique et à la Guadeloupe. On en compte près de 12 000 à la fin du règne tandis que, dans la partie française de Saint-Domingue, la culture du tabac prospère.

Ces efforts sont d'autant plus émouvants qu'ils se heurtent à l'indifférence d'une France rétive occupée, pour l'essentiel, à assurer les récoltes. Dans le domaine des Finances, la guerre de Hollande compromet, à partir de 1672, les efforts entrepris. Les compagnies de commerce, boudées par les capitaux privés, périclitent ou disparaissent dès que l'aide de l'État se fait plus chiche. La Compagnie des Indes occidentales se dissout dès 1674 ; celle du Nord disparaît en 1684 ; celle du Levant est liquidée en 1690. À Saint-Gobain, les premières fabrications ne sont pas couronnées de succès. Même les Gobelins manquent de sombrer. En fait, les Français entreprenants, les Havrais, les Malouins, les Nantais, les Bordelais ou les Marseillais savaient parfaitement ce qu'ils devaient faire pour maintenir ou accroître leurs revenus.

D'autant plus que l'État, toujours à court, avait sans cesse davantage besoin d'eux pour financer ses armées car la politique commerciale de Colbert, inaugurée par des taxes protectrices sur les produits transportés par les navires hollandais, menait tout droit à la guerre avec les Provinces-Unies.

Dès 1668, on pouvait lire dans un mémoire anonyme : « M. Colbert ne prend pas garde qu'en voulant mettre les Français en état de se pouvoir passer de tous les autres peuples, il les conduit à faire la même chose de leur côté, car il est certain qu'ils ont pris une autre route pour aller chercher ailleurs la plupart des choses dont ils se venaient fournir dans nos provinces. » Montrant que la diversité des ressources selon les pays, voulue par Dieu, avait pour conséquence évidente la liberté du commerce, l'auteur poursuivait : « Cela même doit nous faire connaître que la divine Providence n'a établi une telle diversité que pour obliger les hommes par le besoin mutuel qu'ils ont les uns les autres à s'entrecommuniquer toutes les choses qui leur sont nécessaires, et que ce lien de la société civile n'est pas moins ancien que le monde. »

Comme l'écrit, trop durement sans doute, Pierre Goubert : « Hâtivement installée, ne tenant souvent qu'à coup de subventions et d'insistante persuasion, incapable de s'opposer à de trop puissants rivaux, ignorant l'agriculture, ignorant la conjoncture, ignorant les habitudes économiques, financières et peu maritimes des Français, l'œuvre de Colbert, à quelques exceptions près, tombait en porte à faux et était à demi condamnée avant que les dépenses militaires ne viennent l'achever. Dans l'immédiat, Colbert a enrichi surtout quelques affairistes et lui-même, et donné au roi les premiers moyens d'être vainqueur. Mais il a posé des jalons, indiqué des voies qui furent reprises en des temps meilleurs, aidé à réussir de beaux meubles, de belles tentures et de beaux vaisseaux, dont quelques-uns ne furent pas coulés. »

Le « ministre de l'image »

« Surintendant et ordonnateur général des bâtiments, arts, tapisseries et manufactures », Colbert fut aussi et peut-être surtout un véritable « ministre de l'image », le grand prêtre du culte royal chargé de mobiliser les lettres, les sciences et les arts au service du Roi-Soleil.

Posant les bases d'une véritable politique scientifique, il fonde en 1666 l'Académie des sciences et attire à Paris par des pensions élevées les savants étrangers, comme le Hollandais Christiaan Huygens, qui obtient une bourse de 6 000 livres. Construit par Claude Perrault de 1667 à 1672, l'observatoire de Paris a pour premier directeur l'illustre astronome italien Jean-Dominique Cassini, auteur en 1676 d'une spectaculaire *Carte de la Lune*, restée sans rivale jusqu'à l'apparition de la photographie.

Quand, sous la Régence, l'ambassadeur ottoman Mehmed Efendi s'émerveillera devant le matériel accumulé à l'Observatoire, les Français lui diront que Louis XIV, « qui connaissait par lui-même le prix de la science, comblait de bienfaits ceux qui inventaient quelque nouvelle machine et que, lorsqu'on lui en présentait, il les faisait mettre dans l'Observatoire pour l'usage des étudiants ».

Colbert favorise également la création du *Journal des Savants*, dont le premier numéro date du 5 janvier 1665 et qui devient un prestigieux hebdomadaire de vulgarisation scientifique.

Observation de l'espace terrestre et maritime, réalisation des cartes topographiques, mesure d'un degré de méridien entre Paris et Amiens, adoption du principe d'une triangulation géodésique d'ensemble comme canevas d'une carte générale du royaume, missions scientifiques au Danemark, en Acadie, en Guyane, au Cap-Vert, aux Antilles, aux îles de Gorée et San Thomé, autant d'enquêtes et d'explorations qui ont aussi pour ambition de mieux assurer l'emprise du pouvoir sur le royaume, édifier des fortifications, construire des villes, des canaux, des routes et des ponts.

Installés en 1710 dans la Grande Galerie du Louvre, les plans-reliefs qui reproduisent au 1/600 les principales villes fortifiées du royaume avec leur environnement topographique en sont la plus spectaculaire des illustrations.

Ce sont aussi les artistes qui deviennent les prêtres talentueux du culte royal. Tandis que Charles Le Brun, nommé premier peintre du roi en 1662 et chancelier à vie de l'Académie royale de peinture et de sculpture, joue le rôle de metteur en scène du spectacle monarchique, Jean Chapelain, un des premiers membres de l'Académie française fondée par Richelieu en 1635, auteur alors en renom, est chargé de trouver des « trompettes pour les vertus du roi ». Pierre Corneille, « premier poète dramatique du monde », reçoit une pension de 800 livres. Molière, « excellent poète comique », 1 000 livres, Racine, encore débutant, 800 livres, François Eudes de Mézeray, auteur d'une monumentale *Histoire de France*, 4 000 livres, et Chapelain lui-même,

« le plus grand poète français qui ait jamais existé, et du plus solide jugement », 3 000 livres !

À partir de 1671, l'Académie française, chargée de définir les règles de la langue et de l'orthographe, organise aussi un concours pour le meilleur panégyrique du roi, sur un sujet différent chaque année.

Reste à s'interroger sur les perversités inhérentes à l'« État culturel ». En gagnant l'indépendance matérielle, l'écrivain a-t-il perdu la liberté de pensée ? On pourrait le croire à entendre les éloges trop appuyés que Molière glisse dans ses pièces, ou les *Épîtres* que Boileau consacre aux largesses du monarque à partir du moment où il bénéficie de ses « gratifications ».

Ce serait juger avec nos propres valeurs et notre sensibilité des hommes pour qui servir le roi « Très-Chrétien » était la fin suprême de l'art. Les chefs-d'œuvre de Racine et de Molière, l'*Art poétique* de Boileau, les *Maximes* de La Rochefoucauld, les *Oraisons funèbres* de Bossuet, les *Lettres* de Mme de Sévigné, les tableaux de Le Brun, les musiques de Lully traduisent, plus que la flagornerie, la conscience de vivre une grande époque et le sentiment de servir un grand roi.

En fait, la culture « classique », qui est acceptation de règles et de disciplines esthétiques, a fait preuve de singulières audaces. Culte de la nature humaine et de la vérité, conjugaison de l'art et de la morale, recherche dans l'Antiquité d'un idéal d'harmonie et de sagesse, autant de « contraintes » librement acceptées. Dans leur recherche de l'homme, du héros et du tragique, ces écrivains étaient fatalement amenés à croiser le monarque, figure singulière et exemplaire de l'humanité. Certes, en subventionnant des auteurs et des artistes qui n'étaient pas tous conformistes, Louis XIV n'a pas fait œuvre désintéressée. Mais en servant sa gloire, il a en même temps assuré le rayonnement de la culture française en Europe. Le plus fructueux, sans doute, des investissements.

Le spectacle de la guerre

*L*e 26 août 1715, à quelques jours de sa mort, Louis XIV convoque son arrière-petit-fils le dauphin et lui dit : « Mignon, vous allez être un grand-roi, mais tout votre bonheur dépendra d'être soumis à Dieu et du soin que vous aurez de soulager vos peuples. Il faut pour cela que vous évitiez autant que vous le pourrez de faire la guerre : c'est la ruine des peuples. Ne suivez pas le mauvais exemple que je vous ai donné sur cela : j'ai souvent compris la guerre trop légèrement et l'ai soutenue par vanité. »

Cette confession partiellement soufflée par un confesseur dévot à un roi diminué masque le fait que, si la guerre a bien occupé la majeure partie du règne, la « culture de guerre », qu'il est difficile de juger à l'aune de nos propres valeurs, était au siècle de Louis XIV partagée par l'ensemble des princes européens.

La « culture de guerre »

« Sire, dit le renard, vous êtes trop bon roi. Vos scrupules font voir trop de délicatesses. Eh bien, manger mouton, canaille, sotte espèce, est-ce un péché ? Non, non, vous leur fîtes seigneur en les croquant, beaucoup d'honneur. » Cette fable de La Fontaine illustre sans doute mieux que tout la « culture de guerre », une « culture » que partagent tous les souverains européens au siècle de Louis XIV.

Si Louis XIV a été avide de gloire et de conquêtes, il ne l'a pas été plus que les autres, contrairement à ce qu'affirme l'historiographie traditionnelle. S'il a aimé la guerre, c'est qu'à l'époque où il vivait la gloire ne pouvait être que le fruit de la victoire. Comme l'écrit Molière,

Ce sont faits inouïs, grand Roi, que tes victoires !
L'avenir aura peine à les bien concevoir ;
Et de nos vieux héros les pompeuses victoires
Ne nous ont point chanté ce que tu nous fais voir.

Si le règne personnel de Louis XIV, de 1661 à 1715, a compté 29 années de guerre, à la même époque, l'Angleterre en a connu 24, la Suède, 23, l'Espagne, 34, l'Autriche, 36, l'Empire ottoman, 37 et la Pologne, 42.

Surtout, ayant été élevé pour être guerrier, Louis XIV n'a pas été un général de parade. Jusqu'à l'âge de cinquante-cinq ans, il a payé de sa personne, partageant les dangers avec ses hommes, passant la nuit au bivouac, s'exposant dans les tranchées, convaincu que sa présence élevait le moral des combattants et servait son prestige personnel. Comme l'a noté François Bluche, pendant les sept années de la guerre de Hollande, il passera 647 jours avec ses soldats, dont 166 pendant la seule année 1673. « Pour affirmer le repos de ses peuples, s'écrie cette année-là l'académicien Fléchier, il va combattre lui-même [...]. Il croit que c'est une justice qu'il doit à ses sujets, que de leur montrer le chemin de l'honneur, de reconnaître leur valeur par lui-même, et de récompenser le mérite après en avoir été le témoin. Il sait que les yeux du prince répandent je ne sais quelle influence de courage et d'ardeur dans ses armées, et que ces grands corps sont d'autant plus forts et agissants qu'ils reçoivent de plus près les impressions de leurs mouvements et de leur force. » « Il est certain, écrit encore Saint-Simon lors du siège de Namur en 1692, que sans la présence du Roi, dont la vigilance était l'âme du siège, et qui, sans l'exiger, faisait faire l'impossible, tant le désir de lui plaire et de se distinguer était extrême, on n'en serait jamais venu à bout. »

Sous Louis XIV, l'impôt du sang que devait verser l'aristocratie pour justifier son rang a été en fait versé plus que jamais. À Versailles, les rubans couvrent souvent des béquilles.

Au temps de la « réduction à l'obéissance » et de la « maxime de l'ordre », la guerre ne peut plus se limiter aux actions de bravoure et aux batailles désordonnées qu'affectionnaient autrefois les *bellatores* en quête de leur propre gloire. Elle devient celle d'un « roi-cerveau » qui, dans le secret de son conseil, entouré de cartes et de plans, de toises et de compas, décide des stratégies et des actions.

C'est la raison pour laquelle la guerre de siège est devenue au siècle de Louis XIV la guerre par excellence, celle où se manifeste la science des ingénieurs, celle où le roi peut manifester sa présence avec éclat, installé le plus souvent sur une position située en hauteur de laquelle il donne l'ordre d'assaut. « Les sièges me plaisent plus que les autres », a confié dans ses *Mémoires* Louis XIV, qui peut compter sur le talent de Vauban pour amener les places à reddition avec une rapidité qui étonna les contemporains. Maastricht prise en treize jours, Gand surtout prise en six jours, autant de hauts faits d'armes choisis par Charles Le Brun pour illustrer le plafond de la galerie des Glaces à Versailles, autant de symboles d'une monarchie capable de mobiliser à son service une redoutable puissance de feu et de transformer les « malcontents » du début du siècle en « bras » promis à une mort anonyme, autant d'occasions de célébrer des *Te Deum* destinés à insérer la gloire du roi dans les desseins de Dieu. Le 25 août 1673, lors d'un discours à l'Académie, Paul Tallemant déclare : « Louis est la tête qui fait mouvoir tant de bras [...]. Nouveau Jupiter, il lance la foudre, et tous ses Lieutenants, comme autant de bras, font sentir les effets de sa colère [...]. »

Instruments privilégiés de la gloire du prince, les armées ont fait l'objet de toutes les attentions. Tandis que le « clan » Colbert monopolisait les finances, l'économie et les arts, le « clan » Le Tellier-Louvois prenait la guerre en main. Nommé au secrétariat à la Guerre en 1643, Michel Le Tellier, lointain descendant d'un paysan de Chaville, est un travailleur discret, prudent et loyal. Son fils, Louvois, soumis à un dur apprentissage dans les bureaux de son père, lui succède en 1677. Travailleur infatigable, en même temps homme de terrain, brutal et parfois cynique, il mourra à la tâche à cinquante-deux ans. Quand le duc de Luxembourg lui décrit, pendant la guerre de Hollande, la misère des populations, il répond : « Je vous sais le plus mauvais gré du monde de m'avoir si bien instruit de toutes les misères de la Hollande, parce que j'ai été touché au dernier point, et s'il y avait ici des casuistes, je les consulterais pour savoir si je puis, en conscience, continuer à faire une campagne dont l'unique objet est la désolation de mon prochain, et s'ils me conseillaient de la quitter, je m'en retournerais à Paris. Par bonheur pour moi, il n'y a pas de casuistes à la suite de l'armée... » ! À sa mort, en 1691, son fils, le marquis de Barbezieux, lui succédera, assurant ainsi plus d'un demi-siècle de continuité familiale à l'administration de la guerre.

Au lendemain de la paix des Pyrénées, en 1659, l'armée royale n'atteignait pas 50 000 hommes. On en compte 120 000 en 1672, près

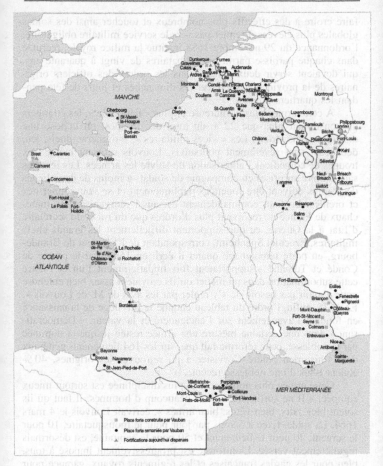

Les travaux de fortification de Vauban.

de 400 000 en 1693. Il faudra attendre la levée en masse de 1793 pour retrouver de tels effectifs. Si le racolage les jours de marché reste le procédé de recrutement le plus courant, suscitant de lourds abus, des fausses promesses aux enrôlements forcés de miséreux et de vagabonds, l'ordonnance de 1667 punit sévèrement les passe-volants, ces faux soldats que les capitaines présentaient lors des « montres » pour faire croire à des effectifs plus nombreux et toucher ainsi des soldes globales plus élevées. Premier pas vers le service militaire obligatoire, l'ordonnance du 29 novembre 1688 institue la milice royale, recrutée dans chaque paroisse parmi les célibataires de vingt à quarante ans, qui devaient servir deux années sous les ordres des officiers originaires de la province et s'exercer les dimanches et jours de fête pendant les quartiers d'hiver.

À cette armée plus nombreuse et plus « nationale », les étrangers ne constituant plus que 22 % du total des troupes, on impose une discipline plus stricte. Les « vices militaires », ivrognerie, duels, jeu, débauche, sont sévèrement poursuivis, Louvois refusant même aux troupes de comédiens l'autorisation de suivre les armées. Les femmes sans emploi surprises en compagnie de soldats à moins de deux lieues des camps doivent être fouettées publiquement et se voir couper nez et oreilles. Le haut commandement est aussi réorganisé. Les maréchaux de France ne reçoivent plus d'ordres que du roi et du secrétaire d'État à la Guerre, ce que supportent difficilement les grands chefs militaires. Ezechiel Spanheim, correspondant de l'Électeur de Brandebourg, en porte témoignage quand il écrit en 1690 que le prince de Condé et Turenne « supportaient fort impatiemment l'un et l'autre cette subordination dans un métier qu'ils croyaient assez bien entendre pour n'avoir pas besoin de s'y régler par les avis de M. de Louvois ». En 1675, enfin, l'ordre du tableau entame le privilège de la naissance en fondant l'avancement sur l'ancienneté et la valeur. « Démocratisant » dans une certaine mesure une armée restée jusque-là dominée par la noblesse, cette réforme fait que, sur les 164 lieutenants généraux dont l'historien André Corvisier a pu retrouver les origines, 40 % étaient issus d'une noblesse récente.

Cette armée plus nombreuse et plus disciplinée est surtout mieux équipée. « Il ne suffit pas d'avoir beaucoup d'hommes, il faut qu'ils soient bien faits, bien vêtus, bien armés », écrivait Louvois le 4 mars 1664. La solde, fixée à 5 sous par jour pour le mousquetaire, 10 pour le sergent, 20 pour le lieutenant et 50 pour le capitaine, est désormais régulièrement versée. L'uniforme est progressivement imposé à tous, bleu pour les gardes françaises et les régiments royaux, garance pour les Suisses et gris-blanc pour le reste de l'infanterie. Les intendants deviennent les principaux responsables des fournitures aux troupes et constituent dès le temps de paix des magasins de vivres et de munitions à proximité des frontières. À partir de 1668, on commence à construire des casernes et des hôpitaux militaires pour les mutilés de guerre. Aux Invalides, qui ouvrent en 1674, chaque soldat recevait par jour 700 grammes de pain, une livre de viande et un quart de vin.

Enfin, techniciens et entrepreneurs sont mobilisés pour améliorer l'efficacité des armes. La grenade, très en vogue, est perfectionnée. L'usage de la baïonnette, fabriquée à l'origine à Bayonne, est généralisé. Le fusil à pierre supplante le mousquet et en 1684 est créé le premier régiment d'artillerie, le Royal Bombardiers. Surtout, en quelques années, Colbert constitue une marine de guerre qui, en 1683, dépasse de quarante-cinq unités la Royal Navy. À Brest, Rochefort et Toulon, les bassins servent de ports d'attache aux flottes du Ponant et aux galères du Levant tandis que les arsenaux construisent les bâtiments que copient bientôt les Anglais. Le Soleil Royal, décoré par Le Brun lui-même, doit affirmer sur les mers la gloire de Louis le Grand.

Louis le Grand

Affirmer hautement la prééminence de la couronne de France, s'imposer comme arbitre international, exiger des excuses du roi d'Angleterre, du Habsbourg de Madrid ou du pape, disputer à l'empereur la gloire de sauver la chrétienté contre les Turcs, occuper la Lorraine sans combat pour punir le duc de « flirter » avec l'Autriche, montrer la nouvelle flotte de guerre dans les Caraïbes, tels sont les gestes de prestige qui attirent l'attention sur « la grande comète qui vient de se lever sur l'Europe. »

Une comète qui, en 1667, trouve l'occasion de « s'amuser à prendre la Flandre », comme l'écrit la marquise de Sévigné. Au lendemain de la mort de son beau-père, le roi d'Espagne Philippe IV, Louis XIV fait publier un *Traité des droits de la Reine* pour exiger une partie de l'héritage espagnol. D'une part, la dot promise en 1659 au traité des Pyrénées pour dédommager Marie-Thérèse d'avoir renoncé à la succession d'Espagne n'a pas été payée. De l'autre, les juristes du roi ont découvert en 1662 une coutume du Brabant selon laquelle, en cas de mariages successifs, l'héritage va aux enfants du premier lit. Dès lors, la reine de France, fille du premier mariage de Philippe IV, devrait hériter du Brabant et des provinces voisines au détriment de Charles II, issu du second lit du roi défunt. C'est, comme autrefois pour la loi salique, étendre abusivement une clause de droit privé aux affaires internationales. « Comme Roi, peut on lire dans le *Traité des droits de la Reine*, [Louis] se sent obligé d'empêcher cette injustice ; comme mari, de s'opposer à cette usurpation et, comme père, d'assurer ce patrimoine à son fils. »

En trois mois d'une brève campagne qui s'ouvre en mai 1667, Charleroi, Tournai, Douai, Cambrai, Lille, Audenarde, Alost sont enlevées par un roi hâlé et aminci qui met quelquefois une demi-heure devant un miroir à arranger sa moustache avec de la cire. Le 2 mai 1668, le traité d'Aix-la-Chapelle donne à la France une douzaine de villes situées principalement en Flandre, Lille, Bergues, Furnes, Armentières, Courtrai, Menin, Douai, Tournai, Audenarde, Ath, Binche, Charleroi. C'est exciter l'inquiétude des puissances maritimes, qui se réconcilient pour s'opposer aux « actes de brigandage » de celui que les pamphlets et les libelles accusent de « rendre la société humaine aussi dangereuse que celle des lions et des tigres ».

En signant avec l'Angleterre et la Suède un traité d'alliance pour s'opposer aux prétentions de la France, les Provinces-Unies ont offert à Louis XIV et à Colbert l'occasion dont ils rêvaient de châtier l'insolence des marchands républicains d'Amsterdam, une insolence que résume en ces termes une médaille de propagande française : « Dès que les Hollandais se virent en état de se passer des secours de la France, ils songèrent à tourner leurs forces contre elle. Ils excitèrent la jalousie des puissances voisines, et conclurent avec l'Angleterre et la Suède le fameux traité connu sous le nom de Triple-Alliance. Alors, sans aucun égard à ce qui avait été réglé avec eux en 1662 touchant le commerce et la navigation, ils défendirent l'entrée de plusieurs marchandises de France, ou les chargèrent d'impôts extraordinaires. Ils osèrent même prendre sur des monuments publics les titres superbes d'arbitres des souverains, de défenseurs des lois, de réformateurs de la religion, de maîtres de la mer ; et il n'y avait point d'occasion où ils ne donnassent au roi des sujets particuliers de mécontentement. »

En fait, tout alors « prédestine » à la guerre entre la France et les Provinces-Unies : la volonté de Colbert d'abattre la première puissance économique de l'Europe et de détourner au profit du royaume le négoce international ; l'irritation d'un roi constamment stigmatisé par les gazetiers d'Amsterdam. L'hostilité du « Très-Chrétien » à ce qui est devenu le bastion du calvinisme. L'orgueilleuse assurance de remporter un succès facile.

Ouverte en 1672 par le brillant passage du Rhin et la reddition en vingt-deux jours de quarante villes, dont Utrecht, la guerre s'avère en fait plus difficile que Colbert et le roi l'avaient imaginé. En ouvrant les digues de Muiden, les Hollandais sauvent Amsterdam, transformée en île. En renversant le modéré Jean de Witt et en élisant stathouder Guillaume d'Orange, ils se donnent pour chef un jeune prince de vingt-deux ans, passionnément patriote, calviniste convaincu et résolument antifrançais. À partir de 1673, presque toute l'Europe se coalise contre la France, qui a définitivement perdu l'alliance des princes « hérétiques » sur laquelle, depuis François Ier, s'étaient appuyés

Valois et Bourbons. La guerre éclair devient alors une guerre d'usure. Turenne bouscule les Impériaux de Montecuccoli mais est tué par un boulet à Sasbach le 27 juillet 1675. Condé sauve l'Alsace menacée d'invasion mais se retire en son château de Chantilly l'année suivante. Pour arracher une paix acceptable, Louis XIV doit frapper un grand coup. En avril 1676, près d'Agosta, en Sicile, la flotte commandée par Duquesne bat l'escadre hollandaise du célèbre Ruyter, blessé mortellement pendant la bataille. Le 12 mars 1678, la prise de Gand, au prix de 40 morts seulement, amène les Hollandais à accepter une paix dont les Espagnols font les frais. Signés en 1678 et 1679, les traités de Nimègue donnent à la France — qui rétrocède Charleroi, Binche, Audenarde, Ath et Courtrai —, la Franche-Comté, Aire et Saint-Omer, Cambrai, Cassel et Ypres, Bouchain, Valenciennes, Condé et Maubeuge. Ainsi, la frontière du Nord, jusque-là discontinue, tend à devenir une ligne que Vauban s'emploie à transformer en « frontière de fer » pour défendre la route de Paris, trop proche des possessions des Habsbourg. Dans un célèbre mémoire daté du 23 novembre 1678, celui qui, dès 1673, avait invité le roi à « faire son pré carré », propose d'installer deux lignes de places fortes qui se soutiendraient mutuellement, « à l'imitation des ordres de bataille », ajoutant que si le roi les avait eues, il aurait pu conquérir le reste des Pays-Bas.

Même si la Ville de Paris décerne au roi le titre de Grand, désormais inscrit sur les monuments, les monnaies et les médailles, même si l'Europe paraît désormais vivre à l'heure française, même si Louis obtient des promesses de voix en Allemagne en cas d'élection impériale, même si ce conflit de six ans a épuisé les finances et brisé l'expansion des Provinces-Unies, la guerre de Hollande semble bien marquer la fin de la « bonne fortune ». À l'issue d'une guerre coûteuse et difficile, Louis le Grand n'a pu vaincre une Hollande qui n'a rien perdu de son territoire et a même obtenu que soit abrogé le tarif douanier français de 1667. Louis XIV semblait alors parvenu « au comble de la gloire », mais il avait sans doute commis sa première erreur.

Le repos du guerrier

Pendant les vingt premières années de son règne, Louis, devenu Grand, a enlevé les places comme il a conquis les cœurs et bousculé les corps. L'homme qui a libéré son autorité des résistances intérieures et des oppositions extérieures a usé de sa puissance de séduction comme Jupiter, multipliant les amours comme les bâtards, qui, tous nés du sexe de l'étalon royal, seront princes et légitimés. Des quatre

FAMILLES LÉGITIME ET ILLÉGITIME DE LOUIS XIV

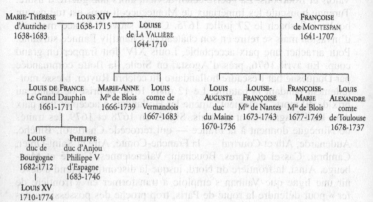

enfants de Louise de La Vallière, pour laquelle il avait organisé notamment en 1664 la fête versaillaise des Plaisirs de l'île enchantée, deux survécurent. Mlle de Blois, née en 1666, légitimée par des lettres patentes de 1667, épousa Louis-Armand de Bourbon, prince de Conti, le neveu du Grand Condé. Le comte de Vermandois, né en 1667, fut fait amiral de France. Des huit enfants que Mme de Montespan, l'éblouissante Françoise Athénaïs de Rochechouart, donna au roi, quatre atteignirent l'âge adulte. Trois furent mariés dans la maison de France, Louis Auguste, duc du Maine, devint grand maître de l'artillerie de France. Françoise-Marie de Bourbon, dite Mlle de Blois, épousa Philippe II d'Orléans, le futur régent. Louis Alexandre, comte de Toulouse, commanda la flotte royale en 1704.

Les historiens, qui pardonnent tout à Louis XIV, citent toujours la « confession » qu'il rédigea pour son fils : « J'aurais pu sans doute, avoue-t-il, me passer de vous entretenir de cet attachement dont l'exemple n'est pas bon à suivre. Mais, après avoir tiré plusieurs instructions des manquements que j'ai remarqués dans les autres, je n'ai pas voulu vous priver de celles que vous pouviez tirer des miens propres. Je vous dirai premièrement que comme le prince devrait toujours être un parfait modèle de vertu, il serait bon qu'il se garantît absolument des faiblesses communes au reste des hommes, d'autant plus qu'il est assuré qu'elles ne sauraient demeurer cachées. » Sachant toutefois que les élans du corps sont difficilement maîtrisables, il faut, ajoute-t-il, que « le temps que nous donnons à notre amour ne soit jamais pris au préjudice de nos affaires, parce que notre premier objet doit toujours être la conservation de notre gloire et de notre autorité [...], qu'en abandonnant notre cœur, nous demeurions maître de notre esprit ; que nous séparions les tendresses d'amant d'avec les résolutions du souverain ; et que la beauté qui fait nos plaisirs n'ait jamais la liberté de nous parler de nos affaires, ni des gens qui nous servent ».

Ernest Lavisse, qui pensait que l'histoire des amours de Louis XIV révélait, autant que l'histoire politique, l'universelle soumission servile, écrivait : « Quant au Roi, il s'y montre glouton d'amour, sans tendresse probablement, engagé par les sens, dégagé par la satiété, dur après l'abandon, égoïste le plus tranquillement du monde. »

François Bluche, qui l'excuse, pense au contraire que les amours du Roi-Soleil, largement pardonnées par le peuple, traduisaient la sensibilité du temps. « La Cour, la Ville et le peuple, écrit-il, retrouvaient, *grosso modo*, à l'égard de Louis XIV, la bonhomie souriante témoignée par leurs pères envers les fantaisies amoureuses de Henri IV. Elles sont belles, Mlle de La Vallière, Mme de Montespan, Mme de Ludres, Mlle de Fontanges. Elles apportent au Roi un bonheur passager, à la cour des plaisirs renouvelés. Elles ne se mêlent point de politique. Elles encouragent les arts. Elles représentent comme une branche des beaux-arts. » Multipliant sur les tableaux baroques le beau visage de Madeleine, la pécheresse relevée par le Christ, l'Église s'accommode aussi du péché à condition qu'il soit suivi de remords, voire de repentir. Louis XIV, qui n'est pas encore totalement dévot, est toutefois un peu Tartuffe.

CHAPITRE 50

Les pièges de l'orgueil

En 1678, le programme iconographique de la galerie des Glaces qui devait être consacré à Apollon est abandonné par le roi, qui, au cours d'une séance du Conseil d'en-haut, « résolut que son histoire sur les conquêtes devait y être représentée ». Achevés en 1684, les vingt-sept tableaux de la voûte expriment l'orgueil d'un roi ivre de louanges qui, seul maître à bord du grand vaisseau de l'État, impose sa loi à l'aigle allemand, au lion espagnol et au trident hollandais. « Ces tableaux et inscriptions qui révoltèrent les nations », comme l'écrit Saint-Simon, traduisent aussi le durcissement d'un monarque qui, peut-être parce qu'il perd ses meilleurs commis et généraux, prend une série de décisions qui, en moins de dix ans, couvrent le soleil de taches.

Le système Versailles

Le 6 mai 1682, Louis XIV quitte définitivement Paris pour Versailles. Jusque-là toujours en mouvement entre le Louvre, Saint-Germain, les Tuileries et Fontainebleau, il décide, à quarante-trois ans, de se fixer dans le château qu'il aime plus que tout pour en faire le cœur politique du royaume et le temple de son culte. Car Versailles n'est pas seulement la résidence de la cour, il devient le théâtre où chaque décor et chaque rite a pour fonction de transformer chaque aristocrate en courtisan, chaque chêne en roseau.

« Ceux-là s'abusent lourdement, écrivait le roi à son fils dans ses *Mémoires*, qui s'imaginent que ce ne sont là que des affaires de cérémonie. Les peuples sur qui nous régnons, ne pouvant pénétrer le fond des choses, règlent d'ordinaire leurs jugements sur ce qu'ils voient audehors, et c'est le plus souvent sur les préséances et les rangs qu'ils mesurent leur respect et leur obéissance. Comme il est important au public de n'être gouverné que par un seul, il lui est important aussi que celui qui fait cette fonction soit élevé de telle sorte au-dessus des autres qu'il n'y ait personne qu'il puisse ni confondre ni comparer avec lui, et l'on ne peut, sans faire tort à tout le corps de l'État, ôter à son chef les moindres marques de la supériorité qui le distingue des membres. »

Ce qui avait été dans les vingt premières années du règne un lieu de fêtes, de rendez-vous galants, de divertissements somptueux donnés en l'honneur des maîtresses successives, devient alors l'expression d'une pensée politique, une énorme entreprise à la gloire du roi, qui surveille tout, impose sa volonté, veille « au détail de tout », de la maçonnerie à la pose d'un buste ou d'une statue. « Ce sera enfin la révolution copernicienne, écrit Emmanuel Le Roy Ladurie, le Roi-Soleil se placera en toute gloire et quiétude au centre de son État. Les mutations d'orbites seront totales : il appartiendra désormais aux courtisans et même aux sujets de tournoyer autour de Sa Majesté, mais non l'inverse. »

Aimable rendez-vous de chasse que Louis XIII avait fait bâtir dans les bois où s'élevait le hameau de Versailles, le château en brique se composait d'un corps de logis et de deux ailes qui formaient les communs. En 1661, Louis XIV, tombé amoureux du refuge de son père et bouleversé par les merveilles de Vaux-le-Vicomte, recrute l'équipe de Fouquet pour conduire les premiers travaux. Le Vau enveloppe d'une construction de pierre prolongée par deux ailes en retrait les bâtiments de Louis XIII que son fils se refuse à faire abattre et construit l'Orangerie. À partir de 1662, l'architecte paysagiste Le Nôtre dessine le parc, organisé autour de deux grands axes, l'un qui longe le château, l'autre, perpendiculaire, qui s'éloigne vers l'horizon dans la perspective du Grand Canal, achevé en 1672. Depuis le château, on peut voir au centre du grand bassin Apollon, le dieu du soleil, assis sur son char. Le Brun ordonne jusque dans les plus petits détails la décoration intérieure. En juillet 1674, pour la première fois, le château peut héberger les invités venus fêter la conquête de la Franche-Comté par Condé. Racine y fait jouer *Iphigénie* dans l'Orangerie. Le *Malade imaginaire* est présenté devant la grotte de Thétis. Lully dirige *Alceste* et, le 31 août, le roi navigue sur le canal. « Dans le profond silence de la nuit, écrit Félibien, l'historiographe des bâtiments du roi, l'on entendait les violons qui suivaient le vaisseau de Sa Majesté. Le son de ces instruments semblait donner de la vie à toutes les figures dont la lumière modérée donnait aussi à la symphonie un certain agrément qu'elle n'aurait point eu dans une entière obscurité. Pendant que les vaisseaux voguaient avec lenteur, l'on entrevoyait l'eau qui blanchissait tout autour ; et les rames qui la battaient mollement, et par coups mesurés, marquaient comme des sillons d'argent sur la surface obscure des canaux. »

En 1678, l'année où Vauban commence la « ceinture de fer » destinée à protéger le royaume, l'île enchantée du plaisir et de l'amour se transforme en grille de lecture du pouvoir absolu. Achevé en 1680, l'escalier des Ambassadeurs, conçu pour éblouir les visiteurs étrangers, illustre, au point le plus élevé du plafond, zone représentant l'immortalité, la réformation de la justice, le rétablissement du commerce, la réception des ambassadeurs, la remise des commandements, la satisfaction reçue de l'Espagne et du Saint-Siège, l'ordre d'attaquer quatre places en même temps, le passage du Rhin et la seconde conquête de la Franche-Comté. Dans les encoignures du plafond, figurent, sous forme allégorique, les quatre vertus royales fondamentales, l'Autorité, la Magnificence, la Force et la Vigilance.

Achevée en 1684, la galerie des Glaces représente les actions d'éclat du monarque et les glorieux épisodes des guerres menées contre la Hollande et l'Espagne. Afin d'être bien sûr que les spectateurs interpréteraient les images comme il fallait, on avait mis des inscriptions sur les peintures. Jugées trop « pompeuses » par Louvois, les « légendes » de Charpentier furent par la suite remplacées par des vers plus simples de Boileau et de Racine, nommés en 1677 historiographes du roi.

Pour la prise de Gand, Louis apparaît dans un nuage, assis sur un aigle, entouré d'une lumière aveuglante, tenant un bouclier d'une main, brandissant la foudre de l'autre. Pour le passage du Rhin, Le Brun a montré la divinité du fleuve « saisie d'effroi » devant ce souverain jupitérien accompagné dans sa traversée par Hercule, Minerve et les allégories de la Gloire et de la Victoire.

Sanctuaire de la royauté où Louis XIV aimait recevoir les ambassadeurs, la chambre du roi, dont le lit est placé exactement au centre du palais, est un lieu de culte quotidien où les levers et les couchers sont l'occasion pour le monarque de prendre sa revanche sur la Fronde.

Architecture modèle d'un pouvoir en représentation, copié dans toute l'Europe, Versailles ne coûta en fait que 80 millions de livres, soit de 2 à 3 % des dépenses annuelles de l'État, l'équivalent de deux ou trois campagnes militaires, finalement 70 % des dépenses de la monarchie pour la seule année 1683 ! Une misère si l'on songe aux bénéfices retirés par une monarchie désormais dispensée de prendre les armes contre tous les « malcontents » qui l'avaient contestée depuis plus d'un siècle. La Fronde a sans doute coûté plus cher à l'État que l'ensemble des travaux du château.

Mis en place par un roi qui voulait déraciner la propension des Grands à la révolte, le système Versailles met en place à tous les instants de la journée un rituel de soumission dont témoigne Ezechiel Spanheim : « La cour de France, sur le pied où elle est sous ce règne, est dans une grande soumission pour son roi, en sorte qu'on ne saurait voir ni plus d'empressement à lui marquer son zèle et à lui faire sa cour, ni plus d'attachement à s'y acquitter, avec une régularité entière et exacte, des fonctions où chacun est appelé. Ce qu'on n'avait pas vu sous les règnes précédents, ni même sous celui-ci durant sa minorité [...]. En sorte que tous les courtisans, jusques aux moindres, se font une application particulière de voir le roi et d'en être vus dans toutes les occasions qui s'en présentent, comme à son lever, quand il sort du Conseil et va à l'église, ou quand il prend ses repas, et ce qu'il fait ordinairement en public. »

Planifiées jusqu'au moindre geste, les actions du roi obéissent à des « rituels » tellement précis que tous peuvent savoir l'heure en les observant ou connaître l'état des relations internationales selon l'ouverture des portes ou l'organisation du cérémonial. En 1701, on n'ouvre qu'un battant des portes pour l'envoyé de l'empereur, la tension entre Paris et Vienne étant à son comble. En 1699, l'ambassadeur du Maroc, reçu dans la chambre royale du grand appartement, doit s'arrêter au bord du tapis, au-dessous et tout contre la marche de l'estrade, le roi assis sur un fauteuil se découvrant seulement un moment et se recouvrant aussitôt. En 1715, pour recevoir Mehemet Reza Beg, l'ambassadeur de Perse, Louis XIV qui « voulait frapper les yeux du plus magnifique souverain d'Orient » et manifester la prééminence du « Très-Chrétien » porte la couronne et un habit couvert de pierreries. Comme l'a fait remarquer le sociologue Norbert Elias dans un ouvrage pionnier, cette « société de cour », mise en place dès Henri III mais poussée à la perfection sous Louis XIV, est un ballet où chaque figurant doit, à tous moments, obéir à des codes stricts fixant les conditions de sa participation au spectacle. Ne jamais tourner le dos au portrait du roi, être assis sur une chaise, sur un tabouret ou rester debout, ne pas entrer dans sa chambre à coucher vide sans faire une génuflexion, rester tête couverte dans la salle où la table était mise pour le dîner du roi, porter des vêtements adaptés aux lieux, aux heures de la journée et aux circonstances, telles sont les règles que le roi de théâtre a fixées pour manipuler les hommes, jouer de leurs jalousies et de leur amour-propre, calmer les passions, établir des normes de sociabilité et transformer les sujets en « vrais singes de la royauté », comme l'écrit La Bruyère, au point de leur faire « tourner la tête » au moindre signe d'attention manifesté par le souverain. Ce n'est pas un hasard si, au même moment, les représentations équestres du souverain s'élèvent à Paris, Rennes, Montpellier, Dijon et Lyon, pour manifester aux yeux de tous l'image d'un roi triomphant qui a renoncé à ses tours de France.

Voltaire, un demi-siècle plus tard, mesure les effets du système Versailles quand il écrit : « Les maisons, les spectacles, les promenades publiques, où l'on commençait à se rassembler pour goûter une vie plus douce, rendirent peu à peu l'extérieur de tous les citoyens presque semblable. On s'aperçoit aujourd'hui, jusque dans le fond d'une boutique, que la politesse a gagné toutes les conditions. Les provinces se sont ressenties avec le temps de tous ces changements. »

Un roi trop chrétien

Le 19 mars 1682, une assemblée extraordinaire du clergé français adopte une déclaration en quatre articles qui ressemble à un coup de tonnerre.

« Article 1. Saint Pierre et ses successeurs, vicaires de Jésus-Christ et [...] toute l'Église n'ont reçu puissance de Dieu que sur les choses spirituelles et qui concernent le Salut, et non point sur les choses temporelles et civiles. En conséquence, les Rois et les Souverains ne sont soumis à aucune puissance ecclésiastique, par l'ordre de Dieu, dans les choses temporelles ; ils ne peuvent être déposés ni directement, ni indirectement, par l'autorité des chefs de l'Église ; et leurs sujets ne peuvent être dispensés de la soumission et de l'obéissance qu'ils leur doivent ou absous du serment de fidélité. [...]

Article 4. Dans les questions de foi, le premier rôle revient au Souverain Pontife. Ses décrets concernent toutes les Églises et chacune en particulier. Mais son jugement n'est pas irréformable, à moins que n'intervienne le consentement de l'Église. »

Rédigés par Bossuet, ces quatre articles qui mettaient en cause le principe de l'infaillibilité pontificale affirmaient hautement l'indépendance de la monarchie à l'égard de Rome. Ils excitaient surtout une querelle de principes qui, à l'heure où se mettait en place le cérémonial versaillais, traduisait la fièvre gallicane du roi « Très-Chrétien ».

Cette querelle avait commencé en 1673, quand Louis XIV avait étendu à l'ensemble du royaume le droit de régale, une coutume d'« usage immémorial », reconnu dans les évêchés du Nord, qui permettait au roi de percevoir les revenus d'un évêché pendant sa vacance. Dès son avènement à la papauté, Innocent XI, pieux, autoritaire et intransigeant, condamne sans ménagements ce « prétendu droit de régale » puis, en riposte à la déclaration des quatre articles, refuse l'investiture canonique aux évêques nommés par le roi. En 1687, le conflit s'envenime encore quand Innocent XI abolit le droit d'asile dont bénéficiait le quartier des ambassades à Rome. Le nouvel ambassadeur de France ayant reçu l'ordre de passer outre est alors considéré par le pape comme excommunié. Une fois de plus, Louis XIV séquestre Avignon et le Comtat venaissin.

Louis est d'autant plus intransigeant à l'égard de Rome qu'il a le sentiment d'être devenu le champion du dogme catholique et le pourfendeur de l'hérésie. En 1679, la persécution a repris contre Port-Royal, dont confesseurs, pensionnaires et novices sont expulsés. C'est également à partir de 1679 que le roi multiplie les vexations contre les protestants. Suppression des chambres mi-parties, interdiction à tout catholique de se faire protestant, conversions des enfants autorisées dès l'âge de sept ans, interdiction des mariages mixtes, pressions sur les mourants, destruction des temples trop proches des lieux catholiques, autant de mesures qui font des huguenots des sujets de seconde catégorie, auxquels on interdit d'être sage-femme, apothicaire, chirurgien, médecin, huissier, notaire, avoué, avocat, expert, interprète, horloger municipal, libraire, épicier, drapier, lingère... ! Il est aussi interdit aux protestants d'avoir des domestiques catholiques et de siéger dans les corps savants.

C'est abandonner la politique de modération que Louis XIV avait tracée quand il écrivait au dauphin, vers 1672 : « Je crus, mon fils, que le meilleur moyen pour réduire peu à peu les huguenots de mon royaume était de ne les point presser du tout par quelque rigueur nouvelle, de faire observer ce qu'ils avaient obtenu sous les règnes précédents, mais aussi de ne leur accorder rien de plus, et d'en renfermer même l'exécution dans les plus étroites bornes que la justice et la bienséance le pouvaient permettre. »

En 1681, la pression s'accentue. L'intendant de Poitiers René de Marillac, qui veut faire du zèle, décide de loger les dragons et les fusiliers chez les huguenots pour accélérer le nombre des « conversions ». Même si les excès de ces « missionnaires bottés » sont dans un premier temps condamnés par le roi et Marillac déplacé, les dragonnades sont bientôt étendues par Louvois au Midi, au Béarn et en Languedoc. C'est à qui présentera à un roi qui se laisse consciemment ou non abuser des chiffres miraculeux de conversions. À la fin de l'été 1685, on en compte 300 000 à 400 000 et Bossuet s'exclame : « Nos pères n'avaient pas vu, comme nous, une hérésie invétérée tomber tout à coup, les troupeaux égarés revenir en foule, et nos églises trop étroites pour les recevoir. »

Le 18 octobre 1685, l'édit de Fontainebleau, qui ne s'applique pas à l'Alsace, révoque l'édit de Nantes, qui n'a plus de raison d'être puisque, précise le préambule : « Nous voyons présentement avec la juste reconnaissance que nous devons à Dieu, que nos soins ont eu la fin que nous nous sommes proposée, puisque la meilleure et la plus grande partie de nos sujets de ladite Religion prétendue réformée ont embrassé la catholique [...]. Nous avons jugé que nous ne pouvions rien faire de mieux pour effacer entièrement la mémoire des troubles, de la confusion et des maux que le progrès de cette fausse religion a causés dans notre royaume, [...] que de révoquer ledit édit de Nantes, [...] et tout ce qui a été fait depuis en faveur de ladite Religion. »

Le culte réformé est interdit. Les ministres protestants doivent quitter le royaume dans les quinze jours. Les écoles protestantes sont fermées. Les protestants doivent faire baptiser leurs enfants par des prêtres catholiques et les hommes qui tenteront de quitter le royaume seront envoyés aux galères. L'article 12 conserve toutefois aux protestants non convertis une certaine liberté de conscience à condition « de ne point faire d'exercice, ni de s'assembler sous prétexte de prières ou de culte de ladite Religion ».

Accueillie dans le royaume par une véritable explosion de joie qui porte à l'extrême la popularité du roi, cette révocation fut sans doute une faute. Malgré son interdiction, l'émigration de 200 000 huguenots, soit peut-être le cinquième des réformés, priva le royaume d'artisans et de marchands qui apportèrent leurs talents aux pays qui les accueillirent. Mais en même temps, cette diaspora instaura par la suite de fructueux échanges entre les protestants du Refuge et ceux restés en France. Si Millau décline, Nîmes prospère comme les ports où les réformés étaient pourtant nombreux. La révocation soude surtout la coalition des puissances protestantes, stimule la résistance intellectuelle à l'absolutisme et suscite la constitution d'un réseau d'espions fort actifs financé par l'Angleterre. Enfin, plus grave peut-être, en amenant les protestants à pratiquer une religion de façade et à manifester leur indifférence en matière de foi catholique, elle a sans doute préparé la déchristianisation du siècle suivant. On ne viole pas impunément les consciences. « C'est un redoutable levain dans une nation », écrivait Fénelon à Bossuet dès le 8 mars 1686.

Pourtant, condamner avec indignation la révocation serait une fois de plus appliquer nos valeurs au passé sans comprendre la sensibilité d'une époque qui nous est largement étrangère. Ce n'est certainement pas l'influence de Mme de Maintenon, la dévote maîtresse épousée en secret au lendemain de la mort de la reine Marie-Thérèse, qui explique cette décision que, par ailleurs, elle réprouva. Ce n'est pas non plus la volonté de prendre sa revanche sur l'empereur qui, en sauvant Vienne du péril turc en 1683, pouvait aussi apparaître comme le champion de la chrétienté. Plus simplement, la dualité de religions au sein d'un même État apparaissait alors, en France mais aussi ailleurs, comme une monstrueuse anomalie. En témoignent assez les persécutions que subissent alors les minorités religieuses en Espagne, en Russie, au Japon, en Scandinavie et en Angleterre, où les catholiques doivent aussi subir expropriations et interdits professionnels. Dans une Europe où quiconque refuse de se conformer à la religion du prince devient un ennemi du pouvoir, dans une France où le roi jurait lors du sacre d'« exterminer » les hérétiques et où l'existence de l'hérésie était vécue comme un véritable sacrilège dans les couches populaires, le roi n'avait pas besoin d'être sous influence pour se convaincre de la justesse de son action. En se disant « persuadé que Dieu consommera à sa gloire l'ouvrage qu'il m'a inspiré », Louis XIV était bien l'homme de son temps.

La guerre froide

Vouloir poursuivre la politique de Richelieu contre les Habsbourg catholiques de Vienne et ceux de Madrid tout en liguant contre lui l'ensemble des États protestants, c'est l'orgueilleux pari que prend Louis XIV à partir de 1679. Seul contre l'Europe avec le belliqueux Louvois comme conseil et le cynique marquis de Croissy, le frère cadet de Colbert, comme secrétaire d'État aux Affaires étrangères à la place du modéré Arnauld de Pomponne, congédié. Convaincu d'être devenu l'arbitre de l'Europe, abusé sans doute par le potentiel démographique et économique du royaume et la crainte qu'inspirent ses armées, Louis XIV utilise alors les artifices du droit et les ruses de la diplomatie pour parfaire la « ceinture de fer » mise en place par Vauban au lendemain de la paix de Nimègue. Inspirée par Colbert de Croissy, qui avait été président à mortier au parlement de Metz, la politique dite des « réunions » consiste à interpréter dans le sens le plus large les articles des traités antérieurs et à exhumer les vieilles chartes pour annexer sans employer la force.

Des « Chambres de réunions » installées à Besançon, Brisach et Metz, rappelant que les traités de Westphalie, d'Aix-la-Chapelle et de Nimègue ont cédé à la France des territoires et des villes « avec leurs dépendances » ou « avec leurs droits et appartenances », « réunissent » ainsi à la couronne la principauté de Montbéliard, les territoires de Germersheim et Lauterbourg, le duché des Deux-Ponts, le bailliage de Pont-à-Mousson, Forbach et les comtés et villes de la Sarre. Plus spectaculaire, plus insolent encore, en septembre 1681, sans tirer un seul coup de mousquet, Strasbourg qui, pendant la guerre de Hollande, avait à plusieurs reprises ouvert le pont de Kehl aux troupes de l'empereur, capitule entre les mains de Louvois. Le 23 octobre, le roi entre dans la ville dans un carrosse doré, fait rétablir l'exercice de la religion catholique dans une ville luthérienne et chanter dans la cathédrale un glorieux *Te Deum*. À Vienne, écrit l'ambassadeur de Venise, « il est proprement impossible de décrire comment les ministres ont été abasourdis et remplis de confusion en se voyant placés au milieu de tant de périls de part et d'autre, redoutant à la fois la puissance considérable du roi de France et la formidable puissance ottomane », un grand empire infidèle considéré avec une bienveillance certaine par le « Très-Chrétien ».

Le jour où les troupes françaises occupaient Strasbourg, d'autres entraient dans Casal, la capitale du Montferrat qu'avait cédée le duc de Mantoue en échange d'une somme de 100 000 pistoles et d'une pension de 60 000 livres. C'était désormais le Milanais espagnol et le Piémont qui étaient surveillés par celui qui, le même jour, avait soumis le Pô et le Rhin.

Autant d'annexions qui, ajoutées aux forteresses que construisent sur le Rhin et la Moselle les ingénieurs du roi, excitent la francophobie de la « nation » allemande. En 1683, en faisant la sourde oreille aux appels du pape qui le pressent d'intervenir pour sauver Vienne menacée par l'armée turque et en laissant l'empereur Léopold remporter au Kahlenberg une victoire éclatante contre Kara Mustapha, Louis XIV commet une nouvelle erreur. Léopold jouit alors d'un prestige qu'il n'avait jamais connu. Une trêve peut bien être conclue à Ratisbonne, le 15 août 1684, pour faire accepter les réunions, le doge de Gênes peut bien venir en personne à Versailles demander pardon pour avoir fourni des galères à l'Espagne, le point culminant de l'expansion française semble bien avoir été atteint l'année où a été révoqué l'édit de Nantes.

Le 9 juillet 1686, la ligue d'Augsbourg, à laquelle se rallient ensuite la Hollande et l'Angleterre, réunit l'Autriche, plusieurs princes allemands et l'Espagne pour défendre ceux qui seraient « attaqués ou inquiétés par des recherches injustes et des demandes illégitimes ». En 1688, la « glorieuse révolution » qui, en Angleterre, détrône le francophile et catholique Jacques II pour le remplacer par sa fille Marie et son gendre Guillaume d'Orange, l'ennemi le plus acharné de Louis XIV, isole totalement la France, qui voit l'ensemble de l'Europe se dresser contre elle. En prenant brusquement l'offensive sur le Rhin en octobre 1688 pour devancer les coalisés et en dévastant systématiquement le Palatinat pour empêcher qu'il serve de base de départ aux armées impériales, Louis XIV soulève contre lui l'indignation de l'opinion publique qui l'assimile à un monstre de l'Apocalypse. Il y a trois vices presque inhérents à l'état des souverains, avait annoncé l'évêque Fléchier dans un sermon prononcé le 25 août 1681 à Saint-Louis-en-l'Île, « un amour-propre qui les attache à leur gloire, à leur intérêt, à leur plaisir, et leur rend tout le reste indifférent ; une imagination d'indépendance qui leur persuade que tout ce qui leur plaît leur est permis ; un esprit du monde, auquel ils tiennent par tant d'endroits, qui les jette dans l'irréligion, ou pour le moins dans la tiédeur ». Dans l'auditoire, il ne manquait que Louis XIV.

L'hiver du règne

*L*e dimanche 1ᵉʳ *septembre 1715, à huit heures un quart du matin, au terme d'un règne de soixante-douze ans, s'éteint le Roi-Soleil. Ses dernières paroles ont été : « Ô mon Dieu, venez à mon aide, hâtez-vous de me secourir. » « Lieutenant de Dieu sur terre », Louis XIV est convaincu qu'il sera jugé sur son « métier de roi » et sur les responsabilités qu'il a eues envers ses sujets qui, sans être devenus les « animaux farouches » décrits par La Bruyère au lendemain de la famine de 1693, ont terriblement souffert en ce grand hiver du règne. Mort, celui qui a été grand partage le sort des plus humbles. C'est ce que souligne Massillon quand il ouvre par ces mots son oraison funèbre devant la cour : « Dieu seul est grand, mes frères. »*

L'épreuve de la guerre

Hormis quelques années de paix entre 1697 et 1702, la guerre qui reprend en 1688 va opposer jusqu'en 1713 la France à l'Europe entière coalisée contre un monarque vieillissant présenté comme un tyran mégalomane qui n'écoute que la voix de son « bon plaisir » et viole à l'envi serments, trêves et édits. En 1689, au lendemain du sac du Palatinat, l'auteur des *Soupirs de la France esclave*, publié à Amsterdam, écrit : « Les Français passaient autrefois pour une nation honnête, humaine, civile, d'un esprit opposé aux barbaries ; mais aujourd'hui un Français et un cannibale, c'est à peu près la même chose dans l'esprit des voisins. » En 1690, Ezechiel Spanheim, représentant du Brandebourg en France, souligne « la passion démesurée et sans bornes pour la gloire » d'un roi qui est « la fatale source des calamités et des guerres qui ont surpris et affligé l'Europe en plusieurs rencontres, et qui la désolent encore aujourd'hui ».

C'est en effet une lutte épuisante qui s'engage, une guerre pour la première fois mondiale et pour la première fois totale. Mondiale car, de Pondichéry au Québec, elle s'étend aux colonies. Totale car elle mobilise des effectifs énormes, plus de 400 000 hommes face-à-face dans les années 1700, se déroule sur terre comme sur mer, épuise les finances des belligérants et provoque des hécatombes sans précédent. De 1688 à 1713, près de 2 millions de soldats sont morts en Europe, fauchés par les nouveaux fusils à tir rapide, les cartouches, les salves plus régulières et les baïonnettes à douille mises au point par Vauban.

« Je n'ai vu nulle part en un si petit espace un nombre aussi considérable de morts, écrivait Des Bournays, un officier présent à la bataille de Malplaquet, en 1709. Ils étaient, du front de la colonne ennemie jusqu'à portée de fusil, entassés jusqu'à deux et trois l'un sur l'autre, et pendant l'attaque, les blessés qui se retiraient formaient comme une procession. » « L'art de détruire, observera Voltaire, est non seulement tout autre de ce qu'il était avant l'invention de la poudre, mais de ce qu'il était il y a cent ans. »

Appelée guerre « de la ligue d'Augsbourg » par les historiens français, « d'Orléans » par les Allemands ou « du roi Guillaume » par les Anglais, la guerre qui s'ouvre, en 1688, par l'offensive de Louis XIV sur le Rhin réduit pour la première fois la France à ses propres forces. « C'est la plus grande guerre qu'aura jamais roi de France sur les bras », affirme bientôt le comte de Bussy-Rabutin.

Victorieuse dans un premier temps à Fleurus, Staffarde, Steinkerque, Neerwinden, Mons et Namur, le dernier siège présidé par Louis XIV, qui, en 1693, quitte le commandement de l'armée, la France voit une partie de sa flotte détruite dans la rade de La Hougue le 2 juin 1692. Même si cette défaite ne fut pas le désastre exagérément grossi par les Anglais, elle fait perdre tout espoir de débarquer en Angleterre pour tenter de restaurer Jacques II Stuart et incite Louis XIV à abandonner la guerre d'escadre pour une guerre de course où s'illustrent Jean Bart, Forbin et Duguay-Trouin.

Le 27 juin 1693, le comte de Tourville, le vaincu de La Hougue, attaque au sud du Portugal un convoi de navires marchands anglais et hollandais et rafle plus de 30 millions de livres. Un an plus tard,

Jean Bart multiplie les prises en mer du Nord et assure la protection des vaisseaux qui transportent les blés polonais dans un royaume éprouvé par une terrible disette. Le 4 mai 1697, le baron de Pointis s'empare de Carthagène des Indes, le plus riche entrepôt de l'Amérique latine, et, au retour de l'expédition qui s'est soldée par un butin de 8 millions de livres, fait sensation en présentant à Louis XIV une émeraude grosse comme le poing. Le 18 juin 1696, Jean Bart, encore lui, surprend un convoi anglo-hollandais de plus de cent navires qui revenait du Sund et en capture la moitié. À l'heure où la France devait aussi lutter contre la Banque d'Amsterdam et la Banque d'Angleterre, fondée en 1694 pour financer Guillaume d'Orange, cette guerre de course, pour être moins glorieuse, était infiniment plus fructueuse, atteignant durement les puissances maritimes qui, aussi exsangues que la France, se décident le 21 septembre 1697 à signer les traités de Ryswick, qui marquent le premier recul de la France.

Louis XIV accepte en effet de restituer les « réunions » des années 1679-1689 à l'exception de Strasbourg. Il renonce aussi à ses conquêtes et rend Luxembourg et Barcelone à l'Espagne, Fribourg et Kehl à leurs princes et la Lorraine sauf Sarrelouis et Longwy à son duc. La France retrouve donc les frontières de Nimègue, moins Fribourg, Brisach et Pignerol mais avec Strasbourg et Sarrelouis.

Les Provinces-Unies se voyaient accorder d'importants avantages commerciaux et, pour assurer leur sécurité, des places fortes dites de « la Barrière », voisines des frontières françaises, à Ath, Charleroi, Courtrai et Mons.

Surtout, suprême humiliation, Louis XIV doit reconnaître Guillaume d'Orange comme roi d'Angleterre et s'engager à ne plus soutenir les prétentions du Stuart en exil au château de Saint-Germain. En revanche, l'Angleterre reconnaît la souveraineté de la France sur la partie occidentale de Saint-Domingue, qui va devenir la perle du commerce colonial de la France au XVIIIe siècle et contribuera aux fortunes de Bordeaux et de Nantes. Au total, ni vainqueur ni vaincu, mais une France qui doit désormais compter avec une Autriche ragaillardie par ses succès sur les Turcs et avec le couple anglo-hollandais. Certes Louis XIV a dû signer un traité que Vauban tient pour « plus infâme que celui du Cateau-Cambrésis » mais, en dépit de ses succès, l'Europe coalisée a dû renoncer à ramener la France à ses frontières de 1648.

Si la modération semble l'emporter à Ryswick, c'est que les diplomates ont en fait les yeux fixés sur le bulletin de santé du roi d'Espagne Charles II, un roi sans enfants dont la mort paraissait imminente. La succession d'Espagne, qui comprenait l'Espagne proprement dite, les îles Baléares, la Sardaigne, la majeure partie de l'Italie, les Pays-Bas catholiques, le Mexique, l'Amérique centrale, l'Amérique du Sud sauf le Brésil, les Philippines et les Mariannes, les côtes du Maroc et les îles Canaries, était bien à l'époque la grande « affaire » qui agitait tous les esprits et suscitait tous les projets de partage.

Parmi tous les « prétendants », deux l'emportaient vraiment, l'empereur Léopold et... Louis XIV lui-même, tous les deux fils et époux d'infantes. Toutefois, à suivre l'ordre naturel de succession, les droits de la maison de France l'emportaient car Marie-Thérèse, femme de Louis XIV, et sa mère Anne étaient aînées de Marguerite Thérèse et de Marie-Anne, femme et mère de Léopold.

Cependant, aucun chef d'État ne pouvait accepter que la totalité des possessions espagnoles revienne à un Bourbon ou à un Habsbourg de Vienne. C'eût été bouleverser l'équilibre des forces en Europe. Avec beaucoup de modération et d'habileté, Louis XIV avait donc pris l'initiative d'entamer des négociations avec ses deux grands ennemis de la veille, l'Angleterre et les Provinces-Unies, pour envisager un partage satisfaisant de la dépouille espagnole. Particulièrement humble, le Roi-Soleil acceptait que l'archiduc Charles, fils de Léopold, devienne roi d'Espagne, à condition qu'il s'engage à ne jamais réunir son royaume aux possessions autrichiennes et accorde des compensations au dauphin français, à chercher en Italie, en Savoie, en Lorraine ou au Luxembourg.

Mais tous ces arrangements sont mis en cause par le testament de Charles II, qui, cédant à la pression de l'orgueilleux sentiment national espagnol, exige le maintien intégral de l'Espagne et de ses possessions et désigne comme héritier Philippe d'Anjou, petit-fils de Louis XIV, et, en cas de refus, l'archiduc Charles. Ce testament, connu au lendemain de sa mort, le 1er novembre 1700, éclate comme une bombe et place Louis XIV devant un choix particulièrement grave : faut-il accepter le testament et se battre à coup sûr contre l'Empire, la Hollande et l'Angleterre, mais avec le désormais « ami » espagnol, ou le refuser et prendre le risque de voir se reconstituer l'empire de Charles Quint ? Au terme d'un conseil des ministres décisif où les différentes hypothèses furent examinées et où l'unanimité se fit en faveur du testament, malgré les réserves d'un Beauvillier qui se disait « persuadé que la guerre, suite naturelle de l'acceptation, causerait la ruine de la France », le roi convoqua le mardi 16 novembre l'ambassadeur espagnol et son petit-fils et dit au premier : « Vous le pouvez saluer comme votre roi. » « Quelle joie ! il n'y a plus de Pyrénées », se serait écrié l'ambassadeur d'Espagne.

Dans ses *Mémoires*, Torcy écrit que « la résolution que le roi prit d'accepter le testament, devenue publique, excita dans l'Europe l'agitation qu'on avait prévue. La Couronne d'Espagne transférée dans la Maison de France, était un des grands événements qui fût arrivé depuis plusieurs siècles et le plus capable de renouveler incessamment une guerre générale ». Une guerre dont Louis XIV précipite l'échéance en prenant une série de décisions inacceptables pour les chancelleries européennes.

Le 1er février 1701, il fait enregistrer par le Parlement de Paris des lettres patentes qui maintiennent les droits du nouveau roi d'Espagne à la couronne de France. Le 6 février, il envoie des troupes françaises occuper les forteresses dites de « la Barrière », dans les Pays-Bas espagnols. Et, à sa demande, Philippe d'Anjou octroie aux marchands français le privilège de l'*asiento*, c'est-à-dire le monopole fructueux de la fourniture d'esclaves à l'Amérique espagnole. Enfin, Jacques II Stuart étant mort, il reconnaît son fils Jacques III comme successeur de « droit » à la couronne d'Angleterre. C'en est trop pour l'empereur, l'Angleterre et les Provinces-Unies qui, le 7 septembre 1701, concluent à La Haye une « Grande Alliance » à laquelle se joignent bientôt le roi du Danemark, l'Électeur de Brandebourg et la plupart des princes allemands.

Jusqu'en 1709, les armées françaises, commandées par des généraux médiocres, accumulent les revers face aux troupes dirigées avec brio par l'Anglais Marlborough et le prince Eugène. En s'emparant de Gibraltar, de la Sardaigne puis de Minorque, les Anglais font de la Méditerranée leur chasse gardée. En s'implantant à Barcelone, l'archiduc Charles, qui se qualifie désormais de Charles III, menace directement Philippe d'Anjou et amène le Portugal à lâcher la France pour s'allier avec les Anglais. Sur le front nord et nord-est, les terribles défaites de Höchstädt, Ramillies et Audenarde menacent la ceinture de fer. En 1708, Lille capitule et c'est la France qui est menacée d'invasion. En Italie, tous les points d'appui tombent les uns après les autres et, après la défaite de Turin, les Français doivent évacuer l'Italie du Nord. Aux ambassadeurs qu'il envoie pour négocier la paix, les Alliés réclament qu'il fournisse des troupes pour expulser d'Espagne son petit-fils et qu'il renonce à Lille, Toul et Verdun.

Dans une lettre adressée le 12 juin 1709 à tous ses sujets, Louis XIV en appelle alors à la « nation » pour expliquer les raisons qui l'amènent à prolonger la guerre : « L'espérance d'une paix prochaine, écrit le vieux roi, était si généralement répandue dans mon royaume que je crois devoir à la fidélité que mes peuples m'ont témoignée pendant le cours de mon règne, la consolation de les informer des raisons qui empêchent encore qu'ils ne jouissent du repos que j'avais dessein de leur procurer. J'avais accepté, pour le rétablir, des conditions bien opposées à la sûreté de mes provinces frontières ; mais plus j'ai témoigné de facilité et d'envie de dissiper les ombrages que mes ennemis affectaient de conserver de ma puissance et de mes desseins, plus ils ont multiplié leurs prétentions [...]. Je passe sous silence les insinuations qu'ils m'ont faites de joindre mes forces à celles de la ligue et de contraindre le roi, mon petit-fils, à descendre du trône, s'il ne consentait pas volontairement à vivre désormais sans États et à se réduire à la condition d'un simple particulier. Il est contre l'humanité de croire qu'ils aient eu seulement la pensée de m'engager à former avec eux une pareille alliance, mais quoique ma tendresse pour mes peuples ne soit pas moins vive que celle que j'ai pour mes propres enfants, quoique je partage tous les maux que la guerre fait souffrir à des sujets aussi fidèles, et que j'aie fait voir à toute l'Europe que je désirais sincèrement de les faire jouir de la paix, je suis persuadé qu'ils s'opposeraient eux-mêmes à des conditions également contraires à la justice et à l'honneur du nom français. »

Cet appel du 12 juin semble galvaniser un sentiment national dont les manifestations sont alors de plus en plus vives. On sait ainsi que la lecture de cette lettre provoqua une vague d'engagements dans la plupart des provinces du royaume et qu'à l'armée, des vivats fusèrent à la fin de sa lecture. À Malplaquet, en septembre 1709, Villars et Boufflers battent en retraite mais en bon ordre après avoir infligé des pertes énormes aux troupes commandées par Marlborough et le prince Eugène. En 1710, Vendôme, envoyé au secours de Philippe d'Anjou, remporte à Villaviciosa une victoire décisive qui fait perdre à l'archiduc Charles ses chances de devenir roi d'Espagne. En septembre 1711, la flotte de Duguay-Trouin, après un raid sur Rio de Janeiro, rapporte à Brest plus de 1 300 kilogrammes d'or. Le 24 juillet 1712, le maréchal de Villars inflige au prince Eugène une lourde défaite à Denain et reconquiert Marchiennes, Saint-Amand, Douai, Le Quesnoy et Bouchain. En 1713, il franchit le Rhin et occupe Fribourg tandis que l'Espagne est complètement libérée après la prise de Barcelone par les forces conjuguées de Philippe d'Anjou et des troupes françaises. Autant de retournements de situation qui permettent à Louis XIV de résister aux exigences des Alliés et de signer à Utrecht, en 1713, et à Rastadt, en 1714, une paix honorable.

Philippe V est reconnu roi d'Espagne mais doit renoncer à la couronne de France et céder à l'empereur les Pays-Bas, le Milanais, la Toscane, Naples et la Sardaigne. La France doit abandonner Ypres, Furnes, Menin et, surtout, Tournai. Dunkerque est démilitarisée mais la possession de Lille, de la Franche-Comté, de Strasbourg, de Landau et de l'Alsace est confirmée. Dans les Alpes, la vallée de Barcelonnette est acquise en échange d'Exilles, de Fenestrelle et de quelques terres en Piémont, et la principauté d'Orange est réunie au royaume.

Pour l'Angleterre, qui a lâché son allié hollandais, Utrecht est remarquable. Louis XIV doit reconnaître l'ordre de succession établi en 1701 en faveur de la branche protestante, s'engager à ne plus donner asile au prétendant catholique, céder à l'Angleterre, qui garde Gibraltar et Minorque, le détroit et la baie d'Hudson, l'Acadie et Terre-Neuve, sous réserve du droit de pêche. Enfin, la France perd le monopole du commerce des esclaves, qui est cédé à la Grande-Bretagne, ainsi que le droit d'envoyer chaque année, en Amérique espagnole, un navire chargé de produits anglais et d'établir des factoreries à La Plata et Buenos Aires.

Même si 1713 confirme l'ascension de la puissance britannique, la reine et ses ministres ont toutefois du mal à faire voter par la Chambre des lords une paix que ces derniers estiment trop favorable à la France. En effet, contrairement aux très nombreux historiens qui ont insisté sur les échecs de Louis XIV en cette fin de règne, ceux qui vivaient l'événement étaient davantage sensibles au fait que le traité de Rastadt avait été rédigé en français, la langue véhicule d'une culture qui s'était imposée aux élites de l'Europe. Assurant en outre la présence d'un Bourbon à Madrid, les traités brisaient définitivement l'angoissante menace d'un encerclement par les Habsbourg et, moyennant la cession de places fortes avancées sans réel intérêt stratégique, assuraient la solidité d'une frontière plus homogène et mieux défendable. Au total, Utrecht et Rastadt sont loin d'être une catastrophe.

Les « années de misère »

En 1694, au lendemain d'une famine qui vient de faire pratiquement autant de morts que la Première Guerre mondiale, mais en deux ans et dans une France moitié moins peuplée, l'archevêque de Cambrai, Fénelon, rédige une lettre implacable qu'il adresse à Mme de Maintenon et au duc de Beauvillier afin qu'ils la montrent au souverain, lequel ne l'a sans doute jamais lue.

« Vos peuples, que vous devriez aimer comme vos enfants, et qui ont été jusqu'ici si passionnés pour vous, meurent de faim. La culture des terres est presque abandonnée, les villes et la campagne se dépeuplent ; tous les métiers languissent et ne nourrissent plus les ouvriers. Tout le commerce est anéanti. Par conséquent vous avez détruit la moitié des forces réelles du dedans de votre État, pour faire et pour défendre de vaines conquêtes au-dehors. Au lieu de tirer de l'argent de ce pauvre peuple, il faudrait lui faire l'aumône et le nourrir. La France entière n'est plus qu'un grand hôpital désolé et sans provision. »

C'était imputer à Louis XIV une calamité qui relève largement d'une dégradation de la conjoncture observable dans toute l'Europe. Le hasard et la malchance ont voulu en effet que les années guerrières de la fin du règne coïncident avec une série d'années noires marquées en particulier par des étés « pourris » et des hivers catastrophiques. Grâce aux travaux de Jean Meuvret et d'Emmanuel Le Roy-Ladurie, on sait aujourd'hui qu'entre 1687 et 1717, l'Europe a connu un « petit âge glaciaire ». Autour de 1690, printemps, étés, automnes, hivers, mesurés par les thermomètres déjà fiables de cette époque, sont plus froids d'un degré qu'ils ne le seront jamais au cours des deux siècles et demi d'observations régulières qui suivront. Une différence énorme qui fait retarder en moyenne les moissons de deux semaines.

Tous les contemporains ont noté ce « dérèglement des saisons » et ces terribles « années de misère ». Le greffier de Saint-Affrique, dans le Rouergue, note dans son registre pour l'année 1693 : « L'on vit en France pendant plus de dix-huit mois, un printemps sans nulle douce température, un été sans chaleur, un fort grand froid pendant des mois, un soleil affaibli et presque éteint, tout cela cause de la famine. »

En ces temps de faible productivité, ce léger dérèglement du climat suffisait pour compromettre le rendement des récoltes et envoyer les plus faibles et les plus démunis au cimetière. Préparée par une série de saisons « pourries », froides et humides, la crise de 1693-1694 a bien été la plus terrible des crises de subsistance. En deux ans, par rapport à la moyenne des années « ordinaires », on compte 1,5 million de décès supplémentaires. Dans la seule année 1693, il y eut sans doute 20 % de morts sur le total de la population adulte. Les plus pauvres survivent en consommant du pain de son, des orties cuites, des chiens et des chats errants, des entrailles de bestiaux ramassées dans l'arrière-cour des étals de bouchers et peut-être pire. C'est l'époque où Charles Perrault écrit *Le Petit Poucet* et où La Bruyère compare les paysans à des « animaux farouches ».

En janvier 1709, sous la pression d'un « grand hyver » qui fait geler la Seine et le vin dans les verres et tomber les oiseaux en plein vol, qui fend les arbres et transforme les plaines en glacières, ce sont encore plus de 600 000 morts supplémentaires qui sont enregistrés. À

Gonesse, le setier de blé vaut en septembre 1709 huit fois plus cher qu'en mars 1708. À Paris, en septembre, on décompte 4 000 malades à l'Hôtel-Dieu et 14 000 personnes à l'Hôpital général. Selon Vauban, le nombre de mendiants et de vagabonds s'accroît tellement qu'il peut alors représenter près du dixième de la population.

Et pourtant, il faut payer davantage encore pour financer la guerre. Comme la « populace » pressurée ne peut guère donner davantage, on réfléchit à un meilleur rendement de l'impôt, la crise excitant, comme toujours, les projets de réforme. Dès 1694, Vauban, confronté quotidiennement à la misère et à la mort dans ses missions d'inspection, présente un *Projet de capitation* qui « doit être imposée sur toutes les natures de biens qui peuvent produire du revenu et non sur les différents étages des qualités, ni sur le nombre des personnes, parce que la qualité n'est pas ce qui fait l'abondance, non plus que l'égalité des richesses, et que le menu peuple est accablé de tailles, de gabelles, d'aides et de mille autres impôts, et encore plus de la famine qui a achevé de l'épuiser ». En 1695, Pierre de Boisguilbert, lieutenant général à Rouen, dénonce les taxes qui réduisent la demande et, condamnant la pensée économique colbertienne, propose une solution libérale en demandant que l'État allège son contrôle des produits et des marchés. En termes actuels, il annonce que c'est la demande solvable qu'il faut encourager pour relancer l'offre. En 1697, un questionnaire mis au point par le duc de Beauvillier et Fénelon, le précepteur du duc de Bourgogne, est envoyé à chaque intendant pour dresser pour la première fois un tableau de la richesse nationale. En 1707, Vauban, encore, fait imprimer, sans autorisation, un *Projet d'une dîme royale qui, supprimant la taille, les aides, les douanes d'une province à l'autre, les décimes du clergé, les affaires extraordinaires et tous les autres impôts onéreux et non volontaires et diminuant le prix du sel de moitié et plus, produirait au roi un revenu certain et suffisant, sans frais et sans être en charge à l'un de ses sujets plus qu'à l'autre, qui s'augmenterait considérablement par la meilleure culture des terres.*

Proprement révolutionnaire, ce projet qui proposait une « contribution générale » proportionnelle à la richesse de chacun sans distinction d'ordres et de privilèges et qui demandait de « ménager » l'ouvrier agricole fut condamné par le Conseil privé « à la saisie et au pilon » parce qu'il contenait « plusieurs choses contraires à l'ordre et à l'usage du royaume ». Dès 1708, un éditeur de Bruxelles imprimait cependant le livre et peu après une traduction paraissait en Angleterre.

Mis à l'index pour ne pas troubler « la maxime de l'ordre », ces réformateurs furent toutefois écoutés. En janvier 1695, préparée par le contrôleur général des Finances Pontchartrain, une déclaration royale institue une « capitation générale » payable par tous, y compris les grands, par tête de chef de famille. Nouveauté remarquable, les contribuables furent répartis non pas en ordres mais en 22 classes qui nous livrent une radiographie exceptionnelle de la société française à la fin du XVIIe siècle. Dans la première classe, imposée à 2 000 livres, on trouve la famille royale ; dans la seconde, imposée à 1 500 livres, les princes, les ducs, les maréchaux de France, les officiers de la couronne, le premier président du Parlement de Paris, les gouverneurs de provinces, les intendants ; la dernière classe, imposée à 1 livre, comprend « les soldats, cavaliers, dragons et matelots, trompettes, timbaliers et fifres, les simples manœuvres et journaliers ».

En octobre 1710, au moment le plus dramatique de la guerre de Succession d'Espagne, Louis XIV se résout à créer le dixième. Inspiré directement des idées de Vauban, ce nouvel impôt prélève 10 % de tous les revenus et oblige le contribuable à faire une déclaration. Un mois plus tard, Nicolas Desmarets, contrôleur général des Finances, fera prélever le dixième à la source pour les gages, appointements, pensions et rentes. Saint-Simon, privilégié parmi les privilégiés, invoque alors le « Créateur » qui aurait toujours été indigné par ces « dénombrements impies » et avoue le « désespoir » de ses pairs d'être « forcés à révéler eux-mêmes le secret de leurs familles ». Une indignation hypocrite promise à un bel avenir !

Au total, toutefois, l'impôt ne suffit pas. En 1683, le déficit s'élevait à 16 millions de livres. En 1715, il atteint 45 millions sans compter les dépenses extraordinaires de guerre qui, pour 1708-1715, atteignent le chiffre effrayant de 1 103 millions. On multiplie alors les « vieilles » recettes. On lance des loteries, on vend des lettres d'anoblissement, on multiplie les offices. « Toutes les fois que Votre Majesté crée un office, dit Pontchartrain au roi, Dieu crée un sot pour l'acheter. » On crée ainsi des contrôleurs de registres, puis des contrôleurs d'extraits de registres, des essayeurs d'eaux-de-vie, de beurres et de fromages. On invente des droits nouveaux sur les jeux de cartes et les perruques, la vente de la glace, du plâtre et des huîtres. On émet des rentes et des emprunts dont on oublie souvent de payer les intérêts. On courtise le banquier-financier huguenot Samuel Bernard, qui parvient à mobiliser des sommes considérables avant de voir ébranlé son crédit. On manipule surtout les monnaies si bien qu'en 1715 le louis d'or vaut environ la moitié de ce qu'il valait en 1686. L'hiver du règne ne fut pas la saison du louis fort. Quand le roi meurt, en 1715, le revenu des impôts jusqu'en 1718 est mangé d'avance et le total de la dette atteint le chiffre vertigineux de deux milliards de livres ! L'État du Roi-Soleil est au bord de la banqueroute.

Le trouble des consciences

Le retour de l'argent corrupteur, les dragonnades qui ont accompagné la révocation de l'édit de Nantes, la violente répression des camisards qui défendent leur protestantisme les armes à la main, la destruction de l'abbaye et du cimetière du Port-Royal, le sac du Palatinat, le viol des tombes princières à Heidelberg, autant de dérives qui troublent les consciences et ternissent l'image d'un vieillard devenu trop dévot dont l'oreille est accaparée par Mme de Maintenon et les jésuites.

En 1713, Louis XIV choque l'opinion gallicane en demandant au pape de condamner le jansénisme par la bulle *Unigenitus*. En 1714, il viole les lois fondamentales du royaume en rédigeant un testament dans lequel il donne le titre de princes du sang à ses deux « bâtards légitimés », les déclare aptes à succéder à la couronne et les introduit dans le conseil prévu pour la régence.

En 1705, dans une lettre, la princesse Palatine décrit la « confusion » qui règne à la cour : « On ne sait plus du tout qui on est. Quand le roi se promène, tout le monde se couvre ; la duchesse de Bourgogne va-t-elle se promener, eh bien, elle donne le bras à une dame, et les autres marchent à côté. On ne voit donc plus qui elle est. Ici, au salon et à Trianon, dans la galerie, tous les hommes sont assis devant M. le dauphin et Mme la duchesse de Bourgogne ; quelques-uns même sont étendus tout de leur long sur les canapés. Jusqu'aux frotteurs, qui jouent aux dames dans cette galerie. On ne se fait plus d'idée comme tout est présentement, cela ne ressemble plus du tout à une cour. » Le 26 août 1709, Nicolas Desmarets, le contrôleur général des Finances, dénonce dans un mémoire « la mauvaise disposition des esprits de tous les peuples ». En 1713, François Marie Arouet, le futur Voltaire, écrit une *Ode sur les malheurs du temps* tandis que l'abbé de Saint-Pierre publie à Utrecht un *Projet pour rendre la paix perpétuelle en Europe*, dans lequel il dénonce « les grands maux que cause la guerre, les prodigieuses dépenses, les chagrins fâcheux des mauvais succès présents, les cruelles inquiétudes sur les événements futurs, la diminution des revenus, la désolation des frontières, la perte de quantité de bons sujets, le cri perçant et perpétuel des peuples qui demandent la fin de leurs malheurs ».

Ce pacifisme qui proclame que la paix, le droit des gens et le bonheur matériel sont supérieurs à la guerre, au principe d'autorité, et à l'honneur traduit un progressif renversement des valeurs.

Quand Bossuet, Molière, Racine et La Bruyère approuvaient tout, Vauban, Fénelon, Beauvillier, Boisguilbert et Saint-Simon stigmatisaient. Alors que les premiers affirmaient que les « Anciens » avaient tout inventé, les autres prétendaient que les « Modernes » étaient aussi grands que ceux d'autrefois et condamnaient l'autorité des premiers au nom de la raison cartésienne, une raison qui trouve ses références dans le *Dictionnaire historique et critique* de Pierre Bayle, publié en 1696.

Déclenchée le 27 janvier 1687 par la lecture à l'Académie du poème de Charles Perrault, *Le Siècle de Louis le Grand*, un poème qui prétendait que l'on pouvait comparer, « sans craindre d'être injuste, le siècle de Louis au beau siècle d'Auguste », la querelle des Anciens et des Modernes, mesquine et « salonnarde » en apparence, annonce en fait le séisme du siècle des Lumières. « À mesure que la raison se perfectionnera, on se désabusera du préjugé grossier de l'Antiquité » annonce Fontenelle, qui ironise en se demandant « si les arbres qui étaient autrefois dans nos campagnes étaient plus grands que ceux d'aujourd'hui ». Quand Guillaume Mauquest de la Motte, médecin à Valognes, publie un *Traité complet des accouchements naturels et contre nature* dans lequel il réfute l'enseignement d'Hippocrate et écrit qu'« il ne faut jamais déférer aveuglément à l'autorité de qui que ce soit » et « qu'il faut, au contraire, laisser à chacun la liberté de penser comme il le trouve à propos », il participe, dans son domaine, à la « querelle des Anciens et des Modernes ». Quand, dans sa bulle *Unigenitus*, le pape Clément XI, sollicité par le roi, condamne les *Réflexions morales sur le Nouveau Testament* du père Quesnel, non seulement parce qu'elles expriment la conception janséniste de la grâce divine, mais aussi parce qu'elles encouragent la traduction en langue française de l'Ancien et du Nouveau Testament, des missels et des bréviaires, il se range délibérément du côté des Anciens et s'aliène tout le bas clergé militant.

Ce n'est pas un hasard si, à la fin de l'année 1715, le curé du village de Saint-Sulpice, près de Blois, écrit dans son registre paroissial : « Louis XIV, roi de France et de Navarre, est mort le 1er septembre du dit an, peu regretté de tout son royaume, à cause des sommes exorbitantes et des impôts si considérables qu'il a levés sur tous ses sujets. Il n'est pas permis d'exprimer tous les vers, toutes les chansons et tous les discours désobligeants qu'on a dits et faits contre sa mémoire. Il a été, pendant sa vie, si absolu, qu'il a passé par-dessus toutes les lois pour faire sa volonté. Les princes et la noblesse ont été opprimés. Les parlements n'avaient plus de pouvoir : ils étaient obligés de recevoir et d'enregistrer tous les édits, quels qu'ils fussent, tant le roi était puissant et absolu. Le clergé était honteusement asservi à faire la volonté du roi : à peine demandait-il quelque secours, qu'on lui en accordait plus qu'il n'en demandait. Le clergé s'est endetté horriblement. Tous les corps ne l'étaient pas moins. Il n'y avait que les partisans et les maltôtiers qui fussent en paix et qui vécussent en joie, ayant en leur possession tout l'argent du royaume. » Une triste oraison funèbre.

L'aimable Régence

*L*a régence de Philippe d'Orléans, établie lors de la minorité de
Louis XV, de 1715 à 1723, a longtemps joui d'une fort mauvaise
réputation. Scandales financiers et fêtes galantes, licence des mœurs et
crapuleries, « le temps de l'aimable Régence où l'on fit tout, excepté Pénitence », écrivait Voltaire, mérite pourtant d'être réévalué. Paix à l'extérieur et apaisement à l'intérieur, essor du commerce et désendettement
paysan, tels sont les acquis d'une période qui prépare les réussites du
« beau XVIIIe siècle ». Maintenir la grandeur de la France et assurer le
bonheur des Français, transmettre à son neveu une puissance royale
intacte mais débarrassée de ses dérives autoritaires, tel fut le pari réussi
par un dilettante de génie, débauché et sceptique, mais intelligent et travailleur.

L'embarquement pour Cythère

Amadouer l'aristocratie que Louis XIV avait exclue du pouvoir,
se concilier gallicans et jansénistes que la bulle *Unigenitus* avait
fédérés, diminuer la charge des endettés sans susciter la révolte des
rentiers, établir la paix avec les puissances protestantes sans désespérer l'Espagne catholique, tel est le programme politique du Régent,
Philippe d'Orléans, un programme qui vise « à détendre à touches
légères les ressorts trop bandés du système sans pour autant rompre

celui-ci », écrit Emmanuel Le Roy Ladurie qui, avec d'autres, s'est employé à « réviser » l'histoire d'une période trop longtemps dénigrée.

Né en 1674 d'un père qui regrettait de ne pas être né fille, Monsieur, et d'une mère qui était un homme manqué, la princesse Palatine, Philippe d'Orléans n'est pas un personnage simple. Travailleur et fêtard, artiste et savant, goûtant l'ancien et prônant le moderne, maniant la ruse et le mensonge, les fausses promesses et les fausses confidences, nonchalant mais obstiné, tournant tout en dérision mais aimant son pays par-dessus tout, il incarne l'esprit de la génération qui a vécu l'hiver du Grand Règne, celle qui s'est délectée à la lecture des *Lettres persanes* et s'est entichée d'Antoine Watteau, sacré par l'Académie « peintre des fêtes galantes ». Ceux qui l'ont connu sont obligés de s'écrier : « *Ô altitudo !* », écrivait Montesquieu, tant sa personnalité hors du commun contrastait avec celle de Louis XIV, ce roi consciencieux et méthodique qui n'aimait guère ce neveu qu'il appelait un « fanfaron du crime » et que l'on soupçonnait d'avoir empoisonné tous les prétendants à la couronne. Dans son entourage, on retrouvait en fait tous ceux que le Grand Roi avait réduits au silence, les nobles de haut rang, comme le duc de Saint-Simon, les libertins en réaction contre le parti dévot, les parlementaires en mal de remontrances qui faisaient du Palais-Royal, la résidence de Philippe d'Orléans, le repère de l'intelligentsia réformatrice dominée par le fils d'un modeste apothicaire de Brive, le « petit abbé » Guillaume Dubois, le futur cardinal, son ancien précepteur, devenu son principal complice et collaborateur.

Aux soupers du Palais-Royal, où chaque convive mettait lui-même la main à la pâte, où l'on mangeait sans retenue les filets de faisan à la financière ou les laitances de carpes au coulis d'écrevisse, où l'on buvait plus que de raison le pommard et le champagne que venait de mettre au point dom Pérignon, on compte aussi ceux que Philippe appelait ses « roués », c'est-à-dire « dignes du supplice de la roue », ses compagnons de « grande bouffe », sa fille, la duchesse de Berry, une gourmande phénoménale, ses maîtresses, Madame de Parabère et Madame de Sabran, des danseuses de l'Opéra et des dames de renom, comme la maréchale de Villars ou la marquise du Deffand. « Les galanteries passées et présentes de la Cour et de la ville, sans ménagement ; les vieux contes, les disputes, les plaisanteries, les ridicules, rien ni personne n'était épargné, écrit Saint-Simon qui a décrit ces "parties". On buvait d'autant, on s'échauffait, on disait des ordures à gorge déployée et des impiétés à qui mieux mieux, et quand on avait fait bien du bruit et qu'on était bien ivre, on s'allait coucher et on recommençait le lendemain. » Tel est l'homme chargé de gérer l'« après-Louis XIV ».

Pour ce faire, il lui faut d'abord mettre en cause le testament rédigé le 2 août 1714 par le Roi-Soleil pour limiter les pouvoirs de son neveu et promouvoir le duc du Maine et le comte de Toulouse, ses bâtards « légitimés ». Seulement président d'un Conseil de régence dont les membres avaient été désignés d'avance, Philippe d'Orléans n'aurait disposé que d'une voix préférentielle en cas de partage des voix, toutes les décisions devant être prises à la majorité. Le 2 septembre 1715, ce testament sur le sort duquel Louis XIV ne se faisait guère d'illusions était vidé de toute substance par les parlementaires de Paris, heureux de prendre leur revanche sur un roi qui les avait systématiquement écartés des affaires de l'État et ravis d'entendre Philippe d'Orléans promettre : « À quelques titres que j'aie droit à la régence, j'ose vous assurer, Messieurs, que je la mériterai par mon zèle pour le service du Roi et par mon amour pour le bien public, surtout étant aidé par vos conseils et vos sages *remontrances* : je vous les demande par avance. » L'édit du 15 septembre 1715 rendait en effet au Parlement ce droit de remontrance qui lui avait été enlevé en 1673 et lui restituait un rôle politique dont il allait abondamment user pendant tout le siècle.

Le même édit du 15 septembre comblait les vœux de la haute aristocratie. Reprenant un plan de gouvernement esquissé par Fénelon, Saint-Simon et l'abbé de Saint-Pierre, le Régent supprimait les ministres et les secrétaires d'État et instituait à leur place sept conseils qui offraient à la noblesse de cour et d'épée l'occasion de prendre sa revanche sur la noblesse de robe, cantonnée dans des fonctions subalternes.

Abandonnée en 1718, cette polysynodie, qui était la forme de gouvernement appliquée en Espagne, apparaissait en fait comme une mesure de circonstance destinée à récompenser ceux qui avaient aidé le Régent à prendre le pouvoir, à calmer les rancunes de la vieille cour et à diviser les factions rivales pour mieux les contrôler. Ainsi, pour la première fois, une régence se faisait sans prise d'armes aristocratique.

Symboliquement aussi, on efface tout ce qui peut rappeler le pesant cérémonial de Versailles. Dès la fin du mois de septembre 1715, le Régent décide que la cour s'installera à Paris. Le père Le Tellier, le confesseur du Roi-Soleil, est exilé en province avec une pension annuelle pour assurer ses vieux jours. Madame de Maintenon s'enferme dans la maison de Saint-Cyr qu'elle avait fondée, on libère de prison un certain nombre de jansénistes et, surtout, on appelle à la présidence du Conseil de conscience le cardinal de Noailles, connu pour son hostilité à la bulle *Unigenitus*. Enfin, par décision du Conseil de régence, en juillet 1717, les bâtards « légitimés » perdent leur qualité de princes du sang et tout droit à la succession au trône. « Je me mourais de joie, écrit alors Saint-Simon, qui exprime la jubilation des ducs et des pairs. J'en étais à craindre la défaillance ; mon cœur dilaté à l'excès ne trouvait plus d'espace à s'étendre. La violence que je me faisais pour ne rien laisser échapper était infinie, et néanmoins ce tourment était délicieux. Je comparais les années et les temps de servitude, les jours funestes où, traîné au Parlement en victime, j'y avais servi de triomphe aux bâtards à plusieurs fois, les degrés divers par lesquels ils étaient montés à ce comble sur nos têtes ; je les comparais, dis-je, à ce jour de justice et de règle, à cette chute épouvantable, qui du même coup nous relevait par la force du ressort. [...] Je triomphais, je me vengeais, je nageais dans ma vengeance ; je jouissais du plein accomplissement des désirs les plus véhéments et les plus continus de ma vie. »

Le temps de la Régence est aussi celui de la réaction, mais une réaction qui n'a toutefois rien de sanguinaire. Moins d'un mois après la mort de Louis XIV, on inaugure dans la salle de l'Opéra, au Palais-Royal, un grand bal public ouvert à tous, trois fois par semaine, de onze heures du soir à quatre ou cinq heures du matin, moyennant six sous l'entrée. Et quand Philippe d'Orléans, venu en curieux, est apostrophé par de joyeux fêtards qui l'invitent à se joindre à eux, il ne se fait pas prier et se mêle aux danseurs. Le 18 mai 1716, les comédiens italiens, expulsés vingt ans auparavant pour avoir représenté la *Fausse Prude*, une pièce jugée insultante pour Madame de Maintenon, s'installent à l'Hôtel de Bourgogne. Les vastes perruques disparaissent au profit des cheveux courts frisés en grosses boucles. Les ceintures et les corsets cèdent devant les robes souples taillées dans les étoffes légères. Les élégantes se fardent de plâtre et se font peindre les veines en bleu. « Chinoiseries » et « singeries » rompent l'austère symétrie des chapiteaux classiques. La fantaisie rococo remplace peu à peu la sévérité de l'art louisquatorzien et l'*Iliade travestie* du jeune Marivaux ou le *Gil Blas* de Lesage illustrent l'ardeur d'un temps nouveau. Après les glaciations de Louis XIV vieillissant, le Régent préside à l'embarquement pour Cythère.

Le renversement des alliances

En 1715, tout le monde s'attendait à la mort prochaine du jeune Louis XV, dont la santé semblait fort fragile. Dans cette éventualité, Philippe d'Orléans devait lui succéder, à condition toutefois que Philippe V, le petit-fils de Louis XIV devenu roi d'Espagne, ne revienne sur sa renonciation au trône de France, qu'il tenait pour extorquée. Saint-Simon lui-même, fidèle compagnon du Régent, lui avait avoué que si le roi d'Espagne entrait en France pour revendiquer ses droits, il le soutiendrait. « Si moi, avait-il ajouté, tel que je suis pour vous, pense et sens de la sorte, qu'espéreriez-vous de tous les autres Français », ces Français qui, trois ans auparavant, suspectaient Philippe d'Orléans d'être responsable de la mort du dauphin, le duc de Bourgogne.

Négocié secrètement par l'abbé Dubois, qui avait quitté Paris le visage grimé, coiffé d'une perruque le rendant méconnaissable, le rapprochement avec l'Angleterre, qui choqua autant la vieille cour que le petit peuple, marque un renversement spectaculaire des alliances. Entre George Ier de Hanovre, le roi d'Angleterre toujours menacé par les jacobites, les partisans de la dynastie « légitime » des Stuarts en exil, et Philippe d'Orléans, dont les droits à une éventuelle succession à la couronne de France étaient contestés, se nouait une « entente cordiale » qui refermait les Pyrénées pour ouvrir le *Channel*. Une convention, signée à Hanovre en octobre 1716 entre le ministre anglais Stanhope et Dubois, se transforma en Triple-Alliance avec la Hollande le 4 janvier 1717, puis en Quadruple-Alliance quand, en août 1718, elle fut étendue à l'empereur d'Autriche.

La France reconnaissait les droits des Hanovre au trône d'Angleterre et acceptait d'expulser le prétendant Stuart. Elle promettait aussi de démanteler Mardyck, un ouvrage fortifié construit sur la côte flamande. En échange, en cas de crise de succession en France, le Régent aurait l'appui de l'Angleterre contre le roi d'Espagne. Fort critiqué par les anglophobes, cet accord consolidé par l'envoi de bouteilles de champagne à George Ier et de quelques pièces rares de vin de Bourgogne à lord Stanhope, assurait toutefois la paix en Europe pour un quart de siècle. Il traduisait surtout l'évolution d'une élite qui s'éloignait des jésuites et des dévots pour se rapprocher de l'Europe libérale et capitaliste.

En janvier 1719, le Régent, malgré ses scrupules, en vint même à déclarer la guerre au petit-fils de Louis XIV qui, poussé par sa seconde femme, l'ambitieuse Élisabeth Farnèse, et le fougueux cardinal Alberoni, voulait retrouver en Italie les possessions que le traité d'Utrecht lui avait enlevées. Menée sans grand entrain, mais avec assez de vigueur pour prendre quelques places en Pays basque espagnol, cette guerre des deux Philippe força le Bourbon d'Espagne à congédier le bouillant Alberoni, à renoncer définitivement à la couronne de France et à rejoindre le système d'alliances élaboré par le couple franco-britannique. La Sicile irait à l'Empereur, qui reconnaissait enfin Philippe V comme roi d'Espagne. Don Carlos, le fils d'Élisabeth Farnèse, aurait plus tard Parme et Florence. George Ier s'engageait à obtenir du Parlement britannique la rétrocession de Gibraltar à l'Espagne et, tandis que l'infante d'Espagne serait fiancée à Louis XV, le prince des Asturies épouserait Mademoiselle de Montpensier, l'une des filles du Régent. Pour une France épuisée par les guerres qu'elle venait de traverser, ce miracle d'équilibre qui assurait la paix avec ses voisins n'était pas une si mince affaire. C'était satisfaire aussi les colombes œcuméniques qui, à travers Fénelon et l'abbé de Saint-Pierre, avaient tant milité pour une diplomatie pacifiste. Décidément, les boutefeux du Grand Siècle ne pesaient plus guère. Pour la génération des « années folles », il était absurde de « mourir pour Mardyck ».

Une salutaire banqueroute

La banqueroute de Law, que les contemporains prononçaient Lass, n'a pas amélioré la réputation du Régent. Spéculation folle, enrichissement des uns et ruine des autres, tel est le « lieu de mémoire » qui a détourné durablement les Français de la banque et du papier-monnaie. Jamais pourtant banqueroute ne fut aussi nécessaire, voire bénéfique.

L'héritage financier du Roi-Soleil était en effet catastrophique. La dette constituée avoisinait 2,1 milliards de livres, auxquels il fallait ajouter plus de 700 millions de dette flottante, ce qui portait la charge annuelle de remboursement à 165 millions de livres, alors que les recettes fiscales ordinaires ne s'élevaient qu'à 69 millions de livres et que les dépenses normales annuelles atteignaient 146 millions de livres. Les revenus des années 1716 et 1717 étaient consommés d'avance, et, dans les caisses, il ne restait plus que 800 000 livres de trésorerie. Président du Conseil de finance, le duc de Noailles écrivait à Madame de Maintenon : « On a trouvé les choses dans un état plus terrible qu'on ne peut le dépeindre, il n'y a guère d'exemple d'avoir vu une monarchie dans une pareille situation. »

Pire, en pratiquant de 1713 à 1715 une politique obstinée de « monnaie forte », alors que l'état de l'économie exigeait au contraire une politique de relance, le contrôleur général Desmarets avait réduit les moyens de paiement en circulation, encouragé l'évasion de capitaux vers Amsterdam et Londres et alangui la consommation. C'était une fois encore favoriser ceux qui « s'enrichissent en dormant » au détriment de ceux qui s'appauvrissent en travaillant. C'était commettre l'erreur souvent reproduite de vouloir redresser l'économie au prix d'une rigueur rétrograde.

Face à cette situation, on usa des expédients traditionnels : diminution des dépenses, avances des financiers et des traitants, réduction des rentes, dévaluation. L'écurie royale fut abaissée à cent chevaux, les frais de table furent divisés par vingt, la musique du roi réduite à vingt-quatre violons et les pensions des courtisans supérieures à 600 livres diminuées de moitié. Classiquement aussi, on stigmatisa « les fortunes immenses et précipitées de ceux qui se sont enrichis par des voies criminelles », on frappa le brasseur d'affaires Antoine Crozat d'une taxe de 6 600 000 livres, on incarcéra les agioteurs les plus crapuleux, on exposa au pilori les « voleurs du peuple », on appela les domestiques à la délation. Comme toujours aussi, la montagne accoucha d'une souris. C'est à peine une centaine de millions que ces procédures firent rentrer dans les caisses de l'État.

C'est dans cette conjoncture fort maussade qu'apparaît un « économiste » écossais qui a sans doute eu tort d'avoir raison trop tôt. Né à Édimbourg en 1671, John Law, fils d'un riche orfèvre, est contraint de fuir l'Écosse après avoir tué en duel un jeune dandy pour une « histoire de femme ». En 1705, de retour au pays, il se fait connaître en publiant *Considérations sur le numéraire et le commerce*, un essai sur la monnaie et le commerce dans lequel il affirme que la prospérité d'un pays dépend de l'abondance de ses liquidités et propose l'émission d'une monnaie de papier indépendante des arrivages capricieux d'or et d'argent des Amériques. De même que le lingot a constitué un progrès par rapport au troc, la pièce par rapport au lingot, de même, affirme-t-il, les billets sont préférables aux pièces quant à la commodité de transport et à la sécurité.

Deux ans plus tard, entre tripots et salons de jeux, il présente au gouvernement français un mémoire démontrant, dans le même esprit, qu'une « espèce de monnaie nouvelle peut être meilleure que l'or et l'argent ». S'appuyant sur les précédents constitués par les banques d'Amsterdam, de Londres et d'Écosse, il propose de créer une institution publique de crédit chargée de centraliser les recettes de l'État, d'émettre des billets pour pallier la rareté des espèces métalliques et de faire baisser les taux d'intérêt pour stimuler les affaires et soulager la misère des pauvres. En substituant à l'or, « cette relique barbare », comme l'écrira au début du XXe siècle John Maynard Keynes, une monnaie de papier dont la création serait à la disposition de l'État, on découragerait l'épargne stérile, on stimulerait l'investissement productif, on éliminerait les traitants et les fermiers de l'impôt et on augmenterait les richesses qui, à terme, permettraient à l'État d'éteindre sa dette. John Law concevait ainsi le premier « système » coordonné d'expansion économique.

« La banque, écrivait-il en décembre 1715 au Régent, n'est pas la seule ni la plus grande de mes idées ; je produirai un travail qui surprendra l'Europe par les changements qu'il portera en faveur de la France, des changements plus forts que ceux qui ont été produits par la découverte des Indes ou par l'introduction du crédit. Par ce travail, Votre Altesse Royale sera en état de relever le royaume de la triste situation dans laquelle il est réduit, et de le rendre plus puissant qu'il n'a encore été, d'établir l'ordre dans les finances, de remettre, entretenir et augmenter l'agriculture, les manufactures et le commerce. [...] Ce grand royaume, bien gouverné, serait l'arbitre de l'Europe sans se servir de la force. C'est sur un commerce étendu, sur le nombre et la richesse des habitants que la puissance de la France devra être fondée. »

Ce « système » qui prétendait que la richesse réside dans le commerce et que le commerce dépend d'une monnaie abondante avait de quoi heurter un pays où la rente était considérée comme la plus sûre des richesses et qui continuait à entretenir vis-à-vis de l'argent un fort sentiment de culpabilité. Il avait par contre de quoi séduire Philippe d'Orléans, qui préférait la paix à la guerre et qui, pour avoir pratiqué l'alchimie, pouvait être tenté de faire de l'or avec du papier.

Avec l'autorisation du Régent, John Law fonde le 2 mai 1716 une banque de dépôt et d'escompte privée au capital de six millions de livres. Très vite, elle rencontre un vif succès tant pour le faible taux qu'elle prend pour escompter les effets de commerce — 6 % puis 5 %, alors qu'auparavant on prélevait fréquemment 30 % — que pour sa ponctualité à échanger, sans réclamer de courtage, des billets contre de l'argent. En avril 1717, elle prend un caractère officieux quand un édit prescrit aux receveurs des tailles d'accepter ses billets en paiement des impôts et de s'en servir pour éviter les transferts de numéraire de la province vers Paris.

Le 23 août 1717, John Law peut mettre à feu le second étage de son « système » en constituant la Compagnie d'Occident, chargée d'exploiter les vastes territoires de la Louisiane cédés par Antoine

Crozat. Au capital de 100 millions de livres divisé en 200 000 actions de 500 livres uniquement payables en billets d'État, la Compagnie recevait pour vingt-cinq ans la propriété de toutes les terres et mines du Nouveau Monde et le monopole du commerce des castors du Canada. Le plan, génial, consistait en fait à transformer les créanciers de l'État en actionnaires de la Compagnie. Le pari, risqué, était de construire un empire commercial avec une mise de fonds dérisoire.

Un nouveau seuil est franchi à la fin de l'année 1718. Le 4 décembre, la banque privée est transformée en banque royale avec privilège de l'émission de papier-monnaie et succursales à La Rochelle, Orléans, Tours et Amiens. En mai 1719, la Compagnie d'Occident devient Compagnie des Indes après avoir absorbé la Compagnie des Indes orientales, obtenu le quasi-monopole du commerce extérieur maritime et l'essentiel des recettes de l'État avec le monopole du tabac, le recouvrement du produit des fermes générales et les droits liés à la frappe des monnaies. Le succès est tel qu'il faut accorder priorité aux actionnaires de la Compagnie d'Occident, qui peuvent souscrire une action de la Compagnie des Indes contre quatre actions de l'Occident, quatre « mères » pour avoir une « fille », disait-on alors.

Quand Law, converti au catholicisme, est nommé, le 5 janvier 1720, contrôleur général des Finances, l'action des « Indes », acquise moyennant un premier versement de 500 livres, cotait 10 000 livres. Rue Quincampoix, où était établi le siège de la banque, la spéculation sur les actions du « Mississippi » se déchaînait à un tel point qu'il fallut fermer la rue avec des grilles, une cloche annonçant l'ouverture et la fermeture de la banque. « La rue Quincampoix fait qu'on ne joue plus à Paris, écrivait la princesse Palatine. C'est une vraie rage ; j'en suis excédée : on n'entend parler que de cela, et il ne se passe pas de jour que je ne reçoive trois ou quatre lettres de personnes qui me demandent des actions ; c'est bien ennuyeux. [...] D'Angleterre, on envoie tous les diamants, tous les joyaux, tous les bijoux : ceux qui ont fait des gains si colossaux avec les actions achètent tout sans marchander. Il se passe d'étranges histoires. Il y a quelques jours, une dame était à l'Opéra. Elle en fit venir une autre fort laide, mais ayant les plus beaux habits du monde et couverte de diamants. La fille de Madame Bégond se met à dire à sa mère : « Ma mère, regardez bien cette dame parée : il me semble que c'est notre cuisinière Marie. » [...] Tout le monde à l'amphithéâtre commence à murmurer : « Marie, la cuisinière ! » Celle-ci se lève et dit tout haut : « Hé bien oui, je suis Marie, la cuisinière de Madame Bégond. Je suis devenue riche, je me pare de mon bien ; je n'en dois rien à personne ; j'aime me parer, je

me pare ; cela ne fait tort à personne. Qu'a donc à redire à cela ? »
Vous pensez comme on a ri. »

Tous les chroniqueurs de l'époque dénoncent cet « insupportable » brassage social que, de tout temps, autorise le jeu spéculatif. Pour tenter de freiner les débordements, une ordonnance du 28 décembre 1719 punit même de sanctions les « maîtres tailleurs, garçons et ouvriers qui se seraient permis d'habiller d'or et de soie la valetaille à l'exception cependant des gens au service des ambassadeurs et des seigneurs étrangers ».

En cette fin d'année 1719, on pouvait toutefois estimer que le « système » fonctionnait. La banque avait émis pour 620 millions de billets dont la convertibilité en or ou en argent était assurée. Les bénéfices tirés de la perception des impôts s'élevaient à près de 100 millions de livres, ce qui permettait de verser aux actions, même à vingt fois leur valeur d'émission, un dividende de 2 %, taux d'intérêt que Law souhaitait progressivement imposer à l'ensemble des prêteurs d'argent.

Mais c'est précisément au moment où l'Écossais parvenait au sommet de sa puissance que le « système » commença à se gripper. En février 1720, deux princes du sang, le duc de Bourbon et le prince de Conti, amis des frères Pâris, des banquiers en vue hostiles à Law, « réalisèrent », c'est-à-dire vinrent spectaculairement se faire rembourser en or leurs billets. Au même moment, le change étranger accusait une perte de 8 % sur la place de Londres et de 10 % sur celle d'Amsterdam. Pour enrayer le mouvement, Law lança alors une véritable bombe en prenant des mesures qui ne visaient rien moins qu'à proscrire l'usage de pièces d'or dans les échanges et même à punir la détention de métal précieux !

Dans une lettre au *Mercure de France* datée du 11 mars 1720, il justifie cette mesure en développant l'argument que nous appellerions aujourd'hui d'intérêt collectif. « L'argent ne nous appartient que par voie de circulation et il ne nous est pas permis de nous l'approprier dans un autres sens. [...] S'imagine-t-on que le peuple plaindra des hommes qui veulent lui arracher sa substance ? Le peuple hait naturellement les riches avares. »

Après une brève période d'accalmie, la tendance se retourne. Law ayant promis le remboursement officiel des actions à 9 000 livres, il lui faut imprimer toujours davantage de billets pour répondre à la demande empressée des actionnaires. Le 21 mai 1720, pendant les fêtes de la Pentecôte et en l'absence du Parlement, en vacances, un arrêt annonce que la valeur des actions et des billets de banque sera réduite de moitié ! Ce sont alors de véritables émeutes qui emportent le « système ». Le 17 juillet, rue Vivienne, nouveau siège de la banque, une bousculade étouffe quinze personnes, selon un témoignage discuté par Edgar Faure, l'historien de cette banqueroute. Enfin, un arrêt du 10 octobre décrète pour la fin du mois la cessation du cours de tous les billets. Le 14 décembre, Law, ruiné, doit s'enfuir à l'étranger. Arrêté en mars 1722, le bilan de la Compagnie des Indes fait état d'un actif de 76 millions et d'un passif de 9 millions...

En fait, on sait aujourd'hui que cette plaie d'argent fut loin d'être mortelle. Si cette expérience en avance sur son temps a renforcé la méfiance des Français envers la banque, la Bourse et le crédit, elle n'a pas eu en fait que des inconvénients. Elle a libéré partiellement l'énorme dette d'un État qui s'est lancé dans une politique de grands travaux dont les bénéfices irrigueront tout le siècle. L'inflation, comme toujours, a développé les affaires. Dans les campagnes, des terres en friche ont été remises en culture. Le maréchal d'Estrées, qui visite la Bretagne pendant l'été 1720, voit des fermes repeintes et des paysans mieux nourris. Les archives des notaires indiquent aussi d'importantes mutations. Surtout, la hausse des prix de vente combinée au désendettement et à la baisse des taux d'intérêt a soulagé bien des misères. Les actes de quittance qui éteignent des dettes datant de Colbert se multiplient en Picardie, en Normandie et en Bourgogne. Unanimement constatée dans les années qui suivirent, l'aisance est bien à mettre en partie au crédit de Law et du Régent. Mais il est rarement populaire de préférer l'intérêt des débiteurs à celui des créanciers.

Une glorieuse croissance

En 1715, John Law avait promis au Régent qu'un bon gouvernement suffirait « à augmenter le nombre des peuples à 30 millions, les revenus généraux à 3 000 millions et les revenus du roi à 300 millions ». Il a eu raison trop tôt. Dans les années 1780, la France compte 28,5 millions d'habitants, le revenu national avoisine 4 000 millions et les recettes de l'État atteignent 500 millions.

Labourant, filant et tissant à tour de bras, « traitant » le « bois d'ébène », vendant le sucre, l'indigo et le café, les Français ont fait du royaume la première puissance économique mondiale et de leurs ports des ruches bourdonnantes. Certes, tous n'ont pas profité au même degré de cette glorieuse croissance, mais tous ont gagné la bataille de la survie et acquis une modeste aisance.

Le recul de la mort

En 1715, la France comptait environ 22 millions d'habitants. Deux générations plus tard, vers 1780, elle en abrite un peu plus de 28 millions. À elle seule, cette croissance de la « peuplade » mesure mieux que tout l'aimable conjoncture du siècle des Lumières. Infranchissable depuis plus de quatre siècles, le plafond des 22 millions d'habitants était pour la première fois « crevé ». Loin d'être en « crise », contrairement à ce que l'on peut encore lire, l'« Ancien Régime », comme on disait autrefois, est saisi par le progrès.

C'est que peste, guerre et famine, les trois grands fléaux qui collaboraient activement pour envoyer au cimetière les populations en excès, ont pratiquement cessé d'exercer leurs funestes effets. La peste de Marseille, apportée le 25 mai 1720 par Le Grand Saint-Antoine, un bateau en provenance de Syrie, marque le dernier assaut de l'épidémie sur le territoire. Selon les comptes généraux de l'Administration, elle aurait fait 120 000 morts, dont 40 000 à Marseille même. Mais les nombreux cordons sanitaires mis en place par les autorités pour isoler les zones contaminées ont évité la propagation dans le royaume. Certes, typhoïde, dysenterie, variole et suette poursuivent toujours leur carrière, mais sans pouvoir remettre en cause l'inexorable triomphe de la vie. À Millau, où les conditions d'hygiène et d'alimentation ne sont pas fameuses, on compte encore douze crises de mortalité entre 1700 et 1789. Cela n'a toutefois pas empêché la population de la ville de passer de 3 000 habitants à 5 500. À Caen, malgré les typhoïdes de 1740 et de 1764-1765, les affections broncho-pulmonaires de 1755-1756, les grippes de 1763, 1767 et 1782, la diphtérie de 1764, la scarlatine de 1776 et la variole en 1769, 1775 et 1785, la population est allègrement grimpée de 26 500 habitants en 1700 à 38 000 en 1789.

Depuis 1713, la France est aussi débarrassée des conflits qui, des guerres de Religion aux guerres de Louis XIV, avaient à plusieurs reprises brisé tout élan démographique. Dans les villes, les remparts tombent pour faire place à des boulevards et des promenades. Enfin, et surtout, la famine a disparu. Même quand les grains sont rares et chers, comme en 1740-1741, on trépasse de dysenterie et non plus de faim.

Ce sont aussi de multiples et infimes progrès qui ont fait reculer la mort. Si la médicalisation reste peu répandue et l'efficacité des traitements faible, les efforts de l'administration sanitaire sont réels. Multiplication et surveillance des hôpitaux, pavage des rues, ramassage des ordures, transfert des cimetières hors des agglomérations et des églises, drainage des marécages, distributions de secours en cas de disette, construction de solides granges en pierre pour stocker les grains, autant de mesures qui ont contribué au mieux-être général. En parcourant les provinces pour enseigner l'art des accouchements et proposer aux futures mères des leçons pratiques grâce à un mannequin qui « représentait le bassin d'une femme, la matrice, son orifice, ses ligaments, le conduit appelé vagin, et l'intestin rectum » et un modèle d'enfant de grandeur naturelle, dont les jointures flexibles permettaient de le mettre dans des positions différentes, Madame Du Coudray a probablement aussi contribué à faire reculer la mortalité des nouveau-nés. Pour l'ensemble de la France rurale, celle-ci serait passée de 350 ‰ au début du siècle à 263 ‰ dans les années 1770 et de 280 ‰ à 240 ‰ pour la France en général. Un progrès léger mais certain qui allonge l'espérance de vie. Une fois passé le cap difficile de l'enfance, on mourait finalement assez « vieux » sous l'Ancien Régime, puisqu'un sexagénaire pouvait encore espérer vivre plus de douze ans.

Comme la mort recule, la vie a plus de prix. Certes, on abandonne beaucoup d'enfants, 25 000 par an, en grande partie amenés à Paris par des filles de la campagne venues y déposer « le fruit de leur faute ». Certes, on met beaucoup en nourrice, avec des risques énormes pour la santé des nourrissons mais, à doses homéopathiques, se diffuse un nouveau modèle maternel où allaitement et puériculture riment avec émancipation et épanouissement.

On en vient même à « tromper la nature » pour contrôler la taille de la famille et mieux espacer la production des héritiers. « Le libertinage pénètre dans les mariages, écrit en 1774 Jean-Baptiste Moheau, secrétaire de l'intendant d'Auvergne. Déjà ces funestes secrets inconnus à tout animal autre que l'homme ont pénétré dans les campagnes ; on trompe la nature jusque dans les villages. » Autrefois tabou, le *coïtus interruptus*, plus fréquemment pratiqué, traduit le fait que pour des maris plus délicats, plus « sensibles », disait-on à l'époque, on peut à la fois maîtriser mieux son corps, respecter davantage son épouse et s'arranger pour ne pas faire paître plus d'un veau à l'herbage, comme diront les paysans normands au XIXe siècle. On traite même de « verrats » les maris jugés trop prolifiques et insoucieux, comme ces Lyonnais qui, impavides, font à leur conjointe un enfant par an pendant la quinzaine d'années de vie commune. À Rouen, en revanche, précocement contraceptive, la descendance des notables, bientôt imités par les boutiquiers puis par les ouvriers et artisans, passe de sept enfants à la fin du XVIIe siècle à quatre entre 1760 et 1789. Dans le Vexin normand, les ménages formés à partir de 1780 acceptent deux, voire trois enfants, rarement plus, car le besoin de remplacer les mort-nés s'est fait moins pressant. Chez les ducs et pairs, on a su avant les autres se « retirer » et enseigner cette virtuosité au personnel de service, éduqué d'autre part par les innombrables prostituées, sans doute 40 000 à Paris, qui compte 600 000 habitants à la veille de la Révolution.

Plus efficace encore, on se marie de plus en plus tard. Mariées en moyenne à vingt et un ans vers 1550, les Normandes convolent à vingt-cinq ans deux siècles plus tard, ce qui se traduit par deux bébés de moins. À Sainghin-en-Mélantois, près de Lille, c'est à vingt-sept ou vingt-huit ans que les jeunes filles se marient à la même époque. « Contamination » du riche au pauvre, transmission de l'urbain au rural ? Ces comportements que l'on ne retrouve alors nulle part en Europe font de la France la première nation du monde à avoir pratiqué le contrôle des naissances. C'est probablement parce que la France des Lumières était déjà un pays de petits propriétaires où il fallait patienter jusqu'à la mort du père pour pouvoir s'« installer » et prendre femme. En attendant, piaffant d'impatience, les jeunes multipliaient les conceptions prénuptiales qui, à Sainghin, passent de 15,2 % du total des naissances à la fin du XVIIe siècle à 36,8 % dans les années 1770 et 1780. Autant de mutations lentes qui traduisent la fermentation d'une société nouvelle, plus malthusienne et plus permissive, plus individuelle et plus tolérante. Autant de « révolutions silencieuses » qui gonflent une classe d'âge qui, approchant la trentaine à la fin des années 1780, réclame vigoureusement sa place au soleil. « C'est l'Émile [de Jean-Jacques Rousseau], écrit à cette époque Restif de La Bretonne, qui nous amène cette génération taquine, entêtée, insolente, impudente, décideuse, qui parle haut, fait taire les vieillards et montre avec une égale audace, tantôt sa folie native, fortifiée par l'éducation, tantôt sa sagesse immature âcre et verte comme le verjus de la mi-août. »

Une révolution de « gagne-petit »

Une population qui augmente de 30 %, une production agricole en hausse d'un peu moins de 40 % du début à la fin du siècle, telle est la modeste arithmétique d'une économie rurale peu productive qui a toutefois trouvé les moyens de nourrir ces bouches plus nombreuses.

Certes, il n'y a eu ni « révolution » agricole, ni « révolution » alimentaire, comme l'a montré l'historien Michel Morineau, mais « une somme de petites acquisitions techniques, une somme de petites trouvailles, une succession d'essais obscurs, persévérés, abandonnés, repris, triomphants ou piteux, l'existence de solutions à portée de la main au grand problème des subsistances, une démarche empirique, capricieuse, irrationnelle » qui ne bouleverse rien, mais atténue le grand « souci des bleds ».

Mieux distribuée par l'allongement du réseau routier, encouragée par la monarchie et les sociétés d'agriculture, valorisée par les élites physiocratiques qui font du laboureur le sel de l'humanité et soutiennent que seule la terre restitue aux hommes plus de matière qu'elle ne reçoit d'eux, la production a permis de fournir au Français moyen, à la veille de la Révolution, une modeste pitance de 1 800 calories par jour, ce qui suffit à éliminer les famines et à espacer les disettes. Le grand progrès du siècle des Lumières est là, dans l'atténuation des oscillations brutales qui décourageaient tous les six ou sept ans l'essor du produit agricole. Après 1710, les crises récurrentes de mortalité font place à de simples difficultés productrices d'émeutes. C'est incontestablement moins dangereux.

À cet égard, zone déshéritée entre toutes, l'Auvergne nous offre le modèle de cette révolution de « gagne-petit ». Des défrichements en montagne, des bêchages en plein champ, des céréales de printemps en lieu et place d'une jachère autrefois biennale, des plantations de vigne pour profiter des bons prix du vin, des prairies artificielles à base de sainfoin, de la pomme de terre cultivée à partir des années 1770, un doublement du nombre des porcs, des moutons pour le marché lyonnais, des bovins pour les marchés de Sceaux et de Poissy, des hommes qui vont s'employer temporairement à Paris et font de la sorte rentrer chaque année entre 1 et 2 millions de livres et surtout beaucoup d'huile de coude, autant de petits progrès qui permettent de gagner la bataille de la survie et de nourrir une population qui augmente de 40 à 50 %.

Stimulés par la croissance des villes, dont la population passe de 3,7 millions d'habitants en 1725 à 5,3 millions en 1789, les échanges de produits commercialisables désenclavent les campagnes et permettent de plus fructueuses spécialisations. Gouffre de viande, avec une consommation de 60 à 80 kilos par an et par habitant, mais aussi consommatrice de bois, de vin et de grains, la capitale, en particulier, crée autour d'elle un large bassin de ravitaillement. Dans le pays de Bray, observe en 1787 le subdélégué de Gournay-en-Bray, « on s'occupe principalement du commerce du beurre. Cette denrée, que la nature du sol donne en excellence, est portée chaque semaine, avec le plus grand soin, à Paris, où elle est justement tant estimée, tant recherchée. On est tellement attaché à cette partie d'agriculture que depuis quelque temps on y a appliqué toutes les terres qui y peuvent [être] propres. Il se fait beaucoup de veaux qui se portent pour la plupart à Pontoise, aux environs de Paris et à Paris même. Il se fait beaucoup de volailles et surtout de dindons, et ces autres comestibles s'exportent à Paris. Il se fait une grande quantité de porcs qu'on conduit aux marchés de Saint-Germain et d'autres lieux. Il se fait encore au marché de Gournay, pour Paris, une très grande quantité d'œufs et, dans la saison, de pigeons, mais ces autres denrées viennent pour la plupart des contrées voisines, même de plus loin. »

En Languedoc, stimulé par le marché toulousain, le maïs, fourrage et céréale à la fois, aliment de l'homme et de la volaille, rogne la jachère et entre largement dans les circuits de l'échange. En 1696, la part du commerce des grains dans l'ensemble du commerce languedocien représentait 1,8 million de livres sur un commerce total de 36 millions (5 %). En 1788, elle est passée à 18 millions de livres sur un commerce total de 72 millions (25 %). Lourmarin, en Provence, qui, dans la décennie 1780, produit 1 609 charges de grain et en consomme 2 949, comble aisément ce déficit céréalier en exportant 300 charges de vin sur les 1 500 produites par les vignes du terroir. À Azereix, en Gascogne, les vignobles passent de 31 hectares en 1692 à 56 hectares en 1767, sarclés et taillés par une population qui s'accroît de 40 % pendant le siècle. La construction du canal du Midi ouvre au bas Languedoc méditerranéen le marché toulousain. En Aunis, en Saintonge et en Angoumois, on travaille pour l'outre-Manche. Les exportations des eaux-de-vie de Cognac et Jarnac doublent des années 1720 aux années 1780. En Île-de-France, on multiplie les cépages pour alimenter en piquette un peuple de Paris raisonnablement méfiant à l'égard de l'eau.

Produit d'économie ouverte, destiné presque totalement à la vente, le vin assure alors le bonheur des campagnes, faisant vivre, selon Lavoisier, plus de 2,5 millions d'individus, soit pratiquement un Français sur dix. Sur les trente-deux généralités que compte alors le royaume, trois seulement, Caen, Lille et Valenciennes, ne sont pas viticoles. Mais, poussant jusqu'en Picardie, en Soissonnais et en Ardenne, pénétrant jusqu'à Paris, l'immense vignoble qui couvre alors la France produit près de 30 millions d'hectolitres. De quoi charger, et au-delà, toute la flotte marchande de l'Empire britannique. De quoi assurer du numéraire au maigre propriétaire parcellaire. De quoi surtout donner du travail à une foule de journaliers. À la fin du règne de Louis XIV, les paysans bourguignons étaient nombreux à coucher sur la paille avec leur cochon. Soixante années plus tard, ils expédient du vin vers Paris, du grain vers Marseille, se nourrissent de 250 à 350 kilos de grain par tête et d'un porc gras par famille et par an.

Autour de Lille, qui fournit à la campagne le fumier de cheval, on jardine à tour de bras, sans jachère, cultivant sans relâche le chou, la betterave et le tabac, le trèfle, les navets et les fèves, avec des rendements céréaliers de 28 à 29 hectolitres à l'hectare. Écuelles en terre et pots en bois sont alors remplacés par de la vaisselle en faïence et en étain, tandis que chenets, casseroles, bouilloires et poêles enrichissent la batterie familiale. Les tenanciers flamands n'ont pas été éclairés par les 1 214 ouvrages agronomiques publiés au siècle des

Lumières mais, comme les paysans chinois, ils ont su fumer leurs modestes parcelles à la cendre et à l'engrais humain. Autant de technologies douces qui économisent une révolution agricole à l'anglaise. N'en déplaise à Arthur Young, ce voyageur britannique qui se déclarait frappé par le retard des méthodes de production et des techniques de l'agriculture française, il a suffi que le rendement à la semence passe de 5 à 5,5 pour 1, un changement imperceptible aux yeux des contemporains, pour assurer plutôt bien que mal la survie de l'immense infanterie paysanne. Gagnante en qualité et en quantité, la production agricole n'a pas perdu la course avec la population.

L'élan de l'industrie

Grande puissance agricole possédant, en gros, le quart des terres arables européennes, la France est aussi devenue une grande puissance industrielle avec, au XVIIIᵉ siècle, un taux de croissance annuel de la production d'environ 1,5 % qui n'est pas loin d'égaler celui de la Grande-Bretagne, une estimation des historiens économistes qui bouleverse un certain nombre d'idées reçues sur le retard et l'archaïsme français. Des années 1700 aux années 1780, la valeur courante du produit industriel et artisanal aurait ainsi quadruplé, passant de 385 millions de livres à 1 574 millions. En fin de siècle, le produit industriel représentait alors 43 % du produit physique total, contre 41 % en Grande-Bretagne...

Certes, la France souffre d'un certain retard technique sur sa grande rivale d'outre-Manche, qui multiplie inventions et « mécaniques », de la navette volante à la machine à vapeur, et de la fonte au coke à la production d'acier au creuset. Mais, spécialisée dans le haut de gamme, alors que la Grande-Bretagne fabrique en série des produits de moindre qualité, elle sait créer une masse énorme de richesses par des procédés anciens et puiser dans son vaste réservoir de main-d'œuvre pour faire l'économie de l'investissement technologique.

Bénéficiant d'une demande élargie et d'un effet de mode diffusé à des couches nouvelles, les industries textiles enregistrent des progressions spectaculaires, produisant 30 millions d'aunes carrées en 1789 contre 17 en 1716. Ouvrant les armoires du peuple de Paris pour en faire l'inventaire, Daniel Roche y a fait d'étonnantes découvertes. Vers 1700, la garde-robe masculine habituelle se composait de quatre ou cinq pièces principales. Vers 1780, elle en compte le double. Au temps de Louis XIV, linge et tabliers étaient coupés dans des toiles frustes, lin et chanvre essentiellement, et les couleurs étaient sombres et uniformes. Au temps de Louis XV, tout a changé. Les bas sont à tous les pieds. Les cols sont dans les deux tiers des armoires, les manchettes dans les trois quarts des commodes. Les caleçons, inconnus vers 1700, sont désormais prisés. Le mouchoir de coton est devenu l'accessoire de propreté indispensable et les rideaux, installés aux croisées, traduisent le besoin fort nouveau d'intimité. Et tandis qu'en 1715, bruns, noirs et gris teintaient 69 % des vêtements portés par les domestiques, en 1775, rouges, blancs, jaunes, verts et bleus en colorent 74 %.

Pour les femmes comme pour les hommes, la chaussure, surtout, est la grande conquête du siècle des Lumières. Observant la révolution, silencieuse une nouvelle fois, des modes féminines, Louis Sébastien Mercier écrit dans les années 1780 : « Tandis que le galon d'or et d'argent entre dans la livrée de la servitude, le sarrau de toile couvre à peine le laboureur et le vigneron. La classe travaillante [paysanne] voit les valets en habit de drap galonné et les femmes de chambre en robe de soie, même avec quelques petits diamants ». Il ajoute, pour s'en désoler : « La Grisette est plus heureuse dans sa pauvreté que la fille des bourgeois. Elle se livre à la licence dans l'âge où ses charmes ont encore de l'éclat ; son indigence lui donne une pleine liberté, et son bonheur vient quelquefois de n'avoir point eu de dot. [...] Aux premiers besoins de la vie se joint celui de la parure : la vanité, non moins mauvaise conseillère que la misère, lui répète tout bas d'ajouter la ressource de sa jeunesse et de sa figure à celle de son aiguille. »

Dans la ville de Grenoble, en 1725, on compte 125 tailleurs et tailleuses d'habits et 239 savetiers et cordonniers pour un peu plus de 20 000 habitants.

Cette conquête fragile des apparences que l'on retrouve aussi dans les paroisses rurales assoit le règne des étoffes. La draperie de Sedan voit son chiffre d'affaires quintupler entre 1732 et 1788. Celle du Languedoc, dispersée en des centaines de villages, des Cévennes aux Pyrénées, connaît un remarquable essor et alimente les marchés du Levant. En Champagne, 30 000 tisserands travaillent dans un rayon de 50 à 80 kilomètres autour de Reims. Sur le plateau picard, entre Amiens, Aumale et Beauvais, on trouve plus de métiers à tisser que de charrues.

L'expansion du « roi-coton » est énorme dans la région de Rouen, où les métiers occupent environ 60 000 personnes. « C'est sur l'industrie que compte la population de cette région, écrit Arthur Young. Tout le pays forme un curieux spectacle ; on voit une grande fabrication, une énorme population laborieuse, qui sont absolument nuisibles à l'agriculture. Tel en a été le résultat dans tout le pays de Caux, dont le sol peut être classé parmi les plus beaux qui soient en France. Si c'eût été un territoire misérablement pauvre, rocheux, stérile, le résultat aurait été avantageux, car l'industrie aurait couvert cette région de cultures. Cependant, les cultivateurs du pays de Caux ne sont pas seulement fabricants ; ils ont aussi le goût pour le commerce ; ceux d'entre eux qui sont riches s'engagent dans des spéculations commerciales au Havre, particulièrement dans le trafic du coton, et quelques-uns même dans celui des Indes occidentales. »

Quand est levée, en 1759, l'interdiction de fabriquer, de vendre et de porter « des toiles de coton peintes en Inde, ou contrefaites dans le royaume », le succès des « indiennes » est effectivement fulgurant. Dès 1730, on prévenait l'intendant de Dijon que « l'usage de ces étoffes [malgré l'interdiction] est si général que les gens de condition en font faire non seulement des ameublements [...], mais que les dames et leurs domestiques mêmes s'en font faire des habillements, que les bourgeoises et les femmes d'artisans, de laboureurs, de vigne-rons, à leur exemple, en font aussi usage. » À la veille de la Révolu-tion, on compte quelque 170 indienneries fondées par de jeunes patrons, anciens ouvriers qualifiés pour près de la moitié, étrangers pour un tiers, la plupart de confession luthérienne ou calviniste, ardents à la besogne, attentifs à l'évolution des techniques comme à celle de la mode.

Fils d'un teinturier wurtembergeois, Christophe Philippe Ober-kampf fonde en 1759, à l'âge de vingt et un ans, une fabrique à Jouy-en-Josas, près de Versailles, avec trois imprimeurs, un capital social de 50 000 livres et des « secrets » jalousement préservés, comme la préparation des couleurs et l'apprêt final des toiles peintes. En 1784, le capital de l'entreprise se monte à 2,64 millions de livres et la fabrique emploie 900 personnes dirigées à la baguette par un « indus-triel », cet « homme nouveau » qui, dans la société, tend à prendre la place du « maître » et exige de plus en plus de « liberté ». « C'est à ceux qui veulent élever des fabriques à calculer sur les possibilités et les difficultés qui s'offrent à leurs projets, écrit en 1783 l'intendant de Rouen. Le gouvernement ne doit pas faire de calculs pour eux. L'inté-rêt personnel voit mieux que l'administration dans ce qui les concerne. Il ne lui faut que de la liberté et c'est de la principale tâche du législa-teur que de la lui accorder. » À cette date, le « colbertisme » est passé de mode.

Investie par la noblesse, qui pouvait la pratiquer sans déroger, l'industrie sidérurgique fabrique aussi bien socs de charrues, lames de couteaux, baïonnettes, lames de sabres que « bouches à feu ». Dans les années 1780, sur 603 maîtres de forge, 304 appartenaient à l'aristocratie qui, possédant forêts, cours d'eau et terres à mine, considère le travail du métal comme une extension normale de ses activités seigneuriales. Le prince de Croÿ et le marquis de Cernay gèrent les mines d'Anzin qui, dans les années 1780, produisent 300 000 tonnes de charbon et emploient 4 000 mineurs. Le duc de Béthune dirige les forges de Cosne. Les Montmorency et les Ségur s'épanouissent à Saint-Gobain, dont les ventes quadruplent de 1725 à 1788. Les usines bretonnes du prince de Condé assurent plus du tiers de la fabrication sidérurgique de la province, et à Belfort, la duchesse de Mazarin possède les usines les plus puissantes de haute Alsace. De Dietrich à Haguenau et les de Wendel à Hayange, des anoblis dynamiques, inaugurent en France la fonte au coke. Fondée en 1782 par des grands financiers de la capitale et installée avec le soutien technique de l'Anglais Wilkinson, Le Creusot fait figure d'usine géante avec ses quatre hauts fourneaux, ses fours à réverbère, ses marteaux, ses fonderies de canons et ses machines à vapeur.

L'appel des marchés

Tandis que l'agriculture nourrit ses hommes et que l'industrie ne cède rien à sa rivale anglaise, le commerce, grand et petit, connaît un véritable âge d'or. L'exemple de l'industrie nîmoise de la soie, qui exporte au Proche-Orient ou en Espagne plus de 70 % de sa production, n'est pas isolé. Le commerce extérieur français qui, avec 155 millions de livres contre 325 millions, sous la Régence, atteignait à peine la moitié de la valeur du commerce anglais, le devance largement à la veille de la Révolution, avec 1 062 millions de livres contre 775 millions. Même s'il est impossible d'en faire l'estimation, le commerce intérieur fait encore mieux. En quatre ou cinq jours, le volume des transactions à la foire de Beaucaire atteint le cinquième de tout le commerce annuel de Marseille.

Grâce aux ingénieurs des Ponts et Chaussées formés par Jean Rodolphe Perronet, aux crédits de l'État qui passent de 770 000 livres dans la période 1683-1700 à 6,9 millions de livres en 1780, et surtout... aux corvées imposées aux paysans, 30 000 kilomètres de routes empierrées, assises sur de solides substructures, bordées de fossés, ombragées par des files d'arbres et vantées par une foule d'écrivains et de voyageurs, de Voltaire au Russe Karamzin, ont permis de doubler l'allure moyenne des voitures et de baisser les coûts de transport. Le voyage de Paris à Lyon, qui exigeait dix à onze jours en 1664, en réclame moins de six en 1760. Paris-Rouen, qui demandait un minimum de trois jours au XVIIe siècle, se fait en un jour et demi à la fin du XVIIIe siècle. Bordeaux est à quinze jours de Paris en 1660, à cinq jours et demi en 1789. À cette date, les voitures des Messageries générales de France parcourent en moyenne 75 kilomètres par jour et transportent soieries, dorures et dentelles à des taux inférieurs à 1 % de leur valeur. « Vous savez que les frais d'ici à chez vous sont bien peu de choses », écrit un négociant lyonnais à son correspondant marseillais en 1753. En Bourgogne, le transport du vin ne représenterait plus que le cinquième ou le sixième du prix de la marchandise, alors qu'il le triplait au XVIIe siècle.

Soutenue par la voie d'eau, encore meilleur marché et qui peut, sur la Seine, entre Paris et Rouen, « porter » jusqu'à 150 tonnes, la route tend à créer un espace de plus en plus « national ». Ainsi, lors de la crise frumentaire de 1740, Paris a pu être ravitaillée par des régions non affectées par la pénurie. Dans ce domaine, la France est en avance sur toute l'Europe. Les hommes, les marchandises, les nouvelles et les pamphlets y circulent toujours plus vite. En 1739, il circulait 1 628 voitures à Vienne, en 1759, 7 378. En 1678, Orléans voyait passer 400 navires ; en 1780, 1 600. En 1738, les recettes des Postes s'élevaient à 3,9 millions de livres, à 15,6 millions en 1768.

C'est toutefois la mer qui, au siècle des Lumières, ouvre à la France un marché étendu aux limites du monde. En 1743, le tonnage global affecté au grand commerce représentait environ 185 000 tonneaux, 426 000 en 1787. C'est le négoce qui assure l'extraordinaire essor des façades maritimes du royaume. C'est le dynamisme des ports, illustré par le peintre Joseph Vernet, qui commande l'activité des arsenaux, la fabrication de voiles et de cordages, le développement des industries alimentaires et fait de la France la plaque tournante du commerce colonial. Le négoce est « l'état d'un vrai citoyen, confie fièrement Jean Joseph de Laborde à son fils. Un négociant qui travaille dans le grand fait mouvoir tous les différents ordres de l'État, en leur faisant recueillir le fruit de son travail. L'agriculture, les manufactures, les artisans, les ouvriers en tout genre, tout se ressent des opérations d'un négociant. J'ai eu jusqu'à dix navires à la pêche à l'Amérique, aux Indes orientales, aux Indes occidentales et en Guinée. Combien de personnes occupées, combien d'argent répandu qui soulage le peuple et le gentilhomme, en leur procurant un débouché avantageux de leur vin et de leur blé dont on fait les farines. »

Plus que tout autre, le commerce avec les Antilles sucrières, surtout Saint-Domingue, connaît une croissance fulgurante. En 1716, les îles d'Amérique procuraient 4,4 millions de livres de produits tropicaux, essentiellement sucre et indigo. Elles en fournissent, avec le café en plus, 193 millions en 1787, assurant à elles seules 32 % des importations françaises, loin devant l'Italie, 13,5 %, l'Allemagne, 10,5 %, et l'Angleterre, 10,3 %. Premier port de France, Bordeaux a vu la valeur totale de son commerce multipliée par 20 de 1717 à 1789. En 1771, année record, le trafic du port a même représenté 40 % du commerce extérieur français. « Cendrillon magnifiquement parée sort de sa citrouille girondine », selon la belle formule d'Emmanuel Le Roy Ladurie. Places, avenues, grand théâtre aux colonnes colossales et palais archiépiscopal de Rohan célèbrent avec faste une prospérité « à l'américaine ».

Premier port négrier français, Nantes affiche sa réussite en décorant ses nouveaux hôtels avec des têtes d'Indiens ou de Noirs, des consoles sculptées et des balcons ventrus sur cariatides. Mais l'ampleur des fortunes accumulées ne doit pas faire oublier leur fragilité. Hautement profitable en cas de succès, le commerce du « bois d'ébène », qui choque tant notre sensibilité, sur le plan strictement économique, est aussi un commerce à haut risque qui nécessite des investissements considérables et exige que tout soit fait pour que la « cargaison » arrive à bon port. Contrairement à une légende fort tenace, le commerce des esclaves a été bien moins meurtrier qu'on ne l'a souvent écrit. Pour les navires nantais, le taux de mortalité au cours du voyage se situerait entre 12 et 15 %, soit un taux inférieur à celui de l'équipage blanc, qui atteint 18 %.

En fait, le Noir d'Afrique, dont le prix est passé en moyenne de 192 livres en 1670 à 480 livres à la fin du siècle, est une « marchandise » qui, parce qu'elle est chère, mérite d'être entretenue. Aux capitaines de navires négriers, les armateurs multiplient les recommandations sur la manière de traiter les esclaves : obligation de leur faire faire de l'exercice, hygiène corporelle, lavages quotidiens des dents... « Aussitôt que les nègres montent le matin, vous donnez à chacun une cuillerée de vinaigre et de l'eau pour le rinçage de la bouche, et de l'eau salée pour laver leurs figures et leurs mains, peut-on lire dans un mémorandum. L'entrepont est gratté tous les deux jours, et les provisions sont examinées régulièrement toutes les semaines, pour voir si elles s'abîment. »

Surtout, loin d'être un piètre marchand, le négrier noir des côtes d'Afrique est un redoutable intermédiaire qui contrôle les flux, connaît la valeur des choses et exige de la « pacotille » de grande qualité, fusils de fabrication danoise, sabres flamands, vins et spiritueux, « articles de Paris », perles de Bohême et de Murano, mouchoirs de Cholet...

Ainsi, au XVIIIe siècle, la traite nantaise aurait mobilisé 450 millions de livres pour 1 424 expéditions recensées. Que des expéditions arrivent au bon moment sur les côtes d'Afrique, fassent la traversée par bon vent, vendent rapidement leur « cargaison » aux Antilles, repartent sans délai et écoulent à un bon prix le sucre ou le café au retour, et les bénéfices peuvent quadrupler la mise de fonds. Mais que le voyage se passe mal, que survienne le calme plat, que les planteurs tardent à payer et c'est la faillite, comme celle qui atteint les de Luynes ou Le Ray de la Clartais, dont les actifs atteignaient pourtant plus de 4 millions de livres l'année précédant leur chute. En moyenne, les bénéfices nantais de la traite se sont élevés entre 5 et 10 %, ce qui, en fin de compte, n'est pas considérable.

Autant dire que pour éviter cette loterie, la plupart des négociants se lancent dans l'achat de terres et de charges anoblissantes et recherchent pour leurs filles des alliances avec la noblesse. Le bourgeois a beau lire l'Encyclopédie, il n'est pas révolutionnaire. Simplement, comme l'écrit dans une brochure Jean-Baptiste Mosneron Dupin, il veut « disperser les fondements de l'édifice gothique » afin que la noblesse n'ait « plus aucun privilège ni exemption ». Au nom de la philosophie qui doit présider à la « régénération de la France », il souhaite que le négociant, à la fois utile et cultivé, devienne la source d'un nouvel ordre privilégié, l'ordre « mitoyen ».

CHAPITRE 54

La société des Lumières

« *Chaque siècle a son esprit qui le caractérise, écrivait en 1771 Diderot à la princesse Dashkoff. L'esprit du nôtre semble être celui de la liberté.* » « *On a commencé par l'érudition, continué par les belles-lettres et fini par la philosophie* », ajoutait d'Alembert, qui préci- sait « *la philosophie pratique, c'est-à-dire cette partie de la philosophie qui proprement en mérite seule le nom* ». C'est qu'au siècle de la glo- rieuse croissance, il est urgent de proposer le « bonheur » aux hommes, le « bonheur » par le « progrès », la liberté d'entreprendre, de faire for- tune, de faire valoir ses mérites, ses talents et son « utilité ». « *Le bonheur est un bien que nous vend la nature, affirmait Voltaire. Il n'est point ici- bas de moisson sans culture.* »

Le sang ou le mérite

En 1756, dans son *Ami des hommes ou traité de la population*, le marquis de Mirabeau, père du célèbre tribun, frappé par la passion d'ascension sociale qui saisissait ses contemporains, écrivait : « On se plaint à bon droit, et l'on regarde comme un vice très nuisible à la construction de la monarchie l'ambition que chacun a en France de faire son fils noble. [...] Le magistrat veut prendre l'épée, parce qu'il est établi que l'état de juger les hommes ne convient pas à la haute noblesse ; le négociant veut devenir magistrat pour faire ensuite le même saut. Le financier à qui l'or fournit la plus brillante et la plus unie des perspectives, prend le plus court, et appellerait volontiers le plus étourdi de ses enfants M. le ministre ou M. le conseiller d'État, comme on désigne quelquefois M. l'abbé dès l'âge de cinq ans. Le fils du paysan devient procureur, et celui du laquais employé. »

Si, au lieu de cela, poursuivait le marquis, « chaque profession élevée dans la modestie et dans une tournure de mœurs uniforme et propre à son état se contentait de faire profiter ses fils des fondements jetés par leurs pères, l'État ne s'en porterait que mieux. Les magistrats donneraient au royaume des Lamoignon ; les financiers, des Jacques Cœur, les manufacturiers, des Van Robais, les paysans d'habiles et industrieux laboureurs et le surabondant de chaque profession fournirait aux portions stériles de la société comme soldats, matelots, etc. »

C'était traduire en termes nostalgiques la déstabilisation de la société d'ordres où chacun avait la place définie par son « état ». C'était condamner le « luxe corrupteur » qui éveillait des « désirs monstrueux jusque dans les réduits les plus reculés où puisse se cacher l'innocence ». « La multiplication des richesses et le désir des jouissances qu'elle entraîne et favorise, ajoutait Gabriel Sénac de Meilhan en 1787, font disparaître les intervalles de la société. »

Remodelée par la croissance, perturbée par l'inflation, déstabilisée par la démographie, travaillée par l'essor de l'instruction, la société d'Ancien Régime est tout sauf immobile. Les « intervalles » ne séparent plus nobles, clercs et bourgeois, mais gagnants et perdants, riches et pauvres, cultivés et incultes, quel que soit l'ordre auquel ils appartiennent.

Évidemment, ce sont les « privilégiés » qui ont été les plus « déstabilisés ». Certes, la noblesse, qui rassemble moins de 300 000 personnes à la fin du siècle, garde encore, et même consolide son prestige. Possédant un cinquième des terres du royaume, infiniment moins toutefois que la gentry britannique, associée souvent aux profits du commerce et de l'industrie, spéculant dans l'immobilier, ayant des intérêts dans la gestion des finances royales et dans les plantations de Saint-Domingue, cueillant à la source grades, pensions et prébendes, elle donne toujours le ton et l'on rêve de l'imiter. Jamais civilisation n'a été aussi « aristocratique » que celle des Lumières. C'est son esprit et ses goûts qui font la « mode ». C'est elle qui montre ses carrosses dans les avenues, ses pur-sang dans les hippodromes, encourage l'édification de théâtres et d'opéras où elle occupe les premières loges, construit des hôtels et des « folies » qu'alimente en objets de luxe une rente foncière qui a largement profité des « bons » prix agricoles.

Pourtant, cette noblesse peine à définir sa place dans la société, hésitant entre libéralisme et réaction. Comme toujours, les « états d'âme » sont les privilèges des nantis. Ayant perdu avec Louis XIV une grande partie de ses pouvoirs traditionnels, séduite par les philosophes qui rejettent ses prétentions contraires au « droit naturel », applaudissant Beaumarchais qui fait dire à Figaro « vous vous êtes donné la peine de naître, et rien de plus », peuplant les loges maçonniques, elle s'épuise en intrigues et cabales et n'arrive plus à proposer une politique qui puisse ranimer une vocation dont elle a perdu le secret et dont elle se contente d'entretenir la nostalgie. N'ayant plus de goût à la fronde, elle se prépare au suicide. C'est le marquis d'Argenson, ministre de Louis XV et ami de Voltaire, qui écrit en 1739 : « Il faut se rapprocher de ce but de l'égalité où il n'y aura plus d'autre distinction entre les hommes que le mérite personnel. »

« Pour nous, jeune noblesse française, avoue dans ses *Mémoires* le comte de Ségur, sans regret pour le passé, sans inquiétude pour l'avenir, nous marchions gaiement sur un tapis de fleurs qui nous cachait un abîme. Riants frondeurs des modes anciennes, de l'orgueil féodal de nos pères et de leurs graves étiquettes, tout ce qui était antique nous paraissait gênant et ridicule. La gravité des anciennes doctrines nous pesait. [...] Entravés dans cette marche légère par l'ancienne morgue de la vieille cour, par les ennuyeuses étiquettes du vieux régime, par la sévérité de l'ancien clergé, par l'éloignement de nos pères pour nos modes nouvelles, pour nos costumes favorables à l'égalité, nous nous sentions disposés à suivre avec enthousiasme les doctrines philosophiques que professaient des littérateurs spirituels et hardis. Voltaire entraînait nos esprits. Rousseau touchait nos cœurs, nous sentions un secret plaisir à les voir attaquer le vieil échafaudage, qui nous semblait gothique et ridicule. Ainsi, quoique ce fussent nos rangs, nos privilèges, les débris de notre ancienne puissance qu'on minait sous nos pas, cette petite guerre nous plaisait. »

Une petite guerre qui se limite toutefois aux épigrammes de salon. On a beau être noble et « éclairé », on n'en est pas moins homme. Certes, on peut recevoir le bourgeois à sa table et afficher du goût pour les Lumières, on n'en milite pas moins pour se réserver les grades de l'armée et les bénéfices des évêchés. Même si cinq à six mille anoblissements ont, pendant le siècle, entrouvert les portes de l'aristocratie, l'ascension est trop lente pour ne pas susciter des impatiences chez les « bourgeois ». Réflexe de survie d'une noblesse provinciale appauvrie qui veut maintenir ses revenus rognés par l'inflation, réflexe de défense de hobereaux méprisés par les grands seigneurs qui tentent de maintenir leur rang, la « réaction nobiliaire », manifestée avec éclat par le règlement du maréchal Henri de Ségur qui, le 22 mai 1781, impose aux futurs sous-officiers de faire la preuve de quatre quartiers de noblesse, compromet l'avènement de cette « bonne société » qui aurait uni naissance, talents et richesse. « C'était mécontenter la haute bourgeoisie et les anoblis dans un empire opulent, se plaint le comte de Tilly, c'était interdire à une classe riche, instruite et bien élevée, une carrière qu'il était juste de ne lui laisser courir qu'après que la noblesse (dont c'est essentiellement le métier, dans un état monarchique) eût été placée. Mais il ne fallait jamais faire une loi de l'État d'une condition. [...] Il était aisé de ne faire que des exceptions. C'est une faute de M. le maréchal de Ségur, une des impérities de son ministère ; c'est l'aperçu d'une vue courte. »

L'argent et le mérite butent donc contre la naissance. En freinant l'ascension d'une roture qui ne demandait qu'à lui être « assimilée », la noblesse finit par faire croire à une « bourgeoisie » jusque-là divisée qu'elle a des intérêts communs. Principale bénéficiaire de l'aimable conjoncture, unie par une solide instruction, frustrée de ne pas être reconnue à son juste mérite, elle aspire à devenir « quelque chose », avec moins de patience qu'elle n'en avait fait preuve depuis des siècles. « Réussir », tel est le maître mot de ceux qui ne bénéficient pas du privilège de la naissance. L'argent, tel est le sésame qui offre à son détenteur le prestige que le sang ne lui assure pas. Financiers, négociants, entrepreneurs, ils sont les conquérants du siècle. Né en 1725 à Gaillac, dans le Tarn, d'un père tonnelier « ne sachant signer », François Lacombe, tonnelier lui-même, devient propriétaire de vignes, négociant en vin, prêteur d'argent, consul de la ville et finit en 1784 par acheter la charge anoblissante de secrétaire du roi à la chancellerie pour devenir, dans les actes notariés, François de Lacombe, sans parvenir toutefois, malgré sa fortune, à convaincre son environnement de son « aristocratie ». De plus grande envergure, Claude Périer, descendant d'un petit marchand, commanditaire d'une société marseillaise spécialisée dans le négoce atlantique, propriétaire d'une plantation de canne à sucre à Saint-Domingue, « indienneur » à Vizille, où travaillent aux toiles peintes 400 ouvriers à la fin du siècle, achète en 1780 le château et les terres seigneuriales de Vizille pour 1 million de livres et se fait appeler « Noble Claude Périer, seigneur de Vizille, Secrétaire du Roy Maison et Couronne de France, homme lige et vassal de sa Majesté ».

Les noms des navires négriers choisis par les négociants nantais montrent aussi à quel point leur désir de paraître l'emporte sur l'« idéologie ». Si une dizaine de noms révèlent des idéaux maçonniques, comme *La Parfaite-Union*, *Les Cœurs-Unis*, la majorité évoque la noblesse « éclairée », comme *Le Marquis-de-Bouillé* ou *Le Duc-d'Orléans*, les monarques bienveillants, comme *Le Henry-Quatre*, les despotes éclairés, comme le *Frédéric-le-Grand* et, surtout, exalte une civilité fort mondaine où se manifeste l'attrait prodigieux exercé par le sentiment d'innocence. Ainsi, le « bois d'ébène » est souvent transporté dans des navires qui portent le qualificatif de « brave », d'« aimable » ou de « jeune » et sont « fidèles », « obligeants » et « gentils ».

Disposant de « folies » dans la campagne nantaise, achetant des terres pour se prévaloir de la particule et disposer d'un banc à accoudoir dans l'église, se faisant appeler *Monseigneur*, accordant à l'argenterie une place essentielle dans leur vaisselle, protégeant peintres et sculpteurs, entretenant parfois danseuses et chanteuses, réunissant des collections d'estampes, se piquant de talents littéraires et artistiques, ouvrant leurs jardins aux essences exotiques, magnolias, camélias, orangers et chênes d'Amérique, sensibles aux nouvelles modes hygiéniques, bidets et chaises de commodité trônant dans les chambres ou dans... les salons, les élites « bourgeoises » paraissent bien saisies du tropisme aristocratique. Pourtant, à Nantes comme ailleurs, la reproduction et l'essor de l'entreprise demeurent leur objectif essentiel. Certes, elles s'entraînent à paraître, mais sans oublier, semble-t-il, la barrière invisible qui les sépare du second ordre. Aussi, la promotion sociale ne leur suffit pas totalement. Dans une société où le profit et le négoce restent méprisés et qui redoute ces « millionnaires » qui traitent les pauvres comme « les nègres d'Afrique », elles peuvent être tentées de faire valoir leur « noblesse », qu'elles appellent « mérite » et « utilité ». C'est le sentiment qu'exprimait Malesherbes quand, en 1785, il écrivait à M. de Montgolfier pour le féliciter de l'anoblissement accordé à son père : « Vous pouvez vous souvenir que lorsqu'on donna à M. votre père des lettres de noblesse, je vous dis que je trouvais que c'était une bien médiocre grâce, non qu'en soi-même ce n'en dût être une grande de faire passer une famille d'un ordre de citoyens à l'ordre le plus élevé. Cette grâce serait la plus flatteuse de toutes si elle n'avait pas été prostituée comme elle l'est. Mais depuis qu'on l'accorde tous les jours aux gens qui y ont le moins de titres, et que même, sans commission du roi, la noblesse s'acquiert à prix d'argent par des charges vénales, je pense que ce n'est plus une récompense digne des hommes qui se sont illustrés par leur mérite. »

C'était espérer une société au sein de laquelle chacun serait classé selon son « importance ». En attendant ce moment, le « bourgeois » n'avait d'autre choix que de mimer la noblesse.

Manifeste à la ville, où s'exprime désormais la déférence sociale, où les *Sieurs* sont toisés de haut par les *Messieurs*, où s'amorce la ségrégration géographique entre quartiers résidentiels et ghettos populaires, la tension sociale est aussi vive à la campagne, où les « coqs » brisent les anciennes solidarités, empiètent sur les communaux et guignent la terre de la noblesse ou du clergé.

Tandis que, porté par la vague démographique, s'y enfle un prolétariat plus ou moins nombreux selon les régions, s'employant au jour le jour ou pour une saison, brassiers, journaliers, manouvriers qui, au lieu de mourir de faim comme ils le faisaient couramment au siècle précédent, tombent parfois dans la mendicité ou le brigandage, se consolide une « classe propriétaire » qui, ayant des surplus à commercialiser, participe aux fastes du « beau XVIIIᵉ siècle ».

Fermiers de terres nobles ou bourgeoises, ayant su arracher à leurs bailleurs des baux favorables, dominant le marché du travail, sachant par cœur les terres, les cheptels et les familles, possédant quelques rudiments dans l'art vétérinaire, ils président les assemblées de communauté, sont le plus souvent exempts de tailles, remplacent leurs coffres par des armoires « normandes », changent régulièrement de chemise, mangent du pain blanc et de la viande, ambitionnent pour leurs enfants une carrière à Paris et seraient prêts à composer avec les seigneurs pour enclore les communaux et promouvoir le profit à la campagne. Considérant, eux aussi, que ce profit est le produit de leurs « risques », ils épousent les lignes de fracture mouvantes qui fissurent sans que l'on y prenne garde l'échafaudage « gothique » de la société d'ordres.

La « vie fragile »

Dans une société où le paupérisme a supplanté le trépas, ceux qui n'ont ni chance, ni talent, ni mérite mènent une « vie fragile », pour reprendre l'expression de l'historienne Arlette Farge qui, à partir des archives judiciaires, nous a révélé les comportements de ceux que la précarité secoue en permanence, qui se révoltent parfois, volent souvent, mais tuent de plus en plus rarement. D'après les registres de l'inspecteur Poussot, affecté au quartier des Halles, à Paris, sur 2 692 personnes arrêtées entre 1738 et 1754, on ne compte que 54 actes de violence, rébellion, assassinats et tentatives d'assassinat, mais 963 vols.

À la campagne, tandis que les salaires des manœuvriers ont peiné à suivre l'inflation, la fécondité non contrôlée des humbles a morcelé leurs maigres propriétés. Écartés des assemblées de paroisses et du bénéfice des premières clôtures, auxquelles ils ont parfois réussi à s'opposer, ils ont, en Auvergne comme ailleurs, complété leurs ressources en s'employant dans l'industrie, en migrant temporairement vers les chantiers urbains, en mendiant ou... en chapardant. Apparaissant comme un élément de contestation sociale, le vol culmine en hiver, quand le travail manque, ou avant la soudure, quand le blé est devenu rare et cher. Cartouche et Mandrin, ces « malfaiteurs » seront plus populaires que les croquants et nu-pieds du siècle précédent. Mais au temps des Lumières, le crime recule partout, sauf en Corse, où les nouvelles armes à feu semblent avoir été fort prisées. Plus sage, plus policée, moins imposée par le fisc, dont les prélèvements deviennent, en valeur réelle, plus légers, la campagne se fait aussi moins rebelle. Certes, on recense encore de nombreuses « émotions » au sujet de la vaine pâture, du ban de vendange du seigneur, des droits d'usage, quelques grèves de moissonneurs menées contre les gros exploitants, quelques braconnages qui manifestent la volonté de démocratiser le droit de tuer le gibier, quelques tutoiements de seigneurs qui sont tout sauf affectueux, mais rien qui ressemble aux grandes rébellions du siècle précédent. Sans doute, le feu couve toujours sous la cendre mais, moins affectés par la peste, la guerre et la famine, les « peuples » sont plus contestataires que révoltés. Plus alphabétisés par le réseau des « petites écoles », capables de lire les livres bleus produits par l'imprimerie de Troyes, les almanachs qui enseignent le jardinage et le savoir-vivre, les « canards » vendus par les colporteurs, sensibles aux aventures du « bonhomme Misère », incarnation de tant d'entre eux, excités par l'insolence de Mandrin, les paysans deviennent plus « modernes ». En contact accru avec les marchés, ils sont moins « farouches » mais plus chicaniers, capables, comme en Bourgogne, de recourir à des procureurs pour défendre leurs droits. Près de la moitié des hommes signent leur acte de mariage à la fin du siècle, contre moins de 30 % au début. « Les leçons de la nouvelle philosophie retentissent jusque dans les ateliers des artisans et sous l'humble toit du cultivateur », se désolent les assemblées du clergé dans la seconde moitié du XVIIIᵉ siècle. C'est parce qu'il est en partie « éclairé » que le peuple discute guerre et paix, dépenses publiques et impôts, spéculation et liberté des grains. Même et surtout à sensation, la presse finit par créer un marché national des nouvelles.

Dans les villes boursouflées par la pression démographique et l'immigration, le climat est plus lourd, plus électrique. À Grenoble, dans les années 1780, 63 % des nouveaux mariés et 54 % des nouvelles mariées sont des immigrés. Rouen fonctionne comme une pompe qui aspire et refoule, absorbant au XVIIIᵉ siècle un tiers d'immigrants et en rejetant également un tiers. « Le peuple de Nancy, écrit un magistrat en 1722, est composé de gens ramassés, la plupart étrangers au pays [...]. C'étaient souvent des gens de suite d'armées, mal disciplinés, violents, ivrognes, et quelque chose de pis, lesquels il n'était pas possible de bien contenir. » À Lyon, dans une grande maison de cinq étages sise au 192, rue de la Barre, vivent en 36 minuscules appartements 36 ménages, dont 10 seulement sont lyonnais.

Plus nécessiteux, ces migrants qui soulagent les campagnes avoisinantes troublent l'ordre et la sécurité. « De partout peut surgir l'esprit de révolte, observe Arlette Farge, des ateliers, des cabarets toujours prompts aux bagarres, des prisons maintes fois troublées pendant le siècle, des assemblées de libertins se tenant dans les faubourgs, des barrières où s'organisent des trafics et où se font agresser les employés des fermes. » Dans des villes qui ne sont plus des mouroirs, on survit, mais pauvrement. La grande vague de hausse des prix a contourné les salaires nominaux, et des années 1720 aux années 1780, le pouvoir d'achat, exprimé en biens de consommation, a peut-être baissé d'un quart, compensé toutefois par la diminution du sous-emploi et le travail des femmes et des enfants. Plus que la misère permanente, c'est la précarité d'une vie fragile qui hante l'univers du travailleur. Étudiant la condition des ouvriers stéphanois, Messance en donnait la mesure quand il écrivait : « Dans le bon temps, ils se nourrissent et se vêtissent comme des bourgeois ; dans le mauvais temps, c'est-à-dire dans l'état de maladie ou lorsque le travail manque, ou que les denrées sont chères [...], c'est le passage d'une vie aisée à l'indigence. » À Lille, sur 65 000 habitants à la fin du siècle, on peut compter 7 000 pauvres qui vivent fièrement et dignement en ne demandant l'aide de personne, mais 20 000 nécessiteux et, parmi eux, 1 650 mendiants, sans compter 3 360 mendiants refoulés chaque année aux portes de la ville.

Qu'un boulanger augmente le prix du pain, qu'un maître cordonnier impose à un compagnon de faire un travail qui ne lui convient pas, qu'un maître serrurier exige le règlement de dettes impayées, et c'est l'atelier, la rue puis le quartier qui s'agitent. Que la police parisienne enlève en pleine rue des enfants et des vagabonds sous prétexte que les uns jouent et que les autres demandent l'aumône et, le 23 mai 1750, quelques hôtels de commissaires sont assiégés et un espion de la police frappé à mort. Qu'en 1756, une petite fille de neuf ans affirme avoir été violée par un garçon marchand de vin et que ses parents, débitants de sel et de tabac rue Saint-Victor, la déclarent enceinte... malgré son âge, et c'est le peuple, les médecins, la dauphine, les bourgeois, la police et le clergé qui défilent, sous les fenêtres de la famille pour assister au prodige jusqu'au jour où la supercherie est découverte.

Rumeurs, peurs et haines, filouteries, prostitution, viols et abandons d'enfants, autant de troubles qui révèlent la poussée de fièvre d'un milieu juvénile et populaire qui rêve de pain, d'argent et de femmes. « Quels sont les instruments de ces calamités publiques ? s'interroge Des Essarts dans son *Dictionnaire universel de police*, dont le premier volume paraît en 1786. Ce sont toujours des hommes dont on ne connaît ni le nom ni la demeure : ce sont des individus qui semblent étrangers dans la ville même qui fournit à leur subsistance, des êtres qui ne dépendent que du moment, et qui disparaissent avec la même facilité qu'ils se sont montrés ; des hommes enfin qui ne tiennent à rien, qui n'ont aucune propriété, et qui fuient avec la rapidité de l'éclair. » Toujours et partout, la faute à l'« étranger » qui trouble une maréchaussée dont les effectifs atteignent seulement 3 300 personnes pour une population de 28 millions d'habitants. On tente bien d'enfermer mendiants et vagabonds dans les hôpitaux généraux puis, en 1767, dans des dépôts de mendicité, qui visent à placer sous contrôle la population flottante n'ayant « exercé ni profession ni métier depuis six mois révolus », précise l'édit, mais sans succès.

Pour l'abbé de Malvaux, qui disserte sur « les moyens de détruire la mendicité en France » au concours organisé par l'académie de Châlons en 1777, « les estropiés n'auront donc pas pour cela le privilège de vivre aux dépens du public. Celui qui n'a qu'une jambe sera occupé au travail des mains ; celui qui n'a qu'un bras le sera à conduire des voitures, à la garde des maisons, des vergers, des vignes, des troupeaux, des pâtures, des fruits, d'un territoire, des forêts. Il n'est pas jusqu'aux aveugles dont on ne puisse tirer un parti avantageux, quand ce ne serait que pour aider au coutelier, en tournant sa roue ; au maréchal, au serrurier, au cloutier, en donnant le mouvement au soufflet, à portée duquel il serait placé. On a imaginé une machine pour occuper même les pauvres qui n'auraient ni bras ni jambe, par la simple inflexion du corps à droite et à gauche, ou en avant et en arrière [...]. Tout homme qui a des yeux, qui a la liberté de ses bras, de ses mains et qui jouit de son bon sens, fût-il mutilé de ses pieds, de ses jambes, de ses cuisses, les culs-de-jatte, à plus forte raison les autres mendiants invalides, peuvent être employés à toutes sortes d'ouvrages manuels et sédentaires. Les imbéciles eux-mêmes et les fous quand ils sont hors de leur accès ne doivent pas rester oisifs [...]. Ce serait violer manifestement les lois de la société de ne pas obliger cette espèce d'hommes à tout le travail dont ils sont capables. »

Conçues pour procurer un minimum de subsistance aux indigents et pour mettre hors de vue une population dont on craignait les « émotions », ces mesures inefficaces ont altéré, dans les années 1770, le lien affectif qui attachait les classes populaires au « roi nourricier ». Phénomène de génération ? Toujours est-il que la société du *baby-boom* traverse une crise d'adolescence qui se traduit, au niveau de l'État comme au niveau des familles, par une opposition plus ou moins dramatique au père. En témoigne assez la multiplication des lettres de cachet pour « affaires de famille », qui permettent aux familles en proie à un conflit grave d'arrêter n'importe lequel de leurs membres sur « ordre du roi » pour éviter le déshonneur d'un procès. « Il y avait peu de familles de Paris, écrit dans ses *Mémoires* le lieutenant de police Lenoir, parmi lesquelles il ne se trouvât personne qui dans un espace de dix à douze années n'eût à recourir au magistrat administrateur de la police générale de cette ville, pour des affaires intéressant son honneur. »

Les philosophes au balcon

« Philosopher, écrivait en 1715 la marquise de Lambert, c'est rendre à la raison toute sa dignité et la faire rentrer dans ses droits, c'est secouer le joug de l'opinion et de l'autorité. »

L'« opinion », telle est la nouvelle « reine des batailles », sacrée par la croissance urbaine et l'instruction élargie. L'« opinion », telle est la cible d'une France « pensante » qui, pour être infiniment minoritaire, n'en diffuse pas moins ses « lumières » par les multiples ruisseaux que sont les sociétés de lecture et les bibliothèques, les clubs et les loges maçonniques, les salons et les académies, les journaux et les cafés, les nouvelles et les pamphlets. « Voyez-les assis sur un banc aux Tuileries, au Palais-Royal, à l'Arsenal, sur les quais des Augustins et ailleurs. Trois fois la semaine, ils sont assidus à cette lecture, et la curiosité des nouvelles politiques saisit tous les âges et tous les états », tels sont les lecteurs de gazettes décrits par Louis Sébastien Mercier. Des lecteurs tellement gourmands qu'en 1778, 1784, 1785 et 1788 sont respectivement lancés 25, 29, 25 et 37 nouveaux journaux. Dans les cafés qui poussent comme des champignons, le beau parleur peut se forger une belle popularité.

« Il y en avait un principalement qui parlait plus haut que les autres, écrit Lesage dans *La Valise trouvée* (1740), et que chacun écoutait comme un oracle. Ce qu'il y a de plaisant, c'est que cet original voulait paraître n'ignorer aucune nouvelle, et s'il en entendait débiter une qu'il n'eût point encore apprise, il interrompait civilement la personne qui l'annonçait, et la faisait taire, en lui disant : "Vous n'en avez pas les gants. J'ai dit cela ici ce matin." Ou bien, si quelqu'un devant lui s'avisait de tirer de sa poche une Lettre, dans laquelle il fût fait mention d'une victoire, par exemple, remportée en Hongrie sur les Turcs, il s'écriait aussitôt à pleine tête : "La date ?" Et si on lui répondait : "Du quatorze de ce mois", il ne manquait pas de répliquer : "Cela est vieux. Nous avons des nouvelles du vingt qui assurent le contraire." »

Moins hâbleurs, les académiciens, près de deux mille cinq cents personnes, dont 37 % de nobles et 43 % de roturiers, forment une « République des Lettres » où tentent de s'associer le savoir-vivre nobiliaire et le savoir-faire bourgeois. Dirigés par les femmes de la haute aristocratie qui se plaisent à marier la robe et l'épée, la plume et la parole, Mme de Lambert et Mme de Tencin, Mme du Deffand ou Mme Geoffrin, les salons deviennent les nouveaux espaces de duels où le bel esprit se plaît à croire qu'il peut tout réformer.

Si Gavroche est tombé par terre, est-ce la faute à Voltaire ? Le nez dans le ruisseau, est-ce la faute à Rousseau ? Cette interrogation, qui soulève le problème de savoir si cette propagation des idées a sapé les fondements de la monarchie et provoqué la Révolution, fait aujourd'hui l'objet de nouvelles réponses. Ni bourgeoises, ni aristocratiques, encore moins populaires, les Lumières n'étaient nullement révolutionnaires. « Le genre humain, tel qu'il est, écrivait Voltaire en 1764, ne peut subsister à moins qu'il n'y ait une infinité d'hommes utiles qui ne possèdent rien du tout ; car, certainement, un homme à son aise ne quittera pas sa terre pour venir labourer la vôtre ; et si vous avez besoin d'une paire de souliers, ce ne sera pas un maître des requêtes qui vous la fera. » Profondément « réformatrices », les Lumières veulent simplement, mais c'est déjà beaucoup, convertir les élites à la raison, au bonheur et à l'idée de progrès, combattre le fanatisme, condamner les privilèges et la monarchie sans contrôle, encourager l'agriculture et abolir la torture, épouser en somme l'élan du siècle sans pour autant faire du passé table rase et sans se préoccuper de faire raisonner la « populace ». Les philosophes n'ont rien « inventé ». Ils ont seulement pris en charge les aspirations diffuses de leur époque pour les transformer en valeurs universelles.

Certes, les œuvres des grands philosophes figurent en bonne place parmi les ouvrages qui ont été « embastillés » après interdiction et confiscation mais, comme le souligne Robert Darnton, l'historien américain qui s'est intéressé à « l'aventure de l'*Encyclopédie* », ce « best-seller du siècle », l'encyclopédisme ne représentait pas une réelle menace pour l'État. Diffusée par les élites et les marquises, les « Lumières » n'étaient pas étrangères aux ministres du roi.

Puisant ses racines dans le doute cartésien et la physique newtonienne, mêlant le goût de l'expérience au principe de l'évidence, le philosophe est devenu un nouveau héros, un « honnête homme qui veut plaire et se rendre utile », un brillant manipulateur d'idées qui peut parler de tout et de rien et doit prendre parti dans toutes les querelles, un mondain qui soupe avec les princes, écrit avec virtuosité et talent que le savoir est préférable à l'ignorance, que la discussion vaut mieux que le fanatisme, qu'il faut bien une religion pour le peuple et que le progrès est capable de mener au bonheur, cette idée fixe qui rend si optimiste le siècle de la glorieuse croissance et de la curiosité scientifique et si hostile à une Église qui prétend que le bonheur n'est pas de ce monde. Même s'il reste « plein de Dieu », le philosophe-physicien n'en finit pas de mettre en défaut les Écritures.

Père de la chimie moderne, refusant toute doctrine d'explication préalable, Lavoisier est peut-être celui qui a le mieux incarné dans sa vie et dans son œuvre l'esprit des Lumières. Né en 1743 d'un père procureur au Parlement de Paris et d'une mère fille de robin et fortunée, il entre au collège Mazarin, où sont élevés gratuitement, aux termes du testament du cardinal, les enfants de gentilshommes ou « principaux bourgeois ». Dans un monde où finance rime avec talent, il s'établit dans l'une des plus hautes puissances d'argent du temps, la Ferme générale, cette « sangsue publique » qui l'amène à déceler les fraudes que pratiquent volontiers les débitants de tabac. Riche, il peut assouvir cette « fureur d'apprendre » qui dévore la société éclairée, concourir au sujet proposé par l'Académie royale des sciences sur « le meilleur moyen d'éclairer pendant la nuit les rues d'une grande ville, en combinant ensemble la clarté, la facilité du service et l'économie », être élu à l'Académie, fréquenter les salons et y trouver femme capable de préparer le thé et de discuter de l'essai de Kirwan sur le phlogistique, qu'elle traduit de l'anglais, s'attaquer à des expériences d'élevage et de cultures dérobées sur ses 600 hectares de Beauce, entreprendre de chiffrer la richesse de la nation, mettre sur pied le projet d'une Caisse d'épargne du peuple pour assurer aux vieillards et aux veuves des secours contre l'indigence, quintupler la production de salpêtre en France et... faire l'analyse de l'air pour identifier l'oxygène et l'azote.

Méditant sur les deux ordres de phénomènes qui ont été la source de ses découvertes, la combustion et la respiration, il écrit : « On dirait que cette analogie qui existe entre la combustion et la respiration n'avait point échappé aux poètes, ou plutôt aux philosophes de l'Antiquité, dont ils étaient les interprètes et les organes. Ce feu dérobé du ciel, ce flambeau de Prométhée ne présente pas seulement une idée ingénieuse et poétique, c'est la peinture fidèle des opérations de la nature, du moins pour les animaux qui respirent. On peut donc dire, avec les anciens, que le flambeau de la vie s'allume au moment où l'enfant respire pour la première fois, et qu'il ne s'éteint qu'à sa mort. » Science, poésie, mythologie et philosophie, tel est bien le souffle des Lumières.

Curieux de tout, de physique et de chimie, de botanique et de zoologie, de mécanique et de conquête de l'air, de médecine et d'électricité, d'agriculture et de voyages, les hommes des Lumières veulent tout connaître. « L'esprit humain n'a point de bornes, déclarait Buffon, qui publie en 1749 ses trois premiers volumes de l'*Histoire naturelle*. Il s'étend à mesure que l'univers se déploie ; l'homme peut donc et doit tout tenter, il ne lui faut que du temps pour tout savoir. »

Du foisonnement d'idées souvent divergentes qui agite la cité des Lumières, se dégagent quelques revendications assez immédiates pour être « politiques ». Au premier rang d'entre elles, la liberté pour les personnes, la tolérance pour les idées, l'égalité devant la loi et la justice. Au moment où à Toulouse, le calviniste Jean Calas était condamné à mort pour un infanticide qu'il n'avait pas commis, au moment où, à Abbeville, le chevalier de La Barre, âgé de dix-neuf ans, était condamné à avoir le poing coupé, la langue arrachée et à être brûlé vif pour être passé près d'une procession sans ôter son chapeau, l'établissement d'un *habeas corpus* apparaissait comme le socle de la liberté politique, « cette tranquillité d'esprit qui provient de l'opinion que chacun a de sa sûreté », écrivait Montesquieu. « Le premier état que l'homme acquiert par la nature, et qu'on estime le plus précieux de tous les biens qu'il puisse posséder, est l'état de liberté, peut-on lire dans l'*Encyclopédie* ; il ne peut ni se changer contre un autre, ni se vendre, ni se perdre ; car naturellement tous les hommes naissent libres, c'est-à-dire qu'ils ne sont pas soumis à la puissance d'un maître, et que personne n'a sur eux un droit de propriété. En vertu de cet état, tous les hommes tiennent de la nature même le pouvoir de faire ce que bon leur semble, et de disposer à leur gré de leurs actions et de leurs biens, pourvu qu'ils n'agissent pas contre les lois du gouvernement auquel ils sont soumis. »

L'égalité fait déjà moins l'unanimité. Si Rousseau, fils d'un modeste horloger de Genève, formule l'idée de la bonté naturelle de l'homme, désigne la propriété comme la source de l'injustice et de la tyrannie et propose un *Contrat social* où le peuple souverain dicterait sa volonté, la plupart des philosophes préfèrent s'en tenir à une société de privilèges fondés sur des services réels et à une monarchie à l'anglaise, forte mais tempérée par le contrôle des corps intermédiaires et le recours à la raison.

Surtout, des *Lettres persanes* du président de Montesquieu au *Candide* de Voltaire, c'est le scepticisme religieux, la volonté d'écraser l'« infâme », de dénoncer l'irrationalité des dogmes et l'obscurantisme des pratiques qui unit ces champions de la tolérance. Si quelques-uns, comme le baron d'Holbach, conçoivent même un univers sans Dieu ni religion, la plupart, déistes, sont attachés à un « Dieu horloger », auteur du monde et garant de l'ordre social. « Je veux que mon procureur, mon tailleur, mes valets croient en Dieu, avoue Voltaire ; et je m'imagine que j'en serai moins volé. »

À elle seule, la diffusion de l'*Encyclopédie*, publiée à partir de 1751 et achevée en 1772, mesure l'influence des Lumières et cerne le marché des idées. Dans le prospectus publicitaire annonçant l'ouvrage, Diderot, le maître d'œuvre avec d'Alembert, écrivait : « Le but d'une encyclopédie est de rassembler les connaissances éparses sur la surface de la terre, d'en exposer le système général aux hommes avec qui nous vivons [...] afin que nos neveux, devenant plus instruits, deviennent en même temps plus vertueux et plus heureux, et que nous ne mourions pas sans avoir bien mérité du genre humain. » Mobilisant 1 500 personnes, depuis les auteurs jusqu'aux typographes, pour une « Somme » de 25 000 pages *in folio* contenant 70 000 articles, elle fut vendue entre 25 000 et 30 000 exemplaires dans toute l'Europe, qui vivait alors à l'heure de Paris. La langue française, qui est déjà celle des diplomates, devient aussi celle des savants, des hommes de lettres et des honnêtes gens. En 1784, l'Académie de Berlin met au concours un sujet sur l'universalité de la langue française, le roi de Prusse Frédéric II écrit dans cette langue son œuvre philosophique et à Saint-Pétersbourg, écrit un voyageur allemand, « même les artisans aisés ont soin que leurs enfants apprennent cette langue, ce qui fait la fortune de plusieurs maîtres et maîtresses de langue de cette nation. »

Ainsi trouve-t-on des lecteurs de l'*Encyclopédie* dans la toundra russe, au-delà de la frontière turque, au cap de Bonne-Espérance et en Amérique. Du moins figure-t-elle en bonne place sur les rayons de la bibliothèque pour afficher le progressisme de son propriétaire ou lui conférer un prestige au même titre qu'un faux blason ou une particule ajoutée. C'est qu'à eux seuls, noblesse et clergé représentent 29 % des acheteurs français. Dans le détail, Besançon, qui compte 28 000 habitants, mais une forte élite de magistrats, achète 338 exemplaires. Lille, avec 61 000 habitants, 28 collections seulement. Dijon, qui rassemble 22 000 habitants, souscrit 152 exemplaires ; Reims, avec 32 000 habi-

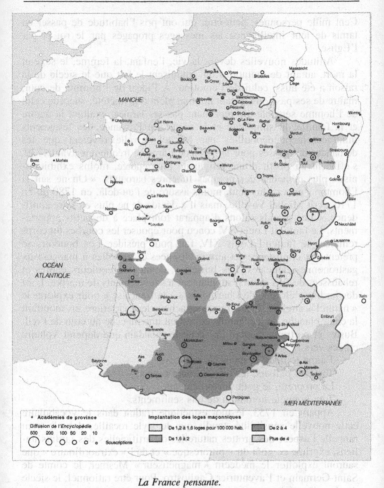

La France pensante.

tants, 24. C'est que négociants et industriels ne pensent guère à la littérature. Ce ne sont pas eux qui ont mis les philosophes au balcon, mais les privilégiés, les « officiers » et les parlementaires, les hommes de loi et les hommes de cour, tous ceux qui pratiquaient l'égalité... des fauteuils dans les académies, les loges et les sociétés de pensée.

Cent mille personnes, peut-être, qui ont pris l'habitude de passer au tamis de leur intelligence les messages propagés par le roi et par l'Église.

Attitudes nouvelles devant la vie, l'enfant, la femme, le sexe et la mort, autant de mutations qui traduisent le fait que le siècle de la raison a été aussi celui de l'émotion. À l'idéal de l'homme de cour, maître de ses passions, galant homme plein d'honnêteté, succède celui de l'homme sensible, ne réprimant pas ses larmes, exaltant la nature et la famille, la simplicité et la vertu. En Provence, les testaments minutieusement dépouillés par Michel Vovelle révèlent que les demandes de messes pour le repos de l'âme, si fréquentes avant 1730, s'effacent au profit d'une religiosité plus épurée, moins exhibitionniste, plus détachée des pompes funèbres baroques. « On ne sait si l'homme s'en va plus seul, moins assuré de l'au-delà, en 1780 qu'en 1710, écrit Michel Vovelle, mais il a décidé de ne plus en faire confidence. » Les grands salons d'apparat font place à de petits appartements. Le fauteuil Louis XV, conçu pour épouser les courbes du corps remplace le fauteuil Louis XIV, fait pour présider. Les boudoirs se prêtent aux confidences et aux médisances et les salles à manger aux gastronomies délicates. Les boiseries, peintes de couleurs claires et rehaussées de fins motifs, supplantent les revêtements de marbre. L'art des jardins s'éloigne de l'harmonie « à la française » pour explorer le « naturel » anglais. Les femmes attachent leur jarretière en montrant la chair blanche de leur jambe et portent une mouche au coin de l'œil. Bustes et portraits mettent en scène le mondain que dépeint Voltaire en ces vers :

J'aime le luxe, et même la mollesse
Tous les plaisirs, les arts de toute espèce
La propreté, le goût, les ornements :
Tout honnête homme a de tels sentiments.

Apparu en 1753, le mot esthétique traduit dans le vocabulaire cette nouvelle sensibilité, tandis que le style rocaille, dont le nom rappelle l'aspect des grottes naturelles ou artificielles des jardins italiens, exprime ce goût du « pittoresque » et de l'« extraordinaire » que sauront exploiter le médecin « magnétiseur » Mesmer, le comte de Saint-Germain et l'aventurier Cagliostro. Pour être rationnel, le siècle des Lumières n'en est pas moins « bizarre ».

CHAPITRE 55

La monarchie en question

Réduire les privilèges pour assurer une justice plus équitable, réformer la fiscalité pour consolider les finances du royaume, imposer le prestige du sacre à un peuple gagné par l'indifférence religieuse, tenir compte d'une « opinion » puissamment travaillée par les philosophes, gouverner un homme de plus en plus « moderne », tel fut le redoutable défi que le siècle des Lumières lança à des monarques qui, gagnés eux aussi à l'esprit du temps, devaient composer avec des forces que leurs prédécesseurs avaient pu ignorer. Construire un État moderne tout en maintenant des principes hérités des temps féodaux, tel était devenu le métier de rois qui, bien ou mal aimés, ont tenté de concilier absolutisme et progrès.

Louis XV, le « mal aimé »

Présent lors de la violation de la sépulture de Louis XV à Saint-Denis, le 10 octobre 1793, Alexandre Lenoir, fondateur du musée des Monuments français, nous a livré dans son *Journal* des impressions qui donnent la mesure de l'impopularité du roi. « Tout ce qui m'a été dit sur la mort de Louis XV, écrit-il, m'invite à ne pas oublier de rapporter ici ce que j'ai vu lors de l'exhumation de son corps. Lors de sa mort, ses ennemis firent mille contes absurdes. J'étais jeune alors et je me rappelle que le bruit courut dans Paris que le prince, mort d'une petite vérole pourpreuse, jetait au loin la peste, qu'il était impossible à tout homme d'en approcher sans être asphyxié. On dit même qu'il ne fut point embaumé parce qu'il avait occasionné la mort de deux chirurgiens qui l'avaient approché. Eh bien ! ce cadavre a été trouvé très conservé et la peau aussi fraîche que s'il venait d'être inhumé. [...] Je dirai plus, il ne se répandit aucune exhalaison à l'ouverture de ce tombeau, tandis qu'à celle d'Henri IV, il s'évapora une exhalaison très forte d'aromates. »

Roi de France au siècle des Lumières, de la même classe d'âge que Diderot, d'Alembert et Rousseau, Louis XV a peut-être été la première victime de l'« opinion » dont le règne se levait en même temps que le sien. On l'accusa de faire enlever à leurs familles des fillettes pour les mener au Parc-aux-Cerfs, une petite maison proche de Versailles qui lui aurait servi de bordel. On assura que Jeanne Antoinette Poisson, « putain royale » devenue marquise de Pompadour, se comportait en Premier ministre et détournait l'argent public pour satisfaire son insatiable frivolité. On rapporta que Jeanne Bécu, comtesse du Barry, qui sut réveiller les prouesses sexuelles d'un roi presque sexagénaire, avait fait l'apprentissage de ses dons chez des maquerelles à la mode. En 1750, enfla la rumeur selon laquelle les enfants errants arrêtés dans Paris avaient été saignés pour la guérison de ce prince « ladre » (lépreux), nouvel Hérode auquel il fallait un bain de sang humain. On chuchota que le roi agiotait et avait amassé des sommes fabuleuses. On assurait que, « spectateur indifférent », il ne se souciait guère des affaires de son royaume et qu'il ignorait tout de ce qui s'y passait. Quand le gouvernement voulut libéraliser le commerce des grains pour stimuler l'agriculture et que le prix du pain augmenta, on parla d'un « pacte de famine » orchestré par le roi pour s'enrichir en organisant la pénurie. Quand le monarque voulut mater les parlementaires qui, sous couvert du « bien public », défendaient leurs privilèges, on cria au « despote », et l'« opinion » prit fait et cause pour les « victimes » d'une réforme louée par Voltaire. Quand, au début du règne, le gouvernement tenta d'imposer silence aux jansénistes dont l'agitation finissait par devenir lassante, une étrange nouvelle se diffusa selon laquelle des malades, en se couchant sur la tombe d'un diacre janséniste, l'abbé Pâris, enterré au petit cimetière de la paroisse de Saint-Médard, étaient « miraculeusement » guéris, tandis qu'un hebdomadaire clandestin, imprimé à cinq mille ou six mille exemplaires, les *Nouvelles ecclésiastiques*, publia jusqu'à la fin du règne des commentaires venimeux, diffusant dans le royaume des documents dérobés jusque dans les bureaux officiels.

Si l'« opinion » condamna avec autant de haine chez Louis XV ce qu'elle avait toléré pour Henri IV et Louis XIV, si l'époque, qui n'était guère austère, joua la comédie de la vertu outragée, si les courtisans, qui vivaient tous avec des maîtresses, se posèrent en parangons de la vertu, c'est que ce roi timide, donc autoritaire, prêtait d'une certaine façon le flanc à la critique, ou du moins à la rumeur.

Né en 1710, orphelin de père et de mère à deux ans, retiré à sept ans à l'affection de « Maman » Ventadour, qu'il chérissait, pour être confié au maréchal de Villeroy, un vaniteux à la tête vide qui aimait l'exhiber comme un singe savant aux bals et le dégoûta des rites de la cour, et au cardinal Fleury qui en fit un étudiant des Lumières, curieux de géométrie et de sciences, de mathématiques et d'astronomie, de médecine et de géographie, un sportif courant sans relâche le cerf et le chevreuil et un manuel formé au métier de tourneur et d'imprimeur, Louis resta toute sa vie un être sensible et inquiet, tiraillé entre la nécessité de faire le roi et sa neurasthénie qui le rendait souvent triste et ennuyé, entre son appétit à courir le jupon et sa foi de charbonnier. Marié à quinze ans à la polonaise Marie Leszczyńska, de sept ans son aînée, il chercha en elle une mère et lui fit dix enfants. « Toujours coucher, toujours accoucher » se plaignait la pauvre reine. Puis, à vingt-trois ans, il partit à la découverte des femmes et amorça le cycle des favorites en titre et des maîtresses obscures. Installé alors dans la « faute », ne jouissant pas de l'adultère épanoui du Roi-Soleil, il en vint à refuser des communions qu'il savait sacrilèges et, pire, à ne plus toucher les écrouelles, un excès de scrupule qui le désigna comme un pécheur public aux yeux de l'« opinion » et banalisa surtout la fonction monarchique en lui faisant perdre son caractère sacré.

« Congénitalement timide, écrit Michel Antoine dans une biographie remarquable, anxieux et secret, naturellement majestueux, il s'est composé un personnage si impénétrable et si indéfinissable que bien peu de ses sujets parvinrent à discerner et à savoir quel prince et quel homme il était et ce qu'il faisait réellement. Dès lors, faute de s'en faire une idée juste, ils furent amenés à accueillir sans discernement les rumeurs, les commérages, les échos plus ou moins vagues, les anecdotes plus ou moins controuvées, les insinuations ou les imputations à partir de quoi ils essaieraient d'imaginer le portrait de leur maître. » Louis XV ne fut pas un homme de « communication ».

« Dual » dans sa vie publique comme dans sa vie privée, il louvoya entre autoritarisme et libéralisme, fit la guerre mais avec beaucoup de remords, vécut à Versailles mais en multipliant les cabinets et les petits appartements pour protéger sa vie privée, changea d'équipes ministérielles pour tenir compte de l'« opinion », hésita entre le néoclassicisme antiquisant et austère et le goût « rocaille », poursuivit les jansénistes et expulsa les jésuites, condamna l'*Encyclopédie* mais donna aux philosophes l'occasion de lancer leurs théories sur le marché des idées, espéra toujours, mais à tort, que la raison l'emporterait.

Ondoyant plus qu'indécis, il épousa l'aimable conjoncture de son temps sans chercher vainement à la violer et présida les fastes du siècle en bâtissant les routes qui colporteront les rumeurs qui feront de lui le « mal aimé ». Un chef d'État « moderne » en somme, muselé et soumis aux humeurs d'un corps qui, pour n'être pas encore électoral, n'en était pas moins « tyrannique ». Il aurait bien voulu établir l'égalité devant l'impôt, abolir les privilèges et réformer la justice mais, n'aimant pas brusquer les choses, il se contenta de favoriser l'évolution qui, à terme, mettait la monarchie en question.

En fait, le tournant du règne se place au milieu du siècle, au moment où se conjuguent l'offensive des philosophes, les « remontrances » des parlementaires et les tentatives avortées de réformes fiscales. C'est à partir de cette date que Louis devient le « mal aimé ». Pendant la première partie du règne, sous le ministériat débonnaire du cardinal André Hercule de Fleury, se prolonge le temps de la Régence, paix à l'extérieur fondée sur l'alliance protestante, prospérité à l'intérieur avec une monnaie stabilisée et un contrôleur des Finances, Philibert Orry, qui parvient même, en 1739 et 1740, à enregistrer plus de recettes que de dépenses, un exploit véritablement historique qui se produit une fois par siècle ! Alors que Louis XIV engageait pendant les dernières années de son règne des dépenses qui se chiffraient à 1 500 ou 1 600 tonnes d'équivalent-argent, de la Régence aux années 1740, elles ne dépassent plus 800 tonnes pour une population plus nombreuse. C'est que, malgré la guerre de Succession de Pologne, destinée à soutenir la candidature du beau-père du roi, la France jouissait d'une paix que désirait ardemment un cardinal qui avait assez connu les guerres du Roi-Soleil pour savoir qu'avec un peu d'habileté et de souplesse, on pouvait éviter le pire en gardant l'essentiel. L'essentiel, ce fut en l'occurrence les duchés de Lorraine et de Bar, offerts à Stanislas Leszczyński en échange de sa renonciation au trône électif de Pologne et qui devinrent français à sa mort, le 23 février 1766. Louis est alors le « Bien-Aimé » pour la guérison duquel le peuple prie avec ferveur quand, en 1744, sa mort est jugée imminente.

Mais deux mauvaises récoltes et le traité d'Aix-la-Chapelle font basculer l'« opinion ». Déclenchée en 1740 à la mort de l'empereur Charles VI, la guerre de Succession d'Autriche, hors de laquelle Louis XV et Fleury auraient souhaité se tenir, marque en fait le tournant du règne. Alors que le roi voulait ne « se mêler de rien » et « demeurer les mains dans les poches » confiait-il en public, il suit le parti anti-Habsbourg et engage la France dans une coalition qui rassemble la Prusse, la Bavière, la Saxe et l'Espagne contre Marie-Thérèse, la fille aînée de l'empereur, soutenue par l'Angleterre et les Pays-Bas. C'en était fini de l'« entente cordiale » avec une Angleterre qui n'était pas mécontente de s'attaquer au commerce français, qui présentait pour elle une sérieuse concurrence. Signée en 1748, la paix d'Aix-la-Chapelle marquait le retour au *statu quo* et indignait une « opinion » qui n'acceptait pas que la France se soit « battue pour le roi de Prusse ». « Tu es bête comme la paix » devint alors une insulte que se lançaient les harengères des Halles. Voulant traiter « non en marchand, mais en roi », Louis XV, qui avait pourtant remporté de belles victoires à Fontenoy, Rocourt et Lawfeld et s'était emparé de Berg-op-Zoom et de Maastricht, rendait toutes ces conquêtes, reconnaissait les droits de Marie-Thérèse à la couronne impériale, chassait de son territoire le populaire Charles Édouard Stuart et laissait au roi de Prusse la Silésie qu'il avait cyniquement conquise. Une « paix blanche » pour une guerre qui avait coûté un milliard de livres et réintroduit le déficit dans le budget. « Il parut plus beau, et même plus utile à la cour de France de ne penser qu'au bonheur de ses alliés que de se faire donner deux ou trois villes de Flandre qui auraient été un éternel objet de jalousie », écrivait alors Voltaire. N'était-il pas philosophe ce roi qui, sur le champ de bataille de Fontenoy, avait ordonné de traiter comme ses propres soldats les blessés ennemis et avait rappelé au dauphin, excité par les pertes anglaises : « Voyez ce que coûte une victoire. Le sang de nos ennemis est toujours le sang des hommes. La vraie gloire, c'est de l'épargner » ?

N'était-il pas « raisonnable » aussi ce roi qui, pour faire face au déficit du budget, décidait en 1749 de créer un impôt nouveau, le vingtième, prélevé sur les revenus de tous, privilégiés ou non. Dans le préambule, Louis XV précisait qu'il avait été amené à décider cette imposition « par la considération qu'il n'y en a pas de plus juste et de plus égale, puisqu'elle se répartit sur tous et chacun de nos sujets dans la proportion de leurs biens et de leurs facultés. »

Cet impôt de 5 % sur les revenus, dont le prélèvement devait être assuré par des contrôleurs dépendant des intendants et non plus par des officiers propriétaires de leurs charges, suscita une « émotion » considérable chez les parlementaires, qui s'appuyèrent sur l'« opinion » pour organiser la résistance, et chez le clergé, dont un membre souligna que son immunité fiscale devait être considérée « comme faisant partie de la religion catholique ». En reculant en 1751, le roi manifestait l'incapacité du pouvoir à imposer la modernisation des finances et cédait aux parlementaires qui n'attendaient que ce signal pour s'ériger en gardiens d'une « Constitution » qui n'existait pas et en porte-parole d'une « Nation » qu'ils ne représentaient pas. En face de cette agitation qui soulignait avec cruauté sa faiblesse, Louis XV lui-même déclarait : « Les "grandes robes" et le clergé sont toujours aux couteaux tirés. Ils me désolent par leurs querelles. Mais je déteste bien plus les "grandes robes". Mon clergé, au fond, m'est attaché et fidèle ; les autres voudraient me mettre en tutelle. [...] Le Régent a bien eu tort de leur rendre le droit de faire des remontrances ; ils finiront par perdre l'État. »

Le temps des « années noires »

Pour en imposer aux privilégiés et faire usage d'une violence qui n'était pas dans la tradition monarchique, il aurait fallu un roi exemplaire, au charisme intact, au caractère trempé et à la légitimité incontestée. Or c'est le moment où la marquise de Pompadour, installée à Versailles, multiplie les maladresses et se fait l'intendante des plaisirs du roi. C'est l'époque où entrent véritablement en scène les philosophes pour exiger la séparation des pouvoirs, faire l'éloge de l'Angleterre, nier le caractère divin de la monarchie, mener campagne contre les abus et la torture et réclamer une justice plus tolérante.

Vers le milieu du siècle, la fracture s'élargit entre un roi paralysé par son impopularité et une France « pensante » qui fait une spectaculaire percée. C'est en rafales que paraissent alors les *Pensées philosophiques*, la *Lettre sur les aveugles* et le premier volume de l'*Encyclopédie* de Diderot, *De l'esprit des lois* de Montesquieu, *Le Siècle de Louis XIV* et *L'Essai sur les mœurs et l'esprit des nations* de Voltaire, le *Discours sur l'origine et les fondements de l'inégalité parmi les hommes* de Rousseau, le *Tableau économique* de Quesnay, le *Traité des sensations* de Condillac. Des édits ont beau être prononcés contre les auteurs et les imprimeurs des publications non autorisées, Diderot a beau être enfermé au donjon de Vincennes, ces mesures stimulent la curiosité de lecteurs alimentés par les imprimeries clandestines et les importations en fraude en provenance de Londres, d'Amsterdam ou de Genève.

C'est en rafales aussi que se succèdent les années « noires ». Engagée en 1756 dans une alliance déroutante avec l'Autriche contre l'Angleterre et la Prusse, la France entame la guerre de Sept Ans par la déroute de Rossbach, qui révèle la faiblesse de son commandement face au génie militaire de Frédéric II. Le 5 janvier 1757, Robert François Damiens, un domestique à l'esprit égaré par les rumeurs des buvettes du palais, tente d'assassiner le roi. En 1759, la flotte française subit des pertes irréparables au sud de Belle-Île, aux îles Cardinaux, et laisse à l'Angleterre la maîtrise des mers. En 1760, malgré les prouesses du chevalier de Lévis, Montréal capitule après Québec. En 1760 toujours, les membres de la Cour des comptes, aides et finances de Rouen s'attaquent au service des Ponts et Chaussées, tentent de paralyser les travaux routiers et réclament le rétablissement des états de Normandie. En 1761, bloqué dans Pondichéry, Lally-Tollendal doit capituler face aux Anglais. C'en est fini de la colonisation française aux Indes.

Au traité de Paris, signé le 10 février 1763, la France cède le Canada à la Grande-Bretagne et la Louisiane à l'Espagne. Même s'il n'affectait guère le commerce colonial, pour lequel Saint-Domingue, l'« île à sucre », comptait bien plus que les quelques « arpents de neige » du Québec, ce traité qui mettait fin à la guerre de Sept Ans affirmait la supériorité de l'Angleterre, la montée en puissance de la Prusse et démontrait qu'une politique extérieure ambitieuse était impossible tant que l'État ne serait pas assuré de son autorité. Ce ne fut pas l'acquisition de la Corse, cédée par la république de Gênes en 1768, qui pouvait compenser cette humiliation politique, même si le duc de Choiseul, secrétaire d'État aux Affaires étrangères, affirmait que l'île de Beauté pouvait « assurer [à Sa Majesté] la domination dans la Méditerranée et que cette île était plus essentielle au royaume que ne l'aurait été une île en Amérique ».

En 1763, encore, quelques mois après la signature du traité de Paris, le roi, influencé par les « lumières » physiocratiques, autorise la libre circulation des « grains, farines et légumes dans toute l'étendue du royaume » et libère leur exportation, ce qui provoque de véritables émeutes dans des dizaines de villes et de villages. En 1764, il sacrifie les jésuites aux parlementaires et à l'« opinion » et les expulse du royaume, une décision qui démontre qu'il était possible d'abattre une institution dont la solidité était réputée.

« Vous venez de donner, Messieurs, un exemple funeste, déclarait le premier président du parlement de Toulouse, celui des suppressions ; vous serez supprimés à votre tour. » En 1765, le parlement de Rennes, mené par son procureur général La Chalotais, entre en conflit avec le duc d'Aiguillon, responsable militaire de la province, et démissionne en bloc, soutenu par les magistrats de Paris et de Rouen. Pourtant, après avoir fait lire au Parlement de Paris, le 3 mars 1766, un discours très dur, dit de « la Flagellation » (du nom de la fête de ce jour), dans lequel il déclare qu'il ne souffrira pas « qu'il s'introduise dans la Monarchie un corps imaginaire qui ne pourrait qu'en troubler l'harmonie » et que « c'est à [lui] seul qu'appartient le pouvoir législatif sans dépendance et sans partage », Louis XV cède, prie d'Aiguillon de démissionner et réinstalle les magistrats de Rennes, qui ouvrent aussitôt le procès de l'ancien commandant militaire.

Mais ce roi qui semblait avoir bu le calice jusqu'à la lie, s'était opposé, en 1765, à ce qu'on célèbre, de quelque manière que ce soit, le cinquantenaire de son avènement et qui avait, en 1766, rédigé son testament, dans lequel il demandait à Dieu d'avoir pitié « d'un grand pécheur », décida en 1770, à l'âge de soixante ans, de frapper un grand « coup de majesté ». Choiseul, aristocrate proche des philosophes et des parlementaires, qui jouait depuis 1758 le rôle de principal ministre, fut disgracié. Maupeou, chancelier depuis 1768, l'abbé Terray, contrôleur général des Finances depuis 1769, et le duc d'Aiguillon, devenu en 1771 secrétaire d'État aux Affaires étrangères, formèrent un « triumvirat » de choc. Trois édits, publiés en février 1771 abolissaient la vénalité des offices et établissaient la gratuité de la justice. Pour « rapprocher les juges et les justiciables » et affaiblir le Parlement de Paris, six conseils supérieurs, composés de magistrats choisis et payés par le roi en fonction « de leurs talents, de leur expérience et de leurs capacités » étaient créés à Arras, Blois, Châlons-en-Champagne, Clermont-Ferrand, Lyon et Poitiers. Les parlements de Rouen et de Douai étaient supprimés et, dans les autres cours, on réduisit les charges inutiles. De son côté, l'abbé Terray spoliait les créanciers de l'État, diminuait les pensions, imposait l'instauration du cadastre et déclarait à ceux qui protestaient qu'« on ne peut parvenir à une perception équitable qu'en laissant à leur taux actuel ceux qui paient suffisamment et en faisant supporter l'augmentation à ceux qui se trouvent dans une trop grande disproportion de ce qu'ils devraient payer. » Une véritable révolution se mettait en place, vivement critiquée par l'« opinion » qui, à travers pamphlets et libelles, vaudevilles et satires, se mobilisait pour sa noblesse, s'en prenait à la du Barry et à celui « qui s'empare de notre blé pour nous le revendre », prétendait un libelle normand rédigé en patois : « *Not' Rouai grippe not' blei pour no l'ervendre.* » Lancé sur la voie du despotisme éclairé, Louis XV semblait vouloir cependant, cette fois, avoir l'audace d'aller jusqu'au bout de sa logique. « Je ne changerai jamais », avait-il proclamé en clôturant le lit de justice du 13 avril 1771, comptant sur le temps pour que les justiciables prennent conscience du bienfait de ce « coup de majesté ».

Louis XVI, le roi malchanceux

Le 10 mai 1774, par un radieux soleil de printemps, les cabarets et les guinguettes ne désemplissent pas. Atteint de la petite vérole, Louis XV le « mal aimé » est mort. Il est enterré à la sauvette pour ne pas affronter la haine de l'« opinion ». Louis XVI, son petit-fils, tout juste âgé de dix-neuf ans, lui succède, salué par le peuple comme un nouvel Henri IV mais fort embarrassé d'avoir à exercer le métier de roi. Dans un billet qu'il adresse alors au comte de Maurepas, un vieillard qu'il appelle auprès de lui pour principal ministre, il avoue : « Monsieur, dans la juste douleur qui m'accable et que je partage avec tout le royaume, j'ai pourtant des devoirs à remplir. Je suis roi : ce seul mot renferme bien des obligations, mais je n'ai que vingt ans. Je ne pense pas avoir acquis toutes les connaissances nécessaires. »

Né le 23 août 1754, Louis XVI a effectivement la « malchance » de devenir simplement roi à une époque où il faudrait à la France un réel souverain. Timide et défiant, mal aimé de sa famille qui lui préférait son frère, mort à quatorze ans et dont les talents faisaient l'admiration de la cour, obèse et peu élégant, solitaire et partageant son temps entre sa bibliothèque et sa forge où il fabrique clés et serrures, lecteur de Voltaire, de l'*Encyclopédie* et de Rousseau, tenant minutieusement ses comptes, notant ses heures de départ et d'arrivée lorsqu'il se déplace, plus passionné de chasse que de tout, dressant une fiche signalétique pour chaque cerf abattu, il donne le sentiment d'être totalement inhibé, comme s'il avait usurpé une place qui n'appartenait qu'à son frère.

La grande affaire de sa jeunesse a été son mariage, à seize ans, avec la plus jeune fille de Marie-Thérèse d'Autriche, l'archiduchesse Marie-Antoinette, une fort jolie jeune fille qui, aristocrate de son temps, rêve de bonheur et de nature, d'aimer et d'être aimée, de plumes et de bijoux. Mais son « prince charmant », qui s'épuise à la chasse et rêve des voyages du capitaine Cook, mettra sept ans à consommer ce mariage, subissant l'humiliation d'un vaudeville commenté dans toute l'Europe. On frappe bientôt des monnaies où son effigie est surmontée d'une corne, et les harengères des Halles crient à ce roi « empêché » : « Fais-nous donc un enfant ! »

« Dans son lit conjugal, écrit Joseph, le frère de la reine appelé en "consultation", il a des érections fort bien conditionnées, il introduit le membre, reste là sans se remuer deux minutes, peut-être, se retire sans jamais décharger, toujours bandant, et souhaite le bonsoir [...] ;

ah si j'aurois pu être présent une fois, je l'aurais bien arrangé, il faudroit le fouetter, pour le faire décharger de foutre comme les ânes. Ma sœur avec cela a peu de tempérament et ils sont deux francs maladroits ensemble [sic]. » C'est peut-être grâce aux bons offices de son beau-frère que Louis pourra, le lundi 18 août 1777, accomplir enfin « la grande œuvre ».

Tel est l'homme qui doit séduire l'« opinion », refaire l'unité de la nation autour du trône et mener les réformes que la société exige mais sans vouloir en faire les frais. Pour l'heure, il suffit d'exiler Madame du Barry, de renvoyer Terray et Maupeou et de rétablir les parlements dans leur forme ancienne pour marquer le « changement ». De sa retraite, Maupeou déclare : « J'avais fait gagner au roi un procès qui durait bien depuis trois siècles. S'il veut le perdre, il est bien le maître. » Pourtant, Louis XVI appelle au Contrôle général des Finances un homme des « Lumières », Anne Robert Jacques Turgot, lecteur assidu des physiocrates et des philosophes, collaborateur de l'*Encyclopédie*, intendant du Limousin depuis 1761. Là, dans l'une des provinces les plus pauvres du royaume, il a fait merveille. Il a réparti plus équitablement la taille, créé des fabriques, amélioré l'agriculture et les voies de communication, introduit la culture de la pomme de terre, créé une école d'accouchement, lutté contre la disette et écrit que « le soulagement des hommes qui souffrent est le devoir de tous et l'affaire de tous ». C'est manifestement l'homme qu'il faut à la monarchie. Une intelligence doublée d'une passion du bien public. Sa lettre, adressée au roi le 24 août 1774, le jour même où il est nommé contrôleur général, a des accents fort contemporains : « Point de banqueroute, point d'augmentation d'impôt, point d'emprunts. [...] Pour remplir ces trois points, il n'y a qu'un moyen. C'est de réduire la dépense au-dessous de la recette, et assez au-dessous pour pouvoir économiser chaque année une vingtaine de millions afin de rembourser les dettes anciennes. Sans cela, le premier coup de canon forcerait l'État à la banqueroute. »

Donnant immédiatement l'exemple en baissant ses appointements de contrôleur général de 142 000 livres à 80 000 livres et en refusant de profiter du pot-de-vin traditionnel de 100 000 écus que versaient à l'occasion de chaque bail les fermiers généraux, Turgot tente une ambitieuse « révolution par le haut » en décrétant la liberté de la circulation et du commerce des grains et des farines afin de « prévenir les inégalités excessives dans les prix », en supprimant les jurandes, maîtrises et corporations, considérées comme des obstacles à l'innovation, en proposant de supprimer les corvées royales et de les remplacer par une « subvention territoriale » acquittée par tous les

propriétaires, privilégiés ou non, en annonçant la création de « municipalités » élues par les propriétaires, chargées de l'administration locale
et d'exprimer leur « opinion » au roi, en songeant à mettre en place
un vrai programme d'instruction nationale et en projetant de rappeler
les protestants exilés en Allemagne ou en Angleterre.

C'était proposer la naissance d'une société nouvelle fondée non
plus sur la naissance et l'esprit de corps mais sur la propriété et la
liberté, ébaucher une « constitution » dont l'application aurait bouleversé les structures politiques du royaume, mettre en question les
« avantages acquis » et faire du « laissez-faire » un mot d'ordre révolutionnaire. C'était véritablement faire « table rase » du passé et mettre
la « raison » au gouvernement. C'était surtout unir les parlementaires
hostiles à toute innovation et le peuple qui, en France, n'a jamais aimé
les programmes « libéraux » et toujours redouté le pain cher. Turgot,
qui avait la tête bien faite et la plume alerte, avait, comme nos
modernes énarques, beaucoup de difficultés à admettre que d'autres
esprits se refusent aux évidences qui étaient les siennes. Comme eux,
il voulait gouverner par des démonstrations et enfoncer sa vérité dans
les cerveaux réfractaires. Necker, un banquier suisse et protestant,
écrivait à cette occasion : « Le pain qui le nourrit, la Religion qui le
console ; voilà ses seules idées [au peuple] : elles seront toujours aussi
simples que sa nature ; la prospérité de l'État, les siècles, la génération
suivante, sont des mots qui ne peuvent le frapper ; il ne tient à la
société que par ses peines, et de tout cet espace immense qu'on appelle
l'avenir, il n'aperçoit jamais que le lendemain ; il est privé par sa
misère d'un intérêt plus éloigné. Aussi, lorsqu'il verra le prix des
grains monter et rendre la subsistance incertaine, comment ne s'élève-
rait-il pas contre l'exportation ou contre toute loi politique à laquelle
il imputerait son malheur et son inquiétude ! [...] Ce Peuple enfant,
qu'on promène avec des lizières, au milieu de l'inégalité des propriétés, et à travers mille objets de privations et d'envie, n'est plus
qu'un lion qui rugit quand il craint pour son nécessaire. » Peu révolutionnaire mais fort lucide.

En avril 1775, au moment de la soudure, éclatait en effet la
« guerre des Farines » provoquée par l'édit sur la libre circulation des
grains pris en septembre 1774 alors que, Turgot ne l'ignorait pas, la
récolte s'annonçait médiocre et que son collègue Bertin l'avait exhorté
« à mettre dans sa marche toute la lenteur de la prudence ». À Dijon,
la foule pille un moulin pour avoir du grain. À Pontoise, elle taxe elle-
même le blé au prix qu'elle a fixé. En Picardie, en Brie, en Beauce,
en Champagne, dans les régions de grande culture, les convois sont
arrêtés et pillés et des fermes attaquées. Le 1er mai, l'émeute éclate à

Saint-Germain. Le 2 mai, elle est à Versailles où elle s'approche du château, le 3 à Paris où des boulangeries sont saccagées. Le 11, le calme est revenu. Pour l'exemple, on condamne à mort deux pauvres garçons accusés d'avoir forcé l'ouverture des boulangeries et d'avoir volé du pain, alors que le roi avait dit : « Si vous pouvez épargner les gens qui n'ont été qu'entraînés, vous ferez fort bien. » Un an après l'avènement de Louis XVI, le peuple avait toutefois compris que l'« état de grâce » était terminé. Considéré depuis des siècles comme le nourricier des petites gens, le roi avait rompu le pacte qui l'unissait à ses sujets. Un an plus tard, le 12 mai 1776, Louis XVI cédait à l'« opinion », « lâchait » Turgot, qui cristallisait tous les mécontentements, et rétablissait corvées et jurandes, à la grande satisfaction du Parlement de Paris qui, en mars, lui avait adressé de « solennelles remontrances » en proclamant que « tout système qui, sous une apparence d'humanité et de bienfaisance, tendrait à établir entre les hommes une égalité de devoir et à détruire les distinctions nécessaires, amènerait bientôt le désordre, suite inévitable de l'égalité absolue, et produirait le renversement de la société ». Le jour de sa disgrâce, Turgot écrivait au roi : « N'oubliez pas, Sire, que c'est la faiblesse qui a mis la tête de Charles Ier [d'Angleterre] sur le billot. »

Le défi américain

Le 4 juillet 1776, quelques semaines après la disgrâce de Turgot, les colons britanniques établis en Amérique du Nord, « insurgés » contre la couronne d'Angleterre qui a multiplié les impôts sans les consulter, se réunissent en congrès à Philadelphie et promulguent une déclaration d'Indépendance qui reprend les principes généraux diffusés par les Lumières. « Nous tenons pour évidentes par elles-mêmes les vérités suivantes, proclame le préambule : tous les hommes sont créés égaux ; ils sont dotés par le Créateur de certains droits inaliénables ; parmi ces droits se trouvent la vie, la liberté et la recherche du bonheur. Les gouvernements sont établis parmi les hommes pour garantir ces droits, et leur juste pouvoir émane du consentement des gouvernés. Toutes les fois qu'une forme de gouvernement devient destructrice de ce but, le peuple a le droit de la changer ou de l'abolir et d'établir un nouveau gouvernement, en le fondant sur les principes et en l'organisant en la forme qui lui paraîtront les plus propres à lui donner la sûreté et le bonheur. »

Ce soulèvement des sujets britanniques contre leur métropole fournissait à la France l'occasion rêvée pour prendre sa revanche sur l'humiliation subie pendant la guerre de Sept Ans et sur le désastreux traité de Paris. Sans songer que l'aide française permettrait d'instaurer dans le Nouveau Monde une république aux principes opposés à la monarchie, sans se préoccuper d'une guerre que Turgot avait déconseillée en estimant que les finances ne la supporteraient pas, Louis XVI, poussé par Vergennes, reconnaissait l'indépendance des treize colonies et signait un traité d'amitié et de commerce avec les États-Unis.

La guerre, soutenue par l'« opinion », qui s'enthousiasmait pour Franklin, ce vieux sage qui avait découvert la nature électrique de l'éclair, pour le marquis de La Fayette, qui s'était engagé aux côtés des Insurgents malgré l'opposition du ministre de la Guerre, et pour les exploits du bailli de Suffren aux Indes, se terminait en 1781 par la victoire de George Washington à la bataille de Yorktown et, en septembre 1783, par la paix de Versailles, qui effaçait la honte du traité de Paris. La France retrouvait le Sénégal, Tobago et Sainte-Lucie aux Antilles, la Louisiane rétrocédée par l'Espagne, les îles Saint-Pierre-et-Miquelon, les droits de pêche à Terre-Neuve et cinq comptoirs aux Indes. Dunkerque, soumise au contrôle de l'Angleterre depuis le traité d'Utrecht en 1713, était libérée de toute tutelle étrangère. Mais cette victoire de prestige avait bien coûté un milliard de livres et aggravé le mal chronique du royaume, les finances. « La dynamique des pouvoirs faibles, écrivait François Furet, est telle que leurs victoires mêmes tournent à leur perte. »

Le fardeau de la dette est d'autant plus insupportable que la conjoncture, décidément perverse, s'est retournée depuis le milieu des années 1770. Louis XVI a la malchance de régner au moment où, après avoir augmenté depuis les années 1720, les prix du grain et du vin baissent, entraînant dans leur sillage l'érosion du profit des fermiers et l'effondrement du revenu des viticulteurs. Après le haut palier de 1770, qui marque l'apogée économique du XVIIIᵉ siècle, commence un long malaise, une « dépression » de moyenne durée qui ravive l'hostilité paysanne contre les prélèvements, jusque-là bien supportés, réveille la haine du vigneron contre l'impôt sur la consommation qui « détruit le commerce » et mécontente le négociant, qui voit s'essouffler le commerce colonial. Ce que l'historien économiste Ernest Labrousse appelait « l'intercycle de contraction », 1778-1787, altère les promesses de la prospérité.

Autant dire que les efforts de la monarchie pour rétablir ses finances lourdement obérées par la guerre d'Amérique arrivent au pire moment. Appelé aux Finances pour remplacer Turgot, Jacques Necker, banquier et philanthrope, qui ne veut pas faire supporter au contribuable les caprices de la conjoncture et aux pauvres la cruauté du marché, multiplie les emprunts émis à 8,5 % puis à 10 % d'intérêt. Les rentiers exultent et l'« opinion » salue ce génie qui sait faire la guerre sans impôts. « C'est un dieu », écrit Mirabeau. Mais cet acharné à plaire est aussi un maladroit qui, en février 1781, fait imprimer un Compte rendu au roi destiné à faire la publicité de sa gestion. Grâce à des chiffres truqués qui masquent un déficit de 80 millions de livres, cet état des finances, appelé bientôt « conte bleu » à cause de la couleur de sa couverture, révèle surtout pour la première fois à l'« opinion », qui s'en délecte, les dépenses de la cour. On connût ainsi les chiffres des pensions et des grâces dont Necker dénonce les excès. Comme nos modernes « Lettre ouverte à... », ce texte de plus de cent pages remporte un succès colossal. On en tire plus de cent mille exemplaires, chiffre alors jamais atteint par quelque texte que ce fût. Le 19 mai 1781, l'auteur imprudent est disgracié, au faîte de sa popularité.

Après Joly de Fleury et Lefèvre d'Ormesson, c'est au tour de Charles-Alexandre de Calonne, intendant de Lille, de jouer les magiciens aux Finances. À son arrivée au Contrôle, il trouve 600 millions de recettes, 176 millions consommés par anticipation, 250 absorbés par le service de la dette et 390 millions de comptes arriérés à solder. Keynésien avant l'heure, Calonne dépense alors sans compter, achète pour la Couronne de grands domaines à Saint-Cloud ou à Rambouillet, développe le port de Cherbourg, crée une bergerie royale de mérinos, fait ouvrir les canaux du Centre et de Bourgogne, subventionne de grands travaux d'urbanisme à Bordeaux, Lyon et Marseille, éteint les dettes des princes et... emprunte 650 millions en trois ans. En 1786, la moitié des recettes de l'année à venir étant dépensée par anticipation, il présente le 20 août au roi un *Précis d'amélioration des finances* qui, reprenant les projets de Machault et de Turgot, propose l'instauration d'un impôt perçu en nature sur toutes les terres sans exception et proportionnel au revenu, le tout étant associé à une pyramide d'assemblées consultatives faisant participer les propriétaires au gouvernement du royaume. Pour faire accepter cette réforme qui n'a aucune chance de « passer » devant le Parlement de Paris, il suggère au roi de réunir une assemblée de notables, nommés par la Couronne. Le 29 décembre 1786, convaincu de la justesse de ce plan qui s'inscrit dans la lignée des précédents, Louis XVI annonce son intention « d'assembler des personnes de diverses conditions et les plus qualifiées de mon État, afin de leur communiquer mes vues pour le soulagement de mes peuples, l'ordre de mes finances et la réformation de plusieurs abus ». En ville, on ne parle pourtant que d'une affaire, celle du collier de près de deux millions de livres que le cardinal de Rohan, grand seigneur fastueux abusé par une intrigante, aurait offert à la reine pour reconquérir ses faveurs au cours d'un rendez-vous. Déféré au Parlement, il est acquitté, et Paris l'acclame. C'est mesurer assez l'« opinion » que l'on se faisait alors de la monarchie.

Le 18 juillet 1652, Omer Talon, l'avocat général qui, quatre ans auparavant, avait prononcé une violente harangue contre les abus du pouvoir royal, dresse, quelques semaines avant son décès, son testament moral. Reconnaissant l'échec de la politique dont il fut l'ardent défenseur, il présente à son fils « [...] la désolation des affaires qui consternent les esprits de tous les gens de bien, parce que l'autorité royale non seulement est diminuée, mais abattue dans Paris, n'étant plus reconnue ni dans sa source, ni dans ses ruisseaux, par le mépris des magistrats, par l'insolence et le soulèvement des peuples, qui peut croître tous les jours, à cause de la disette qui les afflige et de la cherté du pain qui est excessive. »

Critiquant tous ceux qui, comme lui aussi, ont voulu faire entendre les « remontrances » du Parlement, il ajoute : « Il faut éviter toutes sortes de faction, de parti et d'engagement pour se tenir à la défense de l'autorité royale, laquelle ne peut être en deux endroits. Il ne faut jamais faire schisme, ni rompre l'union qui doit être entre le roi et ses officiers, et sous prétexte du bien public et de réformation, être fauteur d'aucune ligue qui s'élève contre le roi, parce que ceux qui suggèrent ces pensées et qui en sont les auteurs n'ont autre dessein que l'intérêt de leur grandeur particulière. » En fait, selon l'heureuse formule d'Alexandre Dumas, « la Fronde qui devait perdre la monarchie, l'a émancipée ». Baroque qui vient de l'espagnol « barruco », déformation de « verruco », « à verrues », « rocailleux », n'est pas une épithète qui convenait à la France. « Le caractère des Français exige du sérieux dans le souverain », écrira encore La Bruyère. Les ovations qui ont accueilli le jeune Louis XIV à chaque fois qu'il est apparu au « public » ont bien montré que la France de 1650 n'est ni l'Angleterre de Charles Ier, ni l'Espagne de Philippe IV. Là, on décapite le roi. Ici l'on doit accepter l'autonomie des provinces qui composent le royaume. En France, par contre, on aspire à l'ordre et les crises se dénouent dans le triomphe de l'absolutisme.

Un absolutisme qui s'épanouit au siècle de Louis XIV et s'affirme encore au temps de Louis XV. Dans son journal, l'abbé de Véri, grand vicaire à Bourges, ami de Turgot et des philosophes des Lumières, écrivait au lendemain de la mort de Louis XV, ce roi « mal aimé » : « Nos esprits sont accoutumés à nommer le siècle de Louis XIV comme l'époque principale et presque unique de la monarchie. Je ne pense pas de même, et je regarde le règne de Louis XV comme l'époque la plus heureuse de notre histoire. [...] Jamais la France n'a été si riche et si abondante en toutes sortes de manufactures, si ornée par la foule de ses savants, si bien cultivée dans les campagnes et si peuplée en habitants que sous le règne de Louis XV. Les armes n'ont pas été si brillantes, je l'avoue, mais elles n'ont pas eu les injustices, l'odieux et les dévastations de son prédécesseur. Aucune guerre civile n'avait versé le sang des citoyens, ni aucun motif de religion ne mit les Français sous la main des bourreaux, pendant cinquante-neuf ans. Nulle époque de la monarchie ne nous présente une paix aussi longue. [...] Les fondateurs de la littérature et les grands généraux ont pris naissance sous Louis XIV ; mais la masse des sciences, de la saine critique, de la vraie philosophie, de la bonne physique et d'une morale saine et humaine, est supérieure à celle qui existait avant l'époque présente. Je veux bien rapporter ces bienfaits au siècle dernier, comme à leur source ; mais leur plénitude s'est fait sentir de nos jours. Buffon, Voltaire et Jean-Jacques Rousseau survivent encore à Louis XV. »

Louanges excessives d'un partisan privilégié ou témoignage de bon sens d'un contemporain conscient de vivre une « belle » époque ?

En fait, « mal aimé » comme le roi Louis XV, le XVIIIe siècle français souffre d'être pris entre le siècle de Louis XIV et la Révolution. Victime de ce que l'historien François Furet appelait le « catéchisme révolutionnaire », il a souvent été présenté comme un siècle de déclin de la monarchie. Pourtant, loin d'être en « crise », le siècle des Lumières fut traversé par des mutations majeures qui en font l'inventeur de notre modernité.

Certes, en 1752, le marquis d'Argenson, ministre des Affaires étrangères, peut écrire dans son *Journal* : « La mauvaise issue de notre gouvernement monarchique absolu achève de persuader, en France, et par toute l'Europe, que c'est la plus mauvaise de toutes les espèces de gouvernement. Tout va de plus en plus à la perte nationale, tout tombe par morceaux. Cependant l'opinion chemine, monte, grandit, ce qui pourrait commencer une révolution nationale. » Certes, en 1787, la monarchie offre le spectacle d'un État au bord de la banqueroute. La conjoncture économique, longtemps favorable, donne des signes d'essoufflement. Aucun ministre ne parvient à imposer les réformes nécessaires. La violence sourd de partout et la noblesse « pense mal », comme en témoigne l'engouement des élites pour *Le Mariage de Figaro*. Certes enfin, Voltaire écrivait en 1764 : « Tout ce que je vois jette les semences d'une révolution qui arrivera immanquablement, et dont je n'aurai pas le plaisir d'être témoin. Les Français arrivent tard à tout, mais enfin ils arrivent ; la lumière s'est tellement répandue de proche en proche, qu'on éclatera à la première occasion et alors ce sera un beau tapage. »

Encore fallait-il que le hasard s'en mêle car, en histoire, rien n'est jamais écrit d'avance.

BIBLIOGRAPHIE

Ouvrages généraux

AGULHON M., *La République de 1880 à 1995*, coll. « Histoire de France », t. V, Paris, Hachette, 1990.

ARIES P. & DUBY G. (dir.), *Histoire de la vie privée*, 2 vol., Paris, Le Seuil, 1985.

BRAUDEL F. & LABROUSSE E. (dir.), *Histoire économique et sociale de la France*, 5 vol., Paris, PUF, 1970.

CARON F., *La France des patriotes (1851-1918)*, Paris, Fayard, coll. « Histoire de France », t. V, 1985.

CORVISIER A. & PEDRONCINI G. (dir.), *Histoire militaire de la France*, 4 vol., Paris, PUF, 1992.

DUBY G. & WALLON A., *Histoire de la France rurale*, 4 vol., Paris, Le Seuil, 1975.

DUBY G., *Histoire de la France urbaine*, 5 vol., Paris, Le Seuil, 1980.

DUBY G., *Histoire de la France*, Paris, Larousse, coll. « In extenso », 1997.

DUBY G., *Le Moyen Âge : de Hugues Capet à Jeanne d'Arc, 987-1460*, t. I, Paris, Hachette, coll. « Histoire de France », 1987.

FAVIER J., *Le Temps des principautés (1000-1515)*, Paris, Fayard, coll. « Histoire de France », t. II, 1984.

FURET F., *La Révolution : de Turgot à Jules Ferry, 1770-1880*, Paris, Hachette, coll. « Histoire de France », t. IV, 1988.

LAVISSE E., *Histoire de France*, Paris, Hachette, 1903-1911.

LE GOFF J. & REMOND R., *Histoire de la France religieuse*, 4 vol., Paris, Le Seuil, 1988.

LE ROY LADURIE E., *L'Ancien Régime, 1610-1770*, Paris, Hachette, coll. « Histoire de France », t. III, 1988.

LE ROY LADURIE E., *L'État royal : de Louis XI à Henri IV, 1460-1610*, Paris, Hachette, coll. « Histoire de France », t. II, 1987.

MEYER J., *La France moderne (1515-1789)*, Paris, Fayard, coll. « Histoire de France », t. III, 1985.

REMOND R., *Notre siècle (1918-1995)*, Paris, Fayard, coll. « Histoire de France », t. VI, 1984.

TULARD J., *Les Révolutions (1789-1851)*, Paris, Fayard, coll. « Histoire de France », t. IV, 1985.

WERNER K.F., *Les Origines (jusqu'à l'an mil)*, Paris, Fayard, coll. « Histoire de France », t. I, 1984.

Aux origines de la France
(– 2 millions / – 4 000 av. J.C.)

BORDES F., *Leçons sur le Paléolithique*, Paris, C.N.R.S., 1984.

CAMPS G., *Introduction à la préhistoire, À la recherche du paradis perdu*, Paris, Le Seuil, Points Histoire, 1994.

CHAUVET J.-M., BRUNEL DESCHAMPS E. et HILLAIRE C., *La Grotte Chauvet à Vallon Pont-d'Arc*, Paris, Le Seuil, 1995.

CLOTTES J. et COURTIN J., *La Grotte Cosquer, peintures et gravures de la caverne engloutie*, Paris, Le Seuil, 1994.

CLOTTES J., *Les Cavernes de Niaux, art préhistorique en Ariège*, Paris, Le Seuil, 1995.

COURAUD C., *L'Art azilien. Origine, survivance*, Paris, C.N.R.S., 1985.

De Néanderthal à Cro-Magnon, Catalogue, Musée de Préhistoire d'Île-de-France, Nemours, 1988.

DELAPORTE H., *L'Image de la femme dans l'art préhistorique*, Paris, Picard, 1979.

DELLUC B. et G., ROQUES M., *La Nutrition préhistorique*, Paris, Pilote 24, 1995.

DEMOULE J.-P. et GUILAINE J., *Le Néolithique de la France. Hommage à Gérard Baillou*, Paris, Picard, 1986.

DEMOULE J.-P., *La France de la préhistoire, mille millénaires, des premiers hommes à la conquête romaine*, Paris, Nathan, 1990.

GOUDINEAU C. et GUILAINE J., *De Lascaux au Grand Louvre. Archéologie et histoire en France*, Paris, Errance, 1989.

GUILAINE J. (éd.), *La Préhistoire, d'un continent à l'autre*, Paris, Larousse, 1989.

GUILAINE J., *La France d'avant la France*, Paris, Hachette, 1980.

GUILAINE J., *Premiers Bergers et Paysans de l'Occident méditerranéen*, Paris, Mouton, 1976.

Le Grand Atlas de l'Archéologie, Paris, Encyclopædia Universalis, 1985.

LEROI-GOURHAN Arlette et ALLAIN J., *Lascaux inconnu*, Paris, C.N.R.S., 1979.

LEROI-GOURHAN A. (éd.), *Dictionnaire de la Préhistoire*, Paris, P.U.F., 1994.

LEROI-GOURHAN A. et al., *La Préhistoire*, Paris, P.U.F., 1985.

LEROI-GOURHAN A., DELLUC B. et G., *Préhistoire de l'art occidental*, Paris, Citadelles & Mazenod, 1995.

LEROI-GOURHAN A., *Le Geste et la Parole*, Paris, Albin Michel. 1964-1965.

LEROI-GOURHAN A., *Les Religions de la préhistoire*, Paris, P.U.F., 1964.

Les Premiers Habitants de l'Europe, 1 500 000 — 100 000 ans, Catalogue, Musée de l'Homme, Paris, 1981.

LUMLEY H. DE et GUILAINE J. (éd.), *La Préhistoire française*, 2 vol., Paris, C.N.R.S., 1976.

MOHEN J.-P. (éd.), *Le Temps de la préhistoire*, Société préhistorique française, Paris, 1989.

PERLÈS C., *Préhistoire du feu*, Paris, Masson, 1977.

ROZOY J.-G., *Les Derniers Chasseurs*, Société archéologique champenoise, Charleville-Mézières, 1978.

RUSPOLI M., *Lascaux*, Paris, Bordas, 1986.

SAINT-BLANQUAT H. DE, *Les Premiers Français*, Paris, Casterman, 1987.

VIALOU D., *L'Art des cavernes-sanctuaires de la préhistoire*, Paris, Le Rocher, 1987.

Le temps des Gaulois
(– 4000 / – 50 av. J.-C.)

L'Art celtique en Gaule, Direction des musées de France, 1983.

AUDOUZE F. et BUCHSENSCHUTZ O., *Villes, villages et campagnes de l'Europe celtique*, Paris, Hachette, 1989.

BREKILIEN Y., *La Mythologie celtique*, Paris, Jean Picollec, 1981.

BRIARD J., *L'Âge du Bronze*, Paris, 1964.

BRIARD J., *L'Âge du Bronze en Europe barbare*, Toulouse, Les Hespérides, 1976.

BRIARD J., *Les Dépôts bretons et l'Âge du Bronze atlantique*, Rennes, C.N.R.S., 1965.

BRIARD J., *Les Tumulus d'Armorique*, Paris, Picard, 1984.

BRUN, P. *Princes et princesses de la Celtique*, Paris, Errance, 1987.

BRUNAUX J.-L., *Les Gaulois, sanctuaires et rites*, Paris, Errance, 1986.

BRUNAUX J.-L. et LAMBOT B., *Guerre et armement chez les Gaulois*, Paris, Errance, 1988.

CAMPS G., *Préhistoire d'une île. Les origines de la Corse*, Paris, Errance, 1988.

Les Celtes, Catalogue de l'exposition de la Fondation Agnelli au Palazzo Grassi à Venise, Milan, 1991.

CÉSAR, *Guerre des Gaules*, édition établie par C. Goudineau, Imprimerie nationale, 1994.

CLAVEL-LÉVÊQUE M., *Marseille grecque*, Marseille, J. Laffitte, 1977.

DUVAL P.-M., *Les Celtes*, Paris, Gallimard, 1977.

DUVAL P.-M., *Les Dieux de la Gaule*, Paris, Payot, 1957, rééd. 1993.

DUVAL P.-M., *Travaux sur la Gaule*, École française de Rome, Paris, De Boccard, 1989.

ÉLUÈRE C., *L'Europe des Celtes*, Paris, Découvertes Gallimard, 1992.

GOUDINEAU C. et PEYRE C., *Bibracte et les Éduens : à la découverte d'un peuple gaulois*, Paris, Errance, 1993.

GOUDINEAU C., *César et la Gaule*, Paris, Errance, 1990.

GRENIER A., *Les Gaulois*, Payot Rivages, 1970, rééd. 1994.

GUILAINE J., *L'Âge du bronze en Languedoc occidental*, Paris, Klincksieck, 1972.

GUYONVARC'H C.-J. et LE ROUX F., *La Civilisation celtique*, Ouest-France, 1990.

HARMAND J., *Vercingétorix*, Paris, Fayard, 1984.

HARRISON R.-J., *L'Âge du Cuivre. La civilisation du vase campaniforme*, Paris, Errance, 1986.

JOFFROY R., *L'Oppidum de Vix et la civilisation hallstattienne finale dans l'est de la France*, Paris, 1960.

JULLIAN C., *Histoire de la Gaule*, 1920-1926, rééd. Hachette 1995.

KRUTA V., *Les Celtes*, Paris, P.U.F., 1976.

LERAT L., *La Gaule romaine*, coll. des Hespérides, Paris, Errance, 1986.

MENIEL F., *Chasse et élevage chez les Gaulois*, Paris, Errance, 1987.

MOHEN J.-P., *L'Âge du bronze dans la région de Paris*, Musées nationaux, 1977.

MOHEN J.-P., *Le Monde des mégalithes*, Paris, Casterman, 1989.

Les Princes celtes de la Méditerranée, Rencontres de l'École du Louvre, Paris, 1989.

PY M., *Les Gaulois du Midi, de la fin de l'Âge du Bronze à la conquête romaine*, Paris, Hachette, 1993.

RAFTERY B., *L'Art celtique*, Paris, Flammarion, 1990.

VRIES J. DE, *La Religion des Celtes*, Paris, Payot, 1963, rééd. 1984.

La Gaule romanisée
(– 50 av. J.C. / 511)

AGACHE R., *La Somme préromaine et romaine*, Société des antiquaires de Picardie, Amiens, 1978.

CONTAMINE Ph., LEBECQ St. & SARRAZIN J.-L., *L'Économie médiévale*, Armand Colin, 1993 (Première partie, « Le premier Moyen Âge »).

CUNLIFFE B., *La Gaule et ses voisins. Le Grand Commerce dans l'Antiquité*, Paris, Picard, 1993.

DELAPLACE C. & FRANCE J., *Histoire des Gaules*, Armand Colin, 1995.

DEMOUGEOT E., *La Formation de l'Europe et les invasions barbares*, t. II, Paris, Aubier, Coll. Historique, 1979.

DUVAL P.-M., *La Gaule jusqu'au milieu du Vᵉ siècle*, Paris, Picard, Coll. Les sources de l'histoire de France, 2 vol., 1971.

DUVAL P.-M., *La Vie quotidienne en Gaule pendant la paix romaine*, Paris, Hachette, 1976.

FUSTEL DE COULANGES N. D., *La Gaule romaine*, éd. de 1981, revue et complétée par C. Jullian, intro. par H. Lavagne, Paris, De Fallois, 1994.

GOUDINEAU C., *César et la Gaule*, Paris, Errance, 1990.

GRIFFE E., *La Gaule chrétienne à l'époque romaine*, 3 vol., Letouzey et Ané, 1965-1966.

GROS P., *La France gallo-romaine*, Nathan, 1991.

HATT J. J., *Histoire de la Gaule romaine (120 av. J.-C.-451 ap. J.-C.)*, Paris, Payot, 1970.

LE GLAY M., *Rome. Grandeur et chute de l'Empire*, Paris, Perrin, Coll. Histoire et Décadence, 1992.

LEBECQ St., *Les Origines franques, Vᵉ-IXᵉ siècles*, t. I de la *Nouvelle Histoire de la France médiévale*, Paris, Seuil, Coll. Points, 1990.

LERAT L., *La Gaule romaine. Textes choisis et présentés*, Paris, Armand Colin, Coll. U2, 1977.

MAURIN L., *Saintes antique*, Saintes, Imprimerie nationale, 1978.

Naissance des arts chrétiens, Atlas des monuments paléochrétiens de la France (dir. N. Duval), t. I, Paris, Imprimerie nationale, 1991.

PELLETIER A., *La Femme dans la société gallo-romaine*, Paris, Picard, 1984.

PERIN P. & FEFFER L. CH., *Les Francs*, t. I, *À la conquête de la Gaule*, t. II, *À l'origine de la France*, Paris, Armand Colin, 1987.

Premiers temps chrétiens en Gaule méridionale, Antiquité tardive et Haut-Moyen Âge, IIᵉ-VIIIᵉ siècle, Catalogue de l'Exposition, Lyon, 1986.

ROUCHE M., *L'Aquitaine des Wisigoths aux Arabes (418-781). Naissance d'une région*, Paris, EHESS et J. Thouzot, 1979.

ROUSSELLE A., *Croire et guérir. La foi en Gaule dans l'Antiquité tardive*, Paris, Fayard, 1990.

Topographie chrétienne des cités de la Gaule, des origines au milieu du VIIIᵉ siècle, 8 vol. parus,

éditée par N. Gauthier et J.-Ch. Picard, Paris, De Boccard.

WOLFRAM H., *Histoire des Goths*, Coll. l'Évolution de l'Humanité, Paris, 1990.

Le royaume des Francs (511 / 814)

BAUTIER R.-H., « Haut Moyen Âge », dans l'*Histoire de la population française* dirigée par J. Dupâquier, t. I, Paris, PUF, 1988.

CARDOT F., *L'Espace et le Pouvoir. Étude sur l'Austrasie mérovingienne*, Paris, Publications de la Sorbonne, 1987.

DE LA RONCIÈRE Ch.-M., DELORT R. & ROUCHE M., *L'Europe au Moyen Âge. Documents expliqués*, t. 1 : *395-888*, Paris, Armand Colin, 1969.

DUBY G., *Guerriers et Paysans (VIIᵉ-XIIᵉ siècle)*, Paris, Gallimard, 1973.

DURLIAT M., *Des Barbares à l'an mil*, Paris, Mazenod, 1985.

ÉGINHARD, *Vie de Charlemagne*, éd. et trad. par Louis Halphen, 4ᵉ éd., Paris, Les Belles-Lettres, 1967.

FOLZ R., *Le Couronnement impérial de Charlemagne*, Paris, Gallimard, 1964.

FOURNIER G., *Les Mérovingiens*, Paris, PUF, 1966.

GRÉGOIRE DE TOURS, *Histoire des Francs*, trad. de Robert Latouche, 2 vol., Paris, Les Belles-Lettres, 1963-1965.

HALPHEN L., *Charlemagne et l'Empire carolingien*, 2ᵉ éd., Paris, Albin Michel, 1968.

HEITZ C., *L'Architecture religieuse carolingienne : les formes et leurs fonctions*, Paris, Picard, 1980.

JAMES E., *Les Origines de la France. De Clovis à Hugues Capet (de 486 à l'an mil)*, Paris, Errance, 1986.

La Christianisation des pays entre Loire et Rhin (IVᵉ-VIIᵉ siècle), colloque de Nanterre, numéro spécial de la *Revue d'histoire de l'Église de France*, 1975.

La Neustrie. Les pays au nord de la Loire de Dagobert à Charles le Chauve (VIIᵉ-IXᵉ siècle), catalogue d'exposition édité par P. Périn et L.-C. Feffer, Rouen, Musées et Monuments départementaux de Seine-Maritime, 1985.

LATOUCHE R., *Les Origines de l'économie occidentale (IVᵉ-XIᵉ siècle)*, Paris, Albin Michel, 1956.

Le Nord de la France de Théodose à Charles Martel, catalogue d'exposition, Musées du Nord-Pas-de-Calais, Aire-sur-la-Lys, 1984.

LEBECQ S., *Marchands et Navigateurs frisons du haut Moyen Âge*, 2 vol., Lille, Presses universitaires de Lille, 1983.

LELONG C., *La Vie quotidienne en Gaule à l'époque mérovingienne*, Paris, Hachette, 1963.

MUSSET L., *Les Invasions*, t. I, *Les Vagues germaniques*, 2e éd., Paris, PUF, 1969.

MUSSET L., *Les Invasions*, t. II, *Le Second Assaut contre l'Europe chrétienne (VIIe-XIe siècle)*, Paris, PUF, 1965.

MUSSOT-GOULARD R., *Charlemagne*, Paris, PUF, 1984.

MUSSOT-GOULARD R., *La Naissance de la France*, Paris, Perrin, 1995.

Paris mérovingien, catalogue d'exposition, Paris (musée Carnavalet), 1981-1982.

PIRENNE H., *Mahomet et Charlemagne*, Paris, PUF, 1970.

Premiers Temps chrétiens en Gaule méridionale. Antiquité tardive et haut Moyen-Âge (IIIe-VIIIe siècle), catalogue d'exposition Lyon, 1986.

RICHÉ P. avec la collaboration de G. Tate, *Textes et Documents d'histoire du Moyen Âge (Ve-Xe siècle)*, 2 vol., Paris, SEDES, 1973-1974.

RICHÉ P., *Éducation et Culture dans l'Occident barbare (VIe-VIIIe siècle)*, 3e éd., Paris, Le Seuil, 1973.

RICHÉ P., *La Vie quotidienne dans l'Empire carolingien*, Paris, Hachette, 1973.

ROUCHE M., *L'Aquitaine des Wisigoths aux Arabes (418-781). Naissance d'une région*, Paris, EHESS et J. Thouzot, 1979.

TESSIER G., *Charlemagne*, Paris, Albin Michel, 1967.

THEIS L., *Dagobert. Un roi pour un peuple*, Paris, Fayard, 1982.

La France féodale
(914 / 1180)

ABÉLARD ET HÉLOÏSE, *Correspondance*, éd. P. Zumthor, Paris, U.G.E., coll. 10/18, 1979.

BARTHÉLEMY D., *L'Ordre seigneurial, XIe-XIIe siècles*, t. III de la *Nouvelle histoire de la France médiévale*, Paris, Le Seuil, coll. Points, 1990.

BLOCH M., *Les Rois thaumaturges*, Paris, Armand Colin, 1924.

BLOCH M., *La Société féodale*, 2 vol., Paris, Albin Michel, 1967/68 (2e éd.).

CONTAMINE P., *La Guerre au Moyen Âge*, Paris, P.U.F., 1980.

DUBY G., *Adolescence de la chrétienté occidentale (980-1140)*, Paris, Skira, 1984.

DUBY G., *L'An Mil*, Paris, Gallimard, 1973.

DUBY G., *Le Chevalier, la femme et le prêtre*, Paris, Hachette, 1981.

DUBY G., *L'Économie rurale et la Vie des campagnes dans l'Occident médiéval*, 2 vol., Paris, Aubier, 1962.

DUBY G., *Guillaume le Maréchal ou le meilleur chevalier du monde*, Paris, Fayard, 1984.

DUBY G., *Le Moyen Âge : de Hugues Capet à Jeanne d'Arc*, Paris, Hachette, 1987.

DUBY G., *Les Trois Ordres ou l'imaginaire du féodalisme*, Paris, Gallimard, 1978.

FLORI J., *L'Essor de la chevalerie*, Genève, Droz, 1986.

FOSSIER R., *Paysans d'Occident (XIe-XIVe siècle)*, Paris, P.U.F., 1984.

FOSSIER R., *L'Éveil de l'Europe, 950-1250*, t. II de *Le Moyen Âge*, Paris, Armand Colin, 1990.

FOURNIER G., *Le Château dans la France médiévale*, Paris, Aubier, 1978.

HELGAUD DE FLEURY, *Vie de Robert le Pieux*, éd. R.-H. Bautier et G. Labory, Paris, Éd. du C.N.R.S., coll. Sources d'histoire médiévale, 1965.

LE GOFF J., *L'Imaginaire médiéval : essais*, Paris, Gallimard, 1985.

LEMARIGNIER J.-F., *Le Gouvernement royal aux premiers temps capétiens (987-1108)*, Paris, Picard, 1965.

LUCHAIRE A., *Les Premiers Capétiens*, Paris, Hachette, 1911 ; et *Louis VII - Philippe Auguste - Louis VIII*, id., t. 2.2 et 3.1 de l'*Histoire de France*, dir. E. Lavisse.

PACAUT M., *L'Ordre de Cluny*, Paris, Fayard, 1986.

PETIT-DUTAILLIS C., *La Monarchie féodale en France et en Angleterre*, Paris, Albin Michel, 2e éd., 1971.

POLY J.-P. et BOURNAZEL E., *La Mutation féodale Xe-XIIe siècle*, Paris, P.U.F., 1980.

SUGER, *Vie de Louis VI le Gros*, Paris, éd. H. Waquet, Les Belles Lettres, coll. « Les classiques de l'histoire de France au Moyen Âge », 1964.

THEIS L., *L'Héritage des Charles, de la mort de Charlemagne aux environs de l'an mil*, t. II de la *Nouvelle histoire de la France médiévale*, Paris, Le Seuil, coll. Points, 1990.

WOLFF P., *L'Éveil intellectuel de l'Europe*, Paris, Le Seuil, coll. Points, 1971.

La France capétienne
(1180 / 1314)

BALDWIN J.W., *Philippe Auguste*, Paris, Fayard, 1991.

BAUTIER R.H. dir., *La France de Philippe Auguste, Le temps des mutations*, Paris, C.N.R.S., 1982.

BEAUNE C., *Naissance de la nation France*, Paris, Gallimard, coll. « Bibliothèque des Histoires », 1985.

CAZELLES R., *Paris de la fin du règne de Philippe Auguste à la mort de Charles V, 1223-1380*, in *Nouvelle Histoire de Paris*, Paris, Diffusion Hachette, 1972.

DUBY G., *Le Dimanche de Bouvines, 27 juillet 1214*, Paris, Gallimard, coll. « Trente journées qui ont fait la France », 1973.

DUBY G., *Le Temps des cathédrales. L'art et la société, 980-1420*, Paris, Gallimard, coll. « Bibliothèque des Histoires », 1976.

DUPÂQUIER J. dir., *Histoire de la population française*, t. 1, *Des origines à la Renaissance*, Paris, P.U.F., 1988.

FARAL E., *La Vie quotidienne au temps de Saint Louis*, Paris, Hachette, 1942.

FAVIER J., *Philippe le Bel*, Paris, Fayard, 1978.

FAVIER J. dir., *La France médiévale*, Paris, Fayard, 1983.

FOURQUIN G., *Les Campagnes de la région parisienne à la fin du Moyen Âge, du milieu du XIIIᵉ siècle au début du XVIᵉ siècle*, Paris, P.U.F., 1964.

GUILLAUME DE LORRIS et JEAN DE MEUNG, *Le Roman de la Rose*, Félix Lecoy éd., Paris, H. Champion, coll. « Les classiques français du Moyen Âge », 1965-1970.

JEAN DE JOINVILLE, *Histoire de Saint Louis*, dans *Historiens et Chroniqueurs du Moyen Âge*, Paris, Gallimard, 1963.

LE GOFF J., *La Bourse et la vie. Économie et religion au Moyen Âge*, Paris, Hachette, 1986.

LE GOFF J., *Les Intellectuels au Moyen Âge*, Paris, Le Seuil, coll. « Points Histoire », rééd. 1985.

LE GOFF J., *Naissance du Purgatoire*, Paris, Gallimard, coll. « Bibliothèque des Histoires », 1981.

LE GOFF J., *Saint Louis*, Paris, Gallimard, coll. « Bibliothèque des Histoires », 1996.

LE ROY LADURIE E., *Montaillou, village occitan, de 1294 à 1324*, Paris, Gallimard, 1975.

LORCIN M.-T., *La France au XIIIᵉ siècle*, Paris, Nathan, coll. « Fac », 1975.

O'CONNELL D., *Les Propos de Saint Louis*, Paris, Gallimard, 1974.

OLDENBOURG Z., *Le Bûcher de Montségur*, Paris, Gallimard, 1959.

Prêcher d'exemples. Récits de prédicateurs du Moyen Âge. Présenté par J.-C. Schmitt, Paris, Stock, coll. « Moyen Âge », 1985.

Recueil des actes de Philippe Auguste, roi de France, éd. Delaborde, F. Henri, J. Monicat, J. Boussard, M. Nortier, *Chartes et diplômes relatifs à l'histoire de France*, publiés par l'Académie des Inscriptions et Belles-Lettres, Paris, 1916, 1943, 1966, 1979.

SIVERY G., *L'Économie du royaume de France au siècle de Saint Louis*, Lille, Presses universitaires de Lille, 1984.

SIVERY G., *Philippe Auguste*, Paris, Plon, 1993.

SIVERY G., *Saint Louis et son siècle*, Paris, Tallandier, coll. « Figures de proue », 1983.

La guerre de Cent Ans (1314 / 1400)

AUTRAND F., *Charles V le Sage*, Paris, Fayard, 1994.

AUTRAND F., *Charles VI*, Paris, Fayard, 1986.

AVOUT J. d', *31 juillet 1358. Le meurtre d'Étienne Marcel*, Paris, Gallimard, coll. « Trente journées qui ont fait la France », 1960.

BIRABEN J.-N., *Les Hommes et la Peste en France et dans les pays européens et méditerranéens*, Paris-La Haye, Mouton, 1975-1976.

CAZELLES R., *Étienne Marcel*, Paris, Tallandier, 1984.

CAZELLES R., *Société politique, noblesse et couronne sous les règnes de Jean le Bon et Charles V*, Genève, Droz, 1982.

CHÂTELET A. et RECHT R., *Le Temps du gothique. Automne et renouveau, 1380-1500*, Paris, Gallimard, coll. « L'univers des formes », 1988.

CONTAMINE P., *La Guerre de Cent Ans*, Paris, P.U.F., coll. « Que sais-je », 1968.

DELUMEAU J. et LEQUIN Y. dir., *Les Malheurs des temps, Histoire des fléaux et des calamités en France*, Paris, Larousse, 1987.

FAVIER J., *La Guerre de Cent Ans*, Paris, Fayard, 1980.

FROISSART J., *Chroniques*, éd. S. Luce, G. Raynaud, L. Mirot, 14 vol., Paris, SHF, 1864-1967.

HUIZINGA J., *L'Automne du Moyen Âge*, Leyde, 1919. Rééd. avec une préface de J. Le Goff, Paris, Payot, 1975.

LEGUAI A., *La Guerre de Cent Ans*, Paris, Nathan, coll. « Fac », 1974.

LEQUIN Y. dir., *La Mosaïque France. Histoire des étrangers et de l'immigration en France*, Paris, Larousse, coll. « Mentalités, vécus et représentations », 1988.

PERROY E., *La Guerre de Cent Ans*, Paris, Gallimard, 1945.

La France restaurée (1400 / 1483)

BASIN T., *Histoire de Charles VII et de Louis XI*, éd. et trad. C. Samaran, Paris, Les Belles Lettres, coll. « Les classiques de l'histoire de France au Moyen Âge », 1963.

BOUTRUCHER R., *La Crise d'une société. Seigneurs et paysans en Bordelais pendant la guerre de Cent Ans*, Strasbourg, Publications de la faculté des lettres, 1963.

CHÂTELET A. et RECHT R., *Le Temps du gothique. Automne et renouveau, 1380-1500*, Paris, Gallimard, coll. « L'univers des formes », 1988.

Chronique de la Pucelle (attribuée à Guillaume Cousinot), réimpression de l'édition de Vallet de Viriville, avec une préface de Fr. Michaud-Fréjaville, Orléans, Paradigme, coll. « Medievalia », 1992.

COMMYNES P. de, *Mémoires*, extraits et présentation par P. Contamine, Paris, Imprimerie nationale, coll. « Acteurs de l'Histoire », 1994.

CONTAMINE P., *Au temps de la guerre de Cent Ans : France et Angleterre*, Paris, Hachette, La vie quotidienne, coll. « Civilisations et sociétés », 1994.

COULET N., PLANCHE A., ROBIN F., *Le Roi René : le prince, le mécène, l'écrivain, le mythe*, Aix-en-Provence, Édisud, 1982.

DEMURGER A., *Temps de crises, temps d'espoirs*, t. V. de la *Nouvelle histoire de la France médiévale*, Paris, Le Seuil, coll. « Points Histoire », 1990.

FRÉDÉRIX P., *La Mort de Charles le Téméraire*, Paris, Gallimard, coll. « Trente journées qui ont fait la France », 1966.

GAUSSIN P.-R., *Louis XI, roi méconnu*, Paris, Librairie A.-G. Nizer, 1976.

GUÉNÉE B., *Un meurtre, une société. L'assassinat du duc d'Orléans, 23 novembre 1407*, Paris, Gallimard, coll. « Bibliothèque des histoires », 1992.

Jeanne d'Arc. Une époque, un rayonnement, colloque d'histoire médiévale, Paris, Éd. du CNRS, 1982.

Journal d'un bourgeois de Paris, 1405-1449, éd. C. Beaune, Paris, Livre de Poche, coll. « Lettres gothiques », 1990.

KENDALL P.M., *Louis XI*, Paris, Fayard, 1974.

LANDES D.-S., *L'Heure qu'il est. Les Horloges, la mesure du temps et la formation du monde moderne*, Paris, Gallimard, coll. « Bibliothèque illustrée des histoires », 1987.

LE ROY LADURIE E., *Les Paysans de Languedoc*, Paris, SEVPEN, 1966, 2 vol.

MOLLAT M., *Jacques Cœur*, Paris, Aubier, 1988.

MONSTRELET E. de, *Chronique (1400-1444)*, éd. L. Douët d'Arcq, Paris, SHF, 1862.

PERNOUD R. et CLIN M.-V., *Jeanne d'Arc*, Paris, Fayard, 1986.

VALE M., *Charles VII*, Oxford, 1974.

La France de la Renaissance (1400 / 1610)

BABELON J.-P., *Henri IV*, Paris, Fayard, 1982.

CHAUNU P., *Église, Culture et Société. Essais sur Réforme et contre-Réforme (1517-1620)*, Paris, SEDES, 1981.

CHEVALLIER P., *Henri III*, Paris, Fayard, 1985.

CLOULAS I., *Catherine de Médicis*, Paris, Fayard, 1979.

CORNETTE J., *Chronique de la France moderne*, t. I : « Le XVIe siècle », Paris, CDU-SEDES, 1995.

CROIX A., *Nantes et le Pays nantais au XVIe siècle. Étude démographique*, Paris, SEVPEN, 1974.

CROUZET D., *Les Guerriers de Dieu*, Paris, Champ Vallon, 1990, 2 vol.

CROUZET D., *La Genèse de la Réforme française, 1520-1562*, coll. « Regards sur l'histoire », Paris, SEDES, 1996.

DELUMEAU J., *Naissance et Affirmation de la Réforme*, Paris, PUF, 1965.

DELUMEAU J., *La Civilisation de la Renaissance*, Paris, Arthaud, 1967.

FEBVRE L., *Le Problème de l'incroyance au XVIe siècle. La religion de Rabelais*, Paris, Albin Michel, 1947.

GARRISSON J., *Protestants du Midi (1559-1598)*, Toulouse, Privat, 1981.

GARRISSON J., *Les Protestants au XVIe siècle*, Paris, Fayard, 1988.

GARRISSON J., *Royaume, Renaissance et Réforme (1483-1559)*, t. I de la *Nouvelle Histoire de la France moderne*, Paris, Le Seuil, coll. « Points Histoire », 1991.

GARRISSON J., *Guerre civile et Compromis (1559-1598)*, t. II de la *Nouvelle Histoire de la France moderne*, Paris, Le Seuil, coll. « Points Histoire », 1991.

GEREMEK B., *Truands et Misérables dans l'Europe moderne (1350-1600)*, Paris, Gallimard, coll. « Archives », 1980.

HATON C., *Mémoires contenant le récit des événements accomplis de 1553 à 1587*, éd. F. Bourquelot, Paris, Imprimerie nationale, 1857, 2 vol.

JACQUART J., *La Crise rurale en Île-de-France (1550-1670)*, Paris, Armand Colin, 1974.

JACQUART J., *François Ier*, Paris, Fayard, 1981.

JACQUART J., *Bayard*, Paris, Fayard, 1987.

JOUANNA A., *Le Devoir de révolte. La noblesse française et la gestation de l'État moderne, 1559-1661*, Paris, Fayard. 1989.

LEBIGRE A., *La Révolution des curés, Paris, 1588-1594*, Paris, Albin Michel, 1980.

LÉONARD E.G., *Histoire générale du protestantisme*, t. I et II, Paris, PUF, 1961.

LE ROY LADURIE E., *Les Paysans du Languedoc*, Paris, SEVPEN, 1966, 2 vol.

LE ROY LADURIE E., *Le Carnaval de Romans, de la Chandeleur au mercredi des Cendres, 1579-1580*, Paris, Gallimard, 1979.

MUCHEMBLED R., *L'Invention de l'homme moderne. Sensibilités, mœurs et comportements collectifs sous l'Ancien Régime*, Paris, Fayard, 1988.

MUCHEMBLED R., *La Sorcière au village*, Paris, Gallimard, coll. « Folio Histoire », 1991.

PERNOT M., *Les Guerres de Religion en France (1559-1598)*, Paris, SEDES, 1987.

VERSORIS N., *Journal d'un bourgeois de Paris sous François Iᵉʳ*, public. P. Joutard, Paris, UGE, 1962.

La naissance de l'absolutisme (1610 / 1661)

ARISTIDE I., *La Fortune de Sully*, Paris, Ministère des Finances,1989.

BAYARD F., *Le Monde des financiers au XVIIᵉ siècle*, Paris, Fayard, 1988.

BERCÉ Y.-M., *La Naissance dramatique de l'absolutisme (1598-1661)*, t. III de la *Nouvelle histoire de la France moderne*, Paris, Le Seuil, coll. « Points Histoire », 1992.

BERCÉ Y.-M., *Croquants et nu-pieds*, Paris, Gallimard, coll. « Folio Histoire », 1991.

BILLACOIS F., *Le Duel dans la société française des XVIᵉ-XVIIᵉ siècles. Essai de psychologie historique*, Paris, EHESS, 1986.

CERTEAU M. de, *La Possession de Loudun*, Paris, Julliard, coll. « Archives », 1970.

CHEVALLIER P., *Louis XIII*, Paris, Fayard, 1983.

DESCIMON R. & JOUHAUD C., *La France du premier XVIIᵉ siècle, 1594-1661*, Paris, Belin, 1996.

DESSERT D., *Argent, Pouvoir et Société au Grand Siècle*, Paris, Fayard, 1984.

DUCCINI H., *Concini*, Paris, Albin Michel, 1991.

DULONG C., *La Fortune de Mazarin*, Paris, Perrin, 1991.

GOUBERT P., *Beauvais et le Beauvaisis de 1600 à 1730*, Paris, EHESS, 1983.

GOUBERT P., *Mazarin*, Paris, Fayard, 1990.

HÉROARD J., *Journal*, éd. M. Foisil, Paris, Fayard, 1990.

JOUHAUD C., *Mazarinades : la fronde des mots*, Paris, Aubier-Montaigne, 1985.

MÉTHIVIER A., *La Fronde*, Paris, PUF, 1984.

MÉTHIVIER A., *L'Ancien Régime en France : XVIᵉ-XVIIᵉ siècle*, Paris, PUF, 1981.

MOUSNIER R., *L'Homme rouge, ou la Vie du cardinal de Richelieu*, Paris, Robert Laffont, coll. « Bouquins », 1992.

MOUSNIER R., *La Vénalité des offices sous Henri IV et Louis XIII*, rééd. Paris, PUF, 1971.

MUCHEMBLED R. dir., *Magie et sorcellerie en Europe du Moyen-Âge à nos jours*, Paris, Armand Colin, 1994.

PERNOT M., *La Fronde*, Paris, Éd. de Fallois, 1994.

PILLORGET R.& S., *France baroque, France classique (1589-1715)*, Paris, Robert Laffont, coll. « Bouquins », 1995.

PORCHNEV B., *Les Soulèvements populaires en France de 1623 à 1648*, Paris, Sevpen, 1963.

RICHELIEU, *Testament politique ou les Maximes d'État de monsieur le cardinal de Richelieu*, Éd. D. Dessert, Paris, Complexe, 1990.

RETZ cardinal de, *Mémoires*, éd. M. Allem, Paris, Gallimard, coll. « Bibliothèque de la Pléiade », 1956.

TAPIÉ V.-L., *Baroque et Classicisme*, rééd., Paris, Librairie générale française, coll. « Pluriel », 1980.

La France de Louis XIV (1661 / 1715)

BLUCHE F. dir., *Dictionnaire du Grand Siècle*, Paris, Fayard, 1990.

BLUCHE F., *Louis XIV*, Paris, Fayard, 1986.

BURKE P., *Louis XIV, les stratégies de la gloire*, Paris, Le Seuil, 1995.

CHASTEL A., *L'Art français*, t. III, « Ancien Régime (1620-1775) », Paris, Flammarion, 1995.

CHAUNU P., *La Civilisation de l'Europe classique*, Paris, Arthaud, 1984.

CONSTANS C., *Versailles, château de la France et orgueil des rois*, Gallimard, coll. « Découvertes », 1993.

CORNETTE J., *Chronique du règne de Louis XIV*, Paris, SEDES, 1997.

CORNETTE J., *Le Roi de guerre. Essai sur la souveraineté dans la France du Grand Siècle*, Paris, Payot, 1993.

CORNETTE J. dir., *La France de la monarchie absolue (1610-1715)*, Paris, Le Seuil, 1997.

DESSERT D., *Fouquet*, Paris, Fayard, 1987.

DESSERT D., *Argent, Pouvoir et Société au Grand Siècle*, Paris, Fayard, 1984.

DUPÂQUIER J. dir., *Histoire de la population française*, t. II, « De la Renaissance à 1789 », Paris, PUF, 1988.

ELIAS N., *La Société de cour*, Paris, Flammarion, coll. « Champs », 1985.

GARRISSON J., *L'Édit de Nantes et sa révocation*, Paris, Le Seuil, 1985.

GAXOTTE P., *La France de Louis XIV*, Paris, Hachette, 1968.

GOUBERT P., *Louis XIV et vingt millions de Français*, Paris, Fayard, nouv. éd. 1991.

HAZARD P., *La Crise de la conscience européenne (1680-1715)*, Paris, Fayard, 1978.

JOUTARD Ph., *Les Camisards*, Paris, Julliard, coll. « Archives », 1976.

LABATUT J.-P., *Louis XIV, roi de gloire*, Paris, Imprimerie nationale, 1984.

LACHIVER M., *Les Années de misère. La famine au temps du Grand Roi*, Paris, Fayard, 1991.

LAVISSE E., *Louis XIV. Histoire d'un grand règne*, avec préface, chronologie, bibliographie et cartes de R. et S. Pillorget, Paris, Robert Laffont, coll. « Bouquins », 1989.

MEUVRET J., *Études d'histoire économique*, Paris, Armand Colin, 1971.

MEYER J., *Colbert*, Paris, Hachette, 1981.

MURAT I., *Colbert*, Paris, Fayard, 1980.

RICHET D., *La France moderne : l'esprit des institutions*, Paris, Flammarion, 1973.

SAINT-SIMON, *Mémoires*, Paris, éd. Y. Coirault, Gallimard, coll. « Bibliothèque de la Pléiade », 1983-1988.

VOLTAIRE, *Œuvres historiques*, éd. R. Pommeau, Gallimard, coll. « Bibliothèque de la Pléiade », 1978.

ZYSBERG A., *Les Galériens : vies et destins de 60 000 forçats sur les galères de France (1680-1748)*, Paris, Le Seuil, 1991.

La France des Lumières (1715 / 1787)

ANTOINE M., *Louis XV*, Paris, Fayard, 1989.

BAKER K. M., *Au tribunal de l'opinion : essais sur l'imaginaire politique au XVIIIe siècle*, Paris, Payot, 1993.

BÉLY L. (dir.), *La France moderne, 1498-1789*, Paris, PUF, 1994.

BUTEL P., *L'Économie française au XVIIIe siècle*, Paris, CDU-SEDES, 1993.

CHALINE O., *La France au XVIIIe siècle, 1715-1787*, Paris, Belin, 1996.

CHARTIER R., *Les Origines culturelles de la Révolution française*, Paris, Le Seuil, 1991.

CORNETTE J., *Histoire de la France : absolutisme et Lumières, 1652-1783*, Paris, Hachette, 1993.

CROUZET F., *De la supériorité de l'Angleterre sur la France. L'économique et l'imaginaire*, Paris, Perrin, 1985.

DARNTON R., *Le Grand Massacre des chats. Attitudes et croyances dans l'ancienne France*, Paris, Robert Laffont, 1985.

DARNTON R., *L'Aventure de l'« Encyclopédie » 1775-1800 : un best-seller au siècle des Lumières*, Paris, Le Seuil, 1982.

DURAND Y., *Les Fermiers généraux*, Paris, Maisonneuve et Larose, 1970, rééd. 1996.

EGRET J., *Louis XV et l'opposition parlementaire*, Paris, Armand Colin, 1970.

FARGE A., *La Vie fragile. Violence, pouvoirs et solidarités à Paris au XVIIIe siècle*, Paris, Hachette, 1986.

FAURE E., *La Banqueroute de Law*, Paris, Gallimard, 1977.

GARDEN M., *Lyon et les Lyonnais au XVIIIe siècle*, Paris, Flammarion, 1970.

GOUBERT P. et ROCHE D., *L'Ancien Régime*, Paris, Armand Colin, 1984.

KAPLAN St., *Le Pain, le peuple et le roi : la bataille du libéralisme sous Louis XV*, Paris, Perrin, 1986.

LABROUSSE E., *La Crise de l'économie française à la fin de l'Ancien Régime et au début de la Révolution*, Paris, PUF, 1943.

LACHIVER M., *Vin, vigne et vignerons en région parisienne du XVIIe au XIXe siècle*, Pontoise, S.H.A., 1982.

LEVER E., *Louis XVI*, Paris, Fayard, 1985.

MEYER J. et alii, *Histoire de la France coloniale*, t. I, Paris, Armand Colin, 1991.

MEYER J., *Le Régent*, Paris, Ramsay, 1985.

MEYER J., *La Noblesse bretonne au XVIIIe siècle*, Paris, Imprimerie nationale, 1966.

MORINEAU M., *Les Faux-Semblants d'un démarrage économique. Agriculture et démographie en France au XVIIIe siècle*, Paris, Armand Colin, 1971.

MORNET D., *Les Origines intellectuelles de la Révolution (1715-1787)*, Paris, Armand Colin, 1933.

PERROT J.-C., *Genèse d'une ville moderne, Caen au XVIIIe siècle*, Paris, Mouton, 1975.

PÉTRÉ-GRENOUILLEAU O., *L'Argent de la traite*, Paris, Aubier, 1996.

ROCHE D., *La France des Lumières*, Paris, Fayard, 1993.

ROCHE D., *La Culture des apparences, une histoire du vêtement, XVIIe-XVIIIe siècle*, Paris, Le Seuil, 1989.

ROCHE D., *Le Peuple de Paris. Essai sur la culture populaire au XVIIIe siècle*, Paris, Aubier, 1981.

SOLNON J.-F., *La Cour de France*, Paris, Fayard, 1987.

VIGUERIE J. de, *Histoire et dictionnaire du temps des Lumières*, Paris, Robert Laffont, coll. « Bouquins », 1995.

VOVELLE M., *Piété baroque et déchristianisation en Provence au XVIIIe siècle. Les attitudes devant la mort*, Paris, Le Seuil, 1973.

WORONOFF D., *Histoire de l'industrie en France, du XVIe siècle à nos jours*, Paris, Le Seuil, 1994.

INDEX

675

Maine (Louis Auguste de Bourbon, duc du), 599
Maintenon (Françoise d'Aubigné, marquise de), 581, 590, 594, 599, 600, 602
Maire (Jean le), 537
Malesherbes (Chrétien Guillaume de Lamoignon de), 625
Malestroit, 338
Malherbe (François de), 506
Malines, 430
Malmédy, 184, 191
Malouins, 561
Malplaquet, 585, 589
Malthus, 343
Malvaux (abbé de), 629
Mandrin (Louis), 627
Mandubiens, 116
Mané-er-Hroeck, 66
Mans (Le), 142, 250, 263, 372, 375, 376, 381
Mansourah, 305
Mantes, 222, 249, 390, 498
Mantoue, 510, 521
Mantoue (Charles III Ferdinand, duc de), 582
Marc (Perrin), 356
Marc Aurèle, 139, 144
Marcel (Étienne), 355 à 358
Marchand (table des), 68
Marche (Hugues, comte de la), 279
Marchiennes, 184, 589
Marco Polo, 287, 314
Marcomans, 139
Marcoul, 397
Marcourt (Antoine), 477
Mardyck, 601, 602
Marguerite (comtesse de Flandre), 369
Marguerite d'Angoulême, 476
Marguerite d'Autriche, 432, 438, 461
Marguerite d'Écosse, 426
Marguerite de Bourgogne, 322, 332
Marguerite de France, 443
Marguerite de France (fille de Philippe III), 336
Marguerite de Provence, 302
Marguerite de Valois (dite la reine Margot), 474, 483
Mariannes (îles), 587
Marie d'Anjou, 423
Marie de Bourgogne, 431, 432
Marie de Clèves, 439, 457
Marie de Luxembourg, 331
Marie de Médicis, 497, 501, 502, 506, 510
Marie II Stuart, 583
Marie Robine, ou Marie la Gasconne, 395
Marie-Antoinette (Marie-Antoinette Joseph Jeanne de Lorraine), 645

Marie-Thérèse d'Autriche, 514, 569, 581, 587, 641, 645
Marignan, 440, 444
Marigny (Enguerrand de), 314, 335
Marillac (Michel de), 509, 517
Marillac (René de), 579, 580
Marius, 107, 140
Marivaux (Pierre Carlet de Chamblain de), 600
Marlborough (John Churchill, duc de), 588, 589
Marle (comté de), 430
Marly, 245
Marmousets, 375
Marmoutier, 153, 489
Marne, 220
Maroc, Marocains, 577, 587
Marolles-en-Hurepoix, 412
Marquenterre, 424
Marseille, Marseillais, 89, 90, 102, 105, 124, 134, 137, 144, 150, 152, 154, 182, 287, 342, 346, 348, 417, 448, 449, 462, 464, 468, 485, 488, 493, 498, 549, 560, 561, 609, 613, 617, 650
Martin (François), 560
Martin (saint), 152, 153, 155, 161, 162, 185, 230
Martinique, 560
Masenx (Guillaume), 467, 468
Massillon (Jean-Baptiste), 584
Maternus, 139
Mathilde de Flandre, 236
Maubeuge, 350, 571
Mauer, 20
Maunoir (Julien), 533, 534
Maupeou (René Nicolas Charles Augustin de), 644, 646
Mauquest de la Motte (Guillaume), 595
Maurepas (Jean Frédéric Phélypeaux, comte de), 645
Maurice (empereur byzantin), 171
Maurille (évêque d'Angers), 183
Maximilien Ier d'Autriche, 432, 437, 438, 440, 441, 447
Mayas, 441
Mayence, 140, 149, 209, 210, 441
Mayenne (Charles de Lorraine, duc de), 490, 493, 502
Mayer (Robert von), 24
Mazarin (duchesse de), 617
Mazarin (Giulio Mazarini, dit Jules), 514, 523 à 527, 539, 542, 543, 545, 553, 554
Meaux, 221, 222, 278, 309, 357, 476, 483
Médicis (Jean de), 541
Médicis (Laurent de, dit Laurent le Magnifique), 455

Médicis (les), 416, 438
Méditerranée, 299, 312
Médoc, 246
Mehemet Reza Beg, 577
Mehun-sur-Yèvre, 392
Meilhan (Gabriel Sénac de), 622
Mello, 358
Melun, 221, 232
Melun (Guillaume de), 366
Ménapes, 106
Menars (Marie Charron de), 553
Menin, 570
Mercier (Louis Sébastien), 615, 630
Mercœur (Philippe Emmanuel de Lorraine, duc de), 493, 532
Mercure, 97, 137
Mérens (col des), 343
Mérobaud, 148
Mérovingiens, 167, 168, 172, 176, 190, 193, 195, 199, 510
Merri, 83
Merveilles (vallée des), 74, 80
Meschinot (Jean), 421
Meslay-le-Vidame, 424
Mesmer (Franz Anton), 636
Mesnil-au-Val, 469
Mésopotamie, 285
Messance (Louis de), 628
Messine, 342
Métezeau (Clément II), 508
Metz, 140, 152, 173, 188, 189, 214, 292, 347, 403, 443, 445, 581, 582
Meung, 397
Meuse, 182, 220, 248
Mexique, 587
Mézeray (François Eudes de), 541, 562
Mézières, 441
Mézières (Philippe de), 365, 366, 378
Michel (Jean), 447
Michelet (Jules), 242, 525
Michelle de France (fille de Charles VI), 378
Milan, Milanais, 105, 209, 380, 397, 425, 437, 439, 440, 442, 455, 559, 582
Millau, 480, 484, 580, 609
Milvius (bataille de), 161
Minorque, 588, 590
Miosson, 354
Mirabeau (Victor Riqueti, marquis de), 621, 650
Miron (Robert), 518
Mississippi, 560, 605
Mithra, 144
Moheau (Jean-Baptiste), 610
Moissac, 262
Molay (Jacques de), 322
Molesmes, 289
Molière (Jean-Baptiste Poquelin, dit), 543, 547, 562, 563, 565, 595

TABLE DES MATIÈRES

collection tempus
Perrin

DÉJÀ PARU

À PARAÎTRE

À PARAÎTRE

Photocomposition Nord Compo
59650 Villeneuve-d'Ascq

Imprimé en avril 2015
sur les presses numériques de l'Imprimerie Maury S.A.S.
Z.I. des Ondes – 12100 Millau
pour le compte des Éditions Perrin
12 avenue d'Italie
75013 Paris

N° d'édition : 1750 – N° d'impression : D15/52172L
Dépôt légal : octobre 2002

Imprimé en France